DILLAVOU and HOWARD'S
Principles of Business Law

Eighth Edition

DILLAVOU and HOWARD'S
Principles of

Prentice-Hall, Inc., Englewood Cliffs, New Jersey

Business Law

WILLIAM J. ROBERT

Professor of Business Law
Head of the Department of Finance
and Business Environment
University of Oregon

ROBERT N. CORLEY

Associate Professor of Business Law
University of Illinois

ESSEL R. DILLAVOU

Professor of Business Law Emeritus
University of Illinois

CHARLES G. HOWARD

Professor of Law Emeritus
University of Oregon

Dillavou and Howard's
Principles of Business Law
Eighth Edition

William J. Robert
Robert N. Corley
Essel R. Dillavou
Charles G. Howard

Previously published under the title of
Principles of Business Law

Printed in the United States of America

Library of Congress Catalog Card No. *67–15188*

Current printing (last digit)
10 9 8 7 6 5 4

PRENTICE-HALL INTERNATIONAL, INC., *London*
PRENTICE-HALL OF AUSTRALIA, PTY. LTD., *Sydney*
PRENTICE-HALL of CANADA, LTD., *Toronto*
PRENTICE-HALL OF INDIA PRIVATE LTD., *New Delhi*
PRENTICE-HALL OF JAPAN, INC., *Tokyo*

Preface

This edition has been prepared and published soon after publication of the alternate 7th edition. There were several reasons for the decision to make an early revision. When the alternate 7th edition was published, only slightly over half of the states had adopted the Uniform Commercial Code, but as of the date of this edition, the Code has been adopted by all but three states. At the time of the previous edition there was a dearth of cases involving the Uniform Commercial Code; the number of such cases interpreting the Code has substantially increased in the past three years. In addition, there have been far-reaching developments in many areas of the law which are of particular importance in the field of commercial law. This is especially true in the field of "products liability" and "long arm statutes," which radically change jurisdictional requirements with respect to out-of-state defendants.

Whereas the previous edition was intended to encompass both the law prior to the Uniform Commercial Code and the Uniform Commercial Code, this edition places primary emphasis upon the Code. References to prior law are included only to provide historical perspective, and in some cases in order to explain the reasons for and meanings of certain Code sections. This has resulted in a shorter, more compact book, and we feel this treatment of the subject matter of the Uniform Commercial Code will be much more meaningful to student and teacher alike.

Those who have previously used this book will note a number of substantial changes, both in the organization of the materials and in the emphasis which is placed upon certain particular subjects. For example, the Uniform Commercial Code is in one "book" and each of the Code articles is discussed. A separate book on "Property" brings together all aspects of the subject in conjunction with complete discussion of the nature of the property concept. The sociological, historical, and philosophical material is spread throughout the book, although major emphasis is in Book I. The book on "Agency" has been expanded to include the subject of employment, as well as background material in labor-management relations. The book on "Contracts" is reorganized, with judicial remedies in the first chapter. A new book has been added entitled "Creditors' Rights." It brings together all aspects of this subject, which is one of the most important to people in business and finance. The Uniform Commercial Code materials are summarized in an introductory chapter, which may be used separately by a professor who does not have the time or inclination to use the comprehensive chapters on the Code which follow. The introductory materials in Book I have been completely revised. There is a comprehensive but understandable discussion of all phases of a legal proceeding; this greatly enhances the ability of the students to grasp the significance of the many cases included as a part of each chapter.

Present users will be pleased to note that this edition continues the basic format maintained by the authors in previous editions. The combination text–case method of presentation is used, selecting cases, as far as possible, that are free from complicated procedural questions but which introduce the student to current problems and procedures confronting business. The book continues a combination of traditional and "environmental" approach. The traditional material is presented in its environment so that the student not only receives an exposure to the legal environment of business but is also able to understand how this legal climate is reflected in the substantive materials which are discussed in detail. To keep the book as up-to-date as possible, we have substituted recent cases of significance for older cases. In addition, other developments in the law and legislative enactments such as the Amendments to the Bankruptcy Law, which did not become effective until October 3, 1966 have been integrated into the text. No effort was spared in an attempt to make this book absolutely current in all areas of the law. The book is designed to satisfy the demands of modern schools of business which emphasize the legal aspects of decision making. We believe the material will make a valuable contribution to the education of tomorrow's business leaders who must be familiar with the legal aspects of business problems.

The authors, of course, are indebted more than we can say to Essel R. Dillavou and to Charles G. Howard for their inspiration, guidance, counseling, and assistance in our efforts to maintain the standards and quality of *their* book. To the extent we are successful, the credit is theirs.

To the extent we fail, the fault is ours. We hope that the tradition of excellence has been maintained.

Paul C. Roberts, Professor of Business Law at the University of Illinois, has long been an author of this text. His contributions over the years have been of major importance. Professor Roberts has now retired from active participation in preparation of the manuscript, but he will continue his interest in the book and his suggestions for improvement will be welcomed by the authors.

We are also indebted to many current and past users of the text for helpful suggestions. These suggestions have been of substantial assistance to the authors in the preparation of this edition, and in helping to produce a text which they feel is an unusually effective teaching tool. We appreciate the assistance of Professor Gaylord A. Jentz, College of Business Administration, University of Texas, and Professor John D. Logsdon, School of Business, University of Kansas, who read the manuscript and offered their suggestions.

We wish to express our gratitude to Betty Hampel, Marcia M. Herndon, and Virginia Nasholm for their typing of the manuscript under difficult conditions.

WILLIAM J. ROBERT
ROBERT N. CORLEY

Contents

BOOK ONE: LAW, ITS FUNCTIONS AND
                    PROCEDURES, *1*

1: Law, *3*
2: Law and Society, *21*
3: Sources of Law, *44*
4: The Judicial System, *63*
5: The Law Suit, *80*
6: Nonjudicial Methods for Resolving Conflicts, *101*

BOOK TWO: CONTRACTS, *107*

7: Introduction to Contracts, *109*
8: The Agreement—Offer and Acceptance, *130*
9: Consideration, *158*
10: Capacity of Parties, *183*
11: Reality of Assent, *200*
12: Illegality, *218*
13: Form of the Agreement, *242*
14: Rights of Third Parties, *264*
15: Performance of Contracts, *281*
16: Discharge of Contracts, *304*

BOOK THREE: THE UNIFORM COMMERCIAL CODE, 319

17: Introduction to the Uniform Commercial Code, 321
18: Sales: The Contract, 331
19: Sales: Performance and Breach: Remedies: Documents of Title: Bulk Sales, 386
20: Introduction to Commercial Paper, 412
21: Commercial Paper: Creation and Transfer, 423
22: Holders and Holders in Due Course, 449
23: Defenses, 464
24: Liability of Parties, 497
25: Commercial Paper: Conditions Precedent, Discharge, 529
26: Bank Deposits and Collections, 556
27: Secured Transactions: The Security Interest, 591
28: Secured Transactions: Priorities, Default and Remedies, 620

BOOK FOUR: AGENCY AND EMPLOYMENT, 651

29: Introduction to Agency and Employment, 653
30: Contractual Liability of Principals and Agents, 663
31: Tort Liabiltiy of Principals and Agents, 686
32: Liability of Third Parties, 707
33: Duties of Principal and Agent to Each Other, 718
34: Termination of Agency, 736

BOOK FIVE: BUSINESS ORGANIZATIONS, 749

PART ONE: PARTNERSHIPS, 750

35: General Principles, 751
36: Rights, Duties and Powers of Partners, 770
37: Dissolution, 781

PART TWO: CORPORATIONS, 793

38: Characteristics, 794
39: Powers of Corporations, 811
40: Stock and Stock Ownership, 824

PART TWO: CORPORATIONS—Continued

41: **Management of Corporations,** *852*
42: **Dissolution of a Corporation,** *866*

PART THREE, *872*

43: **Miscellaneous Business Organizations,** *873*

BOOK SIX: CREDITORS' RIGHTS, *883*

44: **General Rights,** *885*
45: **Suretyship,** *893*
46: **Bankruptcy,** *914*

BOOK SEVEN: PROPERTY, *933*

47: **The Concept of Property,** *935*
48: **Personal Property,** *954*
49: **Real Property,** *972*

APPENDIX, *1005*

GLOSSARY, *1010*

INDEX, *1051*

DILLAVOU and HOWARD'S
Principles of Business Law

BOOK ONE

Law, Its Functions
and
Procedures

1

Law

1-1. Definitions of Law. It is not possible to give a simple or even accurate definition of law. The meaning will frequently depend upon the context in which the word is being used, because "law" expresses a variety of concepts. There have been many definitions throughout history which are worthy of note.

Blackstone, one of the first English legal authorities, defined law as "that rule of action which is prescribed by some superior and which the inferior is bound to obey." The concept of law as a command is operative in many areas of democracy. For example, the income tax law commands that taxes shall be paid to the sovereign and is in the nature of an order by the government of the United States enacted by the people's representatives.

Justice Oliver Wendell Holmes in the case of *American Banana Co. v. United Fruit Co.* (U.S. Supreme Court, 1909) defined law succinctly when he said, "Law is a statement of the circumstances in which the public force will be brought to bear through courts." He considered law simply to be the product of the courts.

Law has also been defined as a scheme of social control. This definition is especially applicable today because law is being used to bring about social, political, and economic changes. For example, law in the form of judicial decisions is being used to integrate schools and to reapportion legislative bodies. These social and political changes also illustrate that law is "an expression of the public will."

Law has also been traditionally defined as the body of principles, standards and rules which the courts apply in the decision of controversies brought before them. Law is made up of three elements: (1) formulated legislation including constitutions, statutes, and treaties, (2) rules of law adopted by the courts, and (3) the system of legal concepts and the traditional legal technique which forms the basis of its judicial action.

The definitions of law which have been used in various cases and at various times in our history are influenced by various schools of legal thought. These schools are developed in the next section and indicate various viewpoints on the nature and origin of law.

1-2. Schools of Legal Thought. There are four generally recognized schools of legal thought—the historical, the analytical, the natural, and the sociological.

a. Historical. ". . . all law is originally formed in the manner in which in ordinary, but not quite correct, language, customary law is said to have been formed, i.e., that it is first developed by custom and popular faith, next by jurisprudence, everywhere therefore by internal silently operating powers, not by the arbitrary will of a law-giver." (Savigny, Friedman, *Legal Theory,* 136, 1953).

Here the scholar in his definition has given weight to the evolutionary process of ideas and formalized them into rules of conduct resting on custom and tradition. The historical aspect has been emphasized and made important. From primitive times community living has required order. Hence, as society developed, there evolved customary and traditional rules of conduct. Law was found in these rules and evolved from them. Custom results from repeated approved usage, and when such usage by common adoption and acquiescence justifies each member of society in assuming that every other member of society will conform thereto, a rule of conduct has been formulated. When such a rule is adopted by a court as controlling in a particular case, or is enacted into legislation, law has been made. Cardozo, in his book *The Paradoxes of Legal Science,* describes this concept as follows:

> When changes of manners or business have brought it about that a rule of law which corresponded to previously existing norms or standards of behavior corresponds no longer to the present norms or standards but on the contrary departs from them, then those same forces or tendencies of development that brought the law into adaptation to the old norms and standards are effective, without legislation, but by the inherent energies of the judicial processes, to restore the equilibrium. My illustrations have been drawn from changing forms of business . . . Manners and customs (if we may not label them as law itself) are at least a source of law. The judge, so far as freedom of choice is given to him, tends to a result that attaches legal obligations to the folkways, the norms or standards of behavior exemplified in the life about him.

Such has been the history of the law of negotiable instruments, partnerships, sales, and many other areas of commercial law. Although the evolution of the law by judicial process may have been somewhat arrested by the legislative enactment of many uniform laws in the commercial field, development has not stopped. Business necessity has brought about amendment and revision, as evidenced by the recent drafting and codification of the Uniform Commercal Code considered in later portions of this text.

b. Analytical. "Law emanates from the sovereign not from its creatures. The sum total of all those rules of human conduct for which there is a state sanction. . . . Law in its essence is made up of those rules of human conduct which are made mandatory by the state upon all its citizens and without which social order and well-being could not exist." (Justice Stone)

Analytical jurisprudence relates to the study and examination of law in terms of its logical structure. The definition above, which is almost identical to Blackstone's, gives weight to the need for certainty and to a system of positive rules logically deduced from fundamental principles dictated by a sovereign state, with power to command. Law here is a rule laid down by a superior power, to guide and regulate those under the power. The state as the lawgiver hands down the law and as sovereign is bound by no overriding superior divine law or principle. Thus, law is a system of principles or rules in the nature of commands. Such commands may be orders of a monarch, or of a totalitarian authority, or they may be legislative enactments, administrative orders, or judicial pronouncements of a democratic state.

This legal theory views the role of government to be limited to the particular purpose of keeping order. Under this philosophy, business activity in the United States was given considerable latitude. With limited governmental interference the individual was free to carry on economic, social, political, and other activities not inconsistent with ordinary police sanction. Providing for public welfare and regulating business were considered outside the province of government. During the nineteenth century this concept, aided by natural law ideas, gave free reign to individualism in business and economy, thus undergirding and stimulating free enterprise. Such terms as *liberty of contract, free competition, individualism,* and *absence of government control* conveyed ideas, defined activities, and expressed policies entitled to protection under the Constitution of the United States.

c. Natural. Law is "a rule of conduct arising out of the natural relations of human beings established by the creator, existing prior to any positive precept, discovered by right, reason and the rational intelligence of man." (Kent)

This definition gives significance to the idea that man by nature seeks an ideal of absolute right and justice as a higher law by which to measure all other rules of conduct.

Law, when set against a background of divine principles, becomes a rule of reason, pronounced by reasonable men for the benefit of mankind and the establishment of the good community. Man as a reasonable being is able to distinguish between good and evil. Above him there exists law resting on reason and divine authority, which validates man-made law. Thus, when the state by legislation or by judicial process lays down rules of conduct that are unfair, unreasonable, or inimicable to the common good, they are in violation of natural and divine law.

Blackstone, the great legal scholar of the fifteen century, in his commentaries, says: "This law of nature being coeval with mankind and dictated by God himself, is of course superior in obligation to any other. It is binding all over the globe in all countries and at all times; no human laws are of any validity if contrary to this . . ."

Natural law, nurtured by the church, softened the rigid common law of England; became the basis of equity; and, finding its way to America, is expressed in the Declaration of Independence in the words "certain unalienable Rights, . . . Life, Liberty and the pursuit of Happiness." Professor Friedman in *Legal Theory* observed:

> Natural law thinking in the United States undoubtedly inspired the fathers of the Constitution and it has dominated the Supreme Court more than any other law court in the world. Such thinking has not prevented the court from vacillating from the unconditional condemnation of legislative regulation of social and economic conditions to its almost unrestricted recognition, from the recognition of almost unrestricted freedom of speech and assembly to virtual outlawing of a political party, and, on the other hand, from the toleration of the most blatant discrimination against negroes to the strong protection given in recent judgments. Yet the American Constitution gives as near an approach to the unconditional embodiment of natural rights as can be imagined.

d. Sociological.   "Law is an experimental process in which the logical factor is only one of many leading to a certain conclusion. . . . Law is a means to an end . . . The Law is both a result of social forces and an instrument of social control." (W. Friedman)

By this definition the writer seeks to find and describe law by what it does, its method, its purpose, and how it functions in balancing conflicting social interests. Many aspects of society are emphasized and made important. In order to find how the law is made, and how it functions, investigations into many areas of society are required. Economic theories, political bias, and religious and social considerations are factors in formulating the law. Under the pressure of conflict of interests, legislators and courts make law. Thus, law, when enacted by legislatures or pronounced by courts, is in the end the result of finding an equilibrium between conflicting interests.

Law is not only generalization deduced from a set of facts, a recognized tradition, a prescribed formula for determining natural justice, but it also consists of rules for social control growing out of the experiences of mankind. Current social mores, political ideologies, international situations and conditions, and economic and business interests are all elements to be investigated and evaluated in making the law and in determining how it operates. In order to find and define the law, facts must be ascertained by an ordered or scientific method. It is advocated that by this method law may be determined, simplified, and better adapted to social needs. Such techniques will permit a determination of what motivates legislators in making legislation and judges in deciding cases. Such emphasis leads to a consideration of statistical studies as to how and what law regulates, what should be regulated and why, and what new rules are required.

In conclusion it may be said that any attempt to find or give a fixed and certain definition of the law is impossible. The law is defined by scholars, judges, legal writers, lawyers, and legislators according to what seem to them the most important, dominant, and significant elements in its nature and purpose.

Thus, in studying law, it is necessary to look behind each definition at the circumstances and conditions which gave rise to its formulation; only then can one understand the author's meaning. In reading legislation, judicial opinions, and other legal materials, an understanding of what jurisprudential theory motivated the writer is of great assistance in determining what idea an author wishes to convey, the intention of a legislature, and why and how a judge reaches his decision.

1-3. Classifications of Law. It is possible to classify the law in many different ways. Many of these classifications are overlapping and interrelated. One of the basic differentiations is *substantive law* as opposed to *adjective* or *procedural law*. Substantive law is the substance of the law—the rules and principles which are applied by the courts in resolving conflicts. It has been defined as that part of the law which creates, defines, and limits rights as contrasted with that branch of the law which establishes the procedures whereby such rights are enforced and protected.

For example, rights which a person has in land are determined by the substantive rules of the law of property. If his rights in the land are invaded, the procedural law would prescribe the method for obtaining redress for such invasion.

Adjective law provides the legal machinery whereby substantive rules are given effect. Included in this category are procedures for instituting legal action and determining the issues to be decided at the trial of a case, the conduct of a trial, the appeal to a higher court, and the enforcement of judgments and decrees issued by the court. The material in Chapter 5 treats these legal procedures in more detail.

Law is also frequently classified into areas of *public* and *private* law. Public law includes those bodies of law which affect the public generally as contrasted with the areas of the law which are concerned with the relationship between individuals.

1-4. Public Law. Public law may be divided into three general categories: (1) *Constitutional law,* which concerns itself with the rights, powers and duties of federal and state governments under the Federal Constitution and the constitutions of the various states; (2) *Administrative law,* which is concerned with the multitude of administrative agencies such as the Interstate Commerce Commission, the Federal Trade Commission, and the National Labor Relations Board. These agencies possess the characteristics of each branch of government, i.e., they possess legislative, executive, and judicial powers (these agencies are more fully discussed in Chapter 3), and (3) *Criminal law,* which consists of statutes and general maxims that forbid certain conduct as detrimental to the welfare of the state and provides punishment therefor.

Criminal actions are prosecuted by either state or federal governments against any person for the violation of a duty prescribed by the common or statutory law. Upon conviction of a crime one of the following punishments may be imposed by society: (1) death; (2) imprisonment; (3) fine; (4) removal from office; (5) disqualification to hold and enjoy any office or vote. Crimes are classified as treason, felonies, and misdemeanors. Treason is defined by the Federal Constitution as follows: "Treason against the United States shall consist only in levying war against them, or in adhering to their enemies, giving them aid and comfort." A like provision is found in state constitutions but these are of questionable importance. Felonies are offenses usually defined by statute to include all crimes punishable by death or by imprisonment in the state prison. Examples are murder, grand larceny, arson, and rape. Crimes of lesser importance than felonies, such as petty larceny, trespass, and disorderly conduct, are called misdemeanors and are usually defined as any crimes not punishable by death or by imprisonment in the state prison, but punishable by fine or confinement in the local jail.

Violation of traffic ordinances, building codes, and similar municipal ordinances where prosecution takes place before a city magistrate are sometimes termed petty offenses or public torts instead of being classified as crimes. The distinction is insignificant because, whether they are called crimes or public torts, the result is the same.

1-5. Private Law. Private law is that body of law which pertains to the relationships between individuals in organized society. It may be separated into certain fields, such as contracts, agency, sales, commercial paper, business organizations, and others. The law in these areas and others pertaining to business law is fully treated in the main text material of this book. The law relating to protection of property and rights in property is especially significant in both the field of commerce and non-commercial areas. Particular attention is called to Chapter 47 of the Book on Property for a general discussion of the concept of property. The next section deals briefly with another field of private law which is not entirely oriented toward business, namely, the law of torts.

1-6. Torts. The *law of contracts* deals with the enforcement of rights and duties arising out of agreements created by the mutual assent of the parties. The *law of crimes* deals with the enforcement of duties imposed by the state. The *law of torts* deals with the enforcement of duties existing between individuals as members of society. A breach of such duties may be both a tort and a crime, for example, assault and battery, trespass, and discriminatory or unfair business practices. Each member of society is entitled to have certain interests protected. Some of these interests are: (1) Freedom from bodily harm or apprehension of bodily harm, or from impairment of movement. Invasions of these interests are called assault, battery, and false imprisonment. (2) Freedom from injury to property. Invasions of this interest are called trespass to goods, conversion of chattels, and trespass to land. (3) Freedom from disparagement of reputation. Invasions of this interest are called defamation, libel, and slander. (4) Freedom from invasion of the right of privacy. (5) Freedom from interference with business relationships. Invasions of this interest are called deceit, threats, and intimidations to customers, inducement of breach of contract, and slander of title and trade name. If any member of society or his agents and servants [1] invades such protected interests of another, the party injured has a right to be reimbursed by such member of society in damages for the wrong committed. Such wrongs are called torts. "Business torts" are discussed separately at the end of this chapter.

Tortious conduct, and especially injuries to persons, may be classified as: (1) Intentional; that is, if the actor intends his conduct to result in injury to another. For example, an assault and battery is an intentional tort. (2) Willful and wanton; that is, if it is in such "reckless and wanton disregard of the safety of others" that the actor should know or have reason to know that harm will likely result. For example, *A* recklessly and knowingly drives through a stop light. *B* is injured. *A* is guilty of willful and wanton misconduct. (3) Negligent; that is, if there is failure to exercise due care. Due care is that which a reasonable man, guided by those circumstances which ordinarily regulate the conduct of human beings, would do or would not do under the circumstances. For example, *A,* a garage owner, or one of his employees, leaves oil-soaked rags and waste near *B*'s stored cars. The rags ignite and burn the cars and adjacent buildings. *A* is liable for loss of the cars and adjacent buildings. *A* was negligent in leaving the highly inflammable material where it might cause damage or because his employee did so. *A*'s lack of knowledge of the dangerous quality of the oily rags is immaterial.

Tort liability is sometimes imposed even though the actor is innocent and exercises reasonable care. This is usually referred to as "strict liability" and is imposed in situations in which harm is caused by dangerous or trespassing animals, blasting operations, and escape of fire. Also, there is a trend in the law to impose strict liability upon manufacturers where persons are injured because of defects in manufactured products such as automobiles and appliances.

Tort liability may also be predicated upon the unreasonable and unlawful use by a person of his own property or on his own unlawful, improper, or indecent activity, which causes harm to another's person, his property, or the public generally. Such conduct is generally described as a *nuisance*. Nuisances may be either private or public. A private nuisance is one that disturbs only the interest of some private

---

[1] Book Four covers this area of the law in detail.

individual, whereas the public nuisance disturbs or interferes with the public in general. The legal theory supporting tort liability in these areas is that an owner of property, although conducting a lawful business thereon, is subject to reasonable limitations and must use his property so as not to unreasonably interfere with the health and comfort of his neighbors, or with their right to the enjoyment of their property. Liability is imposed on business for nuisances even in the absence of negligence. For example, slaughter houses, stables, chemical works, refineries, and tanneries, because of their offensive odors, may interfere with the peaceful enjoyment of property of adjacent landowners. Also, garages, filling stations, rock crushers, and skating rinks may be nuisances because of noise; factories and smelters by reason of the escape of noxious gases. There is a growing body of law relating to pollution of air and water, a problem fraught with economic, social, and political implications as well as legal ones.

The determination of the existence of a nuisance in any case requires a balancing of the equities since society requires that these business activities be conducted somewhere. No rule may be defined to govern these cases since each must be decided on its own facts.

Some fundamental aspects of the tort of *trespass* need to be considered since this tort is a common one and affects both real and personal property. A trespass to personal property—goods and the like, as distinguished from land and buildings—is the unlawful interference by one person with the control and possession of the goods of another. One is entitled to have exclusive possession and control of his personal property and may recover for any physical harm to his goods by reason of the wrongful conduct of another. Closely allied to trespass is the tort of conversion. Conversion is the wrongful disposition and detention of goods of one person by another.

The one in exclusive possession of land is entitled to enjoy the use of the land free from interference of others, either by direct interference or by indirect interference through instrumentalities placed upon the land. Entry upon the land of another is a trespass even though the one who enters is under the mistaken belief that he is the owner by purchase, or has a right, license, or privilege to enter thereon.

BUSINESS TORTS

Control of business conduct by judicial intervention. The businessman, in his competitive practice, is curbed by three forces: first, by his own moral concepts as influenced by the reaction of his business associates; second, by some positive law, legislative or otherwise, making particular conduct a crime or a civil wrong and imposing penalties; and third, by his duty not to injure others in the conduct of his business, for fear of having to pay damages. We are concerned with the third sanction in this section. In addition to the duty imposed by the traditional law of torts, this field of the law includes the duty not to inflict injury by unfair competitive practices. Not only is this a tort defined by common law, but it is also a wrong by virtue of legislation and administrative orders. Such torts are called business torts and are found within conduct labeled as unfair competition, disparagement, inducing breach of contract, and infringement on trade-marks and trade names.

Competition. In general, the right to enter into a business as a competitor of others in the same field is not denied by our economic or political order. Even though the opening of a new enterprise will do serious harm to existing and established businesses, freedom of competition has not been denied. If insufficient demand exists to insure the economic life of all, the law sanctions the economic death of those unable to survive. The facts that old customers are enticed to a new business, that prospective sales dwindle, or that similar wares are offered at lower prices give no cause of action to the old entrepreneur against the new. "The right of a seller to lower his price in good faith to meet the equally low price of a competitor in a sale of goods of like grade and quality is, in reality, the right to compete." Even though one has a sale almost consummated, a competitor, with knowledge of that fact, is at liberty to tempt the customer with a lower price on similar goods.

However, a pricing practice that has for its purpose the elimination of competition is illegal. It may take either of two forms. It may be such as to eliminate competition on the level at which the seller is doing business, or it may be such as to aid the buyer, e.g. a retailer, to eliminate competition in his field. Price discrimination in either area that tends to restrict competition is illegal and subject to such penalties as the law provides. Illustrative is the producer who sells his product at a certain price in one area but cuts that price materially in another locality in an attempt to drive out competitors. It is permissible to discriminate in price to meet competition or to account for differences in transportation costs, but it is no longer proper to use price reductions to destroy a competitor.

It is improper for a producer to offer attractive prices to one buyer in a given area and not to make those prices available to other dealers in the same territory. To give one retailer a material advantage over his competitors, thus making it possible for him to undersell them, tends to force the competitors out of the market. But the manufacturer or producer is allowed to make price concessions in certain instances. He may make different prices to different classes of customers. A jobber may obtain a lower price than a retailer, although the latter is willing to buy as much as the former. It is also proper to make quantity concessions to the large user, provided those concessions are also available to other customers who are willing to purchase in similar quantities. The producer must be in a position to justify the discrimination in price because of the difference in the cost of servicing the quantity user over the cost of supplying the occasional buyer. The question remains pertinent in all price discrimination cases: Has the reduced price a tendency to eliminate competition?

Competition for the primary purpose of injuring another without an intention to benefit himself is illegal.

If a person enters into a competing business for the express purpose of driving his competitor out of business and, having accomplished his purpose, intends to withdraw from the enterprise, he commits an actionable wrong. It is also true that, if one conducts his business in such a manner as to embarrass or harass unduly a competitor without correspondingly promoting his own interests, he may be enjoined from indulging in such tactics. One who injures a competitor commits a wrong unless he can justify it as the lawful exercise of a right.

To these general principles the legislatures have from time to time made exceptions in the case of public utilities. Those industries in which the public has a peculiar interest and which competition most seriously hampers by duplication of facilities and increased costs have been relieved of competition.

Retail price control.   Attempts have often been made by producers to control the price at which their article is sold at the retail level. A contract between the producer and retailer to the effect that the article will not be sold for less than a certain price is illegal at common law. Such an agreement was thought to be contrary to public policy because it eliminated price as a factor in competition between the retailers selling identical products and, hence, robbed society of potentially lower prices. It was also inconsistent to say that title to the article sold passed to the retailer and at the same time permit the seller to have control of the price at which the article was re-sold.

Although a contract containing a retail price-maintenance clause was illegal, manufacturers were able to control prices by selling only to those who maintained the advertised price of the manufacturer, since the sellers were at liberty to select their own buyers. If a retailer were discovered to be cutting the advertised retail price, the manufacturer, by refusing him the privilege of making further purchases, cut off his supply of commodities, thus exercising power to control the resale price. If, however, manufacturers by organization provided for a scheme that caused all price cutters to be reported to a central office and maintained a list of such retailers, such organization was an illegal combination and subject to criminal prosecution.

It has been contended that price cutting has an injurious effect upon the public and also upon the "good will" achieved by the manufacturer's product; thus, many states have passed what are generally called *fair-trade* or *price-maintenance* statutes, which afford protection against the practice of price cutting in the distribution of articles of standard quality having a trade-mark, patent, or name. These state acts have for their purposes the regulation of such unfair competition as price cutting and the elimination of price wars. The remedy authorized by these statutes to protect sellers creates a cause of action in tort against price cutters for unfair competition. Damages or injunctive relief is given against buyers who sell commodities at a price less than that stipulated between the vendor and the vendee.

These state fair-trade laws usually provide as follows:

No contract relating to the sale or resale of a commodity that bears, or the label or content of which bears, the trade-mark, brand, or name of the producer or owner of such commodity, and that is in fair and open competition with commodities of the same general class produced by others, shall be deemed in violation of any law of the state by reason of any of the following provisions which may be contained in such contract:

1. That the buyer will not re-sell such commodity at less than the minimum price stipulated by the vendor.

2. That the buyer will require of any dealer to whom he may resell the commodity an agreement that he will not, in turn, re-sell at less than the minimum price stipulated by the seller.

Such provisions in any contract shall be deemed to contain or imply conditions that such commodity may be re-sold without reference to such agreement in the following cases:

a. In closing out the owner's stock for the purpose of discontinuing dealing in any such commodity: provided, however, that such stock is first offered to the manufacturer of such stock at the original invoice price, at least ten (10) days before such stock shall be offered for sale to the public.

b. When the goods are damaged or deteriorated in quality, and notice is given to the public thereof.

c. By an officer acting under the orders of any court.

Also, most fair-trade laws prohibit "wilfully and knowingly advertising, offering for sale or selling any commodity at less than the prices stipulated in any contract entered into pursuant to the provisions of the act whether the person so advertising, offering for sale or selling is or is *not a party to such contract.*" This so-called "nonsigner" clause adopted in most state price-fixing acts binds persons who are not parties to the contract to control resale prices and provides that a violation is unfair competition and is actionable at the suit of any person damaged thereby. Thus, a distributor or manufacturer and one or more retailers may agree to fix a minimum price; they may by such agreement impose the minimum price fixed upon other retailers in the trade even though such retailers are not parties to the contract.

State fair-trade laws which impose a duty upon "nonsigners" to comply with resale price-maintenance agreements on trade-marked goods in interstate trade were held in the case of *Schwegmann Brothers et al. v. Calvert Distillers Corporation,* 1951, 341 U.S. 384, to be illegal, in violation of the Sherman Anti-Trust Act, and not within the protective provisions of the Miller-Tydings Act which was a federal statute enacted to remove the state laws from the restrictions of the Sherman Act. The Miller-Tydings Act, it was held, did not by its provisions make legal price control contracts against persons who have not signed the agreement. In order to avoid the consequences of the *Schwegmann* case, Congress in 1952 passed what is known as the McGuire Act, which provides that unfair methods of competition in commerce, and unfair or deceptive acts or practices in commerce are unlawful, but that the anti-trust acts shall not render unlawful any contracts or agreements prescribing minimum or stipulated prices, or that require a vendee to enter into contracts prescribing minimum prices for resale of a commodity which bears the trade-mark, brand, or name of the producer or distributor of such commodity, provided such contracts are lawful as applied to intrastate transactions under the statutes of the state.

The purpose of the McGuire Act is to protect the rights of states under the Constitution to regulate their own affairs. It permits states to enact statutes that make legal the contracts prescribing minimum prices for the resale of commodities, and to extend the provisions of such contracts to cover persons who are not parties to such contracts.

This federal legislation has not solved the problem of price control maintenance. At common law and by statute, price-fixing contracts are deemed monopolistic and in restraint of trade. However, under the McGuire Act and state legislation (the fair-trade act), "contracts or agreements" between distributors and one or more retailers to fix prices are legal. These contracts are not regarded as monopolistic schemes of price-fixing. Such contracts are designated as *vertical* price-maintenance agreements, that is, "between producers or manufacturers of a particular commodity and those handling the product, in a straight line down to and including the retailer." Such contracts are to be distinguished from what is termed "horizontal agreements." These are "cross agreements between competitors or between the same class of persons, such as manufacturers, producers, wholesalers or concerns in competition with each other with like commodities." These agreements are monopolistic, restrain trade, and reduce competition.

"Vertical price-fixing maintenance contracts," resting on the voluntary consent of the parties but applicable also to nonsigners were made exempt from federal anti-trust laws, and valid under state statutes, for the avowed purpose of stimulating "fair and open competition with commodities of the same class." Whether this result has been attained has been questioned. Price-fixing by contract in order to stimulate competition presupposes there are sufficient manufacturers and dealers to make competition a reality. Such, however, may not be the case. With the control of trade-marked specialty articles in the hands of a few large corporations, price-fixing agreements might limit rather than stimulate competition.

Also, the effectiveness of the fair-trade acts to stimulate competition and regulate prices has been limited because that portion of the McGuire Act which allows nonsigners to be bound by prices agreed upon between the vendor, manufacturer, distributors, and a retailer has met with constitutional objections. In 18 states the nonsigner clause has been held unconstitutional by the state courts. In 17 states the courts have held the nonsigner clause constitutional.

The reasons given by one court for holding the nonsigner provision of a fair-trade statute invalid include the following:

(1) The statute is an illegal restriction upon the right of contract and disposition of one's own property. Without any purport to declare the business

clothed or affected with a public interest, it destroys the property right of re-tailers to fix the prices at which they will sell their goods. (2) It stigmatizes as unfair an act that is untainted by deceit, oppression or unfair dealing and in-volves no assault upon the good will of the manufacturer. (3) It ignores the motivating purpose of the retailer, which may be merely to shave his margin of profit or otherwise and compels the consuming public to pay tribute to a re-tailer who, as an alert and efficient merchant, does not want to charge the fixed prices, the effect of which goes well beyond what has been called "pred-atory price cutting." (4) It grants special privileges and is an attempt to delegate power to fix prices, a power which the Legislature itself does not have in general, and this is done without laying down any standard or yardstick to be used. (5) It tends to establish a monopoly as it is in restraint of fair trade rather than in promotion of it. (6) It offends constitutional guaranties of a right of personal liberty and private property and allows a citizen to be deprived of his property without due process of law. (7) The right to contract or not contract is a property right protected by constitutional demand of due process of law. (8) It constitutes an unlawful exercise of the police power because the imposition upon a nonsigner to a price fixing contract bears no reasonable relationship to public health, safety, morals or the general welfare. (*General Electric Co. v. American Buyers Cooperative,* Kentucky, 1958, 316 S.W. 2d 354, 358.)

Some of the reasons given in support of the constitutionality of the nonsigner clause are:

(1) The primary object of the statute is to prevent willful assaults upon the manufacturer's good will. (2) The enactment is within the police power of the state to promote the general welfare and does not offend due process or equal protection provisions of the constitutions nor impair freedom of contract. (3) A nonsigner dealer, by virtue of voluntarily deciding to buy and sell the commodity on which a minimum price is fixed by a contract with other parties, elects to be bound by the contract. (4) It is not monopolistic in effect and does not offend constitutional provisions condemning monopolies, for it auto-matically ceases to operate where there is no competition with commodities of the same general class produced by others. (5) It does not delegate legislative power or power to fix a resale price on another's property so as to violate due process. (*General Electric Co. v. Telco Supply,* Arizona, 1958, 325 P. 2d 394.)

Injury to one's business resulting from threats to customers or in-timidation of prospective purchasers is recoverable in damages. If the threats are made by one in good faith who thinks they are legally sound, it may be that no tort has been committed, but an injunction will be issued restraining such conduct in the future. Thus, if the owner of a patent honestly believes that another is infringing on his patent, he may threaten potential purchasers from the alleged infringer with a lawsuit in case they purchase. Should a court later determine that no infringement existed, the party who threatened the buyers is not liable for damages. His threat was made in good faith for the pur-pose of protecting his own interest.

Disparagement.   One who disparages or belittles the goods of another may be enjoined from future misconduct, and in certain instances may be compelled to pay damages to the injured party. There appear to be four distinct elements of disparagement:

1. An express or implied misstatement of fact—as distinguished from words of comparison which indicate merely an opinion. Such expressions as "good" or "bad," "better" or "best" are in effect opinions.

2. The statement must concern the injured party's goods. Merely misrepresenting favorably one's own goods never constitutes disparagement. Some misstatement must be made about goods offered for sale by another.

3. The motive that prompts the statement must be bad. In other words, the statements must be made for the deliberate purpose of injuring the other party.

4. The injured party must allege and show special—as distinct from general—damages. That is, he must be able to prove loss of specific sales as a result of the statements. A general allegation and demonstration that business had declined a certain amount would not be enough.

All four elements must be present in order to recover damages. A showing of the first two elements, however, will entitle one to an injunction against a repetition of such statements.

Disparagement is a business tort that has arisen out of the tort of libel and slander. The defamatory statements concerning the goods may also impute dishonesty, fraud, and questionable business methods to the owner of the goods. If such is the case, then a "libel per se" has been committed. A libellous statement concerning goods alone is called trade libel, and as such is not a "libel per se." In the case of trade libel, special damages must be alleged and proven. Disparagement is recognized as a method of unfair competition which entitles the injured person to a remedy through the Federal Trade Commission or relief in the courts.

Inducing breach of contract. To induce one person to breach his contract with another is to commit a tort. The effect is the same even though the one who induced the breach did so in order to sell his own goods or services.

Mere passive presentation of the merits of one's products which has the net result of causing one to breach a contract and to purchase the goods of another is not actionable. It is only where one is active in persuading another to violate one agreement in order to be free to make another that a tort is committed.

Closely akin to inducing breach of contract are those cases involving boycotts. In general it can be said that an agreement to boycott a certain individual or group of individuals is legal only as long as it is in furtherance of some justifiable objective. Thus, an agreement by retail coal dealers whereby no purchaser may purchase on credit so long as he owes another dealer is legal, because of the protection such an agreement accords all parties to it.

Appropriation of competitor's trade values. Another facet of the security afforded to one's legally protected business interests is that of preserving his rights to somewhat abstract business values.

Wrappers and trade dress used to make merchandise more attractive and convenient to display do not of themselves have an exclusive trade value. No one has an exclusive right to the use of color combinations and package methods. Wrappers and color designs to be protected must be so distinctive as to entitle them to registration under the copyright or trade-mark law. However, if a distinctive wrapper or color design accompanying a distinctive name has by usage acquired a secondary meaning by becoming so identified with the goods that it distinguishes them from others and identifies the origin of the goods, the owner has an exclusive right to their use, and others may be enjoined from the use of the wrapper as an act of unfair competition.

Technically a trade-mark is supposed to be some mark or stamp imprinted upon the product, whereas a name does not have to be attached to the product. So far as the legal rights of the owner are involved, there is practically no difference between the two.

The first user of a trade-mark or name has a right to its exclusive use. The second user of such a mark or name, or of one which is deceptively similar, may be enjoined from its further use. Just how similar the mark, name, or trade dress must appear before relief will be granted presents an interesting problem. In general, it can be said that, whenever the casual observer, as distinct from the careful buyer, tends to be misled into purchasing the wrong article, an injunction is available to the injured party.

A name or mark which is descriptive of the nature of the article sold may not be exclusively appropriated by any one concern. Such terms as "Always Closed" for revolving doors and "Rubberoid" for roofing fall in the descriptive class and may be used by anyone. However, if the words used are so fanciful and remote from a description of the subject matter, such as "floating power" for engine mountings and "stronghold" for ribbed nails, it is appropriate for trade-mark use.

Geographical or place names indicating a specific origin cannot be technical trade-marks. Such words are in the public domain. Every manufacturer or producer has a right to indicate upon his product or article where it is produced. The same is true in the case of proper names. Every individual has a right to make use of his name in connection with his business. Any good will or favorable reputation that attaches to it should not be denied to him. Consequently, one generally cannot exclusively appropriate another's proper name.

The three rules indicated above are subject to one well-recognized exception. If a descriptive, geographical, or proper name has been used so long as to become identified with a certain product, thus having a secondary meaning, the first user will be protected in its use on the principles of unfair competition. Newcomers in the field who desire to use a descriptive term, a geographical location of their plant, or their names in identifying their products will have to qualify the use in such a manner as to avoid possible injury to the first user's good will. The latest cases indicate that such names cannot be identified as the name of the product by the second user, but that the maker's name or location may be placed on the product in some inconspicuous manner. Thus, it is clear that no one by the name of Ford could manufacture an automobile and call it Ford, although the name Ford could undoubtedly be used by the manufacturer in his business.

A trade-mark or name is protected only against infringement on articles of the same class. A first user cannot enjoin a second user from use of a mark or name on an article of an entirely different character. Three tests have been applied by the courts in determining whether articles are of the same class.

1. Are the articles so similar that one can be substituted for the other, as cocoa or chocolate?

2. Are the articles allied products, or are they used together, such as automobiles and automobile tires?

3. An association of ideas test: Does one article call the other to mind? Are they usually associated together in retail establishments? Hats and shoes offer an illustration of this group.

Through the adoption of these tests the courts attempt to prevent the confusion of goods by consumers, attempt to make possible the expansion of a line to include new articles similar in nature, and attempt to protect the good will of a business concern from the assault of a predatory competitor or one attempting to profit from the efforts of another.

A second user who makes an improper use of a trade-mark, name, or wrapper can always be enjoined from using it in the future. In addition, if the user is an intentional wrongdoer—if he intentionally profits from the use of another's good will—the injured party may recover damages or the profits of the wrongdoer. In some courts, including the federal courts, the first user may recover both profits and damages. It should be borne in mind, however, that damages or profits can be recovered only in case of intentional wrongdoing. If the second user copies the mark or name exactly or so nearly as to indicate bad faith, damages or profits are recoverable. If the second user has no knowledge of the first user's name or mark, an injunction is the only remedy available in most of the states.

The user of a trade-mark, which is used in interstate commerce, may have it registered with the federal government. If a trade-mark or name is registered a presumption immediately arises that the party registering the mark or name is the first user. This presumption can be rebutted by another's proof of prior use. The first user is protected regardless of registration. However, if it has been registered and used for a period of five years without protest on the part of another user, it then becomes conclusively presumed that the registered user was the first in point of time to make use of the mark. The marks are registered for use with the specific types of merchandise indicated in the application for registration. Descriptive and geographical names which have been used in business for at least one year may receive a limited amount of protection by registering the name with the government. Registration continues for a period of twenty years unless the user or his assignee has abandoned the use of the mark or it has been canceled.

Procedure is also made available for having the registration renewed for an additional twenty years.

Information about one's trade, customers, processes, or manufacture is confidential in nature. If a competitor can discover this information fairly through research, study, or observation, he may use it freely in the absence of a patent or a copyright. However, if he obtains such information by bribery of an employee of the first concern or by engaging an employee of the first concern with the understanding that he will use this information, the second party may be enjoined from making use of it.

In this connection it should be emphasized that an idea once exposed to the public may thereafter be used by anyone. The forward march of civilization is dependent upon the freedom with which new ideas are adopted. A book or magazine article containing new ideas may be copyrighted, but the ideas set forth therein may be used by anyone so long as the language used is not published by another. One who unfolds to an interested party a plan for financing his product or for merging several industries may discover later that the interested party has made use of these ideas without compensating the originator of them. To forestall such a possibility, the originator of the idea should, before explaining his idea, obtain a promise of payment in case his plan is adopted.

CHAPTER 1
REVIEW QUESTIONS AND PROBLEMS

1. Name and discuss the school of legal thought reflected in each of the following judicial statements:

   a. "If a debtor obtains a discharge under an insolvent act, a subsequent promise to pay the debt is regarded as a new contract, supported by the pre-existing moral obligation, as a consideration for the new promise." (Mr. Justice Harns, *Carshore v. Huyck,* 6 Barb. 583 N.Y., 1849)

   b. "We must weigh the purpose to be served, the desire to be gratified, the excuse for the deviation from the letter, the cruelty of enforced adherence." (Mr. Justice Cardozo, *Jacob & Youngs v. Kent,* 230 N.Y. 239, 129 N.E. 889, 1921)

   c. "There must be power in the states and the nation to remould through experience our economic practices and institutions to meet changing social and economic needs. I cannot believe that the framers of the Fourteenth Amendment, or the States which ratified it, intended to deprive us of the power to correct the evils of technological unemployment and excess productive capacity which have attended the progress of useful arts." (Mr. Justice Brandeis dissenting in *New State Ice Co. v. Liebman,* 285 U.S. 262, 276, 1932)

d. "The principle embodied in this exception was established by the old custom of merchants, which 'before the end of the thirteenth century was already conceived as a body of rules which stood apart from common law.' . . . at that stage these rules were applied merely as the general custom of commercial transactions . . . but later became a part of the common law." (*Leventritt, Referee, Brown et al. v. Perera,* 176 N.Y. Supp. 215, 219, 1918)

e. "The word 'law' imports a general rule of conduct with appropriate means for its enforcement declared by some authority possessing sovereign power over the subject; it implies command and not treaty." (Opinion of the Justices, 262 Mass. 603, 160 N.E. 439, 440, 1928)

2. Distinguish between rules of law and "The Law" as an institution.

3. Does man's way of living create and change the law, or does the law influence and change man's way of living? Discuss from the standpoint of historical and analytical schools of thought.

4. Name four areas of law which are classified as a part of the private law.

5. Law has been defined as a scheme of social control. Can this definition be reconciled with Blackstone's definition? Explain.

6. State *X* enacts an open occupancy law which requires owners of real estate to sell their property to any ready, willing, and able buyer regardless of race, creed, or color. Is this law a part of the public law or the private law? Explain.

7. Name the three general categories of crimes and distinguish them from each other.

8. Magnalectric Corporation, a manufacturer of electrical appliances, entered into a contract with its wholesalers, which had for its purpose the control of resale prices. Under the contract the wholesalers promised not to sell Magnalectric commodities below certain stipulated prices and to refrain from selling commodities to retailers who refused to sign price maintenance contracts. *X* induces these wholesalers who signed contracts with Magnalectric to sell below the stipulated price to nonsigner retailers. Has *X* breached any duty? Has he committed a tort?

Law and Society

1-6. The Role of Law—an Ordered Society. In the preceding chapter, law was discussed from the standpoint of its origin; but to speak of the origin or source of law does not tell what law is. In order to determine what it is, we shall consider "The Law" from two points of view. First, law may be considered as the rules enacted or declared by a sovereign or its agencies to be used as a means to regulate and control man, in his relation to man. Second, we may consider that "The Law" is not the rules, but an ordered society, the result which follows from the operation of "the rules."

Thus "The Law" under the first point of view is that great mass of rules found in constitutions, judicial decisions, legislative enactments, city ordinances, and administrative orders which regulate and control man. Laws are nothing more than the rules promulgated by government as a means to an ordered society.

It must be noted that there are other rules which operate as a means of social control—moral and social rules, religious beliefs, family relations, community mores, custom, etc. Chambers of Commerce, fraternities, unions, churches, trade associations, country clubs, athletic clubs, gangs, and all groups that organize for a definite purpose become entities and regulate their members by rules. Such organizations have their own legislative assemblies, however crude, which make by-laws and rules, establish official positions, and give officers power not only to regulate and control their members but also to influence others who are not members. These "Cohesive and Coercive rules" that maintain and control the entity and its members are not rules of law. The sanction that enforces penalties for breach of the rules is within the unit itself. Fines, expulsion, and other disciplinary actions exercised by the entity are not a matter for the state. If however such enforcement of the entity's rules violates contract relations between the members, or the disciplinary action breaches state criminal law, then legal sanctions must be imposed—the state will enforce rules which are "The Law." It is not enough to use the term "Law" simply to mean rules for the regulation of man.

Under the second point of view "The Law" is something more. In a broad and significant sense, "The Law" is a result, it is an established way of thinking and acting which is produced by the rules. It is "Ordered Society." "The Law" is collective conduct which ends in a result—an adjusted ordered social condition. It is a community of peace and well being. It is "an alternative to chaos."

"The Law" is all-pervading; it is an atmosphere or climate. It overlays and operates in all areas of society—in the home, religion, and business. Even at night when one sleeps, "The Law" is present. It is the orderly behavior of others which contributes to the undisturbed occupation of one's home. During the morning drive to work, the conduct of others in exercising due care and caution for the "use of the traffic and way" assures safe arrival. However, if there is non-compliance with the prescribed traffic pattern, the machinery of control and enforcement imposes sanctions by way of fines and imprisonment. Such control is essential in order that the goal—orderly traffic movement—may be achieved. Where non-compliance occurs, the detailed rules concerning specific conduct—rules of law—come into play. In a traffic accident, not only will speed rules and other motor vehicle regulatory rules be involved, but many other legal rules concerning ownership, due care, negligence, agency, insurance, and so forth, also have relevance. The goal sought is traffic safety and order; it is obtained by compliance with the rules.

In order to distinguish between "The Law" as social order and the detailed rules which produce the social order, an illustration from our national pastime, the baseball game, may be helpful. In order to produce a desired result—the game—predetermined rules which make for a controlled activity are essential. These are the "rules of the game." The rules, however important, are not the most significant element. The most significant feature is the game. The game, the totality of all thoughts, rules, and prescribed activity, is a regulated spectacle. Spectators do not carry rule books; umpires do. The spectators are concerned with a performance; they go to see the game—not to check whether the pitcher's mound is so many feet from the home plate. The game is a living, progressive, regulated spectacle, the conduct of which may be relied upon and predicted. The spectator can expect with certainty that during the game the left fielder will not throw the ball over the fence, the hitting batter will not run to third base, nor the pitcher throw the ball into the grandstands. Such conduct would not produce a ball game, but only chaos.

Thus, a ball game in its totality is a controlled and ordered activity, operating under baseball rules. On a greater scale, our social order is "The Law" operating under rules. The important difference is the sanctions imposed for the breach of the rules. There is no appeal from a decision of a baseball umpire to a state court. However, the baseball game is conducted within the orbit of legal order. If a player or spectator commits assault and battery upon the umpire, not only baseball rules but legal rules are violated.

Business relations are broad and comprehensive. Such relations to be effective must comply with rules and operate in an ordered society. Business has to do with supplying human wants. People must be fed, clothed, housed, transported, entertained, secured, and supplied with a multiplicity of goods and services.

As distinct from other relations, business relations and legal problems are ever-present, urgent, and vital. "Doing business" is an everyday affair. A businessman daily enters into a multiplicity of relations, controlled by legal rules, arising out of contracts, title to goods, security transactions, insurance, labor relations, and business institutions. When a decision has to be made, the proper one is more likely to follow if the businessman has some idea of the implications of the law applicable to the problem. Judgment resting on a previous study of law, its history, and its evolution is more likely to produce a correct decision than one made without this background.

Only in an ordered society can business function. Controls that make an ordered society and are enforced by government are *legal* controls. As stated above, there are many non-legal controls and sanctions arising out of organized group action, as well as ethical considerations, that influence the climate within which business operates.

The businessman, in conducting his business, is always faced with the "dilemma of the times." The uncertainty of the economy, influenced day by day and week by week by domestic and international strife, competition, monopolistic power, government regulation, artificially stimulated consumer demands, and price fluctuation, make flexibility a necessity. In making the adjustments necessitated by changing conditions, the businessman is influenced by the social climate and regulated by the law under which he must operate. These rules change and increase in number and complexity with changes in economic, political, and social growth. Business operating in a simple, rural economy was less affected and restrained than business operating in our present complex, technological age. Large populations living in an urban society under centralized government, with mass communication and rapid transit, have greatly affected business activity. Whether the law as an instrumentality of social control is affected by changes in man's way of living, or whether man's way of living is affected by the law, is not always easy to determine. But the law, with which we are concerned, is the final authority.

Law as a social order has been discussed in order that rules of law may be understood and may be made more purposeful and meaningful. As man becomes more civilized and society more organized and complex, there will be more rules of law. It is true that one cannot know all the rules; yet one can know some of the rules and their purpose. Keeping in mind the end result—an ordered society—it will be our purpose in this book to present and discuss specific rules of law as they are applicable to commercial transactions and controversies which arise out of contract relations; the creation and operation of unincorporated and incorporated institutions; the marketing of goods and services; the extension of credit; agency; labor-management relations; and other business conduct.

1-7. The Historical Role of Law in Business. Political, economic, and social changes have each greatly influenced business, but they have not had as great an impact on the development of our industrial society as has the law. Our business climate today of necessity includes substantial legal controls. A brief examination of the beginning and development of our present industrial and free enterprise system will illustrate the role and importance of law in its development. Such an historical analysis also illustrates the reasons for our current legal environment of business.

The historical development of business evolves into epochs or periods. While the division of these periods is not exact, they may be easily used for study. During the primitive period, man was a hunter and limited agriculturist and had little, if any, industry, market system, or government.

After long years of evolution, man ceased his nomad existence, and upon becoming attached to a particular parcel of land, began to develop better agricultural techniques and more utensils and implements. Permanent location and lack of mobility led to a division of labor. Craftsmen began to process goods out of iron, to weave cloth, and to manufacture other articles, first in the home and then in local shops.

The merchant middleman period. Increased population and a demand for goods and services brought about the next stage of development. In order for the local craftsmen to get their articles to the consumer, the merchant middleman became a necessity. During this period, roughly prior to 1760, industry was operated and controlled by small, independent master craftsmen who employed a few employees, classified by experience and trade as apprentices and journeymen. Such was the business system that prevailed in medieval times. The state sustained, upheld, regulated, and controlled most phases of production and merchandising.

The factory-wage earner period. The next stage in the evolution of business, known as the industrial revolution, produced the factory-wage earner system. Out of this system arose the capitalistic free enterprise economy with which we are familiar.

The invention of the steam engine in 1760, the power loom in 1776, other technological developments, colonial expansion, improved transportation, the development of a money economy, the creation of financial institutions and the corporation brought about great changes in production and distribution methods and in employer-employee relationships, and fostered new economic ideas. Spurred by new concepts of freedom introduced by Adam Smith, and by natural law, medieval restrictions on industry and commerce were loosened, permitting the free enterprise system to come into being.

The period of unlimited free enterprise.—Substantive due process. The proponents of natural law, beginning in the seventeenth and eighteenth centuries, asserted that man is guided by a principle, that he is part of nature, and that, as a rational and intelligent man, he acts in conformity with all of his desires and impulses. Conduct based on these ideas was thought to create rules and regulations for a good society —such moral and just principles were regarded as above any rules of law that may be pronounced by government. Thus, legislation inconsistent with natural law was considered to be invalid. This concept of freedom and individualism opened the way for the industrial revolution. The doctrine declared that a man is a free agent and that it was more natural to be unbound than it was to be bound by state control.

Governmental, planned economy was challenged by Adam Smith, who expounded the doctrine "that each man when seeking selfish advantage is led by an invisible hand to promote an end which is no part of his intention; so that individual selfishness is the best means of fostering social welfare." Thus, Smith contended that business and economic progress limited only by the pursuit of each man's selfish interest would better serve society than would regulation and control by the state.

It was recognized as a basic precept of natural law that if man's acquisitive instinct were given free play in trade, and if business and government restraints were reduced to a minimum, the inevitable result would be competitive conduct between free men. Competitive conduct, stimulated by ". . . personal interest . . . [the profit motive] compels each man vigorously and continuously to perfect and multiply the things he sells." It was asserted that the operation of such economic theory would automatically lead, in a free system, to the stabilization of prices, to the improvement of techniques to make better goods, and to increased production. This, it was contended, would bring about full employment and would equalize the distribution of goods and services, thus creating harmony between capital and labor.

The term *laissez-faire,* applied to these principles, is attributed to a French manufacturer who, in response to a government official's inquiry as to what the government could do for industry, replied: "Laissez-nous faire," which translated means "let us alone." "Laissez-faire," as an economic and political doctrine, advocates a minimum of government interference in business affairs. This doctrine became the dominant controlling economic philosophy in the United States, and, after the Civil War, contributed to great industrial growth. The law resting on natural justice and broad ideas of freedom protected men from interference by the government in the free exercise of their acquisitive instinct. Freedom of contract with few legal restraints became a natural right—the contract itself became the law between the parties which the courts must respect and enforce. The liberty of one person was limited only by the principle of like liberty for other persons. Liberty of contract and private property enjoyed constitutional protection from restrictive federal and state legislation, through a new meaning called "substantive due process" found in the Fifth and Fourteenth Amendments to the Federal Constitution. Although the Declaration of Independence does not use the word *property* as an "inalienable right," the word is so used in the Fifth and Fourteenth Amendments. The Fifth Amendment, as applicable to federal legislation, states: "nor be deprived of life, liberty or property without *due process of law*," and the Fourteenth Amendment, as applicable to state legislation, states: "nor shall any state deprive any person of life, liberty or property without *due process of law. . . .*"

Prior to 1850 the words "due process of law" were limited in meaning to judicial procedural methods. That is, "they [due process of law] mean a course of legal proceedings according to those rules and principles which have been established in our system of jurisprudence for the enforcement and protection of private rights . . . according to the law of the land." The idea that no citizen shall be condemned before trial, and that his life, liberty, and property shall enjoy the protection of the general "law of the land" had its origin in the Magna Carta of 1215, which states that "no freeman shall be taken or imprisoned or disseised or exiled or in any way destroyed . . . except by lawful judgment of his peers and by the law of the land."

The meaning of the words "due process of law" did not remain limited to *procedural due process* but, under the influence of individualism and the prevalent laissez-faire doctrine, the words took on a broader meaning, known as "substantive due process." In tracing the development of "substantive due process," the language used by Mr. Justice Field in his *dissenting opinion* in the famous Slaughter-House cases of 1873, concerning the "privileges and immunities" clause of the Fourteenth Amendment— No state shall make or enforce any law which shall abridge the privileges or immunities of citizens of the United States—is significant. In that case the majority of the court upheld a statute that had been enacted in Louisiana regulating the location and operation of slaughter houses for the purpose of protecting the health of the citizens of New Orleans. Justice Field disagreed with the majority and declared that the term "privileges and immunities" in the Fourteenth Amendment "comprehended protection by the government; the enjoyment of life and liberty with the right to acquire and possess property of every kind and to pursue and obtain happiness . . . that these were the great fundamental rights set forth in the act . . . 'as appertaining to every freeman'."

"Substantive due process" as a judicial theory, in conformity with this dissenting opinion, developed to test the constitutional validity of state and federal legislation, which had for its purpose the regulation and control of private property and business enterprises. Under this doctrine when two parties enter into an agreement, or negotiate to enter into an agreement, the legislature has no right to interfere with the negotiation nor to prescribe the terms or the conditions under which the agreement is made or performed. It was early declared by the Supreme Court of the United States, as a judicial policy, that the determination of the legality of state and federal regulatory legislation was a judicial function, not a legislative function. Legislation to meet the requirements of substantive due process had to be reasonable; that is, reasonable in its purpose, reasonable in its means, not arbitrary, and of such character as not to impose unreasonable or arbitrary limitations on freedom of contract, or to unduly restrict the use of private property. The determination of whether legislation is reasonable or unreasonable or "unduly restricts individual life, liberty or property rights more severely than it gives an advantage to the community is a judicial function."

One of the first judicial pronouncements of "substantive due process" is found in the case of *In re Jacobs* (98 N.Y. 98, 1885). The court held that a law forbidding the manufacture of cigars in tenement houses in cities having a population exceeding 500,000 was invalid and stated:

> Generally it is for the legislature to determine what laws and regulations are needed to protect the public health and secure the public comfort and safety. . . . But they must have some relation to these ends. Under the mere guise of police regulations, personal rights and private property cannot be arbitrarily invaded, and the determination of the legislature is not final or conclusive. If it passes an Act, ostensibly for the public health, and thereby destroys or takes away the property of a citizen, or interferes with his personal liberty, then it is for the courts to scrutinize the Act and see whether it really relates to and is convenient and appropriate to promote the public health. It matters not that the legislature may in the title to the Act, or in its body, declare that it is intended for the improvement of the public health. Such a declaration does not conclude the courts, and they must yet determine the fact declared and enforce the supreme law.
>
> Under the guise of promoting the public health the legislature might as well have banished cigar-making from all the cities of the State, or confined it to a single city or town, or have placed under a similar ban the trade of a baker, of a tailor, of a shoemaker, of a woodcarver, or of any other of the innocuous trades carried on by artisans in their homes. The power would have been the same, and its exercise, so far as it concerns fundamental, constitutional rights, could have been justified by the same arguments. Such legislation may invade one class of rights today and another tomorrow, and if it can be sanctioned under the Constitution, while far removed in time we will not be far away in practical statesmanship from those ages when governmental prefects supervised the building of houses, the rearing of cattle, the sowing of seed, and the reaping of grain, and governmental ordinances regulated the movements and labor of artisans, the rate of wages, the price of food, the diet and clothing of the people and a large range of other affairs long since in all civilized lands regarded as outside of governmental functions. Such governmental interferences disturb the normal adjustments of the social fabric, and usually derange the delicate and complicated machinery of industry and cause a score of ills while attempting the removal of one.

In a 1905 opinion by Justice Peckham, the Supreme Court held unconstitutional a New York statute limiting a work day for bakers to ten hours. (*Lochner v. New York*, 198 U.S. 45) In his opinion he defined the limits of substantive due process and established the principle of judicial supremacy over legislation. Justice Peckham stated:

> The statute necessarily interferes with the right of contract between the employer and employees, concerning the number of hours in which the latter may labor in the bakery of the employer. The general right to make a con-

tract in relation to his business is part of the liberty of the individual protected by the fourteenth amendment of the federal Constitution. Under that provision no state can deprive any person of life, liberty or property without due process of law. . . .

. . . In every case that comes before this court, . . . where legislation of this character is concerned, and where the protection of the federal Constitution is sought, the question necessarily arises: Is this a fair, reasonable, and appropriate exercise of the police power of the state, or is it an unreasonable, unnecessary, and arbitrary interference with the right of the individual to his personal liberty, or to enter into those contracts in relation to labor which may seem to him appropriate or necessary for the support of himself and his family? Of course the liberty of contract relating to labor includes both parties to it. The one has as much right to purchase as the other to sell labor. . . .

There is no reasonable ground for interfering with the liberty of person or the right of free contract, by determining the hours of labor, in the occupation of a baker. There is no contention that bakers as a class are not equal in intelligence and capacity to men in other trades or manual occupations, or that they are not able to assert their rights and care for themselves without the protecting arm of the state, interfering with their independence of judgment and of action. They are in no sense wards of the state. . . .

We think the limit of the police power has been reached and passed in this case. There is, in our judgment, no reasonable foundation for holding this to be necessary or appropriate as a health law to safeguard the public health, or the health of the individuals who are following the trade of a baker. If this statute be valid, and if, therefore, a proper case is made out in which to deny the right of an individual *sui juris*, as employer or employee, to make contracts for the labor of the latter under the protection of the provisions of the federal Constitution, there would seem to be no length to which legislation of this nature might not go. . . .

. . . It is unfortunately true that labor, even in any department, may possibly carry with it the seeds of unhealthiness. But are we all, on that account, at the mercy of legislative majorities? A printer, a tinsmith, a locksmith, a carpenter, a cabinetmaker, a dry goods clerk, a bank's, a lawyer's, or a physician's clerk, or a clerk in almost any kind of business, would all come under the power of the legislature, on this assumption. No trade, no occupation, no mode of earning one's living could escape this all-pervading power, and the acts of the legislature in limiting the hours of labor in all employments would be valid, although such limitation might seriously cripple the ability of the laborer to support himself and his family.

. . . Under such circumstances the freedom of master and employee to contract with each other in relation to their employment, and in defining the same, cannot be prohibited or interfered with, without violating the federal Constitution. . . .

The doctrine of judicial supremacy rests on the two theories: the court's acceptance of Adam Smith's assumption "that realization of private pecuniary motives will result in public gain," and the theory that the will of the people, having been expressed in written constitutions which it is the duty of the court to interpret, is superior to the popular will of the people expressed through legislation.

By the end of the nineteenth century and the beginning of the twentieth century the inevitable consequence of unrestrained free competitive conduct upheld by the constitutional theory of due process as pronounced by the courts, reached its climax. The economic strong became stronger; and the economic weak, weaker. The recognition of the impersonal corporation as a person within the protection of the Fifth and Fourteenth Amendments, and the judicial determination that liberty of contract and the right of property were fundamental absolute rights under the due process clauses, both brought about a condition of inequality of bargaining power by which the economically strong had an excess of liberty of contract and the economically weak had little, if any. Under the Darwinian doctrine of the "survival of the fittest," as applied by Herbert Spencer to economics, this condition of economic unbalance justified and tolerated, both politically and legally, made possible the amassing of vast fortunes, the concentration of wealth into the hands of a few and the development of huge monopolies.

The period of limitation on free enterprise. Public reaction to such inequality manifested itself in the early 1900's in vigorous and strong agrarian and labor movements. The laborer, the farmer, and also the small businessman dominated by monopolies sought legislation as a method to equalize unequal bargaining power. It was argued that if "substantive due process" had for its purpose the protection of the liberty of contract, it must necessarily protect liberty of contract for the weak as well as the strong.

Legislation limiting freedom of contract was not new. In order to safeguard the general welfare and aid the overreached, it had long been considered within the *police power* of the states to prevent by legislation fraudulent, usurious, immoral, and illegal contracts. Such contracts had never been sanctioned under the "due process" clause of the Fourteenth Amendment. Whether these particular contracts were detrimental to the safety, health, morals, and general welfare of the community and were under police power came to be recognized as a matter for legislative judgment—judicial supremacy gave way to such legislative judgment. It was soon discovered that unemployment, long hours of work, low wages, unsafe and unhealthful working conditions, price irregularities, overreaching the consumer, and monopolistic controls of commodities had a deleterious effect upon the general welfare and were a matter of public concern that could be effectively ameliorated only by legislation. By 1937, it was realized "that freedom of contract is a qualified and not an absolute right. There are no absolute rights to do as one wills or to contract as one chooses. The guarantee of liberty does not withdraw from legislative supervision that wide area of activity which consists in making contracts, nor does it deny to government the power to provide restrictive safeguards. Liberty implies absence of arbitrary restraint, not immunity from reasonable regulations and prohibitions imposed in the interests of the community." (Mr. Justice Hughes in *West Coast Hotel Co. v. Parrish,* 300 U.S. 379)

New boundaries were being found for "substantive due process of law." New meanings were given by the courts to the words, by limiting judicial supremacy and by evaluating what the legislature *could do,* not what the Supreme Court thought it should do. Police power through legislative encroachment on business expanded, and constitutional protection by the Supreme Court of freedom of contract retreated. Legislation equalizing bargaining power became recognized as a proper function of the state. Whether the legislation was justified and reasonable was held to be primarily a matter for the state and it was not the function of the court to nullify because in the court's judgment the legislation might be outside the "vague contours of due process."

The question whether social and economic regulatory legislation impinges upon freedom of contract and business activity and is in violation of due process of law, was no longer regarded as an exclusive function of the judiciary. Whether such legislation is reasonable, whether it concerns itself with a fit subject, whether it is economically sound and socially desirable, rests with the legislative branch of government. Of course, if the law is unreasonable, arbitrary, or capricious and the means selected do not have a real and substantial relationship to the object sought to be obtained, such law is not consistent with due process and is constitutionally invalid.

This principle was enunciated as early as 1905 by Mr. Justice Holmes in his famous *dissenting* opinion in the case of *Lochner v. New York* (198 U.S. 45) which, as previously noted, held a New York statute regulating the workday hours for bakers in violation of due process and unconstitutional. Mr. Justice Holmes stated:

> This case is decided upon an economic theory which a large part of the country does not entertain. If it were a question whether I agreed with that theory, I should desire to study it further and long before making up my mind. But I do not conceive that to be my duty, because I strongly believe that my agreement or disagreement has nothing to do with the right of a majority to embody their opinions in law. It is settled by various decisions of this court that state Constitutions and state laws may regulate life in many ways which we as legislators might think as injudicious, or if you like as tyrannical as this, and which, equally with this, interfere with the liberty to contract. Sunday laws and usury laws are ancient examples. A more modern one is the prohibition of lotteries. The liberty of the citizen to do as he likes so long as he does not interfere with the liberty of others to do the same, which has been a shibboleth for some well-known writers, is interfered with by school laws, by the post-office, by every state or municipal institution which takes his money for purposes thought desirable, whether he likes it or not.
>
> The fourteenth amendment does not enact Mr. Herbert Spencer's Social Statics. The other day we sustained the Massachusetts vaccination law. *Jacobson v. Massachusetts,* 197 U.S. 11, 25 S.Ct. 358, 49 L.Ed. 643, 3 Ann.Cas. 765. United States and state statutes and decisions cutting down the liberty to contract by way of combination are familiar to this court. *Northern Securities Co. v. United States,* 193 U.S. 197, 24 S.Ct. 436, 48 L.Ed. 679 . . . Some of these laws embody convictions or prejudices which judges are likely to share. Some may not. But a Constitution is not intended to embody a particular economic theory, whether of paternalism and the organic relation of the citizen to the state or of laissez-faire. It is made for people of fundamentally differing views, and the accident of our finding certain opinions natural and

familiar, or novel, and even shocking, ought not to conclude our judgment upon the question whether statutes embodying them conflict with the Constitution of the United States. . . .

I think that the word "liberty," in the fourteenth amendment, is perverted when it is held to prevent the natural outcome of a dominant opinion, unless it can be said that a rational and fair man necessarily would admit that the statute proposed would infringe fundamental principles as they have been understood by the traditions of our people and our law.

The doctrine expressed in Mr. Justice Holmes' dissenting opinion was gradually adopted by the courts. By 1934 liberty of contract and the right to use one's property as one pleases, even though admitted to be fundamental rights, became amenable to social needs and subject to legislative control. An explanation of this principle and its implication are set out by Justice Roberts in the case of *Nebbia v. People of the State of New York* (291 U.S. 502, 1934), in the following language:

. . . Under our form of government the use of property and the making of contracts are normally matters of private and not of public concern. The general rule is that both shall be free of governmental interference. But neither property rights nor contract rights are absolute; for government cannot exist if the citizens may at will use his property to the detriment of his fellows, or exercise his freedom of contract to work them harm. Equally fundamental with the private right is that of the public to regulate it in the common interest.

The Fifth Amendment, in the field of federal activity, and the Fourteenth, as respects state action, do not prohibit governmental regulation for the public welfare. They merely condition the exertion of the admitted power, by securing that the end shall be accomplished by methods consistent with due process. And the guaranty of due process, as has often been held, demands only that the law shall not be unreasonable, arbitrary, or capricious, and that the means selected shall have a real and substantial relation to the object sought to be attained. It results that a regulation valid for one sort of business or in given circumstances, may be invalid for another sort, or for the same business under other circumstances, because the reasonableness of each regulation depends upon the relevant facts.

The reports of our decisions abound with cases in which the citizen, individual or corporate, has vainly invoked the Fourteenth Amendment in resistance to necessary and appropriate exertion of the police power.

The court has repeatedly sustained curtailment of enjoyment of private property, in the public interest. The owner's rights may be subordinated to the needs of other private owners whose pursuits are vital to the paramount interests of the community. The state may control the use of property in various ways; may prohibit advertising bill boards except of a prescribed size and location, or their use for certain kinds of advertising; may in certain circumstances authorize encroachments by party walls in cities; may fix the height of buildings, the character of materials, and methods of construction, the adjoining area which must be left open, and may exclude from residential sections offensive trades, industries and structures likely injuriously to affect the public health or safety; or may establish zones within which certain types of buildings or businesses are permitted and others excluded. And although the Fourteenth Amendment extends protection to aliens as well as citizens, a state may for adequate reasons of policy exclude aliens altogether from the use and occupancy of land.

Laws passed for the suppression of immorality, in the interest of health, to secure fair trade practices, and to safeguard the interests of depositors in banks, have been found consistent with due process. These measures not only affected the use of private property, but also interfered with the right of private contract. Other instances are numerous where valid regulation has restricted the right of contract, while less directly affecting property rights.

The Constitution does not guarantee the unrestricted privilege to engage in a business or to conduct it as one pleases.

A revised version of "substantive due process of law" which recognizes judicial restraint and gives deference to legislative judgment as advocated in Justice Holmes' dissenting opinion has now become the law of the land. Mr. Justice Black in *Lincoln Federal Labor v. Northwestern Iron & Metal Co.* (335 U.S. 526, 1949) speaking of such new concept of "substantive due process of law," states:

> This Court beginning at least as early as 1934, when the Nebbia case was decided, has steadily rejected the due process philosophy enunciated in the [Lochner] line of cases. In doing so it has consciously returned closer and closer to the earlier constitutional principle that states have power to legislate against what are found to be injurious practices in their internal commercial and business affairs, so long as their laws do not run afoul of some specific federal constitutional prohibition, or of some valid federal law. Under this constitutional doctrine the due process clause is no longer to be so broadly construed that the Congress and state legislatures are put in a straight jacket when they attempt to suppress business and industrial conditions which they regard as offensive to the public welfare.
>
> Appellants now ask us to return, at least in part, to the due process philosophy that has been deliberately discarded. Claiming that the Federal Constitution itself affords protection for union members against discrimination, they nevertheless assert that the same Constitution forbids a state from providing the same protection for non-union members. Just as we have held that the due process clause erects no obstacle to block legislative protection of union members, we now hold that legislative protection can be afforded non-union workers.

Thus the doctrines of judicial restraint and deference to legislative judgment have enlarged the scope of state police power, and have ushered in the new concept of due process.

Federal limitation of free enterprise—interstate commerce. Not only has state police power been enlarged under a new application of due process, but there has also developed a like power in the federal government. In the exercise of powers granted to it by the Constitution, the federal government also exercises powers that are concerned with the welfare, safety, health, and morals of the people.

In the exercise of its constitutional power to regulate and control commerce among the several states, Congress has not only power to protect interstate commerce, but authority to adopt measures "to promote its growth, insure its safety, foster, protect, control, restrain and remove burdens and obstructions at its source" which may interfere with its flow. The burdens and obstructions which interfere with the flow of interstate commerce may be concerned with the health and safety of laborers, the welfare of the community, and the economy of the nation. In sustaining the Federal Fair Labor Standards Act setting standards for hours and wages by excluding from interstate commerce goods manufactured in violation of the Act, the Supreme Court held that the power to regulate commerce among the several states included, in addition to the power to regulate *interstate* commerce, the power to regulate activities *intrastate* which so affect interstate commerce as to make regulation of such intrastate matters appropriate means to the attainment of a legitimate end; the exercise of the granted power of Congress to regulate interstate commerce.[1]

The enlargement of the scope of federal regulatory powers under the extension of the commerce clause covers nearly every aspect of business. For example, the public accommodation provisions of the Civil Rights statute of 1964 were passed under the commerce power rather than the due process clause or the equal protection clause of the Federal Constitution which are usually invoked in civil rights matters. Some legal scholars believe that the federal government may regulate *any* activity under the commerce clause as interpreted by the Supreme Court.

Such is a far cry from the judicial policy advocated by the United States Supreme Court in 1888, in the case of *Kidd v. Pearson,* in which the court stated:

> If it be held that the term (interstate commerce) includes the regulation of all such manufactures as are intended to be the subject of commercial transactions in the future, it is impossible to deny that it would also include all productive industries that contemplate the same thing. The result would be that Congress would be invested, to the exclusion of the states, with the power to regulate not only manufacturing, but also agriculture, horticulture, stock raising, domestic fisheries, mining—in short every branch of human industry.

Federal limitation-taxing power.   In the exercise of the taxing power, Congress has, in addition, regulated the sale of commodities.

Under its power to tax for the general welfare set out in the Constitution, Congress enacted in 1935 the Social Security Act. It was assailed on the ground that the act permitted the federal government to invade the reserved powers of the states, and engage in a function limited to the states. The constitutionality of the act was upheld in *Steward Machine Co. v. Davis*. The court in its opinion found that:

> . . . during the years 1929 to 1936, when the country was passing through a cyclical depression, the number of unemployed mounted to unprecedented heights. . . . The fact developed that the states were unable to give requisite

1 *U.S. v. Darby Lumber Co.,* page 39.

relief and the problem had become national in area and dimension. . . . In the presence of this urgent need for some remedial expedient, the question is to be answered whether the expedient adopted has overleaped the bounds of power.

The court recognized "that every tax is in some measure regulatory" and imposes an economic burden on the activity taxed, and that even though general welfare may be a local burden, the Social Security Act "is an attempt to find a method by which all public agencies may work together for a common end." Said the court, "It is too late today for the argument to be heard with tolerance that in a crisis so extreme the use of moneys of the nation to relieve the unemployed and their dependents is a use for any other purpose narrower than the promotion of the general welfare."

Recent federal legislation. The various sources of Congressional power have been used in the enactment of statutes relating to civil rights, fair housing, voting privileges, jury duty and other activities pertaining to equality of citizenship. Medicare, expanded social security and other social legislation designed to eliminate poverty and stimulate economic and educational opportunities, are additional examples.

These enactments are possible through application of due process, equal protection of the laws, the commerce clause, and the taxing power found in the Constitution of the United States.

1-8. The Contemporary Legal Climate.

Our contemporary legal climate as well as the historical developments of the law and business may be described in terms of bigness—big business, big unions, and big government. Big business as typified by big corporation has developed notwithstanding extensive governmental regulation. Since 1932 national and state legislation affecting almost every aspect of business has been enacted.

Government today has expanded its regulatory power into many areas of business and labor and is no longer limited to enforcing contracts, protecting property, and maintaining order. The growth in size and influence of unions and corporations is one of the important features of the modern legal climate. In reality, however, the most significant problems of the day are reflected more in the interaction of *law* as between government, corporations, and labor than in the status of the large corporation and the role of the big union. One cannot read a newspaper today without noting the gradual evolution of a new role of government in respect to labor and business and the relationships between them.

The present status of the large corporation, however, reflects the newly developing relationships. It is now recognized that the large corporation has evolved into a social as well as economic institution. Business must be concerned with the effect of its decisions on the public; and in the formulation of policy, the public interest must be taken into account.

Big unions. In the last decade labor organizations just as industrial corporations before them have grown to enormous size and great power. Through collective bargaining and legislation at both the state and national levels wages have increased and conditions of employment have improved. In addition many fringe benefits such as medical care, vacation with pay, profit sharing plans and pensions, have been achieved. A national labor policy designed to create equality of bargaining power between management and labor in order that collective bargaining will settle labor-management disputes has resulted in strong and vigorous unions. The development of a strong independent labor movement as a part of our American institutions has made possible the possession, exercise, and control of great economic power by labor leaders. This power has been recognized and frequently criticized. These leaders, it is charged by Raskin in an article entitled "The Squeeze on Unions" which appeared in the *Atlantic Monthly* in 1961: "sit behind lordly desks in glass and marble headquarters of giant unions . . . command huge treasuries; . . . have a controlling voice in investments of billions of dollars of pensions and welfare funds; their strike calls can plunge vital industries into long periods of idleness; their political machinery can influence the democratic process by persuading hundreds of thousands of workers and their families to register and vote." It is asserted also in the *U.S. Code Congressional and Administrative News* (1959), that the abuse of power ". . . by union officers for personal financial advantage under cover of conflicts of interest has corrupted, undermined and weakened the labor movement. . . . The government which vests in labor unions the power to act as exclusive bargaining representatives must make sure that the power is used for the benefit of the workers and not for personal benefit."

Just as business is subject to governmental regulation so also is big labor. For example, in order to correct these abuses, Congress in 1959 passed the Labor Management Reporting and Disclosure Act, known as the "Landrum-Griffin Act" (29 U.S.C.A. Sec. 141-187), "to provide for the reporting and disclosure of certain financial transactions and administrative practices of labor organizations and employers, to prevent abuses in the administration of the trusteeships by labor organizations, to provide standards with respect to the election of officers of labor organizations, establish an advisory committee on ethical practices and permit relationships between the National Labor Relations Board and state agencies. . . ."

Big government. In our early history, it was the policy in the United States that government had for its only object the maintaining of law and order, so that the greatest freedom would be permitted to its citizens. It was felt, since government operated under a system of checks and balances, it could not be an effective instrument for conducting business transactions. On the other hand, since business has for its prime purpose the efficient, economical production and distribution of goods and services, it was asserted that business could, when left free to function, care for the needs of society.

Such, however, was not the result. Monopolistic control of wealth, national emergencies such as wars, economic depressions, and public disasters have brought about great public needs which required government intervention for solution. Since World War I government has assumed many functions previously limited to private organizations and individuals, and in addition many new ones previously thought unnecessary. Government now operates directly, or regulates and controls activities in the fields of land management, transportation, agriculture, manufacturing, distribution, credit, insurance, construction, health, welfare, education, and equal opportunities of employment, housing, Medicare and other areas.

The bigness of government is illustrated by data shown in the *Statistical Abstract of the United States* 1960, wherein the following information is given concerning the operation of "Federal Business-Type Activities." The principal assets and liabilities involved in carrying out such activities for the year 1959 were 112 billion, 448 million dollars. Of these assets, "Public enterprise funds" equal 24 billion, 935 million dollars.[2] These are administered by the Department of Agriculture, Farm Credit Corporation, Housing and Home Finance Agency, Federal Savings and Loan Insurance Corporation, Small Business Administration, Export-Import Bank, Tennessee Valley Authority, Panama Canal Company, Veterans Administration, General Services Administration, Treasury Department, the Post Office, the Interior Department, and the Atomic Energy Commission.

Over the past fifty years there has been a progressive expansion of government regulations and control of business consistent with the growth and expansion of the big corporations and big unions. A partial survey of big government is enough to give some idea of the extent of government bigness and its participation in business decisions: Decisions affecting prices, advertising, mergers, discounts, labor relations, plant locations and even the continued existence of a business are regulated by laws and by governmental activity pursuant to law. Law in all its facets is a partner in the operation of a business and is the tool by which government participates in the management of industrial America.

1-9. Law and Ethics. The contemporary ideas of society with regard to ethics and morality exert a profound influence upon the law. This influence is an integral part of the legal philosophy represented by the Natural Law school of legal thought. Since natural law plays an important part in our law, the issues of whether all that is legal must be moral, or the converse, merits discussion. If an act is legal, is it *ipso facto* moral? If an act is immoral, is it *ipso facto* illegal? The answers to these questions will vary depending on the subject matter. Laws are not the only rules of conduct which govern men. Man also conforms to fashions, to manners, to customs, to conventional standards, and to precepts of morality. Through

---

[2] Subsequent Statistical Abstractions do not carry these totals under the heading "Federal Business-Type Activities."

group pressures people are subject to all kinds of economic ideologies and political theories. These ideologies and theories may express both moral principles and rules of law. Some may be moral rules outside of and concerned with rules of law, and some moral rules may be partially within and partially outside of rules of law. For example, the moral principle, "Thou shalt not steal," is not only a moral rule but a legal rule. Stealing is a crime, which, depending on the value of the property stolen, may be either grand or petty larceny. Gossiping, indolence, and intemperance may be immoral but not necessarily illegal. However, if by gossip slanderous statements are made which injure another, then gossiping becomes illegal. Whether illegal conduct is moral, or moral conduct is illegal, becomes a close question.

What conduct is considered legal and moral or illegal and immoral changes from time to time. Formerly the ownership of slaves and the employment of child labor were regarded by many as neither immoral nor illegal. However, as such conduct took on strong moral implications and met with public disapproval, it likewise became illegal. Segregation and the sale of fireworks offer striking examples of what formerly were considered both moral and legal but now are illegal, although by many not considered immoral. Gambling is by some considered immoral, yet some aspects of gambling are not illegal, though other aspects may be both immoral and illegal. Standards of morality vary from place to place and from time to time. The manufacture and sale of intoxicating liquor is another illustration of conduct that has at different times been moral and legal, immoral and illegal, illegal and moral, and to some immoral although legal. Another illustration of how changing moral standards affect legal standards is found in the law of the sale of goods. In early, less complex society, trading and sales transactions were face-to-face affairs. The seller and buyer, standing before each other with equal bargaining capacity, dickered over the specific article before them. The deal was a duel of cleverness and wits. Equality of bargaining power was always assumed, leaving room for much talk. Out of this "dealers' talk" developed the legal doctrine of *caveat emptor,* "let the buyer beware." Extravagant statements, overreaching, and "pulling a fast deal," were considered accomplishments rather than vices. The range of what was considered fair play was wide, and, as between equally clever parties, fraud and deceit were hard to uncover.

In today's complex technological and machine age, with its great productive capacity accompanied by extensive advertising and mass marketing and distributing systems, the uninformed buyer-consumer does not stand in equal bargaining position with trained sellers and producers. Many buyers today, even upon inspection of the desired article, understand little of the quality, character, construction, and operational capacity of complicated merchandise such as refrigerators, washing machines, television and radio sets, and automobiles; or the content and quality of drugs, cosmetics, and other synthetic materials. By the very nature of the case, equal bargaining power is impossible. Therefore, purchase order forms and printed devices containing schemes to evade liability by way of disclaimer of warranties hidden in fine print in standardized sales contracts take on moral considerations.

The seller of merchandise by implication warrants the merchantability and general fitness of the article sold. Automobile manufacturers and dealers have sought to eliminate this liability by placing in the contract of sale a disclaimer which relieves the manufacturer of liability. In discussing such disclaimer, the court in *Henningsen v. Bloomfield Motor, Inc.* (N.J., 161 A.2d 69, 1960), states:

> The terms of the warranty (disclaimer) are a sad commentary upon automobile manufacturers' marketing practices. Warranties developed in the law in the interest of and to protect the ordinary consumer who cannot be expected to have the knowledge or capacity or even the opportunity to make adequate inspection of mechanical instrumentalities like automobiles and to decide for himself whether they are reasonably fit for the designed purpose. . . . But the ingenuity of the Automobile Manufacturers Association by means of its standardized form has metamorphosed the warranty into a device to limit the maker's liability. . . .
>
> Under modern conditions the ordinary layman on responding to the importuning of colorful advertising has neither the opportunity nor the capacity to inspect or to determine the fitness of an automobile for use; he must rely on the manufacturer who has control of its construction, and to some degree on the dealer who to a limited extent called for by the manufacturer's instructions, inspects and services it before delivery. In such marketing milieu his remedies and those of persons who properly claim through him should not depend upon the intricacies of the law of sales. The obligation should not be based along on the privity of contract. It should rest . . . upon the demands of social justice. . . .
>
> The traditional contract is the result of free bargaining of parties who are brought together by the play of the market, and who meet each other on the footing of approximate economic equality. In such a society there is no danger that freedom of contract will be a threat to the social order as a whole. But in the present day commercial life the standardized mass contract has appeared. It is used primarily by enterprises with strong bargaining power and position. "The weaker party in need of the goods or services is frequently not in position to shop around for better terms, either because the author of the standard contract has a monopoly (natural or artificial) or because all competitors use the same clauses. His contractual intention is but a subjection more or less voluntary to terms dictated by the stronger party terms whose consequences are often understood in a vague way, if at all." . . . Such standardized contracts have been described as those in which one predominant party will dictate its law to an undetermined multiple rather than to an individual. They are said to resemble a law rather than a meeting of the minds. . . . The gross inequality of bargaining position occupied by the consumer in the automobile industry is [thus] apparent. Such control and limitation of his remedies are inimical to public welfare and at the very least call for great care by the courts to avoid injustice through the application of strict common-law principles of freedom of contract.

Dealers' talk and contractual arrangements between sellers and buyers, formerly considered moral and legal, may now be considered deceitful, fraudulent, overreaching, immoral, and illegal. Consumers, no longer equal with sellers, are vulnerable to all types of deceptive merchandising practices: price manipulation; false advertising; extravagant statements about additives in miracle drugs, cosmetics, and food products; undisclosed interest rates and financial charges in installment contracts; and extreme advertising and promotional schemes. Consequently, legal duties founded on moral sanctions are being imposed upon manufacturers, processors, distributors and sellers under the doctrine of *caveat venditor,* "let the seller beware." The old doctrine of *caveat emptor* is passing from the scene.

LAW AND SOCIETY CASE

United States v. Darby Lumber Co.
312 U.S. 100 (1941)

The Darby Lumber Co. was indicted for violating the Fair Labor Standards Act. The Federal District Court quashed the indictment, holding the Act to be unconstitutional and the government appealed directly to the Supreme Court.

The Fair Labor Standards Act contained minimum wage and maximum hour requirements for employees engaged in interstate commerce or the production of goods for interstate commerce. The purpose of the statute was to insure minimum standards of living necessary for health and general well-being for workers.

Defendant was engaged in manufacturing lumber and did pay its employees less than the minimum wage and worked them more than the maximum hours per week without paying overtime. Defendant also did not keep the records required by the Act. The lower court held that manufacturing is not interstate commerce and is therefore beyond the powers of Congress to regulate.

The constitutionality of the statute under the commerce clause of the Constitution as it relates to the manufacture of lumber is the issue before the court.

STONE, J. . . . While manufacture is not of itself interstate commerce, the shipment of manufactured goods interstate is such commerce and the prohibition of such shipment by Congress is indubitably a regulation of the commerce. The power to regulate commerce is the power "to prescribe the rule by which commerce is governed." (*Gibbons v. Ogden,* 9 Wheat. 1, 196) It extends not only to those regulations which aid, foster and protect the commerce, but embraces those which prohibit it. . . . It is conceded that the power of Congress to prohibit transportation in interstate commerce includes noxious articles, . . . , stolen articles, . . . kidnapped persons, . . . and articles such as intoxicating liquor or convict made goods, traffic in which is forbidden or restricted by the laws of the state of destination. . . .

But it is said that the present prohibition falls within the scope of none of these categories; that while the prohibition is nominally a regulation of the commerce its motive or purpose is regulation of wages and hours of persons engaged in manufacture, the control of which has been reserved to the states and upon which Georgia and some of the states of destination have placed no restriction; that the effect of the present statute is not to exclude the proscribed articles from interstate commerce in aid of state regulation . . . , but instead, under the guise of a regulation of interstate commerce, it undertakes to regulate wages and hours within the state contrary to the policy of the state which has elected to leave them unregulated.

The power of Congress over interstate commerce "is complete in itself, may be exercised to its utmost extent, and acknowledges no limitations other than are prescribed in the Constitution." . . . That power can neither be enlarged nor diminished by the exercise or non-exercise of state power. . . . Congress, following its own conception of public policy concerning the restrictions which may appropriately be imposed on interstate commerce, is free to exclude from the commerce articles whose use in the states for which they are destined it may conceive to be injurious to the public health, morals or welfare, even though the state has not sought to regulate their use. . . .

Such regulation is not a forbidden invasion of state power merely because either its motive or its consequence is to restrict the use of articles of commerce within the States of destination; and is not prohibited unless by other Constitutional provisions. It is no objection to the assertion of the power to regulate interstate commerce that its exercise is attended by the same incidents which attend the exercise of the police power of the states. . . .

The motive and purpose of the present regulation are plainly to make effective the Congressional conception of public policy that interstate commerce should not be made the instrument of competition in the distribution of goods produced under substandard labor conditions, which competition is injurious to the commerce and to the states from and to which the commerce flows. The motive and purpose of a regulation of interstate commerce are matters for the legislative judgment upon the exercise of which the Constitution places no restriction and over which the courts are given no control. . . . "The judicial cannot prescribe to the legislative department of the government limitations upon the exercise of its acknowledged power." (*Veazie Bank v. Fenno,* 8 Wall. 533) Whatever their motive and purpose, regulations of commerce which do not infringe some constitutional prohibition are within the plenary power conferred on Congress by the Commerce Clause. Subject only to that limitation, presently to be considered, we conclude that the prohibition of the shipment interstate of goods produced under the forbidden substandard labor conditions is within the constitutional authority of Congress.

In the more than a century which has elapsed since the decision of *Gibbons v. Ogden,* these principles of constitutional interpretation have been so long and repeatedly recognized by this Court as applicable to the

Commerce Clause, that there would be little occasion for repeating them now were it not for the decision of this Court twenty-two years ago in *Hammer v. Dagenhart,* 247 U.S. 251. In that case it was held by a bare majority of the Court over the powerful and now classic dissent of Mr. Justice Holmes setting forth the fundamental issues involved, that Congress was without power to exclude the products of child labor from interstate commerce. The reasoning and conclusion of the Court's opinion there cannot be reconciled with the conclusion which we have reached, that the power of Congress under the Commerce Clause is plenary to exclude any article from interstate commerce subject only to the specific prohibitions of the Constitution.

Hammer v. Dagenhart has not been followed. The distinction on which the decision was rested that Congressional power to prohibit interstate commerce is limited to articles which in themselves have some harmful or deleterious property—a distinction which was novel when made and unsupported by any provision of the Constitution—has long since been abandoned. . . . The thesis of the opinion that the motive of the prohibition or its effect to control in some measure the use or production within the states of the article thus excluded from the commerce can operate to deprive the regulation of its constitutional authority has long since ceased to have force . . . (cases cited). And finally we have declared "The authority of the federal government over interstate commerce does not differ in extent or character from that retained by the states over intrastate commerce." (*United States v. Rock Royal Cooperative,* 307 U.S. 533, 569)

The conclusion is inescapable that *Hammer v. Dagenhart* was a departure from the principles which have prevailed in the interpretation of the Commerce Clause both before and since the decision and that such vitality, as a precedent, as it then had has long since been exhausted. It should be and now is overruled.

There remains the question whether such restriction on the production of goods for commerce is a permissible exercise of the commerce power. The power of Congress over interstate commerce is not confined to the regulation of commerce among the states. It extends to those activities intrastate which so affect interstate commerce or the exercise of the power of Congress over it as to make regulation of them appropriate means to the attainment of a legitimate end, the exercise of the granted power of Congress to regulate interstate commerce. . . .

Congress has sometimes left it to the courts to determine whether the intrastate activities have the prohibited effect on the commerce, as in the Sherman Act. It has sometimes left it to an administrative board or agency to determine whether the activities sought to be regulated or prohibited have such effect as in the case of the Interstate Commerce Act, and the National Labor Relations Act, or whether they come within the statutory definition of the prohibited Act, as in the Federal Trade Commission Act. And sometimes Congress itself has said that a particular activity affects the commerce, as it did in the present Act, the Safety Appliance Act and the Railway Labor Act. In passing on the validity of legislation of the class last mentioned the only function of courts is to determine whether the particular activity regulated or prohibited is within the reach of the federal power. . . .

Congress, having by the present Act adopted the policy of excluding from interstate commerce all goods produced for the commerce which do not conform to the specified labor standards, it may choose the means reasonably adapted to the attainment of the permitted end, even though they involved control of intrastate activities. Such legislation has often been sustained with respect to powers, other than the commerce power granted to the national government, when the means chosen, although not themselves within the granted power, were nevertheless deemed appropriate aids to the accomplishment of some purpose within an admitted power of the national government. . . . A familiar like exercise of power is the regulation of intrastate transactions which are so commingled with or related to interstate commerce that all must be regulated if the interstate commerce is to be effectively controlled. . . .

The means adopted for the protection of interstate commerce by the suppression of the production of the condemned goods for interstate commerce is so related to the commerce and so affects it as to be within the reach of the commerce power. See *Currin v. Wallace, supra,* 11. Congress, to attain its objective in the suppression of nationwide competition in interstate commerce by goods produced under substandard labor conditions, has made no distinction as to the volume or amount of shipments in the commerce or of production for commerce by any particular shipper or producer. It recognized that in present day industry, competition by a small part may affect the whole and that the total effect of the competition of many small producers may be great. . . .

Our conclusion is unaffected by the Tenth Amendment. . . . The amendment states but a truism that all is retained which has not been surrendered. There is nothing in the history of its adoption to suggest that it was more than declaratory of the relationship between the national and state government as it had been established by the Constitution before the amendment or that its purpose was other than to allay fears that the new national government might seek to exercise powers not granted, and that the states might not be able to exercise fully their reserved powers. . . .

From the beginning and for many years the amendment has been construed as not depriving the national government of authority to resort to all means for the exercise of a granted power which are appropriate and plainly adapted to the permitted end. . . .

Reversed.

CHAPTER 2
REVIEW QUESTIONS AND PROBLEMS

1. The meaning of "due process of law" in the Fourteenth Amendment is now fundamentally different from that in 1905. Illustrate by appropriate cases how this difference came about.
2. Distinguish "law" as social order and "law" as detailed rules.
3. During a national emergency the legislature of state *A* passed an act which authorized the district courts of the counties to extend the period of redemption from foreclosure sales, "for such additional time as the court may deem just and equitable." How can this legislation be harmonized with the obligations of contract and due process clauses of the Fourteenth Amendment? (Home Building & Loan Assn. v. Blaisdell, 290 U.S. 398, 1934)
4. An independent contractor enters into a contract to clean windows and do janitor work for a manufacturer who produces articles, part of which are shipped in interstate commerce. The window-washing contractor's employees are employed under conditions less than the minimum required by the Fair Labor Standards Act. A suit is brought to enjoin the contractor from violating the act. Decide the case. (Tobin v. Johnson, 198 F.2d 130, 1952)
5. Are there business activities which are beyond the power of the federal government to regulate? Explain.
6. What factors contributed to the growth of big unions?
7. "The state has power to prevent the individual from making certain kinds of contracts, and in regard to them the Federal Constitution offers no protection." May a state in the exercise of its police power prohibit gambling contracts, contracts for the sale of narcotics, tobacco, fireworks, oleomargarine, birth-control devices, obscene literature, and contracts which include waiver of the warranty for fitness, use and purpose of commodities offered for sale?
8. The words "due process" cannot be defined with exactness. It is certain that these words imply a conformity with natural and inherent principles of justice. To what authority is left the task of determining what are "natural and inherent principles of justice"?
9. "It has never been supposed, since the adoption of the Constitution, that the business of the butcher, the baker, the tailor, the woodchopper, the mining operator, or the miner was clothed with such public interest that the price of his conduct or his wages could be fixed by state regulation." Justify this statement by an economic theory.

chapter 3

Sources of Law

1-10. Introduction. As previously noted, it is not possible to give a simple definition of law or tell exactly from whence it came. Law does not "just happen." It does not spring into existence in full form. Law in its beginning was associated with religion. Its source was thought to be in God or gods. The earliest code of laws appearing over four thousand years ago in Babylon was reputedly handed down by the city god. Likewise, a thousand years later the Hebrew God is said to have given the Ten Commandments to Moses. In Rome the priests were the givers of law, its custodians, and adjudicators of its application. Later it was recognized that law developed out of custom and was said to be man-made in compliance with the Law of Nature.

These indirect or "informal sources" furnished the law which later became formalized into statutes and court decisions. As society became more complex, man found it necessary to make or write his law—this was done by legislative bodies. Such formal law is called *written* law. Law developed by the courts, or judge-made law is formal law although it is sometime called "unwritten" in order to distinguish it from statutory law. It is formal in the sense that the opinions which support and explain the decisions of reviewing courts are written by the judges and bound into volumes so that lawyers may study the principles of law which form the basis of the decisions. This case law, known as "common law," is in effect law created by precedent. The term "common law" is also used to distinguish between the English system of law and the systems of law developed in other sections of the world.

The source of the early American "common law" or judge-made law was the English law. The American colonists were governed by charters granted by the King of England. These charters were general in their nature and left much to be worked out by the people of the colonies. Since most of the colonists were of English origin, they naturally were controlled by the laws and customs of their mother country. In Louisiana, and to some extent in Texas and California and a few other states, the civil law or the Roman law has influenced their legal systems, because the colonies which were the forerunners of these states were founded by French and Spanish peoples. The law of Continental Europe and South America is based more directly upon the Roman law and its modern counterparts—a codified or statutory system of law as opposed to law created by precedents established by the courts. The Civil law is a system of law which is predicated upon a written codification of all the laws so that when a dispute arises the applicable law is found in the massive compilations or codes. The law is determined in advance and is compiled and classified. Of course, much of the law in "common law" countries is statutory. Probably, in simplest terms, it can be said that Civil law operates predominantly on the basis of statutes, while the common law emphasizes law which is created when courts decide controversies in reliance upon precedents.

Another source of law which developed early in this country and which has in recent years become of primary importance is administrative agencies. These agencies which operate at all levels of government make "law" by promulgating rules and regulations as well as by adjudicating matters within their jurisdiction.

In summary, our law comes from written laws such as constitutions, statutes, and ordinances, from so-called "unwritten law" which is judge-made by judicial decision, and from the rules and decisions of administrative agencies. Each of these sources will be more fully discussed in the sections which follow.

WRITTEN LAW

1-11. Constitutions. The Constitution of the United States and the constitutions of the various states are the fundamental written law in this country. Article VI of the Constitution of the United States provides: "This Constitution and the laws of the United States which shall be made in pursuance thereof, and all treaties made, or which shall be made under the authority of the United States, shall be the supreme law of the land; and the judges in every state shall be bound thereby, anything in the Constitution or laws of any state to the contrary notwithstanding." All state laws must conform to, or be in harmony with the Federal Constitution as well as with the constitution of the state.

The Federal Constitution is a grant of power by the states to the federal government whereas the constitutions of the various states basically limit the powers of state government. In other words, the federal government possesses those powers *granted* to it by the states and state governments possess reserved powers, all powers not taken away in the state constitution or specifically denied to them by the United States Constitution. The state constitution is the fundamental written law of the state. Legislative enactments by state legislatures, by cities and towns, and by other smaller governmental units must conform to these constitutions and find in them their authority, either expressed or implied.

There are two legal doctrines based on constitutional provisions which need be noted. These are the doctrine of separation of powers and the doctrine of judicial review. These are discussed in the sections which follow.

1-12. Separation of Powers. Both the federal and state constitutions provide for a scheme of government consisting of three branches—the legislative, the executive, and the judicial. A doctrine usually referred to as the doctrine of separation of powers, ascribes to each branch a separate function and a check and balance on the functions of the other branches. The separation of powers concept has contributed toward stable government. Mr. Justice Frankfurter in a special concurring opinion in *Youngstown Sheet and Tube Co. v. Sawyer* (343 U.S. 579) had occasion to discuss this doctrine. He stated:

A constitutional democracy like ours is perhaps the most difficult of man's social arrangements to manage successfully. Our scheme of society is more dependent than any other form of government on knowledge and wisdom and self-discipline for the achievement of its aims. For our democracy implies the reign of reason on the most extensive scale. The Founders of this Nation were not imbued with the modern cynicism that the only thing that history teaches is that it teaches nothing. They acted on the conviction that the experience of man sheds a good deal of light on his nature. It sheds a good deal of light not merely on the need for effective power, if a society is to be at once cohesive and civilized, but also on the need for limitations on the power of governors over the governed.

To that end they rested the structure of our central government on the system of checks and balances. For them the doctrine of separation of powers was not mere theory; it was a felt necessity. Not so long ago it was fashionable to find our system of checks and balances obstructive to effective government. It was easy to ridicule that system as outmoded—too easy. The experience through which the world has passed in our own day has made vivid the realization that the Framers of our Constitution were not inexperienced doctrinaires. These long-headed statesmen had no illusion that our people enjoyed biological or psychological or sociological immunities from the hazards of concentrated power. It is absurd to see a dictator in a representative product of the sturdy democratic traditions of the Mississippi Valley. The accretion of dangerous power does not come in a day. It does come, however slowly, from the generative force of unchecked disregard of the restrictions that fence in even the most disinterested assertion of authority.

The Framers, however, did not make the judiciary the overseer of our government. They were familiar with the revisory functions entrusted to judges in a few of the states and refused to lodge such powers in this Court. Judicial power can be exercised only as to matters that were the traditional concern of the courts at Westminster, and only if they arise in ways that

to the expert feel of lawyers constitute "Cases" or "Controversies." Even as to
questions that were the staple of judicial business it is not for the courts to
pass upon them unless they are indispensably involved in a conventional
litigation—and then, only to the extent that they are so involved. Rigorous
adherence to the narrow scope of the judicial function is especially demanded
in controversies that arouse appeals to the Constitution. The attitude with
which this Court must approach its duty when confronted with such issues
is precisely the opposite of that normally manifested by the general public.
So-called constitutional questions seem to exercise a mesmeric influence over
the popular mind. This eagerness to settle—preferably forever—a specific
problem on the basis of the broadest possible constitutional pronouncements
may not unfairly be called one of our minor national traits. . . .

The pole-star for constitutional adjudications is John Marshall's greatest
judicial utterance that "it is a *constitution* we are expounding." (*McCulloch
v. Maryland,* 4 Wheat. 316, 407) That requires both a spacious view in applying an instrument of government "made for an undefined and expanding
future" (*Hurtado v. California,* 110 U.S. 516, 530), and as narrow a delimita-
tion of the constitutional issues as the circumstances permit. Not the least
characteristic of great statesmanship which the Framers manifested was the
extent to which they did not attempt to bind the future. It is no less incumbent upon this Court to avoid putting fetters upon the future by needless
pronouncements today.

Marshall's admonition that "it is a *constitution* we are expounding" is
especially relevant when the Court is required to give legal sanctions to an
underlying principle of the Constitution—that of separation of powers. "The
great ordinances of the Constitution do not establish and divide fields of
black and white." (Holmes, J., dissenting in *Springer v. Philippine Islands,*
277 U.S. 189, 209). . . .

The judiciary may, as this case proves, have to intervene in determining
where authority lies as between the democratic forces in our scheme of
government. But in doing so we should be wary and humble. Such is the
teaching of this Court's role in the history of the country. . . .

A scheme of government like ours no doubt at times feels the lack of
power to act with complete, all-embracing, swiftly moving authority. No doubt
a government with distributed authority subject to being challenged in the
courts of law, at least long enough to consider and adjudicate the challenge,
labors under restrictions from which other governments are free. It has not
been our tradition to envy such governments. In any event our government
was designed to have such restrictions. The price was deemed not too high in
view of the safeguards which these restrictions afford. I know no more impressive words on this subject than those of Mr. Justice Brandeis: "The
doctrine of the separation of powers was adopted by the Convention of 1787,
not to promote efficiency but to preclude the exercise of arbitrary power. The
purpose was, not to avoid friction, but, by means of the inevitable friction
incident to the distribution of the governmental powers among three departments, to save the people from autocracy." (*Myers v. United States,* 272 U.S.
52, 240, 293.)

1-13. Judicial Review. Another doctrine which involves separation of
powers and the three branch concept is known as the doctrine of judicial
review. This doctrine and the doctrine of supremacy of the Constitution
were established at an early date in our country's history in the celebrated

case of *Marbury v. Madison.* Chief Justice Marshall stated: "Certainly, all those who have framed written constitutions contemplated them as forming the fundamental and paramount law of the nation, and consequently, the theory of every such government must be that an act of the legislature, repugnant to the constitution, is void. This theory is essentially attached to a written constitution and is, consequently, to be considered by this court, as one of the fundamental principles of our society." Justice Marshall then announced the doctrine of "judicial review" which gives to courts the power to review the action of the legislative and executive branches of government to determine if they are constitutional. This doctrine of judicial review has, to some extent, made the courts the overseer of government, even though Justice Frankfurter questioned this authority. The great power of the judiciary can be seen in the following language in *Marbury v. Madison:*

> It is, emphatically, the province and duty of the judicial department, to say what the law is. Those who apply the rule to particular cases, must of necessity expound and interpret that rule. If two laws conflict with each other, the courts must decide on the operation of each. So, if a law be in opposition to the constitution . . . the court must determine which of these conflicting rules governs the case: this is of the very essence of judicial duty.

1-14. Interpretation of Statutes. The power of courts over legislation is not limited to the doctrine of judicial review. Courts also interpret legislation by resolving ambiguities and filling in the gaps in the statutes. There would be no need to interpret a statute which was direct, clear, and precise. However, most legislation is by its very nature general, and courts are faced with the problem of finding the meaning of general statutes as applied to specific facts. Interpretation is designed to find the intent of the legislature.

One technique of statutory interpretation is to examine the legislative history of an act to determine the purpose of the legislation, or the evil it was designed to correct. Legislative history does not always give a clear meaning to a statute because many of the questions of interpretation which confront courts were never even visualized by the legislature. The real problem often is to determine what the legislature *would have* intended, had it considered the question. There are several generally accepted rules of statutory interpretation which are used by judges in construing legislative intent. Some of the more frequently used rules are:

1. Statutes which are consistent with one another, and which relate to the same subject matter, are *in pari materia* and should be construed together, and effect be given to them all, although they may contain no reference to one another and were passed at different times.

2. Criminal statutes and taxing laws should be strictly construed.

3. Unless contrary intent appears, statutory words are uniformly presumed to be used in their ordinary and usual sense, and with the meaning commonly attributed to them.

4. A thing may be within the letter of the statute and yet not within the statute, because not within its spirit nor within the intention of the makers.

5. Statutes in derogation of the common law are to be strictly construed.

6. Remedial statutes are to be liberally construed.

7. Where a general word in a statute follows particular and specific words of the same nature as itself, it takes its meaning from them, and is presumed to be restricted to the same genus as those words. (A statute naming "ox, cow, heifer, steer, or other cattle" does not include a bull.) This rule is called *ejusdem generis.*

8. Popular words are to be construed in the popular sense and technical words in the technical sense, but if a word has both meanings, its meaning will be determined from the context in which it is used.

9. The meaning of a doubtful word may be ascertained by reference to the meaning of words with which it is associated. (This rule is sometimes referred to as *noscitur a sociis;* it is similar to the rule of *in pari materia* but is applied to sentences and sections of a single statute.)

Many of the above rules conflict with each other and courts frequently use the rule which justifies its selected interpretation.[1]

Such other matters as the objectives of the legislation as stated in preambles and debates; statements by executives in requesting legislation; prior judicial decisions involving the same subject matter; and the title of the act are used as extrinsic aids in judicial interpretations.

In the final analysis it is what the court says that a statute means that determines its effect.

1-15. Uniform State Laws. Since there are 50 states, each of which has its own unique constitution, its statutes enacted by the legislative assembly, and its courts, which in deciding cases have created a body of legal principles which are controlling precedents and form the common law of the state, it is to be expected that there could be a very substantial difference between state laws concerning any given legal proposition. It is important to note that ours is a federal system wherein each state has a good deal of autonomy; thus it can be said that there are really 51 legal systems—a system for each of the states plus the federal legal structure. In many fields of law it does not matter whether the legal principles are uniform throughout the country, especially where the partners to a dispute are citizens of the same state so that the controversy is strictly an *intrastate* one as opposed to one that has *interstate* implications. But when citizens of different states are involved (for example, where a buyer in one state contracts with a seller in another), many difficult problems can arise from the lack of uniformity of laws. Does the law of the buyer's state control or does that of the seller's state? It is true that a body of law called "conflict of laws" relating to the choice of laws in such a situation has developed, but certainly trade between citizens of different

[1] *Jamison v. Encarnacion,* page 58.

states has been impeded and made more difficult because the laws of commerce are not uniform.

Two solutions to the problem are possible: (1) federal legislation governing business law (but this could only apply to interstate transactions and could result in there being two conflicting laws: one applicable to interstate contracts and another to intrastate contracts), and (2) adoption by the legislatures of all the states of the same laws concerning at least certain phases of business transactions. It is the latter procedure which has actually been followed. The first uniform state law, the Uniform Negotiable Instruments Law (NIL), was promulgated in 1896 and subsequently adopted by all the states. Since then many uniform laws concerning such subjects as partnerships, sales of goods, conditional sales, warehouse receipts, bills of lading, stock transfers, and many others have been promulgated and presented to the various state legislatures. The response from the state legislatures has been variable—the uniform laws have been adopted by varying numbers of states.

A great portion of the written law of states which affects or concerns business had its inception with the National Conference of Commissioners on Uniform State Laws which is made up of commissioners appointed by the governors of the states. This national body has for its purpose: "(1) The promotion of the uniformity in state laws on all subjects where uniformity is deemed desirable and practicable; (2) to draft model acts on (a) subjects suitable for interstate compacts, and (b) subjects in which uniformity will make more effective the exercise of state powers and promote interstate cooperation; and (3) to promote uniformity of judicial decisions throughout the United States."

When approved by the National Conference, proposed Uniform Acts are recommended to the state legislatures for adoption. The National Conference within the last sixty years has drafted and approved one hundred and fourteen acts.

The most recent significant development in the field of uniform state legislation has been the *Uniform Commercial Code*. This Code was prepared in cooperation with the American Law Institute. It is the stated purpose of the Code to collect in one body the law that "deals with all the phases which may ordinarily arise in the handling of a commercial transaction from start to finish." "The concept of the present act is that a 'commercial transaction' is a single subject of the law notwithstanding its many facets." Chapter 17 discusses the history of the Code in detail and it is suggested that the material be studied at this time. Book Two on Contracts has several references to Code provisions affecting the law of Contracts.

The Code provisions relating to Contracts are limited to Contracts involving *goods* and many of them are further limited to contracts between *merchants*. The limited scope of the Code must be clearly kept in mind. The Uniform Commercial Code replaces a number of Uniform State Laws but the majority of them are still in effect. The NIL and the Uniform Sales Act have been repealed. An example of a uniform state law which has been widely adopted is the Uniform Partnership Act. It has not been affected by the adoption of the Uniform Commercial Code.

The field of commercial law is not the only area of new codification. Many states are adopting revised criminal codes which contain modern procedures and concepts. In addition, the past few years have seen dynamic changes in both state and federal statutes setting forth civil procedures and revising court systems. The future will undoubtedly bring many further developments to improve the administration of justice. The trend, despite some objection, is to cover more areas of the law with statutes and to rely less on precedent in judicial decisions, or common law, as a source of law.

UNWRITTEN LAW

1-16. The Common Law—*Stare Decisis*. While statutes are an increasingly important source of law in modern times, the common law is the primary source of law in this country. The common law or the law of precedent is based on the doctrine of *stare decisis,* which means "to stand by decisions and not to disturb what is settled."

Thus, when a court of competent jurisdiction has decided a controversy and has in a written opinion set forth the rule or principle which was the basis for its decision, that rule or principle will be followed by the court in deciding subsequent cases. Likewise, subordinate courts in the same jurisdiction will be bound by the rule of law set forth in the decision.

Stare decisis results from the desire for certainty and predictability in the law. In addition, following precedent is expedient. The common law, through precedent, settled many legal issues and brought stability into many areas of the law, such as contracts, enabling individuals to act in reliance upon prior decision, with reasonable certainty as to the results of their conduct. Courts usually hesitate to renounce precedent and generally assume that a principle or rule of law announced in a former judicial decision, if unfair or contrary to public policy, will be changed by legislation. Precedent has more force on trial courts than on courts of review, which have the power to make precedent in the first instance.

1-17. Rejection of *Stare Decisis*. However, the doctrine of *stare decisis* has not been applied in such a fashion as to render the law rigid and inflexible. If a court, and especially a reviewing court, should find that the prior decision was "palpably wrong" it may overrule it and decline to follow the rule enunciated by that case. By the same token, if the court should find that a rule of law established by a prior decision is no longer sound because of changing conditions, it may not consider the rule to be a binding precedent. The strength and genius of the common law is that no decision is *stare decisis* when it has lost its usefulness or the reasons for it no longer exist. The doctrine does not require courts to multiply their errors by using former mistakes as authority and support for new errors. Thus, just as legislatures change the law by new legislation, so also do courts change the law, from time to time, by reversing former precedents. Judges are subject to social forces and changing circumstances just as are legislatures. The personnel of courts change, and each new generation of judges deems it a responsibility to reexamine precedents and to adapt them to the world of the times.

It should be noted, also, that in many cases a precedent created by a decision will not be a popular one and may be "out of step" with the times. The effect of the decision as a precedent can be nullified by the passage of a statute providing for a different result than that reached by the court as to future cases involving the same general issue.

Stare decisis may not be ignored by mere whim or caprice. It must be followed rather rigidly in the daily affairs of men. In the whole area of private law, uniformity and continuity are necessary. It is obvious that the same rules of tort and contract law must be applied in the afternoon as in the morning. *Stare decisis* must serve to take the capricious element out of law and to give stability to a society.

However, in the area of public law, and especially constitutional law, the doctrine is frequently ignored. The Supreme Court recognizes that "it is a constitution which we are expounding, not the gloss which previous courts may have put on it." Justice Douglas, speaking before the Association of the Bar of the City of New York at the Eighth Annual Benjamin N. Cardozo Lectures, expressed this concept when he said:

> A judge looking at a constitutional decision may have compulsions to revere past history and accept what was once written. But he remembers above all else that it is the Constitution which he swore to support and defend, not the gloss which his predecessors may have put on it. So he comes to formulate his own views, rejecting some earlier ones as false and embracing others. He cannot do otherwise unless he lets men long dead and unaware of the problems of the age in which he lives do his thinking for him.
>
> This reexamination of precedent in constitutional law is a personal matter for each judge who comes along. When only one new judge is appointed during a short period, the unsettling effect in constitutional law may not be great. But when a majority of a Court is suddenly reconstituted, there is likely to be substantial unsettlement. There will be unsettlement until the new judges have taken their positions on constitutional doctrine. During that time—which may extend a decade or more—constitutional law will be in flux. That is the necessary consequence of our system and to my mind a healthy one. The alternative is to let the Constitution freeze in the pattern which one generation gave it. But the Constitution was designed for the vicissitudes of time. It must never become a code which carries the overtones of one period that may be hostile to another.
>
> So far as constitutional law is concerned *stare decisis* must give way before the dynamic component of history. Once it does, the cycle starts again. Today's new and startling decision quickly becomes a coveted anchorage for new vested interests. The former proponents of change acquire an acute conservatism in their new *status quo*. It will then take an oncoming group from a new generation to catch the broader vision which may require an undoing of the work of our present and their past. . . .

From age to age the problem of constitutional adjudication is the same. It is to keep the power of government unrestrained by the social or economic theories that one set of judges may entertain. It is to keep one age unfettered by the fears or limited vision of another. There is in that connection one tenet of faith which has crystallized more and more as a result of our long experience as a nation. It is this: If the social and economic problems of state and nation can be kept under political management of the people, there is likely to be long-run stability. It is when a judiciary with life tenure seeks to write its social and economic creed into the Charter that instability is created. For then the nation lacks the adaptability to master the sudden storms of an era. It must be remembered that the process of constitutional amendment is a long and slow one.

That philosophy is reflected in what Thomas Jefferson wrote about the Constitution,

> Some men look at constitutions with sanctimonious reverence, and deem them like the ark of the covenant, too sacred to be touched. They ascribe to the men of the preceding age a wisdom more than human, and suppose what they did to be beyond amendment. I knew that age well; I belonged to it, and labored with it. It deserved well of its country. It was very like the present, but without the experience of the present; and forty years of experience in government is worth a century of book-reading; and this they would say themselves, were they to rise from the dead.

Jefferson's words are *a fortiori* germane to the fashioning of constitutional law and to the lesser lawmaking in which the judiciary necessarily indulges.

It is of great interest to people in America as well as in the British Commonwealth, that the House of Lords, Britain's court of last resort, announced on July 26, 1966, that it is abandoning "the binding force of precedent" in some circumstances in order to make English law more modern and flexible. The importance of this announcement to people in America stems from the fact that English common law formed the basis of our legal system. The impact of the action is lessened somewhat by virtue of the fact that while the House of Lords exempted themselves from the legal principles of previous similar cases, the rule of precedent is still binding on Britain's other courts. The Lords reserved for themselves the right to depart from previous decisions "when it appears right to do so"—a concept applied by our own courts and especially the U. S. Supreme Court in modern times.

Prior to the ruling of the House of Lords, the only English court not bound by precedent was the other major appellate body, the Judicial Committee of the Privy Council, which hears appeals from the courts of the colonies and other parts of the Commonwealth. One of the members of the House of Lords in announcing the action regarding precedent is reported to have said:

> . . . the use of precedent as an indispensable foundation upon which to decide what is the law and its application to individual cases . . . their lordships nevertheless recognize that too rigid adherence to precedent may lead to injustice in a particular case and unduly restrict the proper development of the law.

They propose, therefore, to modify their present practice and, while treating former decisions of this house as normally binding, to depart from a previous decision when it appears right to do so . . .

He also said modernization was a major aim, especially in cases where the lords must "consider that the earlier decision was influenced by the existence of conditions which no longer prevail, and that in modern conditions the law ought to be different."

In the United States, our Supreme Court which early in its history followed the doctrine of judicial restraint, i.e. not deciding matters when it need not decide and leaving questions of policy to other branches of government, now has abandoned judicial restraint in favor of an active role in the solution of the nation's problems. The concept of an "activist" court is consistent with Justice Douglas' view that the court should not be bound by *stare decisis* in the field of constitutional law. Thus we have the Supreme Court rejecting long established precedents in such areas as the criminal law, apportionment of legislative bodies, civil rights and obscenity. It therefore appears that the House of Lords is now following the leadership of the U. S. Supreme Court in its attitude toward *stare decisis* and that the "child" is now leading the "parent" in forming judicial policy.

Frequently, conflicting precedents are presented by the parties to an action. One of the major problems of the courts in such cases is to determine which precedent is applicable or correct, if the cited authorities are in actual conflict. In addition, even today, many questions of law arise on which there has been no prior decision, or in areas where the only authority is by implication.

It should be noted that there is a distinction between precedent and mere dicta. A judicial decision, as authority for future cases, is coextensive only with the facts upon which it is founded and the rules of law upon which the decision actually is predicated. Frequently courts make comments on matters not necessary to the decision reached. Such expressions, called "dicta," lack the force of an adjudication and, strictly speaking, are not precedent which the court will be required to follow within the rule of *stare decisis*. However, dicta or implication in prior cases may be followed if sound and just, and dicta which have been repeated frequently are often given the force of precedent.

1-18. Scope of Precedent. One other problem concerning precedent is: Which state's law is to be applied in cases where the fact pattern involves two or more states? Each state has its own body of precedent, and there is a body of federal precedent for questions of federal law. (However, there is no federal common law and cases tried in a federal court involving matters other than federal questions are decided on the law of the state in which the case is being tried, or the state law which most closely relates to the matter in issue.) Questions involving more than one state frequently arise. For example, a contract may be executed in one state, performed in another, and the parties may live in still others; or an automobile accident may occur in one state involving citizens of different states.

The doctrine of *stare decisis* does not require that one state recognize the precedent or rules of law of other states, although such decisions may be followed and are often cited as authority. Each state is free to decide for itself questions concerning its common law and interpretation of its own constitution and statutes. However, courts will often follow decisions in other states, if they are found to be sound. This is particularly true in cases involving the construction of statutes such as the Uniform Acts where each state has adopted the same statute.

However, there is a body of law known as "Conflicts of Law" which is used to determine the applicable substantive precedent in multi-state cases. For example, the law applicable to a tort is generally said to be the law of the state of place of injury. Thus, a court sitting in state X would follow its own rules of procedure but would use the tort law of state Y if the injury occurred in Y. While it is not the purpose of this text to teach "Conflicts of Law," some of the "conflicts" rules will be noted and the student should be aware that such a body of law exists. The federal courts also follow conflicts rules in determining which state law to apply.

ADMINISTRATIVE LAW

1-19. Administrative Agencies. In a complex industrial society, social and economic problems exist to such an extent that courts and legislative bodies cannot possibly deal with all of them. Legislation must be general in character and someone must fill in the gap. Not only are there too many problems for traditional methods of solution, but interrelationships and conflicting social goals as well as advances in technology require constant changes and the utilization of the administrative agency to lighten the burdens imposed on the executive branch, legislative bodies, and courts by these problems. The multitude of administrative agencies performing governmental functions today encompasses almost every aspect of business operation and, indeed, almost every aspect of our daily lives. These agencies provide flexibility in the law and adaptability to changing conditions.

The direct day-to-day legal impact on business of the many local, state, and Federal administrative agencies is far greater than the impact of the courts and legislative bodies. Administrative agencies create and enforce the greater bulk of the laws which make up the legal environment of business.

The functions of administrative bodies generally are described as (1) rule making, (2) adjudicating, (3) prosecuting, (4) advising, (5) supervising, and (6) investigating. These functions are not the concern of all administrative agencies to the same degree. Some agencies are primarily adjudicating bodies, such as the industrial commissions which rule on workmen's compensation claims. Others are concerned primarily with a special industry such as the Federal Power Commission and still others with a particular phase of business such as the Federal Trade Commission. Others are primarily supervisory, such as the Securities and Exchange Commission which supervises the issue and sale of investment securities. Most agencies perform all the foregoing functions to some degree in carrying out their responsibilities.

In addition to traditional executive functions, the administrative process involves performance of both legislative and judicial functions. Some agencies are best described as quasi-legislative and others are best described as quasi-judicial.

1-20. Legislative Functions. The legislative function in the administrative process is to make rules. The rule-making function is based on the authority delegated to the agency by the legislature. A delegation of legislative authority is valid only if limitations are imposed on the exercise of the power and if standards are prescribed by which a court can determine whether these limitations have been exceeded. The standards set must meet certain minimum requirements before the agency in question is validly empowered to act in a certain area, and the rules promulgated by the agency must follow these standards and limitations imposed by the law establishing it, if they are to be upheld.

Some courts have taken the view that the legislature cannot delegate its law-making function at all, but have concluded that authorizing an administrative agency to "fill in the details" of legislation is valid as not being an exercise of the legislative power. Other courts have stated that the legislature *can* delegate part of its function to an agency as long as sufficient general standards to be used by the agency are included in the grant of authority. The net result is the same.

While there must be standards in the delegation or as Justice Cardozo said, "The delegated power of legislation (must be) canalized within banks that keep it from overflowing," the modern trend of cases is to approve very broad delegations of authority to these agencies. For example, a delegation to make such rules, regulations, and decisions as the public interest, convenience and necessity may require has been held to be a valid standard. Also, directions to be "fair and equitable" constitute a sufficient standard. Today, delegations of legislative authority are in broad terms and business must recognize that actions taken pursuant to such broad authority are in all probability valid.

1-21. Judicial Functions. Administrative agencies almost universally conduct hearings to determine the rights and duties of various parties who may be protected by, or are subject to, their jurisdiction. Based upon evidence submitted to the administrative unit, appropriate orders are issued. These orders have the effect of law and may be enforced in court. The power of courts to change these orders is discussed later in this section.

The rules of procedure for hearings before such administrative bodies are usually formulated by the administrative bodies themselves and are made available to those who may be interested in them. The hearings are usually informal in character, but on the whole they follow the general pattern set by courts. The rules of evidence are not strictly followed since the hearing officer may not have formal legal training. A hearing normally originates with the filing of a petition or complaint, and the interested parties are then notified that a hearing will be held at a stated time, that the interested parties are given an opportunity to file pertinent documents in the interim, and that they will have an opportunity to present evidence at the time of hearing.

The board often appoints a person to conduct the hearing called a hearing examiner to listen to the evidence, submit his findings of the facts, and make his recommendations to the board or commission regarding the disposition to be made in the case. The board studies the report and issues such orders as the law in the case appears to demand.

The quasi-judicial function of administrative agencies is the subject of substantial controversy. Lawyers frequently attack the agencies and the performance of their judicial functions because the procedures are different than in court. It is sometimes onerous to argue law to one not a lawyer, particularly where the laymen's decision is binding. It is often said that administrative agencies make a law, investigate to see if it has been violated, serve as prosecutor, judge, and jury; and then act as appellate court. This multitude of activities by an agency appears to violate the doctrine of separation of powers, but necessity and the other reasons previously discussed for the growth of administrative law have caused this argument to be universally rejected. Other objections to the judicial function of these agencies are:

1. The presence of an inherent "leftist" orientation;
2. A tendency toward totalitarianism, undermining "the rule of law";
3. Bias;
4. Susceptibility to improper influence;
5. Lack of accountability to the people;
6. Some such as the tax court are actually courts and should be part of the judiciary;
7. Many so-called experts are not experts at all.

Notwithstanding the foregoing objections, administrative agencies continue to possess quasi-judicial powers and such powers are expanding.

Perhaps the most important question for businessmen in the field of administrative law is: Under what circumstances will the decision of an administrative agency be changed or reversed by a court?

The decisions of the agency are given great weight on review by the courts. Courts are not likely to overrule an agency's rule of law because courts frequently believe that the agency is better equipped to decide the matter. The courts often suggest that the agency has expert knowledge of the problem or that the legislative intent was to prefer determination of the matter by the agency.

Courts will review the findings and rulings of the agency only after the remedies and review provided within the agency have been exhausted.

Upon review, a court will not reverse the decision of the agency if there is substantial evidence on the record as a whole to support the decision of the agency.[2] If a reasonable result was obtained, the decision will not be changed even though the court on the same evidence would have reached a different conclusion.

Thus, as a practical matter, the decisions of administrative agencies will not be reversed if they are within the delegated authority and are reasonable when the total record of evidence is considered.

SOURCES OF LAW CASES

Jamison v. Encarnacion

281 U.S. 635 (1929)

Plaintiff, a longshoreman, sued defendant, his employer, for personal injuries incurred when he was struck by another employee while loading a barge. The jury awarded plaintiff $2,500 and the defendant appealed, contending that the applicable statutes only created liability for negligence and since the tort was intentional there was no liability. The Court of Appeals of New York held that the word "seamen" in the Federal Employers' Liability Act included "stevedores" and that "negligence" included "misconduct."

BUTLER, J. The question is whether "negligence" as there used includes the assault in question. The measure was adopted for the relief of a large class of persons employed in hazardous work in the service described. It abrogates the common-law rule that makes every employee bear the risk of injury or death through the fault or negligence of fellow servants and applies the principle of respondeat superior (section 1), eliminates the defense of contributory negligence and substitutes a rule of comparative negligence (section 3 (45 U.S.C.A. § 53)), abolishes the defense of assumption of risk, where the violation of a statute enacted for the safety of employees is a contributing cause (section 4 (45 U.S.C.A. § 54)), and denounces all contracts, rules, and regulations calculated to exempt the employer from liability created by the act (section 5 (45 U.S.C.A. § 55)).

The reports of the House and Senate committees having the bill in charge condemn the fellow-servant rule as operating unjustly when applied to modern conditions in actions against carriers to recover damages for injury or death of their employees, and show that a complete abrogation of that rule was intended. The act, like an earlier similar one that was held invalid because it included subjects beyond the reach of Congress, is intended to stimulate carriers to greater diligence for the safety of their employees and of the persons and property of their patrons . . . (cases cited).

The rule that statutes in derogation of the common law are to be

2 *Federal Security Administrator v. Quaker Oats Co.*, page 59.

strictly construed does not require such an adherence to the letter as would defeat an obvious legislative purpose or lessen the scope plainly intended to be given to the measure . . . (cases cited). The act is not to be narrowed by refined reasoning or for the sake of giving "negligence" a technically restricted meaning. It is to be construed liberally to fulfill the purposes for which it was enacted, and to that end the word may be read to include all the meanings given to it by courts, and within the word as ordinarily used. (*Miller v. Robertson*, 266 U.S. 243). . . .

As the Federal Employers' Liability Act (45 U.S.C.A. §§ 51-59) does not create liability without fault (*Seaboard Air Line Ry. v. Horton*, 233 U.S. 492, 501), . . . it may reasonably be construed in contrast with proposals and enactments to make employers liable in the absence of any tortious act, for the payment of compensation for personal injuries or death of employees arising in the course of their employment.

"Negligence" is a word of broad significance and may not readily be defined with accuracy. Courts usually refrain from attempts comprehensively to state its meaning. While liability arises when one suffers injury as the result of any breach of duty owed him by another chargeable with knowledge of the probable result of his conduct, actional negligence is often deemed—and we need not pause to consider whether rightly—to include other elements. Some courts call willful misconduct evincing intention or willingness to cause injury to another gross negligence. . . . And it has been held that the use of excessive force causing injury to an employee by the superintendent of a factory in order to induce her to remain at work was not a trespass as distinguished from a careless or negligent act. (*Richard v. Company*, 79 N.H. 380, 381) . . . While the assault of which plaintiff complains was in excess of the authority conferred by the employer upon the foreman, it was committed in the course of the discharge of his duties and in furtherance of the work of the employer's business. As unquestionably the employer would be liable if plaintiff's injuries had been caused by mere inadvertence or carelessness on the part of the offending foreman, it would be unreasonable and in conflict with the purpose of Congress to hold that the assault, a much graver breach of duty, was not negligence within the meaning of the act. . . .

Judgment Affirmed.

Federal Security Administrator v. Quaker Oats Co.

318 U.S. 218 (1943)

The Federal Security Administrator, acting under the Federal Food, Drug and Cosmetic Act, promulgated regulations establishing "standards of identity" for various milled wheat products. He excluded vitamin D from the defined standard of "farina" and permitted it only in "enriched farina," which was also required to contain vitamin B_1 riboflavin, nicotinic acid, and iron. The question is whether the regulations are valid as applied to respondent. The Court, speaking through Chief Justice Stone, after discussing the history of the statute, the business of the defendant, and the reasons for the actions of the administrator, discussed the weight to be given the action of the administrator and the power of courts over administrative agencies and said in part:

> The court below . . . held that because there was no evidence that respondent's product had in fact confused or misled anyone, the Administrator's finding as to consumer confusion was without substantial support in the evidence. It thought that, if anything, consumer confusion was more likely to be created, and the interest of consumers harmed, by the sale of farinas conforming to the standard for "enriched farina," whose labels were not required to disclose their ingredients, than by the sale of respondent's product under an accurate and informative label such as that respondent was using.
>
> The Act does not contemplate that courts should thus substitute their own judgment for that of the Administrator. As passed by the House, it appears to have provided for a judicial review in which the court could take additional evidence, weigh the evidence, and direct the Administrator "to take such further action as justice may require." (H. R. Rep. No. 2139, 75th Cong., 3d Sess., 11-12.) But before enactment, the Conference Committee substituted for these provisions those which became § 701 (f) of the Act. While under that section the Administrator's regulations must be supported by findings based upon "substantial evidence" adduced at the hearing, the Administrator's findings as to the facts if based on substantial evidence are conclusive. In explaining these changes the chairman of the House conferees on the floor of the House that "there is no purpose that the court shall exercise the functions that belong to the executive or the legislative branches." . . .
>
> The review provisions were patterned after those by which Congress has provided for the review of "quasi-judicial" orders of the Federal Trade Commission and other agencies, which we have many times had occasion to construe. Under such provisions we have repeatedly emphasized the scope that must be allowed to the discretion and informed judgment of an expert administrative body. . . . These considerations are especially appropriate where the review is of regulations of general application adopted by an administrative agency under its rule-making power in carrying out the policy of a statute with whose enforcement it is charged. . . . Section 401 calls for the exercise of the "judgment of the Administrator." That judgment, if based on substantial evidence of record, and if within statutory and constitutional limitations, is controlling even though the reviewing court might on the same record have arrived at a different conclusion.
>
> None of the testimony which we have detailed can be said to be speculative or conjectural unless it be the conclusion of numerous witnesses, adopted by the Administrator, that the labeling and marketing of vitamin-enriched foods, not conforming to any standards of identity, tend to confuse and mislead consumers. The exercise of the administrative rule-making power necessarily looks to the future. The statute requires the Administrator to adopt standards of identity which in his judgment "will" promote honesty and fair dealing in the interest of consumers. Acting within its statutory authority he is required to establish standards which will guard against the probable future effects of present trends. Taking into account the evidence of public demand for vitamin-enriched foods, their increasing sale, their variable vitamin composition and dietary value, and the general lack of consumer knowledge of such values, there was sufficient evidence of "rational probative force" . . . to support the Administrator's judgment that, in the absence of appropriate standards of identity, consumer confusion would ensue. . . .

The standards of reasonableness to which the Administrator's action must conform are to be found in the terms of the Act construed and applied in the light of its purpose. Its declared purpose is the administrative promulgation of standards of both identity and quality in the interest of consumers. Those standards are to be prescribed and applied, so far as is practicable, to food under the common or usual name, and the regulations adopted after a hearing must have the support of substantial evidence. We must reject at the outset the argument earnestly pressed upon us that the statute does not contemplate a regulation excluding a wholesome and beneficial ingredient from the definition and standard of identity of a food. The statutory purpose to fix a definition of identity of an article of food sold under its common or usual name would be defeated if producers were free to add ingredients, however wholesome, which are not within the definition. As we have seen, the legislative history of the statute manifests the purpose of Congress to substitute, for informative labeling, standards of identity of a food, sold under a common or usual name, so as to give to consumers who purchase it under that name assurance that they will get what they may reasonably expect to receive. In many instances, like the present, that purpose could be achieved only if the definition of identity specified the number, names and proportions of ingredients, however wholesome other combinations might be. The statute accomplished that purpose by authorizing the Administrator to adopt a definition of identity by prescribing some ingredients, including some which are optional, and excluding others, and by requiring the designation on the label of the optional ingredients permitted.

Since the definition of identity of a vitamin-treated food, marketed under its common or usual name, involves the inclusion of some vitamin ingredients and the exclusion of others, the Administrator necessarily has a large range of choice in determining what may be included and what excluded. It is not necesssarily a valid objection to his choice that another could reasonably have been made. The judicial is not to be substituted for the legislative judgment. It is enough that the Administrator has acted within the statutory bounds of his authority, and that his choice among possible alternative standards adapted to the statutory end is one which a rational person could have made. . . .

We cannot say that the Administrator made an unreasonable choice of standards . . . We conclude that the Administrator did not depart from statutory requirements in choosing these standards of identity for the purpose of promoting fair dealing in the interest of consumers, that the standards which he selected are adapted to that end, and that they are adequately supported by findings and evidence.

Reversed.

CHAPTER 3
REVIEW QUESTIONS AND PROBLEMS

1. How do you account for the growth of administrative agencies in the last half century?
2. What is the difference in theory between the federal and state constitutions?

3. Why is there a trend toward uniformity in state laws?
4. Under what circumstances may a court reverse the decision of an administrative agency?
5. "We must interpret the constitution, not in the light of what was said but in light of our experience as a country." What is meant by this statement?
6. When may a court refuse to follow precedent? Illustrate.
7. Does precedent or common law vary from state to state? If so, how will a court select the applicable precedent in a case involving more than one state?
8. What is meant by the term "conflict of laws"?
9. Name and illustrate five rules of statutory construction.
10. Is the doctrine of separation of powers violated by an administrative agency which makes a rule, investigates to determine if it has been violated, prosecutes the violator and then serves as finder of fact and hearing examiner? Explain.
11. Does the doctrine of judicial review allow courts to review the actions of the executive branch of government?

The Judicial System

1-22. The Function of Courts. It is essential for the functioning of an ordered society that institutions for resolving conflicts be established and maintained. Our system of government has selected courts for this purpose. The word "courts" is derived from the word "cores" of Latin origin, meaning an open outer space near the king's palace, where disputants came to have their differences adjudicated either by the king himself or his representatives.

Courts settle controversies between persons, and between persons and the state. The court is the judge and the judge is the court. The terms are used interchangeably. In civilized communities controversies are settled by the orderly process of adjudication rather than by the use of force.

The rule of law applied by the court to the facts, as found by the jury or court, produces a decision which settles the controversy. While there are obviously other agencies of government which resolve controversies, it is peculiar to our system that for final decision all controversies must ultimately end up in court.

Organized society has other decision making institutions besides courts. The democratic process permits decision making procedures, through the ballot box, executive orders, and legislation. The following are illustrations of economic, political, and social issues, the solutions for which are made by the legislative and executive processes rather than the judicial: What shall be the policy of the United States toward Cuba, Santo Domingo, and Viet Nam? What kind of tax laws shall be adopted? Shall Town *B* issue bonds to build a new City Hall? Shall "Moche Mix," a vegetable substitute for cream, be taxed in order to protect the dairy industry? What is the responsibility of government for public welfare, schools, transportation safety of automobiles, pollution of water and air, water, power, price regulation, safety, labor, housing, civil liberties, and a host of other social problems?

Such issues are general or universal and may be either transitory or continuous. Whether they get solved does not necessarily threaten the existence or impede the continued activity of society. Town *B* will continue even though it does not immediately acquire a new City Hall. Whether people are denied "Moche Mix" is not crucial. An immediate answer is not an absolute necessity. Such problems are the concern of all the people, though they may be of more concern to one individual than to another. What answers shall be given to such questions is the responsibility of the representatives of the people by the legislative process.

If a conflict between individuals or between an individual and the state arises and continues to the injury of a person or his property, a particular personal controversy is present. If the injured person or state seeks relief through the court, the court is required to make a decision. A decision *must* be made. The court may give the plaintiff relief or it may not—in either case a decision has been made.

Whether Town *B* shall have a new City Hall is an important question, but not an urgent one. But if a citizen alleges the election by which the decision to build the City Hall was improperly conducted and by proper procedure presents the question to the court, a judicial problem is presented which requires an immediate answer. If the election was not held in compliance with the election statutes, the decision to have a new City Hall is illegal and void. To impose taxes upon the plaintiff's property by an unlawful election would be taking his property without due process of law. The question of whether a valid election has been held becomes a particular personal problem. It is a justiciable issue for the court. If the court decides the election was unlawfully conducted, the authority to tax and build the City Hall is not granted, thus a particular personal problem has been solved. The court by a predetermined judicial process conducted in compliance with procedural rules has adjudicated the issue of the legality of the election. A specific question has been answered. The judgment of the court has resolved the question. The result—the judgment has references to the past. What was done by way of the election has gone for naught. This finality of a solution is different from a solution made by the legislative process. Passing an ordinance authorizing the proper officers to issue bonds and build the City Hall pertains to affirmative action in the future. Legislation is law making which is universal in its application and a guide to the future, while adjudication is the interpretation and application of law, retrospective in character which determines a particular issue.

A dramatic illustration of a general social situation which has raised particular personal problems is in the area of civil rights. Discrimination by reason of race has been a general social question for years. But when a particular citizen alleges he has been denied his constitutional rights, either by local law or illegal conduct by others, and for relief presents his cause to the court, a particular issue is raised which the court must decide. A favorable decision, although particular for the plaintiff, redounds to the benefit of all other persons in a similar situation. Past conduct has been determined to be illegal, and past and present rights are restored.

A distinction between issues, controversies and problems that are general, and for solution have relevance to the executive and legislative branches of the government, and those that are personal and particular and are issues for the courts, are not always as clearly defined as those illustrated above.

For example, Congress may pass special appropriations giving relief to particular individuals or groups; or, special legislation may be enacted endowing a particular person with special privileges such as honorary citizenship, or an alien with the right of residence.

A court, in adjudicating a bankrupt business, by decree may enter an order which not only affects the particular parties to the litigation but the future of a large number of other persons, his creditors. Likewise the adjudication of constitutional questions, such as the legality of the use of free textbooks for children in private schools, although limited in its particular application to the parties to the action will nevertheless be an authoritative guide for all school officials.

1-23. State Court Systems. The Judicial System of the United States is a dual system consisting of state courts and federal courts. The courts of the states, although not subject to uniform classification, may be grouped as follows: supreme courts, intermediate courts of appeal (in the more populous states) and trial courts. Some trial courts have general jurisdiction while others have a limited jurisdiction. For example, a justice of the peace has power to hear civil and criminal cases only if the amount in controversy does not exceed a certain sum or the penalty for the crime is restricted.

Law suits are instituted in one of the trial courts. Even a court of general jurisdiction has geographical limitations. In many states the trial court of general jurisdiction is called a circuit court because in early times a single judge sitting as a court traveled the circuit from one county to another.

Each state has courts of limited jurisdiction. They may be limited as to subject matter, amount in controversy, or as to the area in which the parties live. For example, courts with jurisdiction limited to a city are often called municipal courts.

Courts may also be named according to the subject matter with which they deal. Probate courts deal with wills and the estates of deceased persons; domestic relations courts, with divorces, family relations, juveniles, and dependent children; criminal and police courts with violators of state laws and municipal ordinances; and traffic courts with traffic violators. For an accurate classification of the courts of any state, the statutes of that state should be examined.

1-24. The Federal Court System. The courts of the United States are created by Congress under the authority of the Constitution, and their jurisdiction is limited by the grant of power given to the federal government by the states by the Constitution. They are thus courts of limited jurisdiction as will be discussed more fully later. The Constitution creates the Supreme Court and authorizes such inferior courts as the Congress may from time to time ordain and establish. Congress pursuant to this authority has created eleven United States Courts of Appeal, the United States District Courts (at least one in each state), and others such as the Court of Customs and Patent Appeals, the Court of Claims, and the Court of Tax Appeals which handle special subject matter as indicated by the name of the court. The following chart illustrates the federal court system:

FEDERAL COURT SYSTEM

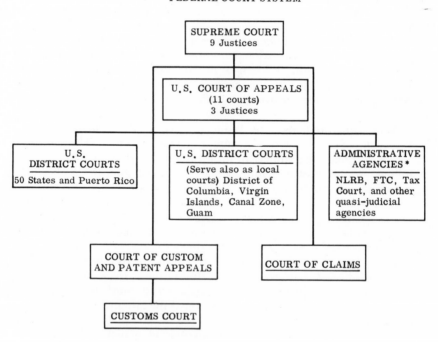

* The federal administrative agencies are not officially part of the Federal Court System but are included in this chart because their rulings can be appealed to a federal court.

The district courts are the trial courts of the federal judicial system. They have original jurisdiction, exclusive of the courts of the states, over all federal crimes, i.e., all offenses against the laws of the United States. The accused is entitled to a trial by a jury in the state and district where the crime was committed. The same facts may constitute a crime against both state and federal authority. For example, robbery of a bank is a crime against both sovereigns. The robber may be tried by both the federal and state courts.

In civil actions the district courts have jurisdiction only where the matter in controversy exceeds the sum or value of $10,000, exclusive of costs or interest, and is based on either diversity of citizenship or a federal question. Diversity of citizenship exists in suits between (1) citizens of different states or (2) a citizen of a state and a citizen of a foreign state. A plaintiff or plaintiffs must be citizens of a different state than any one of the defendants for diversity of citizenship to exist. Diversity of citizenship does not prevent the plaintiff from bringing his suit in a state court, but if the defendant is a citizen of another state, the defendant has the right to have the case removed to a federal court. A defendant, by having the case removed to the federal court, has an opportunity of having a jury selected from a larger area than the county where the cause arose, thus hopefully avoiding the possibility of jurors prejudicial to the plaintiff.

For the purpose of suit in a federal court a corporation is considered a "citizen" of the state where it is incorporated and of the state in which it has its principal place of business. These provisions exclude federal jurisdiction in many cases where one of the parties is a corporation. If any one of the parties on the other side of the case is a citizen of any state in which the corporation is chartered or doing its principal business, there is no diversity of citizenship and thus no federal jurisdiction.

Federal jurisdiction based on a federal question also exists if the controversy involves more than $10,000 and if the law suit arises out of rights granted by the Constitution, laws, or treaties of the United States. For example, a district court has jurisdiction to try a suit in equity brought by persons engaged in sheep raising and living in the same state if the matters in controversy exceed $10,000 and the relief sought is to test the constitutionality of the Taylor Grazing Act, which regulates and controls sheep grazing on federal lands.

The district courts also have jurisdiction of cases arising under the Constitution or federal laws and treaties that involve personal rights without reference to the money value of the controversy. For example, the amount of the controversy is not a jurisdictional question when the suit is brought by the United States or an officer thereof and arises under the Constitution or federal laws and treaties. The civil actions relating to personal rights may involve bankruptcy, setting aside orders of administrative boards—like the Interstate Commerce Commission—matters relating to patents, copyrights, trademarks, taxes, elections, restraint of trade, of federal lands, commerce, and the rights of freedom of speech, press, and religion, the liberty of the individual protected by the Fifth Amendment; also those rights secured to individual citizens by the Fourteenth Amendment. In addition, by statute the district courts now have original jurisdiction to try tort cases involving damages to citizens caused by officers or agents of the federal government, and the power to issue writs of habeas corpus and to grant injunctions in a variety of cases. In cases where injunctions are sought, three judges must hear the case.

Direct appeals from the decisions of the district courts to the United States Supreme Court may be made in several situations, such as: (1) in criminal cases where the decision of the lower court is based upon the invalidity or construction of a statute upon which the indictment or information was founded; (2) where the lower court has held an Act of Congress unconstitutional, and where an agency of the government is a party; (3) where the lower court consisting of three judges has either granted or denied after notice an interlocutory or permanent injunction. However, in most cases, an appeal is taken from a U. S. District Court to the Court of Appeals.

The intermediate courts of appeal from the United States District Courts are called the United States Courts of Appeals. In 1891, because of the heavy burden placed upon the United States Supreme Court, Congress established the Courts of Appeals. The federal judicial districts are divided into eleven circuits, and a Court of Appeals has been established for each circuit. These courts are not trial courts and are limited to appellate jurisdiction. After a case has been decided by a district court, a dissatisfied party may appeal to the Court of Appeals of the circuit in which the district court lies.

In most cases the decisions of the Courts of Appeals are final. The jurisdiction of the court is determined by Congress and it may be changed from time to time. Cases in the Courts of Appeals may be reviewed by the Supreme Court by a writ of certiorari granted upon a petition of any party to any civil or criminal case before or after a judgment or decree in the Courts of Appeals. The writ of certiorari to review a judgment of the Courts of Appeals is within the discretion of the Supreme Court. The writ will be issued where necessary to secure uniformity of decision or to bring cases of grave public concern to the court of last resort for decision.

Court of Appeals decisions may also be reviewed by the Supreme Court in cases in which a state statute has been held unconstitutional and a federal question is presented. Also, the Courts of Appeals may by certification seek instructions from the Supreme Court on any question of law in any civil or criminal case.

The United States District Court and the Courts of Appeals cannot review, retry, or correct the judicial errors charged against a state court. Final judgments or decrees rendered by the highest court of a state are reviewed only by the Supreme Court of the United States. State cases appealed to the United States Supreme Court must concern the validity of a treaty or statute of the United States or must present a question involving the validity of a state statute on the grounds that the statute is repugnant to the Constitution, treaties, or laws of the United States and that the state decision is in favor of the statute's validity. Where a case involves the constitutionality of a state statute or treaty, or when a citizen's rights, privileges, or immunities under the constitution or laws are impaired, the case may be brought to the United States Supreme Court by writ of certiorari. In all other cases the decision of the highest state court is not subject to review.

1-25. Law and Equity. The trial courts in the United States have been frequently divided into two parts—a court of law and a court of equity or chancery. The term equity is peculiar to Anglo-American law. Equity arose because of the failure of the law to give adequate and proper remedy. In early English law the courts could not give remedies for injuries received unless the king's original writs covered the particular remedy sought. Consequently, the proceedings at law were so limited that it was often impossible to obtain justice in the king's courts.

In order that justice might be done, the person seeking a remedy sought redress from the king in person. Since the appeal was to the king's conscience, he referred such matters to his spiritual adviser, the chancellor. Such an individual was usually a church official, and in giving a remedy he usually favored the Ecclesiastical law and the Civil law.

By such method there developed a new system of procedure and new rules. Actions involving these rules were said to be brought in "chancery" or in "equity," in contradistinction to suit "at law" in the king's courts. Courts of equity were courts of conscience and recognized many rights which were not recognized by common law courts.

For example, trusts in lands were recognized; rescission was allowed on contracts created through fraud; injunction and specific performance were developed.

In a few states, courts of equity are separate and distinct from courts of law. In most states the equity and law courts are organized under a single judge who has two dockets—one in law, the other in equity. Whether the case is in equity or in law is determined by the remedy desired. Modern Civil Practice Acts have abolished the common law names heretofore used to distinguish different forms of actions at law and in equity, but pleadings usually must denote whether the action is legal or equitable because as a general rule there is no right to a jury trial of an equitable action.

By statute in some states a jury may be had to hear the evidence. The determination of the jury in these cases is usually advisory only and is not binding on the court. The judge passes upon questions of both law and fact and he may decide the case upon the pleadings without the introduction of oral testimony. If the facts are voluminous and complicated, the judge often refers the case to another person, called a master, to take the testimony. This is the usual procedure where a complicated accounting is required. The master hears the evidence and reports back to the judge his conclusions of fact and law. Sometimes the master's duty is confined only to the hearing and reporting of testimony.

Courts of equity use maxims instead of strict rules of law. There are no *legal* rights in equity, for the decision is based on moral rights and natural justice.

Some of the typical maxims of equity are:

1. "Equity will not suffer a right to exist without a remedy."
2. "Equity regards as done that which ought to be done."
3. "Where there is equal equity, the law must prevail."

4. "He who comes into equity must do so with clean hands."
5. "He who seeks equity must do equity."
6. "Equity aids the vigilant."
7. "Equality is equity."

These maxims serve as guides to the chancellor to use in exercising his discretion. For example, the clean hands doctrine (no. 4) prohibits a party who is guilty of misconduct in the matter in litigation from receiving the aid of the court.

The decision of the court in equity is called a decree. A judgment in a court of law is measured in damages, whereas a decree of a court of equity is said to be "in personam," that is, it is directed to the defendant, who is to do or not to do some specific thing.

Decrees are either final or interlocutory. A decree is final when it disposes of the issues in the case, reserving no question to be decided in the future. A decree quieting title to real estate, granting a divorce, or ordering specific performance is usually final. A decree is interlocutory when it reserves some question to be determined in the future. A decree granting a temporary injunction, appointing a receiver, and ordering property to be delivered to such a receiver would be interlocutory.

Failure upon the part of the defendant to obey a decree of a court of equity is contempt of court because the decree is *in personam*. Any person in contempt of court may be placed in prison or fined by order of the court.

Equity jurisprudence plays an ever-increasing role in our legal system. The movement toward social justice requires more reliance on the equitable maxims and less reliance on rigid rules of law. This also contributes to the further decay of the doctrine of *stare decisis*.

1-26. The Jurisdiction of Courts. Jurisdiction means the power given to a court by the constitution or the legislature to adjudicate concerning the subject and parties, to determine the cause, to render a judgment, and to carry such judgment into effect. For example, "probate courts" have the original jurisdiction of all probate matters, namely, the settlement of estates of deceased persons by administration and the probate of wills, the appointment of guardians and conservators, the settlement of their accounts, the regulation of all matters relating to apprentices and the supervision of the sale of real estate of deceased persons for the payment of debts.

Jurisdiction which is original is frequently also exclusive. This means that no other court has the *power* to hear such cases. For example, the Supreme Court of the United States has original and exclusive jurisdiction in all controversies between two or more states, all proceedings against ambassadors, public ministers, consuls, and domestics of foreign states, all controversies between the United States and a state, and all actions by a state against citizens of another state or country.

Jurisdiction refers to two matters, jurisdiction over the subject matter and jurisdiction over the person. Jurisdiction over the subject matter means that it is of the type which the court has the power to hear and the actual subject matter of the case must come within the limits of the court. For example, a probate court would not have jurisdiction to determine questions of law involving a civil suit for damages, and a circuit court in one county would have no jurisdiction to determine title to the land lying within the boundaries of another county. Courts may also be limited by the amounts of money involved as noted in the federal jurisdictional amount of $10,000.

Jurisdiction over the person refers to jurisdiction over the parties—the plaintiff and defendant. Jurisdiction over the plaintiff is obtained by the filing of the lawsuit. A plaintiff voluntarily submits to the jurisdiction of the court when he files his complaint.

Jurisdiction over the defendant is accomplished by a summons that issues out of the court in which the case is to be tried and is delivered to a sheriff or other person to be served upon the defendant in the suit; or in some cases by publishing a notice in a newspaper. This latter is possible in a limited number of cases involving status such as a suit for divorce or cases involving real estate where the "thing" involved is of sufficient importance that notice by publication is deemed sufficient to actually notify the defendant. Publication may also be accompanied by proper attachment proceedings, in which case service by publication brings under the court's jurisdiction all attached property of a nonresident which lies within the territorial limits of the court, so that such attached property is liable for the judgment debt and may be used to satisfy the judgment. Most cases, however, require the actual service of a summons on the defendant in order to give him notice of the suit.

For many years, it was felt that a summons could not be served beyond the borders of the state in which it was issued. Recently, however, this concept has changed.

Historically, the jurisdiction of courts to enter judgment against a person required actual personal service of the summons on the defendant. This was necessary in order to give the defendant notice of the suit and an opportunity to defend. Since the jurisdiction of courts is limited to geographical areas such as a state or a county, power to issue and serve summons beyond the borders of the state or county did not exist. To extend judicial jurisdiction across a state boundary for the purpose of acquiring jurisdiction over the person of a nonresident was a denial of due process of law. To remove a person from his own state or county to another state or county for trial imposed undue burdens on the defendant and denied him of his right to fair play and a fair trial. (*Pennoyer v. Neff,* 95 U.S. 714, 1878.)

Such limitation of jurisdiction is now no longer tenable. Personal jurisdiction over nonresidents has been expanding—modern transportation and communication facilities, technological progress, the increased flow of interstate commerce, federal highways, automobiles, and population movements have minimized the inconveniences of a trial against a nonresident, while at the same time they have had the effect of denying a local citizen a remedy in local courts for an injury caused by a nonresident. Under the old law nonresident motorists, for example, were not subject to suit in the state where the accident occurred unless they were served with summons while in the state or unless they owned property in the state which could be attached, as previously explained. In most cases the injured person was left without a remedy, unless he could afford to bring action in the motorist's home state. To correct the situation most states have passed statutes which generally provide that a nonresident by using the state highways has automatically appointed a designated state official, usually the Secretary of State, as his agent to accept service of process for any actions arising out of an injury caused by the operation of his automobile on the state highways.

These nonresident motorist statutes opened the door for adoption of other statutes called "long arm" statutes, which further extend the jurisdiction of courts over nonresidents, whether they are individuals or corporations. The nonresident motorist statutes are limited to actions to recover for injuries arising out of automobile accidents; however, more recent statutes extend the jurisdiction to cover situations in which a *tort*-injury has been caused by a nonresident "doing business" in the state or owning property, either personal or real property, situated in the state. Thus a nonresident individual or corporation may be subject to suit for injuries if either has certain "minimal contacts" within the state, so long as the maintenance of the suit does not offend "traditional notions of fair play and substantial justice."

What "minimal contacts" and activities are necessary to bring the "corporate presence" into a state is a fact question depending upon each particular case. Whatever the basis for the action may be, either in contract or tort, the court can acquire jurisdiction over the defendant. Thus, an action to recover damages for personal injury arising out of a defective goods manufactured in one state and sold and delivered in another can be maintained at the place of injury irrespective of the theory upon which the action was brought.[1]

1-27. Venue. As stated above, the term jurisdiction defines the power of the court to hear and adjudicate the case. The term jurisdiction includes the court's power to inquire into the facts, apply the law to the facts, make a decision, and declare and enforce a judgment. Venue relates to and defines the particular territorial area within the state, county, or district in which the civil case or civil prosecution should be brought and tried. Matters of venue are determined by statute. Venue statutes usually provide that actions concerning interests in land must be commenced and tried in the county or district in which the land is located. Actions for the recovery of penalties imposed by statute against public officers must be commenced and tried in the county or district where the cause of action arose. Suits for divorce must be commenced and tried in the county in which one of the parties resides. All other suits or actions must be commenced and tried in the county in which the defendants or

[1] *Singer v. Walker*, page 73.

one of them reside or may be found at the commencement of the action or in which the transaction or occurrence happened. For example, a tort action may be commenced and tried either in the county or district where the tort was committed or where the defendant resides or may be found. If the defendants are nonresidents, and assuming that proper service can be made upon them under a "long arm" statute, the suit may be commenced and tried in any county which the plaintiff designates in his complaint.

The judge may change the place of trial at the request of either party when it appears from an affidavit of either party that the action was not commenced in the right county, or that the judge has an interest in the suit or is related to any parties to the action or has manifested a prejudice so that he cannot be expected to conduct a fair and impartial trial. A change of venue may be requested when the inhabitants of the county manifest a prejudice which makes a fair trial doubtful. The convenience of witnesses and the parties may also justify a change of venue.

THE JUDICIAL SYSTEM CASE

Singer v. Walker

1964, 250 N.Y.S.2d 216

BREITEL, J. The issue in this personal injury action is whether the courts of this State may exercise personal jurisdiction over defendant foreign corporation under CPLR § 302, and subject to the applicable constitutional limitations. Special Term held there was no such jurisdiction and plaintiffs appeal.

At Special Term, it was held that, because defendant corporation was not doing business in this State and the cause of action did not rise from any tortious act or from transaction of business in this State by defendant, the new statute (section 302) did not confer jurisdiction. While it is true that defendant does not do business in the State, and this has been judicially determined in a prior action brought by plaintiffs, the new statute authorizes jurisdiction over a non-domiciliary where a cause of action against him arises from the commission of a tortious act within the State. Because, under the complaint, defendant was responsible for a continuous tortious act, namely, the circulation in New York of a defective hammer, always bearing its mislabeling, a tortious act occurred in this State from which the cause of action arose; for the hammer would not have been acquired in New York except for the undisclosed defect and the mislabeling, and the occurrence of the harm in Connecticut was incidental for jurisdictional purposes. Notably, the statute is not defined in terms of requiring that the cause of action arise in the State, but only that it arise from the commission of a tortious act in the State. This is within constitutional limits, and therefore, there is personal jurisdiction over defendant, and the order setting aside service of the summons and complaint should be reversed and defendant's motion denied.

The complaint contains two causes of action, one in breach of warranty and the other in negligence. It alleges that a geologist's hammer, marked as unbreakable, broke while being wielded in rock-breaking by infant plaintiff, then 10 years old, resulting eventually in the loss of his eye. The hammer had been manufactured in Illinois by defendant corporation, and shipped, f.o.b. Rockford, Illinois, to a New York dealer. He had purchased it by a direct mail order, using a catalogue which had been mailed to him by defendant. The boy's aunt purchased the hammer from the New York dealer in February, 1960, and presented it to the boy. Plaintiffs, father and son, are residents of New York, but in April, 1960 they were in Connecticut on a field trip when the hammer broke and the son's injury sustained. The complaint also alleges that the hammer, if defective, had dangerous propensities and was an imminently as well as an inherently dangerous instrument.

Plaintiffs brought a prior action, but the service of process was set aside twice: first, on the ground that the service was not made on a proper person, and second, on the ground that defendant was not doing business in the State. The determinations were made under the old statute and before the jurisdiction over non-domiciliaries was enlarged by section 302. . . .

The new statute, effective September 1, 1963, provides in relevant part:

§ 302. Personal jurisdiction by acts of non-domiciliaries
    (a) Acts which are the basis of jurisdiction.

        A court may exercise personal jurisdiction over any non-domiciliary, or his executor or administrator, as to a cause of action arising from any of the acts enumerated in this section, in the same manner as if he were a domiciliary of the state, if, in person or through an agent, he:

        1. transacts any business within the state; or

        2. commits a tortious act within the state, except as to a cause of action for defamation of character arising from the act; or

        3. owns, uses or possesses any real property situated within the state.

The tort cause of action arose in Connecticut, under traditional analysis; but as already stated the statute is not cased in terms of where the cause of action arose. The modern trend is to reject the old cause of action test, both as a matter of fairness and because of the definitional problems which follow in the wake of that test (cf. Uniform Interstate and International Procedure Act, § 1.03 incl. Commr's Notes, 9B Uniform Laws Ann. 1963 Suppl., pp. 75-78). It suffices that a tortious act is committed within this State, albeit the harm, and, therefore, the cause of action, arose in Connecticut.

A breach of warranty resulting in harm is now characterized as also a tortious wrong (*Goldberg v. Kollsman Instrument Corp.*, 12 N.Y.2d 432, 436, 240 N.Y.S.2d 592, 594, 191 N.E.2d 81, 82-83; *Randy Knitwear, Inc. v. American Cyanamid Co.*, 11 N.Y.2d 5, 10-11, 226 N.Y.S.2d 363, 365-367, 181 N.E.2d 399, 400-402; Prosser on Torts (2nd ed.) pp. 493-496). Hence, both causes of action are in tort. That a tortious act was committed by defendant corporation in New York would appear from the physical delivery and circulation in the New York market of the defective hammer, a particularly dangerous instrument because of its function and the false labeling which it bore with respect to its unbreakability (Restatement, Torts, Second (Tent. Draft #10, April 20, 1964) § 402A). The fact that the hammer was shipped by the seller, f.o.b. Rockford, Illinois, is significant in sales law for determining the risk of loss in transit and the like. Nonetheless, it is still the seller, defendant corporation, which sent the mislabeled defective hammer into the New York market knowing that it would be circulated there for sale.

To be sure, cases analyzing in traditional fashion the tortious act as compared with the complete tort hold generally that the duty of proper manufacture was breached in the manufacture or production of a defective product and, therefore, occurs only at the place of manufacture. (Uniform Interstate and International Procedure Act, § 103 incl. Commr's Notes, 9B Uniform Laws Ann. 1963 Suppl., pp. 75-78, *supra*) (The analysis is then carried further to allow of jurisdiction *in personam* where the harm occurred, because the cause of action arose there, even if not at the place of manufacture or production.) But there are some breaches of duty which create a continuing condition of hazard to users, very much like an enjoinable nuisance which may ground a cause of action short of the harm having yet occurred (66 C.J.S. Nuisances § 110; Anno. Injunction—Threatened Nuisance, 26 A.L.R. 937; 55 A.L.R. 880). In the case of an instrument defective in construction or dangerous because mislabeled the hazard persists wherever and so long as the product circulates. To be sure, if there had not been any contact with the user in a place where the product has circulated (in this case, New York) but only in the place where the harm occurred (in this case, Connecticut), it could not be said that the cause of action arising from the harm had any practical relation to the events in the place where the product had merely circulated (New York). Hence, in that instance, it could not be said that the cause of action arose from any act in the place of circulation (New York). That, however, is not this case.

In this case the acquisition by the infant plaintiff of the defective hammer occurred in New York and occurred in New York only because the defendant was responsible for the circulation in New York of the defective hammer which, being mislabeled, increased the hazard. It is alleged that there was reliance by the aunt and plaintiffs on the representations. The fact that the infant plaintiff obtained possession of the hammer in New York is an essential nexus to sustain jurisdiction. By the same token, the place or places to which the infant plaintiff took the hammer in his use of it is of less relevance. Thus, it happened that it was in Connecticut that the defective hammer broke under the strain to which it was subjected and caused the harm. It could just as well have been in New York or in any other place that this would have happened.

On this view, the tortious act, namely, the circulation in New York of the dangerous instrument mislabeled, was proximately connected with the acquisition and continued possession by the infant plaintiff and his resulting injury. This should suffice, therefore, to satisfy the requirements of subdivision (a), par. 2 of section 302 and also to satisfy the constitutional limitations which require some contacts within the state in which the action is brought in order to sustain personal jurisdiction.

Until recently, products liability cases had been restrictively affected by the "doing business" or "presence" doctrine of jurisdiction in the selection of forums in which the foreign manufacturers might be sued. Under the impact of the newer jurisdiction-expanding cases in the Supreme Court, the restrictions have been substantially removed (*International Shoe Co. v. Washington,* 326 U.S. 310, 66 S.Ct. 154, 90 L.Ed. 95, *McGee v. International Life Ins. Co.,* 355 U.S. 220, 78 S.Ct. 199, 2 L.Ed.2d 223; 2 Frumer and Friedman, Products Liability, § 45.01, supra).

It has been recognized that, assuming some causal nexus, jurisdiction, as distinguished from the application of the appropriate law, may rest upon events (contacts) in between the manufacture of a harmful product and the occasion of harm. Whatever other reasons exist for the rarity of cases involving this intermediate situation, a principal cause would be that there was no opportunity to entertain such cases so long as the old "doing business" or "presence" doctrine prevailed. (For a subtle and considered discussion of the problem see Ehrenzweig on Conflict of Laws, 114-118, 587-592.) Restatement, Conflicts, Second, in stating the rules to cover the enlarged judicial jurisdiction over non-domiciliaries says of a foreign corporation in part:

> A state has judicial jurisdiction over a foreign corporation as to causes of action arising out of (1) an act done, or caused to be done, by the corporation in the state or resulting in consequences there . . ." (Tent. Dr. #3 (1956) § 91a; cf. id. § 84 incl. Comments).

While the Restatement does not go as far in its comments as does Ehrenzweig in his analysis, its language, it would seem, is sufficiently broad to embrace the same concepts.

A recent and influential case, albeit distinguishable, in the field of jurisdiction is *Erlanger Mills, Inc. v. Cohoes Fibre Mills,* 239 F2d 502 (4th Cir. 1956). There the court struck down as unconstitutional the application of a very broad North Carolina jurisdiction statute:

The pertinent part of the statute reads:

> Jurisdiction over foreign corporations not transacting business in this State —(a) Every foreign corporation shall be subject to suit in this State, by a resident of this State or by a person having a usual place of business in this State, whether or not such foreign corporation is transacting or has transacted business in this State and whether or not it is engaged exclusively in interstate or foreign commerce, on any cause of action arising as follows: . . .
>
> (3) Out of the production, manufacture, or distribution of goods [which] are to be used or consumed in this State and are so used and consumed, regardless of how or where the goods were produced, manufactured, marketed, or sold or whether or not through the medium of independent contractors or dealers. (G.S. § 55-38.1)

Plaintiff sued in federal court in North Carolina against a New York corporation for the sale to it of inferior goods. The order for the goods had been placed in New York by plaintiff and accepted in New York, and the goods were then shipped f.o.b. New York. That case, of course, did not involve the present situation. In this case the goods were ordered from New York by a New York dealer from defendant's catalogue which had been sent into New York by defendant, and the goods were then shipped into New York. Moreover, unlike the Erlanger case, defendant corporation, although short of being present in the jurisdictional sense, does a great deal of business directly in the New York area, sending its salesmen and its catalogues into the city. In the Erlanger case it was a first transaction for the defendant with the North Carolina firm, and all arrangements for the purchase had been made in New York by plaintiff. Withal, the Erlanger decision has not been without its adverse critics (see 1 Weinstein, K. & M., *op. cit. supra,* ¶ 302.03 at pp. 3-33 to 3-34). But there is a further distinction to be made between the Erlanger case and this one. The Erlanger case involved but an ordinary breach of warranty in contract resulting in a claim of lesser value. This case is in tort and involves an instrument dangerous to human beings if defective. (Restatement, Conflicts, Second [Tent.Dr. #3, 1956] § 84, Comment c.)

Supportive of the analysis here, and in its facts going well beyond the necessities of this case, is *Gray v. American Radiator & Sanitary Corp.* (22 Ill.2d 432, 176 N.E.2d 761). That case involved a statute very similar to section 302. Under it the court sustained jurisdiction over a defendant manufacturer located in Ohio which had sold its product to a manufacturer in Pennsylvania, who assembled it into a water heater. The heater was sold in Illinois and exploded there injuring plaintiff Gray. The case, of course, presents difficult problems since the manufacturer's contact with the State of Illinois was slender, indeed, it having done little in Illinois except to be responsible for its defective part having been incorporated into an assembly which, in turn, was sent and delivered into Illinois by another. (For an analysis of the Gray case, see 1 Weinstein, K. & M., *op. cit. supra,* ¶ 302.10.)

It would seem, therefore, that the New York statute comes well within the constitutional limitations. It is not necessary to determine in this case whether the New York statute exhausts the possibilities within the constitutional limitations. Of paramount importance, no doubt, is the fact that an instrument dangerous to human life and health, if defective, is involved. Due process considerations would undoubtedly be more restrictive if there were involved simply a dispute of commercial dimensions between parties to a commercial contract. Where one introduces into a state a dangerous instrument the expectation of responsibility should be greater. Of little consequence except, perhaps, for purposes of determining the applicable conflict of law rules, is the fact that a cause of action in the traditional sense arose in Connecticut. Whatever it was that defendant corporation did, it did not only in the State of Connecticut, but it did the same in the State of New York. Once it is found that a tortious act occurred in this State it is only reasonable that the actor should be responsible in New York to its residents with respect to any cause of action arising from such activity.

Accordingly, the order granting defendant corporation's motion to set aside the service of the summons and complaint should be reversed on the law, without costs to plaintiffs-appellants.

Order, entered on November 21, 1963, unanimously reversed, on the law, without costs, and the motion to vacate service of the summons and complaint denied.

CHAPTER 4
REVIEW QUESTIONS AND PROBLEMS

1. Name and classify the various federal courts. By what authority is the United States Supreme Court created? How does it differ from the lower federal courts?
   Name four state courts of limited jurisdiction.
2. Over what must the courts have jurisdiction in order to render a judgment? Has one court any jurisdiction over a matter arising in another county? May a court render a judgment against a person who is not found in the county?
3. What are "long arm" statutes? Do all states always have jurisdiction over interstate businesses? If not, what is the test to determine if a business is subject to a court's jurisdiction?
4. Why were courts of equity created? Do the reasons still exist?
5. Name five equitable maxims and illustrate situations in which they might be used.
6. What is the difference between jurisdiction and venue?
7. Name three reasons which would justify a change of venue.
8. What is meant by diversity jurisdiction?
9. If X, a citizen of state Illinois sues Y, a citizen of Indiana, and Z, a citizen of Illinois, does a federal court have jurisdiction?
10. What is the jurisdictional amount in the federal courts?
11. A, a citizen of Illinois, sues the XYZ Co., for breach of contract in the Federal District Court. XYZ Co. is incorporated in Delaware but has its principal place of business in Illinois. Does the Federal Court have jurisdiction?
12. X, a citizen of Alabama, sues Y, a citizen of Mississippi, in the Alabama State Courts. Jurisdiction is obtained by service of process in Mississippi. Can Y have the case removed to the Federal Courts?
13. X and Y are discussing a matter and disagree on the legality of proposed action. X suggests that a suit be filed to determine the legality of the proposed conduct. Will a court settle their dispute?

14. What agencies of government other than courts settle controversies? Give an example for each agency.
15. What types of matters are heard and decided in Probate courts?
16. Is the Supreme Court of the United States a court of general jurisdiction? Explain.
17. In what types of cases in the Federal Courts is the jurisdictional amount not involved?

chapter 5

The Lawsuit

1-28. The Need for Adjective Law. As previously noted, there are two kinds of law; "substantive law" and "procedural law" or "adjective law." "Substantive law" defines the rights and duties of citizens—it is the result of legislative action or judicial action. It defines the legal relations between citizens and between the citizen and the state. Procedural or adjective law specifies the method, means, and way the substantive law is made, enforced, and administered by legislators, administrators, judges, and citizens. Legislative procedure consists of the rules of order by which legislation is made, for example, "a majority vote of the assembly is required for the passage of a bill." Administrative procedures prescribe the rules of order by which administrative boards such as the Federal Trade Commision and the National Labor Relations Board shall function.

Judicial procedure is concerned with the rules by which a law suit is conducted so that a fair and impartial trial may be had. There are two kinds of judicial procedure—criminal and civil. Criminal procedure prescribes the rules of law for the apprehension, prosecution, and fixing of punishment of persons who have violated the criminal law. Such procedure is initiated by the State. Civil procedure prescribes the rules by which parties to a law suit use the courts to settle their disputed claims. The law of procedure called adjective law is the legal mechanism by which a substantive law question is presented to the court in order that a decision may be made. Procedure is a means of accomplishing a legal result through the proper application of rules of substantive law. It is the method by which an aggrieved person who claims to have suffered injury to his property or person is able to get the person who committed the alleged wrong into court and compel him to pay damages or make restitution. Likewise, it enables one against whom a contract has been breached to obtain redress.

Procedural rules prescribe the method by which the lawyer, the court and the jury resolve the conflict between the parties. If the complaining party were permitted to present his side of the case in his own way and no orderly process was followed, confusion would be added to confusion. Without such rules one's substantive rights would be of no value.

Law does not operate in a vacuum. It must be applied. There must first be a dispute; the court is not designed to simply answer legal questions. In order to settle the dispute, it must be presented to the court. Procedure is the method by which the court "gets the case."

The procedural rules compel the parties, by their attorneys, to find the basis of the dispute, present the issues to the court, and exclude from the conflict all matter not relevant to the controversy. Procedural rules have for their objective the elimination, as far as possible, of passion, exaggeration, improper evidence, overreaching, partiality, falsehood, and unfairness.

The disputants by the use of procedural rules must clearly define the issues of the dispute; otherwise the court may not know what it is to settle. Whether the dispute is over what are the facts, or what evidence is relevant to prove the facts, or what rule of law applies to the facts, the dispute must be resolved. The procedure prescribed to settle each of these questions is different. Thus, if the dispute is over the legal validity of the claim or the kind of evidence required to prove the claim procedural rules provide that these are questions of law for the judge. If there is a dispute as to what are the facts about the claim, rules of procedure will require a trial, and place the duty of finding the facts on the jury under proper instructions from the judge.

An orderly method for settling disputes by an impartial third party is the prime function of any legal system. As a substitute for force, judicial procedure has been found the most effective method for resolving disputes.

1-29. Pleadings. The purposes of pleadings in civil actions are to define the issues of the lawsuit, and to notify the adverse party of the pleader's contentions and position. This is accomplished by each party making allegation of fact and the other party either admitting the allegations or denying them. The process is commenced by the plaintiff filing with the clerk of the court a pleading usually called a "complaint" or a "declaration" or "petition." The clerk issues a summons which, together with a copy of the complaint, is served on the defendant by leaving it either with him personally or with some member of his family, if the law so provides. The summons notifies the defendant of the date he is required to file a pleading in answer to the allegations of the complaint or some other pleading attacking the complaint. If the defendant does not attack the pleading on points of law, he will file an answer or his appearance in the suit. The defendant's answer will either admit or deny each allegation of the plaintiff's complaint and may also contain affirmative defenses which if proved will defeat the plaintiff's claim. The answer may also contain causes of action the defendant has against the plaintiff, called "counterclaims." Upon receipt of the defendant's answer, the plaintiff will, unless the applicable rules of procedure do not so require, file a reply which specifically admits or denies each allegation of the defendant's answer. Thus the allegations of each party are admitted or denied in the pleadings.

The first pleading (complaint) must clearly and accurately allege facts sufficient to set forth a right of action or right to legal relief in the plaintiff. The defendant's attorney, after studying the complaint, may choose one of several different ways to challenge its legal sufficiency instead of answering. By motion to the court, the defendant may object to the complaint, pointing out specifically its defects. If the complaint is legally insufficient, the court will dismiss the action, but will also give the plaintiff an opportunity to amend. The defendant's attorney, through such motion, admits for purposes of argument all of the facts alleged in the complaint by arguing that those facts are not sufficient to give the plaintiff a cause of action. Such motion, called a *demurrer* at common law, raises questions of law, not questions of fact. If the court finds that the complaint does set forth facts sufficient to give the plaintiff a cause of action, it will deny the motion. The defendant will then be granted leave to answer the complaint; should he fail to do so within the time limit set by the court, a judgment by default will be entered for the plaintiff. If the court finds, however, that the complaint fails to state facts sufficient to give the plaintiff a cause of action against the defendant, the court will allow the motion, dismiss the suit, and grant leave to the plaintiff to amend his complaint. The plaintiff will thus be given an opportunity to restate his facts so that he may be able to set forth a cause of action.

In addition to a motion to dismiss for failure to state a cause of action, a defendant may also move to dismiss the suit for reasons which as a matter of law prevent the plaintiff from winning his suit. Such matters as a discharge in bankruptcy, lack of jurisdiction of the court to hear the suit, or expiration of the time limit during which the defendant is subject to suit may be raised by such a motion. These are matters of a technical nature which raise questions of law for the court's decision.

Most states and the federal courts have procedures where either party may submit the case for final decision by procedures known as "motions for summary judgment" or "motions for judgment on the pleadings." In these hearings, the court examines all papers on file in the case, including affidavits that may have been filed with the motion or in opposition to it, to see if a genuine material issue of fact remains. If there is no such question of fact, the court will then decide the legal question raised by the facts and find for one party or the other.

If a defendant subject to the jurisdiction of the court fails to file an answer either originally or after his motions have been overruled, he is in default and a court of law may enter a default judgment against him.

A court of equity would enter a similar order known as a decree *pro confesso*.

1-30. Pre-trial Stage. During the pleading stage and in the interval before the trial, the law provides for procedures called "discovery" procedures which are designed to take the "sporting aspect" out of litigation and to ensure that the results of lawsuits are based on the merits of the controversy and less on the ability, skill, or cunning of counsel. Without these procedures an attorney with no case on the facts or law might win a lawsuit through surprise—by keeping silent about a fact or by concealing his true case until the trial. Lawsuits should not be based on the skill or lack thereof of counsel, but on the relative merits of the controversy. Discovery practice is designed to ensure that each side is fully aware of all the facts involved in the case and of the contentions of the parties, prior to trial. Another of its avowed purposes is to encourage settlement of suits and to avoid actual trial.

Discovery practices include the taking of the deposition of other parties and witnesses, the serving of written questions to be answered under oath by the opposite party, compulsory physical examinations by doctors chosen by the other party, orders requiring the production of exhibits, documents, maps, photographs, etc., and the serving by one party on another of demands to admit facts under oath. Some courts even allow the discovery of the amount of insurance coverage possessed by the defendant in a personal injury case. The Federal Rules of Civil Procedure illustrate the trend and scope of discovery procedures. They allow discovery of

> any matter, not privileged, which is relevant to the subject matter involved in the pending action, whether it relates to the claim or defense of the examining party or to the claim or defense of any other party, including the existence, description, nature, custody, condition and location of any books, documents, or other tangible things and the identity and location of persons having knowledge of relevant facts. It is not ground for objection that the testimony will be inadmissible at the trial if the testimony sought appears reasonably calculated to lead to the discovery of admissible evidence. . . .

Just prior to the trial a pre-trial conference between the lawyers and the judge will be held in states with modern rules of procedure. At this conference, the pleadings, results of the discovery process and probable evidence are reviewed in an attempt to settle the suit. The issues may be further narrowed and the judge may even give his prediction of the outcome in order to encourage settlement. It is significant that a very substantial number of all lawsuits which are filed are settled sometime prior to trial. Discovery procedures contribute significantly to these settlements.

1-31. The Trial. Not all cases can be settled even under modern procedures. Some must go to trial on the issues of fact raised by the pleadings which remain after the pre-trial conference. If the only issues are a question of law, the court will decide the case without a trial by a ruling on one of the motions previously mentioned. If the case is at law and either party has demanded a jury trial, the cause will be set for trial and a jury empaneled. If the case is in equity or if no jury demand has been made, it will be set down for trial before the court or possibly a Master in Chancery. For purposes of discussion the following assumes trial before a jury.

The first step of the trial is to select the jury. Prior to the calling of the case, the clerk of the court will have summoned prospective jurors. They will be selected at random from lists of eligible citizens and twelve of them will be called into the jury box for the conduct of *voir dire* examination. (Section 1-33 explains this process in greater detail.) *Voir dire* examination is a method by which the court and the attorneys for each party examine the jurors as to their qualifications to be fair and impartial jurors. Each side in the lawsuit may challenge or excuse a juror for cause, e.g. for bias, prejudice or relation to one of the parties. In addition, each side will be given a certain number of challenges known as "preemptory challenges" for which no cause need be given. Each side is given an opportunity to question the prospective jurors and either to accept them or reject them until his challenges are exhausted. The prospective jurors are sworn to give truthful answers to the questions on *voir dire*. The processes continue until the full jury is selected.

After selecting the jurors, the attorneys make opening statements. An opening statement is not evidence but is only used to familiarize the jury with the essential facts in the case which each side expects to prove in order that the jury may understand the over-all picture of the case and the relevancy of each bit of evidence as presented. After the opening statements, the plaintiff presents his evidence.

Evidence is presented in open court by means of examination of witnesses and the production of documents and other exhibits. The party calling a witness has a right to examine that witness and ask him questions to establish the facts of which he is familiar about the case. As a general rule, a party calling a witness is not permitted to ask "leading questions," questions in which the desired answer is indicated by the form of the question. After the party calling the witness has completed his direct examination, the other party is given the opportunity to cross-examine the witness. Matters inquired into on cross-examination are limited to those matters which were raised on direct examination. After cross-examination, the party calling the witness again has the opportunity of examining the witness and this examination is called redirect examination. It is limited to the scope of those matters gone into on cross-examination and is used to clarify matters raised on cross-examination. After redirect examination, the opposing party is allowed re-cross-examination again, with the corresponding limitation as to scope of the questions. Witnesses may be asked to identify exhibits. Expert witnesses may be asked to give their opinion, within certain limitations, about the case and sometimes experts are allowed to answer hypothetical questions.

In the conduct of a trial, the rules of evidence govern the admissibility of testimony and exhibits, and establish which facts may be presented to the jury and which facts may not. Each rule of evidence is based on some policy consideration and the desire to give each party an opportunity to present his evidence and contentions without unduly taking advantage of the other party. Rules of evidence were not created to serve as a stumbling block to meritorious litigants or to create unwarranted roadblocks to justice. On the contrary, the rules of evidence were created and should be applied to ensure fair play and to aid in the goal of having controversies determined on their merits.

To illustrate the policy considerations which form the basis of the rules of evidence, an examination of the rules relating to privileged communications is helpful.

The policy behind the Fifth Amendment's privilege against self-incrimination is obvious. There are other communications, such as between husband and wife, doctor and patient, clergy and penitent, and attorney and client, which are also considered privileged by the law in order that these communications can be made without fear of their subsequent use against the parties involved. Fair play requires that an attorney not be required to testify as to matters told him in confidence by his client. The preservation of the home requires that a spouse not be required to testify against the other spouse regarding confidential communications. Some matters are privileged, such as the existence of insurance coverage of a party, because of the great effect that knowledge of the existence of insurance would have on a jury. Matters which are privileged are matters which by the rules of fair play should not be admitted into evidence. Similar policy considerations support all rules of evidence. Each rule is designed to assist in the search for truth.

A basic rule of evidence is that a party cannot introduce evidence unless it is competent and relevant to the issues raised by the pleadings.

After the plaintiff has presented his evidence, the defendant will often make a motion for a directed verdict. This motion asks the court to rule as a matter of law that the plaintiff has failed to establish a right against the defendant and that judgment should be given to the latter. The court can only direct a verdict if the evidence taken in the light most favorable to the party resisting the motion establishes as a matter of law that the moving party is entitled to a verdict. The defendant argues that the plaintiff has failed to prove each allegation of his complaint. Just as a plaintiff must *allege* certain facts or have his complaint dismissed by motion to dismiss, he must have some *proof* of each essential allegation, or lose his case on a motion for a directed verdict. If he has some proof of each allegation, the motion will be overruled.

In cases tried without a jury, either party may move for a finding in his favor. Such a motion will be allowed during the course of the trial if the result is not in doubt. While the judge on such motions weighs the evidence, he may end the trial only if there is no room for a fair difference of opinion as to the result.

If the defendant's motion for directed verdict is overruled, the defendant then presents his evidence. It should be noted that a party calling a witness vouches for his credibility and is not allowed to impeach or attempt to discredit a witness whom he has called. After the defendant has presented all his evidence, the plaintiff may bring in rebuttal evidence. When neither party has any additional evidence, the attorneys and the judge retire for a conference to consider the instructions of law to be given the jury.

The purpose of the jury instructions is to acquaint the jury with the law applicable to the case. Since the function of the jury is to find the facts and the function of the court is to determine the applicable law, there must be a method to bring them together in an orderly manner that will result in a decision. At the conference, each attorney submits to the court the instructions which he feels should be given to the jury. The court examines these instructions and confers with the attorneys. He then decides which instructions will be given to the jury. A typical jury instruction in a case where a minor is seeking to recover money paid by him in purchase of an item is as follows: The court instructs the jury that contracts of minors may be avoided by the minor upon return of so much of the consideration received by the minor as he had left, providing the consideration is not a necessity. If you find from the evidence that the plaintiff was a minor, that the consideration received by him was not a necessity and that he has returned so much of what he received as he has left, then your verdict will be for the minor, plaintiff.

In this instruction, the court is in effect saying that the plaintiff must prove that he was a minor, that the contract does not involve necessities and that he has returned all of what he received that he had. Thus the law of minors is applied to the facts and the jury is instructed as to the result to be returned if they find certain facts.

After the conference on jury instructions, the attorneys argue the case to the jury. The party with the burden of proof, usually the plaintiff, is given an opportunity to open the argument and to close it. The defendant's attorney is only allowed to argue after the plaintiff's argument and is only allowed to argue once. After the arguments are completed, the court reads the instruction to the jury.

In the federal courts and in some state courts, the judge while giving instructions may comment on the evidence. He may indicate the importance of certain portions of evidence, the inferences that might be drawn therefrom, point out the conflicts, and indicate what statements are more likely to be true than others and state why. The court, however, is duty bound to make clear to the jury that it is not obligated to follow his evaluation of the evidence and that it is its duty to determine the facts of the case. The jury then retires to deliberate upon its verdict.

There are two kinds of verdicts. A "general verdict" and a "special verdict." A general verdict is one in which the jury makes a complete finding and single conclusion on all issues presented to it. First it finds the facts, as proven by the evidence, then applies the law as instructed by the court and returns a verdict in one conclusion that settles the case. Such verdict is reported as follows: "We the jury find the issues for the plaintiff (or defendant, as the case may be) and assess his damages at One Thousand Dollars." The jury does not make a separate finding of fact, or report what law is applied.

By a special verdict the jury is limited to finding the facts. It is the duty of the court to apply the law to the facts as found by the jury. Such verdict is not a general settlement of the case; it settles only the specific questions of fact. Since the jury finds only the facts it receives no instructions from the court as to the law. This duty is left to the court. Under what circumstances general or special verdict may be used is controlled by statute.

Upon reaching a verdict the jury returns from the jury room, announces its verdict, and judgment is entered. Judgments are either *in rem* or *in personam*. A judgment *in rem* is an adjudication entered against a thing—property, real or personal. The judgment is a determination of the status of the subject matter. Thus a judgment of forfeiture of goods for the violation of a revenue law is a judgment *in rem*. Although a judgment *in rem* is limited to the subject matter, it nevertheless affects the rights and duties of persons. For example, while a decree dissolving a marriage seriously affects persons, it is nevertheless a judgment *in rem* because it affects a "status," the marriage relation. A judgment *in rem* is binding not only on the persons previously concerned with the status or thing but all other persons.

A judgment against a particular person is a judgment *in personam*. It is limited in its application to such person only, whereas a judgment *in rem* is conclusive on all persons.

After judgment is entered, the losing party starts the procedure of post-trial motions, which raise questions of law concerning the conduct of the lawsuit. These motions seek such relief as a new trial or a judgment notwithstanding the verdict of the jury. A motion seeking a new trial may be granted if the judge feels that the verdict of the jury is contrary to the manifest weight of the evidence. The court may enter a judgment opposite to that of the verdict of the jury if the judge finds that the verdict is, as a matter of law, erroneous. To reach such a conclusion, the court must find that reasonable men viewing the evidence could not reach the verdict returned. For example, a verdict for the plaintiff may be based on sympathy instead of evidence.

From the ruling on the post-trial motion, the losing party may appeal. It should be noted that lawsuits usually end by a ruling on a motion, either before trial, during the trial, or after the trial. Motions raise questions of law which are decided by the court. The right to appeal, which is discussed in a subsequent section, is absolute if perfected within the prescribed time. Before discussing appeals, a look at the function, duties, and role of judges and the jury is helpful in understanding the trial of the lawsuit.

1-32. The Judge. "Judges ought to be more learned than witty, more reverent than plausible, more advised than confident. Above all things, integrity is their portion and proper virtue." (Bacon)

The judge, by virtue of his office, is in his personal conduct under a duty to the state, its people, the litigants, the law, the witness, and the jury. He must remember that the court is for the litigants, not the litigants for the court. He must observe and apply constitutional limitations and guarantees. A judge should be temperate, attentive, patient, impartial, studious, diligent, industrious, and prompt in ascertaining the facts and applying the law. He should organize his court with a view to the prompt and convenient dispatch of its business. He should be courteous, civil, and considerate of jurors, witnesses and others in attendance upon the court, but should criticize and correct unprofessional conduct of attorneys. He should appoint all court personnel with a view solely to their character and fitness and not act in a controversy where he or a near relative have an interest. He should not be swayed by public clamor or consideration of personal popularity nor be apprehensive of unjust criticism. He should not improperly interfere in the conduct of a trial except to prevent waste of time and clarify obscurity. He should be mindful of the general law and administer justice with due regard for the integrity of the legal system. He should not compel a person brought before him to submit to humiliating acts or discipline of his own making. He should abstain from making personal investments in enterprises which are apt to be involved in litigation in the court and should not participate in partisan politics or contribute to party funds. He should not, and in many states by law cannot, engage in the private practice of law. He should not accept gifts or favors from litigants or lawyers whose interests are likely to be submitted to him for judgment. He should conduct the court proceedings so as to reflect the importance of ascertaining the truth.

Such are the virtues required of the trial judge, who renders his decisions at a level which deals directly with the people. It is in the trial courts where the law is made alive and its words are given meaning. Trial judges see and deal intimately with persons in conflict. Whatever provocations may disturb him personally, the judge is burdened with the task of upholding the dignity of the courts and maintaining respect for the law. Appellate judges reviewing the cold words of the record of the trial below, seeking to determine the presence or absence of error as a basis for affirmation or reversal, are insulated from the live drama of the trial. Of the thousands of criminal and civil cases which are filed, only a small portion are tried, and less than one-third of the cases tried are appealed. Therefore, it is apparent that the effective function of the law must lie largely upon the character and training of the trial judge.

1-33. The Jury. In Anglo-American law, the right of trial by jury, particularly in criminal cases, is traced to the famous "Magna Carta" issued by King John of England in 1215, wherein it is stated:

> . . . that no freeman shall be taken or imprisoned or disseised or outlawed or exiled . . . without the judgment of his peers or by the law of the land. . . .

In early English legal history the juror was a witness, that is, he was called to tell what he knew, not to listen to others testify. The word "jury" comes from the French word *juré* which means "sworn." The jury gradually developed into an institution to determine facts. Thus today a juror must come to a trial with an open mind; otherwise his previous knowledge might prejudice him in evaluating the testimony presented at the trial. The jury system as brought to the colonies from England was adopted as a matter of right in the Constitution of the United States. The Sixth and Seventh Amendments to the United States Constitution guarantee the right of trial by jury in both criminal and civil cases: in addition, the Fifth Amendment provides for indictment by a grand jury for capital offenses and infamous crimes. In civil cases the right to trial by jury is preserved in suits at common law when the amount in controversy exceeds twenty dollars. State constitutions have like provisions guaranteeing the right of trial by jury in state courts.

The persons who are selected to serve on trial juries are drawn at random from lists of qualified voters in the county or city where the trial court sits. Most states by statute have listed certain occupations and professions such as doctors, dentists, pharmacists, embalmers, policemen, firemen, lawyers, and newspapermen who are exempt from jury duty. When a case is called for trial, those selected as noted above will appear as the jury panel and unless excused by the judge for personal reasons will be available to serve as jurors. Twelve persons will be selected by drawing, and *voir dire* examination will be conducted to select the jury in a particular case. Serving on the jury is an important civic duty. It is one significant way in which a citizen can take part in his government and participate in the administration of justice.

For many years the jury system has been subject to criticism. It is contended that most jurors are not qualified to distinguish fact from fiction, that they are easily influenced by public opinion, vote their prejudices, and are too easily emotionally moved by persuasive trial lawyers. Admitting the frailties of men, the average American still believes in the "right to be tried by a jury of his peers" in criminal cases. Safeguarded by the rules of trial procedure it is felt by most members of the bench and bar that the jury system is as fair and effective a method of ascertaining the truth and giving an accused "his day in court" as has been devised.

In most states the decision of the jury except in particular stituations prescribed by constitution or statute must be unanimous. It is expected that in most cases the jury's verdict "will be a total assertion." It is asserted that the truth is more nearly to be found and justice rendered if the jury acts only on one common conscience, on what is almost immediately obvious, not on what is elaborated by a little group. It operates in "the native way of deciding an issue," that is, "to discuss it until there is unanimity of opinion or until the opposition feels it is no longer worthwhile to argue its point of view." Statutes and constitutions provide the number of jurors who must concur for a verdict in other cases. In some states the concurrence of three-fourths of the jurors is required in civil cases.

A jury is not permitted to take notes as a general rule and is not permitted to give reasons for its decision. Actually, it would be impossible for the jury to give reasons for its verdict. A controversy must have finality as to the facts. In our democratic judicial process this is the function of the jury. Reason does not support facts. Judges are required to give reasons for their decisions, because their conclusions are part of a public record. Judicial decisions must give as far as possible certainty and continuity to the law, and rest on logic and rationality. In reaching a decision, a judge is concerned with two aspects of the case—the law and the facts. Bringing these elements together by the very nature of the intellectual process requires reason, but the jury is not engaged in such process. It is interpreting other persons' impressions of what are the facts. The jurors are not seeking to render a judgment—they are evaluating "patterns of behavior."

1-34. The Lawyer. English law was not only the source of the common law but also the direct ancestors of the common law lawyers were persons hired as "champions" in trial by battle in early English "litigation." In criminal actions a defendant was required to establish his innocence by defeating the plaintiff or his champion. In civil actions the bout was waged by champions, not by the parties themselves, because if either party to the case was killed the suit would end and no judgment could be taken.

"Trials" of this sort were later abolished in England, and trial by jury was substituted. However, the idea of a "contest" survived, so that today a trial is in a sense a contest between the lawyers, as advocates for their clients, like champions in olden times. The court acts as referee, within an adversary system so conducted as to fairly persuade a jury toward a just result. In early England, after William the Conqueror, land law and pleadings became so complex that there developed of necessity a class of legal advisers increasingly experienced and competent.

Since biblical times, the lawyer has always been the subject of criticism and sometimes derision. In the late 1700's four states even went so far as to abolish the legal profession. In 1917 the profession in Russia was destroyed by governmental fiat, but it did not stay dead. An ordered society makes necessary men learned in the law.

The lawyer uses his knowledge of the law in many ways. For the client he is a confidant and adviser. He assists the client by the preparation of legal documents, mediates disputes, and as advocate represents the client in court. The lawyer as a policy maker contributes to public order not only by participating personally in the legislative and judicial functions of government, but also when as a legal consultant to decision makers both in business and government he advises them as to a proper and legal course of action.

To the layman the lawyer presents a contradictory picture. It is difficult for a layman to evaluate the many activities and duties of the lawyer, and make a fair judgment concerning his conduct and usefulness to society. A lawyer's duties are diverse, in that his responsibilities are by the very nature of the profession fourfold. A lawyer's first duty is to the state as a licensed official and a citizen. Secondly, he is an officer of the court, and an aid in the administration of justice; thirdly, he is a trustee and fiduciary for his client; and fourthly, he is obligated to deal honestly and fairly with other lawyers and the public in maintaining the honesty and integrity of the profession.

It is not always easy to properly keep in balance these obligations. The lawyer cannot give his sole attention to one of these obligations and neglect the others. In his zeal to assist his client he cannot be dishonest to the court. The court assisted by the lawyer is the public instrument for the administration of justice. Justice cannot be done if the court's decisions rest upon false proof and misquoted law. To be dishonest with the court is not only to be dishonest to the client but also dishonest to the state and his fellow lawyers. The lawyer must perform each of these four duties without neglecting the others.

The adversary system within which the lawyer operates makes for many different impressions about his duties. By tradition and definition a lawsuit is a place of strife. The modern lawsuit is a substitute for the ancient physical combat; the lawyer today is in a sense a "combatant" for his client. Instead of using physical force, a lawyer today represents his client in litigation by the use of words. Through pleadings, persuasion, cleverness, psychology, and argument, he represents his client in a forum called a court room. The lawyer's problem is not only what is or is not the law, but what law—case or statute—should be applied to the particular circumstances with which he has to deal.

A lawyer's conduct is governed by forty-seven Canons of Legal Ethics touching every aspect of a lawyer's duty: his duty to the court, his client, the public, the jury, the profession, as well as his professional conduct in relation to advertising, unjustifiable litigation, fees, witnesses, newspapers, and the unauthorized practice of the law.

The contesting lawyers as partisan advocates, operating within the rules of procedure and evidence, and supervised by the court, make possible the exploration of every aspect of the case. It is the general belief of the legal profession that a single arbiter acting as judge, advocate, and jury would by the very nature of the method used find himself prematurely reaching a fixed opinion which would continue and become a guide or standard that would foreclose further consideration of the case and color his final decision. Such preconceived judgments will not prevail under the adversary system. The narrowing of issues by the rules of procedure, preparation and presentation of the case to the jury by partisan advocates, examination and cross-examination of the witnesses, argument by counsel, and the control, supervision, and instruction by the judge make premature conclusions impossible. During the process of a trial, the court or jury has the benefit of seeing both sides of the issue, clearly defined, and they are able to arrive at a just conclusion. Settling private contentions by a public adversary system, manipulated by intelligent advocates, operating under an orderly process supervised by a neutral third party—the judge—is believed to be one of the most important institutions of American democracy.

However, there are many critics of the adversary process. That such system is best able to find the truth and render justice is questioned by scholars, laymen, and members of the bench and bar. It is believed by many that the adversary system is greatly abused; that it permits the lawyers to overreach witnesses, mislead the jury, use rules of evidence to cover up facts rather than disclose the truth; that it also makes it possible for a clever experienced lawyer to dominate the proceedings to such an extent that the other less experienced party has "not had his day in court." Certainly there is much public misunderstanding of the nature and purpose of the jury trial and the lawyer's function therein.

It is especially important that the businessman have a clear understanding of the lawyer's role since he will undoubtedly have occasion to avail himself of the services of a lawyer. Lawyers agree that the greatest service a lawyer can render for his client is to practice "preventive law"—to give counsel in anticipation of potential legal difficulties so that there will be no need for litigation. Businessmen can ill afford the time which they must spend away from their businesses during the time-consuming process of a trial, let alone the expense involved. In order that a businessman can obtain maximum value from his lawyer, he must, therefore, be able to confer efficiently with him and in a sense "educate" the lawyer to the specific problems likely to arise in connection with his particular business. The businessman should be able to recognize in a general way that a potential legal problem is in the offing and at that time consult the lawyer. He should recognize that his attorney needs the "facts" and will soon acquire the ability to communicate these efficiently to the lawyer.

In spite of efforts to avoid legal involvements, it is inevitable that some will develop. The client will consult his attorney who will elicit all of the facts so that he will be in a position to serve as advocate in his client's behalf. The lawyer will make every effort to negotiate a settlement for his client and will resort to a lawsuit only when all reasonable efforts to settle have failed.

Actually, most of the services rendered by a lawyer do not involve the court room at all. Most cases are settled—only a few ever come to trial. In a way, more effort is expended in preparing appellate court briefs in appeals of cases from trial courts than in the trial thereof. The bulk of most lawyers' time is spent in preparing contracts and other legal instruments and in giving advice. The growth of administrative law, governmental regulation and the complexities of laws of taxation make it likely that most people in business will seek the out-of-court services of their lawyer.

1-35. Appeals. A dissatisfied party, plaintiff or defendant, has a right to appeal the decision of the trial court to a higher court providing he proceeds promptly and in the proper manner. It should be noted that the cases collected and abstracted in this text with a few exceptions are decisions of an appellate court which reviews cases that were tried in a lower court. Whether he is plaintiff or defendant, the person who appeals is called the appellant and the opposite party is called the appellee, or respondent. The appellant is often named first in the title of the case or appeal and therefore care must be used in reading reported cases in order to properly identify each party as a plaintiff or defendant.

Appellate procedures are not uniform among the states and the appellant must comply with the appropriate statute and rules of the particular court. Appeals are usually perfected by the appellant giving "notice of appeal" to the trial court and opposing parties. Statutes provide that appeals must be taken within a certain number of days from the entry of the judgment, such as 30, 60, or 90 days, and these limitations refer to the time of giving the "notice of appeal." The filing of the notice of appeal and its entry upon the journal of the court where the trial was held give the appellate court jurisdiction of the case. After the appellate court has acquired jurisdiction, it may dismiss the appeal upon its own motion or that of the respondent if there are any statutory omissions in perfecting the appeal.

Most states require that within at least ten days after giving notice of appeal the appellant must file an appeal bond which, in effect, guarantees that the appellant will pay all damages, costs, and disbursements that may be awarded against him on the appeal. This is to protect the respondent so that he may collect his judgment and costs if the appellant loses on appeal.

The statutes usually require that within a specified time after the appeal is perfected, the appellant shall file with the clerk of the appellate court what is known as a *transcript*. The transcript consists of a copy of the judgment, decree, or order appealed from, the notice of appeal, the proof of service upon the respondent, the appeal bond, the pertinent portions of the stenographic transcript of the evidence, and such other papers as are required by the rules of the court. The record also includes all dispositions and other papers filed with the clerk in the lower court. The respondent, or appellee, receives a copy of the evidence and if he feels that additional parts of the record are pertinent, he may file an additional transcript.

Some states require, in addition, the filing of a bill of exceptions. A bill of exceptions is a written instrument in which are set out the objections or exceptions made and taken by the attorneys during the trial to the decisions, rulings, and instructions of the trial judge. The rulings excepted to are stated with an enumeration of as much evidence as is necessary to explain the exceptions. Sometimes the bill of exceptions may include all of the testimony, including the exhibits offered, received, or rejected, and the instructions to the jury, given or refused. In these states, the bill of exceptions must be agreed to by the parties, "settled" or "allowed," signed by the trial judge, and filed with the clerk of the trial court. When this is done, it becomes a part of the record of the case.

The transcript alone is not enough to present the case to the appellate court. The appellant must prepare and file a "brief" which contains a statement of the case, a list of the assignment of errors upon which the appellant has based his appeal, his legal authorities and argument.

A statement of the legal points and authorities relied upon for reversal and the appellant's arguments in written form which are set forth in the "brief" are illustrated by the following:

a. The court, upon the examination of witness X, erred in failing to sustain the objection to the admission of testimony in response to the following questions: (Here in the brief are set forth the questions, the objections, the answers given, and so forth.)

b. The court erred in denying a motion for a nonsuit or directed verdict. (Here are set out the exact motion and the court's ruling.)

c. The court erred in giving or in failing to give the following instructions: (Here are set out the instructions, the objections made, and so forth.)

d. The court erred in its decision because the statute under which the action was brought is unconstitutional. (Here are set out the statute and the reasons for its unconstitutionality.)

The next division of the brief sets out the points and authorities relied upon by the appellant relating to the particular assignments of error. In this section the attorney also presents the particular propositions he seeks to establish. Statutes and previously decided cases will be cited as authority for the propositions proposed.

The brief contains the arguments on both fact and law by which the attorney attempts to show how the court below committed the errors alleged.

The appellee (respondent) files a brief of like character setting out his side of the case with points, authorities, and arguments. By such procedure the case on the issues raised gets to the appellate court for decision.

The appellate court upon receipt of the case will place it on the calendar for hearing. The attorneys will be notified of the time and will be given an opportunity for oral arguments. After the oral arguments there is deliberation by members of the court and an opinion will be written stating the law involved and giving the court's reasons for its decision. The court by its decision may affirm or reverse the court below, or the court may send the case back for a new trial. At the end of each published opinion found in the reports, there will appear in a few words the result of the court's decision. Such words may be "affirmed," "reversed," "reversed and remanded," and so forth, as the case requires.

1-36. Enforcements of Judgments and Decrees. After a case has been finally determined, judicial action may be necessary to enforce the decision. In most cases, the losing party will voluntarily comply with the decision and satisfy the judgment or otherwise do what the judgment or decree requires him to do, but the assistance of the court is sometimes required.

If a judgment for dollar damages is not paid, the judgment creditor may apply for a writ of execution. This writ directs the sheriff to seize property of the judgment debtor and to sell enough thereof to satisfy the judgment and to cover the costs and expenses of the sale. If the judgment debtor's property does not sell for enough to pay the judgment and costs, the adjustment creditor may at a later date have execution issued for the deficiency against such property as the debtor may then own. Execution may also be levied against intangible property, such as bank accounts, which may be taken in satisfaction of the judgment. Wages may be garnisheed in satisfaction of a judgment but statutes closely regulate the amount of wages that can be garnisheed and otherwise restrict the use of this remedy. It should be noted that certain property of a judgment debtor is by statute exempt from execution. For example, most statutes provide for a homestead exemption and also exempt necessary household items, clothing, and the tools used by a person in his trade, as well as a certain amount of personal property.

In many states the unsatisfied judgment becomes a lien upon the real property owned by the judgment debtor at the time of the judgment, or any real property acquired by him during the life of the judgment. Thus, the judgment debtor could not convey a clear title to such property unless the judgment lien were satisfied.

In addition to the remedies available to obtain enforcement of a judgment, other procedures are available to a person who has instituted legal action by filing a complaint. These are discussed fully in the chapter on Creditor's Rights. One of these ancillary remedies is attachment of property belonging to the defendant. As previously discussed, such attachment will serve to acquire *in rem* jurisdiction over a case involving a non-resident defendant. It may also be used by a plaintiff in a contract action who may have had property of the defendant seized pending the outcome of the trial. This is called "attachment" and the procedures controlling its use are governed by statutes which vary among the states. The attaching plaintiff-creditor must put up a bond with the court for the protection of the defendant and the statutes provide methods whereby the attachment may be vacated by the defendant. If the plaintiff receives a judgment against the defendant, the attached property will be sold to satisfy the judgment.

1-37. The Nature of the Judicial Process. The court procedures involved in the pre-trial, trial, and review of cases have been discussed in the preceding sections. The procedures are important in bringing into play the substantive rules of law and in determining whether a case merits trial but they reveal to us only "how" a court reaches a decision; not why it reaches a particular decision. The great power of courts which results from the doctrine of judicial review, from the function of the court to interpret and apply statutes, and from the concept of *stare decisis* has been noted but the questions remain: What causes a court to reach one decision rather than another? What type of reasoning is used by courts— what factors influence the courts in their decisions? Of course, no absolute answers can be given to these questions, but a consideration of them is essential to an understanding of the legal process.

      Judicial reasoning. After a court of review decides a case, the court prepares and publishes an opinion which states the reasoning on which the decision is based. In many cases, the general character of such reasoning is deceptively simple; the court determines that some rule or rules of law are applicable, and decides the case accordingly.

Such reasoning has been characterized as syllogistic in form. According to this view, the applicable rule of law is stated as the major premise, the facts to which the rule applies as the minor premise, and the court's determination as the conclusion. Thus, to illustrate from an actual case: "No woman is entitled to recover damages against a party who has seduced her spouse" (major premise), "the plaintiff is a woman" (minor premise), "therefore the plaintiff is not entitled to recover" (conclusion).

Although the structure of most judicial opinions may be cast in syllogistic form, the student must not conclude that legal reasoning which exhibits this form is sound reasoning. Reasoning may be syllogistic, or "logical," but at the same time quite unsound as a basis for practical decision. Thus, in the foregoing illustration, the reasoning is "logical," but is not sound because the major premise is based on what Justice Cardozo called an "assumption of a bygone inequality. . . ." Early in the development of the common law, women occupied a lower status than men. This was reflected in decisions establishing the rule that a man could recover damages for the seduction of his wife because, it was said, a man had a property interest in the body of his wife. But a woman could not recover for the seduction of her husband, since she had no such property interest in the body of her husband. However, as Justice Cardozo said in the case of *Appenheim v. Kridel,* by 1920, "Social, political, and legal reforms [have] changed the relations between the sexes, and put woman and man upon a plane of equality. Decisions founded upon the assumption of a bygone inequality [are] unrelated to present-day realities, and ought not to be permitted to prescribe a rule. . . ."

Obviously, judicial reasoning must be sound as well as "logical." That is, both major and minor premises must be true in the light of "present-day realities." The most difficult task an appellate court confronts in each case is to establish sound premises for a decision. However, judicial opinions seldom reflect any effort by judges to ascertain the existence of some valid formal relationship between premises and conclusion such as that exemplified in the syllogism. Justice Cardozo has described the role of the appellate judge as follows:

> The judge is to scrutinize the aggregate of social facts of which "the juridical norm" is to be regarded as a product. Chief among these are "the positive laws, the usages actually obeyed, the economic needs, the aspirations toward the realization of the just." But the scrutiny, though an essential part of his function, is not the whole. The judge interprets the social conscience, and gives effect to it in law, but in so doing he helps to form and modify the conscience he interprets. Discovery and creation react upon each other.

In most cases, the pertinent legal rule or rules (major premise) have been authoritatively formulated. Accordingly, most judicial reasoning revolves around establishment of what, in syllogistic terms, is called the minor premise. Consider the following reasoning: "An offer and an acceptance are required to form a contract" (major premise), "*D*'s statement to *P* did not constitute an acceptance" (minor premise), "therefore no contract was formed" (conclusion). Here, the principal task of the court was to determine whether *D*'s statement to *P* constituted an acceptance of *P*'s offer. By establishing the minor premise that it did not, the court by the application of the major premise formulated and applied a legal rule that an offer and an acceptance must coincide in order to form a contract.

Several kinds of reasoning ordinarily influence a court in determining the application of a legal rule or rules. A court may base its determination upon the literal meaning of words appearing in the rule, upon the purpose of the rule, upon similarities between the facts of the case to be decided and the facts of decided cases, or upon considerations of social policy. Thus, reasoning may be literal, purposive, precedent-oriented, or policy-oriented. Adherents of the different schools of jurisprudence discussed in Chapter 1 above may be identified in term of which of these "approaches" to judicial decision they emphasize or prefer. Thus, members of the historical school would emphasize precedent-oriented analysis. Some positivist legal scholars would emphasize the literal approach. Adherents of sociological and natural law jurisprudence would prefer the purposive and policy-oriented approaches.

Literal reasoning, or what has also been characterized as the literal approach, may be illustrated by the following hypothetical case: Congress, having jurisdiction over the District of Columbia, passed a law providing that vehicles should not be taken into parks in Washington, D.C. Pursuant to this law, appropriate signs were posted at park entrances. *D* entered one of the parks pushing his bicycle, and was arrested and convicted of violating the law. *D* appealed, and his conviction was upheld on the basis that, as *D*'s bicycle had all the physical characteristics of a vehicle, it constituted a "vehicle"; therefore, *D* had violated the statute.

A court adopting a "purposive approach" to the issue presented by the foregoing hypothetical case might have decided *D*'s appeal differently. If, upon inquiry into the purpose of the law, it appeared that Congress was only attempting to reduce risk of harm to pedestrians in the park, such a court might have refused to uphold *D*'s conviction upon the basis that as he did not ride the bicycle into the park, he did not expose pedestrians to any significant risk of harm, and therefore did not violate the statute.

Few principles are more firmly established in Anglo-American law than the principle of *stare decisis,* which requires that like cases be decided in like manner. Accordingly, many judicial decisions are precedent-oriented, and in nearly every case lawyers and judges expend considerable time and energy analyzing and discussing similarities and differences between the facts of decided cases and the facts of the case to be decided.

The great mass of cases are decided within the confines of *stare decisis.* Yet there is a steady evolution, for it is not quite true that there is nothing new under the sun; rarely is a case identical with the one that went before. Courts have a creative job to do when they find that a rule has lost its touch with reality and should be abandoned or reformulated to meet new conditions and new moral values. And in those cases where there is no *stare decisis* to cast its light or shadow, the court must hammer out new rules that will respect whatever values of the past have survived the tests of reason and experience and anticipate what contemporary values will best meet the tests. The task is not easy—human relations are infinitely complex and subtlety and depth of spirit must enter into their regulation. Often legal problems elude final solution and courts there can do more than find what Cardozo called the least erroneous answer to insoluble problems. (Traynor, Judge, 2 Univ. of Ill. Law Forum 232, 1956)

Policy considerations influence the decision of many cases. Such considerations often influence a court to apply or refuse to apply an existing rule, and are usually of paramount significance in those relatively infrequent cases in which a court is called upon to resolve problems not heretofore adjudicated by that court. Policy-oriented reasoning may be illustrated as follows: *P* claimed damages for harm to an eye due allegedly to *D*'s negligent failure to place safety guards over a grindstone. Immediately after the harm to *P* occurred, *D* placed safety guards over the grindstone. At the trial, *P* sought to introduce evidence of *D*'s action for the purpose of showing that *D* had, by placing the guards over the grindstone, admitted that he had been careless. *D* objected to the admission of this evidence, but the court overruled his objection, and the jury rendered a verdict for *P*. On appeal, the appellate court decided that admission of this type of evidence was error. The court stated that there was a strong policy to encourage employers to establish and maintain optimum safety conditions at all times. The admission of the proffered evidence would frustrate this policy because an employer would, after an accident, hesitate to improve safety conditions for fear that this might be used against him in a lawsuit by the injured employee.

The literal, the purposive, the precedent-oriented, and the policy-oriented approaches to determining the application of legal rules may each influence the decision of a particular case. Sometimes these approaches point in different directions. Thus, in those cases in which the courts refused to apply the doctrine that the consumer of defective food could recover for breach of warranty only against the seller and not against the manufacturer, the courts adopted a policy-oriented approach and chose to protect the health of consumers rather than follow the precedents which had established the non-liability of manufacturers.

When a court decides a case primarily upon the basis of what is here called policy-oriented reasoning, a choice between conflicting policies is often required. Thus, the immediately preceding illustration may also be viewed as posing a conflict between the policy of protecting consumer health and the policies underlying the doctrine of *stare decisis*. The cases in which one party claims that another has infringed a trademark usually pose a conflict between the policy of protecting an established property right and the policy of fostering competition. The illustrations could be multiplied by numerous cases in which the courts carefully weigh all factors in determining which approach is to be decisive.

Occasionally, a case arises presenting issues that have been decided differently by different courts. The court must then choose between conflicting precedents. This choice is frequently made primarily on the basis of an evaluation of the policy considerations supporting each precedent. Often, courts also consider other factors, such as the standing of the tribunals which decided the conflicting precedents.

When reading assigned cases, the student should attempt to analyze the court's reasoning in terms of the discussion in this section. The student will thereby enhance his comprehension of the cases and also improve his own reasoning powers.

CHAPTER 5
REVIEW QUESTIONS AND PROBLEMS

1. What is the first step in a suit at law? What is a court summons? Who serves it? Upon whom may it be served?
2. What is meant by a judgment by default or a decree "pro confesso"?
3. What is meant by the term "framing the issues"? Why is framing the issues necessary? Describe the steps used in framing the issues.
4. What relationship exists between the framing of the issues and the introduction of evidence? Why?
5. Who is an appellant; an appellee?
6. Give the steps by which a case is appealed from a trial court to a court of appeals.
   What is a "transcript"? A "bill of exceptions"?
   What does an attorney include in his brief?
7. What is the purpose of the "pre-trial" conference?
8. Give the qualifications for a judge. Considering these qualifications, how should judges be chosen—by appointment or by election? Discuss.
9. Give the constitutional authority for the use of the jury. Who serves on the jury and what is its function?
10. Does the jury have to give reasons for its verdict? If not, why not?
11. Why are there strict rules about how, when, and why a witness may testify?
12. What are instructions for the jury and why are they necessary? Who finds the facts and who pronounces the law?
13. Distinguish between a verdict, a judgment, and remedies.
14. Name three discovery procedures and explain the possible uses of each.

15. What is the purpose of a pre-trial conference?
16. What is voir dire examination and what is its purpose?
17. What is demurrer? What is its function?
18. What is a motion for directed verdict? What is its function?
19. What procedures are available to enforce a judgment?
20. Illustrate judicial reasoning that is deductive and inductive? What is the purposive approach to a judicial decision?

chapter 6

Nonjudicial
Methods for
Resolving Conflicts

1-38. Introduction. There are situations in which it is not advantageous to settle business disputes by judicial proceedings. The amount involved, the necessity for a speedy decision, the nature of the contest, the uncertainty of a legal remedy, the unfavorable publicity, and the expense entailed are factors in avoiding a court trial.

Since proceedings in judicial tribunals are by law the authorized legal method to adjudicate controversies, other methods have been few and limited. Compromise by accord and satisfaction (an agreement to accept a substituted performance followed by such performance), self-help, and arbitration are possible remedies. Accord and satisfaction is not adequate to avoid litigation unless satisfaction, performance of the accord, is obtained. If the agreement for an accord is broken, resort to the court is necessary to enforce the promise to give substituted performance. Self-help is not satisfactory because the aggressor is likely to create more difficulties than he settles, although it may be authorized in case of "repossessions."

1-39. Arbitration. Arbitration as an extra-judicial procedure is the most inexpensive, speedy and amicable method of settling disputes and avoiding litigation. Arbitration has been defined as a contractual proceeding, whereby the parties who have a dispute agree, often in advance of the dispute, to a final disposition of the matter involved, select judges of their own choice and by consent submit their controversy to such judges for determination in place of tribunals provided by ordinary process of law. *Arbitration* is a contractual method or a proceeding prescribed by statute to settle disputes "out of court." Arbitration, like litigation, has for its purpose settling a controversy but its proceedings are somewhat different. Arbitration may be called a quasi-judicial proceeding. Its rules and regulations are set by statute or stipulated by contract. Upon notice, a hearing is held, testimony taken, deliberations had, and a decision called an award rendered by the arbitrators without the necessity for written pleadings, motions, rules of evidence, and other formal requirements of a law suit.

Arbitration has long been recognized at common law. Its use and effectiveness, however, have been limited by a negative attitude on the part of some courts. Agreements to submit existing and future controversies to arbitrators have met judicial opposition, because it is alleged such agreements "oust the courts of jurisdiction." It is argued that disputes are not private matters, but matters of public concern; courts are public institutions to settle controversies; citizens ought not be permitted to deprive themselves or others of the protection of public tribunals and well established procedures. Furthermore, the opposition to arbitration contends that to permit individuals to create tribunals and to provide for their procedures by contract in order to settle their disputes, constitutes an indirect repeal of that legislation which provides for judicial process. It is argued that this is particularly true as to future disputes and that a person should not bind himself in advance to remove his right to judicial process and appeal before he is aware of the nature of the controversy—courts are institutions to redeem wrongs and settle controversies and their power to function ought not be contracted away.

Such ideas, however, have not prevailed. It is contended by many that there never was "any factual basis for holding that an agreement to arbitrate 'ousted' jurisdiction. It has no effect upon the jurisdiction of any court. Arbitration simply removes a controversy from the arena of litigation. It is no more an ouster of judicial jurisdiction than is a compromise and settlement . . . or a convenant not to sue. Each disposes of issues without litigation. One no more than the other ousts the court of jurisdiction."

Even though arbitral agreements may not "oust" the court's jurisdiction, at common law they were not a very effective method for settling controversies for several reasons. First, on the assumption that arbitrators are the agents of the parties, their authority could be canceled at any time, thus making the stability of the arbitral procedure rest upon the continued consent of the parties. Second, either party at any time might revoke the agreement by giving notice of refusal to comply, leaving only a remedy for damages for the breach of the contract to arbitrate. Since a party always has the power to breach a contract, an arbitral agreement was no different from any other agreement for which a judicial proceeding is necessary to recover for a breach. A person who has broken a contract to arbitrate is not precluded from defending the action thereon.

1-40. Statutory Aspects. The inadequacy of common law arbitration led to remedial legislation. In nearly all states, arbitration is now subject to statute. These statutes vary greatly, depending upon their purpose. When the statute provides for a definite arbitration procedure, strict compliance is necessary, otherwise the proceedings are null and void. It has been held, however, that even though strict statutory compliance has not been made, a proceeding at common law may be conducted, provided the parties have not previously contracted what particular method shall be used.

In many states, statutes are merely declaratory of the common law. In others, statutes are enacted to make arbitral proceedings more effective; they eliminate the necessity for a suit on the award, by allowing the award to be entered as a judgment in the court upon which an execution may issue; by removing the common law right of revocation, by compelling specific performance of the agreement to arbitrate and by judicial enforcement of the award. Some jurisdictions have statutes which provide for compulsory arbitration in certain situations, but it has been held that statutes compelling parties to submit to arbitration are in violation of the constitutional right to trial by jury and that they violate the Fourteenth Amendment to the Constitution if the statute makes the decision of the arbitrators final and closes the courts to litigants. However, if there is an appeal to the courts from the arbitrator's award, no constitutional rights have been denied.

Since statutes vary widely, no attempt will be made to discuss these differences. By way of illustration, however, some of the provisions of a typical statute are here listed:

1. Persons may submit any controversy to *commercial arbitration* except disputes concerning the title to real estate and conditions of employment under collective bargaining agreements.

2. By written contract there may be arbitration of any controversy arising from a contract, or from a refusal to perform the whole or any part of a contract. Likewise, an agreement in writing may be made to submit to arbitration any controversy existing between the parties.

3. Any party aggrieved by the failure, neglect, or refusal of the other party to perform under a contract, or to submit a dispute to arbitration, may petition the court for an order directing that the arbitration be carried out according to the terms of the agreement. Upon hearing, if the court finds that making the contract to arbitrate or submission to arbitrate is not an issue, the court shall direct the parties to proceed to arbitrate according to the terms of the agreement.

4. If, however, there is doubt as to the making of the contract or submission, the court shall try the issue, either with or without a jury. If it is found that no contract was made, the petition shall be dismissed. If it is found that a contract to arbitrate or to submit was made, and there was a default, the court will issue an order directing the parties to proceed with arbitration according to the contract.

5. After an award has been made, it is filed with the clerk of the court and after twenty days, if no exceptions are filed, it shall become a judgment upon which an execution may be issued for satisfaction, as if a judgment had been entered in a civil action.

6. Exception to an award may be made for the following causes: corruption, fraud, partiality, misconduct, exceeding power, and mistake, or upon an award resting on matters not within the statute.

7. Appeals from the judgment may be taken as in any legal action, and such appeals cannot be denied by contractual provisions.

8. If it appears that the award should be vacated, the court may refer it back to the arbitrators, with instructions for correction and rehearing. If the arbitrators do not act, the court has jurisdiction to try the case.

Arbitration as a "substitute for the courts for settling controversies" is an excellent procedure if it works. But if it does not work and there is resort to the courts, the very end sought is not accomplished. In spite of the uncertainty of the law about arbitration, the procedure for arbitration has been a successful method for settling differences within trade groups and associations. There has been sufficient experience in the field for the publication of standard contract clauses, rules, and procedures.

The previous attitude of the courts, the question of whether arbitration is a matter of contract concerned with substantive law, or a matter of procedure regulated by contract or statute, makes for conflict both at common law and in statutes. Therefore, the student is advised to refer to local decisions and statutes for complete information.

It should also be noted that public pressure may have the effect of coercing disputants to compromise or arbitrate their dispute. The inconvenience resulting from prolonged strikes in vital industries such as transportation will so affect the public interest that the pressure of public opinion may force labor and management into a settlement. By the same token, Congress may require by legislation settlement of labor disputes by compulsory arbitration particularly in prolonged strikes involving transportation and other industries having large public interest characteristics.

CHAPTER 6
REVIEW QUESTIONS AND PROBLEMS

1. What is the difference between arbitration and mediation?
2. Name four situations in which business may want to include an arbitration provision in a contract.
3. X Co., by contract with Y labor union, agreed to submit disputes to arbitration. An employee was paid Workmen's Compensation under a settlement contract as a result of being permanently disabled. X refused to allow the employee to return under a contract provision that allowed it to do so. The union objected and demanded arbitration. The company refused, contending that there was nothing to arbitrate since the contract terms were not in dispute and the employee ad-

mitted his disability. Must the company submit the dispute to arbitration?

4. What are the advantages of arbitration over a judicial decision?

BOOK TWO

Contracts

Introduction
to Contracts

2-1. Nature and Importance of the Contractual Relationship. The law of contracts is concerned with creation, transfer, and disposition of property through promises. Property in this sense refers to a "bundle of rights" which the law will enforce and protect. The "bundle of rights" concept is discussed in detail in Chapter 44. A contract is a promise or a set of promises for the breach of which the law gives a remedy or the performance of which the law recognizes as a duty. In other words, a contract is a legally enforceable promise.

The law of contracts forms the oldest branch of the law relating to business or to commercial transactions. In one form or another it has existed from the beginning of organized society. Just as the safety of person and of property depends upon the rules of criminal law, so the security and stability of the business world are dependent upon the law of contracts. It is the legal mechanism by which the free enterprise capitalistic system has developed and been made to operate. It is the tool by which promises are made and expectations created to the end that there will be a continuous flow of goods and services to meet man's economic needs.

To a very high degree, our whole philosophy of personal liberty, with its concept of private property—the right to acquire and to dispose of property freely with provision for individual business enterprise—has as one of its main structural supports the law of contracts. The freedom to contract as well as the sanctity of and respect for contracts form a highly important feature of our cultural life.

Capital and wealth are evidenced by promises. The greater the number of enforceable promises, the greater the wealth. In order for a contract to serve as an instrument to create wealth and enhance the economic good, freedom to contract, accompanied by legal machinery for the enforcement of promises, is essential.

By contract the parties, by mutual assent either expressed or implied, "fix their own terms and set bounds upon their liabilities." Thus, it may be said that the parties freely create for themselves their own law, leaving it only to the state to set up the machinery for the interpretation of the contract and the enforcement of the promises.

Although the parties to a contract "fix their own terms and set bounds upon their liabilities," they are subject to limitations. To create a valid contract, there must be compliance with specific rules of law. The expression of "the terms" must be in compliance with stated rules of law. The expression of "the terms" must be promissory in character and must create a legal obligation. What promises are legally binding depend upon how and to whom they are expressed and whether there are present the other elements which the law requires, such as consideration, capacity of the parties, and a legal purpose in light of sound public policy.

This latter requirement recognizes that in our society, parties do not possess absolute freedom of contract. For example, the public interest demands that parties not be allowed to enter into contracts limiting competition or in restraint of trade. Inequality of bargaining power between the parties requires action by legislative, judicial, and administrative bodies to control the terms and provisions of contracts. As a result, we have statutes which limit freedom of contract in such areas as marketing, the employer-employee relationship, insurance, and transportation. We have administrative agencies such as the National Labor Relations Board in the field of labor and the Federal Trade Commission in the field of marketing which regulate the parties and terms of contracts in these areas. Finally, the judicial power of courts includes the power to declare contracts or provisions thereof to be illegal as contrary to public policy or unenforceable because they are unconscionable. Thus it must always be recognized that the law of contracts while a branch of the private sector of the law is clothed with many aspects which make it a part of the public law. Indeed one trend in the law today is to consider that more and more contracts are sufficiently connected with the public interest to warrant more and more governmental participation in setting their terms.

Since the law of contracts furnishes the foundation for other branches of commercial law, a study of the general rules applicable to contract law precedes the invasion of other fields. The particular rules of law pertaining to agency, sales, commercial paper, corporations, partnerships, and secured transactions are all superimposed upon the general principles of contract law.

Contracts are made so frequently and have become so much a part of our everyday life that we often fail to realize when they are made or, once made, when they are performed. Purchasing groceries, dropping money into the coin box of a bus, paying for a ticket to the theater, and signing a written agreement to buy real estate are equally illustrative of the myriad of daily contract transactions. The principles of law in the chapters which follow are generally applicable to all contracts.

2-2. Classification of Contracts. For certain purposes it is desirable to classify contracts according to characteristics which they possess. They may well be classified as follows:

1. Valid, voidable, or unenforceable.[1]
2. Executed or executory.
3. Bilateral or unilateral.
4. Express or implied (in fact or in law).

An *executed* contract is one that has been fully carried out by the contracting parties. An *executory* contract is one that is yet to be performed. An agreement may be executed on the part of one party and executory on the part of the other. For example, a contract for the purchase of a suit of clothes on credit, followed by the delivery of the suit, is executed on the part of the dealer and executory on the part of the purchaser.

As discussed in the next chapter, most contracts grow out of an offer made by one party to another and accepted by the latter. A *bilateral* contract involves two promises, one made by each of the parties to the agreement. To illustrate, let us assume that *A* offers to sell to *B* certain merchandise at an established price. *B*, after receiving the offer, communicates his acceptance to *A* by promising to buy the merchandise and to pay the price set forth in the offer. After the promises are exchanged, it becomes the duty of each party to carry out the terms of the agreement. Most contracts are bilateral in character.

A *unilateral* contract consists of a promise for an act, the acceptance consisting of the performance of the act requested rather than the promise to perform it. An unsolicited order for merchandise sent by a retailer to a manufacturer, asking for prompt shipment of the goods ordered, illustrates a unilateral offer. The buyer requests and desires shipment, rather than a promise to ship. Until the goods are shipped, the retailer is at liberty to withdraw his offer. Further discussion of these contracts will be found in the next chapter.

A contract may result from an agreement either oral or in writing in which event it is said to be an express contract. On the other hand, a contract may be entirely implied from conduct and acts of the parties, the acts being such that a contract may be inferred from them. In other instances, the contract may be, and often is, partially expressed and partially implied. Thus, an employee may be engaged to perform certain work without any clear agreement as to the compensation to be received. When the service has been rendered, the courts impose a duty upon the employer to pay a reasonable sum for the benefit received. This duty to

---

[1] To be discussed in detail in chapters which follow.

pay is implied from the nature of the situation and the type of service rendered.

A contract is also implied in fact whenever one person, without protest, knowingly accepts a benefit at the expense of another under circumstances which negate the possibility of a gift. The person who accepts the benefit implicitly promises to pay the fair value of the benefit that he receives, but no implied promise to pay arises where the person who receives a benefit is totally unaware that such a benefit is being conferred. It is the acceptance of benefits at a time when it is possible to reject them that raises the implied promise to pay for them. To illustrate: *A*, by mistake, and during the absence of *B*, made certain repairs on *B*'s residence. Upon his return *B* was under no duty to pay for the repairs, although he of necessity made use of them in connection with his occupancy of the property. The use of the house created no implied promise to pay for the repairs, since *B* had never had the opportunity to reject them. However, where *B* is present and watches the repairs being made, his silence may well be deemed an acceptance of an offer, obligating him to pay the reasonable value of the improvement.

2-3. Quasi Contract. A contract implied in fact must be distinguished from a contract implied in law, generally known as *quasi contract*. The former is a true contract, created by inference from facts and circumstances which show the assent and intention of the parties. The latter arises in situations in which courts, to do justice and to avoid unjust enrichment, impose a duty upon a party and consider the duty as arising from a contract for the purpose of establishing the existence of a legal remedy. The remedy of quasi contract is a legal fiction dictated by reason, justice, and equity to prevent fraud, wrongdoing, or one person from being unjustly enriched at the expense of another.[2] The law presumes a promise by a party to do what in equity and good conscience he ought to do even though he does not want or intend to do it. The remedy of quasi contract is generally not available where there is an action for breach of an express contract. To establish a right to the remedy of quasi contract, the plaintiff must prove that a benefit has been conferred on the defendant, that the defendant has accepted and retained the benefit, and that the circumstances are such that to allow the defendant to keep the benefits without paying for them would be inequitable. A typical case would involve the receipt or payment of money improperly. The defendant improperly receiving the money would have a duty to return it and since no actual contract existed, the law would imply one.

Quasi contract, as a remedy, is used in several types of situations where one person, unofficiously and without fault or misconduct, confers a benefit upon another, for which the latter in equity and good conscience ought to pay. Among such situations are those in which money is improperly paid or received, property is wrongfully appropriated or converted,

[2] *Anderson v. Copeland*, page 118.

money or property is obtained by trespass, fraud, or duress, or necessities of life are furnished a person under legal disability. In each of these situations, there is no contract but one person would be unjustly enriched if he were not required to pay for the benefits received.

2-4. Elements of a Contract. A contract has been defined as "an agreement enforceable by law." A more complete definition follows: A contract is an agreement (expression of mutual assent) between two or more competent persons, having for its purpose a legal object, wherein each of the persons acts in a certain manner or promises to act or to refrain from acting in such a manner. This definition breaks up logically into four component parts:

1. The *Agreement* which consists of an *offer* by one party and its *acceptance* by the other.
2. *Consideration,* which is the price paid by each party to the other or what each party receives and gives up in the Agreement.
3. *Competent parties,* which means that the parties must possess legal capacity to contract (be of legal age and sane).
4. A legal purpose consistent with law and sound policy.

These elements are all essential in an enforceable agreement and will be considered in detail in the chapters that follow. The word "promise" when used in the law of contracts means an undertaking, however expressed, either that something shall happen, or that something shall not happen in the future.

The sections which follow in this chapter are concerned with the legal remedies available to a victim of a breach of contract and the rules of law used by courts in interpreting contracts. For purposes of studying these matters, you may assume that a valid contract possessing the required elements exists.

2-5. Judicial Remedies for Breach of Contract. There are three judicial remedies which are generally available to a party injured by a breach of contract. First of all, he may seek *dollar damages* for the injuries he sustained. Secondly, he may, in certain situations, invoke the aid of a court of equity and seek *specific performance* of the contract. These two remedies are discussed in the sections which follow.

The third remedy frequently involved in contract litigation is *rescission*. This remedy is used to cancel or avoid the contract and to return the parties to their original position. For example, rescission may be used by a person who has been the victim of fraud, misrepresentation, and by minors or others lacking legal capacity in order to return themselves to the original status quo. A party who discovers facts which warrant rescission of his contract has a duty to act promptly and, if he elects to rescind, to notify the other party within reasonable time so that rescission may be accomplished at a time when parties may still be restored, as nearly as possible, to their original positions.[3] He must return what he received in substantially as good a condition as when he received it. This remedy is an equitable one and is subject to the usual maxims of courts of chancery.

DAMAGES

2-6. Theory of Damages. The purpose and indeed the theory of damages is to make the injured party whole or to place him in the same position as he would have been had the breach of contract not occurred.[4] The fundamental basis is just compensation for the losses which necessarily flow from the breach. These are the damages that arise naturally from the breach itself and were within the contemplation of the parties at the time of making the contract as those that might arise in the event of a breach. The injured party is not entitled to a profit from the breach of the transaction but is limited to being placed in the same position he would have been had the contract been carried out. Unusual and unexpected damage resulting from peculiar facts unknown to both parties at the time the agreement was entered into should not influence the amount of the recovery.

The question as to the amount of damages is usually one of fact for the jury. While a jury may not speculate or guess as to the amount of damage, the fact that the amount is not capable of exact computation will not prevent a recovery. Justice and public policy require that a wrongdoer bear the risk of uncertainty which his wrong may have created. In such cases, a reasonable basis of computation is used but damages which are uncertain, contingent, remote, or speculative cannot be used as a basis for recovery. Loss of profits may be included if they can be computed with reasonable certainty from tangible competent evidence.

The plaintiff is not entitled to recover the amount which he expends for attorney's fees, unless the contract so provides or special legislation permits it in the particular case. Court costs, however, which include witness fees, filing costs, and so forth, are usually assessed against the losing party.

2-7. Special Types of Damages. There are several terms used to describe special types of damages and matters relating thereto. First of all, the term "nominal damages" is used to describe the situation in which no actual loss is incurred and a small and inconsequential sum, usually $1.00, is awarded to denote that a technical breach had occurred.

The term "liquidated damages" or "liquidated damage clause" is used to describe the situation in which the parties in the contract provide for the damages to be awarded in the event of a breach. These provisions are legal and will be enforced so long as the court does not consider the stipulation to be a penalty for failure to perform, rather than compensation for damages. Should the court find the term to have been inserted

---

3 *Galati v. Potamkin Chevrolet Co.*, page 119.
4 *White Const. Corp. v. Jet Spray Cooler, Inc.*, page 121.

primarily to force actual performance and not to compensate for probable injury, it will not be enforced.[5] In order to be construed as liquidated damages and not a penalty, the amount of recovery agreed upon must bear a reasonable relation to the probable damage to be sustained by the breach. Once having arrived at the conclusion that the parties intended to compensate for possible damages, the court will not permit either of them to introduce evidence showing the amount of actual damages; recovery is allowed for the amount agreed upon by the parties, although actually the damages suffered may vary somewhat from those agreed upon in the contract.

The Code also seeks to avoid the fixing of unreasonably large liquidated damages by declaring them to be void as a penalty. To be valid under the Code, a liquidated-damages clause must be reasonable in light of the anticipated or actual harm caused by the breach, the difficulties of proof of loss, and the inconvenience or nonfeasibility of otherwise obtaining an adequate remedy.[C1] The Code further attempts to avoid penalties by allowing a buyer who is in breach of contract to obtain from a seller who has rescinded the contract because of the buyer's breach, restitution of part of his payments if they exceed (1) the amount stated in the liquidated-damage clause or (2), if there is no liquidated-damage clause, 20 per cent of the contract or $500, whichever is smaller.[C2] Thus a buyer who has made part payment will not be penalized by breaching the contract, and the seller is prohibited from receiving a windfall in excess of $500 or the amount stated as liquidated damages of the seller and any benefit actually received by the buyer.

The terms punitive or exemplary damages refer to damages awarded to one party in order to punish the other for his conduct. While it is not the purpose of a civil proceeding to punish a party, punitive damages are allowed in cases of intentional torts such as fraud or libel. These are allowed in the interest of society to deter the commission of these acts. Punitive damages may be awarded only where actual damage is shown.

2-8. Rules Concerning Damages. There are other matters relative to the awarding and amount of damages that need be noted. First of all, there is a general duty on the part of the injured party to mitigate the damages. This duty requires that he take whatever steps are necessary to reduce the actual loss to the lowest possible point. He cannot add to his injury or permit the damages to be enhanced when it is reasonably within his power to prevent such occurrence. An employee who has been wrongfully discharged cannot sit idly by and expect to draw his pay.[6] A duty is imposed upon him to seek other work of the same general character.

Frequently, the distinction between a willful and unintentional breach becomes significant. Contracts that are willfully and substantially breached after part performance has taken place may or may not confer

---

5 *King Motors v. Delfino,* page 122.
6 *McKenna v. Commissioner of Mental Health,* page 123.

C1 *U.C.C.* 2-718(1).   C2 *U.C.C.* 2-718(2)(3).

some benefit on the promisee. Even though a benefit has been conferred, it may be such a one as the promisee may or may not be able to return to the other party. For example, in construction contracts and other contracts of similar nature, in which the benefit received from partial performance cannot be returned, the person entitled to performance is not required to pay for the benefit conferred upon him. The other party is penalized to that extent because of his failure to perform. Where the breach is unintentional—resulting from a mistake or a misunderstanding—the party must pay for the net benefit which he has received on a theory of quasi contract. In any event, such net benefit is automatically taken into account if the damages allowed are the cost of completing the contract.

In those contracts where partial performance confers benefits of such a nature that they can be returned, the recipient must either return the benefits or pay for their reasonable value. In contracts for the sale and purchase of goods, the buyer who receives only a portion of the goods contracted for and still has them when he learns of the breach, must either pay their reasonable value, less the damages resulting from the failure to receive the balance of the goods, or return the goods received. He cannot keep the goods and at the same time refuse to pay for the benefits received from them.

2-9. Specific Performance. The legal remedy of dollar damages and the equitable remedy of rescission are sometimes inadequate to provide the remedy to which the party injured by a breach of contract should be entitled. In these cases, the only adequate remedy is to require the party in breach to perform the contract. This equitable remedy is known as specific performance.[7]

Specific performance, being an equitable remedy, is never granted as a matter of right but is only allowed when the chancellor or judge in the exercise of his discretion, determines that equity and good conscience require performance of the contract because dollar damages are an inadequate remedy. Dollar damages are inadequate and specific performance is the usual remedy where the subject matter of the contract is unique. Since each parcel of real estate differs from every other parcel of real estate, all land is unique and courts of equity will specifically enforce contracts to sell real estate where the terms are equitable. Examples of unique personal property are antiques, race horses, heirlooms, and the stock of a closely held corporation. The latter is unique because each share of stock has significance in the power to control the corporation. The Code takes a more liberal viewpoint and allows specific performance in situations where commercial needs makes it equitable to do so.[C3]

2-10. Arbitration. Parties frequently desire to avoid litigation as a means of resolving disputes because of the cost and time delays involved. Litigation may take up to several years and cost more than could be recovered.

[7] *Hogan v. Norfleet,* page 125.

[C3] *U.C.C.* 2-709, 2-716.

One common method of resolving disputes over contracts is known as arbitration. This method is very often used in connection with labor-management contracts and is becoming more common in other areas of the law of contracts.[8]

Arbitration is the submission of a dispute for a binding decision to one or more reasonable, competent and trustworthy individuals. Instead of submitting a dispute to a person selected by society called a judge, the parties submit it to a person or persons selected by them for a binding decision. In some states, this decision has the effect of a judgment of a court and a party can be enjoined from suing on a contract containing an arbitration clause. Since the people involved will not have the crowded docket of a court, the matter can usually be quickly and less expensively decided.

If the parties can agree on a single arbitrator, he is selected and the evidence presented to him. If they cannot agree, each party selects one arbitrator and the two arbitrators so selected, select a third and the three hear the case.

Arbitration is now an accepted method of resolving business conflicts. It has less formality than a judicial hearing, creates less animosity and allows the decision makers greater latitude in obtaining a fair and just decision. It is of growing importance and a provision requiring the arbitration of disputes should be considered in the preparation of a contract.

2-11. Construction and Interpretation of Contracts. The purpose of construing or interpreting a contract is to determine the intent of the parties or the meaning of the words used. If the language is unambiguous, construction is not required and the obvious intent will be followed. When the language of a contract is ambiguous, imperfect, or obscure, courts use certain established rules of construction in order to ascertain the intention of the parties.[9] However, these rules cannot be used to make a new contract for the parties or to rewrite the old one, even if the contract is inequitable or harsh. They are simply used to make the contract as agreed upon certain.

The general standard of interpretation is to use the meaning which the language has to a reasonably intelligent person with common sense and understanding familiar with the circumstances in which the language was used. Thus, language is judged objectively, rather than subjectively, and is given a reasonable meaning. What one party meant or thought he was saying or writing is immaterial when words are given effect in accordance with their meaning to a reasonable man in the circumstances of the parties.

In determining the intention of the parties, it is the expressed intention which controls and this will be given effect unless it conflicts with some rule of law, good morals, or public policy. The language is judged with reference to the subject matter of the contract, its nature, objects, and

[8] *Brennan v. Brennan,* page 126.
[9] *Smith v. Russ,* page 127.

purposes. The motives of the parties may be examined. Language is usually given its ordinary meaning but technical words are given their technical meaning. Words with an established legal meaning are given that legal meaning. Doubts are resolved in favor of legality and the law of the place of making is considered to be a part of the contract. Isolated language is not considered but instead the contract is considered as a whole to ascertain the intent of the parties. If one party has prepared the agreement, the contract will be construed against him since he had the chance to eliminate the ambiguity. As an aid to the court in determining the intention of the parties, business custom, usage and prior dealings between the parties are usually considered, especially under the Code.[C4]

INTRODUCTION TO
CONTRACT CASES

Anderson v. Copeland

1963 (Okla.) 378 P.(2) 1007

PER CURIAM.   This is an appeal from the District Court of Cotton County. The parties will be referred to in this Court as they appeared in the court below.

Plaintiff, Jack Copeland, doing business as Copeland Equipment Company, brought this action against defendant, Walter Anderson, to recover for the rental value of a tractor owned by plaintiff which was in defendant's possession for approximately two weeks.

The facts giving rise to this claim were for the most part undisputed. Defendant orally agreed to purchase a used tractor from plaintiff for the sum of $475.00. For eleven days thereafter defendant attempted to borrow money to cover the purchase price but was unable to, and so advised plaintiff. Plaintiff asked defendant to return the tractor, which was done within a few days. The only dispute appears to be in that defendant says the sale was conditioned on defendant's ability to borrow money to pay for it, while plaintiff says the sale was final and without conditions. In any event, both parties agree that the sale contract was rescinded when plaintiff asked that the tractor be returned.

The case was tried to a jury which returned a verdict for plaintiff in the amount of $50.00. Defendant's motion for new trial was overruled and he appeals.

It appears from the facts that the parties, instead of attempting to enforce such rights as they may have had under the sale contract, rescinded it. The parties were then in the same position as before the agreement was made, except that defendant had had the use of plaintiff's tractor without paying for it. Under those circumstances the law would imply a contract for defendant would be unjustly enriched.

C4 1-205, 2-208.

In the first paragraph of the syllabus in *Piggee v. Mercy Hospital,* (199 Okl., 411, 186 P.2d 817), we held:

> Contracts implied by law, or more properly quasi or constructive contracts, are a class of obligations which are imposed or created by law without regard to the assent of the party bound, on the ground that they are dictated by reason and justice, and may be enforced by an action *ex contractu.*

Defendant contends that there cannot exist at the same time an express contract and an implied contract between the same parties covering the same subject matter. This statement of law is not applicable in the instant case for the reason that the subject matter of the express contract was a sale, whereas the subject matter of the contract implied in law was a rental. The case of *Berry v. Barbour* (Okl., 279 P.2d 355) is somewhat similar. In that case a contractor was employed to make improvements and repairs of the owner's building. During the owner's absence in Europe, the roof of the building was partially destroyed by fire without the fault of the contractor who made necessary repairs of the fire damage, without knowledge of the owner. We held that a quasi contract arose obligating the owner to reimburse the contractor for the reasonable cost of material and labor furnished.

Defendant further contends that the trial court's instructions to the jury were erroneous. The instruction requested by defendant, however, covered contracts implied in fact. Such instruction was not applicable. In *First Nat. Bank of Okmulgee v. Matlock* (99 Okl., 150, 226 P.328, 36 A.L.R. 1088) we distinguished between contracts implied in fact and contracts implied in law. In the former the intention of the parties is ascertained and enforced. We believe that the instructions to the jury in the instant case sufficiently covered the law to be applied to the facts. There was ample evidence in the case to support the verdict of the jury and the trial court's judgment rendered thereon.

Affirmed.

Galati v. Potamkin Chevrolet Co.

1962 (Penn.) 198 Pa. Super. 533, 181 A.2d 900

Plaintiff, an automobile purchaser, brought suit in equity against the seller to rescind an installment sales contract for an automobile. Plaintiff alleged that defendant filled in the blanks on the contract in an amount of $427.42 more than agreed upon. Plaintiff, who discovered the excess charge on August 1, 1957, made a payment on August 18, 1957 and monthly thereafter through the August 1958 installment which was paid October 10, 1958. On May 17, 1958 Plaintiff had a discussion with the salesmen where he was told that no adjustment would be made. On November 10, 1958 the auto was repossessed for non-payment of the September 1958 installment. On August 7, 1959 Plaintiff sued to rescind the contract. The trial court found for the plaintiff despite defendant's contention that Plaintiff had lost his right to rescind because of the delay and defendant appealed.

FLOOD, J.   When a party discovers facts which warrant rescission of his contract, it is his duty to act promptly, and, if he elects to rescind, to notify the other party within a reasonable time so that the rescission may be accomplished at a time when the parties may still be restored, as nearly as possible, to their original positions. In the present case prompt restoration of the parties to their original positions would have permitted the defendant to reacquire possession of the vehicle, and would have prevented plaintiff's using the vehicle rent-free for a period of from five to fifteen months. The grafting of new equities upon a transaction by the passage of time is one of the reasons why the right of rescission must be asserted within a reasonable time after the discovery of the fraud.

A buyer is not entitled to a return of the price unless promptly after knowledge of the breach he returns or offers to return what he has received in substantially as good condition as when it was transferred to him. (Restatement, Contracts, § 349(1)) None of the exceptions to this rule, contained in § 349(2), are applicable here. Illustration 2 to § 349(1) reads:

> *A* sells an automobile to *B* for cash. After driving it for a few hundred miles, *B* learns of such a substantial breach of warranty by *A* as justifies rescission; and he at once tenders the return of the machine and demands his money back, the tender being conditioned on repayment. The slight use of the machine by *B* did not substantially affect its physical condition, although it considerably reduced its market value. *B* can get judgment for restitution of the price paid. Had *B* continued to make use of the machine after knowledge of the breach, he could not get judgment for his money back.

In *Ajamian v. Schlanger,* (20 N.J.Super. 246, 89 A.2d 702 (App. Div. 1952)), the relevant facts of which are similar to those in the instant case, the plaintiff sought rescission on the ground of fraud. In ruling that he had forfeited his right to rescind, the court stated (Id. at page 249, 89 A.2d at page 704):

> A party entitled to rescission on the ground of fraud may either avoid the transaction or confirm it; he cannot do both; and once he elects, he must abide by his decision. When he has discovered the fraud, or has been informed of facts and circumstances from which such knowledge would be imputed to him, he must thereupon act with diligence and without delay if he desires to rescind; and the transaction will be deemed ratified if he does any material act which assumes the transaction is valid. His continued dealing with the property purchased, after knowledge of the fraud, as if the contract were subsisting and binding, is evidence of an election to treat the contract as valid; so, also, is the payment of purchase money after such knowledge. . . . Since this plaintiff, with full knowledge of the alleged fraud, continued for more than six months to deal with the property as his own, and made the monthly payments on the purchase price, his actions afford plenary evidence of an election to abide by the contract; and once made, this election is irrevocable.

Certainly it was up to the plaintiff here to rescind within a reasonable time after May 17, 1958, when he learned that his dispute with the defendant could not amicably be resolved. Far from doing so, the plaintiff retained the automobile, continued to make payments on it and continued to use it for a period of more than five months. Whatever the effect was of plaintiff's conduct before, his conduct subsequent to May 17, 1958 constituted a binding election to affirm his transaction with the defendant, barring rescission. Therefore, the plaintiff's recovery, if any, must be limited to the difference between the amount which he would have been obligated to pay if the contract had been completed properly and the amount due under the instrument as filled in by the defendant, a sum in the neighborhood of $400.

The decree of the court below is reversed and the record is remanded for further proceedings consistent with this opinion.

White Const. Corp. v. Jet Spray Cooler, Inc.

1962 (Mass) 183 N.E.2d 719

Plaintiff and defendant entered into a bilateral contract for the construction of a building on a cost plus 10 percent basis. Defendant breached the contract by constructing the building itself. At the trial, plaintiff failed to establish the actual cost of the construction and was awarded $1.00 as nominal damages. Plaintiff appeals.

WILLIAMS, J. We think that there was no error. The jury was warranted in finding that the parties entered into a bilateral contract at the time DeCillis and Jacobs shook hands by which the plaintiff agreed to construct the warehouse with the architect's plans as a basis when they were complete, and the defendants agreed to pay the cost of construction plus 10 per cent; that the plaintiff stood ready to perform until Jacobs informed DeCillis that the defendants were going to act as their own general contractor; and that this action by the defendants prevented performance by the plaintiff and was a material breach of the contract.

If the plaintiff had performed its contract it would have been entitled to a sum equal to the cost of the material and labor required for the performance and in addition a fee amounting to 10 percent of the cost.

The established rule for ascertaining damages for breach of a building contract is stated in *John Hetherington & Sons, Inc. v. William Firth Co.* (210 Mass. 8, 21-22, 95 N.E. 961, 964):

[T]he injured party shall be placed in the same position he would have been in, if the contract had been performed, so far as loss can be ascertained to have followed as a natural consequence and to have been within the contemplation of the parties as reasonable men as a probable result of the breach, and so far as compensation therefor in money can be computed by rational methods upon a firm basis of facts. . . . [R]ecovery can be had where loss of profits is the proximate result of the breach, . . . and where it can be determined as a practical matter with a fair degree of certainty what the profits would have been. But profits cannot be recovered . . . when they are remote, or so uncertain, contingent, or speculative as not to be susceptible of trustworthy proof. They must be capable of ascertainment by reference to some definite standard, either of market value, established experience or direct inference from known circumstances. . . . This is simply a concrete application of the wider principle . . . to the effect that the complaining party must establish his claim upon a solid foundation in fact, and cannot recover when any essential element is left to conjecture, surmise or hypothesis.

Since the recoverable profits would be a percentage of the actual cost to the contractor of constructing the building, it was essential for the plaintiff to prove with substantial certainty what that cost would have been. This it failed to do. All that appears are estimates made by DeCillis at various times. At one time he estimated that the actual cost of the work would be less; at another, $156,810; and again, that the actual cost of the work would be $142,000.

It is contended that evidence that the cost of the completed building including engineering services was $161,000 is sufficient proof that it would have cost the plaintiff a similar amount, but it was not shown that the building as erected by Jacobs was like or similar to the contemplated structure which DeCillis purported to estimate. We are constrained to hold that the plaintiff's claim for damages rests on surmise and conjecture. The judge rightly instructed the jury that if they found a breach of contract only nominal damages could be awarded. . . .

So ordered.

King Motors v. Delfino
1960 (Conn.) 72 A.2d 233

MALTBIE, C. J. The question presented in this case is whether a provision in a contract for the payment of a certain sum of money constituted one for liquidated damages, as stated in it, or one for a penalty. The trial court gave judgment for the plaintiff to recover upon the former basis and the defendant has appealed.

The plaintiff is an automobile dealer. It has a franchise to sell Cadillac cars which provides, in effect, that if a new car it sells becomes the property of a person not in its territory within a six-month period from the date of the sale, it has to pay a commission to the dealer in the territory where the owner resides. On July 13, 1948, it sold and delivered to the defendant a new 1948 Cadillac car for $3,935.48, $1,675 of which was represented by the trade-in value of the defendant's Buick car. At the time of the sale the defendant executed and delivered to the plaintiff a "Contract for Repurchase" which provided that the defendant would not sell or transfer the Cadillac for a period of six months without first offering it to the plaintiff for purchase at the price at which it was sold to the defendant less 3 per cent per month for depreciation and less cost of necessary repairs. The contract then went on to provide: "It is further understood and agreed by and between the parties that if the said Purchaser shall violate any of the terms of the Contract, expressed above, then the said Purchaser shall owe the said Dealer the sum of Three Hundred Dollars ($300.00) in current money of the United States, as liquidated damages, which amount shall be immediately due and payable." The only term of the contract to which the quoted provision could apply is that which required the defendant to offer the plaintiff the option of repurchase. On July 19, 1948, the defendant sold the Cadillac to another person for $5,450 without first offering to sell it to the plaintiff in accordance with the agreement for repurchase. At that time new used cars were selling in excess of the retail price of new cars. No legal reason existed which would have prevented the plaintiff from realizing a profit on the sale of the Cadillac had the defendant re-sold it to the plaintiff.

As a general rule parties can contract to liquidate their damages, and courts have not interfered with such contracts where the proof of damages would be uncertain or difficult and the amount agreed upon is reasonably commensurate with the extent of the injury. The conditions for recovery on such a contract are . . . (1) the damages to be anticipated as resulting from the breach must be uncertain in amount or difficult to prove; (2) there must have been an intent on the part of the parties to liquidate them in advance; and (3) the amount stipulated must be a reasonable one, that is to say, not greatly disproportionate to the presumable loss or injury. "If the provision was inserted for the purpose of deterring the defendant from breaching his contract and of penalizing him for doing so, instead of specifying a sum which the parties in good faith agreed upon as representing the damages which would ensue from a breach, it is to be regarded as imposing a penalty . . . In such a case recovery will be limited to the actual damage and if no damage is proven no recovery may be had." (*May v. Young*, 125 Conn. 1, 9)

If the agreement had contained no provision for liquidated damages, the plaintiff's damages on the breach of the defendant's agreement to offer the car to it for repurchase would have been properly measured by the profits it would probably have made on a resale of the car. But what that profit might be was not capable of anticipation, particularly as the provision covered a period of six months after the sale; and the trial court might well have considered that, looking forward from the date of sale, $300 was not a sum clearly disproportionate to the probability of loss through the plaintiff's inability to have the car for resale. The words of the contract clearly express the intent of the parties that the sum is to be "liquidated damages"; and the factual situation is such that the trial court could reasonably conclude that those words fairly meant that, and not merely a penalty designed to compel the defendant not to make default. . . .

There is no error.

McKenna v. Commissioner of Mental Health

1964 (Mass.) 199 N.E.2d 686

REARDON, J. This is a petition for a writ of mandamus to compel the Commissioner of Mental Health and the superintendent of Cushing Hospital to restore the petitioner to his position at the Cushing Hospital without loss of compensation. On July 30, 1963, a judge of the Superior Court ordered the writ to issue and the petitioner was reinstated.

On September 18, 1963, the judge ordered further that McKenna be reinstated as of December 11, 1962, and be paid his salary by "the respondent" at the rate of $15.65 a day from the date of discharge to that of his return to work, for a total of $2,566.60. From this latter order, the respondents appealed.

The petitioner, a veteran, who had been a special attendant at Cushing Hospital for more than three years, was discharged by letters as of December 11, 1962, for dereliction of duty. Because he was not given a copy of G.L. c. 31, §§ re, 45, and 46A, or a hearing before the appointing authority, the judge ruled the discharge to have been in violation of G.L. c. 30 § 9A.

The petitioner was reinstated as of July 27, 1963. In proper circumstances a petitioner can recover back salary incident to a writ of mandamus ordering reinstatement to employment. At the trial, however, McKenna admitted on cross-examination that he had made no effort to procure any employment following his discharge. For that reason, the respondents contend, he cannot recover for loss of salary.

> Where one is under contract for personal service, and is discharged, it becomes his duty to dispose of his time in a reasonable way, so as to obtain as large compensation as possible, and to use honest, earnest and intelligent efforts to this end. He cannot voluntarily remain idle and expect to recover the compensation stipulated in the contract from the other party.

A succinct statement applicable to the status of the employee who has been discharged has been made in Corbin, Contracts, § 1039:

> It is not infrequently said that it is the "duty" of the injured party to mitigate his damages so far as that can be done by reasonable effort on his part. Since there is no judicial penalty, however, for his failure to make this effort, it is not desirable to say that he is under a "duty." His recovery against the defendant will be exactly the same whether he makes the effort and mitigates his loss, or not; but if he fails to make the reasonable effort, with the result that his injury is greater than it would otherwise have been, he cannot recover judgment for the amount of this avoidable and unnecessary increase. The law does not penalize his inaction; it merely does nothing to compensate him for the loss that he helped to cause by not avoiding it. . . .

Our cases have indicated however, that the employer has the burden of proof on the issue of mitigation of damages. The overwhelming weight of authority elsewhere places that burden upon the employer. We adopt that rule. McKenna is entitled to recover his back salary less what he did in fact earn following his discharge or in the exercise of proper diligence might have earned in another employment. While the respondents showed that McKenna made no effort to secure other employment, they failed to show what he could have earned in other similar work. He, therefore, is entitled to recover from the Commonwealth the sum of $2,566.60. As so modified the order is affirmed.

So ordered.

Hogan v. Norfleet

1959 (Fla. App.) 113 S.2d 437

MOODY, J. Appellant, plaintiff below, brought a suit for specific performance after exercising his option to purchase a franchised bottled gas business. The appellee, defendant below, filed a motion to dismiss and, upon hearing, the court dismissed the complaint, or in the alternative, granted plaintiff leave to file a suit on the law side of the court. To this order plaintiff filed interlocutory appeal.

Defendant is the owner of Norfleet Gas and Appliance, a bottled gas business based on a franchise covering a particular territory. The complaint alleges that in October, 1951, defendant induced the plaintiff to enter his business stating that he needed help in his business and planned to retire; that if the plaintiff would work for him the defendant would sell his business to the plaintiff and that in furtherance thereof, in December 1952, the parties signed a written option setting forth the price and terms under which the plaintiff could purchase said business if such option were exercised. The complaint further alleges plaintiff exercised his option in October, 1957, but that the defendant has failed and refused to transfer said business to the plaintiff; that said business is prosperous; that it is the type of business and franchise which cannot be obtained in the open market; that the plaintiff fully performed his part of the agreement, and, that defendant should be required to convey all of the assets of said business including the franchise and privileges of such business.

The sole point argued on appeal and the only point covered in this opinion is whether or not specific performance should be granted for the sale of the business as set forth in the complaint. The general rule is that, although the remedy of specific performance is available to enforce contracts for the sale of realty, specific performance of contracts relating to personal property will not be enforced for the reason that ordinarily compensation for breach of contract may be had by way of an action at law for damages. Such an action would be regarded as fully adequate.

The apparent reluctance of equity to grant specific performance of [a] contract relating to personalty does not arise from any less regard for contracts involving contracts for personalty than for those involving realty, but is simply a corollary of the principle upon which equity acts in decreeing specific performance, namely, the inadequacy of the remedy at law for damages. . . .

Our Florida courts have held that specific performance of a contract is a matter of equitable cognizance as applied both to real and personal property, and where, in the case of personal property, it is of a peculiar character and value, specific performance will be granted. . . .

In the case now before us, it appears the contract of sale involves a going business including good will and an operating franchise covering a particular territory. Obviously, such a franchise would not be available in the open market and its value would be very difficult, if not impossible, to ascertain. The value of good will or of a going business is an intangible asset of an indefinite, speculative or uncertain value. The contract executed in 1952 provides the method of determining the purchase price. However, the measure of damages in an action at law would entail the determination of the *present* value of such business which involves elements of going business value, good will and prospective profits. Certainly these are matters which cannot be readily ascertainable or fixed and could not conform with the rule in a law action that any recoverable damages must be susceptible to reasonable ascertainment.

For the reasons stated the decree is reversed and the cause is remanded for further appropriate proceedings.

Brennan v. Brennan

1955 (Ohio) 128; N.E.(2) 89

Plaintiff sued defendant for amount due him for sale of corporate stock. The contract provided for sale at book value to be determined by accountants who were to include machinery at depreciated values. Certain equipment was shown on the books at $7,108.65 but was fully depreciated for tax purposes. The accountants included this equipment at $1,810.31 but Plaintiff contended that they should have been valued at $7,108.65. The contract provided that the accountants decision was to be final and conclusive. Trial court found for plaintiff and defendant appealed.

STEWART, J. . . . As was said by Judge Zimmerman in the case of *Campbell v. Automatic Die & Products Co.* (162 Ohio St. 321, 329, 123 N.E.2d 401, 405):

> It is the policy of the law to favor and encourage arbitration and every reasonable intendment will be indulged to give effect to such proceedings and to favor the regularity and integrity of the arbitrator's acts.

As far back as 1835, this court, in the case of *Ormsby's Adm'rs v. Bakewell and Johnson* (7 Ohio 99), held that, where arbitrators are substituted for parties, the award of the arbitrators is final and cannot be impeached for error; and that nothing but fraud in the parties or in the arbitrators can be alleged to avoid the award. . . .

It seems to be the universal law that where a matter is submitted by parties to an arbitrator for decision, with an agreement that the arbitrator's decision shall be binding upon the parties, they are bound by such decision provided there is no fraud or bad faith upon the part of the arbitrator and he acts according to the instructions given him.

Therefore, the question for us to decide is whether the accountants followed the directions given to them in the contract. Those directions are that they should proceed promptly to make an examination of the property, books, accounts and assets of the company and prepare a statement showing the book value of the shares of stock of the company. . . .

We hold that, under the contract, between plaintiff and defendant, the accountants, who were the arbitrators whose decision was to be final and conclusive, did follow the directions in the contract and did employ ordinary and usual methods of accounting in determining the value of machinery and equipment of The Brennan Company at the depreciated value thereof. They were not told to find the actual value of such items, and if they had made an appraisement and done so, either one of the parties who had been harmed thereby could have questioned the accountants' statement because an appraisement of actual value would have been a departure from the directions in the contract. . . .

Therefore, when the accountants valued the machinery on a depreciated cost basis at $1,717.85, and the office equpiment on the same basis at $92.54, and stated that those values were not necessarily the present true values, they acted only in accordance with the instructions given them, and, by their contract with each other, plaintiff and defendant are bound by such determination.

It follows that the judgment of the Court of Appeals must be, and it hereby is, reversed, and final judgment rendered for defendant.

Judgment reversed.

Smith v. Russ

1959 (Kansas) 339 P.(2) 286

Plaintiff-landlord brought an ejectment action against defendant-tenant. Defendant claimed to have extended his lease and to have a right to possession. The original lease first contained a provision that the tenant should not sublease premises or assign lease or renew the same without the written consent of the landlord. The next paragraph gave tenant the option of extending the lease for an additional five years upon certain conditions. The tenant exercised his option without the consent of the landlord but complying with the stated conditions.

SCHROEDER, J. The principal question is whether the tenant may at his option extend the lease without the written consent of the landlord. . . .

Courts generally endeavor to ascertain the intention of the parties where a controversy arises concerning a written instrument and there is ambiguity or uncertainty involved. The general rule is that these instruments are to be interpreted from their "four corners." That is to say, that all the language used anywhere in the instrument should be taken into consideration and construed in harmony with other portions of the instrument.

The difficulty in applying the foregoing rule to the facts in the case presently before the court is that we find it impossible to reconcile the two provisions which are repugnant.

Appellees rely on *Burchfield v. Brinkman* (92 Kan. 377, 140 P. 894) And see 81 A.L.R. 1058. The lease there provided: " 'It is further agreed that after the expiration of this lease the party of the second part shall have the option for a further period of five years from that date, provided that the terms and conditions are *satisfactory to both parties* of this lease.' " (Emphasis added.) (92 Kan. at page 379, 140 P. at page 895) Such cases have no application to the facts presently before the court. Likewise, provisions in a lease giving a lessee the right " '. . . to the first option in case they may desire to continue to occupy said premises under a new lease after the expiration of the present term . . .' " as in *Landowners Company v. Pendry* (151 Kan. 674, 675, 100 P.2d 632, 633, 127 A.L.R. 890), were held merely to give a preferential right to release in the event the lessor did not desire to sell or occupy the premises, and have no application here.

Resort to two familiar rules of construction control the decision herein. First, where there is an uncertainty between general provisions and specific provisions, the specific provisions ordinarily qualify the meaning of the general provisions. (Restatement of Law, Contracts, Volume 1, § 236[c], p. 330; and 12 Am. Jr., Contracts, § 244, p. 779) It is a reasonable inference that specific provisions express more exactly what parties intend than broad or general clauses which do not necessarily indicate that the parties had the particular matter in thought.

Second, where words or other manifestations of intention bear more than one reasonable meaning, an interpretation is preferred which operates more strongly against the party from whom they proceed. (Restatement of Law, Contracts, Volume 1, § 236[d], p. 330) Since one who speaks or writes can, by exactness of expression, more easily prevent mistakes in meaning, than one with whom he is dealing, doubts arising from the ambiguity of language are resolved against the former in favor of the latter. This rule has been given specific application to a farm tenancy lease in *Christenson v. Ohrman* (159 Kan. 565, 156 P.2d 848), where it was held as a general rule, in construing the provisions relating to renewals or extensions of leases between landlord and tenant, where there is an uncertainty, the tenant is favored and not the landlord. (32 Am. Jr., Landlord and Tenant, § 962, p. 809) Here it is conceded counsel for the appellees prepared the farm lease in question.

Upon application of the foregoing rules of construction we hold the general provision [1] in the lease here under consideration, requiring the written consent of the landlord for a renewal of the lease, must yield to the specific provision [2] giving to the tenant an option to extend the lease for an additional period of five years, and that the trial court erred in entering judgment for the appellees.

The judgment is reversed.

CHAPTER 7
REVIEW QUESTIONS AND PROBLEMS

1. *P* sued *D*, a contractor, for breach of a contract to build a house. If built in accordance with the plans and specifications, the house would have been worth $20,000. As completed it was worth $10,000 and $5,000 of labor and materials would be required to complete work and eliminate defects. How much is *P* entitled to collect?

2. *X*, a college faculty member, had a contract of continuing employment with *Y* college. *Y* college dismissed *X* and he sued for specific performance of the contract contending that his services were unique. What result?

3. *P* sued *D* in quasi contract for the fair value of work done on two houses which were substantially completed in accordance with the contract but which contracts were not completely performed in that the water pipes were not sealed and other small items were not performed. *D* contended that the case should not have been submitted to a jury. What result?

4. *W* sued *H* in quasi contract for ½ the value of property acquired by *H* during a period in which *W* cohabited with *H* and rendered services as housekeeper, cook. and homemaker. What result?

5. *P* sued *D* in quasi contract for the increased value of certain real estate which *D* had orally agreed to sell *P* but which *D* repudiated. *P* had improved the premises prior to *D*'s repudiation of the oral agreement (assume that it is unenforceable). What result?

6. *X* sued *Y* for back wages. *X* had been wrongfully discharged from his job. *Y* proved that *X* made no effort to find another job but offered no evidence as to what *X* might have been able to earn. What result?

7. *X* sued *Y* for breach of a contract by which *Y* agreed to purchase yarn. The contract price was $2.15 per pound. The market price at the time of breach was $1.90. *Y* failed to accept 16,000 lbs. How much is *X* entitled to recover assuming the cost of manufacture to be $1.00 per pound?

8. *P*, a country club, sued *D*, a former member, for the balance of *D*'s yearly dues. *D* had paid the dues until the date of his withdrawal but the membership application provided that withdrawing members had to pay the entire year's dues even if someone else took over for him. *D* alleges that the agreement is unenforceable as a penalty and in the alternative that he is entitled to offer proof in mitigation of damages. What result?

9. *P*, who was injured in an automobile accident, sued *D* to recover damages based upon her having to give up her chosen and intended occupation as a physical education teacher. *P* had been trained as such a teacher but had not begun teaching. Is she entitled to collect for the difference in salary between that of a physical education teacher and the job she was able to accept?

10. *X* agreed to sell 1000 shares of the *XYZ* company, a closely held corporation to *Y*. *X* then refused to carry out the agreement and *Y* sued for specific performance. What result?

11. What are the advantages of arbitration to businessmen?

12. Name 3 remedies for breach of contract.

chapter 8

The Agreement—
Offer and
Acceptance

FORMATION OF OFFERS

2-12. The Offer. The first requirement of a valid enforceable contract is an "agreement" between the parties. The agreement is usually created by one party making an offer and the other party accepting it. Offer and acceptance have been described as the acts by which the parties have a "meeting of minds." An offer is the communication by one party, known as the offeror, to another party, called the offeree, of the former's willingness to act or to refrain from acting as specified if the latter will act or promise to act or refrain from acting as requested. In other words, it is a communication of what each party is willing to do or not to do for a stated consideration.

Not all communications that invite future business transactions are so worded as to constitute offers. Many are of a preliminary character, being transmitted primarily for the purpose of inducing the person to whom they are addressed to respond with an offer.[1] Within this class of communications fall most catalogs, circulars, advertisements, estimates, proposals in which major terms are not included, and oral statements of general terms, where it is understood that the detailed terms will be reduced to writing and signed before the agreement is to be binding. Such communications may, however, constitute an offer.

The chief reason why proposals of the kind indicated do not qualify as offers is that the parties making them have no intention of entering into a binding agreement on the basis of the terms expressed. The party

[1] *McGinn v. American Bank Stationery Co.*, page 142.

making the statement, as the other party should reasonably understand, does not intend that any legal consequences necessarily flow from his action, sometimes because major terms are lacking and sometimes because of the circumstances under which the statements are made. With a few exceptions under the Code later discussed, an offer must be definite, and the proposal must be made under such circumstances that the person receiving it has reason to believe that the other party is willing to deal on the terms indicated.

One of the reasons for this requirement of definiteness is that courts may have to determine at a later date whether or not the performance is in compliance with the terms. Consequently, if the terms are vague or impossible to measure with some precision, or if major terms are absent, no contract results. It is noted that time for performance is not necessarily a major term, since in the absence of a time clause, the court assumes performance is to take place within a reasonable time. Price is usually a major term, although where one person has performed under the agreement, the court will assume that a reasonable price was intended. An executory agreement, however, in which price is absent, will normally not be enforced.

The Code recognizes that parties often do not include all of the terms of the contract in their negotiations and contract. It provides that even though one or more terms are left open, a contract for sale of personal property does not fail for indefiniteness if the parties have intended to make a contract and there is a reasonably certain basis for giving an appropriate remedy.[C1] It further provides that an agreement which is otherwise sufficiently definite to be a contract is not made invalid by the fact that it leaves particulars of performance to be specified by one of the parties.[C2] The specification must be made in good faith and within limits set by commercial reasonableness. Unless otherwise agreed, specifications relating to assortment of the goods are at the buyer's option and those relating to shipment are at the seller's option.[C3]

2-13. Communication. An offer is not effective until it has been communicated to the offeree. For example, an offer to remain open 10 days mailed on March 1 and received on March 3 would remain open until March 12, or 10 days from receipt. An offer is effective even though it be delayed in reaching the offeree. Since the delay normally results from the negligence of the offeror's agent or his chosen means of communication, he should bear the loss resulting from the delay. However, if the delay is apparent to the offeree, his acceptance will be good only if it becomes effective within a reasonable time after the offer would normally have been received.

The unexpressed desire to enter into an agreement can never constitute an offer. The writing of a letter embodying a definite proposition will also prove futile unless the letter is mailed and reaches the offeree.

C1 *U.C.C.* 2-204.
C2 *U.C.C.* 2-311(1).

C3 *U.C.C.* 2-311(2).

An offer can be effectively communicated only by the offeror or his duly authorized agent. If the offeree learns of the offeror's intention from some outside source, no offer results—it must be communicated through the medium or channel selected by the offeror.

An offer to the public may be made through the newspapers or the posting of notices, but it is not effective so far as a particular individual is concerned until he learns that the offer has been made.

2-14. Construction of Offers. Courts have often stated that there must be a "meeting of the minds" of the parties on the subject matter and terms of the agreement or no contract is created. Difficult questions as to the existence of the contract frequently arise because of ambiguous language in the contract or because of extrinsic facts known to only one party. For example, if X offers to pick Y's corn for $30.00 per acre and Y states that he will pay "half of it," no contract results (assuming that either $15.00 per acre or half the corn is reasonable) since there was no meeting of the minds. The same result occurs when Jones offers to sell his used Chevrolet car to Brown for $750.00 and Brown agrees to buy it, if Jones, who has two such cars, was thinking of one and Brown had in mind the other. In reality they failed to reach an agreement; their negotiations resulted in no bargain because Jones offered to sell Car X and Brown promised to buy Car Y. The rule that the minds of the parties must be in accord is limited in one important respect; namely, that the intention of the parties is to be determined by their individual conduct—and what each leads the other reasonably to believe—rather than by their innermost thoughts, which can be known only to themselves. It is the objective manifestation of intent rather than the subjective which controls. Thus, the courts hold the minds of the parties to have met when a written agreement is signed. Each person possessing legal capacity to contract who signs a written document with the idea of entering into a contract is presumed to know the contents thereof. Since the act of signing manifests a person's intention to be bound by the terms contained in the writing, he is in no position at a later date to contend effectively that he did not mean to enter into the particular agreement. All contracts should be read carefully before they are signed.

Offers clearly made in jest or under the strain or stress of great excitement are usually not enforced, as one is not reasonably justified in relying on them. Whether an offer is made in jest is determined by applying the objective standard previously discussed.

OFFERS IN SPECIAL SITUATIONS

2-15. Auctions and Advertisements for Bids. When articles are sold at public auction, the offer is said to be made by the bidder and accepted by the seller at the drop of the auctioneer's hammer. Because of this rule, the seller can withdraw his article from sale at any time during the auction. The purchaser may withdraw his bid at any time before the auctioneer has concluded the sale. Naturally, the seller may, by statements in the circulars relating to the sale or by statements made on the part of the auctioneer, prescribe the conditions under which the contract is to be concluded. Thus, an auction advertised "without reserve" means that the property will be sold to the highest bidder. In such a case each bid is an acceptance unless or until a higher bid is received or the bid is retracted. A retraction of a bid does not revive a previous bid.

Unless it is announced before the sale, the seller has no right to bid at his own sale. For him to bid or have an agent do so would amount to fraud, the potential buyers having the right to presume that the sale is held in good faith. If an auctioneer knowingly accepts a bid on the seller's behalf or the seller makes or procures such a bid without giving notice of such bidding, the buyer may at his option avoid either the sale or take the goods at the price of the last good faith bid prior to his bid.

When one advertises that bids will be received for construction work, it is held that the person calling for bids makes no offer, but that the party who submits a bid is the offeror.[2] The one calling for the bids may reject any or all of them, and in the absence of some statute, the bidder is free at any time to withdraw his bid until it has been accepted. The same is true of public construction. Although the statutes of most states provide that public work must be let to the lowest responsible bidder, courts hold that all bids may be rejected.

2-16. Tickets. Tickets purchased for entrance into places of amusement or as evidence of a contract for transportation often contain matter in small print that attempts to limit or define the rights of the holder. Some conflict exists relative to the effectiveness of these stipulations, but it is generally held that they become a part of the offer and are accepted by the holder if he is aware of the printed matter even though he does not read it. There are some cases, such as those involving steamship tickets, in which the purchaser is presumed to know about the printed matter even though his attention is not called to it at the time the ticket is delivered because the ticket purports on its face to be a contract.

If a ticket is received merely as evidence of ownership and is to be presented later as a means of identification, the provisions are ineffective unless the recipient's attention is specifically directed to them at the time the ticket is accepted.[3] Thus, tickets given at checkrooms or repair shops are received usually as a means of identifying the article to be returned rather than setting forth the terms of the contract.

Printed material often found on the back of contract forms and occasionally on letterheads, unless embodied in the contract by reference thereto, generally is not considered to be a part of any contract set forth on such a form or letterhead.

2-17. Options and Firm Offers. An option is a contract based upon some consideration to hold an offer open for an agreed period of time. It offers

2 *O. C. Kinney v. Paul Hardeman, Inc.,* page 143.
3 *Kergald v. Armstrong Transfer Exp. Co.,* page 144.

the holder of the option a choice to accept or reject a continuing offer within a specified time. Quite often the offeree pays, or promises to pay, money in order to have the offer remain open, but the consideration may be any other thing of value. The significant fact is that the offer has been transformed into a contract of option based upon consideration supplied by the offeree. It is now irrevocable for the period of the option.

Frequently an option is part of another contract. A lease may contain a clause that gives to the tenant the right to purchase the property within a given period at a stated price, or a sale of merchandise may include a provision that obligates the seller to supply an additional amount at the same price if ordered by the purchaser within a specified time. Such options are enforceable, since the initial promise to pay rent serves as consideration for both the lease and the right to buy, and the original purchase price of goods serves as consideration for the goods purchased and the option to buy additional goods.

The Uniform Commercial Code contains a provision which in effect creates a limited option without consideration when a merchant [C4] in an offer states that the offer will remain open for a stated period. This is called a firm offer and in such case, the merchant may not withdraw the offer during the stated period provided it does not exceed three months, or for a reasonable length of time not exceeding three months if no period is stated. The offer must be a signed written offer and in the event the offer is on a form supplied by the offeree, it must be separately signed by the offeror in addition to his signature as a party to the contract.[C5] Thus the offeree can rely upon the continuing legal obligation of the offer and can make other commitments on the strength of it.

DURATION OF OFFER

2-18. Duration. An offer that has been properly communicated continues until it lapses or expires, is revoked by the offeror, is rejected by the offeree, becomes illegal or impossible by operation of law, or is accepted by the offeree.

2-19. Lapse. An offer does not remain open indefinitely, even though the offeror fails to withdraw it. If the offer stipulates the period during which it is to continue, it automatically lapses or expires at the end of that period. An attempted acceptance after that date can amount to no more than a new offer being made to the original offeror by the offeree of the original offer. An offer that provides for no time limit remains open for a reasonable time—a reasonable time being such period as a reasonable person might conclude was intended. Whether an offer has lapsed because of the passage of time is usually a question of fact for the jury after it has given proper weight to all related circumstances, one such being the nature of the property. For example, an offer involving property the

C4 *U.C.C.* 2-104(1)(3).　　　　　　　　C5 *U.C.C.* 2-205.

price of which is constantly fluctuating remains open a relatively short time in comparison with property the price of which is more stable.[4] Other factors that should be considered are: the circumstances under which the offer is made, the relation of the parties, and the means used in transmitting the offer. For example, an offer made orally usually lapses when the conversation ends unless the offeror clearly indicates that the proposal may be considered further by the offeree.

2-20. Revocation. With the exception of merchants who have made firm offers under the Code, an offeror may revoke an offer at any time before it has been accepted. This is true even though the offeror has promised to hold his offer open for a definite period. As long as it is a mere offer and not an option, the offer can be withdrawn legally even though morally or ethically such action seems unjustified in many instances.

A few recent decisions, however, have held that it is too late to withdraw an offer after the offeree, in reliance on it, has changed substantially his position; particularly if the offeror promised to hold it open for a certain period. This situation is well illustrated by general contractors who submit bids for improvements in reliance upon bids made to them by subcontractors or suppliers of material. This doctrine, commonly referred to as the doctrine of promissory estoppel,[5] is discussed in detail in the next chapter. Promissory estoppel is in effect a substitute for consideration and when applied it is legally sufficient to create a valid contract to keep the offer open.

As was previously noted in the discussion of options and firm offers, the Code reaches the same result in connection with offers by merchants as does the theory of promissory estoppel in contracts generally.[C6] The Code's firm offer does not require a material change of position by the offeree, however.

The revocation of an offer becomes effective only when it has been communicated to the offeree. The mere sending of a notice of revocation is insufficient. It must be received by the offeree or have reached a destination where it would have been available to him.

Communication of a revocation is effective when actually received regardless of how or by whom it is conveyed. If the offeree obtains knowledge from any source of the offeror's conduct clearly showing an intent to revoke, the offer is terminated. Direct notice of revocation is not required because it would be unjust to let the offeree knowingly take advantage of the offeror's position. To illustrate: an offeree who learns from some source that an industrial site offered for sale has been sold by the offeror to a third party cannot thereafter accept the offer. The offer is revoked as soon as the offeree learns of the sale, regardless of the source of his information.

---

[4] *Minnesota Linseed Oil Co. v. Collier White Lead Co.*, page 144.

[5] *Drennan v. Star Paving Company*, page 145.

[C6] *U.C.C.* 2-205.

An offer made to the public presents a special problem to an offeror who desires to revoke the offer. It would be impossible to give personal notice of revocation to all persons who may have learned of the offer. Because of this fact, the offeror may withdraw his offer by giving the same general publicity to the revocation that he gave to the offer. A public offer made through the newspapers in a certain locality may be withdrawn through the same medium. As a result, it is possible for such an offer to be withdrawn without every offeree's having actually learned of the withdrawal.

2-21. Rejection. Rejection by the offeree causes an offer to terminate even though the original offer was to have remained open for a longer period. The offeree cannot, after his rejection, change his mind and accept the offer. An attempt to do so will, at best, amount to a new offer which must be accepted by the original offeror in order to create a contract. For example, if *B* has paid *S* for a ten-day option to purchase property at a given price, but on the seventh day tells *S* that he does not want it, *S* is immediately free to sell to another buyer.

With one exception under the Code,[C7] which is discussed later in this chapter (Section 2-28), an attempted acceptance which departs from the terms of the offer is a rejection of the offer and is in effect a counteroffer, since it implies that the original terms are not acceptable.[6] This rule is subject to the rule of reason and a recognition that there are certain implied provisions in every contract, which, if mentioned in the acceptance, will not establish a rejection.[7] The effect of a counteroffer as a rejection may be avoided if the offeree uses language making it clear that he is not rejecting but is still considering the original offer.

An acceptance embodying terms other than those contained in the offer should be distinguished from a mere request for additional information. This distinction is especially necessary when the request for further information suggests that the original offer is still being considered.

Rejection of an offer is not effective until it has been received by the offeror or by his chosen agent or is available to him at his usual place of business. Consequently, a rejection which has been sent may be withdrawn before delivery to the offeror and such action does not bar a later acceptance.

2-22. Operation of Law. There are several events which will terminate an offer as a matter of law. Notice of the happening of these events need not be given or communicated as the offer ends instantaneously upon the happening of the event or occurrence. Such events include the death or insanity of either party or the destruction of the subject matter of the offer. These events eliminate one of the requisites for a contract, then

---

[6] *Banks v. Crescent Lumber & Shingle Co.,* page 147.
[7] *Department of Public Works v. Halls,* page 149.

[C7] *U.C.C.* 2-207.

making its creation impossible. The same effect results from the action of a law-making body declaring certain contracts to be illegal. If the subject matter of the contract becomes illegal, the legal object requirement would be missing making the continued existence of the contract impossible.

It should be emphasized that death or insanity terminates an offer and not a contract. As a general rule, death does not excuse performance of contracts although an exception obviously exists for contracts of personal service.

To illustrate the effect of a death of one of the parties, assume that Adams offers to sell to Barnes a certain electronic computer for $15,000 and that Barnes, after Adams' death but without knowledge of his decease, mails his acceptance to Adams and immediately enters into a contract to resell the computer to Curtis for $17,000. The estate of Adams has no duty to deliver the machine, even though Curtis may have a claim against Barnes for breach of contract if Barnes fails to deliver it to Curtis. Had the acceptance of Barnes become effective before the death of Adams, the executor of Adams' estate would have been obligated to deliver the computer.

ACCEPTANCE

2-23. Definition. A contract consists of an offer by one party and its acceptance by the person or persons to whom it is made. Figuratively speaking, an offer hangs like a suspended question, and the acceptance should be a positive answer to that question. The offeror, in effect, says "I will sell you this article for $200. Will you buy it?" The offeree-acceptor answers the question in the affirmative. An acceptance is an indication by the offeree of his willingness to be bound by the terms of the offer. It may, if the offer permits, take the form of an act (unilateral offer), a promise communicated to the offeror (bilateral offer) or the signing and delivery of a written instrument. This latter method is the most common in situations of substantial importance and in more formal transactions. Where a written contract is the agreed method of consummating the transaction, the contract is formed only when it has been signed by both parties and has been delivered. However, delivery may be conditioned upon the happening of some event, and unless it occurs, no contract exists.

2-24. Acceptance of Unilateral Offer. As indicated previously, contracts are either unilateral or bilateral, depending upon whether the offer must be accepted by an act on the part of the offeree or whether a promise to perform will create the contractual relation. Most contracts are bilateral in nature, and, in case the offers are ambiguous, the courts tend to construe them as bilateral. The fact remains, however, that many contracts are unilateral in form. The offeror in such cases does not require, in fact does not desire, a promise or assurance of performance, but insists on substantial completion of the act requested before a contract is created.

Since a unilateral offer is not accepted until completion of the requested act, the offeror is at liberty to withdraw his offer at any point prior to the time when substantial performance has been rendered. If only partial performance has occurred prior to withdrawal, and if it has benefitted the offeror, he must pay for the benefit conferred on a theory of a quasi contract, but by the prevailing view he is not obligated to permit the offeree to complete his performance. If substantial completion of performance has occurred prior to the attempted withdrawal, the offeror has lost his right to withdraw. However, expense incurred in preparation for performance does not affect the offeror's right to revoke his offer or afford any remedy to the offeree. A revocable offer contemplating a series of independent contracts by separate acceptances may be effectively revoked so as to terminate the power to create future contracts, even though one or more of the proposed contracts has been formed.

A promise of continuous guaranty made to a creditor to insure payment of future purchases by a debtor is of this kind. It may be terminated by proper notice at any time, thus relieving the guarantor of liability for debts contracted thereafter. (See Section 2-73, Chapter 13)

The distinction between bilateral and unilateral contracts is further illustrated by the following typical situations: A hardware merchant who is approached by a salesman of a manufacturer signs a purchase order for certain goods, the order being subject to the approval by the manufacturer's home office. At common law acceptance was effective as soon as that approval had been communicated to the merchant, because the offer was bilateral in nature and was to be accepted by a promise to ship. It could have been accepted by shipment of the goods also.[8] Until notice of acceptance was received or the goods were received, the offeror was at liberty to withdraw his offer. On the other hand, if a merchant was immediately in need of several items of merchandise and mailed a letter to a certain concern asking for immediate shipment of the articles listed, the offer was unilateral at common law. It was accepted by the act of shipment, even though the buyer had no actual knowledge of the acceptance. The buyer could withdraw prior to delivery to the carrier even though the seller might have incurred some expense in anticipation of delivery by way of procuring, assembling, or packing the goods for shipment.

Under the Code, such an offer may either be treated as a unilateral offer and accepted by shipment or it may be treated as a bilateral offer and accepted by a promise to ship.[C8] The seller is thus afforded an opportunity to bind the bargain prior to the time of shipment if he wants to do so. However, in the event that the seller elects to ship, the buyer may treat the offer as having lapsed unless notification of acceptance is made within a reasonable length of time. Commencing performance is a rea-

---

8 *Lewis and Lewis v. Root and Root,* page 151.

C8 *U.C.C.* 2-206.

sonable mode of acceptance, but notice will still be required if an unreasonable length of time will pass prior to delivery of the goods to the offeror. If the seller ships goods which do not conform to the order, he may seasonably notify the buyer that the shipment is not an acceptance but is only offered as an accommodation to the buyer. This is in effect a counteroffer which the buyer may accept or reject.

2-25. Bilateral Offer. A bilateral offer is accepted by a promise to do the acts or conduct requested by the offer. The promise must be communicated to the offeror or his agent and may consist of any conduct which unequivocally evinces an intention to be bound by the conditions prescribed in the offer. In construing the language of a purported acceptance, the usual rules of construction including the principle that ambiguous language is construed against the person using it are applied.[9] The acceptance may take the form of a signature to a written agreement or a nod of the head. No formal procedure is required by the law of contract. If the offer is made to a group of people in the aggregate, the acceptance is not complete until each person of the group has indicated his acceptance. Until all have responded, the offeror is at liberty to withdraw.

Where the agreement takes the form of a written instrument, the acceptance is effective only when the document has been signed and delivered, unless it was clearly the intention of the parties that the earlier verbal agreement be binding and that the writing act merely as a memorandum or evidence of their oral contract.

2-26. Silence as Assent. As a general rule, the offeror cannot force the offeree to speak. In most cases, therefore, mere silence by the offeree does not amount to acceptance, although the offeror in his offer may have stated that a failure to reply would constitute an acceptance. A previous course of dealing between the parties or the receipt of goods under certain circumstances might well raise a duty upon the part of the offeree to speak in order to avoid contractual relationship.[10] Silence of itself never constitutes an acceptance, but silence with intent to accept may do so. For example, the receipt of a renewal fire insurance policy retained by the insured with intent to keep and pay for it constitutes acceptance of the offer to insure for the new period. Mailing out the renewal policy constituted the offer to insure and the retention of the policy was the acceptance if the offeree intended to avail himself of the insurance protection.

The Code provides that a buyer has accepted goods when he fails to make an effective rejection or does any act inconsistent with the seller's ownership.[C9] Failure to reject will not be construed as an acceptance unless the buyer has had a reasonable opportunity to examine the goods.[C10]

---

[9] *Hill's Inc. v. William B. Kessler, Inc.,* p. 152.
[10] *Hendrickson v. International Harvester Co. of America,* page 153.

[C9] *U.C.C.* 2-606.   [C10] *U.C.C.* 2-606.

2-27. Acceptance by Offeree. Only the person to whom the offer is made can accept the offer. An offer cannot be assigned to a third party. Quite often goods are ordered from a firm that has discontinued business, and the goods are shipped by its successor. In such case the offeror is under no duty to accept the goods. If he accepts the goods knowing that they were shipped by the successor, he then by implication agrees to pay the new concern for them at the contract price. If he does not know of the change the liability is in quasi contract for the reasonable value of the goods.

Offers to the public may be accepted by any member of the public who is aware of the offer. Option contracts, although a form of offer, are usually assignable and may be accepted by the assignee.

2-28. Acceptance Must Follow Offer. In contracts which do not come within the provisions of the Code, an acceptance to be effective must conform exactly to the terms of the offer. As was discussed in Section 2-21, if the acceptance contains new terms or conditions or deviates in any manner from the terms of the offer, it is a counteroffer and constitutes a rejection of the offer, unless the offeree states that it is not to be considered a rejection. A provision in an offer relating to time, place, or manner of acceptance must be strictly complied with by the offeree. Any deviation from these terms will be construed to be a counteroffer and a rejection.

After the parties have either orally or by informal writings reached an agreement, one of them may acknowledge the contract or send a memorandum stating its terms and in addition may add new terms not previously discussed. The situation is a commonplace one and results largely from the widespread use of printed forms by merchants, both in ordering goods and in accepting orders. It is natural that there would be variations between the two forms, yet businessmen would expect that their exchange of forms would result in a binding contract. In keeping with its basic philosophy, the Code recognizes that a contract may result but within well defined limits. The Code makes it clear that the contract does not include the new terms but they are considered as proposals or additions to the contract which may be accepted or rejected by the other party.[11]

A similar situation arises when a party in reply to an offer states that he accepts the offer but adds new terms such as "rush" or "ship immediately." Again, the acceptance is effective without the new terms. However, if the correspondence is between merchants, the new terms are included if they are not material (minor terms) unless the offeror promptly rejects them or the offer states that the acceptance is limited to the terms of the offer.[c11] An example of a change which would be material and not accepted by silence would be a clause eliminating warranties. On the other hand, a clause requiring notice of breach of warranty within a reasonable time would be considered minor and this

11 *Roto-Lith Ltd. v. F. P. Bartlett & Co.*, page 154.

c11 *U.C.C.* 2-207.

would become a part of the contract unless notice of objection is season-ably given.[C12]

The Code further recognizes that conduct by the parties which recog-nizes the existence of a contract is sufficient to establish the contract for sale even though the writings do not establish the contract. In such a case, the terms on which the writings agree are part of the contract together with the other agreements of the parties.[C13]

2-29. Time of Taking Effect. A bilateral offer is accepted upon commu-nication of the acceptance to the offeror. A conflict has long existed in the law on the issue as to whether or not the acceptance is effective to create a contract at the moment the communication is deposited in the mail or whether its effectiveness is delayed until received the same as other communications associated with contracts such as revocations and rejections. In early English law, a case known as "Adams v. Lindsell" established the "deposited acceptance rule" which held that an acceptance was effective when deposited in the offeror's channel of communication or the one indicated by him to be used by the offeree. If none was indi-cated or used by the offeror, it was effective when deposited with the post or mail.[12] This rule has been challenged on the ground that there could actually be no meeting of the minds upon deposit of the acceptance be-cause the offeror would not know that it had been deposited. In recent years, postal rules have authorized a withdrawal of a letter and this change has been the basis of further attacks on the "deposited acceptance rule." Notwithstanding the strength of these arguments, most courts still adhere to the rule of "Adams v. Lindsell" and as a general rule an ac-ceptance is considered effective when deposited in the offeror's channel of communication or the mail if no other channel is indicated. If a dif-ferent means of communication is used, it is not effective until received.

The Code has adopted the deposited acceptance rule and has even extended it. Under the Code, acceptance by any reasonable means of communication is effective as soon as placed with the communicating agency unless the offeror in the offer specifies a particular means to be used in communicating the acceptance.[C14] An offer is construed as invit-ing acceptance in any manner and by any medium reasonable under the circumstances.[C15]

The deposited acceptance rule has the effect of placing on the offeror any possible loss resulting from a failure on the part of the communicat-ing agency to deliver the acceptance. A contract may exist although a letter of acceptance is lost in the mails. The offeror, in such cases, is duty bound to perform even though he may have entered into other contracts as a result of his failure to receive a reply. He can avoid this result only by stating in his offer that the acceptance shall be ineffective until it is actually received by him.

---

[12] *Falconer v. Mazess,* page 156.

[C12] *U.C.C.* 2-207(2).
[C13] *U.C.C.* 2-207(3).

[C14] *U.C.C.* 1-201(38)(26).
[C15] *U.C.C.* 2-206, 2-207.

OFFER AND ACCEPTANCE CASES

McGinn v. American Bank Stationery Co.

1963 (Maryland C.A.) 195 A.20 615

SYBERT, J. The plaintiff below appeals from a decree granting a motion for a summary judgment in favor of the defendants. The appellant [McGinn, the plaintiff] had filed an equity suit against the appellees, American Bank Stationery Company and its president, J. Wilford Sheridan, to enforce an alleged contract to sell 100 shares of the corporation's treasury stock at $50.00 per share.

Appellant claims that a contract arose in the following manner. In June 1960 the board of directors of the corporation passed a resolution authorizing the sale of stock "to such persons as may be selected by the President." At a subsequent meeting of all the salesmen of the corporation, including the appellant, a company official stated that treasury stock was being made available for sale to them, and that if they desired to purchase some, they should make a written request to the president. The salesmen were informed that if the requests exceeded the number of shares which the company intended to sell, then the stock would be prorated on the basis of the amount requested.

The appellant subsequently wrote the appellee Sheridan stating that he would like to buy 100 shares at $50.00 each. At a later conference with Sheridan, according to the appellant's own testimony, Sheridan did not indicate whether the corporation would sell "100 shares or any amount." Thereafter the appellant was told that 100 shares would not be made available to him, apparently because of the large number of subscriptions, but that he could buy a lesser amount if he so desired. He never requested fewer shares. Later the appellant asked Sheridan when he could expect to get the stock and was told that the corporation did not need money at that time but that the appellant would be informed when it did. No note or memorandum of the alleged contract was ever signed. Appellant never tendered payment in any amount because, to use his own words, "how could I, not knowing how much stock I was going to get or when?" The appellees' principal defense was that the evidence disclosed no contract.

We think the summary judgment was properly granted. The pleadings and the testimony of the appellant show that there was no genuine dispute as to any material fact and that the appellees were entitled to judgment as a matter of law. In order to create a valid contract there must be both an offer and an acceptance. The appellant contends that the statement made at the meeting of the salesmen, that stock would be made available for sale to them, was an offer and his written request for 100 shares was an acceptance thereof. However, we agree with the Chancellor that the statements made at the meeting constituted only an invitation to submit offers, and that the appellant's response requesting 100 shares was merely an offer to buy, which was never accepted. There was never any meeting of minds as to the number of shares to be sold to the appellant.

"A contract, to be final, must extend to all the terms which the parties intend to introduce, and material terms cannot be left for future settlement. Until actual completion of the bargain either party is at liberty to withdraw his consent and put an end to the negotiations." (*Peoples Drug Stores v. Fenton Realty Corp.*, 191 Md. 489, 62 A.2d 273, 276 (1948)). No contract having arisen between the parties, the appellees' motion for summary judgment was properly granted.

Affirmed.

O. C. Kinney, Inc. v. Paul Hardeman, Inc.

1963 (Colo.) 379 P.2d 628

Plaintiff was low bidder on a certain job related to construction of an Air Force base. Defendant, the prime contractor, who had solicited bids, did not award contract to plaintiff but gave it to another contractor as part of a two-site bid and this suit for damages resulted. The trial court granted a summary judgment for defendants.

SUTTON, J. . . . In the instant case the record discloses no meeting of the minds to create an express contract nor can one be implied from proof of custom and usage or from the circumstances shown here. A bid is normally considered only as an offer until such time as it is accepted. Mere notification or knowledge that one's bid is low cannot of itself create a contract between the parties.

Even if defendant's uncommunicated desire to have bids submitted could be relied upon by plaintiff, it is obvious that, at best, it was merely an invitation to bid and not an operative offer. Plaintiff's bid itself constituted the offer and it would take defendant's acceptance to complete a contract.

Plaintiff's assertion that here there was no provision in the specifications reserving the right to defendant to reject any and all bids makes no difference, for it has been held that an owner is under no obligation to accept any bid. Of course, the express terms and conditions of a call for bids might alter that rule, but we are not faced with that situation here.

The depositions here also show that even if plaintiff's dollar amount had been acceptable to defendant, other material provisions of a written contract, including conditions and bonding terms, would have had to be agreed upon. The bid submitted by plaintiff in this case was not capable of being acted upon without reference to these matters so could not be considered complete in any event.

Plaintiff's theory that it was a trade custom for low bids to be automatically accepted is not helpful to plaintiff. The applicable rule, correctly applied by the trial court, is that evidence of a trade custom, where such in fact exists, is admissible only to show the terms with reference to which parties in a trade are presumed to agree in a contract actually entered into, and is not admissible where no contract has been first shown to exist.

We find no merit in any of plaintiff's grounds urged as error.

The judgment is affirmed.

Kergald v. Armstrong Transfer Exp. Co.

1953 (Mass.) 113 N.E.2d 53

LUMUS, J. This is an action of contract, begun by writ dated August 26, 1949, in which the plaintiff sues for the loss of her trunk and its contents. The defendant is an intrastate common carrier. There was evidence that the plaintiff arrived with her trunk at the South Station in Boston late in an evening in May, 1949, and went to the defendant's office there. She was not asked the value of her trunk, but was given a small pasteboard check by the defendant which was not read to her and which she did not read, but put in her purse. The trunk was to be delivered at her home in Boston. The defendant failed to deliver her trunk, and admitted that it had been lost. The small check had on one side the order number and the words "Read contract on reverse side," and on the other the words, "The holder of this check agrees that the value of the baggage checked does not exceed $100 unless a greater value has been declared at time of checking and additional payment made therefor . . ."

The judge instructed the jury, over the exception of the defendant, that the plaintiff is bound by that limitation if she had knowledge of it when she took the check, and otherwise is not. The jury returned a verdict for the plaintiff for $1,700, and the defendant brought the case here.

Where what is given to a plaintiff purports on its face to set forth the terms of a contract, the plaintiff, whether he reads it or not, by accepting it assents to its terms, and is bound by any limitation of liability therein contained, in the absence of fraud. . . .

On the other hand, whereas in this case what is received is apparently a means of identification of the property bailed, rather than a complete contract, the bailor is not bound by a limitation upon the liability of the bailee unless it is actually known to the bailor. (Cases cited.)

The cases in this Commonwealth so clearly show the law applicable to the facts of this case that we need not discuss decisions elsewhere. But we may say that our conclusions are supported by well-reasoned cases in New York as well as other jurisdictions.

Judgment for plaintiff affirmed.

Minnesota Linseed Oil Co. v. Collier White Lead Co.

1876, Fed. Cas. No. 9,635, 4 Dill. 431

The defendant, Collier White Lead Co., is being sued for $2,150 which it admits is owing to the plaintiff for linseed oil previously shipped. It has refused to pay because it maintains the plaintiff failed to ship oil under a second contract, thus causing it damages which should be deducted from the $2,150. The facts regarding the second contract are that on July 31, plaintiff by telegram offered to sell a certain amount of linseed oil to defendant at a certain price. Although this telegram was transmitted late in the evening of July 31, it was not delivered to defendant until the morning of August 2. On August 3 defendant accepted plaintiff's offer by depositing a telegram with the telegraph office in his city and shortly thereafter upon the same day defendant received a telegram from the plaintiff revoking plaintiff's offer. The market price on linseed oil was very unstable.

NELSON . . . In the case at bar the delivery of the message at the telegraph office signified the acceptance of the offer. If any contract was entered into, the meeting of minds was at 8:53 of the clock, on Tuesday morning, August 3rd and the subsequent dispatches are out of the case. . . . Conceding this, there remains only one question to decide, which will determine the issues: Was the acceptance of defendant deposited in the telegraph office Tuesday, August 3rd, within a reasonable time so as to consummate a contract binding upon the plaintiff? . . .

The better opinion is, that what is, or is not, a reasonable time, must depend upon the circumstances attending the negotiation, and the character of the subject matter of the contract, and in no better way can the intention of the parties be determined. If the negotiation is in respect to an article stable in price, there is not so much reason for an immediate acceptance of the offer, and the same rule would not apply as in a case where the negotiation related to an article subject to sudden and great fluctuations in the market. *Parson on Contracts* (Volume 1, p. 482) says: " . . . If no definite time is stated, then the inquiry as to a reasonable time resolves itself into an inquiry as to what time it is rational to suppose the parties contemplated; and the law will decide this to be that time which as rational men they ought to have understood each other to have had in mind." Applying this rule, it seems clear that the intention of the plaintiff, in making the offer by telegram, to sell an article which fluctuates so much in price, must have been upon the understanding that the acceptance, if at all, should be immediate, and as soon after the receipt of the offer as would give a fair opportunity for consideration. The delay, here, was too long and manifestly unjust to the plaintiff, for it afforded the defendant an opportunity to take advantage of a change in the market and to accept or refuse the offer as would best subserve its interests.

Judgment will be entered in favor of the plaintiff for the amount claimed. The counterclaim is denied. Judgment accordingly.

Drennan v. Star Paving Company

1958 (Cal.) 333 P.2d 757

Drennan, the plaintiff, was a general contractor and in preparation for submitting a bid on a school job requested the defendant to submit a bid for certain paving which was involved. The defendant offered to do the work for $7,131.60, and the plaintiff used this subcontractor's offer in making his bid. The contract was awarded to plaintiff, but as he approached the defendant, he was notified that it could not perform as it had made an error in its calculations. The plaintiff got another to do the work at a cost of $10,948.60 and seeks to recover this difference of the defendant. The lower court gave judgment for plaintiff in the amount of $3,817.00.

TRAYNOR, J.   . . . There is no evidence that defendant offered to make its bid irrevocable in exchange for plaintiff's use of its figures in computing his bid. Nor is there evidence that would warrant interpreting plaintiff's use of defendant's bid as the acceptance thereof, binding plaintiff, on condition he received the main contract, to award the subcontract to defendant. In sum, there was neither an option supported by consideration nor a bilateral contract binding on both parties.

Plaintiff contends, however, that he relied to his detriment on defendant's offer and that defendant must therefore answer in damages for its refusal to perform. Thus the question is squarely presented: Did plaintiff's reliance make defendant's offer irrevocable?

Section 90 of the Restatement of Contracts states: "A promise which the promisor should reasonably expect to induce action or forbearance of a definite and substantial character on the part of the promisee and which does induce such action or forbearance is binding if injustice can be avoided only by enforcement of the promise." . . .

Defendant's offer constituted a promise to perform on such conditions as were stated expressly or by implication therein or annexed thereto by operation of law. (See 1 Williston, *Contracts* [3rd ed.], § 24a, p. 56, § 61, p. 196.) Defendant had reason to expect that if its bid proved the lowest it would be used by plaintiff. It induced "action . . . of a definite and substantial character on the part of the promisee."

Had defendant's bid expressly stated or clearly implied that it was revocable at any time before acceptance we would treat it accordingly. It was silent on revocation, however, and we must therefore determine whether there are conditions to the right of revocation imposed by law or reasonably inferable in fact. In the analogous problem of an offer for a unilateral contract, the theory is now obsolete that the offer is revocable at any time before complete performance. Thus section 45 of the Restatement of Contracts provides: "If an offer for a unilateral contract is made, and part of the consideration requested in the offer is given or tendered by the offeree in response thereto, the offeror is bound by a contract, the duty of immediate performance of which is conditional on the full consideration being given or tendered within the time stated in the offer, or, if no time is stated therein, within a reasonable time." In explanation, comment *b* states that the "main offer includes as a subsidiary promise, necessarily implied, that if part of the requested performance is given, the offeror will not revoke his offer, and that if tender is made it will be accepted. Part performance or tender may thus furnish consideration for the subsidiary promise. Moreover, merely acting in justifiable reliance on an offer may in some cases serve as sufficient reason for making a promise binding (see § 90)."

Whether implied in fact or law, the subsidiary promise serves to preclude the injustice that would result if the offer could be revoked after the offeree had acted in detrimental reliance thereon. Reasonable reliance resulting in a foreseeable prejudicial change in position affords a compelling basis also for implying a subsidiary promise not to revoke an offer for a bilateral contract.

The absence of consideration is not fatal to the enforcement of such a promise. It is true that in the case of unilateral contracts the Restatement finds consideration for the implied subsidiary promise in the part performance of the bargained-for exchange, but its reference to section 90 makes clear that consideration for such a promise is not always necessary. The very purpose of section 90 is to make a promise binding even though there was no consideration "in the sense of something that is bargained for and given in exchange." (See 1 Corbin, *Contracts* 634 et seq.) Reasonable reliance serves to hold the offeror in lieu of the consideration ordinarily required to make the offer binding. . . .

When plaintiff used defendant's offer in computing his own bid, he bound himself to perform in reliance on defendant's terms. Though defendant did not bargain for this use of its bid neither did defendant make it idly, indifferent to whether it would be used or not. On the contrary it is reasonable to suppose that defendant submitted its bid to obtain the subcontract. It was bound to realize the substantial possibility that its bid would be the lowest, and that it would be included by plaintiff in his bid. It was to its own interest that the contractor be awarded the general contract; the lower the subcontract bid, the lower the general contractor's bid was likely to be and the greater its chance of acceptance and hence the greater defendant's chance of getting the paving subcontract. Defendant had reason not only to expect plaintiff to rely on its bid but to want him to. Clearly defendant had a stake in plaintiff's reliance on its bid. Given this interest and the fact that plaintiff is bound by his own bid, it is only fair that plaintiff should have at least an opportunity to accept defendant's bid after the general contract has been awarded to him.

It bears noting that a general contractor is not free to delay acceptance after he has been awarded the general contract in the hope of getting a better price. Nor can he reopen bargaining with the subcontractor and at the same time claim a continuing right to accept the original offer. (See *R. J. Daum Const. Co. v. Child,* Utah, 247 P.2d 817, 823) In the present case plaintiff promptly informed defendant that plaintiff was being awarded the job and that the subcontract was being awarded to defendant. . . .

Judgment for plaintiff affirmed.

Banks v. Crescent Lumber & Shingle Co.

1963 (Wash.) 379 P.2d 203

Plaintiff is a corporation which operates a lumber mill and defendant is a lumber broker. Over a three-week period, defendant executed in triplicate and mailed to plaintiff 67 orders for lumber. Each order was numbered separately and was a separate transaction. Upon receipt, plaintiff changed the orders in several respects, including price, marked them accepted, and returned one copy to defendant. Plaintiff shipped 54 carload orders which defendant accepted and then resold to his customers. Defendant paid for 34 at the price and terms as modified by the plaintiff and paid for the other 20 carloads as provided in the original orders. The second count of plaintiff's claim is based on the difference between the original price and the changed price on these 20 carloads.

Subsequently, the lumber market declined. May 27, 1959, defendant wrote plaintiff concerning 13 orders previously placed as follows:

> . . . We therefore must ask that you suspend all shipments until further notice . . . We recognize that this may be inconvenient for you and you may cancel the (13) remaining orders if you wish. If that is not your choice, *we can discuss the balance of the orders* just as soon as the current situation is cleared up . . .

July 6, 1959, defendant wrote plaintiff:

> When you were in Seattle last month you mentioned to the writer that you had sold the unshipped stock elsewhere when we asked you to hold up the shipment until we could move some of our transit cars. In view of this we will consider the remaining orders canceled.

Plaintiff's first cause of action is based upon the alleged breach of the 13 contracts of purchase. The trial court found for plaintiff on both counts and defendant appeals.

WEAVER, J. . . . Applicable to both causes of action is *Owens-Corning Fiberglass Corp. v. Fox Smith Sheet Metal Co.,* (56 Wash.2d 167, 170, 351 P.2d 516, 518 (1960)) where this court said:

> An acceptance of an offer must always be identical with the terms of the offer or there is no meeting of the minds and no contract . . .

Defendant's offers to purchase lumber were not accepted by plaintiff. The terms of the offers were changed, thus becoming counteroffers to sell upon plaintiff's terms . . .

Defendant's exercise of dominion over the subject-matter by the sale of the 20 carloads of lumber to others is an unambiguous acceptance of the terms of plaintiff's counteroffer.

In Restatement, *Contracts,* § 72, it is stated:

> . . . (2) Where the offeree exercises dominion over things which are offered to him, such exercise of dominion in the absence of other circumstances showing a contrary intention is an acceptance. . . .

In the comment on this section (Comment b.), it is stated:

> The duty that is imposed on the offeree . . . is not a quasi contractual duty to pay a fair value, but a duty to pay or perform according to the terms of the offer.
>
> Frequently, services are rendered under circumstances such that the party benefited thereby knows the terms on which they are being offered. If he re-

ceives the benefit of the services in silence, when he had a reasonable opportunity to express his rejection of the offer, he is assenting to the terms proposed and thus accepts the offer. (1 Corbin, *Contracts,* § 75)

The 13 unfilled orders that were not shipped by plaintiff present the same general problem: Did defendant accept plaintiff's counteroffers? We think not.

The acceptance by defendant of previous orders did not constitute an acceptance of the 13 orders in dispute; for, as the court said in *Excelsior Knitting Mills v. Bush,* (38 Wash.2d 876, 233 P.2d 847 (1951)):

> We think this is a case where both parties made tentative offers and both parties acted without confirmation of the other party. *That some goods were shipped, received and paid for throws no light on the existence or absence of a contract with regard to the other items refused.*

Nor do we believe that defendant's letters of May 27 and July 6, 1959, quoted *supra,* constitute an unconditional acceptance of plaintiff's counteroffers. The most that can be said for them is that they might be construed as a conditional acceptance; but, as this court pointed out in Bond v. Wiegardt, *supra,* ". . . conditional acceptances are counter-offers and reject the original offer." This conclusion is fortified by defendant's statement that ". . . we can discuss the balance of the orders just as soon as the current situation is cleared up . . ."

As this court said in Excelsior, *supra,*

> The parties acted upon the assumption that there was a contract between them. However, *they never agreed upon what the contract was.* . . .

In summary:
The judgment for $2,510.04, based upon plaintiff's first cause of action, is reversed. The judgment for $438.93, based upon plaintiff's second cause of action, is affirmed.

Department of Public Works v. Halls
1965 (Ill.A.C.) 210 N.E.2d 226

SMITH, J. While the pleadings and the number of parties would seem to indicate numerous complexities, only one question is presented for review and it can be simply stated: Was an option to purchase real estate properly exercised? It reads:

> 7. AND, IT IS HEREBY FURTHER AGREED by and between said parties, that lessee shall have the right and option to purchase said above described premises for the sum of TWENTY-FIVE THOUSAND DOLLARS ($25,000.00), at any time during the term of this lease.

Lessee decided to purchase the premises and notified lessor as follows:

> YOU ARE HEREBY NOTIFIED that I have elected to exercise the option to purchase the real estate described in that certain lease dated the 23rd day

of June, A.D. 1955 by and between Vera A. Garowski as lessor and the under-signed Charles Jordan, as lessee, the real estate being more particularly de-scribed as follows: (Describing same) the said lease providing that the option could be exercised at any time during the term of the lease, which was a period of ten (10) years from the 1st day of July, 1955, at the purchase price of Twenty-five Thousand ($25,000.00) Dollars.

The abstract should be submitted to my attorney, Charles R. Young, 500 McMullen Building, Danville, Illinois, for examination, and the purchase price will be available upon the furnishing of a merchantable abstract of title and warranty deed.

For a proper exercise, lessee must accept in toto the conditions contained in the option and he cannot add new ones of his own. Lessor [defendant] says he did, indeed, add new ones—that she furnish a merchantable abstract of title and warranty deed—and hence she need not perform. With this the trial court agreed, and lessee appeals.

An option is defined as a right acquired by contract to accept or reject a present offer within the time limited. If an optionee does signify his acceptance of an offer within the time limited and upon the terms stated, the obligations become mutual and are capable of enforcement at the instance of either party. Nothing is said expressly in this option as to the character of the deed, or for that matter *any* deed, nor is there any allusion apropos of a merchantable abstract of title. Should lessee, in exercising this option, have signified his acceptance and delivered $25,000.00 to lessor and let it go at that? What if after lessee had done just that but fee simple title had not been immediately put in him, could he have changed his mind? Or what if after a conveyance of some sort, lessee had discovered that his title was something less than fee simple, could he have backed away, or would lessor be given a reasonable time to remedy the defect? By these few questions, and we could posit many more, we are suggesting, what we all know, that all agreements, options included, have implied promises or conditions, even including those that purport to cover every conceivable situation, and indeed, say so. As Chief Judge Cardozo remarked in *Wood v. Lucy, Lady Duff-Gordon,* (222 N.Y. 88, 118 N.E. 214 (1917)):

> The law has outgrown its primitive stage of formalism when the precise word was the sovereign talisman, and every slip was fatal. It takes a broader view today. A promise may be lacking, and yet the whole writing may be "instinct with an obligation," imperfectly expressed.

It is true, of course, that lessor did not promise in so many words that she would give a deed or furnish merchantable abstract of title, but we think that such, or their equivalents, can fairly be implied. To put legal, as opposed to equitable title, in lessee, requires some type of legal con-veyance. The fact that lessee happened to request a warranty deed, in our opinion, does not provide lessor with a convenient loophole to avoid her promise. We are not saying that lessor need furnish a warranty deed as such—only that she find some legal vehicle to get the job done. It is an implied promise or condition. So too, with regard to furnishing a merchantable abstract of title. Her promise was to put fee simple title in lessee and she can give him such assurance in any reasonable way she can find. She is not bound, however, to do it this way, but she must do it. It is also an implied condition or promise. Lessee's so-called "counterconditions," are in reality only suggested ways and means by which his purchase of the premises can be appropriately effected by lessor. They are not iron-bound and double riveted pre-conditions that must be met by lessor. By the same token, assuming performance by lessor by some other way, their lack would not prevent her from enforcing payment by lessee.

.   .   .

We think lessee properly exercised the option and we view lessor's stance as strained. The option reads that the lessee can purchase the premises. We cannot agree that lessee in any way added new conditions to the option by suggesting to lessor appropriate avenues to that end.

.   .   .

. . . We think the option reasonably implies some sort of conveyance and some sort of evidence of ownership; that such was within the reasonable contemplation of the parties; and that the type of deed and the evidence of ownership related to suggested means to a performance of the contract to sell and not to a conditional acceptance of the option.

Accordingly, the order appealed from is reversed and the cause remanded with directions to enter judgment for the lessees and for such further orders not inconsistent with this opinion.

Reversed and remanded with directions.

Lewis and Lewis v. Root and Root

1959 (Wash.) 337 P.2d 52

Plaintiff, Lewis and Lewis, placed an order, through a broker for 1,000 squares of No. 1-5x green centigrade shingles at $11.75 per square, the purchaser requiring a minimum of one truck load a week and preferably two. The defendant received the order which said "please confirm this order with Lewis and Lewis." The defendant did not confirm the order but in time made three shipments at the price indicated. It now, having refused to make further shipments, denies there was any acceptance of the offer. The lower court awarded damages to the plaintiff in its suit to recover on the contract.

HUNTER, J. . . . In the case of *Pillsbury Flour Mills, Inc. v. Independent Bakery, Inc.,* 1931, (165 Wash. 360, 5 P.2d 517, 8 P.2d 430, 10 P.2d 975), which is similar on the facts to the instant case, we said:

This appeal presents for determination only one question, which we state as follows: Where an order for a quantity of goods to be delivered in installments is given to a salesman subject to the seller's written approval, does that order become a binding contract on the seller's delivery of a number of the installments, without communication by the seller to the buyer of acceptance of the order? The question was answered in the affirmative, and we stated:

The contracts were for delivery by installments. One contract was for the shipment of fifteen hundred barrels of flour; the other for four hundred and fifty barrels of flour. It was not contemplated—in fact, it was agreed otherwise —that all of the flour would be delivered in one shipment. Under that arrangement, as soon as one installment of flour was delivered and accepted the contracts became binding on the parties. Thereafter the appellant was bound to perform by delivering the remainder of the flour called for in the contracts. A corresponding obligation was imposed upon the respondent of accepting the remainder of the flour under the contract. Failure of performance on the part of either would entitle the other party to recover for the damages by the breach of the contract.

In the present case, as soon as the first shipment of shingles was delivered by the appellants and accepted by the respondents, in pursuance of the order of July 7, 1955, the contract became binding upon the parties. By their failure to deliver the balance of the shingles, as called for in the purchase order, the appellants were answerable to the respondents for their damages suffered as a result of the breach . . .

Finding no error in the record, the judgment of the lower court is affirmed.

Hill's, Inc. v. William B. Kessler, Inc.

1952 (Wash.) 246 P.2d 1099

Action by Hill's, Inc., against William B. Kessler, Inc., for breach of contract. The Superior Court, King County, Hugh C. Todd, J., rendered the judgment for plaintiff, and defendant appealed.

MALLERY, J.   The plaintiff, Hill's, Inc., ordered thirty-four men's suits from the defendant, using a printed form supplied by defendant through its salesman.

The printed form provided that the order would not become a binding contract until it had been accepted by an authorized officer of the defendant at its office in Hammonton, New Jersey.

The defendant's salesman procured the order on May 16, 1950, and on May 23, 1950, the defendant by form letter, advised the plaintiff that "You may be assured of our very best attention to this order." What occurred next is shown by the trial court's finding of fact:

> . . . but notwithstanding, on or about July 18, 1950, defendant intentionally and deliberately, at the instigation of a large store selling defendant's clothing in the downtown Seattle area, wrongfully cancelled said order and breached its agreement with plaintiff to deliver said suits as ordered, or at all. That at the time defendant cancelled said order and breached its agreement, the period for placing orders for delivery of fall suits had passed, and it was impossible for plaintiff to thereafter procure comparable suits from any other source to meet its fall trade. . . .

Thereupon, plaintiff brought this action for loss of profits in the amount of a 66⅔ per cent markup aggregating $815.83.

From a judgment in favor of the plaintiff, the defendant appeals.

The defendant contends that its letter of May 23, 1950, in which it said "You may be assured of our very best attention to this order," was not an acceptance of the plaintiff's order.

In *Bauman v. McManus* (75 Kan. 106. 89 P. 15, 18, 10 L.R.A., N.S., 1138) the court said:

> . . . The promise that the order shall receive prompt and *careful* attention seems to imply something more than that the manufacturers will quickly and cautiously investigate the advisability of accepting it. The care they might expend in that direction—in looking up defendants' financial standing, for instance—is not presumably a matter in which any one but themselves would be greatly interested. The engagement to use care seems more naturally to relate to the manner of filling the order than to the settling of a doubt whether to fill it at all. The expression of thanks for the favor has some tendency in the same direction. We incline strongly to the opinion that the letter standing by itself was as effectual to close a contract as though in set phrase it had said that the goods would be shipped; that to permit any other construction to be placed upon it would be to countenance the studied use of equivocal expressions, with a set purpose, if an advantage may thereby be derived, to keep the word of promise to the ear and break it to the hope.

Judgment is affirmed for plaintiff.

Hendrickson v. International Harvester Co. of America

1927, 100 Vt. 161, 135 Atl. 702

Action by Peter Hendrickson against the International Harvester Company of America to recover damages on account of the defendant's failure to deliver to him a broadcast seeder. The defendant's agent took the order for the machine, which order was retained by the defendant an unreasonable time and, until this controversy arose, without indicating that it either accepted or rejected the offer of the plaintiff to buy the seeder mentioned.

Powers, J. . . . The order was subject to approval. . . . The fact that the defendant kept the order without approving it or notifying the plaintiff of its disapproval would amount to an acceptance.

True it is that it takes two to make a bargain, and that silence gives consent . . . only when there is a duty to speak. And true it is that it is frequently said that one is ordinarily under no obligation to do or say anything concerning a proposition which he does not choose to accept; yet we think that, when one sends out an agent to solicit orders for his goods, authorizing such agents to take such orders subject to his (the principal's) approval, fair dealing and the exigencies of modern business require us to hold that he shall signify to the customer within a reasonable time from the receipt of the order his rejection of it, or suffer the consequences of having his silence operate as an approval.

Judgment for plaintiff.

Roto-Lith, Ltd. v. F. P. Bartlett & Co.

1962 (U.S.C.A.) 297 F.2d 497

ALDRICH, J. Plaintiff-appellant Roto-Lith, Ltd., is a New York corporation engaged *inter alia* in manufacturing, or "converting," cellophane bags for packaging vegetables. Defendant-appellee is a Massachusetts corporation which makes emulsion for use as a cellophane adhesive. This is a field of some difficulty, and various emulsions are employed, depending upon the intended purpose of the bags. In May and October 1959 plaintiff purchased emulsion from the defendant. Subsequently bags produced with this emulsion failed to adhere, and this action was instituted in the district court for the District of Massachusetts. At the conclusion of the evidence the court directed a verdict for the defendant. This appeal followed.

.   .   .

On October 23, 1959, plaintiff, in New York, mailed a written order to defendant in Massachusetts for a drum of "N-132-C" emulsion, stating "End use: wet pack spinach bags." Defendant on October 26 prepared simultaneously an acknowledgment and an invoice. The printed forms were exactly the same, except that one was headed "Acknowledgement" and the other "Invoice," and the former contemplated insertion of the proposed, and the latter of the actual, shipment date. Defendant testified that in accordance with its regular practice the acknowledgment was prepared and mailed the same day. The plaintiff's principal liability witness testified that he did not know whether this acknowledgment "was received, or what happened to it." On this state of the evidence there is an unrebutted presumption of receipt. The goods were shipped to New York on October 27. On the evidence it must be found that the acknowledgment was received at least no later than the goods. The invoice was received presumably a day or two after the goods.

The acknowledgment and the invoice bore in conspicuous type on their face the following legend, "All goods sold without warranties, express or implied, and subject to the terms on reverse side." In somewhat smaller, but still conspicuous, type there were printed on the back certain terms of sale, of which the following are relevant:

1. Due to the variable conditions under which these goods may be transported, stored, handled, or used, Seller hereby expressly excludes any and all warranties, guaranties, or representations whatsoever. Buyer assumes risk for results obtained from use of these goods, whether used alone or in combination with other products. Seller's liability hereunder shall be limited to the replacement of any goods that materially differ from the Seller's sample order on the basis of which the order for such goods was made.

7. This acknowledgment contains all of the terms of this purchase and sale. No one except a duly authorized officer of Seller may execute or modify contracts. Payment may be made only at the offices of the Seller. *If these terms are not acceptable, Buyer must so notify Seller at once.*

It is conceded that plaintiff did not protest defendant's attempt so to limit its liability, and in due course paid for the emulsion and used it. It is also conceded that adequate notice was given of breach of warranty, if there were warranties. The only issue which we will consider is whether all warranties were excluded by defendant's acknowledgment.

The first question is what law the Massachusetts court would look to in order to determine the terms of the contract. Under Massachusetts law this is the place where the last material act occurs. Under the Uniform Commercial Code (Mass. Gen. Laws Ann. (1958) ch. 106, § 2-206) mailing the acknowledgment would clearly have completed the contract in Massachusetts by acceptance had the acknowledgment not sought to introduce new terms. Section 2-207 provides:

(1) A definite and seasonable expression of acceptance or a written confirmation which is sent within a reasonable time operates as an acceptance even though it states terms additional to or different from those offered or agreed upon, unless acceptance is expressly made conditional on assent to the additional or different terms.

(2) The additional terms are to be construed as proposals for addition to the contract. Between merchants such terms become part of the contract unless:

(a) the offer expressly limits acceptance to the terms of the offer;

(b) they materially alter it; or

(c) notification of objection to them has already been given or is given within a reasonable time after notice of them is received.

Plaintiff exaggerates the freedom which this section affords an offeror to ignore a reply from an offeree that does not in terms coincide with the original offer. According to plaintiff defendant's condition that there should be no warranties constituted a proposal which "materially altered" the agreement. As to this we concur. (See Uniform Commercial Code comment to this section, Mass. Gen. Laws Ann., *supra*, paragraph 4) Plaintiff goes on to say that by virtue of the statute the acknowledgment effected a completed agreement without this condition, and that as a further proposal the condition never became part of the agreement because plaintiff did not express assent. We agree that section 2-207 changed the existing law, but not to this extent. Its purpose was to modify the strict principle that a response not precisely in accordance with the offer was a rejection and a counteroffer. Now, within stated limits, a response that does not in all respects correspond with the offer constitutes an acceptance of the offer, and a counteroffer only as to the differences. If plaintiff's contention is correct that a reply to an offer stating additional conditions unilaterally burdensome upon the offeror is a binding acceptance of the original offer plus simply a proposal for the additional conditions, the statute would lead to an absurdity. Obviously no offeror will subsequently assent to such conditions.

The statute is not too happily drafted. Perhaps it would be wiser in all cases for an offeree to say in so many words, "I will not accept your offer until you assent to the following: . . ." But businessmen cannot be expected to act by rubric. It would be unrealistic to suppose that when an offeree replies setting out conditions that would be burdensome only to the offeror he intended to make an unconditional acceptance of the original offer, leaving it simply to the offeror's good nature whether he would assume the additional restrictions. To give the statute a practical construction we must hold that a response which states a condition materially altering the obligation solely to the disadvantage of the offeror is an "acceptance . . . expressly . . . conditional on assent to the additional . . . terms."

Plaintiff accepted the goods with knowledge of the conditions specified in the acknowledgment. It became bound.

Falconer v. Mazess

1961 (Pa.) 168 A.2d 558

Plaintiff brought suit to recover $1000 held by defendant in escrow under an agreement between plaintiff and one Bain. Defendant counter claimed for commissions due on sale. By a letter dated August 13, 1953 plaintiff offered to purchase the common stock of Maine Forwarding Co., settlement to be made under one of two options contained in the written offer. The offer also provided "It is a condition of this offer that it be accepted in writing, within five days from the the the date hereof. . . ." On August 18, 1953, defendant through a duly authorized agent, by letter dated August 17, 1953, mailed to plaintiff an acceptance. This letter arrived in plaintiff's city on August 19 but was not delivered until August 20, 1953. The parties stipulated that the 20th was beyond the five-day period and that if the acceptance was effective when deposited, there was a contract, but if it was effective upon receipt, there was no contract.

BELL, J. . . . The trial Judge ruled that defendant's offer was not accepted until it was actually delivered to plaintiff. Plaintiff lived in Pittsburgh, and the defendant lived in Philadelphia. Plaintiff's letter-offer of August 13 did not expressly state how it was to be accepted, but under the circumstances of this case the use of the mails as a means of acceptance was impliedly authorized. As this Court said in *Meierdierck v. Miller* (394 Pa. 484, 487, 147 A.2d 406, 408):

> . . . Where the use of the mails as a means of acceptance is authorized or implied from the surrounding circumstances, the acceptance is complete by posting the letter in normal mail channels, without more. (Restatement, *Contracts* § 66; 1 Williston, *Contracts* § 83 (3d ed. 1957)). There is no requirement of receipt unless expressly provided for. . . .

For this reason alone the judgment would have to be reversed.

CHAPTER 8
REVIEW QUESTIONS AND PROBLEMS

1. X submitted a bid for certain brick work to C, who used it as a basis for a general contract bid on a certain job. C's bid was accepted, and he notified X he had been successful and would have a form contract ready soon. When the form arrived, it contained two or three new terms and X refused to sign or to perform. Is X liable to C?

2. X Co., engaged in the development of a real estate project, needed a good construction foreman. It employed A, promising to pay him $125 a week and a fair share of the profits made on the project. X Co. later refused to pay any of the profits. The court held the agreement to be unenforceable. Why?

3. O parked his car in a parking lot, paid 35 cents and received a ticket which stated the operator of parking lot was not liable for contents. O did not notice the ticket provision; the car was stolen, but was later found without contents. Has O a good cause of action against the operator?

4. O offered in writing to lease property to T for three years at a monthly rental of $700. T accepted in writing with three minor modifications to the offer and mailed his check of $700 for the first month's rent. O cashed the check, and T moved in at considerable expense. O now contends the contract is unenforceable because of changed terms. What result?

5. X, a contractor, agreed with Y to remodel an old dwelling into a rooming house at a cost not to exceed $10,000, and parties agreed that as required plumbing, heating or electrical wiring became necessary, such items would be contracted for at most reasonable price available. Y refused to allow X to proceed with the performance of the contract. If X sues Y for breach of contract, what result?

6. H applied for life insurance on himself and his family. Insurer issued a contract of insurance with an amendment to the application deleting one child. H did not sign the new application. The insurer sues to have the policy declared null and void. What result?

7. D sent a letter to several persons stating that he had clover seed for sale and was asking 24 cents per pound. P requested a firm offer and a lower price. D then replied stating "I am asking 23 cents per pound. Have an offer of 22¾." P then replied accepting D's offer. Is there a contract?

chapter 9

Consideration

2-30. Introduction. Many promises are not legally enforceable. For example, a father says to his son, "I promise to give you $15,000 on your eighteenth birthday." Historically, our courts have refused to enforce such a promise unless it were a written promise under seal or unless it was supported by consideration. At common law, the presence of a seal imported consideration or at least a seal served as a substitute for consideration. Today, many states have altered the effect of a person adding a seal to his signature to the effect that the presence of a seal only creates a presumption of consideration, while still others have provided that adding a seal is ineffective to create a binding contract if the promise is unsupported by consideration. The Code adopts the latter view.[C1]

Consideration has been defined as the price bargained for and paid for a promise. It usually takes the form of some benefit to the promisor or a detriment to the promisee.[1] Benefit does not refer to tangible benefits but means that the promisor has in return for his promise acquired some legal right to which he otherwise would not have been entitled and detriment means that the promisee has forborne some legal right which the promisee otherwise would have been entitled to exercise. Consideration has also been defined as the surrender or promise to surrender a legal right at the request of another. An even more succinct definition is "consideration is what each party to bargain gives to the other." By all definitions, the performance or the promise to perform an act or the surrender or promise to surrender a right as requested by the promisor

[1] *Stelmack v. Glen Alden Coal Co.*, page 166.

[C1] *U.C.C.* 2-203.

supplies the consideration to make the promise enforceable. Without this "benefit" or "detriment," the promisor might be morally obligated to carry out his promise, but the law would consider it to be *nudum pactum* and legally unenforceable.

There are exceptions to the general rule which requires consideration before a promise is legally enforceable. Frequently, the courts do not consider these to be exceptions but simply find consideration to exist in a somewhat different form or find a substitute for consideration. A notable exception to the rule requiring consideration is *promissory estoppel*. This equitable doctrine enforces a promise in the absence of actual consideration where the promise is such that the promisor should reasonably expect the promisee to take some substantial action or forbearance in reliance on the promise and the promisee does materially change his position in reliance on the promise to such an extent that injustice can be avoided only by enforcing the promise.[2] Promissory estoppel thus either serves as a substitute for consideration or is regarded as a form of action or forbearance as is discussed in the Feinberg case, *supra*. Consideration which may take the form of an act, forbearance, or change of legal relationship, usually takes the form of a return promise. Thus a promise for a promise creates a binding contract.

Another exception in some states is created by a statute which provides that all written modifications of contracts and written releases need not be supported by consideration.

2-31. Adequacy of Consideration. It is not the function of law to make value or economic judgments concerning contracts voluntarily entered into by the parties. Thus, as a general rule, courts do not attempt to weight the consideration received by each party to determine if it is adequate in light of that which the party gave. It is sufficient in law if a party receives something of value providing the "something" is that which he agreed to accept. The law is only concerned with the existence of consideration, not with its value. Of course, if the contract is merely to exchange sums of money, whose value is exactly fixed, the law requires equal consideration. This is further discussed in section 35 which follows. In the usual case however, any inadequacy is for the person to judge at the time the contract is created and not for determination by the courts at the time of enforcement. In the absence of fraud, oppression, undue influence, or statutory limitation, a party may make any contract he pleases and the fact that it is onerous or improvident is immaterial.

It must be kept in mind that a promise to make a gift is unenforceable. The fact that the recipient of a proposed gift must take certain steps to place himself in a position to receive it cannot be substituted for consideration. If, however, the promisee is requested to act in a certain manner and the action is considered to be the price paid for the promise, the taking of such action as is requested will function as consideration.

---

2 *Feinberg v. Pfeiffer Company,* page 168.

Care must be used in determining whether the offeree's conduct acted as consideration or merely as a move to meet the conditions for a gift.

For example, a promise by a relative to give a family heirloom does not become enforceable just because the promisee goes to visit the relative making the promise. It should be noted that a gift, once it has been executed, cannot be set aside by the donor because of the lack of consideration. Once a gift has been completed, the property involved belongs to the donee.

A statement that a nominal consideration exists or is promised is not consideration unless it is the thing bargained for and performance is expected. Quite often a promise is made stating that it is given for $1 in hand paid and other good and valuable consideration, there never having been any intention to pay the dollar.[3] Under the circumstances, no consideration is present unless, in fact, some other consideration was provided. The statement that consideration was given is a mere pretense and without foundation in fact or in contemplation of the parties and a court may properly inquire as to the existence of a valid consideration. In states which have not abolished the seal, however, a recital of consideration with a seal is conclusive. It should also be noted that the recital will stand in the absence of evidence to the contrary and of course, $1 may be good consideration in a given case. Just as a court may examine a contract where consideration is recited, it may also receive evidence of consideration where none appears on the face of the agreement.

2-32. Forbearance. Consideration which usually takes the form of an action may take the opposite form, forbearance from acting. The law considers the waiver of a right or the forbearance to exercise a right to be sufficient consideration for a contract.[4] The right which is waived or not exercised may be enforceable at law or in equity and may exist either against the promisor or someone else. The forbearance may take the form of a promise to forbear suit, generally referred to as the giving of a covenant not to sue or a release. Forbearance to sue is good consideration for a promise regardless of the actual validity of the claim if the one who forbears has reasonable and sincere belief in its validity. Giving up the right to litigate is something of value and a detriment even though it is ultimately discovered that the claim is worthless or the assertion unreasonable. However, if the claim is frivolous, vexatious, unlawful, or the claimant knows it is not well founded, forbearance to sue is not good consideration.

Forbearances other than to sue have been held to constitute consideration. For example, the relinquishment of all rights in an estate or the right to enforce a lien are actually forbearances which serve as consideration for a promise. In addition, mutual promises to forbear are sufficient to support each other.

---

3 *Allen v. Allen,* page 170.
4 *Grombach v. Oerlikon Tool and Arms Corporation of America,* page 171.

SPECIAL CONCEPTS

2-33. Existing Obligations. In addition to the general rules concerned with the concept of consideration, adequacy of consideration, and forbearance, previously discussed, there are several special situations which involve the law of consideration and special rules relating thereto. The first of these is concerned with the adequacy of consideration when the promisee has an existing obligation which has been created either by contract or statute. As a general rule, an agreement that offers for its consideration the performance of an existing obligation by one of the parties is unenforceable, performance being nothing more than the courts would compel him to do. He has surrendered no legal right. Hence, an owner who promises a contractor an additional sum to complete a job already under contract is not legally bound to pay the additional sum. If, however the promisee agrees to do anything other than, or different from, what the original contract demanded, ample consideration is provided. The contractor who agrees to complete his work at an earlier date or in a different manner may recover on a promise of the owner to pay an additional amount. The cancellation of the original contract and the formation of an entirely new agreement is always possible.

Many obligations which prevent an act which otherwise would serve as consideration from doing so involve a statutory duty. For example, a promise to appear as a witness at a trial or a promise by a public officer to make an arrest will not support a promise to pay money therefor. However, if the party promises to go beyond what the law demands, then he has waived a legal right and consideration has been given.

Some conflict exists in those cases in which a third party promises added compensation to one of two contracting parties if the latter will complete his contract. The majority of the courts hold that a promise made to a third party to perform an existing contractual obligation offers no consideration although the more recent judicial decisions appear to favor the promisee. Thus, a promise by a third party to a contractor to pay an additional sum upon the latter's completion of a certain construction job is unenforceable in most of the states. It is unenforceable even when the contractor fulfills his contract only because of the promise of the additional sum. Here also, if anything new or different is requested, the contract becomes binding because of the new consideration.

As we have seen, the general rule is that consideration is required to modify a contract. However, the Uniform Commercial Code has eliminated consideration as a requirement to modify a contract for the sale of goods.[C2] In such contracts, terms favorable to one party may be changed to more burdensome provisions by mutual agreement without any consideration being given by the other party. The contract may specify:

[C2] *U.C.C.* 2-209(1).

"This agreement may not be modified or rescinded except by a signed writing." Such a provision will be given effect, but if it appears in a contract between a merchant and a consumer the provision must be separately signed by the latter—that is, in addition to his signature as a party he must sign again in such fashion as to indicate that he is aware of the provision.[C3] This restriction is not applicable in transactions between merchants.

The fact that the Code does not require consideration to modify a contract involving the sale of personal property, while consideration is required to modify other contracts, illustrates the effect of changing public attitudes toward the law. The strict requirements of contract law are yielding to moral and ethical considerations as well as business practice. We recognize that the parties do not cancel the old contract and execute an entirely new one each time a change or modification is required. Some courts, in their desire to reach a just result, will examine the reason for the change of terms and conclude that additional consideration was not required or was present under the circumstances of the particular case. The next section illustrates this approach.

2-34. Unforeseen Difficulties. A promise to pay additional compensation for the completion of a contract is deemed binding by some courts where unforeseen difficulties are encountered after the original agreement is executed.[5] In such a case the result is most often justified on the theory that, in effect, the parties rescinded the old agreement, because of the new circumstances, and formed a new one. Even in such cases, however, it is prudent for the party under duty to furnish some new consideration or to have the old agreement rescinded and a new one executed. Unforeseen difficulties are those which seldom occur and are extraordinary in nature. Price changes, strikes, bad weather, and shortage of material are of frequent occurrence and are not unforeseeable. It must be emphasized that even though difficulties are unforeseen, the promisor is obligated to perform at the original contract price unless the other party indicates a willingness to make an adjustment.

2-35. Discharge of Debts and Claims. As was previously noted, there is one exception to the general rule relating to adequacy of consideration. If the consideration on each side involves money—money given to satisfy a money debt or to support a promise to pay money in the future—the consideration given must equal in value the promise made. Because of this rule, an agreement between a debtor and his creditor to have the debt discharged upon the payment of a sum less than the amount agreed to be owing is unenforceable.[6] In most states, even though the lesser sum has been paid, the unpaid portion is collectible. The payment of the lesser sum is the performance of an existing obligation and cannot act

[5] *Pittsburgh Testing Lab. v. Farnsworth & Chambers Co., Inc.,* page 172.
[6] *Monroe v. Bixby,* page 174.

[C3] *U.C.C.* 2-209(2).

as consideration for a release of the balance. Naturally, if there is evidence that the creditor made a gift of the balance to the debtor, no recovery may be had by the creditor. A receipt which states that the payment is in full satisfaction of the account is in many states an indication that a gift was intended. Furthermore, where the debt consists of a note or written agreement, the cancellation and return of the evidence of indebtedness will act to discharge the debt. In states which have not abolished the seal, a release under seal discharges the debt.

Payment of a lesser sum, where accompanied by additional consideration, will discharge a larger liquidated sum. Since the value of consideration is ordinarily unimportant, the added consideration may take any form. For example, payment in advance of the due date, payment at a place other than that agreed upon, surrender of the privilege of bankruptcy, and the giving of a secured note for less than the face of the debt have all been found sufficient to discharge a larger amount than that paid.

The mere giving of a negotiable note for a lesser sum than the entire debt will not release the debtor of his duty to pay the balance. The note is merely a promise to pay, and consequently the mere promise to pay less than is due will not discharge the debt.

As was noted in section 32, a promise to forbear from prosecuting a claim is sufficient consideration to support a release as also is the compromise of a claim. In each case, the parties are surrendering their right to litigate the dispute. Therefore, when one party has a claim against another party which is disputed, uncertain in amount and unliquidated whether arising from a dispute which is contractual in nature such as one involving damaged merchandise[7] or is tortious in character such as one arising from an automobile accident, a bona fide settlement of the claim or demand between the high demanded and the low admitted to be due operates as a contract to discharge the claim known legally as an accord and satisfaction. The dispute must be in good faith or the rules for unliquidated debts are applicable.

Both liquidated and unliquidated debts may also be discharged in a composition of creditors. This occurs when the creditors agree with each other and the debtor to accept a percentage of their claims in full satisfaction. The consideration for the discharge is the promise by each creditor not to file a petition in involuntary bankruptcy or to enforce their claims in other legal proceedings. The consideration in theory flows from creditor to creditor and the debtor receives the benefit of their contract for his promise and forbearance.

2-36. Moral Obligation and Past Consideration. A mere moral obligation or conscientious duty unconnected with any legal obligation is not valid consideration for an executory promise.[8] The law will not enforce an obligation resisting only on ethical or moral principles but instead insists on the presence of a legal benefit or detriment to create enforceable con-

---

7 *Nardine v. Kraft Cheese Co.,* page 176.
8 *Pascali v. Hempstead,* page 177.

tracts. The doctrine of promissory estoppel is sometimes used to make a promise which appears to be based on merely moral consideration enforceable. For example, X promises his church $1,000 to be used to construct a new church. The church in reliance on X's and other promises undertakes the construction project. While some courts may refer to the moral obligation theory, X's promise is actually binding because he induced the church to materially change its position in reliance on his promise which it did. It is equally clear that if his $1,000 promise were to be used to discharge an existing mortgage, it would be unenforceable for lack of consideration because the church did not change its position in reliance on the promise. Thus, the moral obligation theory is rarely if ever actually used.

Past consideration is insufficient to support a present promise. The consideration must consist of some present surrender of a legal right. Some act that has taken place in the past will not suffice. Hence, an express warranty concerning real property sold, when made after the sale has taken place, is unenforceable [9] and a promise to pay for a gift previously received cannot be enforced. It must be noted that many businesses do perform such contracts as a matter of good business practice and ethics but they may not be compelled to do so.

A seeming exception to this rule exists in those cases in which one person requests another to perform some work for him without definitely specifying the compensation to be paid. After the work is completed, the parties agree upon a certain sum to be paid for the work. It appears as if the work done in the past furnishes the consideration to support the promise made later to pay a definite sum, but this analysis is erroneous. As soon as the work is completed, the party performing it is entitled to reasonable compensation. Later he surrenders this right in consideration of a promise to pay a definite sum. The cancellation of the contract for a reasonable wage is the consideration for the new contract.

There are a few exceptions to the rules of law concerning moral and past consideration in addition to promissory estoppel. For example, a new promise to pay a debt that has been discharged in bankruptcy is enforceable without any added consideration. The promise to pay must be expressed. Acknowledgment or part payment cannot import a promise to pay the creditor. Most states by statute require the new promise to be in writing, which promise may be to pay only a part of the debt or to pay it only when certain conditions are satisfied.

A creditor who has given a voluntary and binding release of part of a debt may not enforce a later promise by his debtor to pay the balance. The release of the unpaid portion is considered in the nature of a gift, and promise to pay for a gift previously received is unenforceable.

In a few isolated cases, courts have enforced a promise where in equity and good conscience the promisee ought to perform. These cases sometimes refer to a moral obligation but most of the results could be justified by equitable estoppel theory. For example, A promises X University

---

[9] *James v. Jacobsen,* page 178.

money for a new building. If construction is commenced, the promise is enforceable.

2-37. Mutuality of Consideration. A major problem area in the law of consideration is the area of mutuality of consideration or illusory promises. Mutual promises as a general rule furnish a sufficient consideration to support a valid enforceable contract. However, these mutual promises must be valuable, concurrent, certain, and not impossible of performance or they will not suffice as consideration. If one party is not bound by his promise, neither is bound. A promise is valuable if it meets the benefit-detriment test previously discussed. It is concurrent if made at the same time. Promises made at different times on the same day are not sufficient. The requirement that a promise be definite and certain involves the same issues as previously discussed in the chapter on Offer and Acceptance. A promise which cannot by any means be accomplished is not a binding promise and does not constitute consideration. However, a promise which is dependent on a condition which is a remote possibility is nevertheless binding.

The law requires mutuality of consideration, not mutuality of obligation. As was previously noted, the law is not concerned with the adequacy of the consideration, only with its actual existence. To determine if mutuality of consideration is present or if the purported promise is illusory, a careful examination of the language is required. For example, an agreement that gives to one of the parties the right to cancel the contract at any time prior to the time for performance is not binding and is illusory. However, if the right to cancel is not absolute, but is conditioned upon the happening or nonhappening of some event, the contract is such that neither party may avoid it unless the condition occurs and it is not illusory. Mutuality does not require that a contract be definite in all details or that there be reciprocity or a special promise for each obligation. Neither does it require mutuality of remedies between the parties.

Many promises that appear to assure something of value, but when fully understood, do not embody such an assurance, are illusory promises because real mutuality is lacking.[10] Let us consider the following agreement: *B,* a trucker, promises to purchase from *S* all he *wants* of *S*'s gasoline at 20 cents a gallon plus taxes, and *S* promises to sell all that *B wants* at that price Careful analysis of this agreement makes it clear that *B* has not agreed to buy any gasoline. He has promised to purchase only in case he wants it, which is equivalent to no promise at all. Since *B* has thus given *S* no consideration for his promise, *B*'s promise being illusory, *S* is at liberty to withdraw, and his withdrawal becomes effective as soon as notice thereof reaches *B*. Until withdrawn by *S,* the above agreement stands as a continuing offer on his part, and any order received prior to revocation must be filled at the quoted price.

In the above case, if *B* had agreed to buy his gasoline needs from *S*

---

10 *Streich v. General Motors Corporation,* page 179.

for a period of one year, the agreement would have been binding. Whenever the buyer is certain to have needs or requirements, an agreement to purchase all of one's needs or requirements will support the promise to supply them even though the amount is uncertain, since past experience will, in a general way, aid the seller in estimating the amount required.

The Code provides that a term which measures the quantity by the output of the seller or the requirements of the buyer means such actual output or requirements as may occur in good faith.[C4] In addition, no quantity unreasonably disproportionate to any stated estimate or in the absence of a stated estimate to any normal or otherwise comparable prior output or requirement may be tendered or demanded.[C5] In other words, quantity must bear a reasonable relationship to estimates given or to past outputs or requirements under the Code.

An illusory contract may be cured by performance of the illusory promise. Lack of mutuality is not defense to an executed contract as it becomes binding upon the promisor after performance by the promisee.

CONSIDERATION CASES

Stelmack et al. v. Glen Alden Coal Co.
1940 (339 Pa. 410) 14 A.2d 127

Plaintiffs brought suit against defendant to recover the cost of repairs to their building which was damaged as a result of mining operations of the defendant. Plaintiffs purchased the surface rights subject to a reservation and condition in a prior deed in the chain of title by which defendant had disclaimed any liability for damage to the surface caused by mining and the parties agreed that defendant had no liability except by reason of certain promises made in 1927. Defendant by a duly authorized agent made an oral agreement that if plaintiffs would permit the coal company's employees to enter upon their land and prop up their building to prevent its collapse, or to minimize any damages which might occur, the company would make all repairs necessary to restore the property to its original condition.

Plaintiffs permitted the ties and supports to be erected about their building which rendered it "unsightly" and resulted in some loss of rents, although it is not contended that the work was performed negligently. As the operations continued during the period from 1928 to 1935, it became necessary, according to plaintiffs, to reconstruct the building, due to the further subsidence of the surface. From time to time the defendant made repairs to the property, but later refused to restore it to its previous condition.

The lower court excluded all evidence of the oral agreement, upon the ground that plaintiffs had failed to show that it was supported by a consideration, and directed a verdict in favor of the defendant. From

C4 *U.C.C.* 2-306.   C5 *U.C.C.* 2-306.

the order of the court *in banc* refusing a new trial, and entering judgment for the defendant, plaintiffs appeal.

BARNES, J.   . . . Plaintiffs contend that (1) there was consideration for the oral agreement because of the detriment suffered by them in permitting the defendant to enter upon their land and place props and ties about their building; (2) the promise to repair was supported by a "moral consideration"; and (3) they are entitled to recover under the doctrine of promissory estoppel.

That consideration is an essential element of an enforceable contract is one of our fundamental legal concepts, and there are but few exceptions to the rule. "Consideration is defined as a benefit to the party promising, or a loss or detriment to the party to whom the promise is made." (*Hillcrest Foundation, Inc. v. McFeaters,* 332 Pa. 497, 503, 2 A.2d 775, 778) The terms "benefit" and "detriment" are used in a technical sense in the definition, and have no necessary reference to material advantage or disadvantage to the parties.

It is not enough, however, that the promisee has suffered a legal detriment at the request of the promisor. The detriment incurred must be the "quid pro quo," or the "price" of the promise, and the inducement for which it was made. "Consideration must actually be bargained for as the exchange for the promise." (Restatement, *Contracts,* Section 75, Comment (b)); . . . If the promisor merely intends to make a gift to the promisee upon the performance of a condition, the promise is gratuitous and the satisfaction of the condition is not consideration for a contract. . . .

In the present case it clearly appears that the defendant's offer to repair the plaintiffs' building was entirely gratuitous. The permission to enter upon the land and erect props and ties was sought by defendant merely for the purpose of conferring a benefit upon plaintiffs as a voluntary act, and not as the price or consideration of its alleged promise to restore the building to its original condition. The placing supports about the structure was of no conceivable advantage to the defendant, for, as we have seen, it had no liability whatever "for any injury or damage that may be caused or done to the said surface or right of soil, or to the buildings or improvements" under the provisions of the deeds in plaintiff's chain of title. The interest of plaintiffs alone was served by the defendant's efforts to prevent the collapse of the structure and to minimize the damages resulting from the mining operations. As this was done at the expense of the defendant, and solely for the protection of the plaintiffs, we are unable to see how it could have constituted a consideration for the defendant's promise, and have converted a purely gratuitous undertaking into a binding contract.

Here there was no pre-existing legal or equitable obligation which could serve as the foundation of a moral obligation. The plaintiffs and their predecessors in title were fully compensated, as expressly stated in the original deed, for any loss which might result from the withdrawal of surface support by the owner of the mining rights. The possibility of damage was reflected in the reduced purchase price paid for the property.

Plaintiffs accepted the deed with full knowledge of the reservations and waiver of damages, and with the express stipulation that defendant should have no liability whatsoever for a subsidence of the land.

Nor can plaintiffs' final contention that the defendant should be estopped from repudiating its promise be sustained. The doctrine of promissory estoppel, upon which they rely, may be invoked only in those cases where all the elements of a true estoppel are present, for if it is loosely applied, any promise, regardless of the complete absence of consideration, would be enforceable. The principle involved is defined in the Restatement, *Contracts,* Section 90, in the following terms:

> A promise which the promisor should reasonably expect to induce action or forbearance of a definite and substantial character on the part of the promisee and which does induce such action or forbearance is binding if injustice can be avoided only by enforcement of the promise. . . .

Here no action was taken by plaintiffs in reliance upon the defendant's promise which resulted in disadvantage to them. They did not alter their position adversely or substantially. They have suffered no injustice in being deprived of a gratuitous benefit to which they have no legal or equitable right. We are satisfied there is nothing in the present record to bring this case within any recognized exception to the well established principle of contract law, that a promise unsupported by consideration is nudum pactum, and unenforceable.

The judgment of the court below is affirmed.

Feinberg v. Pfeiffer Company

1959 (Mo.) 322 S.W.2d 163

Plaintiff, a former employee of the defendant, brought suit on an alleged contract whereby defendant agreed to pay the plaintiff $200 per month for life upon her retirement. Plaintiff had been employed by defendant for 37 years when the Board of Directors at an annual meeting passed a resolution increasing her salary and affording her the privilege of retiring at any time she may elect to do so at $200 per month. Eighteen months later plaintiff retired and commenced to receive her pension. Approximately seven years later and after a change in management, the defendant attempted to reduce the pension to $100 per month and considered the payment to be a mere gift. The trial court awarded judgment for the plaintiff and the defendant appealed.

DOERNER, Commissioner. . . . We come, then, to the basic issue in the case. . . . whether plaintiff has proved that she has a right to recover from defendant based upon a legally binding contractual obligation to pay her $200 per month for life.

It is defendant's contention, in essence, that the resolution adopted by its Board of Directors was a mere promise to make a gift, and that no contract resulted either thereby, or when plaintiff retired, because there was no consideration given or paid by the plaintiff. It urges that a promise to make a gift is not binding unless supported by a legal consideration; that the only apparent consideration for the adoption of the foregoing resolution was the "many years of long and faithful service" expressed therein; and that past services are not a valid consideration for a promise. Defendant argues further that there is nothing in the resolution which made its effectiveness conditional upon plaintiff's continued employment, that she was not under contract to work for any length of time but was free to quit whenever she wished, and that she had no contractual right to her position and could have been discharged at any time.

Plaintiff concedes that a promise based upon past services would be without consideration, but contends that her change of position, i.e., her retirement, and the abandonment by her of her opportunity to continue in gainful employment, made in reliance on defendant's promise to pay her $200 per month for life. . . . We must agree with plaintiff. By the terms of the resolution defendant promised to pay plaintiff the sum of $200 a month upon her retirement. Consideration for a promise has been defined in the Restatement of the Law of Contracts, Section 75, as:

(1) Consideration for a promise is
    (a) an act other than a promise, or
    (b) a forbearance, or
    (c) the creation, modification or destruction of a legal relation, or
    (d) a return promise, bargained for and given in exchange for the promise.

As the parties agree, the consideration sufficient to support a contract may be either a benefit to the promisor or a loss or detriment to the promisee. . . .

Section 90 of the Restatement of the Law of Contracts states that: "A promise which the promisor should reasonably expect to induce action or forbearance of a definite and substantial character on the part of the promisee and which does induce such action or forbearance is binding if injustice can be avoided only by enforcement of the promise." This doctrine has been described as that of "promissory estoppel." . . .

Was there such an act on the part of the plaintiff, in reliance upon the promise contained in the resolution, as will estop the defendant. and therefore create an enforceable contract under the doctrine of promissory estoppel? We think there was. . . .

The fact of the matter is that plaintiff's subsequent illness was not the "action or forbearance" which was induced by the promise contained in the resolution. As the trial court correctly decided, such action on plaintiff's part was her retirement from a lucrative position in reliance upon defendant's promise to pay her an annuity or pension. In a very similar case, *Ricketts v. Schothorn,* (57 Neb. 51, 77 N.W. 365, 367, 42 L.R.A. 794), the Supreme Court of Nebraska said:

> . . . According to the undisputed proof, as shown by the record before us, the plaintiff was a working girl, holding a position in which she earned a salary of $10 per week. Her grandfather, desiring to put her in a position of

independence, gave her the note accompanying it with the remark that his other grandchildren did not work, and that she would not be obliged to work any longer. In effect, he suggested that she might abandon her employment, and rely in the future upon the bounty which he promised. He doubtless desired that she should give up her occupation, but, whether he did or not, it is entirely certain that he contemplated such action on her part as a reasonable and probable consequence of his gift. Having intentionally influenced the plaintiff to alter her position for the worse on the faith of the note being paid when due, it would be grossly inequitable to permit the maker, or his executor, to resist payment on the ground that the promise was given without consideration.

The Commissioner therefore recommends, for the reasons stated, that the judgment be affirmed.

PER CURIAM. *The foregoing opinion by* DOERNER, C., *is adopted as the opinion of the court. The judgment is, accordingly, affirmed.*

Allen v. Allen

1957 (D.C.) 133 AT1.2d 116

HOOD, J.   In 1898 by deed of conveyance from an aunt, appellees, who are brother and sister, became tenants in common of certain improved real estate. The conveyance was subject to the condition that appellees provide their father and mother a comfortable home on the premises for as long as they lived, unless the mother became the wife of another husband. By 1938 the father had died and the family consisted of appellees, their mother, and three brothers who were born after the 1898 conveyance. In that year appellees at the request of the mother, entered into a written agreement with her whereby "in consideration of the sum of One ($1.00) Dollar to them paid by Julia A. Allen (the mother), the receipt whereof is hereby acknowledged," they promised and agreed that in the event of the sale of the property during their lifetime, they would divide the proceeds equally among themselves and their three brothers.

The mother died in 1951 and in 1953 appellees sold the property for $15,000. These suits were then brought by one of the three brothers, one suit being on his own behalf and the other as administrator of a deceased brother's estate, each claiming one-fifth share of the $15,000. The original 1938 agreement had either been lost or misplaced, but a copy thereof was received in evidence. While the agreement recited that appellees and the mother "have hereunto set their hands and seals," the copy did not disclose anything purporting to be a seal after the signatures of the parties.

The trial court found that the agreement was a simple contract not under seal, and ruled that the consideration of one dollar was "grossly inadequate" to support the contract. Judgment was entered for appellees and these appeals followed.

. . .

Appellant next argues that it was error for the trial court to question the adequacy of the consideration recited in the agreement. In ruling that the consideration was grossly inadequate, the trial court relied on our case of *Sloan v. Sloan* (D.C. Mun.App., 66 A.2d 799), wherein we held that, although generally a court will not inquire as to the adequacy of the consideration, where there is an agreement to exchange unequal sums of money and the sums are grossly disproportionate, the agreement will not receive the sanction of the courts. We agree with appellant that the Sloan case is inapplicable here. This was not an exchange of unequal sums of money. Appellees' promise was that should the property be sold during their lifetime they would divide the proceeds equally with their three brothers. If the property were not sold, they were not bound to pay anything; and they were not obligated to sell unless they so desired.

However, we think the trial court's denial of recovery was sound for another reason, and in the discussion of this reason will be found the answer to appellant's final contention that the recital of receipt of one dollar consideration estopped appellees from showing the real consideration or lack thereof.

The testimony was that the one dollar mentioned in the agreement as consideration was never paid by the mother to appellees and they received no consideration whatever for signing, that they signed in order to please their mother, and that one of appellees even paid the lawyer's fee of $10 for preparing the agreement. We think it is plain from this testimony, and implicit in the trial court's reference to the "stated payment of One ($1.00) Dollar" as the only consideration, that the one dollar not only was not paid but was never intended to be paid.

As stated in the Sloan case, adequacy of consideration is not required; and if one dollar is intended as the consideration and paid and accepted as such, it is sufficient consideration. However, a stated consideration which is a mere pretense and not a reality is not sufficient; because if in fact no consideration was intended and none given, recital of a consideration cannot make the promise enforceable. . . .

The recital in the agreement of a consideration and acknowledgment of payment thereof was evidence that such consideration was agreed upon by the parties and that payment was actually made; but such evidence was not conclusive. Recital of consideration in an unsealed instrument may be contradicted by parol evidence. On the evidence here the court found no actual but only a stated consideration. We conclude, therefore, that the promise of the appellees was without consideration and unenforceable.

Affirmed.

Grombach v. Oerlikon Tool and Arms Corp. of America
1960 (U.S.C.A.) 276 F.(2) 155

The plaintiff and defendant had a written contract by which the plaintiff would serve as a public relations representative for the defendant. The employer had the right to cancel the contract by giving written notice of cancellation before May 1, 1953. The period of performance extended for several years in the event of no cancellation by that date. On April 27, 1953 the employee agreed to an extension of the cancellation option to June 30, 1953. On June 24, 1953 the employer exercised the option and cancelled the contract. Plaintiff-employee sues the defendant-employer contending among other things that the period of cancellation had expired because the extension of the cancellation option was invalid due to lack of consideration.

BARKSDALE, D. J. . . . We cannot agree with plaintiff's belated contention that this agreement to extend the time within which the contract of February 10, 1953, might be canceled, was invalid because not supported by a valuable consideration. As set out in paragraph VI(a) of the contract, Buehrle had the right to cancel the contract by giving written notice before May 1, 1953. By cable, on April 27, 1953, Grombach agreed to an extension of the cancellation option to June 30, 1953. The crux of the situation is that Buehrle requested, and Grombach agreed to, the extension of the time in which the option to cancel might be exercised, within the period during which, according to the terms of the written contract, Buehrle had the unquestioned option to cancel. Buehrle's forbearance to cancel at a time when he, by the terms of the contract, had the undoubted right to do so, constituted consideration for the extension of time.

> The waiver of a right or forbearance to exercise the same is a sufficient consideration for a contract, whether the right be legal or equitable, or exists against the promisor or a third person, provided it is not utterly groundless. (17 C.J.S. *Contracts* 103, p. 456)

In the case of *Millikan v. Simmons* (244 N.C. 195, 93 S.E.2d 59), it was held that an agreement to extend an option for the purchase of real estate made before the expiration of the original option, was valid, the agreement to forego the right to close the transaction at once, constituting sufficient consideration to support the agreement to extend the option.

See also *Brown v. Taylor* (174 N.C. 423, 93 S.E. 982, 984, L.R.A.1918B, 293), where the principle is stated as follows:

> There is a consideration if the promisee in return for the promise, does anything legal which he is not bound to do, or refrains from doing anything which he has the [legal] right to do, whether there is any actual loss or detriment to him or actual benefit to the promissor or not.

Affirmed.

Pittsburgh Testing Lab. v. Farnsworth & Chambers Co., Inc.

1958, 251 F.2d 77

MURRAH, C. J. This is an appeal from a judgment of the District Court invalidating, for lack of consideration, an oral contract to pay additional compensation for services rendered in connection with the performance of an antecedent written contract. Jurisdiction is based upon diversity of citizenship and requisite amount in controversy.

According to the unchallenged findings of the trial court, the appellant, Pittsburgh Testing Laboratory, entered into a written subcontract with the appellee, Farnsworth & Chambers, Inc., under the terms of which the Testing Company agreed to do all of the testing and inspection of materials required under a master contract between Farnsworth and the Douglas Aircraft Corporation for the construction of concrete ramps and runways at Tulsa, Oklahoma. The consideration for the performance of the service was $24,450, to be paid in seven monthly installments, less ten per cent retainage until completion of the contract. In the preliminary negotiations, Farnsworth estimated that the job would be completed in seven months, or October 15, 1952, on the basis of a ten-hour day, sixty-hour work week, and that the Testing Company's work would be concluded about November 1. While these representations undoubtedly formed the basis for Pittsburgh's proposal and for the lump sum compensation in the contract, there was no guarantee of a completion date or hour work week. Before the end of the seven months period, and in September 1952, it became manifest that the contract would not be completed within the estimated time, due principally to the necessity of moving 1,200,000 tons of dirt or material instead of the estimated 600,000 tons. A controversy thereupon arose between the parties as to Pittsburgh's obligation under the written contract and Farnsworth's liability for overtime compensation to Pittsburgh's personnel for work in excess of the sixty-hour week. Pittsburgh was told by Farnsworth's representatives that if it would continue to perform its services, it would be compensated. When, however, no payments were made in December 1952, Pittsburgh refused to proceed unless a new contract was entered into providing payment for the remaining work at the rate of $3,492.85 per month from November 1 until the completion of the work, plus time and one-half for all man hours worked over sixty hours per week. On December 20, the parties entered into an oral contract to that effect and Pittsburgh continued to perform the same service and to submit invoices for the monthly compensation, and separate invoices for overtime pay in excess of the sixty hours per week. Although Farnsworth did not remit for the invoices or reply to Pittsburgh's persistent statements, it made no protest or objection to either the statements for the stipulated additional compensation or the separate statements for the overtime. After the work was completed in the Spring of 1953, and Pittsburgh had been paid the balance of the retainage under the original contract, Farnsworth finally repudiated the oral agreement and this suit followed.

The trial court specifically found that at the time of making the oral contract to pay additional compensation, plus overtime, a bona fide dispute existed between the parties concerning their respective obligations under the written contract. The trial court also specifically found, however, that the Testing Company performed no services pursuant to the oral contract which it was not already bound to do by the terms of the written contract. Based on these findings, the trial court finally concluded that the oral contract was unenforceable for want of consideration, and that Farnsworth was not estopped to defend on that basis.

It is the general rule, followed in Oklahoma where this contract was made and performed, that a promise to pay additional compensation for the doing of that which the promisee is already legally bound to do or perform, is insufficient consideration for a valid and enforceable contract. . . .

Another more widely accepted exception might properly be called the "unforeseeable difficulties exception," under which the courts have recognized the equities of a promise for additional compensation based upon extraordinary and unforeseeable difficulties in the performance of the subsisting contract. In these circumstances, the courts generally sustain the consideration for the new promise, based upon standards of honesty and fair dealing and affording adequate protection against unjust or coercive exactions. . . .

As far as we can determine, Oklahoma courts have not had occasion to embrace or reject what seems to us a salutary exception to the rule. But, there can be no doubt that the oral contract was made in the face of unforeseen and substantial difficulties—circumstances which were not within the contemplation of the parties when the original contract was made, and which were recognized when the subsequent oral contract was entered into. The performance of the contract took more than twice as long as the parties estimated. Pittsburgh's primary cost was expensive skilled labor, and the consideration for the contract was necessarily based upon the estimated time required for performance. We should be content to sustain the contract on the assumption that the Oklahoma courts would recognize and apply the so-called unforeseen difficulties exception in a case like ours. But the contract need not rest upon that ground alone. There can be no doubt that an agreement which compromises a bona fide dispute concerning duties and obligations under a subsisting contract, is supported by valid consideration and is enforceable. . . . The trial court's specific finding in that regard is amply supported by the evidence, and we hold the contract valid and enforceable.

The judgment is accordingly reversed.

Monroe v. Bixby

1951 (330 Mich.) 353, 47 N.W.2d 643

BOYLES, J. Plaintiff, Monroe, the owner of a house and lot on Clancy Street in the city of Grand Rapids, on September 1, 1937, entered into a written land contract to sell it to her daughter, the defendant, for $4,000. $60.60 * was paid on the purchase price and the balance of $3,039.40,* with interest at the rate of 6 per cent per annum, was to be paid in monthly instalments of $30 or more per month the first year, then $35 or more each month. Defendant's then-husband was also named as a vendee but some time later defendant and her husband were divorced

_____

* Apparently an error in the record.

and assignment of his interest in the contract was made to the defendant. Plaintiff shows that some time later defendant asked to have the monthly payments and the interest reduced. Plaintiff drew up a purported agreement which is as follows:

Agreement

First party, Anna V. Wiley Monroe; Second party, Hazel May Bixby;

First party agrees to accept 5% interest on contract. The first party agrees to accept Thirty ($30.00) Dollars a month payment instead of Thirty-five ($35.00) Dollars a month. The first party agrees to give the second party a deed when the first party has received Twenty-Five Hundred ($2,500.00) Dollars from September 1, 1939.

The second party is not to transfer the contract unless the first party agrees to the transfer.

(s) Mrs. Anna V. Wiley Monroe

Subscribed and sworn to
before me this 5th day
of November, 1940.

(s) Catherine M. May,
Notary Public,
My comm. expires

(Seal)

Nov. 23, 1940

This paper was signed by plaintiff but not by defendant. After it was executed by the plaintiff, the defendant made monthly payments until January 25, 1950, when defendant refused to make further payment.

Plaintiff claims when the $2,500 was paid upon the contract she was to give a deed and have a mortgage to secure her for the balance of the $4,000 purchase price. Defendant claims that she was entitled to a deed after paying the $2,500 upon the contract and was under no obligation to pay the balance of the $4,000 purchase price.

When the contract showed an unpaid balance of $1,178.08, defendant refused to pay more, and plaintiff filed the instant bill of complaint praying for a foreclosure of the land contract and an accounting for certain furniture. She claimed that the aforesaid "agreement" was invalid because of lack of consideration and failure to comply with the statute of frauds. After a hearing on the merits, the court entered a decree dismissing plaintiff's bill of complaint but decreeing that there was $32.08 still due her on the contract and directing plaintiff to execute a deed to defendant upon payment of that amount, as prayed for by the defendant in her cross bill. Plaintiff appeals.

Assuming that defendant's position was supported by the proofs, and that the plaintiff had agreed to accept less than the full amount of the purchase price, such an agreement must be considered as unenforceable for lack of consideration. Plaintiff's claim of $1,178.08, balance of the purchase price and interest, was a liquidated demand, and any agreement to accept less than the full amount could not be considered as a compromise and settlement of an unliquidated or doubtful claim.

Under the law in this state there is no doubt that a payment of less than the full amount of a past-due liquidated and undisputed debt, although accepted and receipted for as in full satisfaction, is only to be treated as a partial payment, and does not estop the creditor from suing for and recovering the balance. (*People for use of Zeeland Brick Co. v. Fidelity & Deposit Co.,* 195 Mich. 738, 162 N.W. 338, 340)

We have many times held that part payment of a past-due, liquidated and undisputed claim, even though accepted in full satisfaction thereof, does not operate to discharge the debt, but constitutes a payment *pro tanto* only. (*Aston v. Elkow,* 279 Mich. 232, 271 N.W. 742, 743) . . .

We conclude that the claimed "agreement" to accept less than the amount due for principal and interest on the contract, being without consideration, was void. That being true, there is no occasion to consider the claim that it also was void because of the statute of frauds.

Judgment for plaintiff.

Nardine v. Kraft Cheese Co.

1944 (Ind. App.) 52 N.E.2d 634

FLANAGAN, J.   For several years prior to August 24, 1941, the appellant, Lattie Nardine, a resident of Vincennes, Indiana, had operated a grocery in Lexington, Kentucky, under the name of Standard Market. During that time she had been an open account customer of appellee. In July 1941 she purchased from appellee 515¾ pounds of longhorn cheese. After a short time a dispute developed as to this cheese. Appellant said it was spoiled when received and that appellee should take it back. Appellee said that appellant spoiled it trying to force cure it and therefore it could not be returned. This dispute continued until after appellant closed her business on August 24, 1941.

Thereafter letters were exchanged between the parties concerning settlement of appellant's account, whereby it developed that there were other differences as to items in the account. About October 1, 1941, appellee's Lexington manager went to Vincennes to discuss the account with appellant but they were unable to agree as to the amount appellant owed. The dispute concerning the shipment of longhorn cheese above referred to was continued at that conference.

On October 30, 1941, appellant wrote appellee the following letter:

Enclosed please find check in the amount of One Hundred Forty Six Dollars and one cent ($146.01) which according to our records pays my account in full.

You will notice that I have taken a 10¢ per lb. deduction on the 515¾ lb. bad longhorn cheese, that I received from you. We are still at quite a loss on this cheese, as we really had to sacrifice it to get rid of it.

In regard to the balance on your statement of overcharges and deductions, I wish to advise that I find it impossible to check upon this as they are so old. I feel that if the deductions were not in order, that I should have been notified at the time they were taken from the checks. As you told me, these were left over from before the time you took over this account.

We are sorry to have had to make the above deductions, but I really feel that it is a just one. It has been a pleasure to do business with the Kraft Cheese Company at Lexington, and I want to thank you for all past favors.

With best regards to you, I remain,

Enclosed with the letter was a check for $146.01, marked, "This pays my account in full to date." After receiving the letter and check appellee mailed the check to the Vincennes bank on which it was drawn for certification. The bank certified the check and returned it to appellee who still retains it.

Thereafter appellee brought this action against appellant seeking to recover on account for the balance it claimed due after deducting the sum of $146.01. Appellant answered among other things that there had been an accord and satisfaction. Trial resulted in judgment for appellee in the sum of $87.88 and this appeal followed. The sufficiency of the evidence is properly challenged.

When the holder of a check has it certified by the bank on which it is drawn, the drawer is discharged and the debt becomes that of the bank. . . . If it was tendered in full payment of a claim which was unliquidated or concerning which a bona fide dispute existed, the acceptance of the check discharged the debt. . . .

Appellee says that there was no dispute because the trial court found that the longhorn cheese which appellant claims was spoiled when it arrived was in fact spoiled by appellant in trying to force cure it. The trial court could, and undoubtedly did, find that appellant spoiled the cheese. But in determining whether there was an accord and satisfaction we are not concerned with the question as to who was right and who was wrong in an existing dispute. We are concerned only with the question as to whether a good faith dispute existed at the time the check was tendered in full payment. (*Neubacher v. Perry, supra.*) The evidence on this question by both parties was all to the effect that such a dispute did exist.

It is true as appellee contends that the question of accord and satisfaction is ordinarily a question of fact, but where the controlling facts requisite to show accord and satisfaction are undisputed the question becomes one of law. . . .

Our conclusion is that the facts in this case show an accord and satisfaction of the claim sued upon.

Judgment for defendant Nardine.

Pascali v. Hempstead

1950 (N.J.) 73 A.2d 201

EASTWOOD, J. A. D.   Defendant appeals from a judgment entered in favor of plaintiff by the Bergen County District Court, sitting without a jury, in the sum of $125.01. The court found for the plaintiff in the sum of $143.51 and in favor of the defendant for $18.50 on his counterclaim. Plaintiff has not filed a brief nor did he appear at the argument.

In the first count of plaintiff's complaint, he alleges negligence on the part of defendant in the performance of certain work on his automobile, a 1941 Plymouth sedan, causing damage thereto; in his second count, he alleges that defendant admitted that said work was negligently performed and promised to pay the cost of repairs. Defendant's answer denied the plaintiff's allegations.

Defendant conducts what is generally known as a "gas service station" and does not undertake expert mechanical motor vehicle repairs. Plaintiff entrusted his vehicle to defendant for the sole purpose of having its spark plugs cleaned and adjusted. This is the only work that was done on the car. When plaintiff returned for his car, he discovered that it would not start. Although defendant installed a new battery, the motor could not be started until employees of the defendant rocked the vehicle and "unjammed" the starter; a "rattling noise" was then heard in the engine. Subsequently, the vehicle was towed to Decker Brothers garage where it was repaired. . . .

. . . Plaintiff testified that the defendant promised to pay the cost of the repairs and deduct same from the wages of the employee allegedly responsible for the damage. It is now well settled that a mere moral obligation or conscientious duty arising wholly from ethical motives or a mere conscientious duty unconnected with any legal obligation, perfect or imperfect, or with the receipt of benefit by the promisor of a material or pecuniary nature will not furnish a consideration for an executory promise. (12 Am.Jur., *Contracts*, Sec. 97, p. 590.) "A moral obligation which has at no time been a legal duty will not, according to the great weight of authority, afford a consideration for a promise." (13 C. J., *Contracts*, 219(10), p. 358) . . . In view of the fact that defendant was not liable to plaintiff, the promise to pay was unenforceable.

The judgment of the trial court in favor of the plaintiff is reversed and the judgment in favor of the defendant on his counterclaim in the sum of $18.50, representing the price of the battery, is affirmed.

James v. Jacobsen

1956 (Ga. App.) 91 S.E.2d 527

Jacobsen brought an action against James, defendant, to recover for alleged breach of warranty to the effect that the property purchased was free of termites. The warranty was given after the contract of sale had been signed.

GARDNER, J.   The record reveals that this is an action ex contractu and not ex delicto. This leads us to consider first whether or not the instrument regarding termite infestation was a legal and binding contract with sufficient consideration to vary the terms of the original contract of sale and contract of purchase. It is our understanding of the law that where the vendor of realty stipulates the terms upon which the property is offered for sale and such offer is accepted by a proposed purchaser, such contract between them is executed within the terms of the agreement. The contract of sale set up certain specifications, all of which were fulfilled by the vendor and the purchaser within the specified time. Before the consummation of the sale there was executed an instrument in which the seller guaranteed to the purchaser, in writing, that the premises in question were free of termite infestation and free of damage due to any previous termite infestation. . . .

The original contract was based on legal consideration and was valid and enforceable. The original contract of sale here, as the record reveals, was executed on January 14, 1955 and the express warranty with regard to termites was given by the defendant on February 10, 1955. The sale had not taken place and no delivery of the property had been made and the parties had not yet done what the original contract obligated them to do. (See *Woodruff v. Graddy & Sons,* 91 Ga. 333, 17 S.E. 264) Where, as here, the termite instrument is relied upon as a part of the original contract of sale, there are decisions to the effect that such a reliance is not tenable but is nudum pactum. . . .

Judgment for defendant.

Streich v. General Motors Corp.

1955 (5 Ill.) App.2d 485, 126 N.E.2d 389

The plaintiff, Streich, as seller sues for breach of what he contends is a contract to supply the defendant with its requirements for certain air magnet valves from September 1, 1948 to August 31, 1949. This would have been approximately 1,600 units based on previous requirements. The so-called contract consisted of a purchase order reading as follows:

> This Purchase Order is issued to cover shipments of this part, to be received by us from September 1, 1948, to August 31, 1949, as released and scheduled on our 48 'Purchase Order release and Shipping Schedule.'

It described the valves and set a price of $13.50 each, and on the reverse side the order said it constituted the final agreement between buyer and seller. It called itself a contract, but said, "Deliveries are to be made both in quantities and at times specified in schedules furnished by Buyer."

The defendant contended there was no contract since no goods had been ordered, although the plaintiff spent considerable sums of money for machinery and tooling in preparation for production.

McCormick, J. . . . There is no question but that under the law a contract properly entered into whereby the buyer agrees to buy all its requirements of a commodity for a certain period, and the seller agrees to sell the same as ordered, is a valid and enforceable contract and is not void for uncertainty and want of mutuality. . . . The contract in the instant case is not such a contract. Purchase Order No. 11925 states that it is issued to cover "shipments of this part, to be received by us from Sept. 1, 1948 to August 31, 1949 as released and scheduled on our series 48 'Purchase Order release and Shipping Schedule' No. 478412 attached and all subsequent Purchase Order releases." . . . Reading and construing the two documents together, notwithstanding the detailed provisions contained on the reverse side of the purchase order, the result is an agreement on the part of the seller to sell a certain identified valve at a certain fixed price in such quantities as the buyer may designate, when and if it issues a purchase order for the same. The word "release" as used throughout these documents is treated by both parties as equivalent to "order."

In *Corbin on Contracts,* Vol. 1, § 157, the author says:

> In what purports to be a bilateral contract, one party sometimes promises to supply another, on specified terms with all the goods or services that the other may order from time to time within a stated period. A mere statement by the other party that he assents to this, or 'accepts' it, is not a promise to order any goods or to pay anything. There is no consideration of any sort for the seller's promise; and he is not bound by it. This remains true, even though the parties think that a contract has been made and expressly label their agreement a 'contract.' In cases like this, there may be no good reason for implying any kind of promise by the offeree. Indeed, the proposal and promise of the seller has the form of an invitation for orders; and the mode of making an operative acceptance is to send in an order for a specific amount. By such an order, if there has been no previous notice of revocation, a contract is consummated and becomes binding on both parties. The standing offer is one of those that empowers the offeree to accept more than once and to create a series of separate obligations. The sending in of one order and the filling of it by the seller do not make the offer irrevocable as to additional amounts if the parties have not so agreed.

(See also *Williston on Contracts,* Rev. Ed., Vol. 1. 104A)

Here, the buyer proffers purchase order 11925, with its twenty-five or more clauses, to the seller for acceptance. In the instrument it makes no promise to do anything. On the surface it appears to be an attempt to initiate a valid bilateral contract. The seller accepts, and as by a flash of legerdemain the positions of the buyer and the seller shift. The buyer now becomes the promisee and the seller the promisor. The promise of the seller to furnish identified items at a stated price is merely an offer and cannot become a contract until the buyer issues a release or order for a designated number of items. Until this action is taken the buyer has made no promise to do anything, and either party may withdraw. The promise is illusory, and the chimerical contract vanishes. "An agreement to sell to another such of the seller's goods, wares, and merchandise as the other might from time to time desire to purchase is lacking in mutuality because it does not bind the buyer to purchase any of the goods of the seller, as such matter is left wholly at the option or pleasure of the buyer. . . ."

The agreement in question is an adaptation of what was termed an "open end contract," which was used extensively by the federal government during the late war. However, it was used only in cases where the commodities dealt with were staples and either in the possession of or easily accessible to the seller. In this case the use of the contract is shifted and extended to cover commodities which must be manufactured before they are available for sale. According to the admitted statements in the complaint, special tools had to be manufactured in order to produce the item herein involved. The seller here, misled by the many and detailed provisions contained in purchase order No. 11925 and ordinarily applicable to an enforceable bilateral contract, undoubtedly, as he alleged in his complaint, did go to considerable expense in providing tools and machines, only to find that by the accepted agreement the buyer had promised to do absolutely nothing. A statement of expectation creates no duty. Courts are not clothed with the power to make contracts for parties, nor can they, under the guise of interpretation, supply provisions actually lacking or impose obligations not actually assumed. . . .

The agreement contained in purchase order No. 11925 was artfully prepared. It contains, in print so fine as to be scarcely legible, more than twenty-three clauses, most of which are applicable to bilateral contracts. It has all the indicia of a binding and enforceable contract, but it was not a binding and enforceable contract because the promise was defective. Behind the glittering façade is a void. This agreement was made in the higher echelons of business, overshadowed by the aura of business ethics. To say the least, the agreement was deceptive. In a more subterranean atmosphere and between persons of lower ethical standards it might, without any strain of the language, be denominated by a less deterged appellation.

Nevertheless, as the law is today, on the pleadings in the instant case, the trial court could do nothing but sustain the motion to dismiss the complaint. The judgment of the Circuit Court is affirmed.

Judgment for defendant affirmed.

CHAPTER 9
REVIEW QUESTIONS AND PROBLEMS

1. X sold an apartment building to Y but the sale was conditioned on Y finding satisfactory tenants. X refused to perform contending lack of mutuality. Is X bound?

2. W's brother Q had been seriously ill and had incurred a substantial bill while in the hospital. As Q was being released from the hospital, W promised to pay the bill, but later refused to do so. Is he obligated to pay?

3. D was indebted to C in the amount of $10,000 and the indebtedness was past due. C told D if the latter would raise $8,000 and pay him within ten days, he would cancel the debt. Five days later he received D's check for $8,000 marked "Paid in Full" and cashed it. He now desires to recover the remaining $2,000. May he do so?

4. F promised to give his adult son, S, a birthday present of $5,000.

Relying on *F*'s promise, *S* contracted to buy a Thunderbird for $5,500, paying $500 down and promising to pay the balance in one month. When *F* learned of this purchase, he had an argument with *S* and refused to pay *S* the $5,000. Is *F*'s promise enforceable?

5. *A* had a written contract to manage *P*'s hotel for two years at $18,000 a year. At the end of three months *A* received a better offer, whereupon *P* in writing agreed to pay *A* an additional $5,000 if *A* remained the full two year period. At the end of two years, is *P* liable for the $5,000 if *A* remained and did an excellent job during the period?

6. *S* sold *B* 5,000 squares of roofing at $4.75 a square. After the roofing was received but prior to payment, *B* discovered no warranty had been obtained, so he wrote to *S*. *S* by letter guaranteed the roofing for a ten year period, whereupon *B* paid for it. Is the warranty enforceable?

7. *X* pledged $1,000 to State University in a campaign to obtain funds from alumni. Under what circumstances would a court enforce such a pledge?

8. *X* agreed to sell and *Y* agreed to buy 5,000 pairs of shoes at $6.00 per pair. Prior to delivery, *X* notified *Y* that he would be unable to deliver unless *Y* would pay $6.50 per pair which *Y* agreed to do. How much is *X* entitled to receive per pair?

9. *X* purchased a used automobile from *Y* on credit, the original debt being $1,000. *X* discovered that the car had a cracked valve and demanded that *Y* correct it. When *Y* refused to do so, *X* sent *Y* a check for $750 marked paid in full of account. Should *Y* cash the check?

10. *V* agreed with *P* to supply all the coal that *P* desired to buy for one year for *P*'s business, at a price of $20 per ton. The price of coal went up, so *V* notified *P* that *V* would not be able to perform. Nevertheless *P* ordered his normal monthly needs of 200 tons of coal from *V*. If *V* refuses to perform, what rights has *P* against *V*?

10

Capacity of Parties

2-38. Introduction. This chapter is primarily concerned with the legal problems of infants and their parents. Since infants' contracts are voidable, this subject is a portion of the law of voidable contracts, the remainder of which is discussed in the next chapter.

A voidable contract is one that for some reason such as lack of capacity, fraud, misrepresentation or mutual mistake may be disaffirmed by a party. The judicial remedy used by a party to disaffirm or avoid the contract is known as rescission. Rescission is an equitable concept designed to restore the parties to their original position. Voidable contracts should not be confused with illegal contracts or with unenforceable contracts, each of which will be discussed in a subsequent chapter. This latter term refers to situations in which a court will not require a party to perform a contract which is contrary to a statute, violates public policy, or fails to meet the statutory requirements as to the form of the agreement.

The Uniform Commercial Code incorporates the law relative to capacity to contract, fraud, misrepresentation, duress, and mistake as supplementary to its provisions.[C1] Therefore, the materials contained in these chapters on voidable contracts are applicable to all contracts including those under the Code.

2-39. Competent Parties. As previously noted, one of the requirements of a binding contract is competent parties, or parties possessing legal capacity to contract. At common law, married women lacked capacity to contract but this has been changed by statute so that today only infants,

---

C1 *U.C.C.* 1-103.

insane persons, and intoxicated persons are said to lack the legal capacity to contract. It should be noted that corporations may lack capacity or power to enter into certain contracts, which subject is discussed with the materials on Business Organizations. Persons who lack capacity are allowed to avoid their contracts as a matter of social policy to protect such persons. The validity of this policy as it relates to emancipated minors (those freed from parental control) is subject to debate today.

This chapter dealing with capacity is primarily concerned with cases involving minors since such cases predominate and the law concerning insane persons and drunkards is similar to that which governs the rights of infants. It will be considered separately only in those cases in which the rules differ.

2-40. Infant's Contracts. In most states, an infant or minor reaches majority at age 21 although some states have provided that females attain majority at 18. Majority for the purpose of contracting should not be confused with other state statutes which provide for a minimum voting age, drinking age, or age to hold public office. In absence of a statute to the contrary, a person reaches a given age on the day preceding the anniversary of his birth. It must be recognized at the outset that a contract between an infant and an adult is voidable only by the infant; the adult finds his obligation enforceable unless the infant desires to disaffirm.

The law grants minors the power to disaffirm their contracts in order to promote justice and to protect minors from their immaturity, lack of judgment and experience, limited will power, and imprudence.[1] An adult deals with a minor at his peril because the right of a minor to disaffirm a contract is practically absolute, although there are a few statutory exceptions. A minor's only liability is for necessities furnished to him as is discussed in section 2-44 of this chapter. The right to disaffirm exists, irrespective of the fairness or favorability of the contract, and whether or not the adult knew he was dealing with a minor. It even extends to contracts involving two minors. Legislation in many states has altered in a limited way the right of minors to avoid their contracts. Some statutes take away the minor's right to avoid after he marries, and a few give the courts the right to approve freedom of contract upon a showing of maturity. These, and other exceptions to the general rule, may be found in some few states, but in most states the rule allows the minor the right to avoid any contract made during his minority.

A minor's participation in certain business transactions creates difficult questions of conflicting policy. For example, an eighteen-year-old minor appoints his fifty-year-old father to serve as his agent. Should the minor be able to enter into such contracts and, if so, should he be allowed to disaffirm these contracts? The traditional view has been that the appointment of an agent by an infant is absolutely void and that contracts entered into by such an agent have no effect. The tendency of the courts at present, however, seems to be to place contracts of this nature in the

---

[1] *Harvey v. Hadfield,* page 189.

same category as any other agreement of the minor, thus requiring the infant to avoid contracts made by his agent in order to evade liability.

Another difficult problem arises when an infant joins a partnership. The current view is that he may withdraw from the partnership at any time, regardless of the terms of the agreement, and avoid liability in damages to his partners. The capital which he has invested is nevertheless subject to firm debts; therefore, to the extent of the capital which he has invested, he cannot avoid the payment of firm creditors.

2-41. Requirements and Right to Disaffirm. If the contract is purely executory, any act on the part of the infant that clearly indicates an intent to disaffirm the agreement will serve to avoid the contract. Any subsequent suit by the adult will fail as the act will operate as an avoidance of the contract as a matter of law. Even if the contract is fully or partially executed, the infant still has the right to avoid the contract and obtain a return of his consideration. If the infant is in possession of the consideration that has passed to him, he must return it to the other party, as he cannot disaffirm the contract and at the same time retain the benefits. If the minor has the consideration received by him but in a different form—for example, if he has traded it for something else—he is bound to return the consideration which he has, as a basis of his disaffirmance. Since the minor's right to disaffirm is based on equity, he will be considered to be trustee of the consideration until it is returned. Any burdens imposed by the contract upon the infant must continue to be met until he decides to disaffirm the agreement.

The states are somewhat in conflict concerning those cases in which the infant has spent or squandered what he received and is, therefore, unable to return it. The majority of the states hold that the infant may disaffirm the contract and demand the return of the consideration with which he has parted, even though he is unable to return that which he received. Hence, an infant may purchase an automobile, and, after driving it for a year or two, rescind his contract and demand the full amount which he paid for it,[2] or, after having an accident that demolishes it, he may follow the same procedure. A few of the courts, however, hold that if the contract is advantageous to the infant and if the adult has been fair in every respect, the contract cannot be disaffirmed unless the infant returns the consideration which he received.

If a contract involves real property, the right of the infant to disaffirm and regain his property extends to third persons. For example, if a minor sells his farm to Y who in turn sells it to Z, the minor may disaffirm against Z and obtain his farm back. This power to disaffirm against innocent third parties has been eliminated by the Code in cases involving sales of personal property by a minor.

There is a conflict of authority among the courts of the various states as to the effect of a minor misrepresenting his age at the time of the contract. Some states distinguish between contract and tort liability of

2 *Wooldridge v. Hill,* page 190.

minors because they are based on different principles and involve different measures of recovery. In these states if an infant is liable for his torts generally he is liable for deceit in misrepresenting his age in negotiating a contract. In these states, the view is that the deceit does not involve the subject matter of the contract and that the recovery allowed is for the damage resulting to the defrauded person by virtue of the minor's deceit. Therefore the infant is not held liable on the contract in form or substance, but rather because of his tort.

These states regard the common law as a growing institution, keeping pace with social and economic conditions, and believe that the purpose of the rule relating to rescission of contracts of minors is to shield minors against their own folly and inexperience, and against unscrupulous persons. The rule, however, is not designed to give "old" minors a sword with which to wreak injury upon unsuspecting adults. The necessity to protect adults against depredations by minors who knowingly employ fraudulent methods, outweighs the interests of such minors, and, therefore, adults should have available for their protection the remedies not founded on contract.

Other states, however, deny any recovery against the minor because it is felt that the enforcement of the tort liability has the indirect effect of enforcing the contract.[3]

A minor is not deprived of the right to rescind by reason of the fact that he is in business, has all the appearances of an adult, or possesses a business acumen beyond that of the average adult, except as these situations may have been modified by statute in a few states.

A minor is not permitted to avoid a contract in part only, as disaffirmance must be in total or not at all.

2-42. Time of Disaffirmance. With the exception of sales of real estate by a minor, an infant may avoid his contract at any time during his minority and demand the return of any consideration with which he has parted. This right continues for a reasonable time after he becomes of age providing he has performed no act of ratification after he has reached majority. What constitutes a reasonable time depends upon the nature of the property involved and upon the surrounding circumstances. In the case of real estate sold by the infant, it may be as long as two years in some states.

A minor cannot disaffirm a sale of his real estate and recover his title until after he reaches his majority. This provision is based on the fact that the land will always be there and therefore he cannot be materially injured by being forced to wait until he becomes of age. He may, however, prior to disaffirmance, enter into possession and take over the management of the property, thus appropriating to himself the income from it while title rests in the adult. Where the minor does not avail himself of this protection, many states will permit him at the time of disaffirmance of the sale of real estate to recover from the adult the income received from the property while the minor has been out of possession.

[3] *Lesnick v. Pratt*, page 192.

2-43. Ratification. An executed contract is ratified by a person who entered into it as a minor, when he retains the consideration received for an unreasonable time after he reaches majority. Ratification also results from acceptance of the benefits incident to ownership, such as rents, dividends, or interest; a sale of the property received; [4] or from any other act, after he becomes of age, which clearly indicates his satisfaction with the bargain made during his minority. A contract which is wholly executory is disaffirmed by continued silence or inaction by the former minor after majority.

A majority of the states hold that ratification is impossible unless the minor knows of his right to disaffirm at the time of the alleged act of ratification but inaction for an unreasonable length of time will constitute a ratification of an executed contract irrespective of knowledge of the right to disaffirm. In no state is ratification possible until the minor reaches his majority, since action prior to that date could always be avoided.

2-44. Liability for Necessaries. As previously noted, a minor is liable for necessaries furnished to him. Some courts state that a minor is bound on contracts for necessities [5] indicating that his liability is at the contract price, but the better view is that the minor's actual liability is in quasi contract for the reasonable value of necessities actually received. Whether a given contract involves a necessity is a question of law for the court and will not be submitted to a jury as a question of fact. Necessaries within the rule include such things as clothing, food, lodging, medical care and a certain amount of education.

In determining if a given item is a necessity, the court must consider the needs of the minor and it is possible for a contract to involve an item which is usually a necessity but which in a particular case is not. For example, if an infant is already possessed of four suits of clothes and his station in life does not demand more, or if he is adequately supplied with clothes by a parent or a guardian, another suit cannot be considered a necessary, although, as a general rule, clothing falls within the list of necessaries.

While in the Mitchell case, *supra,* the court held that an automobile was not a necessity, there are situations in which a court might hold to the contrary. As more and more "infants" are married, the scope of necessities is gradually being broadened by the courts. For example, an automobile or farm machinery which is used by a minor to earn his living may be held to be a necessity.

Modern legal concepts have by decision and statute broadened some areas of contractual liability for minors. For example, most states have statutes which provide that life insurance contracts entered into by infants, and contracts with universities for room and board, are binding obligations. However, the general rule still exists that minors are not

---

[4] *Camp v. Bank of Bentonville,* page 193.
[5] *Mitchell v. The Campbell and Fetter Bank,* page 194.

liable for business contracts such as for money borrowed. Adults dealing with minors should do so only through a properly authorized guardian.

2-45. Parent's Liability for Infant's Contract. Many persons labor under a misapprehension concerning the parent's liability for the contracts of an infant. The parent is liable on a contract made by a minor only when the minor is acting as the duly authorized agent of the parent or when the parent becomes a party to the contract. It should also be noted that the parent has a duty to support his minor children, and having failed in this duty, he is responsible for any necessaries furnished the infant by third parties. For example, a parent is responsible for medical care furnished a minor child. It should be noted also that the parent is entitled to any compensation which an infant earns unless the parent has in some manner surrendered this right. Payment to the infant does not discharge this duty owed to his parent unless the parent has authorized the payment or has left the minor to support himself. (This is very important in the settlement of tort claims for loss of income during minority. Any release must come from the parent.) This latter is known as emancipation, and the minor, having assumed the obligation to support himself, is entitled to the compensation earned by his services.

2-46. Infant's Torts. An infant may be held liable for his own torts depending in part on his age and the nature of the tort involved.[6] If the tort is intentional, he has liability at all ages unless some necessary element of the tort is necessarily lacking in the child. At common law and in many states, a child under the age of seven is conclusively presumed to be incapable of negligence and from ages seven to ten a child is presumed to be incapable but the presumption may be rebutted. If the child is older than ten, he is treated as any other person in so far as his torts are concerned. Some states use the age fourteen instead of ten for these rules.

Another area of substantial misunderstanding of the law is concerned with parents' liability for the torts of their children. As a general rule, a parent is not responsible for the torts of his child; he is liable only if the child is acting as an agent of the parent or if the parent is himself at fault. For example, the parent is responsible for his children's torts if they are committed at his direction or in his presence when the children should have been controlled.[7] In addition, some states have adopted the family purpose doctrine which provides that when an automobile is maintained by the owner for the pleasure and convenience of his family, a member of the family including an infant who uses it for his own pleasure or convenience is the owner's agent and the owner is responsible for his negligence. This is a minority view, however.

2-47. Other Persons Lacking Capacity. Contracts of insane persons, according to the view of most courts, are voidable much the same as those of infants. There is a tendency to go a step further and hold that, pro-

[6] *Jorgensen v. Nudelman,* page 196.
[7] *Gissen v. Goodwill,* page 197.

vided the contract is reasonable and no advantage has been taken of the disabled party's condition, an insane person cannot disaffirm unless he can return the consideration received. The appointment of a conservator for an insane person vests the conservator with full control over the property of his charge. For this reason any contracts made by a lunatic after such an appointment are absolutely void and not merely voidable.

If a person becomes so intoxicated as to be incapable of understanding the effect of his action, he is thereby incapacitated, and his contracts are voidable. They differ from those of the infant and the insane person in that these contracts cannot be disaffirmed against a third party who has subsequently in good faith purchased the property which was sold by such an intoxicated person. Drunkards, like infants, are liable in quasi contract for necessaries.

CAPACITY OF PARTIES CASES

Harvey v. Hadfield
1962 (Utah) 372 P.2d 985

CROCKETT. J.   Plaintiff, a minor, sues by his guardian *ad litem* to recover $1,000 he had advanced defendant under a proposed contract to buy a house-trailer. From adverse judgment he appeals.

Plaintiff, a student attending college at Logan, turned 19 years of age on the 13th day of October, 1959. A few days after his birthday he quit school and got a job. In the latter part of October he went to the defendant's lot and selected a trailer he liked. He told the defendant of the above facts, of his plans to be married, and of his desire to buy the trailer. The defendant advised him that he would have to get his father's signature to get financing through the defendant.

Plaintiff responded that he thought he could arrange financing and that he could raise a thousand dollars as a down payment. He paid $500 on November 6 and another $500 on November 13 and applied for financing at the bank. The bank finally refused to accept his application for a loan because of his minority and because his father would not sign with him.

After plaintiff's plans failed to materialize, he asked the defendant to return his money. Defendant refused but finally did agree to a statement which the plaintiff typed up and which both signed. It released the trailer in question for sale and granted plaintiff $1,000 (plus interest) credit on a trailer of his choice the next spring. About February 1, 1960, plaintiff's attorney sent a letter to the defendant disaffirming the contract and demanding the return of his money. Upon refusal, this suit was commenced.

Since time immemorial courts have quite generally recognized the justice and propriety of refusing to enforce contracts against minors, except for necessities. It is fair to assume that because of their immaturity they may lack the judgment, experience, and will power which they should have to bind themselves to what may turn out to be burdensome and long-lasting obligations. Consequently, courts are properly solicitous of their rights and afford them protection from being taken advantage of by designing persons, and from their own imprudent acts, by allowing them to disaffirm contracts entered into during minority which upon more mature reflection they conclude are undesirable. We agree that justice requires that minors have such protection. It is the responsibility of our courts to so safeguard their rights until they have attained their majority and thus presumably have the maturity of judgment necessary to deal with opposing parties on equal terms so that it is fair and equitable to bind them by their acts. Accordingly, adults dealing with minors must be deemed to do so in an awareness of the privilege the law affords the minor of disaffirming his contracts. The rule relating to disaffirmance is codified in our law, Sec. 15-2-2, U.C.A.1953:

> A minor is bound not only for reasonable value of necessaries but also by his contracts, unless he disaffirms them before or within a reasonable time after he attains his majority and restores to the other party all money or property received by him by virtue of said contracts and remaining within his control at any time after attaining his majority.

Defendant advances the following propositions which he claims exclude this case from the general rule allowing a minor to disaffirm:

. . . That even if the contract be disaffirmed, he is entitled to an offset of the actual damages he has sustained from loss of sale of the trailer from the $1,000.

. . . Defendant urges that from the fact that the plaintiff was "on his own," living away from home, working, and contemplating marriage, he could reasonably regard him as "engaged in business as an adult" and that he was therefore capable of entering into a binding contract. The defendant's position is not sound. . . .

Our statute cannot be construed to support the defendant's contention that the disaffirming minor must compensate him for damages he may have incurred. Sec. 15-2-2, U.C.A.1953, hereinabove quoted, requires only that the minor restore "to the other party all money or property received by him by virtue of said contracts and remaining within his control at any time after attaining his majority." The trailer was left in the possession of the defendant. That fulfills the requirement of the statute.

The plaintiff minor having disaffirmed the contract is entitled to the return of his money. *The judgment is reversed. Costs to Plaintiff (appellant).*

Wooldridge v. Hill

1953 (Ind. App.) 114 N.E.2d 646

The plaintiff, Wooldridge, sued to recover from the defendant $530 which he had paid the latter on the price of an automobile, the plaintiff being 17 years of age at the time of sale. Six months after the purchase he notified defendant of his desire to rescind and returned the auto. The lower court gave plaintiff judgment for $280 only and he appealed.

CRUMPACKER, J. . . . A careful examination of the record reveals testimony to the effect that at the time of the occurrences in question the appellant was a hired hand on the appellee's farm. He was still in high school and during the school year the appellee paid him $10 per week, room, board and laundry. During vacations in the summer his cash wages were increased to $20 per week. He had, on occasions, told the appellee of his desire to buy an automobile so that "I wouldn't have to depend on the other fellows to take me all the time." As a result of these conversations the appellant and appellee, on October 4, 1950, went to the place of business of a man named Alexander who owned the automobile here involved. The appellee told the appellant on the occasion that if he wanted the car he would buy it for him and that he could pay for it at the rate of $5 per week and when he got it paid for he, the appellee, would transfer title to him but in the meantime he would retain title in himself. That was agreeable to the appellant and the appellee bought the car from Alexander for $1,350 and delivered it to the appellant under the above arrangement. The appellant thereupon gave the appellee his check in the sum of $400, designated "car payment," which the appellee subsequently cashed. Thereafter the appellant made weekly payments aggregating $130 to April 7, 1951, when he left the appellee's employ and delivered the car into his possession. On May 5, 1951, he gave the appellee written notice of his disaffirmance of the contract between them and demanded his money back. . . .

This brings us to the consideration of appellant's right to a new trial because of the contention that the amount of his recovery was too small or because there is no evidence upon which the court could fix his damage at $280. It was held in *McKee v. Harwood Automotive Co.* (1932, 204 Ind. 233, 183 N.E. 646), that where an infant 19 years old rescinded his contract to purchase an automobile and returned the same to the seller, in the absence of any evidence showing that it was a "necessary" or used in gaining a livelihood, the infant's liability to pay the contract price was thereby extinguished and the court approved the infant's recovery of all monies paid on the contract.

There is no contention in this case that the automobile involved was a "necessary" or that it was used by the appellant in gaining his livelihood, and, in view of the fact that there is no dispute that he paid the appellee $530 under the purchase agreement, it is difficult to understand the basis upon which the court assessed his damages at $280. There is no evidence in the record, direct or inferential, upon which such a recovery can be sustained. We suspect, however, that the court concluded that these proceedings, though brought in law, should be determined under equitable principles and as the appellant had had the use of the automobile for approximately six months he ought, in good conscience, to pay something for its use and the natural wear and tear incidental thereto as in no other way could both parties be placed in statu quo. Equitable as such a decision may be it is not sanctioned by the law of

Indiana. This court, in *Story & Clark Piano Co. v. Davy* (1918, 68 Ind. App. 150, 119 N.E. 177, 180), quoted with approval the following excerpt from *McCarthy v. Henderson* (1885, 138 Mass. 310):

> It is clear that, if the plaintiff had made no advance, the defendants could not maintain an action against him for the use of the property. The contract, express or implied, to pay for such use is one he is incapable of making, and his infancy would be a bar to such suit. We cannot see how the defendants can avail themselves of and enforce, by way of recoupment, a claim which they could not enforce by a direct suit.

It is our considered judgment that the decision of the court in this case is contrary to law. *It is therefore reversed and the cause remanded to the Rush Circuit Court with instructions to sustain the appellant's motion for a new trial.*

Lesnick et al. v. Pratt

1951 (Vt.) 78 A.2d 487

CLEARY, J.   . . . This is an action of tort for fraud and deceit involving the sale of an automobile to the plaintiff by the defendant (Pratt). The defendant pleaded infancy. Trial was by the court with judgment for the plaintiffs. Both parties excepted.

The findings of fact show that at the time of the sale on January 20, 1949, the defendant falsely and fraudulently represented that the automobile was fully paid for and was free of liens and encumbrances and on September 13, 1949, the plaintiffs were obliged to pay the balance owing on a conditional sale contract which the defendant had signed when he purchased the automobile on January 10, 1949. The defendant was born on July 29, 1928, so when he bought the automobile and when he sold it to the plaintiffs he was a minor.

Thus it is clear that the cause of action arises out of a contract and, as this court said in *West v. Moore* (14 Vt. 447, 450): "It is for us to declare the law as we find it." In that case, which was trespass on the case for false warranty in the sale of a horse, this Court held: "Though an infant is liable for positive wrongs, and constructive torts, or frauds, yet, to charge him, the fraudulent act must be wholly tortious. If the matter arises from contract, though the transaction is infected with fraud, it cannot be turned into a tort to charge the infant by a change in the form of action."

In *Gilson v. Spear* (38 Vt. 311), another case for deceit, or fraudulent concealment of unsoundness in the sale of a horse, and a plea of infancy, where both the English and American cases on the subject are collected and discussed, this Court held 38 Vt. at page 315: "We think that the fair result of the American as well as of the English cases is that an infant is liable in an action *ex delicto* for an actual and wilful fraud only in cases in which the form of action does not suppose that a contract has existed; but that where the gravamen of the fraud consists in a transaction which really originated in contract the plea of infancy is a good defense. For

simple deceit on a contract of sale or exchange, there is no cause of action unless some damage or injury results from it, and proof of damage
could not be made without referring to and proving the contract. An
action on the case for deceit on a sale is an affirmance by the plaintiff of
the contract of sale, and the liability of the defendant in such an action
could not be established without taking notice of and proving the contract." That case then repeats and adopts the principle as stated in *West
v. Moore, supra.* . . .

We are governed by the law we have quoted. If modern youth has become so sophisticated that he no longer needs protection from his contracts or public opinion demands that the long recognized rule be
changed, it can be done by statute. We are constrained to hold that the
plea of infancy in the present case was a full defense. Therefore, it is unnecessary to consider other questions raised by the exceptions.

*Judgment reversed and judgment for the defendant to recover his
costs.*

Camp v. Bank of Bentonville

1959 (Ark.) 323 S.W.2d 556

McFADDIN, J.   Jerry Lee Camp appeals from a decree of the
Chancery Court which found that Camp, now of lawful age, had ratified
a debt which he made while a minor. The question is whether Camp's
acts under the circumstances here shown were sufficient to support the
decree holding that there had been ratification.

On January 9, 1957, Camp executed his note to A. V. Bright, doing
business as "Bright's Used Cars," for $3,000 [probably for the truck], pay-
able $125 per month until paid in full. The note was secured by a chattel
mortgage covering: (a) one 1952 2-ton Chevrolet truck; (b) one 1954
Plymouth sedan; (c) miscellaneous stock of automotive parts valued at
$500; and (d) eleven cows and increase. Bright immediately and uncon-
ditionally transferred the note and mortgage to the appellee, Bank of
Bentonville (hereinafter called "Bank"). The payments made to the Bank
on the note were:

Date	Amount	Nature of Payment
2/25/57	$ 50.00	Cash.
3/20/57	100.00	Cash.
4/20/57	800.00	Proceeds of sale of Plymouth car.
5/ 1/57	47.52	Return of insurance premium cancelled when Plymouth car was sold.
7/ 1/57	51.00	Probably cash.
11/ 8/57	102.00	To be discussed later in this opinion.
12/ 9/57	100.00	To be discussed later in this opinion.
12/13/57	56.00	To be discussed later in this opinion.

When Camp defaulted, the Bank filed suit for judgment and foreclosure of the mortgage. Camp's defense was: that he was not 21 years
of age until August 19, 1957; that the three payments credited on the note

thereafter (i.e. November 8th, December 9th, and December 13th) were not sufficient to constitute ratification; and that he now disaffirmed the entire transaction. The said three payments came about in this manner: each was made to the Bank by A. V. Bright from money due by him to Camp, and each payment was made with Camp's implied consent. The $100 on December 9, 1957, was part of the proceeds of the sale of a car. The payments of November 8th and December 13th were for money that Bright owed Camp for work. Camp was doing considerable hauling of some kind for Bright, and Bright, with Camp's implied consent, made the two payments on the dates mentioned.

The Chancery Court held that Camp, after reaching full age, had ratified the note and mortgage; and under all the facts and circumstances here existing, we cannot say that the Chancery Court was in error. . . .

From our own cases, and from all of the foregoing [cases in other states], we are not willing to hold that payment after reaching full age is, in itself, sufficient to constitute ratification as a matter of law: rather, we think the better rule is, to examine each case on its own facts and determine whether payment, along with all the other facts and circumstances, constitutes ratification. We have done that in the case at bar. There is no claim of any kind that Bright ever imposed on Camp when the note and mortgage were executed on January 9, 1957. Camp was working for Bright all along; and thought he was of full age, as he considered eighteen to be the lawful age. It was not until after this suit was filed and he had consulted an attorney that he ever had any idea of disaffirmance of any part of the trade. This is the case of a man who was doing his own work, carrying on his own business, making trades in which there is no claim that he was imposed on, and who, after reaching 21, continued to make payments on the obligation, with no thought of disaffirming the transaction. Under all these facts and circumstances, we reach the conclusion that Camp, after reaching full age, ratified the particular transaction here involved.

Affirmed.

Mitchell v. The Campbell and Fetter Bank

1964 (Ind. A.C.) 195 N.E.(2) 489

Appellees sued the appellant, a minor, to recover the balance due on a conditional sales contract for the purchase of an automobile. The bank had purchased the conditional sales contract from the car dealer to whom the appellant, Mitchell, has represented that he was 21 when in fact his true age was 19. Mitchell seeks to avoid his liability because of his minority and in addition seeks to recover back the auto traded in to the car dealer and his down payment. The plaintiff contends that Mitchell appeared to be an adult, was about to be married, and that therefore the automobile was a necessity. The lower court held for the bank and Mitchell appeals.

KELLEY, J. Adhering to the long established rule in this state, we have just recently held in *Bowling etc. v. Sperry etc.* (1962, 133 Ind.App. 692, 184 N.E.2d 901), that

> . . . the contracts of minors are voidable and may be disaffirmed. It is not necessary that the other party be placed *in statu quo,* nor is it necessary that the minor tender back the money or property he has received before suing for the value or possession of the money or property given by him to the adult.

However, a minor is bound on his contract for necessaries furnished to him. Whether the goods contracted for or furnished to the minor are necessaries is a question of law for the court. . . .

In the case of *Bowling etc. v. Sperry etc., supra,* we were confronted with the question of whether the automobile purchased by the minor appellant was a necessity. We therein set forth the definition of necessaries as provided in § 58-102, Burns' 1961 Replacement:

> Necessaries in this section means goods suitable to the condition in life of such infant or other person, and to his actual requirements at the time of delivery.

We quoted the definition found in *Price et al. v. Sanders et al.* (1878, 60 Ind. 310, 314):

> "Necessaries," in the technical sense, mean such things as are necessary to the support, use or comfort of the person of the minor, as food, raiment, lodging, medical attendance, and such personal comforts as comport with his condition and circumstances in life, including a common school education; but it has been pithily and happily said, that necessaries do not include "horses, saddles, bridles, liquors, pistols, powder, whips and fiddles."

Further, we made adoptive reference to the statement concerning necessaries which appears in 27 Am.Jur., Infants, § 17, pp. 760, 761, as follows:

> Aside from such things as are obviously for maintenance of existence, what are or what are not necessaries for an infant depends on what is reasonably necessary for the proper and suitable maintenance of the infant in view of his social position and situation in life, the customs of the social circle in which he moves or is likely to move, and the fortune possessed by him and by his parents. It has been said that articles of mere luxury or adornment cannot be included but that useful articles, although of an expensive and luxurious character, may be included if they are reasonable in view of the infant's circumstances. The necessities to be procured by the contract must be personal necessities, that is, for the living or personal well-being of the infant . . . What is furnished to the infant must be suitable, not only to his condition in life, but also to his actual requirements at the time—in other words, the infant must not have at the time of delivery an adequate supply from other sources. To be liable for articles as necessaries, an infant must be in actual need of them, and obliged to procure them for himself.

There being no evidence to support any finding that the automobile was a necessity, the judgment is reversed and a new trial ordered.

Jorgensen v. Nudelman
1963 (Ill. A.C.) 195 N.E.(2) 422

ENGLISH, P. J.   The complaint, brought on behalf of a nine-year-old girl, alleged that defendant, a six-year-old boy, struck her with a stone, causing loss of sight in one eye. Defendant's motion for summary judgment was allowed and the complaint was dismissed by the trial court which held that defendant as a matter of law was conclusively presumed not responsible for his alleged tortious conduct because he was less than seven years of age. . . .

We shall first consider Count II of the complaint which charges that the act of throwing the stone was negligent. In *Seaburg v. Williams* (23 Ill.App.2d 25, 30, 161 N.E.2d, 576) in a somewhat different setting, the court said:

> [W]e would have no hesitancy in holding that a minor under the age of seven years is conclusively presumed to be incapable of negligent conduct for the same reasons assigned for holding that a minor of the same age is conclusively presumed to be incapable of contributory negligence.

.   .   .

Plaintiff concedes that Illinois has long recognized the common law rule that a child under seven is conclusively presumed to be incapable of contributory negligence. Plaintiff argues, however, that this rule is arbitrary—with which we agree—and that it should, therefore, not be applied as a shield on behalf of a defendant—with which we do not agree.

The basis for the contributory negligence rule is the concept that in a child of such tender years his capacity for reasoning is inadequately developed for the task of sorting out the consequences of his actions. Surely this condition of immaturity is a fact which must be related to the acts of the child regardless of whether, as a litigant, he is to be called plaintiff or defendant. . . .

Count I alleges that defendant "wrongfully and unlawfully, with force and arms . . . assaulted the plaintiff" by hitting plaintiff with a stone. We believe this alleges a non-negligent or intentional tort. . . . The Seaburg plaintiff alleged that a five-year-old boy burned down his garage. The Appellate Court reversed the dismissal of the cause, holding the complaint to be sufficient. The basis for its holding apparently was the rule for which support was found at the common law: a child is civilly liable for torts, unconnected with his contracts, unless in the commission of the tort there is required to exist some element which the infant is presumed not to possess.

The court believed, as we do, that no element of an intentional tort was necessarily lacking in the child. It was a question of fact whether the particular child had the capacity to intend the act and possessed that intention.

The court in *Ellis v. D'Angelo* (116 Cal. App.2d 310, 253 P.2d 675 (1953)), held that a count for battery of a babysitter by a four-year-old boy was legally sufficient.

In *Garratt v. Dailey* (46 Wash.2d 197, 279 P.2d 1091, 1094 (1955)), suit was brought against a five-year-old child for injuries caused to plaintiff when defendant removed a chair from the place where plaintiff was about to sit down. In remanding for clarification of facts the Supreme Court held that "[a] battery would be established if, in addition to plaintiff's fall, it was proved that, when [defendant] moved the chair, he knew with substantial certainty that the plaintiff would attempt to sit down where the chair had been."

The reason for the distinction between the two types of torts arises from the different degrees of maturity required to appreciate the consequences of negligence as against intentional harm. We believe that while a six-year-old child is incapable of realizing that his carelessness might foreseeably lead to another's injury, the same child may have the capacity to intend an injurious act. . . .

Affirmed in part, reversed in part, and remanded with directions.

Gissen v. Goodwill

1955 (Florida) 80 S.2d 701

Gissen, the plaintiff and appellant, sued the defendant for injuries sustained from acts of the defendant's daughter. The lower court gave judgment for defendant and plaintiff appealed.

KANNER, J. . . . It is averred in the second amended complaint that at the time of the appellant's injury, he was employed as a clerk at the Gaylord Hotel in the City of Miami Beach, Florida, and the appellees were residing as business invitees at the same hotel; that the minor child, Geraldine Goodwill, 8 years of age, "did wilfully, deliberately, intentionally and maliciously" swing a door "with such great force and violence against the plaintiff so that the middle finger on plaintiff's left hand was caught in the door and a portion of said finger was caused to be instantaneously severed and fell to the floor. . . ."

It is a basic and established law that a parent is not liable for the tort of his minor child because of the mere fact of his paternity. However, there are certain broadly defined exceptions wherein a parent may incur liability: 1. Where he intrusts his child with an instrumentality which, because of lack of age, judgment, or experience of the child, may become a source of danger to others. 2. Where a child, in the commission of a tortious act, is occupying the relationship of a servant or agent of its parents. 3. Where the parent knows of his child's wrongdoing and consents to it, directs, or sanctions it. 4. Where he fails to exercise parental control over his minor child, although he knows or in the exercise of due care should have known that injury to another is a probable consequence.

Analyzing this problem in the light of the exceptions for parent liability enumerated, one may note that the exceptions relating to instrumentality intrusted to a child, to master and servant or agent relationship, and to parental consent or sanction of a tortious act by the child do not bear upon the circumstances here involved. It is only the fourth category which may be logically analyzed for the purpose of determining whether legal culpability might be attached to the parents of the child here concerned, and it is on this exception to the general rule that the appellant relies. . . .

An analysis of cases related to or bearing upon the type of case that we have here is necessary in order to determine whether the second amended complaint states a cause of action or whether it is deficient for the reason urged by the appellees.

In the case of *Bateman v. Crim* (D.C. Mun. App., 34 A.2d 257), the question concerned the liability of the parents of two boys, 10 and 12 years of age, who, while playing on the sidewalk with a football, collided with plaintiff, injuring her. The court instructed verdict for the parents, which verdict was affirmed on appeal. Plaintiff claimed that a parent's failure to exercise proper supervision, notwithstanding lack of evidence of prior unrestrained conduct, renders liability to parents for acts of a minor which would have been averted through adequate supervision and that whether proper supervision had been employed was in such case a question of fact for the jury. Nevertheless, the court stated that there was no evidence that either boy had previously played with a football on public streets or conducted himself in a disorderly manner; and that in order to attribute to a parent responsibility for injuries resulting from his minor child's wrongful deed, parent's negligence in exercising parental restraint must have some *specific relation to the act complained of,* and that such was lacking in this case. . . .

One common factor from the foregoing case appears salient in the assessment of liability to the parents, that the child had the habit of doing the particular type of wrongful act which resulted in the injury complained of. In the instant case, the cause of action sought to establish fails in that the negligence charged with relation to parental restraint is not claimed to flow from the commission of an act or course of conduct which the child habitually engaged in and which led to the appellant's injury. It is nowhere claimed that the child here involved had a propensity to swing or slam doors at the hazard of persons using such doors. The deed of a child, the enactment of which results in harm to another and which is unrelated to any previous act or acts of the child, cannot be laid at the door of the parents simply because the child happened to be born theirs. However, a wrongful act by an infant which climaxes a course of conduct involving similar acts may lead to the parents' accountability. A deed brought on by a totally unexpected reaction to a situation which is isolated in origin and provocation could not have been foretold or averted and hence could not render the parents responsible.

Therefore, from the allegations of the second amended complaint, it is not made to appear that the injury claimed to have been sustained by the appellant was a natural and probable consequence of negligence on the part of the appellee parents.

The judgment of the court below is affirmed.

CHAPTER 10
REVIEW QUESTIONS AND PROBLEMS

1. *M,* a minor, purchased and paid $93 on a diamond engagement ring, *J* being the seller. The engagement was later terminated, but the girl refused to return the ring to *M*. *M,* nevertheless, seeks to avoid his contract with *J* and recover the down payment. Is he entitled to do so?

2. A minor purchased a car by giving his age as 23. After making one payment in addition to the down payment, he defaulted and the seller repossessed. May the minor rescind and recover the payments made?

3. *A* entered into a contract to convey his farm Blackacre to *B,* a minor, for $10,000 payment to be in equal installments of $1,000 for 10 years. After *B* had paid two installments, *A* learned *B* was a minor, refused to accept the third installment, and informed *B* he was going to terminate the contract. *B* sued for specific performance. What result?

4. *M,* a minor, purchased and paid for a radio, the price being $350. Thirty days later, an electrical storm severely damaged the radio and *M* desires to return it and obtain the purchase price from the seller. Is he entitled to do so?

5. *M,* a minor, paid $900 for a three year policy of term life insurance. At the end of three years, *M* seeks to rescind and recover the $900. May he do so?

6. *M,* a minor, contracted to buy a truck from *A* Co. for his transfer business, paying for it in thirty-six installments. He became of age on March 1 and on March 2 paid his sixth installment. On March 10, *M* seeks to avoid the contract by offering to return the truck. May he do so?

7. *X,* a minor, driving the family car to a high school social event, negligently injures *Y*. *Y* sues *X*'s parents for the tort. What result?

8. *H* and *W,* minors, are married college students. The *X* grocery store allowed them to charge groceries and when *H* and *W* failed to pay their account, *X* brought suit for the total amount against their parents. What result?

9. *M* purchased a suit from the *X* clothing store that had to be altered. *M* paid for the suit at the time of purchase. When *M* stopped to pick up the suit he decided that he didn't like it and demanded his money back. Is he entitled to it?

11

Reality of Assent

2-48. Introduction. The preceding chapter was concerned with the rights and liabilities of persons lacking capacity and especially the right of minors to disaffirm or avoid contracts. There are several additional reasons or situations in which one party or the other may avoid or disaffirm a contract. In addition to lack of capacity, the other grounds for avoiding contracts are fraud, misrepresentation, bilateral mistake, and lack of free will of one of the parties. These matters are discussed in this chapter.

FRAUD

2-49. Definition. Fraud and misrepresentation possess the same legal characteristics and requirements except one, and are therefore discussed concurrently. Fraud consists of an intentional misstatement of a material existing fact which is justifiably relied upon by another to his damage.[1] Fraud may be present, however, in situations which involve no direct misstatement of fact. For example, concealment or suppression of material facts is as fraudulent as is a positive direct misstatement. Fraud must be proven by the party alleging it by clear and convincing evidence and is never presumed. The sections which follow discuss each element of actionable fraud and misrepresentation. Every element must be present before appropriate relief is available.

[1] *Channel Master Corporation v. Aluminum Limited Sales, Inc.,* page 206.

2-50. Intention to Mislead. Intention to mislead, *scienter,* is the characteristic which distinguishes fraud from unintentional misrepresentation, usually referred to simply as misrepresentation. Intention to mislead is based on the state of mind of the party allegedly guilty of fraud. The legal term *scienter* is frequently used by courts to describe this element of fraud, *scienter* being defined as "knowingly making a false statement." Intention to mislead may also be established by showing that a statement was made with such reckless disregard as to whether it is true or false that intention to mislead may be inferred.[2] This is usually present where there is a special duty of care running from the representor to the representee. Reckless disregard for the truth is thus made the equivalent of scienter.

Intention to mislead is the one element which distinguishes fraud from misrepresentation; otherwise the same legal principles apply to both and the discussion which follows is therefore applicable to each.

2-51. Misstatement of Fact. An actual or implied false representation of a matter of fact relating to the present or to the past and which is material to the transaction is the gist of fraud. False statements of opinion, of conditions to exist in the future, or of matters promissory in nature will not, even if the other elements are present, constitute fraud.[3] Every failure to perform a promise obviously is not fraudulent but failure to perform the promise justifies a suit for breach of contract. However, if the promisor never intended to carry out his promise at the time he made it, he misstated his intention and fraud results. This misstatement of fact must be material or significant to the extent that it has a moving influence upon the contracting party but it need not be the sole inducing cause for entering into the contract.

False statements as to matters of opinion such as the representation as to value of property are not considered actionable. Whether a particular statement is one of fact or opinion is a question of fact for the jury. If there is a confidential or fiduciary relationship between the seller and the buyer the ordinary doctrine of "puffing" does not apply.

The misstatement may be oral and may in fact be true in part. A half truth or partial truth which has the net effect of misleading may form the basis of fraud just as if it were entirely false. The untruth may be the result of a series of statements, the net result of which is to mislead. Although each statement, taken alone, may be true, there is fraud if all of them, taken together, tend to mislead the party to whom the statements are made. A partial truth, in response to a request for information, becomes an untruth whenever it creates a false impression and is designed to do so.

An intentional misrepresentation of existing local or state law affords no basis for rescission, since the law is, presumably, a matter of common knowledge, open and available to all who desire to explore its mysteries. A misstatement as to the law of another state or nation, however, is one of fact and may be used as a basis for redress.

2 *Wire & Textile Machinery, Inc. v. Robinson,* page 207.
3 *Barrett Associates, Inc. v. Aronson,* page 208.

As was previously noted, a misrepresentation may be made by conduct as well as by language. Any physical act which has for its ultimate object the concealment of the true facts relating to the property involved in a contract is, in effect, a misstatement. One who turns back the speedometer on a car, fills a motor with heavy grease to keep it from knocking, or paints over an apparent defect—in each case concealing an important fact—asserts an untrue fact as effectively as though speaking. Such conduct, if it misleads the other party, amounts to fraud and makes rescision or an action for damages possible.

2-52. Silence as Fraud. In the absence of a fiduciary relationship—one of trust and confidence, such as exists between principal and agent or guardian and ward—neither party to an agreement is under any duty to inform the other party of special facts and circumstances that might vitally affect the value of the subject matter under consideration and are known only to him. In other words, silence, of and by itself, does not constitute fraud. To this rule exceptions exist: For example, it is the duty of the vendor of property who knows of a latent defect [4]—one which is not apparent upon inspection—to inform the purchaser of the defect; also, a person who has misstated an important fact on some previous occasion is obligated to correct the statement when negotiations are renewed or as soon as he learns about it.

The gist of these exceptions is that one of the parties rests under the erroneous impression that certain things are true, whereas the other party is aware that they are not true and also knows of the misunderstanding and it therefore becomes his duty to disclose the truth. There is a tendency to hold that fraud exists under these circumstances. A typical illustration involves the sale of farm land for a lump sum when the buyer indicates that he thinks there are 80 acres in the tract. If the seller knows that there are only 60 acres in the particular property, he is duty-bound to notify the buyer of that fact. Similarly, if there had previously been a house on the tract, but, unknown to the buyer, it had been destroyed, the seller, provided he is in possession of the information, should make known such fact to the buyer. This does not mean that a potential seller or buyer has to disclose all the factors about the value of property that are in his possession. It is only where he knows that the other party to the agreement is harboring a misunderstanding relative to some vital matter that the duty to speak arises.

2-53. Justifiable Reliance. Before a false statement of fact can be considered fraudulent, the party to whom it is made must reasonably believe it to be true, must act thereon to his damage, and in so acting must rely on the truth of statement. If an investigation is made which reveals the falsity, fraud is not present. The cases are somewhat in conflict as to the need to investigate. Some courts have indicated that, if all the information is readily available for ascertaining the truth of statements,

[4] *Bryant v. Troutman,* page 209.

reliance upon the misrepresentation is not justified. In such a case the party is said to be negligent in not taking advantage of the facilities available for confirmation of the untrue statement.

Thus, if a party inspects property, he is not misled if a reasonable investigation would reveal untruths with regard to its condition even though his investigation is inadequate. On the other hand, some courts have stated that one who by misrepresentation has induced another to act to the other's prejudice cannot impute negligence to the other merely because of the other's reliance on the misrepresentation. Nor can he relieve himself of liability in advance by a disclaimer. However, all courts generally agree that reliance is justified except where no substantial effort or expense is required to determine the true facts.

2-54. Injury or Damage. In order to establish fraud, the party relying upon the misstatement must offer proof of resulting damage. Normally such damage is proved by evidence which indicates that the contract would have been more valuable provided the statements had been true but actual proof of damage must be shown in an action at law for deceit. Injury results where the party is not in as good a position as he would have been had the statements been true. Where fraud is established, a party may rescind all related contracts with the other party as fraud is said to vitiate all contracts between the parties.

2-55. Remedies. Fraud gives to the injured party a choice of two basic remedies—a tort action of deceit for damages and rescission. In addition, if the contract is executory, he may plead fraud as a defense in the event action is brought against him. Where the contract has been executed, he may demand a rescission and a return of the consideration parted with, in which case he must offer to restore the consideration which he has received,[5] or he may bring a tort action of deceit to recover the dollar damages he has suffered by reason of the fraud.

It should be noted that rescission is permitted only in case the defrauded party acts with reasonable promptness after he learns of the fraud. Undue delay on his part effects a waiver of his right to rescind, thus limiting the defrauded party to recovery of damages. Ignorance of the right to rescind does not prevent his conduct from constituting an election to retain the benefits of a contract which might have been rescinded for fraud. A victim of fraud may in effect ratify the agreement if, after having acquired knowledge of the fraud, he manifests an intention to affirm or exercises dominion of things which he would have to give up in order to avoid the contract.

Under the Code, neither rescission of the contract for sale, nor rejection or return of the goods by the buyer is a bar to a suit for dollar damages because of the fraud.[C1] Thus both remedies are available.

The remedy for unintentional misrepresentation is rescission. Since

[5] *Cherry v. Crispin,* page 211.

[C1] *U.C.C.* 2-271.

the gist of the tort action of deceit is "scienter" and this element is missing in misrepresentation, the action at law for dollar damages is unavailable.

The action available as a remedy for fraudulent deceit can be brought against a person who is not a party to the contract, if the elements of fraud are present. The non-contracting third party who makes statements of fact which he could reasonably expect would be relied upon and which are made intentionally or recklessly is liable in deceit.

MISTAKE

2-56. Bilateral Mistake. Cases involving mistake are of two types—those in which both parties are mistaken, called bilateral mistake, and those in which only one party is mistaken, called unilateral mistake. Bilateral mistake exists when parties enter into a contract on the assumption of a material fact which assumption is in fact false. This mutual assumption, called mutual mistake of fact, arises in two situations: one in which the minds of the parties fail to meet so that no contract results [6] and the other in which the mistake merely makes the agreement more onerous for one of the contracting parties and therefore renders it voidable at his option.

Typical of the first type are those cases in which the subject matter of the contract has been destroyed prior to the date of the agreement and cases in which the language used in the contract is clearly subject to two interpretations and each party construes it differently. In either case no contract results since there was no valid offer and acceptance or meeting of the minds. (See Chapter 8.) The second type is illustrated by the sale of floor covering for a certain room at a lump-sum figure on the assumption by both parties that only a certain number of square feet were involved. If the area is greater than both parties thought to be true, the contract is voidable at the instance of the party who would suffer a loss because of the mistake.

In the transaction of business, it is customary in many situations to dispose of property about which the contracting parties willingly admit that all of the facts are not known. In such instances, the property is sold without regard to its quality or characteristics. Such agreements may not be rescinded if it later appears that the property contains properties which neither of the parties had reason to suspect or otherwise differs from their expectations. Under such conditions, the property forms the subject matter of the agreement, regardless of its nature. Thus, *A* sells *B* a farm, and shortly thereafter a valuable deposit of ore is discovered on it. Such an agreement could not be rescinded by the seller on the ground of mutual mistake.

2-57. Unilateral Mistake. A contract entered into because of some mistake or error on the part of only one of the contracting parties usually affords no basis for relief to such party. The majority of such mistakes

[6] *Hollywood Credit Clothing Co. v. Gibson,* page 212.

result from carelessness or lack of diligence on the part of the mistaken party, and should not, therefore, affect the rights of the other party.

This rule is subject to one well-recognized exception. Where a mistake has been made in the calculation or transmission of the figures which form the basis of a contract and prior to acceptance such mistake is clearly apparent to the offeree, the contract may be avoided by the offeror.[7] Hence, a contractor who arrives at, or transmits his estimates for a bid on construction work, using the wrong figure, may be relieved of his contract if the error was so great as to become apparent to the offeree prior to the latter's acceptance. The courts, in such a case, refuse to allow one party knowingly to take advantage of another's mistake.

2-58. Reformation of Written Contracts. Another common example of mutual mistake is that in which an error is made in reducing the oral agreement to a written contract. Frequently, the draftsman or typist makes an error which is not discovered prior to signing the contract and the party benefiting from the error seeks to hold the other party to the agreement as written. Courts of equity provide a remedy known as reformation for such situations. Reformation is only available where there is clear and positive proof of the drafting error. Courts frequently justify this remedy on the basis that the contract is not being changed; that only the written evidence is being corrected. This problem can be prevented by a careful reading of contracts before execution.

LACK OF FREE WILL

2-59. Duress and Undue Influence. Equity allows a party to rescind an agreement that was not entered into voluntarily.[8] The involuntariness or lack of free will may take the form of duress or undue influence and is predicated on the equitable concept that a person who has obtained property under such circumstances should not in good conscience be allowed to keep it. A person may lose his free will because of duress— some threat to his person, his family or property—or it may result from a more subtle pressure where one person overpowers the will of another by use of moral, social, or domestic force as contrasted with physical or economic force. Cases of undue influence arise frequently in situations involving the elderly. In those cases where free will is lacking some courts hold that the minds of the parties did not meet. At early common law, duress would not be present where a courageous man would have possessed a free will in spite of a threat, but modern courts do not require a standard of courage or firmness as a condition to exercise of the equitable remedy. If the pressure applied in fact affected the individual involved to the extent that the contract was not voluntary, there is duress. If a person has a free choice, there is no duress even though some pressure may have been exerted upon him.

---

[7] *Rushlight Auto Sprinkler Co. v. City of Portland,* page 213.
[8] *Kolias v. Colligan,* page 215.

REALITY OF ASSENT CASES

Channel Master Corporation v. Aluminum Limited Sales, Inc.

1958 (4 N.Y.) 2d 403, 151 N.E.2d 833

FULD, J.   On this appeal, here on questions certified by the Appellate Division, we are called upon to determine the sufficiency of a complaint in a tort action for damages based on fraud and deceit.

The plaintiff, a manufacturer and processor of aluminum, requires for its business a dependable supply of aluminum ingot in large quantity. The defendant is engaged in the business of selling that metal. The amended complaint states two causes of action.

In the first cause of action, the plaintiff alleges that in April, 1954, the defendant represented that "its available and uncommitted supplies and productive capacity of aluminum ingot, then existing, were such as rendered it then capable of selling to the plaintiff 400,000 pounds per month and that it had entered into no binding commitments with other customers which could in the future reduce such available and uncommitted supplies and productive capacity." The complaint then recites that such representations were made "with the intention and knowledge that plaintiff should rely thereon and in order to induce the plaintiff to refrain from entering into commitments with other suppliers and to purchase the greater part of its requirements from the defendant," that the plaintiff acted in reliance on the representations, and that they were false and known by the defendant to be so. In truth and in fact, the complaint further asserts, the defendant had previously entered into long-term contracts with other customers which committed all of the defendant's supplies and productive capacity for many years to come. By reason of the defendant's fraudulent misrepresentations and the plaintiff's reliance thereon, the complaint continues, the plaintiff refrained from securing commitments for future supplies from others and was thereby injured in its business. . . .

To maintain an action based on fraudulent representations, whether it be for the rescission of a contract or, as here, in tort for damages, it is sufficient to show that the defendant knowingly uttered a falsehood intending to deprive the plaintiff of a benefit and that the plaintiff was thereby deceived and damaged. . . .

The essential constituents of the action are fixed as representation of a material existing fact, falsity, *scienter*, deception and injury. . . . Accordingly, one "who fraudulently makes a misrepresentation of . . . intention . . . for the purpose of inducing another to act or refrain from action in reliance thereon in a business transaction" is liable for the harm caused by the other's justifiable reliance upon the misrepresentation. (3 Restatement, Torts, § 525, p. 59).

As examination of the complaint demonstrates, it contains all the necessary elements of a good cause of action, including statements of existing fact, as opposed to expressions of future expectation. The representations allegedly made, that the defendant had "available and uncommitted supplies and productive capacity of aluminum ingot" sufficient to render it then capable of selling to the plaintiff 400,000 pounds a month and that it had entered into no binding commitments which could in the future reduce such available and uncommitted supplies and productive capacity and that it was its intention to make available and to sell to the plaintiff the number of pounds specified for a period of five years, related to the defendant's present intention. A person's intent, his state of mind, it has long been recognized, is capable of ascertainment and a statement of present intention is deemed a statement of a material existing fact, sufficient to support a fraud action.

Judgment for plaintiff.

Wire & Textile Machinery, Inc. v. Robinson

1955 (Mass.) 125 N.E.2d 403

The plaintiff, acting through Kenner, its president, sold to Mohawk Wire Co., acting through Robinson, its president, certain machinery at a price of $6,000. The buyer paid only $1,000 in cash and the conditional sale contract provided that plaintiff retain title to the machinery as security for the balance payable in installments. For the security to be good at bankruptcy it was necessary to record it in the city where the business was located. Plaintiff asked Robinson for the address and was told, "Court Street Road, Syracuse, N.Y." The contract was recorded there, but the true address was Salina, N.Y., a city adjacent to Syracuse. Mohawk became a bankrupt, the plaintiff lost its security because of improper recording, and plaintiff sued the defendant in tort for fraud. Robinson contends he made the statement in good faith believing it to be true. The lower court gave judgment for plaintiff and defendant appeals.

SPALDING, J. . . . The defendant argues that the plaintiff has not made out a case because the evidence would not warrant a finding that his representations were consciously false. It is true that the evidence does not show that the defendant knowingly stated what was false. On the contrary such evidence as there was on that issue tends in the opposite direction. The defendant testified that he was executive vice president of a corporation which had its principal place of business in Brooklyn, New York, and visited the Mohawk plant only once or twice a month; that the post office address of Mohawk had always been Syracuse; that Syracuse had always been designated for freight and other shipments; that he had never heard of Salina until the conditional sale agreement was questioned in the bankruptcy court; and that the street on which Mohawk's plant is located runs into the downtown section of Syracuse and is called Court Street in Salina and Court Street in Syracuse. This testimony, of course, might be disbelieved but such disbelief would not establish scienter.

But proof that the representations were consciously fraudulent was not essential to the plaintiff's case. The rule deductible from the New York decisions is that a representation made as of one's own knowledge when knowledge there is none, a reckless misstatement, or an opinion based on grounds so flimsy as to lead to the conclusion that there was no genuine belief in its truth, are all sufficient upon which to base liability for deceit. . . . Tested by these principles we are of the opinion that the evidence was sufficient to warrant a finding for the plaintiff on the count for deceit. The judge could have found that when the defendant made the representation to Kenner he was making a statement of fact of his own knowledge concerning a matter that was susceptible of knowledge with the intention that it would be used in connection with the drafting and recording of the conditional sale agreement. In fact the statement was not true. The evidence amply warranted a finding that the defendant had never ascertained and did not know the location of Mohawk. Despite what he believed, he ran the risk of liability for deceit if he did not know and spoke as if he did. Giving the appearance of knowledge where there is none, without heed to the consequences, would, as we read the New York decisions, support a finding for deceit.

As stated above the judge found that the plaintiff relied on the defendant's representation concerning Mohawk's address. . . .

Judgment for plaintiff affirmed.

Barrett Associates, Inc. v. Aronson

1963 (Mass.) 190 N.E.2d 867

SPALDING, J. The plaintiff, Barrett Associates, brought an action for fraud and deceit setting forth its cause of action in three counts or separate charges. The trial court ruled that two of the counts were insufficient to justify a recovery from the defendants. The plaintiff appealed from this ruling.

The material averments of the second count are as follows: In April, 1960, the defendants Aronson and Levitt organized a corporation called Hollywood Lanes of Walpole, Inc. (Hollywood). Levitt was president and treasurer of the corporation and Aronson was its clerk. Levitt represented to the plaintiff that both he and Aronson "then intended to take no salary or other funds, directly or indirectly," from Hollywood until it was actually operating in business and earning a profit. Levitt further represented that if Hollywood failed in business he stood to lose about $250,000 "as a result of actions he took for the benefit" of Hollywood, so he had "set aside and was then holding a reserve of $50,000.00 of his own funds" to be used if Hollywood encountered financial difficulty or needed further funds. These representations were false and were made to the plaintiff "to cause . . . [it] to rely upon . . . [them] and so induce it to purchase a minority stock interest" in Hollywood, by purchasing eighty shares of no par stock from Hollywood, which was then owned solely by Levitt and Aronson. Relying on these representations and believing them to be true, the plaintiff purchased eighty shares of stock from Hollywood for which it paid $25,000. As "a result of the foregoing statements by . . . Levitt, the plaintiff suffered substantial damage in that the said stock . . . was worth substantially less than . . . $25,000.00."

The allegations in the third count are substantially the same except that the representations are alleged to have been made by the defendant Aronson. . . .

Even though this declaration is somewhat inartistically drawn, it does allege facts in skeleton form which, if proved, establish the elements of an action in tort for deceit.

> To recover for that intentional fraudulent conduct of which the plaintiff complains, he must allege and prove that the defendant made a false representation of a material fact with knowledge of its falsity for the purpose of inducing the plaintiff to act thereon, and that the plaintiff relied upon the representation as true and acted upon it to his damage. (Citing cases).

In support of the decision below, the defendants argue that the representations were promissory. Statements promissory in nature, of course, are not actionable. While the representations concerning salary and withdrawal of funds have a promissory flavor, they are, on analysis, representations of present intent. "Present intention as to a future act is a fact. It is susceptible of proof. When such intention does not exist, . . . it is a misrepresentation of a material fact. . . . The statement of fact as to present intention of the defendant, being susceptible of actual knowledge and being a fact alleged to have been false, may be made the foundation of an action for deceit." *(Feldman v. Witmark,* 254 Mass. 480, 481-482, 150 N.E. 329. Restatement, Torts, § 530). The allegation of falsity, taken with the allegation of present intention, if construed as we think they can be, as meaning also that the defendants were withdrawing or later withdrew salary and funds, asserted facts which, if proved, might affect the value of the shares.

The allegation as to damage (without which an action for deceit must fail), although stated somewhat summarily, was sufficient. . . .

Reversed in favor of the plaintiff.

Bryant v. Troutman
1956 (Ky.) 287 S.W.2d 918

SIMS, J. Appellants, plaintiffs below, sued appellees for $4,066.10 damages the complaint alleged they sustained by reason of fraudulent representations appellees made in reference to a house in Louisville, which appellants purchased from appellees for the sum of $12,250. Appellees filed motion for a summary judgment. . . . The court sustained the motion, dismissed the complaint, and this appeal followed.

The complaint averred the property was purchased on June 27, 1953, and that appellees willfully and knowingly concealed material facts concerning defective conditions of the house, which defects were unknown to appellants and could not have been discovered by them by the exercise of reasonable care in the inspection of the property. After this general averment of fraud on the part of appellees, appellants specifically set out fourteen defects in the house and the amount they were damaged by each defect.

The affidavit supporting the motion for summary judgment averred the house was built by affiant and was completed prior to June 27, 1953, the date the parties entered into the written contract for the sale of the property. The affidavit further averred all the parties to this action signed the contract of sale, which contained this sentence:

> We have read the entire contents of this contract and are not relying on verbal statements not contained herein. We further certify that we have examined the property described hereinabove; that we are thoroughly acquainted with its condition and accept it as such.

Appellants insist the sentence just quoted does not relieve appellees from any fraud they practiced on appellants. Appellees contend that under the sentence just quoted from the contract appellants cannot introduce testimony of contemporaneous parol agreements unless the contract is reformed for fraud or mutual mistake. . . .

In the sale of real estate, the intentional suppression of facts known to the seller and unknown to the purchaser is ground for an action for deceit if the purchaser was damaged by reason of the fraudulent concealment. Where there is a latent defect known to the seller and he remains silent with the knowledge that the buyer is acting on the assumption that no defect exists, the buyer has a cause of action against the seller for an intentional omission to disclose such latent defect. However, mere silence does not constitute fraud where it relates to facts open to common observation or discoverable by the exercise of ordinary diligence, or where means of information are as accessible to one party as the other.

If appellees in selling this property to appellants intentionally omitted to disclose to appellants latent defects in the property, of which the latter were not aware and they were thereby induced to enter into the contract to purchase, then the sentence in the contract which is quoted in the third paragraph of this opinion will not relieve appellees of their fraud. One cannot contract against his fraud. It was written in *Ganley Bros. v. Butler Bros. Building Co.* (170 Minn. 373):

> The law should not, and does not, permit a covenant of immunity to be drawn that will protect a person against his own fraud. Such is not enforceable because of public policy. . . . Language is not strong enough to write such a contract. Fraud destroys all consent. It is the purpose of the law to shield only those whose armor embraces good faith. Theoretically, if there is no fraud, the rule we announce is harmless. If there is fraud, the rule we announce is wholesome.

It is patent from what we have said that the court erred in granting summary judgment in favor of appellees. He should have required them to answer and if an issue be raised, then proof should be heard. However, on the fourteen specific defects set out in the complaint, it would appear some of them are of such nature that appellants could have discovered them upon using ordinary care in inspecting the property. As above pointed out, appellants should not be permitted to recover on such apparent defects.

The judgment is reversed for proceedings consistent with this opinion.

Cherry v. Crispin

1963 (Mass.) 190 N.E.(2) 93

Plaintiffs brought suit in equity seeking rescission of a conveyance of real estate alleging fraud and misrepresentation on the part of the defendants. The defendants have appealed from a final decree granting, in effect, rescission of the conveyance.

The defendants sold a parcel of land with a dwelling and garage thereon to the plaintiffs for $21,000. The agreement provided that the sale was contingent upon the plaintiffs' acquiring a so-called "G. I." mortgage. . . . An essential condition to such approval was satisfaction of the Veterans' Administration's (V.A.) requirement that "The Seller shall furnish Veteran Purchaser prior to settlement a written statement (or certification) from a recognized exterminator that there is no evidence of termites or other wood-boring insects in the property." Defendant through the real estate broker communicated with an exterminator, whom he had engaged on prior occasions, and requested "the usual certificate" from him. The examination and inspection of the premises by this exterminator "was done, if at all, in a very careless manner." Although there was extensive and obvious evidence of "termite and woodborer activity in various parts of the house, inside and out," on February 4, 1960, the day he claims to have made the examination, he stated in a letter addressed to Crispin, but sent to Matthews: "There is no evidence of termite or wood-borer activity in the structures." On February 10, 1960, papers were "passed" in the office of the bank's lawyers. The exterminator's letter was referred to in the presence of the defendant during this closing, and read by Cherry who "relied upon its contents in going through with the sale." At the closing and at the time the purchase and sale agreement was executed, the defendants "had reason to believe that termites and wood-borer insects had infested parts of the house." They "knowingly permitted and acquiesced in the false representation made at the passing of papers to the effect that there was 'no evidence of termites or wood-borer insects.' " The Home Savings Bank was relying upon the V. A. approval in making the loan, and the V. A. would not have approved the mortgage without the certificate from the recognized exterminator.

The plaintiffs moved into the house on March 11, 1960, and, within a few days, saw evidence of termites and "wood-borer insects." The . . . work necessary to relieve the premises of termites and wood-borers and install termite control will cost $1,500. Since acquiring the property the plaintiffs have spent about $40 on the garage and painted the inside of the house.

SPIEGEL, J. One who has relied upon a misrepresentation as to a material fact, intentionally made and knowingly false, is entitled to rescission of the disputed transaction. "The test is the same as that applied in actions of tort for deceit." The defendants make no contention that the evidence fails to support the finding that they knowingly acquiesced in the false representation upon which the plaintiffs relied. They argue, rather, that the plaintiffs have suffered no "legal damage" because the misrepresentation merely "induced them to do what they were already legally bound to do," i.e., perform the purchase and sale agreement. They point out that the contingency of V. A. approval of the mortgage was satisfied, thus requiring the plaintiffs to accept conveyance of the deed. We are unable to agree with this line of reasoning. The contingency of V. A. approval of the mortgage was "a condition inserted in the contract for the benefit of the buyer." (*deFreitas v. Cote,* 342 Mass. 474, 477, 174 N.E.2d 371, 373.) The plaintiffs were bound to accept the deed only if the V. A. approved. They had the right to expect that this "approval" would be untainted by the fraudulent representation later found to have existed. The judge found that the V. A. would not have "approved the mortgage" had the true condition of the premises been known. The V. A. and the plaintiffs relied upon the representation that the real estate was free from "termite or wood-borer activity" and without this representation the sale would not have taken place. In completing the purchase the plaintiffs were damaged and they are entitled to relief by means of rescission of the conveyance.

Although rescission is an appropriate remedy on the facts found, the final decree entered must be modified. Ordinarily one seeking rescission of a transaction must restore or offer to restore all that he received under it. The final decree before us orders, *inter alia,* a reconveyance from the plaintiffs to the defendants, payment of the full purchase price with interest to the plaintiffs by the defendants, and also reimbursement for the $40 expended by the plaintiffs on the garage. No mention is made, however, of payment to the defendants of the fair rental value of the premises during the plaintiffs' occupancy, a consideration necessary for full restoration of the status quo. Such restoration also requires a determination of amounts to be credited to either of the parties by way of adjustments of taxes paid, improvements made, and so forth. The court has the power to impose such equitable conditions upon the relief granted the plaintiffs as will amply protect the rights of the defendants. In the accounting which must follow, reconsideration of the $225.62 payment ordered in paragraph five of the final decree is necessary as there does not appear to be any support for it in the record.

The case is remanded to the Superior Court and the final decree is to be modified after further proceedings consistent with this opinion.

So ordered.

Hollywood Credit Clothing Company v. Gibson

1963 (D.C.) 188 A.2d 348

HOOD, C. J.   This appeal is from a judgment denying appellant recovery of the purchase price of a television set. The testimony of appellee, largely uncontradicted and evidently accepted by the trial court, was that two days before Christmas he went to appellant's store and looked at a television, that appellant's salesman told him the price was $189, and he agreed to buy it at that price; that a conditional sales contract was filled in and he signed it; that when he arrived at home with the set he looked at his account book (apparently he was not given a copy of the conditional bill of sale) and saw that the stated price was $298, instead of $189, which with carrying charges made a total cost to him of $354.35. As soon as the store reopened after the Christmas holidays appellee returned the set to the store, explaining that the cost was more than he agreed to pay. When the store personnel refused to take back the set, appellee left it there. He paid nothing on account and appellant brought this action for the full amount of $354.35. Trial resulted in a finding for appellee. In denying appellant's post-trial motion for judgment or a new trial, the trial court stated there had been a mutual mistake of fact as to the correct price of the set.

Appellant argues that appellee signed the contract and is bound thereby even if he failed to read it before signing it. Appellant urges us to rule that in his jurisdiction "a contract is still a contract." It is, of course, the general rule that one who signs a contract has a duty to read it and is obligated according to its terms. It is also a general rule that no relief can be afforded for a bad bargain or an extravagant purchase improvidently made. But another rule requires mutual assent or agreement as an essential element of a contract; and a contract in form may be avoided by a showing that assent was obtained by fraud or even misrepresentation falling short of fraud. If it is shown that the minds of the parties did not meet "honestly and fairly, without mistake or mutual misunderstanding, upon all the essential points involved," there is no contract. (*Cunningham Mfg. Co. v. Rotograph Co.*, 30 App.D.C. 524, 527, 15 L.R.A., N.S., 368.)

The trial court by its finding indicated that it believed that appellee had been told that the price was $189, that this representation was a material factor in inducing him to sign the contract, and that he signed the contract believing the price to be $189. This was a sufficient basis for denying recovery to appellant.

Affirmed.

Rushlight Auto Sprinkler Co. v. City of Portland

1950 (180 Or.) 194, 219 P.2d 732

The plaintiff, in submitting its bid to the defendant City of Portland for a certain sewage and disposal project, hurriedly submitted a bid of $429,444.20 and issued its certified check of $21,472.21 to be retained by the city in event plaintiff failed to enter a contract after notice that his bid had been accepted. When the bids were opened, it was discovered that the next lowest bid was $671,600. All were quite concerned because plaintiff's bid was exceedingly low and plaintiff discovered that it had omitted an item for steel of $99,225.68. Plaintiff requested that its bid be withdrawn, but it was accepted and the certified check was cashed when plaintiff refused to proceed with the work, the contract being let to another. Plaintiff seeks to recover the amount of the check. The lower gave judgment for plaintiff and defendant appealed.

ROSSMAN, J. . . . As we said, the City concedes the mistake concerning the steel item which the plaintiff's officers, to their manifest embarrassment, described. The plaintiff prays that its mistake be deemed excusable; the City insists that the error was a culpable one. . . .

So far as we can ascertain, the plaintiff's bid was compiled by an adequate staff of estimators. No one challenged the competence of the estimators nor questioned the methods they pursued. The record shows that one of the estimators, after having calculated the amount of earth that would have to be moved in one phase of the construction work, called upon a member of the City Board of Engineers for the purpose of comparing his estimate with that made by the board. He found that the two were virtually the same. That fact and an occasional other one mentioned in the record tend to show that the estimators were careful. . . .

We believe that it is manifest from the evidence that the difference between the plaintiff's bid and the next higher was so large that all of those concerned with the undertaking were rendered uneasy. The plaintiff's officers at once returned to their work sheets, fearing that they must have committed a mistake. The City Engineer, according to his own words, found the variation so great that it "scared us to death." A member of the Board of Engineers, who seemingly expressed himself in wary words, described the plaintiff's bid as "a very low" one and termed the difference between it and the City's estimate "a very decided difference." The bid aroused suspicion in all minds. We think that the difference apprised the City that a mistake had probably occurred.

It is true, as already indicated, that the steel item accounts for only $99,225.68 or 41 per cent of the total disparity of $242,155.80 between the plaintiff's and the next higher bid. Therefore, it alone did not provoke the misgivings. The $99,225.68 was a substantial part of the total difference. The variation between the second and third high bids was only $2,232.06. The difference between the second and the fourth high bids was $13,291.50. The material fact is that the omission of the steel was a substantial factor in reducing the bid to such a low amount that the city officials surmised that it was too good to be true. . . .

From *Williston on Contracts* (rev. ed.), § 1573, the following is taken:

> In two classes of cases, mistake of one party only to a contract undoubtedly justifies affirmative relief as distinguished from a mere denial to enforce the contract specifically against him;
> (1) Where the mistake is known to the other party to the transaction. . . .

Section 503, Restatement of the Law, Contracts, says: "A mistake of only one party that forms the basis on which he enters into a transaction does not of itself render the transaction voidable; . . ."

The Reporters' Notes to that section cites many illustrative decisions and some treatises. From the notes, we take the following: "Where one party knows or has reason to know that the other party has made a basic mistake (see Comment *c*) restitution is granted. This situation has frequently arisen where there has been an error in the price given. In this case rescission is ordinarily allowed. . . ."

We believe that in this State an offer and an acceptance are deemed to effect a meeting of the minds, even though the offeror made a material mistake in compiling his offer, provided the acceptor was not aware of the mistake and had no reason to suspect it. But if the offeree knew of the mistake, and if it was basic, or if the circumstances were such that he, as a reasonable man, should have inferred that a basic mistake was made, a meeting of the minds does not occur. The circumstances which should arouse the suspicions of the fairminded offeree are many, as stated in § 94 of *Williston on Contracts* (rev. ed.): ". . . And the same principle is applicable in any case where the offeree should know that the terms of the offer are unintended or misunderstood by the offeror. The offeree will not be permitted to snap up an offer that is too good to be true; no contract based on such an offer can then be enforced by the acceptor. . . ."

It is unnecessary to state once more that the proof in cases of this kind must possess a high degree of cogency. The bidder must prove, not only that he made a material mistake, but also that the offeree was aware of it. In this case, the facts which we have mentioned are unchallenged.

It is our belief that although the plaintiff alone made the mistake, the City was aware of it. When it accepted the plaintiff's bid, with knowledge of the mistake, it sought to take an unconscionable advantage of an inadvertent error. Equity is always prepared to grant relief from such situations.

The decree of the Circuit Court is affirmed.

Kolias v. Colligan

1959, (Cal. App.) 342 P.2d 265

DRAPER, J. This action arises out of a construction contract. Knowing that a commercial concern desired to lease a building built to its specifications, defendant Colligan negotiated with plaintiff, who owned vacant land in an industrial section of San Francisco. By letter, Colligan offered to plan, build, finance and lease a building for plaintiff for $67,500. Plaintiff accepted the offer. Long-term financing in the sum of $50,000 would not be available until completion of the building. As part of his "package deal" Colligan arranged for Mrs. Waegemann (named as a defendant herein but not served) to provide the interim financing, and also to loan $17,500 on security of a second deed of trust. To secure Mrs. Waegemann's advances for the interim financing, plaintiff's property was transferred to her, to be reconveyed to plaintiff when the building was completed and the long-term loans were made. Plaintiff asked that the location of the building on the lot be changed somewhat from that planned by Colligan. The latter notified plaintiff that this would require additional work and, some four months before completion, sent a letter advising plaintiff of this fact and specifying the amounts to be charged for a portion of this extra work. Plaintiff did not sign an approval of this letter until shortly after completion of the building. At about the time of this acceptance, Colligan sent plaintiff a bill detailing all extras, in an amount totalling some $9,000. Seven months later, plaintiff paid the charges for extras in full. One day less than two years after payment, he brought this action to recover $8,455.74 paid for extra work. Defendant cross-complained for interest and rents amounting to $3,431.80 which he claims was erroneously omitted from his bills to plaintiff. After trial without a jury, the court awarded plaintiff $2,629 on the complaint, granted cross-complainant $1,271, and entered judgment in favor of plaintiff for the net amount of $1,358. Defendant appeals.

Appellant next asserts error in the admission of any evidence relating to the reasonable value of the extra work. The argument is that respondent voluntarily paid these charges, and that payments voluntarily made are not recoverable. But in overruling appellant's single objection to such evidence, the court pointed out that he would be allowed to offer evidence as to the claimed voluntary character of the payment. Much evidence on this issue was in fact introduced by both parties. At most, the objection raised a question as to the order of proof. We find no abuse of discretion in the ruling. In any event, appellant was in no way prejudiced, since the issue was fully tried and was determined against him.

There is substantial evidence that neither respondent's acknowledgment of the charges nor his payment of them was voluntary. Appellant's joint venturer, Mrs. Waegemann, held title to respondent's property. There is evidence that she and appellant would not reconvey to respondent until he acknowledged and paid the charges for extra work. It follows that the acknowledgment and payment here were made under compulsion, and were not voluntary. Whether respondent, as a reasonably prudent person, acted under compulsion is a question of fact for the trier of fact, which has, on substantial evidence, resolved it against appellant. . . .

Judgment in favor of plaintiff affirmed.

CHAPTER 11
REVIEW QUESTIONS AND PROBLEMS

1. *S* sold goods on credit to *B*, the latter being asked to indicate how he stood financially. He said he had $3,000 in his business assets but neglected to say he had liabilities of $2,100. *S* seeks to avoid the contract and recover the goods sold. Has he a right to do so?

2. *P*, a prospective purchaser of land presently leased for a long time to the government at rather nominal rental, knew that the government was to terminate the lease in the near future. Since this fact was unknown by *H*, the owner, *P* was able to purchase the property much cheaper than would otherwise have been possible. If *H* had made inquiry of the government he could have known of its intention. *P*

had acted as the agent of *H* in managing the property. Was fraud present?

3. *P* sued *D* to cancel a release and to recover for personal injuries. The release was given some five weeks after rear-end collision and five months before *P* felt tingling sensation in fingers and was preceded by no negotiations or discussion of personal injuries but was given for exact amount of property damage. *P* had a ruptured cervical disc. What result?

4. *P* sued *D* (who sold him a house) for fraud and deceit. During an inspection of the property and at the time of closing the contract, *D* stated when asked about a creek at the rear of the house, "it would come over its banks in heavy rain but it never came near the house." The creek had overflowed four times prior to the sale, each time entering the house. The creek overflowed after the sale, doing extensive damage. What result?

5. *P* purchased a large pile of storage batteries from *D*. *D* told *P* that there were at least 3000 batteries in the lot but there were only 1786. *P* did not count the batteries. If *D* knew that there were less than 3000 batteries, did *D* commit fraud?

6. *P* agreed to build a fence for *D*. The area to be fenced in was 484 feet long and *D* wanted it 10 feet high. A mistake was made in reducing the contract to writing in that the typist doubled the ground feet, thus reducing the cost 50 per cent. If *P* seeks to reform the contract, will a court of equity allow him to do so?

7. *P* sued *D* for fraud based on false representations concerning some stock. *P* offered no evidence as to the actual value of the stock at the time of purchase but did prove the purchase price. Is *P* entitled to damages?

8. *P* bought a certain lot from *D*, alleging that the purchase price was based on a square foot valuation and that the number of total square feet was misrepresented. *P* was told that the lot contained 27,300 square feet when in fact it only contained 25,116 square feet. If *D* knew the exact area, was fraud present?

9. *D* agreed to construct a house for *P* according to plans and specifications. *D* did not fully complete the house according to the plans and a dispute arose between the parties. *P* then sued to cancel the contract on the ground of fraud. What result?

10. *P* purchased a house from *D*. The contract contained a recital that *P* had inspected the house and accepted it in its current condition. There were several serious defects which an inspection would not reveal. If *D* knew of these defects, is he guilty of fraud?

11. *P*, when buying land from *D*, was told by *D*'s agent that the land was capable of producing an income of $2300 per year. If it is not, is *P* entitled to rescind?

Illegality

2-60. Concept of Illegality. The final requirement for a valid contract is that it have a lawful purpose or object. Contracts which do not have a legal object are illegal and void notwithstanding the fundamental concept of freedom of contract which is basic to a free society. The term void is not accurate as what is really meant is that such contracts are unenforceable in a court. The law does not grant complete freedom of contract and if a contract or a provision thereof is specifically prohibited by statute, contravenes the express rules of the common law, or is contrary to public policy, courts will declare that it is illegal. A contract provision is contrary to public policy if it is injurious to the interests of the public, contravenes some established interest of society, violates the policy or purpose of some statute,[1] or tends to interfere with the public health, safety, morals, or general welfare. Contracts which contravene common law principles and those which are against public policy are often inseparably blended so that it is difficult to tell which is involved. Thus all agreements are subject to the paramount power of the sovereign and to the judicial power to declare contracts void if they are contrary to law, morality, or public policy. However, contracts are not to be lightly set aside on the grounds of public policy and doubts will be resolved in favor of legality.

Illegality may take the form of illegal consideration or illegal performance. The purpose of the parties to a contract usually indicates the presence of illegality and illegality is measured by what is intended rather than by what is accomplished. Legal contracts are not rendered illegal by

---

[1] *Elephant Lumber Co. v. Johnson,* page 225.

illegal acts of performance if legal performance is possible or was intended.

Illegality frequently arises when a contract has the net effect of circumventing or indirectly avoiding a constitutional or statutory policy. If the statute imposes a penalty for its violation, contracts which defeat the policy of the statute are illegal.

As was previously noted, freedom of contract is subject to the limitation that the agreement must not be against public policy. If a contract is contrary to the welfare of society, it is not necessary that a statute prohibit it as courts will protect society and prevent injury to the public as part of their general responsibilities. The term "public policy" is vague and variable and changes as our social, economic, and political climates change. As society becomes more complex, courts turn more and more to statutory enactments in search of current public policy. A court's own concept of right and wrong as well as its total philosophy will frequently come into play in answering complex questions of public policy. Some of the cases in the sections which follow may be in conflict with each other and may state questionable rules of public policy. Care should be taken to ascertain the reason behind each rule and each result and any indicated trends in the law noted.

2-61. Freedom of Contract and the Public Interest. The law early declared that absolute freedom of contract existed in a barter situation because of the equal bargaining position of the parties. Each party could agree to the offered exchange or could reject it and the law would not interfere. At the other extreme are the contracts with public utilities in which there is no equality of bargaining power between the parties because of the existence of a monopoly. The law therefore denies freedom of contract to utilities in return for the monopoly power and government regulates all contractual provisions including rates. The need for this regulation is readily apparent. For example: imagine the problem if bargaining over the price of water were possible.

The difficulty today is that most contracts do not fall within these two extremes. There are many contracts which are entered into between parties with unequal bargaining power. When the subject matter of the contracts involves items of everyday necessity, courts frequently hold that one of the parties is a quasi public institution and that such institutions are not entitled to complete freedom of contract because freedom of contract is not in the public interest. Thus, all contracts or parts of the contracts of such institutions may be held illegal where the quasi public institution has taken advantage of its superior bargaining power, and executed a contract or included a provision in a contract which in the eyes of the court excessively favors the quasi public institution to the detriment of the other party and the public. A typical example is an exculpatory clause in which one party seeks to disclaim liability for his own negligence. Such contracts are discussed in the next section. There are numerous other situations in which the public interest or public policy determines the legality of a private agreement or a part thereof. This is true in cases where to allow the contract provision to stand would have a harmful effect on the public generally. Many areas of heretofore private law and contract are becoming or have become at least in part affected with the public interest in recent years thus reducing freedom of private contract.

2-62. Exculpatory Clauses. An exculpatory clause is a provision of a contract which relieves a party of liability for his own negligence. These disclaimers of liability are not favored by the law, are strictly construed against the party relying on them and are frequently declared to be illegal by courts as contrary to public policy.[2] Some states have by statute declared these clauses in certain types of contracts such as leases to be illegal and void.

The judicial decisions which declare such contracts to be illegal usually involve a duty owed to the public or cases where the duty owed is private but involves the public interest. The public interest is involved in cases of private contract where the subject matter of the contract is an everyday necessity and there is inequality of bargaining power between the parties. For example, a parking lot might seek to avoid its liability for damages to cars caused by its negligence but such contract would be illegal because parking is an everyday necessity and there is inequality of bargaining power between drivers and parking lot operators. In addition, a public carrier such as a railroad may not disclaim its liability for negligence.

2-63. Contracts in Restraint of Trade. Government in the United States by statute on several occasions has attempted to insure a competitive economic system. These statutes beginning with the Sherman Antitrust Act in 1890 have attempted to prevent monopolistic practices and declared contracts which involve conspiracy to restrain trade to be illegal. Subsequent to the Clayton Act in 1914, the Robinson-Patman Amendment in 1936, and the Celler-Kefauver Amendment in 1950, each of which was designed to clarify and make more effective this policy of free competition and the prevention of activities in restraint of trade. While the details of these various statutes cannot be covered here, it must be recognized that these laws provide three legal sanctions to be used in the event of a violation: a criminal penalty with fine and imprisonment; the equitable sanction of injunction; and the legal sanction of a suit by the victim of a violation for treble damages. In addition, the administrative agency (F.T.C.) may issue a cease and desist order. Some of the terms of contractual obligations covered by these statutes are prices, including specific provisions on quantity discounts and promotional allowances, provisions which tie one product to another or provide for exclusive arrangements and provisions relating to the acquisition of the stock or assets of another company. These terms are involved in possible violations of the laws where the effect of the contract provision may be to substantially

---

2 *Hunter v. American Rentals, Inc.*, page 226.

lessen competition or where it may tend to create a monopoly. Other contract terms covered by these statutes are the so called "fair trade" provisions and other attempts at resale price maintenance. Many states have "loss-leader" statutes and other laws affecting competition. Without a detailed study, it may be stated that any contract provision which is expressly prohibited by these statutes or which is contrary to the policy of these statutes is illegal.[3] Courts will attempt to insure that the policy of these laws is not defeated by the imagination of clever lawyers and businessmen. The section which follows discusses one type of contract in partial restraint of trade which may be legal.

2-64. Agreements Not to Compete. Contracts in partial restraint of trade are valid if such restraint has reference to and is ancillary [4] to the sale of property, the creation or sale of a business interest or a profession, or to the discontinuance of employment, and if such restraint is reasonably necessary for the protection of the purchaser, the remaining member of the business, or the employer. Such agreements will be enforced in a court of equity, provided that they are (1) reasonable in point of time, (2) reasonable in the area of restraint, (3) necessary to protect goodwill, (4) do not place an undue burden on the covenantee and (5) do not violate the public interest. Each agreement will be examined by the court, not a jury, from the standpoint of reasonableness to both parties and to the general public. The court in making the examination will have to examine the business and look at such factors as uniqueness of product, patents, trade secrets, type of service, employee's contact with customers, and other goodwill factors. It is difficult to determine which factors will influence any particular court to decide what is or what is not in the public interest; but certainly in the employment situation whether or not the employee will become a burden on society and whether or not the public is being deprived of his skill, etc., will usually be considered. If the restriction exceeds what is reasonably necessary, a few courts will reform the contract so as to make the restrictions reasonable, but most courts hold that the entire limiting clause is illegal, thus leaving the person to be benefited by the restriction without protection. It must be recognized that the law will look with more favor on these contracts if they involve the sale or creation of a business interest than it will in the case of such a provision included in an employment contract. In fact, an agreement not to compete may even be presumed in the case of a sale of business and its goodwill and the seller must not thereafter directly or by circular solicit business from his old customers, although he may advertise generally.[5] The reason courts are more likely to hold the agreements between a buyer and seller or partners valid as contrasted with employer-employee contracts is that in these situations there is more equality of bargaining power than in the case of the employer and employee. A seller or a partner could readily refuse to sign, whereas an

[3] *Simpson v. Union Oil Company of California*, page 228.
[4] *Hayes v. Parklane Hosiery Company, Inc.*, page 230.
[5] *Terminal Vegetable Company, Inc. v. Beck*, page 232.

employee seeking a job might have to sign almost anything to gain employment. The law generally sympathizes with persons whose bargaining power is not equal to that of the other party and provides relief for them. In addition, it is clearly evident that there is a goodwill factor involved in the sale of a business and that goodwill as an asset deserves protection. In many employee-employer situations, it is not readily evident that the employee is able to create goodwill, or take it with him upon termination of his employment.[6] It should be noted here and kept in mind that some states have by statute or by their constitutions, declared such agreements illegal as a matter of public policy. However, there are only a few such states.

One further word of caution is necessary. Quite often a valid employment contract whereby the employee agrees not to compete or work for a competitor after separation is prepared, the employee signs it, leaves the employer and violates his contract by either working for a competitor or going into competition directly. The employer, not desiring the publicity and the inconvenience of a law suit, does nothing for six months or perhaps even a year, hoping that in the meantime the former employee will not adversely affect his business. It is then discovered that the employee's competition is creating an adverse effect and the former employer decides to institute action against his former employee. When suit is started to enjoin the employee from this competitive activity, the employee contends that by failing to raise the issue immediately when the breach occurred, the employer has waived his rights. The point may be a good one since an employer should not allow his former employee to expend large sums of money or otherwise materially alter his position, by establishing a business and then seek to prevent his action by attempting to enforce the original contract. The doctrines of estoppel and waiver can thus frequently be used by an employee to prevent the use in equity of the contract rights to which the employer would otherwise have been entitled. Equity does not favor a party who "sleeps on his rights" and the failure to promptly seek enforcement of the agreement may very well preclude its enforcement. As was previously noted, similar restrictions are often imposed in leases and sales of real estate. So long as the vendor or lessor does not desire to have competition on property that he controls, he may avoid such competition by contract. Since other property in the community may be used for competitive purposes, the agreement is binding. If a lease is made, however, for the express purpose of taking an industry out of competition, the lease is unenforceable in that it unduly limits competition.

2-65. Unconscionable Bargains. Courts of equity, being courts of conscience, have always refused to grant equitable relief where it would be unconscionable to do so. Thus, where one party to an agreement has obtained unfair advantage over the other, equitable relief and especially

[6] *Beltone Electronics Corporation v. Smith*, page 234.

suits to complete performance of the contract have failed. Traditionally, however, courts of law have awarded dollar damages in cases in which equitable relief was denied. The trend to apply equitable principles to cases at law has been manifested in the Code which provides that if an agreement or a clause thereof is found by a court to be unconscionable as a matter of law, it is unenforceable and in effect illegal.[C1] The code does not define an unconscionable bargain, but evidence as to the commercial setting, purpose, and effect of the contract or clause may be used by the court in making the determination.

2-66. Usury. Most states limit the amount of interest that may be charged upon borrowed money or for the extension of the maturity of a debt. Any contract by which the lender is to receive more than the maximum interest allowed by the statute is illegal.[7] In the majority of the states the lender is denied the right to collect any interest in such cases, although one state has recently denied collection of even the principal. A few of the states permit recovery of interest at the legal rate. The law against usury is generally not violated by collection of the legal maximum in advance or by making, in addition to the maximum interest charge, a service fee that is no larger than reasonably necessary to cover the incidental costs of making the loan—inspection, legal, and recording fees. It is also allowable for a seller to add a finance or carrying charge on long-term credit transactions even though the charge exceeds the maximum interest rate. Many of these exceptions are created by statute. Other exceptions allow special lenders such as pawn shops, small loan companies or credit unions to charge in excess of the otherwise legal limit. In fact, the exceptions to the maximum interest rate in most states far exceed the situations in which the general rule is applicable. It must be noted that the laws relating to usury which were designed to protect debtors from excessive interest have been largely nullified by these exceptions so that little protection is actually available.

The purchase of a note at a discount greater than the maximum interest is not usurious, unless the maker of the note is the person who is discounting it. A note is considered the same as any other personal property and may be sold for whatever it will bring upon the market. There are some courts, however, which hold that if the seller of the note indorses the negotiable paper and thus remains personally liable on it, a discount greater than the legal rate of interest is usurious. This is particularly true if the paper is considered worthless except for the indorsement. In such a case the sale of the paper is regarded as actually being a loan for the period the note has yet to run.

As long as one lends the money of others, he may charge a commission in addition to the maximum rate. A commission may not be legally charged when one is lending his own funds, even though he has to

7 *The Bankers Guarantee Title and Trust Company v. Fisher,* page 236.

C1 *U.C.C.* 2-302.

borrow the money with which to make the loan and expects to sell the paper shortly thereafter.

2-67. Other Illegal Agreements. There are an endless variety of other contracts which may be against public policy. For example, wagering agreements, contracts to affect the administration of justice, such as to conceal evidence or suppress a criminal investigation, and contracts to influence legislative or executive action or to interfere with or injure public service are frequently declared illegal by statute or are illegal as being contrary to public policy. Of course, lobbying is legal so long as it does not amount to bribery or undue influence.

Contracts quite similar to those involving the relation of one to his government are those which involve the relation of an employee to his employer. Any attempt by contract to persuade an employee to violate his duty to his employer is illegal.

2-68. Effect of Illegal Contracts. It is incorrect to say that illegal contracts are void. They are merely unenforceable either at law or in equity. The courts, in such cases, simply refuse to grant any relief because the court will not allow itself to be used to consummate an illegal act. Although one of the parties has fully carried out his part of the agreement, he may neither demand performance nor force a return of his consideration. The court leaves the parties just as it finds them in order to deter others from entering into like contracts; fully or partially executed contracts are left undisturbed.

To this general rule there are several exceptions. If the refusal to grant affirmative relief has the indirect effect of enforcing the illegal contract, the court may give the necessary aid to relieve the injured party from further performance of the illegal agreement. Where the situation is such that the contract should be enforced, the court will see that the terms of the agreement are carried out. Thus, a contract whereby a bank loans to a customer more than the law permits is illegal; however, the interests of other depositors being involved, the borrower must repay what he has borrowed. Where certain contracts are made illegal to protect society, or a certain segment of it, the injured party is usually granted relief by statute if he is one of the group which the law was designed to protect. Statutes frequently provide other exceptions to the general rule.

Also, a party who performs an illegal contract, in ignorance of the fact that it is illegal because certain important facts are not revealed to him, may recover the reasonable value of his performance in quasi contract.

Contracts that contemplate the performance of various acts, some legal and some illegal, may be enforced to the extent that they are legal, especially when the illegal part is executory. This is true only in those cases in which the contract, by nature, may be so divided that the legal portion can be segregated from the illegal portion.

ILLEGALITY CASES

Elephant Lumber Co. v. Johnson
1964 (Ohio C.A.) 202 N.E.2d 189

COLLIER, P. J.   The Elephant Lumber Company, a corporation, plaintiff-appellee, herein designated the plaintiff, brought this action on June 10, 1963, in the Chillicothe Municipal Court to recover for
services rendered the defendant-appellant, Helen Johnson, herein referred to as the defendant, in preparing and drawing plans, specifications
and material lists for the erection of a building to be used as a nursing
home. The allegations of the petition are:

> Defendant agreed and promised, in consideration of plaintiff's preparing
> such plans, specifications and material lists, that defendant would either
> procure and purchase, or cause to be procured or purchased from plaintiff,
> all the lumber and other building materials and supplies for the construction
> of such building; and if all of such lumber and other building materials and
> supplies were not so procured and purchased from plaintiff, then defendant
> agreed and promised to pay plaintiff for such plans, specifications and material
> lists the sum of $1,000.00.

No answer or other pleading was filed by the defendant and, on July
15, 1963, a default judgment was entered in favor of plaintiff for the full
amount claimed in the petition. . . . The defendant now seeks a reversal
of that judgment.

The defendant's contentions are that the petition does not state a
cause of action for the reason it is not alleged in the petition that the
plaintiff is an architect or has as its employee an architect authorized to
draw and furnish plans and specifications and to charge for such services;
that the alleged contract is in violation of statute and therefore void;
that a valid default judgment may not be rendered upon such defective
petition. Section 4703.18, Revised Code, provides:

> No person shall enter upon the practice of architecture, or hold himself
> forth as an architect or registered architect, unless he has complied with
> sections 4703.01 to 4703.19, inclusive, of the Revised Code, and is the holder
> of a certificate of qualification to practice architecture issued or renewed and
> registered under such sections. . . .

Ohio is one of the many states that have enacted statutes regulating
architects in the practice of their profession. It is generally held that designing a building for another, or furnishing the plans and specifications
for such a building for another, constitutes architectural services. It is
also well settled that such legislation is a proper exercise of the police
power.

The general rule is that a contract entered into by a person engaged in
a business without taking out a license as required by law is void and un-

enforceable and that where a license or certificate is required by statute as a requisite to one practicing a particular profession, an agreement of a professional character without such license or certificate is illegal and void. It is also a well established rule that a contract which cannot be performed without a violation of a statute is void. . . .

Plaintiff does not allege in its petition that any of its employees was licensed or registered as an architect under the laws of Ohio. It is elementary that in an action of this kind the petition must allege a binding enforceable contract. In the case of *McGill v. Carlos*, (Ohio Com. Pl., 81 N.E.2d 726), a very well considered Common Pleas Court decision, it was held that preparing plans and specifications for the construction of a dwelling house estimated to cost $12,800, was engaging in the practice of architecture and precluded recovery for such services. In the instant case the building was designed to be used as a nursing home, which is regulated by statute and subject to inspection and would require more expert knowledge and skill in preparation than an ordinary dwelling. (Chapter 3721, Revised Code). The factual situation in the McGill case is identical with the present case except that in the former, the contractor prepared the plans and in the case before us, the materialman is the plaintiff.

Our conclusions are that the plaintiff's claim is for services rendered as an architect; that to practice the profession of architecture in Ohio and to recover in an action for such services, it is necessary to obtain a license as prescribed by law; that a contract for such services entered into by one who is not so licensed and registered is void. . . .

Judgment reversed and final judgment for defendant.

Hunter v. American Rentals, Inc.

1962 (Kansas) 371 P.2d 131

This was a tort action of negligence for damages brought by Everett L. Hunter, plaintiff (appellee), against American Rentals, Inc., defendant (appellant). Plaintiff rented a trailer and hitch from defendant. Defendant's agents attached the trailer and hitch to Plaintiff's car and advised Plaintiff that the trailer was ready for travel. Plaintiff paid the rental charges and while driving the car, the trailer hitch broke, leaving the trailer and automobile attached only by the safety chain. This chain had been attached by the defendant's agent in such a manner that it permitted the trailer to start moving from one side of the highway to the other. This caused plaintiff's car to overturn, and plaintiff received personal injuries and damaged the automobile.

By its answer defendant sought to avoid liability, contending that the plaintiff entered into a written rental agreement which contained the following clause absolving the defendant of any liability:

The renter hereby absolved the AMERICAN RENTALS of any responsibility or obligation in the event of accident, regardless of causes or consequence, and that any costs, claims, court or attorney's fees, or liability

resulting from the use of described equipment will be indemnified by the
renter regardless against whom the claimant or claimants institute action. . . .

AMERICAN RENTALS makes no warranty of fitness or usage, express
or implied. The undersigned received said property in its present condition
and waives all claims present and future against AMERICAN RENTALS
including those resulting from defects, latent or apparent.

Plaintiff contended that the above provisions were void as being contrary to public policy. The trial court held that the contract terms did
not constitute a valid defense and held for the Plaintiff. The Defendant
appeals.

WERTZ, J. . . . Contracts for exemption for liability from negligence are not favored by the law. They are strictly construed against
the party relying on them. The rule is unqualifiedly laid down by many
decisions that one cannot avoid liability for negligence by contract. The
rule against such contracts is frequently limited to the principle that
parties cannot stipulate for the protection against liability for negligence
in the performance of a legal duty or a duty of public service, or where
the public interest is involved or a public duty owed, or when the duty
owed is a private one where public interest requires the performance
thereof. There is no doubt that the rule that forbids a person to protect
himself by agreement against damages resulting from his own negligence
applies where the agreement protects him against the consequences of a
breach of some duty imposed by law. It is, of course, clear that a person
cannot, by agreement, relieve himself from a duty which he owed to the
public, independent of the agreement. An analysis of the decisions indicates that even under the view that a person may, under some circumstances, contract against the performance of such duties, he cannot do so
where the interest of the public requires the performance thereof.

. . . The defendant, being engaged in the business of renting trailers
to the general public, including trailer hitches and other attendant equipment necessary to connect the rented trailers to the automobiles, owed a
duty, not only to the plaintiff but also to the general public, to see that
the trailer hitch was properly installed and the trailer properly attached
thereto in order that the same might be safely driven on the highway for
the purpose and use for which it was intended; and defendant, by contract, could not relieve itself from its negligent acts of failing to make
those safe connections and installations. The contract on the part of the
defendant to relieve itself from such negligent liability is against the
public policy of this state and void.

An agreement is against public policy if it is injurious to the interests
of the public, contravenes some established interest of society, violates
some public statute, or tends to interfere with the public welfare or
safety.

For the reasons stated, this court is of the opinion that the contract
pleaded, being in contravention of the statute and the public policy of
this state, is void and unenforceable and constitutes no defense to plaintiff's cause of action.

Affirmed.

Simpson v. Union Oil Company of California

1964, 84 S.Ct. 1051

Mr. Justice DOUGLAS delivered the opinion of the Court.

This is a suit for damages under § 4 of the Clayton Act, (38 Stat. 731, 15 U.S.C. § 15), for violation of §§ 1 and 2 of the Sherman Act, (26 Stat. 209), as amended, (50 Stat. 693, 15 U.S.C. §§ 1, 2), The complaint grows out of a so-called retail dealer "consignment" agreement which, it is alleged, Union Oil requires lessees of its retail outlets to sign, of which Simpson was one. The "consignment" agreement is for one year and thereafter until canceled, is terminable by either party at the end of any year and, by its terms, ceases upon any termination of the lease. The lease is also for one year; and it is alleged that it is used to police the retail prices charged by the consignees, renewals not being made if the conditions prescribed by the company are not met. The company, pursuant to the "consignment" agreement, sets the prices at which the retailer sells the gasoline. While "title" to the consigned gasoline "shall remain in Consignor until sold by Consignee," and while the company pays all property taxes on all gasoline in possession of Simpson, he must carry personal liability and property damage insurance by reason of the "consigned" gasoline and is responsible for all losses of the "consigned" gasoline in his possession, save for specified acts of God. Simpson is compensated by a minimum commission and pays all the costs of operation in the familiar manner.

The retail price fixed by the company for the gasoline during the period in question was 29.9 cents per gallon; and Simpson, despite the company's demand that he adhere to the authorized price, sold it at 27.9 cents, allegedly to meet a competitive price. Solely because Simpson sold gasoline below the fixed price, Union Oil refused to renew the lease; termination of the "consignment" agreement ensued; and this suit was filed. The terms of the lease and "consignment" agreement are not in dispute nor the method of their application in this case. The interstate character of Union Oil's business is conceded, as is the extensive use by it of the lease-consignment agreement in eight western States.

. . . The District Court, concluding that "all the factual disputes" had been eliminated from the case, . . . granted the company's motion for summary judgment . . . holding that Simpson had not established a violation of the Sherman Act and, even assuming such a violation, that he had not suffered any actionable damage. The Court of Appeals affirmed. . . . The case is here on a writ of certiorari.

. . . If the "consignment" agreement achieves resale price maintenance in violation of the Sherman Act, it and the lease are being used to injure interstate commerce by depriving independent dealers of the exercise of free judgment whether to become consignees at all, or remain consignees, and, in any event, to sell at competitive prices. The fact that a retailer can refuse to deal does not give the supplier immunity if the arrangement is one of those schemes condemned by the antitrust laws.

There is actionable wrong whenever the restraint of trade or monopolistic practice has an impact on the market; and it matters not that the complainant may be only one merchant.

> Congress has, by legislative fiat, determined that such prohibited activities are injurious to the public and has provided sanctions allowing private enforcement of the antitrust laws by an aggrieved party. These laws protect the victims of the forbidden practices as well as public.

The fact that, on failure to renew a lease, another dealer takes Simpson's place and renders the same service to the public is no more an answer here than it was in Poller v. Columbia Broadcasting System, (368 U.S. 464, 473, 82 S.Ct. 486, 7 L.Ed.2d 458). For Congress, not the oil distributor, is the arbiter of the public interest; and Congress has closely patrolled price fixing whether effected through resale price maintenance agreements or otherwise. . . .

. . . A supplier may not use coercion on its retail outlets to achieve resale price maintenance. . . .

Consignments perform an important function in trade and commerce, and their integrity has been recognized by many courts, including this one. Yet consignments, though useful in allocating risks between the parties and determining their rights *inter se,* do not necessarily control the rights of others, whether they be creditors or sovereigns. Thus the device has been extensively regulated by the States. Congress, too, has entered parts of the field. . . .

One who sends a rug or a painting or other work of art to a merchant or a gallery for sale at a minimum price can, of course, hold the consignee to the bargain. A retail merchant may, indeed, have inventory on consignment, the terms of which bind the parties *inter se.* Yet the consignor does not always prevail over creditors in case of bankruptcy, where a recording statute or a "traders act" or a "sign statute" is in effect. The interests of the Government also frequently override agreements that private parties make. Here we have an antitrust policy expressed in Acts of Congress. *Accordingly, a consignment, no matter how lawful it might be as a matter of private contract law, must give way before the federal antitrust policy.* Thus a consignment is not allowed to be used as a cloak to avoid § 3 of the Clayton Act. Nor does § 1 of the Sherman Act tolerate agreements for retail price maintenance. . . .

Dealers, like Simpson, are independent businessmen; and they have all or most of the indicia of entrepreneurs, except for price fixing. The risk of loss of the gasoline is on them, apart from acts of God. Their return is affected by the rise and fall in the market price, their commissions declining as retail prices drop. Practically the only power they have to be wholly independent businessmen, whose service depends on their own initiative and enterprise, is taken from them by the proviso that they must sell their gasoline at prices fixed by Union Oil. By reason of the lease and "consignment" agreement dealers are coercively laced into an arrangement under which their supplier is able to impose noncompetitive prices on thousands of persons whose prices otherwise might be competitive. The evil of this resale price maintenance program, . . . is its inexorable potentiality for and even certainly in destroying competition in retail sales of gasoline by these nominal "consignees" who are in reality small struggling competitors seeking retail gas customers.

To allow Union Oil to achieve price fixing in this vast distribution system through this "consignment" device would be to make legality for antitrust purposes turn on clever draftsmanship. We refuse to let a matter so vital to a competitive system rest on such easy manipulation.

Hence on the issue of resale price maintenance under the Sherman Act there is nothing left to try, for there was an agreement for resale price maintenance, coercively employed.

. . . we hold . . . that resale price maintenance through the present, coercive type of "consignment" agreement is illegal under the antitrust laws, and that petitioner suffered actionable wrong or damage. . . .

Reversed and remanded.

Hayes v. Parklane Hosiery Co., Inc.

1963, 24 Conn. Sup. 218, 189 Atl.2d 522

COTTER, J. The plaintiffs seek to enforce a covenant not to compete, contained in an agreement executed August 8, 1957, among the plaintiff Albert Hayes, the defendant and other persons not parties to this action. The defendant has demurred, stating that the complaint fails to set forth a cause of action because the restrictive convenant sought to be enforced is invalid and unenforceable because (1) it is in restraint of trade and against public policy, and (2) there was no consideration for defendant's promise.

The convenant is contained in an agreement for the sale of 60,000 dozen pairs of hosiery by plaintiff Hayes to defendant and security for payment therefor and for payment of a cash balance owed Hayes by defendant. It is contained in paragraph ninth, which provides:

Ninth: Upon condition that Parklane duly performs all of the terms and provisions of this agreement Hayes covenants and agrees that he, or any firm or corporation in which he is financially interested, will not establish and operate a retail store for the sale of hosiery within a radius of five blocks from any such store presently operated by Parklane. Hayes shall have the full and unrestricted right to sell hosiery at the prevailing wholesale prices to any retail store selling hosiery, or to any other person, firm or corporation, whether located within the aforesaid areas or elsewhere. Parklane, Slotkin, Somekh, Yaffee and Schulman, and each of them, jointly and severally, covenant and agree that none of them, nor any person with whom, or firm or corporation in which, any of them or any of their wives are financially interested, shall establish and operate a retail store for the sale of hosiery within a radius of five blocks from any existing store being operated by Hayes or under the name "Albert's."

The complaint alleges the agreement was entered into for "the considerations therein stated." The facts contained in the complaint and exhibit *A* allege that the plaintiff Hayes is engaged in the business of selling ladies' hosiery wholesale and is the owner of the trade name "Albert's," which he has licensed certain hosiery retailers to use. Plaintiff Patrick operates a retail hosiery store under the trade name "Albert's" on Main Street in Hartford. Patrick was not a party to the agreement of August 8, 1957. It was operating the store at that time. Defendant operates a chain of retail hosiery stores in various states. On April 12, 1962, defendant opened a retail hosiery store on Main Street in Hartford across the street from Patrick's store. Five months later, on September 14, 1962, plaintiffs commenced this action to enjoin the operation of defendant's store.

Section 515 of the Restatement of Contracts provides in part: "A restraint of trade is unreasonable, in the absence of statutory authorization or dominant social or economic justification, if it . . . (e) is based on a promise to refrain from competition and is not ancillary either to a contract for the transfer of goodwill or other subject of property or to an existing employment or contract of employment." A covenant limiting competition such as the one plaintiffs seek here to enforce, which is not ancillary to a contract for the transfer of goodwill or other subject of property by the promisor, has been held in *Domurat v. Mazzaccoli,* (138 Conn. 327, 84 A.2d 271), to be a covenant against public policy and unenforceable in this state. The court stated (p. 330, 84 A.2d p. 272): "It is basic that a covenant restricting the covenantor from engaging in a competing enterprise is one in restraint of trade and therefore is against public policy if the restraint is unreasonable. It is not valid unless it is ancillary either to a contract for the transfer of goodwill or other subject of property or to an existing employment or contract of employment." New York has found such a covenant invalid and unenforceable. "An agreement in restraint of trade is unreasonable if based upon a promise to refrain from competition where the promise is not ancillary either to a contract for the transfer of goodwill or other subject of property or to an existing employment or contract of employment." (*Paramount Pad Co. v. Baumrind,* 4 A.D.2d 944, 168 N.Y.S.2d 215, aff'd, 4 N.Y.2d 393, 175 N.Y.S.2d 809, 151 N.E.2d 609).

Cases cited to support the injunction involve employment contracts and ones which would satisfy the requirement of the Restatement and other authorities. "Ancillary" has been defined to mean "[a]iding; . . . attendant upon; . . . describing a proceeding attendant upon or which aids another proceeding considered as principal." (Black, Law Dictionary (3rd Ed.)). The mere sale of 60,000 dozen pairs of hosiery cannot carry with it a valid restrictive covenant such as that which the plaintiff would like to enforce. A contract imposing a restraint must be ancillary or incidental to, or in support of, another contract or a sale by which the covenantee acquires some interest in the business needing protection. Contracts which have for their object merely the removal of a rival or competitor in business are unlawful under the circumstances. The restraint must be reasonable. In the instant case, there was no transfer of goodwill or other subject of property and no existing employment or contract of employment.

The question of consideration need not be considered in view of the above.

The demurrer is sustained.

Terminal Vegetable Co., Inc., v. Beck

1964 (Ohio C.A.) 196 N.E.2d 109

SKEEL, C. J.   This appeal comes to this court on questions of law from a judgment entered for defendants on defendants' demurrer by the Court of Common Pleas of Cuyahoga County. The action is one for money damages for breach of plaintiff's rights under a contract whereby the plaintiff purchased the wholesale vegetable business of the defendants, Russell H. and Anna L. Beck, for the wrongful interference with plaintiff in the conduct of the business purchased.

The petition alleges that in December of 1959, plaintiff purchased from the defendants, Anna L. Beck and Russell H. Beck, under the terms of a written agreement, the Becks' Wholesale Vegetable business which they (the Becks) were then operating. It further alleges that as an inducement to persuade the plaintiff to enter into the purchase of said going business, the Becks promised that if the plaintiff would agree to employ Russell H. Beck during the summer of 1960 that he (Russell H. Beck) would retire from the wholesale produce business. It is alleged that except for such assurances, the plaintiff would not have entered into the purchase agreement.

In 1961, it is alleged Russell H. Beck made a demand to the plaintiff that it reemploy him for the summer (of 1961), the demand including the threat that if said employment was not agreed to on Beck's terms, he would accept employment from the defendant, The Cleveland Growers Market, whose place of business was next door to the plaintiff's business address. (The Cleveland Growers Market is a competitor, transacting like business with that of the plaintiff.) It is further alleged that upon plaintiff's refusal to reemploy Beck on the terms he demanded, the defendant, Russell H. Beck, in violation of his obligations under the sale, entered into employment with the defendant, The Cleveland Growers Market, the latter being fully informed of the fact that Beck, in entering its employ for the year 1961, was violating his obligations to the plaintiff. It is alleged that for the benefit of his new employer, who was fully advised of plaintiff's rights to the goodwill of Beck's former business for its benefit, Russell H. Beck solicited his former customers, informing them that he was to be affiliated with defendant, The Cleveland Growers Market, thereby attempting to induce the customers with whom he once had done business when operating the business he sold to plaintiff, and, as a consequence, a great many of plaintiff's customers transferred their business to Russell H. Beck and his new employer, The Cleveland Growers Market, to plaintiff's damage.

The defendants Beck demurred to plaintiff's amended petition, stating as the grounds for the demurrer that the petition did not state a cause of action. It needs no citation of authority to declare that the demurrer admits for the purposes of the demurrer all of the well pleaded allegations of the petition. By giving the allegations their most favorable interpretation in favor of the pleader, it must be concluded that the sale of the "business" must have included the "goodwill" it had generated under the management of the Becks. The sale was of the business as a going concern.

The inducement to enter into the contract, as pleaded, was made on behalf of the present owners, for their benefit. It was not an employment contract. We are not, therefore, concerned with the law dealing with restrictive covenants as a part of employment agreements. Nor is the question here presented, as argued in the briefs, one concerning a restrictive covenant not to compete with plaintiff after the sale of a business. No such claim is pleaded. The legal claim presented is whether or not the defendant, Russell H. Beck, and his new employer, may attempt to destroy or purposely minimize the value of the goodwill of a business which he has sold, by aggressive competition within a time necessarily needed by the plaintiff to obtain the benefits of the goodwill purchased under the assurances pleaded. There is no time alleged within which the defendants Beck agreed (by his promise to retire) not to interfere with the goodwill of the business sold. It must be concluded that a reasonable time within which to possess the advantages of the commercial relationship between the plaintiff and the former customers of the defendants Beck must pass before Beck can seek, without violating plaintiff's rights in the goodwill purchased, to do business with his former customers.

The meaning of the term "goodwill" is clearly set out in Black's Law Dictionary and is, in part, as follows:

> . . . The advantage or benefit which is acquired by an establishment, beyond the mere value of the capital, stocks, funds, or property employed therein, in consequence of the general public patronage and encouragement which it receives from the constant or habitual customers, on account of its local position. . . .

In the case of *Snyder Manufacturing Co. v. Snyder,* (54 Ohio St. 86, on page 91, 43 N.E. 325, on page 326, 31 L.R.A. 657), the court in defining "goodwill" states:

> Without attempting an accurate or exhaustive definition of the good will of a business, it may be said that it practically consists of that favorable reputation it has established creating a disposition or inclination of persons to extend their patronage to the business on that account; and, as the business is always associated with the name under which it is conducted, the name becomes a part, and often an important part of its good will.

Also, in the case of *Lima Tel. & Tel. v. Public Utilities Comm. of Ohio,* (98 Ohio St. 110, 120 N.E. 330), the court said that the goodwill value of any business enterprise is the value that results from the probability that old customers will continue to trade with the established concern.

It must be concluded that the goodwill transferred to a buyer is a property right that must be respected by the seller for a sufficient time to permit the buyer to make the business customers his own. In the case of *Suburban Ice Mfg. & Cold Storage Co. v. Mulvihill*, (21 Ohio App. 438, 153 N.E. 204), the court said in the third paragraph of the syllabus:

> 3. Seller of ice business, including good will, cannot impair good will by soliciting business of old customers before buyer has time to make them his own.

And in the case of *Soeder v. Soeder*, (82 Ohio App. 71, 77 N.E.2d 474), the court said in the fourth paragraph of the syllabus:

> 4. While the vendor of a business with goodwill included in the sale cannot impair the goodwill by directly soliciting the old customers of the business before the buyer has had time to make them his own, nevertheless, a period of three years must be considered a sufficient time to attach goodwill to the buyer and make it his own.

The time which must be allowed a purchaser to make the customers of the purchased business "his own" is a question of fact for the determination of the jury or the court in the event a jury is waived on the allegations set out in the petition. Certainly to accept employment by a competitor who joins with him in active solicitation of his former customers that he had developed when he owned the business sold to the plaintiff, thus diminishing the value of the goodwill of such business, requires the defendant to show as a defense that sufficient time had elapsed under the surrounding circumstance for the plaintiff to make the customers his own unless the time elapsing between the sale and defendants subsequent acts can be said as a matter of law to be sufficient to protect the plaintiff to the extent necessary in the enjoyment of that which he purchased. The facts coming within "the circumstances to be considered"—in addition to the sale of a going business—is the fact that the defendant, Russell H. Beck, continued as an employee of plaintiff during the summer of 1960, striving to maintain the goodwill of plaintiff's business and then attempted to destroy it by accepting employment with plaintiff's next door competitor in 1961 by soliciting the same customers for his new employer.

The judgment of the trial court is, therefore, reversed as contrary to law and the cause is remanded to the trial court with instructions to overrule the demurrer and for further proceedings according to law.

Beltone Electronics Corporation v. Smith
1963 (Ill. App.) 194 N.E.2d 21

BURKE, Presiding Justice.   Victor G. Smith appeals from the order for a temporary injunction restraining him, a former employee, from disclosing or using at any time, any secret or confidential information or knowledge attained or acquired by him while employed by Beltone Electronics Corporation and from directly or indirectly performing at any time on or before February 1, 1964, any services for or continuing or accepting employment by or association in any capacity with Zenith Radio Corporation. The Chancellor rejected the recommendations of a Master in Chancery that the application for preliminary injunction be denied.

On May 13, 1957, defendant was hired by Beltone as chief industrial engineer. His initial task was to set up an industrial engineering department and assume responsibility for production control. At the time defendant ceased employment with Beltone he was manager of manufacturing. Smith's duties were largely administrative. He was not an inventor, designer or chemist. When Smith joined Beltone he signed an employment agreement with his employer which states that Smith, "shall not disclose or use at any time, either during or subsequent to his employment by Employer, any secret or confidential information or knowledge obtained or acquired by Employee while in Employer's employment; . . . that he will not, at any time within one (1) year subsequent to the termination of his employment with Employer, however occurring, directly or indirectly perform any service or be employed by, or become associated in any capacity with, any person, firm or corporation engaged in the manufacture or sale of hearing aids or hearing aid accessories or audiometers or be engaged on his own behalf in the manufacture or sale of any such products; . . . that for a violation by Employee of any of the covenants of this Agreement, Employer may have an injunction restraining Employee therefrom." The agreement was not limited as to its geographic scope.

The defendant, in the fall of 1961, began putting out "feelers," answering advertisements and mailing out résumés. He had interviews with Zenith Corporation in December 1962 and was employed by it on January 8, 1963. His position with Zenith Corporation was that of director of hearing aid production. Defendant left Beltone on February 1, 1963. Prior to his termination of employment with Beltone he was warned against taking employment with a competitor. He commenced to work for Zenith on February 18, 1963. An announcement of his retention by Zenith appeared in the Chicago press on February 26, 1963 and shortly thereafter the instant complaint was filed.

The 1931 case of *Parish v. Schwartz* (344 Ill. 563, 176 N.E. 757, 78 A.L.R. 1032), has spelled out the general Illinois rule with respect to enforcement of restrictive covenants in employment contracts. Where a covenant places restrictions upon a party not to engage in subsequent competitive employment or in a competitive line of trade, these restrictions must be reasonably related to safeguarding the employer without putting unreasonable restraints upon trade. An employee, after severing connections with his employer may compete with the former employer in his new position unless restricted by contract. While limitations may be placed upon an employee's freedom of action these limitations must conform to a test of reasonableness which will be stricter in the case of employment contracts.

The Restatement of Contracts, Secs. 313 to 315, 1932, states a test for the validity of post-employment restraints. Such restraining covenants are reasonable if (1) the restraint is no greater than that required for the protection of the employer, (2) they do not impose undue hardship on the employee, and (3) these are not injurious to the public. It does not appear that the activities of the defendant while performing his duties for the plaintiff were such as to require a covenant which would prevent him from obtaining subsequent employment with a competitor for a period of 1 year. From the nature of Smith's work at Beltone and his non-technical position, the restraint upon his engaging in any other employment within 1 year would not be likely to produce corresponding benefits for the plaintiff. The covenant in prohibiting defendant's employment by anyone engaged in the manufacture or sale of hearing aids by anyone in any place goes farther than necessary to protect the plaintiff. Defendant by the covenant cannot be employed in a non-hearing aid capacity by firms employed in the manufacture or sale of other products as well as hearing aids. . . .

The business of plaintiff is highly competitive. The burden of business risks, inherent in its operation, however, cannot be allocated to the employee by placing such wide restrictions upon his right to future employment. . . .

We feel that the covenant falls within the rule announced by the Supreme Court in *Parish v. Schwartz*, (344 Ill. 563, 176 N.E. 757, 78 A.L.R. 1032) and followed by us in *Brunner & Lay, Inc. v. Chapin*, (29 Ill. App.2d 161, 172 N.E.2d 652). The order granting the temporary injunction is reversed.

Order reversed.

The Bankers Guarantee Title and Trust Company v. Fisher

1965 (Ohio) 204 N.E.2d 103

ROSSETTI, J. The plaintiff filed a law suit against the defendants claiming that there is due the plaintiff from the defendants Fisher the sum of Eighty-nine hundred ninety-eight dollars and ninety-six cents ($8998.96) with interest from February 1, 1962. Defendants Fisher filed an answer requesting that the interest of the plaintiff and the defendants be determined. . . .

The defendants, Daniel Arthur Fisher and Dorothy L. Fisher, entered into a written contract with William J. Savage and Mildred E. Savage to purchase certain premises in Louisville, Ohio. The plaintiff loaned the Fisher defendants Ninety-one hundred and fifty dollars ($9150.00) and accepted a note and mortgage for that amount.

A closing of this transaction was held in the office of the plaintiff and certain costs were paid by the Fisher defendants, among which was Item F in the fourth stipulation in the amount of Ninety-one dollars and fifty cents ($91.50) designated as "origination charge," which is one per cent of the loan.

Another cost item paid by the Fisher defendants is the so-called loan discount fee of Eight hundred twenty-three dollars and fifty cents ($823.-50) which is nine (9) per cent of the face amount of the loan. This was authorized to be deducted from the sales price by the sellers of the property.

The item of Eight hundred twenty-three dollars and fifty cents ($823.50) has been referred to as a loan discount fee, and again in the plaintiff's brief it has been referred to as "points." Whatever it is called, the simple fact is that nine (9) per cent of the loan was deducted and retained by the plaintiff bank, amounting to Eight hundred twenty-three dollars and fifty cents ($823.50). However, as between the plaintiff bank and the defendant borrowers this sum or item was not deducted which means that the bank received in addition to the regular interest charged on the loan of Ninety-one hundred and fifty dollars ($9150.00) the sum of Eight hundred twenty-three dollars and fifty cents ($823.50), plus the origination charge.

The Fisher defendants claim that they should not pay any more to the plaintiff than what plaintiff paid out, and consequently the plaintiff bank is only entitled to recover the sum of Eighty-three hundred twenty-six dollars and fifty cents ($8326.50) plus interest and less any payments made.

One of the questions in this case is as follows:

> When the payee of a promissory note in the amount of Nine thousand one hundred fifty dollars ($9,150.00) pays to and disburses for the maker of said note the sum of Eight thousand three hundred twenty-six dollars and fifty cents ($8,326.50), how much can the payee recover from the maker?
> . . .

The next question is whether the transaction in this case was a shift or device to evade the usury law. The evidence shows that the only contract was between the plaintiff and the Fisher defendants and that was as a result of the note and mortgage. The note and mortgage clearly indicates that the subject of the loan was the property in question.

The Court must, therefore, examine all disbursements made by the plaintiff and deductions held by the plaintiff to determine whether or not the plaintiff violated the usury statute and whether or not the plaintiff collected more than the legal rate of interest allowed in Ohio.

The evidence shows that the plaintiff received the following for making the loan to the Fisher defendants:

1. Origination charge, $91.50 or 1 per cent.
2. Interest on the $9150.00 note or 5¼ per cent.
3. Loan discount fee of $823.50 or 9 per cent.

Thus we find that the plaintiff bank actually disbursed the sum of Eighty-three hundred twenty-six dollars and fifty cents ($8326.50) of the Ninety-one hundred fifty dollar loan for the Fisher defendants. That simply means, the plaintiff bank realized an additional profit of Eight hundred twenty-three dollars and fifty cents ($823.50) for making a loan to these defendants in addition to the interest and origination charge.

An early case dealing with this question is *Spalding v. Bank of Muskingum,* (12 Ohio 544), which held:

> An agreement between a bank and contractors on the public works, for the bank to make a loan to the state, to be applied to the public improvements on which they were engaged, and charge the contractors five per cent commission is an illegal shift and device by the bank to obtain more than six per cent interest on its loans. Such a contract would not be enforced in favor of the bank against the contractors.

The Court further said:

> Whatever pretense may be set up to retain the amount in controversy, as commissions in the sums allowed, it is very clear it is one of those illegal shifts and devices to which the inordinate money-lender resorts to acquire to himself gains by an evasion of the wholesome provisions of the laws of the state, and it is much to be regretted that such efforts are but too frequently successful.

In the case of *Rose v. Baxter,* (67 Ohio App. 1, 34 N.E.2d 1011), the Court held:

> Whenever an agent, with the knowledge and consent of the lender, exacts from the borrower a bonus or commission for procuring the loan, which bonus or commission is deducted from the amount of the loan and paid by the lender direct to his agent or attorney and only the balance left, after such deduction, is paid to the borrower, by the great weight of the authorities that which is paid as bonus or commission to the agent or attorney of the lender is considered as being a charge for the use of the money. Such bonus will be added to the amount of interest contracted for by the provisions of the note in determining whether or not such note is usurious.

The law against usury was made necessary and originated by reason of evil practices that prevailed to a large degree in the loaning of money, and out of that condition came the prohibition by express statute, Section 1343.01, Ohio Revised Code, which reads as follows:

> The parties to a bond, bill, promissory note, or other instrument of writing for the forebearance of payment of money at any future time, may stipulate therein for the payment of interest upon the amount thereof at any rate not exceeding eight per cent per annum payable annually.

Referring to Item F of the closing cost of this case the evidence does not show the purpose of the so-called origination charge of Ninety-one dollars and fifty cents ($91.50) which is exactly one (1) per cent of the face amount of the note. There is no explanation of what value or benefit is rendered to the Fisher defendants by this charge. This Court must consider this charge as interest on the loan.

Again the evidence does not show the purpose of the loan discount fee which was a matter between the plaintiff bank and the seller of the property. It appears to this Court that this is a matter of the seller of the property reducing the sales price of the property, and in that event the purchaser is entitled to receive the full benefit of the reduction of the sales price.

The question is not what the parties called the transaction herein, but what the transaction requires the Court to call it. It, therefore, is necessary for this Court to scan the transaction carefully to ascertain its real substance with a purpose of determining whether it is a disguised loan or something else.

The question in this case is not what price the Fisher defendants paid for their house, but rather what did the plaintiff receive for making this loan to the Fisher defendants. Therefore, is the plaintiff lender exacting an interest rate greater than eight (8) per cent in making this loan to the borrowers? What is the plaintiff receiving for making the loan in this case? There can be no question but what the plaintiff is receiving 15¼ per cent of the loan which is in excess of the legal rate of eight (8) per cent.

Having in mind, therefore, the purposes of the statute in its inception and the need for a rule understandable by laymen as well as the courts the Court expresses the following rule for determination of usury:

> If the total amount contracted to be paid by a borrower before or after the use of money actually received as a loan for the period of time it is used, regardless of the names used for the various charges, is in excess of eight per cent per annum, then the excess is usurious.

This was the purpose and intent of the law. This is a rule easily followed and understood by all. This Court is not concerned with the proposition of whether or not eight (8) per cent is sufficient money to receive by way of return in lending money. This is a matter to be determined by the state legislature.

The Court cannot close its eyes to the pretense between lenders and the sellers of real estate who agree on circumstances which will result in a lender's receipt of interest in an amount greater than its legal rate of eight (8) per cent. This Court cannot approve a transaction which is merely a shift or device to evade the usury law.

The evidence in this case fails to show that plaintiff rendered any additional service to the Fisher defendants which would justify the plaintiff retaining the sum of Eight hundred twenty-three dollars and fifty cents ($823.50).

The Court finds that the plaintiff only disbursed or paid out for the Fisher defendants on the Ninety-one hundred and fifty dollar ($9150.00) note, the sum of Eighty-three hundred twenty-six dollars and fifty cents ($8326.50).

The Court finds that the Fisher defendants paid interest to the plaintiff on Ninety-one hundred fifty dollars ($9150.00).

The Court finds from the evidence that the note and mortgage provides a rate of interest within the law; however, the Court further finds that the plaintiff did receive a bonus, points, or loan discount fee of

Eight hundred twenty-three dollars and fifty cents ($823.50), which together with the rate of interest constituted a usurious transaction in violation of the law.

The motion of the plaintiff for summary judgment is sustained. Judgment is rendered to the plaintiff for Eighty-three hundred twenty-six dollars and fifty cents ($8326.50), plus interest, and less any credits or payments made on said note.

CHAPTER 12
REVIEW QUESTIONS AND PROBLEMS

1. X Council of tne Boy Scouts of America admitted boys to its summer camp program only if the boys and their parents signed an agreement releasing the camp of all liability for injury even though camp officials were careless. F was injured and brought suit. Is the exculpatory clause illegal?

2. M was purchasing a residence from S on installments at a price of $20,000. After payment of $5,000, M needed money, so W paid the remaining $15,000 to S, took title and resold the property to M for $21,000 on installments. M is now in default and W seeks to foreclose the contract of sale. M insisted that the resale was nothing more than a loan to M of $15,000 and the $6,000 added was in reality usurious interest and that there is no contract for the sale of real estate but rather a loan, secured by real estate which is involved. Is M correct?

3. A finance company loaned money directly to the buyer of a car and added to the loan a finance or carrying charge which was greatly in excess of the legal rate of interest. Was usury present?

4. O sued W for injuries resulting from the carelessness of W in failing to maintain the premises leased to O. The lease contained language relieving the landlord of liability for any negligence on his part. Is this provision enforceable?

5. The X oil company leased its service stations to Y and sold its gasoline by consignment. Y sold gasoline below the price suggested by X and X canceled the lease. Y sues X for damage under the Clayton Act. What result?

6. Three doctors formed a medical clinic. As a part of the agreement forming the clinic each doctor agreed that if he left the clinic, he would not practice medicine for 5 years in the county in which the clinic operates. X left the clinic and the others sought to enforce the agreement. X contended that the agreement was illegal as contrary to public policy since there was a shortage of doctors in the county. What result?

7. The promoters of a new corporation had each subscriber of the stock sign an agreement which authorized the promoters to select the persons to be elected directors of the company at the first meeting of shareholders. Is the agreement binding?

8. *O* leased space in his office building to *T*. The lease contained a clause exempting *O* from liability if *T* or his invitees were injured while using the elevator in the building. Is the clause enforceable?

9. *X* operated a branch office of the *ABC* Loan Co. As a part of his contract of employment, *X* agreed not to work for any other loan company in any state in which *ABC* operated for one year. If *X* goes to work for a competitor in violation of the agreement, may *ABC* enjoin his action?

10. *X* stole *Y*'s car and wrecked it. *X* signed a note payable to *Y* in return for *Y*'s promise not to prosecute *X*. If *X* fails to pay, can *Y* collect the note by legal proceedings?

11. A partnership agreement contained the usual buy and sell provisions and a special provision which provided that if any partner filed a suit concerning the agreement, he would forfeit his interest. If this latter provision is illegal, is the remainder of the partnership agreement enforceable?

12. A manager of a department store agreed in his contract of employment that if his employment were terminated for any reason he would not engage in a similar business activity for two years within a 25 mile area surrounding the store. Is the contract enforceable?

13. A city ordinance prohibited the operation of a movie theater within 200 feet of a church. *X* and *Y* entered into a contract by which *X* agreed to construct and operate a theater for *Y* next door to a church. If *X* fails to perform, is the contract enforceable?

14. *X* assigned his interest in his grandfather's estate to *Y* for 23 per cent of the face amount of the value of his interest in the estate. *X* later wishes to cancel the assignment and tenders back the money received. May he do so?

15. *X* signed a $500 note payable to *Y* and received $500. How much does *X* owe *Y*?

13

Form of the
Agreement

2-69. Introduction. As has been previously noted, a contract may arise
from oral or written communications between the parties, from a combination of such communications or it may be created by the execution of
a written document. As a general rule, an oral agreement is just as valid
and enforceable as a written one even though the parties intend to later
reduce their agreement to writing; but as a practical matter, written
contracts are more desirable.[1] It is much easier to establish the existence
and terms of a written agreement and the terms cannot be varied by oral
evidence. Written agreements do not require proof of contract terms,
thus reducing the scope of any litigation concerning alleged breaches of
the contract. The parol evidence rule, which is discussed in the next
section, is a rule of contract law which is used by courts as a rule of
evidence in trials of contract cases to prevent the use of oral testimony to
alter or vary the terms of a written agreement.

Not only are written agreements highly desirable, but a writing is
frequently required in order to make the contract enforceable. Our legal
system has recognized the need for written evidence of the existence of a
contract in certain types of agreements. This need has been met by
statutory enactments usually known as the Statute of Frauds which create
exceptions to the general rule that a contract may be either oral or
written. These exceptions are discussed later in this chapter.

A few states have statutes which require that certain types of contracts
be executed with formality. These statutes require a seal on contracts
involving land or may require that the signatures of the parties be

1 *Federal Security Insurance Company v. Smith,* page 251.

acknowledged before a notary public in certain classes of contracts. Some statutes, such as those relating to wage assignments by an employee may require that the contract of assignment be on a sheet of paper which is separate from other contracts to which the assignment is related. The trend in the law generally, however, is to reduce the legal requirements relating to the form of contracts. Consultation with an attorney is necessary to determine the form requirements for a contract in any given state.

2-70. Parol Evidence Rule. The parol evidence rule prevents the introduction of oral testimony to alter or vary the terms of a written agreement.[2] Thus, a party to a contract or other witness may not introduce testimony about oral statements of the parties prior to or contemporaneous with the written agreement if such statements are in conflict with the written agreements. The written contract is the only evidence of the agreement since all matters which were agreed upon prior to its execution are presumed to have been incorporated or integrated in the written agreement. All negotiations and oral understandings are said to have merged in the agreement.

The applications of the parol evidence rule are predicated on this concept of merger and on general principles of equity. There are exceptions to the rule which allow the introduction of oral testimony for certain purposes. Parol evidence is admissible to establish modifications agreed upon subsequent to the execution of the written agreement and also to establish cancellation of the contract by mutual agreement. It must be remembered that if the contract is one of those within the purview of the Statute of Frauds, any modification or cancellation must be in writing.

There are several other exceptions to the parol evidence rule which find their basis in equity, good conscience, and common sense. Evidence of fraudulent misrepresentation, lack of delivery of an instrument where delivery is required to give it effect, and errors in drafting or reducing the contract to writing are admissible under some of the many exceptions to the rule.

The Code contains provisions relating to the parol evidence rule in cases involving construction or interpretation of an agreement for the sale of goods. The Code recognizes that terms of an agreement may be explained or supplemented by a prior course of dealing between buyer and seller, or usage of trade, or by the course of performance. Thus in the latter situation if a contract of sale involves repeated occasions of performance by either party with knowledge of the nature of the performance and opportunity for objection to it by the other, any course of performance of the agreement accepted or acquiesced in, without objection by the other party is relevant in determining the meaning of the agreement. If there is an inconsistency, express terms will prevail over an interpretation based on the course of performance and the course of performance will prevail over an interpretation predicated upon either the

2 *Grubb v. Rockey*, page 252.

course of dealing or usage of trade. In addition, the Code allows the admission of oral evidence of consistent additional terms unless the court finds the writing to have been intended as a complete and exclusive statement of the terms of the agreement.

While the application of the parol evidence rule is a problem for judges and lawyers, businessmen should recognize the importance of the protection afforded them in connection with their written agreements by this rule.

STATUTE OF FRAUDS

2-71. Historical Development. In 1677, "An Act for Prevention of Frauds and Perjuries" was enacted in England. This statute was designed to prevent fraud by excluding legal actions on certain contracts unless there was written evidence of the agreement signed by the defendant or his duly authorized agent. The contracts covered by the statute of frauds were (a) special promises by the personal representative of a deceased to pay claims against the estate of the deceased out of such representative's own estate, (b) guaranty contracts, (c) agreements made upon consideration of marriage, (d) contracts involving real estate, and (e) agreements not to be performed within one year from the date of making.

Another English statute later made a part of the statute of frauds provided that any contract for the sale of personal property involving more than ten pounds sterling required a writing in order to be enforceable.

The need for these statutes arose out of the peculiar rules of evidence used by English courts during the seventeenth century. A party was not allowed to testify in his own behalf and law suits were frequently tried with either professional witnesses or with testimony of friends of the parties. Perjury was commonplace, and in the law of contracts it soon became apparent that defendants were at a distinct disadvantage because of the difficulty of proving a negative that no contract in fact had been made. For example, suppose that A sued B and alleged that B orally agreed to sell a certain land for £100. C testified that he heard B agree to the sale. Would it help B any to have D testify that D didn't hear B enter into the agreement? Obviously not. This difficulty was overcome by requiring written evidence that a contract actually had been entered into in contracts of substantial importance. Since the purpose of the statute was to prevent fraud and the use of perjured testimony, it became known as the Statute of Frauds.

All the states have enacted the Statute of Frauds in essentially the same format as the early English statute. Some states have added other provisions relating to real estate covering such matters as the appointment of an agent to sell real estate or the creation of a trust with real estate as the corpus or subject of the trust. Some states have provisions requiring that a promise by a bankrupt to pay a debt discharged in bankruptcy be in writing. The rules of evidence were subsequently changed to allow parties to contracts to testify, but the Statute of Frauds remained essentially intact. Today, the Statute may be used as a defense even though there is no factual dispute as to the existence of the contract or to its terms. A contract that requires a writing comes into existence at the time of the oral agreement but it is unenforceable until written evidence of the agreement is available. The agreement is valid in every respect except that proper evidence of its existence is lacking. Except for contract for the sale of goods under the Code which is discussed later, the Statute creates an immunity from suit for the breach of oral contracts if such contracts are covered by its provisions. The Code retains the Statute of Frauds concepts but drastically limits its application, thus taking a major step toward modernization of this old English statute.[C1] A substantial argument can be made for repeal of the Statute of Frauds in light of modern trial techniques such as discovery procedures. The sections which follow discuss the modern version of the classes of contracts covered by the Statute of Frauds in most states.

2-72. Contracts of Executors or Administrators. The personal representative of a deceased is in legal effect two entities—his own self and the estate which he represents. Assume that he promises a creditor of the estate that a debt of the deceased will be paid. In which capacity was the promise made? Because of the difficulties inherent in this factual situation, it is apparent that such a promise must be in writing if the personal representative is promising personally to pay the debt as contrasted with the normal procedure which is to pay it from the estate.

2-73. Guaranty Contracts. A guaranty contract is one in which one party becomes responsible for the debt, default, or miscarriage of some third person. For example, *B* promises *A* that if *A* will sell to *C* on credit he will pay *C*'s debt to *A* if *C* fails to pay. In such case, *C* is primarily liable to *A* and *B* is secondarily liable or liable only in the event that *C* fails to pay. However, if the agreement is such that the obligation of the principal debtor, *C*, is cancelled or merges in the agreement of the third party to pay; or if the promise is to pay out of money held for, or owing to, the principal debtor, *C*, by the party who makes the promise, no guaranty results. Such promise is an original one and no writing is required. In addition, if credit is extended directly to *B* or is extended in part to *B*, the oral agreement is binding as where *B* says to *A:* "Sell to *C* on credit and charge it to me."

An agreement which has for its object the substitution of one debtor for another does not fall within the statute and no writing is required. Thus, if *A* says to *Y*, "If you will release *B* from his liability to you, I will pay the same," and *Y* consents, the agreement is binding, although made orally, because it is a primary promise of *A* and is not secondary to *B*'s promise, as is required in a guaranty contract.

In case a guarantor agrees to become responsible for the default or debt

---

C1 *U.C.C.* 1-206, 2-201.

of another because of some material advantage that he may gain from the transaction, no writing is required.[3] Thus, an oral guaranty by a *del credere agent*—a consignee who sells consigned goods on credit, but who guarantees to the consignor that the buyers will pay for the goods purchased—is enforceable. Since the agent obtains a commission for selling the merchandise, his pecuniary interest in the consignment disposes of the necessity of a writing, and the consignor may collect from the consignee on the oral guaranty if the purchaser fails to pay.

2-74. Contracts Involving Real Property. Contracts involving interests in land have always been considered important by the law and therefore it is not surprising that such contracts are within the coverage of the Statute of Frauds. In addition to contracts involving a sale of an entire interest, the Statute is applicable to contracts involving interests for a person's life time, called life estates, to mortgages, to easements and even to leases[4] for a period in excess of one year.

Contracts involving such items as growing crops, timber, minerals or other items which may appear to be a part of or attached to the real estate create a special problem in the application of the Statute.[5] These items during their existence may be either real property or personal property, depending on whether or not they are attached to the real estate. The question as to the applicability of the Statute can not be answered by simply deciding the status at the time of the contract. It can only be answered by the question "What does the contract involve, real property or personal property?" This question in turn is answered by an examination of the agreement to ascertain when the title to the property passes to buyer. If the title passes while the property is reasonably permanently attached to the land, the contract involves real estate. If the title passes after the property is severed from the land, the contract involves personal property.

A contract that imposes a duty upon the seller to sever and deliver rather clearly suggests that title is to pass later, and the contract will be considered a contract for the sale of goods with no sale of real property involved. The Code contains special provisions relating to the sale of such property.[C2] Where the buyer is to enter, sever, and effect delivery, the cases are somewhat in conflict. If the right to enter and take is one that can be exercised in a relatively short period of time, it is likely to indicate an intention to sell personal property as distinct from realty. To illustrate: *A* orally contracts to deliver to *B* 100 twelve-inch trees from certain timber land. Later he refuses to deliver the trees and denies any liability. Inasmuch as it is apparent that title was to pass only after the trees were severed from the land, the agreement involves personal property rather than real estate. Once this decision is made, it is then

---

[3] *Hayes v. Guy*, page 254.
[4] *First National Bank of Boston v. Fairhaven Amuse. Company*, page 255.
[5] *Sutton v. Wright & Sanders*, page 256.

[C2] *U.C.C.* 2-107.

necessary to examine the personal property provisions of the Statute to determine if these prevent a suit on the oral agreement.

Frequently, a buyer under an oral contract involving real estate will partially perform the contract, either by making part payment, taking possession, or making last improvements. This situation imposes a dilemma for courts. A fully executed contract is enforceable as being beyond the scope of the Statute of Frauds and a fully executory contract is clearly unenforceable. The partially executed contract could be either, depending on the extent of the performance. For many years, most courts held that part performance by the buyer of real estate did not make the contract enforceable. The writing was not dispensed with merely because the buyer has made a down payment. If the seller refused to carry out the oral agreement, the buyer had as his only remedy the right to recover all payments made and the reasonable value of all improvements that have been added by him. If the buyer refused to perform, he could not recover the payments he had made or the value of the improvements.

In recent years as equitable concepts have tended to prevail over strict rules of law, some courts have recognized that a buyer may progress to a point where mere return of payments made by him and compensation for improvements added by him prove unfair and inequitable. Courts of equity, to handle such situations fairly, have disregarded this section of the Statute of Frauds and enforced the oral contract. Courts still are not entirely in agreement as to what is required to remove the case from the Statute, but mere part payment or mere entry into possession, standing alone, is still not enough. Where both take place and cannot be explained on any basis other than a contract for sale, most courts will enforce the oral agreement. This is also true if, in addition, the buyer makes substantial improvements or has placed himself in a position where he cannot be restored to his prior position. It would seem that oral contracts partially performed should be enforced since there is no danger of fraud, especially where the parties admit the existence of the oral agreement.

2-75. Contracts of Long Duration. An oral contract which by its terms is not possible of full performance within one year from the date of its creation is unenforceable under this section of the Statute of Frauds. For example, an agreement to work for another for a period of years or a contract by a manufacturer that gives to a retailer exclusive territory for eighteen months is not enforceable if made orally. Performance may in fact extend for more than one year without affecting enforceability if full performance was *possible* within the one year period.[6]

For illustration, assume that *A* contracted orally to sell to *B* 15,000 tons of steel at $185 a ton, *B* being free to order it out as he saw fit within a period of fifteen months. One thousand tons were ordered out and paid for, after which *A* refused to ship the balance. The contract was enforceable even though the remaining balance was ordered out fourteen months

[6] *Haveg Corporation v. Guyver,* page 258.

after the contract was made, completion having been possible within one year at the time the contract was made. Thus, if the time for performance is of uncertain duration, being dependent upon the happening of a contingency such as death, the act of one of the parties, the arrival of a certain ship, or the sale of certain property, no writing is required, despite the fact that actual performance extends over several years. Since it is *possible* for such contingencies to occur within a year, the contract falls outside of the statute. Attention should also be called to the fact that the year is figured from the date of the agreement, and not from the time performance is to begin. A contract to work for one year at a certain salary, employment to begin two days later, would have to be in writing.

In contracts that provide for performance over a period in excess of one year, full performance of all obligations by one of the parties, which has been accepted by the other, makes the agreement enforceable. Thus, if a present sale of goods is made, followed by delivery, the oral agreement is binding although the buyer is to make his payments over a period of 18 months. Some few states go even further and hold that where the contract calls for complete performance by one of the parties within a year, the oral agreement is effective.

2-76. Contracts Involving the Sale of Personal Property. The Statute of Frauds provisions relating to the sale of personal property are part of the Code. Prior to the Code and in those few states which have not adopted the Code, these provisions are a part of the Uniform Sales Act. The Code contains separate Statute of Frauds provisions relating to the sale of goods,[C3] the sale of securities,[C4] and the sale of other personal property which does not fall within the other two categories.[C5] This latter general provision provides that a contract for the sale of personal property is not enforceable by way of action or defense beyond $5,000 in amount or value of remedy unless there is some writing which indicates that a contract for sale has been made between the parties at a defined or stated price, reasonably identifies the subject matter, and is signed by the party against whom enforcement is sought or by his authorized agent.[C6]

Contracts for sale of goods are governed by a special section dealing with the necessity for a writing.[C7] The basic requirement of written proof is retained but is substantially modified. A contract for sale of goods for the price of $500 or more is not enforceable unless there is some writing sufficient to indicate that a contract for sale has been made between the parties.[7] The writing must be signed by the party against whom enforcement is sought, but it may be quite informal. It is important to keep in mind that the basic purpose of the requirement is simply to establish that there is in fact a contract for sale and purchase. The details, such as price,

---

[7] *Acuri v. Weiss,* page 259.

C3 *U.C.C.* 2-201. C6 *U.C.C.* 1-206.
C4 *U.C.C.* 8-319. C7 *U.C.C.* 8-319.
C5 *U.C.C.* 1-206.

time, and place of delivery, and the like may be omitted. The quantity of goods, however, should be explicitly expressed in the writing.[C8]

An oral contract of sale is nevertheless enforceable if there are other circumstances present which are indicative of the existence of a contract. If the goods are to be specially manufactured for the buyer, and the seller has made a substantial beginning of their manufacture for the buyer, a writing is not required.[C9] Likewise receipt and acceptance of either the goods or of the price makes it enforceable to the extent of such acceptance.[C10] Also, if a suit is brought on an oral contract and the defendant admits in the court proceeding that he did enter into a contract, the contract will be enforceable, but only to the extent of the quantity of goods admitted by the defendant.[C11]

A special provision is applicable if the oral transaction is *between merchants.* Assuming an oral contract for sale, one merchant may send a written confirmation of the contract to the other. The merchant receiving the confirmation may not defend on the ground of the lack of writing unless he gives written notice of his objection within ten days after he receives the confirmation.[C12] (It is to be noted that the only effect is to take away from the party who fails to object the defense of the Statute of Frauds; the other party still has the burden of proving that the oral contract was, in fact, made and the terms of the alleged contract.)

The provision of the Statute of Frauds pertaining to securities applies to all sales of securities regardless of dollar amount. It requires a writing signed by the party to be charged or his authorized agent or broker. However, delivery of the security or payment therefore renders a contract for sale enforceable. This section of the Code also contains a provision on confirmations of and a provision for establishing the contract by admissions in legal proceedings or pleadings similar to the provisions in the sale of goods section.[C13]

One further problem concerning the sale of personal property must be noted. In determining whether the value of property is such as to cause it to fall within the statute, it often becomes necessary to decide how many contracts have been entered into. Thus, *A* orders from *B* $400 worth of one item to be delivered at once and $200 of another item to be delivered ten weeks later. Either item considered alone is worth less than $500; both items total over $500. If the parties intended only one contract, the Statute of Frauds is applicable; however, if two contracts were entered into, no writing is required. The intention of the parties in these cases is gleaned from such factors as the time and the place of the agreement, the nature of the articles involved, and other surrounding circumstances.

2-77. A Contract Involving Two or More Sections of Statute. A single contract often involves two or more sections of the statute. In such a case, all sections of the statute that are involved must be complied with or the

---

[C8] *U.C.C.* 2-201(1).
[C9] *U.C.C.* 2-201(3)(a).
[C10] *U.C.C.* 2-201(3)(c).

[C11] *U.C.C.* 2-201(3)(6).
[C12] *U.C.C.* 2-201(2).
[C13] *U.C.C.* 8-319.

contract is unenforceable. Thus, a single integrated oral contract may be entered into involving an agreement to sell both real and personal property, followed by delivery of some of the personalty. Since only one contract is involved and real property requires a written memorandum, no part of the contract is enforceable.

An oral contract for the sale of personal property may be so drawn that it cannot be completed within a period of one year, in which case receipt and acceptance of part of the property does not eliminate the necessity for a writing. If a contract is unenforceable for any reason, it is entirely unenforceable.

2-78. Nature of the Writing. The writing required by the Statute of Frauds is not a formal written document signed by both parties. Except in cases under the Code which are even more liberal,[C14] the law merely requires that some note or memorandum concerning the transaction be signed by the party sought to be bound by the agreement but the memorandum must contain the basic terms of the contract.[8] A situation exists in which one party may be bound by an agreement although the other party is not bound since only the party who resists performance need sign. Such a result may be explained on the theory that the agreement is legal in all respects, but proper evidence of such an agreement is lacking unless the person sought to be charged with the contract has signed a writing. Any kind of note or memorandum that describes the property involved, that sets forth the major terms, and that indicates the parties to the agreement is sufficient. If one memorandum is incomplete, but it is clear that two or more writings relate to the same subject matter, they may be joined to supply the necessary written evidence. This is true only if it is clear that the writings relate to the same agreement. If, prior to the time when suit is started, the party sought to be held signs any statement that indicates the existence of such a contract he furnishes the necessary evidence. Other evidence of the agreement, regardless of how authentic it may be, will not suffice to establish the agreement. The Statute of Frauds is complied with only by securing some note or memorandum in writing signed by the proper party. Of course, the Code provision concerning pleadings and testimony greatly reduces the use of the defense in cases involving sales of personal property.[C15]

The signature may be quite informal and need not necessarily be placed at the close of the document. It may be in the body of the writing or elsewhere, so long as it identifies the writing with the signature of the person sought to be held.

2-79. Concepts Applicable to All Provisions. There are certain rules of law which are general in nature and apply to all sections of the Statute of Frauds. For example, the defense of the Statute of Frauds is personal to the parties to the contract and cannot be used as a defense by strangers

---

8 *Custis v. Valley National Bank of Phoenix,* page 260.

C14 *U.C.C.* 2-201.   C15 *U.C.C.* 2-201(3)(b).

to the agreement. In addition, a defendant will be estopped from asserting the defense where he would be thus allowed to perpetrate a fraud. However, nothing short of fraud itself will operate to create the estoppel.[9]

FORM OF THE AGREEMENT CASES

Federal Security Insurance Company v. Smith
1958, 259 F.2d 294

PICKETT, J.　Joseph L. Smith brought this action for an accounting of insurance commissions alleged to be due him from the defendant, Federal Security Insurance Company, under the provisions of an oral General Agency insurance contract. The Insurance Company admitted in its pleadings that it entered into a verbal contract whereby plaintiff was to sell its policies in the State of Idaho, but denied that the commission schedule as claimed by the plaintiff was agreed to or that plaintiff was to act as a General Agent. . . . Judgment was entered for the plaintiff in the sum of $38,346.60. . . .

The trial court found that, on or about January 1, 1953 the parties entered into a verbal agreement by the terms of which plaintiff agreed to sell insurance for the defendant in the State of Idaho and to serve as Exclusive General Agent for the defendant's insurance business in that state; that on all policies sold by the plaintiff he was to receive a commission of 90 per cent of the first year's premiums, $17\frac{1}{2}$ per cent of the second year's renewal premiums, and $7\frac{1}{2}$ per cent of the renewal premiums from three to ten years; that on policies sold within the State of Idaho for the defendant by other persons, the plaintiff was to receive 10 per cent of the first year's premiums and $2\frac{1}{2}$ per cent on renewal premiums from two to ten years. The court also found that the agreement was effective as of January 1, 1953, and was terminated on the 8th day of February, 1954. The question presented is whether there is substantial evidence to sustain these findings.

While it is agreed that there was a verbal arrangement whereby plaintiff was to represent the defendant in Idaho, there was a sharp conflict between the parties as to some of the terms. The plaintiff testified that early in January, 1953, he met A. A. Timpson, Vice-president and General Manager of the defendant company, in Salt Lake City, Utah, for the purpose of negotiation with defendant company a General Agency contract for the State of Idaho. After stating to Timpson that he would not accept any contract except that of a General Agent, he was advised to return later for a decision. The gist of plaintiff's testimony is that upon his return a few days later, Timpson agreed to a General Agency contract with commissions as stated in the Court's findings.

The plaintiff stated that the contract was to commence immediately and was to be reduced to writing and forwarded to him in Idaho. . . .

[9] *Ozier v. Haines*, page 261.

In March, the plaintiff, with the consent of Timpson, opened a bank account in Idaho for the company. Timpson testified that the plaintiff was the only agent working for the company throughout its various territories who was authorized to withdraw funds from the company's bank account. After obtaining an Idaho license, plaintiff and agents selected by him sold and continued to sell defendant's insurance in Idaho. Timpson testified that it was quite likely that the company advised the Idaho Insurance Commissioner that plaintiff was the designated person to hire and discharge its agents in Idaho. In July of 1953 Timpson forwarded a form of contract to plaintiff, which was substantially different from that which Smith testified had been agreed upon. Plaintiff did not sign it and there was no change in his method of handling the company's business prior to the termination of his services in February of 1954. The trial court accepted plaintiff's version of the contract, which satisfies the substantial evidence rule.

The fact that the parties intended that their agreement should later be reduced to writing does not affect the validity of the oral arrangement. It is quite evident that the parties did not intend that the effectiveness of the contract was to be delayed until reduced to writing as actual performance began and continued for several months before a written form was submitted, which admittedly was not the same as the original understanding. The rule is that the mere intention to reduce an oral or informal agreement to writing is not of itself sufficient to show that the parties intended that until such formal writing was executed the contract should be ineffective. In the absence of a contrary intention, where the terms of a contract have been agreed upon, the failure to later execute a contemplated written instrument does not prevent the contract from becoming an obligation of the parties. . . .

As to the date upon which the contract was to become effective, we do not believe that the evidence supports the finding that it was to be effective as of January 1, 1953. It is without conflict that negotiations between Smith and Timpson began after the first of the year and continued for several days. The record does not disclose the date upon which Smith arrived in Idaho. An Idaho license was obtained by plaintiff about February first. . . .

The case is remanded for determination of the date upon which plaintiff qualified as an agent for defendant in Idaho, for an accounting from that date, and a modification of the judgment accordingly.

Grubb v. Rockey

1951, (Pa.) 79 A.2d 255

BELL, J.   Plaintiffs filed a bill in equity for specific performance of a written contract to sell real estate. The contract provided that the purchase price for the real estate or farm was $10,000, which plaintiffs proved they had paid on or before March 1st. Mr. Rockey alleged and testified over the vigorous objection of counsel for plaintiffs that an oral agreement was made for "the sale of said farm for $11,200, and a reservation to the defendants of the wheat crop" after March 1st; and that this oral agreement induced the written agreement. The chancellor found that the purchase price orally agreed upon was $11,200, and consequently refused specific performance. The narrow but very important question raised in this appeal is whether evidence of an oral contemporaneous inducing agreement is admissible to vary and contradict (1) a comprehensive written agreement, and (2) the purportedly real consideration set forth therein.

The parties hereto entered into a complete, comprehensive and carefully prepared written agreement drawn by Mr. Taylor, defendants' attorney. . . .

Defendants attempted to both vary and contradict the written contract by the aforesaid oral agreement which they alleged induced the written contract. . . .

The modern Pennsylvania Parol Evidence Rule is . . .

> Where parties, without any fraud or mistake, have deliberately put their engagements in writing, the law declares the writing to be not only the best, but the only, evidence of their agreement. All preliminary negotiations, conversations and verbal agreements are merged in and superseded by the subsequent written contract . . . and unless fraud, accident or mistake be averred, the writing constitutes the agreement between the parties, and its terms cannot be added to nor subtracted from by parol evidence.

In the leading case of *Gianni v. R. Russell & Co., Inc.,* (281 Pa. 320, at page 324, 126 A. 791), at page 792, we thus stated the test to be applied in cases of this character: "In cases of this kind, where the cause of action rests entirely on an alleged oral understanding concerning a subject which is dealt with in a written contract it is presumed that the writing was intended to set forth the entire agreement as to that particular subject.

" 'In deciding upon this intent [as to whether a certain subject was intended to be embodied by the writing], the chief and most satisfactory index . . . is found in the circumstances whether or not the particular element of the alleged extrinsic negotiation is dealt with at all in the writing. If it is mentioned, covered, or dealt with in the writing, then presumably the writing was meant to represent all of the transaction on that element; . . .'." The wheat crop was clearly an issue or profit of the farm and both it and the purchase price of $10,000 were clearly and specifically mentioned and dealt with—adversely to the defendants—in the written agreement.

But the defendants further contend, and the chancellor found, that "parol evidence may always be introduced to prove the true consideration or purchase price . . . ."

No logical or sound reason has been suggested why, in a case like this, the purchase price or consideration set forth in an executory written contract for sale of real estate should be treated differently from any other term or provision therein, or, more particularly, why it should be excluded from the Parol Evidence Rule. The old rule probably originated in connection with deeds which frequently recited a consideration of $1 or other nominal consideration, and which did not purport to show the true consideration or the real purchase price which the parties had actually agreed upon. The language so broadly asserted by the Court in such cases was loosely and perhaps unwittingly repeated in and applied to all cases in which the parties sought to prove by parol evidence the alleged actual or true consideration. We are convinced that there exists no more reason for excepting in an agreement of sale of real estate the purportedly real purchase price or consideration from the Parol Evidence Rule than there would be for excepting from said Rule any other term or provision of the written contract.

We therefore hold that where the purchase price set forth in a written agreement purports to be not merely a nominal, but the real or actual amount agreed upon, then in the absence of fraud, accident or mistake, evidence of an alleged contemporaneous oral agreement (on the faith of which the written contract was allegedly executed), is inadmissible to add to or subtract from or contradict or vary the purchase price or consideration set forth in said written contract.

Decree reversed and record remanded to court below, with directions to enter in accordance with this opinion. Costs to be paid by appellees.

Hayes v. Guy

1965 (Mass.) 205 N.E.2d 699

SPALDING, J.   The plaintiff brought this action against Roland D. Boulay (Boulay) and Nathaniel Guy (Guy) for materials supplied and labor performed. Boulay was the general contractor for the construction of a dwelling house for Guy. The plaintiff was a subcontractor for electrical work. The basis of the action is a claim for rough wiring against both Guy and Boulay. The judge found against Boulay on the claim for rough wiring. . . .

Facts found by the judge include the following: Boulay and Guy entered into a contract for the construction of a house which was to be completed within four months of July 28, 1959. Boulay, in turn, hired the plaintiff to do the rough wiring. While the plaintiff assumed he had been hired to do the entire electrical job, there was no definite agreement for anything other than the rough work. It was understood that the plaintiff was to be paid by Boulay when the wiring was completed and Boulay had received his payment under the progress payment clause of his contract with Guy. On February 25, 1960, Guy ordered the plaintiff to make changes which departed from the plans furnished the plaintiff by Boulay. Boulay was never a party to the arrangement, nor was he notified of the changes in accordance with his contract with Guy.

In March, after the rough wiring was done, "Guy wished to have the electrical service hooked up." Under his contract with Boulay, the time for doing this had not arrived. Guy, who was "having trouble with Boulay," approached the plaintiff and "asked him to put in the electrical service for which he would pay him." Guy also promised to pay for the rough wiring if the plaintiff "would put in the service."

The principal question is whether this oral promise to pay for the rough wiring is within the Statute of Frauds. We are concerned with that portion of the Statute which provides that oral contracts based "upon a special promise to answer for the debt, default, or misdoings of another" are unenforceable.

The plaintiff contends that Boulay was in debt to him for rough wiring. Hence, it is argued, by the defendant, Guy, that Guy's oral promise to pay the plaintiff was within the statute.

There is a well established exception which takes an oral promise out of the statute "where the promisor receives something from the promisee for his own benefit." *(Paul v. Wilbur,* 189 Mass., 48, 52, 75 N.E. 63, 64, and cases cited). "The theory . . . is that if the promisor is himself acquiring property or other pecuniary benefit, he is engaging not to pay the debt of another, but his own." (Williston, Contracts (3d ed.) § 472). An unqualified statement of the exception, however, is misleading. It has received a more limited interpretation. The basic question is one of determining whether this case "falls within a class of cases in which the essence of the transaction is . . . the obtaining of some . . . benefit, by the promisor from the promisee, and the payment of the continuing debt of a third person in accordance with the promise is merely incidental and not the real object of the transaction." The rule, while easy to state, is often difficult to apply.

Applying this test to the case at bar, . . . Guy's promise to pay for the rough wiring comes within the exception. The findings indicate that his purpose was to get electrical service "hooked up" prior to the time it was to be done under his contract with Boulay; this was a direct benefit to Guy. The plaintiff was under no obligation to either Guy or Boulay to perform this work. The fact that Boulay's debt would be extinguished was purely incidental. We see no merit to Guy's argument, which finds no support in the findings or the evidence, that the real objective of his promise was to keep the contract going for the benefit of all. . . .

Affirmed.

First Nat. Bank of Boston v. Fairhaven Amuse. Co.

1964 (Mass.) 197 N.E.2d 607

SPALDING, J. The pertinent evidence most favorable to the plaintiff was as follows: On July 22, 1958, the defendants made an oral agreement with the plaintiff. Under its terms, the defendants were to bid at least $135,000 at a judicial foreclosure sale for personal property on which the plaintiff held a chattel mortgage and for the interest in a ten year lease of real estate which had been assigned to the plaintiff. The property had been used in connection with the operation of a drive-in theatre in Newington, Connecticut. The sale was held on February 6, 1959, in Connecticut pursuant to an order of the Superior Court of Hartford County, but the defendants failed to bid. The property, consisting of personal property and the leasehold interest, was sold to one Poland, the highest bidder, for $85,000. On February 16, 1959, the sale was confirmed by the court.

The plaintiff brought this action of contract to recover the sum of $50,000, the difference between the amount realized at the sale and the amount the defendants agreed to bid for the property. The defendants pleaded the Statute of Frauds. At the conclusion of the evidence the judge directed verdicts for the defendants on the ground that the agreement concerned an interest in land and, not being in writing, was within the Statute of Frauds.

. . . The plaintiff argues that the agreement was to bid at a judicial sale, that such sales are not within the Statute of Frauds and that, therefore, the agreement to bid at the sale, although oral, is also not within the statute.

The plaintiff urges that unlike an ordinary auction, execution, or foreclosure sale, a judicial sale should not be within the statute of frauds because it is conducted under the superintendence of a court of equity which is well equipped to prevent the mischief which the statute of frauds was designed to prevent. Although recognizing that this court has never passed on the question, the plaintiff cites cases from other jurisdictions which hold that judicial sales do not come within the statute. Whether we would so hold need not be decided. The validity of the preliminary contract is not necessarily determined by the ultimate contract. Here the oral agreement sought to be enforced was not arrived at under the aegis of a court and consequently was not clothed with such protection from fraud as would attend a judicial sale. . . .

The plaintiff also argues that the agreement to bid $135,000 at the sale for the leasehold and personal property was not "a contract for the sale of lands, tenements or hereditaments or of any interest in or concerning them." (G.L. c.259, § 1, Fourth). The leasehold was an interest in land and subject to the statute of frauds. The bid price was indivisible and made no allocation of value between the interest in land and the personal property, and thus brought the entire agreement within the statute.

The judge rightly directed verdicts for the defendants.

Exceptions overruled.

Sutton v. Wright & Sanders

1926, (Tex. Civ. App.) 280 S.W. 908

This suit was instituted by Sutton to recover damages because the defendant failed to take and pay for 100,000 cubic yards of sand at 12½ cents a yard. The plaintiff owned land upon which there was a substantial deposit of sand and gravel, and the defendant contracted to buy the amount indicated, being given license to enter on the land and remove it. The buyer was to have five years in which to remove it, but was to remove not less than 1,000 cubic yards a month. The plaintiff alleged it was possible for the defendant to have removed all of the sand within one year. The defendant set up the Statute of Frauds as a defense, and the lower court ordered the jury to return a verdict for the defendant.

COBBS, J. . . . In this case it will be noted by the oral contract there was no intention, express or implied, to sell land per se, but the sale of gravel thereon only. There was no intention to pass ownership or title to the land, and only a permission was given to enter thereupon in order to excavate and remove 100,000 cubic yards of gravel therefrom. Of course, a contract for any interest in land is widely different from a contract to remove a commodity therefrom, because a sale of the land, as such, would carry the gravel with it, but sale of the gravel, as such, would not include or pass title to the land in which it was situated, or any part thereof. (*Anderson v. Powers*, 59 Tex. 214).

It is urged that the gravel could be moved in one year, and a proper construction of the contract so indicated. If such was the effect to be given to the contract or intention of the parties, and was so found by the jury, it would not be in violation of the Statute of Frauds. It may be that the issue as to the time of performance should go to the jury. If the contract was to be performed within one year, that would not take beyond the time provided for in the Statute of Frauds, and the contract would be in harmony therewith. Does the option to perform the contract to remove the gravel all in five years bring it within the statute, and thus subject it to be denounced by the statute?

The evidence showed no limit was fixed as to the time within which all the gravel should be removed. It did provide that some should be removed each month, and it was agreed that not less than 1,000 cubic yards should be taken out per month, and the "pay to be not less than $125 a month as a minimum."

The contract on its face does not show that it was not to be performed within one year, but was ambiguous in that particular. It was a question of fact whether it was to be and could be performed within one year which, if so, would not on its face render it void per se. If two constructions to a contract can be given, one legal and the other illegal, the court will give that construction to the contract that will make it legal. It was ambiguous in the particulars referred to, and was not determinable on its face as a question of law. It is true that the testimony showed a verbal contract for the sale of an interest in land, but a severance of the commodity within a year would not render it obnoxious to the Statute of Frauds. Clearly it was a contract for the sale of gravel, a merchantable commodity, such as trees or other products of the land, and is real estate only by an arbitrary construction of a rule of law. The title to the land itself did not pass, and the land, as such, still remained in its locus, and title to the land upon which the gravel lay was not affected. We hardly think that five years, given as the ultimate date for removal, will have much effect in the determination of the question as to performance. As stated, we think gravel on the natural soil stands with the same relation to it as the growing trees. . . .

The court's charge created fundamental error, as the record showed the existence of controverted material facts, and for the reasons given *the judgment is hereby reversed and the cause remanded for another trial.*

(The amount involved did not violate the Texas statute concerning the sale of personal property.)

D   P

Haveg Corporation v. Guyer

1965 (Del.) 211 A.2d 910

This is an action by the seller for breach of five alleged oral contracts. The plaintiff, Guyer, agreed to furnish all the requirements for cutting and sewing certain nylon phenolic tape used by the defendant corporation in its business. It was agreed that the contracts were exclusive and were not to terminate until the defendant had no further requirement for the services involved. The defendant defended by, among other things, stating that the alleged contracts violated the Statute of Frauds. The defendant moved for a summary judgment and when the trial court denied the motion it appealed.

HERRMANN, J.   The question for decision in this facet of the case is whether a contract contemplating continued performance for an indefinite period of time comes within the Statute of Frauds.

The majority rule is that an oral promise of a long-extended performance, which the agreement provides shall come to an end upon the happening of a certain condition, is not within the Statute of Frauds if the condition is one that may happen in one year. There is a minority rule to the contrary.

The Superior Court applied the majority rule and held that, since the defendants' requirements for the services to be rendered under the alleged contracts may have actually and finally terminated within a year, the Statute of Frauds does not apply.

We agree with the Superior Court's conclusion on this point. It has been the law in Delaware for many years that the Statute of Frauds does not apply to a contract which may, by any possibility, be performed within a year. In *Devalinger v. Maxwell,* (4 Pennewill 185, 54 A. 684, 686 (1903)), this court approved the following statement of the rule:

> . . . the statute (of frauds) does not extend to an agreement which may by any possibility be performed within a year, in accordance with the understanding and intention of the parties at the time when the agreement was entered into. And if the specific time of performance be not determined upon at the time of the making of the contract, yet, if by any possibility it may be performed within a year, the statute does not apply, and such an agreement need not be in writing. And likewise when the performance of the agreement rests upon a contingency which may happen within a year.

And in *Duchatkiewicz v. Golumbuski,* (12 Del. Ch. 253, 111 A. 430 (1920)), the Chancellor stated:

> In this state the law is settled authoritatively that if any agreement by any possibility may, under the contract, be performed within one year it is valid notwithstanding the statute (of frauds); or rather, unless it appear that the contract could not possibly be performed within one year from the making thereof, its enforcement is not prohibited by the statute. . . .

We approve and adhere to the rule as thus stated and restated.

Since the defendants were unable to show that the alleged contracts could not possibly be performed within a year, we affirm the conclusion of the Superior Court that the alleged agreements are not within the Statute of Frauds.

It follows that the order denying the defendants' motion for summary judgment is affirmed insofar as it is based upon the ruling that the alleged contracts are not within the Statute of Frauds; and insofar as the appeal attempts to present the other issues discussed herein, it is dismissed.

buyer
P   D seller of business

Acuri v. Weiss

1962 (Penn. S.C.) 184 Atl. 2d 24

Plaintiff sued to recover $500 deposit made on tentative purchase of a restaurant business. Plaintiff had given the defendant a check with following notation on left side of check: "Tentative deposit on tentative purchase of 1415 City Line Ave., Phila. Restaurant, Fixtures, Equipment, Goodwill." An inventory was subsequently prepared by defendant's attorney and accountant to which the terms of the contract were added and the agreement was sent to plaintiff. Plaintiff then refused to complete transaction and sued for his deposit. Defendant contended that the contract of sale was enforceable and plaintiff relied upon the Statute of Frauds to establish that the agreement was unenforceable. The jury returned a verdict the defendant and plaintiff appealed.

WATKINS, J. . . . Appellant's (plaintiff) first question: "Does the Statute of Frauds of the Uniform Commercial Code, 1953, . . ., render the defense to the claim insufficient as a matter of law?". . . The pertinent portions of the section are:

(1) Except as otherwise provided in this section a contract for the sale of goods for the price of $500 or more is not enforceable by way of action or defense unless there is some writing sufficient to indicate that a contract for sale has been made between the parties and signed by the party against whom enforcement is sought or by his authorized agent or broker. A writing is not insufficient because it omits or incorrectly states a term agreed upon but the contract is not enforceable under this paragraph beyond the quantity of goods shown in such writing. . . .

(3) A contract which does not satisfy the requirements of subsection (1) but which is valid in other respects is enforceable

(a) if the goods are to be specially manufactured for the buyer and are not suitable for sale to others in the ordinary course of the seller's business and the seller, before notice of repudiation is received and under circumstances which reasonably indicate that the goods are for the buyer, has made either a substantial beginning of their manufacture or commitments for their procurement; or

(b) if the party against whom enforcement is sought admits in his pleading or otherwise in court that a contract for sale was made; or

(c) with respect to goods for which payment has been made and accepted or which have been received and accepted. . .

The writing upon which the appellee relies to satisfy the requirement of the statute is the check with the marginal notation. We cannot escape the clear meaning of the key words in this notation, "Tentative deposit on tentative purchase." The word tentative is not an uncommon word in the English language and has been defined thusly: "Of the nature of an attempt, experiment, or hypothesis to which one is not finally committed." Antonyms being: definite, final, conclusive. In fact, when Weiss read the notation the warning flag immediately went up, and when he inquired as to their purpose he was told that was just until the formal papers were made up. This writing does not satisfy the requirement of the statute.

Since this is the first appellate decision touching upon this question we feel some comment is needed. The purpose of the Uniform Commercial Code, which was written in terms of current commercial practices, was to meet the contemporary needs of a fast moving commercial society. It changed and simplified much of the law which it has supplanted but it also sets forth many safeguards against sharp commercial practices. This section we feel is one such safeguard. While it does not require a writing which embodies all the essential terms of a contract, and even goes so far as to permit omission of the price, it does require some writing which indicates *that a contract for sale has been made.* [Emphasis writer's.]

. . . *Judgment reversed and judgment n.o.v. not withstanding the verdict entered for appellant.*

Custis v. Valley National Bank of Phoenix
1962 (Ariz.) 375 P.2d 558

Plaintiff sued defendant for breach of contract alleging that defendant agreed to sell Plaintiff all of the stock in Flagstaff Cheshire Motors, Inc., a Chevrolet dealership, and to lease the premises occupied by the firm to Plaintiff. The parties had sent a letter to the Chevrolet Division of General Motors setting forth the details of the sale and requesting approval thereof. Defendant pleaded the Statute of Frauds and the trial court entered judgment for defendant holding that the letter was an insufficient memorandum to satisfy the Statute of Frauds.

BERNSTEIN, C. J.   A memorandum sufficient to satisfy the requirements of the Statute of Frauds need not be a writing intended by the parties to be the integration of their agreement. It may be an informal writing, such as a letter, and may be addressed to a third party. It must, however state with reasonable certainty the subject matter to which the contract relates and the terms and conditions of all of the promises constituting the contract. The essentials of a memorandum include, in an agreement of sale, the identity of the buyer and seller, the price to be paid, the time and manner of payment, and the property to be transferred, describing it so it may be identified. In a memorandum of an agreement to lease real property the essentials include the identification of the property to be leased, the term of the lease, and the rental agreed upon.

The memorandum under consideration discloses an agreement for the sale and purchase of stock in Flagstaff Cheshire Motors, a corporation, and for a lease by defendant of the "present Dealership Buildings" to the Corporation. While the letter is sufficient in several respects it fails to specify the term of the lease. The authorities appear to be unanimous that a memorandum of a lease agreement which makes no mention of the length of the term is insufficient. Where a written memorandum is deficient for the reason that essential terms are omitted, parol evidence is not admissible to supply these missing terms.

Plaintiff has argued that the agreement to lease the premises is severable from the agreement to sell the stock, and that for this reason an action may be maintained upon the agreement to sell the stock. The learned trial judge did not accept this argument, nor can we. It is clear to us that a fundamental part of the consideration for the agreement to transfer an interest in this going business operation was the lease, on favorable terms, of the business property owned by defendant. Plaintiff has not suggested that there is any evidence that Cheshire would have agreed to the sale of the stock on the terms indicated apart from the agreement to lease his buildings. Since the contract was indivisible it follows that no action can be maintained because of the insufficient memorandum. . . .

Because we hold that the alleged oral contract is within the provisions of the Statute of Frauds, and is therefore unenforceable, it is unnecessary to consider the other assignments of error.

The judgment of the trial court is affirmed.

Ozier et al. v. Haines

1951, 343 Ill. App. 400, 99 N.E.2d 395

O'CONNER, J. Plaintiffs (Ozier and Others) filed complaint in the Circuit Court of Piatt County, which alleged in substance that the plaintiffs operated a grain elevator, that the defendant was a farmer who came to the elevator and verbally sold plaintiff 5,000 bushels of corn for $1.24 per bushel. While the defendant was in the office, the plaintiffs, relying upon the contract of sale, called a grain broker on the telephone and resold the grain. The complaint alleged that the defendant knew that the plaintiffs resold the grain, and knew that the plaintiffs resold the grain in reliance upon the defendant's agreement, and that the defendant is estopped to defend against his acts, representations and contract.

The complaint further alleged that it was the custom of the trade, which custom was well known by all the parties and relied upon by them, to buy and sell grain upon verbal contracts, and for the purchasing elevator company to resell said grain to grain brokers immediately upon such verbal sale being made.

Thereafter the defendant refused to deliver the corn and the plaintiffs had to purchase corn on the open market at a higher price and bring this suit to recover the difference in price at which the corn was purchased on the open market and the price at which the defendant had agreed to sell to the plaintiffs.

Defendants filed a motion to dismiss, which trial court granted. The plaintiffs elected to stand by the complaint and a final judgment was entered for the defendant. Plaintiffs appeal from this ruling of the trial court.

The defendant in his motion pleaded the Statute of Frauds. Plaintiffs contend the defendant is estopped from relying on the Statute.

A situation similar to this was before this court in the case of *Ludlow Cooperative Elevator Company v. Burkland,* (338 Ill. App. 255, 87 N.E.2d 238). In that case we held that the Statute of Frauds, as set forth in Section 4 of our Sales Act, (Chap. 121½ Ill. Rev. Stats. 1947), was a good defense and the plaintiff could not recover. We recognized that one may be estopped under certain circumstances from asserting the Statute of Frauds, but pointed out that the moral wrong of refusing to be bound by an agreement because such an agreement does not comply with the Statute of Frauds, does not authorize the application of the doctrine of equitable estoppel.

The section of the Sales Act quoted in the *Ludlow* case, *supra,* is still in force and unchanged (Chap. 121½, Ill. Rev. Stats. 1949, Sec. 4).

Our Supreme Court laid down the rule in *Lowenberg v. Booth,* (330 Ill. 548, 162 N.E. 191, 195), that in order to invoke the principle of equitable estoppel six elements must appear, the first of which is: "Words or conduct by the party against whom the estoppel is alleged, amounting to a misrepresentation or concealment of material facts."

We cannot find a misrepresentation or concealment of material facts by the defendant. Promises as to future action are not misrepresentations of existing fact. Action taken in reliance on such promises, as distinguished from action taken in reliance on a misrepresentation of existing facts, cannot raise an estoppel. While it is true that equity will not allow the Statute of Frauds to be a shield to shelter a fraud, the breach of a promise which the law does not regard as binding, is not a fraud. There does appear to be a moral wrong, but if we attempted to right this moral wrong under these conditions, the Statute would be rendered nugatory. The plaintiffs are presumed to know the law, and they could easily have protected themselves by making a part payment on the contract, or by preparing a written memorandum of the contract.

We have carefully examined all the cases cited by the plaintiffs. No one of them sustains the position taken by the plaintiffs here. It may well be that this section of the Statute is an anachronism, but this argument should be addressed to the legislature and not to this court.

The judgment of the trial court is affirmed.

CHAPTER 13
REVIEW QUESTIONS AND PROBLEMS

1. *A,* the father of *B,* aged 22, orally promised the *X* fraternity that he, *A,* would pay *B*'s house bill. When *B* failed to pay it *X* contacted *A,* who also refused. *X* sues *A* for breach of contract. What result if *A* asserts the Statute of Frauds as a defense?

2. *C* on December 29, 1965 orally leased an office to *D* for the period January 15-December 31, 1966, for the rental of $505. *D* refused to take possession and was sued by *C* for breach of contract. What result if *D* asserts the Statute of Frauds as a defense?

3. *E* orally sold *F* an uranium deposit in New Mexico. *F* had the option of mining the ore or leaving it in the ground and re-selling it at a future date. *E* later wishes to keep the ore and refuses to allow *F* to mine it. *F* sues *E* for breach of contract and *E* raises the defense of the Statute of Frauds. What result?

4. On June 15, 1965, *G* orally promised *H* that he, *G,* would work for *H* as an architect until January 1, 1970, or until the project was completed. On January 1, 1967, *G* resigned his position and refused to finish the project. *H* sues *G* for breach of contract. What result? (Assume that *G* uses the Statute of Frauds as a defense.)

5. *K*, a tailor of custom clothes, orally agreed to make three suits of clothes for *J* at a price of $185 each. *K* finished and attempted to deliver the first suit to *J*, who refused to accept delivery because of a lack of funds. *K* sues *J* for the profit he would have made on the second and third suits plus the cost of the first suit. What result, assuming the Statute of Frauds is used as a defense?

6. *X* and *Y* entered into a written contract which provided that *Y* would be paid $10,000 per year for his services. Prior to the execution of the agreement *X* had told *Y* that his salary would be $12,000. In a suit by *Y* for the remaining $2,000, will the court allow *Y* to testify concerning *X*'s oral statement?

7. *P* contracted to do certain construction work for *G,* the written contract providing that no additional work was to be done unless agreed to in writing. Later *G* made several requests for added work at specified rates orally, but after the work was completed, he refused to pay because the requests were not in writing. Is *P* permitted to recover?

8. *P* orally agreed to sell *A* a one-half interest in his business for $10,000. He later refused to sell to *A*, selling the entire business to *X* for $29,-000. Has *A* any recourse against *P*?

9. *A* made an oral contract with *B* whereby *A* was to convey certain real estate to *B* for the price of $6,000. In reliance upon the oral agreement, *B* hauled certain fertilizer to the farm, piped water to the feed lots, and made cement platforms for feeding livestock. Under these conditions was the oral agreement enforceable?

10. *X* purchased a pressure cooker from *Y*. *Y* warranted that the cooker would not explode. The cooker exploded 3 years after the purchase. When sued for breach of warranty *Y* defended, using the Statute of of Frauds. What result?

11. *X* orally sold his house to *Y*. *Y* made a down payment, sold his old residence, moved to the house and made substantial improvements thereon. Is *X*'s contract enforceable?

14

Rights of
Third Parties

ASSIGNMENTS

2-80. Nature of Assignment. As has been previously discussed, a legal contract creates rights for each party and imposes corresponding duties or obligations. Each party's right is to have the other perform his duty. Frequently, a party may desire to transfer his rights, his duties or both to another party. A party *assigns* his rights and *delegates* his duties. The term assignment is used to describe the situation where both rights and duties are transferred as well as the situation in which only the right is transferred. The transferor is known as the *assignor,* whereas the one receiving the assignment is called the *assignee.* The other or non-assigning party to the contract is called the obligor when the right is assigned because he has the obligation to perform the duty that is the subject matter of the assignment (the right which is being transferred). When a duty is delegated, the other party is the obligee because his right is to receive performance of the duty which was delegated. In a contract each party is both an obligor and an obligee regardless of assignment.

2-81. Requisites of Assignment. No particular formality is essential to an assignment. Consideration, although usually present, is not required. However, an assignment without consideration, where the right involved has not been realized through the collection of money or receipt of other performance, may in most states be rescinded by the assignor upon notice to the debtor or obligor.

Unless the contract assigned deals with real or personal property covered by the Statute of Frauds, an assignment may be either oral or written, although it is better to have a written assignment. Any contract, including the rights arising therefrom, may be assigned provided both parties to the agreement are willing. The more important question deals with the effect of an assignment where the other party to the original contract refuses to respect it. In the section which follows the particular legal principles which are helpful in determining which rights and contracts may not be assigned over the objection of the other party are set forth.

2-82. Unassignable Contracts. Of the several classes of contracts which may not be transferred without the consent of the other party, the most important are contracts which involve personal rights or personal duties. A personal right or duty is one in which personal trust and confidence is involved or one in which the skill, knowledge, or experience of one of the parties is important. In such cases, the personal acts and qualities of one or both of the parties form a material and integral part of the contract. For example, a lease contract where the rent is a per cent of sales is based on the ability of the lessee and would be unassignable without the consent of the lessor. Likewise, an exclusive agency contract would be unassignable.[1] The Code provides that rights cannot be assigned where the assignment would materially change the duty of the other party, or increase materially the burden or risk imposed on him by his contract, or impair materially his chance of obtaining return performance.[C1]

There are some duties which appear to be personal in nature but which are not considered so by the courts. For example, a building contractor is not expected to do all the work on any particular building, it being understood that he will delegate responsibility for certain portions of the structure. If the construction is to be done according to agreed specifications, the agreement to build is assignable. It is presumed that all contractors are able to follow specifications, and since the duties are mechanical in nature, the owner is bound to permit the assignee to build.

It must be kept in mind that the contractor must substantially complete the building according to the plans and specifications or he will not be entitled to payment.

Another example of an unassignable contract is one in which an assignment would place an additional burden or risk upon the obligor that was not contemplated at the time he made the agreement. Such appears to be true of sales of merchandise on credit. Most states hold that one who has agreed to purchase goods on credit may not assign his right to purchase the goods to a third party since the latter's credit may not be as good as that of the original contracting party—the assignor.

This reasoning is questionable because the seller could hold both the assignor and assignee to the agreement but the inconvenience to the seller in collecting has influenced most courts to this result. However, in contracts where the seller has security such as retention of title or a

---

[1] *Wetherell Bros. Co. v. U. S. Steel Co.*, page 270.

[C1] *U.C.C.* 2-210.

mortgage, the seller's protection is in the security and the right to buy on credit is assignable.

Finally, it is customary for certain contracts to contain a provision that they are nonassignable. The majority of the states strictly enforce such a provision. A few hold an assignment of such a contract to be valid, although allowing the other party to recover damages for a breach of this provision.

Under the Code, a prohibition of assignment of "the contract" is construed as only prohibiting the delegation of the assignor's duties, unless the circumstances of the case clearly indicate that the rights are also not assignable.[C2] A claim for damages for breach of a whole contract is always assignable.

2-83. Claims for Money. All claims for money, due or to become due under existing contracts, may be assigned. For example, employees frequently assign a portion of their wages to a creditor when obtaining credit. In this connection, it should be borne in mind that an assignment is more than a mere authorization or order directed to the debtor since an authorization or order leaves the option of payment to the debtor as to payment to the assignor or the assignee. In a true assignment, the obligor must pay the assignee—payment to the assignor would not discharge the obligation to pay the assignee.

A question often arises concerning the liability of the assignor in case the assignee is unable to collect from the debtor-obligor. If the assignee takes the assignment merely as security for a debt owing from the assignor to the assignee, it is clear that, if the assigned claim is not collected, the assignor is still liable to pay his debt. On the other hand, it should be equally plain that if the assignee purchases a claim against a third party from the assignor he should have no recourse against the assignor unless the claim proves invalid for some reason or unless the claim is sold expressly with recourse. Otherwise, the mere inability of the debtor-obligor to pay or his unwillingness to do so does not give the assignee recourse against the assignor.

In any event, the assignor warrants that the claim which he assigns is a genuine claim. In case there is a defense available to the third party debtor and for this reason the claim cannot be collected, the assignor must return to the assignee the amount he received from him.

2-84. Rights of the Assignee. Unless the contract assigned provides otherwise, the assignee receives the identical rights of the assignor. Since the rights of the assignee are neither better nor worse than those of the assignor, any defense of the third party available against the assignor is available against the assignee.[2] For example, part payment, fraud, duress or incapacity can be used as a defense in a suit brought by the assignee as well as in one brought by the assignor. Because of this it is becoming

[2] *American Bridge Company v. City of Boston,* page 272.

[C2] *UC.C.* 2-210(4).

customary to insert a clause in contracts of sale that the buyer waives any defense he may have against the seller in case the seller assigns the contract to a third party. The Code provides that subject to any statute or decision relating to special protection of buyers of consumer goods such clauses may be enforced by the assignee. However, the buyers may assert real defenses—infancy, illegality, extreme duress, etc.—even though the sale contract includes such a clause.

If the assignee buys a claim which is subject to a defense, the assignee has a claim against the assignor on a theory of breach of warranty. The assignor of a claim impliedly warrants that the claim assigned is a genuine one and free from defenses and he breaches this warranty if the obligor has a defense.

2-85. Duties of the Assignee. Failure on the part of the assignee to perform the duties delegated to him by an assignment gives rise to a cause of action in favor of the obligee. In the majority of the states he can elect to sue either the assignor or the assignee, provided the assignee has agreed, expressly or by implication, to assume the burdens of the contract. Except in those contracts under the Code,[C3] the mere assignment of a contract which calls for the performance of affirmative duties by the assignor, with nothing more, does not impose those duties upon the assignee,[3] although there is a decided trend to hold that an assignment of an entire contract carries an implied assumption of the liabilities. It is only where the assignee undertakes to perform as a condition precedent to enforcement of the rights, or has assumed the obligation to perform as part of the contract of assignment, that he has any liability for failure to perform. To illustrate: If a tenant assigns a lease, the assignee is not liable for future rents if he vacates the property prior to expiration of the lease unless he expressly assumes the burdens of the lease at the time of the assignment. To the extent that an assignee accepts the benefits of a contract, he becomes obligated to perform the duties which are related to such benefits. If he merely receives the assignment of a right to purchase or to lease as in an option, he is not liable for the purchase price or the rental unless he demands title to, or possession of, the realty.

Under the Code, an assignment of a contract or of all the rights under a contract is a delegation of duties.[C4] The assignee assumes the duties or burdens unless the contract provides otherwise or the assignment is given as security for a debt. If there has been a delegation of performance, the other party, if he feels insecure as to performance, may demand that he be adequately assured by the assignee that the latter will in fact render proper performance.[C5]

The assignor, of course, is not released by an agreement on the part of the assignee to assume the burdens of the contract. In such a case, the third party has his choice of holding either the original contracting party

---

3 *Chatham Pharmaceuticals, Inc. v. Angier*, page 273.

C3 *U.C.C.* 2-210(4)   C5 *U.C.C.* 2-210(5), (2-609).
C4 *U.C.C.* 2-210(4).

or the assignee. He cannot be denied his claim against the assignor without his consent.

2-86 Notice. Immediately after the assignment, the assignee should notify the third party, obligor or debtor, of his newly acquired right. This notification is essential for two reasons:

1. In the absence of any notice of the assignment, the third party is at liberty to perform—pay the debt or do whatever else the contract demands—for the original contracting party, the assignor. In fact, he has no knowledge of the right of anyone else to require performance. Thus, the right of the assignee to demand performance can be defeated by his failure to give this notice. The assignor who receives performance under such circumstances becomes in turn a trustee of funds or of property received and can be compelled to turn them over to the assignee. As soon as notice is given, however, the third party must perform for the assignee.

2. The notice of assignment is for the protection of innocent third parties. The assignor has the power, although not the right, to make a second assignment of the same subject matter. If notice of the assignment has been given, it has much the same effect as the recording of a mortgage. It furnishes protection for a party who may later consider taking an assignment of the same right. One considering an assignment should, therefore, always confirm that the right has not previously been assigned by communicating with the debtor. If the debtor has not been notified of a previous assignment, and if the assignee is aware of none, the latter can, in many states, feel free to take the assignment. He should immediately give notice to the debtor. In other words, the first assignee to give notice to the debtor, provided he has no knowledge of a prior assignment, will prevail over a prior assignee in most states.[4]

In some other states, it is held that the first party to receive an assignment has a prior claim, regardless of which one gives notice first on the theory that the assignor has parted with all interest by virtue of the original assignment. In all states, however, the party who is injured by reason of the second assignment has a cause of action against the assignor to recover the damages which he has sustained.

CONTRACTS FOR BENEFIT OF THIRD PARTIES

2-87. Nature of Such Contracts. Contracts are often made for the express purpose of benefiting some third party. The most typical example of such an agreement is the contract for life insurance in which the beneficiary is someone other than the insured. The beneficiary in such case is in effect receiving a gift from the insured and is therefore known as a donee beneficiary.

---

[4] *Boulevard National Bank of Miami v. Air Metal Industries,* page 274.

Another illustration may be taken from mortgages. Real property is often conveyed with an outstanding mortgage against it, and in such cases it is customary for the purchaser to assume and agree to pay the mortgage debt. Indirectly, at least, the holder of the mortgage stands in a position to benefit from this promise and since he is a creditor, he is referred to as a creditor beneficiary.

A third party beneficiary frequently needs to bring suit to enforce his rights as beneficiary.[5] Since he is not a party to the contract a legal theory is required which will enable him to bring the suit. The law operates on the agreement of the contracting parties and creates a duty by implying a promise or obligation to the third party beneficiary.

2-88. Legal Requirements. A third party beneficiary is not entitled to enforce a contract unless he can establish that the parties actually intended to make the contract for his benefit. The intent to benefit the third party must appear from the terms of the contract,[6] but such intent is easily inferred in creditor beneficiary situations. The third party need not be named as an individual in the contract if he can show that he is a member of a group for whose benefit the contract was made. The fact that the actual contracting party could also sue to enforce the agreement will not bar a suit by the beneficiary if he was intended to directly benefit from the contract.

If the benefit is only incidental, the beneficiary can not sue. Thus, an orphanage lost a suit which was based on an agreement between several merchants to close their places of business on Sunday with a provision that each one keeping open was to pay one hundred dollars to the orphanage. The court stated that the contract was entered into primarily to benefit the contracting parties, and the orphanage was only indirectly to be a beneficiary. Contracts of guaranty which assure the owner of property that contractors performing construction contracts for him will properly complete the project and pay all bills have been held in many states to benefit the material men and laborers. A few states have held otherwise, indicating their belief that the agreement was made primarily to protect the owner.

In most states, a contract made for the express purpose of benefiting a third party may not be rescinded without the consent of the beneficiary after its terms have been accepted by the beneficiary. The latter has a vested interest in the agreement from the moment it is made and accepted. For example, an insurance company has no right to change the named beneficiary in a life insurance policy without the consent of the beneficiary, unless the contract gives the insured the right to make this change. Until the third party beneficiary has either accepted or acted upon provisions of contract for his benefit, the parties to the contract may abrogate the provisions for third party's benefit and divest him of the benefits that would otherwise have accrued to him under contract. Minors, how-

---

[5] *Wesley v. Electric Auto-Lite Company,* page 276.
[6] *Hamilton and Spiegel, Inc. v. Board of Education of Montgomery County,* page 278.

ever, are presumed to accept a contract upon its execution and such contract may not be changed so as to deprive the minor of its benefits.

One who seeks to take advantage of contract made for his benefit takes it subject to all legal defenses arising out of contract. Thus, if the obligee has not performed or satisfied the conditions precedent to the other party's obligation, the third party would be denied recovery.

The rules on rescission of a contract for the benefit of a third party apply equally to donee and creditor beneficiaries. If the party obligated to perform for a creditor beneficiary retains the consideration which he has received for the original promise, the contract cannot be cancelled. For example, if X assumes Y's mortgage obligation to Z, the obligation is enforceable by Z against X so long as X retains the mortgaged property.

CASES ON RIGHTS OF THIRD PARTIES

Wetherell Bros. Co. v. United States Steel Co.

1952, 105 F. Supp. 81

Wetherell Bros. Co., a Massachusetts corporation, had held a contract since 1930 with the defendant whereby it had the exclusive right in the New England states to sell cold, rolled steel strips on a 5 per cent commission and stainless steel products on a 7 per cent commission. The contract was to run indefinitely except as it might be terminated by two years notice. On March 1, 1950, the Massachusetts corporation liquidated and ceased to function, but sold some assets to Penn Seaboard Iron Co., a Pennsylvania corporation, and so far as possible sought to assign to the latter their right to represent United States Steel Co. in New England. The Pennsylvania corporation changed its name to Wetherell Bros. Co., but refrained from giving notice of the assignment to the defendant. Learning of the new arrangement, however, the defendant notified the parties of the immediate termination of the sales relationship. Plaintiff, the Pennsylvania corporation, brings suit for breach of contract.

McCarthy, D. J. . . . The plaintiff seeks to hold the defendant liable because of its action in terminating the contract between it (defendant) and Wetherell-Massachusetts. Since admittedly no contract was ever entered into between the plaintiff and the defendant, the question of law is whether the duties of the Wetherell-Massachusetts under the contract could be effectively assigned to plaintiff without the consent of the defendant. The conclusion is inescapable: the assignment to the plaintiff of the duties of Wetherell-Massachusetts under its sales agency contract without the consent of the defendant was ineffective for the purpose of substituting the plaintiff for the "assignor" corporation with whom the defendant contracted.

This was a contract for a sales agency within a particular geographical area, an exclusive agency in that only the principal could compete with Wetherell-Massachusetts in obtaining customers for the defendant's products.

In a contract for a sales agency the personal performance of the agent is practically always a condition precedent to the duty of the principal and employer. The performance of the agent's duty cannot be delegated to a substitute. The assignee of the agent's right must fail, therefore, in his attempt to enforce it if he merely tenders a substituted performance.

The claim has been made also that it is only in a technical sense that these two companies could be called distinct entities. They had the same capital stock and practically the same stockholders, officers and agents; the Maine company had taken over all the assets and assumed all the liabilities of the other, and was carrying on the same business, at the same stand, in the same manner and under the same management. The master has found that for practical purposes the two companies were the same. Accordingly, the plaintiff claims that an agreement with the one is the same as an agreement with the other, that the defendant's ignorance of their separate identity was immaterial, that the agreement may be treated as made with either company indifferently, was capable of enforcement by either or at least by the Maine company, and is valid in the hands and for the benefit of the plaintiff. But we cannot assent to this reasoning. These are two distinct corporations, created by the laws of two different states. The powers of each corporation are limited and controlled by the statutes of the state which created it, and it is scarcely conceivable that the statutes of the two states are the same or that the franchises and powers of the two corporations are identical. But if this were so, it would remain true that they are the creation of two different governments, the offspring of different parents, and not only distinct legal entities, but having separate and distinct existences. . . .

The contract in this case is one requiring a relationship of particular trust and confidence, and such a contract cannot be assigned effectively without the consent of the other party to the contract. The grant of an exclusive agency to sell one's goods presupposes a reliance upon and confidence in the agent by the principal, even though the agent be what is frequently called a large "impersonal" corporation. It is apparent that the principal in this case must have relied upon the "legal equation" represented by the corporation which it chose as its sole sales representative in a large area; otherwise, the surrender of the right to grant additional agencies is illogical.

The plaintiff has argued that the fact that the assignment is made from one corporation to another alters the rule of non-assignability of the agent's duties under the contract. The New York Court of Appeals met this argument in an early phase of the *New York Bank Note Company* litigation.

The plaintiff was not only technically but substantially a different entity from its predecessor. It is true that in dealing with corporations a party cannot rely on what may be termed the human equation in the company. The personnel of the stockholders and officers of the company may entirely change. But though there is no personal or human equation in the management of a corporation, there is a legal equation which may be of the utmost importance to parties contracting with it. In dealing with natural persons in matters of trust and confidence, personal character is or may be a dominant factor. In similar transactions with a corporation, a substitute for personal character is the charter rights of the corporation, the limits placed on its power, especially to incur debt, the statutory liability of its officers and stockholders. These are matters of great importance when, as at present, many states and territories seem to have entered into the keenest competition in granting charters; each seeking to outbid the other by offering to directors and stockholders the greatest immunity from liability at the lowest cash price. . . .

Judgment must be entered for the defendant.

American Bridge Co. et al. v. City of Boston

1909, 202 Mass. 374, 88 N.E. 1089

The plaintiffs had received an assignment of all money due or to become due by the City of Boston to one Coburn under two contracts and now seek to recover the amount authorized by two architects' certificates. Shortly after they were issued Coburn defaulted, and the city desires to recoup the damages resulting from the breach and deduct it from the amount of the two certificates. The default took place, however, after the city had received notice of the assignment. This is an action by the assignee to recover.

HAMMOND, J. . . . The assignment of a chose in action conveys, as between assignor and assignee, merely the right which the assignor then possesses to that thing; but as between the assignee and the debtor it does not become operative until the time of notice to the latter, and does not change the rights of the debtors against the assignor as they exist at the time of the notice.

It becomes necessary to consider the exact relation between the defendant and Coburn, the assignor, at the time of notice. The auditor has found that written notice of the assignments was given to the defendant on November 14, 1902, before the service of any trustee process. At that time there does not seem to have been any default on the part of Coburn. At the time of the notice what were the rights between him and the defendant, so far as respects this contract? He was entitled to receive these sums, but he was also under an obligation to complete his contract. This right of the defendant to claim damages for the nonperformance of the contract existed at the making of the contract and at the time of assignment and of notice, and the assignees knew it, and they also knew that it would become available to the defendant the moment the assignor should commit a breach. Under these circumstances it must be held that the assignees took subject to that right. . . . Even if the sums were due and payable in November, 1902, at the time of notice, still if this action had been brought by the assignor after the default, there can be no doubt but that the defendant would have had the right to recoup the damages suffered by his default. And the assignees who seek to enforce this claim can stand in no better position in this respect than the assignor.

Judgment for defendant.

Chatham Pharmaceuticals, Inc. v. Angier Chemical Co., Inc., et al.

1964 (Mass.) 196 N.E.2d 852

SPIEGEL, J. This is a bill to establish the amount due from the defendant corporation Angier and to reach and apply the alleged obligations of the noncorporate defendants (the assignees) "to assume the obligations and liabilities" of the defendant corporation. A final decree was entered favorable to the plaintiff Chatham from which only the assignees appealed . . .

The trial judge made a report of material facts, which we summarize. On September 1, 1957, the plaintiff and the defendant Angier Chemical Co., Inc. (Angier), entered into an agreement. Under the terms of this agreement, the plaintiff was granted an exclusive license "to manufacture, use and sell the product, use or process covered by United States Letters Patent No. 2,688,585." The plaintiff agreed to pay royalties to Angier and to purchase Angier's then existing inventory of the licensed product, and Angier agreed that "if the license granted should be terminated or surrendered . . . it would buy back from the . . . plaintiff, at the same cost, any part of said inventory then remaining in the possession of the . . . plaintiff." Pursuant to this agreement, the plaintiff purchased Angier's inventory. On February 24, 1958, Angier assigned "all its right, title and interest in said agreement" to the assignees, who accepted the assignment. On January 18, 1960, the plaintiff terminated the agreement, but Angier has refused to repurchase said remaining inventory.

The assignees contend *inter alia* that the 1958 assignment was an assignment of rights only and not of obligations and that they are not obligated to perform any of Angier's duties under the licensing agreement. Although there is a paucity of cases in point, it is the law of this Commonwealth that "an assignment of what is due, or is to become due, under a contract is not an assignment of both the duty of performing the contract and receiving payment therefor." . . .

Where, however, "the contract, as a whole, is assigned, there is no separation between the benefits and burdens." See Restatement: Contracts, § 164, which treats the assignment of a whole contract, still partly executory, "in the absence of circumstances showing a contrary intention, as an assignment of the assignor's rights under the contract and a delegation of the performance of the assignor's duties." In the present case, whether the assignees impliedly promised to perform the assignor's duties thereunder is a question of interpretation of the assignment, read in the context of the circumstances.

There is nothing in the ambiguous instrument of assignment to indicate that Angier intended the assignees to assume any obligations under the agreement. There is no express assumption by the assignees of obligations under the licensing agreement. It appears to be undisputed that the assignees were Angier's shareholders and that Angier was heavily indebted to them. . . . There remained few duties to be performed by Angier under the licensing agreement. In these circumstancs, it is particularly dubious that the assignees also assumed duties. The use of the words "right, title and interest" does not necessarily show that the assignment was intended to include obligations. . . .

We are constrained to hold that construing the instruments in the light of those circumstances which are essentially undisputed, the assignees did not assume the obligations under the agreement. . . .

Accordingly, the final decree is to be modified by dismissing the bill as against the assignees with costs of appeal, and as so modified is affirmed.

So ordered.

Boulevard Nat. Bank of Miami v. Air Metals Indus.

1965 (Fla.) 176 So. 2d 94

Plaintiff Bank sued several defendants including a contractor (Tompkins-Beckwith) on a construction project which had a subcontract with Air Metals Industries, Inc., also a defendant. On January 3, 1962, Air Metal procured performance bonds and as security for said bonds assigned to the bonding company (American Fire) all monthly, final or other estimates and retained percentages; pertaining to or arising out of or in connection with any contracts performed or being performed or to be performed, such assignment to be in full force and effect as of the date hereof, in the event of default in the performance of—any contract as to which the surety has issued, or shall issue, any surety bonds or undertakings.

On November 26, 1962, the bank lent money to Air Metal and to secure the loans Air Metal purported to assign to the bank certain accounts receivable it had with the contractor which arose out of subcontracts being done for that contractor.

In June 1963, Air Metal defaulted on contracts covered by the performance bonds and on July 1, 1963, the bonding company notified the contractor of its assignment. On August 12, 1963, the bank notified the contractor of its assignment. On October 9, 1963, the contractor paid all funds due to the bonding company and the bank filed suit. The trial court found for the defendants because the notice of the bonding company preceded the notice by the bank. The District Court of Appeal affirmed.

WILLIS, C. J.   . . . The "question" is whether the law of Florida requires recognition of the so-called "English" rule or "American" rule of priority between assignees of successive assignments of an account receivable or other similar chose in action. Stated in its simplest form, the American rule would give priority to the assignee first in point of time of assignment, while the English rule would give preference to the assignment of which the debtor was first given notice. Both rules presuppose the absence of any estoppel or other special equities in favor of or against either assignee. The English rule giving priority to the assignee first giving notice to the debtor is specifically qualified as applying "unless he takes a later assignment with notice of a previous one or without a valuable consideration." The American rule giving the first assignee in point of time the preference is applicable only when the equities are equal between the contending assignees, and if a subsequent assignee has a stronger equity than an earlier one, he would prevail.

In the case here there are no special equities and no rights, such as subrogation, which would arise outside of the assignments.

.   .   .

The American rule for which petitioner contends is based upon the reasoning that an account or other chose in action may be assigned at will by the owner; that notice to the debtor is not essential to complete the assignment; and that when such assignment is made the property rights become vested in the assignee so that the assignor no longer has any interest in the account or chose which he may subsequently assign to another.

The English rule (holds) that in the case of a chose in action an assignee must do everything toward having possession which the subject admits and must do that which is tantamount to obtaining possession by placing every person who has an equitable or legal interest in the matter under an obligation to treat it as the assignee's property. It was stated:

> For this purpose you must give notice to the legal holder of the fund; in the case of a debt, for instance, notice tantamount to possession. If you omit to the debtor is, for many purposes, to give that notice you are guilty of the same degree and species of neglect as he who leaves a personal chattel, to which he has acquired a title, in the actual possession, and, under the absolute control, of another person.

It is undoubted that the creditor of an account receivable or other similar chose in action arising out of contract may assign it to another so that the assignee may sue on it in his own name and make recovery. Formal requisites of such an assignment are not prescribed by statute and it may be accomplished by parol, by instrument in writing, or other mode, such as delivery of evidences of the debt, as may demonstrate an intent to transfer and an acceptance of it. . . .

It seems to be generally agreed that notice to a debtor of an assignment is necessary to impose on the debtor the duty of payment to the assignee, and that if before receiving such notice he pays the debt to the assignor, or to a subsequent assignee, he will be discharged from the debt. To regard the debtor as a total non-participant in the assignment by the creditor of his interests to another is to deny the obvious. An account receivable is only the right to receive payment of a debt which ultimately must be done by the act of the debtor. For the assignee to acquire the right to stand in the shoes of the assigning creditor he must acquire some "delivery" or "possession" of the debt constituting a means of clearly establishing his right to collect. The very nature of an account receivable renders "delivery" and "possession" matters very different and more difficult than in the case of tangible personalty and negotiable instruments which are readily capable of physical handling and holding. However, the very principles which render a sale of personal property with possession remaining in the vendor unexplained fraudulent and void as to creditors applies with equal urgency to choses in action which are the subject of assignment. It would seem to follow that the mere private dealing between the creditor and his assignee unaccompanied by any manifestations discernible to others having or considering the acquiring of an interest in the account would not meet the requirement of delivery and acceptance of possession which is essential to the consummation of the assignment. Proper notice to the debtor of the assignment is a manifestation of such delivery. It fixes the accountability of the debtor to the assignee instead of the assignor and enables all involved to deal more safely.

We do not hold that notice to the debtor is the only method of effecting a delivery of possession of the account so as to put subsequent interests on notice of a prior assignment. The English rule itself does not apply to those who have notice of an earlier assignment. The American rule is not in harmony with the concepts expressed. It seems to be based largely upon the doctrine of caveat emptor which has a proper field of operation, but has many exceptions based on equitable considerations. It also seems to regard the commercial transfers of accounts as being the exclusive concern of the owner and assignee and that the assignee has no responsibility for the acts of the assignor with whom he leaves all of the indicia of ownership of the account. This view does not find support in the statute or decisional law of this State.

After examining the authorities we conclude . . . that "as between successive assignments of the same right the assignee first giving notice prevails."

. . .

We concur in the decision of the district court of appeal in this case.

Wesley v. Electric Auto-Lite Co.

1959, (Common Pleas, Ohio) 155 N.E. 2nd 713

LEIS, J.   This is an action brought by Ransom Wesley against the Electric Auto-Lite Company for wages allegedly due him from the defendant. Plaintiff is an employee of the defendant and is a member of the Local 68, Metal Polishers, Buffers, Platers and Helpers International Union. Plaintiff stands in the shoes of a third party beneficiary to a contract entered into between defendant and plaintiff's bargaining unit, said Local 68, and for his claim avers that defendant corporation has breached said contract, thereby resulting in a loss to plaintiff of some fifty-six hours of work at $2.60½ per hour.

The demurrer of the plaintiff to defendant's amended answer having been overruled, the case was tried before the Court, a jury having been waived. . . . By way of background, it should be stated that the defendant corporation was engaged in the manufacture of various electric auto accessories, including automotive lamps. While defendant produced for various customers, the Chrysler Corporation accounted for approximately eighty-five per cent of the volume of production (R. 49). The evidence shows that beginning in December of 1955, the orders to defendant from its chief customer, Chrysler, were cut severely by what counsel for defendant aptly described as a "blizzard of cancellations." . . . At the time of the cancellations, the plant was working a five day week. Due to the order cancellations, the decision was made by defendant corporation to cut down to a four day week without a reduction in working force. (R. 72.) As a result, plaintiff was laid off seven consecutive Fridays from February 10, 1956 to March 25, 1956, although he reported for work each of the seven Fridays in question. (R. 39-40.) Therein lies the crux of this lawsuit.

It is the claim of plaintiff that being third man in seniority in his union (R. 39), he was entitled under Local 68's contract with defendant corporation, to continue his full time work week, until probationary employees, and those employees with less seniority than he were laid off first.

Both parties cite the agreement of July 11, 1955, between the Electric Auto-Lite Company Lamp Division and the Metal Polishers, Buffers, Platers and Helpers International Union in support of their positions.

There are three pertinent parts of this Agreement to which the Court will refer.

The first part is Article III (A) "Working Hours":

(A) *Eight* (8) *consecutive hours, except for the lunch period, shall constitute a normal work day, and forty* (40) *hours of five consecutive days* (Monday, Tuesday, Wednesday, Thursday, and Friday) *shall constitute a normal week's work* except when a holiday occurs on these days, in which event thirty-two (32) hours shall constitute a week's work. [Emphasis added.]

The next part is Article VI (G) which the Court will label the "seniority clause":

(G) *When it becomes necessary to reduce the working force of a department, probationary employees will be laid off first. Thereafter, layoffs will be made according to seniority to provide normal eight* (8) *hours per day and forty* (40) *hours per week for employees in the polishing and buffing departments;* . . .

To put it simply, plaintiff says that under the seniority clause he is entitled to a forty hour week until all those with less seniority than he are laid off first. . . .

Upon the evidence and law, the Court finds that plaintiff is a third party beneficiary to the contract of July 11, 1955, between The Electric Auto-Lite Company Lamp Division and the Metal Polishers, Buffers,

Platers and Helpers International Union; that plaintiff being third man on the seniority list has a contractual right under the seniority clause VI(G) to have those with less seniority laid off first; that plaintiff's employment was reduced contrary to the provisions of the seniority clause and that plaintiff is entitled to recover therefor.

Judgment for the plaintiff.

Hamilton and Spiegel, Inc. v. Board of Education of Montgomery County
1963 (Md.) 195 ATL. 2d 710

HAMMOND, J. Technical Engineers and Contractors, Inc. (Technical) agreed by a written contract to build a school for the Board of Education of Montgomery County (the Board). The United States Fidelity and Guaranty Company (the Bonding Company) became surety on the payment bond required by Code. Appellant, Hamilton and Spiegel, Inc. (Hamilton), a roofing and sheet metal contractor, supplied material and labor for the school building at the request of the prime contractor.

To recover a claimed unpaid balance of $3,501.82, Hamilton brought suit against Technical, the Bonding Company and the Board. . . . Hamilton says it is a creditor beneficiary under the contract between Technical and the Board (although not named therein). . . .

The Board demurred to the declaration against it on the grounds that no cause of action was stated and the contract under which the balance due was claimed was one between Technical and the Board only, so that there was no privity between the claimant and the board. Judge Shook sustained the demurrer without leave to amend and the appeal followed.

This Court has recognized the right of a third party beneficiary to avail himself of the benefits intended for him by a contract to which he is not a party, and has adopted the definitions of such beneficiaries set out in Restatement Contracts.

Sec. 133 says that where performance of a promise will benefit a person other than the promisee that person is a donee beneficiary "if it appears from the terms of the promise in view of the accompanying circumstances that the purpose of the promisee . . . is to make a gift to the beneficiary or to confer upon him a right against the promisor to some performance neither due nor supposed or asserted to be due from the promisee to the beneficiary," and that person is a creditor beneficiary "if no purpose to make a gift appears . . . and performance of the promise will satisfy an actual or supposed or asserted duty of the promisee to the beneficiary . . ."

Appellant makes no claim to being a donee beneficiary. It argues it is a creditor beneficiary in that the performance (to the extent of $3,501.82, the amount Hamilton claims it is due) of the Board's promise to pay will benefit it and satisfy a duty of the Board to it.

In determining whether one is a creditor beneficiary (as is true in the case of a donee beneficiary) the intention of the contract, revealed by its terms, in the light of the surrounding circumstances is the controlling determinative.

It is not enough that the contract may operate to the benefit of the one claiming to be a beneficiary. "[I]t must be shown that the contract was intended for his benefit; and, in order for a third party beneficiary to recover for a breach of contract it must clearly appear that the parties intended to recognize him as the primary party in interest and as privy to the promise. An incidental beneficiary acquires by virtue of the promise no right against the promisor or the promisee." (Citing cases). "In order to recover it is essential that the beneficiary shall be the real promisee; i.e., that the promise shall be made to him in fact, though not in form. It is not enough that the contract may operate to his benefit."

By virtue of Code, requiring binding performance and payment bonds before a contract for a public building, work or improvement is awarded by the State or any political subdivision thereof, the contract between the Board and Technical provided for a payment bond for (in the words of paragraph (a) (2) of the statute) "the protection of all persons supplying labor and materials to the contractor or his subcontractor."

The purpose of the bond has been said to be to protect subcontractors and materialmen on State or other public projects where they have no lien on the work done.

The statutory direction that each public construction contract include the furnishing of a payment bond for the protection of materialmen and subcontractors refutes the claim that the contract between the Board and the prime contractor intended to make suppliers or subcontractors beneficiaries "in fact though not in form," entitled to demand payment direct from the Board. From the requirement of a payment bond there may soundly be inferred a legislative intent, written into each public construction contract, that the State or other public body is not to have a duty to pay or to see to the payment of materialmen or subcontractors beyond the furnishing of the payment bond.

The requisite intent to make the appellant a creditor beneficiary of the contract was lacking, and it cannot prevail on its theory that it was one. . . .

Judgment affirmed, with costs.

CHAPTER 14
REVIEW QUESTIONS AND PROBLEMS

1. *H* held a life insurance policy in *N* Company which had lapsed but which carried a cash surrender value of $500. *H* assigned the policy right to *M*. *M* demanded payment from *N* Company, but it paid *H*. May *M* recover of *N* Company?

2. *L* Co. issued a life insurance policy upon the life of *A*, it providing

that the policy could not be assigned without the consent of *L* Co. The right to money under the policy had matured, and *A* assigned the money claim to *M*. When the company refused to pay, *M* brought suit. The court allowed *M* to recover. Why?

3. *X*, a contractor, assigned his claim for work being done to *Y*, a bonding company. *Y* did not notify the obligor. *X* later assigned his claim to *Z* who did notify the obligor. To whom should the obligor make payment?

4. *X* assigned his claim against *Y* to *Z*. *X* later assigned the same claim to *A*. *A* had knowledge of the assignment to *Z* but claimed priority because *Z* had charged *X* usurious interest on the assigned debt. Does *A* or *Z* have the prior right to payment by *Y*?

5. *X* leased his drugstore to *Y* for 5 years at a monthly rental of $1,000. The rent was to be paid to the City Hospital. Later *X* and *Y* agreed to reduce the rent to $500 in return for *Y*'s installing new fixtures. City Hospital objects to the rent reduction and sues *Y* for the balance of the rent. What result? Could *X* cancel the hospital's rights and direct that the rent be paid to him?

6. A contractor agreed with a municipal body to pay, at contractor's expense, for all injuries arising out of the construction. *X* suffered injuries as a result of an explosion. Can *X* collect from the contractor without proving negligence?

7. *M*, the mother of *X*, an illegitimate child, entered into a contract with *F* for the support of the child and for an insurance policy on the life of *F* payable to *X*. *M* later married and informed *F* that he no longer needed to support *X*. *X* later sued *F* for the payments which were not made. What result?

8. *X* purchased an automobile from *D*. *D* agreed to procure "full coverage" insurance from *X* but did not do so. *X* negligently injured *P*. *P* sues *D* on the contract for the personal injuries. What result?

9. *P* assigned its accounts receivable to *D* for collection. *D* acted as *P*'s agent and notice of the assignments was not given. *D* misappropriated the funds and when sued by *P*, defended on the ground that the assignments were invalid due to lack of notice. What result?

10. *P* employed *A* to work, the latter agreeing to a reasonable restraint from competing when employment terminated. *P* sold his business to *T*, and assigned the contract. *A* quit and began to compete immediately in the area. Has *T* a good cause of action against *A*, who urged such a contract could not be assigned?

11. *A* contracts with *B* to build a house for *B*. *A* assigns the contract to *C*, who substantially performs the contract but commits several minor breaches. From whom can *B* collect?

chapter 15

Performance of Contracts

CONDITIONS

2-89. Introduction. This chapter is concerned with the law relating to performance of contracts including such matters as the order of performance and excuses for nonperformance. As was discussed in Chapter 7, there are three basic remedies for breach of a contract. The victim of the breach can always bring suit for dollar damages, and in addition, in certain situations may rescind the contract or may sue to have it specifically enforced. The material in this chapter indicates those breaches which are limited to dollar damages and those which justify rescission as a remedy.

As a general rule, if the breach of contract is of minor significance, the the only remedy is damages. However, in an executory contract where the provision is one of vital importance and the breach of it is material, rescission of the agreement may be obtained. To illustrate: *A* agrees to build a brick house for *B*, according to agreed specifications, for $20,000 and to have it completed by a certain date. *A* is ten days late in finishing the house. The breach being of minor importance, *B* must accept the house and pay the contract price less any damages sustained by reason of the delay. On the other hand, let us assume that the breach consisted in building a five-room house instead of a seven-room house called for by the contract. Unquestionably, the breach of such an important provision would justify *B* in rescinding the agreement.

Those terms of a contract, the breach of which justifies rescission, are called *conditions*. Conditions may be *precedent, concurrent,* or *subsequent*. For purposes of our discussion, only the first two will be considered in detail. *Conditions subsequent* establish events, the occurrence of which take away otherwise vested rights. An insurance policy which takes away the right to recover for a fire loss, unless notice of the loss is given to the insurer within a stated period, has included a condition subsequent. Failure to give notice causes the insured to lose his right to recover.

2-90. Conditions Precedent. A provision of a contract which one party must perform before he obtains a right to performance by the other party is called a condition precedent. Since one party must perform before the other has a duty to perform, it follows that the failure of the first party to perform permits the other party to refuse to perform or in effect to rescind the contract. To illustrate a condition precedent, assume that *A* agrees to work for *B* one month for $400. *A*'s work for the month is a condition precedent to his right to recover the $400.

Not all of the terms which impose a duty of performance on a person are of sufficient importance to constitute conditions precedent. As a general rule, if a provision is relatively insignificant, its performance is not required before recovery may be obtained from the second party. In such cases, the party who was to receive performance merely deducts the damages caused by the breach before performing on his part. Judging whether the breach of a particular provision is so material as to justify rescission, often presents a problem.[1] If damage caused by the breach can be readily measured in money, or if the nature of the contract has not been so altered as to defeat the justifiable expectations of the party entitled to performance, the clause breached is generally not considered a condition precedent. To illustrate, assume that *R*, a retail grocer, contracts to buy from *S* 10,000 pounds of Ole's oleo at 15 cents a pound, *R* to pay for the oleo within thirty days and *S* to send a salesman to display and assist in selling the oleo. If *S* fails to send a salesman and the oleo fails to sell, must *R* pay for it or may he return it and rescind the contract? In other words, was the provision for sending a salesman a condition precedent to *R*'s duty to pay? Whether the provision is an important one would doubtless depend in part on whether *R* had previously sold oleo and upon whether Ole's brand was new to the trade. If the brand is a new one and needs special promotion, and if *R* is a somewhat inexperienced grocer, it seems likely that the breach would be substantial as to justify the rescission. On the other hand, it would not be substantial in the usual situation. Where it is difficult to measure with any degree of accuracy the money damage resulting from the breach, the provision is a condition precedent.

A condition precedent need not be completely performed to entitle the party to performance by the other party. Whenever there has been substantial performance of the condition precedent, the promisee becomes obligated to perform, less damages for minor deficiencies.[2]

---

[1] *Bonadelle Construction Co. v. Hernandez,* page 291.
[2] *Surety Development Corp. v. Grevas,* page 292.

2-91. Time as a Condition Precedent. When is the provision relating to time of performance a condition precedent? When may a party rescind a contract because the other party fails to perform within the agreed time? The answer to these questions depends upon the type of contract involved. The time provision establishing the exact time for performance of a contract that involves primarily the expenditure of labor and materials or the production of a commodity of little value to anyone other than the contracting party is normally not considered of major significance. Thus, the failure of a contractor to complete a house by the date set in the contract would not justify rescission by the owner. He could, however, deduct from the contract price such damages as resulted from the delay.

A clause calling for performance within a certain time found in a contract for the sale of marketable goods is usually held to be a condition precedent[3] to the extent that substantial compliance is required. In contracts whereby retailers purchase goods that are normally bought and sold in the market, performance by the seller on the exact date specified is considered quite important. Sales promotion campaigns and provisions for the normal needs of customers are built around delivery dates. To replace merchandise not received promptly, other sources must be tapped. Failure to comply in detail with the time provisions of such contracts usually justifies the buyer in rejecting an offer to perform at a later date.

An extended delay eventually becomes material in the performance of any contract and ultimately justifies rescission. If partial performance has not taken place, a relatively short delay may justify rescission, whereas if performance is under way and time is not of the essence, a delay of some time may be required before rescission is justified. If the contract does not provide a specific date for performance, it is implied that performance will take place within a reasonable time, the length of time being dependent upon the nature of the commodity involved and the surrounding circumstances.

In those contracts in which time for performance normally is deemed not to be a condition precedent, performance on time may be made a condition precedent by adding a clause that "time is of the essence in this agreement." The parties may stipulate that something shall be important in a particular contract which ordinarily is not considered so. In such a case, failure to perform on time affords ground for rescission, unless the court construes the time clause to be a penalty provision and therefore unenforceable.

2-92. Concurrent Conditions. Many contracts are so drawn that the parties thereto are to act simultaneously as to certain matters. An agreement that calls for a conveyance by *A* of a certain farm upon payment of $60,000 by *B* is illustrative of such a situation. The deed is to be delivered at the time payment is made. Those terms of a contract that

---

[3] *Sunshine Cloak & Suit Co. v. Roquette* et al., page 294.

require both parties to the agreement to perform contemporaneously are designated *concurrent conditions.* Under the terms of such an agreement, neither party is placed in default until the other has offered to perform. Such offer on his part is called a tender, and actual performance is unnecessary to place the other party in default. For this reason *B* could not successfully sue *A* for failure to deliver the deed until he had offered to make the payment required. Actual payment is not required unless *A* offers to deliver the deed; tender of payment is sufficient.

2-93. Money Tender. Frequently, one party will tender the money due the other party and the payment will not be accepted for any number of reasons. Usually, there is a dispute as to the amount due or a party may feel that his legal rights will be affected by accepting payment. For example, a judgment debtor may tender the amount of the judgment to the judgment creditor who refuses to accept because he plans to appeal due to dissatisfaction with the amount of the judgment. What then is the legal effect of such a tender?

A tender obviously does not pay or discharge the debt. It does have three important legal effects: (1) it extinguishes any security interest such as a mortgage or pledge that secures the debt, (2) it stops interest from accruing thereafter, and (3) in case the creditor later brings suit recovering no more than the amount tendered, he must pay the court costs.

A valid tender consists of an unconditional offer to pay in legal tender the proper amount at the proper time to the creditor or his agent. A tender before the maturity of an obligation is not a proper tender, and the creditor is under no duty to accept it. Tender of payment in something other than legal tender—such as a check—is good unless the creditor refuses it because it is not legal tender. If he refuses it for some other reason, a proper tender has been made.

There are two aspects to tender under the Code.[C1] Unless otherwise agreed, tender of payment by the buyer is a condition to the seller's duty to tender and complete any delivery.[C2] Such tender may be made by any means or in any manner current in the ordinary course of business unless the seller demands payment in legal tender and gives a reasonable extension of time to procure it.[C3] Thus payment by check is quite customary but such payment is conditional—it is defeated if the check is dishonored.[C4] Tender or delivery by the seller [C5] is also provided for in the Code and is discussed in the chapters on Sales.

2-94. Anticipatory Breach. Breach of contract usually occurs when a party fails to perform at the time agreed upon. A party may, however, announce his intention not to perform prior to the time of the agreed performance. This is called an anticipatory breach. While the general rule is that an action for damages or restitution cannot be maintained

[C1] *U.C.C.* 2-503; 2-511.   [C4] *U.C.C.* 2-511(3).
[C2] *U.C.C.* 2-511(1).   [C5] *U.C.C.* 2-507(1).
[C3] *U.C.C.* 2-511(2).

until performance is due and there is a failure to perform, an exception exists in the case of anticipatory breach. If one party announces positively, clearly and unequivocally that he will not or cannot fulfill the contract, the opposite party may bring suit without awaiting the day set for performance. It must be kept in mind that the statement constituting anticipatory breach must be more than a mere implication that a party will not perform.[4]

However, an anticipatory breach is nullified as a basis of action for damages if repudiated or withdrawn before the opposite party brings his action or otherwise materially changes his position. If the opposite party after notice of the anticipatory breach, insists upon performance and takes no further action, he may lose his right to sue for dollar damages until the actual time of performance arrives. Also, if a suit for specific performance is brought after notice of anticipatory breach, the right to collect dollar damages may be lost altogether.

Assume that a seller of goods notifies a buyer that he will be unable to perform. If the buyer then "covers" the contract by purchasing o her goods from another seller, the buyer has changed his position and the original seller cannot withdraw or repudiate his anticipatory breach. In addition, in cases under the Code, an anticipatory breach may not be withdrawn if the opposite party gives notice of cancellation of the contract or notice that he considers the notice of breach final.[C6] In cases which do not fall under the Code, as previously noted, the anticipatory breach may be withdrawn unless suit is commenced or there is a material change of position.

The rules of law relating to anticipatory breach are a corollary of the duty to mitigate damages. When the victim of the breach is notified of the anticipatory breach, the law assumes that he should promptly attempt to enter into another agreement and thus minimize his damages. Since this reasoning does not apply to anticipatory breaches of promises to pay a money debt, the rule is not applicable to these promises. For example, if a debtor before maturity denies that he will pay the debt when it falls due, the creditor must nevertheless wait until maturity before bringing suit because it is not essential that he take action immediately in order to reduce the damages that might otherwise accrue.

2-95. Divisible and Installment Contracts. While many contracts are completely performed at one time, there are many situations where the contract is to be performed in stated installments. In addition, installment contracts are created by clauses providing that each delivery is a separate contract. Where a contract is to be performed on more than one occasion, two important questions arise: (1) Is the contract divisible on both sides, so that the second party is under a duty to perform in part after the first party performs an installment? (2) Does material breach of any installment justify a rescission of the balance of the agreement?

---

[4] *Diamos v. Hirsch,* page 295.

[C6] *U.C.C.* 2-610, 2-611.

Diamos v. Hirsch, page 295.

The Code contains provisions relevant to both inquiries in respect to sales contracts. Unless otherwise agreed, all of the goods called for by the contract must be tendered in a single delivery at which time payment is due, but where the circumstances give either party the right to make or demand delivery in lots, the price, if it can be apportioned, may be demanded for each lot.[C7] Thus if the price can be determined for each lot, the buyer must pay for each lot as it is delivered and the contract is treated as divisible.

Insofar as Question 2 is concerned, the Code provides that if the default on an installment is so substantial that it impairs the value of the whole contract, the buyer may treat the breach as a breach of the whole and rescind the whole contract.[C8] The value would be impaired where the breach indicates the seller's inability to perform, or his unreliability. A buyer will be held to have reinstated the agreement by accepting a non-conforming installment without giving notice of cancellation or by demanding conforming performance of the agreement.[C9] Thus, in a divisible contract, a buyer may waive a breach and demand full performance or may rescind the agreement on substantial breach of an installment.

EXCUSES FOR NONPERFORMANCE

2-96. In General. Even though the contract is silent on the point, a party may be relieved from performing a provision of the contract including conditions precedent, or his liability for breach of contract may be eliminated, if he is legally excused from performance of the contract. As noted previously performance by one party is excused where the other party has failed to perform a condition precedent or when a defense such as fraud or lack of capacity is present. In addition there is no liability for breach of contract where (1) one party has waived performance by indicating that he does not intend to hold the other party to the terms of the contract; (2) one party has prevented the other party from carrying out the agreement or (3) performance of the contract has been frustrated; or (4) the contract has become impossible of performance as contrasted with performance merely becoming more burdensome for one of the parties.

In addition, the Code allows substituted performance where the agreed carrier or other facilities have become unavailable or the agreed manner of delivery becomes commercially impracticable, and where the agreed means or manner of payment fails because of some governmental regulation.[C10] In such cases, a reasonable substitute or equivalent method of performance will discharge the contract. The Code also gives sellers an excuse if performance has become impracticable by the failure of presupposed conditions.[C11]

[C7] *U.C.C.* 2-307.
[C8] *U.C.C.* 2-612.
[C9] *U.C.C.* 2-612(3).

[C10] *U.C.C.* 2-614.
[C11] *U.C.C.* 2-615.

2-97. Waiver. The essence of waiver is conduct that indicates an intention not to enforce certain provisions of the agreement. It usually occurs after a breach and is established by some statement or conduct indicating a willingness by the injured party to forgive the breach. A waiver may be retracted by reasonable notice unless the retraction would be unjust because of a change of position in reliance on the waiver.

As a general rule the party who has waived a breach or a provision of the contract may still recover damages unless consideration or conduct amounting to an estoppel, is present. This is especially true of a waiver of a contractual right which constitutes a substantial portion of the contract.[5] Conditions precedent may be waived the same as other provisions and acceptance either express or implied of performance differing from the required performance generally constitutes a waiver. Acceptance does not constitute a waiver if the breach is a latent one, not readily discoverable by the other party.

2-98. Prevention. It is obvious that a person may not recover for nonperformance of a contract if he is responsible for the nonperformance. If a party creates a situation where it is impossible for the other party to perform, the other party is excused. It is an implied condition of every contract that either party will not prevent performance by the other.

Prevention often occurs when one party by his conduct prevents or hinders the occurrence or fulfillment of a condition in the contract.[6]

2-99. Additional Hardship. As a general rule, in the absence of a provision so providing, circumstances which impose additional hardship on one party do not constitute an excuse for breach of contract. Therefore, most contracts provide that manufacturers, suppliers, or builders shall be relieved from performance in case of fire, strikes, difficulty in obtaining raw materials, or other incidents over which it has no control. To be effective, however, it is generally held that such provisions must be included in the body of the agreement. It should be recognized that the facts or circumstances creating additional hardships are frequently those which may be insured against or involve situations in which the liability may be passed to someone else as in the case of the failure of a supplier.

2-100. Impossibility of Performance—Generally. Actual impossibility of performance is a valid excuse for breach of contract and releases a party from his duty to perform. As was noted in the prior section, the impossibility must be real and more than mere additional hardship or inconvenience.

The difficulty in applying the foregoing rule to actual cases is that the alleged impossibility usually arises subsequent to the execution of the contract. At early common law, the impossibility had to exist at the time the

---

[5] *Mead v. Collins Realty Co.*, page 296.
[6] *Overton v. Vita Food Corporation*, page 298.

contract was made or it could not be used as an excuse but the modern trend is to liberalize the rule. Some courts have even found impossibility in some cases where only an extreme hardship exists.[7] The liberalizing trend has been developed on the basic premise that if a situation develops which a promisor had no reason to anticipate and for the presence of which he is not at fault create impossibility, then the promisor in equity and good conscience ought to be discharged. Thus many cases state that in order to constitute impossibility there must be a fortuitous or unavoidable occurrence which was not reasonably foreseeable. In addition, such occurrence must not be caused by the promisor or by developments which he could have prevented, avoided or remedied by corrective measures. For this reason, the failure of a third party such as a supplier to make proper delivery does not create impossibility. Impossibility will not be allowed as a defense where the obstacle was created by the promisor or was within his power to eliminate.

In some cases the ability to perform is the essence of the contract, it having been contemplated at the time of the agreement that performance may or may not be possible. A promisor who knowingly accepts the risk of performance under such circumstances is in no position to ask for relief when it is later determined that he will be unable to perform.

Let us assume that *A* contracts to sell and deliver 500 bales of cotton from a *certain* plantation, delivery of cotton from any other source not being permitted by contract terms. *A* actually raises only 200 bales, and seeks to be released of his duty to deliver the balance. Naturally, if his inability to deliver has developed out of the fact that he failed to plant a sufficient acreage or was careless in his planting, cultivation, or harvesting of the crop, *A* should not be relieved of his duty to deliver. However, if he planted enough to have produced 800 bales under normal conditions, but the weather or other factors were such as to decrease the yield materially below that which was normally grown, failure to perform would be excused. In such a case, he is obligated to deliver the 200 bales at the contract price, providing the buyer desires such partial performance. Had the parties at the time of making the contract taken into account such contingencies and *A* had nevertheless promised performance, impossibility could not be effectively urged by him as a defense. It is because people seldom take such factors into consideration when making a contract that relief is provided when impossibility develops.

2-101. Impossibility of Performance—Specific Cases. There are four situations in which impossibility of performance is frequently offered as an excuse for nonperformance. The first of these deals with situations in which performance becomes illegal because of the enactment of some law or some act on the part of the government. Illustrative of this situation are instances in which a manufacturer is prevented from making delivery

---

[7] This is frequently explained on a theory of frustration as is discussed in Section 2-103.

of merchandise because the armed forces make a superior demand for it. However, governmental action which merely makes an agreement more burdensome than was anticipated does not afford a basis for relief.

The second is death or incapacitating illness of one of the contracting parties. This is not deemed to be a form of impossibility unless the nature of the contract is such as to demand the personal services of the disabled or deceased person. Ordinary contracts of production, processing, and sale of property are unaffected by the death or illness of one or both of the parties. In the event of death, it is assumed that the contract will be carried out by the estate of the deceased. However, if a contract is one for personal services or is of such a character as clearly to imply that the continued services of the contracting party are essential to performance, death or illness will excuse nonperformance.[8] If an artist contracts to paint a portrait or an architect agrees to draw plans and specifications for a building, the death or illness of the artist or architect concerned renders performance impossible. The nature of the service to be rendered by them is such as to demand their personal attention. In contracts for personal services, illness excuses a laborer for his inability to perform, but it does not bar the employer from terminating the contract of employment, provided the employee's absence constitutes a material breach. In contracts for personal services—one in which the employer-employee relationship exists—death of the employer, as well as of the employee, terminates the relation. The estate of the employer is not liable to the employee in damages for prematurely terminating the contract in such a case.

Many agreements involve certain subject matter the continued existence of which is essential to the completion of the contract. The third rule is that destruction of any subject matter that is essential to the completion of the contract will operate to relieve the parties from the obligations assumed by their agreement. Another somewhat analogous situation arises where property that one of the parties expected to use in his performance is destroyed. If a factory from which the owner expected to deliver certain shoes is destroyed by fire, performance is not excused, inasmuch as performance is still possible, although an undue hardship may result. The shoes needed to fill the order can be obtained from another source. Had the contract stipulated that the shoes were to be delivered from this particular factory, however, its destruction would have operated to excuse a failure to perform. Stated in other language, the destruction of the source from which one of the parties *expects* to make performance does not relieve him. He is still under duty to obtain the property from some other source. A destruction of the source from which he has *agreed* to make delivery will excuse him, for he is not at liberty to use any other source.

As was previously noted, there has been a liberal trend based on the theory of implied conditions which holds that where both parties *under-*

8 *Wasserman Theatrical Enterprise, Inc. v. Harris*, page 299.

stood delivery was to be made from a certain source, even though it was not expressly so agreed, destruction of the source of supply will relieve the obligor from performing.

The last form of impossibility is where there is an essential element lacking. It has never been very satisfactorily defined. Apparently, where some element or property which the parties assumed existed or would exist is in fact lacking, the agreement may be rescinded. This is said to be a form of impossibility at the time of making the contract and courts have always tended to consider the contract null and void in such cases. Mere additional burden or hardship is not sufficient to relieve the party from the duties imposed by the agreement. It must be definitely proved that performance is substantially impossible because of the missing element. For example, *A* contracts to build an office building at a certain location. Because of the nature of the soil, it is utterly impossible to build the type of building provided for in the agreement; the agreement must therefore be terminated. The missing element is the proper condition of the soil. In other words, from the very beginning the contract terms could not possibly have been complied with, and in such cases the courts are prone to release the contracting party.

2-102. Right to Recover for Part Performance—Impossibility. Often impossibility of performance becomes apparent only after the agreement has been partially performed. One coat of paint is placed upon a house before it is destroyed. In such cases, is the loss of the work already completed to fall upon the one doing the work or upon the party who was to have the benefit of the labor? Most states permit the person who has partially performed to recover the value of the benefit the other party would have received had impossibility not arisen. This is simply another way of saying that the recipient of the work must pay for all labor and material expended up to the date of impossibility, provided the labor and material had attached to the property of the one for whom the work was being done. However, there are many states which do not allow any recovery.[9]

Care should be taken in such cases, however, to differentiate between impossibility and mere additional burden. The destruction of a partially completed building does not make recovery impossible for the work done. Performance is still possible by starting construction anew, although the cost will be greater than was anticipated. The additional cost in the latter case must be borne by the contractor.

2-103. Frustration. Frequently, an event occurs which does not create actual impossibility but does prevent the achievement of the object or purpose of the contract. In such cases, the courts may find an implied condition that certain developments will excuse performance. Commercial frustration has the effect of excusing nonperformance and arises where there is an intervening event or change of circumstances which is

---

[9] *Hipskind Heating & Plumb. Co. v. General Industries,* page 302.

so fundamental as to be entirely beyond that which was contemplated by the parties and which results in extreme hardship. Frustration is not impossibility but is more than mere hardship. It is an excuse created by law to eliminate liability where a fortuitous occurrence has defeated the reasonable expectations of the parties. For example, assume that X agrees to sell property to Y, delivery to be made in a foreign country. If the foreign country goes to war or denies entry of the product, the contract is frustrated and the parties excused.

2-104. Impracticability. The Uniform Commercial Code allows substituted performance in shipment or payment in certain situations.[C12] In addition, the Code has rejected the strict requirements of the law of impossibility and has recognized the modern viewpoint that parties to a contract do make certain basic assumptions which, if they later prove to be incorrect, result in one party as a practical matter being unable to perform the agreement. The Code provides that failure of a seller to deliver, or to deliver on time, is not a breach of contract if his performance has been made impracticable by the occurrence of a contingency, the nonoccurrence of which was a basic assumption on which the contract was made.[C13] He is also excused if performance is made impracticable by compliance with governmental regulations.[C14] If only a portion of the seller's capacity is affected, he must allocate his production in a reasonable manner among his customers.[C15] Sellers are required to notify buyers of the delays and the allocations. Buyers are allowed to terminate the whole contract upon receipt of notice of allocation, or they are allowed to negotiate modifications of the agreement. Failure to modify within 30 days of the notice causes the contract to lapse insofar as affected deliveries are concerned.[C16]

PERFORMANCE OF CONTRACTS CASES

Bonadelle Construction Co. v. Hernandez
1959 (Cal. App.) 337 P.2d 85

      GRIFFIN, J. This is an action for specific performance or damages. On January 9, 1957, respondents (a young war veteran and his wife) signed a deposit receipt for the purchase of a described lot and a house to be erected thereon, according to "Plan 3-H" (corner). The foundation had already been laid. It was orally agreed it would be in accord with the requirements of the Veterans' Administration and similar in appearance to a model house located near-by which was shown to defendants by plaintiff's agent. . . . "Seller hereby agrees with the purchaser that the proposed construction shall be completed in accordance with the plans and specifications submitted to the V.A. under Master C.R.V." Application for the loan was made by defendants and it was

---

[C12] *U.C.C.* 2-614.   [C15] *U.C.C.* 2-615(b).
[C13] *U.C.C.* 2-615.   [C16] *U.C.C.* 2-615(c).
[C14] *U.C.C.* 2-615.

duly processed and the house was constructed. Plaintiff executed a grant deed to the property which was placed in escrow about March 15, 1957. Within two days after the exterior color coat stucco of the house had been applied by means of a spray gun, defendants noticed it was streaked and blotched over a great area. Defendants notified the salesman of plaintiff company who negotiated the deal that the house was unsatisfactory and not acceptable to them in that condition. The agent told them to wait about a week and it would dry out in even color. They waited and it was still streaked and blotched. No steps were taken by plaintiff to correct the condition. Several demands were made by defendants to have them do so and each time plaintiff insisted defendants take possession and they would correct the condition afterwards. . . . Defendants refused to accept and orally rescinded the contract. Plaintiff then brought this action. After trial, the court found generally in accordance with the defendants' evidence, as above related, and found, in addition, that the defect was a material one; that plaintiff had ample time and ample notice to correct it, and the failure to do so was willful and intentional. . . .

In this connection it is argued that the failure of a building contractor to comply strictly with construction specifications in some minor matter is not necessarily such failure of performance as would warrant rescission by the owner, and that there is no evidence of plaintiff's failure to perform being willful or intentional. . . .

As said in *Connell v. Higgins,* relied upon by plaintiff, "The definition of substantial performance is difficult to give in general terms. It is usually a question to be determined in each case with reference to the existing facts and circumstances." And quoting from 2 *Elliott on Contracts,* Par. 1607, it is said at page 912: "Substantial performance means that there has been no willful departure from the terms of the contract, no omission of any of its essential parts, that the contractor has in good faith performed all of its substantive terms. . . . Whether, in any case, such defects or omissions are substantial, or merely unimportant mistakes that have been or may be corrected, is generally a question of fact."

A partial failure of consideration resulting from the willful failure of plaintiff to perform a material part of the contract is sufficient to justify defendants' rescission. . . . The judgment in favor of defendants was justified. The motion for new trial was properly denied.

Judgment affirmed.

Surety Development Corporation v. Grevas

1963 (A.C. Ill.) 192 N.E.2d 145

SMITH, Justice. When is a house a home? In our context a house is a home when it can be lived in. But when is that: When substantially completed or completely completed? We posit the question, because the answer is decisive.

Plaintiff sells prefabricated houses. Defendants selected one of their models, styled "Royal Countess, elevation 940". A contract was signed. The cost was $16,385.00; completion date September 27, 1961. Around

4:00 P.M. on that date defendants refused to accept the house asserting non-completion. Plaintiff then sued for the balance due and defendants counter-claimed for their down payment. Both alleged performance by them and non-performance by the other. The issue is therefore relatively simple: Who performed and who didn't? The facts are more elusive— plaintiff at times says one thing, defendants another. We narrate them briefly.

On the morning of the twenty-seventh, "Royal Countess, elevation 940" was far from being a house, let alone a home. Racing the clock, plaintiff initiated a crash program. When defendants arrived on the scene at 4:00, at plaintiff's behest for final inspection, the crash program was still crashing—workmen were all over the place, slapping on siding, laying the floors, bulldozing the yard, hooking up the utilities, and so on. Defendant's tour was not a success, to put it mildly. Instead of a home, they found, to their dismay, a hive buzzing with activity. They did not tarry, in spite of the foreman's assurances that all would be right by 5:30. Nor did they come back. They should have. Believe it or not, the foreman was right. The job *was* substantially completed by 5:30, with only a service walk, some grading and blacktopping left undone.

The trial court found that the house had been substantially completed and concluded that there had been, therefore, substantial compliance with the contract and with this we agree. But because the house was not completely completed, it found that there had not been *complete* compliance. With this, too, we agree, but such finding is beside the point. Substantial—not complete—compliance in a construction contract is all that is required. By 5:30, there had been just that, in other words, substantial performance of the contract. Plaintiff's contretemps in having inspection set for 4:00 o'clock was hardly the way to make friends and influence people, but such happenstance is of no moment in determining whether or not there had been substantial compliance, unless such can be said to indicate bad faith. We do not think that it does. What it indicates is bad timing, not bad faith.

That substantial performance or compliance is the key needs no extensive citation. In *Bloomington Hotel Company v. Garthwait*, (227 Ill. 613, 81 N.E. 714), it was said:

Literal compliance with the provisions of a contract is not essential to a recovery. It will be sufficient if there has been an honest and faithful performance of the contract in its material and substantial parts, and no willful departure from or omission of the essential points of the contract.

In 12 Ill.Law & Practice Contracts, (§ 402, p. 547), it is said:

In building contracts a literal compliance with the provisions of the particular contract, and the plans, specifications and drawings, is not necessary to a recovery by the contractor. It is sufficient that there is a substantial performance in good faith or that there is an honest and faithful performance of the contract in its material and substantial parts, with no willful departure from, or omission of, the essential points of the contract.

No substantial sum was required to complete the items left undone. Nor were they of so essential a character that defendants could not have been ensconced in their new home that night if they had so desired. We have thus answered our question: A house is ready to be lived in, to become a home, when it has been substantially completed.

Defendants make one further point. By motion they assert that plaintiff waived its right of appeal by having paid the judgment on the counter-claim. The court conditioned such payment upon a reconveyance by defendants of title to the premises which they had held so that a mortgage could be obtained. Their argument is that this constituted an acceptance by plaintiff of the benefits of the adverse judgment, if such a thing is possible. No waiver occurred. The appeal is not rendered moot by payment, conditioned though it was on reconveyance. Plaintiff's choice was either to pay or to seek a stay. The judgment is therefore appealable regardless of their choice and so long as they made it in time. This they did.

The issue of damages was never reached except on the counter-claim. Since the court should have found for plaintiff and against defendants, there must be a determination apropos thereof. Accordingly, the judgment below is reversed and remanded with directions to enter judgment for plaintiff on their complaint and against defendants on their counter-claim and thereafter to determine plaintiff's damages.

Reversed and remanded with directions.

Sunshine Cloak & Suit Co. v. Roquette et al.

1915, 30 N.D. 143, 152 N.W. 259

Sunshine Cloak & Suit Company brought an action to recover $173.25 alleged to be due for certain ladies' cloaks and coats. The evidence indicated that defendant ordered the goods with the understanding that they were to be shipped by August 15, they being fall goods. They were shipped on September 28 and arrived October 12. They were immediately returned to the plaintiff. Lower court gave judgment for the plaintiff.

CHRISTIANSON, J. . . . It is doubtless true, as appellant contends, that time is never considered as the essence of a contract, unless by its terms it is expressly so provided. . . . But, although it is true that time is never considered as the essence of the contract, unless it is so provided by the terms thereof, still it is not necessary to declare in so many words that "time is of the essence of the contract," but it is sufficient if it appears that it was the intention of the parties thereto that time should be of the essence thereof.

The Supreme Court of Iowa, in considering this question in *Bamberger Bros. v. Burrows*, (145 Ia. 441, 450) said: "In the law of sales it is a settled rule that time may be of the essence of the contract; and, when a time for delivery is fixed it is generally so regarded. Therefore, if the seller fails to make delivery on the date so fixed, the buyer may rescind or recover damages for the seller's breach of contract." . . .

In *Cleveland Rolling Mill Co. v. Rhodes,* (121 U.S. 255), that court said: ". . . In the contracts of merchants time is of the essence. The time of shipment is the usual and convenient means of fixing the probable time of arrival, with a view of providing funds to pay for the goods, or of fulfilling contracts with third parties." . . . We are satisfied that the agreement to ship on August 15th was a condition precedent.

Judgment reversed.

Diamos v. Hirsch

1962 (Ariz.) 372 P.2d 76

Plaintiff commenced suit to recover damages sustained as a result of an alleged breach of contract by anticipatory repudiation. Defendants filed a counterclaim alleging the breach was by the plaintiff. The trial court found for the defendants.

On November 20, 1956, plaintiff and defendants entered into an agreement the terms of which provided that plaintiff would construct a building on land owned by him and lease it to defendants for ten years. The rent clause of the agreement set forth a mathematical formula, the purpose of which was to establish the total amount payment for the 10 year period. There was a mistake in the written provision which both parties acknowledged. Defendants were to give plaintiff a letter setting out the correct rent but instead gave plaintiff an addendum to the contract which in addition to the rent provision, contained four additional items to which the plaintiff refused to agree. The addendum was not signed and all further discussions were by the attorneys. Plaintiff offered to carry out the original contract with the rent as corrected in the unsigned Addendum. When defendants did not answer, plaintiff commenced suit for expenses incurred by reason of defendants alleged breach of the agreement. Defendants filed a counterclaim alleging that plaintiff had breached the agreement by failing to construct the building. Thereafter plaintiff filed an amended complaint alleging that on or about January 28, 1957, defendants repudiated the agreement and refused to perform any of the conditions therein. . . .

STRUCKMEYER, J. Plaintiff's first assignment of error directs our attention to the question of whether the trial court erred in directing a verdict against plaintiff on his claim of repudiation. . . .

Plaintiff in his amended complaint alleged that defendants repudiated the agreement on January 28, 1957, when defendant Hirsch met with plaintiff and submitted the addendum. Plaintiff further contends . . . , that in any event the letter written by defendant's attorney on February 13, 1957, constituted a repudiation of the agreement.

We have recognized that an action may be maintained for breach of contract based upon the anticipatory repudiation by one of the parties to the contract. It is well established that in order to constitute an anticipatory breach of contract there must be a positive and unequivocal manifestation on the part of the party allegedly repudiating that he will not render the promised performance when the time fixed for it in the contract arrives. And as succinctly pointed out in § 319 of the Restatement of the Law of Contracts, the effect of a repudiation is nullified:

> (a) Where statements constituting such a repudiation are withdrawn by information to that effect given by the repudiator to the injured party before he has brought an action on the breach or has otherwise materially changed his position in reliance on them.

At the conclusion of plaintiff's case the trial judge upon defendants' motion for a directed verdict reviewed the evidence and concluded that there was insufficient evidence to support plaintiff's contention that there had been a repudiation and that if defendants had repudiated, the repudiation had been nullified thereafter.

We have examined the evidence and are of the opinion that the trial court did not err in granting defendants' motion. George Nick Diamos, son of plaintiff, was present at the January 28th conference and testified (plaintiff did not testify) that Hirsch implied that he wanted plaintiff to sign the addendum or defendants would not perform. However, this witness, the only witness who testified on behalf of plaintiff on this point, admitted on cross-examination and on re-direct that he couldn't recall what Hirsch said in this respect and further admitted that Hirsch never made a positive statement that defendants would not perform unless plaintiff agreed to the addendum. Viewing this evidence in the light most favorable to plaintiff it is clear that it falls far short of the requisite proof that in order to constitute a breach by anticipatory repudiation there must be a positive and unequivocal refusal to perform.

Plaintiff's further contention that defendants' letter of February 13, 1957, repudiated the agreement is equally without merit. This letter merely clarified defendants' position and expressed their willingness to have plaintiff proceed to erect the building since defendants considered the terms of the agreement as signed binding upon the parties. Nowhere in this letter is there contained any statement which could reasonably be construed to be a positive and unequivocal repudiation of the agreement. In view of our conclusion it is unnecessary to determine whether defendants subsequently nullified the claimed repudiation. . . .

For the foregoing reasons the judgment of the court below is affirmed.

Mead v. Collins Realty Co.

1950 (Del.) 75 A2d 705

Plaintiffs purchased houses from Defendants under a contract which provided in part that homes would contain a Westinghouse electric range. Another and cheaper model was substituted and Plaintiffs seek to recover the difference in value. Defendants answer pleaded waiver based upon payment for house and acceptance with knowledge of all facts.

LAYTON, J. There is authority for the proposition that where one party to a contract commits a minor breach in its performance which is brought to the attention of the other party, who deliberately excuses it, then the latter is deemed to have waived his right of action for damages. The Restatement, together with the illustrations, has this to say:

> The duty of a party to a contract to make compensation where he has committed a breach insufficient to discharge the other party, is itself discharged if the injured party, knowing or having reason to know the facts, manifests assent to discharge the duty on accepting subsequently from the wrong-doer some performance under the contract.

ILLUSTRATION

> *A* contracts to build a house on *B*'s land and *B* contracts to pay *A* $25,000 for it. *A* fails in some particulars to build the house according to plans and specifications. *B* takes possession of the house and says to *A:* "I don't care about these defects in your performance; on the whole you have done pretty well, and I am satisfied with the house." *A*'s duty to make compensation is discharged. It is immaterial that *B* has completely paid for the house before *A* has finished the work, and the contract has thus been fully performed on one side.

In *Bye v. George W. McCaulley & Son Co., supra* (76 A. 622), Plaintiff brought an action to recover from Defendant for work and labor in constructing a porch. Defendant raised the defense that the porch when completed was not satisfactory. Plaintiff, on the other hand, maintained that the Defendant, knowing all the facts, accepted the work unconditionally and waived the defects. The Court charged the jury, in part, as follows:

"The defendants claim, on the other hand, that the defects resulted from the bad and unskilled manner in which the work was done; that by reason thereof the porch and steps were of no value whatever to them. If you should find this to be true, from the evidence, the defendants would be entitled to your verdict, unless the defendants waived the defects and accepted the work unconditionally. If the completed porch and steps were accepted by the defendants . . . such acceptance would amount to a waiver of the defects and entitle the plaintiff to your verdict. And in like manner, if you should find from the evidence that the defendants promised to pay the claim, with a full knowledge of such defects, it would amount to a waiver."

Webster v. Beebe, supra was an action by Plaintiff to recover for repairs made to Defendant's boat which Defendant resisted because the work was not done in accordance with the contract. Again the Court charged the jury that

> . . . if there were defects in the materials furnished and work done, if the defendant accepted the boat and failed to give notice to the plaintiff of such defects, after he had had a reasonable opportunity to discover such defects, the plaintiff would in such event be entitled to recover. (77 A. 770)

However, it is difficult to reconcile such a result, though desirable, with accepted principles of contract law. According to Williston, (Vol. 3, Sec. 690, page 1995), the only instances in which a waiver of a breach of a contract will be held to bind the injured party are when there are facts indicating an estoppel or where some new consideration is given the injured party for waiving his right of action for damages.

And in *Duval v. Metropolitan Ins. Co.*, (1903, 82 N.H. 543, 136 A. 400, 403, 50 A.L.R. 1276), the Supreme Court of New Hampshire said in this same connection:

> While a waiver is sometimes spoken of in a loose way, which might indicate the idea that it would bind the party granting it simply upon proof that it was offered, the true rule is that, in the absence of an estoppel, it stands like any other undertaking. It must be supported by a consideration, or it is not binding upon the party making it. (See also *Colbath v. H. B. Stebbins' Lumber Co.*, 127 Me. 406, 144 A. 1, 5).

Strictly speaking, then, it would appear that when a party to a contract breaches it in some minor respect and upon the tender by him of performance the other party, knowing of the defect, deliberately acquiesces, then the purported waiver of the right so accrued is not binding in the absence of consideration.

Now in the case before me the breach of contract to supply a Westinghouse stove was presumably not known to Plaintiffs until the houses were completed and offered to Plaintiffs for occupancy, thus precluding the possibility of an estoppel. Moreover, nothing in the pleadings reveals that the claimed assent or waiver by Plaintiffs to the substitution of another and cheaper type of range was based upon some new consideration for it is useless to argue that the acceptance of the houses by Plaintiffs rather than having no home at all imports a new consideration in view of the fact that Defendant was legally obligated to furnish, and Plaintiffs had a legal right to receive, a home supplied with a Westinghouse range. It would appear, therefore, that in conformity with the strict principles of law here reviewed the Plaintiffs could not be held to be bound by their purported waivers.

However, the thought of one party to a contract with full knowledge of the facts deliberately excusing some minor breach in performance and thereafter bringing an action for damages is repugnant. The Restatement bars a right of action in such case and, more importantly, the decisions of this State are in accord. The Bye case and the Webster case, above referred to, have been the law of this State for many years and I feel I should regard them as binding me here. Plaintiff's may test their correctness on appeal.

Plaintiff's motion to strike is denied.

Overton v. Vita-Food Corporation
1953 (Calif. C.A.) 210 P.2d 757

Plaintiff sued defendant to recover compensation for services under the terms of a written contract. The contract provided in part that plaintiff would not earn a salary if the plants of the defendant were out of production from causes incident to our resulting from the present and prospective emergent conditions, or other causes beyond the control of the defendant such as transportation delays, strikes, and acts of God. Defendant plant ceased production because it sold its trade-mark to another company. The trial court held that plaintiff was entitled to recover his salary and that the "out of production" clause was not an excuse. Defendant appeals.

VALLÉE, J. Appellant [defendant] argues that we must determine as a matter of law that respondent's employment was suspended in 1945 and 1946 because the evidence is without conflict to the effect that the "plant or plants" were out of production as the term is defined in the contract. Assuming the evidence to be without conflict in this respect, that fact does not settle the question. The contract says that the employment shall be suspended if the plant or plants are out of production "from causes incident to or resulting from the present and prospective emergent conditions, or other causes beyond the reasonable control of the Corporation, such as, but without limitation to, transportation delays or interruptions, strikes, and acts of God." The court, in the light of the evidence, interpreted "emergent conditions" to mean war conditions. No contention is made here that the evidence in aid of interpretation of the contract was inadmissible. The court found on substantial evidence that the fact that appellant was out of production in 1945 and 1946 was not due to "emergent conditions" but was due to the fact that appellant by selling a trade-mark for $200,000 "voluntarily placed it out of its power to meet the provisions of the so-called 'production clause.'" Having voluntarily placed itself out of production so as to prevent its performance of the contract, appellant will not be permitted to deny liability. A party to a contract cannot take advantage of his own act or omission to escape liability thereon. Where a party to a contract prevents the fulfillment of a condition precedent or its performance by the adverse party, he cannot rely on such condition to defeat his liability. Whether appellant voluntarily placed it out of its power to meet the production clause of the contract, and whether respondent waived the breach, were questions of fact for the determination of the trial court and not questions of law for this court, as appellant appears to contend. Since appellant was not out of production from one of the causes specified in the contract, respondent's employment was not suspended. . . .

Affirmed.

Wasserman Theatrical Enterprise, Inc. v. Harris

1950, 137 Conn. 488, 77 A.2d 329

BROWN, C. J. The plaintiff brought this action to recover damages for the defendant's failure to produce a theatrical performance as provided in a written contract between the parties. The court rendered judgment for the defendant and the plaintiff has appealed.

These facts are not in dispute: On October 30, 1946, the plaintiff entered into a contract with the defendant (Harris) whereby the latter agreed to present Walter Huston in a theatrical performance entitled

"The Apple of His Eye" at Worcester, Massachusetts, on the night of December 16, 1946. The contract contained this provision: "(T)his agreement and the terms hereof shall be subject to the customs governing uncontrollable circumstances, such as . . . illness of any of the chief artists of the said attraction and the like, and . . . upon the happening of any such events no claim for compensation or damages shall be made by either party as against the other." The plaintiff which had been engaged in theatrical productions in Worcester for some eleven years, had reason to anticipate a profit from the production and went to considerable expense and effort in preparing to stage it. On December 12, 1946, the defendant canceled the performance on the ground of Huston's illness. At the same time, bookings for Ithaca, Springfield and Rochester, scheduled to follow that for Worcester, were also canceled. The plaintiff has received nothing for its loss incident to the cancellation of the performance and has been at all times ready, able and willing to perform its obligations under the contract. The show, with Huston as leading man, had been on the road since the early fall of 1946. After eight performances a week had been given for four weeks in Boston, it opened in New Haven on December 12, 1946, for four performances and closed on December 14. As scheduled, the show opened for a month in Chicago on December 25. Huston participated in every performance given and had no understudy.

The defendant alleged as a special defense the provision of the contract quoted above, that Huston was the chief artist and essential performer in the production, and that by reason of his illness performance of the contract on December 16, 1946, was rendered impossible on the part of the defendant. Whether the court was warranted in sustaining this defense and, in reliance thereon, rendering judgment for the defendant is the question for determination. "One who engages for performance of such personal character that it can be performed only by a particular person is excused from liability by the physical incapacity of that person, before breach of the contract unless he has clearly assumed the risk of such incapacity. . . . Generally it is the promisor himself who is to render the personal services, but the principle is applicable to contracts where the promisor has agreed that a third person shall render such services and the latter becomes physically unable to do so. . . ." (6 Williston, Contracts (Rev. Ed.) § 1940). The quoted provision of the contract therefore is substantially declaratory of the condition which arises by implication in an agreement of this nature. An agreement for personal services, in the absence of a manifested contrary intention, is always subject to the condition, implied by law, that the person who is to render the services shall be able to perform at the appointed time. . . .

In the view which we take of the case, the only conclusion of the court requiring consideration was that Huston's apprehension as to the state of his health was reasonable and reasonably justified the defendant in canceling the performance. The rule quoted is amplified by this further principle: "Where a promisor apprehends before . . . the time for performance of a promise in a bargain . . . that performance will seriously jeopardize his own life or health or that of others, he is not liable, unless a contrary intention is manifested or he is guilty of contributing fault, for failing to begin . . . performance, while such apprehension exists, if the failure to begin . . . performance is reasonable. . . ." Restatement, 2 Contracts Section 465. "Out of regard for human welfare the rule is often applicable . . . though performance is not only practicable but is not increased in difficulty. The possible consequences of performing may be so injurious as to free the promisor; and the fact that it later appears that no harmful consequences would have ensued does not alter the rule. The promisor is not bound to perform so long as failure to perform is reasonable because of existing ground for apprehension. . . ."

The further facts established by the finding as corrected and material upon this issue, which is sufficiently raised by the special defense, may be thus summarized: While playing in Boston, Huston, for some two weeks prior to December 12, experienced a tickling sensation in his throat, and during this time the condition became progressively worse. As often as two or three times during a performance he experienced a tightening of his throat. Although use of a medication afforded him temporary relief, he had similar difficulty while performing on the stage in New Haven on December 12, 13, and 14. His throat condition was a continuous and increasing cause of worry to him for he was constantly in fear during a performance that he would be unable to finish it. This fear did not affect him in social intercourse off the stage, but because of his apprehension that he could not go on with the show in the face of the recurring throat sensation he wanted to find out definitely the nature of his ailment. Had he kept the engagement in Worcester, and had his throat tightened, he probably could have completed the performance with the aid of lozenges. He had consulted a doctor in New York three or four times in the spring of 1946. The only doctor Huston consulted during November and December, 1946, was Dr. Loyal Davis, his personal friend, who, after hearing his symptoms, though no examination was made, advised him to go to Chicago for a complete and thorough examination and to have the condition attended to. Huston's throat attacks were becoming more frequent and he felt impelled to do something about them without delay. While he believed he could complete the New Haven engagement, he insisted upon canceling all performances for the week of December 16 in order to look after his throat condition immediately, for he believed it would be impossible for him to continue after concluding in New Haven. He was gravely concerned over the consequences of any delay in procuring medical attention.

From New Haven he proceeded to Chicago. A minor operation was performed on his throat at a hospital there and specimens of tissue were taken. The report that these disclosed no malignant condition relieved his mind, and he was able to resume his next scheduled performances in Chicago, where he played every performance. Huston was a man with a sincere desire to carry out his obligations. During his entire theatrical career of forty-five years, the only request which he had made for the cancellation of a performance was for the one at Worcester. The court's conclusion that Huston's fear and apprehension that his illness was of such a nature that it would, in the absence of immediate expert medical attention, seriously jeopardize his health and particularly his voice was a reasonable one and was warranted upon the facts set forth in the preceding paragraph.

There is no error. Judgment for defendant affirmed.

Hipskind Heating & Plumb. Co. v. General Industries
1965 (Ind.) 204 N.E.2d 339

ARTERBURN, C. J.   This case is before us on petition to transfer from the Appellate Court . . .

In this case a building in the process of repairs by the installation of a sprinkler system was destroyed by fire. The destruction of a building which is the subject of the contract for repairs excuses the performance of the remainder of the contract as to each party. The majority rule is that an event unforeseen which creates an impossibility of performance by reason of the destruction of the subject matter of the contract will excuse the performance thereof by each of the parties.

However, that is not the exact question here. The question here is: may a contractor who was originally obligated to perform a contract with reference to repairs on a building which has been destroyed by fire recover for partial work done not on the expressed contract but on *quantum meruit*? The authority on the latter question is divided in this country.

However, in Indiana it seems under the authority of *Krause v. Board, etc.* (1904, 162 Ind. 278, 70 N.E.2d 264, 65 L.R.A. 111), this Court has said that it leaves both parties as it finds them in a case such as this and that neither can recover from the other if each is "equally blameless and irresponsible for the accident by which the property is destroyed."

Petition to transfer is denied.

CHAPTER 15
REVIEW QUESTIONS AND PROBLEMS

1. *A* Co. installed and leased to *E* at his restaurant a burglar alarm system for five years at a certain rental, *A* Co. to maintain and repair said system as needed. The state condemned *E*'s property for public use. *A* Co. sued for rental falling due thereafter, and *E* claimed impossibility as a defense. What result?

2. *C* contracted to do a considerable amount of work on improving *O*'s residence, part of the work involving the addition of millwork. After some of the work had been done, the residence was destroyed by fire, leaving *C* with $2,000 of millwork on hand that he was to use on the

job but that has little value for use elsewhere. *C* seeks to recover of *O* for the value of the millwork. Should he succeed?

3. *H* Co. agreed to repair the refrigeration system on *M*'s ship and to test it for effectiveness at cost of $4,700. The work was done, but before *H* Co. could test it, *M* took the ship on a trip. *M* claims to have suffered damages because the work was not effective. In spite of this, the court allowed recovery by *H* Co. What defense did *H* Co. have against *M*'s claim of poor workmanship?

4. *W* sued *S* for loss of value of a boat which *S*, an experienced operator in salvaging submerged boats, had agreed to raise and keep afloat until it reached harbor. Before *S* could begin operation the boat slipped off the reef and sank in deep water, making it impossible to raise it. The court held this did not relieve *S* of liability. Is the decision sound?

5. *O* leased property, which the latter expected to use in sale of automobiles, to *T* for five years. War intervened, automobiles were not available, and *T* desires to be released of his contract. Is the contract binding?

6. *S* sold a truckload of pork to *B*. *S* was to deliver on 12/26 but did not tender delivery until 12/29 at which time *B* refused to accept the hogs because of the delay. Did *S*'s breach justify rescission?

7. *X* obtained a judgment against *Y*. *Y* tendered payment of the judgment debt but *X* refused and appealed contending that the judgment should have been greater. On appeal, the original judgment was affirmed. Is *X* entitled to interest on his judgment until it is paid?

8. *S*, a securities dealer, contracted to sell stock of *D*, an Ohio Co., in Ohio. After the contract, the sale became illegal because of the federal securities law. *S* sues *D* for the commission he would have earned. What result?

9. *X* leased premises to *Y* at a rental of $250 per month plus a percentage of profits. *Y* ceased operations but continued to pay the $250 per month. *X* sued *Y* for the percentage of anticipated profits. What result?

10. *A* sold *B* a lot with a house and 2 small buildings at the rear. One building was a small shed which encroached on a neighbor's land by 1.2 feet. The neighbor required that 20 inches of the shed be sawed off and refinished. Does this breach justify *B* in refusing to consummate the sale?

chapter 16

Discharge of
Contracts

2-105 Introduction. The rights and duties created by a contract exist until the contract is discharged. Of course, the usual and intended method of discharge is by performance of the contract as agreed. After full performance by both parties, the life of the contract is over and the parties are automatically discharged. Another method of discharge is an intentional cancellation or alteration of the written evidence of the agreement. This situation arises most frequently with commercial paper where an intentional material alteration avoids the instrument.

The final act of performance in many contracts is the payment of money; there are three questions about payment that deserve special treatment. What constitutes payment? Which of several items has been paid? What is good evidence of payment?

In answer to the first question, there is no doubt that the transfer of money acts as payment, but the receipt of the debtor's check,[1] his note, or an endorsed check or note of someone else is not payment unless the creditor expressly receives such items payment. They are considered as conditional payment, payment becoming final only when the instruments are honored. The same appears to be true of the assignment of an account receivable. Unless otherwise agreed, the assignment is received as collateral for the principal indebtedness, and unless the assigned claim is collected, the debtor is still obligated to pay his indebtedness.

As to the second question, a debtor who owes several obligations to his creditor is free at the time of payment to stipulate which of the several obligations he is paying, and the creditor who receives such payment is

[1] *Tuckel et al. v. Jurovaty*, page 307.

obligated to follow the instructions. In the absence of any intructions, the creditor may apply the payment on any one of several obligations that are due or he may credit a portion of the payment upon each of several obligations. The creditor may apply a payment against a claim that has been outlawed. However, this will not cause the outlawed claim to revive as to the balance. If the source of a payment is someone other than the debtor and this fact is known to the creditor, the payment must be applied in such a manner as to protect the third party who makes the payment. Hence, if a surety supplies the money for the payment and the creditor knows it, he is bound to apply the payment on the obligation for which the surety was secondarily liable. Finally, if the creditor fails to make a particular application prior to the time the issue is raised in court, the payment is applied against the debtor's obligations in the order of their maturity, except where the creditor holds both secured and unsecured obligations, in which event the courts are inclined to apply it on an unsecured obligation which has matured. Similarly, if both principal and interest are due, the court considers the interest to be paid first, any balance being credited on the principal.

The third question can be answered by stating generally that a receipt is acceptable evidence of payment, although it may be rebutted by evidence showing it to be in error or to have been given under mistake. A check is evidence of payment, but the evidence is more conclusive where the purpose for which it is given is stated on the check.

There are several events other than performance which will discharge the contract and release the parties from their obligations. These include the legal concepts of accord and satisfaction, novation, the running of the Statute of Limitations, and discharge in bankruptcy. These matters are discussed in the sections which follow. In addition, a contract may be discharged by another contract which replaces it or by a mutual agreement that the original contract is discharged. As discussed in the chapter on Consideration, if the contract is executory, the release of each party by the other supplies the consideration and the contract of discharge is valid. If on the other hand, one party has performed, there is no consideration to support the release of the other party and the purported contract of discharge is a nullity. However, a contract which is fully performed by one party may be discharged if the release is found to be a gift by the party making the discharge.

2-106 Accord and Satisfaction. An accord consists of an agreement between contracting parties whereby one of them is to do something different by way of performance than that called for by the contract.[2] This accord is *satisfied* when the substituted performance is completed. The cashing of a check marked "paid in full" when it is tendered to settle a disputed claim is an accord and satisfaction.[3] Both accord and satisfaction must take place before the old obligation is discharged, unless it is ex-

---

[2] *W. H. McCune, Inc. v. Revzon*, page 309.
[3] *Burgamy v. Davis*, page 310.

pressly stated that it is being substituted for the old. Otherwise, the new agreement of itself does not terminate the old agreement. To illustrate: *A* purchased a used car from *B* and agreed to pay him $600 within sixty days. *A* failed to pay *B* at the end of the period, and agreed to paint *B*'s building in full payment of the debt. At any time before *A* commences to perform, *B* may recover upon the original contract. The painting of the building constitutes the satisfaction of the accord, and thus discharges the original contract.

2-107 Novation. *Novation* is an agreement whereby an original party to a contract is replaced by a new party. In order for the substitution to be effective, it must be agreed to by all of the parties. The remaining contracting party must agree to accept the new party and at the same time consent to release the withdrawing party.[4] The latter must consent to withdraw and to permit the new party to take his place. The new party must agree to assume the burdens and duties of the retiring party based on consideration received by him. If all of these essentials are present, the withdrawing party is discharged from the agreement. To illustrate: *A* purchases an automobile from *B*, making a small down payment, and agreeing to pay the balance of $400 within six months. Finding times somewhat hard, *A* sells the car to *C*, who agrees to pay the balance to *B*. Both parties notify *B* of this arrangement. As yet no novation is completed because *B* has not agreed to release *A* and to look to *C* for payment. If *B* releases *A*, then *A* is discharged from any duty arising under the original agreement, and a novation is created.

2-108 Statute of Limitations. The Statute of Limitations prescribes a time limit within which suit must be started after a cause of action arises. An action for breach of any contract for sale of personal property under the Code must be commenced within four years.[C1] The Code further provides that the parties in their agreement may reduce the period of limitation to not less than one year but may not extend it.[C2] Where contracts are not controlled by the Code, and in those states which have not adopted the Code, there is a wide variety of limitation periods, the most common being six years. Some states distinguish between oral and written contracts, making the period longer for the latter. The purpose of a statute of limitations is to prevent actions from being brought long after evidence is lost or important witnesses have died. A contract action must be brought within the prescribed period after the obligation matures or after the cause of action arises.

Any voluntary[5] part payment made on a money obligation tolls the statute, starting it to run anew. Similarly, any voluntary part payment, new promise or clear acknowledgment of the indebtedness[6] made after the claim has been outlawed reinstates the obligation and the statute

---

[4] *Strunk Chain Saw, Inc. v. Williams*, page 311.

[5] *Nilsson et al. v. Kielman et al.*, page 313.

[6] *Whale Harbor Spa, Inc. v. Wood*, page 314.

[C1] *U.C.C.* 2-725.   [C2] *U.C.C.* 2-725.

commences to run again. No new consideration is required to support the reinstatement promise. If the old obligation has been outlawed, a new promise may be either partial or conditional. Since there is no *duty* to pay the debt, the debtor may attach such conditions to his new promise as he sees fit or may promise to pay only part of the debt. A few states require the new promise or acknowledgment to be in writing particularly where the original obligation was in writing. The Code does not alter the law on tolling of the Statute of Limitations.[C3]

The period during which a debtor removes himself from the state or the period during which the debtor or creditor is incapacitated by minority or insanity is usually totally or partially eliminated from the period prescribed by statute. In other words, the debtor's absence from the state extends the period within which an action may be brought against him, and a minor usually has a short time in which to bring action after he reaches his majority, although the full period set by statute has expired earlier.

2-109 Bankruptcy and Composition of Creditors. Congress by statute has provided procedures which if followed will cause debts to be discharged. The discharge is in the nature of a defense which may be pleaded in the event suit is brought on the claim and may be waived and the debt may be revived by a new promise to pay, as noted above.[7]

A discharge in bankruptcy may result from the debtor voluntarily petitioning the court that his debts be discharged, or may result from a petition filed by his creditors called involuntary bankruptcy. There are numerous rules of law concerning these petitions and other matters such as debts which are not discharged, recoverable preferences, and priority of claims. These matters are discussed in Chapter 46.

A composition of creditors is an agreement by the creditors agreeing to accept a less than full payment in return for the discharge of the debt. This usually occurs when the debtor is insolvent and the creditors wish to avoid further losses and expenses which would be involved in formal bankruptcy proceedings. A part of the consideration for such contracts is the promise by each creditor not to file a petition in involuntary bankruptcy and a promise by the debtor not to file voluntary bankruptcy. The assets of the debtor are prorated among the creditors and they accept their allocated amount in full discharge of the debtor.

DISCHARGE OF CONTRACTS CASES

Tuckel et al. v. Jurovaty
1954 (Conn.) 109 A. 2d 262

BALDWIN, J. The plaintiffs brought suit to recover the balance due on sale of a television set to the defendant. They have appealed from a judgment for the defendant.

---

7 *Domestic Loan, Inc. v. Peregoy*, page 315.

C3 *U.C.C.* 2-725(4).

Stated briefly, the facts are these: the plaintiffs were engaged in the business of selling radio and television sets. On November 30, 1950, they sold a television set to the defendant (Jurovaty) for the agreed price of $340. The defendant paid $85 in cash, took the set and agreed to pay the balance of the purchase price within thirty days. On December 22, 1950, the defendant gave to the plaintiffs' agent an additional $85 in cash and indorsed to the plaintiffs and delivered to their agent a check for $170, drawn to the order of the defendant by Joseph Irving. The plaintiffs presented the check to the bank for payment but it was returned for insufficient funds. Three to four weeks later the plaintiffs notified the defendant that the check had not been honored. The question presented is whether the acceptance of the check and the marking of the bill as paid discharged the defendant's obligation.

In the absence of a special agreement to the contrary, the giving of a check by a debtor to his creditor does not discharge the debt until the check is paid. In the case at bar, the defendant was the indorser and not the drawer of the check. This does not alter the situation. The dishonored check leaves the defendant's obligation to the plaintiffs still outstanding. The indorsement of the check made it negotiable in the hands of the defendant but it did not convert it into money. The check still retained its character as a written promise to pay in accordance with its terms.

The decision of this case turns upon whether the facts found spell out a special agreement by the parties that acceptance of the check and $85 in cash, representing the balance due on the purchase price, constituted payment in full. The defendant argues that the court has so found. We do not so interpret the finding. The court concluded from the subordinate facts found that "[t]he acceptance of the check . . . and the marking of the defendant's bill 'paid in full' constituted payment of the $170.00 balance due the plaintiffs." This was no more than a conclusion drawn from subordinate facts. It is not a finding that there was a special agreement. In the giving and acceptance of a check to pay a debt, it is presumed that the parties intended only a conditional payment. "Ordinarily the parties act, and the great volume of trade proceeds, upon the assumption that the condition will in due course be fulfilled. Thus the merchant who sells goods and receives a check therefor often credits the amount upon his books and perhaps issues a receipt purporting to show that the charge for them has been paid; or the holder of a note upon receipt of a check or draft offered in payment of it may surrender the note; but these and like facts in themselves will not destroy the presumption that only conditional payment has been made. They are the results of the assumption that the check or draft will ultimately be paid, rather than the evidence of its acceptance in absolute payment." (*Bassett v. Merchants' Trust Co.*, 118 Conn. 586, 595, 173 A. 777). Something more than the facts found is required to demonstrate that the intention of the parties was otherwise. Nor does the fact that the plaintiffs retained the check three to four weeks after it had been returned unpaid alter the presumption that the check was accepted only as a conditional payment of the amount it represented. The plaintiff is not suing the defendant on the check. He is suing upon the defendant's promise to pay for the television set.

There is error, the judgment is set aside and a new trial is ordered.

W. H. McCune, Inc. v. Revzon

1963 (Conn.) 193 A. 2d 601

SHEA, J.   In September, 1957, the plaintiff sent the defendant a bill for work done and materials furnished during the preceding four months. The defendant made payments on account until December, 1957; the balance then due was $1482.82. At that time, the parties had some conversation about the bill. Later, the defendant claimed that the plaintiff had agreed to accept $1000 in full payment, but the trial court found that the amount of the bill was not in dispute, that the conversation about the bill was "talk" designed to induce the plaintiff to accept less than the amount actually due and that there was no compromise. In January, 1958, the defendant by his check paid $300 on account. On February 11, 1958, the defendant personally delivered to the plaintiff a check for $200. On the lower left-hand corner of the face of this check, the defendant had written "bal. $500.00." The plaintiff told the defendant that the notation on the check was not correct and, before depositing it, crossed out the "$500.00" and substituted "$982.82." A few days later, the plaintiff did a small job for the defendant amounting to $4.50, and this sum was added to the defendant's bill. On February 28, 1958, the defendant personally delivered to the plaintiff a check for $250 on which the defendant had written "bal. $250.00 to date." Again, the plaintiff orally disputed the correctness of the notation on the check. He kept it, however, and, in the absence of the defendant, changed the notation to read: "Bal. $737.32 to date." The defendant was willing to pay the plaintiff an additional $250 if the plaintiff would give him a receipt marked "paid in full." At the trial, the defendant conceded that the original bill rendered by the plaintiff was correct.

The plaintiff brought this action to recover the balance of $737.32. The defendant denied that this sum was due and alleged, by way of further defense, that the parties had reached an accord as to the balance due, that the defendant had tendered the balance, and that the tender had been refused. The court found the issues for the plaintiff and rendered judgment in the amount of $737.32. The defendant appealed to the Appellate Division of the Circuit Court, which construed the defense as alleging that the parties had entered into an accord and satisfaction, found error and remanded the case "with direction to enter judgment for the plaintiff to recover of the defendant the balance of $250.00 due under the terms of the accord and satisfaction."

An accord is a contract between creditor and debtor for the settlement of a claim by some performance other than that which is due. Satisfaction takes place when the accord is executed. The defendant does not claim, nor has he pleaded, that his debt has been paid in full. He has alleged an accord executory. "[A]n accord is an agreement; but there is no agreement, without a consideration; and receiving part only, is no consideration for an agreement not to collect the rest; it is a nude pact." (*Warren v. Skinner,* 20 Conn. 559, 561). Where the claim is unliquidated, however, any sum, given and received in settlement of the dispute, is a sufficient consideration. Where one of two different sums is due, if there is a dispute as to which is the proper amount, the demand is unliquidated. Here, the trial court found that there was no dispute as to the amount of the debt. In fact, the defendant conceded during the trial that the bills presented by the plaintiff were correct. Nor was there any controversy about payments which had been made on account. The mere assertion that a compromise has been made is not sufficient to convert the claim into an unliquidated one. The question whether the claim is liquidated or disputed is generally a question of fact to be determined by the trier. The facts found by the trial court fully supported the conclusions reached by it, and the trial court did not err in rendering judgment as it did.

There is no error in the judgment of the trial court, and the judgment of the Appellate Division is set aside.

In this opinion the other Judges concurred.

Burgamy v. Davis

1958 (Tex. C.A.) 313 S.W. 2d 365

RENFRO, J. Appellant Burgamy, as plaintiff, sued appellee Davis for the sum of $328.73 and foreclosure of a mechanic's and materialmen's lien. Defendant pleaded accord and satisfaction. Trial, without a jury, resulted in judgment for defendant.

Findings of fact and conclusions of law were filed by the trial court.

The court found: Appellant and appellee entered into an oral contract by the terms of which appellant was to furnish material and labor, on a cost plus basis, for plumbing modifications in a house owned by appellee. Prior to completion of the contract, appellant made demand on appellee for the sum of $328.73, which appellee paid on March 19, 1957. About the 22nd of March, appellant completed the job and made demand for an additional $537.45. About the first of April, a dispute in good faith arose between appellant and appellee as to the amount due appellant. Thereafter, while the dispute still existed, appellee delivered a check in the sum of $208.73 to appellant, with the words, "Payment of account in full," written on the check. The check was intended to be in full payment of the disputed claim. Appellant accepted and received the amount of the check.

. . . The dispute had not been settled when appellee sent the check of April first. Appellant admitted that, without communicating with appellee, he marked out the words, "Payment of account in full," and wrote on the check the words, "Paid on account," endorsed the check and deposited it to his account. . . .

Sufficient consideration for accord may inhere in or arise out of a dispute as to liability upon a liquidated claim. This presupposes that denial of liability, in whole or in part, is not merely factitious or *mala-fides.*

The test is not whether the debtor was correct in his contention, in that he really had a legal or equitable defense to the claim in whole or in part, but consists in the fact that he in good faith urged or asserted a defense which he really believed was substantial.

If the one who is sought to be held liable in good faith urges a defense which he believes to be substantial, and which he claims will defeat the demand in whole or in part, and in good faith raises a controversy and dispute as to his liability, a settlement and compromise of the demand, based upon such contention, will not be disturbed. Existence of a dispute of that character affords a good consideration for the new agreement of accord.

In *Firestone Tire & Rubber Co. v. White,* (Tex. Civ. App. 274 S.W.2d 452, 454), the court recognizes the rule " 'where a claim is unliquidated or disputed, the cashing of a check marked "in full payment" is a binding accord and satisfaction and extinguishes the claim. . . . The cashing of the check is held to constitute an acceptance even though the words "in full payment" are erased by the creditor before he cashes the check.' "

It is well settled that when an account is made the subject of a bona fide dispute between the parties as to its correctness, and the debtor tenders his check to the creditor upon condition that it be accepted in full payment, the creditor must either refuse to receive the check or accept the same burdened by its attached condition. If he accepts the check and cashes the same, he impliedly agrees to the condition, although he may expressly notify the debtor that he is not accepting the same with the condition, but is only applying the same as a partial payment on account.

When appellant, knowing appellee was disputing in good faith the amount of the claim, received the check marked "Payment of account in full," he was given the option either to accept the check as full payment or to return the check to appellee, unaccepted, and hold appellee for his full claim. He chose to accept and deposit the check to his account. Under the findings of the trial court, there was a valid accord and satisfaction.

The judgment of the trial court is affirmed.

Affirmed.

Strunk Chain Saws, Inc. v. Williams

1959, (La.), 111 So.2d 195

This is an action against defendant, Williams, to collect $500, the balance of an account. The defendant asserts novation as a defense. The plaintiff had difficulty collecting a $2430.72 account from defendant for merchandise sold when a partnership, S & F Repair Service, offered to take defendant's assets and assume the obligation, payable in monthly installments. It paid $500 on account and gave its notes for the balance, defendant's name not appearing on the notes. S & F became insolvent, leaving $500 of the amount unpaid, and plaintiff seeks to recover of the defendant. The lower court gave judgment for defendant, implying that the taking of another's note indicated a release of the original party.

GLADNEY, J. . . . The only defense urged herein is a plea of novation, in which it is contended defendant's obligation was extinguished by plaintiff's substitution of a new obligation for the original debt, and a new debtor for the defendant. The plea was sustained by the trial judge.

Novation is defined and explained in the following articles of the LSA-Civil Code:

> Art. 2185 Novation is a contract, consisting of two stipulations; one to extinguish an existing obligation, the other to substitute a new one in its place.
> Art. 2189 Novation takes place in three ways:
> 1. When a debtor contracts a new debt to his creditor, which new debt is substituted to the old one, which is extinguished.
> 2. What a new debtor is substituted to the old one, who is discharged by the creditor.
> 3. When by the effect of a new engagement, a new creditor is substituted to the old one, with regard to whom the debtor is discharged.
> Art. 2192 The delegation, by which a debtor gives to the creditor another debtor who obliges himself towards such creditor, does not operate a novation, unless the creditor has expressly declared that he intends to discharge his debtor who has made the delegation.

Counsel for appellant earnestly insists novation does not take place by the substitution of one debtor for another unless there is an express declaration by the creditor to discharge the debtor who has made the delegation. The evidence as presented, it must be admitted, does not show that by oral or written expression plaintiff stipulated the release of the defendant from his original obligation. But we are of the opinion our jurisprudence has accorded a more liberal construction to the above-quoted articles and a debtor may be discharged where the intent of the creditor to novate is clearly indicated. . . .

We deem it unnecessary to attempt a review of the jurisprudence relating to the application of Articles 2189 and 2192, LSA-C.C. This has been excellently done in an article entitled "The Requisites and Effects of Novation: A Comparative Survey," written by Walter L. Nixon, Jr., *Tulane Law Review,* Volume 25, page 100. The author therein, page 113, concluded:

> Despite the fact that Article 2192 of the Louisiana Civil Code provides that express intention on the part of the creditor is requisite to novation by the substitution of a new debtor for the old one, the Louisiana jurisprudence indicates that acts tanamount [sic] to an express declaration will suffice. . . .

As observed above, our courts have not adhered to the strict construction contended for by appellant but have ruled a release or discharge

can be evidenced by acts of a creditor clearly disclosing an intent to no
longer look to the original debtor for payment.

*For the reasons herein assigned, the judgment from which appealed is
affirmed at appellant's cost.*

Nilsson et al. v. Kielman et al.

1945, 70 S.D. 390, 17 N.W.2d 918

Action by M. T. Nilsson and E. P. Nilsson against Ethel E. Kielman
and L. T. Nilsson on a note. The note matured in 1926 and the statute
of limitations had run against it unless certain payments indorsed thereon
had extended the life of the note. One payment resulted from the sale
of certain property pledged as security and a second payment was the
result of the collection of a note which had been assigned as collateral.
Ethel E. Kielman made no payments and the security for the note had
been given plaintiff many years before the money was realized and the
credit given on the note.

ROBERTS, J. . . . It appears from the provisions of SDC33.0213 that
an acknowledgment or promise to be effectual to interrupt the running
of the statute of limitations must be in writing and signed by the party
to be charged, but this requirement does not alter or take away the effect
of a part payment. It is the settled law of this state that a part payment to
be effectual to interrupt the running of the statute must have been made
voluntarily and must have been made and accepted under circumstances
consistent with an intent to pay the balance. . . . Payments made by a
joint debtor bind only the person making the payments and do not operate to interrupt the running of the statute as to the other debtors not
participating or acquiescing in the payments. . . . The principle on
which part payment operates to take a debt without the statute is that the
debtor by the payment intends to acknowledge the continued existence
of the debt.

The agreement with reference to the amount of credit on January 19,
1940, constitutes neither a new promise in writing nor a part payment as
of that date. It is the fact of voluntary payment made by the debtor, and
not entry of credit, that interrupts the running of the statute. Nor did the
collection of the account amounting to $74.40 give new life to the debt.
Plaintiffs were authorized to collect the accounts and apply the proceeds
to payment of the debt, but this did not have the same effect as if made
personally by the defendants. There is no vital distinction between such a
case and one where money received by the payee of a note from collateral
security such as notes and mortgages of third parties pledged by the
maker is credited on the principal note. Such payment does not interrupt
the running of the statute. . . . The underlying reason for the doctrine
is that a creditor is not an agent of the debtor to such an extent as to
make an act done by him in the name of the debtor operate as a new
promise to himself without which element the payment cannot operate
to interrupt the statute.

Judgment for defendant affirmed.

Whale Harbor Spa, Inc. v. Wood

1959, 266 F.2d 953

JONES, J.   The appellant, Whale Harbor Spa, Inc., is a Florida corporation. Its stock was owned in equal shares by Dorothy W. Wood and Al B. Luckey. The corporation was managed by Luckey. The Luckey and Wood families had been close friends over a period of many years. Between May 1, 1946, and October 14, 1948, Mrs. Wood made six open loans aggregating $24,750 to the corporation. These loans were not evidenced by promissory notes or other written obligation. On July 10, 1950, Mrs. Wood loaned the corporation $5,000 upon its demand note. On April 7, 1947, the corporation paid Mrs. Wood $3,000 on account. The amount of the advances unpaid remains at $26,750. The indebtedness was set up on the corporation's books and was carried as a liability of the corporation to Mrs. Wood. On July 10, 1950, the corporation, by an endorsement on a letter from Mrs. Wood's agent, acknowledged the existence of the indebtedness and the amount of it. From at least as early as November, 1952, and at intervals of never more than six months, the bookkeeper of the corporation, at the direction of Luckey, sent to Mrs. Wood or her agent profit and loss statements and balance sheets of the corporation. The balance sheets showed an indebtedness to Mrs. Wood of $26,750. After the death of both Mrs. Wood and Luckey, the executor of Mrs. Wood brought suit against the corporation for the amount of the unpaid advances. The corporation did not deny that the loans had been made nor did it contend that payment had been made. Its sole defense is that the indebtedness is barred by the Florida statute of limitations. The plaintiff, as executor of Mrs. Wood's estate, contended that the balance sheets were written acknowledgements of the debt sufficient to toll the statute, and further contended that the corporation was equitably estopped to plead the statute of limitations. The court, after a trial without a jury, determined that no part of the debt was barred by the statute of limitations and entered judgment against the corporation. It has appealed.

It is not questioned that the period of limitation has run and that the statute of limitations is a bar to decovery unless the statute has been tolled or the corporation is estopped to assert it. The Florida statute requires that "Every acknowledgment of or promise to pay a debt barred by the statute of limitations, must be in writing and signed by the party to be charged." (F.S.A. § 95.04.) This statute does not apply to promises made before the expiration of the period of limitations, and verbal promises made before the cause of action had run will take the cause of action out from the operation of the statute. . . . Where there is a distinct acknowledgment in writing of the debt, a promise to pay it will be inferred. . . .

The precedents of the decided cases point to a rule, which we think is sound in principle, that the requirement of an acknowledgment of an indebtedness which will interrupt the running of the statute of limitations is met by a balance sheet of a corporate debtor where the obligations in question are listed as liabilities of the corporation.

No error is shown in the judgment of the district court for the appellee. That judgment is affirmed.

Domestic Loan, Inc. v. Peregoy

1962 (Ohio) 184 N.E.2d 457

Plaintiff obtained a judgment for $509.94 against defendant on a promissory note. Defendant then filed a petition in voluntary bankruptcy and was adjudged a bankrupt. Plaintiff and defendant then entered into a "Revivor Agreement" by the terms of which the defendant agreed to pay the plaintiff $250.00 at the rate of $15 per month. The defendant failed to make these payments and plaintiff seeks to enforce the original judgment as revised by the agreement. The trial court held for the defendant.

KOVACHY, J. . . . The appellant claims that under this agreement defendant appellee revived the judgment against him even though it was listed as a dischargeable debt in the bankruptcy proceeding and authorized it to execute on the same upon default of the terms contained in the "Revivor Agreement."

The defendant appellee contends that the "Revivor Agreement" constituted a new promise which superseded the judgment and gave the plaintiff a new remedy—a right of action for defaulted payments, and that it must sue anew on such cause of action.

The law with respect to a discharge of a debt or a judgment in bankruptcy is well-settled. The debt or judgment is not paid, satisfied, extinguished or cancelled. The bankrupt is merely afforded the privilege to interpose the discharge as a defense against the enforcement of the debt or judgment. And, since the matter is personal with the bankrupt, he has the choice of either interposing such defense to an action on the debt or judgment or of waiving the same, as he sees fit.

Remington on Bankruptcy, Vol. 8, page 133, "Revival of Discharged Debts" states the following in Section 3288:

> A discharge in bankruptcy although it is a "release" of liability on provable debts generally, is a defense against the liability rather than an annihilation of it and as a defense it can be waived. The obligation or liability still has vitality. . . . The moral obligation is still there and it can be adequate consideration for a new promise to pay.

The Supreme Court, in a case decided in 1851, held that a *new promise* to pay a debt discharged in bankruptcy was adequate consideration to sustain a cause of action on the *old debt* for the reason that the bar to a recovery of a debt discharged in bankruptcy is "strictly a personal privilege" and is waived by a subsequent promise.

The syllabus of *Turner v. Chrisman,* (Admr. of Moore, 20 Ohio 332, 333), reads:

A new promise is, in law, available to sustain a recovery upon an old contract, against a plea of bankruptcy.

The "bar" arising from the bankruptcy is strictly a personal privilege and is "waived" by the subsequent promise.

When the "bar" is "waived" by a new promise to pay an old debt, it is competent to declare on the old liability without suing on the new promise.

. . . The "Revivor Agreement" entered into recites in plain language that the defendant revives his liability to Domestic Loan, Inc. *in the partial sum of $250.00,* that such revivor covers the obligation of a note and chattel mortgage executed October 21, 1959, that it applies to all claims, warrants of attorney and/or judgments which Domestic Loan, Inc. may hold or have against the defendant by virtue of the above described note and chattel mortgage, and that Domestic Loan, Inc. *shall be authorized to proceed against him upon said judgments* in the event of his failure to comply with the terms contained in the agreement.

It seems to us, therefore, that the defendant in the use of such clear and unmistakable language revived his obligation to the plaintiff in the sum of $250.00 and at the same time authorized the plaintiff in case he (the defendant) defaulted on his new promise, to execute on the judgment standing against him in the Cleveland Municipal Court. The default was with respect to monthly payments beginning February 17, 1961.

We accordingly hold that the plaintiff had the right to institute proceedings in aid of execution on the existing judgment and to enforce such payments and that it is entitled to recover a total sum not exceeding $250.00 from the date of his adjudication in bankruptcy which occurred on January 5, 1961.

CHAPTER 16
REVIEW QUESTIONS AND PROBLEMS

1. *M* and *X* were co-makers of a note. After maturity, *M* made some payments, and a question arose as to whether the payments extended the period of *X*'s liability. Is the liability of *X* outlawed, or was it extended by the payments of *M*?

2. *L & B,* a partnership, sued *W* for services rendered and *W* urged accord and satisfaction as a defense. *W* claimed the bill to be excessive and mailed a check for a lesser amount marked "in full of account." *L & B* drew a line through the statement and cashed the check. Was this an accord and satisfaction?

3. *A* sold a printing machine to *B* on the installment plan. *B* sold the machine to *C,* who agreed to pay the balance of the purchase price. Both parties notified *A* of the arrangement. *C* failed to make the payments, and *A* now seeks to hold *B*. May he do so?

4. On April 1, *B* purchased a typewriter on credit at a price of $150 and on July 1 he purchased bookkeeping machines at a cost of $325, both items being purchased of *C*. On August 1 *B* mailed his check of $200 to *C* and instructed him to apply it on the $325 item. Assuming a five-year Statute of Limitations, how much will *C* be able to recover of *B* as of June 1 five years after the typewriter was purchased?

5. *D* owed Bank a $4,000 note, and long after it was due the bank credited a small bank balance of $1.41 owing to *D* on the note. Did this toll the Statute of Limitations?

6. *B*, a buyer, and *S*, a seller, had a dispute over a sales contract. A settlement agreement was signed which provided that the seller's promised performance will complete and cancel the remaining contract. Did the settlement agreement discharge the original contract?

7. *D* signed a statement that he owed *P* $750. There was a five-year Statute of Limitations on oral contracts and a ten-year Statute of Limitations on written contracts. *P* sued to collect 6 years from the date of the statement and *D* interposed the Statute of Limitations as a defense. What result?

8. *P* sent *D* a letter which stated that a statement of account was enclosed. *D* replied that the statement had not been enclosed but this was immaterial since *D* would not pay the amount claimed due to a dispute. *P* then sent the statement to which *D* replied by sending a partial payment marked paid in full. *P* cashed the check and sued for the balance. What result?

BOOK THREE

The Uniform
Commercial Code

chapter 17

Introduction
to the Uniform
Commercial Code

3-1. History of "Commercial Law." The rules and principles of commercial law are of ancient origin. Throughout the centuries merchants engaged in trade and commerce have recognized many customs and usages which regulate and control their conduct and their relationships with one another. Gradually over the years a body of law developed based upon the practices of merchants—the *lex mercatores,* or law merchant. The disputes between merchants were resolved by application of recognized principles derived from custom and usage in special courts established by the merchants themselves. The greater part of commercial activity in England was conducted at great fairs to which all merchants came, both foreign and local, to display their wares. At each of these fairs a court sat to adjust differences between buyers and sellers. The very nature of the situation demanded speedy and permanent termination of the disputes. These special mercantile courts were called "The Courts of Piepoudres" (pieds poudrés—"dusty feet"), so called because justice was administered as the dust still fell from the litigants' feet. These courts were later created by statute and continued as separate bodies until about 1756. Through royal prerogative the King's court, by this time jealous of the administration of justice by others, gradually won its way and absorbed the merchants' court. However, in deciding commercial cases, the King's court continued to apply the law merchant. When determining suits between merchants, or when a merchant was a party to the suit, before the court would recognize the law merchant, the party pleading such custom and usage was under duty to show himself to be a merchant. This rule prevailed until about one hundred years ago. The absorption of these merchants' courts by the King's courts wove the law merchant into and made it a part of the common law. The practice of permitting the proof of custom and usage of the merchants in the common law courts made possible the development of separate rules which became established rules of law. The union of these mercantile customs with the legal system already in operation resulted in the formation and further development of the law merchant by judicial action. Cases decided in the common law courts created precedents and for many years the law relating to the sale of goods and other areas of the law merchant was found largely in the reports of judicial decisions. In these judicial decisions previous usage and custom were interpreted and applied according to the prevailing and established usage of the particular community. This situation led to varying interpretations and the consequent lack of uniformity. In order to find the law, it was necessary to examine many decisions. The result of such search was often futile, owing to the conflicts and contradictions of important rules. Consequently, in England, in 1893, Parliament enacted what is known as the Sale of Goods Act. The Act completely codified the law as found in the decisions and harmonized the existing rules in as complete and comprehensive a manner as possible. Thus, in England the law relating to the sale of goods was governed by a body of rules and principles which were in a large measure extracted from the cases involving sales problems. In the United States a very similar effort at codification resulted in the promulgation in 1906 of the Uniform Sales Act, patterned very closely upon its English counterpart. The same situation in the field of negotiable instruments led to the earlier enactment in England of the Bills of Exchange Act in 1882.

In 1895, in the United States, under the leadership of the American Bar Association and the American Bankers Association, a commission was appointed for the purpose of revising and codifying the law merchant in the United States. This committee, taking the English Bills of Exchange Act as a model, derived with modifications, the Uniform Negotiable Instruments Law (NIL). This Act was completed in 1896, and was submitted to the legislatures of the various states with recommendation for adoption. The Act was adopted by every state, with some changes being made in states seeking to make the Act more suitable for their purposes.

Over the ensuing years other uniform laws were promulgated in other areas of commercial law and were adopted by varying numbers of states. These laws relate to warehouse receipts, bills of lading, transfers of corporate securities, and devices for utilizing personal property as security for the financing and sale of goods.

Notwithstanding these uniform laws, the rules of law pertaining to business transactions varied from state to state. Variances were created by judicial decisions in areas not covered by statute and by judicial decisions interpreting statutes differently from state to state. In addition, many of the states changed provisions of the Uniform Statutes so that they were not truly uniform.

As more and more business transactions were conducted on a nationwide basis with buyers and sellers from all parts of the country dealing with each other, the search for uniformity gained momentum. The wide variations were causing problems for businessmen and were creating a business climate which was uncertain and in which the legal effects of any given act were not entirely predictable.

One solution to the problem of uncertainty in the legal climate of business was to provide a modern code of laws relating to all aspects of the business or commercial transaction, in keeping with modern business practices and technology, which would be uniform throughout the country. As a result, the Commissioners on Uniform State Laws and the American Law Institute with the assistance of scholars, businessmen and bankers prepared the Uniform Commercial Code. At first, the Uniform Commercial Code, usually referred to simply as the Code, did not gain legislative acceptance. However, in the late 1950's a number of states gave legislative approval and by the middle sixties all but three of the states have adopted the Code. It appears likely that at least two of the remaining states will adopt it in the near future.

It must be noted that even under the Code complete uniformity is lacking in that (1) the legislatures of some of the states have altered certain sections of the Code in line with local economic and financial factors, (2) the Code provides certain alternative sections wherein the legislatures make a choice as to the alternative best suited to the state, (3) the Code purposely has left certain areas open to further development by the courts and has left room for continued expansion as new methods of doing business and new media of communication come into use, (4) some areas were deemed better suited to local regulation in keeping with social problems and other conditions which can best be handled at the individual state level, (5) it is possible that the courts in interpreting the various sections of the Code and applying them to factual situations may reach somewhat varying conclusions. This is especially true of some sections which appear to be ambiguous. It is anticipated that revisions will be made to eliminate this latter factor, which impinges upon uniformity.

Note, for example, the case of *Commonwealth Loan Co. v. Downtown Lincoln-Mercury Co.* which appears on page 642 in relation to Secured Transactions. In that case the court points out an ambiguity of the Code in respect to priorities between a finance company which held a security interest in an automobile and a garageman who had repaired the automobile.

The continually expanding use of electronic data processing equipment may require a reappraisal of some Code sections and amendments thereof in the near future. Certainly, problems have arisen and will arise which may be difficult to resolve under the existing Code provisions. This is especially true of the Articles on Commercial Paper, Bank Deposits and Collections, and Investment Securities.

It has been suggested that the check, which is the primary subject matter of Articles 3 and 4 of the Code may soon be passé, and that we will live in a "checkless society." It is estimated that approximately 250 computer centers located throughout the country could handle the process of settlement and deposit accounting. Through the use of a data communications network, the computers at such centers will electronically transfer funds from payor to payee's accounts.

At the present time all of the large banks and many small ones make extensive use of EDP (electronic data processing) in conjunction with MICR (magnetic ink character recognition) in handling the collection and handling of checks. Banks currently using EDP hold over 60 per cent of all commercial bank deposits. The absolute need for some better method of handling and expediting the transfer of funds from payor to payee accounts is illustrated by the following statistics:

1952—8 billion checks were written,
1960—13 billion checks were written,
1970 (estimate)—22 billion checks will be written.

The impact of this increase in checks written (called by bankers the "paper tiger") is magnified by the fact that an average check must pass through two and one third banks and be handled up to twenty times before being returned to the check writer.

In view of the legal problems resulting from the use of EDP and MICR, the National Automation Conferences have sought suitable amendments to Article 4—Bank Deposits and Collections—of the Uniform Commercial Code. This effort has not been successful as yet in obtaining changes in the Code. One example of the problems which are likely to arise is that of mistakes made in MICR encoding of the amount of a check. Business transactions always involve the risk of human error, but such errors are usually caught in visible systems. Such is not always the case when the errors are committed in the form of electronic impulses on magnetic tape.

The number of cases interpreting and applying the Code is not large. Many states have only recently adopted it and some have postponed its effective date. In the normal course there is a substantial lapse of time between the transaction which gives rise to the dispute and the final determination by an appellate court. It is to be noted, also, that many transactions which took place prior to adoption of the Code and which are now before the courts will be governed by pre-Code law. In this situation the courts in applying the old law will often refer to the Code and indicate what different result might have obtained under the Code— several of the cases in this Book are of this nature. Such judicial observations are instructive and shed additional light on the full implications of the Code. The uniform laws which have been repealed and replaced by the Code in states which adopted it will be mentioned briefly in ensuing sections. It should be noted that there are many "Uniform Laws," besides the Commercial Code, including some related to business, which are not affected by the Code and continue to be effective in *all* states that have adopted them. An example is the "Uniform Partnership Act."

3-2. Purposes of the Code. The purposes of the Code are to simplify, clarify, and modernize the law governing commercial transactions; to permit the continued expansion of commercial practices through custom, usage, and agreement of the parties; and to make uniform the law among the various jurisdictions.[C1]

To effectuate these purposes, the effect of provisions of the Code may be *varied by agreement* of the parties, with the exception that the obligations of good faith, diligence, reasonableness and care prescribed by the Code may not be successfully disclaimed. However, the parties may by agreement determine the *standards* by which the performance of such obligations is to be measured if such standards are not manifestly unreasonable.[C2] Thus, the parties to a transaction can, within limits, tailor their agreement to suit their needs. The Code provides the rules and principles which will apply if the parties have not otherwise agreed.

In order to accomplish the aforesaid purposes, the concept of the Code is, that a "commercial transaction" is a single subject of the law, notwithstanding its many legal relations.

> "Commercial transaction" is a single transaction which may very well involve a contract for sale, followed by a sale, the giving of a check or draft for a part of the purchase price, and the acceptance of some form of security for the balance. The check or draft may be negotiated and will ultimately pass through one or more banks for collection. If the goods are shipped or stored, the subject matter of the sale may be covered by a bill of lading or warehouse receipt or both. Or, it may be that the entire transaction was made pursuant to a letter of credit either domestic or foreign.
>
> Obviously, every phase of commerce involved is but a part of one transaction, namely, the sale of and payment for goods.

Thus the Code, to effectuate its purposes, purports to deal with all the phases which may ordinarily arise in the handling of a commercial transaction, from start to finish. The component parts of the Code are briefly discussed in the next section.

3-3. Scope of the Code. It is important to note that the Code is restricted to transactions involving various aspects of the sale, financing, and security in respect to *personal property*—tangible and intangible. It relates only tangentially to *real property*—land and interests in land—in a few isolated circumstances. It does not cover contracts other than those mentioned. The Code contains nine Articles, of which eight deal with specific aspects of the commercial transactions in detail and one contains General Provisions applicable to the whole body of Code law. The content of these Articles is discussed generally in material which follows in this chapter and in detail in the ensuing chapters.

    General provisions. Article 1—General Provisions—sets forth certain rules which are applicable in general to all of the other eight Articles, including rules of construction and interpretation, 46 separate definitions of generally applicable terms, and a *general* "Statute

---

[C1] *U.C.C.* 1-102.   [C2] *U.C.C.* 1-102.

of Frauds." This general section, which requires a writing for an enforceable contract for the sale of personal property involving sums of five thousand dollars or more, is *not* applicable to sales of goods or securities or to security agreements.[C3] Article 2–Sales, Article 8–Investment Securities, and Article 9–Secured Transactions, contain sections dealing with the requirement of a writing for these specific transactions. The provision in Article 1 is designed to "fill the gap" by providing the writing requirements for transactions involving the sale of royalty rights, for example, which would not fall within any of the other Articles. Obviously, it is of very limited application.

While the Code contains rules which provide for most situations likely to arise in a commercial transaction, Article 1 provides:

> the principles of law and equity, including the law merchant and the law relative to capacity to contract, principal, and agent, estoppel, fraud, misrepresentation, duress, coercion, mistake, and bankruptcy supplement its provisions.[C4]

Sales.   Article 2–Sales is restricted to transactions involving the sale of "goods," which are defined generally as "movable" physical property. This definition excludes intangible items of property such as contract claims and also excludes contracts for sale of investment securities—stocks and bonds.[C5] In many instances the sale of goods is the underlying transaction which brings into play the other Articles relating to protection of the seller by means of security for the sale, financing, and the like. Article 2 replaces the Uniform Sales Act.

Commercial paper.   Article 3–Commercial Paper is limited to instruments which satisfy the formal requirements of negotiability as set forth in the Article; drafts, checks, certificates of deposit and notes. These instruments are generally short-term credit paper designed to be utilized as a part of a transaction such as a sale of goods and not intended for purposes of investment. Article 3 does *not* apply to money, documents of title or investment securities.[C6] In its application to drafts, checks, certificates of deposit and notes it replaces the Uniform Negotiable Instruments Law.

Bank deposits and collections.   Article 4–Bank Deposits and Collections is related to Article 3 and sets forth the rules for the negotiable instruments specified in Article 3 as they pass through banking channels in the collection process. Article 4 prescribes the relationship between a bank and its customer in such matters as overdrafts, stop-payment orders, duties with respect to forgeries, and the like. Article 4 is not limited to transactions involving checks or other "commercial paper" but also covers collections of bonds and like instruments handled by banks. Article 4 is in general a codification of the well-recognized and defined patterns of banking operations.

[C3] *U.C.C.* 1-206.
[C4] *U.C.C.* 1-103.

[C5] *U.C.C.* 2-102.
[C6] *U.C.C.* 3-103.

Letters of credit. Article 5–Letters of Credit covers a device which has long been used in international trade to facilitate sales of goods between remote buyers and sellers. It is expected that it will now be used more extensively in domestic transactions. Basically, a letter of credit is an engagement whereby one party, usually a bank, agrees in advance to honor a draft (order to pay) drawn upon it by another party (a seller of goods) upon compliance with certain conditions—most commonly the presentation to the bank of documents, such as bills of lading, and other documents which represent and relate to goods sold. The letter of credit furnishes a financing device which substitutes the financial responsibility of a bank vis-à-vis the seller of goods for that of a buyer of goods. The main commercial function of the letter of credit is to facilitate sales of goods and to afford proper protection to all parties concerned. The buyer is protected because the bank with which he has made the arrangements for the letter of credit will not honor drafts drawn against it by the seller except upon the latter's presentation of documents which assure that the goods are available to the buyer. The seller is protected because the bank has obligated itself to honor drafts drawn by him for payment for the goods. It is important to note that banks dealing with letters of credit are primarily concerned with *documents* and not with enforcing the underlying sales contact. Thus, if the documents are in order the bank will pay the seller without regard to the condition of the goods which have been bought and sold.

A letter of credit is typically used when a person wishes to purchase goods from a seller with whom he has not previously established his credit. Such person will make arrangements with a bank whereby the latter agrees to honor drafts drawn upon it by a prospective seller of goods. The letter of credit constitutes the bank's promise and the bank will require the potential buyer to post collateral sufficient to protect the bank. The buyer will now contract with the seller for the purchase of goods and the seller on the strength of the letter of credit will ship the goods. He will send the bill of lading and other documents to the bank along with a draft for payment of the goods. The bank will examine these documents and if they are in good order will pay or accept the draft and surrender the documents to the buyer so that he can obtain the goods from the carrier. The buyer will then in most cases sell the goods and pay the bank. If the bank has merely *accepted* the draft which is payable at a later date the buyer will reimburse the bank prior to its having paid any money. In such case the bank is truly "lending its credit" to the buyer.

The terminology of Article 5 can be simply described: the buyer (customer of the bank) makes an arrangement with his bank (issuer) whereby the bank agrees to honor drafts drawn upon the bank by the seller (beneficiary) in payment for goods sold to the buyer, when the seller presents proof that he has in fact complied with the terms of his agreement with the buyer.[C7]

[C7] *U.C.C.* 5-103.

Article 5 deals with the duty of the bank to honor drafts drawn under the terms of the letter of credit and all of the aspects of the letter of credit transactions; the formal requirements of a letter of credit; the relations between issuer and customer, issuer and beneficiary, and customer and beneficiary; and the rights and duties of other parties who participate as intermediaries, including banks other than the issuing bank. In general, the beneficiary or a non-issuing bank which relies upon the letter of credit will be protected. The Article is new in the field of codification—letters of credit were not previously covered by uniform legislation. It is predicated to a large extent on the "Uniform Customs and Practice for Commercial Documentary Credits," of the International Chamber of Commerce and applies many of these customs and practices to domestic transactions.

Bulk transfers. Article 6–Bulk Transfers relates to sales or transfers "in bulk and not in the ordinary course of the transferor's business, of a major part of the materials, supplies, merchandise or other inventory of an enterprise subject to this Article." [C8] Typically, a sale of an entire retail store would be a "bulk transfer." The Article, which replaces a variety of divergent state statutes, provides protection for unsecured creditors of the seller against the possibility that he might "sell out" and not make provision to pay his creditors.

Documents of title. Article 7 deals with commodity paper—paper which may be negotiable and which represents goods or commodities in storage or transportation. Such paper is to be distinguished from "commercial paper" which represents an obligation to pay *money*— a document of title enables the holder to obtain *goods*. Both have the characteristic of *negotiability* and holders of either have a degree of protection not available to holders of non-negotiable instruments.[C9] This Article replaces the Uniform Warehouse Receipts Act and the Uniform Bills of Lading Act.

Investment securities. Article 8 also relates to instruments which have negotiable characteristics, and deals with the transfer of securities and the protection afforded to the transferee. Such instruments as stock certificates and corporate bonds are within the purview of this Article which is a sort of negotiable instruments law dealing with securities.[C10] The instruments are, however, usually long-term rather than short-term credit instruments, and are intended not as a medium of exchange but as a medium of investment. The Article replaces the Uniform Stock Transfer Act.

Secured transactions. Article 9 applies to any transaction which is intended to create *a security interest* [C11] in personal property— goods, documents, instruments, accounts receivable, and other items.[C12] A retailer may sell an article and retain an interest in the article as security for the payment of the purchase price; he may borrow money against his

---

C8 *U.C.C.* 6-102.
C9 *U.C.C.* 7-104.
C10 *U.C.C.* 8-102.

C11 *U.C.C.* 1-201.
C12 *U.C.C.* 9-102.

inventory; he may borrow against the security of his accounts receivable, or against notes payable to him. There are a great variety of security arrangements. The above are but a few examples. The Article also covers the outright *sale* of accounts receivable and certain other intangibles. It replaces the Uniform Trust Receipts Act and the Uniform Conditional Sales Act and a great variety of other security devices, including the chattel (personal property) mortgage.

3-4. Overlapping of Articles. While each Article is restricted to a specialized area, it is recognized that in certain situations more than one Article could be applicable. The Code makes provision for such overlapping as follows: (1) an instrument may qualify as "negotiable" under Article 3 and also as "negotiable" under Article 8. If it is intended as a "security" [13] it will be controlled by Article 8, although it satisfies the formal requirements of Article 3.[14] (2) If an instrument such as a check is in the process of collection, the provisions of Article 4 would control,[15] (3) If commercial paper is pledged as security for a debt, the provisions of Article 9 would control over Article 3.[16] (4) To the extent that items in the banking process (Article 4) are also within the scope of Article 3 or Article 8, they are *subject to the provisions* of those Articles, but in the event of conflict Article 8 has priority over Article 4.[17] Thus, the more specialized functional article will take precedence to the extent that there are conflicting provisions between the two. This will become more clear as the various Articles are studied in detail.

CHAPTER 17
REVIEW QUESTIONS AND PROBLEMS

1. The comment to the U.C.C. in describing the preparation of the Code states that frequent consultations were had with "practicing lawyers, hard-headed businessmen and operating bankers who contributed generously of their time and knowledge. . . ." What insight does this give as to the nature of the Code?
2. In view of the years of intensive study which went into the preparation of the Code, is it to be anticipated that it will be revised in the near future?
3. At a recent professional meeting, a paper was presented on the topic: "The Non-uniform Commercial Code." How do you account for the lack of uniformity?
4. Does the Code relate to all contracts and activities involving business-legal relationships?

[13] *U.C.C.* 8-102.
[14] *U.C.C.* 8-102(1)(b), 3-103(1).
[15] *U.C.C.* 3-103(2), 4-102(1).
[16] *U.C.C.* 3-103(2).
[17] *U.C.C.* 4-102(2).

5. *A* and *B* are negotiating a contract for the sale and purchase of goods. To what extent does the Code impose limitations on the terms and conditions which can be included in their contract?

6. Does the Code preempt the entire law of commercial transactions to the exclusion of all other legal rules and principles?

7. *A* and *B* have entered into a contract for the sale of "goods." Article 2 of the Code deals with such a contract. What other articles of the Code might have a bearing on this transaction?

8. What is the function of a bank in a transaction involving a letter of credit? What must a seller of goods furnish to the bank in order to obtain the benefit of the letter of credit?

9. *A* is arranging to sell his hardware store to *B*. The sale is to include all the assets of the business. What problem might this sale present to creditors of *A*? What provisions of the Code would be particularly applicable to this transaction?

10. The Code contains articles which deal separately with several types of negotiable instruments. What is meant by "negotiable"? Why are separate Code articles provided rather than one article dealing with all such instruments?

11. A merchant, *A*, wishes to sell goods to *B* but desires to protect himself against the possibility of *B*'s default in payment and the exposure of the goods to claims of other creditors of *B*. How may he accomplish this result?

12. Merchant *A* is in need of "working capital," as he has engaged in many credit sales and has numerous outstanding accounts receivable. His present inventory is substantial, but he wishes to expand it. Advise *A* as to how he might arrange for the needed money and inventory.

13. *A* is the holder of a negotiable promissory note. He wishes to borrow money from *B* and pledge the note as security. Can this be accomplished? What articles of the Code would govern this transaction?

14. *A* forged *B*'s name to a check drawn on *X* Bank. The check was made payable to the order of *C*. *C* indorsed the check to *D*. *D* presented the check to *X* Bank and received payment. What articles of the Code would come into play in determining which party must bear the loss resulting from the forgery?

15. *A* sold a car to *B* on an installment contract and retained a security interest in the car. *B* later took the car to *X* for repairs. *B* was unable either to pay for the repairs or to continue his installment payment to *A*. How would the rights of *A* and *X* in the car be determined?

chapter 18

Sales:
The Contract

3-5. The Sales Article. The Sales Article applies to transactions in "goods" and particularly to the "contract for sale" of goods. It does not apply to sales of other types of property or to transactions in goods which may appear to be a sale but which are intended only as a security transaction. This latter subject is covered by a separate article and is discussed in Chapters 27 and 28. The coverage of the Sales Article is thus limited but its provisions cover all of the aspects of the sales transaction.[C1]

    General principles: definitions. The Article is premised upon certain fundamental concepts which relate to many phases of the contract for sale and condition many of the rights, duties, and obligations of the parties. Throughout are many references to transactions in which one or both of the parties are "merchants." [C2] This designation is of great importance and is recognition of a professional status for businessmen, justifying the application of different standards to their conduct than to "nonprofessionals." In a sense it is a modern application of the special treatment afforded merchants in the early development of the law merchant. The Code defines a merchant as a "person who deals in goods of the kind or otherwise holds himself out as having knowledge or skill peculiar to the practices or goods involved in the transactions. . . ." [1] Closely related is the concept of "good faith," which applies to all parties and in the case of a merchant means honesty in fact and the observance of reasonable commercial standards of fair dealing in the trade.[C3] An-

---

[1] *Cook Grains, Inc. v. Fallis,* page 347.

[C1] *U.C.C.* 2-102.
[C2] *U.C.C.* 2-104(1).

[C3] *U.C.C.* 2-103(1)(b), 1-201(19).

other basic concept is the underlying policy of the Article to give recognition to the existence of a contract whenever the parties have indicated their intention to be bound, even though all of the terms and particulars have not been expressed.

The technicalities of traditional contract law relating to offer and acceptance, consideration, seals, and other principles, have been deemed inappropriate in many respects in the sales picture. Substantial modifications of traditional contract law have been made as discussed in the Book on Contracts. Rather than considering Sales as simply a branch of contract law, the Code treats the contract for sale as a unique tool for which a specially designed set of rules is necessary in order to meet the needs and expectations of merchants and others engaged in buying and selling goods. Thus, many agreements which would fail to meet the rigid requirements of ordinary contract law will be upheld and enforced under the Code. For example, a contract for sale of goods may be made in any manner sufficient to show agreement;[C4] an acceptance of a unilateral offer to purchase goods may be either a promise to ship or a shipment; [C5] no consideration is required to make a "firm offer" by a merchant irrevocable; [C6] and an acceptance may be effective even though it is at variance with the terms of the offer.[C7] For other significant changes in the law of contracts for the sale of goods, see Book Two.

Definitions of terms are an important part of the Article and are therefore to be stressed in setting the stage for the cases and materials that follow. Basically, "goods" means all things which are movable—i.e., items of personal property or chattels which are of a tangible, physical nature.[C8] The definition excludes investment securities, such as stocks and bonds, and things in action, such as negotiable instruments. The limitation of coverage to "goods" necessarily excludes sales of real property. However, the sale of timber, minerals, or a building which is to be removed from the land is a sale of goods within Article 2 *if these things are to be severed* by the seller.[C9] Growing crops are also included within the definition of goods whether they are to be removed by the buyer *or* the seller.[C10] This is in recognition of the fact that such crops are frequently sold prior to harvesting.

A "sale" involves the passing of title to the goods from the seller to the buyer for a price, and the full interest in goods cannot pass from seller to buyer unless and until the goods are in existence and have been "identified" as the specific goods which will be utilized in the transaction.[C11] Goods which are not in existence, or which have not been so identified, are "future goods." [C12] They may be the subject of a "contract to sell" goods at a future time; but obviously not of a "present sale" which is a sale accomplished by the making of a contract.[C13] The Code uses the designation "contract for sale" to encompass both a present sale and a

---

[C4] *U.C.C.* 2-204.
[C5] *U.C.C.* 2-206
[C6] *U.C.C.* 2-205.
[C7] *U.C.C.* 2-207.
[C8] *U.C.C.* 2-105(1).

[C9] *U.C.C.* 2-107(1).
[C10] *U.C.C.* 2-107(2).
[C11] *U.C.C.* 2-106(1).
[C12] *U.C.C.* 2-105(2).
[C13] *U.C.C.* 2-106(1).

contract to sell goods at a future time. In general, the rights of the buyer and seller do not vary according to whether the transaction is a present sale or a contract to sell, but there are some specific provisions in which the distinction *is* significant. The "seller" is a person who either sells or contracts to sell goods and a "buyer" is a person who either buys or contracts to buy goods.[C14] Other significant definitions will be discussed in later sections.

       Contract principles. Recognition in the Code that traditional principles of contract law are not sacred has led to a thorough reappraisal of simple contract rules from the standpoint of their utility and effectiveness in the commercial arena of sales. As a result, many contract rules which were previously applied to all contracts have been modified by the Code in order to achieve a commercially desirable result. It must always be borne in mind that these changes and modifications are restricted to contracts involving sales of goods and that traditional principles are still applied in other contractual situations. Rules and principles of contract law which may achieve a desirable result in a transaction for the sale or construction of a building or in a contract between an employer and an employee would not necessarily produce a good result in a contract for the purchase and sale of goods. Hence, Article 2–Sales of the Uniform Commercial Code has "tailored" the law of contracts to fit the pattern of the sales transaction.

Also, the drafters of the Code recognized shortcomings of the prior law of sales as set forth in the Uniform Sales Act (repealed in Code states) and cases decided under the old act and the common law. This is especially true of the "title concept" of the Sales Act under which a substantial number of sales problems were resolved on the basis of the location of the "title" to the goods at a particular time. Thus, under the old law the risk of loss followed title so that if goods were destroyed prior to delivery the loss would fall upon the party who had the title at the time of damage or destruction of the goods. Likewise, the remedies available to buyers and sellers for breaches of the sales contract were dependent upon the title factor and in general title was stressed as a very important element in the law of sales.

The Code takes a quite different approach and de-emphasizes the "passage of title." The old law emphasized the supposed intention of the parties with regard to when title was to pass. The Code, on the other hand, stresses the contractual aspects of a sales agreement—what each party is obligated by contract to do—and sets forth rules which specify these obligations.[C15]

It is very seldom that parties to a sales contract indicate any intention with regard to the matter of title or its passage, or, for that matter, that they consciously consider the title concept as such. Accordingly, the Code sets forth specific provisions with regard to the rights and duties of the buyer and seller such as risk of loss, remedies, and the like and does not tie these in to the factors of ownership. Therefore, under the Code

---

C14 *U.C.C.* 2-103(1).   C15 *U.C.C.* 2-401.

one does not initially make a search for title in answer to question on these points, but rather looks for specific Code provisions relating to the particular problem. Only if the Code does not provide an answer to the problem does the title become important. Since the Code is comprehensive in the area of Sales, it is to be expected that most problems will be resolved without recourse to the title concept. It must be noted, however, that title has significance under the Code to govern questions which are not resolved by any section of the Code and in those instances where a Code provision refers to title.

The following sections relate to the formation of a sales contract, its interpretation and other aspects.

3-6. Formation of the Contract. As in any contract, a contract for sale involves an offer and an acceptance. The basic premise of the Code is that the existence of a contract should be recognized whenever it is clear that the parties have intended to make a contract and there is a reasonably certain basis for giving an appropriate remedy for a breach of the contract.[C16] This concept underlies and undergirds the sales article in the area of the contract for sale and the related rights, duties, and obligations of parties to sales transactions. The Code has to a large extent eliminated technical "tricks" or maneuvers which enabled a party to a sales transaction to avoid contractual liability—it places offeror and offeree on reasonably equal terms and closes many of the "loop-holes" which permitted a party to rely, for example, upon the element of "indefiniteness" to avoid responsibility. The parties may leave various terms of their agreement "open" yet the Code will recognize that the agreement is valid despite the missing terms "if the parties have intended to make a contract and there is a reasonably certain basis for giving an appropriate remedy." [C17]

The offeror, whether he is buyer or seller, can control his offer but unless he clearly indicates to the contrary his offer shall be construed as inviting an acceptance in any reasonable manner and by any reasonable medium of communication. Thus, an offer sent by mail could be accepted by telegram, teletype, etc. as well as by mail. In the case of a unilateral offer, e.g., an order "ship 1000 X-50 tubes at once," the offeree can accept the offer by either a prompt promise to ship or by a prompt shipment of proper goods. [C18]

The Statute of Frauds section of the Code provides that a contract for the sale of goods for the price of $500 or more is not enforceable unless it is evidenced by "some writing" sufficient to indicate that a contract for sale has been made between the parties. [C19] The writing must be signed "by the party against whom enforcement is sought or by his authorized agent or broker." It is *not* required that both parties sign. The problem of a writing or a sufficient writing arises when one of the parties—buyer

---

[C16] *U.C.C.* 2-204.
[C17] *U.C.C.* 2-204(3).

[C18] *U.C.C.* 2-206(1)(b).
[C19] *U.C.C.* 2-201.

or seller—to an alleged contract refuses to perform. If the party who refuses to perform has not signed a writing, the contract is not enforceable; if he has signed a proper writing, the contract is enforceable whether the party seeking to enforce it has signed or not.

The provisions relating to the sufficiency of the written memorandum are very broad and are in keeping with the spirit of the Code which is to avoid technical obstructions to enforcement of agreements made between sellers and buyers. The writing need not be a formal instrument; it does not have to state all of the terms agreed upon by the parties; the incorrect statement of a term agreed upon will not vitiate the writing. Bear in mind that the purpose of the requirement is primarily to establish that a contract does exist—the terms and conditions are subject to being proved and established, but this is not a Statute of Frauds problem. All that is required is that the written statement afford a basis for believing that the oral evidence which is offered to establish the terms rests on a real transaction. There is one significant proviso, however, with relation to the *quantity* term of the contract. The contract is not enforceable beyond the quantity of goods expressed in the writing.

A contract for the sale of goods is ordinarily the outcome of negotiations between a buyer and a seller. Obviously, questions may be raised as to whether the parties have actually reached an agreement or whether they are still in the negotiation stage. One or the other of the parties may contend that no definite agreement had been reached while the other will claim that such an agreement had been reached. The Statute of Frauds is concerned with this type of conflict. It is recognized that many sales contracts are entered into on the basis of oral agreements and the Code does not entirely preclude the enforcement of such agreements *between merchants.*

Either merchant can write to the other confirming the oral contract in a writing—e.g. a letter—sufficient to satisfy the requirements of the Statute as against the sender. Such confirmation will satisfy the requirement of a writing as against the merchant receiving the letter unless he gives written notice of objection to its contents within 10 days after it is received. Thus the recipient of the confirmation will be deprived of the Statute of Frauds defense unless he makes a timely objection.[C20] However, the person sending the letter still has the burden of proving that a contract was in fact made.

In keeping with the basic purpose of the writing requirement, the Code recognizes that the existence of a contract can be established by other means than a writing.[C21] There are several substitutes for a written memorandum. Thus, where a contract calls for goods which are to be specially manufactured for the buyer and are not suitable for sale to others in the ordinary course of the seller's business, a contract will be enforceable if: (1) the circumstances reasonably indicate that the goods are for the buyer and (2) the seller has either made a substantial begin-

[C20] *U.C.C.* 2-201(2).   [C21] *U.C.C.* 2-201(3).

ning of their manufacture or has made commitments to procure the goods. [C22]

Another indication that a contract exists is the receipt of goods by the buyer and his acceptance of the goods. This is regarded as a clear admission by both parties that a contract exists. Likewise if the seller has received payment for goods and has accepted the payment, he can be required to deliver such goods as are covered by the payment.[C23]

Since the requirement of a writing is simply to establish that buyer and seller have entered into a contract, the necessary evidence that there was in fact a contract can be adduced in the course of litigation. The defendant against whom enforcement is sought may admit in his pleadings—e.g., answer to the complaint—that there was a contract; or he may in the course of the trial make such an admission in his testimony. Such admissions would make the contract enforceable but only to the extent of the quantity of the goods admitted. [C24]

Reference has been made in the Book on Contracts to variance between the terms of the offer and the terms of the acceptance. The acceptance may contain terms additional to or different from those contained in the offer. A confirmation of an oral agreement may state terms additional to or different from those agreed upon. Nevertheless, the parties may be held to a contract. In many cases the variations result from the use of "forms" by both the offeror and the offeree. The buyer may use an order form which states that the order is subject to certain terms; the seller may "accept" by means of a form which provides that the order is accepted subject to certain conditions. While a conflict in terms would preclude the formation of a contract under ordinary contract law, such is not the case under the Code unless the acceptance expressly stipulates that it is not effective unless the offeror assents to the additional or different terms. Absent such a stipulation, the expression of acceptance is operative and the additional terms are simply construed as proposals for an addition to the contract.[C25] If the transaction is *between merchants,* the additional terms become part of the contract unless the offer expressly provides that acceptance is limited to the terms of the offer or the additional terms are so significant that they materially alter the contract. Also, the merchant offeror can preclude the incorporation of non-material additional terms by notifying the other party within a reasonable time of his objection to them.[C26] Both parties are given an opportunity to bring about a clear "meeting of the minds." However, the offeree, who has created a potential problem by virtue of his nonconforming "acceptance" is the party who must ultimately bear the burden. He is bound by all the terms of the offer and his additional terms may be rejected by the offeror. The offeree, if he considered the additional terms important to him, would be well advised to reject the original offer and make a clear-cut counteroffer.

When does an additional term "materially alter" a contract so that it

[C22] *U.C.C.* 2-201(3)(a).
[C23] *U.C.C.* 2-201(3)(c).
[C24] *U.C.C.* 2-201(3)(b).

[C25] *U.C.C.* 2-207.
[C26] *U.C.C.* 2-207(2).

would not become a part of it unless expressly assented to by the offeror? It is suggested that a clause negating standard and customary warranties would be material whereas one which simply excused timely performance by a seller in the event that a strike impeded transportation of the goods would not be. The test would be whether there would be an element of unreasonable surprise to offeror if the additional term were included in the contract so that the term ought to be excluded even though he had not made a timely objection to it.

Another acceptance problem relates to unilateral contracts. The offeree can accept a unilateral offer by beginning performance but this will be an effective acceptance only if he notifies the offeror of his acceptance within a reasonable time. This notice requirement is designed to prevent the offeree from beginning performance and then having a broad latitude in time as to whether he wishes to complete performance or not. The offeror, unless he receives timely notice of acceptance can treat the offer as having been rejected and thus be free to make other arrangements.[C27]

3-7. Obligation of the Parties. The contract for sale imposes obligations on both the buyer and the seller. The seller is obligated to transfer and deliver ("tender delivery") and the buyer is obligated to accept and pay in accordance with the contract.[C28] In general, the parties to a contract can agree upon any terms and conditions which are mutually acceptable. There are, of course, some limitations and these are set forth explicitly in the Code. An all-pervading limitation is found in the concept of *unconscionability*.[C29] If the court as a matter of law finds the contract, or any clause of the contract, to have been unconscionable at the time it was made, the court may refuse to enforce the contract, or it may enforce the remainder of the contract without the objectionable clause; or it may temper the effect of the unconscionable clause. The significance of this provision is that a court may strike unfair and overreaching clauses in a contract for sale if it feels that the clauses involved are so one-sided as to be improper when tested in the light of the general commercial background and the commercial needs of the particular trade or case.[2]

The factor of fairness is very significant in connection with the warranty obligation. This is one of the most important obligations of the sales contract—certainly a very substantial portion of the litigation relating to sales of goods involves warranties. In its broadest sense, a warranty involves a representation made by the seller to the buyer with respect to the goods which are the subject of their contract. Warranties of goods are classified as either express warranties or implied warranties.

3-8. Warranties. Express warranties are those which are negotiated by the parties in connection with their individual bargain and are tailored to fit the particular transaction. A clear distinction exists between express

---

2 *Williams v. Walker Thomas Furniture Co.,* page 380.

C27 *U.C.C.* 2-206(2).   C29 *U.C.C.* 2-302.
C28 *U.C.C.* 2-301, 2-503(1).

warranties on the one hand and what is referred to as "puffing" or "seller's talk." The latter relates to commendatory remarks made by the seller, statements which reflect simply the seller's opinion and statements concerning the value of the goods. A buyer is not justified in relying upon such statements, and they do not become a part of the bargain and are not warranties. On the other hand, factual statements made by the seller or promises made by him relative to the goods create an express warranty that the goods will conform to the statement or promise.[3] The [C30] Code speaks of such statements or promises as becoming a part of the "basis of the bargain between buyer and seller." If a *description* of the goods is made a part of the basis of the bargain, there is an express warranty that the goods shall conform to the description; if a *sample* or a model is made a part of the basis of the bargain, there is an express warranty that all of the goods shall conform to the sample or model. In net effect, a seller is responsible if the goods do not conform to the standards that the parties have agreed upon as a part of their bargain.

It is not necessary to the creation of an express warranty that the seller use formal words such as "warrant" or "guarantee" or even that he have a specific intention to make a warranty.[C31] The seller's conduct and words which are made a part of the basis of the bargain produce the result regardless of his specific intention; the objective manifestations control. However, as noted above, a seller does have considerable latitude in that an affirmation merely of the value of the goods or a statement which merely commends the goods or expresses the seller's opinion of the goods does not create a warranty.

The person claiming breach of warranty has the burden of proof that the warranty was in fact breached.[4]

Implied Warranties. Whereas express warranties come into existence by virtue of stipulations which the parties include in their bargaining, implied warranties come into being without any bargaining and as an integral part of the normal sales transaction. Express warranties are said to rest on "dickered" aspects of the bargain between seller and buyer; implied warranties are automatically included unless clearly negatived. The implied warranties are warranties of title, fitness for a particular purpose and merchantability.

The seller warrants that he is conveying a good title to the buyer.[C32] This means that there are no liens or encumbrances against the goods other than those actually known to the buyer. This warranty can be excluded only by specific language or circumstances surrounding the sale which make it clear that the seller is not vouching for the title. Judicial sales and sales by executors of estates would not necessarily imply that the seller guaranteed the title. A seller who is a merchant regularly dealing in goods of the kind that are the subject of the sale makes an addi-

---

[3] *Q. Vandenberg & Sons v. N. V. Siter,* page 348.
[4] *Strauss v. West,* page 350.

[C30] *U.C.C.* 2-313.   [C32] *U.C.C.* 2-312.
[C31] *U.C.C.* 2-313(2).

tional warranty. He warrants that no third person has a rightful claim; that no third party rights have been infringed, e.g. that the goods sold violate a trade-mark or patent held by a third party. The seller does not make this warranty if he manufactures goods in accordance with specifications furnished by the buyer. In the latter case, the buyer must protect the seller against claims that the goods manufactured infringe upon the rights of others.[C33]

An implied warranty for fitness for a particular purpose is created if the seller is aware of the purpose which the buyer has in mind with respect to the use to be made of the goods, and knows that the buyer is relying on him to select goods suitable for that purpose.[C34] The buyer need not specifically tell the seller his purpose if the seller is otherwise aware of the facts.[5] The obligation of the seller is to supply goods reasonably fit for the particular purpose which the buyer has specified to him. Some question had arisen as to whether a buyer who specifies a product by a patent or trade name can be said to rely on the seller's skill and judgment in providing goods fit for the buyer's particular purpose. The warranty may still exist but the fact that a trade name was specified is a fact to be taken into account, along with others, to determine whether or not he actually *relied* on the seller's skill and judgment to supply him with suitable goods.

An implied warranty of merchantability arises in a contract for the sale of goods if the seller is a merchant in goods of the kind called for under the contract.[C35] Merchantability as defined by the Code includes a requirement that the goods sold are at least of such quality that they are fit for the ordinary purposes for which such goods are used.[6] If fungible goods (those sold by weight or measure) are involved, they must be of fair average quality as designated by their description in the contract. Should the sale involve packaged goods, the goods must be properly packaged and labeled and must conform to any statements which are made on the label or container concerning their quality. Thus, the warranty may be said to extend to both container and contents. Other warranties may arise from a course of dealing or usage of trade. If foods or drinks are served for consumption, either on the premises or elsewhere, the transaction is a sale and is covered by this warranty.[7]

The above warranties, both express and implied extend to and benefit the members of the buyer's family, and guests in his home, if any such person could be reasonably expected to use the product purchased and is injured in person by the breach of the warranty.[C36]

Implied warranties can be excluded or modified but rigid rules apply to such disclaimers.[8] The implied warranty of merchantability can be excluded only by language expressly mentioning "merchantability" and

[5] *Southwest Distributors Inc. v. Allied Paper Bag Corp.*, page 352.
[6] *Corneliuson v. Arthur Drug Stores, Inc.*, page 354.
[7] *Ray v. Deas*, page 356.
[8] *Delta Air Lines, Inc. v. Douglas Aircraft Co.*, page 356.

[C33] *U.C.C.* 2-312(3).   [C35] *U.C.C.* 2-314.
[C34] *U.C.C.* 2-315.   [C36] *U.C.C.* 2-318.

if the disclaimer is in writing it must be conspicuous. The exclusion of the warranty of fitness must be in writing and conspicuous but the latter warranty can be excluded by such language as "There are no warranties which extend beyond the description on the face thereof." [C37]

There are additional circumstances under which warranties are totally or partially excluded. The seller may sell the goods "as is" or "with all faults." These and similar expressions would make it clear that there is no implied warranty. Where a buyer has had full opportunity to examine the goods before entering into the contract, there is no implied warranty as to defects which this examination ought to have revealed to him. Likewise, if he has refused to examine he cannot claim breach of warranty as to defects that an examination would have revealed. A course of dealing between the parties or usages of the trade can also be the basis for exclusion or modification of implied warranties.[C38]

Another warranty problem relates to the situation in which warranties whether express or implied appear to be inconsistent with one another. The rule of construction is that such overlapping warranties be construed as consistent with each other and cumulative unless such interpretation would be unreasonable. If unreasonable, the intention of the parties will determine which warranty is dominant. The Code specifies rules to be applied in ascertaining that intention.[C39]

3-9. Product Liability. A topic closely related to warranty is that of product liability. When a product is sold and placed in the stream of commerce it may, if defective, cause injury to a person or to his property. The person injured may have had no contractual dealings with either the retailer who sold the product or the manufacturer who produced it. In most cases, the injured party will have dealt only with the retailer. Thus, the problem is raised as to what relief will be afforded to the person and against whom he may seek damages.

There is no problem as the right of the injured person or, as noted above, members of his family, to recover damages from the *retailer* who sold the product, assuming that the sale carried implied warranties of fitness and/or merchantability which were clearly breached. The problem which is difficult to resolve is whether an action can also be maintained against the *manufacturer* or *producer,* and related is the question of whether a *third party* who had no dealings with either the manufacturer or retailer, but who was injured because of the defective product, can sue either or both of them. Is "privity of contract"—a contractual relationship—a requisite to maintaining an action?

The liability for a defective product has been imposed on manufacturers or producers on the basis of several theories, not all contractual, applied by the courts. Some courts have held a manufacturer or producer liable on the tort theory of negligence—failure to use reasonable care in the manufacture of the product. The burden is upon the injured party

[C37] *U.C.C.* 2-316.
[C38] *U.C.C.* 2-316(3).

[C39] *U.C.C.* 2-317.

to establish such lack of due care, and frequently he also has the burden of establishing his freedom from any negligence that contributed to the injury. Other courts have imposed liability on the basis of the implied warranty of fitness and merchantability—extending the warranties of the manufacturer to a third party with whom the manufacturer had not had any contractual relationships. Negligence is not an element and the plaintiff must simply establish that the product was defective and that the defect was the proximate cause of his injury. A third theory and the one of most recent development is that of "strict liability." The manufacturer or producer is liable without any requirement of warranty or negligence. Some states have imposed strict liability by statute and in others it has been imposed by judicial decision.[9]

The major question in product liability, therefore, is whether or not a contractual relationship—privity of contract—is required in order to maintain a suit. Negligence theories do not require privity of contract since the action is in tort rather than contract. However, suits for breach of warranty have traditionally required privity of contract. Thus, when a consumer purchased an article from a retailer, and a hidden defect in that article then appeared, the consumer had no right of recovery against the manufacturer, packer, or grower because of no privity of contract. The only recourse of the consumer was to look to the retailer upon express or implied warranties. The retailer in turn could look to the manufacturer.

The law gradually developed exceptions to the privity rule. First of all, if the article or product sold is one that, if defective, would prove dangerous to human life while being used in the normal way, courts tend to permit the ultimate consumer to recover from the manufacturer, packer, or grower, as well as from the retailer. This exception is most usually applied in cases where the product sold consists of food, beverages, or drug preparations, although some decided cases involve other products. Some courts took the position that warranties, express or implied, extend to the consumer irrespective of privity of contract,[10] on the fiction that the warranty runs with goods. Other theories have been resorted to at times to reach the same result.[11]

The law in connection with products liability shows a definite trend in the direction of imposing "strict liability" upon manufacturers and rendering them liable to consumers by direct action. This has been accomplished by enlarging tort liability, by eliminating to a large extent the strict privity requirement for breach of implied warranties, and by statute.

It is to be noted that the Code does not make provision for a direct action against manufacturers. The Code remains neutral, preferring to allow the trend, already evident in court decisions, to continue to develop.[12] The only Code provision relating to the privity requirement is

---

[9] *Wright v. Massey-Harris Inc.*, page 359.
[10] *Suvada v. White Motor Co.*, page 361.
[11] *Chairaluce v. Stanley Warner Management Corp.*, page 363.
[12] *Lonzrick v. Republic Steel Corp.*, page 366.

the one noted above—extending warranties to members of the purchaser's family and his guests. This means, only, however, that if the purchaser was entitled to warranties, his guests and family members would also have the benefit of such warranties.

While the requirement of privity is becoming less and less significant, there are still many situations in which it is required and some jurisdictions in which it must be established in order to state a cause of action against a defendant.[13] It is therefore necessary to look to the law of the individual states in order to determine the status of the law in that particular jurisdiction.

There are many facets to the growing body of cases relating to products liability and many unique fact situations have been presented to the courts. It has been held that implied warranties do not exist in favor of one who receives a blood transfusion; that services rather than goods are here involved. One who leased defective equipment to another has been held liable to employees of the latter who were injured because of defects in the equipment leased to the employer.[14] It has been held that a particular consumer's susceptibility to harm may relieve the manufacturer of liability.[15] Other fact patterns will be presented to the courts in the future as this growing area of the law continues to develop. One significant question is the degree of proof which must be presented by a plaintiff in order to establish that the manufacturer was actually responsible for the condition of the product that caused the injury.[16] Since both the retailer and manufacturer make implied warranties, questions have arisen as to whether a retailer is liable to a consumer for injuries resulting from a defective *container*.[17] As might be expected, the courts do not express a unanimity of opinion on these and other questions.

3-9. Construction of Sales Contracts. When is a contract for sale subject to contradiction, explanation, or supplementation in the event of a dispute between the parties as to its terms? If it appears that the writing was intended to be the final expression of the agreement between the parties—that no further negotiations were contemplated—its terms may not be contradicted by oral evidence.[C40] However, the writing may be *explained* or *supplemented* by showing that in past dealings between the parties certain "ground rules" had been established, or that a usage of the trade was to be considered as part of the agreement, although not expressed.[18] In substance, the rules are designed to ascertain the true understanding of the parties as to the agreement and to place the agreement in its proper perspective. The assumption is that prior dealings between the parties and the usages of the trade were taken for granted when the

[13] *Kuschy v. Norris*, page 369.
[14] *Greeno v. Clark Equipment Co.*, page 371.
[15] *Corneliuson v. Arthur Drug Stores, supra*, page 354.
[16] *Sundet v. Olin Matheson Chemical Corp.*, page 374.
[17] *Foley v. Weaver Drugs, Inc.*, page 374.
[18] *Associated Hardware Supply Co. v. Big Wheel Distributors*, page 377.

[C40] *U.C.C.* 2-202.

contract was worded.[C41] Often a contract for sale involves repetitive performance by both parties over a period of time. The course of performance is indicative of the meaning which the parties by practical construction have given to their agreement and is relevant to its interpretation.

One underlying purpose of the Code is to recognize the existence of a contract for sale in a realistic and practical manner. The conduct of the parties may be sufficient to establish the existence of an agreement without the necessity of a formal arrangement. The parties may leave many terms of their contract "open," yet the agreement may be valid in law. The test is whether the parties intended to make a contract, despite the missing terms, and whether a court could have a proper basis for granting a remedy in event of a breach.[C42] An agreement may thus be a mere skeleton with the flesh to be added later on by the parties.

3-10. The Terms of the Contract—in General. The parties to a contract for sale are privileged to specify in detail the terms of their agreement relating to the price to be paid, the quantity of goods involved, the details of delivery of the goods, the time for performance, the time for payment, any provisions for inspection of the goods by the buyer, and provisions for the protection for the seller. Often, however, the parties do not specify all of these terms and the Code accordingly sets forth rules which are applicable to interpret the contract *in the absence of specific provision in the contract.*[C43]

The price term. The price term of the contract can be left open with the price to be fixed by later agreement of the parties, or some agreed market or other standard may be designated.[C44] It may even be agreed that the buyer or the seller shall fix the price in which event he is obligated to exercise good faith in doing so. If the contract says nothing as to price, or if for some reason the price is not set in accordance with the method agreed upon, the price will be determined as a reasonable price at the time for delivery. It is important to note that parties can bind themselves even though the price is not settled if it appears that it is their intention to do so. Obviously, the absence of any definite price term might indicate that no deal has really been concluded, but such is not necessarily the case. The parties always have the privilege of stipulating expressly either (1) that they intend to be bound even though the price is not settled or (2) that they do not intend to be bound until the price is fixed.

The quantity term. The Code allows flexibility in the quantity term of the contract. There may be an agreement to purchase the entire output of the seller, or the quantity may be specified as all that is required by the buyer.[C45] There are limitations imposed by the Code in order to insure fair dealing between the parties where the quantity is specified in this fashion. The parties may in their agreement express an estimate as to the quantity involved, and no quantity which is unreason-

C41 *U.C.C.* 2-208.
C42 *U.C.C.* 2-204.
C43 *U.C.C.* 1-102(3)(4).
C44 *U.C.C.* 2-305.
C45 *U.C.C.* 2-306.

ably disproportionate to the estimate will be enforced. If the parties have
not agreed upon an estimate, the Code implies a quantity which is in
keeping with normal or other comparable prior output or requirements.

The delivery term.   As to delivery, the place for delivery is
the seller's place of business, or if he has none, his residence—unless the
goods are known to both parties to be at some other place, in which event
that place is the place for their delivery.[C46] The seller is required to
tender the goods in a single delivery rather than in installments over a
period of time, and the buyer's obligation to pay is not due until such a
tender is made.[C47] The Code recognizes that in some situations the seller
will not be able to deliver all of the goods at once or that the buyer may
not be able to receive the entire quantity at one time, in which event
more than a single delivery will be allowed. The time within which the
goods are to be delivered is a reasonable time if the parties have not otherwise specified.[C48] The parties may have entered into an agreement which
calls for delivery of goods at stated intervals without specifying the duration of the agreement. Such an agreement will be valid for a reasonable
time, subject, however, to being terminated at any time by either party
upon proper notice to the other party. In this connection it is possible
that the parties may have been carrying on under such an arrangement
for a matter of several years, in which event it is suggested that the contract would not terminate until notice was given.[C49] The buyer's obligation to pay for the goods arises at the time he is to receive the goods, and
this is true even though the place of shipment is the place of delivery.[C50]
The delivery terms of the contract for sale are particularly important
since they determine to a large extent which of the parties has the risk
of loss during shipment, as well as which of them is obligated to pay the
costs of shipping.

3-11. Special Terms.   The Code defines a number of terms commonly used
in connection with contracts for sale, and sets forth the particular attributes of each. It is thus very convenient for the parties to use these terms
without the necessity of specifying in great detail the provisions which
are governed by the terms. "F.O.B." a named place, such as "$500 F.O.B.
Eugene, Oregon" is a delivery term of the contract. If Eugene, Oregon, is
the place of shipment, the seller is required to put the goods in the possession of a carrier at that place at his expense and risk.[C51] If the term is
F.O.B. the place of destination, the obligation of the seller is to provide
transportation to that place at his own risk and expense.[C52] If the term
is also "F.O.B. vessel, car, or other vehicle," the seller must, in addition,
at his own expense and risk load the goods on board.[C53] Another delivery
term, "F.A.S. vessel" (Free alongside) at a named port requires the seller
at his own expense and risk to deliver the goods alongside the vessel in

C46 *U.C.C.* 2-308.
C47 *U.C.C.* 2-307.
C48 *U.C.C.* 2-309.
C49 *U.C.C.* 2-309(2)(3).

C50 *U.C.C.* 2-310.
C51 *U.C.C.* 2-319(1).
C52 *U.C.C.* 2-319(1)(b).
C53 *U.C.C.* 2-319(1)(c).

the manner usual in the port, or on a dock designated and provided by the buyer.[C54] "C.I.F." means that the price includes in a lump sum the cost of the goods and the insurance and freight to the named destination. The seller's obligation is to load the goods, make provision for payment of the freight, and also obtain an insurance policy in favor of the buyer.[C55] Risk of subsequent loss or damage to the goods passes to the buyer upon shipment if the seller has properly performed all his obligations with respect to the goods. Generally the C.I.F. term means that the parties will deal in terms of the documents which represent the goods and that the seller performs his obligation by tendering the proper documents, which would include a negotiable bill of lading and an invoice of the goods. The buyer is required to make payment against the tender of the required documents. The contract may provide that the price will not be definitely arrived at until the goods have arrived.[C56] Another term in common usage is "no arrival, no sale." Under this term the seller is relieved of liability for *non-delivery* if the goods are destroyed or lost as a result of the hazards of transportation. This term is used in connection with overseas contracts and leaves the risk of loss on the seller but exempts him from liability for damages resulting from non-delivery.[C57]

In many cases it is known to both the buyer and the seller that the seller in the transaction is reselling goods which he has bought from someone else and that the goods are to be shipped by the person from whom the seller is buying. Under these circumstances since the seller is not under obligation to make the shipment himself, he is entitled to a clause which exempts him from payment of damages for non-delivery if the goods do not arrive, or if the goods which actually do arrive are not in conformity with the contract. This may be accomplished by using the term "No arrival, no sale."

Sale on approval: sale or return. The arrangement made between the buyer and the seller may be such that the buyer has the privilege of returning the goods which have been delivered to him. If the goods are delivered primarily for use, as in the case of a consumer purchase, the transaction is designated a "sale on approval" whereas if the goods are delivered primarily for resale, it is called a "sale or return." [C58] The distinction is an important one because goods held on approval are not subject to the claims of the buyer's creditors until the buyer has indicated his acceptance of the goods, whereas goods held on "sale or return" are subject to the claims of the buyer's creditors while in the latter's possession. A delivery of goods on consignment, such as a transaction in which a manufacturer or a wholesaler delivers goods to a retailer who has the privilege of returning any unsold goods, is a "sale or return." The goods in the possession of the buyer are subject to the claims of the buyer's creditors unless the seller makes it known that he has an interest in the goods or complies with the filing provisions of

C54 *U.C.C.* 2-319(2).
C55 *U.C.C.* 2-320.
C56 *U.C.C.* 2-321.

C57 *U.C.C.* 2-324.
C58 *U.C.C.* 2-326.

Article 9 dealing with secured transactions.[C59] Another characteristic of
the sale on approval is that risk of loss does not pass to the buyer until
he accepts the goods.[C60] A failure to seasonably notify the seller of his
decision to return the goods will be treated as an acceptance. After notification of election to return, the seller must pay the expenses of the
return and bear the risk, but the buyer, if he is a merchant, must follow
any reasonable instructions given him by the seller with reference to the
return of the goods. In contrast, the return of the goods is at the buyer's
risk and expense under a sale or return.[C61]

3-12. Rights of Third Parties in Goods Sold. Creditors. Reference has
been made to the rights of creditors of the *buyer* in goods which have been
consigned by the seller or delivered to the buyer on a sale or return
basis. Another situation relates to the rights of creditors of the *seller* in
goods which have been "sold" to a buyer, but which were allowed to
remain in the seller's possession. The law in the various states is not uniform, but in many states such retention of possession is presumed to be
fraudulent as against the seller's creditors as giving an appearance of continuing ownership in the seller. The Code recognizes this local law and
its continued application, but provides that the retention of possession in
good faith by a merchant seller for a reasonable time after sale is not to
be considered fraudulent.[C62] The rights of creditors of a seller *are* protected in cases where there is fraudulent transfer of goods by a seller or
where the transfer is made by him outside the current course of trade in
satisfaction of a pre-existing debt. The rights of the creditors to reach the
goods in the hands of a transferee who acquired the goods in such fashion
are definitely superior to those of the transferee. The foregoing relates
to unsecured creditors of the seller. If the creditor has a security interest
in the goods in conformity with the provisions of Article 9–Secured
Transactions, his rights of course are not impaired.

Purchasers. As a general proposition, the purchaser of goods
obtains only the title of the person who transferred the goods to him. As
noted above, a creditor may assert rights against goods which do not
belong to his debtor in some situations, and by the same token one who
has a voidable title to goods may transfer good title to a good faith purchaser for value.[C63] A voidable title is one which can be set aside because
of some irregularity in connection with its transfer. Article 2 has codified
the principle that considerable protection be afforded to a "purchaser"
by stipulating that he obtains good title although the person *from whom
he purchased* had acquired the goods, 1) by fraud, 2) in return for a dishonored check, 3) by deceiving the transferor as to his identity, or 4)
under an agreement that the title would not pass until the price was
paid. Obviously, this means that a loss under these circumstances will
fall upon the person who dealt with the original purchaser. The sale of
goods by a thief does not, however, deprive the owner of his title, and

C59 *U.C.C.* 2-326(3).
C60 *U.C.C.* 2-327.
C61 *U.C.C.* 2-327.

C62 *U.C.C.* 2-402.
C63 *U.C.C.* 2-403.

a good faith purchaser from a thief would not be protected. In addition, persons who buy in the ordinary course of business from a merchant are protected, although the goods sold by the merchant do not belong to him by reason of a consignment arrangement; a security interest in the inventory retained by the person who furnished the inventory to the seller; or other restrictions upon the authority to dispose of the goods.[19]

SALES: THE CONTRACT CASES

Cook Grains, Inc., v. Paul Fallis

1965 (Ark.) 395 S.W. 2d 555

The plaintiff, a grain dealer, brought action against defendant, a farmer, for breach of a contract to sell soybeans. The parties had negotiated for the sale of 5000 bushels and there was conflicting testimony as to whether or not an agreement had been reached. The grain company had sent a proposed written contract to the defendant and had stipulated that it would be bound if the defendant signed it. The defendant neither signed nor returned the contract. The plaintiff contended that the defendant's failure to indicate disapproval resulted in a contract, while defendant claimed that no obligation was imposed on him because the Statute of Frauds had not been satisfied. The trial court entered a judgment for the farmer-seller-defendant and plaintiff appealed.

ROBINSON, J.   The appellant grain company concedes that ordinarily the alleged cause of action would be barred by the statute of frauds, but contends that here the alleged sale is taken out of the statute of frauds by the Uniform Commercial Code. Ark. Stat. Ann. Sec. 85-2-201 (1961 Addendum) is relied on.

> Formal requirements—Statute of Frauds.—(1) Except as otherwise provided in this section a contract for the sale of goods for the price of $500 or more is not enforceable by way of action or defense unless there is some writing sufficient to indicate that a contract for sale has been made between the parties and signed by the party against whom enforcement is sought or by his authorized agent or broker. A writing is not insufficient because it omits or incorrectly states a term agreed upon but the contract is not enforceable under this paragraph beyond the quantity of goods shown in such writing.
> (2) Between merchants if within a reasonable time a writing in confirmation of the contract and sufficient against the sender is received and the party receiving it has reason to know its contents, it satisfies the requirements of subsection (1) against such party unless written notice of objection to its contents is given within ten (10) days after it is received. . . .

Thus, it will be seen that under the statute, if appellee (farmer) is a merchant he would be liable on the alleged contract because he did not, within ten days, give written notice that he rejected it.

The solution of the case turns on the point of whether the appellee

---

[19] *Independent News Co. v. Williams,* page 383.

Fallis is a "merchant" within the meaning of the statute. Ark. Stat. Ann. Sec. 85-2-104 (1961 Addendum) provides:

> "Merchant" means a person who deals in goods of the kind or otherwise by his occupation holds himself out as having knowledge or skill peculiar to the practices or goods involved in the transaction or to whom such knowledge or skill may be attributed by his employment of an agent or broker or other intermediary who by his occupation holds himself out as having such knowledge or skill. . . .

There is not a scintilla of evidence in the record, or proffered as evidence that appellee is a dealer in goods of the kind or by his occupation holds himself out as having knowledge or a skill peculiar to the practices or goods involved in the transaction, and no such knowledge or skill can be attributed to him.

The evidence in this case is that appellee is a farmer and nothing else. He farms about 550 acres and there is no showing that he has any other occupation. . . .

If the General Assembly had intended that in the circumstances of this case a farmer should be considered a merchant and therefore liable on an alleged contract to sell his commodities, which he did not sign, no doubt clear and explicit language would have been used in the statute to that effect. There is nothing whatever in the statute indicating that the word "merchant" should apply to a farmer when he is acting in the capacity of a farmer, and he comes within that category when he is merely trying to sell the commodities he has raised. . . .

Judgment affirmed.

Q. Vandenberg & Sons, N. V. v. Siter

1964 (Pa.) 204 A. 2d 494

The plaintiff, a bulb grower in Holland, sold hyacinth bulbs to the defendants. The defendants claimed that the bulbs were not healthy and when sued for the price presented a counterclaim for breach of warranty. Defendant sought to introduce testimony relating to the condition of the bulbs at a time more than eight days after delivery. Defendant contended that it took some time for the defects to show up. The lower court excluded the testimony and a judgment was entered for the plaintiff. The defendant appealed.

Flood, J. The contract contained the following clause of warranty:

> "The seller warrants the goods to be sound and healthy at the time of shipment but does not *otherwise* warrant flowering or other planting, growing or forcing results. . . . All claims hereunder shall be deemed waived unless presented within eight (8) days after receipt of the goods."

In limiting the warranties as he did, the trial judge ignored the word "otherwise" in the express warranty. We repeat the important language: "The seller warrants the goods to be sound and healthy at the time of shipment but does not otherwise warrant flowering. . . ." While this means that flowering is not warranted unless the failure to flower results from an unsound or unhealthy condition of the bulbs at time of shipment, it is equally obvious that the seller does warrant that at the time of shipment the bulbs were capable of flowering properly. Since the defendants' evidence was that failure to flower properly resulted from a condition which existed at the time of shipment because the bulbs had grown beyond their capacity in Holland, the failure falls within the terms of the express warranty if the jury believes this evidence.

It is true that nothing which occurred after delivery which made the bulbs unfit or unmerchantable would be a breach of either the express or implied warranties. There was, however, no evidence that the damage to the bulbs involved in the suit occurred in transit. On the contrary, as we have noted, the defendants offered expert testimony tending to show that the defect for which the counterclaim is laid occurred prior to delivery and existed at the time of delivery.

The express warranty herein is not inconsistent with an implied warranty of merchantability under § 2-314 of the Uniform Commercial Code of April 6, 1953. . . . nor with an implied warranty of fitness for a particular purpose, under § 2-315 of the Code. Indeed the express warranty coincides with such implied warranties in so far as the express warranty covers sound and healthy bulbs and warrants flowering capacity at shipment. Consequently the expert testimony as to these implied warranties should not have been stricken.

While the defendants did not present their claim until several months after they received the bulbs, it was for the jury to say, under proper instructions, whether the eight day limitation is reasonable and binding upon them under the circumstances. Several provisions of the Uniform Commercial Code affect this question. Section 2-607 provides that the buyer must give notice of the breach of the contract of sale "within a reasonable time after he discovers or should have discovered any breach. . . ." Section 2-608 provides: "(2) Revocation of acceptance must occur within a reasonable time after the buyer discovers or should have discovered the ground for it . . ." Finally, § 1-204 provides: "(1) Wherever this Act requires any action to be taken within a reasonable time, the agreement may fix any time which is not manifestly unreasonable. (2) What is a reasonable time for taking any action depends on the nature, purpose and circumstances of such action."

Under the defendants' evidence which was stricken out by the court below, the defects in the bulbs which prevented flowering, though existing at the time of delivery, were latent, and not known to the defendants at the time of planting and could not be discovered thereafter by the buyer until flowering time. The defendants argue that this makes the eight day limitation unreasonable under § 1-204 of the Code, *supra*.

Undoubtedly the parties may by their contract limit the time for the buyer's notice of claim for breach of warranties, but the limitation must be reasonable. A limitation which renders the warranties ineffective as regards latent defects, literally covered by the warranty but not discoverable within the limitation period of the contract, is manifestly unreasonable and therefore invalid under § 1-204 of the Code. The evidence offered by the defendants on the question of the timeliness of the notice under the circumstances should have been received and left for the jury's consideration, along with the countervailing evidence of the plaintiff.

Where the facts are in dispute, the question of the reasonableness of the time when notice of breach of warranty was given is for the jury. . . . This is particularly true when the defect is not discoverable upon an ordinary inspection. Thus, it has been held that where a defect is discoverable only by microscopic examination the question of time for notice of a claim based on an alleged breach of warranty was for the jury under all the facts. . . . In *Victorson v. Albert M. Green Hosiery Mills, Inc.,* (202 F.2d 717 (3d Cir., 1953), 41 A.L.R.2d 806, 811), the court said: "The latent-defect cases constitute a well-recognized, separate category in the Pennsylvania decisions construing reasonable time,". . .

While in most of the cases just cited there was no time limitation in the contract, the question whether the time limitation is "manifestly unreasonable" under § 1-204 of the Code is, under the circumstances of this case, clearly for the jury under proper instruction. . . .

The rulings of the court below striking out defendants' evidence on the defense and counterclaim and rejecting defendants' offer of proof under the counterclaim were erroneous and require a new trial. The result of the court's rulings referred to was that the issues involved in the defense and counterclaim were not defined or presented to the jury. Both the question as to whether the bulbs were healthy and sound as regards flowering capacity at delivery, and the question whether the defendants gave notice of the alleged breach of warranty within a reasonable time, were for the jury.

*Judgments reversed with **a procedendo.** (i.e. the case is returned to the trial court to proceed in accordance with this opinion.)*

Strauss v. West

1966 (R.I.) 216 A.2d 366

POWERS, J. This is an action of assumpsit to recover the agreed consideration for the sale of a race horse which, after delivery, the defendant rejected for an alleged breach of warranty. The case was tried to a superior court justice, sitting without a jury, and resulted in a decision for the plaintiff. It is before us on the defendant's exceptions to the decision and to an evidentiary ruling.

The uncontradicted evidence discloses that plaintiff was the owner of a race horse stabled at Belmont Park, a race track located in New York, when on April 27, 1962 it was purchased by defendant and at the latter's request was shipped over the road for delivery at Suffolk Downs in Massachusetts.

On the day of the sale defendant was accompanied by John D. Canzano, a professional horse trainer with twenty-three years' experience, who assisted him in negotiating the purchase. The horse was shown to them by

Lawrence Gieger, a public horse trainer who was acting as agent for plaintiff.

Mr. Gieger refused to have the horse galloped for the reason that it had raced the previous day, but he assured defendant and his agent that the horse was sound. The horse was brought from the stable, walked in the presence of defendant and his trainer, and examined by the latter who found nothing wrong with the animal.

The plaintiff's agent accepted defendant's check in the sum of $1,800 payable to plaintiff, whereupon the parties agreed title passed to defendant.

Thereafter, pursuant to defendant's request, plaintiff's trainer made arrangements to ship the horse by motor van which left on the evening of April 28, 1962 and arrived at Suffolk Downs, a distance of some 215 miles, about six o'clock the following morning.

The defendant's trainer testified that within an hour and a half after the horse arrived, he had it saddled and mounted to observe how it galloped, and that when it started to gallop it almost fell down. After some adjustments another attempt was made but again, after a shorter gallop, the horse almost fell.

He further testified that he then examined the horse's front legs and found a bowed tendon in the left leg, and that on April 29 and April 30 he made seven or eight telephone calls to New York in an unsuccessful effort to speak to the trainer Gieger. Thereupon on May 1, 1962, defendant stopped payment on the check and on May 3, trainer Canzano shipped the horse back to New York.

The plaintiff's trainer testified that there were several possible ways by which a horse might sustain a bowed tendon and included traveling in a van for a considerable distance as one of them.

The trial justice found as a fact that the horse was sound at the time it was purchased and rendered decision for plaintiff in the sum of $1,800 with interest.

In support of his exception to the decision, defendant argues that the case is controlled by the provisions of the Uniform Commercial Code, (G.L. 1956, §§ 6A-2-313, 6A-2-513 and 6A-2-601). These sections set forth the conditions on which a warranty is established, the buyer's right to inspect and his right to reject for breach of warranty, respectively.

He contends that the facts in the instant case disclose an express warranty, an inspection of the horse on delivery, and rejection thereof within a reasonable time after it was discovered that the horse was not sound as warranted. In support of this contention he cites several Rhode Island cases. These are of no assistance to defendant, however, for the facts on which they rest are not present here.

Here the trial justice found that the horse was sound as warranted when purchased by defendant and delivered to him in New York. That it was found to have a bowed tendon subsequent to delivery was immaterial. There was no breach of warranty, if the trial justice's finding that the horse was sound when purchased can be supported by the evidence on which such finding was made. It is well settled that the findings of a trial justice sitting without a jury are given great weight and will not be disturbed unless he has misconceived or overlooked material evidence in making them. . . .

The question before us then is whether in making the finding of fact on which his decision is predicated, the trial justice misconceived or overlooked material evidence. We have carefully reviewed the record before us and conclude that he did not. It becomes readily apparent that the trial justice gave great weight to the testimony of plaintiff's trainer as to the condition of the horse at the time of the sale. Further, he emphasized with particularity his impression of defendant's trainer's skill and manifestly concluded that if a bowed tendon were present at the time Canzano examined the horse at Belmont Park, he would have discovered it. The defendant's exception to the decision therefore is without merit.

All of the defendant's exceptions are overruled, and the case is remitted to the superior court for entry of judgment on the decision.

Southwest Distributors, Inc. v. Allied Paper Bag Corp.

1964 (Mo.) 384 S.W.2d. 838

SPEERY, Commissioner.   Plaintiff sued defendant for damages growing out of the breach of an implied warranty of fitness for intended use. Defendant counterclaimed. Trial to the court resulted in a judgment for plaintiff, on its petition, for $3,200.00, and for plaintiff on defendant's counterclaim. Defendant appeals.

Plaintiff has its offices in Kansas City. It is engaged in the business of manufacturing and selling mixed feeds, fertilizers, and other products. It maintains a plant in Verdun, Nebraska, where it processes corncobs for various commercial uses. Among its corncob products is a mulch which is adapted to agricultural uses. It is beneficial to soil, as an aid to moisture retention, aeration, fertilization, and the addition of humus. It is a dry, bulky material and is shipped, as are other products of plaintiff, in fifty (50) pound paper bags. Prior to the occurrence of this controversy, plaintiff had purchased bags from defendant for shipment of its other products, and the bags furnished were satisfactory.

Defendant was engaged in the business of manufacturing and selling bags for use in the shipment of various commercial products. Its factory and place of business is located in Kansas City.

Sometime prior to June, 1959, defendant's salesman called on Mr. Harris (plaintiff's manager). Mr. Harris stated that he told the salesman about the new product that he intended to produce, the name of which was "Magic Mulch." He stated that he told him, generally, of its nature and purposes; that he wanted to bag it for shipment in "nice, new, fancy bags;" that the bags were to contain fifty (50) pounds of the product, to be sold chiefly in California, where there was a good demand because of the nature of the climate and soil; that he asked defendant to produce a "dummy" sample that could be shown to California customers engaged in distributing such products; that the defendant produced such a sample bag; that witness went to Los Angeles; where he contacted one Cal Erwin and sold him two carloads of the product. He also sold an order to another dealer at Van Nuys, California. He stated that, upon his return, he interviewed defendant's agent and told him that such products were, universally, stored in the open, on the ground, in California; that defendant's representative then recommended that the bag should contain an inner liner of asphalt, so as to protect its contents from moisture; that plaintiff ordered five thousand (5,000) bags; that plaintiff did not specify to the defendant any quality required of the bags except size—that they weigh fifty (50) pounds when filled, that they were to be stored outside of sheds, and the lettering that was to go on them; that he wanted them as quickly as possible because he had orders ready to be filled; that, before the bags were made, plaintiff saw and inspected the plate (the lettering) and changed one word therein; that he was present when an extra workman, at defendant's plant, was ready to print the lettering on the bags; that the workman was having trouble with the ink; that the workman said the trouble was with the steam; that the workman, eventually, told him that they had the matter corrected; that witness left the plant after having seen some bags that "looked good." He stated that the bags were shipped to Nebraska, where they were filled and shipped to dealers in California, in box cars; that he did not see the bags prior to their shipment; that he left the making of the bags to the judgment of defendant, who was skilled in that business.

Mr. Harris stated that, about four (4) weeks after shipment, he received telephone complaints from dealers regarding the bags; that they were fading; that Mr. Erwin, a customer who had ordered and received two carloads, had then only paid for one car; that he went to California to see Erwin to collect, but that he could not collect; that, later, he made another trip to California and brought back samples of the bags, one of which was placed in evidence as an exhibit. It is before us. The advertising matter appears in red, green, and black. The red and green coloring is badly faded and the colors have "run," so that the entire bag is unsightly. It gives the appearance of being stale, shopworn. Mr. Harris stated that several hundred bags sold to Erwin were in this condition; that he had previously purchased from defendant from five to ten times the number of bags herein involved, which were used for shipment of ground corncobs and which were stored in the open by purchasers, particularly oil well driller; that these bags had been satisfactory and had been paid for. He also stated that one shipment of "Magic Mulch" went to B. & E. Enterprises, Van Nuys, California; that the customer refused to pay therefore, because of the above conditions, and that plaintiff took the shipment back; that Erwin had returned to him much of this merchandise that they had sold; that the complaints were based on colors fading and running; that at no time did plaintiff suggest or specify the type of ink to be used in the printed matter on the bags.

Mr. Erwin's deposition was in evidence. His testimony fully corroborated that of Mr. Harris.

Plaintiff ordered these bags from defendant for the specific purpose of shipping its "Magic Mulch" to customers in California. Plaintiff told defendant, generally, what type and size of container it wanted. It wanted an attractive bag printed in multicolors, describing the contents and stating its purposes and uses. It wanted bags that could safely be stored in the open. It was not in the business of manufacturing bags but only produced merchandise for shipment therein. It had no facilities for chemically testing the paints, inks, and other materials that went into or on the bags. It left all of that to the judgment and discretion of defendant who specialized in that business and had access to such information. It had previously ordered many thousands of bags from defendant for shipment of similar merchandise under similar conditions.

Defendant is bound by the well settled law on this subject, to wit: that a manufacturer-seller of an article for a particular purpose impliedly warrants that such article will be reasonably fit for that purpose for which it is intended to be used, *if the buyer communicates to the manu- facturer-seller the specific purpose for which he wants the article, and if he relies, and has reason to rely, on the producer-seller's skill, judgment and experience to produce an article that will answer the purpose.*

The doctrine does not apply to well known or commonly used articles. It rests in part upon the principle of superior knowledge and experience of the producer-seller. However, if the purchaser has, or acquires by testing and analysis, knowledge equal to that of the seller the rule does not apply because the seller has no superiority of knowledge of the facts.
. . .

The evidence in this case supports the court in its finding of the issues for plaintiff against defendant. The evidence was to the effect that plaintiff relied wholly on defendant to produce bags for a specific purpose; that that purpose was communicated to defendant; that plaintiff did not specify the types of materials to be used but relied on defendant's judgment and skill in producing an article reasonably fit for its purposes; that plaintiff had reason to rely on defendant's skill and judgment to produce for it a bag reasonably fit for its intended use; that the bags produced were not reasonably fit for that use; and that by reason thereof, plaintiff suffered damages as adjudged by the court.

Defendant contends that the judgment is excessive because it includes freight charges on merchandise shipped to California which charges were, in fact, paid by buyers to whom plaintiff shipped the merchandise. The evidence is to the effect that plaintiff is obligated to make its customers in California whole as to their losses, the merchandise having proved to be unmarketable because of the defective containers.

This contention is denied.

The judgment is affirmed.

Corneliuson v. Arthur Drug Stores, Inc., et al.

1965, (Conn.) 214 A.2d 676

The plaintiff brought suit to recover damages for breach of warranty of fitness of a home permanent waving lotion sold by the defendants. The plaintiff purchased a hair waving lotion known as Ogilvie Sisters

Home Permanent from the defendants, and she claimed that, as a result of her use of the lotion, she sustained a severe dermatitis with concomitant physical and neurotic injuries. The jury returned a verdict for the plaintiff and the defendants have appealed.

HOUSE, A. J. In *Crotty v. Shartenberg's-New Haven, Inc.* we had occasion to consider the development of the law in the field of products liability and analyze the provisions of the Connecticut state on implied warranties. . . .

In that case, . . . we noted that some jurisdictions hold that if the article sold can be used by a normal person without injury, there is no breach of the implied warranty of reasonable fitness, while others adopt the theory that the seller is not absolved from liability under the implied warranty created by the statute by the mere fact that only a small proportion of those who use the product suffer injuries from its use. We concluded . . . that the term "reasonable fitness" must, of necessity, be considered one of degree and that the term must be "related to the subject of the sale." Rejecting the rule limiting the application of the term "reasonable fitness" to a class or group designated as normal persons, we adopted the test of injurious effect to "an appreciable number of people." We held that not only the causal connection between the product and the injury must be established but also the plaintiff must be a member of a class who would be similarly affected by the product, identifying that class as an appreciable number of people. . . .

Proof of the harmful propensities of the substance and that it can affect injuriously an appreciable number of persons is essential to his (plaintiff's) case. . . . If a buyer has knowledge, either actual or constructive, that he is allergic to a particular substance and purchases a product which he knows or reasonably should know contains that substance, he cannot recover damages for breach of an implied warranty. Nor can he recover if he suffers harm by reason of his own improper use of the article warranted. . . .

Viewed in the light most favorable to the plaintiff, there was evidence before the jury that all permanent waving lotions, including Ogilvie Sisters, now contain as a principal ingredient ammonium thioglycolate, a chemical compound which varies in degree of alkalinity according to the relative strength of the ammonia. An alkali is an irritant to the skin, depending on the degree of alkalinity. . . .

In short, although there was evidence from which the jury could find that the Ogilvie Sisters lotion did cause injury to the plaintiff, there was no evidence from which they could find that this lotion as compounded had a tendency to affect injuriously an appreciable number of people. Proof of both injury to the plaintiff and such injurious tendency are necessary for the plaintiff to prevail. . . .

We must conclude, therefore, that the plaintiff has failed to sustain her burden of proving a breach of implied warranty, and the trial court should have granted the defendants' motion to set aside the verdict.

Judgment set aside and a new trial ordered.

Ray v. Deas

1965, (Ga.) 144 S.E.2d 468

Plaintiff ate a hamburger sandwich at defendant's restaurant. She broke a tooth on a hard object in the sandwich and sued the defendant for damages. The defendant demurred to the complaint. The demurrer was overruled and defendant appealed.

FRANKUM, J.   Prior to the enactment of the Uniform Commercial Code it was the settled law in Georgia that a restaurateur who furnished unwholesome food or food containing a foreign substance or dangerous object to a customer who was injured thereby was not liable upon the theory of an implied warranty. . . . The rule of law thus announced and applied in the Georgia courts was clearly based upon the proposition that the furnishing of food by a restaurateur for consumption on the premises did not amount to a sale, but was in fact the rendition of a service solely for the purpose of satisfying the customer's immediate desires and need to be fed. . . . However, the plain, unambiguous, and express language of 2-314 of the Uniform Commercial Code . . . provides: "Unless excluded or modified . . . a warranty that the goods shall be merchantable is implied in a contract for their sale if the seller is a merchant with respect to goods of that kind. Under this section the serving for value of food or drink to be consumed either on the premises or elsewhere is a sale." The legislature has thus evidenced a manifest intention of abrogating and repealing the substantive rule of law announced by the courts. . . .

Judgment affirmed.

Delta Airlines, Inc., v. Douglas Aircraft Company, Inc.

1965 (California) 47 Cal.Rptr. 518

Action for breach of warranty in sale of a commercial airplane. Delta purchased a new DC-7 from Douglas for $2,250,000. Two days after delivery, while the pilot was attempting to land the plane after a check flight, the nose wheel failed to function and the plane veered off the runway and caused considerable damage to the plane although no personal injuries. The contract for the sale of the plane contained an *exculpatory clause* releasing Douglas from any liability except that contained in the contract which read:

> The warranty provided in this article and the obligations and liabilities of Seller thereunder are in lieu of and Buyer hereby waives all other warranties, guaranties, conditions or liabilities, express or implied, arising by law or otherwise (including without limitation any obligation of the Seller with respect to consequential damages) and whether or not occasioned by Seller's negligence and shall not be extended, altered, or varied except by a written instrument signed by Seller and Buyer; provided, that in the event the provision relieving Seller from liability for its negligence should for any reason be held ineffective, the remainder of this paragraph (E) shall remain in full force and effect.

The jury returned a verdict for Delta and Douglas appealed.

KINGSLEY, Justice. The first issue raised herein pertains to the breadth of the exculpatory clause (Paragraph E of the above quoted warranty provision). It is argued by Delta that the clause does not disclaim liability for negligence as a tort concept but only disclaims liability for contractual liability, i.e., a negligent breach of an express or implied warranty. The general rule in California and in other states is that exculpatory or indemnity clauses which attempt to free an actor from liability for his own negligence are basically valid but must be strictly construed and that failure to state an attempted exculpation or indemnity in plain, unambiguous and clear terminology will result in an interpretation that the clause was not intended to exempt the actor from liability for his own negligence. Notwithstanding this rule of strict interpretation, the contract must be interpreted by the court and the intent of the parties determined. (citation) The present clause includes within its provisions a statement that the buyer "waives all other . . . conditions or liabilities . . . arising by law or otherwise . . . whether or not occasioned by Seller's negligence. . . ." The reference to negligence can have no meaning unless it refers to tort negligence, for an action based on warranty may be maintained whether or not there is negligence; that is its function. Even though disclaimer clauses are to be strictly construed, still we find that this clause covers not only contractual warranty liability but also tort liability.

Next, Delta claims that, assuming the exculpatory clause is construed so as to apply to the facts of this case, it is void as against public policy.

As we have said above, the law does not, in general, prohibit a clear and express contract absolving an actor from his own negligence. Civil Code section 1791, as in force at the times herein involved, provided that "Where any right, duty or liability would arise under a contract to sell or a sale by implication of law, it may be negatived or varied by express agreement. . . ." In *Burr v. Sherwin Williams Co.* ((1954) 42 Cal.2d 682, 693, 268 P.2d 1041), the court stated: "The statutory implied warranties of quality can, of course, be disclaimed by the seller, provided the buyer has knowledge or is chargeable with notice of the disclaimer before the bargain is complete." The present disclaimer clause is sufficiently broad to disclaim the implied warranty of fitness for the purchaser's purpose upon which Delta bases its breach of warranty cause of action.

Furthermore, a contract which exempts one from liability for his own negligence is not necessarily invalid. In *Tunkl v. Regents of University of California* ((1963) 60 Cal.2d 92, 96, 32 Cal. Rptr. 33, 383 P.2d 441), the court reviewed a number of exculpatory clause cases and concluded that an exculpatory provision is valid if it does not affect the "public interest."

However, Delta argues that modern law, in what is commonly referred to as the field of products liability, has shown a movement away from the traditional doctrine that a manufacturer has an absolute freedom of contract and may disclaim his liability in all circumstances. Conceding that recent cases have imposed limits on the freedom to impose exculpatory clauses, we do not regard the instant case as within either the letter or the spirit of the authorities relied on.

Unlike *Greenman v. Yuba Power Product, Inc.* ((1963) 59 Cal.2d 57, 27 Cal. Rptr. 697, 377 P.2d 897): *Tunkl v. Regents of University of California, supra* ((1963) 383 P.2d 441), and *Henningsen v. Bloomfield Motors, Inc.* (161 A.2d 69), this case involves no element of personal injury; and, also, unlike Greenman and Henningsen, involves no issue of "privity of contract."

Perhaps more important, the case at bench involves none of the elements of inequality of bargaining on which the cited cases, and other recent cases of the same sort, have laid their stress.

The difference between the contract before us and those involved in the cases relied on by Delta becomes apparent from the language of the leading California case on the point. In *Tunkl v. Regents of University of California, supra* . . . the court set out the kind of transaction in which exculpatory provisions will be held invalid:

> It concerns a business of a type generally thought suitable for public regulation. The party seeking exculpation is engaged in performing a service of great importance to the public, which is often a matter of practical necessity for some members of the public. The party holds himself out as willing to perform this service for any member of the public who seeks it, . . . As a result of the essential nature of the service, in the economic setting of the transaction, the party invoking exculpation possesses a decisive advantage of bargaining strength against any member of the public who seeks his services. In exercising a superior bargaining power the party confronts the public with a standardized adhesion contract of exculpation, and makes no provision whereby a purchaser may pay additional reasonable fees and obtain protection against negligence. Finally, as a result of the transaction, the person or property of the purchaser is placed under the control of the seller, subject to the risk of carelessness by the seller or his agents.

. . . The fact that Delta is a regulated enterprise and carries passengers has no relevance to the present decision. The upholding of the exculpatory clause will not adversely affect rights of future passengers. They are not parties to the contract and their rights would not be compromised. They retain their right to bring a direct action against Douglas for negligence. *(MacPherson v. Buick Motor Co. (1916) 111 N.E. 1050, L.R.A. 1916F, 696)* Also, their right to bring an action against Douglas for breach of implied warranty would not be interfered with because the passengers were not a party to the contract containing the exculpatory clause.

In short, all that is herein involved is the question of which of two equal bargainers should bear the risk of economic loss if the product sold proved to be defective.

Judgment reversed with directions to enter a judgment in favor of Douglas.

Wright v. Massey-Harris Inc.

1966, (Ill.) 215 N.E. 2d 465

The plaintiff was injured while operating a self-propelled corn picker, which had been manufactured by the defendant, and which had been purchased from an implement dealer by the plaintiff's employer. The plaintiff alleged in his complaint that the cornpicker did not have a reasonably safe shield over that part of the machine from which jammed corn ears were manually extracted. Plaintiff's injury occurred when extracting a jammed ear. The trial court dismissed the complaint and plaintiff appealed.

MORAN, J. . . . Defendant claims that the foregoing complaint does not state a cause of action because (1) there are no facts alleged sufficient to show that the machine in question was inherently dangerous when put to the use for which it was intended, and (2) the complaint fails to allege facts sufficient to demonstrate that there was any hidden or latent defect in them, but on the contrary, the complaint shows that the danger would be obvious to anyone placing his hands in the corn husking rollers while the machine was in operation and the complaint therefore shows on its face that there is no liability to the plaintiff for the occurrence alleged.

While this cause was pending in this court, the Supreme Court of Illinois rendered a landmark decision in the case of *Suvada v. White Motor Company et al.*, (32 Ill.2d 612, 210 N.E.2d 182), in which it not only shattered the privity defense in Illinois in actions against manufacturers, sellers, contractors, those who hold themselves out to be manufacturers, assemblers of parts, suppliers and manufacturers of component parts, but also held these same parties to strict privity-free liability for any injury or damage caused by any unreasonably dangerous products which one or all of them might place into the stream of commerce.

The Court based its holding solely on the same public policy which had heretofore motivated the Illinois Courts to impose strict liability on the sellers and manufacturers of food . . .

The rationale underlying the cases cited and law scholars quoted by the Supreme Court in Suvada is succinctly stated by Prosser on Torts, Third Edition, Chapter 14, at page 509:

> . . . The problem is dealt with as one of allocating a more or less inevitable loss to be charged against a complex and dangerous civilization, and liability is placed upon the party best able to shoulder it. The defendant is held liable merely because, as a matter of social adjustment, the conclusion is that the responsibility should be his.

We have refrained from extended comment on any cases pre-dating Suvada because we believe that Suvada inaugurates a new era in products liability law in Illinois to such an extent that almost all of the cases preceding this decision are completely outmoded. In our opinion, the language of Suvada is plain and unambiguous. Hereafter, manufacturers of unreasonably dangerous products are strictly liable in tort to the hapless victims of their machines or products.

The wisdom of Suvada is well illustrated by the result reached in the case of *Murphy v. Cory Pump & Supply Company* (47 Ill.App.2d 382, 197 N.E.2d 849), relied upon by the defendants. Plaintiff, a seven year old child, lost her leg by falling in front of a power mower with a rotary blade which was being operated by her eleven year old sister. The negligence charged was that the mower was inherently dangerous in that the rotary blade would be likely to injure and maim children and that although the rotary blade appeared to be covered, it lacked a safety screen or bar.

The Appellate Court upheld the action of the trial court in allowing a motion for summary judgment in favor of the defendant, giving as its reason that the manufacturer of this mower owed no duty to the plaintiff.

Murphy illustrates a typical result which Suvada seeks to remedy by placing the losses caused by unreasonably dangerous machines or products on those who have created the risk and reaped the profit rather than on an innocent seven year old child.

The desirability of reaching an opposite result from that which was reached in Murphy is illustrated by a cogent statement from another field of learning. McClure, Power Lawn Mower Injuries, 25, *The American Surgeon,* 70 (1959) says:

> It would be wise . . . to point out that approximately 30 per cent of all power lawn mowers are made by companies whose primary objective is to turn out a lower priced, sometimes poorly constructed, machine for a profit. These companies have given little or no consideration to safety features of their products and some do not bother to caution the buyer of the machine about its inherent dangers. The low cost of these mowers make them attractive to the unsuspecting customer. On the other hand, some of the more reputable manufacturers have attempted to construct mowers which meet rigid safety standards. These also usually attach a card or booklet of instructions regarding proper operation of the machine and emboss special warnings at the danger points on the machine housing.

In discussing a manufacturer's duties, Harper and James say in Volume II at page 1540:

> . . . His specific obligations may be roughly divided into two categories: the first concerns the design, plan, structure, and specifications for the product; the second concerns miscarriages in the process of manufacture because of which the product is not what was intended—it is "defective" in some respect. It is not suggested that this dichotomy has any automatic or uniform legal significance. Certainly the two classes merge imperceptibly into one another.

The present case involves a claimed defect in design rather than a defect in manufacture and we interpret Suvada to mean that the strict liability imposed upon a manufacturer includes injuries which arise from defects in design as well as defects in manufacture.

Whether the design defect in the present case is of a nature upon which liability can be imposed involves the factual question of whether it creates an unreasonably dangerous condition, or, in other words, whether the product in question has lived up to the required standard of safety.

We believe that the complaint in the present case states a good cause of action in negligence and also a good cause of action in strict liability if we treat all of the allegations in excess of those required by Suvada as surplusage.

For the foregoing reasons the judgment of the trial court in favor of the defendants is reversed. We remand the case for further proceedings not inconsistent with this opinion.

Reversed and remanded.

Suvada v. White Motor Company
1964 (Ill.) 201 N.E.2d 313

A truck belonging to the plaintiffs, partners in a milk distributing business, collided with a bus as a result of the failure of the brakes on the truck.

In 1957 plaintiffs purchased from White the 1953 motor vehicle for use in plaintiffs' business of distributing milk. White installed a brake system in the reconditioned motor vehicle which brake system was manufactured and supplied by Bendix. The plaintiffs allege that the collision was caused by an inherently dangerously made brake system in the tractor-trailer, and that the unit was purchased from White and the brake system was manufactured by Bendix; that as a result of the collision the tractor-trailer unit was damaged and numerous persons were injured; that plaintiffs expended money for investigation of the collision and in the defense of law suits arising out of the collision; that they made compromise settlements of some of the personal injury claims and property damage claims, and that they expended money in repair of their tractor-trailer. The complaint alleges that the failure of the braking system to operate was because of an inherently dangerous and defectively made linkage bracket. The plaintiffs sued both the seller, White, and manufacturer of the brake system, Bendix, for recovery of property damage to their tractor-trailer unit and, additionally, for indemnification of expenditures made by them in settlement, investigation and defense of claims that arose out of the collision.

Burke, J.   Plaintiffs state that the amounts paid by them for settlement, investigation and defense of personal injuries and property damage claims constitute proper elements of damage for indemnification from defendants; that these expenditures are reasonably probable and foreseeable as a direct result of the sale and manufacturing of an inherently dangerous or defectively made product and that the expenditures under the facts pleaded do not make them volunteers.

In the recent case of *Goldberg v. Kollsman Instrument Corp.*, (12

N.Y.2d 432, 240 N.Y.S.2d 592, p. 594, 191 N.E.2d 81, p. 82), the court said: "A breach of warranty, it is now clear, is not only a violation of the sales contract out of which the warranty arises but is a tortious wrong suable by a noncontracting party whose use of the warranted article is within the reasonable contemplation of the vendor or manufacturer. . . . As we all know, a number of courts outside New York State have for the best of reasons dispensed with the privity requirement. . . . Very recently the Supreme Court of California (*Greenman v. Yuba Power Prods., Inc.,* 59 Cal.2d 67, 27 Cal. Rptr. 697, 377 P.2d 897 (1963), *supra*) in a unanimous opinion imposed 'strict tort liability' (surely a more accurate phrase) regardless of privity on a manufacturer in a case where a power tool threw a piece of wood at a user who was not the purchaser. The California court said that the purpose of such a holding is to see to it that the costs of injuries resulting from defective products are borne by the manufacturers who put the products on the market rather than by injured persons who are powerless to protect themselves and that implicit in putting such articles on the market are representations that they will safely do the job for which they were built." The majority of the judges of the New York Court of Appeals decided that for the present they did not think it necessary to extend the rule to hold liable the manufacturer of a component part. The majority thought that adequate protection is being provided for the passengers of the airplane by casting in liability the airplane manufacturer which put into the market the completed aircraft.

The cases in Illinois appear to follow the thinking of the New York court; *Rotche v. Buick Motor Co.* (258 Ill. 507, 193 N.E. 529) cites *MacPherson v. Buick Motor Co.,* (217 N.Y. 382, 111 N.E. 1050, L.R.A. 1916F, 696) in support of the proposition that the manufacturer who places in the stream of commerce a product that becomes dangerous to life and limb of the public is liable to a subpurchaser because of the nature of the product and that the liability is not based upon a contractual relationship. In *Lindroth v. Walgreen Co.,* and *Knapp-Moncharch Co.,* (329 Ill. App. 105, 67 N.E.2d 595), the court held that where the product is inherently dangerous a cause of action by the subpurchaser against the manufacturer exists in the absence of privity. See also *Biller v. Allis Chalmers Mfg. Co.,* (34 Ill. App.2d 47, 180 N.E.2d. 46). Today's manufacturer, selling to distributors or wholesalers, is still interested in the subsequent sales of the product. His advertising is not aimed at his distributors. The historical relative equality of seller and buyer no longer exists. A product that is inherently dangerous or defectively made constitutes an exception to the requirement of privity in an action between the user of the product and its manufacturer. We cannot say from the allegations of the complaint that Bendix is beyond the immediate distributive chain. The complaint alleges that Bendix manufactured an inherently dangerous or defectively made brake system which was installed by White into a motor vehicle as part of its renovation. Bendix is charged with manufacturing and supplying that brake system. The complaint does not charge that the brake system was reconditioned.

The exception to the privity requirement is not superseded nor is it modified by the provisions of the Uniform Commercial Code. In Comment 3 to Sec. 2-318 of the Code, (Ill. Rev. Stat. 1963, c.26, 2-318), the drafters state that: "The section is neutral and is not intended to enlarge or restrict the developing case law on whether the seller's warranties, given to his buyer who resells, extend to other persons in the distributive chain." In *Henningsen v. Bloomfield Motors, Inc.,* (32 N.J. 358, 161 A2d. 69, 75 A.L.E.2d. 1), the court held that the subpurchaser is entitled to recover from a manufacturer of an automobile that is inherently dangerous or defectively manufactured in the absence of privity. The court said that it could find no distinction between an unwholesome food case and a defective car. This position was taken in *B. F. Goodrich Co. v. Hammond,* (269 F.2d. 501 (10th Circuit Kansas). In that case the administrator of an estate of a subpurchaser and wife who were occupants of an automobile sued the tire manufacturer for breach of implied warranty. Goodrich sold blowout proof tires. The mishap resulted because of a defect in the manufacture of a tire that caused a sudden blowout. In deciding that the subpurchaser and his wife had a cause of action against the manufacturer based upon breach of warranty, the court said, (269 F.2d. p. 502): "(P)rivity is not essential where an implied warranty is imposed by law on the basis of public policy."

A motor vehicle that is operated on the highways with a braking system that is inoperative is obviously dangerous to life and limb. The State of Illinois recognizes the necessity for a proper braking system in motor vehicles and has declared it to be public policy of the State that all motor vehicles manufactured and sold within the State shall be equipped with brakes adequate to control the movement of the vehicle. The manufacturer of the braking system is in the best position to provide and insure an adequate braking system of motor vehicles that are driven on the public highways. (Ill. Rev. State. 1963, Chap. 95½, 211.) We think that the court erred in striking the counts based on the theory of an implied warranty.

For these reasons the judgment is reversed and the cause is remanded with directions to reinstate the counts that were dismissed and for further proceedings not inconsistent with these views.

Judgment reversed and cause remanded with directions.

Chairaluce v. Stanley Warner Management Corp. et al.

1964, 236 F.Supp. 385

ZAMPANO, J.   The defendant, The Wise Shoe Company, Inc., hereinafter designated as "Wise," has moved . . . for an order dismissing the second count of plaintiff's amended complaint for failure to state a claim upon which relief can be granted. Specifically, the question presented is whether this cause of action against Wise, which is predicated upon breach of express and implied warranties, must be dismissed because plaintiffs have failed to allege privity of contract or reliance on defendant's representations or advertising.

This action was brought to recover damages for injuries sustained by the wife-plaintiff when she fell on a stairway in a theater owned by the defendant, The Stanley Warner Management Corp. At the time of the accident she was wearing for the first time a pair of new shoes which were manufactured by Wise and purchased by the plaintiff from the mail-order retail store of the defendant, Spiegel, Inc. She alleges her fall was caused by the breaking of a defective heel on one of these shoes.

. . . The second count . . . is founded upon the breach of express and implied warranties in the manufacture and sale of the defective shoe. . . . The plaintiffs merely contend there was a breach of "the warranties and duties which were owed to the plaintiff under the laws of the State of Connecticut."

Wise claims that absent allegations of representations through advertising by which the plaintiffs were misled, lack of privity between manufacturer and ultimate consumer bars recovery based upon breach of implied warranty. The Connecticut state courts have not yet ruled directly on this issue and, therefore, this Court must examine the effect of the recent far-reaching change in the Connecticut law of warranties. . . .

The Supreme Court of Errors of Connecticut in *Hamon v. Digliani* (148 Conn. 710, 174 A.2d 294 (1961)), stressing consumer reliance on a manufacturer's misleading advertising, ruled for the first time that privity of contract was not prerequisite to liability for breach of express warranty. In a searching inquiry into the relevant policy considerations, the Court commented:

> The maxim "caveat emptor" has become a millstone around the necks of dealer and customer. While the customer may maintain an action under the Sales Act against the retailer for breach of implied warranty, the dealer in turn must sue his supplier to recoup his damages and costs where the customer prevails. Eventually, after several separate and distinct pieces of costly litigation by those in the chain of title, the manufacturer is finally obliged to shoulder the responsibility which should have been his in the first instance.

(148 Conn. at 717, 174 A.2d at 297). Continuing at page 718, (174 A.2d at page 297), the Court established the following rules:

> The manufacturer or producer who puts a commodity for personal use or consumption on the market in a sealed package or other closed container should be held to have impliedly warranted to the ultimate consumer that the product is reasonably fit for the purpose intended and that it does not contain any harmful and deleterious ingredient of which due and ample warning has not been given. . . . Where the manufacturer or producer makes representations in his advertisements or by the labels on his products as an inducement to the ultimate purchaser, the manufacturer or producer should be held to strict accountability to any person who buys the product in reliance on the representations and later suffers injury because the product fails to conform to them.

Wise contends the Hamon case merely carved out an exception to the long-standing rule of privity in circumstances where a sealed package is involved or where the manufacturer's express representations are relied upon by the consumer. Wise urges, in effect, that the Hamon holding not be extended beyond the narrow factual circumstances there presented.

The obvious trend of the Connecticut law on the subject militates against defendant's position. Under the old Sales Act, § 42-16 of the Connecticut General Statutes, the protection of implied warranty of fitness of food and drink was extended to all persons for whom the purchase was intended. In 1961, the legislature enacted the Uniform Commercial Code which, by its § 42a-2-314, §42a-2-315 and § 42a-2-318, further expands an implied warrant of merchantability and fitness for a particular purpose to any person in the family or household of the buyer, or who is a guest in his home. Recent amendments to the statutes now allow an action for wrongful death based on breach of warranty. (Conn.Gen. Stat. § 52-555 (Rev. 1958)). In *Simpson v. Powered Products of Michigan, Inc.* (24 Conn.Sup. 409 (1963)), the plaintiff was not the buyer but his lessee, and the Court permitted the cause of action in warranty to stand against the seller of a defective golf cart which allegedly caused plaintiff's injuries.

These recent statutory changes and cases, coupled with the broad language and a review of the citations of authorities in Hamon, indicate to this Court that giant steps toward the inevitable demise of the privity requirement have been taken in Connecticut. The heights attained in this field by the legislature and judiciary in Connecticut should not now serve as pinnacles from which this Court backslides toward resuscitation of the privity doctrine. Sound public policy requires that a manufacturer be held strictly accountable to a plaintiff who, using his product in a way it was intended, is injured as a result of a defect in manufacture of which plaintiff was not aware.

Moreover, discarding the privity bugaboo in such cases harmonizes with the modern trend in other states and with the views of learned scholars in the field. The Court of Appeals for this Circuit, in two recent cases, supported the principle of strict liability against manufacturers who placed defective articles in the stream of commerce. . . . The Courts stressed the role of public policy in protecting innocent buyers from the harm of manufacturers' defective articles. The Third Circuit's approach to the issue is expressed in *Mannsz v. Macwhyte Co.*, (155 F.2d 445 (3 Cir. 1946)), wherein the Court, at page 450, noted:

> The abolition of the doctrine (privity) occurred first in the food cases, next in the beverages decisions and now it has been extended to those cases in which the article manufactured, not dangerous or even beneficial if properly made, injured a person because it was manufactured improperly.

Under the facts in the instant case, the reasoning of the Court in *Greenman v. Yuba Power Products, Inc.*, (59 Cal.2d 57, 27 Cal.Rptr. 697, 377

P.2d 897 (1963)) is directly in point. There the Court recognized a plaintiff's right of action based on express warranty and went on to hold that

> . . . it should not be controlling whether plaintiff selected the machine because of the statements in the brochure, or because of the machine's own appearance of excellence that belied the defect lurking beneath the surface, or because he merely assumed that it would safely do the jobs it was built to do. . . . To establish the manufacturer's liability it was sufficient that plaintiff proved that he was injured while using the Shopsmith in a way it was intended to be used as a result of a defect in design and manufacture of which plaintiff was not aware that made the Shopsmith unsafe for its intended use. (59 Cal.2d at 64, 27 Cal.Rptr. at 701, 377 P.2d at 901).

Professor Fleming James, Jr., noting that several cases "have stressed the extensive advertising" in holding a manufacturer liable, comments: "It would be a pity if they should emerge as requirements or limitations on liability under implied warranty. If injury from defective products is properly a risk of the producer's enterprise, it would be so whether he advertised or not and whether or not there was a conscious need to rely on his skill." James, Products Liability, (34 Texas L.R. 192 (1955)). . . .

These views are shared by Dean Prosser who deplores the "expensive, time-consuming, and wasteful process" of the privity requirement and advocates a "blanket rule which makes any supplier in the chain liable directly to the ultimate user, and so short-circuits the whole unwieldy process." Prosser, The Assault Upon the Citadel (Strict Liability to the Consumer), 69 Yale L.J. 1099, 1124 (1960). . . .

In light of the evident trend of the law in Connecticut and elsewhere, this Court concludes that the plaintiffs have alleged facts sufficient to state a claim upon which relief may be granted.

Accordingly, defendant's motion to dismiss is denied.

Lonzrick v. Republic Steel Corp.

1965 (Ohio) 205 N.E.2d 92

SKEEL, J. This appeal comes to this court from a judgment entered for the defendant by the Court of Common Pleas of Cuyahoga County. The action is one for money only. The plaintiff alleges in his petition that he suffered certain personal injuries when "steel bar joists" manufactured by the defendant, which had been placed in a building, collapsed and fell down upon him. The plaintiff was a construction worker employed by a *sub-contractor,* the Valley Steel Erectors, Inc. The joists were purchased from the defendant by the *general contractor.* The cause of action, as stated by the plaintiff, is based on a claim of a breach of the duty imposed by law on the defendant to furnish *merchantable* joist to the general contractor. *No claim of privity between the plaintiff and defendant is stated in the petition,* and under the facts stated no such claim could be made.

We are, therefore, confronted with the question whether the petition states a cause of action.

This question requires a survey of the rapidly changing theory of "product liability." The earlier rule, requiring privity between buyer and seller as a basis for creating liability under an express warranty grew out of the proposition that no such obligation was created until a promise was separately made upon the request of the buyer. Such a warranty was said to be collateral in character and enforceable by an action in tort. As then understood, a breach of such a promise did not breach the contract of sale, and, without such a collateral promise, the doctrine of *caveat emptor* applied. The transition of product liability from caveat emptor to strict tort liability, regardless of privity, where the manufacturer or dealer induces the sale under the law of express warranty, is set out in the case of *Rogers v. Toni Home Permanent Co.,* (105 Ohio App. 53) from . . . which statement of the law we hereby adopt without quoting at length.

An implied warranty is one imposed by law which under the Uniform Commercial Code dealing with sales, . . . writes into an agreement of sale certain obligations imposed upon the seller by law and requires the seller to be responsible for certain qualities to be possessed by the goods sold unless clearly negated by the sales contract. *This statute does not deal with the rights of third persons not parties to the sale who come into possession of the goods and use them in the manner intended by the manufacturer and are thereby injured by reason of the faulty condition of the goods latent in character due to improper manufacture or the use of faulty materials.* The rule, *as developed by the cases,* was clearly stated by the Supreme Court of West Virginia in the case of *Peters v. Johnson, Jackson & Co.* (1902). . . .

The theory of liability of the manufacturer or producer of chattels to the ultimate consumer without privity for negligence in producing the property, which negligence proximately caused injury or damage to the ultimate consumer while in the proper use of the property, is now almost universally accepted. Only the difficulty of proving negligence in the manufacturing process prevents such remedy from giving adequate relief to the ultimate consumer injured as a proximate result of the lack of care in producing the good purchased. However, with the right to pursue the manufacturer for damages due to dangers created by the negligent manufacture of his product, based on negligence, it was to be expected that the law would expand carrying the responsibility of a manufacturer for the negligent or careless manufacture of his goods, which carelessness created a danger to the consumer when using them in a proper manner, even further and find (as is true as to all persons whose negligence proximately causes injuries to others) grounds for enforcing strict tort liability against the producer whose negligence or lack of reasonable care in producing the goods is the direct cause of injury to the consumer. The source of such an obligation, when recognized, is created by law and has no dependence whatever on contractual relations between the parties. The soundness of this result is established by the weight of authority in recent decisions by many of the courts of last resort in the several states.

In the case of *Randy Knitwear, Inc., v. American Cyanamid Co.,* (11

N.Y.2d 5, 226 N.Y.S.2d 363, 181 N.E.2d 399), the plaintiff claimed a breach of an express warranty by the defendant (resin manufacturer) for damages resulting from the use of its product which is used by textile manufacturers to prevent shrinking of fabrics. The plaintiff purchased fabrics from mills licensed by the defendant to treat and sell them under the defendant's label and with the guaranty that the clothes would not shrink when they were "Cyana" finished. The defendant had advertised that the use of its product would make the goods so treated shrinkproof. After the issues were joined a motion for summary judgment was filed on the basis that there was no privity between the plaintiff and defendant. The court denied the motion, holding that substantial fact issues precluded summary judgment for defendant notwithstanding lack of privity between it and the garment dealer (plaintiff). The court said on page 12 of 11 N.Y.2d, page 367 of 226 N.Y.S.2d, page 402 of 181 N.E.2d:

> The world of merchandising is, in brief, no longer a world of direct contract; it is, rather, a world of advertising and, when representations expressed and disseminated in the mass communications media and on labels (attached to the goods themselves) prove false and the user or consumer is damaged by reason of his reliance on those representations, it is difficult to justify the manufacturer's denial of liability on the sole ground of the absence of technical privity. . . .

From the foregoing authorities it is clear that one who is injured as a result of the use of a defective chattel may look to the producer for redress. Privity is not a necessary element of such an action. Such liability is imposed by rule of law as pronounced by the highest judicial authority. The world of merchandising is no longer a world of direct contract. Goods are produced to be used by ultimate purchasers, and the representations of the manufacturer through and by the production thereof for use in the channels of commerce, at least, impliedly intend to induce their use in the justifiable belief that, when used as intended, there will be no danger of injury to others. . . .

There are, therefore, three methods by which one who suffers injury or damage in using a chattel delivered by the manufacturer or the vendor in a defective condition may proceed to seek redress against the manufacturer:

1. Where the ultimate purchaser stands *in a contractual relation* with the producer or vendor, an action (if justified by the facts) for breach of express or implied warranty may be maintained as provided by the Uniform Commercial Code.
2. By an action charging *negligence* in producing the chattel . . . *regardless of privity.*
3. By an action seeking to enforce *strict tort liability without privity.* . . .

In the case now before us, the plaintiff states facts which show that he had no contractual relations with the defendant and that he bases his claim on "strict tort liability." While the words "implied warranty" are used, they are intended to mean and describe the duty and representation of a producer of chattels to the buying public that his goods may be used for the purposes intended without danger to the purchaser from latent defects making their use dangerous to the user. The use of the word "warranty" is probably improper; however, the courts, in describing causes of action for strict tort liability in product cases, seem to have continued to use it for want of a better word, not intending it to mean anything more than the manufacturer putting his goods into the stream of commerce, thereby representing that they are of merchantable quality, unless a different intention is clearly expressed.

For the foregoing reasons, the judgment of the Court of Common Pleas sustaining the defendant's demurrer and entering judgment for the defendant is reversed, and the cause is remanded with instructions to overrule the demurrer and for further proceedings.

Judgment reversed.

Kuschy v. Norris

1964, (Conn.) 206 A.2d. 275

THIM, J. These allegations of fact are contained in the complaint: On January 3, 1964, the defendant, Harry L. Norris, Jr., purchased a used automobile from the defendant Cochrane Chevrolet Company, a dealer in new and used automobiles. On the same day, the daughter of Norris, while driving the above-mentioned automobile, collided with an automobile driven by John J. Kuschy. As a result of injuries sustained in the accident, Kuschy expired. The plaintiff, administratrix of Kuschy's estate, claims that the Norris automobile at the time of the accident contained a defective braking system. In the third count of the complaint, the plaintiff alleges that the defect was a breach of an expressed or implied warranty of merchantability and warranty of fitness made by Cochrane when the automobile was sold to Norris.

The pending demurrer attacks the legal sufficiency of the cause of action alleged against Cochrane in the third count on the sole ground that the plaintiff has no cause of action based on the theory of a breach of warranty. The issue is this: May an automobile motorist, injured on a public highway by another operator of a motor vehicle, maintain a cause of action for breach of warranty for injuries sustained against the person who sold the vehicle to the other party involved in the accident?

The complaint fails to disclose that the plaintiff's decedent was in privity of contract with Cochrane. Prior to the decision of *Hamon v. Digliani*, (148 Conn. 710, 174 A.2d. 294), the law in our state was clear that no action could be maintained for injuries arising out of an alleged breach of warranty without the essential element of privity of contract existing between the plaintiff and the defendant. In Hamon, the court held that lack of privity did not bar a cause of action based on a breach of warranty. However, the factual situation in that case is substantially different than the facts alleged in the plaintiff's complaint. In Hamon, the plaintiff was burned and injured when the contents of a nationally advertised product spilled on her. She sought recovery against the manufacturer of the product. In holding that the plaintiff had alleged a valid cause of action, our court said (p. 718, 174 A.2d. p. 207):

> The manufacturer or producer who puts a commodity for personal uses or consumption on the market in a sealed package or other container should be held to have impliedly warranted to the ultimate consumer that the product is reasonably fit for the purpose intended and that it does not contain any harmful and deleterious ingredient of which due and ample warning has not been given. . . . Where the manufacturer or producer makes representations in his advertisements or by the labels on his products as an inducement to the ultimate purchaser, the manufacturer or producer should be held to strict accountability to any person who buys the product in reliance on the representations and later suffers injury because the product fails to conform to them. . . . Lack of privity is not a bar to suit under these circumstances.

In the instant case, Cochrane sold a used automobile and, according to the allegations of the complaint, Cochrane made warranties to the purchaser at the time of the sale. It is these warranties that the plaintiff is attempting to enforce on behalf of a person who was not in privity with Cochrane at the time of the accident. To allow the warranty to run to members of the public such as persons who are in the path of harm from a defective automobile, the court would have to conclude that privity should be entirely disregarded.

Extending the benefits of an implied warranty to persons who, in the reasonable contemplation of the parties to the warranty, might be expected to be a user of the property has developed under both our case law and our statutory law. Although such cases as *Henningsen v. Bloomfield Motors, Inc.* (32 N.J. 358, 161 A.2d. 69, 75 A.L.R.2d 1), *Hamon v. Digliana, supra,* and *Connolly v. Hagi* (24 Conn. Sup. 198, 188 A.2d 884) have extended the right of other persons to claim under a warranty, no reported cases can be found which extend the benefits to members of the public. The Connolly case extended the warranty to all those who could reasonably be expected to use, occupy or service the operation of the chattel. The activity of the decedent at the time of the accident did not bring him within the purview of the extension of the rule in the Henningsen case or even with the more liberal rule followed in the Connolly case. When the contract of sale in the instant case was entered into, Kuschy was not a person who, in the contemplation of the parties to the contract, might be expected to use, occupy or service the used automobiles.

Sound reasons justified modification of the strict rule of privity in such cases as *Hamon v. Digliani, supra, Henningsen v. Bloomfield Motors, Inc., supra,* and *Connolly v. Hagi.* However, the rule should not be extended to allow a member of the public to recover from a used-car dealer on a breach of warranty claim under the allegations as alleged in the third count of the pending complaint.

For the aforesaid reasons, the demurrer is sustained.

Greeno v. Clark Equipment Company

1965 237 F.Supp. 427

The plaintiff was injured when a fork lift truck which he was operating while working for his employer failed to operate properly due to an alleged defect. He brought an action for damages against the manufacturer of the truck which had been leased by his employer from an equipment handling company. He claimed to be entitled to relief on the basis of strict liability of a manufacturer. The defendant moved to dismiss the complaint.

ESCHBACH, J. This opinion will consider the theory of strict liability only in the context of products liability. When so confined, its least ambiguous definition appears in Restatement (Second), Torts 402A (Approved May 1964), set out as follows:

> 402A. Special Liability of Seller of Product for Physical Harm to User or Consumer.
> (1) One who sells any product in a defective condition unreasonably dangerous to the user or consumer or to his property, is subject to liability for physical harm thereby caused to the ultimate user or consumer, or to his property, if
>   (a) the seller is engaged in the business of selling such a product, and
>   (b) it is expected to and does reach the user or consumer without substantial change in the condition in which it is sold.
> (2) The rule stated in Subsection (1) applies although
>   (a) the seller has exercised all possible care in the preparation and sale of his product, and
>   (b) the user or consumer has not bought the product from or entered into any contractual relation with the seller.

Without attempting an exhaustive explanation, it may fairly be said that the liability which this section would impose is hardly more than what exists under implied warranty when stripped of the contract doctrines of privity, disclaimer, requirements of notice of defect, and limitation through inconsistencies with express warranties. . . . The conditions of liability which may not be self-evident in the above text are a "defective condition" at the time the product leaves the seller's control and which causes harm to a user or consumer. A "defective condition" is a condition not contemplated by the consumer/user and which is "unreasonably dangerous" to him or his property, that is, more dangerous than would be contemplated by the ordinary consumer/user with the ordinary knowledge of the community as to its characteristics and uses. (Restatement, *supra,* comment at 351-52). An axe is not unreasonably dangerous because, as in negligence law, users would contemplate the obvious dangers involved. But a farm combine with a weak lid over the auger would constitute an unreasonable danger because such a danger is beyond the contemplation of ordinary users. The same basis applies in Indiana negligence law for the determination of whether a latent defect exists. *J. I. Case Co. v. Sandefur,* (197 N.E.2d 519 (Ind. 1964)). The difference between strict liability and the law of Sandefur is that in the former the care or lack of care of the manufacturer in causing a defect is irrelevant. But the plaintiff-user's conduct is very much in question under the doctrine of strict liability. Recovery in strict liability is not conditioned on privity of contract, or reliance or notice to the seller of a defect, and the seller cannot disclaim or by contract alter a duty which the law would impose upon him. Nor can inconsistent express warranties dilute the seller's duty to refrain from injecting into the stream of commerce goods in a "defective condition."

It is generally recognized that implied warranty is more properly a matter of public policy beyond the power of the seller to alter unilaterally with disclaimers and inconsistent express warranties. . . . Where there is implied in law a certain duty to persons not in contract privity, it seems preposterous that the seller should escape that duty by inserting into a non-contractual relationship a contractual disclaimer of which the remote injured person would be unaware. Even as between parties to a contract, where the law would imply in a sale the reasonable fitness of the product for ordinary purposes, it seems unconscionable that the seller should by disclaimers avoid the duty of selling merchantable products or shift the risk of defect, unless the total circumstances of the transaction indicate the buyer's awareness of defects or acceptance of risk. This warranty imposed by law, irrespective of privity and based on public policy is more aptly called "strict liability." . . .

As the Indiana courts have escaped the rigors of privity in negligence through the doctrine of "imminently dangerous," other courts have invoked various exceptions which in time have devoured the requirement of privity in both negligence and implied warranty. Some cases, . . . hold that privity is not required in a products liability case based on implied warranty, while others reach the same result by expanding the old common law concept of privity. . . . Food and beverages are well known products where privity is no longer required. . . . In the recent case of *Putman v. Erie City Manufacturing Co., supra,* the Court of Appeals for the Fifth Circuit extended to all defective products unreasonably dangerous to the user the reasoning of Decker & Sons, Inc. v. Capps, . . . The latter was an implied warranty food case which dispensed with privity on the grounds that implied warranty arises from public policy rather than contract and that the rights and duties it creates cannot be limited to the contracting parties. *Henningsen v. Bloomfield Motors, Inc., supra,* did likewise, stating at p. 379 of 32 N.J., at p. 80 of 161 A.2d, at p. 17 of 75 A.L.R.2d,

> The limitations of privity in contracts for the sale of goods developed their place in the law when marketing conditions were simple, when maker and buyer frequently met face to face on an equal bargaining plane and when many of the products were relatively uncomplicated and conducive to inspection by a buyer competent to evaluate their quality. See Freezer, "Manufacturer's Liability for Injuries Caused By His Products," (37 Mich.L.Rev.

1 (1963)). With the advent of mass marketing, the manufacturer became remote from the purchaser, sales were accomplished through intermediaries, and the demand for the product was created by advertising media. In such an economy it became obvious that the consumer was the person being cultivated. Manifestly, the connotation of "consumer" was broader than that of "buyer." He signified such a person who, in the reasonable contemplation of the parties to the sale, might be expected to use the product. Thus, where the commodities sold are such that if defectively manufactured they will be dangerous to life or limb, then society's interests can only be protected by eliminating the requirement of privity between the maker and his dealers and the reasonably expected ultimate consumer.

The reasoning of *Henningsen,* of *Spence v. Three Rivers Builders & Mason Supply, Inc.,* (353 Mich. 120, 90 N.W.2d 873 (1958)), and of *Putman, supra,* and the many other cases striking down the requirement of privity in implied warranty seems eminently sound. As Judge Wisdom so aptly recognized in *Putman, supra,* at 919 of 338 F.2d, "Since 1958, almost every court which has considered the question has expanded the doctrine of strict liability to cover all defective products, regardless of lack of proof of negligence." (See footnotes 18 and 19). Various means have been applied to reach this result without naming the rule "strict liability" and without the furor which that label has created.

The direction of the law is clear. Again drawing on the language of and authorities cited by Judge Wisdom in *Putman, supra,* at 919-920 of 338 F.2d, we find that "Part of the impetus has come from an almost unanimous call from the authorities in the field of torts." If the Restatement correctly states the conditions of recovery now in practice, let those elements have a fresh name and abandon the old entanglements of "warranty."

Already the Restatement, *supra,* is being followed and shaped. *(Putman, supra).* The recent case of *Delaney v. Towmotor Corp.,* (339 F.2d. 4, 2d Cir., December 3, 1964), held the Restatement word "sells" is merely descriptive and that the product need not be sold, if it has been placed "in the stream of commerce by other means." The operator of a "demonstrator" model lift truck was injured when a defective overhead guard collapsed; facts somewhat similar to those at bar. The defendant manufacturer in the instant case is alleged to have sold the fork lift truck in question and the plaintiff's employer is alleged to have leased the equipment from a company other than the manufacturer. Thus, the Delaney issue is not before this court. It could not seriously be contended that the lease would prevent the instant plaintiff from being a consumer or user.

The question is now squarely before this court and must be decided. It is perhaps fortuitous that the Indiana Supreme Court has not yet passed on this issue, but doubtlessly that forward-looking court would embrace the Restatement (Second), Torts 402A, and the many recent cases and authors who have done likewise, as eminently just and as the law of Indiana today.

Accordingly, defendant's motion to dismiss . . . is hereby denied.

Sundet v. Olin Matheson Chemical Corp.

1966, (Neb.) 139 N.W.2d 368

SMITH, J.   While plaintiff was firing his rifle which contained in its chamber a cartridge allegedly manufactured by defendant, an explosion of the rifle injured him. This action for breach of warranty was dismissed by the district court on motion of defendant at the close of plaintiff's evidence-in-chief. We affirm the judgment on the ground of insufficient evidence that any defective condition of the cartridge existed at the time the cartridge case left defendant's control.

Shortly before the accident plaintiff purchased from a retailer twenty .264-caliber cartridges in an unsealed box. Both the box and the rims of the cartridge cases indicated manufacture by defendant. The explosion occurred on April 21, 1961, while the first cartridge was being used.

Plaintiff may have purchased cartridges with cases which someone else had reloaded. There were grayish discolorations on several cases and plier or vise marks on two bullets. Plaintiff, who repaired firearms and sold equipment for reloading cartridge cases, testified that in the reloading process the neck of a case is crimped against a bullet. Defendant manufactured a product for the box on September 8, 1960, but it knew neither the date of shipment nor the place of delivery. The retailer did not testify. The condition of the product at the time it left defendant's control or the treatment which the product received up to the time of purchase by plaintiff is unknown.

If there was a defect in the cartridge, the defect must be found from these facts and a stipulation excluding the parts and assembly of plaintiff's rifle from the legal cause of injury; but it is unnecessary for us to consider the sufficiency of the evidence on this point.

In a products liability case against a manufacturer the plaintiff must show that the offending condition existed when the product left defendant's control.

We find no basis for a reasonable inference that defendant manufactured these cartridges. The unsealed box contained earmarks of reloaded cases, and without additional evidence a trier of the facts cannot infer reasonably that defendant was in the business of reloading spent cases. Even if we assume that plaintiff purchased cartridges with unused cases, a reasonable conclusion cannot be drawn that any defect at the time of the retail sale represented a preexistent condition of defendant's making. The evidence is insufficient to carry the issue of warranty to a jury, and the district court correctly dismissed the action.

The judgment is affirmed.

Foley v. Weaver Drugs, Inc.

1965, (Fla.) 177 So.2d 221

ROBERTS, J.   The record shows that, on October 17, 1959, James S. Foley purchased from Weaver Drugs, Inc., the respondent here, at one of its retail stores, a bottle of Revlon reducing pills, better known as "Thin Down," for use by his wife, Rose M. Foley. The pills were packed in a glass bottle which closed with a screw-on top. The day after the purchase Mrs. Foley attempted to open the bottle by unscrewing the top when the bottle broke, fragmented, and one piece thereof lacerated her right wrist.

Predicated upon these facts the Foleys instituted an action against Revlon, Inc., the manufacturer, *and Weaver Drugs, Inc., the retail-seller,* [Emphasis supplied] setting forth the facts and their respective damages, and alleging causes of action for negligence and for breach of implied warranty of fitness and merchantability against each defendant.

Weaver Drugs, Inc., moved to dismiss and strike from the complaint every theory of action against it. . . . At the pre-trial conference the court struck all allegations relating to implied warranty as against the defendant Weaver Drugs, Inc., the effect of which was to hold that neither of the plaintiffs had a cause of action against the retailer based on an implied warranty.

A motion for summary judgment filed by the defendant Revlon, Inc., was denied.

On appeal by plaintiffs to the District Court of Appeal, Third District, the court affirmed, without opinion, the actions of the trial court with respect to the defendant Weaver Drugs, Inc., thereby holding, in effect, that neither of the plaintiffs had a cause of action against the defendant retailer for breach of an implied warranty of fitness and merchantability, and also holding, in effect, that they were not entitled to damages on the theory of negligence; but the action of the appellate court in this respect is not complained of in the instant proceeding.

As noted above, the plaintiffs have invoked this court's "conflict jurisdiction" to review the adverse decision of the appellate court, alleging that it directly conflicts with a decision of the District Court of Appeal, Second District, in *Canada Dry Bottling Co. of Florida, Inc. v. Shaw,* (Fla.App.1960, 118 So.2d 840). In that case the injured party purchased a bottle of Canada Dry soda from a retail grocer, Food Fair, and took it home. Shortly thereafter, while attempting to open the bottle on a wall opener in the usual manner, it broke and injured her hand. She filed suit against both the bottler, Canada Dry, and the retailer, Food Fair, on the theory of breach of implied warranty of fitness. A jury verdict and judgment against both defendants was appealed and was affirmed by the appellate court. The rationale of the appellate court's decision was that the strict liability of the retailer for breach of an implied warranty of wholesomeness and fitness applicable to products sold for human consumption, sold by him should be extended to include the bottle, as well as its contents, in a case of this kind. . . .

The court said that it would not, at that time, extend the doctrine of implied warranty to all containers of food, but that "in this case the bottle and its contents are so closely related that it is difficult—if not impossible—to draw a distinction."

It is clear that the decision in the instant case, holding that the plaintiffs had no cause of action against the retailer for breach of an implied warranty of fitness and merchantability, is in direct conflict with the Canada Dry case, insofar as the plaintiff husband, who was in privity with the retailer, is concerned. Thus, we have jurisdiction to determine the question of the implied warranty liability, in general, of a retail-seller of a product sold in a container for injury caused by the container.

This exact question has not heretofore been presented to this court. . . . other than in the case of foodstuffs, we know of no decision of this court imposing liability upon a retail seller of a product upon the theory of implied warranty, except under established commonlaw principles. . . .

The rationale of our decisions extending to the retail-seller of food products the absolute liability imposed upon the manufacturer of such products, upon the theory of an implied warranty of fitness and wholesomeness, is that neither the retail-purchaser nor the retail-seller can discover that a particular item of food enclosed in a sealed container is defective; that the retail-seller is in a superior position to that of the consumer since he is experienced in buying from the manufacturers, is acquainted with the products and the manufacturers and relies upon the reputation of the manufacturers in stocking such food items; so that, in this area of wholesome food which is of vital concern to the public, the retailer should be held to the same liability as the manufacturer as a matter of public policy. (See *Sencer v. Carl's Market, supra,* 45 So.2d 671). It was pointed out, in a specially concurring opinion, that in many cases the manufacturer of a food product was located in a foreign country beyond the reach of the consumer, that the retailer has a right of indemnity against the manufacturer if compelled to pay damages to a consumer because of the unwholesomeness of the food product, and the retailer "can avoid placing himself in a position wherein he could not, in turn, sue the manufacturer by electing to purchase only from responsible manufacturers within the jurisdiction of the courts in which he might enter suit." (45 So.2d at p. 673).

Assuming for the purpose of this argument that the reducing pills, being for human consumption, would fall within the same category as foodstuffs, insofar as the retailer's liability upon an implied warranty is concerned, the question then becomes: Does public policy dictate that the retailer be held to the same liability for the merchantability and fitness of the container of food products as is imposed upon him for the food products themselves? We confess that we can see no more reason for holding the retailer liable for a defect in a container of foodstuffs (when such defect is unrelated to and has no deleterious effect upon the food product itself) than for a defect in or the non-merchantability of the container of other non-food products which he sells at retail. The public interest in having a non-defective, merchantable container would seem to be the same, regardless of whether it encloses a food product or any other product.

We are not persuaded that considerations of public policy require us to extend to food containers the "implied warranty" liability of retailers as to the food contained theerin; on the contrary, we are of the opinion that it would be unreasonably burdensome to extend liability in this respect. . . .

Accordingly, the Third District Court of Appeal was eminently correct in affirming the judgment of the trial court in the instant case insofar as it could be construed as holding that the complaint failed to state a cause of action, upon the theory of breach of implied warranty, against the defendant retailer, Weaver Drugs, Inc. This being so, it is unnecessary to decide whether the plaintiff-wife's suit would have been barred, had a cause of action existed, because of her lack of privity with the defendant, Weaver Drugs, Inc.

Our examination of the record in this cause reflected prima facie jurisdiction because of the alleged conflict with the decision of another district court of appeal, in *Canada Dry Bottling Co. of Florida v. Shaw, supra,* (118 So.2d 840). For the reasons stated, the decision of the appellate court in the Canada Dry case is disapproved, that of the appellate court in the instant case is approved, so the decision under review will not be disturbed and the writ is discharged.

It is so ordered.

Associated Hardware Supply Co. v. Big Wheel Distributing Co.

1965 236 F.Supp. 879

DUMBAULD, J. Plaintiff creditor [Associated Hardware Supply Co.] seeks to recover $40,185.62 as the balance of an open unpaid account for merchandise sold and delivered, together with interest.

Defendant debtor [Big Wheel Distributing Co.] pleaded fraud and counterclaimed, alleging overpayment, and failure of plaintiff to furnish certain promotional assistance in merchandising the goods for profitable resale.

After extensive *discovery proceedings,* plaintiff on November 5, 1964 filed a motion to dismiss the counterclaim, for judgment on the pleadings and for summary judgment for the amount of the debt and interest. . . .

When the voluminous verbiage with which this case has been surrounded is penetrated and disentangled, the issue is seen to be one of price. Defendant contends that the goods were to be sold at cost plus 10 per cent, whereas plaintiff billed them at dealers' catalogue price (representing a 20 per cent mark-up) less 11 per cent. Defendant's counterclaim is based upon a recomputation at defendant's assumed price of all past transactions between the parties, and much of defendant's voluminous discovery aims to determine plaintiff's costs, which enter into the price as defendant would compute it. Defendant's allegations of fraud and misrepresentation are based on the lack of identity, allegedly asserted by plaintiff, between prices computed under plaintiff's method and defendant's method.

What was the contract between the parties, as shown by the undisputed facts in the record?

Plaintiff in a letter of February 9, 1962 (Ex. A. to Complaint) made an offer, subject to a volume of $5,000 per week at catalogue price less 11 per cent discount. Defendant being a new corporate operation, personal liability of Mr. Irving Molever was insisted upon in the letter, together with a request for acknowledgement and signature. Apparently Molever did not sign the letter, but considered himself personally liable and later secured a release from such liability after defendant established a satisfactory payment history.

However, dealings between the parties went ahead. Defendant ordered, received, retained, and paid for a large volume of merchandise, billed at catalogue price less 11 per cent discount.

As calculated in plaintiff's brief, defendant's purchases from February 1962 through May 1964 aggregated $860,000. This figure apparently includes the unpaid amount of $40,185.62, to collect which the present suit was brought. Over $800,000 of merchandise was thus bought and paid for under billings computed under plaintiff's method.

What effect did these dealings of the parties have upon their legal rights, in the light of the Uniform Commercial Code?

We conclude as a matter of law, after consideration of numerous provisions of the Code, that there was a contract between the parties, and that the price was governed by plaintiff's formula.

The alleged misrepresentation or fraud on plaintiff's part we are unable to consider as anything more than normal commercial "puffing" which could not have misled an astute trader such as defendant's negotiator, Mr. Molever. We conclude that defendant simply later decided that its bargain was not a good one and decided not to pay because the agreed price was too high.

Obviously, to say that cost plus 10 per cent is the same as catalogue price less 11 per cent is to indulge in approximation, and the mathematical relationships were as obvious to defendant as to plaintiff. We compute the price on defendant's theory as 1.1 times plaintiff's costs, whereas under plaintiff's system the price would be 1.068 times plaintiff's costs. Whether these are to be treated as substantially identical is obviously a matter of commercial judgment or opinion, and a contract duly negotiated on an assumption that the two methods are to be considered as equivalent can not be set aside for "fraud."

Turning to the Code provisions involved, we begin with 12A P.S. 1-103 that "Unless displaced by the particular provisions of this Act, the principles of law and equity, including . . . the law relative to . . . fraud, misrepresentation, duress, coercion, mistake . . . or other validating or invalidating cause shall supplement its provisions." This section merely invites us to look to more specific provisions of the Code to determine whether a contract arose between the parties, and what its terms were.

Section 1-201(3) defines "Agreement" as "the bargain in fact as found in the language of the parties or in course of dealing or usage of trade or course of performance or by implication from other circumstances."

Section 1-201(11) defines "Contract" as "the total obligation in law which results from parties' agreement as affected by this Act and any other applicable rules of law."

Section 1-205(1) says: "A course of dealing is a sequence of previous conduct between the parties to a particular transaction which is in fact fairly to be regarded as establishing a common basis of understanding for interpreting their words and conduct."

Section 1-205(3) provides: "The parties to a contract are bound by any course of dealing between them."

Section 1-205(4)(a) declares that "Unless contrary to a mandatory rule of this Act: (a) A course of dealing . . . gives particular meaning to and supplements or qualifies terms of the agreement."

Section 2-104(1) and (3) defines "merchants" and "between merchants," and we consider both parties to this litigation as knowledgeable merchants.

Section 2-106(2) defines "goods or conduct including any part of a performance" as "conforming" when in accordance with the obligations under the contract.

Section 2-201(1) reads: "Except as otherwise provided in this section a contract for the sale of goods for the price of $500 or more is not enforceable by way of action or defense unless there is some writing sufficient to indicate that a contract for sale has been made between the parties and signed by the party against whom enforcement is sought."

Section 2-201(2) provides that: "Between merchants if within a reasonable time a writing in confirmation of the contract and sufficient against the sender is received and the party receiving it has reason to know its contents, it satisfies the requirements of subsection (1) against such party unless written notice of objection to its contents is given within ten days after it is received."

Section 2-201(3)(c) provides: "A contract which does not satisfy the requirements of subsection (1) but which is valid in other respects is enforceable (c) with respect to goods for which payment has been made and accepted or which have been received and accepted."

Section 2-202(a) provides that a writing "may be explained or supplemented . . . by course of dealing."

Section 2-204(1) says: "A contract for sale of goods may be made in any manner sufficient to show agreement."

Section 2-204(2) provides that: "Conduct by both parties which recognizes the existence of a contract is sufficient to establish a contract for sale even though the moment of its making cannot be determined."

Section 2-204(3) provides: "Even though one or more terms are left open a contract for sale does not fail for indefiniteness if the parties have intended to make a contract and there is a reasonably certain basis for giving an appropriate remedy."

Section 2-206(1) says: "Unless the contrary is unambiguously indicated by the language or circumstances (a) an offer to make a contract shall be construed as inviting acceptance in any manner and by any medium reasonable in the circumstances."

Section 2-206(3) provides that "The beginning of a requested performance can be a reasonable mode of acceptance."

Section 2-208 provides: "Where the contract for sale involves repeated occasions for performance by either party with knowledge of the nature of the performance and opportunity for objection by the other, any course of performance accepted without objection shall be relevant to determine the meaning of the agreement or to show a waiver or modification of any term inconsistent with such course of performance."

Review of the foregoing Code provisions shows that the Code attaches great weight to the course of dealing of the parties, even in the absence of a written agreement with respect to every term of the contract. Weighing in the light of the Code the conduct of the parties here, it seems clear that the mode of calculating price set forth in plaintiff's letter of February 9, 1962, although not accepted formally by signature of a copy, was adhered to by both parties during an extensive course of dealing, during which defendant received, accepted, and paid for over $800,000 worth of merchandise. This course of dealing must be held applicable and governing with respect to the remaining merchandise which has been received and accepted but not paid for. Judgment should be rendered for plaintiff for the amount due.

There is no genuine dispute of fact with regard to any legally relevant circumstance.

The disputed facts concerning which defendant by discovery and otherwise seeks to inquire extensively relate to matters which are not pertinent, *since the law gives effect to the contract recognized by the parties in their course of dealing, regardless of other provisions which the parties might have adopted during their negotiations if they had seen fit to do so.*

It is ordered, adjudged and finally determined that plaintiff's motion to dismiss defendant's counterclaim be and the same hereby is granted, and that said counterclaim be and the same hereby is dismissed, and that judgment be and it hereby is entered in favor of plaintiff, Associated Hardware Supply Co., a corporation, and against defendant, The Big Wheel Distributing Company, a corporation, in the amount of $40,185.62, together with interest and costs.

Williams v. Walker-Thomas Furniture Company

(1965) 350 F.2d 445

Plaintiff, Walker-Thomas Furniture Company operated a retail furniture store in the District of Columbia. During the period from 1957 to 1962 the defendant purchased a number of household items from Walker-Thomas, for which payment was to be made in installments. The terms of each purchase were contained in a printed form contract which set forth the value of the purchased item and purported to lease the item to defendant for a stipulated monthly rent payment. The title would remain in Walker-Thomas until the total of all the monthly payments made equaled the stated value of the item, at which time purchaser could take title. In the event of a default in the payment of any monthly installment, Walker-Thomas could repossess the item.

The contract further provided that

the amount of each periodical installment payment to be made by (purchaser) to the Company under this present lease shall be inclusive of and not in addition to the amount of each installment payment to be made by (purchaser) under such prior leases, bills or accounts; *and all payments now and hereafter made by (purchaser) shall be credited pro rata on all outstanding leases, bills and accounts due the Company by (purchaser) at the time each such payment is made.*

The effect of this provision was to keep a balance due on every item purchased until the balance due on all items, whenever purchased, was liquidated. As a result, the debt incurred at the time of purchase of each item was secured by the right to repossess all the items previously purchased by the same purchaser, and each new item purchased automatically became subject to a security interest arising out of the previous dealings.

On April 17, 1962, Williams bought a stereo set of stated value of $514.95. She defaulted shortly thereafter, and plaintiff sought to replevy all the items purchased since December, 1957. (At the time of this purchase her account showed a balance of $164 still owing from her prior purchases. The total of all the purchases made over the years in question came to $1,800. The total payments amounted to $1,400.) The Court of General Sessions granted judgment for plaintiff. The District of Columbia Court of Appeals affirmed, and an appeal was taken to the Court of Appeals.

WRIGHT, J. . . .

Appellant's principal contention, rejected by both the trial and the appellate courts below, is that these contracts, or at least some of them, are unconscionable and, hence, not enforceable. In its opinion . . . the District of Columbia Court of Appeals explained its rejection of this contention as follows:

> Appellant's second argument presents a more serious question. The record reveals that prior to the last purchase appellant had reduced the balance in her account to $164. The last purchase, a stereo set, raised the balance due to $678. Significantly, at the time of this and the preceding purchases, appellee was aware of appellant's financial position. The reverse side of the stereo contract listed the name of appellant's social worker and her $218 monthly stipend from the government. Nevertheless, with full knowledge that appellant had to feed, clothe and support both herself and seven children on this amount, appellee sold her a $514 stereo set.
>
> We cannot condemn too strongly appellee's conduct. It raises serious questions of sharp practice and irresponsible business dealings. A review of the legislation in the District of Columbia affecting retail sales and the pertinent decisions of the highest court in this jurisdiction disclose, however, no ground upon which this court can declare the contracts in question contrary to public policy. . .

We do not agree that the court lacked the power to refuse enforcement to contracts found to be unconscionable. In other jurisdictions, it has been held as a matter of common law that unconscionable contracts are not enforceable. While no decision of this court so holding has been found, the notion that an unconscionable bargain should not be given full enforcement is by no means novel. In Scott v. United States . . . the Supreme Court stated:

> . . . If a contract be unreasonable and unconscionable, but not void for fraud, a court of law will give to the party who sues for its breach damages, not according to its letter, but only such as he is equitably entitled to. . . .

Since we have never adopted or rejected such a rule, the question here presented is actually one of first impression.

Congress has recently enacted the Uniform Commercial Code, which specifically provides that the court may refuse to enforce a contract which it finds to be unconscionable at the time it was made. (28 D.C. Code 2-302). . . . The enactment of this section, which occurred subsequent to the contracts here in suit, does not mean that the common law of the District of Columbia was otherwise at the time of enactment, nor does it preclude the court from adopting a similar rule in the exercise of its powers to develop the common law for the District of Columbia. In fact, in view of the absence of prior authority on the point, we consider the congressional adoption of 2-302 persuasive authority for following the rationale of the cases from which the section is explicitly derived. (See Comment, 2-302, Uniform Commercial Code (1962). Compare Note, 45 Va.L.Rev. 583, 590 (1959), where it is predicted that the rule of 2-302 will be followed by analogy in cases which involve contracts not specifically covered by the section.) Accordingly; we hold that where the element of unconscionability is present at the time a contract is made, the contract should not be enforced.

Unconscionability has generally been recognized to include an absence of meaningful choice on the part of one of the parties together with contract terms which are unreasonably favorable to the other party. Whether a meaningful choice is present in a particular case can only be determined by consideration of all the circumstances surrounding the transaction. In many cases the meaningfulness of the choice is negated by a gross inequality of bargaining power. The manner in which the contract was entered is also relevant to this consideration. Did each party to the contract, considering his obvious education or lack of it, have a reasonable opportunity to understand the terms of the contract, or were the important terms hidden in a maze of fine print and minimized by deceptive sales practices? Ordinarily, one who signs an agreement without full knowledge of its terms might be held to assume the risk that he has entered a one-sided bargain. But when a party of little bargaining power, and hence little real choice, signs a commercially unreasonable contract with little or no knowledge of its terms, it is hardly likely that his consent, or even an objective manifestation of his consent, was ever given to all the terms. In such a case the usual rule that the terms of the agreement are not to be questioned should be abandoned and the court should consider whether the terms of the contract are so unfair that enforcement should be withheld.

In determining reasonableness or fairness, the primary concern must be with the terms of the contract considered in light of the circumstances existing when the contract was made. The test is not simple, nor can it be mechanically applied. The terms are to be considered "in the light of the general commercial background and the commercial needs of the particular trade or case." (Comment, Uniform Commercial Code 2-307.) Corbin suggests the test as being whether the terms are "so extreme as to appear unconscionable according to the mores and business practices of the time and place. . . ." We think this formulation correctly states the test to be applied in those cases where no meaningful choice was exercised upon entering the contract.

Because the trial court and the appellate court did not feel that enforcement could be refused, no findings were made on the possible unconscionability of the contracts in these cases. Since the record is not sufficient for our deciding the issue as a matter of law, the cases must be remanded to the trial court for further proceedings.

So ordered.

Independent News Co. v. Williams
1961, 293 F.2d 510

McLaughlin, C. J.   Can a second-hand periodical dealer who purchases cover-removed comics from waste paper dealers be enjoined . . . from marketing them as reading material? . . . Plaintiff, Independent News Co., Inc., is the distributor of the comics. . . . The defendant, Harry Williams, is a Philadelphia distributor of second-hand books and magazines.

The critical facts involve the distribution system used in marketing the comics. The distributor, Independent, pursuant to a written contract, sells the comics to the wholesaler. The comics are to be offered for sale during a period specified by the publisher. The wholesaler then sells them to the various retail outlets with the same restriction. At the end of the sales period, the wholesaler reacquires from the retail outlets all unsold comics and gives the retailer full credit. In turn, the wholesaler is entitled to full credit from Independent. However, instead of returning the entire comic, the agreement provides that unless otherwise directed, the wholesaler need only return the covers. As to the remaining portion of the comic, the wholesaler is obligated to, ". . . destroy or mutilate the remaining portions so as to render them unsalable as publications.". . .

[Here the court points out that the contract required that the destroyed or mutilated copies were to be disposed of or sold only as waste paper, and that the wholesaler should obtain a written agreement from a purchaser of such copies that he would use them only for waste, and not resell them. The defendant purchased cover-removed comics from waste paper dealers and resold them. No written commitment not to resell was obtained from the waste paper dealers, and it appeared that the defendant had no knowledge that the waste paper dealers were required to sell the coverless comics as wastepaper only. This action is brought to enjoin defendants from selling these comics as reading material.]

. . . Under the Uniform Commercial Code, adopted in Pennsylvania, Section 2-403 (2), . . . provides "(2) Any entrusting of possession of goods to a merchant who deals in goods of that kind gives him power to transfer all rights of the entruster to a buyer in ordinary course of business."

That section of the Code has broadened the protection of buyers in the ordinary course of business and has changed prior Pennsylvania law. . . . In the case at bar, plaintiffs ". . . conceded that plaintiffs have 'entrusted' the magazines in question to the Wholesaler-Agent." However, they dispute the applicability of Section 2-403 (2) stating: "(a) Wholesaler-Agent is not a 'merchant who deals in goods of that kind' . . . and "(b) neither the waste paper house nor the defendant is a 'buyer in the ordinary course of business' as defined by the Code."

The first assertion seeks to distinguish between the Wholesaler ". . . selling new publications prior to or during the publication period," and the wholesaler selling the cover-removed magazines. The argument is specious. The wholesaler deals in comics, and the fact that the covers are present or not is irrelevant. His regular business is dealing with comics and as such he is a "merchant who deals in goods of that kind."

The interrelated second contention, namely, that neither the waste paper dealer nor the defendant are buyers in the ordinary course of business is equally without merit. . . . Section 1-201 (9) of the Code, . . . provides: "(9) 'Buyer in ordinary course of business' means a person who in good faith and without knowledge that the sale to him is in violation of the ownership rights or security interest of a third party in the goods buys in ordinary course from a person in the business of selling goods of that kind. . . ."

. . . There is no evidence in the record . . . that shows that the waste paper dealers had any notice of any restriction whatsoever on the cover-removed comics purchased from the wholesaler. It follows, that when the wholesaler sold these coverless comics to the waste paper dealer, the waste paper dealer, under Section 2-403 (2) of the Code, obtained the totality of property rights in the comics, which included the right to use or sell them as reading material. . . .

The judgment of the district court will be affirmed.

CHAPTER 18
REVIEW QUESTIONS AND PROBLEMS

1. *A* sold *B* a car which had been mortgaged to *X* Finance Co. *B* was not aware of the mortgage. The contract contained a clause which excluded all warranties. If *X* Finance Company repossesses the car, does *B* have any rights against *A*?

2. *A* purchased diving equipment from *B*. He told *B* that he intended to dive to depths of 200 feet. *B* selected the gear from his stock. *A* suffered from the "bends" when he dove to that depth. Can *A* recover damages from *B*?

3. *A* sold *B* a gasoline-driven garden tractor. While mowing the lawn *C*, *B*'s employee, was injured when the throttle stuck and the tractor

overturned. Can *C* recover from *B* on the basis of a breach of warranty?

4. *A* of Eugene, Oregon, entered into a contract to purchase magnesium flares from *B*, whose plant is in Elgin, Illinois. The contract calls for delivery F.O.B. Eugene. While the flares were enroute, a bolt of lightning struck the car and the flares were destroyed. Who must bear the loss?

5. *A* received beauty treatments at *B*'s Beauty Parlor. The treatments consisted of the application of products manufactured by *X* Co. The treatments caused *A*'s hair to fall out and she sued both *B* and *X* Co. for breach of warranty. Should *A* win the lawsuit?

6. *A* delivered record racks and phonograph records to *B*, a music store owner, on consignment. Can *B*'s creditors reach these items? Can *A* protect himself from claims of *B*'s creditors?

7. *A* purchased a refrigerator from *B*, a dealer. The purchase order provided in large type: "All orders accepted are subject to the following." There followed in small type a disclaimer of all warranties. If the refrigerator fails to maintain a proper temperature, can *A* recover damages from *B*?

8. *P* was employed by *X* Manufacturing Co. He was injured when steel roof joists, which had been manufactured by *D* Co., gave way and the roof collapsed on him. Does *P* have a cause of action against *D* Co.?

9. *A*, a child, was injured when a "Hot Shot" vaporizer spurted boiling water on him. The vaporizer had been purchased from *X* Pharmacy by *A*'s aunt, who lived next door. Does *A* have a cause of action against *X* Pharmacy? Against the manufacturer of the vaporizer?

10. *A* purchased cherries from *B* Fruit Co. *B* had previously sent *A* a sizing card containing holes cut in perfect circles. The circles bore numbers which denoted size categories used by the cherry industry. The contract called for "Row 12" cherries. The cherries delivered were not all of the exact size of the Row 12 hole. Must *A* accept the cherries?

11. *P* is a wholesale distributor of beer and has for many years purchased beer from *D* Brewery. In 1965 *P* and *D* entered into an oral agreement wherein *D* contracted to sell beer to *P* for cash at an agreed price schedule. No period of time was stipulated. In 1966 *D* arbitrarily terminated the contract. *P* brought action for specific performance of the contract. The court ruled that *P* had not stated a cause of action against *D*. Was this ruling correct?

12. *A*, in Omaha, ordered a carload of lumber from *B* in Portland. The terms were C.I.F. Omaha. *B* shipped the lumber and forwarded the bill of lading and other documents to *A*. *A* contends that he does not have to pay until the lumber is unloaded in Omaha. Is this correct?

chapter 19

Sales: Performance and Breach: Remedies: Documents of Title: Bulk Sales

3-14 In General. The preceding chapter dealt with matters relative to the contract between the buyer and the seller; the general obligations of the parties; and rights of third parties. In this chapter the general context is the performance of the contract and breaches by either party. It is to be stressed that the parties can provide for various contingencies in their contract and that such provisions will in general be controlling. The ultimate expectation of both the buyer and the seller is that the contract will be duly performed and that all rights in the goods will pass from the seller to the buyer.

3-15 Title to Goods: Risk of Loss. The concept of "title" to goods is somewhat nebulous and it frequently does not enter into the framework of thinking of business people. Most people who engage in sales transactions focus their attention upon the results to be obtained rather than the legal theories which lead to these results. As a consequence, Article 2–Sales does not emphasize title. It provides, rather, that in the main the rights, obligations, and remedies of the seller, the buyer, purchasers from either or other third parties, are determined without reference to the location of title.[1] [C1] Although "title" is not emphasized, the Code does state that a sale consists "in the passing of *title* from the seller to the

[1] *Park County Implement Co. v. Craig*, page 406.

[C1] *U.C.C.* 2-401.

buyer for a price," [C2] and since title does have some significance, the Code makes provisions relating to its passage. The Code specifies that: "Insofar as situations are not covered by the other provisions of . . . (Article 2–Sales) and matters concerning title become material the following rules [respecting title] apply:" [C3] Title to goods cannot pass until the goods have been "identified" to the contract but identification does not automatically pass title.[C4] Identification is the process whereby the particular goods which are to fulfill the requirements of the contract are designated.[C5] If the goods are in existence and are specified when the sale is made, identification has been accomplished without any further steps. If the contract is for sale of future goods (Section 3-5), identification occurs when the goods are shipped to the buyer or when they are marked or otherwise designated by the seller as the goods to which the contract refers. Upon identification, the buyer obtains what the Code refers to as a "special property" and an "insurable interest" in the goods—an interest less than title.[C6] The whole interest in the goods called title passes to the buyer at the time and place the seller completes his performance with reference to the physical delivery of the goods.

The rules for determining when such performance is completed depend upon the nature of the seller's obligation to deliver and the location of goods. Title passes to the buyer at the time and place of *shipment* if the contract does not require delivery at destination; if the contract does require delivery at destination, title passes on *tender* there.[C7] If delivery is to be made without moving the goods, i.e., where they are in possession of a bailee, or if the seller is to deliver a document of title, so that the buyer can obtain the goods, title passes upon *delivery of the documents.* Title passes at the *time and place of contracting* if no documents are to be delivered and the goods at the time of contracting are already identified.[C8]

If the buyer should reject the goods, or otherwise refuse to receive or retain them, title to the goods revests in the seller.[C9] It is to be noted that the buyer obtains an insurable interest in the goods upon identification of them and prior to the passage of title. Likewise, the seller retains an insurable interest in the goods so long as he still has title so that in many instances both buyer and seller will have an insurable interest in the goods which are the subject of the transactions.

The seller can reserve a security interest in goods which have been shipped or delivered to the buyer and the retention or reservation of title by the seller is limited to such security interest. The security interest gives the seller security for payment of the price but its reservation does not prevent passage of title to the buyer.[C10]

Risk of loss. A related area to that of title is risk of loss to goods. The Code enumerates a number of rules for determining which

C2 *U.C.C.* 2-106(1).

C3 *U.C.C.* 2-401.

C4 *U.C.C.* 2-401.

C5 *U.C.C.* 2-501.

C6 *U.C.C.* 2-501.

C7 *U.C.C.* 2-401(2).

C8 *U.C.C.* 2-401(3).

C9 *U.C.C.* 2-401(4).

C10 *U.C.C.* 2-401(2).

party to a sales contract must bear the risk of loss or damage to goods. The approach is contractual rather than title-oriented. Two basic situations are encompassed: (1) where no breach of contract is involved; [C11] (2) where there is a breach.[C12]

If the contract has been breached, the loss will be borne by the party who has breached. If a seller has tendered or delivered nonconforming goods which the buyer has a right to reject, the risk of loss remains on the seller until such time as he has cured the nonconformity (e.g. makes necessary repairs) or the buyer has accepted the goods. If the buyer revokes his acceptance for good cause, the risk is that of the seller to the extent that the buyer's insurance does not cover the loss. The seller thus has the benefit of any insurance carried by the buyer—the party most likely to carry insurance. The loss may occur while the goods are under the seller's control and before the risk of loss has passed to the buyer. If the buyer repudiates or is otherwise in breach as to conforming goods which have already been identified to the contract for sale, the seller can impose the risk of loss on the breaching buyer for a commercially reasonable time and to the extent that the seller's insurance does not cover the loss. The title usually does not pass to the buyer until the goods are delivered to him, but the buyer's breach shifts the risk of loss to him.[C13]

Where there has been no breach of contract the risk of loss is determined in accordance with several basic fact patterns.

Where the contract between buyer and seller provides for shipment by carrier the risk of loss passes to the buyer when the goods are delivered to the carrier if it is a shipment contract; if it is a destination contract risk of loss does not pass to the buyer until the goods arrive at the destination and are made available to him so as to take delivery. A shipment contract is one which requires only that the seller make the necessary arrangements for transport while a destination contract imposes upon the seller the obligation to deliver at a destination. At this point the mercantile shipping terms discussed in Sec. 3-12 have further significance. Thus F.O.B. the place of destination is a destination contract; C.I.F. contracts are shipment contracts. Since the shipping terms are clearly defined in the Code their use would preclude problems as to the point at which risk of loss passes. When the parties do not use these symbols or otherwise make provision for risk of loss it will be necessary to determine whether a contract does or does not require the seller to deliver at a destination.[C14] The presumption is that a contract is one of shipment and that the seller is not obligated to deliver at a specified destination and bear the risk of loss until arrival unless he has either specifically agreed to do so or the items used indicate such an obligation.

Often the goods will be in the possession of a bailee such as a warehouse and the arrangement is for the buyer to take delivery at the warehouse. If the goods are represented by a negotiable document of title such as a warehouse receipt the risk of loss passes to the buyer when

---

[C11] *U.C.C.* 2-510.
[C12] *U.C.C.* 2-509.

[C13] *U.C.C.* 2-510.
[C14] *U.C.C.* 2-509(1).

the seller tenders such document to the buyer. Also, if the seller obtains an acknowledgment from the bailee that the goods are now being held on behalf of the buyer who has the right to possession risk of loss passes to the buyer. The tender of a non-negotiable document of title delays passage of risk of loss until the buyer has had a reasonable time to present it to the bailee.[C15] A refusal by the bailee to honor the document defects the tender.

If the goods are not to be shipped and are not held by a bailee to be delivered without being moved, the passage of risk to the buyer depends upon the status of the seller. If the seller is a merchant, risk of loss will not pass to the buyer until he *receives* the goods.[C16] Receipt of goods means taking physical possession of them.[C17] A non-merchant seller can impose risk of loss on the buyer by *tendering* delivery. A tender of delivery requires that the seller make conforming goods available to the buyer and give him reasonable notice to enable him to take delivery.[C18]

The foregoing rules are subject to any reasonable agreement between the parties with reference to allocation of the risk of loss. Also, the effect of a breach by either party, as noted previously, is to place the risk on the party who has breached.[C19]

3-16 Performance—in General. The contract for sale imposes obligations on both the buyer and the seller. The seller is obligated to transfer and deliver the goods, and the buyer is obligated to accept and pay in accordance with the contract.[C20]

While initially both the seller and the buyer anticipate that each will perform his obligations under the contract and that nothing will prevent a successful conclusion to their transaction, it is a known fact that these expectations are often frustrated. Frequently the parties do not take into account the vicissitudes—what will happen if performance is not forthcoming—and make no provision therefore in their contract.

The events or circumstances which may stand in the way of the fulfillment of the expectations of either party are numerous. Some unexpected event may occur which renders performance by one of the parties impossible or impractical. One of the parties may repudiate the contract —state in advance that he does not intend to perform. The seller may tender goods which do not meet the specifications of the contract or which do not arrive on time or which are defective. The buyer may unjustifiably or capriciously reject goods tendered by the seller, or refuse to pay the price of the goods. Either the buyer or the seller may become insolvent during the course of the transaction. The Code makes provision for all of these eventualities and provides appropriate remedies for both the seller and the buyer.

Both parties are required to act in "good faith" in their dealings with each other. Thus, while a buyer has the right to reject goods tendered by the seller if they do not meet the specifications of the contract, he must

---

C15 *U.C.C.* 2-503.
C16 *U.C.C.* 2-509(3).
C17 *U.C.C.* 2-103.

C18 *U.C.C.* 2-503.
C19 *U.C.C.* 2-509(4).
C20 *U.C.C.* 2-301.

act fairly in doing so. If the rejection is for a relatively minor deviation from the contract requirements the seller must be given an opportunity to "cure" the defective performance. He may accomplish this by notifying the buyer of his intention to cure, and by then tendering proper or conforming goods if the time for performance has not expired.[C21] If the time for performance has expired, as for example, when the buyer makes a last-minute rejection, the seller, if he had reasonable grounds to believe that the goods would be acceptable in spite of the nonconformity, will be granted further time to substitute goods which are in accordance with the contract.[C22] The main purpose of this rule allowing "cure" is to protect the seller from being forced into a breach by a surprise rejection at the last moment by the buyer. The seller, in order to take advantage of this privilege, must notify the buyer of his intention to cure.

The provision for "cure" by the seller does not detract from his obligation to render a performance which "conforms" to the contract. The seller is obligated to tender and the buyer is entitled to receive the goods as specified in the contract. If the goods are not "conforming" the buyer may reject them—such nonconformity constitutes a breach of the contract by the seller.[C23]

As a basic premise each party is entitled to receive performance in strict accordance with the terms of a contract for sale and a variety of remedies are afforded to the buyer and seller if such performance is not forthcoming or is otherwise defective. The nature of these remedies will be discussed later, following a brief résumé of some general principles which bear upon the matter of performance or the lack thereof.

3-17 Excuses of Performance. Both parties may be relieved of their obligations under a contract for sale if the goods suffer casualty—are damaged, destroyed, or have deteriorated, without fault of either party, prior to delivery.[C24] Avoidance of the contract will result only if 1) the casualty occurs prior to the time when the risk of loss passes to the buyer, and 2) the goods have been "identified to the contract." If the loss is only partial, the buyer can either treat the contract as avoided or accept the remaining goods with due adjustment of the contract price to allow for the deficiency.[C25] The avoidance principle applies whether the goods were already destroyed at the time of contracting without the parties' knowledge or whether they were destroyed subsequently but before risk of loss passed to the buyer. The protection afforded to the seller is quite limited since he is still under an obligation to perform if the contract did not require for its performance specific goods identified when the contract was made.

The seller is also excused from timely *delivery* of goods where supervening circumstances not within the contemplation of the parties at the time of contracting have made his performance impracticable.[C26] Thus, if an unforeseen event occurs which adversely affects the ability of the

C21 *U.C.C.* 2-508.
C22 *U.C.C.* 2-508(2).
C23 *U.C.C.* 2-601, 2-106.

C24 *U.C.C.* 2-613.
C25 *U.C.C.* 2-613.
C26 *U.C.C.* 2-615.

seller to perform, he may be relieved of the normal consequences resulting from a late delivery, a partial delivery or no delivery at all. The
seller is excused only if 1) the non-occurrence of the contingency was a
basic assumption upon which the contract was made, and 2) its occurrence made the agreed performance commercially impracticable. The
Code does not elaborate on these matters, but it seems clear that increased
costs and a rise or collapse of the market are basic business risks which
would not in themselves justify a seller's failure to perform. On the other
hand, if it were understood that a particular source would supply the
seller with the goods to be used in fulfillment of the contract, and, due
to casualty, the supplier could not furnish such goods, then the seller
would be relieved. If the seller's capacity to perform is only partially cur-
tailed, he is obligated to allocate the available goods among his customers
in a fair and reasonable manner. The seller must give proper notice to
the buyer that there will be a delay or nondelivery, and when, in the
case of partial curtailment, allocation is required, he must furnish the
buyer an estimate of the quota available to the buyer. The buyer, upon
receiving such notification, may terminate the contract as to any delivery
concerned, or he may agree to modify the contract and take his available
quota.[C27]

3-18 Anticipatory Repudiation. Either a buyer or a seller may in advance
of the date when final performance is due indicate by word or action that
he will not continue with his performance. The aggrieved party who has
been informed of such repudiation may 1) treat the contract as having
been breached and resort to any remedy for breach, or 2) await performance by the repudiating party for a commercially reasonable time, and
3) in either case suspend his own performance.[C28] The repudiating party
can retract his repudiation and reinstate his rights under the contract
unless the aggrieved party has indicated that he considers the repudiation final as by cancelling or by materially changing his position on the
basis of the repudiation.[C29]

3-19 Adequate Assurance. A problem analogous to anticipatory repudiation is one in which circumstances arise which give either party cause
for concern as to whether or not the other will *actually render* the performance due. It is not enough to give either party—buyer or seller—
a right to sue and collect damages for the ultimate breach. There is need
for some protection to be afforded to the party whose reasonable expectation that he will receive due performance is jeopardized. The Code
grants such protection by providing that the contract for sale imposes an
obligation on each party that the other's expectation of receiving due
performance will not be impaired. A party who has reasonable grounds
for insecurity as to the other's performance can demand in writing that
the other offer convincing proof that he will in fact perform. Having

[C27] *U.C.C.* 2-616.   [C29] *U.C.C.* 2-611.
[C28] *U.C.C.* 2-610.

made such demand, he may then suspend his own performance until he receives such assurance. If none is forthcoming within a reasonable time, not to exceed thirty days, he may treat the contract as repudiated.[C30] Two factual problems are presented: What are reasonable grounds for insecurity and what constitutess an adequate assurance of performance? The Code does not particularize but does provide that as between merchants commercial standards shall be applied to answer these questions.

RIGHTS, REMEDIES AND OBLIGATIONS OF THE BUYER

3-20 In General. The buyer is entitled to receive from the seller a performance which is in conformity with the contract. A variety of remedies are available to him if the seller breaches or repudiates the contract. Thus if the goods do not conform, are not in accordance with warranties, express or implied, or the seller is otherwise in default, several remedies are available to the buyer. Also, it must be noted that the buyer has certain *obligations* to the seller over and above the obligation to accept conforming tender or performance and to pay the price. For example, the buyer has obligations with respect to the care, custody, and disposition of goods which have been tendered to him and rejected by him.[C31]

In general the buyer has the right to inspect the goods at any reasonable time and place before accepting them or paying for them.[C32] However, the buyer does not have this privilege if the contract provides for delivery "C.O.D." (Collect on Delivery) or if he is to pay against documents of title, unless in the latter case, the contract provides that payment is not due until the goods arrive.[C33] If the contract requires the buyer to pay before inspection, his rights and remedies are not affected if subsequent inspection discloses that the contract has not been properly performed by the seller. Payment under such circumstances does not constitute an acceptance of the goods.[C34] *no inspection*

3-21 Rejection. If the seller's performance is deficient as, for example, where the goods tendered or delivered do not conform to the contract, the buyer has the right to reject such goods. As noted, this right is tempered somewhat by the seller's right to cure a tender rejected for nonconformity—that is, the seller has a limited privilege to correct the defective performance by substituting goods which do conform.

Several options are available to the buyer to whom nonconforming goods have been tendered or delivered. He may reject the whole or he may accept either the whole or any commercial unit or units and reject the rest.[C35] A commercial unit is one that is generally regarded as a single whole for purposes of sale and which would be impaired in value if

---

[C30] *U.C.C.* 2-609.
[C31] *U.C.C.* 2-602(2)(b).
[C32] *U.C.C.* 2-602(2)(b).

[C33] *U.C.C.* 2-513.
[C34] *U.C.C.* 2-512.
[C35] *U.C.C.* 2-601.

divided.[C36] Thus the buyer could accept those portions of the goods that would be satisfactory to him so long as he did not thereby break up a unit. The buyer, whether he accepts the whole or any unit, does not impair his right of recourse against the seller, provided he notifies the seller of the breach within a reasonable time.[C37] He may still pursue his remedy for damages for breach of contract.[C38]

The ordinary buyer in possession of rejected goods is under a duty to hold them with reasonable care for a sufficient time to enable the seller to remove them.[C39] A merchant buyer who has possession of rejected goods is under a greater obligation. He is required to follow reasonable instructions from the seller with respect to disposition of the goods and in the absence of such instructions to sell them for the seller's account if they are perishable, or threaten speedily to decline in value.[C40] If the merchant buyer sells the goods under these circumstances, he is entitled to reimbursement from the seller for his reasonable expenses in caring for and selling the goods.[C41] Generally, if the seller upon receipt of notice of rejection does not give any instructions to the buyer as to disposition of the goods, the buyer may store the rejected goods for the seller's account or reship them to him, or resell them for the seller's account with reimbursement.[C42]

Notice of rejection. The notice of rejection may be simply to the effect that the goods are not conforming without particular specification of the defects relied upon by the buyer. If, however, the defect could have been cured by the seller if he had had notice, then the failure to particularize will take away from the buyer the right to rely upon the defect as a breach justifying a rejection. Special rules govern the notice which is required in transactions between merchants upon the assumption that particularization of defects is more important to a merchant seller. Therefore, the merchant seller is entitled to require that he be furnished a full and final written statement of all of the defects and if the statement is not forthcoming the buyer may not rely upon such defects to justify his rejection or to establish that a breach has occurred.[C43]

Notice of breach—"accepted goods." Another phase of the notice requirement pertaining to breach is one in which the buyer has accepted the goods in spite of their nonconformity. Such acceptance of course cuts off his right to reject but does not result in a denial of other remedies. The buyer will have to pay for the goods which he has accepted but he can set off against the price damages resulting from the nonconformity. However, failure to give such notice of nonconformity and breach will result in a denial of any other remedies.[C44]

Acceptance. The buyer has "accepted" goods, if after a reasonable opportunity to inspect them, he indicates to the seller that the goods are conforming or that he will take or retain them in spite of

C36 *U.C.C.* 2-105.
C37 *U.C.C.* 2-607.
C38 *U.C.C.* 2-714.
C39 *U.C.C.* 2-602(2)(b).
C40 *U.C.C.* 2-603.

C41 *U.C.C.* 2-603.
C42 *U.C.C.* 2-604.
C43 *U.C.C.* 2-605.
C44 *U.C.C.* 2-607.

their nonconformity, or if he has failed to make an effective rejection of the goods.[2] [C45]

In many instances, the buyer will have accepted nonconforming goods because either 1) the defects were not immediately discoverable, or 2) the buyer reasonably assumed that the seller would cure by substituting goods which did conform. In either of these events the buyer has the privilege of "revoking his acceptance" by notifying the seller of this fact. The revocation of acceptance must take place within a reasonable time after the buyer has discovered, or should have discovered the reason for it. If a buyer revokes his acceptance, he is then placed in the same position with reference to the goods as if he had rejected them in the first instance.[C46]

Installment contracts. Frequently, the contract will authorize or require delivery in stated lots or installments to be separately accepted rather than one delivery of all the goods. The buyer's right to reject a nonconforming installment is restricted in two ways: 1) the nonconformity must substantially impair the value of that installment and 2) must be one that could not be cured by the seller. The buyer can treat the defective performance of the installment as a breach of the whole contract if it can be said to substantially impair the value of the whole.[C47]

3-22 Remedies of Buyer. The buyer is afforded a variety of remedies against a seller who has failed to comply with his obligations under the contract for sale. Some of these remedies come into play when the seller has failed to make delivery or has repudiated the contract and when the buyer has for good reason either rejected the goods or has revoked his acceptance. There is a four year statute of limitations for actions for breach of any contract for sale.[3] [C48] The basic remedy is to cancel—put an end to the contract because of breach. Cancellation, which is optional, does not preclude the buyer from pursuing his remedies against the seller, and whether the buyer cancels or not he is entitled to recover whatever he had already paid to the seller.[C49]

The remedies of the buyer are classified as to those permitting the recovery of money damages and those which permit reaching the goods. The nature of the remedies available to the buyer is dependent on whether 1) he has rejected or has revoked his acceptance, or 2) has finally accepted the goods.

Cover: damages—goods not received. The buyer who has not received the goods he bargained for may "cover"—arrange to purchase goods from some other source in substitution for those due from the seller. He is allowed to recover from the seller as damages the difference

---

2 *Park County Implement Co. v. Craig, supra,* page 406.
3 *Rufo v. Bastion-Blessing Company,* page 407.

C45 *U.C.C.* 2-606.	C48 *U.C.C.* 2-725.
C46 *U.C.C.* 2-608.	C49 *U.C.C.* 2-711.
C47 *U.C.C.* 2-612.	

between what he paid for the substitute goods and the contract price. Cover is optional with the buyer; he can elect to recover net damages for nondelivery or repudiation.[C50] The measure of damage in this instance is the difference between the market price when the buyer learned of the breach and the contract price.

Damages—acceptance of nonconforming goods. The buyer who has accepted nonconforming goods and who does not have the right to revoke his acceptance is also entitled to damages, provided he has given proper notice of breach to the seller. He must credit the seller for the value of the accepted goods and his loss will be measured in general by the difference between the actual value of the goods and the value they would have had if they had conformed to the contract.[C51] If there has been a breach of warranty, the measure of damages is the difference between the value of the goods and the value they would have had had they been as warranted.[4] [C52] The buyer must pay for the goods, but he can recoup the amount of his damages by deducting them from any part of the price still due.[C53] In each instance the buyer is allowed in addition to his ordinary damages, "incidental and consequential damages" which encompass, 1) expenses incurred in connection with caring for the goods and effecting cover and 2) particular losses occasioned by the breach where the seller had reason to know of special needs of the buyer as where the buyer lost a resale opportunity because the goods were not made available to him. Also, if a breach of warranty is the cause of injury to person or property, such damages are recoverable.[C54]

Right to goods. Under proper circumstances the buyer has rights in and to the goods. The Code provides that the remedy of specific performance is available where the goods are unique and also where other circumstances make it equitable that the seller render the required performance.[C55] It would appear that in order to invoke this remedy the buyer must have been unable to "cover." While the Code does not define "unique," it is fair to assume that it would encompass output and requirement contracts where the goods are not readily or practically available from other sources. The choice of specific performance as a remedy is not exclusive in that a court may also award damages or other relief.

Another remedy is that of replevin, the right to obtain the goods which are identified to the contract. This remedy is available only if the buyer is unable to cover.[C56]

Seller's insolvency. A related remedy which reaches the goods from a somewhat different standpoint is the buyer's right to recover the goods if the seller becomes insolvent. The right rises only if 1) the buyer has an insurable interest, i.e., the goods have been identified to the contract, 2) the seller becomes insolvent within 10 days after he received

---

[4] *Babcock Poultry Farm, Inc. v. Shook*, page 408.

[C50] *U.C.C.* 2-712.
[C51] *U.C.C.* 2-714.
[C52] *U.C.C.* 2-714(2).
[C53] *U.C.C.* 2-717.

[C54] *U.C.C.* 2-715.
[C55] *U.C.C.* 2-716.
[C56] 2-716(3).

the first installment payment from the buyer.[C57] Absent such factors, the buyer is relegated to the position of a general creditor of the seller.

If the buyer can recover the goods from the trustee in bankruptcy, for example, he is in a much better position than he would be as a general creditor for the amount of the price already paid.

RIGHTS, REMEDIES AND OBLIGATIONS OF THE SELLER

3-23 In General. The remedies available to a seller are classified under the Code into two basic categories. The first relates to the seller's remedies where the buyer: 1) wrongfully rejects or revokes acceptance of goods, or 2) fails to make a payment due on or before delivery, or 3) repudiates the contract. In general, these remedies relate to the situation in which the goods have not been received or accepted by the buyer. The second category covers the remedies of the seller where the buyer *has accepted* the goods. Other provisions of the Code relate to the seller's remedies when the buyer has become insolvent and where there has been a casualty to goods after the risk of loss has passed to the buyer. It will be noted that the remedies afforded to a seller are in a large number the counterparts of the remedies which the Code provides to a disappointed buyer. The remedies available to the seller under the first category will be first discussed.

3-24 Remedies Where Buyer Not in Possession.
      Stoppage of goods. The seller is given the right to withhold delivery of goods to the breaching buyer. If the goods are in the possession of a carrier or other bailee, he may by appropriate action stop the delivery of the goods. The right arises if he discovers the buyer to be insolvent, if the buyer repudiates, or if for any other reason the seller has a right to withhold or reclaim goods.[C58] Unless the stoppage is based upon the buyer's insolvency the right of stoppage is limited to carload, truckload, planeload, or larger shipments. This right of stoppage is, of course, no longer available if the goods have been received by the buyer. Likewise if a warehouseman or any bailee other than a carrier acknowledges to the buyer that he is holding the goods on the buyer's account, the right of stoppage is no longer available. If a negotiable document of title, such as a bill of lading or warehouse receipt, has been negotiated to the buyer, the seller cannot withhold or reclaim the goods.[C59] To the extent that the right to stop delivery does exist, the seller must give proper and timely notice to the bailee and if a negotiable document of title has been issued for the goods, such document must be surrendered to the bailee before he is required to obey the stop order.[C60] The importance of the seller's right to stop delivery of goods and to withhold possession of goods

[C57] 2-502, 2-402.
[C58] *U.C.C.* 2-705.

[C59] *U.C.C.* 2-705(2).
[C60] *U.C.C.* 2-705(3).

is a very valuable one, as he is in a much stronger position if he can prevent the goods from reaching the control of the buyer. The Code makes it clear that after an effective stoppage the seller's rights in the goods are the same as if he had never made a delivery. If the stoppage was unjustified the seller will be liable to the buyer and the buyer can take advantage of the several remedies discussed previously.

Resale.   The exercise of the right to withhold goods or to stop delivery of goods does not preclude the seller from also recovering any damages which he may have suffered because of the buyer's conduct or insolvency. As in other cases where the buyer has breached the seller is allowed to make a reasonable resale of the withheld or rejected goods and recover from the buyer the difference between the price for which the goods were sold at resale and the price called for in the contract together with incidental damages.[C61] This right exists whether or not title had passed to the buyer. In general, the seller has broad discretion in accomplishing the resale and the seller is not accountable to the buyer for any profit made on any resale. The resale may be made at either a public or private sale and in either event the seller must give reasonable notice to the buyer of his intention to resell. If the resale is at a public sale, the seller must inform the buyer as to the time and place of the resale, except where the goods are perishable or threaten to decline in value speedily. The seller can himself buy at a public sale.[C62]

Damages.   The seller is not required to resell the goods and can instead, if he chooses, retain the goods and bring an action for damages for nonacceptance or repudiation.[C63] The measure of damages is the difference between the market price at the time and place for tender and the unpaid contract price together with any incidental damages.[C64] However, if this measure of damages leaves the seller in less favorable position than he would have been in had the buyer accepted the goods, the measure of damages will be the profit which the seller would have made from full performance by the buyer.[C65]

In computing profit the reasonable overhead of the seller is to be taken into account. This remedy recognizes that a seller may have suffered a loss even though he receives on resale the same amount that he would have received from the buyer. He has "lost a sale" and the profit on that sale should be a factor taken into account. Thus, a dealer in office furniture may have entered into a contract for the sale of a number of desks, chairs, and filing cabinets to the buyer at a price of $15,000. He has a warehouse which contains hundreds of each items and maintains at all times a large inventory. If the buyer were to refuse to accept the items contracted for or repudiate the contract, the seller could, and would of course ultimately, sell these items to other parties, but the fact remains that as a result of the breach the seller has lost the profit which he would have made had the buyer properly performed.

C61 *U.C.C.* 2-706, 2-710.   C64 *U.C.C.* 2-710.
C62 *U.C.C.* 2-706(3)(4).   C65 *U.C.C.* 2-708(2).
C63 *U.C.C.* 2-708.

Recovery of the price. If the contract specifies the time at which payment of the price is due, and the buyer fails to so pay, the seller is allowed to recover from the buyer the contract price for the goods together with incidental damages, if the goods cannot be effectively resold.[C66] Note that this remedy by way of recovery of the contract price is restricted to goods accepted by the buyer although in the seller's possession, or identified to the contract and that the seller must be unable to resell the goods. Thus if the seller cannot resell the goods he can push them off on the buyer and recover the price.

Identification and salvage. However, the seller who has on hand finished goods which conform to the contract can proceed to identify them to the contract whether they are resalable or not.[C67] After such identification, he may exercise his resale remedy, or if the goods are not resalable he can utilize his remedy by way of an action for the price or damages. As to unfinished goods, the seller may within the bounds of reasonable commercial judgment: 1) complete their manufacture and identify the goods to the contract, or 2) cease manufacture and resell for scrap or salvage value, or 3) proceed in any other reasonable manner.

3-25 Remedies Where Buyer has Accepted. If the buyer has accepted the goods the remedy of the seller is to bring an action for the price together with any incidental damages. His limited right to reclaim the goods if the buyer is insolvent is discussed in the next section. The problem of the seller becomes acute if the buyer is insolvent. He does not ordinarily have any right to reclaim the goods unless he has a security interest in them as provided in Article 9.

3-26 Other Remedies of Seller.

Loss or damage. If the goods conform to the contract and are lost or damaged before receipt by the buyer but within a commercially reasonable length of time after the risk of loss has passed to the buyer, the seller can maintain an action for the price.[C68] This contemplates a situation in which the goods are damaged while in transit or otherwise prior to the delivery to the buyer.

In addition to damages specifically designated the seller is entitled to "incidental damages"—to be reimbursed for expenses reasonably incurred by him as a result of the buyer's breach.[C69] Included are expenses in connection with stopping delivery, transportation, care and custody of the goods subsequent to the buyer's breach, and the like.

Insolvency of the buyer. Insolvency of the buyer poses particular problems for his seller. He is given a variety of remedies which are designed primarily to allow him to retain or reclaim the goods. Upon discovering the buyer's insolvency he may refuse to make delivery except for cash and may insist upon payment for all goods previously furnished under the contract as a condition to delivery.[C70] He may stop delivery by a carrier,

---

[C66] *U.C.C.* 2-709.
[C67] *U.C.C.* 2-704.
[C68] *U.C.C.* 2-709(i)(a).

[C69] *U.C.C.* 2-710.
[C70] *U.C.C.* 2-702, 2-705.

warehouseman or other bailee and recover the goods. If the goods were sold on credit and the buyer was insolvent at the time he received the goods, the seller can reclaim them from the buyer provided he makes a demand for them within 10 days of the buyer's receipt.[C71] If the buyer has made a false statement as to his solvency in writing to the seller within three months before delivery, the 10 day limitation does not apply. If the seller is successful in reclaiming the goods, he has no further remedy. The importance of this limited opportunity of the seller to reclaim the goods should be stressed. If he is not able to reclaim the goods, they are then subject to the claims of other creditors of the buyer, and in the event of the buyer's bankruptcy would be possessed by the trustee in bankruptcy and the seller would be relegated to the status of a general creditor of the bankrupt without any preference with regard to these goods.

3-27 Limitation of Actions. With regard to the time within which an action must be commenced for any breach of a contract for sale, the Code provides that:

> An action for breach of any contract for sale must be commenced within four years after the cause of action has accrued. By the original agreement the parties may reduce the period of limitation to not less than one year but may not extend it.
> A cause of action accrues when the breach occurs, regardless of the aggrieved party's lack of knowledge of the breach. A breach of warranty occurs when tender of delivery is made, except that where a warranty explicitly extends to future performance of the goods and discovery of the breach must await the time of such performance, the cause of action accrues when the breach is or should have been discovered.[C72]

It will be noted that this section takes sales contracts out of the general laws limiting the time for commencing contractual actions. The four year period was selected because this is the normal commercial record-keeping period. State law relating to the tolling of the Statute of Limitations continues to be controlling under the Code.

DOCUMENTS OF TITLE

3-28 General Concepts: Definitions. The most common documents of title are warehouse receipts and bills of lading. Documents of title are covered by Article 7 of the Uniform Commercial Code. However, there are numerous statutes, both state and federal, which regulate the business of carriers and warehousemen and the Code does not displace these statutes. The Federal Bills of Lading Act, for example, controls bills of lading covering foreign exports and interstate shipment of goods.

[C71] *U.C.C.* 2-702(2).
[C72] *U.C.C.* 2-725.

The subject of documents of title is presented at this point in the text because of the close relationship of such documents to sales transactions. It should be noted, however, that these documents are also significant in connection with other transactions; particularly Secured Transactions— Article 9.

These documents play an important role in modern commerce and facilitate the shipment and storage of merchandise as well as serving to integrate these functions with various aspects of sales and financing transactions. The use of such documents dates back many centuries—it was recognized at an early date that a written instrument could represent goods and stand in their place and stead. Thus when goods are stored with a warehouseman or delivered to a carrier for shipment, a receipt is issued; and this receipt can be treated as a token of the goods shipped or stored. In a sense the piece of paper can represent the goods and can be transferred, sold or pledged as representative of the goods described therein.

The documents of title can thus serve a dual function. They serve as a receipt for goods stored or shipped and they also are emblems of the goods. In the latter capacity they are most useful in financing commercial transactions. In addition the document is the contract for storage or shipment as the case may be.

The definition of a document of title includes commonly used instruments in addition to bills of lading and warehouse receipts. The Code defines a document of title as including bills of lading, dock warrants, dock receipts, warehouse receipts, or orders for the delivery of goods.[C73] Any other document which in the regular course of business or financing is treated as adequately evidencing that the person in possession of it is entitled to receive, hold and dispose of the document and the goods it covers also falls within the definition. The document must represent that it is issued by a bailee (e.g. warehouse or carrier) or be addressed to a bailee and must purport to cover goods in the bailee's possession which are properly identified.[C74]

A bill of lading is a document evidencing the receipt of goods for shipment issued by a person engaged in the business of transporting or forwarding goods. An airbill is included within this definition.[C75] A warehouse receipt is a receipt issued by a person engaged in the business of storing goods for hire.[C76]

Documents of title may be negotiable or non-negotiable. The concept of negotiability is discussed in Chapter 20 (sec. 3-33) in connection with negotiable instruments—commercial paper. The basic philosophy of the concept is to render certain written instruments capable of free movement in commerce. In order to accomplish this such instrument must be readily transferable, acceptable by merchants, and must afford substantial security and protection to the holder. There are similarities but also substantial differences between documents of title as negotiable instruments and commercial paper. Commercial paper is payable in money—it is in a sense a substitute for money and symbolic of money. Documents of title are symbols of goods and the particular goods must be identified.

There are are significant differences between negotiable and non-negotiable documents of title. The former more effectively represents the goods since the bailee is not entitled to deliver the goods unless the document is surrendered.

3-29 Negotiation and Transfer. A warehouse receipt, bill of lading or other document is negotiable if by its terms the goods are to be delivered to the "bearer" or to the "order of" a named person.[C77] A document not containing these "words of negotiability" is not negotiable.[C78] Thus, a bill of lading which states that goods are consigned to "John Doe" would not be negotiable; one ordering delivery to "the order of John Doe" or to "bearer" would be negotiable. Either a negotiable or a non-negotiable document can be transferred but the method of transfer is different. A non-negotiable document can be "assigned"—the assignee acquires only the rights of the assignor and is subject to all defenses which are available against the assignor. The assignee is burdened with all defects in the assignor's title. "Negotiation"—the process whereby negotiable documents are transferred—places the transferee in a much more favorable position. If there is "due negotiation" the transferee is free from the defects of the tranferor's title and the claims of third persons.[C79] His rights are superior and he enjoys a favored position as transferee-holder of a negotiable document.

There are two methods of negotiating a document of title depending upon whether it is an "order" document or a "bearer" document. The former is accomplished by indorsement and delivery; the latter by delivery alone. An indorsement consists of the transferor's (indorser) signature on the document—usually the back side. The indorser's signature without more is called a "blank indorsement" and the document can now be further negotiated by delivery. The result obtains if the indorsement includes the clause: "Deliver to bearer." However, if the indorsement is special—the indorsee's name is specified—the indorsement of the special indorsee would be required for further negotiation. Thus an indorsement by John Doe: "Deliver to Richard Roe" would require further indorsement by Roe if he wished to negotiate the document. If the instrument specifies on its face that it runs to bearer no indorsement is required for negotiation. A thief can thus negotiate a bearer document—one that specifies on its face that it runs to bearer or one which is indorsed in blank. It must be noted that the last indorsement is controlling—if it is special, further indorsement is required; if blank, it can be further negotiated by delivery.[C80]

In order for the holder of a negotiable document of title to have the preferred status mentioned above there must have been a "due negotia-

C77 *U.C.C.* 7-104.   C79 *U.C.C.* 7-501, 7-502.
C78 *U.C.C.* 7-104.   C80 *U.C.C.* 7-501(3).

tion" which means not only any necessary indorsement and/or delivery but also that the holder satisfy certain requirements. He must have purchased the document in good faith, without notice of a defense against or claim to it on the part of any person. He must have paid value for it and the negotiation must have been in the regular course of business or financing. One to whom a document is negotiated in satisfaction or payment of a prior debt has not paid value.[C81]

If there has been "due negotiation" the holder acquires title to the document, title to the goods and the "direct obligation of the issuer" (carrier or warehouseman) to hold or deliver the goods according to the terms of the document and free from any defense or claim of the issuer other than those afforded him by Article 7.[C82] The holder's rights cannot be defeated by any stoppage of the goods or surrender of them by the bailee.[C83] His rights are not impaired "even though the negotiation or any prior negotiation constituted a breach of duty or even though any person has been deprived of possession of the document by misrepresentation, fraud, accident, mistake, duress, loss, theft or conversion; or even though a previous sale or other transfer of the goods or document has been made to a third person." The foregoing is premised upon a rightful bailment of the goods in the first instance. A thief or unauthorized person cannot pass title to stolen or misappropriated property by delivering it to a public warehouse and then negotiating the warehouse receipt which he receives therefor. The owner of the goods would prevail against the holder of the document of title.[C84]

The position of a transferee of a non-negotiable document or of a negotiable one which has not been duly negotiated is that of an assignee. His rights are subject to being defeated by certain creditors of the transferor, by a purchaser of the goods from the transferor or by the bailee who has dealt in good faith with the transferor.[C85] Likewise, his rights may be defeated by a stoppage of delivery as described in Section 3-24 on rights of sellers.[C86] It is to be noted that the transferee of a negotiable document in order form to whom the document was transferred without indorsement, has a specifically enforceable right to such indorsement.

3-30 Liability of Indorser or Transferor. The indorser or transferor of a document of title makes three warranties to his immediate purchaser.[C87]

(1) He warrants that the document is genuine. One who purchases a forged document of title may, upon discovery of the forgery, recover from the person who sold it to him.

(2) He warrants that he has no knowledge of any facts which would impair its validity or worth.

(3) He warrants that his sale of the document is rightful and fully effective with respect to the title to the document and the goods it repre-

---

[C81] *U.C.C.* 7-501(4).
[C82] *U.C.C.* 7-502.
[C83] *U.C.C.* 7-502.
[C84] *U.C.C.* 7-503.

[C85] *U.C.C.* 7-504.
[C86] *U.C.C.* 7-504.
[C87] *U.C.C.* 7-507.

sents. However, unless he also has sold the goods, he does not make any additional warranties as to the goods. If he is also the seller of the goods, he makes the warranties previously presented in the discussion on sales contracts. The indorser of a document of title does not warrant performance by the bailee or against default by any previous indorser.[C88]

His warranties are satisfied when the purchaser obtains a good right against the warehouseman or carrier. If the bailee has misappropriated the goods or refuses to surrender them, the holder of the document has, as his only recourse, an action against the bailee who issued the document.

If a bank or other person has been authorized to deliver a document of title, acting as an agent for this purpose, the delivery of the document creates no warranty by the agent as to the document itself. The bank or other agent does, however, warrant that it is acting in good faith and has the authority to deliver the document.[C89] Thus, no liability would be assumed by any such agent if the document were not genuine.

3-31 Obligations of Bailee. A public warehouse which issues a negotiable receipt is not at liberty to surrender the goods to the original bailor unless he surrenders the receipt for cancellation. The receipt represents the goods and must be surrendered before the goods may be obtained. The warehouse that surrenders goods without the return of the receipt may be called upon for the goods by someone who has purchased the document. The goods should be delivered only to the person in possession of the receipt and then only if it has been properly indorsed when such indorsement is required. Much the same can be said of a common carrier or any other organization which issues a negotiable document of title.

However, the bailee may refuse to deliver the goods called for by the document until the payment of his just charges have been made, if the bailee requests such payment to be made, or where applicable law prohibits delivery without payment.[C90]

A bailee is responsible for documents, which are issued when no goods are delivered. Thus, an agent of a bailee who fraudulently issues a negotiable document of title without receiving any goods makes it possible for an innocent purchaser of the receipt to hold the warehouseman according to the terms. If the receipt was complete when issued, but was later altered without authority, the warehouse's liability is determined by the original term of the document. If a receipt was issued with blanks, a good faith purchaser of the completed receipt may recover from the warehouse that issued the incomplete receipt.[C91]

A warehouse receipt, even though it has been properly negotiated, will, in one situation, be inferior to the rights of a buyer of the goods represented by the receipt. The Code provides that a buyer in the ordinary course of business, who buys fungible goods from a warehouseman who also is engaged in the business of buying and selling such fungible goods, takes the goods free of any claim under the receipt.[C92] A typical case

[C88] *U.C.C.* 7-505.

[C89] *U.C.C.* 7-508.

[C90] *U.C.C.* 7-209, 7-210.

[C91] *U.C.C.* 7-208.

[C92] *U.C.C.* 7-205.

would involve the purchase of grain from an elevator by a farmer. In such a case, the holder of the receipt would have no claim to the grain purchased by the farmer.

It will be recalled that this same concept is consistent with the result in a similar situation, previously discussed involving the sale of goods, entrusted to him for some other purpose, by a merchant who deals in such goods. Other obligations of issuers of documents of title—warehousemen and carriers and other aspects of their rights and duties are discussed in Chapter 48.

BULK TRANSFERS

3-32 The Bulk Transfer Problem. The subject of bulk sales is covered by a separate article of the Uniform Commercial Code rather than by Article 2–Sales. Article 6–Bulk Transfers is devoted to this topic. The discussion is included at this point in the text, however, because it does present a problem in connection with the sale of goods. It is also significant in connection with Creditors Rights–Book Six.

The problem which Article 6 resolves is that of creditors of a businessman who suddenly sells his entire business, converts everything to cash and departs without paying the creditors. The creditors had presumably extended credit on the strength of his assets to which they could look for satisfaction of their claims if he did not pay them. When this sale occurs the creditors are deprived of any meaningful source of payment.

To remedy this situation the various states enacted "Bulk Sales Laws" which in effect provided that a sale of an entire business was void as to the seller's creditors unless they had been given advance notice of the impending sale and thus would have an opportunity to protect their interests. If the parties to the sale did not comply with the various requirements of the bulk sales laws, creditors of the seller could reach the property sold and subject it to their claims. Thus the purchaser of the business, even though he was himself innocent of any actual wrong, would be deprived of the assets he had purchased to the extent that the claims of the seller's creditors were satisfied from these assets. The various state laws were far from uniform and Article 6 brings uniformity as well as simplification to the law of bulk transfers. However, it continues the basic purpose and procedures which were included in the state laws which it replaces.

A "bulk transfer" encompasses more than the sale of an entire business. (Do not confuse bulk transfer with a sale of fungible goods, for example, which are sold by weight or measure rather than in packaged form.) It is defined as "any transfer in bulk and not in the ordinary course of the transferor's business of a major part of the materials, supplies, merchandise, or other inventory of an enterprise subject to this article." [C93] Also, a transfer of a substantial part of the equipment of an

[C93] *U.C.C.* 6-102.

enterprise is a bulk transfer if it is made in connection with a bulk transfer of inventory, but not otherwise. The businesses covered by the bulk transfer article are those "whole principal business is the sale of merchandise from stock." A manufacturing concern would not ordinarily be included but would be if the concern maintained a retail outlet. Enterprises which manufacture what they sell, such as certain bakeries, for example, would be included. Enterprises whose principal business is the sale of services rather than merchandise are not included.

In order to fall within the provision of Article 6 the transfer must be out of the ordinary course of business and of a "major part" of the materials, supplies, merchandise or other inventory.[C94]

Requirements for compliance. At the outset it is to be noted that if there is full compliance with the bulk transfer requirements, the transfer will not be subject to attack by creditors of the seller. It is only when compliance is lacking that the creditors can reach the goods in the hands of the transferee-purchaser of the business.

Basically, there are two requirements: (1) a scheduling of the property and a listing of the creditors of the seller; (2) a notification of the proposed sale to the seller's creditors.[C95] An optional provision of Article 6 provides for application of the proceeds of the transfer to the debts of the transferor. The states are free to adopt this provision which gives additional protection to the seller's creditors or not as they desire.

It is the duty of the *transferee* to obtain from the transferor a schedule of the property transferred and a sworn list of the transferor's creditors, including their addresses and the amount owed to each. The transferee can rely on the accuracy of this listing. The transferee must keep this information for six months and have it available for creditors, or in the alternative, file it at the designated public office.

The *transferee* must then give notice personally or by registered mail to all persons on the list of creditors and all other persons known to the transferee to assent claims against the transferor.[C96] The notice must be given at least 10 days before the transferee takes possession of the goods or pays for them (whichever happens first) and must contain the following information: (1) that a bulk transfer is about to be made; (2) the names and business addresses of both transferor and transferee; (3) whether the debts of the creditors are to be paid in full as a result of the transaction and if so the address to which the creditors should send their bills. If no provision is made for payment in full of the creditors the notice must contain the following additional information: (1) estimated total of transferor's debts; (2) location and description of property to be transferred; (3) address where creditor list and property schedule may be inspected; (4) whether the transfer is in payment of or security for a debt owing to transferee and if so, the amount of the debt; (5) whether the transfer is a sale for new consideration and if so, the amount of the consideration and the time and place of payment.

[C94] *U.C.C.* 6-102.
[C95] *U.C.C.* 6-104.
[C96] *U.C.C.* 6-107.

The optional provision provides that the transferee is obligated in effect, to see that the creditors are paid in full or pro rata from the "new consideration" paid by the transferee.[C97]

If the required procedure has been followed, the transferor's creditors will have had ample opportunity to take any steps required to protect their interests. If the Code has not been followed, the transfer is ineffective as to the creditors, and they may use any appropriate remedy for the payment of their debts.[C98] The creditors must then act within six months after the transferee took possession unless the transfer was concealed, in which case they must act within six months after they learn of the transfer.[C99] A purchaser who buys for value and in good faith from the transferee obtains the property free of objection based on noncompliance with the Code.

SALES: PERFORMANCE AND BREACH CASES

Park County Implement Co. v. Craig

1964 (Wyo.) 397 P.2d 800

Mr. Chief Justice PARKER delivered the opinion of the court.

Plaintiff sued defendants for the amount due on a purchase of a truck chassis and cab. . . . (T)he court entered a summary judgment for defendants, from which judgment this appeal is taken.

On February 16, 1962, defendants ordered a 1962 International A-162 chassis and cab from plaintiff, which advised that one was not on hand but should be in the area. Three days later defendants were informed that such a vehicle was at the International Harvester Company in Billings, Montana, whereupon defendant Holler drove to Billings and there received the vehicle from that company, asking the International employee from whom the vehicle was received for a statement of origin, title certificate, or some evidence of title. The employee responded that the company did not have the same. The agreed selling price was approximately $3,150 delivered in Cody, Wyoming, or approximately $3,115 if defendants took delivery of the truck at Billings. . . . defendants brought the vehicle to Cody, put it in their shop, and were installing a hoist and dump bed when a fire occurred March 1, destroying the chassis and cab. Defendants said they had made request of plaintiff's manager for statement of origin or other title papers to no avail, but plaintiff's manager said a statement of origin was tendered to defendants on March 2 and was refused. . . .

At the inception of the synthesis, we note that the Uniform Commercial Code–Sales had been adopted in Wyoming January 1, 1962, and was in effect at the time of the transaction, and further that this Code has been held as applicable to motor vehicles. . . .

We hold, therefore, that the transaction in this case was within the

C97 *U.C.C.* 6-106.   C99 6-111.
C98 6-105.

Uniform Commercial Code–Sales. The buyers accepted the goods under the provisions of 34-2-606(1)(c), . . . "Acceptance of goods occurs when the buyer does any act inconsistent with the seller's ownership," when they began installing a hoist and dump bed on the vehicle. At that time the buyer became liable under the provisions of 34-2-607(1), "The buyer must pay at the contract rate for any goods accepted."

Even if there is merit in defendants' contention concerning the pertinency of various provisions of the motor vehicle law requiring certificates of title to be issued under certain circumstances, the rights of the parties under the Code do not depend upon title. As is noted in the official comment:

> This Article (Uniform Commercial Code–Sales) deals with the issues between seller and buyer in terms of step by step performance or nonperformance under the contract for sale and not in terms of whether or not "title" to the goods has passed. . . . (Uniform Commercial Code (U.L.A.) 2-401, p. 190 1962)).

In the instant case, there were no issues of fact before the court except the question of whether or not the plaintiff offered statement of origin to defendants on March 2 and this point is not material. Under the admitted facts the defendants accepted the goods at an agreed price. The summary judgment granted to defendants was in error; the motion of plaintiff for summary judgment should have been granted. The cause is reversed with instructions to enter judgment for plaintiff.

Reversed.

Rufo v. Bastian-Blessing Company

1965, (Pa.) 207 A.2d 823

      COHEN, J.   This is an appeal from an order dismissing plaintiff's complaint in assumpsit for damages arising from the alleged breach of implied warranties of the fitness for intended purpose and merchantable quality.

The complaint was filed July 12, 1960. It alleged that in March of 1956, in Philadelphia, plaintiff, Clementino Rufo, purchased from one J. F. Martin a refilled, portable cylinder of liquified gas for use in a torch in connection with his work, that defendant, Bastian-Blessing Company, manufactured a valve connected with such cylinder, that defendant impliedly warranted to plaintiff the fitness of the valve for said purpose, its merchantability, and its possession of all the qualities required by usage of trade, that plaintiff relied on defendant's skill and judgment and had no knowledge to the contrary, and that the breach of these warranties resulted in an explosion on December 8, 1957, when gas escaped from the valve and caught fire, causing personal and property damage to plaintiffs.

The lower court held that the complaint on its face showed that plaintiffs' action was barred by the statute of limitations.

In affirming, we find it necessary to discuss only one issue. The complaint was properly dismissed because it is apparent on its face that it was originally filed beyond the period permitted by the applicable statute of limitations.

By this action in assumpsit plaintiffs seek to recover consequential damages arising from breaches of implied warranties in connection with the sale of goods under the Uniform Commercial Code–Sales. The Code provides:

> (1) An action for breach of any contract for sale must be commenced within four years after the cause of action has accrued. . . . (2) A cause of action accrues when the breach occurs, regardless of the aggrieved party's lack of knowledge of the breach. A breach of warranty occurs when tender of delivery is made, except that where a warranty explicitly extends to future performance of goods and discovery of the breach must await the time of such performance the cause of action accrues when the breach is or should have been discovered. . . .

Notwithstanding the fact that plaintiffs are claiming personal injuries, the suit is in assumpsit, based upon warranties; therefore, with an exception not here applicable, it must be brought within four years of the breach of warranty, as the statute provides, regardless of the time of the accident directly giving rise to the damages claimed. . . . Applying the statute, the latest time that the alleged breaches of implied warranties could have occurred and, therefore, the latest time that the cause could have accrued was when Rufo took delivery of the allegedly defective cylinder in March of 1956. Because the complaint was filed more than four years later, in August of 1960, it was too late.

Order affirmed.

Babcock Poultry Farm, Inc. v. Shook

1964, (Pa.) 203 A.2d 309

WOODSIDE, J.   This is an appeal from a judgment entered in an assumpsit action in the Court of Common Pleas of Mercer County after the court refused the plaintiff's motions for judgment *non obstante verdicto* and for a new trial. (See glossary.)

The plaintiff, Babcock Poultry Farm, Inc. (Babcock), a wholesaler of baby chicks, sued John E. Shook, Jr., a poultry farmer, in assumpsit to recover $507.99, the balance due on the sale of baby chicks under a written agreement entered into in 1960. Shook, admitting this claim, filed a counterclaim for $4,489.40 alleging the breach of an express warranty made in conjunction with an oral agreement entered into by the parties in 1959. The jury allowed Babcock's uncontested claim in full, but returned a verdict for Shook on his counterclaim in a net amount of $3,014.81.

Babcock contends that the lower court erred . . . because the evidence did not establish (1) the existence of an express warranty; (2) that Babcock had received notice of the alleged breach of warranty "within a reasonable time," as required by the Uniform Commercial Code . . . or (3) that Shook had relied upon the express warranty.

Shook, an experienced poultry farmer, entered into a written agreement in 1958 with Babcock providing for his participation in an experimental testing program designed to evaluate a new strain of chicks developed by it. For his part Shook bought 2200 experimental chicks which he then raised, keeping and submitting to Babcock detailed records on their egg production. Babcock paid Shook for the records.

In 1959 Shook advised the wholesaler that he would no longer participate in the testing program because the egg production of the chicks involved was inferior to that of a strain known as Barbara chicks which he had been using. Whereupon, Babcock invited Shook and his wife to its Ithaca, New York, office for a conference. At this conference the parties entered into an oral agreement providing that Shook would remain in the testing program, that is, raise the experimental chicks and continue to submit records on their egg production, while Babcock agreed to furnish without cost to Shook both experimental chicks and some Barbaras for control purposes, and in addition, to assist Shook with compiling the required records.

At the trial Babcock contended that the offer to supply free Barbara chicks which were allegedly in short supply was the means by which it secured Shook's promise to continue in the program. Shook, testifying that he could have obtained Barbaras from another source, contended that Babcock induced him to enter into the oral agreement and thus remain in the testing program, by guaranteeing or warranting that the experimental chicks would average, egg production-wise, as "good or better" than the Barbara chicks to be sent as a control flock. Babcock through its employees denied that such a warranty was made, testifying that experimental chicks could not by their very nature be warranted or guaranteed.

Pursuant to the oral agreement, Babcock shipped three flocks of birds totalling 2459 chicks of which 106 were Barbaras and the rest were of the experimental strain. Babcock admits that the latter did not perform as well as the Barbaras.

The evidence was conflicting, but in considering a motion for judgment n.o.v. [notwithstanding the verdict], the verdict winner, in this case the counterclaiming defendant, must be given the benefit of the evidence which is most favorable to him, together with all reasonable inferences therefrom. . . . Viewed in this light, there was sufficient evidence as summarized above to take the case to the jury. The question of whether or not a warranty had been made by Babcock was resolved by the jury in Shook's favor, and we cannot say that there was insufficient evidence to support that finding.

On the question of notice of the breach, the jury could infer that Babcock was aware that its warranty was breached through the periodic reports required to be submitted to it by Shook which showed the inferior egg production of the experimental chicks.

On Babcock's appeal from the refusal of the court to grant a new trial, it contends that there was insufficient evidence for the jury to apply the proper measure of damages. Babcock complains that Shook's damages should be limited to *the difference between the value of the experimental chicks accepted and the value they would have had if they had been as warranted,* citing the Uniform Commercial Code, supra, 2-714(2). . . . This argument overlooks the nature of the warranty found by the jury to have been made by Babcock. If the egg production of the experimental chickens was warranted to average "as good or better" than the control flock of Barbaras, evidence as to the loss in production and the market value of the difference was the correct measure of damages. Shook introduced such evidence, as well as evidence that he had purchased eggs during the period in question at a wholesale egg auction in order to supply his larger customers and thereby retain them as future customers. In effect he showed the amount of the loss, the value thereof, and that he could have sold the eggs if the experimental chicks had produced as warranted.

Judgment affirmed.

CHAPTER 19
REVIEW QUESTIONS AND PROBLEMS

1. *A* contracted to deliver to *B*'s factory 520 bushels of No. 1 tomatoes by June 25. On June 15 *A* delivered the tomatoes but it was discovered that 200 bushels were damaged by frost. *A* told *B* that he would replace them, but *B* stated that he would refuse to accept them. If *A* replaces the damaged tomatoes, must *B* accept them?

2. *A* contracted to buy 5000 bushels of corn from *B*. Just before harvest a hail storm destroyed the crop. Is *B* relieved from the obligation of the contract?

3. *A*, a clothing manufacturer, contracted to buy 500 gross of fancy buttons from *B* for delivery on July 25. On June 1, *B* notified *A* that because of a shortage of mother-of-pearl he would not deliver the buttons on the date specified. *A* promptly made arrangements to satisfy his button requirements from *X*. Shortly thereafter *B* stated that he would make delivery. Advise *A* as to his rights in this situation.

4. *A* Furnace Company on June 1, 1963, sold a furnace to *B* and warranted that it would heat well in sub-zero weather. *B* brought action for breach of warranty on November 1, 1967. Was the action timely?

5. *A* Lumber Co. had been selling materials to *B* Window Co. over a period of time. *B* was behind in his payments, and *A* refused to make further shipments until some of the payments in arrears were made.

B promised to send a check, and *A* accordingly shipped the goods. The check was never sent and *B* filed a petition in bankruptcy. Can *A* recover the goods?

6. *A* contracted to purchase lumber of a certain grade and dimension from *B*. The lumber was delivered and stored in *A*'s warehouse. Some time later *A* discovered that the lumber was of an inferior grade. Does he have any remedy?

7. *A*, a clothing manufacturer, had a contract to purchase all of his wool cloth requirements from *B*. *B* repudiated the contract. Can *A* require *B* to abide by the terms of the contract?

8. *A* contracted to purchase goods from *B* and made a down payment of $10,000. Shortly thereafter, *B* was adjudicated a bankrupt. The goods were never delivered. What is the position of *A*?

9. *A* shipped merchandise to *B*. He then discovered that *B* was insolvent. What remedy is available to *A*?

10. *A* contracted to manufacture specially designed valves for *B*. After he had manufactured a considerable number and at a time when others were being assembled, *B* repudiated the contract. What should *A* do?

11. *X* owns and operates a hardware store. He has negotiated a sale of the entire business to *Y*. Describe the procedures to be followed by *Y* to obtain maximum protection in this transaction.

12. *A* sold goods to *B*. At the time of the sale the goods were in storage at *X* warehouse. *X* had given *A* a negotiable warehouse receipt. *A* indorsed the warehouse receipt to *B*. Before *B* removed the goods from the warehouse a creditor of *A* notified *B* that he had a judgment against *A* and was about to seize the goods in storage. What is *B*'s position?

13. *A* ordered 500 tables from *B*. *B* crated the tables awaiting shipping instructions from *A*. *B* wishes to know if he should carry insurance on these tables. Advise him.

14. *A* sold goods to *B* under a contract which required *B* to pick up the goods at *A*'s place of business and which allowed *B* 30 days in which to pay for the goods. When *B* came to get the goods, *A* refused to let *B* have them unless he paid cash. Under what circumstances would *A*'s conduct be justified?

chapter 20

Introduction to Commercial Paper

3-33 History. The term "commercial paper" is used by the Code to describe certain particular types of negotiable instruments. The adjective "negotiable" has long been used to describe special types of written contracts used to represent credit and to function as a substitute for money. The term is derived from the Latin word *negotiatus,* consisting of the prefix, *neg,* meaning *not* or *negation,* plus the root *otium,* meaning leisure—making the combination *not-leisure* or *non-leisure*—plus the suffix *able,* meaning capable of. This idea was easily applicable to business and came to mean the capacity of certain kinds of paper to pass, like money, from person to person. Paper designated as "negotiable" became a medium of exchange.

The overwhelming importance of negotiable instruments to our business community and to our economy is readily apparent. It is obvious that business could not expand and develop its full potential if it were necessary to rely only upon money—coin and currency—for its transactions. Checks are used in settling about nine-tenths of all business transactions. Accumulations of wealth in the form of commercial paper far exceed wealth represented by actual money.

Commercial paper consists of two types of instruments—promissory notes and bills of exchange (drafts). The historical development of each is pertinent to their modern usage.

3-34 The Promissory Note. The origin of the modern promissory note may be traced to an early writing called *scripta obligatoria* or *writing obligatory.* The debtor made a promise, formally under seal or informally without a seal, to pay a sum of money to the creditor, his attorney, or a nominee. The attorney or nominee of the creditor could thus sue the debtor. Sometimes the paper would read "payable to the creditor or the producer of the document." Early cases tried in the "Fair Courts" in England in the sixteenth century disclose suits by persons other than the original creditor, such as an attorney or assignee or the "bearer or producer of the paper." Thus the idea of a transferable writing, either as order or bearer paper, was conceived. In buying and selling goods and wares from overseas, *bills of debt* or *billes obligatories* were given for merchandise by one merchant to another merchant. By transferring the "billes obligatories," the merchant as creditor could empower another to collect a debt, or the merchant as debtor could use the paper to pay a debt owed by him to another. Thus these notes served as a medium of exchange and to discharge debts. By statute and a recognition of the law merchant by the king's court, these written obligations took on many of the present characteristics of negotiable promissory notes.

Bills obligatory were not only used to pay for goods but were issued by goldsmiths to merchants who left their surplus funds for safe keeping with the goldsmiths. These instruments were transferable; it may be said that they were the forerunners of our modern bank notes.

Bank notes issued by an individual goldsmith as a banker were subject to the risk of the bankruptcy of the goldsmith. It was not until 1694, when the Bank of England was established, that a quasi-government institution gave credit to bank notes. The Bank of England was authorized to issue "bills obligatory and of credit"—bank notes—which would pass from one person to another, by assignment or indorsement, for the payment of debts.

In 1704, Parliament passed a statute known as the Promissory Note Act which gave to promissory notes the attributes of negotiability according to the custom of merchants.

Another early source of modern promissory notes now recognized as government obligations, such as bonds and paper money, was the English Exchequer Bill. The English government was authorized by statute in 1696 to borrow money and issue interest-bearing demand bearer bills therefor. The act authorized that these bills pass from one person to another and be accepted for the payment of debts. Soon, by necessity, these instruments—as government paper money—took on all the attributes of negotiability.

3-35 The Bill of Exchange. The origin or source of the bill of exchange rests in antiquity. There is evidence of its use in ancient Assyria, Egypt, Greece, and Rome. The bill of exchange was invented for the purpose of effecting an exchange of money—coin, silver, and gold—in distant parts without running the risk of its physical transportation. Italian merchants are said to have introduced the efficient use of modern bills of exchange. As trade and commerce increased, a safe and effective method for the exchange of money became a necessity. Goldsmiths and money exchangers in the different countries established a system whereby a merchant who owed money in a foreign country could pay his debt. The merchant delivered his money to his local exchanger, and the local exchanger drew a bill upon his foreign correspondent, directing that the creditor merchant be paid or that the foreign merchant collect from the foreign correspondent exchanger. The exchangers met from time to time at the local merchant fairs and settled the accounts. The type of instrument used by the exchangers is the ancestor of our modern bill of exchange, bank draft, and check.

Not only were drafts drawn on money exchangers, acting as bankers, but merchants in foreign countries also became drawees when their credit was well established. The following situation illustrates how the modern trade acceptance developed: *D*, a silk merchant in London, had his purchasing agent *A*, in Brussels, purchase silk from a merchant in Brussels. In order to pay for the silk, *A* drew a bill of exchange on *D* in London, payable to the order of the Brussels merchant. The Brussels merchant cashed the bill with a money exchanger, who sent it, in turn, to London for collection. Instead of making the seller in Brussels the payee, *A* might, "by way of exchange, as is done by common custom of merchants," cash the bill of exchange with an exchanger and pay the Brussels seller with coin. By the close of the seventeenth century, these instruments were in general use but not yet recognized by the common law courts of England.

Thus, the law of negotiable instruments developed first in the law merchant based upon customs and usages of the merchant. Later it was absorbed by the common law and a great body of case law developed which was replete with conflicts and contradictions. Subsequently, it was codified by the Uniform Negotiable Instruments Law (NIL) and finally the NIL was replaced by Article 3–Commercial Paper–of the Uniform Commercial Code.

3-36 The Concept of Negotiability. The legal theory which forms the basis for the use of commercial paper to represent credit and as a substitute for money must be understood prior to an examination of the details of Article 3. The theory is the same under the Code as it was under the law merchant or the N.I.L. and was developed primarily because a party to an instrument may have a defense when sued on the instrument. The theory can best be explained by noting the distinction between an assignment of a contract and the negotiation of a negotiable instrument.

As was discussed in Chapter 14, Book Two, on Contracts, contract rights are transferable by assignment. For example, suppose *A* owed *B* $100 for goods sold by *B* to *A*, or for services rendered by *B* for *A*. *B* has a right that *A* pay him $100. *A* is under duty to *B* to pay this $100. This type of contract right owned by *B* is called a chose in action. *B* may sell to *C* his right to collect $100 from *A*. Assume that *A* has a defense in the nature of a counterclaim against *B* for $35, either because the goods sold were not as required by contract or the services rendered by *B* were not satisfactory. The right that *C* purchased from *B* would be subject to *A*'s defense of failure of consideration and *C* could collect only $65 from *A*.

C, the assignee, would secure no better right against *A* than the original right held by *B*, the assignor.[1]

In the example given above, if the evidence of the debt is not a simple contract for money but a negotiable promissory note given by *A* to *B* and it is properly negotiated to *C*, *C* is in a superior position to that which he occupied when he was an assignee. Assuming that *C* is a purchaser in good faith and that he is otherwise qualified, *C* has a better title because he is free of the personal defenses that are available against *B*, the original party to the paper. Therefore, *A* cannot use the defense of failure of consideration and *C* can collect the $100 note.

Transfer of the instrument free of personal defenses is the very essence of negotiability. There are four requirements which must be met before a party is free from a defense. First, the commercial paper must be negotiable, i.e., it must comply with the formalities and language requirements of Article 3. An instrument that does not qualify is nonnegotiable and any transfer is an assignment subject to defenses. These requirements are discussed in the next chapter.

Second, the instrument must be properly negotiated. Nonnegotiable paper is transferred only by assignment, whereas negotiable contract rights may be transferred either by negotiation or assignment. In either case, if the transfer is an assignment, the defenses available may be used when the assignee seeks to collect. The method of negotiation depends upon whether the instrument is payable to "bearer" or payable to "order." If the former, it is negotiated by mere delivery; if the latter, an indorsement is required. The person who negotiates an instrument assumes responsibilities in connection with it that far surpass the responsibilities of one who assigns or transfers a nonnegotiable instrument or contract right. These matters are also discussed in the next chapter.

Third, the party to whom negotiable commercial paper is negotiated must be a holder in due course or have the rights of a holder in due course as contrasted with his status as a mere holder or an assignee. A holder is a person to whom a negotiable instrument is negotiated. But a holder in due course is a holder who qualifies as a good faith purchaser of the instrument before its maturity date. This concept is fully discussed in Chapter 22.

Fourth, the defenses eliminated by negotiation to a holder in due course are called personal defenses. Real defenses, on the other hand, may be asserted against anyone, including a holder in due course. Real defenses include forgery and fraud in the execution, that is, defenses that go to the very existence and enforceability of the instrument. Personal defenses involve only such matters as failure of consideration, fraud or other defenses to a valid negotiable instrument.

Thus, under the Code, a holder in due course of a properly negotiated negotiable instrument is not subject to personal defenses of the original parties, thus making commercial paper free to pass as money from person to person, fulfilling the purpose for which it was created. Business con-

[1] *Universal C.I.T. Credit Corp. v. Hudgens,* page 402.

venience requires this characteristic; it is the very reason for which the paper is created. A businessman is not willing to take a note, a check, a draft, or certificate of deposit from a payee if he thereby incurs all of the risk of an assignee of an ordinary contract right.

It should be noted that a result comparable to negotiability can be obtained if the indebted party by express provision in a written instrument agrees to waive defenses as against assignees and thus give protection to bona fide purchasers. Even though the language of the instrument does not comply with the formal requisites of the Code, if the parties have by contract expressed such intention, the courts have recognized such provisions to the extent that a bona fide purchaser would take the paper free from the defenses of failure or lack of consideration, fraud in the inducement, set-offs, and breach of warranty.

3-37 Scope of Article 3. Article 3–Commercial Paper is restricted in its coverage to the draft (bill of exchange), the check, the certificate of deposit, and the note. A writing which complies with the requirements of this Article is:

(a) a "draft" (bill of exchange) if it is an order;
(b) a "check" if it is a draft drawn on a bank and payable on demand;
(c) a "certificate of deposit" if it is an acknowledgment by a bank of receipt of money with an engagement to repay it;
(d) a "note" if it is a promise other than a certificate of deposit.[c1]

These negotiable instruments can be conveniently classified according to the number of parties to the paper. A note is two-party paper as is the certificate of deposit. The draft (bill of exchange) and the check are three-party paper. The parties to a note are the maker, who promises to pay, and the payee to whom the promise is made.

A draft presupposes a debtor-creditor relationship between the *drawer* and the *drawee* or some other obligation. The drawee is the debtor; the drawer the creditor. The drawer-creditor orders the drawee-debtor to pay money to a third party who is the payee. The mere drawing of the draft does not obligate the drawee on the paper. His liability on the paper arises when he formally accepts in writing and upon the draft itself and by so doing he becomes primarily liable on the paper. Thereafter the drawee is called an acceptor and his liability is similar to the liability of the maker of a promissory note. A check is a draft drawn on a bank (drawee-creditor) to the order of a payee. Of course, checks are customarily paid by the bank in due course without an acceptance in the usual sense, but the holder of a check may have it certified which is the equivalent of an "acceptance" by the bank.

3-38 Types and Use of Negotiable Instruments. There are a great variety of negotiable instruments which are tailored to meet the needs of par-

[c1] *U.C.C.* 3-104.

ticular types of business transactions and to serve particular needs as credit devices and substitutes for money. A few are discussed in this section.

Checks.   A check drawn by a bank upon itself is a *cashier's* check. A *certified* check is a check that has been accepted by the drawee bank. *Traveller's checks* are like cashier's checks in that the financial institution issuing such instruments is both the drawer and the drawee. Such instruments are negotiable instruments under Article 3 when they have been completed by the identifying signature.

Drafts.   A *bank draft* is a banker's check; that is, it is a check drawn by one bank on another bank, payable on demand. Such drafts are often used in the check collection process and are called "remittance instruments" in this connection. As noted, Article 4–Bank Deposits and Collections deals with this phase of commercial paper.

Drafts are often used as an instrument for payment of goods shipped by a seller to a buyer—e.g., a manufacturer shipping goods to a distributor. The draft in payment for the goods may be drawn on the buyer's bank and may provide, for example, that it is payable in 90 days. The bill of lading may be attached to the draft with instructions to the bank to surrender the bill of lading to the buyer after the bank has "accepted" the draft. The name given to this arrangement is *banker's acceptance.*

The business situation in which a banker's acceptance is used may be described as follows: The seller of goods often refuses to deliver to the buyer upon the buyer's credit alone; or the seller of the goods may wish to secure in payment for his goods a negotiable instrument that has a ready sale. A draft accepted by a bank would have stronger credit than a check or a trade acceptance. *B* informs his banker that he expects to purchase goods from *S* and requests the bank to accept a draft drawn on it by *S*. *B* presents collateral to the bank or agrees to keep a certain amount on deposit in order that the bank will be assured of funds at the time of payment. The collateral may consist of other notes, shipping documents, warehouse receipts, and bills of lading. By this means the bank does not make a loan, but merely lends its credit to the buyer and thus gives selling capacity to the paper. *S* can dispose of his paper more readily and on better terms than if the negotiable instrument were a trade acceptance accepted only by the original buyer, *B*.

The above arrangement may be formalized through the use of a *letter of credit* as provided in Article 5 and the *documentary draft* as explained in the previous chapter. The documentary draft is one which can be honored by the issuer of the credit (bank) only upon presentation of documents such as bills of lading as specified in the agreement between the bank and its customer.

A draft drawn by the seller in reliance upon a *letter of credit* creates a binding obligation of the bank. Letters of credit, although used in domestic trade, are more frequently employed in international trade. In domestic commerce, letters of credit are employed in automobile marketing to assure the manufacturer of prompt payment by the distributor.

Such paper is also used to assist in securing credit to finance the manufacture of articles which are made for a particular buyer.

The trade acceptance is another type of draft used largely by manufacturers and merchants. A trade acceptance is taken by the seller as payment for goods purchased at the time of the sale. The seller draws on the purchaser to his own order for the goods sold. When the draft is accepted by the purchaser, it becomes his primary obligation. The buyer, having acknowledged the debt by his acceptance, cannot later dispute the debt as against a holder of the trade acceptance. The seller often *discounts* trade acceptances at the bank or uses them as collateral for loans.

The process of discounting is extremely important in business and commercial transactions. Typically it involves the situation in which the holder of a trade acceptance desires to obtain money on the strength of the instrument prior to the time when it matures. Thus, the holder may be in need of funds presently, and if he is the owner of a trade acceptance which matures six months in the future, he may by discounting obtain funds for his present needs. If the trade acceptance is discounted at a bank, for example, the bank would compute the interest that would accrue during the life of the trade acceptance, subtract this amount from the face of the instrument, and pay the borrower the net sum.

Promissory notes. Notes may be used in many different ways. The purpose for which they are used and the nature of the security for the promise given by the maker to support his promise are often used to designate the type or kind of note. A note which on its face carries only the promise of the maker and is limited to his personal security may be called a simple promissory note. However, business convenience often requires a high degree of certainty that the money promised will be paid; hence the personal promise of the maker is often supported by other contracts which make available property as collateral security or contracts which enumerate various remedies that may be used by the payee or holder in case of default by the primary obligor. In addition to property as security, the payee may require the promise of another person. Such person may be a cosignor or an accommodation party.

A note may be secured by personal property in the nature of other notes, bonds, stock certificates, chattel paper, and other security devices, temporarily placed within the control of the payee or holder. The property transferred is called collateral, and such a note a *collateral note.* Many kinds of property may be used as collateral security for a note.

The maker may sign a contract as additional security, which contract gives a remedy to the payee or holder to confess a judgment against the defaulting maker or primary obligor, without a trial. This form of note is called a *judgment note.*

In order to secure the payment of a note given for the sale of merchandise, the contract of sale may be set forth upon the face of the note. The contract usually provides that title to the chattel sold shall remain with the payee-vendor until the note given is paid in full, and, in addition, that in case of default in payments as shown upon the note, the vendor may repossess the chattel. A note in this form is called a *conditional sale note*.

A security contract separate from the simple promissory note is illustrated by the mortgage. There are two kinds of mortgages, depending upon the character of the property used as security. When the maker conveys to the payee as security a right in the title of chattels, the note so secured is called a *chattel mortgage note*. When the right in the title conveyed is in real property, the note so secured is called a *real estate mortgage note*.

It is noted that the Code (Article 9) has consolidated all security devices involving personal property into a device known as the "security interest." However, the terms chattel mortgage and conditional sales contract are still used as security for promissory notes. For more complete information concerning such instruments see Article 3 and Article 9 of the Code. Article 3 sets out the requirement of negotiability and Article 9 determines the rights of the parties as holders of a security interest.

Certificate of deposit. The classification of different types of promises to pay money is sometimes controlled by the character of the maker. This is true of the certificate of deposit and of the bond. A certificate of deposit is given by a bank to a depositor, as a receipt for the deposit, the bank engaging to repay the amount to the depositor. Care must be taken to distinguish certificates of deposit from the usual receipt given by the bank when a depositor deposits sums to his checking account. This receipt is called a "deposit slip," which evidences the contract of deposit. There is no uniformity in this type of paper. The language used does not satisfy the requirements for negotiable paper; consequently such deposit slips are not negotiable.

3-39 Other Negotiable Instruments. The negotiable attributes of a *bond* are covered by Article 8 of the Code. A bond is a very formal instrument and in general is so worded as to satisfy the requirements of negotiability. However, since the bond is used as an investment instrument for the purpose of loaning money over a long term, it necessarily carries on its face much language referring to the nature of security and the remedies permitted in case of default. For this reason a bond would not be negotiable under Article 3 although in form it is comparable to a promissory note.

As noted previously, there are many instruments which are negotiable but whose characteristics are determined by other articles of the Code. Included in addition to the bond are other investment securities, bills of lading and warehouse receipts. Attention is now being given only to those instruments which fall within Article 3–Commercial Paper. The material in the next chapter is descriptive of such instruments.

INTRODUCTION TO THE LAW OF
COMMERCIAL PAPER CASE

Universal C.I.T. Credit Corporation v. Hudgens

1962, 234 Ark. 668, 356 S.W.2d 658

SMITH, J.   On May 21, 1959, the appellees, Anson Hudgens and his daughter, bought a used Ford car from E. W. Mack, doing business as West Memphis Auto Sales. The conditional sales contract executed by the purchasers was transferred by Mack to the appellant finance company the next day. None of the monthly payments were made by the purchasers, who insist that they were defrauded. The appellant brought this action in replevin to recover the car. The case was transferred to equity, where the chancellor canceled the contract for fraud in its procurement and for usury. We do not reach the issue of usury, for we have concluded that the decree must in any event be affirmed upon the finding of fraud.

It should be stated at the outset that the appellant does not and cannot invoke the protection afforded to the holder of a negotiable instrument. No promissory note is involved, and the conditional sales contract is not negotiable, as it does not contain an unconditional promise payable to order or bearer. *Gale & Co. v. Wallace,* (210 Ark. 161, 194 S.W.2d 881). Hence, as we held in the case cited, the appellant holds the contract subject to defenses available against the original seller.

If the execution of the contract was induced by fraud it was properly canceled. *Gentry v. Little Rock Road Mach. Co.,* (232 Ark. —, 339 S.W.2d 101). Here, as in the Gentry case, the purchasers testified that the seller represented the vehicle to be in good condition, when in fact it needed extensive repairs. Mack's salesman gave the appellees a signed memorandum stating that the seller had given a 30-day guarantee on the motor, transmission, and rear end; but when the dissatisfied purchasers brought the car back within a few days Mack refused to repair it unless the buyers would bear half the expense.

A more serious charge of fraud is the appellees' assertion that Mack's salesman, Harris, induced them to sign the contract in blank and then filled it in for $300 more than the agreed purchase price of $1,095. As a witness for the appellant, Harris admitted that the contract was signed in blank and was left with him for completion, but he insisted that the figure which he inserted as the purchase price, $1,395, was in accordance with the parties' agreement.

No useful purpose would be served by a detailed discussion of the conflicting testimony. Hudgens, his daughter, and his son were all present when the car was bought, and all three testified to facts amply supporting the charge of fraud. Their version of the matter is contradicted only by the salesman, Harris. After studying the record we cannot say that the evidence adduced by one side is essentially more credible than that adduced by the other. The chancellor had the great advantage of observing the witnesses as they testified. His findings do not appear to us to be against the weight of the evidence.

Affirmed.

CHAPTER 20
REVIEW QUESTIONS AND PROBLEMS

1. *A* sold *B* a TV set on an installment contract. *A* then sold the contract to *X*. When *X* sought to recover the payments from *B*, *B* refused to pay on the ground that the set was defective. Can *B* successfully defend on this ground? Does *X* have any recourse against *A*?

2. *M* executed a note payable to the order of *P*. *P* indorsed the note to *H* at a time when the note was overdue. Does the late transfer affect *H*'s rights against *M*?

3. *A* is the holder of a note which provides: "I promise to pay $500 to *A* or bearer." The note is stolen from *A* and sold by the thief to *B*. Can *A* recover the note from *B*?

4. *M* executed a note: "I promise to pay $500 to *P* on June 1, 1966." *P* indorsed the note to *A* in payment for goods. If *M* is unable to pay the note, can *A* hold *P* liable?

5. *A* purchased a car from *B* and gave a negotiable note in payment. The note provided that title to the car would remain in *B* until the note was paid. If the car were destroyed without fault of *A* prior to maturity of the note, would *A* be relieved of liability?

6. *A* is indebted to *B* in the amount of $500. *B* drew a draft on *A* in that amount payable to the order of *P*. *P* presented the draft to *A* for payment and *A* refused to pay. Can *P* sue *A* on the draft?

7. *A* is the holder of a check drawn by *B* on *X* Bank. Under what circumstances might *A* wish to have the check certified?

8. How is the letter of credit used in financing sales of goods?

9. *S*, Seller, drew a trade acceptance on *B*, buyer, for the price of goods sold. *B* accepted the instrument and *S* then discounted it at *X* Bank. The goods were never delivered to *B*. Can *X* Bank force *B* to pay the amount of the acceptance?

10. *M* executed a note in favor of *P* and also delivered corporate stocks to *P* as security. What may *P* do with the stocks if *M* fails to pay the note at maturity?

chapter 21

Commercial Paper: Creation and Transfer

LANGUAGE AND WORDS REQUIRED TO CREATE NEGOTIABLE PAPER

3-40 In General. In order that an instrument may be negotiable it must conform to certain requirements. If it does not satisfy these requirements, it will not be negotiable and the transferee will be subject to all defenses of prior parties; its transfer will be an assignment. The Code provides that in order to qualify as a negotiable instrument, a writing must (a) be signed by the maker or drawer; (b) contain an unconditional promise or order to pay a sum certain in money; (c) be payable on demand or at a definite time; and (d) be payable to order or to bearer.[C1] These are the basic requirements. The sections which follow discuss these requirements in detail.

3-41 Writing and Signature. The requirement of the Code is simply that there be a writing signed by the maker or drawer. It is not required that any particular type or kind of writing be used, nor is it necessary that the signature be at any particular place upon the instrument. The instrument may be in any form which includes "printing, typewriting, or any other intentional reduction to tangible form." [C2] A symbol is a sufficient signature if it was "executed or adopted by a party with present intention to authenticate a writing." [C3] The use of the word "authenticate" in the definition of "signed" makes it clear that a complete signature is

[C1] *U.C.C.* 3-104(1).
[C2] *U.C.C.* 1-201(46).
[C3] *U.C.C.* 1-201(39).

not required. The authentication may be printed or written and may be placed on the instrument by stamp.

3-42 The Necessity of a Promise or Order. One of the basic requirements of a negotiable note is that it must contain a *promise* to pay. It is not required that the exact word "promise" be used; it is necessary, however, that in absence of the word promise, the language used shall manifest an undertaking or promise. A promise must be derived from the language, not from the fact that a debt exists. For example, the words in an instrument "due *X*, $500 for value received" would not satisfy the requirement of a promise. A mere acknowledgment of a debt in writing is not promissory.[C4] The simplest form of an instrument which merely acknowledges a debt is an I.O.U. Though such a written memorandum is sufficient to evidence and create a valid enforceable instrument upon which recovery may be had by the creditor or his assignee against the debtor, such instruments are not negotiable notes. In order to constitute a promise, there must be an undertaking to pay and the mere acknowledgment that an obligation exists would not be sufficient.

A draft must contain an *order* to pay. The purpose of the instrument is to order the drawee to pay money to the payee, and it is therefore necessary that plain language be used to show an intention to make an order. The language must signify more than an authorization or request. It must be a direction to pay.[C5] Thus, an instrument in the following form would not be negotiable: "To John Doe. I wish you would pay $1,000 to the order of Richard Roe. (Signed) Robert Lee." This would nevertheless be a valid authorization for John Doe to make payment to Richard Roe.

3-43 The Promise or Order Must be Unconditional. Negotiable instruments serve as a substitute for money and as a basis for short-term credit. Negotiable instruments thus stand for money which is to be paid in the future. If these purposes are to be served, it is essential that the instruments be readily accepted and that they be freely transferable. Conditional promises or orders would defeat these purposes for it would be necessary for every transferee to make a determination with regard to whether or not the condition had been performed prior to accepting a transfer. The instruments would therefore not freely circulate. In recognition of the functions which are served by negotiable instruments, and the need for certainty if the instruments are to serve as a substitute for money and a basis for credit, the Code requires that the promise or order be unconditional. If the promise or order is a conditional one, the instrument would not be negotiable even though it satisfied all of the other requirements.

The question of whether or not the promise or order is conditional arises when the instrument contains language in addition to the promise or order to pay money. The Code specifies those situations in which the additional language renders the promise or order conditional, and also

---

[C4] *U.C.C.* 3-102(1)(c).   [C5] *U.C.C.* 3-102(1)(b).

sets forth a number of situations in which the additional language does not impair negotiability.[C6]

The promise or order is conditional if the language upon the face of the paper says that payment is controlled by or subject to the terms of some other agreement.[C7] Clearly a promise or order is conditional if reference to some other agreement is *required* and payment is *subject to* the terms of another contract. It would be necessary to refer to such contract in order to determine the exact nature of the promise or order before payment. However, a mere *reference* to some other contract or agreement does not condition the promise or order and does not impair negotiability.[C8] A distinction, then, is to be drawn between additional language which imposes the terms of some other agreement and that which simply gives information as to the transaction which gave rise to the instrument. Thus, the use of the words *subject to contract* conditions the promise or order, while the words *as per contract* would not render the promise or order conditional.[C9] The latter is informative rather than restrictive. A recital "as per contract" might disclose an executory promise as the return for which an instrument was given. The Code states specifically that implied or constructive conditions such as the implication that no obligation would arise until the executory promise had been performed do not render a promise or order conditional.[1] [C10]

Statements of the consideration for which the instrument was given and statements of the transaction out of which the instrument arose are simply informative and are not conditional. A draft may have been drawn under a letter of credit and a reference to this fact does not impose a condition. Notes frequently contain a statement that some sort of security has been given, such as a mortgage on property or that title to goods has been retained as security for the payment of the note. In either case the purpose is to make clear to the holder that the promise to pay is secured by something in addition to the general credit of the maker and as a consequence a mere reference to the security does not destroy negotiability.

Notes given in payment for property purchased on installment often provide that title to such property shall not pass to the maker of the note until all payments called for have been made. A statement to this effect in a note does not condition the promise to pay.

3-44 The Particular Fund Concept. A statement that an instrument is to be paid only out of a particular fund imposes a condition.[C11] Such an instrument does not carry the general personal credit of the maker or drawer and is contingent upon the sufficiency of the fund on which it is drawn. An illustration of such promise or order is as follows: "To *A*. Pay to *B* or order $500 out of the proceeds of the sale of my store building.

---

1 *Gordon Supply Co. v. South Sea Apts.*, page 441.

C6 *U.C.C.* 3-105.
C7 *U.C.C.* 3-105(2)(a).
C8 *U.C.C.* 3-105(1)(c).

C9 *U.C.C.* 3-105(1)(6).
C10 *U.C.C.* 3-105(1)(a).
C11 *U.C.C.* 3-105(2)(b).

(Signed) *Y."* Even though there is a sufficient fund in existence when the instrument falls due, the instrument is non-negotiable.

There are two exceptions to the foregoing rule with regard to a limitation to payment out of a particular fund.[C12] An instrument issued by a government or government agency is not deemed non-negotiable simply because payment is restricted to a particular fund. Second, an instrument issued by or on behalf of a partnership, unincorporated association, trust, or estate may be negotiable, although it is limited to payment out of their entire assets.

A mere reference to a particular fund does not impair negotiability.[C13] Such references are often made for purposes of record keeping and accounting, and do not in any way limit liability to the fund mentioned. Thus, a check which provides "charge to agent's disbursing account" would not be deemed to contain a conditional order, but would simply indicate the account to be debited.

3-45 The Sum Must be Certain. The language used in creating commercial paper must be certain with respect to the amount of money promised or ordered to be paid.[C14] Otherwise, its value at any period could not be definitely determined. If the principal sum to be paid is definite, negotiability is not affected by the fact that it is to be paid with interest, in installments, with exchange at a fixed or current rate, or with cost of collection and attorney's fee in case payment shall not be made at maturity. If at any point of time during the term of the paper its full value can be ascertained with certainty, the requirement that the sum must be certain is satisfied. The obligation to pay costs and attorney's fees is part of the security contract, separate and distinct from the primary promise to pay money and does not, therefore, affect the requirement as to a sum certain. The certainty of amount is not affected if the instrument specifies different rates of interest before and after default; neither is the certainty affected by a provision for a stated discount for early payment or an additional charge if payment is made after the date fixed.[C15]

3-46 Instruments Must be Payable in Money. An instrument, to be negotiable, must be payable in money.[C16] Instruments payable in chattels, such as one hundred bushels of wheat or one ounce of gold, are therefore not negotiable. "Money" is defined as "medium of exchange authorized or adopted by a domestic or foreign government as a part of its currency." The amount payable may be stated in foreign as well as domestic money, provided the medium specified has government approval. An instrument is payable in money if the medium of exchange in which it is payable is money at the time the instrument is made. Thus, the amount payable may be stated in sterling, francs, lire, or other foreign currency. If the sum payable is stated in foreign currency, the instrument may be satisfied by payment of the dollar equivalent, that is, the number of dollars that

[C12] *U.C.C.* 3-105(1)(g).
[C13] *U.C.C.* (1)(f).
[C14] *U.C.C.* 3-106.

[C15] *U.C.C.* 3-106.
[C16] *U.C.C.* 3-107.

could be purchased by the foreign currency at the "buying sight rate" on the day payable, or if it is demand paper at the rate on the date of demand. However, if it is specified in the instrument that a foreign currency is the medium of payment, payment would have to be made in that currency. An instrument expressed in terms of foreign currency but payable in dollars is negotiable, even though the exchange rate fluctuates. It might be argued that the sum is not certain since the number of dollars required to satisfy the instrument could not be determined until the date of payment or demand, but what is really involved is simply the "buying power" of money.

Negotiable instruments are sometimes made payable in "currency" or "current funds." Such terms mean that the instrument is payable in money.

TIME OF PAYMENT MUST BE CERTAIN

3-47 In General. As a substitute for money, negotiable instruments would be of little value if the holder were unable to determine at what time he could demand payment. It is necessary, therefore, that there be certainty as to the time of payment. A negotiable instrument must be payable on demand or at a "definite time."

3-48 Demand Paper. An instrument is payable on demand when it so states, when payable at sight or on presentation, or when no time of payment is stated.[C17] In general, the words "payable on demand" are used in notes and the words "at sight" in drafts. If nothing is said about the due date, the instrument is demand paper.[2] A check is a good illustration of such an instrument. The characteristic of demand paper is that the holder of such paper can require payment at any time by making a demand upon the person who is obligated on the paper.

3-49 Payable at a Definite Time. The requirement of a definite time is in keeping with the necessity for certainty in instruments.[C18] It is important that the value of an instrument at any given time be capable of determination. This value will be dependent upon the ultimate maturity date of the instrument. If an instrument is payable only upon an act or event the time of whose occurrence is uncertain it is not payable at a definite time even though the act or event has occurred. Thus, an instrument payable "thirty days after my father's death" would not be negotiable.

The requirement of certainty as to the time of payment is satisfied if it is payable *on or before* a specified date.[3] Thus, an instrument payable on June 1, 1968, is payable at a definite time, as is one payable "on or before" June 1, 1968. In the latter situation, the obligor on the instrument

---

[2] *Liberty Aluminum Products Co. v. John Cortis, et ux.,* page 441.
[3] *Ferri v. Sylvia,* page 442.

[C17] *U.C.C.* 3-108.　　　　　　　　　　　　[C18] *U.C.C.* 3-109.

has the privilege of making payment prior to June 1, 1968, but is not required to pay it until the specified date. An instrument payable at a fixed period after a stated date, or at a fixed period after sight, is payable at a definite time. The expressions "one year after date" or "sixty days after sight" are definite as to time.

There are two types of provisions appearing on the face of instruments which affect the definite time. The first is called an acceleration clause.[C19] An acceleration clause hastens or accelerates the maturity date of an instrument. Accelerating provisions may be of many different kinds. One kind, for example, provides that in case of default in payment of interest or of an installment of the principal, the entire note shall become due and payable. Another kind gives the holder an option to declare the instrument due and payable when he feels insecure with respect to ultimate payment. An instrument payable at a definite time subject to *any acceleration* is negotiable.[C20] If, however, the acceleration provision permits the holder to declare the instrument due when he feels insecure, time of payment is made indefinite unless the holder acts in good faith in the honest belief that the likelihood of payment is impaired and not forthcoming.[C21] The presumption is that the holder has acted in good faith, placing the burden on the obligor-payor to show that such act was not in good faith.

The second type of provision affecting time is an extension clause. An extension clause is the converse of the acceleration provision. It provides for the extension of the time for payment beyond that specified in the instrument.[C22] For example, a note payable in two years might provide that the maker has the right to extend the time of payment six months. An instrument is payable at a definite time if it is payable "at a definite time subject to extension at the option of the holder, or to extension to a further definite time at the option of the maker or acceptor, or automatically upon or after a specified act or event." [C23] It is to be noted that in an extension at the option of the holder, no time limit is required. The holder always has the right to refrain from undertaking collection. An extension at the option of the maker or acceptor, or an automatic extension, must provide for a definite time for ultimate payment.

PAYABLE TO ORDER OR BEARER

3-50 Words of Negotiability. A basic requirement is words of negotiability. Such words clearly express the intention to create negotiable paper. The words of negotiability are "order" and "bearer." Although these exact words are not required, words of equivalent meaning must be used. However, in order to avoid questions as to whether equivalent words impart negotiability it is desirable to always use the words "order" or "bearer." In the absence of words of negotiability, an instrument will

---

C19 *U.C.C.* 3-109(1)(c).
C20 *U.C.C.* 3-109(1)(c).
C21 *U.C.C.* 1-208.

C22 *U.C.C.* 3-109(1)(d).
C23 *U.C.C.* 3-109(1)(d).

ordinarily lack the capacity to pass as money. An instrument which is not payable to order or bearer, but which satisfies the other requirements of negotiability, may be treated in many respects as though it were negotiable. The Code does not preclude the recognition of certain attributes of negotiability to such instruments—that is, instruments lacking words of negotiability. Courts can arrive at a result similar to negotiability by estopping the obligor of a non-negotiable contract (a mercantile specialty or "almost negotiable" instrument) from asserting his defenses against a bona fide purchaser, and thus bring the law into conformity with commercial and banking practice. Thus, a check which provides simply "Pay to *A*" is recognized as a check under Article 3.

The maker of a note, made payable to "*X* or order" may be said to make two promises. The maker promises to pay *X* if *X* holds the paper; he also promises to pay any other person that *X* may order him to pay. A drawer of a draft orders the drawee to pay the named payee, or any person named by the payee.

3-51 Order Paper. Indorsement for negotiation is a distinguishing characteristic of order paper, whereas bearer paper is negotiated by delivery. An instrument is payable to order when by its terms it is payable to the order of any person therein specified with reasonable certainty, or to him or his order.[C24]

An instrument may be payable to the order of the maker or drawer, the drawee, or a payee who is not a maker, drawer, or drawee. It may be payable to two or more payees together or in the alternative. An instrument payable to the order of "*A* or *B*" may be negotiated by the indorsement of either of the parties.[C25] It may be drawn payable to the order of "*A* and *B*" in which event the indorsement of both would be required.[C26]

An instrument may be payable to the order of:

> An estate, trust, or fund, in which case it is payable to the order of the representative of such estate, trust, or fund or his successors; or
>
> An office, or an officer by his title as such in which case it is payable to the principal but the incumbent of the office or his successors may act as if he or they were the holder; or
>
> A partnership or unincorporated association, in which case it is payable to the partnership or association and may be transferred by any person thereto authorized.[C27]

Thus, an instrument payable to the order of the estate of a decedent is payable to the order of the estate representative. Likewise, if an instrument is payable to the order of a fund such as the "Development Fund," it is payable to the representative thereof, or his successors. An instrument payable to the order of an officer or an office as for example, the "Treasurer of the Traffic Club" runs to the present officer (treasurer) or his

---

C24 *U.C.C.* 3-110.
C25 *U.C.C.* 3-116(a).

C26 *U.C.C.* 3-116(b).
C27 *U.C.C.* 3-110(1)(e)(f)(g) .

successors in that office. An instrument payable to the order of a partnership or an unincorporated association, such as a labor union, may be indorsed or transferred by an authorized person.

In addition, an instrument may be drawn payable to the order of a *named* person with *additional words* describing such designated person.[C28] The descriptive words show that the payee is an agent of a named principal or an officer of a specified company or organization—"John Smith, Treasurer of X Corp." They indicate that he is a fiduciary for a specified person or entity—"Henry Rose, Trustee of the Ford Trust." The words may, on the other hand, simply describe the status of the payee without tying in any other specified person—"John Doe, Agent." In the first example the instrument is payable to the company—the additional words are not merely for identification—and the officer is named only for convenience in enabling him to cash the check.

In the second example, "Henry Rose, Trustee," the instrument by reason of the law of fiduciaries is payable to the individual named. He is the real party in interest. He has power to negotiate, enforce, or discharge the paper. As a trustee he is liable for breach of trust, but this does not impinge upon his power to negotiate. It should be noted here that purchasers of paper which discloses on its face a trust situation, are put on notice of the fiduciary position of the payee. Such purchasers will not be holders in due course and thus will be subject to the rights of the beneficiary if the trustee negotiated the instrument in breach of trust, and they have notice of such breach. Such notice would be imparted if the fiduciary negotiated the instrument in payment of a personal obligation.[C29]

In the last example, "pay to John Doe, Agent," where the descriptive words do not disclose a principal or beneficiary, the person named is the payee and real party in interest. Such person may negotiate, enforce, or discharge the paper. Any person dealing with such payee may in effect disregard the description and will be protected unless he has notice of some irregularity.[C30]

An instrument which is not payable to order may contain a statement such as "payable upon return of this certificate properly indorsed." [C31] Since the purpose of such language is usually to have the indorsement serve as a receipt, the addition of such clause does not make the instrument payable to order and the instrument would not be negotiable. Paper which is on its face payable to order becomes bearer paper if it is indorsed in blank—by signature alone without specification of the indorsee.[C32]

When an instrument is drawn payable to the order of any one of several payees, such are called *alternative payees*. Thus "payable to the order of *A* or *B* or *C*" means pay to any of the three. However, when it is intended to make the instrument payable to *A* and *B* and *C* together, such instrument is payable to a *unit* or *joint payees*.[C33] An instrument payable in the alternative designates the payee with reasonable certainty,

[C28] *U.C.C.* 3-117.
[C29] *U.C.C.* 3-304(2).
[C30] *U.C.C.* 3-117(c).

[C31] *U.C.C.* 3-110(2).
[C32] *U.C.C.* 3-204(2).
[C33] *U.C.C.* 3-117.

and an indorsement and delivery by any one of the payees passes title. Much difficulty arises when one of the payees dies. Does the survivor or the deceased payee's personal representative succeed to the deceased payee's interest? The question here is not one of negotiability or who is holder, but who is the owner of the paper. Normally, an instrument payable to "*A and B*" is intended to be payable to the two parties as tenants in common and there is no right of survivorship whereby the surviving party becomes the sole owner in the absence of express language to that effect. To assure the right of survivorship, the relationship should be spelled out thus: "pay to *A and B* or the survivor."

An instrument payable to the order of joint payees can be negotiated only by the indorsement of all of the payees or by the authorization of one to sign for the other. Payment by the obligor to one of the payees will not otherwise discharge the obligation toward the others.

If an instrument is payable to *A* and/or *B* it is payable to *A* or to *B*, or to *A* and to *B* together, and it may be negotiated, enforced, or discharged by any one payee or by both the payees.

It sometimes happens that in filling in a printed form a person will execute an instrument in such form as "Pay *to the order of* John Smith or bearer," without noticing the word "bearer," and the underscored words are typed or written by the person drawing the instrument. This is considered as order paper because the insertion of the name of the payee shows such an intent.[C34] On the other hand, if the word "bearer" is added either in typewriting or handwriting, this indicates an intent that the instrument be payable to bearer.

3-52 Bearer Paper. An instrument is payable to bearer and can be negotiated by delivery if it is payable to:

(a) bearer or the order of bearer; or

(b) a specified person or bearer; or

(c) "cash" or the order of "cash," or any other indication which does not purport to designate a specific payee.[C35]

The basic characteristic of bearer paper as distinguished from order paper is that it can be negotiated by delivery—no indorsement is required. Bearer paper is determined by what appears on the face of the paper and by indorsements. A bearer negotiable instrument specially indorsed—that is, the indorsee's name is specified—becomes order paper—payable to the order of the special indorsee.[C36] Paper on its face payable to order and indorsed in blank—simply signed by the indorser becomes payable to bearer until specially indorsed. Indorsement determines whether paper is order paper or bearer paper.

Under the Code a check is bearer paper when it "does not purport to designate a specific payee." [C37] This language means an impersonal or inanimate designation of a payee such as "cash," "bills payable," "Ship

C34 *U.C.C.* 3-110(3).
C35 *U.C.C.* 3-111.
C36 *U.C.C.* 3-204(1).
C37 *U.C.C.* 3-111(c).

Fortune," or "Twenty Tons of Steel." Since such designated payee cannot indorse the paper, the maker clearly intended title should pass by delivery only and it is therefore bearer paper.

ADDITIONAL TERMS: OMISSIONS

3-53 Terms and Omissions Not Affecting Negotiability.[C38] Mention has already been made of various provisions which can be included in an instrument in connection with the requirements of sum certain, time, and unconditional promise. Certain other language can be added without impairing negotiability. Statements relating to collateral given to secure the obligation including the right to sell such collateral in case of default are permitted, as is a provision for maintaining the collateral or giving additional collateral. A provision authorizing a confession of judgment has no effect on negotiability, although many states by statute do not permit enforcement of such clauses. A party may waive without impairing negotiability the protection of any law designed for his protection, such as a homestead exemption statute. It will be noted that all of the above are designed to give additional rights or protection to a holder. A provision inserted for the protection of a drawer—that the payee by cashing or indorsing acknowledges full satisfaction of an obligation of the drawer—is also permitted.

The Code suggests certain formal language to be used in order to give an instrument its negotiable character. Nevertheless, the instrument need not include the exact language of the Code, but may use any terms that clearly indicate an intention to conform to the requirements of the Code. Many words which would appear to be essential are, in fact, nonessential. The validity and negotiable character of an instrument otherwise negotiable are not destroyed by the fact that it is not dated, that the words "value" or "value received" are omitted, or that it does not state what consideration was given for it.

3-54 Date. The dating of an instrument is not an essential of negotiability.[C39] Whether there is no date, an antedate, or a postdate is not important from the standpoint of negotiability. Any date which does appear on the instrument is presumed correct until evidence is introduced to establish a contrary finding. Even though the date on the instrument is not proper, it has no effect on the negotiability. Any fraud or illegality connected with the date of the instrument does not affect its negotiability, but merely gives defenses to the parties as provided for under other Code sections.

If a date is necessary in order to ascertain maturity an undated instrument is an incomplete instrument. The date, however, may be inserted by the holder under rules set forth in the next section.

If an instrument is payable on demand or at a fixed period after

C38 *U.C.C.* 3-112.   C39 *U.C.C.* 3-114.

date, the date which is put on the instrument is the date of the instrument even though it is antedated or postdated.

3-55 Incomplete Instruments. A person may sign an instrument which is incomplete in that it lacks one or more of the necessary elements of a complete instrument. Thus a paper signed by the maker or drawer in which the payee's name or the amount is omitted, is incomplete. A blank paper containing only a signature, however, cannot later be completed for the purpose of creating a negotiable instrument. However, a person who signs a blank *form* may be held liable.[4] Assuming that blank spaces on forms are provided for the insertion of the missing information, such an incomplete instrument cannot be enforced until it is completed.[C40] If the blanks after signatures are subsequently filled in by any person in accordance with the authority or instructions given by the party who signed the instrument, in its incomplete state, it then is effective as completed. A person might, for example, leave blank signed checks with an employee with instructions to complete the checks as to amounts and payee in payment of invoices as goods are delivered. When the employee completes the checks in accordance with these instructions, they are perfectly valid.

A blank date can be supplied in similar fashion and this may be important in order to constitute a "complete instrument," e.g., where it is payable "sixty days after date."

If the completion of the blanks is not in conformity with the signer's authority, the unauthorized filling-in is treated as a material alteration of the instrument.[C41] A holder in due course can enforce the instrument as completed, even though the instrument has been initially taken from the signer and delivered with his permission. The loss is placed upon the person who signed the blank paper because he made wrongful completion possible. A person not a holder in due course is subject to the defenses of improper completion.

3-56 Instruments "Payable Through" a Bank—"At a Bank." Instruments representing insurance payments, payroll checks, dividends, and other instruments used to transfer credit are sometimes made "payable through" a designated bank. The words, "payable through," do not make the bank the drawee; they do not authorize or order the bank to pay the instrument out of funds in the account of the drawee; neither do they order or require the bank to take the paper for collection.[C42] The bank's agency authority in this situation is extremely limited; the bank is merely a funnel or collecting means through which the paper is to be properly presented to the drawee or maker.

A related situation is that in which a note or acceptance of a draft contains the language: "Payable at" a bank. In recognition of varying

4 *Century Appliance Co. v. Groff,* page 443.

C40 *U.C.C.* 3-115.   C42 *U.C.C.* 3-120.
C41 *U.C.C.* 3-115(2).

banking practices in different sections of the country, the Code provides two alternatives either of which may be adopted by a state:

> *Alternative A*—A note or acceptance which states that it is payable at a bank is the equivalent of a draft drawn on the bank payable when it falls due out of any funds of the maker or acceptor in current account or otherwise available for such payment.
>
> *Alternative B*—A note or acceptance which states that it is payable at a bank is not of itself an order or authorization to the bank to pay it.[C43]

The Code thus accepts either of two positions, namely, (1) that a note or an acceptance of a draft "payable at a bank" *is* like a draft on the bank, and upon its due date the bank is authorized, without consultation, to make the payment out of any available funds of the maker or acceptor; or (2) such words *are not* an order or authorization, but a mere direction for the bank to request instructions from the maker or acceptor.

3-57 Other Writings Affecting Instrument. Often a transaction will involve both a negotiable instrument and another contract where both are executed as a part of the same transaction. The separate written agreement may be a conditional sale contract for consumer goods, a contract for the purchase of a house by way of a cash down payment accompanied by a note for the balance secured by a mortgage, or a contract for the purchase of heavy machinery. Such contracts are legion and out of them arise promises to pay money.

Negotiable instruments are also contracts between the immediate parties such as the maker and the payee. Under a general rule of construction, courts will look to the entire contract and all writing executed as part of the same transaction, and construe them as a single agreement. Therefore, if the separate writing (separate from the note) provided for an acceleration of payment, a court would construe the acceleration as applicable to the note.[C44] Of course if the terms of the note and the terms of the other writing are in direct conflict, the note would not be affected and its terms would prevail.

A separate agreement does not affect the negotiability of the note or other negotiable instrument, although if the note states that it is "subject to" or governed by any other agreement it is not negotiable under Article 3.[C45] As noted previously, a mere reference to the other agreement has no effect on negotiability.[5] The basic concept is that negotiability is always determined by "what appears on the face of the instrument alone." Thus, a purchaser of the paper who does not know of the separate writing is not affected by it.

Protection is afforded to the holder in due course because he is not affected by any limitation of his rights arising out of the separate

---

[5] *D'Andrea v. Feinberg,* page 444.

[C43] *U.C.C.* 3-121.
[C44] *U.C.C.* 3-105(1)(c).

[C45] *U.C.C.* 3-105(2)(a).

written agreement if he had no notice of the limitation when he took the instrument. With this limitation it is clear that the terms of a negotiable instrument may be modified or affected by any other written agreement executed as part of the same transaction.[C46] There is no reason why the principle of construing note and separate writing together should not apply, if the paper is in the hands of a transferee.

3-58 Ambiguous Terms and Rules of Construction. Since negotiable commercial paper passes current as money, it must mean the same thing to different persons at different times and in different places. The language should be clear, distinct, and unambiguous. A holder should feel free to negotiate and takers encouraged to accept. In order to eliminate as much as possible the use of parol evidence in case of doubt or ambiguity, except to reform the paper as created, the rules of the Code are so drafted as to give faith to holders and purchasers that valid negotiable paper has been made and can circulate free from defenses. The rules are:

(a) Where there is doubt whether the instrument is a draft or a note, the holder may treat it as either. A draft drawn on the drawer is effective as a note.

(b) Handwritten terms control typewritten and printed terms, and typewritten control printed.

(c) Words control figures except that if the words are ambiguous, figures control.

(d) Unless otherwise specified, a provision for interest means interest at the judgment rate at the place of payment from the date of the instrument, or if it is undated from the date of issue.

(e) Unless the instrument otherwise specifies two or more persons who sign as maker, acceptor or drawer or indorser and as a part of the same transaction, are jointly and severally liable even though the instrument contains such words as "*I* promise to pay."

(f) Unless otherwise specified, consent to extension authorizes a single extension for not longer than the original period. A consent to extension, expressed in the instrument, is binding on secondary parties and accommodation makers. A holder may not exercise his option to extend an instrument over the objection of a maker or acceptor or other party who . . . tenders full payment when the instrument is due. A meaning cannot be given the paper which is inconsistent with these rules.[C47]

These rules are self-explanatory. However, the phrase "extension of time" (see Sec. 3-49) merits some consideration. In order to retain and continue the liability of primary and secondary parties, co-makers, and indorsers, the following clause is often found in commercial paper, particularly in notes: "The makers, indorsers, and other secondary parties of this note consent that it may be extended without notice to them." Under suretyship law, extension of an obligation by a creditor with-

---

[C46] *U.C.C.* 3-119.   [C47] *U.C.C.* 3-118.

out the consent of the sureties discharges the sureties. Consent to such extension binds the secondary parties—sureties—such as indorsers, in spite of the extension of time, and the presence of the extension clause implies the consent. Where the instrument provides for an extension but does not specify the duration, only one extension is permitted and it is limited to a period no longer than that of the original period. If payment is tendered on the due date and not accepted, the holder cannot extend the period and thereby keep interest running. Refusal of the tender will also result in discharge of the indorsers. (See Sec. 3-121.)

TRANSFER AND NEGOTIATION

3-59 In General. The rights which a person has in an instrument may be transferred to another by "negotiation" or "assignment." Transfer is an encompassing word which means the process by which the owner of the property delivers it to another intending thereby to pass his rights in it to the other. The Code provides that the transfer of an instrument vests in the transferee such rights as the transferor has.[C48] Negotiation is defined as a specific type of transfer of such form that the transferee becomes a "holder." [C49] A "holder" is a person who is in possession of an instrument "drawn, issued, or indorsed to him or to his order or to bearer or in blank."

A person must first qualify as a holder before he can be a holder in due course. A holder in due course, as previously discussed, occupies a preferred status of not being subject to personal defenses, and must satisfy other requirements in addition to being a holder.

3-60 Negotiation.[C50] There are two methods of negotiating an instrument so that the transferee will become a holder. If the instrument is payable to bearer, it is negotiated by delivery alone which means that a thief or finder can pass bearer paper.

The indorsement in the case of order paper must be written on the instrument itself or on a paper so firmly affixed to it as to become a part thereof. Such paper is called an *allonge*. The indorsement must be made by the holder or by some one who has the authority to do so on behalf of the holder.

The indorsement must be for the entire amount of the instrument. *A* cannot indorse to *B* $50 out of a $100 check; he must indorse the whole amount to *B* or it is not a negotiation. If it is not for the entire amount, such transfer is effective only as a partial assignment. The rights of a partial assignee are to be determined under local contract law. An indorsement "Pay *A* one-third and *B* two-thirds" is not effective as a negotiation and neither *A* nor *B* is a holder. However, an indorsement to "*A* and *B*" is effective. The only instance in which a

C48 *U.C.C.* 3-201(1).
C49 *U.C.C.* 3-202.

C50 *U.C.C.* 3-202.

negotiation of a part interest can be made is when such part interest is the entire remaining unpaid balance of the instrument. In case part of an instrument has been paid, it can be indorsed as to the *residue*.

Sometimes an indorser will add words to his indorsement such as "I hereby assign all my right, title, and interest in the within note." The Code provides: "Words of assignment, condition, waiver, guaranty, limitation or disclaimer of liability, and the like accompanying an indorsement do not affect its character as an indorsement." Thus, if an indorser adds the words "I guarantee payment" to his indorsement, he is nevertheless negotiating the instrument.[C51]

If the name of the payee is misspelled, the payee may negotiate by indorsing either in the name appearing on the instrument or in his true name, or both. A person who pays the instrument or gives value for it may require that both names be indorsed. The desirable practice is to indorse in both names.[C52]

It sometimes happens that an order instrument, or one which is specially indorsed, is transferred without indorsement. Thus a purchaser may pay for an instrument in advance of the time when it is delivered to him and the seller either inadvertently or fraudulently may fail to indorse the paper. Of course, an indorsement would be necessary for negotiation. If the transferee has given value for the instrument, and if there was no contrary agreement between the parties, the transferee has a specifically enforceable right to an indorsement. However, the negotiation is not effective until the indorsement is given. The transferee is not a holder. He cannot qualify as a holder in due course if he receives notice of a defense or claim prior to obtaining such indorsement. Until the indorsement is given the transferee is not entitled to the presumption that he is the owner, which means that he must establish his right to the unindorsed paper by proof of the transaction by which he acquired it.[C53]

NEGOTIATION BY INDORSEMENT

3-61 Kinds of Indorsement. Indorsements are either *special* or *blank*.[C54] These are the ordinary indorsements used in negotiating order paper. If other terms are added which condition or inhibit the indorsement, it is referred to as a *restrictive* indorsement.[C55] Such terms restrict the indorsee's *use* of the paper. The indorser may limit or qualify his *liability as an indorser* by adding such words as "without recourse." This *qualified* indorsement has the effect of relieving the indorser of his contractual liability as an indorser—that he will pay if the primary obligor refuses to do so.[C56] However, he does make warranties as to the quality of the paper indorsed. (See Sec. 3-99.) These indorsements are discussed in the sections which follow.

C51 *U.C.C.* 3-202(4).   C54 *U.C.C.* 3-204.
C52 *U.C.C.* 3-203.   C55 *U.C.C.* 3-205.
C53 *U.C.C.* 3-201(3).   C56 *U.C.C.* 3-417(3).

3-62 Blank Indorsement. A blank indorsement consists of the indorser's name written on the instrument, or the paper formerly affixed thereto for that purpose, and is a form of indorsement commonly used. It does not specify any particular indorsee.[C57] If an instrument has been drawn payable to order and is indorsed in blank, it becomes payable to bearer and may be negotiated by delivery, without indorsement. However, if such instrument is thereafter indorsed specially, it reverts to its status as order paper and the indorsement is required for further negotiation. The blank indorsement thus changes order paper to bearer paper when it is the only or last indorsement. For example, a check on its face payable to "Henry Smith or order," if indorsed "Henry Smith," carries a blank indorsement. By this indorsement and delivery, Henry Smith relinquishes all rights to the instrument even though he has not directed payment to any particular person. Consequently, as long as it is bearer paper, it can be negotiated by mere delivery and a thief or finder could by such delivery pass title to the instrument. On the other hand, if the person to whom Henry Smith has indorsed the paper in blank had himself indorsed it specially, a further indorsement would be required for negotiation.

3-63 Special Indorsement. A special indorsement specifies the person to whom or to whose order it makes the instrument payable.[C58] When an instrument is specially indorsed, it becomes payable to the order of the special indorsee and requires his indorsement for further negotiation. Thus an indorsement "pay to Henry Smith" or "Pay to the order of Henry Smith" is a special indorsement and requires the further indorsement by Henry Smith for negotiation.

A blank indorsement of paper payable to order makes it payable to bearer. The special indorsement of a bearer instrument requires further indorsement by the indorsee. The underlying philosophy of this provision is that the special indorser is the owner of the paper and, even though the paper on its face is payable to bearer, the owner has the right to require the indorsement of his indorsee as evidence of the satisfaction of his own obligation.

The holder of an instrument may convert a blank indorsement into a special indorsement by writing above the blank indorser's signature "any contract consistent with the character of the indorsement." [C59] Thus, Richard Roe, to whom an instrument has been indorsed in blank by John Doe, could write above Doe's signature "Pay to Richard Roe." The paper would now require Roe's indorsement for further negotiation.

3-64 Restrictive Indorsements. A person who indorses an instrument may impose certain restrictions upon his indorsement, that is, the indorser may protect or preserve certain rights in the paper and limit the

---

[C57] *U.C.C.* 3-204(2).   [C59] *U.C.C.* 3-204(3).
[C58] *U.C.C.* 3-204(1).

rights of the indorsee. There are four types of restrictive indorsement. The most important one is used in the *deposit* and *collection* of instruments.[C60] Thus, checks may be indorsed "For collection" "For Deposit" or "Pay any Bank." In addition there is the *conditional* indorsement which invokes limitations on the indorsee and obligor with respect to payment—"Pay John Doe only if Generator XK-711 arrives by June 1, 1968." In the third type the indorser stipulates that the transfer is for the benefit or use of the indorser or some other designated person—"Pay John Doe in trust for Richard Roe." The Code also lists a fourth type—an indorsement which *purports* to prevent further transfer—"Pay John Doe *only*." Such an indorsement does *not* prevent transfer and presumably mention of it is made simply because such indorsements occasionally are used. The Code specifies that "no restrictive indorsement prevents further negotiation or transfer of the instrument." [C61]

The effect of restrictive indorsements is substantially limited as applied to banks which are involved in the process of deposit and collection of instruments. This process is described in Article 4–Bank Deposits and Collections. The process and terminology can best be illustrated by considering a typical banking transaction.

> *D* owes $100 to *P* for an article of merchandise which he has purchased from *P*. *D* draws a check on the bank ("payor bank") of which he is a "customer" and mails it to his creditor in another city. The creditor ("depositor") deposits the check in his own bank ("depositary bank"). *P*'s bank then forwards the check to *X* Bank which may in turn forward it to *Y* Bank. *X* Bank and *Y* Bank are called "intermediary banks" and along with the depositary bank are called "collecting banks." *Y* Bank ("presenting bank") presents the check to the payor bank. The payor bank honors the check, charges it to the customer's account and finally returns it to the customer along with his other cancelled checks and monthly statement. Even a simple transaction such as this involves a multiplicity of legal relationships.

The usual practice is for the depositary bank to credit the account of the depositor at the time of deposit. Each collecting bank likewise credits the account of the previous collecting bank (or remits to that bank) and finally when the check reaches the payor bank that bank debits the drawer's account. The payor bank then credits the account of the presenting bank, remits to it, or, if both the presenting bank and payor bank belong to the same "clearing house," includes the check in its balance at such clearing house. A clearing house is defined as "any association of banks or other payors regularly clearing items." Each of the foregoing transactions is referred to as a "provisional settlement" because until final settlement it is not known whether or not the check is good. If the payor bank honors the check, the settlement is final; if it dishonors the check, each provisional settlement is revoked and the depositary bank which had given provisional credit

---

[C60] *U.C.C.* 3-205(c).　　　　　[C61] *U.C.C.* 3-206.

for the deposit cancels the credit. Because of the tremendous volume of such transactions and the bulk handling of items, banks do not have any practicable opportunity to consider the effect of restrictive indorsements. Therefore the Code provides that *intermediary banks* or a *payor bank* which is not a depositary bank can disregard any restrictive indorsement *except* that of the bank's immediate transferor.[C62] This limitation does not affect whatever rights the restrictive indorser may have against the first bank in the collection process or his rights against parties outside the bank collection process.

The purpose of the indorsement for deposit or collection is to assure that payment on the instrument will be applied consistently with the indorsement.

An indorsement by *A*—"Pay to *T* in trust for *B*"—imposes upon *T*, the trustee, an obligation to apply any proceeds of the instrument in favor of *B*, the beneficiary of the trust. If *T* sells and negotiates it to *X* in breach of the trust, *X* will be protected if he bought in good faith. The only recourse would be against the trustee who did not properly apply the value given.

3-65 Negotiation Subject to Rescission. Negotiation by an infant or other person lacking in contractual capacity is effective to transfer the instrument notwithstanding the lack of capacity.[C63] This is true also in the case of a corporation where the transfer exceeds its powers. In addition, the transfer is effective even though it was obtained by fraud, duress, or mistake; in violation of a duty on the part of the transferor; or as part of an illegal transaction. This reflects the philosophy of negotiability that "any person in possession of an instrument which by its terms runs to him is a holder and that anyone may deal with him as a holder." Thus, the indorsee who has received the instrument under the above circumstances is nonetheless a holder and can in turn negotiate the paper as long as he is in possession of it. Certainly the party who lacks capacity or who was imposed upon can rescind the transfer but until he does so the transferee is in a position where he can negotiate the paper to a holder in due course.[C64] The right to rescind is not available against a holder in due course, but may be exercised against other parties.[6] The remedies available against such parties are determined by local law—e.g., the law relating to an infant's rights. It is to be noted that the foregoing relates only to the effectiveness of the transfer and does not impose liability on the infant or other party negotiating the instrument.[7] Such party may take advantage of various defenses which are available under the Code and which will be discussed later in Chapter 23.

[6] *Snyder v. Town Hill Motors,* page 445.
[7] *Wyoming Discount Corp. v. Harris,* page 446.

[C62] *U.C.C.* 3-206(3).   [C64] *U.C.C.* 3-207(2).
[C63] *U.C.C.* 3-207.

CREATION AND TRANSFER CASES

Gordon Supply Co. v. South Sea Apts., Inc.

1965, (N.Y.) 257 N.Y.S.2d 237

The defendant company, South Sea Apts., had executed a note in payment for services rendered by the payee to whose order the note was made payable. The note was indorsed by the other defendants and was negotiated to the plaintiff, Gordon Supply. The note was not paid at maturity and the defendants assert as a defense that the payee had agreed to repair defective items and that the note would not be payable unless such repairs were made. It was alleged that the plaintiff, holder, was aware of this condition when the note was negotiated to him. The lower court granted judgment for the plaintiff and an appeal was taken.

MEMORANDUM BY THE COURT.

Plaintiff is a holder in due course of the note, having obtained title thereto for value about January 24, 1963. The defense is that, shortly before the making of the note on January 24, 1963, the payee agreed that before the maturity of the note on April 24, 1963, it would repair all the defective work it had allegedly done theretofore; that, unless the repairs were thus properly made, the note would not be paid; that plaintiff took the note about January 24, 1963 with knowledge of this agreement; and that thereafter the payee failed to perform its promise. These facts, even if proved, would not constitute a defense (*Petroleum Acceptance Corp. v. Queen Anne Laundry Service,* 265 App.Div. 692, 40 N.Y.S.2d 495; *Eaton v. Laurel Delicatessen Corp.,* 5 N.Y.2d 1029, 185 N.Y.S.2d 551, 158 N.E.2d 251).

Affirmed.

Liberty Aluminum Products Company v. John Cortis Et Ux.

1958 (Pa.) 38 Wash. 223, 14 D.&C.2d 624.

The plaintiff, holder of a note executed by the defendants obtained a judgment on the note. The defendants filed a motion to have the judgment set aside on the ground that the note did not contain a schedule of installments and set out no date of maturity.

CUMMINS, J. . . . The first alleged deficiency is the one which must be explored a little further. The defendants' motion to strike completely overlooks the Uniform Commercial Code. . . . This Code states categorically that "instruments payable on demand include those payable at sight or on presentation and *those in which no time for payment is stated*" (italics added)—that under the Commercial Code this instrument is a demand note by virtue of its tenor.

Even if this were not so, the logic of the situation compels this conclusion. The parties have the right to use a blank and tailor it to their needs. And the failure to include installment payments simply and clearly means that none were intended.

It is our opinion that the motion to strike the judgment should be denied for the reason that it must be decided solely on the face of the record, as is indicated by the cases and the statutes cited above.

The face of the record will support the judgment.

Ferri v. Sylvia
1965, (R.I.) 214 A.2d 470

JOSLIN, J.   The question is whether the note is payable at a fixed or determinable future time. If the phrase "within ten (10) years after date" lacks explicitness or is ambiguous then clearly parol evidence was admissible for the purpose of ascertaining the intention of the parties. . . .

At the law merchant it was generally settled that a promissory note or a bill of exchange payable "on or before" a specified date fixed with certainty the time of payment. . . . The same rule has been fixed by statute first under the negotiable instruments law . . . and now pursuant to the uniform commercial code. The code in 6A-3-109 (1) reads as follows: "An instrument is payable at a definite time if by its terms it is payable (a) on or before a stated date or at a fixed period after a stated date. . . ."

The courts in the cases we cite were primarily concerned with whether a provision for payment "on or before" a specified date impaired the negotiability of an instrument. . . .

On principle no valid distinction can be drawn between an instrument payable "on or before" a fixed date and one which calls for payment "within" a stipulated period. . . .

We . . . equate the word "within" with the phrase "on or before." So construed it fixes both the beginning and the end of a period, and insofar as it means the former it is applicable to the right of a maker to prepay, and insofar as it means the latter it is referable to the date the instrument matures. We hold that the payment provision of a negotiable instrument payable "within" a stated period is certain as well as complete on its face and that such an instrument does not mature until the time fixed arrives.

For the foregoing reasons it is clear that the parties unequivocally agreed that the plaintiff could not demand payment of the note until the expiration of the ten-year period. It is likewise clear that any prior or contemporaneous oral agreements of the parties relevant to its due date were so merged and integrated with the writing as to prevent its being explained or supplemented by parol evidence. . . .

Judgment for the defendants.

Century Appliance Company v. Groff

1958, (Pa.) 56 Lanc. Rev. 67

The defendant executed an installment note which contained a confession of judgment clause and was payable to the order of the Fulton National Bank. The note was given for the purchase of a soft water system from the Century Appliance Company. The bank indorsed the note to the plaintiff who obtained a judgment thereon. The defendant seeks to open the judgment and contends that he had been told that the amount of the installation would not exceed $350; that the note was blank as to amount at the time he signed it; and that it was not until after the judgment was confessed that he learned that the real debt was $538.55.

WISSLER, J. . . . The gravamen of the defendant's contention is that he signed the note in blank; that the whole amount would not exceed $350.00; and that the job was unsatisfactory.

As to the contention of signing the note in blank, the Uniform Commercial Code of April 6, 1953, (P.L. 3, 12A PS 3-115), provides as to incomplete instruments as follows:

> (1) When a paper whose contents at the time of signing show that it is intended to become an instrument is signed while still incomplete in any necessary respect it cannot be enforced until completed, but when it is completed in accordance with authority given it is effective as completed; (2) if the completion is unauthorized the rules as to material alterations apply (Section 3-407) even though the paper was not delivered by the maker or drawer; but the burden of establishing that any completion is unauthorized is on the party so asserting.

Section 1-201, paragraph 8 of the Uniform Commercial Code, "Burden of establishing" a fact means the burden of persuading the triers of fact that the existence of the fact is more probable than its nonexistence.

The work for which the note was given was completed February 26, 1957. On the same date defendant signed an application for a property improvement loan to be made by the Fulton National Bank of Lancaster, Pennsylvania, and the amount of credit sought was $500.00, which amount was written in the upper left part of the application and approved by the defendant. Defendant then on February 27, 1957, signed the note in question in blank which was later filled in by the Fulton National Bank in the amount of $538.55 after it had ascertained the correct amount of the loan, including interest and insurance charges. Defendant also signed a Borrower's Completion Certificate whereby he certified that all articles and materials had been furnished and installed and the work satisfactorily completed on premises indicated in his application to the Fulton National Bank. It is not denied by defendant that in March, 1957, the Fulton National Bank sent him a Payment Coupon Book which indicated the amount of the note as being

$538.55 and which he returned to the bank with a memorandum stating that Clifford C. Lehman would take care of this. All of this clearly indicates that the note in question was completed in accordance with authority given and that the defendant has not met the burden of establishing that the completion of the note was unauthorized. . . .

The rule to show cause why judgment should not be opened . . . is discharged.

D'Andrea v. Feinberg

1965, (N.Y.) 256 N.Y.S.2d 504

JOHN J. DILLON, J.   The plaintiff as a holder in due course of a promissory note in the face amount of $4,000. has moved for summary judgment. . . . The maker of the note is Sain Builders, Inc. and the note is executed on behalf of the maker by Samuel Feinberg as President. The note is endorsed by Samuel Feinberg in his capacity as President of the corporation and individually. The action was commenced against the corporation and against Samuel Feinberg individually. The note was duly presented for payment, was dishonored and protested. The corporate defendant is involved in bankruptcy proceedings in the Federal District Court and in connection therewith an order has been signed staying all actions against it until a final decree has been entered in the bankruptcy proceedings. Accordingly, the motion for summary judgment as against the corporation is denied.

On behalf of the individual defendant, it is urged that plaintiffs are not holders in due course because at the time they acquired the note they were aware of the existence of a contract between the corporate defendant and the payee of the note. This fact cannot be disputed because the note itself has endorsed thereon, in the lower left hand corner the legend "as per contract." It is argued that the endorser should not be held liable on the note until such time as the primary obligation between the maker and the payee has been resolved. The court is thus faced with two questions: (1) whether the note is a negotiable instrument; and (2) whether the plaintiffs are holders in due course.

The note meets all the requirements of section 3-104 of the U.C.C. with the possible exception that it does not contain an unconditional promise because of the legend "as per contract." Section 3-105(1)(c) expressly states that an unconditional promise "is not made conditional by the fact that the instrument (c) refers to or states that it arises out of a separate agreement or refers to a separate agreement for rights as to prepayment or acceleration."

The official comment on the above quoted provision . . . is that it was "intended to resolve a conflict, and to reject cases in which a reference to a separate agreement was held to mean that payment of the instrument must be limited in accordance with the terms of the agreement, and hence was conditioned by it." The court is satisfied that the legend "as per contract" does not affect the negotiability of an instrument as would a statement that the instrument "is subject to or governed by any other agreement" (Uniform Commercial Code, Sec. 3-105(2) (a); Enoch v. Brandon, 249 N.Y. 263, 164 N.E. 45).

The court determines that the note being sued upon is a negotiable instrument and that the plaintiffs are holders in due course. Since a cause of action against "an indorser of any instrument accrues upon demand following dishonor of the instrument" (Uniform Commercial Code, Sec. 3-122(3)), it is clear that the plaintiffs need not first recover judgment against the maker as the individual defendant urges.

Snyder v. Town Hill Motors, Inc.

1960, 193 Pa. Super. 578, 165 A.2d 293

A minor (Snyder) entered into a contract with a friend (Rhea) whereby he agreed to trade his 1946 Pontiac plus $1,000 for the Rheas' Chrysler. The two thereupon went to the place of business of the defendant (Town Hill Motors) where Rhea negotiated for the purchase of a Lincoln. Rhea instructed Snyder to assign the title of the Pontiac to the Motor Company and to indorse to the company a $1,000 check which was payable to Snyder's order and drawn by a third party, as the down payment by Rhea on the Lincoln. (Snyder had intended to use the check in payment for the Chrysler.) Snyder complied with Rhea's instructions and Rhea gave him a receipt:

"Received of Richard Snyder one-thousand dollars and 1946 Pontiac coupe in exchange for a 1955 Chrysler Windsor."

Snyder accepted delivery of the Chrysler, but a month or so later he returned it to the motor company and demanded the return of his Pontiac and the $1,000. He contended that Rhea had misrepresented the amount of the encumbrance against the Chrysler.

The motor company which had cashed the check and received the proceeds refused his demand. Snyder then sued the motor company for $1,000 on the theory that he had the right to rescind the negotiation of an instrument. The jury returned a verdict for the defendant and Snyder appealed.

MONTGOMERY, J. . . .

Appellant's . . . theory is . . . without merit. The rescission of a negotiable instrument by an infant against a subsequent holder in due course is not permitted by Section 3-207 of the Uniform Commercial Code, on which appellant relies. Having received the instrument by negotiation from Rhea for value, in good faith, and without notice that it was overdue or had been dishonored or that there was any defense against it, the Motor Company was a subsequent holder in due course. The jury has found that there were no dealings between Snyder and the appellees.

Appellant's argument that the Motor Company was not a "subsequent" holder in due course is not supported by the evidence. The fact that the check was not manually transferred from Snyder to Rhea and then to the Motor Company would be immaterial under the definition of "delivery" contained in the Negotiable Instruments Law of 1901

. . . which provides that transfer of possession may be actual or constructive. Although the Uniform Commercial Code repealed the Negotiable Instruments Law, it nevertheless did not prescribe any new definition of the term delivery. We are of the opinion, therefore, that the established definition should prevail. The generally recognized meaning of "delivery" set forth in Corpus Juris Secundum is as follows: "What constitutes delivery depends largely on the intent of the parties. It is not necessary that delivery should be by manual transfer. A constructive delivery is sufficient if made with the intention of transferring the title, and this rule is recognized by the definition of delivery in Negotiable Instruments Act . . . as the transfer of possession, 'actual or constructive.' ". . .

The facts previously stated show clearly the intention of these parties. Together, Snyder and Rhea took the check to the Motor Company, where it was exhibited and where Rhea exercised dominion over it by directing Snyder to hand it over to the Motor Company. Snyder agreed to this and accepted Rhea's receipt, which acknowledged that Rhea had received the proceeds of the check. This was sufficient to constitute constructive delivery from Snyder to Rhea and "subsequently" from Rhea to the Motor Company.

Orders affirmed. . . .

Wyoming Discount Corporation v. Harris

1964, (Wyo.) 397 P.2d 799

PER CURIAM.   Plaintiff sued defendant for principal and interest on a note, alleging defendant to have been under the age of twenty-one at the time of signing the instrument and having knowingly made a false statement as to his age with intention to deceive. After trial before the court without a jury, judgment was entered finding generally for defendant and against plaintiff; this appeal has resulted.

It is asserted by the appellant that the court made an oral statement that defendant had represented his age to be twenty-one and that the plaintiff did not rely on defendant's representation of full age in giving the loan complained of; however, no such findings are included in the record. It is unquestioned and stipulated that the defendant was only sixteen years of age at the time that he made application for the loan of some three hundred and thirty dollars with which to complete payment on an automobile.

We find no merit in the only contention of the appellant, that there was no substantial evidence in the record to support the judgment. Plaintiff's representative, who made out the loan application, testified that defendant in response to his question concerning age answered that he was twenty-one and that the lender relied on the age representation in making the loan. However, the defendant testified that at the time of the application for loan there was no conversation concerning his age. He said further that his birth date was not asked and that he did not see, and was not asked to sign, the application for loan which erroneously listed his birth date.

The trier of fact was the sole judge of the credibility of the witnesses and entitled to give conflicting testimony such weight as was deemed proper. There was substantial evidence to warrant the judgment.

Affirmed.

CHAPTER 21
REVIEW QUESTIONS AND PROBLEMS

1. *M* executed a note to *P* in the sum of $500. The note did not contain words of negotiability. Can *P* recover on the note from *M*? If *P* transferred the note to *X*, could *X* recover from *M*?

2. A note contained a provision: "This note is payable from the proceeds of the sale of the Douglas Building." Is the note negotiable?

3. A note provides: "Payable on January 1, 1967, or sooner in the event that the *A-B* partnership is dissolved." Is the note negotiable?

4. *M* contracted to purchase irrigation equipment from *P* and executed a note on March 1, 1967, payable to the order of *P* "When my wheat crop is harvested." *P* immediately sold the note to *X*. The equipment was never delivered to *M*. Can *X* recover on the note from *M*?

5. A draft provided: "Pay to Albert Prince $250 on return of this instrument properly indorsed." Prince indorsed to Harold Boyd for value. Boyd sought to recover from the drawer who had a defense. Should Boyd prevail?

6. *M* executed a note payable to the order of *P* on a printed form which contained blank spaces to be filled in, setting forth a schedule of installment payments. These spaces were left blank. No maturity date was specified. When is the note due and payable? If *P* indorsed to *H*, would *M* be able to assert the defense of failure of consideration?

7. A check was drawn payable to "Smith and/or Jones or order." Smith cashed the check at the bank after indorsing his name only. Smith then departed with the money and Jones seeks recovery from the bank. Should he succeed? What would your answer be if the check were payable to the order of "Smith and Jones"?

8. A negotiable note provides that it is "payable at the Last National Bank." If it is presented at the bank for payment, what is the bank obligated to do? What would the bank's obligation be if the clause were "payable through the Last National Bank"?

9. *M* signed a note to the order of *P* payable "within 10 years after date"

on April 1, 1965. One year later *P* sought to recover on the note. *M* contended that he was not required to pay prior to the expiration of ten years. Is this contention correct?

10. *A* is the indorser of a note which contains a stipulation for payment of attorney's fees if suit is brought on the note. The maker did not pay and the holder sues *A*. Is *A* obligated to pay attorney's fees?

11. *P* signed a check but left the designation of the payee in blank. The check was stolen and the word "cash" inserted in the blank. The check was honored by the bank. *P* seeks to recover the amount of the check from the bank. What result?

12. By fraudulent misrepresentations, *P* induced *M* to execute a note payable to the order of *P*. *P* indorsed the note to *A*, who had no notice of the fraud when he first acquired the note but subsequently learned of the fraud and thereafter indorsed to *B*, a holder in due course. *A* then repurchased the note from *B*. Can *A* enforce the note against *M*?

13. *P*, the payee of a note given in payment for a TV set, indorsed it "without recourse" to *A*. *A* sought to recover from *M*, the maker of the note. *M* refused to pay and contended that *P* had never delivered the set. Is this a good defense? Could *A* hold *P* for the amount of the note?

14. *M* made a note payable to the order of *P*. *P* indorsed to *A* by writing his name "*P*" on the back of the note. *A* transferred the note to *B* without indorsement. Can *B* be a holder in due course?

15. *H*, the holder of a check, wishes to protect himself against its loss or theft. It has been indorsed to him in blank. How may he gain this protection?

16. *A* purchased merchandise from *B* Chemical Co. and "accepted" a trade acceptance drawn to the order of *B* Chemical Co. The company indorsed the instrument to *F* Finance Co. *F* Finance Co. now seeks to recover on the instrument, which states, "The transaction which gives rise to this instrument is the purchase of goods from the drawer by the acceptor." *A* claims the merchandise was defective. Is this defense good against *F*? Does *F* have recourse against *B* Chemical Co.?

chapter 22

Holders and Holders in Due Course

3-66 Definitions. A "holder" is "a person who is in possession of a document of title or an instrument or an investment security drawn, issued or indorsed to him or to his order or to bearer or in blank." [C1] One who is the holder of an instrument may transfer or negotiate it and with certain exceptions may discharge it or enforce payment. A person may be a holder even though he does not own the instrument. A person in possession of a negotiable instrument may occupy two very different positions. A holder may be in no better position than the assignee of any simple contract right. That is, he may be subject to any personal defenses that the maker or drawer may have against the payee. This holder usually referred to as a simple holder is subject to the same defenses as if the instrument were non-negotiable. He may be a holder free from such personal defenses where his rights against the primary party are superior to those possessed by the former holder or owner of the instrument. Such a holder is said to be a *holder in due course*.[C2] For a holder to occupy such a position he must satisfy very definite requirements.

3-67 Requirements for a Holder in Due Course. Such a holder must have taken the instrument for value and in good faith. In addition he must not have notice that the instrument is overdue, that it has been dishonored, that any other person has a claim against it, or that any other person has a defense to it. If a holder can satisfy all of these

[C1] *U.C.C.* 1-201(20). [C2] *U.C.C.* 3-302.

requirements, he will be able to qualify as a holder in due course.[C3]
A holder does not become a holder in due course of an instrument:

(a) by purchase of it at judicial sale or by taking it under legal process; or

(b) by acquiring it in taking over an estate; or

(c) by purchasing it as part of a bulk transaction not in regular course of business of the transferor.[C4]

The foregoing is a codification of the law as it stands under existing cases. The person purchasing or acquiring the paper is merely succeeding to the interest of the prior holder and acquires only the rights of such prior holder. However, if the prior holder was a holder in due course the purchaser may acquire the rights of a holder in due course as is discussed in section 3-68.

Examples of Subsection (a) above are purchases at execution sales and bankruptcy sales. Subsection (b) applies to an executor or administrator who takes over the instrument as part of an estate. Subsection (c) is illustrated by the situation in which as a part of a corporate consolidation one corporation takes over all of the assets of the other corporation or in a bulk transfer as discussed in Sec. 3-32 of Chapter 19. In all of these situations the Code recognizes that circumstances do not warrant granting to a holder the status of a holder in due course.

A purchaser of a limited interest can be a holder in due course only to the extent of the interest purchased. The import of this provision is that the purchaser of a limited interest does not have protection as a holder in due course to the *full value* of the paper.[C5] For example, if a negotiable instrument is transferred to a holder as a security interest for a loan to the holder, the transferee may be a holder in due course, but he takes the instrument free of defenses only to the extent of the debt which is secured by the pledge of the instrument.

A payee may be a holder in due course. Since the payee of an instrument usually deals directly with the primary party, he ordinarily has notice of any defense that the maker or drawer may have. However, if the payee is able to satisfy the requirements he may become a holder in due course in the same fashion as any other holder.[C6] There are a variety of situations in which the payee may qualify as a holder in due course.

To illustrate, assume that M signs his name to an instrument complete except for the amount, payable to the order of P, and directs his agent, A, to purchase a certain quantity of merchandise from P and pay for the same by filling in the proper amount. The agent, A, in violation of this authority, completes the check in a larger sum than authorized, delivers it to P complete and regular upon its face, obtains the merchandise, and appropriates the balance. P is not immediate to M in the transaction and has no knowledge of the unauthorized act of M's agent. P has satisfied all of the requirements of a holder in due

[C3] *U.C.C.* 3-302(1).
[C4] *U.C.C.* 3-302(3).
[C5] *U.C.C.* 3-302(3).
[C6] *U.C.C.* 3-302(4).

course in that he has taken the check in good faith, for value, and without notice.

3-68 Holder from a Holder in Due Course. Since a transferee obtains the rights of a transferor, a person who does not himself qualify as a holder in due course but who derives his title through a holder in due course has the same rights and privileges as a holder in due course.[1] This is often referred to as the "shelter provision." [C7] While this may seem to detract from the basic holder in due course philosophy, it is in reality in keeping with the underlying concept of marketability of commercial paper. The shelter provision which affords an extension of the holder in due course benefits is designed to aid the holder in due course so that he may readily dispose of the paper. The paper in the hands of the holder in due course is free from personal defenses and such holder should have the privilege of transferring all of his rights in the paper. Thus the transfer of an instrument vests in the transferee such rights as the transferor has therein.

The "shelter provision" is subject, however, to the limitation that a person who formerly held the paper cannot improve his position by later reacquiring it from a holder in due course.[C8] If a former holder was himself a party to any fraud or illegality affecting the instrument, or if he had notice of a defense or claim against it as a prior holder, he cannot claim the rights of a holder in due course by taking from a later holder in due course. This reflects the philosophy that a holder in due course should have a free market for his paper but one who was a party to any fraud or who had notice of a claim or defense against an instrument should not be allowed to improve his status by repurchasing from a later holder in due course. A person should not be allowed to wash the paper clean by passing it into the hands of a holder in due course and then repurchasing it.

A *reacquirer* may reissue or further negotiate the instrument. He is not, however, entitled to enforce payment against any intervening persons to whom he was liable. Such intervening indorsers are also discharged as to subsequent parties except subsequent holders in due course.[C9] A person may reacquire an instrument for the purpose of eliminating the liability of an intervening party and this is usually accomplished by striking out such party's indorsement. If the indorsement is so stricken, that indorser will be discharged even as against a subsequent holder in due course.

The following examples illustrate the shelter provision. *P* fraudulently induces *M* to execute a note payable to the order of *P*. (1) *P* indorses to *A* who takes in good faith and otherwise satisfies the requirements of a holder in due course. *A* indorses in blank and delivers it to *B* who has notice of the fraud but did not participate in it. *B* de-

---

[1] *Blow v. Ammerman,* page 456.

[C7] *U.C.C.* 3-201(1).
[C8] *U.C.C.* 3-201(1).

[C9] *U.C.C.* 3-208.

livers the note to *C* as a gift and *C* delivers it to *D* after maturity. *B*, *C*, and *D* each obtained the rights of *A*, the holder in due course. Each could collect from *M* when they held the instrument, notwithstanding the fact that they were not holders in due course, because each had the rights of a holder in due course. (2) *P* indorses to *A* who has notice of the fraud. *A* negotiates it to *B* who takes without notice of the fraud and is a holder in due course. *A* repurchases the note from *B*. *A* remains subject to *M*'s defense of fraud and does not acquire *B*'s rights as a holder in due course.

The following sections cover the requirements of a holder in due course in detail.

3-69 Value.[C10] A holder must take for value in order to qualify as a holder in due course. One who receives an instrument as a donee, for example, is thus not a holder for value. A holder takes the instrument for value to the extent that the agreed consideration for the transfer has been performed or that he acquires a security interest in or a lien on the instrument otherwise than by legal process. Value is also given when he takes the instrument in payment of or as security for an antecedent claim against any person whether or not the claim is due; or when he gives a negotiable instrument for it or makes an irrevocable commitment to a third person.

An *executory* promise to give value does not make the holder a holder for value. It is required in general that the consideration agreed upon by the parties must actually have been given. When an instrument is negotiated presently under an arrangement that the transferee will pay for it later or perform the required services at a later date, such transferee has not given "value." If a purchaser has not yet paid value when he becomes aware of a defense to the instrument, he does not have to pay for it but is free to rescind the transaction. Accordingly, there is not the same necessity to give him the standing of a holder in due course, free from claims and defenses, as in the case of a holder who has actually parted with value. A holder who purchases an instrument for less than its *face value* can be a holder in due course to the full amount of the instrument; but, if the discount is exceedingly large, it may, along with other factors, be evidence of bad faith on the part of the holder.

The provision that a mere promise to pay for negotiable paper does not make one a holder for value is of particular importance in banking transactions. A bank will often give provisional credits to its customers on items which are deposited, pending collection of such items. If the bank learns of defenses to these items before they are collected and before the customer has withdrawn the funds represented by the deposits, the provisional credits will not be regarded as value and the bank will not be free of claims and defenses in connection with the paper so deposited. Of course, if the bank has collected an item and the customer has with-

[C10] *U.C.C.* 3-303.

drawn the funds for which provisional credit was given, the bank could qualify as a holder for value. It therefore becomes necessary to determine the point of time at which the customer has been paid the proceeds of an item left with the bank for collection. The courts have applied different theories in making this determination and in tracing the funds against which payment has been made. In many cases the courts in determining whether the item arising from the deposited paper has been drawn upon, apply the "first in, first out" theory. Under this theory the earliest credits are deemed to have been absorbed by the earliest debits. The Code does not spell out the tracing rules which are to be applied, and it would appear that the common law on this subject is still applicable.

A holder who takes an instrument in payment of an antecedent claim is a holder for value. The same is true of a holder who takes the instrument as security for an antecedent debt. Thus if *A* owed *B* $500 on a past due account and transferred a negotiable instrument to *B* in payment of such account or as security for its payment, *B* would qualify as a holder for value. In this regard it is to be noted that "value" is not synonymous with consideration. Consideration is significant in determining whether an obligation can be enforced against a party whereas value is relevant on the question of the qualification of a holder as a holder in due course.[C11]

As noted above a mere promise to pay for negotiable paper does not make one a holder for value. If the promise to pay is *negotiable in form*, however, the purchaser immediately becomes a holder for value.[C12] For example, a drawer who issues his check in payment for a negotiable note which he is purchasing from the holder, becomes a holder for value even before his check is cashed. The reason for this rule is that there is a possibility that the check or other negotiable instrument might be negotiated to a holder in due course in which event the party giving it could not refuse to pay. By the same token an irrevocable commitment to a third person would leave the holder no alternative but to live up to his commitment. In these circumstances the holder has placed himself in a position where he could be required to perform and is thus in much the same position as a person who has actually paid.

3-70 Good Faith and Without Notice. In order that a person may qualify as a holder in due course he must have taken in good faith. The test of good faith is a subjective one—the state of mind of the person who claims to be a holder in due course.[C13] As noted previously, there are certain transactions in which a person cannot become a holder in due course regardless of his state of mind or "good faith." [C14] Also, there are other circumstances in which the very nature of the situation precludes a person from becoming a holder in due course. A person cannot be a holder in good faith and in due course unless he has taken the paper:

C11 *U.C.C.* 3-408.
C12 *U.C.C.* 3-303(c).

C13 *U.C.C.* 1-201(19).
C14 *U.C.C.* 3-302(3).

(1) Without notice of any claim or defense against the instrument.
(2) Without notice that it is overdue or has been dishonored.

If a person has notice of either of the foregoing he would not be a
holder in due course. A person has notice of a fact when he has actual
knowledge of it, has received a notice or notification of it although he
has not actually seen the notice, or from all the facts and circumstances
known to him at the time in question he has reason to know that it
exists.[2] [C15]

A purchaser has notice of a *claim* or *defense* if the instrument is so
incomplete, bears such visible evidence of forgery or alteration, or is
otherwise so irregular as to call into question its validity, terms, or ownership or to create an ambiguity as to the party to pay. Also, notice of a
claim or *defense* is given if the "purchaser has notice that the obligation of
any party is voidable in whole or in part, or that all parties have been
discharged." The "voidable" obligation does not refer to a set-off or
counter-claim which the maker of a note might have against the payee
but is limited to a situation in which a party such as the maker of a note
has the right to avoid his original obligation on the instrument, as in the
case of a fraud perpetrated by the payee. Notice that *one party* has been
discharged is not notice of any lack in the obligation of the remaining
parties.

A purchaser has notice of a *claim* against the instrument if he is aware
that a fiduciary such as a trustee or agent has negotiated the instrument in
payment of or as security for his own debt or in any transaction for his
own benefit.[C16] Thus, if a trustee negotiates a trust instrument in payment
of his own personal debt, this would give notice of misappropriation of
the funds. However, the mere fact that a purchaser has knowledge of the
fiduciary relation would not in itself prevent him from being a holder in
due course. One is entitled to assume that the fiduciary acted properly in
the absence of the circumstances set forth above. Knowledge that the
negotiation was in breach of the fiduciary's duty would prevent the
transferee from being a holder in due course.

There are a number of situations in which knowledge of certain facts
does not of itself give the purchaser notice of a defense or claim.[C17]

Knowledge that an instrument is antedated or postdated does not
prevent a holder from taking in due course.

Notice of a defense or claim is not imparted by virtue of knowledge
that an instrument was issued or negotiated in return for an executory
promise or that the instrument was accompanied by a separate agreement,[3] nor does the fact that the purchaser of the instrument was engaged
in financing the payee of the instrument.[4] Of course if the purchaser is
aware that the contract has been breached or repudiated or that the

---

[2] *Norman v. World Wide Distributors, Inc.*, page 457.

[3] *First Natl. Bk. of Phil. v. Anderson*, page 459.

[4] *Commercial Credit Equipment Corp. v. Reeves*, page 461.

[C15] *U.C.C.* 1-201(25).   [C17] *U.C.C.* 3-304(4).
[C16] *U.C.C.* 3-304(2).

separate agreement has been violated he would not qualify as a holder in due course. While mere notice that there is an executory promise or separate agreement will not deprive one of holder-in-due-course status, if he has notice of a default in connection therewith which raises a defense or claim against the instrument, he is on notice to the same degree as would be furnished by any other information.[C18]

Knowledge that an incomplete instrument has been completed does not give notice of a defense or claim. However, if the purchaser has notice that the completion was improper, he cannot be a holder in due course.

The filing or recording of a document does not of itself constitute notice to a person who would otherwise be a holder in due course.[C19]

To be effective notice must be received at such time and in such manner as to give a reasonable opportunity to act on it.[C20] For example, a notice received by the president of a bank one minute before the bank's teller cashes a check is not effective to prevent the bank from becoming a holder in due course.

3-71 Before Overdue.[C21] A holder in due course must be a holder who has purchased the paper before it is due. The law presumes that every person under a duty will perform on the date that performance is due, and, if such person fails to perform—that is, fails to pay the instrument— it is presumed that he has some defense or valid reason for not performing. Consequently, a purchaser of overdue paper would be charged with knowledge that some defense may exist. Where an instrument is payable on a fixed date, any purchaser thereafter would not be a holder in due course.

Where the instrument is due upon a fixed date, but subject to an early maturity by reason of an accelerating clause, the instrument would not be overdue until the option to mature the paper had been exercised by the holder. If an acceleration of the instrument has been made, the purchaser with notice of such fact is a purchaser of overdue paper; notice that acceleration of the instrument has been made and accordingly, that payment has not been made is notice that an instrument is overdue.[C22] However, a purchaser may take accelerated paper as a holder in due course if he takes without notice of the acceleration.

If the instrument is payable on demand, it is said to be overdue an unreasonable length of time after issue. A purchaser has notice that an instrument is overdue if he has reason to know "that he is taking a demand instrument after demand has been made or more than a reasonable length of time after its issue." Thus a purchaser may take as a holder in due course, a demand instrument on which a demand has actually been made, only if he takes without notice of the demand. What is a reasonable or an unreasonable time is determined by a consideration of the nature of the instrument, the usage of the trade or business, and all of the circumstances and facts involved in each case. With regard to a

C18 *U.C.C.* 3-304(4)(b).
C19 *U.C.C.* 3-304(5).
C20 *U.C.C.* 3-304(6).

C21 *U.C.C.* 3-304(3).
C22 *U.C.C.* 3-304(3)(b).

check, however, the time is specified. "A reasonable time for a check drawn and payable within the states and territories of the United States and the District of Columbia is presumed to be thirty days." [C23] "Presumption" or "presumed" mean that "the trier of fact must find the existence of the fact presumed unless and until evidence is introduced which would support a finding of its nonexistence."

If an instrument is payable in installments it may be transferred at a time when one or more of the installments is past due. A purchaser who has reason to know of an overdue installment on principal has notice that the instrument is overdue and therefore could not be a holder in due course. Past due interest, on the other hand, does not impart notice of any defect in the instrument. It is recognized that interest payments are frequently in arrears without a defense existing.

HOLDERS AND HOLDERS IN DUE COURSE CASES

Blow v. Ammerman
1965 350 F.2d 729

PER CURIAM.   Mary Kuhn, for whom appellants [executor] were substituted in the District Court after her death, gave two notes of $25,000 each to Baron Johann von Liedersdorff on April 25, 1963. Two paintings were the consideration for the notes. The day following its issuance note 1 was transferred by the Baron to the Pinnacle Investment Corporation in part payment for certain realty and for cash. Pinnacle is wholly owned by the appellee Wheeler. He took the note from Pinnacle in exchange for one of his own of $24,000 on October 24, 1963, the day before it was due. Appellee Ammerman acquired note 2 directly from the Baron.

Mrs. Kuhn was sued on the notes by Wheeler and Ammerman after nonpayment on their due dates. It was claimed in defense that the paintings are fraudulent. The trial court gave summary judgments in favor of appellees.

We are satisfied that on the basis of the record before the District Court Pinnacle was shown to be a holder in due course and that no genuine issue of material fact appears in that regard. Accordingly, when Wheeler took the note he met the requirements of D.C.Code § 28-408: [nil]

> a holder who derives his title through a holder in due course, and who is not himself a party to any fraud or illegality affecting the instrument, has all the rights of such former holder in respect of all parties prior to the latter.

The rule would seem to apply even if Wheeler had actual knowledge of prior defenses (*Cover v. Myers,* 75 Md. 406, 23 A. 850). Nothing in the record suggests that Wheeler was a party to the original fraud, if such it was. We accordingly affirm the judgment in his favor.

[C23] *U.C.C.* 3-304(3)(c).

2. As a result of separate transactions with the Baron after transfer to Pinnacle of note 1, Wheeler became aware "in June or July" that other paintings of the Baron's were not authentic. Wheeler thereafter arranged for Ammerman to take note 2 from the Baron. Ammerman required security from the Baron in the form of other paintings and took the note on June 22, 1963 at a $5,000 discount. It also appears that written on both notes was the consideration for which they were given, namely, two paintings by Monet and Renoir.

There is an issue of fact whether Ammerman when he took the note actually knew of (1) Wheeler's collateral dealings with the Baron and (2) Wheeler's conclusion "in June or July" that some of the paintings transferred by the Baron to him were frauds. Bearing upon the issue is appellants' allegation that a close relationship existed between Wheeler and Ammerman. This and all the circumstances surrounding the negotiation and transfer of the note as they appear on the present record were sufficient to raise a jury issue as to bad faith on the part of Ammerman. (See *Commercial Trust Co. of New Jersey v. Kealey,* 92 F.2d 397, 402 (4th Cir.))

Liberally construed (see *Palmer v. Associates Discount Corp.,* 74 App.D.C. 386, 387, 124 F.2d 225, 226) appellants' pleadings and papers satisfy D.C.Code § 28-409 that "when it is shown that the title of any person who has negotiated the instrument was defective, the burden is on the holder to prove that he or some person under whom he claims acquired the title as a holder in due course." The burden of proof thus being on Ammerman and there being sufficient question as to possible bad faith (see *Hazen v. Van Senden,* 43 App.D.C. 161, 165) it was error to grant summary judgment in his favor.

3. Should it be decided that there was an original failure of consideration for note 2 and that Ammerman was a holder in due course, there remains for decision whether the loss to the innocent Mrs. Kuhn, whose interests are now represented by appellants, could at least be reduced by either subtracting from the recovery of Ammerman the value of paintings he received as security from the Baron, or by requiring those paintings to be transferred to the estate of Mrs. Kuhn upon payment of Ammerman's judgment.

The summary judgment in favor of the holders of the notes was reversed as to note 2 and affirmed as to note 1. [The case was decided under the NIL since the Code did not become effective in the District of Columbia until after the events of this case. The same result would obtain under the "shelter provision" of the Code.]

Norman v. World Wide Distributors, Inc. et al.

1963, (Pa.) 195 A.2d 115

A representative of World Wide Distributors, Inc. called upon the plaintiffs and outlined to them a "program for direct advertising." He said that if they would purchase a breakfront he would pay them $5 for each letter they wrote to a friend urging the friend to buy a breakfront and $20 for each sale made to such person—the so-called "referral plan."

He persuaded the plaintiffs to sign, without reading, an "Owner's Participation Certificate," a purchase agreement, and an attached judgment note *in blank*. The note was subsequently filled in for $1,079.40 in 30 monthly installments of $35.98. (The fair retail price was about one-fifth that amount.) The note was also filled in so as to be payable to "H. Waldran T/A *State Wide Products* at the office of Peoples National Fund," and was sold to *Peoples National Fund* for $831. A judgment was obtained against the plaintiffs on the note by Peoples National Fund, holder, and plaintiffs brought action to have the judgment declared null and void and to rescind the transaction. A judgment was rendered in their favor. World Wide had failed to pay for most of the letters mailed by plaintiffs in accordance with the agreement. A judgment was rendered in favor of plaintiffs setting aside the judgment previously entered against them and Peoples National Fund, Inc. appealed.

WOODSIDE, J. It is hardly necessary to add that World Wide is now nowhere to be found. Within approximately a year its principals, unnamed in the record, had operated first under the name of Carpet Industries, then under State Wide, and finally under World Wide Distributors. The appellant [Peoples National Fund] dealt with all three companies and purchased notes from all three of them. The vice president of Peoples testified that he "had knowledge of the referral plan," although he claimed that he was not familiar with the details of the plan. Immediately after the plaintiffs received a $50 check from World Wide for the first ten names furnished under the agreement, the vice president of Peoples called the plaintiffs to inquire whether they were satisfied with the transaction. He told them Peoples had nothing to do with the referral plan.

The referral plan was a fraudulent scheme based on an operation similar to the recurrent chain letter racket. It is one of many sales rackets being carried on throughout the nation which are giving public officials serious concern. The plaintiffs introduced evidence to show that at the end of 20 months of operation, it would require 17 trillion salesmen to carry on a referral program like World Wide described to the plaintiffs.

Peoples contend that even though World Wide may have been guilty of fraud, it can collect on the note because *it was a holder in due course*.

"A holder in due course is a holder who takes the instrument (a) for value; and (b) in good faith; and (c) without notice that it is overdue or has been dishonored or of any defense against or claim to it on the part of any person." 3-302(1) of the Uniform Commercial Code. . . .

Section 1-201(19) of the code defines "good faith" as meaning "honesty in fact in the conduct or transaction concerned." Thus, to be a holder in due course Peoples must have acted in good faith.

The freedom from the defense of prior equities afforded to a holder in due course is an extraordinary protection, which, although having its origin in the law merchant, is closely akin to similar protection given in other types of cases by courts of equity; and running through all the authorities dealing with holders in due course we find the principle, not always stated, perhaps, that he who seeks the protection given one in that position must have dealt fairly and honestly in acquiring the instrument in controversy and in regard to the rights of all prior parties, this is, the kind of good faith which the law demands, and the principle is closely analogous to the equitable doctrine of clean hands. (*Fehr v. Campbell,* 288 Pa. 549, 558, 137 A. 113, 116, 52 A.L.R. 506 (1927).)

He who seeks protection as a holder in due course must have dealt fairly and honestly in acquiring the instrument as to the rights of prior parties, and where circumstances are such as to justify the conclusion that the failure to make inquiry arose from *a suspicion that inquiry would disclose a vice or defect in the title,* the person is not a holder in due course. . . .

When the defense of fraud appears to be meritorious as to the payee, the burden of showing it was a holder in due course is on the one claiming to be such. . . .

The appellant here had knowledge of circumstances *which should have caused it to inquire* concerning the payee's method of obtaining the note. Peoples knew enough about the referral plan to require it to inquire further concerning it. The fact that the appellant's vice president called the makers of the note and denied any connection with the referral plan, indicates his own suspicion concerning it. The frequency with which the principals changed the name under which they were operating—three times in approximately one year—should have added to his suspicion. Furthermore, the appellant paid $831 for a $1,079.40 note payable three days after date. . . . Under all the circumstances, Peoples was bound to inquire further into the operation of the seller of these notes, and having made no inquiry, *it is held as though it had knowledge of all that inquiry would have revealed.* . . .

The appellant argues that the plaintiffs are estopped from raising against it any defenses which they might have raised against World Wide, because they did not complain to the appellant when its vice president called them. The appellant's hands are not clean enough to raise this point. Estoppels are used in law as a means to prevent fraud, and never to become its instruments. . . .

Decree affirmed.

The First National Bank of Philadelphia v. Anderson

1956 (Pa.) 7 D. & C. 2d 661, 6 Bucks 287.

The defendant entered into a contract with the Atlantic Storm Window Co. for the installation of twelve jalousie windows. A judgment note signed by the defendant appeared on the same sheet of paper as the contract. The note was indorsed for value to the plaintiff bank. The defendant claims that the note was signed in blank; that it was to be in the amount of $744; that it was completed in the amount of $895.32; and that the work was improperly done and the windows were not as represented. When the bank notified the defendant that payments on the note were to be made to it, he complained of the defective work and refused to pay. The bank entered judgment against him and defendant seeks to have it set aside on the above grounds, asserting also that he did not have sufficient opportunity to examine the note and contract before signing.

BIESTER, J. J.   . . . It is the position of plaintiff that it was a holder in due course for value, without notice, and that it is, therefore, not subject to the various defenses and objections raised by petitioners.

Our first inquiry must be of determination of the question of whether, under the facts revealed by the record before us, plaintiff is a holder in due course.

Section 3-302 of the Uniform Commercial Code . . . the provisions of which govern the proceeding before us, states that:

(1) A holder in due course is a holder who takes the instrument
   (a) for value; and
   (b) in good faith including observance of the reasonable commercial standards of any business in which the holder may be engaged; and
   (c) without notice that it is overdue or has been dishonored or of any defense against or claim to it on the part of any person.

It is our understanding that, as to these provisions, defendant contends that the bank was not a holder in due course in that it did not take the instrument in good faith, on the theory that it became incumbent upon plaintiff to communicate with the payee and/or the makers of the note to determine whether the work had been satisfactorily completed before accepting the note. We find no merit in this contention. (The court cites pre-Code cases.) . . .

Although these cases are decided under the Negotiable Instruments Law of May 16, 1901, P. L. 194, we find no provision in the Uniform Commercial Code making any change in the good faith concept. True, Section 1-201 defines good faith as being honesty in fact and under Section 3-302 good faith includes the observance by reasonable commercial standards of any business in which the holder may be engaged. No evidence was presented, however, indicating that the failure to make inquiry of the payee or the maker of the note as to the satisfactory completion of the contract was in any sense a divergence from common banking or commercial practice. On the contrary, if a holder of an instrument were required to investigate in each instance whether the contract had been completed satisfactorily before accepting it, the burden placed on the free flow of negotiable paper would be almost insurmountable.

We, therefore, find that plaintiff bank accepted the paper in good faith and is a holder in due course. . . .

As to the alleged alteration of the judgment note in that it is said to have completed contrary to the original agreement of the parties, Section 3-407 of the Uniform Commercial Code appears to clearly control the situation. It provides, inter alia, that when an incomplete instrument has been completed the subsequent holder in due course may enforce it as completed. Without holding that there was a material alteration of the instrument, we do find that even if there was such an alteration it would not be effective as a defense against the holder in due course.

As was said in the recent and remarkably similar case of *Newark Trust Co. v. Herr,* (54 Lanc. pp. 31, 34):

> The difficulty with defendants' position is that all the acts of infirmity alleged in the petition to open the judgment existed between the immediate parties to the note and not between the parties and the plaintiff as a holder in due course, and as there is no allegation that plaintiff had notice of any infirmities at the time it was negotiated to it, the defendants cannot avail themselves of such alleged infirmities as against the plaintiff as a holder in due course.

Petition to open the judgment is refused.

Commercial Credit Equipment Corporation v. Reeves

1964 (Ga.) 139 S.E.2d. 784

The defendant, Reeves, purchased several items of farm equipment from an implement company and gave his note in payment. The note contained a title retention provision. Several of the items were never delivered and those which he did receive were not satisfactory. The plaintiff, Commercial Credit, received the note from the implement dealer. The defendant refused to pay the note and the plaintiff finance company brought action on the note. The lower court ruled in favor of the defendant and the plaintiff appealed.

FELTON, J. The contracts in this case were executed before the effective date of the Uniform Commercial Code, January 1, 1964. "A holder in due course is a holder who has taken the instrument under the following conditions: . . . (3) That he took it in good faith and for value; . . .

The only condition which is questioned is (3), above. The fact "(t)hat the plaintiff had knowledge of the consideration of the notes did not carry with it any notice of the failure of consideration nor was it bound to make inquiry as to whether the consideration had or would fail." (Cases cited). To constitute bad faith by a purchaser of a negotiable instrument before maturity he must have acquired it with actual knowledge of its infirmity or with a belief based on the facts or circumstances as known to him that there was a defense or he must have acted dishonestly. (Cases cited). The evidence showed that the plaintiff did not have notice of the defects or the nondelivery of the machinery until February of 1961—2 and 3 months after the notes were transferred to it. Even if the evidence is construed to indicate that the plaintiff financed the sale of the machinery from the manufacturer to the seller, as well as the sale from the seller to the defendants, this is not sufficient to demand a finding that the plaintiff had such relationship with the manufacturer or the seller as to impute to it knowledge of any defects or nondeliveries. There is no evidence of any facts which would put the plaintiff on notice that either the manufacturer or the seller was unreliable or dishonest, or which would show that the plaintiff was a party to any acts of fraud. On the contrary, it appeared that the plaintiff was merely the financing agency which happened to have financed both transactions, which fact, in itself, was not inconsistent with good faith. "The necessities of commercial life have impelled the courts to resort to the fiction that when a negotiable instrument is transferred, the legal title to it passes, so that the purchaser can sue on it in his own name and is therefore unaffected by defenses against it in the hands of the former owner. . . . it is better that there should be an occasional instance of hardship than to have doubt and distrust hamper a common method of making commercial exchanges" (Cases cited). The absence or failure of consideration is a matter of defense only as against a person not a holder in due course. (Citations.) Likewise, inadequacy of consideration does not prevent the holder of a note from enjoying the protection of a bona fide holder. (Citation.)

The verdicts and judgments were not authorized by the evidence.
Judgments reversed.

CHAPTER 22
REVIEW QUESTIONS AND PROBLEMS

1. *M* bought a logging tractor from *P* and gave a negotiable note in payment. *P* sold the note to *X* Bank. *M* later discovered that the tractor was subject to a security interest of *Y*. Can *X* Bank recover from *M* on the note?

2. Jones induces Smith to sign a note in payment for worthless securities which Jones fraudulently claimed had great value. Jones indorses the note to Black in payment of a long-standing obligation. Black indorses to White, who has knowledge of the fraud, having read about it in a newspaper account of the criminal prosecution of Jones. Can White recover on the note from Smith?

3. *M* executed a note to *P*, who promised to paint *M*'s building. *P* indorsed the note in blank to *H*. *H* sued *M* on the note and *M* alleged that the building had not been painted. He also alleged that *H* knew that the note had been given in return for *P*'s promise to paint. *H* contends that he is entitled to a judgment because *M* has not alleged a valid defense. Decide.

4. *A* gave *B* a check in the amount of $500 in payment for linoleum installed in *A*'s home. The check was dishonored, and *B* brought action to recover on the check. *A* contended that the linoleum was not satisfactory. The trial judge instructed the jury that the check was not subject to any defenses arising from claimed breaches of the contract. Was this instruction correct?

5. *A* signed notes in blank at the request of a business associate. He was informed that they would not be negotiated. The notes were completed and negotiated. Can the holders of the notes recover from *A*?

6. *A* purchased a garden tractor from *B* on an installment contract. The contract contained a clause waiving all claims and defenses as against an assignee of the contract. *B* assigned the contract to *C*. *C* brought action on the contract against *A*, and *A* defends on the ground of breach of warranty. What result?

7. *A* purchased goods from *B* and accepted a trade acceptance for the amount of the purchase price. The acceptance stated that it was given in connection with goods to be delivered by *B*. *B* indorsed the instrument to Equitable Discount Corporation. *B* never delivered the goods. Equitable did not make inquiry from *A* as to whether the goods had been delivered. Can Equitable be a holder in due course?

8. The *X* Finance Co. furnished a dealer with printed forms of notes and contracts. The dealer, after making sales to customers and using these forms, would sell the paper to the finance company. On one such note the customer-maker of the note refused to pay, contending that the merchandise he bought was defective. Is this defense good against *X* Finance Co.?

9. *M* executed a note as a gift to *P*. *P* indorsed the note to *H* for value. Can *H* enforce the note against *M*? Would the result be different if *H* knew of the gift nature of the note when it was indorsed to him?

10. *A* fraudulently induced *B* to execute a check for $2495. *B* discovered the fraud and stopped payment on the check. In the meantime *A* cashed the check at Perfect's Market. The market seeks to recover from *B*. How would you decide?

11. *M* drew a check to the order of *P* in payment for goods. The goods were defective, and *M* stopped payment on the check. *P* indorsed the check to *A* in payment of an old debt. When the check was returned to *A* because of the stop order, *A* brought action against *M*. Should he prevail?

12. *A* bought automatic automobile washing equipment on a conditional sales contract from *B* and executed a note. *B* indorsed the note to *C* after maturity. The equipment was faulty, and cars of *A*'s customers were damaged. *A* informed *B* that he would have to remove the equipment. Can *C* collect on the note?

13. *M* executed a note to *P* for siding which *P* agreed to furnish and install on *M*'s home. *M* delivered part of the siding, but failed to deliver the balance and did no installation. *P* indorsed the note to *G* bank, which had been placed on notice that precaution should be taken in purchasing notes from *P*. To what extent can the bank recover on the note?

chapter 23

Defenses

3-72 Introduction. The defenses which a party may have in relation to his obligations on commercial paper may be classified into real defenses and personal defenses. The real defenses can be asserted even against a holder in due course. The holder in due course is free from personal defenses but these, along with real defenses, can be asserted against one who is not a holder in due course or who does not have the rights of one under the "shelter" provision. It is to be noted that certain defenses may be either real or personal depending upon local state law. It is important to bear in mind that this section relates only to *defenses* which can be asserted by a party.

A *negotiation* by a person who has these defenses even though they are real defenses, cannot be rescinded as against a holder in due course. Thus, for example, a maker can defend on the ground of infancy but an infant indorser of an instrument payable to his order cannot recover the instrument from a holder in due course.[C1]

It should be noted that in addition to being free of personal defense, a holder in due course takes the instrument free from all *claims* to it on the part of any person, which means freedom from both legal and equitable claims of third parties.[C2]

A holder who does not qualify as a holder in due course takes the instrument subject to the rights of other persons in the paper.[C3] These include all valid claims to it on the part of any person including not only claims of legal title, but all liens, equities, or other claims of right

C1 *U.C.C.* 3-305(2)(a), 3-207(2).   C3 *U.C.C.* 3-306.
C2 *U.C.C.* 3-305(1).

against the instrument or its proceeds. It includes claims to rescind a prior negotiation and to recover the instrument or its proceeds. However, the claim of a third person to the instrument is not available as a *defense* to any party liable thereon unless the third person himself defends the action for such party. The primary party is required to pay the holder and is protected in doing so in spite of the third party's claim unless such party himself is made a party to the case. It should be noted, however, that the defense that the holder (plaintiff) or a person through whom he holds the instrument, acquired it by theft can be asserted.

The real defense in most states are (1) forgery, (2) material alteration, (3) infancy, to the extent that it is a defense to a simple contract, (4) other incapacity, (5) duress, (6) illegality of the transaction, which renders the obligation of the party a nullity, (7) such misrepresentation as has induced the party to sign the instrument with neither knowledge nor reasonable opportunity to obtain knowledge of its character or its essential terms,[1] and (8) discharge in insolvency proceedings.

The personal defenses in most states include (1) lack of or failure of consideration, (2) nonperformance of any condition precedent, (3) nondelivery whether the instrument be complete or incomplete, (4) delivery for a special purpose, (5) payment, (6) fraud in the inducement or consideration, (7) theft by the holder or a person through whom he holds the instrument, (8) violation of the terms of a restrictive indorsement, (9) claims of third persons, and (10) other defenses to a simple contract.

The sections which follow discuss most of these defenses in detail.

3-73 Forgery. A person whose signature is forged has a real defense and is thus not liable on the instrument unless his conduct is such as to prevent him from asserting the defense. Conduct amounting to an estoppel may be predicated on negligence.[2]

A forged signature may be ratified or adopted and such ratification is retroactive to the time when the forgery occurred. If the person whose name was forged obtains and retains the benefits of the transaction with knowledge of the forgery, the principle of ratification will apply. Likewise an estoppel may apply where there has been a representation by the person whose name was forged to an innocent purchaser that the signature is genuine.

The liability in the case of a forgery is on the wrongdoer—the forger or agent. He is bound to the full amount of the instrument to a party who takes the instrument or pays it in good faith. For a further discussion of liability, see the next chapter.

3.74 Material Alteration. The Code prescribes what constitutes a material alteration and the effect of such alteration on the liability of the parties, both as to holders in due course and to others who do not have that status.[c4]

[1] *Equitable Discount Corp. v. Fischer,* page 472.
[2] *Huber Glass Co. v. First Nat. Bank,* page 475.

[c4] *U.C.C.* 3-407.

Any alteration of an instrument is *material* which changes the contract of any party thereto in any respect, including any such change in the number or relations of the parties; or an incomplete instrument, by completing it otherwise than as authorized; or the writing as signed, by adding to it or by removing any part of it.

As a general rule, a person should not be charged on a contract he has not made. However, certain words may be added or deleted which do not affect the paper or in any way affect the contract of any previous signer. For example, addresses of parties may be changed or information about the parties added without any legal operative effect.

Changes in the amount of money due, adding persons as additional payees, changing the interest rate, unauthorized completion of blanks, mutilating or cutting away nonperforated related contracts are illustrations of material alterations which change the legal effect of the instrument and make a different contract than that originally intended.

Commercial paper is often printed as part of formal written contracts. Such instrument may or may not provide for the detachment of the commercial paper. To evidence implied authority to detach, perforations or dotted lines are set out between the negotiable portion and the contract. In absence of authority to detach either expressed or implied, unauthorized detachment from a formal written contract constitutes a material alteration. A holder in due course of a detached instrument, however, may recover according to the original tenor of the paper as it was with the contract attached.

The *effect* of a material alteration is dependent upon a number of factors: who made the alteration; the intent of such party; whether the alteration affected the contract of any given party; whether the present holder is a holder in due course. Material alteration is a "real defense" to the extent of the alteration—but a holder in due course can enforce the instrument according to its original tenor. Thus a check which has been "raised" from $50 to $500 can be enforced by a holder in due course in the original amount $50. If an incomplete instrument has been completed in excess of the authorized amount the holder in due course can enforce it as completed.

Otherwise, it can be said in general that a material alteration results in a discharge of the person whose contract is changed. However, for this result to obtain, the alteration must have been made by a holder and for a fraudulent purpose. Interference with the paper by third party strangers can in no way affect the holder's rights nor impair the instrument in its original form. Likewise, if an alteration is made innocently with an honest belief that it is authorized or for the benefit of an obligor, such note is not discharged. If the alteration is not material, no party is discharged. Thus a discharge of a party results only from a fraudulent, material alteration by a holder which affects the contract of the party claiming the discharge—only the party whose contract was changed can assert this defense.

Alterations which do not qualify under the above specifications will not result in the discharge of any parties and the altered instrument may be enforced against them in accordance with its original tenor. If the instrument was incomplete and thereafter wrongfully completed, it can be enforced in accordance with the authority in fact given.

The defense of discharge by alteration is quite restricted and a party whose contract would have been discharged may nevertheless be bound if he has previously assented to the alterations or his conduct has been such as to estop him from asserting this defense.

3-75 Lack of Capacity, Duress, Illegality. The defense of infancy may be asserted against a holder in due course. The laws of the various states differ with regard to the degree of protection afforded an infant and the Code does not attempt to state the conditions under which infancy is available as a defense. These questions are to be resolved under local law in accordance with each state's policy with regard to protecting infants.[C5]

Incapacity includes mental incompetence, guardianship, *ultra vires* acts of a corporation, or lack of corporate capacity to do business. As in the case of infancy, state laws determine the effect of contracts entered into by persons lacking capacity to contract. In some states the law merely renders the obligation of the instrument *voidable* at the election of the obligor. In such states the defense of incapacity cannot be asserted against a holder in due course. In other states the effect is to render the obligation of the instrument *null and void* in which event the defense is considered real.

Duress. Duress is a matter of degree and it may be either a real [3] or a personal defense.[4] An instrument signed at the point of a gun is void even in the hands of a holder in due course. On the other hand, one signed under threat to prosecute the son of the maker for theft may be merely voidable so that the defense is personal. Thus in each case it will be necessary to determine the degree of duress in order to decide whether or not the person imposed upon can assert the defense against a holder in due course.

Illegality. There are many state statutes relating to illegal transactions and the effects thereof. Gambling and usury are two of the most common. Contracts involving usury in particular are treated quite differently in different jurisdictions. If the local law makes obligations of a usurious nature *null and void,* the defense of usury can be asserted against a holder in due course. If the statute does not have this effect, the defense would be personal.

3-76 Fraud and Misrepresentation. A distinction exists between fraud in the *inducement* or *consideration* and fraud in the *inception*.[C6] The former pertains to the consideration for which an instrument is given. The primary party intended to create an instrument, but was fraudulently induced to do so. Such a defense is personal and is not available

---

[3] *Smith v. Lenchner,* page 479.
[4] *Acker v. First Federal Savings & Loan Assn.,* page 480.

[C5] *U.C.C.* 3-305(2)(a).   [C6] *U.C.C.* 3-305(2)(c).

against a holder in due course. Fraud in the *inception* exists where a negotiable instrument is procured from a party when circumstances are such that the party does not know that he is giving a negotiable instrument.[5] Fraud in the inception, sometimes called fraud in the *factum,* may be available as a defense against a holder in due course.[6] The theory is that since the party primarily to be bound has no intention of creating an instrument, none is created. For example: *A,* intending to sign a lease at the request of *B,* unknowingly, and by trickery on the part of *B,* signs a negotiable instrument. *B* negotiates the instrument to *C,* a bona fide purchaser. Upon presentation of this instrument by *C* to *A* for payment, *A* may have a real defense against *C.* Carelessness on the part of the maker which facilitates the fraud will deprive him of this defense against a holder in due course. Thus, in the above illustration, if *A* had signed the so-called lease without reading it and had allowed himself to be deceived into thinking the negotiable instrument he signed was a lease, he would have been liable to a holder in due course of the instrument. In such a case he cannot throw the loss occasioned by his negligence on the holder in due course.

3-77 Discharge. A person who is unable to meet his obligations may become involved in bankruptcy or other insolvency proceedings.[07] " 'Insolvency proceedings' include any assignment for the benefit of creditors or other proceedings intended to liquidate or rehabilitate the estate of the person involved." A discharge in bankruptcy or other insolvency proceedings will be available as a defense against a holder in due course. Thus, if *A* owed *B* $500 on a negotiable note and thereafter filed a petition in bankruptcy and received his discharge, *A* could assert his discharge in bankruptcy as a defense against *B,* or a holder in due course to whom *B* had negotiated the note.

       Other discharge of which holder has notice. As noted previously, a purchaser is not a holder in due course if he has notice that all the parties to an instrument have been discharged. However, if the notice does not include all of the parties, the holder may still be a holder in due course. Suppose that *M* has made a note payable to the order of *P. P* has indorsed to *A, A* has indorsed to *B,* and *B* has indorsed to *C.* If *C* discharges *B* from his liability as an indorser and then negotiates the paper to *H, H* could be a holder in due course and could hold the maker and prior indorsers liable. If he does not have notice of the discharge of *B,* such discharge would not be effective against him and the discharge is treated as a personal defense.

3-78 Lack and Failure of Consideration. Consideration is essential to make promises binding in commercial paper and its want or failure is a

---

5 *Heating Acceptance Corp. v. Patterson,* page 481.

6 *Talcott, Inc. v. Kolberg,* page 482.

07 *U.C.C.* 3-305.

defense as against all persons except holders in due course.[7] Unlike general contract law, consideration is *not* required in connection with the issuance or transfer of commercial paper if the paper is given in payment of or as security for an antecedent obligation such as payment of an existing debt.[8] This applies also to accommodation parties.[9]

As noted in connection with the requirements for a holder in due course, another term, *value* is used in the law of negotiable instruments.[C8] The two terms must be distinguished. "Consideration" has significance only in determining whether a binding contractual obligation has been created—it refers to what the obligor—e.g., maker of a note—has received for his obligation and is important only in its bearing on the question of whether his obligation is enforceable against him. "Value" is used to determine whether a holder has given something in payment for an instrument as an element of his acquiring the status of a holder in due course. To illustrate: *M* executes a note in favor of *P* in return for merchandise which is never delivered. As against *P, M* has a defense of failure of consideration. *P* indorses the note to *H* in payment of an obligation. *H* has furnished value and can enforce the note against *M* in spite of his defense. Want or failure of consideration is only a personal defense.

A holder in due course takes free from the defense of failure or absence of consideration. However, want or failure of consideration is a defense between immediate parties[10] and against nonholders in due course. Partial failure of consideration is not a complete defense but may be set up pro tanto.

Local statutes should be examined to ascertain under what circumstances consideration is not required.

3-79 Lack of Delivery.[C9] The defenses of nondelivery, conditional delivery, or delivery for a special purpose may be asserted against one who is not a holder in due course, but a holder in due course takes the instrument free of these personal defenses. For example, *A* executed a note in favor of *B* intending to deliver it to *B* only after *B* had performed certain services. *B* managed to obtain possession of the note without *A*'s knowledge and negotiated it to *C. A* can assert the defense of nondelivery against *C* only if *C* is not a holder in due course. As between immediate parties and parties other than holders in due course, the delivery may be shown to be conditional or for some special purpose only. To illustrate: *A* drew a check in favor of *B* and delivered it to him with the express understanding that it was to be negotiated only on condition that *B* first redecorate the main floor of *A*'s department store. *B* nego-

---

[7] *Greater Valley Terminal Corp. v. Goodman*, page 483.

[8] *Insdorf v. Wil-Avon Merchandise Mart, Inc.*, page 483.

[9] *Umani v. Reber*, page 484.

[10] *Bankers Guaranty Trust Co. v. Fisher*, page 485.

[C8] *U.C.C.* 3-303.   [C9] *U.C.C.* 3-306.

tiated the check to *C* in violation of this understanding. If *C* is not a holder in due course, *A* can assert the conditional delivery and *B*'s failure to perform as a defense against *C*.

3-80 Theft.[C10] A person who is not a holder in due course is subject to the defense that he acquired the instrument by theft or that a person through whom he holds the instrument acquired it by theft. Of course, a person who acquired by theft could not be a holder in due course. One who is a holder in due course is free of the defense that a person through whom he holds acquired the instrument by theft. Also a holder who does not have the rights of a holder in due course takes subject to the defense that there is a restrictive indorsement on the paper and that payment would not conform to such indorsement.

3-81 Claims of Third Persons.[C11] A holder in due course is not subject to the defense that a third party has a claim to the instrument. He is entitled to be paid in spite of such claim. One who does not have the rights of a holder in due course is subject to the defense that such claims exist with reference to instruments acquired by theft and failure to comply with restrictive indorsements but other third party claims are not available as a defense unless the third person who has the claim to the instrument defends the action in which enforcement of the instrument is sought. The reason for this limitation is set forth in the Code official comment:

> The contract of the obligor (e.g., maker of a note) is to pay the holder of the instrument and the claims of other persons against the *holder* are generally not his concern. He is not required to set up such a claim as a defense, since he usually will have no satisfactory evidence of his own on the issue; and the provision that he may not do so is intended as much for his own protection as for that of the holder. The claimant who has lost possession of an instrument so payable or indorsed that another may become a holder has lost his rights on the instrument which by its terms no longer runs to him. . . . Nothing in this section is intended to prevent the claimant from intervening in the holder's action against the obligor (e.g., maker) or defending the action for the latter, and assenting his claim in the course of such intervention or defense.

Thus the claimant is given an opportunity to establish his claim without burdening the defendant (maker or other obligor) with the duty to assent and establish it on behalf of the claimant.

3-82 Burden of Proof.[C12] Each signature on an instrument is admitted unless specifically denied in the pleadings. When the effectiveness of a signature is in issue, the party claiming under it has the burden of establishing its genuineness and authority but these matters are presumed except where the purported signer is dead or incompetent.

When the signatures are admitted or established, production of the in-

---

[C10] *U.C.C.* 3-306(d).   [C12] *U.C.C.* 3-307.
[C11] *U.C.C.* 3-306(d).

strument entitles a holder to recover on it unless the defendant establishes a defense. After a defense is shown to exist and if it is a personal defense, (a real defense could be used in all cases) the plaintiff has the burden of proving that he or some person under whom he claims is in all respects a holder in due course.[11]

The foregoing rules are in conformity with the Code policy to encourage the free movement of commercial paper. Maximum protection is given to the holder of the paper yet the basic rights of a defendant are also protected. The following principles are to be noted: there is a general presumption that a signature is genuine or authorized;[12] that the defendant has the burden of establishing any and all defenses; and that it is only when a defense has been established, that the holder has the burden of proving his holder-in-due-course status—that he is himself a holder in due course or that some person through whom he claims is a holder in due course. Unless and until a defense is shown to exist, the holder-in-due-course question is not in issue.[13]

3-83 Negligence as a Factor in Asserting Defenses.[C13] Negligence of a party will reduce a real defense to a personal defense. Negligent conduct is frequently present in situations of fraud and material alteration. For example, in the case of material alteration, that which otherwise might have resulted in a discharge will not have that result if the negligence of the party claiming the discharge contributed to or facilitated the alteration. Thus one who writes a check and leaves a large blank space in front of the amount of the check renders it easier for a wrongdoer to "raise" the check and constitutes negligence reducing the defense to a personal one.

Likewise, a person may not be able to assert that his signature was forged or otherwise unauthorized as a defense if his negligence facilitated such wrongful acts.

Negligence precludes the careless party from asserting his defense against a holder in due course or asserting the defense against a drawee or payor such as a bank who pays the instrument in good faith and "in accordance with the reasonable commercial standards of the drawee's or payor's business."

Negligence in failing to detect forged indorsements may deprive the person whose indorsement was forged from relief, unless outweighted by the negligence of the indorser.[14]

The reasoning behind the negligence rule is that if checks or other commercial paper are to pass current as money, the careless creator of paper should suffer the loss as against holders in due course and the innocent drawees and other payors who pay the instrument in good faith.

---

[11] *Pitillo v. Demetry,* page 488.
[12] *Altex Aluminum Supply Co. v. Asay,* page 489.
[13] *United Securities Corporation v. Bruton,* page 491.
[14] *Gresham State Bank v. O & K Construction Co.,* page 493.

[C13] *U.C.C.* 3-406.

How negligent and careless the drawer must be is a fact question but the negligence must be *substantial.*

Insofar as checks are concerned, the debtor-bank is under a duty to pay checks drawn by the depositor in accordance with the contract. It is therefore proper that the depositor should be bound to exercise care in drafting checks in order to prevent the bank from being deceived. Drawing a check in a manner which facilitates fraud constitutes a breach of duty to the bank. For example, *A* as a practice has permitted his secretary to issue checks by means of a mechanical device and rubber stamps. Unauthorized checks issued and delivered by reason of the careless control and supervision of such equipment would prevent *A* from denying liability. Likewise, inadvertency in mistakenly mailing checks, particularly to persons of the same name as the intended payee, is negligent conduct contributing to the use of an unauthorized signature, so that the loss must be borne by the drawer. The question is, what conduct is "negligent" so that it can be said that it has "substantially contributed to a material alteration" or to the making of "an unauthorized signature." It is believed that reasonable care would not demand the use of sensitized paper, fast inks, and "checkographs" by drawers in order to avoid negligent conduct.

A person placing current paper in the channels of business owes a duty to future users to so create paper that it cannot be altered. The holder, drawee, and other good faith takers should not be deterred in its use. The negligent drawers and makers must seek recovery from the wrongdoer. Of course when the instrument has been altered by a mechanical process or erasure or chemical change another instrument has been created, and no negligent conduct can be attributed to the issuer of the paper.

DEFENSES CASES

Equitable Discount Corp. v. Fischer

1957 (Pa.) 12 D. & C. 2d 326., 55 Lanc. 381

JOHNSTONE, J.   The plaintiff seeks to recover in this action in assumpsit the sum of Six Hundred ($600.00) Dollars, together with interest, on three trade acceptances, each in the sum of Two Hundred ($200.-00) Dollars, executed and delivered by the defendant to Sterling Materials Company, Inc., and transferred by indorsement to the plaintiff. At the close of the trial of this case, the court entered a directed verdict in favor of the plaintiff and against the defendant on motion of counsel for the plaintiff. The defendant has filed a motion for a new trial and assigned two reasons in support thereof. Argument was heard by the court *en banc* and counsel for the parties have submitted briefs.

The testimony reveals that the defendant admittedly signed three trade acceptances, each in the sum of Two Hundred ($200.00) Dollars, all dated July 25, 1955, all payable to the order of Sterling Materials Company, Inc., at The First Columbia National Bank at Columbia, Pa., and serially due on December 1, 1955, January 1, 1956, and February 1, 1956. These trade acceptances were delivered by the defendant to Sterling Materials Company, Inc., in payment of certain roofing materials, which the defendant later refused to accept. On August 10, 1955, in the regular course of its business, the plaintiff purchased the three trade acceptances from Sterling Materials Company, Inc., for the sum of Four Hundred Twenty ($420.00) Dollars and they were transferred to the plaintiff by unrestricted indorsements. Notice of the purchase of the three trade acceptances by the plaintiff from Sterling Materials Company, Inc., was given to the defendant by the plaintiff by letter dated August 10, 1955. Subsequently, the three trade acceptances were forwarded through regular channels to the paying bank on their respective due dates and payment was refused. Purchase of the trade acceptances was made by the plaintiff without knowledge of any defense on the part of the defendant and without knowledge that the defendant had not received the materials purchased.

The defendant, an electrical contractor, agreed to purchase a quantity of roofing materials from a representative of Sterling Materials Company, Inc., and to pay therefor the sum of Six Hundred ($600.00) Dollars. The defendant was requested to pay cash for the materials but he arranged to make three monthly payments of Two Hundred ($200.00) Dollars each. The Sterling representative had the defendant sign the three trade acceptances, telling him they were in the nature of a note and would be put through a bank. The record discloses that the defendant had had no experience with trade acceptances and did not know what they were, but had experience in writing checks. No effort was made by the defendant to obtain any advice before signing the trade acceptances and he knew when he signed them that he would have to pay them on their respective due dates. The day after signing the trade acceptances the defendant went to his bank and asked the bank to check Dun & Bradstreet on the reputation of Sterling Materials Company, Inc. Following the receipt from the bank of the report, the defendant cancelled the order and refused to take delivery of the materials. No testimony was offered as to the method used to cancel the order or the time of the cancellation.

The question to be determined here is whether the court properly directed a verdict for the plaintiff or should have permitted the jury to pass on whether the defendant had a defense under Section 3-305 (2) (c) of the Uniform Commercial Code (12 A. P. S. Section 3-305). The record clearly discloses the plaintiff to be a holder in due course of the three trade acceptances. They were purchased for value, before their due dates and in the regular course of business. The trade acceptances had not been dishonored and the plaintiff had no notice of any defense on the part of anyone, including the defendant. Under these circumstances, the plaintiff meets the requirement of a holder in due course as defined by the Code. As such a holder, the plaintiff took the trade acceptances free from all defenses on the part of the defendant, with whom the plaintiff had no dealings, except those set forth in Section 3-305 of the Code. In the present case, the only possible defense available to the defendant is set forth in Section 3-305 (2) (c). This section of the Code reads, a holder in due course takes the instrument free from all defenses of any party to the instrument with whom the holder has not dealt except "(c) such misrepresentation as has induced the party to sign the instrument with neither knowledge nor reasonable opportunity to obtain knowledge of its character or its essential terms." By directing a verdict for the plaintiff, the court determined at the time of the trial that the defendant had not produced testimony which justified submitting to the jury the question of whether the defendant had brought himself within the exception to the general rule. After further deliberation and careful study of the record, we are convinced that the defendant failed to show he was induced to sign the trade acceptances by misrepresentations, with neither knowledge nor reasonable opportunity to obtain knowledge of their character or essential terms and that the directed verdict was proper.

This particular part of the section of the Code is new but follows the majority of the decisions which recognized the defense of fraud in the essence or fraud in the factum against a holder in due course. The circumstances of the present case do not bring it within the class of cases where the maker is tricked into signing. In *Resh v. First National Bank of Allentown* (93 Pa. 397), the defendant signed a note but was told he was signing a receipt and there the court held the instrument invalid even in the hands of a holder in due course. Here the defendant signed the three trade acceptances after being told they were in the nature of a note and would be put through a bank. The defendant knew he was signing three obligations which he would be required to pay on their several due dates. The record is devoid of any testimony that any misrepresentations were made by the Sterling representative before or at the time the defendant signed. The defendant knew that he had agreed to purchase certain roofing materials and that he would have to pay for the materials at the rate of Two Hundred ($200.00) Dollars per month for three months. He said he thought he was signing something in the nature of a check and he could hardly have been more correct.

However, paragraph (c) of subsection (2) of Section 3-305 of the Code extends the defense to an instrument of which the signer had neither knowledge nor reasonable opportunity to obtain knowledge of its character or its essential terms. In other words, was the defendant excusably ignorant of the contents of the writing he signed and had he no opportunity to obtain such knowledge? In our opinion the defendant was not ignorant of what he signed. He knew the three trade acceptances were obligations which required him to pay definite amounts of money on certain dates. He admitted being told the trade acceptances were like a note and would be put through a bank. He testified he thought he was signing something in the nature of a check, which he was accustomed to signing, and knew or must have known that a check is an order to pay money to some named person. It is true that he did not know the meaning of the word negotiable but he knew that checks which he issued might get into the hands of someone other than the payee. The defendant may have given no thought at the time of signing to the possibility of the instruments getting into the hands of someone other than Sterling Materials Company, Inc. but he knew he had promised to pay definite sums of money on definite dates. The defendant was not only aware of the character of the instruments signed but also understood the essential terms of the three trade acceptances.

The defendant made no effort to ascertain from any outside source the meaning or implications of the instruments he signed. The Sterling representative did not refuse to permit the defendant to make inquiries, since no such request was made and the defendant apparently understood what he was doing and needed no help. It was the defendant who suggested that payment for the materials be spread over a three months' period. The defendant also testified that he never saw the Sterling representative before and had no reason to place any confidence in anything he said. The defendant had been in business for almost forty years and obviously considered himself capable of transacting business without the aid or assistance of anyone else.

The facts of this case are even weaker than those in *First National Bank vs. Anderson* (7 D. & C. 2d, 661), where the court refused to open a judgment entered on a warrant of attorney signed by three persons who had not read the contract and note and made no effort to seek advice before signing.

The motion for a new trial is dismissed.

Huber Glass Co. v. First National Bank of Kenosha

1965 (Wisc.) 138 N.W.2d 157

Huber Glass Co. maintained a checking account with First National Bank of Kenosha. R. C. Huber, president, and his wife Bertha, were the only ones authorized to sign checks. Kenneth Miller, bookkeeper for the company since 1959, was discharged in 1963 and committed suicide the next day. It was later discovered that certain checks signed "R. C. Huber" and made out to and indorsed by Miller had been drawn on the account since August, 1960. Huber denied actually signing any of the checks. Huber Glass Co., plaintiff, brought suit against the bank, defendant, to recover $23,875.42, which had been paid within the prior year on the checks allegedly forged by Miller. (The statute outlawed claims on checks more than a year old.) Judgment was rendered for plaintiff and the defendant bank appealed.

WILKIE, J.   The law concerning the duty of a bank towards its depositor was summarized in *Wussow v. Badger State Bank.* Since their relationship is grounded in contract, a bank can only make payments from a depositor's account in accordance with proper authorization and is bound to restore any amount paid out on forged checks. A bank can only avoid this strict liability where the "depositor is in equity estopped to assert that the bank is absolutely liable." To do this successfully, the bank must show (1) that it was without fault in failing to detect the forgeries, and (2) that the depositor was negligent in causing the money to be paid. In the instant case the trial court found as a matter of fact that (1) the bank "was negligent in not detecting the forgeries," and (2) that the depositor "was not negligent." To enable the bank to prevail against the depositor's claim it must, on this appeal, demonstrate that both of these findings are against the great weight and clear preponderance of the evidence.

Thus, the two issues presented on this appeal are:

1. Is the finding of negligence on the part of the bank against the evidence?

2. Is the finding of no negligence on the part of the depositor against the evidence?

The Bank's Negligence.

Two bank officials, George Gehring and Rudolph Scuglik, explained the procedures employed by the bank when a check was presented for payment. When checks come in, they are totaled, listed, and sorted alphabetically in the proof department and are then routed to the bookkeeping department. There an employee, who is responsible for a particular alphabetical segment of accounts, examines each check for signature, date, amount, payee, and endorsement, and posts it to the appropriate account. The checks are then photographed, perforated, filed with others charged against the same account, and, at the end of the month, returned to the depositor. Every bookkeeping department employee has a file containing signature cards for each of their depositors and are trained to recognize the various signatures. The checks are actually compared with the cards until the employee becomes sufficiently familiar with the signature. The head of the bookkeeping department is notified in case of a discrepancy. Scuglik, who was in charge of the bookkeeping department, could not say that each of the checks in question was processed according to the prescribed manner, but he assumed that this was done as a matter of routine. There was no testimony which would even suggest that there was a breakdown of this system in regard to the checks in question. As to the forgeries themselves, an examination of the bogus checks, respondent's signature card, and several genuine checks which were introduced into evidence, demonstrates that "each forged signature was a reasonable facsimile of the genuine signature."

The record establishes that the bank used a reasonable method to inspect and process the checks presented to it, and that the forgeries were not palpable or flagrant, as was the case in *Wussow*, where the bank was found to be negligent for failing to detect the obvious discrepancy in signatures. Thus, unless the mere fact that the forgeries did escape detection of itself raises an inference of negligence, the bank, in the absence of any affirmative evidence to the contrary, has sustained the burden of showing that it acted reasonably and with "due diligence."

(*Wussow v. Badger State Bank, supra,* . . . It should be noted that the rule as to who has the burden of proving that the bank was free of negligence *has been changed by the Uniform Commercial Code, Section* 404-406(3), *Stats., pro-*

viding that the burden is on the depositor to prove negligence by the bank as distinguished from the rule, applicable to the case at bar, that requires the bank to prove itself free of negligence.)

Consequently there is no evidence to support the finding that the bank was negligent.

Negligence of Depositor.

Even if the bank is not guilty of negligence in failing to uncover the forgery, the depositor is nonetheless entitled to a restoration of the funds paid out in the absence of negligence on its own part. Thus, the crucial question here is whether or not the depositor was negligent.

A depositor is bound to examine the checks and statements returned by the bank, and this duty is violated when it neglects to do those things dictated by ordinary business customs and which, if done, would have prevented the wrongdoing.

In *Wussow,* the court held that the depositor had a duty

to examine his checks and the statement and discover whether the balance stated was correct and whether any forgeries were included and report any discrepancies in balance and any forgeries to the bank at once.

It had been held that the reconciliation should include, as a minimum, the following steps: (1) A comparison of the cancelled checks with the check stubs, (2) a comparison of the statement balance with the checkbook balance, and (3) a comparison of the returned checks with the checks listed on the statement.

There is no question that in the case at bar the procedure employed by the respondent [plaintiff] in checking the returned checks and bank statements did not comply with these suggested steps. On the contrary, the undisputed evidence showed that the checks returned to respondent by appellant were received by Miller who made a preliminary examination of the statement. Presumably, the forged checks were removed from the others at this point. Then another employee of the bookkeeping department listed the checks numerically and determined the ones that were outstanding. After this, Miller would reconcile the bank statement with the check ledger. Huber got the checks at this point, but he testified that he never attempted to reconcile the bank statement with the books but left this task entirely up to Miller. When asked:

Q. . . . You could have yourself taken the number of checks that were there, taped them, and added to it the outstanding checks, and subtracted that from your total deposit and determined whether there was any discrepancy, could you not?

Huber replied:

A. I could have, but this is what I hired Mr. Miller to do.

Miller advised Huber that the accounts were in balance. Between April 2, 1962, and April 19, 1963, respondent's account was overdrawn on 14 different occasions. Although appellant mailed respondent a notice of overdraft each time, Huber did not recall having seen any of them. However, he did learn of the overdrafts from the monthly statement.

Miller's methods were such that a comparison of the statement balance with the checkbook balance or a matching of the cancelled checks with the actual charges on the statement would have quickly disclosed a discrepancy. Likewise, a perusal of the cancelled checks, which were numbered consecutively, would have revealed that certain checks were missing and had been missing for some time. Yet Huber admittedly never complied with any of the suggested reconciliation practices, and, in fact, left full responsibility to Miller.

No other employee was assigned to verify Miller's work. That there were 14 overdrafts in a year should have prompted Huber to investigate the state of his books even if ordinary business practices did not so persuade him. Under the circumstances, entrusting Miller alone with the job of reconciling the statements for three years, when a simple spot check of the records would have uncovered the forgeries, was unreasonable and the trial court's finding of no negligence is contrary to the great weight and clear preponderance of the evidence. Huber, however, takes the position that the president of a company which employs between 50 and 75 people, and which writes almost 13,000 checks a year, cannot be expected to personally examine and/or reconcile the books. But the president himself is not required to do this; the task can be delegated to another employee. Modern business practice dictates at least some semblance of internal control. Estoppel from claiming against the bank is the price of blind reliance on a single employee.

The earliest checks forged on the depositor's account by Miller appeared in August in 1960. Respondent's negligence in failing to employ proper reconciliation methods preceded the one-year period—April, 1962-1963—embraced by the depositor's claim, and he is estopped from asserting a claim against the bank for any check embraced in the lower court's judgment.

Other courts have arrived at the same conclusion upon similar facts. In *Clarke v. Camden Trust Co.* the depositor never made an attempt to reconcile his bank statement himself but left this job entirely to his trusted secretary. After the secretary mysteriously disappeared, it was learned that she had forged 41 checks over a four-year period. The depositor was precluded from recovering from the bank because "any kind of reasonable examination" would have detected the forgeries. In *Morgan v. United States Mortgage & Trust Co.*, a clerk who made deposits, wrote out checks, and received the cancelled checks and statements from the bank forged several checks on a trust account. As an examination, the trustees matched the genuine checks, which the clerk submitted to them, with the checkbook. The court held that the trustees-depositors failed in their duty of examination by not at least comparing the cancelled checks with the statement or passbook returned by the bank.

Judgment reversed.

Smith v. Lenchner
1964 (Pa.) 205 A.2d 626

WRIGHT, J.   . . . The note in question is dated July 6, 1962, in amount of $1,200.00 payable on demand, and is under seal. The petition . . . alleges that the maker of the note is not indebted to the payee, and requests that the judgment be opened because (a) the note was given "under duress of a threat made by the plaintiff to maliciously and falsely interfere with and disrupt a business transaction which petitioner was then negotiating"; and (b) no consideration was received for the execution and delivery of the note. Appellant's answer denies that the note was given under duress of a threat, and avers to the contrary that the note was voluntarily negotiated as "the result of a good-faith, arms-length business transaction." The answer further denies want of consideration, and alleges to the contrary (1) that the presence of the seal imports consideration and (2) that the transaction which gave rise to the note "was a sale of stock by plaintiff to defendant.". . . A brief summary of this testimony is as follows:

Joseph S. Lenchner, the appellee, testified that he was a college graduate, admittedly experienced in business transactions. In the month of June, 1962, negotiations were pending for the sale of the Lenchner-Corvato Company, a security business in which he was financially interested. Martin B. Smith, [plaintiff] an employe and owner of one share of stock, demanded the sum of $1,200.00, "and if I didn't give it to him he was going to try to do everything and anything he could to kill our deal . . . I suggested a note which he agreed to take." Although he had ample time to do so, Lenchner did not consult his attorney before the note was executed and delivered.

Martin B. Smith, the appellant, testified that he was manager of the underwriting department of Lenchner-Corvato Company, and had paid $1,200.00 for the one share of stock which he owned. He had doubts as to the financial status of the proposed purchaser of the business, and objected to the sale "because I didn't think we'd ever get paid." He proposed that Lenchner buy his share of stock for the cost price. Lenchner did not have the cash available, and said "that he would give me a note." The stock certificate was endorsed, but was retained as collateral. Smith flatly denied making any threats, and testified that the transaction was purely a business deal.

We perceive no merit in appellee's contention that he was under duress when he executed and delivered the note in question. The threat purportedly made by appellant was not of physical violence or of criminal process, indeed not even of civil process. The case of *McDermott v. Bennett* (213 Pa. 129, 62 A. 637) cited in the brief, involved the relationship of client and attorney and is readily distinguished. Duress has been defined as that degree of restraint or danger, either actually inflicted or threatened and impending, which is sufficient in severity or apprehension to overcome the mind of a person of ordinary firmness. The quality of firmness is assumed to exist in every person competent to contract, unless it appears that by reason of old age or other sufficient cause he is weak or infirm. Where persons deal with each other on equal terms and at arm's length, there is a presumption that the person alleging duress possesses ordinary firmness. Moreover, in the absence of threats of actual bodily harm, there can be no duress where the contracting party is free to consult with counsel.

Appellee also contends that he may raise his alleged defense of want of consideration despite the fact that the note was executed under seal. Reliance is placed upon Section 3-113 of the Uniform Commercial Code, which reads as follows: "An instrument otherwise negotiable is within this Article even though it is under a seal." It is argued that the Code Comment under this section, as well as the Pennyslvania Bar Association Notes, indicate that the defense of want of consideration is now available despite the presence of a seal. This question was raised but expressly not decided in *Thomasik v. Thomasik* (413 Pa. 559, 198 A.2d 511). Howbeit, the note in the instant case is not "an instrument otherwise negotiable" because it *authorizes confession of judgment as of any term.* Prior to the enactment of the Code, a note containing a warrant of attorney to confess judgment at *any time* was held to be a non-negotiable instrument. This rule was applied to a demand note. The same result has been reached in cases subsequent to the enactment of the Code. Since the instant note is *non-negotiable,* it follows that the seal imports consideration.

We should perhaps here mention that Section 3-112(1) of the Code provides that the negotiability of a note "is not affected by . . . (d) a term authorizing a confession of judgment on the instrument if it is not paid when due." The Pennsylvania Bar Association Notes under the section point out that most judgment notes in use in this Commonwealth are not negotiable because judgment may be entered before the amount is due. To the same effect is the Code Comment that "paragraph (d) is intended to mean that a confession of judgment may be authorized only if the instrument is not paid when due, and that otherwise negotiability is affected." The Code did not change prior law in this respect.

Appellee contends finally that appellant may not rely upon the seal because he affirmatively pleaded independent consideration. It is argued that appellant "should now be estopped from relying upon the seal as a substitute for consideration." The doctrine of estoppel has no application in the instant case. We perceive no reason which would prevent appellant from utilizing both theories.

Order reversed.

Acker v. First Fed. Savings & Loan Assn. of St. Petersburg
1965, (Fla.) 173 So.2d 170

On December 31, 1961, the defendant wrote a check on the Madeira Beach Bank to John B. Peters which was dated January 4, 1962. On the next business day after the check was written the defendant stopped payment on this check. Peters deposited this check in his account in a different bank, plaintiff, on January 3, 1962, and later withdrew these funds.

Peters' bank received notice of the stop payment order on January 9, 1962.

The defendant has alleged that she made this check out under great fear of bodily injury, although it is not disputed that she actually signed the check. It was not alleged, however, that the plaintiff-bank had any notice of this duress.

The plaintiff bank, which had allowed Peters to withdraw against the deposit of the check, obtained a garnishment order against the defendant's account in the Madeira Beach Bank. The defendant, Acker appealed from the judgment in favor of the garnishor, First Federal.

SHANNON, J.   When an instrument is in the hands of a holder in due course, it is conclusively presumed that there was a valid delivery by all parties prior to the holder. (Fla.Sta. Sec. 674.18, F.S.A.) While the defense of duress would be available against Peters, it would not be available against the bank, which did not have notice of the duress.

Other questions raised by the defendant were settled in the case of *Sorrells Bros. Packing Co. v. Union State Bank* (Fla.App. 1962, 144 So.2d 74) which held that when a bank honors a depositor's check withdrawing the amount deposited by another check, the bank becomes a holder in due course of the check deposited if it has no notice of any defect in the instrument. Ample authority is cited in that opinion, a repetition of which would serve no useful purpose . . .

Affirmed.

Heating Acceptance Corporation v. Patterson

1965 (Conn.) 208 A.2d 341

KING, J.   The plaintiff sued as the endorsee of a promissory note given by the defendant to the payee, Holland Furnace Company, hereinafter referred to as Holland, in payment for a furnace purchased from it and installed in the defendant's six-family dwelling house in Bridgeport. The note was executed and delivered to Holland's agent in Bridgeport on or about November 12, 1958, but was made payable at Holland's home office in Holland, Michigan. On or before December 30, 1958, the note was endorsed and negotiated by Holland to the plaintiff, apparently in Michigan. The defendant claimed, in effect, that the furnace was defective and improperly installed by Holland; that she knew nothing about the note and signed it as a result of fraud in the factum on the part of Holland; and that the plaintiff was not a holder in due course. From a verdict for the plaintiff the defendant has appealed.

The defendant offered evidence to prove that she signed the note in question in reliance upon the representation of the seller that it was a credit application. Since there was abundant, although controverted, evidence that the plaintiff finance company was a holder in due course, it became important to determine whether the facts testified to by the defendant, if credited, would constitute fraud in the *factum*, available against a holder in due course, or merely fraud in the *inducement*. It seems best to adopt as a common-law definition of fraud in the factum, for use under the Negotiable Instruments Law, which contains no definition, the codification of the common-law definition in Uniform Commercial Code, General Statutes 42a-3-305(2) (c), which is: "(S)uch misrepresentation as has induced the party to sign the instrument with neither knowledge of its character or its essential terms." The defendant was entitled to a charge defining fraud in the factum together with its application to her claims of proof. Nothing along this line was given, although such a charge was requested.

There is error, the judgment is set aside and a new trial is ordered.

James Talcott, Inc. v. Kolberg
1965, 344 F.2d 119

PER CURIAM. Plaintiff-appellant brought suit in the District Court upon a promissory note claimed to have been signed by appellees [defendants], who are husband and wife. They defended on the ground that the wife's signature on the note was a forgery; that the alleged signature of the husband was not established by the evidence; and, that, if he did sign, his signature was obtained by fraud. On judgment entered by the District Court of no cause of action, appellant [plaintiff] seeks review.

It was contended by appellant that appellee Kolberg and his wife executed the note, payable to The Affiliated Laundry Sales, and delivered it to one Lou Lakos, as part of a transaction which involved a chattel mortgage covering laundry equipment sold to appellees. Lakos, purporting to act for the mortgagee, The Affiliated Laundry Sales, subsequently assigned the note to appellant company. It is submitted by appellant company that it received the note in good faith for a valuable consideration without notice of any infirmity.

Appellees planned to open a laundromat business in a shopping center, and it was for this purpose that they wanted to secure the laundry equipment. A certain amount of the equipment was delivered, but only a portion thereof; and it was not installed, as provided by the agreement. The mortgage was later foreclosed, the property repossessed, and, on sale thereof, the amount of $8,500 was realized; and appellant company sued for the deficiency. Appellant company had theretofore secured a judgment, in the full amount of the note, against Lakos, based upon his liability as an endorser. Lakos did not appear in order to defend this suit against himself, and, apparently, none of the parties could locate him, in order to secure his presence as a witness on the hearing of the instant case, although he was the one witness, other than the defendants, who could testify about the original transaction, and as to whether appellees, or either of them, had signed the note.

After hearing, the District Court found that the alleged signature of appellee Bonnie N. Kolberg was a forgery; but there was no finding as to who committed the forgery. Further, the District Court found that not only was the claimed signature of Raymond F. Kolberg not established by a preponderance of the evidence, but that even if he did, in fact, sign the note, his signature was procured by trickery, fraud, and misrepresentation. Moreover, the court found that no negligence on the part of Raymond F. Kolberg precluded his making such a defense as against a bona fide purchaser of the paper. Accordingly, a judgment of no cause of action was entered.

The case is unusual, because of the defense of forgery and fraud in the procurement of a note, and no evidence is forthcoming from any witness to the transaction to dispute any of the testimony of the defendants.

An examination of the record is convincing that the findings of the District Court, as set forth in the opinion of Judge Roth, were sustained by the evidence; and no error of law appearing, the judgment of the District Court is affirmed.

Greater Valley Terminal Corp. v. Goodman

1962, 405 Pa. 605, 176 A. 2d 408

COHEN, J.   ABC Federal Oil & Burner Co. (ABC) owed substantial debts to Greater Valley Terminal Corporation (plaintiff) and P. J. Goodman (defendant) for unpaid oil deliveries. Plaintiff was exerting pressure upon ABC for payment and had refused to sell any more oil to that firm unless paid for on delivery and unless the past debt was liquidated.

Defendant recognized that if plaintiff proceeded to enforce collection of the debt owed plaintiff by ABC, ABC would not be able to pay and its credit position would be so endangered that it would be forced to discontinue operations. Consequently, numerous meetings were held by parties representing plaintiff, defendant and ABC. As a result of these meetings, ABC gave plaintiff its note for $325,306.92 payable in eighteen weekly installments. Executed contemporaneously was defendant's signed statement written on the bottom of the note: "For value received, the undersigned hereby guarantees payment of the within Note." Defendant at the same time also delivered to plaintiff his personal financial statement indicating thereon the said statement was given by the defendant to induce plaintiff to accept defendant's guarantee of the note given by ABC to plaintiff. ABC defaulted in the terms and payment of the note and plaintiff brought this action on defendant's guarantee.

Since an inference of consideration may be drawn where surety is given contemporaneously with the principal obligation, the plaintiff could have properly rested its case after having proved, in addition to the principal agreement, defendant's contemporaneous endorsement and nonpayment. . . .

Judgment for plaintiff affirmed.

Insdorf v. Wil-Avon Merchandise Mart, Inc.

1958, (Pa.) 8 Ches. Co. Rep. 341

The defendant executed a check payable to the order of the plaintiff in settlement of accounts owing to the plaintiff. The check was made and delivered on January 11, 1958, but dated January 23, 1958. The plaintiff presented the check after January 23, but the bank refused payment because the defendant had stopped payment. The plaintiff attempted to recover the amount of the check and the defendant resisted claiming that the plaintiff's complaint failed to allege with particularity the accounts between the parties for which the check was allegedly given in payment.

GAWTHROP, J. . . . Defendant's second contention is without merit. Under the Negotiable Instruments Law . . . Section 24, every negotiable instrument was deemed, prima facie, to have been issued for valuable consideration. There was no necessity to plead in detail the terms of the contract in connection with delivery of a check . . . The Uniform Commercial Code, . . . Section 3-408, supplies and replaces, inter alia, Section 24 of the Act of 1901, and by its terms provides that "no consideration is necessary for an instrument or obligation given in payment of or as security for an antecedent obligation of any kind." We cannot conclude that the enactment of the Code has altered the law or the practice to require Plaintiff to aver the details of the contract which gave rise to making the check. Moreover, Section 3-408 of the Code, by making consideration unnecessary where the instrument is given for an antecedent obligation, makes it equally unnecessary to plead consideration in such circumstances. Therefore, the averment may be regarded as surplusage.

Furthermore, the same section of the Code makes want or failure of consideration a matter of defense as between the original parties. Both such defenses must . . . be pleaded under New Matter in Defendant's Answer, and if not so pleaded are waived. . . . In our view the detailed nature of the consideration pleaded need not be set forth, especially since Defendant must make any defense of want or failure of consideration by pleading it affirmatively as New Matter.

The preliminary objection is dismissed. Defendant is allowed twenty days to file an answer.

Umani v. Reber

1959, 191 Pa. Super. 185, 155 A. 2d 634

Umani leased a hotel to Reber and also transferred the hotel liquor license with the understanding that the license would be returned upon termination of the lease. Later Reber threatened to surrender the license for cancellation unless Umani reimbursed him for losses resulting from operation of the hotel. He claimed that the amount of past revenue had been misrepresented in order to induce him to lease. He set his losses at $5000 and demanded this sum for return of the license. Umani executed two checks to Reber for a total of $5000 and placed them in escrow pending approval of the license transfer by the Liquor Control Board. Approval was forthcoming but Umani immediately told the escrow agent not to deliver the checks to Reber. The escrow agent deposited the checks with the court and the court awarded a judgment in favor of Reber.

ERVIN, J. . . . Appellant also argues that it was error for the trial court to enforce an oral agreement which lacked consideration because the parties were already obligated to perform under a prior agreement. The $5,000, represented by the two certified checks deposited by Mrs.

Umani with Parke in escrow, was being paid to Reber, not for the re-transfer of the liquor license but to compensate Reber for losses which he claimed to have sustained because of false information given to him by Joseph Umani concerning the previous money revenue from the operation of the hotel under Umani. Reber claimed these representations were false and induced him to enter into a bad bargain. The checks were to be turned over to Reber upon the retransfer of the license but they were actually given to settle his claim for losses. The testimony of Parke on this subject is quite clear. There was, therefore, a new and good consideration for the payment of the $5,000 and the cases cited by the appellant in this connection are not applicable to the facts in the present case. . . .

Orders affirmed. . . .

Bankers Guarantee Title and Trust Co. v. Fisher

1965, (Ohio) 204 N.E.2d 103

ROSSETTI, J. The plaintiff filed a law suit against the defendants claiming that there is due the plaintiff from the defendants Fisher the sum of Eighty-nine hundred ninety-eight dollars and ninety-six cents ($8998.96) with interest from February 1, 1962. Defendants Fisher filed an answer requesting that the interest of the plaintiff and the defendants be determined.

The defendants, Daniel Arthur Fisher and Dorothy L. Fisher, entered into a written contract with William J. Savage and Mildred E. Savage to purchase certain premises in Louisville, Ohio. The plaintiff loaned the Fisher defendants Ninety-one hundred and fifty dollars ($9150.00) and accepted a note and mortgage for that amount.

A closing of this transaction was held in the office of the plaintiff and certain costs were paid by the Fisher defendants, among which was Item F . . . the amount of Ninety-one dollars and fifty cents ($91.50) designated as "origination charge," which is one percent of the loan.

Another cost item paid by the Fisher defendants is the so-called loan discount fee of Eight hundred twenty-three dollars and fifty cents ($823.-50) which is nine (9) percent of the face amount of the loan. This was authorized to be deducted from the sales price by the sellers of the property.

The item of Eight hundred twenty-three dollars and fifty cents ($823.-50) has been referred to as a loan discount fee, and. . . . Whatever it is called, the simple fact is that nine (9) percent of the loan was deducted and retained by the plaintiff bank, amounting to Eight hundred twenty-three dollars and fifty cents ($823.50). However, as between the plaintiff bank and the defendant borrowers this sum or item was not deducted which means that the bank received in addition to the regular interest charged on the loan of Ninety-one hundred and fifty dollars ($9150.00) the sum of Eight hundred twenty-three dollars and fifty cents ($823.50), plus the origination charge.

The Fisher defendants claim that they should not pay any more to the plaintiff than what plaintiff paid out, and consequently the plaintiff bank is only entitled to recover the sum of Eighty-three hundred twenty-six dollars and fifty cents ($8326.50) plus interest and less any payments made.

One of the questions in this case is as follows:

> When the payee of a promissory note in the amount of Nine thousand one hundred fifty dollars ($9,150) pays to and disburses for the maker of said note the sum of Eight thousand three hundred twenty-six dollars and fifty cents ($8,326.50), how much can the payee recover from the maker?

It is to be noted that the parties to this law suit are the original maker and payee on said note. The plaintiff is not a holder in due course. A holder in due course can collect the base amount of the note although he purchases the same at a discount.

It is well established as a rule that, as between the original parties to an instrument, the consideration may be inquired into.

Again the evidence does not show the purpose of the loan discount fee which was a matter between the plaintiff bank and the seller of the property. It appears to this Court that this is a matter of the seller of the property reducing the sales price of the property, and in that event the purchaser is entitled to receive the full benefit of the reduction of the sales price.

The question is not what the parties called the transaction herein, but what does the transaction require the Court to call it. It, therefore, is necessary for this Court to scan the transaction carefully to ascertain its real substance with a purpose of determining whether it is a disguised loan or something else.

The question in this case is not what price the Fisher defendants paid for their house, but rather what did the plaintiff receive for making this loan to the Fisher defendants. Therefore, is the plaintiff lender exacting an interest rate greater than eight (8) per cent in making this loan to the borrowers? What is the plaintiff receiving for making the loan in this case? There can be no question but what the plaintiff is receiving $15\frac{1}{4}$ per cent of the loan which is in excess of the legal rate of eight (8) per cent.

Having in mind, therefore, the purposes of the statute in its inception and the need for a rule understandable by laymen as well as the courts the Court expresses the following rule for determination of usury:

> If the total amount contracted to be paid by the borrower before or after the use of money actually received as a loan for the period of time it is used, regardless of the names used for the various charges, is in excess of eight per cent per annum, then the excess is usurious.

This was the purpose and intent of the law. This is a rule easily followed and understood by all.

It, therefore, follows that a person who is not a holder in due course may not collect the full amount thereon if there is a defense.

Want of consideration is a defense in an action by the original payee of a note against a maker thereof. In this case since the plaintiff is the original payee and not a holder in due course, then the defense of failure or lack of consideration may be raised by the defendants against this plaintiff.

The next question is whether the transaction in this case was a shift or device to evade the usury law. The evidence shows that the only contract was between the plaintiff and the Fisher defendants and that was as a result of the note and mortgage. The note and mortgage clearly indicates that the subject of the loan was the property in question.

The Court must, therefore, examine all disbursements made by the plaintiff and deductions held by the plaintiff to determine whether or not the plaintiff violated the usury statute and whether or not the plaintiff collected more than the legal rate of interest allowed in Ohio.

The evidence shows that the plaintiff received the following for making the loan to the Fisher defendants:

1. Origination charge, $91.50 or 1 per cent.
2. Interest on the $9150.00 note or 5¼ per cent.
3. Loan discount fee of $823.50 or 9 per cent.

Thus we find that the plaintiff bank actually disbursed the sum of Eighty-three hundred twenty-six dollars and fifty cents ($8326.50) of the Ninety-one hundred fifty dollar loan for the Fisher defendants. That simply means, the plaintiff bank realized an additional profit of Eight hundred twenty-three dollars and fifty cents ($823.50) for making a loan to these defendants in addition to the interest and origination charge.

In the case of *Rose v. Baxter* (67 Ohio App. 1, 34 N.E.2d 1011), the Court held:

> Whenever an agent, with the knowledge and consent of the lender, exacts from the borrower a bonus or commission for procuring the loan, which bonus or commission is deducted from the amount of the loan and paid by the lender direct to his agent or attorney and only the balance left, after such deduction, is paid to the borrower, by the great weight of the authorities that which is paid as bonus or commission to the agent or attorney of the lender is considered as being a charge for the use of the money. Such bonus will be added to the amount of interest contracted for by the provisions of the note in determining whether or not such note is usurious.

The law against usury was made necessary and originated by reason of evil practices that prevailed to a large degree in the loaning of money, and out of that condition came the prohibition by express statute.

Referring to Item F of the closing costs of this case the evidence does not show the purpose of the so-called origination charge of Ninety-one dollars and fifty cents ($91.50) which is exactly one (1) per cent of the face amount of the note. There is no explanation of what value or benefit is rendered to the Fisher defendants by this charge. This Court must consider this charge as interest on the loan. This Court is not concerned with the proposition of whether or not eight (8) per cent is sufficient money to receive by way of return in lending money. This is a matter to be determined by the state legislature.

The Court cannot close its eyes to the pretense between lenders and the sellers of real estate who agree on circumstances which will result in a lender's receipt of interest in an amount greater than its legal rate of eight (8) per cent. This Court cannot approve a transaction which is merely a shift or device to evade the usury law.

The evidence in this case fails to show that plaintiff rendered any additional service to the Fisher defendants which would justify the plaintiff retaining the sum of Eight hundred twenty-three dollars and fifty cents ($823.50).

The Court finds that the plaintiff only disbursed or paid out for the Fisher defendants on the Ninety-one hundred and fifty dollar ($9150.00) note, the sum of Eighty-three hundred twenty-six dollars and fifty cents ($8326.50).

The Court finds that the Fisher defendants paid interest to the plaintiff on Ninety-one hundred fifty dollars ($9150.00).

The Court finds from the evidence that the note and mortgage provides a rate of interest within the law; however, the Court further finds that the plaintiff did receive a bonus, points, or loan discount fee of Eight hundred twenty-three dollars and fifty cents ($823.50), which together with the rate of interest constituted a usurious transaction in violation of the law. . . .

Judgment is rendered to the plaintiff for Eighty-three hundred twenty-six dollars and fifty cents ($8326.50), plus interest, and less any credits or payments made on said note.

Pitillo v. Demetry

1965, (Ga.) 145 S.E.2d 702

The defendant made a note payable to one Barwick who indorsed it in blank to plaintiff. The note was dishonored and defendant alleged that the note was given in return for a promise to construct a parking area; that the construction was never completed; and that plaintiff was not a holder in due course. The lower court granted a summary judgment to the plaintiff on the ground that defendant's answer did not set forth a valid defense. Defendant appealed.

FELTON, J. [The] Code . . . provides as follows: "After it is shown that a defense exists a person claiming the rights of a holder in due course has the burden of establishing that he or some person under whom he claims is in all respects a holder in due course." The defense alleged by the answer is failure of consideration. If the plaintiff was not a holder in due course, he took the instrument subject to this defense. . . . There is no allegation in the petition that the plaintiff was a holder in due course, nor was such allegation necessary to state a prima facie cause of action on the note, since a holder who is not a holder in due course nevertheless has a prima facie right of action on the note, subject only to the claims and defense provided in (the) Code. . . . Assuming, however, that the plaintiff was claiming the rights of a holder in due course, his prima facie right of action on the note was challenged by the allegation that the defense of failure of consideration exists, which thereby casts the burden on him "of establishing that he or some person under whom he claims is in all respect a holder in due course." The defenses which may be alleged and shown to exist cannot be restricted merely to those which are available only against holders in due course, since this would mean that the statute . . . would require the plaintiff holder to assume the burden of establishing that he is a holder in due course even though his proof of that fact would not free him from such defense. The law does not require a man to do a useless act. The only possible construction of this statute, then, is that the showing of any defense provided by (the) Code . . . against holders in due course as well as holders not in due course, is what is required to cast the burden on the plaintiff holder. The allegation of the defense of failure of consideration in the answer in the present case was therefore adequate to cast on the plaintiff holder the burden of establishing himself as a holder in due course by showing, inter alia, that he took the instrument without notice of any defense against it on the part of any person. . . .

Although the allegation in the answer, that the plaintiff is not a holder in due course, does not state why this is true and is hence merely a conclusion, this does not prevent the answer from raising an issue of fact, since the allegation of the defense of failure of consideration was what served to cast the burden on the plaintiff and raised the issue of whether or not he was a holder in due course, hence not subject to the alleged defense. There being this genuine issue of material fact to be resolved in the case, the court erred in its judgment granting the summary judgment.

Judgment (for plaintiff) reversed.

Altex Aluminum Supply Co. v. Asay

1962, 72 N.J. Super. 582, 178 A. 2d 636

Home Specialists, Inc. was payee of a note executed by the defendant. The payee by its president indorsed the note to plaintiff, Altex Aluminum Supply. The defendant contends that Home Specialists, Inc. had agreed to hold the note and that defendant was to pay off the note by giving additional business to the payee. He testified that he did secure a siding job for Home Specialists, Inc. and that his share of the contract price was more than sufficient to pay the note. The lower Court ruled in favor of the plaintiff.

SULLIVAN, J. A. D. . . . Defendant, testifying in his own behalf, admitted signing the note and delivering it to Home Specialists, Inc., the payee. He said, however, that the payee was supposed to hold the note and "to do nothing with the note," and that defendant would give the payee additional business to pay off the note. He further testified that he did secure a siding job for Home Specialists, Inc., and that his share of the contract price was more than sufficient to pay the note. The payee, however, refused to return the note to him although he made repeated demands for it. Defendant did not claim that plaintiff had any knowledge of these arrangements. The foregoing, of course, would be no defense against a holder in due course. . . .

We find that the proofs support the judgment in favor of plaintiff. As to defendant's claim that plaintiff did not receive the note "for value," it is clear from the evidence that the note was received by plaintiff in connection with the account of Home Specialists, Inc. It is settled law that a party taking a negotiable note in payment of, or as security for, an antecedent debt, is a holder in due course (cases cited). This is so even though satisfaction of the *antecedent debt* is conditioned on actual payment of the note (cases cited). . . .

Defendant's other point is that plaintiff did not prove the genuineness of the signature of the payee nor was there any proof of the authority of the president of the corporate payee to endorse and deliver the note to plaintiff. For these reasons, argues the defendant, the trial court erred in allowing the note to be marked in evidence. We do not agree. Plaintiff's witness testified that the note was delivered to him at the payee's office by the president and other officers of the payee corporation and that the president signed the endorsement on the back of the note in the presence of plaintiff's witness. We are in accord with the finding of the trial court that the "endorsement of the instrument was proved by direct testimony."

Defendant, however, claims that his mere denial of the corporate payee's endorsement puts plaintiff to its proof not only that the endorsing signature of the corporate officer is genuine but also that such officer was actually authorized to execute such endorsement. He cites *Van-Syckel v. Egg Harbor Coal and Lumber Co.,* 109 N.J.L. 604, 162 A. 627, 85 A.L.R. 300 (E. & A. 1932), in support of his argument. *Van-Syckel,* though, dealt with a situation where the note was payable to the order of an individual payee and the endorsement of the note purported to be signed by a third person under a power of attorney. There the court set aside a judgment for the plaintiff because it found there was no evidence that the signature upon the back of the note was the payee's, or that the agent purporting to sign the same was authorized to do so.

The New Jersey cases dealing with the authority of corporate officers to endorse checks or notes emphasize that they must be read in the light of the facts of the particular case (cases cited).

A corporation has the general power to make and endorse negotiable paper. (*O'Connor v. First Bank & Trust Co.,* 12 N.J. Super. 281, 287, 79 A. 2d 687 (App. Div. 1951)). The authority of the president to execute an endorsement of a promissory note on behalf of the corporation in the normal course of business must be presumed; otherwise the negotiability of the commercial paper would be seriously impaired. To become a holder in due course one is not required to satisfy himself of the actual authority of such officer. (10 C.J.S. Bills and Notes Section 506(h); 19 C.J.S. Corporations Section 1224(b)). A corporate endorsement of a negotiable instrument will pass the property therein to the endorsee notwithstanding that from want of capacity the corporation may incur no liability thereon. R.S. 7:2-22, N.J.S.A.

It is to be noted that the Uniform Commercial Code, adopted in New Jersey (L. 1961, c. 120), effective January 1, 1963, in Article 3, revises and clarifies the Negotiable Instruments Law, R.S. 7:1 et seq., N.J.S.A. Section 3-307 thereof provides as follows:

(1) Unless specifically denied in the pleadings each signature on an instrument is admitted. When the effectiveness of a signature is put in issue
  (a) the burden of establishing it is on the party claiming under the signature; but
  (b) the signature is presumed to be genuine or authorized except where the action is to enforce the obligation of a purported signer who has died or become incompetent before proof is required.

The comment on this section made in Uniform Laws Annotated, Uniform Commercial Code, 1958 official text, includes the following:

> The question of the burden of establishing the signature arises only when it has been put in issue by specific denial. "Burden of establishing" is defined in the definitions section of this Act (Section 1-201). The Burden is on the party claiming under the signature, but he is aided by the presumption that it is genuine or authorized stated in paragraph (b). "Presumption" is also defined in this Act (Section 1-201). It means that until some evidence is introduced which would support a finding that the signature is forged or unauthorized the plaintiff is not required to prove that it is authentic. The presumption rests upon the fact that in ordinary experience forged or unauthorized signatures are very uncommon and normally any evidence is within the control of the defendant or more accessible to him. He is therefore required to make some sufficient showing of the grounds for his denial before the plaintiff is put to his proof. His evidence need not be sufficient to require a directed verdict in his favor, but it must be enough to support his denial by permitting a finding in his favor. Until he introduces such evidence the presumption requires a finding for the plaintiff. Once such evidence is introduced the burden of establishing the signature by a preponderance of the total evidence is on the plaintiff.

Here, plaintiff is the holder of the note and produced testimony that the note was delivered to plaintiff by the officers of the payee-corporation before it was overdue in partial payment of a debt owed by the payee to plaintiff, that the note was delivered at the corporate office and that the president of the payee-corporation executed the endorsement. It is undisputed that the note is regular on its face and that defendant is the maker thereof. Under these circumstances, plaintiff has established that it is a holder in due course and is entitled to judgment. . . .

Affirmed. . . .

United Securities Corporation v. Bruton

1965 (D.C.) 213 A.2d 892

HOOD, J. Appellee purchased two wigs from The Wig Shoppe, Inc. and in payment therefor gave her promissory note for $322.98. Two weeks later she returned one of the wigs to The Wig

Shoppe, and complained of defects in its workmanship. After paying approximately one-half of the note she refused to make further payments. This action was brought by United Securities Corporation, to whom The Wig Shoppe had sold the note two days after its execution, for the balance of the note.

The trial court found that United Securities was not a holder in due course, and gave judgment for appellee. On this appeal United Securities asserts that it relies upon Title 28, Section 409, of the District of Columbia Code, 1961 ed., which provides that: "Every holder is deemed prima facie to be a holder in due course . . ." and claims it was denied the benefit of the statutory presumption.

Appellant overlooks the fact that Title 28, Section 409, of the 1961 Code has been superseded by D.C.Code 1961, § 28:3-307 (Supp. IV, 1965), a part of the Uniform Commercial Code, effective in this jurisdiction since January 1, 1965. Section 28:3-307(3) provides:

> After it is shown that a defense exists a person claiming the rights of a holder in due course has the burden of establishing that he or some person under whom he claims is in all respects a holder in due course.

Although the entire transaction occurred prior to the effective date of the Uniform Commercial Code, the trial occurred after the effective date, and the burden of proof, a procedural matter, was controlled by the law existing at date of trial. There is no vested right in a rule of evidence, and a statute relating solely to procedural law, such as burden of proof and rules of evidence, applies to all proceedings after its effective date even though the transaction occurred prior to its enactment. Procedural statutes are the exception to the general rule against retroactive application, if indeed the application can be considered retroactive. The savings clause of the Act under consideration preserves the "rights, duties and interest" of the parties to transactions entered into prior to its effective date, but we do not construe this as an intention by Congress that procedural changes made by a statute should not apply in court proceedings for the enforcement of such rights, duties and interests.

In the case before us a defense of defective workmanship in the article sold was shown. Appellant [plaintiff] made no attempt to meet the merits of that defense, but sought to avoid the defense by its claim of being a holder in due course. Under present law the burden was on appellant to prove that it was "in all respects a holder in due course." The only evidence offered by appellant to establish its status as a holder in due course was that it "purchased" the note on the date shown on the endorsement. It offered no evidence of the price paid and no explanation why the note was payable at its office, or why the note was purchased so promptly after its execution, or what was the relationship between it and the payee. Under these circumstances the court could, as it did, find that appellant had failed to sustain its burden of proving it was a holder in due course. [Emphases supplied.]

Affirmed.

Gresham State Bank v. O & K Construction Co.

1962, 231 Or. 106, 370 P. 2d 726 (Rehearing denied, June 13, 1962, 372 P. 2d 187)

F. C. McKenna was employed by O & K Construction Company as a bookkeeper. He was authorized to receive checks payable to the company and to deposit these checks in the First National Bank of Gresham. The company furnished him with a rubber stamp, "For deposit only at the First National Bank." The office supplies also included another stamp, "O & K Construction Co., Route 1, Gresham, Oregon," which was intended to be used in marking statements and other items. During the years 1957, 1958, 1959, McKenna indorsed 30 checks which had been made payable to the company and cashed them at Zimmerman's store. He indorsed the checks with the latter rubber stamp followed by his own name and the designation, "Office Manager" or "Bkpr." Zimmerman's store deposited the checks in its account in the plaintiff bank. The checks were sent through the regular banking channels and paid by the drawee banks. In May, 1959, McKenna's defalcations were discovered. The construction company obtained the cancelled checks from the various drawers and made a demand for payment from all of the drawee banks. These banks in turn made demand upon the plaintiff bank. As these demands were made on it the plaintiff withdrew from the account of Zimmerman's Store an amount equal to the check and placed it in a "suspense account." After the last check had been presented, the bank filed an interpleader suit naming O & K Construction Co. and Zimmerman's Store as defendants. The bank paid the money represented by the checks into court and was discharged from liability. The lower court entered a judgment for Zimmerman's Store.

O'CONNELL, J. . . . The defendant O & K Construction Company relies upon the rule that one who makes payment upon an unauthorized endorsement of the payee's name is liable to the payee for conversion.

Defendant Zimmerman contends that the loss falls upon the defendant construction company on the basis of any one of the following grounds: (1) that McKenna had implied or apparent authority to endorse the checks and to present them to Zimmerman's for payment on behalf of the construction company; (2) the construction company is precluded from recovery by its negligence; (3) where one of two innocent parties must suffer the loss should fall upon the one whose acts made the loss possible.

The third contention adds nothing to the first two. There is no legal principle which places the loss upon one of two innocent parties merely because one acted and the other did not. The law makes the choice upon the basis of fault or some other consideration warranting the preference. In the present case we must decide upon some such rational ground which of the two defendants should be favored.

We begin with the well established rule that one who obtains possession of a check through the unauthorized endorsement of the payee's name acquires no title to it and is liable to the payee for the amount of the check unless the payee is precluded from setting up the want of authority. . . .

The mere fact that an employee has charge of a company's office does not entitle third persons dealing with the employee to assume that he has the authority to execute or endorse the company's negotiable paper. We find no evidence to support a finding that McKenna was clothed with apparent authority.

The contention that defendant O & K Construction Company was precluded from recovery because of its negligence presents a more difficult legal problem. There was evidence to support a finding that Osburn and Kniefel were negligent in failing to scrutinize the records of the company over the three-year period during which the defalcation occurred. They made little individual effort to examine their books during that period and no audit was made. . . .

The pattern for decision in cases such as the one before us is found in Section 3-406 of the Uniform Commercial Code which was adopted by the enactment of Oregon Laws 1961 . . . to be effective on September 1, 1963. That section . . . provides as follows:

> Any person who by his negligence substantially contributes to a material alteration of the instrument or to the making of an unauthorized signature is precluded from asserting the alteration or lack of authority against a holder in due course or against a drawee or other payor who pays the instrument in good faith and in accordance with the reasonable commercial standards of the drawee's or payor's business.

Although this section is not operative until September 1, 1963, it expresses the legislative view as of the time of its enactment. There is no existing Oregon statute or adjudicated case which announces a contrary principle. As we have already indicated the cases in other jurisdictions are in conflict. We are, therefore, free to adopt the principle which, in our opinion, will comport with the needs of the business community in dealing with commercial paper under circumstances such as we have here. We believe that Section 3-406 of the Uniform Commercial Code expresses the appropriate principle. We therefore adopt it. . . .

It is apparent that this section requires a weighing process in choosing between the owner of the forged instrument and the payor in allocating the loss. Translating the section in terms of the factual situation before us, the O & K Construction Company is not precluded from asserting McKenna's lack of authority unless two conditions exist: (1) That O & K Construction Company's negligence "substantially contributes" to the making of the unauthorized signature and, (2) that Zimmerman made payment on the instrument in good faith "and in accordance with the reasonable commercial standards of the . . . payor's business."

Ordinarily the customary practices of a business must be established by evidence. However, it has been judicially recognized in many adjudicated cases that one who cashes a check indorsed by an agent has the duty to inquire as to the agent's authority to make the indorsement. We can, therefore, take judicial notice of this duty to make inquiry as a part of the "reasonable commercial standards" of a business. . . .

In testing Zimmerman's conduct by the standard of ordinary commercial practice, it is to be noted that the checks were not cashed by McKenna in connection with any purchase of items in the store on behalf of the construction company. McKenna received the whole amount of the check. Moreover, the amounts paid to him were substantial, including several checks for $300 or more.

Ordinarily, it is the usual practice for a company to deposit checks received by it and to pay for its expenditures by checks drawn on its own account. . . .

We hold that, as a matter of law, Zimmerman did not make payment of the checks in accordance with the reasonable commercial standards of his business. . . .

We hold that, because of defendant Zimmerman's negligent failure to act in accordance with the reasonable commercial standards of its business, the defendant O & K Construction Company, although negligent, is not precluded from recovering upon the forged checks. Oregon Laws 1961, Ch. 726, Section 73.4060 indicates that the payor's failure to act in accordance with reasonable commercial standards might bar him from setting up the owner's negligence no matter how gross it might be. It is not necessary for us to decide whether the statute will be so interpreted. In the present case the negligence of the O & K Construction Company was clearly outweighed by that of Zimmerman.

We hold that, under these circumstances, Zimmerman cannot rely upon the construction company's negligence to bar the latter's recovery. . . .

Reversed and remanded.

[The U.C.C. became effective in Oregon on September 1, 1966.]

CHAPTER 23
REVIEW QUESTIONS AND PROBLEMS

1. *B* purchased a used car from *V* and gave him a check in payment. *V* cashed the check at *P* Bank. *B* stopped payment on the check because *V* had made fraudulent misrepresentations about the car. *P* Bank seeks to collect the amount of the check from *B*. What result?

2. *M* executed a check in the amount of $1000 to the order of *P*. *P* "raised" the check to $10,000 and indorsed it to *A*. How much can *A* collect on the check?

3. *S*, a dealer, sold an automobile to *B* on a conditional sale contract. The contract contained a note, and *B* signed both. *S* cut off the note and indorsed it to *X*. The automobile did not function properly, and

the motor and transmission had to be replaced. *S,* who is now insolvent, refused to make repairs. Can *X* recover on the note from *B?*

4. *M* executed a note to *P* with interest at the rate of 25 per cent. *P* indorsed the note to *H*. Can *H* enforce the note against *M?*

5. *M,* the maker of a note, filed a petition in bankruptcy. Prior to bankruptcy he had executed a note in the amount of $10,000 to *A,* and *A* had indorsed it to *H*. Can *H* recover on the note from *M?*

6. *M* arranged to have a new furnace installed in her home and signed several papers including a note, at the request of *P,* a heating contractor, without knowledge or reason to believe that any one of the papers was a note. *P* indorsed the note to *X* Bank. *M* never received the furnace. Is *M* liable to the bank?

7. *M* signed a note in blank and left it on his desk. *A,* an employee of *M,* stole and completed the instrument. He then negotiated it to *H*. *H* sues *M* on the note. What result?

8. *M* is the maker of a note. *H* is the holder. *M* has a defense of fraud in the inception. Can this defense be asserted against *H* if *H* is a holder in due course?

9. *M* is the drawer of a check. He has given the check to *P* in payment for merchandise. He has discovered that the merchandise is worthless. To what extent can *M* protect himself by stopping payment on the check?

10. *P* is the payee of a check executed by *M*. *P* transferred the check to *H* in payment of a past-due account, but did not endorse the check. What are *H's* rights?

11. The *X* Finance Co. furnished an automobile dealer with printed forms of notes and contracts and did credit investigations prior to approval of a transaction. The dealer, after making sales to customers and using these forms, would sell the paper to the finance company. The form for assignment was a part of the contract. Are defenses of car purchasers good against *X* Finance Co.?

12. *A* drew a check in favor of *B* for $50 and presented it to *B* as a gift. *B* indorsed the check to *C* in payment of a debt that *B* owed *C*. *A* stopped payment on the check. Can *C* recover from *A?*

chapter 24

Liability of Parties

3-84 Introduction. The liability of a party on a negotiable instrument may arise out of the nature of the transaction, the manner of its execution, or the status of the parties. Liability or lack thereof may be dependent on the signature of the party, the authority of an agent, or the intent of the parties. The Code also provides that liability is determined by the relationship of the parties and certain liabilities are created by operation of law. The discussion of these liabilities in this chapter must be considered in light of the preceding materials on defenses; it must be remembered that a real defense may be asserted against anyone and that a personal defense may not be asserted against a holder in due course. For purposes of this chapter except when otherwise noted, we shall assume that no defense exists on behalf of the party being sued.

LIABILITY BASED ON SIGNATURES

3-85 In General. No person is liable *on an instrument* unless his signature appears thereon.[C1] A person signing a contract which gives rise to a negotiable instrument is liable on the contract, but his obligation is not measured by any negotiable instrument related thereto unless he signs such instrument. Drawees who orally accept and purported indorsees who never sign the paper are not liable *on the paper*. Any liability that might arise by reason of warranties and breaches thereof is not covered by this portion of the Code. A signature may be made by an agent or other

---

[C1] *U.C.C.* 3-401(1).

representative and if such person is authorized to sign paper on his principal's behalf the principal will be bound. (See Book 3, Agency.) If the agent does not have authority to sign for or on behalf of his principal, his signature is treated as an unauthorized signature and would not in most instances bind the principal.

3-86 Signature by Authorized Representative.[C2] Most business is conducted by agents or representatives on behalf of principals. Principals may be individuals, partnerships acting under an assumed name, corporations, and other legal entities. The business relationship that exists between the principal and the agent in most cases presupposes that the acts and conduct of the agent bind the principal only. In creating commercial paper on behalf of the principal, an authorized agent may execute the instrument in many different ways. An authorized agent may by proper signature avoid personal liability on the paper. However, if he does not sign in the proper fashion he may be personally liable on the paper.

An authorized agent or representative who signs his own name to an instrument *is* personally obligated:

(1) if the instrument does not name the person represented or fails to show that the representative signed in a representative capacity;

(2) if the instrument names the person represented but does not show that the representative signed in a representative capacity; or

(3) if the instrument does not name the person represented even though it shows that the representative signed in a representative capacity. However, as between the immediate parties—the agent and the person with whom he deals—the status of the agent can be established and the agent will not be personally liable.

The name of an organization preceded or followed by the name and office of an authorized individual is a signature made in a representative capacity.

A purchaser of a negotiable intrument is entitled to know by looking at the face of the paper whose obligation is evidenced by the paper. When a purchaser looks at an instrument and finds two or more names on the paper, it may not be easy from inspection of the paper to determine whether there is a principal-agent relationship or whether the purported agent intended to bind himself, or only his principal, or both.

Assuming that the agent has authority to bind the principal, the way in which the agent signs the paper may justify a purchaser in believing that the agent intends to be jointly liable with the principal.[1] The problem is the same whether the kind of signature in question is that of an agent signing for a maker, drawer, indorser, or acceptor.

The different ways in which an agent may sign are numerous. The following examples will illustrate the problems involved.

1. An agent may sign only his own name, without showing the name of his principal and that he is signing in a representative capacity. Thus,

---

[1] *In re Laskin,* page 515.

C2 *U.C.C.* 3-403.

he may sign simply, "John Doe." The agent here is personally liable and extrinsic evidence is not admissible to avoid liability. Since the principal's name does not appear on the paper, he cannot be liable on the paper.

2. An authorized agent may sign the name of his principal only. Thus, "Roy Roe." The principal here is personally liable. The authority granted by the principal to the agent, orally or by a separate agreement, relieves the agent in an action between the principal and agent.

3. An agent may sign the instrument, "John Doe, Agent." Here he has not disclosed a principal, but he has disclosed that he is acting in a representative capacity. Since the term, "agent," is merely descriptive, doubt is raised in the mind of a purchaser as to who is obligated. A holder in due course should be free from the burden of ascertaining for whom John Doe is an agent.

If evidence were admissible to ascertain whose instrument has been created, negotiability would be impaired. The mere addition of words describing the signer "as agent" does not exempt the agent from personal liability. Parol evidence is inadmissible to show that the agent did not intend to be bound except as between the immediate parties. For example, corporate officers have been held personally liable on a note signed in the corporate name as maker and also signed by *A, B,* and *C,* corporate officers where they did not disclose that they signed in a representative capacity. However, an agent is permitted to use parol evidence in litigation between *immediate parties* if the paper on its face shows he signed in a representative capacity without naming the principal, or if the principal is named but the language does not show a representative capacity.[2]

The Comment to the Code gives the following illustration:

Assuming "Peter Pringle" is a principal and "Arthur Adams" is his agent, an instrument might for example bear the following signatures affixed by the agent:

(a) "Peter Pringle" or
(b) "Arthur Adams" or
(c) "Peter Pringle by Arthur Adams, Agent" or
(d) 'Arthur Adams, Agent" or
(e) "Peter Pringle
      Arthur Adams" or
(f) "Peter Pringle Corporation
      Arthur Adams"

The form set out in (a) does not bind the agent Arthur Adams; the signature in (b) does personally bind Adams even though he is the agent. He cannot introduce evidence to show he was such agent. The principal would be liable on the paper under (a) but would not be *liable on the paper* under (b) since his name does not appear.

The most desirable way is to sign as in (c) where not only is the

---

2 *Leahy v. McManus,* page 516.

principal disclosed but the agent's representative capacity is clearly indicated also.

Where the agent signs as in (d), (e), and (f), the principal is obligated and the agent has the right to introduce parol evidence to establish his freedom from liability—to prove that he signed in a representative capacity—in litigation between immediate parties. As to all other persons the agent is personally liable.

3-87 Signature is Ambiguous–Capacity.[C3] It is sometimes difficult to determine the status on the paper of a person who signs commercial paper. The rule for resolving ambiguous signatures is that unless the instrument clearly indicates that a signature is made in some other capacity it is an *indorsement.*[3]

This rule applies in cases where the signer does not place his name on the paper in the usual place. If the place of signature clearly indicates that the signer intended to be bound other than as an indorser, parol evidence is not admissible to show that he intended to be an indorser. However, if the signer's name appears on the front of the paper after the word "indorser," he is an indorser in spite of the fact that he signed on the face of the paper. For example, a note might provide: "I, John Doe, promise to pay . . ." and be signed by both John Doe and Richard Roe. This would indicate that Roe signed as an indorser even though his signature is on the face of the paper.

The intention to be bound in some capacity other than that of indorser must be clearly indicated by the language used. Thus the signatures "John Jones, Maker," "Henry Brown, Acceptor," "Pete Smith, Surety" clearly indicate an intention to be bound, but not as indorsers. Where the *back* of an instrument contained a long list of notations of interest payments followed by an entry, "Interest paid to Aug. 1, 1968, J. B. Brown." Brown's indication of the purpose for which his signature was placed on the paper, namely, receipt for an interest payment, clearly indicates that he did not sign as an indorser or intend any liability on the paper.

3-88 Unauthorized Signatures.[C4] The general rule is that an unauthorized signature is not operative as the signature of the person whose name is signed. The limitations of the rule relate to ratification of the unauthorized signature and to circumstances under which the person whose name is signed is estopped from asserting the lack of authority.

The term "unauthorized signature" encompasses signatures by agents who exceed their authority, actual or apparent, and forgeries. The person whose signature is forged is not bound on the instrument unless his conduct is such as to prevent him from asserting the forgery or other unauthorized signature as a defense. However, the wrongdoer—forger or

[3] *Grange Natl. Bank v. Conville,* page 518.

[C3] *U.C.C.* 3-118, 3-402. [C4] *U.C.C.* 3-404.

agent—is himself bound to the full amount of the instrument to a party who takes the instrument or pays it in good faith.

To illustrate the foregoing, suppose that *A*, an agent, executes an instrument and that he lacks the authority to do so. He signs the instrument in the name of his principal, *P*, by "*A*, agent." The principal, *P*, is not bound (absent ratification or estoppel), but *A* is liable to the holder.

As previously noted, a forged or unauthorized signature may be ratified. In such case, the actual signer or forger is liable to the person whose name was signed and he may also be subject to criminal action for the forgery notwithstanding the ratification.

3-89 Bank's Liability. A special problem exists in connection with forgeries in so far as banks are concerned. Checks presented to drawee banks for payment may bear forged signatures of drawers or forged indorsements. If the bank pays on such paper it incurs liability to the person whose name was forged. If the drawer's signature was forged the bank that honors the check has not followed the order of the drawer, and cannot charge his account. If charged, it must be recredited. Likewise, the bank will have to make restitution to the holder whose name was forged on the check as an indorsement. In either case the loss initially is that of the bank and in the case of a forged drawer's signature, the so-called "*Rule of Price v. Neal*" precludes the bank from shifting the loss to the person who received payment or to persons who indorsed the paper.[4] This is subject to the limitation that recovery may be had from the person who dealt with the forger if it can be established that he was negligent.[5] Also, the person whose name was forged will suffer the loss if his negligence made the forgery possible. See Section 3-83 of Chapter 23 for the effect of negligence on defenses.

Banks may also cash checks indorsed by agents who lack authority. In such cases, the bank will be held liable to the payee if the bank is charged with knowledge of the lack of authority and the principal can recover from the bank the amount paid out on such indorsements, which are, in effect, forgeries. Just as in the case of forgery by a stranger, the drawer can insist that the drawee recredit his account with the amount of any unauthorized payment.

Two problems relating to the liability of banks and sometimes other persons in regard to forgery need to be mentioned. These refer to imposters and fictitious payees.

3-90 Imposters: Fictitious Payees.[C5] A situation which is comparable to forgery arises when an instrument is made payable to a fictitious person or where one person impersonates another and the instrument is made payable to the imposter in the name he has assumed. In each of these

---

4 *First Natl. Bk. of McAlester v. Mann,* page 519.
5 *White v. First Natl. Bk. of Scotia,* page 520.

C5 *U.C.C.* 3-405.

situations the drawer's signature is genuine but the instrument is *indorsed* in the fictitious name or the name of the person who is being impersonated. Who should bear the loss under the following circumstances?

(a) an impostor by the use of mails or otherwise has induced the maker or drawer to issue the instrument to him or his confederate in the name of the payee; or

(b) a person signing as or on behalf of a maker or drawer intends the payee to have no interest in the instrument; or

(c) an agent or employee of the maker or drawer has supplied him with the name of the payee intending the latter to have no such interest.

Imposter. An example of a fraudulent scheme is one in which a person poses as someone else and induces the drawer to issue a check payable to the order of the person who is being impersonated. In such situations the indorsement by the imposter is effective and the loss falls on the drawer rather than the person who took the check or the bank which honored it.[6]

The Code rejects prior decisions which distinguished between face-to-face imposture and imposture by mail and held that where the parties dealt by mail, the *dominant intent* of the drawer was to deal with the name rather than with the person so that the resulting instrument could have been negotiated only by indorsement of the payee whose name had been taken in vain. The result of these distinctions had been to throw the loss in the mail imposture case forward to a subsequent holder or to the drawee.

Since the maker or drawer believes the two to be one and the same, the two intentions cannot be separated, and the "dominant intent" was a fiction. The position of the Code is that the loss, regardless of the type of fraud which the particular impostor has committed, should fall upon the maker or drawer.

"Impostor" refers to impersonation, and does not extend to a false representation that the party is the authorized agent of the payee. The maker or drawer who takes the precaution of making the instrument payable to the principal is entitled to have his indorsement.

Fictitious payee. A typical situation of a fictitious payee is one in which a dishonest employee is either authorized to sign his employer's name to checks or draws checks which he presents to his employer for the latter's signature. Thus the employee may draw payroll checks or checks payable to persons with whom the employer would be expected to do business. He either signs the checks or obtains his employer's signature and then cashes the checks indorsing the name of the payee. If he is in charge of the company's books, he is able to manipulate the books when the cancelled checks are returned and may thus avoid

[6] *Davis v. West. Union,* page 522.

detection. The Code imposes this loss on the employer—the dishonest employee can effectively indorse in the payee's name.

The sections which follow discuss the liability of the parties in more detail. The liability is contractual in nature but created and governed by statute.

LIABILITY BASED ON STATUS

3-91 In General. The Code determines the liability of the various parties by statute because the parties would ordinarily not do so themselves. The parties are divided into two groups—primary parties and secondary parties. The primary parties are the makers of notes and the acceptors of drafts. These parties have incurred a definite obligation to pay and are the parties who, in the normal course of events, will *actually* pay the instrument.[C6] They understand that this is their responsibility and that no conditions need be satisfied as a prerequisite to this responsibility. A primary party engages that he will pay the instrument according to its tenor—the terms of the instrument—at the time of his engagement. The maker thus assumes an obligation to pay the note as it was worded at the time he executed it, and the acceptor assumes responsibility for the draft as it was worded when he gave his acceptance. As noted previously, if an instrument is incomplete at the time the maker signs it or the acceptor accepts it, and is thereafter completed, it is enforceable against such party in its completed form by a holder in due course. On the other hand, material alteration is a real defense in the absence of negligence.

There are some instances in which makers and acceptors are treated to some extent as secondary rather than primary parties. This relates to what is called "domiciled paper," i.e., an instrument which is payable at a particular place on the date of its maturity. In most instances "domiciled" notes and drafts are made payable at a specified bank—the bank specified is the place where the note or draft must be presented for payment.

The secondary parties are drawers of drafts, drawers of checks, and indorsers of either.[C7] These parties do not *expect* to pay the instrument but assume rather that the primary parties will fulfill their obligations. The drawer and indorsers expect that the acceptor will pay the draft. The indorsers of a note expect that the maker will pay when the note matures. Drawers and indorsers have a secondary responsibility; i.e., an obligation to pay if the primary parties do not, *provided* that certain conditions precedent are satisfied. The drawer and the indorser are, in effect, saying that they will pay if the primary party—acceptor or maker —does not, but only if the party entitled has made proper demand upon the primary party, and due notice of the primary party's dishonor of the instrument has then been given to them—the secondary parties.

[C6] *U.C.C.* 3-413.   [C7] *U.C.C.* 3-413, 3-414.

THE CONTRACTUAL LIABILITY OF PARTIES

3-92 Liability of Drawee-Acceptors. The drawee of a draft, by accepting it, assumes liability as a primary party.[C8] By accepting he has agreed to honor the draft as presented to him. By accepting the instrument he engages that he will pay according to the tenor of his acceptance; and admits (1) the existence of the drawer; (2) the genuineness of the drawer's signature; (3) the drawer's capacity and authority to draw the instruments; (4) the existence of the payee, and (5) his then capacity to indorse. The instrument may be drawn by the drawer and negotiated before its acceptance by the drawee.[C9] The instrument may be accepted by the drawee before it is signed by the drawer or completed. This, of course, involves some risk on the part of the drawee-acceptor.

One who draws a draft (drawer) is usually a creditor of the drawee or has arranged with the drawee for authority to draw on him. Some creditor-debtor arrangement ordinarily exists between the drawer and drawee. For instance, John Doe enters into an agreement with the First National Bank whereby the latter agrees to accept drafts for a certain amount drawn on the bank by John Doe. The bank is not liable to the payee of the draft until it "accepts" the draft. If the bank refuses to accept, it is liable to John Doe, the drawer, for breach of its contract to accept. It is only after acceptance that the bank is liable to the payee.

The acceptance must be in writing on the draft and signed by the drawee-acceptor.[C10] Acceptance is usually made by the drawee's writing or stamping the word "Accepted," with his name and the date, across the face of the instrument. Promises to accept and acceptances upon separate instruments and other collateral acceptances are not effective *as acceptances.* Danger of separation from the draft or check and ambiguous language leading to dispute as to whether an acceptance was or was not made dictate the necessity for certain and accurate evidence of the drawee's liability. However, in spite of this rule the issuer of a letter of credit has an obligation to pay in accordance with a previously issued letter of credit.

The drawee's signature as acceptor on incompleted paper binds him to all subsequent parties to the extent of its completion as authorized—he is subject to the risks and duties imposed by the Code as to wrongful completion and, if by his negligent conduct he contributes to materially altered paper which gets into the stream of commerce, he is liable to any person with the rights of a holder in due course for all loss caused by such negligence. It is to be noted that the acceptance relates to the instrument as it was at the *time of acceptance.* If the draft were "raised" or otherwise altered before acceptance, the acceptor is bound to pay the

C8 *U.C.C.* 3-410.   C10 *U.C.C.* 3-410(1).
C9 *U.C.C.* 3-413.

raised amount—his responsibility is not limited to the original tenor of the draft. However, as noted in a later section, the acceptor would have recourse against the party who presented the paper for acceptance since that party warrants that the draft has not been materially altered.

A check or other draft does not of itself operate as an assignment of any funds in the hands of the drawee and the drawee is not liable *on the instrument* until he *accepts* it.[C11]

Drawees of a draft or check occupy an unusual position. They are debtors or potential debtors of the drawer. The drawer by the instrument orders the drawee to pay money to the payee or holder. Before such duty on the paper arises the drawee must accept the paper. Previous contracts between the drawer and drawee, such as a depositor-bank relationship, may give the drawer *power* to draw a check or draft on the drawee. Likewise, a drawer-buyer might, by reason of a previous contract for the sale of goods, draw a draft on his purchaser-debtor-drawee by way of payment.

Even if the drawee by previous contract is under a duty to accept, such duty gives no cause of action to a *holder* upon refusal of the drawee to pay. The drawee's liability is to the drawer. The failure of the drawee to accept or his breach of other arrangements with the drawer, will expose the drawee to liability to the drawer, but not to a holder. A drawee bank's refusal to pay a check which thereby impairs the credit of the drawer may subject the bank to tort liability to the drawer for failure to comply with its obligation to him as may its failure to live up to other promises to pay or accept. However, the drawee who fails to accept may be liable to *either a drawer or a holder* for breach of the terms of a *letter of credit* or any other agreement by which he is obligated to accept.

It is the acceptance of the paper by the drawee that gives rights to the holder *on the paper*. The acceptance makes the drawee-acceptor the primary obligor; the drawer and all other parties become secondary parties. By such method paper is created which can function freely in the channels of commerce as a substitute for money.

Thus the holder of an unaccepted draft has no right against the drawee on the paper until it has been accepted. His recourse, if acceptance is refused, is against the drawer or any prior indorsers. Unlike an assignment, the draft does not give the holder any direct interest in funds in the drawee's possession. Another significant point related to the non-assignment feature of a draft or check is that the drawer can, for example, stop payment on a check and thereby possibly defeat the holder's expectations.

3-93 Certification of Checks.[C12] Related to acceptance is the responsibility of a bank with respect to the certification of checks. When the bank upon which a check is drawn accepts or certifies it, such an act operates as an appropriation of as much of the drawer's deposit as is required to pay the instrument. Sufficient funds out of the drawer's account are set aside for the purpose of paying the check when it is later presented.

[C11] *U.C.C.* 3-409.   [C12] *U.C.C.* 3-411.

The certification of a check by the bank upon which it is drawn, at the request of a holder, is equivalent to an acceptance. The bank thereby becomes the principal debtor upon the instrument. The liability of the bank is the same as the liability of an acceptor of any other draft. The bank admits that the drawer's signature is genuine; that the depositor's account contains sufficient funds to pay the check; and that the money will not be withdrawn.

The certification must be in writing and signed by the proper officer of the bank. A certification adds much to the saleability of the paper, as it carries with it the strength and credit of the bank.

The certification may or may not change the legal liability of the parties upon the instrument. When the *drawer* has a check certified, such a certification merely acts as additional security and does not relieve the drawer of any liability. On the other hand, when the *holder* of a check secures certification by the drawee bank, he thereby accepts the bank as the only party liable thereon. Such an act discharges the drawer and all prior indorsers from liability. The effect of such certification is similar to a payment by the bank and redeposit by the holder. Note that in the case of other drafts acceptance does not ordinarily give a discharge to the drawer or indorsers.

The refusal of a bank to certify a check at the request of a holder is held not to be a dishonor of the instrument. The bank owes the depositor a duty to pay but not necessarily the duty to certify checks which are drawn on it, unless there is a previous agreement to certify. A drawer cannot countermand a check after the bank has certified it.

A check may also come to the drawee bank without proper indorsement. The bank *may* certify the check before returning the same through channels for indorsement, in order to relieve the drawer from liability that might arise because of loss occurring before the check is returned. Such certification discharges the drawer.

The nature of the acceptance.[C13] As previously stated, the right to draw a draft or check usually rests upon a previous contractual understanding between the drawer and drawee. The drawer is a creditor, the drawee a debtor. The depositor-bank contract gives the depositor the right to draw a draft-check upon the bank, which instrument as negotiable paper is used by the drawer to pay an obligation to the payee. The drawer orders the bank to pay by cash or accept the check in such manner as to discharge the drawer's obligation. The situations are numerous under which a creditor may draw a draft on his debtor. When a draft is created and placed in the channels of trade, the payee and all future holders are entitled to an *unqualified acceptance* by the drawee. Any other acceptance changes the original contract between the parties. Thus when the drawee offers an acceptance which in any manner varies or changes the direct order to pay or accept the holder may refuse the acceptance.[C14] The paper is dishonored, and upon notice of dishonor or protest the holder may hold all prior parties on the paper back to and

[C13] *U.C.C.* 3-410.   [C14] *U.C.C.* 3-412.

including the drawer. An acceptance is at variance with the order when the drawee-acceptor accepts for only a part of the specified sum, or specifies a different time of *payment* from that required by the draft. If the drawee places a condition on his obligation to pay or stipulates that he will perform a service in payment of the draft in lieu of a money payment, he has deviated from the duty to pay money as ordered by the drawer.

Tender of a different kind of acceptance by the drawee is an offer to give a substituted performance. If the holder wishes to accept such nonconforming performance, he may do so. This however creates a new contract, and all prior parties including the drawer are discharged unless a consent for substituted performance has been given. If the drawee refuses to perform the varied acceptance, he is liable for breach of contract to the holder.

The draft is not varied by an acceptance to pay at a particular bank or place in the United States unless acceptance states that the draft is to be *paid* only at such bank.

3-94 Liability of Maker and Acceptor.[C15] The maker of a note and the acceptor of a draft are primarily liable. Each is obligated to pay the instrument according to its terms. If a maker signs an incomplete note, such note when thereafter completed can be enforced against him. On the other hand if an instrument is materially altered after it is made, the maker has a real defense in the absence of negligence. The maker admits as against all subsequent parties the existence of the payee and his capacity to indorse. The foregoing applies also to acceptors of drafts.

3-95 Liability of the Drawer.[C16] The drawer engages that upon *dishonor* of the draft and any necessary notice of dishonor or protest he will pay the amount of the draft to the holder or to any indorser who takes it up. In effect, the drawer assumes a conditional liability on the instrument— that he will pay if the instrument is dishonored and he is properly notified of this fact. Such liability can be disclaimed, however, if the draft is drawn "without recourse." The party who draws a draft or check like one who makes a note or accepts a draft, admits as against all subsequent parties the existence of the payee and his then capacity to indorse.

3-96 Liability of Indorsers.[C17] Indorsers are secondarily liable on instruments by virtue of their *contract* of indorsement. If an indorser adds the words "without recourse" to his indorsement, he thereby disclaims liability on the *indorsement contract.*[7] The contract of indorsement is conditional, that is, the indorser obligates himself to pay only if the instrument is properly presented to the primary party, is dishonored and notice of dishonor is given to him. This obligation of the indorser runs

[7] *Union Bk. of Mobilla,* page 522.

[C15] *U.C.C.* 3-413.
[C16] *U.C.C.* 3-413(2)(3).

[C17] *U.C.C.* 3-414.

to any holder and to a subsequent indorser who has reacquired the instrument. The engagement of the indorser is to pay the instrument according to its tenor at the time of his indorsement. The indorser of an altered instrument thus assumes liability as indorser on the instrument as altered.

As noted previously, a person who indorses in a representative capacity can indorse in such terms as to negative personal liability.

In addition to this conditional liability, an indorser, if he is a transferor, makes *warranties* with reference to the instrument which is transferred. Thus the indorser in addition to his conditional contract liability has unconditional liability as a warrantor.

Unless they otherwise agree, indorsers are liable to one another in the order in which they indorse. This is presumed to be the order in which their signatures appear on the instrument, but parol evidence is admissible as between indorsers to show that the indorsers did not actually indorse in the order in which their names appear or that they may have agreed among themselves as to the nature and order of their liability.[8]

3-97 Liability of Accommodation Parties.[C18] One who signs an instrument for the purpose of lending his name and credit to another party to the instrument is an "accommodation party."[9] An accommodation party is always a surety or guarantor. He may be an indorser or he may be a maker or an acceptor. As an indorser he does not indorse for the purpose of transferring the paper but rather to lend security to it.[10] He may indorse for the accommodation of the holder or for the accommodation of the indorser from the holder.[11] If he is a maker or acceptor, he has assumed the obligation for the purpose of giving security.

The obligation of an accommodation party as a surety is determined by the capacity in which he signs. Thus an accommodation maker or acceptor is bound as a party to the instrument without the necessity of proceeding against the principal, the party accommodated. An accommodation indorser is liable only after presentment and notice of dishonor.

The Code on accommodation parties deals with the interrelations between the law of commercial paper and the law of suretyship. (Chapter 45 treats the law of suretyship in detail.) A surety under the law of suretyship has certain special defenses not available to other persons and the accommodation party may take advantage of such defenses. Oral proof is admissible as against a person who is not a holder in due course to show that one signed as an accommodation party. Oral proof of accommodation status, however, is not admissible against a holder in due course who had no notice of the accommodation and assumed that the party was a regular maker or indorser as the case may be.

Since a surety's status is somewhat different from that of the contracting

---

[8] *Niebergall v. A.B.A. Contracting & Supply Co.*, page 523.

[9] *Ibid.*

[10] *General Refrigerator Co. v. Fry*, page 524.

[11] *Dollak v. Educational Aids Co.*, page 526.

[C18] *U.C.C.* 3-415.

parties, it is important to note than an irregular or anomalous indorsement—one which is not in the chain of title—gives notice to all subsequent parties that such indorsement was for accommodation.

The law of suretyship provides that if a surety is required to pay his principal's obligation he can recover such payments from his principal. This rule of suretyship applies to commercial paper and the accommodation party who pays is subrogated to the rights of the holder to whom payment was made with the right of recourse against the accommodated party on the instrument.

3-98 Contract of Guarantors.[C19] The preceding sections dealt with the contract of the maker, the drawer, the acceptor, the indorser, and the accommodation party. This section relates to a guarantor's contract and to the effect to be attributed to *words* of guaranty. This should be distinguished from the accommodation situation in which the obligation arises without express words designating its specific nature.

If the words "Payment guaranteed" or their equivalent are added to a signature, the signer engages that if the instrument is not paid when due he will pay it *without previous resort by the holder to other parties on the paper.* If the words "Collection guaranteed" are added to a signature, the signer becomes secondarily liable on the instrument and can be required to pay only if the holder has obtained a judgment against the primary party and execution on the judgment has been returned unsatisfied, unless the primary party has become insolvent or "it is otherwise apparent that it is useless to proceed against him."

If words of guaranty are used but it is not specified whether "of payment" or "collection," they will be deemed to constitute a guaranty of payment.

Words of guaranty by a sole maker or acceptor are without effect; but if such words are added to the signature of one of two or more makers or acceptors such words create a presumption that the party who added such words signed for the accommodation of the others.

If an indorser guarantees payment he waives the conditions precedent of presentment, notice of dishonor, and protest. The words of guarantee do not affect the indorsement as a means of transferring the instrument, but impose upon such indorser the liability of a co-maker. If the indorser guarantees collection, he likewise waives the performance of the conditions precedent.

THE WARRANTY LIABILITY

3-99 In General.[C20] The preceding sections dealt with the contract liability of parties to instruments; the following sections deal with warranty liability. Contract liability and warranty liability often overlap. Both are imposed for the same basic purpose, to promote the free flow of com-

[C19] *U.C.C.* 3-416.   [C20] *U.C.C.* 3-417.

mercial paper by giving assurance and protection to those who take it.

A negotiable instrument not only represents contracts, but is also a type of property which is sold and exchanged. Just as implied warranties with respect to title, description, and quality are made in the sale of chattels, such warranties also attach to the sale of negotiable instruments.

There are two basic types of warranties in the law of commercial paper; warranties on presentment and warranties on transfer. Presentment warranties set forth the undertaking of a person who receives payment or obtains acceptance of an instrument to the person who pays or accepts the instrument. Transfer warranties are given by one who transfers the paper, as distinguished from one who presents it for payment or acceptance.

3-100 Presentment Warranties.[C21] Warranties or assurances are given by persons when they present instruments for payment or acceptance. Thus, when the holder seeks to obtain payment or acceptance of an instrument, he is asserting that he is legally entitled to receive such payment or acceptance. After a drawee pays or accepts a draft or a maker pays a note, he may discover that his name was forged, that an indorser's name was forged, that the drawer's name was forged, or that the instrument had been materially altered. The payor or acceptor will then desire to recover his payment from either the party to whom payment was made or some other party to the paper. The rights of the payor and acceptor are governed by the warranties made upon presentment and the breach thereof. The responsibility of a bank which honors a forged check has already been discussed.

A person who presents a note to the maker for payment or a draft to the drawee for payment or acceptance warrants to the maker or drawee who pays or accepts: (1) that he has good title to the instrument—i.e. no indorsements are forged, (2) that he has no knowledge that the signature of the maker or drawer is forged or unauthorized, and (3) that the instrument has not been materially altered—e.g. "raised" in amount. Note that if any of these warranties have been breached, the party who pays or accepts will not have discharged his obligation—he will not have paid the right person. These warranties are also made by prior transferors in favor of the person who accepts or pays.

The person who pays or accepts can "charge back" against the person who received payment and any prior transferor if the signature of an indorser has been forged or if the instrument has been materially altered. However, no charge back is allowed where the drawer's signature is forged unless the presenting party had *knowledge* of that fact. Otherwise the drawee who pays or accepts must stand the loss.

If the person making the presentment is a holder in due course acting in good faith, he does not warrant as to this lack of knowledge to an acceptor of a draft provided: (1) he took the draft after the acceptance, or (2) he obtained the acceptance without knowledge that the drawer's

---

[C21] *U.C.C.* 3-417(1).

signature was unauthorized. It would thus appear that a holder in due course could proceed to obtain payment on an accepted draft if he finds out about a forgery of the drawer's signature *after* he has obtained the acceptance. The acceptor could not recover the payment from the holder in due course but he could recover from any prior transferor who had knowledge of the forgery.

Likewise a holder in due course acting in good faith does not warrant against material alteration to: (1) the maker of a note or the drawer of a draft (these parties are expected to recognize their own paper), (2) the acceptor of a draft with respect to (a) an alteration made *prior* to the acceptance if the holder in due course took the draft *after* the acceptance, or (b) an alteration made *after* the acceptance. Thus the holder in due course can retain money paid to him by an acceptor even though the draft has been raised. Suppose that a check drawn on X Bank in the amount of $1,000.00 is certified by the bank and subsequently raised to $10,000. Thereafter, the check is negotiated to A who presents it to the bank and receives $10,000.00. The bank cannot recover from A even though the certification provided "payable as originally drawn." Of course, if the bank had noticed the alteration it would not have paid out the money in the first instance.

The warranty as to good title is breached if there is a forged *indorsement* in the chain of title. Since no title passes by a forged indorsement, the person who was in possession of the paper has no right to retain money paid to him. This is true even though he has no knowledge of the forged indorsement. The party whose name was forged as an indorser may recover from the party who collected on the paper or from the payor. The party who pays or accepts may recover the payment or avoid the acceptance on the theory that he is not in a position to verify the signatures of indorsers. On the other hand, if a *drawer's* signature is forged, a drawee who accepts or pays may not be allowed to recover his payment. As stated in the Comment to this section: "The justification for the distinction between forgery of the signature of the drawer and forgery of an indorsement is that the drawee is in a position to verify the drawer's signature by comparison with one in his own hands, but has ordinarily no opportunity to verify an indorsement."

In contrast to the warranty of good title, the warranty made to a *maker* or *drawer* with regard to the signature of the maker or drawer is merely that the presenting party has no knowledge that such signatures are not genuine, since the drawer and maker should be able to recognize their own signatures. The same applies to presentment to an *acceptor* who is in a position to verify the drawer's signature. The holder in due course does not warrant to the acceptor lack of knowledge as to the genuineness of the signature of the drawer if he takes the instrument after the drawee's acceptance, or if he obtained the acceptance without knowledge that the drawer's signature was forged nor does he warrant such lack of knowledge to a maker or drawer.

A person who pays a materially altered instrument can recover the payment in excess of the amount for which originally drawn, and a drawee who accepts such an instrument can disavow his acceptance. However, the warranty against material alteration is not imposed upon a holder in due course in favor of a *maker* or *drawer*. Such parties are presumed to know the provisions of the instrument as of the time when they signed. As noted, a holder in due course can retain money received from an acceptor on the theory that the holder relied in good faith on the acceptance. If the alteration is made after acceptance, the holder in due course is also exempt from the warranty on the theory that the drawee could have checked its prior records before making payment. It is again to be noted that a holder who takes through a holder in due course will have the same rights as a holder in due course if he acts in good faith. The warranties in this section may be avoided by a disclaimer agreement between the immediate parties.

3-101 Transfer Warranties.[C22] Just as one who presents an instrument for acceptance or payment makes warranties, so does one who *transfers* an instrument. He is liable for warranties with regard to the nature and character of the instrument transferred.

Any person who transfers an instrument and receives consideration warrants to his transferee and if the transfer is by indorsement to any subsequent holder who takes the instrument in good faith that

(a) he has a good title to the instrument or is authorized to obtain payment or acceptance on behalf of one who has a good title and the transfer is otherwise rightful; and

(b) all signatures are genuine or authorized; and

(c) the instrument has not been materially altered; and

(d) no defense of any party is good against him . . .

It will be noted that the transfer warranties are quite similar to the presentment warranties. However, they come into play in different circumstances; their requirements are somewhat different; there are additional warranties; and the warranties are made to a party other than a maker, drawer, drawee or acceptor. The transferor warrants that all signatures *are* genuine or authorized—not merely that he has no knowledge to the contrary. The holder in due course does make this warranty and also warrants against material alteration.

A transferor warrants that no defense of any party is good against such indorser or transferor. One who transfers "without recourse" merely warrants that he has *no knowledge of a defense*. Except for this limitation the indorser "without recourse" has the same *warranty* liability as other indorsers. It will be recalled that an indorser "without recourse" effectively disclaims *contract* liability on his indorsement. The provision relating to insolvency proceedings does not mean that a transferor warrants against collection difficulties but simply that if insolvency proceedings have been instituted against the primary party—maker or acceptor

C22 *U.C.C.* 3-417(2).

—or the drawer of an unaccepted draft, and the transferor has knowledge of such fact and conceals the same, a fraud has been perpetrated on the transferee.

The warranties upon transfer are made whether the transfer is by delivery, by qualified indorsement ("without recourse") or by unqualified indorsement. In the case of delivery, warranties extend only to the transferee. If the transfer is by indorsement, warranties run to any subsequent holder who takes in good faith. An accommodation indorser is not liable on warranties since "only a person who transfers an instrument and receives consideration" is a warrantor.

The Code provides that a selling agent or broker who does not disclose his agency capacity is bound by warranties. However, if he discloses his capacity, he merely warrants his good faith and his authority to make the transfer.

3-102 Finality of Payment or Acceptance.[C23] As a counterpart of the preceding section, the Code provides:

> *Except* for recovery of bank payments as provided in the Article on Bank Deposits and Collections (Article 4) and *except* for liability for breach of warranty on presentment under the preceding section, *payment* or *acceptance* of any instrument is final in favor of a holder in due course, or a person who has in good faith changed his position in reliance on the payment.

Under this section a drawee who accepts or pays an instrument which bears the forged signature of the drawer is bound on his acceptance and is not permitted to recover his payment. The rationale of this rule is that "it is highly desirable to end the transaction on an instrument when it is paid rather than reopen and upset a series of commercial transactions at a later date when the forgery is discovered." The provisions of this section also apply to makers of notes and other parties who pay an instrument to either a holder in due course or "a person who has in good faith changed his position in reliance on the payment." This section applies to overdrafts or any other error as to the state of the drawer's account. The drawee is responsible for knowing the state of the account before he accepts or pays. The finality is restricted to good faith takers. The mere negligence of a holder in taking the paper does not justify recovery from the holder by the paying party. The Code stresses the finality of the acts of paying or accepting an instrument.

This section requires reference to the warranties made by one who receives payment or acceptance and to the provisions of Article 4–Bank Deposits and Collections—which permit a bank to recover payment of items which have been improperly paid. The bank has a very limited right as to both time and nature.

3-103 Conversion of Instrument: Forged Indorsements.[C24] In tort law, a conversion is any act in relation to personal property inconsistent with

[C23] *U.C.C.* 3-418.   [C24] *U.C.C.* 3-419.

the owner's interest in the goods. The refusal of a drawee to accept a draft which has been delivered to him for *acceptance* is designated as a conversion. Refusal to return any instrument presented for *payment*, including a note, is a conversion. Likewise the payment of an instrument which bears a forged *indorsement* is a conversion of property belonging to the person whose indorsement was forged. The person who pays on a forged indorsement, of course, has recourse against the person who received payment and indorsers subsequent to the forgery. However, he must "make good" to the true owner—the person whose indorsement was forged. The application of the concept of conversion in these three situations is predicated upon the fact that an instrument is property and a refusal to return an instrument after a demand therefor, or the payment of an instrument that belongs to someone else, is certainly inconsistent with the owner's interest in it. It is to be noted that the cause of action granted to the owner is not on the instrument itself but rather in tort for conversion. The measure of damages for the tort is the face amount of the instrument in an action against the *drawee* and is presumed to be the same as against other parties. Where an action is brought against someone other than the drawee, such party can introduce evidence that the instrument is worth less than face value because of insolvency, the existence of a defense, or for any other reason.

If an agent, such as a depositary or collecting bank or a broker, deals with an instrument on behalf of one who is not the owner, such representative is not liable in conversion to the true owner. The representative must have acted in good faith and "in accordance with the reasonable commercial standards applicable to the business of such representative. . . ." However, the representative may be required to account to the true owner for any proceeds remaining in his hands, or if he still has the instrument to return it to the true owner. The purpose of these rules is to protect a party who is performing a service for his customer and assumes that such customer is honestly in possession of the item which is being collected. Such persons are insulated from liability because they are mere "funnels" to facilitate passage of the paper to the drawee.

An intermediary bank or a nondepositary payor bank will not be liable in conversion to the beneficial owner of an instrument "solely because of the fact that the proceeds of an item indorsed restrictively are not paid or applied consistently with the restrictive indorsement of an indorser other than its immediate transferor." A payor bank is one upon which an instrument is drawn and an intermediary bank is one to which an item is transferred in the course of collection. The payor bank is the drawee and items drawn on such bank by its customers may likewise be deposited in the same bank by other customers who are holders of such items. In this situation the payor bank is also a depositary bank. On the other hand many checks are drawn, for example, on *A* Bank and deposited by the holder in *B* Bank. *B* Bank sends the checks to *C* Bank in the process of collection. In this case *A* Bank is a non-depositary payor (drawee) bank and *C* Bank is an intermediary bank.

LIABILITY OF PARTIES CASES

In re Laskin

1962, 204 F.Supp. 106

GRIM, S. D. J.   The problem here presented is the construction of a promissory note:

> $15,426.50   March 31, 1959
> Sixty days after date .... promise to
> pay to the order of INDUSTRIAL RAYON CORPORATION
> Fifteen Thousand Four Hundred Twenty-Six and
> 50/100 ......Dollars payable at Cleveland, Ohio
> with interest at 6% per annum. Value received.
> LASKIN BROS. OF PHILA. INC.
>
>   Harold Laskin
>   K-71730   Due May 30, 1959

Harold Laskin being bankrupt, the question here is whether this note constitutes the holder, Industrial Rayon Corporation, a creditor of the bankrupt. The referee held that the bankrupt was not liable on the note and that the holder was not his creditor. The holder has petitioned for review of the referee's action.

The question is governed by Section 3-403 of the Uniform Commercial Code: . . .

(1) A signature may be made by an agent or other representative, and his authority to make it may be established as in other cases of representation. No particular form of appointment is necessary to establish such authority.

(2) An authorized representative who signs his own name to an instrument is also personally obligated unless the instrument names the person represented and shows that the signature is made in a representative capacity. The name of an organization preceded or followed by the name and office of an authorized individual is a signature made in a representative capacity.

It is helpful as well as proper . . . to refer to the Uniform Code Comment on Section 3-403 prior to the 1959 amendments.

. . . The rule here stated is that the representative is liable personally unless the instrument itself clearly shows that he has signed only on behalf of another named on the paper. If he does not sign in such a way as to make that clear the responsibility is his . . .

Clearly and obviously, the signature "Harold Laskin" on the Industrial Rayon note, without one word to indicate that it was affixed to the note in a representative capacity, makes him individually liable on the note. . . .

The 1959 amendment to Section 3-403 of the Uniform Commercial Code provides:

(2) An authorized representative who signs his own name to an instrument . . .

  (b) *except as otherwise established between the immediate parties,* is personally obligated if the instrument names the person represented but does not show that the representative signed in a representative capacity. (emphasis added)

The Pennsylvania Annotation to the Code's 1959 amendment states:

> Section 3-403. Signature by Authorized Representative.
> Subsection (2). This subsection of the 1953 Code has been divided into two subsections. The revised subsection (2) changes the rule of the 1953 Code that a signing agent was personally liable unless the instrument both named the principal and disclosed the agency relationship. Under the revised Code it is open to the agent who has complied with one of the two requirements to show the other by evidence aliunde the instrument, as between the immediate parties. Insofar as the 1953 Code appeared to change the rule in Pennsylvania, the revised subsection is a reversion to the pre-Code rule (cases cited) . . .

Since the note is dated prior to the 1959 amendment and evidence outside of the note is not admissible to show that Laskin was not liable personally on the note, and since the acts and orders of the Referee were based on the premise that such evidence was admissible, *those orders will be all vacated and the record returned to the Referee for proceedings consistent with this opinion. . . .*

Leahy v. McManus

1965, (Md.) 206 A.2d 688

OPPENHEIMER, J.   This appeal is from a judgment absolving the individual appellee (McManus, defendant) from *personal liability* on a note of the corporate appellee, (Multi-Krome) on the ground that the former signed in a representative capacity.

The note dated April 15, 1957, reads:

> —Four months after date we promise to pay to order of A. Hamilton Leahy —One Thousand and no/100—Dollars Payable at .... Without defalcation, value received, with interest.

There follows authority to confess judgment. The note bears the stamped name of Multi-Krome Color Process, Inc. (the corporation); immediately below are the signatures and seals of the individual appellee, C. E. McManus, Jr. (McManus) and C. E. Delauney (Delauney), without designation of any representative capacity. A. Hamilton Leahy (Leahy), the payee of the note, died on October 10, 1962, and suit on the note was brought in the Circuit Court for Baltimore County by his executrix, the appellant (plaintiff) herein. Judgment by confession was entered against both the corporation and McManus; McManus filed *a motion to vacate the judgment,* stating under oath that he had signed the note solely as an officer of the corporation; testimony was taken on the motion, and Judge Turnbull *vacated the judgment against McManus,* setting the case to be heard *on the merits.*

Certain facts, adduced at the two hearings, are undisputed. The $1,000 represented by the note went into the corporation's funds. At the time the note was executed, Leahy was a stockholder and director of the corporation. McManus was chairman of the Board, and Delauney was the corporation's treasurer. On October 24, 1956, when the corporation was in some financial difficulties, although not insolvent, the corporation's board of directors passed a resolution requiring the counter-signature on all the corporation's checks of either McManus or one Ralph Bolgiano, in addition to the already authorized signatures of the treasurer (Delauney), the president, or the vice-president. Delauney prepared the note here involved. The corporation, at the time of suit, had discontinued operations and was insolvent. Leahy never made demand on the corporation *or* McManus for payment of the note during his lifetime.

At the hearing on the motion to vacate, Bolgiano testified that the corporate resolution as to signing of checks was meant to and did apply to the signing of *all corporate obligations.* McManus testified to the same effect at the hearing on the merits. The resolution had not been prepared by the corporation's counsel. At the time of the second hearing, Bolgiano was deceased, as were all the other persons involved, other than Mc-Manus. McManus testified that he had made advances to the corporation, and that Leahy had lent money to Delauney, whose estate, at the time of his death, was insolvent. McManus also stated that he signed the note "as a result of the new set-up" of the corporation, under which he was authorized to sign for the corporation. *He was not permitted to testify as to any conversations* with Leahy about the note, because of the Dead Man's Statute, Code (1957) Art. 35, Section 3, but on cross-examination, stated that the "we" in the note referred to the corporation, as "a collective group," and that he signed in a *representative capacity.*

At the conclusion of the testimony, the lower court held that there was a *prima facie* case against McManus, but found that, on the evidence, Leahy *knew* that McManus and Delauney were signing in *representative* capacities and accepted the note as the obligation of the corporation alone. The court's verdict was for McManus; *the judgment against the corporation remained undisturbed.*

The appellant's [plaintiff] principal contention is that the lower court erred in finding that McManus signed the note only in a representative capacity. It is clear, as the appellant contends, that an endorsement can be written anywhere on the instrument; that a person may endorse a negotiable instrument in a representative capacity in such terms as to negative personal liability; and that, in the absence of such express negation, the endorser is liable to a holder for value. ⹁ . . It has been held that ordinarily a corporation may validly sign an instrument by stamp. . . . Even though no holder for value is here involved, absent permissible evidence that McManus signed only in a representative capacity, he would be liable as a *maker* or an *endorser.*

As between the parties, in this State, while a person who signed a note made by a corporation is *prima facie* liable to the payee, if there is conflict in the evidence relative to the circumstances, the individual who signed that note is not liable if he affirmatively shows an understanding between him and the payee that there was to be no personal liability. . . . *While the Uniform Commercial Code was not in effect at the time of the transaction here involved, the Code embodies this principle.* (Code (1957) Art. 95B, Sections 3-402, 3-403.)

In this case, there was ample evidence of ambiguity in the evidence as to the circumstances under which the note was executed. While there was no testimony of conversations between Leahy and McManus, the relationship of Leahy to the company, the fact that Delauney who also signed the note, was one of the officers whose signature was required to bind the corporation, and Leahy's failure to attempt to hold McManus personally liable for over four years, were factors supporting McManus' contention of an understanding with Leahy that he, McManus, signed only in a representative capacity. We have considered all the evidence and do not find the judgment of the lower court was clearly erroneous. (Maryland Rule 886a.)

Judgment affirmed; costs to be paid by appellant.

Grange National Bank v. Conville

1956 (Pa.) 8 D & C. 2d 616, 5 Lyc. 170

The plaintiff bank entered a judgment by confession against John P. Conville, Doris E. Conville, and the Hughesville Manufacturing Company, Inc. on two notes. The defendants sought to set aside the judgments against themselves as individuals and assert that liability should be assessed only against the Hughesville Manufacturing Company.

GREEVY, J. . . . John P. Conville and Doris E. Conville have petitioned this Court to open the judgments. In support of their petition they aver that by a mutual mistake of the Plaintiff and the Defendants the notes were improperly executed and signed as follows: . . .

Hughesville Mfg. Co.
John P. Conville
Doris E. Conville

Whereas, they should have been executed as follows: . . .

Hughesville Mfg. Co. Inc.
John P. Conville, President
Doris E. Conville, Secretary

Plaintiff, in its answer, denies that there was any mutual mistake . . .

The Pennsylvania Uniform Commercial Code, Section 3-402, provides: "Unless the instrument clearly indicates that a signature is made in some other capacity it is an indorsement.". . . Under this section any ambiguity as to capacity in which a signature is made must be resolved that it is an endorsement. The question is to be determined from the face of the instrument alone and unless the instrument itself makes it clear that he has signed in some other capacity, the signer must be treated as an endorser.

Section 3-403 (2) provides: "An authorized representative who signs his name to an instrument is also personally obligated unless the instrument names the person represented and shows that the signature is made in a representative capacity. The name of an organization preceded or followed by the name and office of an authorized individual is a signature made in a representative capacity."

Under this section a representative is liable personally unless the instrument itself clearly shows that he signed only on behalf of another named on the paper. If he does not sign in such a way as to make that clear, the responsibility is his.

Under these sections any doubts are to be resolved against the representative and the Court is required to look to the four corners of the instrument and construe the writing, and the question is not for the jury. . . .

Evidence of a mistake must be clear, precise and indubitable, otherwise relief will not be granted. The mistake must be such that would warrant a court of equity to reform the contract and in the main it must be a mutual mistake as to a material fact. The remedy of reformation is never granted on a probability or mere preponderance of evidence. Relief, by the way of reformation, will be denied where the evidence is loose, equivocal, or contradictory, or where it is open to doubt or opposing presumptions.

From this record, being the depositions, we find that the testimony as to a mistake is not clear, precise and indubitable and is not of such weight and directness as to carry conviction to the mind, and that if there was a mistake it was not mutual but unilateral and was due to no fault of the plaintiff but to the petitioners' own negligence and reformation of the note would not be justified.

The testimony taken on the rule is insufficient to justify a chancellor reforming the note and likewise is insufficient to justify the submission of the question to a jury. In accordance therewith we find that petitioners do not have a meritorious defense to the claims upon which the judgments were based and the judgments should not be opened.

Judgment against individual defendants affirmed.

First National Bank of McAlester v. Mann

1965 (Oklahoma) Okl. 410 P.2d 74

This is an action by the depositor, Mann, against the bank to recover for payment of money from his account on forged checks. Mann had for many years operated a business called Mann's Flower Shop and was a customer of the bank. Mann had employed Lloyd Puckett, operator of a bookkeeping service, to keep his books, make tax returns and handle related business. Puckett employed Morrison who handled Mann's account. From 1955 to 1958 Morrison embezzled $26,725.00 from the Mann account. Eventually the embezzlement was discovered and Mann demanded [that] the bank reimburse him for the loss. When the bank refused to reimburse him Mann brought this action to recover. The jury returned a verdict for Mann and the bank appealed.

BERRY, J. . . . Defendant insists that where a series of forgeries are involved there are two classes of checks to be considered and different rules of law are to be applied: (1) checks paid and returned with the first monthly statement after the forgeries begin; (2) other checks similarly and subsequently forged. As this case arose before the Uniform Commercial Code . . . became effective, it is governed by 48 O.S. 1961, Section 43, which provides:

> Where a signature is forged or made without authority of the person whose signature it purports to be, it is wholly inoperative, and no right to retain the instrument, or to give a discharge therefor, or to enforce payment thereof against any party thereto, can be acquired through or under such signature, unless the party, against whom it is sought to enforce such right, is precluded from setting up the forgery or want of authority. . . .

The general rule is that a drawee bank is required to know the signature of its depositors, and pay only such checks as have genuine signatures. (Citation) The exceptions to what may be denominated an unvarying rule arise only where the bank can invoke principles of negligence or estoppel against the depositor. *National Bank of Commerce v. Fish et al.,* (67 Okl. 102, 169 P. 1105, L.R.A.1918F 278) (other citations) states the rule in this language:

> A bank is under an obligation to its depositor to use care in scrutinizing checks paid in order to detect forgeries, and to render its accounts to prevent the perpetration of frauds upon its depositors. . . . Or, stating the rule in terms of negligence, a bank which is guilty of negligence in failing to discover an alteration or forgery cannot avoid liability on the ground that the depositor was negligent in failing to examine his balanced passbook, statement of account, or returned checks. . . .

Plaintiff's evidence showed that substantial sums had been paid out of his account on forged checks, and demand for repayment had been refused by defendant. This showing made out a *prima facie* case and plaintiff was not required to go further and show himself free from negligence. The burden was upon defendant to prove itself free from negligence since it had paid the forged checks at its own peril. . . .

Judgment for plaintiff affirmed.

White v. First National Bank of Scotia

1964, (N.Y.) 254 N.Y.S.2d 651

REYNOLDS, J. Stanley G. White, who had a joint checking account with his wife, Emma C. White, in appellant bank, purportedly wrote his name as "S. G. White" and included his address on the *back* of one of his *blank* checks and gave it to a stranger. Thereafter someone allegedly filled out the *face of the check* in the amount of $300.00 naming Emma J. White as *payee* and S. G. White as *drawer*. On the reverse side of the instrument appears the name of the payee, Emma J. White, above that of S. G. White. The instrument in this form was cashed at the Ticonderoga branch of the State Bank of Albany and forwarded to the appellant [defendant-drawee bank] which paid the State Bank and charged White's account. When the cancelled check was received by White he immediately notified appellant and demanded reimbursement to his account. The appellant refused and White brought an action to recover the balance in his account including the disputed $300 debited therefrom by appellant. The court below granted summary judgment for White and this determination is brought here on appeal. *Appellant in turn commenced a third-party action against the State Bank of Albany.* [Cashing bank] The State Bank without answering appellant's complaint moved to dismiss it on the grounds it did not state facts sufficient to constitute a cause of action. The instant appeal is also brought from an order granting this motion and the subsequent judgment dismissing appellant's complaint.

We do not think respondent White was entitled to summary judgment. While it is true that *as a general rule a bank which makes payment on forged paper cannot debit its depositor's account for the amount improperly paid out . . . it is also true that conduct of the depositor may preclude his recovery. . . .* Here White alleges that his signature as drawee is also forged and that his "endorsement" was not intended as such. At least the last and perhaps, most crucial of these assertions, however, is exclusively within his knowledge and clearly not within the knowledge of appellant. Under these circumstances summary judgment should not have been granted. . . . *If the record as finally developed supports White's assertions he may well be entitled to recovery.* However, appellant is entitled to subject him to cross examination in the hope of eliciting a variance in his account of what transpired which might preclude his recovery.

With respect to the third-party action, it is clear that appellant would be entitled to a recovery from the State Bank of Albany except for the long established rule of *Price v. Neal* (3 Burrows 1354) that the drawee cannot recover payment when it has paid on the forged signature of its depositor, . . . This doctrine, however, is subject to the exception that the drawee may recover from a presenter or cashing bank which itself acts in bad faith or negligently. . . . It should be noted that *the Uniform Commercial Code while retaining the bad faith exception abandons unanswered questions of fact as to respondent's conduct in receiving the check which requires a plenary trial.* Appellant may well be able to establish that respondent contributed to the fraud by its negligence in purchasing the check from a stranger or other third person without adequate inquiry, although in good faith and for value. . . .

Judgments and orders reversed, on the law and the facts, and motions denied, without costs.

[The case was returned to the trial court for a trial at which time the defendant bank will be allowed to offer proof concerning the "indorsement" and negligence on the part of the Albany Bank.]

Davis v. Western Union Telegraph Co.

1954, (Pa.) 4 D. & C. 2d 264

The Plaintiff, Davis, received what purported to be a request from his son in California for money. He wired the money and it was paid over to a person, who posed as the son. The imposter had a Marine Corps identification card which had been stolen from the son. The plaintiff did not ask for a "test question" or other method to identify the person entitled to the money. The plaintiff seeks to collect the money from defendant.

CUMMINS, J. . . . In *Real Estate Land Title & Trust Company v. United Security Trust Company,* 303 Pa. 273 (1931), the Supreme Court said (page 278): "The characteristic feature of these cases was . . . that the money was in fact paid to the person to whom the plaintiff by its actions showed it intended the money should be paid. . . ."

. . . The Supreme Court termed this line of cases cited hereinabove as the so-called impostor cases, defining such as those "which hold that a bank is not liable for the payment of a check on a forged indorsement where the person who committed the forgery and received the money was in fact the person to whom the drawer delivered the check and whom he believed to be the payee named.". . .

It is interesting to note that this will still be the law under the Pennsylvania Uniform Commercial Code. See Section 3-405 (1) (a).

. . . It is immaterial that the impostor posed through the mail is one of these cases.

Judgment for defendant.

[This case was decided under the NIL.]

The Union Bank v. Joseph Mobilla

1959 (Pa.) 43 Erie Co. Leg. J. 45

LAUB, J. . . . On January 15, 1958, the defendant, a used car dealer, represented to the plaintiff bank that he had sold a used Ford automobile to one Theresa Piotrowski of 650 East 24th Street. For finance purposes, he exhibited an installment sales contract and a judgment note allegedly signed by Theresa Piotrowski as maker. There was nothing on the face of either instrument to indicate that the signatures had not been placed there by the maker or that either had been signed by someone else acting in the maker's behalf. . . . The note which was payable to defendant was endorsed by him "without recourse," and the security agreement, which was in defendant's favor as a seller of a chattel, was assigned to the bank. Both instruments, as well as the title to the vehicle in question, were turned over to the bank as part of the finance transaction.

. . . After default the bank importuned both the purported maker and the defendant to discharge the obligation but without avail, the maker having denied executing either document or having bought the vehicle from the defendant. In consequence, plaintiff instituted this action, alleging that defendant is guilty of a breach of warranty, and as part of its action, alleging a written warranty in the security agreement "that the above instrument is genuine and in all respects what it purports to be." Plaintiff also claims upon an implied warranty of the genuineness of the note.

The defendant in his answer admits that he endorsed the note and assigned the security agreement to the plaintiff. He also admits that the maker did not sign either document. It is his defense, however, that Theresa Piotrowski's signature was affixed by an authorized agent named Edward Rogalia and that he (the defendant) is not liable in any event because his indorsement of the note was "without recourse."

We can see not merit whatever in the defenses offered and consider that plaintiff is entitled to the judgment which it seeks. The defendant's conception of the litigation as being a suit against an endorser who signed "without recourse," misses the point. Plaintiff is not suing on the note, but, as noted above, is claiming upon a breach of warranty. If it were true that the suit was against the defendant on the sole basis that he was an endorser, there might be some value to the defenses offered, but the pleadings reveal an entirely different situation. As the pleadings now stand, it is admitted on the record that the defendant in writing warranted the security agreement to be all that it purported to be, and it is clear that it was not. Further, the admission that defendant endorsed the note as part of his finance dealings with the plaintiff and that the note was not signed by the maker is a clear admission of a breach of the implied warranty which accompanies situations of this character. While no statute is required to establish the common sense conclusion that one who presents a document for discount or otherwise impliedly warrants its genuineness when he accepts a consideration for its transfer, the Uniform Commercial Code has such a provision. In Section 3-417 (2) (a) of that Act . . . it is provided that the transferor of an instrument for consideration warrants, among other things, that all signatures are genuine or authorized. This certainly does not imply that a transferor, with knowledge that a signature is not that of the person it purports to belong to and there is no qualifying or descriptive language indicating that the signature was made by someone other than the maker, may remain silent and suppress such knowledge to the detriment of the transferee.

Judgment for the Plaintiff.

Niebergall v. A.B.A. Contracting & Supply Co.

1965 N.Y. 263 N.Y.S. 2d 589

Harvey K. Niebergall was holder of a note which he wished to use as collateral for a loan from the bank. Accordingly the defendant, Merle, indorsed the note as an accommodation to Niebergall so that he might obtain the loan. Niebergall then indorsed the note to the bank and subsequently paid it off. Thereafter Niebergall died. It is now contended that Merle as a prior indorser is liable to subsequent indorsers or their representatives. The lower court ruled in favor of Merle and the plaintiff appealed.

REYNOLDS, J.   Appellants-Plaintiffs seek to recover $10,000.00 from the Respondent-Defendant, Merle, a prior indorser of a note which the decedent Harvey K. Niebergall, a subsequent indorser, redeemed during his lifetime. While "indorsers are *prima facie* in the order in which they indorse; . . . evidence is admissible to show that as between or among themselves they have agreed otherwise." (Negotiable Instruments Law, § 118, see also, U.C.C. § 3-414 [2].) The trial court has found that there was here sufficient evidence to establish that Merle signed solely as an *accommodation* to Niebergall to facilitate his securing bank acceptance of the loan and that it was understood between them that Merle would not be liable to Niebergall in case of default. We concur in this determination and also the finding of the court below that since there was no evidence to the contrary such intent was carried forward to renewals of the note . . .

Judgment affirmed with costs.

General Refrigerator and Store Fixture Company v. Fry

1958, 393 Pa. 15, 141 A.2d 836

MUSMANNO, J.   Edward Mueller of Philadelphia sought a loan of $5,000 from David Fogel, owner of the General Refrigerator and Store Fixture Company of the same city. When Fogel refused to lend the money unless Mueller could supply surety, Mueller prevailed upon a friend, Wm. O. Fry, to sign, with him, a judgment note in the sum of $6,750. Mueller then asked Fogel to make out two checks, one for $2,504.50 payable to Mueller and the other payable to Mueller and Fry in the amount of $2,495.50. Later, Mueller returned to Fogel with the two checks, the $2,495.50 one purportedly having been endorsed by Fry. Mueller asked Fogel to sign his name to the checks so they could be cashed since the bank knew Fogel but did not know Mueller. Fogel so signed the checks and Mueller cashed them but gave none of the proceeds to Fry, his signature, as well as that of his wife's, having been forged.

Fogel recorded the judgment note, Mueller absconded, and Fry was left holding the fi fa.

Fry refused to pay the amount of the note. . . . Fry contended that, since he was a payee on one of the checks but received none of the $5,000, a failure of consideration resulted and he, therefore, was not liable on the note. He accordingly filed a petition in the Court of Common Pleas of Philadelphia to open the judgment. The petition was granted but later rescinded by the Court and judgment confirmed in the name of Fogel in the amount indicated. Fry appealed.

From the time that man learned to communicate thought by means of writing, he has been expressing approval of things which he later repudiated. Whether he chiseled his name to a stone, scribbled it on parchment, or penned it to twentieth century bond paper, he has found reasons to regret his signature and has appealed to some tribunal to be excused from the obligation he voluntarily assumed. Thus William Fry asserts that he is not liable under the judgment note because he signed as an obligor and not as a surety. But the Court below found, from depositions which were taken, that Fry never expected to receive any of the proceeds of the two checks. Therefore, it was of no consequence that his name had been unauthorizedly added to one of the checks as payee. The Court concluded, from all the evidence, that Fry signed the judgment note as an accommodation maker and was responsible for the face value of the note since the original obligor had failed to honor the primary obligation.

Fry asserts on this appeal that he had many defenses to the note: (1) that he did not know what he was signing; (2) that the judgment note was blank when he signed it; (3) that in any event he could not be regarded as an accommodation maker since his name appeared on one of the checks as payee and his name was forged to the check; (4) that Fogel was negligent in the entire transaction. . . .

Although Fry did not dispute his signature to the judgment note, he testified that he was unaware that the paper he signed was a judgment note. At first he asserted that the blank lines on the note had not been filled in when he attached his signature to the document but later he declined to say "positively" that the blanks had not been filled in. The most that he could assert with assurance was that the note carried no date. He admitted that though he could read, he had not read the instrument but merely "glanced" at it. This is rather thin ice on which to skate to the shores of non-liability. We said in *Commonwealth, to Use of Liberty Nat. Bank of Pittston v. Gudaitis*, (323 Pa. 110, 111, 186 A. 82, 83):

> As long ago as when Shephard's Touchstone was written (1648), the law was as follows (page 56): "If a party that is to seal the deed can read himself and doth not, or being illiterate or blind, doth not require to hear the deed read or the contents thereof declared, in these cases albeit the deed is contrary to his mind, yet it is good and unavoidable." In language not quite so quaint, we repeated this principle in *Re Greenfield's Estate*, (14 Pa. 489, 496), adding that one who so signs a document "is guilty of supine negligence which . . . is not the subject of protection, either in equity or at law." We have never deviated from this ruling, one of our latest cases being *O'Reilly v. Reading Trust Co.* (262 Pa. 337, 343, 105 A. 542).

The whole business structure of America would become a shambles if signers were to be allowed to repudiate their obligations on the basis that they did not know what they were signing. The ever-constant possibility of such disavowal would turn into water the adhesive mortar of legal responsibility holding together the bricks of every contractual wall; such an accepted possibility would wreck every business dealing at the slightest touch of the repudiator.

And then, it was not established in the case at bar that Fry did not know what he was signing. He testified that when he signed the note he took for granted that "it was a *reference for a loan.*" (Emphasis supplied.) He testified further:

> (Q) What was the reference supposed to be for? (A) To borrow money. (Q) Why was he borrowing money? (A) I don't know. (Q) Are you related to him? (A) No. (Q) Are you a friend of his? (A) Yes.

When asked if he was seeking a loan from Fogel, Fry replied:

> No. If I wanted to get a loan—it was my corporation—I could go to a bank and make a loan as far as that goes. As I said, I never heard of this Mr. Fogel or the General Refrigerator and Store Fixtures Company, and I am sure I would not have gone there. I know other people who I could go to to get a loan if I needed one.

As the lower Court indicated, Fry has not averred any fraud. A review of the entire record establishes quite clearly that Fry got himself into his present troubles through what this Court has already well denominated as "supine negligence." The person who willingly lies down so that others may step on him will have a difficult time convincing the world that he has not contributed in large measure to his own misfortune.

Even so, we believe that since the Frys were only sureties and received no part of the loan of $5,000, the costs in the case should be divided equally between the appellants and the appellee. *Thus, with that qualification, the judgment is affirmed. . . .*

Dollak v. Educational Aids Company

1965, (D.C.) 214 A.2d 481

Plaintiff company, Educational Aids, supplied wholesale merchandise to retail stores including Dixie Dime Stores, Inc. of which defendant J. Dollak, was president. Defendant's company was in arrears in its payments and plaintiff refused to deliver any more merchandise unless the balance of the account was paid. However, plaintiff agreed to accept a promissory note provided that defendant would personally indorse it. Accordingly, the note was signed by Dollak both in his capacity as president and personally. The note was discounted at a bank which retained it for collection. The note was not paid and was returned to plaintiff. Action was brought against Dollak and a jury returned a verdict for plaintiff. Defendant appealed.

MYERS, A. J. . . . At trial appellant maintained he had endorsed the note merely as accommodation for appellee [Educational Aids Co.] to assist in discounting it at the bank and not in his individual capacity for the purpose of securing further extension of credit and additional merchandise for his own corporation. This presented a question of fact which could not be decided by the trial judge as a matter of law but was for the determination of the jury.

We find no error in the action of the trial judge in overruling appellant's motions for directed verdicts and in submitting the factual questions under proper instructions to the jury. They were resolved adversely to appellant [Dollak]. When a jury performs its function under proper instruction, we are without authority to set aside its resolution of the factual issues or to substitute our own views.

Affirmed.

CHAPTER 24
REVIEW QUESTIONS AND PROBLEMS

1. *A* is an agent of *P* with limited authority to sell goods. *A* executes a note in *P*'s name and makes it payable to *X* in payment for an automobile. Can *X* hold *P* liable on the note?

2. A promissory note was signed:
   "*A* and *B* Distributing Inc.
   Albert Jones"
   The payee of the note seeks to collect from Jones. Can Jones introduce evidence that he signed only on behalf of *A* and *B* Distributing Inc.?

3. Checks drawn on *X* Bank and payable to the order of *A* were stolen from him, and his name was forged as an indorser. Those checks were accepted by the bank and the accounts of the drawers were debited. *A* contends that the bank will have to pay him the amount of these checks. Is *A* correct?

4. *A* was an accommodation maker of a note executed by *D* Corporation to *X* Bank. *A* paid the amount of the note to the bank and the note was surrendered to him. The note was secured by a mortgage on corporate property. *A* seeks to foreclose on the mortgage. Persons who have liens on the property for improvements made by them claim priority over *A*. What result?

5. A negotiable note which provided: "I, John Smith, promise to pay . . ." was signed by John Smith and Willard Green. The note was indorsed to John Black who presented it to Smith for payment one month after maturity. Smith refused to pay. Can Black recover from Green?

6. *A,* the holder of a note, indorses it to *B* "without recourse." The maker of the note had filed a petition in bankruptcy prior to the indorsement. Can *B* hold *A* responsible for the payment of the note?

7. *M,* the bookkeeper for *X* Corporation, prepared payroll checks to the order of persons not on the payroll. The checks were presented to the company's treasurer, who signed them as a matter of course. *M* indorsed the checks in the name of the purported payees and cashed

the checks at various stores. The checks were honored by the drawee bank. *X* Corporation seeks to recover from (1) the stores which cashed the checks (2) the drawee bank. How would you decide this case?

8. Smith introduced himself to Brown as "Professor Weinstein," a noted psychologist, and claimed to be raising funds for a study of juvenile delinquency. Brown drew a check for $10,000 payable to the order of "Professor Weinstein." Smith (alias Weinstein) indorsed the check in the name of Weinstein and cashed it at the bank. Is the bank liable to Brown?

9. *A* drew a check in such fashion that enough room was left at the left margin to insert the words, "One thousand" in front of the word "Fifty" (the actual amount of the check). A person who obtained possession of this check thus altered it to read "One Thousand Fifty and no/100 Dollars." The check was then negotiated to *H*. How much can *H* recover on the check?

10. *M* made a note payable to the order of *P* and delivered it blank as to amount. *P* agreed to fill in the amount which his books would show as the balance owed by *M*. Instead, he filled in the amount for ten times the obligation and indorsed the note to *H*. How much can *H* recover from *M*?

11. *D* drew a check payable to the order of *P*. *P* indorsed to *A*, *A* indorsed to *B*, and *B* indorsed to *H*. *H* obtained certification of the check after which the drawee bank failed. What are *H*'s rights against *D*, *P*, *A*, and *B*?

12. *M* was induced by the fraud of *P* to execute a note payable to the order of *P* as an accommodation to *P*. *P* indorsed the note to *H*. Can *M* introduce evidence that he was induced by fraud to enter into the transaction and that he is only an accommodation party?

13. *H* holds a note which, unknown to him, has been forged. He, by an indorsement "without recourse," indorses it to *A*, a holder in due course. It is presented and payment is refused. *A* desires to hold *H* liable on his indorsement. May he do so?

14. *M* gave *P* a note for a debt owed. Three months later *F*, *M*'s father, signed on the face of the note below *M*'s name. The note was not then due, and *F* had had no part in the prior transactions. Can *P* collect from *F* if *M* doesn't pay at maturity?

15. *M* conducts a used car business. *X* came to *M*'s car lot with a Chevrolet sedan he had stolen from *P*. *X* had the registration certificate in *P*'s name and *P*'s driver's license. Upon the strength of the papers and *X*'s oral representations that he was *P*, *M* drew a check payable to "*P* or order" and handed it to *X*. *X* indorsed the check in *P*'s name and presented it to the drawee bank and received payment. Can *M* recover from the drawee bank for paying the check out of his account?

chapter 25

Commercial Paper: Conditions Precedent, Discharge

PRESENTMENT, NOTICE OF DIS-HONOR, AND PROTEST

3-104 Introduction. In the preceding sections the liability of the second-ary parties, namely, drawers and indorsers of negotiable paper was dis-cussed. It was pointed out that their conditional (contractual) liability to the holder does not arise until the performance of certain *conditions precedent,* namely, due presentment for payment, dishonor by the pri-mary party, and the giving of due notice of dishonor to the drawer or indorser. In this connection it must be remembered that these conditions may be waived by the parties to a negotiable instrument. A waiver set forth in the body of a note is effective as to all parties whose names appear on the instrument, while a waiver which is part of an indorsement ap-plies only to the particular indorser, unless the language used is broad enough to cover later indorsers.[C1] *Protest* is a very formal act or procedure for complying with the conditions precedent.

The importance of presentment and notice of dishonor should be stressed—failure to comply may result in either the complete or the par-tial discharge of the secondary parties. Thus, a holder who fails to properly present a note to the primary party-maker will have thereby dis-charged the indorsers from their conditional liability. If the maker does not pay, the holder will not have recourse against the indorsers. The Code specifies that performance of conditions precedent "is necessary to charge secondary parties" unless excused.

[C1] *U.C.C.* 3-511(6).

It must be remembered that secondary parties also have *unconditional liability* which stems from the warranties which they make upon transfer of an instrument. Such warranty liability exists without regard to the performance of conditions precedent. Likewise it must be noted that even though a secondary party is discharged from his liability as a secondary party, he may still be liable on the underlying obligation which was the basis of the transfer of the instrument. (See Sec. 3-124 for a discussion of this concept.) Thus a secondary party may incur liability on his contract as indorser or drawer, his warranty obligation, or the underlying obligation.

Performance of conditions precedent is not necessary to impose liability on a primary party—maker or acceptor except as noted hereafter for "domiciled paper"—notes and drafts payable at a bank. The secondary parties, however, engage to pay only if there has been presentment, dishonor, and any necessary notice of dishonor or protest.

Attention will now be given to the various conditions precedent that normally must be fulfilled to establish secondary liability. It is necessary to carefully distinguish drawers from indorsers and also to differentiate between drawers of drafts as compared to drawers of checks. A distinction is also to be noted as between indorsers of notes on one hand and indorsers of checks and drafts on the other.

3-105 Presentment in General. Presentment is defined as a "demand for *acceptance* or *payment* made upon the maker, acceptor, drawee or other payor by or on behalf of the holder." [C2]

The Code does not make exhibition of the instrument an essential element of a proper presentment nor does it matter in general where or how the demand for payment is made. Presentment, demand for payment or acceptance, may be made by mail, by telephone or in any other way. If the presentment is made by mail, it is effective on the date when the mail is *received*. Presentment may be made through a "clearing house," an association of banks in a community. It may be made to any person who has authority to make or refuse the payment or acceptance. If there are two or more makers, acceptors, drawees or other payors, presentment can be made to any one of them. [C3]

An instrument may be presented for payment (in the case of a note or draft) or may be presented for acceptance (in the case of a draft). Thus there are two basic types of presentment—for acceptance and for payment.

3-106 Presentment for Acceptance. Presentment for acceptance is not applicable to promissory notes, but it is often *required* in the case of drafts. The drawee of a draft is not bound upon the instrument as primary party until he accepts it. The holder will, in most cases, wait until maturity and present his draft to the drawee for payment, but he may present it to the drawee for acceptance before maturity in order to give credit to the instrument during the period of its term. The holder may

[C2] *U.C.C.* 3-504(1).   [C3] *U.C.C.* 3-504(2).

present the draft to the drawee for acceptance at any time. The drawee is under no legal duty to the *holder* to accept; but if he refuses, the draft is dishonored by non-acceptance; a right of recourse arises immediately against the drawer and the indorsers, and no presentment for payment is necessary.

When presentment for acceptance required.[C4] In most instances it is not necessary to present an instrument for *acceptance*. Presentment for *payment* alone is usually sufficient, but in the following cases *presentment for acceptance must be made in order to charge the drawer and indorsers of a draft.*

1. Where the *draft* expressly stipulates that it must be presented for acceptance.
2. Where the *draft* is payable elsewhere than at the residence or place of business of the drawee. Otherwise the drawee may not know of his obligation to be present at the place designated for payment.
3. Where the date of payment depends upon such presentment. Where the draft is payable after sight; for example, "Thirty days after sight pay to the order of X," the draft must be presented to the drawee for acceptance in order to determine the maturity date of the instrument.

The privilege of presenting for *acceptance* does not apply to a *demand draft* for it is contemplated that the holder is entitled to immediate payment and there is no need for acceptance.

3-107 Presentment for Payment.[C5] Such presentment is required to charge *"any indorser"* and he will be completely discharged on the instrument if such presentment is not properly made. However, there is a limited discharge for such failure in the case of *drawers* of *drafts* and *checks*. The limited discharge also applies to *makers* and *acceptors* of "domiciled paper" who are treated to this extent as "secondary parties."

Presentment is necessary to charge secondary parties. However, in the case of any drawer (check or draft) and the acceptor of draft or the maker of a note *payable at a bank,* failure to make presentment results in only a partial discharge of these parties.[C6] The foregoing parties receive a discharge only to the extent that the delay in presentment caused them a loss. If the bank becomes insolvent subsequent to the date upon which presentment should have been made, the loss resulting from such insolvency will fall on the tardy holder. In the event of such insolvency of the bank, these parties can discharge their liability

by written assignment to the holder of his rights against the drawee or payor bank in respect of such funds, but such drawer, acceptor or maker is *not otherwise discharged.*[C7]

For example, suppose that on March 1, 1967, *A* draws his check on *D* bank, payable to *P*. *P* negotiates the check to *X*. *X* does not present the

C4 *U.C.C.* 3-501(1)(a).
C5 *U.C.C.* 3-501(1)(b).

C6 *U.C.C.* 3-501(1)(c).
C7 *U.C.C.* 3-502(1)(b).

check for payment within a reasonable time as specified by the Code. The check is dishonored by *D* Bank; *X* gives notice to *A*, the drawer, and *P*, the indorser. Although the check has been presented for payment late, *A* is still liable, because he suffered no loss on account of the delay. However, if between the date when presentment should have been made and the date of presentment by *X*, the bank had become insolvent and *A* had lost 60 per cent of the money he had on deposit in the bank, *A* would be discharged on the check held by *X* to the extent of 60 cents on the dollar. *P*, the indorser, is discharged completely in either case.

Thus the following general rules on presentment are to be noted: drawers of drafts and checks are not completely discharged but receive a discharge only to the extent of any loss they may suffer; presentment is to a limited degree required to charge primary parties, i.e., where notes on drafts are payable at a bank ("domiciled paper"); and presentment is not necessary to charge primary parties (makers of notes and acceptors of drafts) where such instruments are not payable at banks.

3-108 How Presentment is Made.[C8] As noted the Code is very liberal as to the mechanics of presentment.[1]

The place of presentment is usually immaterial, but a draft accepted or a note made payable at a bank must be presented at such bank. If the place of payment or acceptance is specified in the instrument, presentment may be made at such place. If no place is specified, it may be made at the place of business or residence of the party who is to accept or pay. If there is no one authorized to accept or pay "present or accessible" at the place of payment specified, or at the place of business or residence of the party to accept or pay, presentment is excused. Ordinarily, presentment would be made at the place of business of the primary party or drawee, but the Code is extremely liberal both as to place of presentment and mode of presentment.

Though the Code in most cases does not require that presentment be made at any particular place and does not require that the person making the presentment exhibit the instrument to the party who is to pay or accept, it does provide a safeguard for the rights of the latter.

> The party to whom presentment is made may without dishonor require that the instrument be produced for acceptance or payment at the place specified in it, or if there be none at any place reasonable in the circumstances.[C9]

Thus the party to pay or accept may not be imposed upon by a holder who presents at an unusual or inconvenient place.

Article 4—Bank Deposits and Collections—provides further rules with respect to the manner of presentment with particular reference to the rights and duties of banks.

---

[1] *Batchelder v. Granite Trust Co.*, page 545.

[C8] *U.C.C.* 3-504.   [C9] *U.C.C.* 3-505.

3-109 Time of Presentment.[C10] In general an instrument must be presented on the date of maturity. However, the actual time of presentment depends upon several factors including the nature of the instrument. The following basic rules apply to *any* presentment:

> Where any presentment is due on a day which is not a full business day for either the person making presentment or the party to pay or accept, presentment is due on the next following day for both parties. Presentment to be sufficient must be made at a reasonable hour, and if at a bank during its banking day.

This provision gives recognition to the increasing practice of closing businesses on Saturday.

If the instrument expresses the time for presentment, such expression controls. Otherwise, the time for presentment is determined as follows: [C11]

1. Where an instrument is payable at or a fixed period after a stated date, any presentment for *acceptance* must be made on or before the date it is payable.
2. When an instrument is payable after sight (or on demand) it must either be presented for *acceptance* or *negotiated* within a *reasonable time* after the date on the instrument or the date of issue, whichever is later.
3. Where an instrument shows the date on which it is payable it is to be presented for *payment* on that date.
4. If the maturity date of an instrument is accelerated presentment for *payment* is due within a reasonable time after the acceleration. This presumably means that the specified maturity date is controlling where the holder was not aware that maturity had been accelerated. Persons who have not received notice of the occurrence of the event which accelerated payment are not charged with knowledge of the earlier maturity of the paper.
5. In order to fix liability on any secondary party presentment for *acceptance or payment* of any other instrument is due *within a reasonable time after such party becomes liable thereon*, e.g., after his indorsement. This relates to demand instruments such as demand notes and demand drafts which do not fall within any of the prior classifications. Thus a secondary party is discharged if the presentment is not made within a "reasonable time" after he indorsed or transferred the instrument.

Note that presentment within a "reasonable time" is required in those situations where a definite maturity date is not included in the instrument—i.e., sight and demand instruments. Certain rules are to be applied in determining what constitutes a "reasonable time." "A reasonable time for presentment is determined by the nature of the instrument, any usage of banking or trade and the facts of the particular case." Though this is of some help in resolving the question of reasonableness—and possibly as much as can be accomplished by statute—it was deemed desirable to provide more definite rules for checks. Also, most of the problems

[C10] *U.C.C.* 3-503.   [C11] *U.C.C.* 3-503.

arising concern the ordinary (uncertified) check. The Code accordingly provides that—

> in the case of an uncertified check which is drawn and payable within the United States and which is not a draft drawn by a bank the following are presumed to be reasonable periods within which to present for payment or to initiate bank collection:
> (a) with respect to the liability of the *drawer,* thirty days after date or issue whichever is later; and
> (b) with respect to the liability of an *indorser* seven days after his indorsement.[C12]

Thus the drawer must "back up" a check for a longer period than an indorser, but the drawer having issued the check is not being imposed upon by the requirement that he keep funds on hand for thirty days to cover it. Thirty days is also the period after which a purchaser has notice of the staleness of a check. But an indorser is in a different position and is entitled to more prompt notice so that he may take adequate steps to protect himself against his transferor and prior parties, if the check is dishonored. In addition the drawer of a check is protected as to funds on deposit by Federal Deposit Insurance.

3-110 Rights of Party to Whom Presentment is Made.[C13] The party to whom presentment is made may without dishonor require the exhibition of the instrument, and reasonable identification of the person making presentment and evidence of his authority to make it if made for another. In addition, he may require that the instrument be produced for acceptance or payment at a place specified in it, or if there be none at any place reasonable in the circumstances, and he has the right to a signed receipt on the instrument for any partial or full payment and its surrender upon full payment.

If the primary party does not avail himself of these rights, the presentment is perfectly valid no matter how the presentment is made or where it is made. If he does require that the presentment be made in accordance with the above provisions, a failure to comply invalidates the presentment and the instrument is not dishonored. However, the time for presentment is extended to give the person presenting a reasonable opportunity to comply. The requirement of identification of the presenting party applies to bearer paper as well as order paper.

3-111 Dishonor.[C14] The party who presents an instrument is entitled to have the instrument paid or accepted as the case may be. If the party to whom the instrument is presented refuses to pay or accept (except as stated in the preceding section), the instrument is dishonored. The presenting party then has recourse against indorsers or other secondary parties provided he has given proper notice of such dishonor.

C12 *U.C.C.* 3-503(2). C14 *U.C.C.* 3-507.
C13 *U.C.C.* 3-505.

An instrument is dishonored when presentment is duly made and acceptance or payment is refused or cannot be obtained within the prescribed time. In case of bank collections if the instrument is seasonably returned by the midnight deadline it is dishonored; these rules apply to both optional and necessary presentment. An instrument is also dishonored when presentment is excused and the instrument if not duly accepted or paid.

Upon dishonor, the holder has an immediate right of recourse against secondary parties subject to any necessary *notice of dishonor* or *protest.* In keeping with general banking and commercial practices, the return of an instrument for lack of proper indorsement does not indicate an intention to dishonor and is not so treated.

The Code also makes provision for drafts which contain a provision for *representment* following an initial dishonor. Thus a draft or an indorsement thereon may provide that the presenting party is allowed to present the draft to the drawee *again* if it is dishonored upon the first presentment. The requirement is that a stated time must be set forth within which such representment may be made. This concession is limited to (1) dishonor by *nonacceptance* if it is a time draft; (2) dishonor by *nonpayment* if it is a sight draft. Thus, when such a provision is found in a draft or indorsement the holder may waive the initial dishonor, and present it again within the specified time without thereby discharging any secondary party upon whom the provision for representment is binding.

3-112 Time Allowed for Acceptance or Payment.[C15] As to the amount of time allowed to a party to whom an instrument is presented within which to accept or pay it, the Code covers both the time allowed to the primary party on presentment for *payment,* and presentment for *acceptance,* as follows:

(1) *Acceptance* may be deferred without dishonor until the close of the next business day following presentment. The holder may also in a good faith effort to obtain acceptance and without either dishonor of the instrument or discharge of secondary parties allow postponement of acceptance for an additional business day.   *next day okay*

(2) Except as a longer time is allowed in the case of documentary drafts drawn under a letter of credit, and unless an earlier time is agreed to by the party to pay, *payment* of an instrument may be deferred without dishonor pending reasonable examination to determine whether it is properly payable, but payment must be made in any event before the close of business on the day of presentment.   *Before close*

Thus a holder may allow one extra day in an effort to obtain acceptance, but he may not otherwise extend the time for payment without discharging secondary parties. The reference to letters of credit means that the time allotted is determined by Article 5–Letters of Credit–which con-

[C15] *U.C.C.* 3-506.

trols as to documentary drafts that are drawn under a letter of credit.

As to payor banks, Article 4–Bank Deposits and Collections–controls with regard to the bank's right to recover tentative settlements made by it on the day an item is received.

3-113 Notice of Dishonor.[C16] In the preceding sections two of the conditions precedent to the enforcement of liability against secondary parties have been discussed—presentment and dishonor. This section deals with the third requirement.

When an instrument has been dishonored on proper presentment, the holder must give prompt notice of the dishonor and by so doing has an immediate right of recourse against the secondary parties who have been notified. Failure to give prompt and proper notice of dishonor results in discharge of indorsers, and drawers of checks are discharged *pro tanto* as in the case of slow presentment. The same applies to makers, drawers, and acceptors of "domiciled paper" who are entitled also to notice of dishonor but are released only to the extent that they are injured by the failure of the holder to give prompt notice of dishonor.

By whom and to whom notice may be given.[C17]   Generally, notice is given to secondary parties by the *holder* or by an indorser who has himself received such notice. The Code permits any party who may be compelled to pay the instrument to notify any party who may be liable on it. An indorser *may* give notice to another indorser who is *not* liable to the one who gives notice in the hope that such indorser will pay.

If the party presenting the instrument is an *agent* of the owner or a bank, such agent or bank upon dishonor can "give notice to his principal or customer or to another agent or bank from which the instrument was received."

Time within which to give notice of dishonor.[C18]   Except for banks, notice must be given before midnight of the third business day after dishonor. In the case of a person who has received notice of dishonor and wishes to notify other parties, notice must be given by him before midnight of the third business day after *receipt* of the notice of dishonor. This Code provision is intended to give a person sufficient time to determine what he is supposed to do and then get out a business letter in relation thereto.

In the case of banks any necessary notice must be given before its "midnight deadline"—before midnight of the next banking day following the day on which a bank receives the item or notice of dishonor.

Article 4 provides further exceptions with respect to collecting banks, which are discussed in Chapter 26.

How notice is given.[C19]   Notice may be given in any reasonable manner, which would include oral notice, notice by telephone, and

C16 *U.C.C.* 3-508.   C18 *U.C.C.* 3-508(2).
C17 *U.C.C.* 3-508(1).   C19 *U.C.C.* 3-508(3).

notice by mail. Such notice must identify the dishonored instrument and state that it has been dishonored. The Code approves the general banking practice of returning the instrument bearing a stamp that acceptance or payment has been refused as a sufficient notice of dishonor.

Written notice is effective when *sent* although it is not received, assuming proper address and postage.[2] Note that when *presentment* is made by mail, the time of *presentment* is determined by time of *receipt* of mail.

Notice to one partner is deemed to be notice to the firm even though the firm has been dissolved. When any party is dead or incompetent notice may either be sent to his last known address or given to his personal representative.

If a party to whom notice is to be given is involved in insolvency proceedings, e.g., assignment for benefit of creditors, the notice may be given either to such party or the representative of his estate.

Effect of notice.[C20]   Proper notice preceded by any necessary presentment and dishonor imposes liability upon secondary parties to whom such notice of dishonor is given, including makers and acceptors of "domiciled paper." Proper notice operates for the benefit of all parties who have rights on the instrument against the party notified. Thus it is only necessary to notify a party once for his liability to be fixed. For example, if *A, B, C,* and *D* are indorsers in that order, and the holder gives notice only to *A* and *C, C* will not be required to give additional notice to *A* and if *C* is compelled to pay, he would have recourse against *A. B* and *D* are discharged if they are not notified by the holder or one of the indorsers.

3-114 Indorsers after Maturity.[C21] Neither presentment, notice of dishonor, nor protest is necessary to charge an indorser who has indorsed an instrument *after maturity.* The reason for this is that few people would think to present an overdue instrument for the purpose of charging an indorser and the provision in the prior law requiring presentment and notice had become "little more than a trap, for those not familiar with the Act." Accordingly, indorsers after maturity are not entitled to performance of conditions precedent. Like primary parties they remain liable for the period of the statute of limitations.

3-115 Protest.[C22] Protest is a *certificate* which sets forth that an instrument was presented for payment or acceptance, that it was dishonored, and the reasons, if any, given for refusal to accept or pay. It is a formal method for satisfying the conditions precedent. The Code confines the requirements of protest to drafts which are drawn or payable outside the United States. The protest requirement was retained by the Code as to international drafts "because it is generally required by foreign

[2] *Durkin v. Siegel,* page 546.

[C20] *U.C.C.* 3-507(2).
[C21] *U.C.C.* 3-501(4).

[C22] *U.C.C.* 3-509.

law, which this Article cannot affect." In other cases protest is optional with the holder.

3-116 Evidence of Dishonor and Notice of Dishonor.[C23]

Protest serves as evidence both that presentment was made and that notice of dishonor was given; and it creates a presumption that the conditions precedent were satisfied. The Code recognizes two other types of admissible evidence which create a presumption of dishonor and notice of dishonor. One is "any book or record of the drawee, payor bank, or any collecting bank kept in the usual course of business which shows dishonor. . . ." The second is "The purported stamp or writing of the drawee, payor bank or presenting bank on the instrument or accompanying it stating that acceptance or payment has been refused for reasons consistent with dishonor." A stamp "Indorsement missing" or "Forgery" is not evidence of dishonor. However, a stamp "N.S.F." (insufficient funds) or "Payment stopped" is consistent with dishonor and creates a presumption of dishonor. If any of these types of evidence—protest, stamp or writing, or book or record—indicates that notice of dishonor has been duly given, it creates a rebuttable presumption that such notice was in fact given.

3-117 Unexcused Delay: Discharge.[C24]

An unexcused delay in making any *necessary* presentment or in giving notice of dishonor discharges secondary parties—indorsers and drawers. Indorsers are completely discharged by such delay but as noted in previous sections, drawers, makers of notes payable at a bank, and acceptors of drafts payable at a bank receive only a *pro tanto* discharge.

The rationale of the Code provision which grants the *pro tanto* discharge is simply that if the holder had acted properly and presented the instrument promptly it would have been paid and the obligor would have been discharged. If during the delay the drawee or payor bank becomes insolvent, the resulting loss is caused by the holder and should be borne by him. The obligor party is not likely to be in a good position to prevent the loss for he feels obliged to leave his funds with the drawee or payor bank to cover the instrument. On the other hand, it is equally clear that there should be a limit on his discharge. The drawer, acceptor, or maker has not yet paid anything by virtue of having given the instrument and he has probably received some benefit because of his engagement. For example, *A* gives a check to *B* in payment for a new automobile and *B* delays unreasonably in presenting the check to the bank upon which it is drawn. When *B* presents the check it is dishonored because the bank in the meantime has become insolvent. It would be unfair to let *A* keep the automobile while giving nothing to *B*. Consequently, the Code provides that *A* will be discharged if he makes an assignment to *B* of his rights against the drawee bank.

C23 *U.C.C.* 3-510.   C24 *U.C.C.* 3-502.

The Code provides that where *protest* is necessary, *and* is delayed beyond the time when due, *any drawer or indorser* is discharged. Thus a complete discharge is given, where protest is required, to all drawers as well as indorsers.

3-118 When Conditions Need Not be Performed. [C25] There are many rules with respect to waiver of the conditions precedent necessary to charge secondary parties; excuses for failure to perform such conditions; and excuses for delay in complying with the conditions. In some situations satisfaction of the conditions is "excused" and in others performance is "entirely excused."

Delay in presentment, protest, or notice of dishonor is excused when the party is without notice that it is due or when the delay is caused by circumstances beyond his control and he exercises reasonable diligence after the cause of the delay ceases to operate.

Delay in making presentment, in giving notice of dishonor, or in making protest is excused when the holder has acted with reasonable diligence and the delay is not due to any fault of the holder. He must, however, comply with these conditions or attempt to do so as soon as the cause of the delay ceases to exist. Also, delay in complying with the conditions precedent is excused if the holder did not know that the time for compliance had arrived. Thus, if an instrument has been accelerated but the holder did not know of this fact, his late presentment would be excused. Likewise, where a demand had been made by the party from whom he received the instrument immediately before his purchase, the holder's delay in presenting would be excused. He would not in either case know that the time for presentment had arrived.

Presentment or notice or protest are entirely excused:

1. If the party to be charged, e.g. the indorser, upon whom liability is sought to be imposed, has *waived* the condition either before or after it is due. The waiver may be express as where it is set forth in the instrument or in the indorsement or it may be by implication. Where such waiver is stated on the face of the instrument it is binding on all parties; where it is written above the signature of the indorser it binds him only.

Implied waivers are not defined but the test evolved by the courts is whether the secondary party's (e.g. indorser) conduct was such as to induce the holder to forego the usual procedures to fix liability on the indorser or was such as to otherwise indicate an intention to waive.

The words "Protest Waived" contained in an instrument mean that presentment, notice of dishonor, as well as technical protest are waived. This is true even though technical protest is not required.

2. The performance of the conditions precedent is entirely excused if "the party to be charged has himself dishonored the instrument or has countermanded payment or otherwise has no reason to expect or right to require that the instrument be accepted or paid." This provision is illustrated by the situation in which a drawer of a check has stopped payment on the check. Such drawer is aware that the bank will dishonor the check in accordance with his order and certainly is not in a position to complain about slow presentment or any lack of notice of dishonor. Similarly, the rule applies to an accommodated party who has failed to pay. Even though he may nominally appear as an indorser he is in reality a primary party and the accommodation maker is really a surety.

3. Performance of the condition precedent is also entirely excused if "by reasonable diligence the presentment or protest cannot be made or the notice given." This means that if the circumstances which gave rise to the "excuse" persist, the performance of the conditions is "entirely excused."

The foregoing rules relate to dispensing with the requirements of *any or all* of the conditions precedent. In addition there are two rules which relate to excuse of *presentment* only.

1. If the maker, acceptor, or drawee of any instrument is dead or is involved in insolvency proceedings instituted after the issue of the instrument, *presentment* is not required. (This provision does not apply to documentary drafts.) The rule is predicated upon the theory that there is no reason to require a useless thing to be done. The holder is permitted to have immediate recourse upon the drawer or indorsers leaving to them the right to file a claim against the estate in probate or in the insolvency proceedings.

2. *Presentment* is dispensed with if "acceptance or payment is refused but not for want of proper presentment." Here again if the primary party has definitely refused to pay for reasons which do not relate to presentment, it would be a useless ceremony to make a later presentment—he has already indicated that he won't pay and that presentment would be futile.

Draft dishonored by non-acceptance.[C26]   "Where a draft has been dishonored by *non-acceptance* a later presentment for *payment* and any notice of dishonor and protest for non-payment are excused *unless in the meantime the instrument has been accepted.*" (Emphasis supplied.) This means that a holder who has presented a draft for *acceptance* is not, if acceptance is refused, required to make a subsequent presentment for *payment*. The refusal to accept is in itself a dishonor of the instrument.

DISCHARGE

3-119 In General. The discharge of *any party* to a negotiable instrument may be accomplished in a variety of ways. The Code classified the

[C26] *U.C.C.* 3-511.

grounds for discharge in terms of whether (1) an individual party to an instrument receives a discharge or whether (2) all of the parties to the instrument are discharged. The Code proceeds on the theory that an instrument is simply a piece of paper—that strictly speaking, it cannot itself be discharged. Rather the parties are discharged from their liability on the instrument.

The following are methods whereby "any party" may be discharged from liability on an' instrument.[C27]

1. By payment or satisfaction.
2. By tender of payment.
3. By cancellation or renunciation.
4. By impairment of right of recourse or collateral.
5. By reacquisition of the instrument by a prior party.
6. By fraudulent and material alteration.
7. By certification of a check.
8. By acceptance varying a draft.
9. By unexcused delay in presentment or notice of dishonor or protest.

In addition to the foregoing "any party is also discharged from his liability on an instrument to another party by any other act or agreement with such party which would discharge his simple contract for the payment of money." This is in recognition of the fact that insofar as the discharge of any one party is concerned a negotiable instrument differs from other contracts only in the special rules arising out of its character (as enumerated above) and in the effect of a discharge on a subsequent holder in due course. No discharge of any party is effective against a subsequent holder in due course unless such holder has notice of the discharge when he takes the instrument. Thus the defense of discharge is only a personal defense which is cut off when a subsequent holder in due course takes without notice. For example, if an instrument is paid without surrender and is then negotiated to a holder in due course, such a subsequent purchaser cuts off the defense of payment.

3-120 Payment or Satisfaction.[C28] The obligor can safely pay the holder even though he is aware that some third party claims an interest in the paper. This is subject, however, to the privilege of the adverse claimant to (1) bring court action to enjoin the payment or (2) to supply the obligor with indemnity against double liability. If either of these steps is taken the obligor is protected in his refusal to pay the holder. If the adverse claimant does not take either course of action, the obligor is protected in paying the holder except in two cases:

1. A party who in bad faith pays a holder who acquired the instrument by theft is not protected. Likewise the obligor is not protected if he

---

[C27] *U.C.C.* 3-601.   [C28] *U.C.C.* 3-603.

in bad faith pays a holder (unless he has the rights of a holder in due course) who holds through a thief.

2. A party, with the exception of banks in certain situations, will not be discharged from liability if he pays the holder of a restrictively indorsed instrument in a manner not consistent with the terms of the restrictive indorsement. The person who is to make payment cannot refuse to pay a *holder in due course* on the ground that a third party claim exists because payment or satisfaction to such holder would be inconsistent with the terms of a restrictive indorsement. The restrictive indorser's recourse would be against the indorsee who did not act in accord with the indorsement.

Payment by a "stranger to an instrument" can accomplish a discharge. Payment may be made with the consent of the holder by any person, including one who is not a party to the paper. Thus a third party may intervene to protect the drawer's credit and at the same time preserve his own rights. When the instrument is surrendered to the third party, he obtains the rights of a transferee.

3-121 Tender of Payment.[C29] A tender is an offer to pay or perform a contractual obligation. A tender does not discharge the debt or obligation, but it does stop the running of interest. If the creditor thereafter brings legal action to recover the amount of the debt, the costs of suit and attorney's fees will be imposed on him.

This generally accepted rule of tender is adopted by the Code to give a limited discharge to the obligor on an instrument. If he tenders to the holder full payment when or after it is due, "he is discharged to the extent of all subsequent liability for interest, costs and attorney's fees."

The Code further provides that where the maker or acceptor is ready and able to pay at every place of payment specified in the instrument (when the instrument is due), an equivalent of tender has been made. This does not apply to demand instruments. Thus makers and acceptors of notes and drafts payable at a bank have made a proper tender if they maintain an adequate balance in the bank as of the due date of the instruments. As previously noted, failure to make a proper presentment in the case of "domiciled paper" results in a pro tanto discharge of drawers and makers in the event of the insolvency of the bank.

If the holder refused to accept a proper tender, *indorsers* and other parties who have a right of recourse against the party making the tender are discharged.

Thus, if the maker of a note tendered payment which was refused by the holder, indorsers prior to the holder would be discharged because they have a right of recourse against the maker.

C29 *U.C.C.* 3-604.

3-122 Cancellation and Renunciation.[C30] Cancellation and renunciation are only personal defenses and like other discharges cannot be asserted against a holder in due course.

The holder of an instrument may even without consideration discharge any party in any manner apparent on the face of the instrument or the indorsement. This can be accomplished by intentionally cancelling the instrument or the party's signature by destruction or mutilation, or by striking out the party's signature. He can renounce his rights by a writing signed and delivered or by surrender of the instrument to the party to be discharged. Neither cancellation nor renunciation without surrender of the instrument affects the title thereto. The instrument might still be negotiated to a holder in due course.

3-123 Impairment of Right of Recourse or of Collateral.[C31] It will be recalled that certain principles of the law of suretyship with reference to discharges are significant in the law of negotiable instruments. Mention has been made of this in connection with accommodation parties and defenses available to them. Under the law of suretyship a surety is discharged if the creditor releases the principal debtor; a surrender by the creditor of security furnished by the principal to the creditor, discharges the surety; a binding agreement between the creditor and the debtor to extend the time of payment by the principal debtor discharges the surety. These suretyship concepts are based upon the rationale that a surety is assuming liability to the creditor for the principal debtor's performance of a contractual obligation to the creditor. If the creditor increases the surety's risk by extending the time for the principal debtor's performance, or deprives the surety of the benefit of collateral, the surety is discharged. If the creditor releases the principal debtor he must also intend to release the surety—otherwise the creditor could sue the surety who in turn could demand reimbursement from the principal debtor.

Placed in the context of the law of negotiable instruments a holder is a creditor; the primary party—maker or acceptor—is the principal debtor; and the secondary party—indorser or drawer—is the surety. In the case of an accommodation party who is a maker, these rules for discharge would be applicable since such a party is a surety. The "suretyship defenses" are not limited to parties who are secondarily liable.

Another basic principle of suretyship law is that a creditor may release the principal debtor or grant him a binding extension of time without thereby discharging the surety if the surety consents to the release or extension. Also the creditor who releases or grants a time extension to the principal debtor can preserve his rights against the surety by "reserving his rights" against the surety. If rights are reserved, the surety is privileged to satisfy the obligation to the creditor and then proceed against the principal debtor for reimbursement. The application of this concept to commercial paper is set forth in the Code which provides:

[C30] *U.C.C.* 3-605.   [C31] *U.C.C.* 3-606.

. . . By express reservation of rights against a party with a right of recourse [against the obligor] the holder preserves

(a) all his rights against such party as of the time when the instrument was originally due; and
(b) the right of the party to pay the instrument as of that time; and
(c) all rights of such party to recourse against others.

Note that the party—e.g. indorser—against whom rights are reserved, can in effect defeat the attempt by the holder to grant relief to another party against whom the indorser has recourse. He can pay the instrument and proceed immediately against the party—e.g. maker—to whom the release or covenant not to sue was given. Timely notice of reservation of rights should be given to the parties against whom such rights are reserved.

3-124 Discharge of Underlying Obligation.[C32] In most situations involving the issuance or transfer of an instrument, there is an obligation involved for which the instrument was issued or transferred. It is the usual understanding of the parties that the *obligation* itself is not discharged until the instrument is paid and that action on the debt or obligation is simply held in abeyance pending the exhaustion of efforts to collect on the instrument.[3] By the same token the parties could agree otherwise—that is, that the instrument *is* received as final payment. However, it is not often that the parties spell out their intention in this regard. An instrument is said to be only conditional payment—the person who receives it gives up the right to sue on the obligation until the paper is due, but if it is not paid upon proper and timely presentment, the right to sue on the obligation is reinstated.[4] (See Section 2-93 in the Book on Contracts.)

While it is generally true that the underlying debt is not discharged by the execution or transfer of a negotiable instrument, there is one exception. If the instrument which is transferred is one executed by a bank, the underlying obligation is discharged.

Otherwise, where an instrument is taken for an underlying obligation the obligation is suspended until the instrument is due; and if it is dishonored, action can be brought either on the instrument or the obligation.[5]

A question arises as to the position of the parties where an instrument has been indorsed to another and the holder was late in presenting the instrument or in giving notice of dishonor. Here the holder initially had rights against the indorser on the indorsement contract and the underlying debt. If because of slow presentment or tardy notice of dishonor, the indorser is discharged from the former is he also discharged from the latter? The Code provides that "discharge of the underlying obligor on

---

[3] *Visnov et ux. v. Levy,* page 548.
[4] *Mansion Carpets, Inc. v. Marinoff,* page 549.
[5] *In re Eton Furniture Co.,* page 550.

[C32] *U.C.C.* 3-802.

the instrument also discharges him on the obligation." As noted previously, failure to satisfy the conditions precedent discharges indorsers of checks, drafts and notes irrespective of any injury to them. On the other hand, *drawers* are discharged on the instrument only to the extent of injury caused by the delay, so that they would continue to be liable on the underlying obligation except to the extent that the delay caused them a loss. Therefore, if the holder of a check indorses it to a creditor in payment of an underlying obligation and the creditor does not make a proper presentment the indorser is discharged *both* on the instrument and on the underlying debt. The indorser does not have to prove any injury. If a person draws a draft or a check in payment of an obligation he remains liable on the underlying obligation in the event of dishonor of the check or draft in spite of late presentment.

These provisions emphasize the importance of proper compliance with the conditions precedent.

3-125 Lost, Destroyed or Stolen Instrument.[C33] The Code provides a method of recovering on lost, destroyed or stolen instruments as follows:

The owner of an instrument which is lost, whether by destruction, theft, or otherwise, may maintain an action in his own name and recover from any party liable thereon upon due proof of his ownership, the facts which prevent his production of the instrument and its terms. The court may require security indemnifying the defendant against loss by reason of further claims on the instrument.[6]

Since it is possible that the instrument might at a later date actually turn up in the hands of a holder in due course, the court may require security to indemnify the obligor against double liability.

CONDITIONS PRECEDENT, DISCHARGE CASES

Batchelder v. Granite Trust Co.

1959, 339 Mass. 224, 157 N.E. 2d 540

The plaintiff was the holder of a note which it placed in the defendant's hands for collection. Plaintiff alleged that the defendant failed to make proper presentment to the maker (now bankrupt) and that a financially responsible indorser was thereby discharged. The bank had sent notice by mail ten days prior to maturity, notifying the maker that the note would become due and that the bank held it for collection. The lower Court ruled in favor of the defendant.

SPALDING, J. . . . The questions for decision arise out of exceptions taken by the plaintiff to certain rulings on evidence and to the denial of his fourth request for ruling. The fourth request asked the judge to rule that the defendant did not make proper presentment of the third note.

[6] *Dluge v. Robinson*, page 551.

[C33] *U.C.C.* 3-804.

Inasmuch as the facts relating to presentment were agreed this presents a question of law. The request was rightly denied.

Prior to the adoption of the negotiable instruments law in 1898, it was well settled in this Commonwealth in situations similar to this that a written demand mailed by a bank to the maker of a note to pay the note at the bank on the due date was sufficient to make the offices of the bank the place of payment (cases cited). And it has been said that "such previous notice to the promisor, and neglect on his part to pay the note at the bank, are a conventional demand and refusal, amounting to a dishonor of the note" (Cases cited). . . .

It could be argued that a strict construction of Section 96 [of the NIL] would call for different presentment procedure than that employed by the defendant. But we are not disposed to construe that section as abrogating a rule which has been so deeply embedded in our law. Our common law rule arose from the custom of merchants, the development of which was described by Chief Justice Shaw in these terms: ". . . the custom of the banks of Massachusetts, of sending a notice to the maker of a note to come to the bank and pay it, and treating his neglect to do so during bank hours, on the last day of grace, as a dishonor, and all parties acquiescing in, and consenting to, such neglect as a dishonor, has become so universal and continued so long, that it may well be doubted, whether it ought not now to be treated as one of those customs of merchants, of which the law will take notice, so that every man, who is sufficiently a man of business to indorse a note, may be presumed to be acquainted with it, and assent to it, at least, until the contrary is expressly shown." If conformity to custom need be shown, it was not lacking. The bank followed its usual practice in dealing with this note. Its practice was similar to that of the other local banks. The payee, maker and indorsers of this note were acquainted with this practice, since it was followed in making demand for payment of the two earlier notes, and they acquiesced in its use with regard to them.

It is worthy of note that the Uniform Commercial Code, which became law in this Commonwealth on October 1, 1958, although not applicable here, would sanction the presentment procedure followed by the defendant. . . .

Exceptions overruled. . . .

[This case was decided under the NIL.]

Durkin v. Siegel

1960, (Mass.) 165 N.E. 2d 81

CUTTER, J.   . . . Promissory notes signed by one Browne were indorsed by the defendant. They were protested for nonpayment and notice of dishonor was sent on January 17, 1957, "by the plaintiffs' attorney by certified mail, return receipt requested, properly stamped and addressed to the defendant at his home . . . [in] Brookline. . . . The letter, unopened, was returned by the post office . . . with the notation 'refused' . . . across the face of the envelope. The defendant testified that he was in Canada at the time." The defendant in each of these two actions presented a motion for a directed verdict, which was denied. Certain of the defendant's requests for instructions were also denied. There were verdicts for the plaintiffs. The only question argued raised by the bill of exceptions is whether it was good notice of dishonor of promissory notes under Sections 119 and 128 (both now repealed), to send a letter, otherwise in order, by certified mail, return receipt requested, rather than regular mail, where the letter was returned unopened and undelivered, marked "refused," with the blank form of post office receipt unsigned.

The Negotiable Instruments Law . . . applies to this case, because these events occurred prior to October 1, 1958, the effective date of the Uniform Commercial Code. The holder of a dishonored negotiable instrument must give prompt notice of dishonor to those secondarily liable. The provision here controlling is Section 128 . . . which reads, "Where notice of dishonor is duly addressed and deposited in the post office the sender is deemed to have given due notice, notwithstanding any miscarriage in the mails." Registered and certified mail, return receipt requested, are usually regarded by careful people as preferred methods of ensuring delivery. No exception is made in Section 128 with respect to these or other types of first class mail. The section has been carried over into the Uniform Commercial Code in somewhat different language but without attempt to change its meaning. See . . . Section 3-508, which in par. (3) provides that "[n]otice may be given in any reasonable manner" and that "[i]t may be oral or written," and in par. (4) states, "Written notice is given when sent although it is not received." The comments of the draftsmen show that no changes in . . . the Negotiable Instruments Law (. . . Sections 119 and 128) were intended (cases cited). . . .

In the light of the foregoing considerations, we hold that Section 128 makes reasonable use of any form of first class mail (not excluding registered or certified mail) for a properly addressed notice of dishonor the equivalent of actual notice. Section 128 is not merely an application of the principle that the "mailing, postage prepaid . . . of a properly addressed letter is *prima facie* evidence of its receipt by the addressee" (cases cited). . . .

Persons who become secondarily liable upon negotiable instruments are not unfairly burdened if they are held bound by notices sent to them by any generally used form of first class mail at a usual address. They can protect themselves by stipulating (see Section 131) that a particular address be used and by arranging at that address during any absence to have their mail received, opened, forwarded and collected (in the event of the receipt of a notification from the postal authorities that it has not been possible to deliver to them a piece of registered or certified mail). That use of ordinary mail might have ensured delivery (see *Fields v. Western Millers Mut. Fire Ins. Co.*, 182 Misc. 895, 897-898, 50 N.Y.S. 2d 70) is completely irrelevant in view of Section 128. Refusal of a registered or certified letter, of course, would not protect an indorser from the effect of notice (case cited).

Certain decisions in other States, dealing with different types of notices, have held that use of registered mail may have obstructed delivery of a notice, thus making the notice insufficient. We put to one side cases arising under statutes or court rules requiring actual receipt of a notice or document (cases cited). . . .

Although some cases (see *Saffold v. Fellows,* 128 Misc. 422, 424, 220 N.Y.S. 200; but see Id., 219 App. Div. 865, 221 N.Y.S. 197) intimate that the senders of certain types of notice are not entitled to require a receipt, it is not unreasonable for the holder of a dishonored negotiable instrument to ask for a postal receipt when he gives notice of dishonor to one who has become secondarily liable on that instrument.

The defendant's motions for directed verdicts could not have been granted. *His requests for instructions were properly denied.* . . .

[This case was decided under the NIL.]

Visnov Et Ux v. Levy

1955, (Pa.) 2 D. & C. 2d 686

FLOOD, J.   Judgment was entered in ejectment for the leased premises in the above case for failure to pay rent when due. The lease, dated June 1, 1953, provided that the rent should be payable in lawful money of the United States on the first of each month and that time was of the essence. The rent due April 1, 1954, was paid by check dated that day and received by plaintiff on April 2nd. The check was deposited by plaintiffs in their own bank on April 6th. On April 13th they received from their bank a notice, dated April 12, 1954, that the check had been returned marked "N.S.F." On April 18th defendant received a letter from plaintiff, dated April 16th, giving defendant 90 days' notice to quit under the lease for failure to pay rent as required under the lease.

The rent had been paid by check consistently from the beginning of the lease and therefore any requirement to pay in cash had long since been waived by the course of performance between the parties.

This reduces the question before us to whether the facts set forth constitute so substantial a breach as to warrant a forfeiture of the lease, carrying with it defendant's option to purchase. We do not believe that it was. A check was received by plaintiffs on the second day of the month and was not deposited in their own bank until the sixth. We have no information in the stipulation as to the status of defendant's account with the drawee bank between April 2nd and April 6th. There is a serious question as to whether the drawer of the check would not have been discharged by the delay in presentation. It was plaintiff's duty as the law stood in April 1954, to present the check promptly to the drawee, although Section 3-503 (2a) of the Uniform Commercial Code of April 6, 1953, P. L. 3, which became effective thereafter, provided that presentation within 30 days is presumed to be within a reasonable time. It is clear that defendants' obligation to plaintiffs would have been completely discharged if anything had happened during that period which made it impossible for drawee to pay the check through no fault of defendant. While we do not hold that it is necessarily negligent on the part of the holders not to present the check within the period when it would have operated as a discharge in the case of failure of the drawee, yet it has some bearing upon plaintiff's right to declare a forfeiture when the check was dishonored.

We do not know when the check was dishonored, except that it was sometime between April 6th when the check was deposited at plaintiff's bank and April 12th when plaintiffs' bank wrote to the plaintiffs that the drawee had returned the check marked "N.S.F." *It is to be noted that it is now the law under the code, section 3-802, that where a check is taken for an underlying obligation, here the obligation to pay the rent in cash, the obligation is suspended* pro tanto *until the presentation of the check.* This presumably was law in Pennsylvania before the code. (See Pennsylvania Bar Association notes, Section 3-802 of the code, 12-APS Section 3-802.) This would indicate that the crucial date is not earlier than April 12th since on the question of forfeiture we must take all intendments in favor of defendant. It may have been on any date up to April 11th for all we know. When we add to this the fact that a new and good check was forthcoming promptly upon notice, we do not believe that forfeiture should be decreed. This is a situation in which plaintiff's position is not even as strong as it was in *Feinstein v. Siskin et al.* (69 D. & C. 90, 1949) where the judgment of forfeiture was opened. We think the matter should be fully explored and the facts determined after a full hearing before a default judgment of forfeiture should be allowed to stand.

And now, January 27, 1955, the rule to open judgment is made absolute.

[This case was decided under the NIL.]

Mansion Carpets, Inc. v. Marinoff

1965, (N.Y.) 265 N.Y.S.2d 298

Per curiam. . . . Plaintiff sued to recover upon a check issued by defendants for carpeting and floor tile installed by plaintiff in defendants' residence. Defendants counterclaimed for breach of warranty based on work not encompassed by the check. At the time of trial, plaintiff's claim on the check had been reduced to $415 by payment made after suit was begun. In defense, defendants offered proof of failure of consideration. The jury found for plaintiff on the $415 claim and awarded defendants $200 on their counterclaim. There must be a new trial because of the *reversible error committed in instructing the jury that the check represented an unconditional promise to pay and was not subject to any defenses arising from claimed breaches of the contract pursuant to which payment was made by check.* The requirement of the Uniform Commercial Code, 3-104(1) (b) that a check contain an unconditional promise to pay applies only to the matter of the *form* of a negotiable instrument. *As between the original parties payment by check is conditional* (UCC 2-511); and if the instrument is dishonored, action may be maintained *on either the instrument or the obligation* (UCC 3-802 (1) (b). [Emphases added.] Want or failure of consideration is a defense as against any person not having the rights of a holder in due course (UCC 3-408). Although UCC

3-302 (2) states a payee may be a holder in due course, it is obvious that plaintiff herein does not fall within the category of the type of payee contemplated by that Section. Thus, the jury should have been permitted to consider defenses to the check based upon the original transaction. It would, however, be appropriate for defendants to amend their answer to plead failure of consideration as a defense. Moreover, the jury was apparently confused by the charge for it originally returned to announce a verdict for defendants on plaintiff's cause of action and for defendants on their counterclaim in the sum of $100. Only after the Trial Judge reiterated his direction that plaintiff was entitled to a verdict on the cause of action based on the check and sent the jury back for further deliberation, did the jury return with the verdict appealed from. In view of our conclusion as to the prejudicial effect of the erroneous charge, we are of the opinion that the interests of justice dictate a new trial as to defendants' counterclaims as well. Submission of the case on an erroneous theory may well have influenced the jury in its deliberations on the entire case.

Reversed and remanded for new trial.

In Re Eton Furniture Co.

1961, 286 F. 2d 93

The general manager of the Eton Furniture Company, Huntington, on several occasions borrowed money from the bank, giving his personal note to the bank, and arranged for the proceeds to be credited to Eton's account. When Eton's deposits produced a balance deemed to be sufficiently ample, the bank appropriated Eton's funds to pay off the loans. On November 6, 1957, Eton was adjudged a bankrupt and the trustee in bankruptcy asked for a turnover order against the bank alleging that the bank had in its possession $6,600 belonging to the bankrupt estate. The trustee contended that "the loans negotiated by Huntington from the bank, and for which he gave his personal notes to the bank were loans to Him and not to Eton." His position was that the money in the account was Eton's and that as an asset of the estate it should be turned over to him as trustee. The bank, in effect, contended that the loan was really to Eton and that the amount in the account, therefore, could be set off against Eton's deposit account thereby satisfying Eton's debt to the bank. The referee and the lower court held that the primary obligation was that of the company and ruled in favor of the bank.

BIGGS, C. J. . . . It was argued that Eton received the proceeds of the loans from Huntington and not from the Bank, and that therefore the satisfaction of the obligations from Eton's account with the Bank constituted an unjustified appropriation of Eton's funds by the Bank to pay the debts of another. . . .

The single issue which this court must determine is whether Eton was indebted to the Bank in the amounts of the loans negotiated by Huntington, its general manager. The trustee makes two arguments which we must consider. First, relying on Section 3-401 (1) of the Uniform Commercial Code, applicable in Pennsylvania, 12A P.S. Section 3-401 (1), he contends that *since Huntington's signature alone appears on the notes* given by him to the Bank, Huntington alone can be held liable by the Bank for repayment of the loans. Second, he argues that Huntington was not authorized to borrow money for Eton and that therefore, regardless of any understanding that may have existed between Huntington and the Bank, Eton, not being bound, could not be liable for repayment of the loans. . . .

Section 3-401 (1) provides that "[N]o person is liable on an instrument unless his signature appears thereon." On the basis of this provision the trustee contends that Eton, not having signed the notes given to the Bank, cannot be held liable for repayment of the loans. This argument finds no support in the words of the statute which provides merely that one who does not sign a note cannot be liable *on the note.* Contrary to the trustee's argument, the provision quoted cannot be read to mean that no person is liable on a debt whose signature does not appear on a note given as collateral security for that debt. Indeed, it has long been settled in Pennsylvania and elsewhere that the one to whom money is loaned or property advanced is liable for the debt regardless of the fact that his name may not appear on the security taken if that security was regarded by the parties purely as collateral. That Section 3-401 (1) was not intended to change this rule is demonstrated clearly by the comment to that section which states in pertinent part: "Nothing in this section is intended to prevent any liability arising apart from the instrument itself. The party who does not sign may still be liable on the original obligation for which the instrument was given—". . . .

In the present case, the evidence of Huntington, adopted "as verity" by the referee, similarly shows that the loans were for Eton's use, that the Bank, Eton and Huntington understood this to be so, and that the money was in fact used by the Company for its own benefit. We hold that the finding of the referee and that of the court below that the debts were incurred by Eton is supported by the evidence and that their rulings are in accordance with the applicable law. . . .

The judgment of the court below will be affirmed.

Dluge v. Robinson
1964 (Pa.) 204 A.2d 280

FLOOD, J.   This is an appeal from a judgment for the plaintiffs in an action against J. Robinson as endorser of two checks, brought by Isaac Dluge, the endorsee. The checks were dishonored by the drawee bank because of insufficient funds in the maker's account. Dluge died after instituting suit and the executors of his estate have been substituted as plaintiffs.

The complaint sets forth that immediately after the bank refused payment and returned the checks to Dluge, he returned them to the defendant with a demand for payment which the defendant refused. The defendant, both in his answer and on the witness stand, denied any demand for payment at the time Dluge returned the checks. When called by the plaintiffs for cross examination, Robinson testified that the checks had been returned to him by Dluge "for insufficient funds, to give them back to Mr. Wapner [the maker]" and that he turned them over to Wapner and never got them back. Wapner testified that he paid the amount of the checks to Dluge and then tore them up. The trial judge, who heard the case without a jury, overruled an objection to the admission of Wapner's testimony at the trial, but later reconsidered that ruling. Concluding that Wapner was an incompetent witness under the Dead Man's Act she excluded his testimony from consideration in reaching the decision that plaintiffs were entitled to recover on the checks.

If the plaintiffs [executors of Dluge estate] were holders in due course, they would have to prove only (1) that the defendant [Robinson] endorsed the checks and delivered them to Dluge, and (2) that they had been presented to the endorser for payment within a reasonable time. (Uniform Commercial Code, § 3-501(1) (b).) In the case of an uncertified check this is presumed to be within seven days after the endorsement. (U.C.C., § 3-503(1)(e), § 3-503(2)(b).)

> Presentment is a demand for acceptance or payment . . . by or on behalf of the holder. (U.C.C., § 3-504(1).)

The only evidence of any demand was the admission by defendant that he received a letter from Dluge's attorney demanding payment. The defendant did not state when he received this letter. The plaintiffs did not offer the letter in evidence and there is no way to determine from the record when it was sent except that it was presumably sent before the complaint was filed on September 12, 1960, seven months after the checks were dishonored by the drawee bank. Since the defendant denied any demand at the time the checks were returned to him, and the record is otherwise barren of any evidence of demand within seven days, or any reasonable time, after endorsement, the plaintiffs did not establish any right to recover even if they had been holders in due course.

The plaintiffs are not holders in due course. Dluge gave the checks to the defendant without any demand for payment, so far as the record shows, and was not in possession of them when the suit was brought. Therefore he was not the holder. "'Holder' means a person who is in possession of a document of title or an instrument or an investment security drawn, issued or endorsed to him or to his order or to bearer or in blank." (U.C.C., § 1-201(20).) A fortiori, he was not a holder in due course. (U.S.C., § 3-302(1).)

The plaintiffs argue that they may nevertheless recover from the defendant, as the endorser of a "lost" check owned by them, under § 3-804 of the Uniform Commercial Code. This section provides: "The owner of an instrument which is lost, whether by destruction, theft or otherwise, may maintain an action in his own name and recover from any party liable thereon upon due proof of his ownership, the facts which prevent his production of the instrument and its terms. . . ."

There is, however, neither allegation nor proof that the checks were destroyed, stolen, or otherwise lost. If the plaintiffs had proved that Dluge had returned the checks with a demand for payment, or that they later demanded that defendant return the checks, they might argue that his failure either to pay or return them constituted a theft or a *conversion*. (U.C.C., § 3-419.) There was no evidence of such demand and therefore no proof of conversion or theft. The maker, Wapner, testified that he paid Dluge and then destroyed the checks. This testimony was stricken from the record, following the plaintiffs' objection. Therefore there is no evidence in the record of the destruction of the checks. Finally, there is no evidence that they were otherwise lost. "A note cannot be considered to have been lost so as to permit action on it as a lost note if the party in possession of it is known to plaintiff and the ownership is in dispute." (54 C.J.S. Lost Instruments § 1.) "An article is 'lost' when the owner has lost the possession or custody of it, involuntarily and by any means, but more particularly by accident or his own negligence or forgetfulness, and when he is ignorant of its whereabouts or cannot recover it by an ordinary diligent search." (*Black's Law Dictionary*, 4th ed., p. 1096 and cases cited.)

Moreover, to recover under § 3-804 of the Code, the plaintiffs must prove ownership of the checks. Such proof of ownership must be clear and convincing. In the absence of possession, ownership would usually depend upon proof that the holder did not voluntarily surrender possession unless he did so conditionally upon payment of the checks. Surrender of the checks to a prior party, without payment, and without even a demand for payment, tells against the retention of ownership, and indicates, if anything, an intention not to hold such party liable on the instrument. (Cf. U.C.C., § 3-605(1)(b).)

The plaintiffs did not prove that the checks were "lost" as that word is used in § 3-804 of the Code, or that they were still the owners of the checks when suit was brought. More importantly, there is no proof of *demand for payment* by the plaintiffs when the checks were returned to the defendant. Plaintiffs have therefore failed to prove their right to recover against Robinson whether they are holders or owners of the checks.

The burden upon one not a holder who seeks to recover on a negotiable instrument is a heavy one. The plaintiffs have not sustained it. They must recover, if at all, upon the underlying obligation for which the checks were given.

Judgment reversed and entered for the defendant n.o.v. [Notwithstanding the verdict.]

CHAPTER 25
REVIEW QUESTIONS AND PROBLEMS

1. *M* executed a check to the order of *P* on June 15. *P* indorsed to *A* on June 18 and *A* indorsed to *B* on June 21. *B* presented the check to the drawee bank on July 30. The check was dishonored. What are *B*'s rights?

2. *M* made a note payable to the order of *P*. *P* indorsed to *A*; *A* indorsed to *B*; *B* indorsed to *H*. *H* presented the note to *M* who refused to pay. *H* promptly notified *B* of the dishonor. What should *B* do upon receipt of this notice?

3. *A* performed services for *P* and gave him in payment a third party note of which *P* was payee. *P* indorsed the note to *A* "without recourse." If the note is not paid, does *A* have any remedy against *P*?

4. *A* drew a check in favor of *B* as payee. *B* delayed in presenting the check to the drawee bank, and upon presentation the check was returned to him marked "insufficient funds." Can *B* hold *A* liable on the check? Would *B* be required to give notice of dishonor to *A*?

5. *M* draws a demand bill of exchange upon *D* in favor of *P*. *P* holds the bill for six months and then negotiates it to *A*. *A* holds the bill for a year and then negotiates it to *H*, who immediately presents it to *D*. *D* is insolvent and unable to pay. Upon giving proper notice of dishonor, may *H* recover from either *P* or *M*?

6. *A* is the holder of a bill of exchange drawn by *X* on *Y*. *A* presents the instruments to *Y* for the acceptance and *Y* refuses to accept. What should *A* do to protect his rights? May he wait until the bill matures before taking any action?

7. *A* executed a note in favor of *B*. The note was indorsed by *B* to the holder. Prior to the maturity of the note, *A* became insolvent and for this reason the holder did not present the note to *A* for payment. Is *B* relieved of his liability as an indorser?

8. *A* executed a note in favor of *B*, the note containing an automatic acceleration clause. Several days after the event which accelerated payment had occurred, the holder of the note presented it to *A* for payment. Payment was refused. Can the holder look to *B* as indorser?

9. Contractor mailed a check to Subcontractor in payment for work performed. Subcontractor contended that check was not in proper amount and so notified Contractor. After repeated efforts to contact Contractor, Subcontractor mailed the check back, but the letter was returned unopened. Contractor claims that failure to promptly present the check for payment discharged his liability. Is this correct?

10. *X* Corporation borrowed money from *Y*, and the president of *X* Corporation indorsed the note. When the note fell due, *Y* extended the time of payment. Thereafter *X* Corporation became bankrupt and *Y* sought to recover from the president. Should he succeed?

11. *A* Bank sued *C*, accommodation indorser, on a renewal note. *C* contended that there was no consideration for the note because the bank had not cancelled the old notes. Is *C*'s contention correct?

12. *A* is the maker of a note drawn in favor of *B*. *B* indorses to *C*, and *C* indorses to *H*. *H* presents the note to *A* and receives a worthless check in payment. Is the note discharged?

13. *H* is the holder of a negotiable bill of exchange upon which there are six indorsers. *H* desires to release the fourth on the list. If he does, what will be the effect?

14. *H* holds a negotiable note upon which there are three indorsers. The maker is unable to pay it at maturity and desires additional time. *H* consents to give him an additional thirty days in which to make payment. At the end of thirty days the note is not paid. Assuming that *H* made proper presentment and gave notice of dishonor at the maturity date, may he recover from the indorsers?

15. *A* is a co-maker with *M* of a negotiable note, although he is merely acting as surety. This fact is known to the holder. Do the rules of suretyship apply?

16. At the office of a real estate broker *X*, *M* gave his negotiable note and mortgage to *P* in return for the conveyance of land. *M* paid annual interest on the note to the broker *X* under *P*'s instructions. A year later, *P* assigned the note to *H* but did not deliver the same. Thereafter *M* paid all the principal and interest in a lump sum to *X*, *X* retaining possession of the note. *X* absconded with the payments. Whose loss?

chapter 26

Bank Deposits
and Collections

3-126 Introduction. Article 4 of the Uniform Commercial Code is entitled "Bank Deposits and Collections." It is not possible in this text to
consider in detail the numerous provisions of this Article. Attention is
directed rather to those provisions which most closely relate to the law of
commercial paper, particularly checks.

Article 4 provides uniform rules to govern the collection of checks and
other instruments for the payment of money. It also sets forth rules which
govern the relationship of banks with depositors in the collection and payment of "items." (An item is any instrument for the payment of money
whether it is negotiable or not.) This Article covers items which are also
within Article 3—Commercial Paper, and Article 8—Investment Securities. In the event of a conflict the provisions of Article 4 govern those of
Article 3, but the provisions of Article 8 govern those of Article 4.

The significance of Article 4 is set forth in the comment to the first
section:

> The tremendous number of checks handled by banks and the country-wide
> nature of the bank collection process require uniformity in the law of bank
> collections. Individual Federal Reserve banks process as many as 1,000,000
> items a day; large metropolitan banks average 300,000 a day; banks with less
> than $5,000,000 on deposit handle from 1,000 to 2,000 daily. There is needed
> a uniform statement of the principal rules of the bank collection process with
> ample provision for flexibility to meet the needs of the large volume handled
> and the changing needs and conditions that are bound to come with the years.
>
> The American Bankers Association Bank Collection Code, enacted in eight-
> een states, has stated many of the bank collection rules that have developed,
> and more recently Deferred Posting statutes have developed and varied further

rules. With items flowing in great volume not only in and around metropolitan and smaller centers but also continuously across state lines and back and forth across the entire country, a proper situation exists for uniform rules that will state in modern concepts at least some of the rights of the parties and in addition aid this flow and not interfere with its progress.

This Article adopts many of the rules of the American Bankers Association Code that are still in current operation, the principles and rules of the Deferred Posting and other statutes, codifies some rules established by court decisions and in addition states certain patterns and procedures that exist even though not heretofore covered by statute.

Article 4 does not substantially change the law in the banking area. In the main it codifies existing case law, statutes, and banking and commercial practices. Article 4 is flexible in that, within certain limits, the provisions of the Article can be varied by agreement between the depositor and his bank. Likewise the banks in the chain of collection of an item can make special agreements. The Code specifies that Federal Reserve Regulations and operating letters, clearing house rules, and the like are part of each agreement.

The typical banking transaction involving the collection checks has been described previously (See Section *3-64*) wherein the steps in the process were traced. Following a discussion of certain basic concepts, the various aspects of banking as related primarily to checks will be discussed: first, from the standpoint of the relationships between a bank (depositary bank) in which a check is deposited by a holder and *collecting* banks through whose hands the check passes on its way to the bank upon which it was drawn—the drawee or payor bank. As previously noted, the check may have been handled by a number of *intermediary* banks in this process before it is finally presented to the payor bank by the *presenting* bank at which time the payor bank will be required to take some action—either pay the check or dishonor it and return it.

The second subject to be treated will be the obligations and responsibilities of the payor bank, and the last will be the nature of the relationship between a bank and its customers.

Certain initial observations will aid in understanding this material. It will be recalled that as provided in Article 3, a holder of a check should present it to the drawee-payor bank or initiate the collection process without delay; that a check becomes "stale" after 30 days; and that to charge indorsers, presentment must be made within 7 days. Since "timing" is very important, there are two time elements which are stressed: (1) A *banking day* means "that part of any day on which a bank is open to the public for carrying on substantially all of its banking functions." A bank is permitted to establish a "cut-off" hour of 2 P.M. or later in order that the bank may have an opportunity "to process items, prove balances and make the necessary entries to determine its position for the day." If an item is received after the cut-off hour, if one be fixed, or after the close of the banking day, it may be treated as having been received at the opening of the next banking day. (2) *Midnight deadline* with respect to a bank means midnight on its next banking day following the banking day on which the bank receives the check or notice with regard to it.

Another important term is "clearing house," which means an association of banks which engages in the clearing or settling of accounts between banks in connection with checks.

A customer who deposits an item for collection should indorse it, but it happens quite frequently that a customer overlooks doing so. The depositary bank *may* supply the missing indorsement. If the bank states on the item that it was deposited by a customer or credited to his account, such a statement is effective as the customer's indorsement. This is a practical rule intended to speed up the collection process by making it unnecessary to return to the depositor any items he may have failed to indorse.[C1]

3-127 Collection of Items: Depositary and Collecting Banks. The collection process is initiated when the customer deposits a check in his account; his account is credited by the bank at that time. The check then passes through the collecting banks, each of which credits the account of the prior bank (or remits to that bank) and finally when the check reaches the payor (drawee) bank, that bank debits the drawer's account. The payor bank then credits the account of the presenting bank, remits to it, or if both belong to the same clearing house, includes the check in its balance there. Transactions prior to this final settlement by the payor bank are called "provisional settlements" because, until final settlement it is not known whether the check is "good." If the payor bank honors the check, the settlement is final; if it dishonors the check, each provisional settlement is *revoked* and the depositary bank which had given its provisional credit to the customer for the deposit cancels it.

Unless a contrary intent clearly appears, a collecting bank is an agent or subagent for the owner of a check.[C2] As a practical matter, the continuing agency status of the bank until its settlement is or becomes final is important in that the depositor bears the risk of loss as owner of the check in the event of nonpayment of the check or insolvency of one of the collecting banks before final settlement. The original depositor thus continues to be the owner of the check until it is paid by the bank upon which it is drawn and final settlement is made to the depositary bank in which he has his account.

Responsibility for collection.[C3] When a bank has received a check for collection, the Code imposes upon it the duty to use ordinary care in performing its collection operations.[1] These operations include presenting the check or forwarding it for presentment, sending notice of dishonor or nonpayment or returning the check after learning that it has not been paid, and settling for the check when it receives final payment.

[1] *Hydrocarbon Processing Corp. v. Chemical Bank,* page 567.

[C1] *U.C.C.* 4-205.
[C2] *U.C.C.* 4-201.
[C3] *U.C.C.* 4-202.

Should the collecting bank fail to use ordinary care in handling a check or other item, the depositor can recover damages from such bank.

The Code also contains provisions with reference to the time within which the collecting bank should perform the above mentioned operations. If the bank takes proper action before its "midnight deadline" following receipt of an item, notice, or payment, it has acted seasonably. Thus if a collecting bank receives a check on Monday and presents it or forwards to the next collecting bank any time prior to midnight Tuesday, it has acted seasonably.

A limited extension of these time limits is allowed. A collecting bank may allow a period not in excess of one additional banking day in a good faith effort to obtain payment of an item. Such extension does not discharge secondary parties nor does it impose any liability on the transferor or any prior party.

Warranties of customer and collecting bank.[C4] Each customer or collecting bank who obtains payment or acceptance of an item makes certain warranties to the payor bank. These warranties made by customers and collecting banks are in general the same as those provided in Article 3–Commercial Paper with reference to warranties on presentment and transfer.

Security interest of collecting bank.[C5] A security interest is an interest in personal property which gives protection by way of an interest in such property to guarantee payment or performance of an obligation. The Code recognizes the right of a bank in the collection process to claim a security interest in an item or its proceeds to protect the bank, with respect to advances and payments it has made in connection with the item, as against the depositor and his creditors. Where an item has been deposited in an account the bank has a security interest to the extent that withdrawals have been made against the credit. This is true even though the depositary bank does not own the item—it may nevertheless hold the item as security as against the depositor or his creditors.

Where the item has not been *deposited* in an account but has, for example, been *discounted* and the bank has given credit to the transferor which is available for withdrawal, the bank also has a security interest.[2]

The security interest exists even though the credit is not actually drawn upon and the bank has a right to charge back in the event of dishonor of the item.

Likewise, a security interest is given when the bank makes an advance to its customer against an item which has been deposited.

Where a single credit is given for several items, such as a number of checks, the security interest on all of the deposited items continues though only a part of the credit given is withdrawn. In determining whether there has been a withdrawal against a particular credit the Code

---

2 *Citizens Natl. Bk. of Englewood v. Fort Lee S. & L.*, page 569.

C4 *U.C.C.* 4-207.   C5 *U.C.C.* 4-208.

provides that "credits first given are first withdrawn." This is often referred to as the "first in, first out rule."

The security interest continues until the bank receives a final settlement or surrenders the instrument for purposes other than collection.

Collecting bank as holder in due course.[C6] The Code provides that for purposes of determining the status of a bank as a holder in due course, a security interest constitutes value. Thus, if a bank satisfies the other requirements as set forth in Article 3, it can qualify as a holder in due course and can enforce an instrument even though its depositor or other transferor could not.[3] In this connection it is to be noted that an intermediary bank or a payor bank which is not a depositary bank is not affected by a restrictive indorsement except that of the bank's immediate transferor. Notice of claim or defense is not imparted by such indorsement. Depositary banks, however, may be liable to the owner of an item who had indorsed it restrictively.

Right of charge-back or refund.[C7] If an item has been dishonored, as in the case of an "N.S.F." check, the presenting bank will revoke its "provisional settlement" and charge the item back to the account of the next prior collecting bank. Likewise, other banks in the chain of collection will charge back. The final step is a charge-back to the customer's account by the depositary bank. Each of the collecting banks must return the item or send notification of the facts by its midnight deadline. The right to charge back by the depositary bank is not affected by the fact that the depositor may have drawn against the provisional credit.

Final payment of item by a payor bank.[C8] The Code sets forth the rules for determining the point of time at which an item is finally *paid* by a payor bank; when provisional debits and credits become *final*; and when credits become *available for withdrawal*. As stated in the Comment: ". . . final payment of an item is the 'end of the line' in the collection process and the 'turn around' point commencing the return flow of proceeds."

A depositor does not have the right to draw against uncollected funds. Accordingly, he is not entitled to draw against an item payable by another bank until the provisional settlement which his depositary bank has received becomes final.

Where the deposit is an item *on which the depositary bank is itself the payor* ("on us" items), the credit becomes final on the second banking day following receipt of the item.

Insolvency and preference.[C9] The Code section on problems resulting from the failure of a bank in the collection process is applicable only to state banks. Practically, the Federal Deposit Insurance Regulation that each owner of a collection item, for the payment of which a closed bank has become obligated will be recognized as a depositor of the closed bank, has greatly diminished the significance of this problem.

---

3 *Sandler v. United Industrial Bank,* page 571.

C6 *U.C.C.* 4-209.   C8 *U.C.C.* 4-213.
C7 *U.C.C.* 4-212.   C9 *U.C.C.* 4-214.

3-128 Collection of items: Payor banks. The previous section has dealt with depositary and collecting banks in the collection process. This section treats *payor* banks.

        Deferred posting: recovery of payments by return of items: time of dishonor.[C10]   When an item is presented to a payor bank for payment *over the counter,* it must be paid or dishonored before the close of business on the day of presentment. Most items, however, will be presented through a clearing house or by mail and the payor bank will make a *provisional settlement* for them on the day they are received. In this event, it has until final payment of the check but not later than midnight deadline on the following day to decide whether or not the item is good. Within this time the bank may revoke the settlement and return the item or, if this is not possible, send written notice of dishonor or nonpayment. This enables the bank to defer posting as described in the following comment:

> Deferred posting and delayed returns is that practice whereby a payor bank sorts and proves items received by it on the day they are received, e.g. Monday, but does not post the items to the customer's account or return "not good" items until the next day, e.g. Tuesday. The practice typifies "production line" methods currently used in bank collection and is based upon the necessity of an even flow of items through payor banks on a day by day basis in a manner which can be handled evenly by employee personnel without abnormal peak load periods, night work, and other practices objectionable to personnel. Since World War II statutes authorizing deferred posting and delayed returns have been passed in almost all of the forty-eight states. This section codifies the content of these statutes and approves the practice.

Where a check drawn by one customer of a bank is *deposited by another customer* of the same bank for credit on its books, the bank may return the item and revoke any credit given at any time on the following day. If the payor bank decides that such check should not be paid, it has a sufficient time in which to return the check to its customer or send him notice of dishonor.

        Responsibility for late return.[C11]   The foregoing relates to the time limits within which a bank must take action when it receives an item drawn on it or payable by it. This section relates to the rights of the owner of a check who deposited an item if a bank *fails to take action* within the prescribed time limits. A payor bank may be held accountable to the person who deposited a check although the check is not paid and the drawer of the check did not have sufficient funds to cover it. This liability is imposed if (1) the bank retains a check presented to it by another bank beyond midnight of the day of receipt without settling for it or (2) does not pay or return the check or send notice of dishonor within the period of its midnight deadline.[4] If the payor bank is also the depositary bank, i.e., the check deposited by the customer is one

---

4 *Rock Island Auction Sales v. Empire Packing Co.,* page 572.

C10 *U.C.C.* 4-301.   C11 *U.C.C.* 4-302.

which is drawn on his bank, settlement on the day of receipt is not required, but the bank must return the check or send notice of dishonor before its midnight deadline. Thus failure on the part of the payor bank to take the necessary action within the proper time renders it liable to the depositor even though the check was not properly payable.

Notice, stop orders, legal process or set-off, order of payment.[C12] Following the receipt of a check the payor bank must process it. This involves a series of acts which are initiated by receipt of the check from the clearing house, by mail, or over the counter. The check passes to the sorting and proving departments after which it may be photographed. It then moves to the bookkeeping department where it is examined as to form and signature. Here it is determined also whether the drawer's account is sufficient to cover it. If it is found to be proper in all respects it will be posted to the drawer's account. The entire process may require considerable time and may extend into the next banking day.

During the period of processing or prior thereto, the payor bank may receive notice or acquire knowledge concerning the check or other item. Such knowledge or notice may be that the drawer has filed a petition in bankruptcy; that the drawer has stopped payment on a check; that the drawer's account has been attached by a creditor. These circumstances raise questions as to (1) when stop order becomes effective so that the bank is under a duty to refuse to pay the check and (2) when an attachment is effective so as to preclude the bank from paying checks which are drawn on the account. The payor bank is in somewhat of a dilemma because if it disregards the attachment or other legal proceedings or stop order and honors the checks, the attaching creditor or trustee in bankruptcy[5] or the customer who placed the stop order may seek to impose liability upon the bank. By the same token, if the bank *refuses* to honor the checks, the owners who are seeking to collect on them may claim that payment was effected prior to the time when the stop order, attachment, or other legal notice became effective. A related problem is that of a set-off by a bank whereby the bank charges its customer's account to satisfy an obligation owed by the customer to the bank. When does the set-off (or stop order, legal process, or notice) come too late to prevent payment and the charge to the customer's account? Under prior law the position of a bank was uncertain due to the fact that the court decisions on this subject were in conflict.

The Code provides definite rules to govern situations involving any notice, stop order, legal process, or any set-off exercised by the bank;[6] provides that any notice or stop order received by a bank, or any legal process such as attachment served on it, or any set-off exercised by the bank, comes too late to prevent payment of a check by the bank if the bank has done any one of the following:

---

[5] *Bank of Marin v. England,* page 574.
[6] *Gibbs v. Gerberich,* page 576.

[C12] *U.C.C.* 4-303.

(1) accepted or certified the item,

(2) paid the item in cash,

(3) settled for the item without reserving or having the right to revoke the settlement,

(4) completed the posting of the check to the customer's account or otherwise has evidenced its *decision* to pay the check by examining the customer's account and has taken some action to indicate in *intention to pay.*

(5) become liable for the check or other item because of failure to settle for or return the check in time.[C13]

Clearly, if a bank has paid a check in *cash,* an attachment of the drawer's account, for example, would come too late, and the funds represented by that check would not be available to the attaching creditor. Such attachment would also come too late if the bank has prior thereto indicated its *decision* to pay a check presented to it for payment, or completed its posting process. Thus a check may well be considered as beyond the reach of an attachment or stop order even though it has not yet been literally "paid." The check may still be subject to return by the payor bank to the collecting bank, but for these other purposes it is treated as paid. It is to be expected that the use of central computers in connection with banking functions will present some problems on the question of when a check is paid.

Still another problem relates to the *order of payment* of checks. The Code provides that there is no priority as among checks drawn on a particular account and presented to a bank on any particular day. The account on which the checks are drawn may not have a sufficient balance to pay all of these checks. As a result some of the checks will be dishonored and others will be paid and charged to the customer's account. The checks and other items ". . . may be accepted, paid, certified or charged to the indicated account of its customer in any order convenient to the bank." The unfortunate owners to whom checks were returned "N.S.F." (not sufficient funds) will not have recourse against the drawee bank on the ground that other checks received by the bank on the same day were honored and paid while their checks were not honored.

3-129 Relationship Between Payor Bank and Its Customer. Several important problems arise in connection with the rights, duties, and obligations as between a bank and its customer.[7] Previous sections have treated the collection of items with reference to the relationships between depositary and collecting banks and the role of payor banks. This section deals with the relationships between *payor* bank and customer.

When bank may charge customer's account.[C14]   It is basic to the banking function that upon proper payment of a draft or check the drawee (payor bank) may charge the account of the drawer (customer).

---

[7] *Stone & Webster Engineering Corp. v. First National Bank & Trust Co.,* page 578.

[C13] *U.C.C.* 4-303.   [C14] *U.C.C.* 4-401.

This fundamental proposition applies even though the check or draft is an *overdraft,* since the check itself authorizes the payment for the drawer's account and carries with it an implied promise to reimburse the drawee.[8] The Code specifically grants the bank the right to charge its customer's account with any check otherwise properly payable even though such charge creates an overdraft.

It will be recalled that Article 3–Commercial Paper contains a provision protecting a *holder in due course* against the personal defense of discharge by reason of material alteration and permits him to enforce the instrument according to its original tenor. Likewise, protection is afforded to a *drawee* who pays a subsequently completed instrument in good faith according to the instrument as completed. These concepts are applied to the banking situation so that if a bank in good faith makes payment to a holder it may charge the account of its customer according to (1) the original tenor of the altered check or (2) the tenor of a completed item. Thus, if a check is raised, the bank can charge its customer's account with the original amount of the check. In addition, if a person signs his name to a check in blank and loses it, after which an unauthorized person completes it and it is paid by the drawee bank, the bank may charge the customer's account the full amount of such check, if it pays in good faith and does not know that the completion was improper. A bank is not liable simply because an employer misuses funds obtained from cashing a check.[9]

Wrongful dishonor—bank's liability to customer.[C15] A bank is under a duty to honor checks drawn by its customers when there are sufficient funds in his account to cover the checks. If a bank wrongfully dishonors a check, it is liable in damages to its customer for damages proximately caused by the wrongful dishonor.

The Code both defines the extent of a bank's liability to its customers for wrongful dishonor and specifies the damages which may be recovered. When the dishonor occurs by mistake, as distinguished from malicious or willful dishonor, liability is limited to the *actual damages* proved. Provision is also made for *consequential* damages proximately caused by the wrongful dishonor and may include damages for arrest or prosecution of the customer. The Code rejects decisions which have held that if the dishonored item were drawn by a merchant he is defamed in his business because of the reflection on his credit and accordingly could recover substantial damages on the basis of defamation per se without proof of actual damages.

Customer's right to stop payment.[C16] The Code provides that a customer has the right to stop payment on checks drawn on his account. Only the drawer has this right—it does not extend to holders— payees or indorsees. In order to be effective such order must be "received at such time and in such manner as to afford the bank a reasonable op-

---

[8] *National Bank of Slatington v. Derhammer,* page 580.
[9] *Peoples Savings Bank et al. v. Playdium Lanes, Inc.,* page 582.

[C15] *U.C.C.* 4-202.   [C16] *U.C.C.* 4-403.

portunity to act on it prior to an action by the bank with respect to the item. . . ."

If a check has been certified, the depositor cannot stop payment whether he, or the payee, procured the certification.[10]

The Code provides that an oral stop order is binding on the bank for only 14 days unless confirmed in writing within that period. A written order is effective for only six months unless renewed in writing.

If a bank pays a check upon which payment has been stopped, it will be liable to its customer for resulting damages. However, the burden is on the customer to prove the fact and amount of loss. If the customer cannot prove that he has suffered a loss he cannot recover against the bank for paying the check.

If the stop order agreement contains a provision relieving the bank from responsibility for *negligently* disregarding a stop order, such provision is invalid under the Code.

Stale checks. The Code provides that a bank is not *obligated* to pay a check that is over six months old. The bank, however, is entitled to pay a check which has been outstanding more than six months and may charge it to the customer's account.

Certified checks do not fall within the six months rule—they are the primary obligation of the certifying bank and the obligation runs directly to the holder of the check.

Death or incompetence of customer. As a general proposition the death or incompetency of a person terminates the authority of others to act on his behalf. If this principle were applied to banks, a tremendous burden would be imposed upon them to verify the continued life and competency of drawers. Accordingly, the Code provides that the death of a customer does not revoke the bank's authority to pay checks drawn by him until the bank knows of the death and has a reasonable opportunity to act on it. The same rule applies to an adjudication of incompetency.

Even though the bank knows of the death of its customer it *may* pay or certify checks for a period of ten days after the date of his death. This is intended to permit holders of checks drawn and issued shortly after death to cash them without the necessity of filing a claim in probate. This is subject to the proviso that a stop order may be made by a relative or other person who claims an interest in the account.

Duty of customer to bank.[C17] A bank generally makes available to its customer a statement of his account and his cancelled checks. The customer is under a duty to examine his bank statement and cancelled checks for forgeries of his signature and for raised checks, within a reasonable time after they are returned to him or made available to him. He is further obligated to report any irregularities to the bank. While the bank does not have the right to charge his account with forged checks, the customer's failure to examine and notify will prevent him from assert-

[10] *Malphrus v. Home Savings Bank of City of Albany,* page 583.

[C17] *U.C.C.* 4-406.

ing the forgery (or alteration) against the bank, if the bank can establish that it suffered a loss because of this failure. Thus, the bank may be able to prove that a prompt notification would have enabled the bank to recover from the forger.

The Code does not specify the period of time within which the customer must report forgeries or alterations, but it does specify that if the same wrongdoer commits successive forgeries or alterations, the customer's failure to examine and notify within a period not to exceed fourteen days after the first item and statement were available to him, will bar him from asserting the forgeries or alterations of subsequent checks by the same person paid by the bank in good faith. This rule is intended to prevent the wrongdoer from having the opportunity to repeat his misdeeds. If the customer can establish that the bank itself was *negligent* in paying a forged or altered item, the bank cannot avail itself of a defense based upon the customer's failure to promptly examine and report.[11]

A customer is precluded from asserting a forged signature or alteration on a check after one year from the time the check and statement are made available to him even though the bank is negligent. Forged indorsement must be reported within three years. If a payor bank as a matter of policy or public relations waives its defense of tardy notification by its customer, it cannot thereafter hold the collecting bank or any prior party for the forgery.

Subrogation rights of payor bank.[C18]   In some situations a payor bank is subrogated to or takes over the rights of other parties in order to prevent unjust enrichment and to prevent loss to the bank by reason of its payment of a check or other item. This right arises in those cases where the bank has made an improper payment such as a payment in violation of a stop order. Three aspects of a payor bank's subrogation rights are important.

(1) The bank is subrogated to the rights of any holder in due course on the item against the drawer. When a bank is sued for wrongful payment over a stop order, it can assert the defense that its customer, the drawer, did not suffer a loss because he would have been liable to a holder in due course whether the stop order was obeyed or not. Thus, even if payment had been stopped, the drawer would have had to make good to a holder in due course. To the extent necessary the Code places the bank in the position of such holder as against the drawer.

(2) The bank is subrogated to the rights of the payee or any other holder of the item against the drawer, customer. This relates to rights of the payee in the check or his rights under the transaction for which the check was issued. Again, assuming payment of a check over a stop order, the payee may have received the check in payment for defective goods. If the drawer retains the goods he is probably obliged to pay at least a part of the agreed price. If the bank has paid the check, it is subrogated to the

---

[11] *Jackson v. First National Bank of Memphis, Inc.*, page 585.

[C18] *U.C.C.* 4-407.

payee's claim against the drawer for a portion of the contract price and can recoup its loss to this extent.

(3) The bank is subrogated to the rights of the drawer against the payee or any other holder in connection with the transaction which gave rise to the item. Here the bank, having improperly paid a check, takes over the rights of its own customer—the drawer—against the payee. If the drawer had been defrauded by the payee, for example, the bank, upon reimbursing the drawer, is subrogated to the latter's right to get back his money from the fraudulent payee.

BANK DEPOSITS AND COLLECTIONS CASES

Hydrocarbon Processing Corp. v. Chemical Bank N.Y.T. Co.

1965. 16 N.Y.2d 147, 262 N.Y.S.2d 482

The plaintiff sold goods to a customer in Cuba and drew a sight draft on the customer in order to obtain payment. The draft was deposited with the defendant bank for collection in September, 1959. It forwarded the draft to a Cuban bank, Continental Cubano, (Banco) and that bank obtained the funds. However, the Cuban bank was nationalized—taken over by the Cuban government—and the nationalization decree merged the banks assets and liabilities into Banco Nacional de Cuba, (Nacional) which is wholly owned, dominated and controlled by the Republic of Cuba. The same decree nationalized the Cuban Electric Company (Electric), a Florida Corporation operating as a public utility in Cuba, which, at the time of nationalization, was indebted to the defendant bank, Chemical Bank, on matured loans totalling $750,000. In November of 1960, the defendant bank received a cable from the Whitney National Bank of New Orleans, Louisiana, instructing it to charge Whitney's account, maintained with the defendant, in the sum of $38,607.43, and to credit Banco with a like amount at the defendant's branch office in London, England. The defendant complied and then, on its own initiative, (1) charged the Banco account in London for $38,607.43, credited the same amount to Nacional at its main office, and (2) charged the $38,607.43 against Nacional as an offset against Electric's debt to itself. In other words, by treating Electric, Banco, and Nacional as a single entity (Cuba) as a result of the nationalization, the defendant secured payment of a portion of Electric's debt to itself.

The plaintiff, Hydrocarbon Processing Corp., claims that the defendant had no right to offset the Banco credit against the Electric debt; that the plaintiff does have such a right; and that the defendant, as the plaintiff's agent for collection, was obligated to either set off for the plaintiff or to give the plaintiff notice of the Banco credit so that the plaintiff might act for itself. Plaintiff claims that failure to give this notice makes defendant liable for the amount of the draft. The lower court ruled in favor of the plaintiff and defendant appealed.

DYE, J. . . . The effect of the Cuban nationalization and the propriety of the defendant's act in appropriating the Banco credit to the Electric debt are irrelevant to the present question. The parties stipulated that payment by Banco to the defendant was subject to the prior approval of the Currency Stabilization Fund in Cuba. If the situation is to be altered as a result of the nationalization, it must be because the nationalization, in fact, nullified the possibility of obtaining the export permit and merged, as the parties agreed it did, all the assets and liabilities of Banco into Nacional.

If this be the case, then Electric, whose assets and liabilities were assumed by the same act, also became part of the same entity. In short, the plaintiff cannot take advantage of the confiscation to reach an otherwise unavailable Banco fund, and at the same time disown it to prevent the defendant from doing the same thing. Moreover, if the defendant acted improperly in appropriating the Banco credit, that wrong was a wrong against Banco or Cuba, and they are not parties to this suit. If the plaintiff is to recover from the defendant, it must show that the defendant, in its role as an agent for collection, breached a duty which it owed to the plaintiff, and it is of no avail to merely show that the defendant has improperly appropriated an unrelated fund.

A collecting bank owes its principal "ordinary care" in the discharge of its duty . . . (Uniform Commercial Code, 4-202). It is responsible for presenting an item or sending it for presentment, sending notice of dishonor or nonpayment or nonacceptance, settling for an item, making necessary protest, and notifying its transferor of any loss or delay in transit within a reasonable time after discovery thereof (Uniform Commercial Code 4-202). The defendant bank fulfilled these requirements and, subject thereto, subdivision (3) of Section 4-202 of the Code provides that "a bank is not liable for the insolvency, neglect, misconduct, mistake or default of another bank or person or for loss or destruction of an item in transit or in the possession of others."

Since drafts do not, of themselves, operate as an assignment of the funds of the drawee in the hands of a third party, . . . it remains only to consider whether an extra-statutory obligation is properly applicable to these funds in the defendant's hands or whether the defendant's conduct with respect to these funds constitutes less than "ordinary care" within the meaning of Section 4-202 of the Code. Numerous factors militate against such a holding. As was pointed out in the dissenting opinion below, "To so hold would in effect prevent any collecting bank from doing its routine business if, by the law of the sovereignty having jurisdiction over it, it is prevented from remitting after the collection of a draft. Such a holding would (not) be conducive to free international commercial intercourse." More significant difficulties are readily perceived. Each bank in the collecting chain would, in effect, become a guarantor of the draft—at least to the extent that they had possession of, or access to, other funds of a prior party who received payment. Due care for the protection of their own financial dealings with a drawee would often impel them to decline a part in the collection process, to say nothing of the difficulties inherent in correlating every collection item with their own accounts. The collection process does not lend itself to such a conclusion and cases have so held (cases cited). Nor is this a case in which the facts tend to establish collusion or bad faith by the defendant. . . . In *Thack v. First Nat. Bank,* (206 F.2d. 183), the court stated the principle thusly:

> "Although, as collecting agent for the drafts, the appellee bank owed appellants the duty of due diligence, good faith, and impartiality, appellee was not necessarily precluded thereby from collecting its own debt by lawful means, so long as it was guilty of no bad faith. It owed appellants no duty to notify them that it was also a creditor of (the drawee) unless suppression of that fact would amount to bad faith, which, in the circumstances here present, it does not. Having acted in good faith and with due diligence in the performance of its duties as collecting agent, and being unable to pay appellants' drafts because the drawee had not accepted them, appellee was at liberty to apply (the drawee's) available funds to the payment of his debt to the bank."

So in the present case, there is no question but that the appellant bank acted properly throughout the collection process and that the fund in dispute came into their possession in "good faith" through a transaction unrelated to the agency relationship. If, then, the defendant could properly apply the money to its own debt, at least as opposed to the plaintiff, there would be no purpose in requiring the bank to notify the plaintiff of the funds' existence, and no liability would flow from the failure to do so.

The order of the Appellate Division should be reversed, with costs in this court and in the Appellate Division, and judgment entered in favor of the defendant.

Citizens National Bank of Englewood v. Fort Lee Savings and Loan Association et al.

1965 New Jersey 213 A.2d 315

This is an action to recover monies advanced against a check which was deposited with the plaintiff, Citizens National Bank, for collection, but was later dishonored. One George Winter had agreed to sell a house in Fort Lee to defendant Jean Amoroso and her husband. On the same day Amoroso requested her bank, Fort Lee Savings and Loan Association, to issue the bank's check to her order for $3,100 to be used as a deposit on the contract for sale. Amoroso indorsed and delivered the check drawn on the Fort Lee Trust Co. to Winter, who deposited the check in his account at the plaintiff bank. After the check was deposited the bank cashed a $1,000 check for him against his account. In addition the bank processed four other checks for Winter totaling $291.76. Amoroso then discovered that Winter had previously sold the property to a third party by agreement which had been recorded. Amoroso immediately asked Winter to return her money. He agreed to return the money but when Mrs. Amoroso and her husband reached Winter's office they learned that he had attempted suicide. He died shortly thereafter. The Amorosos then requested Fort Lee Savings to stop payment on the check. The bank issued a written stop payment order which reached the Fort Lee Trust Company, the drawee, the next day. Notice was then transmitted to the plaintiff. The Plaintiff contends it is entitled to recover the monies Winter charged to his account from the drawer and payee-endorser of the check and that under the Code it is a holder in due course to that extent.

BOTTER, J. S. C.   The central issue is whether plaintiff bank is a holder in due course, since a holder in due course will prevail against those liable on the instrument in the absence of a real defense. Of course, it must first be determined that plaintiff is a "holder" if plaintiff is to be declared a holder in due course. . . . The definition of "holder" includes a person who is in possession of an instrument indorsed to his order or in blank (N.J.S. 12A:1-201(20), N.J.S.A.) It is clear that the bank is a holder of the check notwithstanding that it may have taken the check solely for collection and with the right to charge back against the depositor's account in the event the check is later dishonored. . . .

To be a holder in due course one must take a negotiable instrument for value, in good faith and without notice of any defect or defense. . . . Amoroso contends that Plaintiff did not act in good faith or is chargeable with notice because it allowed Winter to draw against uncollected funds at a time when his account was either very low or overdrawn. Winter's account was low in funds. However, this fact, or the fact that Winter's account was overdrawn, currently or in the past, if true, would not constitute notice to the collecting bank of an infirmity in the underlying transaction or instrument and is not evidence of bad faith chargeable to the bank at the time it allowed withdrawal against the deposited check. . . .

Lacking bad faith or notice of a defect or defense, plaintiff will be deemed a holder in due course if one additional element is satisfied, namely, the giving of value for the instrument. Prior to the adoption of the Uniform Commercial Code the general rule was that a bank does give value and is a holder in due course to the extent that it allows a depositor to draw against a check given for collection notwithstanding that the check is later dishonored. . . .

This result is continued by provisions of the Uniform Commercial Code which give plaintiff a security interest in the check and the monies represented by the check to the extent that credit given for the check has been withdrawn or applied. . . .

It would hinder commercial transactions if depositary banks refused to permit withdrawal prior to clearance of checks. Apparently banking practice is to the contrary. It is clear that the Uniform Commercial Code was intended to permit the continuation of this practice and to protect banks who have given credit on deposited items prior to notice of a stop payment order or other notice of dishonor. . . .

It is also contended that liability on the check is excused because N.J.S. 12A:4-403, N.J.S.A. gives Fort Lee Savings the right to order Fort

Lee Trust Company to stop payment on the check. However, U.C.C. Comment 8 under this section makes it clear that the stop payment order cannot avoid liability to a holder in due course. "The payment can be stopped but the drawer remains liable on the instrument to the holder in due course . . . ." . . .

Plaintiff's status as a holder in due course insulates it from all personal defenses of any party to the instrument with whom it has not dealt, although real defenses may still be asserted. . . . The defense raised here is fraud in inducing Amoroso to enter into the contract. There is no suggestion that either defendant signed the check without knowledge of "its character or its essential terms.". . . Therefore the fraud is a personal defense available only against Winter and cannot be asserted against plaintiff. . . .

Judgment for plaintiff.

Sandler v. United Industrial Bank

1965, (N.Y.) 256 N.Y.S.2d 442

MEMORANDUM BY THE COURT. This action was brought by appellant, Rose Sandler, as administratrix of the estate of her husband, Sidney Sandler, to recover $9,127.60 and interest from defendant, a commercial bank with which she and her husband had maintained a joint checking account. The Bank asserted, as a separate and complete defense, that it had properly offset said amount against its indebtedness to Sidney Sandler, deceased, arising from the deposit in such joint account.

It appears that on May 7, 1962 the husband, who had a separate checking account of his own in another bank, Chemical Bank New York Trust Company, drew a check on that account in the amount in suit, payable to the order of James A. Brancato & Co., which deposited the check the same day in its account in the respondent bank United Industrial. The respondent bank gave Brancato immediate credit for the check by applying $6,421.33 of it to repay that sum which was overdrawn and by applying the balance to other items presented for payment against the Brancato account that day.

The husband, Sidney Sandler, died on the evening of the same day (May 7, 1962), and thereafter the check was returned unpaid to the respondent bank by the Chemical Bank with the notation "maker deceased." There were then insufficient funds in the Brancato account to cover the check, but there was more than enough in the Sandler joint account. Respondent bank offset the amount of the unpaid check, $9,127.60, against the Sandler account; this suit ensued.

The Sandler account being a joint account in a commercial bank, there is a presumption that when one of the joint tenants dies the amount on deposit belongs to the survivor. That presumption is rebuttable, however, upon a showing that the depositors' purpose or intent was other than to create a joint tenancy. . . .

It is not disputed that the plaintiff wife, as administratrix, has a right to maintain this action to establish the right, if any, of her husband's estate to the fund. Since respondent bank became the holder for value of decedent's check prior to his death (Uniform Commercial Code, 4-201 et seq.) . . . it thereby acquired a matured claim against him which it had the right to offset against his deposit in its hands while he lived. . . .

Now, after the death of decedent, this right of setoff or "banker's lien" pertaining to the check, presently a claim against his estate, may be applied against the deposit if it belongs to his estate. . . . However, if the fund belongs to the plaintiff "individually," the lien may not be asserted by another; both must mutually exist between the same parties. . . .

Accordingly, since the respondent bank has the right to offset the amount of the unpaid check against so much, if any, of the amount on deposit as belongs to the husband's estate, the order of the Appellate Term was proper. . . .

Judgment for defendant bank affirmed.

Rock Island Auction Sales v. Empire Packing Co.

1965, (Ill.) 204 N.E.2d 721

SCHAEFER, J. . . . On Monday, September 24, 1962, the plaintiff, Rock Island Auction Sales, Inc., sold 61 head of cattle to Empire Packing Co., Inc. and received therefor Empire's check in the sum of $14,706.90. The check was dated September 24, 1962, and on that day the plaintiff deposited it in the First Bank and Trust Company of Davenport, Iowa. It was received by the payor bank, Illinois National Bank and Trust Company of Rockford, Illinois, on Thursday, September 27, 1962. Empire's balance was inadequate to pay the check, but the payor bank, relying upon Empire's assurances that additional funds would be deposited, held the check until Tuesday morning, October 2, 1962. It then marked the check "not sufficient funds", placed it in the mail for return to the Federal Reserve Bank of Chicago, and sent notice of dishonor by telegram to the Federal Reserve Bank. The depositary bank, the First Trust and Savings Bank of Davenport, received the check on October 4, 1962. The check was never paid. On November 7, 1962, bankruptcy proceedings were instituted against Empire and on December 13, 1962, it was adjudicated a bankrupt.

On February 15, 1963, the plaintiff instituted this action against Illinois National Bank and Trust Company of Rockford. The trial court entered judgment for the plaintiff for the face amount of the check, and the defendant appealed. The plaintiff's case against Illinois National Bank and Trust Company of Rockford (hereafter "defendant") rests squarely on the ground that as the payor bank it became liable for the amount of the check because it held the check without payment, return or notice of dishonor, beyond the time limit fixed in Section 4-302 of the Uniform Commercial Code.

The defendant relies upon several alternative defenses. It first asserts that Section 4-302, properly construed, does not make it liable for the face amount of the check, and that if the section is construed to impose that liability it violates the principle of separation of powers and deprives the defendant of due process of law and equal protection of the laws.

Section 4-302 of the Uniform Commercial Code provides: "In the absence of a valid defense such as breach of a presentment warranty . . . settlement effected or the like, if an item is presented on and received by a payor bank the bank is accountable for the *amount of* a demand item . . . if the bank . . . retains the item beyond midnight of the banking day of receipt without settling for it or . . . does not pay or return the item or send notice of dishonor until after its midnight deadline. . . ." Section 4-104(h) of the Code defines the "midnight deadline" of a bank as midnight on the banking day following the day on which it received the item.

The important issues in the case involve the construction and validity of Section 4-302. The defendant argues that the amount for which it is liable because of its undenied retention of the check beyond the time permitted by Section 4-302 is not to be determined by that section, but rather under Section 4-103(5) which provides that "(t)he measure of damages for failure to exercise ordinary care in handling an item is the amount of the item reduced by an amount which could not have been realized by the use of ordinary care. . ." Its position is that the word "accountable" in Section 4-302 means that "the defendant must account for what it actually had (which is zero because there were not funds on deposit sufficient to pay the check) plus the damages (as measured by Section 4-103(5)) sustained by the plaintiff as the result of the failure to meet the deadline, but for no more."

But the statute provides that the bank is accountable for the amount of the item, and not for something else. "Accountable" is synonymous with "liable" (Webster's New Twentieth Century Dictionary Unabridged, Second Edition; Webster's Dictionary of Synonyms), and Section 4-302 uses the word in that sense. The word "accountable" appears to have been used instead of its synonym "liable" in order to accommodate other sections of Article 4 of the Code which relate to provisional and final settlements between banks in the collection process, and to bar the possibility that a payor bank might be thought to be liable both to the owner of the item and to another bank. The circuit court correctly held that the statute imposes liability for the amount of the item.

This construction does not create an irrational classification and so cause the statute to violate constitutional limitations. Defendant's contention to the contrary is based upon the proposition that Section 4-302 is invalid because it imposes a liability upon a payor bank for failing to act prior to its midnight deadline that is more severe than the liability which Section 4-103(5) imposes upon a depositary bank or a collecting bank for the same default. Of course there are no such separate institutions as depositary, collecting, and payor banks. All banks perform all three functions. The argument thus comes down to the proposition that the failure of a bank to meet its deadline must always carry the same consequence, regardless of the function that it is performing.

But the legislature may legitimately have concluded that there are

differences in function and in circumstance that justify different consequences. Depositary and collecting banks act primarily as conduits. The
steps that they take can only indirectly affect the determination of
whether or not a check is to be paid, which is the focal point in the collection process. The legislature could have concluded that the failure
of such a bank to meet its deadline would most frequently be the result
of negligence, and fixed liability accordingly. The role of a payor bank
in the collection process, on the other hand, is crucial. It knows whether
or not the drawer has funds available to pay the item. The legislature
could have considered that the failure of such a bank to meet its deadline
is likely to be due to factors other than negligence, and that the relationship between a payor bank and its customer may so influence its conduct
as to cause a conscious disregard of its statutory duty. The present case
is illustrative. The defendant, in its position as a payor bank, deliberately
aligned itself with its customer in order to protect that customer's credit
and consciously disregarded the duty imposed upon it. The statutory
scheme emphasizes the importance of speed in the collection process. A
legislative sanction designed to prevent conscious disregard of deadlines
can not be characterized as arbitrary or unreasonable, nor can it be said
to constitute a legislative encroachment on the functions of the judiciary.
   Judgment affirmed.

Bank of Marin v. England, Trustee
352 F.2d 186 (1965)

   Between August 27, 1963 and September 17, 1963, Marin Seafoods
drew five checks in favor of Eureka Fisheries, payee, upon its account
with the Bank of Marin, drawee-defendant, totalling $2,318.82. On Sep-
tember 26, before these checks had been presented for payment, Marin
Seafoods filed a voluntary petition in bankruptcy. John M. England was
appointed Receiver and subsequently Trustee in bankruptcy. He is the
plaintiff in this law suit.

   On the date of the filing of the petition, sums of money in excess of
$3,200 were due and owing Marin Seafoods from customers for mer-
chandise previously delivered. Beginning on the day after the filing of
the petition, and continuing for several days, Marin Seafoods collected
portions of these outstanding accounts receivable and deposited them in
the company's commercial account at the bank. On October 2, 1963, the
checks which Marin Seafoods had drawn and delivered to Eureka Fisheries prior to the filing of the petition were duly presented to the bank by
Eureka Fisheries for payment and were paid.

   At the time the bank paid these checks it had received no notice and
had not otherwise obtained knowledge of the filing of the petition in
bankruptcy. The bank was not informed of the pending bankruptcy
proceeding until October 3, 1963, when it received a letter, dated October
2, 1963, from the Receiver (England, plaintiff). This was one day after
the bank had honored the checks referred to above.

   The trustee applied to the Referee for a "turn-over order" to require the bank to pay over to him the amount paid to Eureka on October 2, or in the alternative to require Eureka to pay this amount. The Referee held that the bank and Eureka were *jointly liable*. Eureka *paid* and demanded *contribution* from the bank. The bank appealed from the Referee's ruling.

HAMLEY, J.   In seeking recovery of the stated amount from the bank, the trustee relied upon section 70, sub. a of the Act, (52 Stat. 879 (1938)), as amended, (11 U.S.C. 110, sub. a (1964)). This section provides, in pertinent part, that, upon his appointment and qualification, a trustee in bankruptcy shall be vested "by operation of law" with the title of the bankrupt as of the date of the filing of the petition initiating a proceeding in bankruptcy, with exceptions not here material, to described kinds of property wherever located. Among the kinds of property so described, the statute includes:

> . . . (5) property, including rights of action, which prior to the filing of the petition he (bankrupt) could by any means have transferred or which might have been levied upon and sold under judicial process against him, or otherwise seized, impounded, or sequestered: Provided, . . . (not here material).

This provision of the Act, considered by itself, would appear to support the trustee's application for a turnover order against the bank. The bank, however, contends that notwithstanding this statute, *it should be held that a bank is not liable to a trustee in bankruptcy when, in good faith, and without actual knowledge of the bankruptcy proceedings, it honors the checks of a bankrupt depositor in the regular course of business after the adjudication of bankruptcy.*

The bank also contends that, in California, a trustee in bankruptcy must give a bank notice of the bankruptcy by complying with Section 952 of the California Financial Code before he can hold the bank liable for honoring checks of the bankrupt.

Section 952 provides that notice of an *adverse claim* to bank deposits may be disregarded until the *adverse claimant* obtains a restraining order, injunction or other court order against the bank; without such an order the bank may honor checks drawn by the depositor or allow withdrawals by him without incurring liability to the *adverse claimant*. The bank contends that since the Bankruptcy Act makes no provision for notice to banks, state law should apply to fill this gap. The trustee gave no notice in this case, nor did he make any attempt to comply with Section 952.

A claim of this kind, made by the trustee in bankruptcy for a bankrupt depositor, is *not* an "adverse claim," within the meaning of such a statute. . . . Thus, even overlooking inconsistencies between Section 952 and the Bankruptcy Act, the California statute does not undermine the district court order under review.

The bank further argues that a court of bankruptcy is governed by equitable principles and, applying those principles to this case, must protect the bank from incurring liability for honoring checks of a depositor where it had no notice of the bankruptcy of the depositor.

Under the trustee's theory of the case the bank must, in order to avoid liability, keep itself informed of the possibility of bankruptcy proceedings involving a depositor. According to the bank, this will require it to keep advised momentarily of bankruptcy filings. This burden is enhanced by the fact that filing in any district court in the United States will have the same effect. The steps demanded for protection are cited as *impractical and otherwise burdensome.*

Upon considering the respective arguments, we think the bank makes out a strong case for hardship and impracticability insofar as the timely discovery of bankruptcy proceedings involving depositors is concerned. We are not as certain that the problem is one which threatens great and unprotectable financial liability. The fact that our case, and Rosenthal, appear to be the only reported cases dealing with this particular problem is some indication that it is not one which will frequently confront banks. Moreover, it would seem that the risk, such as it is, may ordinarily be taken into account *as a cost of the business and financed as such.*

It is true that courts of bankruptcy exercise certain equity powers. But there is no room for equitable relief of a kind which is expressly foreclosed by the Act.

The bank characterizes its position as analogous to a garnishee who has paid his creditor without notice of garnishment. A garnishee is not liable to the garnishor in such circumstances. . . . But, the analogy is inapplicable in our case because, in bankruptcy proceedings, the filing of the petition and the adjudication is deemed *notice to the world,* except where the Act requires more specific notice.

Affirmed.

Gibbs v. Gerberich

1964, Ohio 203 N.E.2d 851

The defendants, realtors, had sold property belonging to the plaintiffs but had allegedly failed to account to the plaintiffs for the proceeds of the sale. The money had been deposited in an escrow account at the bank. Plaintiffs brought suit for an accounting and the appointment of a receiver. The court issued an order on the bank restraining it from making payment from the escrow account. Prior to notice of the restraining order the bank had received a check drawn on the account payable to one Hewit. This check was for the entire balance of the account. The bank had charged the check to defendant's account but upon receipt of the restraining the bank restored the credit to the account. Hewit's check was returned to him unpaid. The lower court ruled that Hewit's check had not been paid and that the money in the escrow account belonged to the receiver for the purposes of distribution to the plaintiff and other creditor clients of the realtors.

Doyle, J.   In brief, we must determine whether a certain check cleared The First National Bank of Wadsworth, Ohio, and was or was not paid within the meaning of the provisions of the Uniform Commercial Code adopted by the Ohio Legislature; . . .

In the appeal of Hewit, the first assignment of error relates to this check. It is claimed that: "The check for . . . $9,579.76 was paid by the bank to the Hewits within the meaning of the Uniform Commercial Code of Ohio prior to the receipt of the restraining order and the receiver, therefore, has no right to said funds.". . .

The Ohio Code further provides:

(A) An item is finally paid by a payor bank when the bank has done any of the following, whichever happens first:

(3) completed the process of posting the item to the indicated account of the drawer, maker, or other person to be charged therewith; . . . .

As we view the statutes in their bearing upon the assignment of error, the question for decision appears to be whether the check was paid prior to the bank's notice of the restraining order of the court, and one of the measuring points for determining whether the check was paid is whether the "process of posting" was completed.

In Section 4-109 of the Uniform Commercial Code—Bank deposits and collections (not incorporated in the Ohio Code)—the experts, whose combined talents created the Code, gave the following definition:

The "process of posting" means the usual procedure followed by a payor bank in determining to pay an item and in recording the payment including one or more of the following or other steps as determined by the bank:

(a) verification of any signature;

(b) ascertaining that sufficient funds are available;

(c) affixing a "paid" or other stamp;

(d) entering a charge or entry to a customer's account;

(e) correcting or reversing an entry or erroneous action with respect to the item.

It is generally thought, and this court so holds, that the "process of posting" involves two basic elements: (1) a decision to pay, and (2) a recording of the payment.

In brief summary, we find that the check had been charged against the Gerberich escrow account undoubtedly prior to the receipt of the restraining order, but that before any decision to pay was made by the bank, the restraining order was served, and the bank then recredited the account. The check had not been perforated or otherwise cancelled.

Under these circumstances, we conclude that the check had been posted, but that the "process of posting" had not been completed, as there is no evidence indicating a decision of the bank to pay. The mere debiting of a customer's account does not per se indicate a decision to pay. The key point in a bank's completion of the "process of posting" is the completion of all of the steps followed in the particular bank's payment procedure. In the instant case, the "posting run" was not completed, and the day's posting had not been found to be in balance prior to the receipt of the restraining order. The check had not been "voided or cancelled," as it would have been if the "process of posting" had been completed. It appears, therefore, that the statutory "process of posting" had not been completed, and, as a consequence, the check had not been paid.

We reject the claim of the appellant Hewit "that the restraining order was of no avail and that this money belongs to the Hewits just as though it had been paid to them in cash over the counter."

It is obvious from the foregoing that we affirm that part of the trial court's judgment holding that this fund belongs to the receiver for the purposes of distribution.

Stone & Webster Engineering Corp. v. First National Bank & Trust Co. of Greenfield

1962, (Mass.) 184 N.E.2d 358

Between January 1, 1960, and May 15, 1960, plaintiff was indebted at various times to Westinghouse Electric Corp. for goods and services. Plaintiff drew three checks on its checking account in the First National Bank of Boston payable to Westinghouse in the total amount of $64,755.44. Before delivery of the checks to Westinghouse an employee of the plaintiff in possesssion of the checks forged the indorsement of Westinghouse and "cashed" the checks at the defendant bank. The defendant forwarded the checks to the First National Bank of Boston and received full payment. The latter bank charged the account of the plaintiff and has refused to recredit the plaintiff's checking account. The drawer, Stone and Webster, sued the "cashing bank," defendant. The lower court sustained a demurrer to the complaint.

WILKINS, C. J. . . . The plaintiff contends that "First National paid or credited the proceeds of the checks to the defendant and charged the account of the plaintiff, and consequently, the plaintiff was deprived of a credit, and the defendant received funds or a credit which 'in equity and good conscience' belonged to the plaintiff."

In our opinion this argument is a non sequitur. The plaintiff as a depositor in First National was merely in a contractual relationship of creditor and debtor. . . . The amounts the defendant received from First National to cover the checks "cashed" were the bank's funds and not the plaintiff's. The Uniform Commercial Code does not purport to change the relationship. (See G.L. c. 106, Sections 1-103, 4-401 to 4-407), Section 3-409 (1) provides: "A check or other draft *does not of itself operate as an assignment of any funds in* the hands of the drawee available for its payment, and the drawee is not liable on the instrument until he accepts it." This is the same as our prior law, which the Code repealed . . . Whether the plaintiff was rightfully deprived of a credit is a matter between it and the drawee, First National.

If we treat the first count as seeking to base a cause of action for money had and received upon a waiver of the tort of conversion—a matter which it is not clear is argued—the result will be the same. In this aspect the question presented is whether a drawer has a right of action for conversion against a collecting bank which handles its checks in the bank collection process. Unless there be such a right, there is no tort which can be waived.

The plaintiff relies upon the Uniform Commercial Code, G.L. c. 106, Section 3-419, which provides, "(1) An instrument is converted when . . . (c) it is paid on forged indorsement." This, however, could not apply to the defendant, which is not a "payor bank," defined in the Code, Section 4-105 (b), as a "bank by which an item is payable as drawn or accepted.". . .

A conversion provision of the Uniform Commercial Code which might have some bearing on this case is Section 3-419 (3). This section implicitly recognizes that, subject to defenses, including the one stated in it, a collecting bank, defined in the Code, Section 4-105 (3), may be liable in conversion. In the case at bar the forged indorsements were "wholly inoperative" as the signature of the payee, Code Sections 3-404 (1), 1-201 (43), and equally so both as to the restrictive indorsements for deposits, see Section 3-205 (c), and as to the indorsement in blank, see Section 3-204 (2). When the forger transferred the checks to the collecting bank, no negotiation under Section 3-202 (1) occurred, because there was lacking the necessary indorsement of the payee. For the same reason, the collecting bank could not become a "holder" as defined in Section 1-201 (20), and so could not become a holder in due course under Section 3-302 (1). Accordingly, we assume that the collecting bank may be liable in conversion to a proper party, subject to defenses, including that in Section 3-419 (3). . . . But there is no explicit provision in the Code purporting to determine to whom the collecting bank may be liable, and consequently, the drawer's right to enforce such a liability must be found elsewhere. Therefore, we conclude that the case must be decided on our own law, which, on the issue we are discussing, has been left untouched by the Uniform Commercial Code in any specific section. . . .

We state what appears to us to be the proper analysis. Had the checks been *delivered* to the payee Westinghouse, the defendant might have been liable for conversion to the payee. The checks, *if delivered,* in the hands of the payee would have been valuable property which could have been transferred for value or presented for payment; and, had a check been dishonored, the payee would have had a right of recourse against the drawer on the instrument under Section 3-413 (2). Here the plaintiff drawer of the checks, which were *never delivered* to the payee . . . , had no valuable rights in them. Since, as we have seen, it did not have the right of a payee or subsequent holder to present them to the drawee for payment, the value of its rights was limited to the physical paper on which they were written, and was not measured by their payable amounts (cases cited).

The enactment of the Uniform Commercial Code opens the road for the adoption of what seems the preferable view. An action by the drawer against the collecting bank might have some theoretical appeal as avoiding circuity of action. . . . It would have been in the interest of speedy and complete justice had the case been tried with action by the drawer against the drawee and with an action by the drawee against the collecting bank. . . . So one might ask: if the drawee is liable to the drawer and the collecting bank is liable to the drawee, why not let the drawer sue the collecting bank direct? We believe that the answer lies in the applicable defenses set up in the Code.

The drawer can insist that the drawee recredit his account with the amount of any unauthorized payment. Such was our common law (cases cited). This is, in effect, retained by the Code Sections 4-401 (1), . . . 4-406 (4). But the drawee has defenses based upon the drawer's substantial negligence, if "contributing," or upon his duty to discover and report unauthorized signatures and alterations. Sections 3-406, 4-406. As to unauthorized indorsements, see Sections 4-406 (4). . . . Then, if the drawee has a valid defense which it waives or fails upon request to assert, the drawee may not assert against the collecting bank or other prior party presenting or transferring the check a claim which is based on the forged indorsement. Section 4-406 (5). . . . See Am. Law Inst. Uniform Commercial Code, Official Text with comments, Section 4-406, Comment 6, which shows that there was no intent to change the prior law as to negligence of a customer. . . . If the drawee recredits the drawer's account and is not precluded by Section 4-406 (5), it may claim against the presenting bank on the relevant warranties in Sections 3-417 and 4-207, and each transferee has rights against his transferor under those sections.

If the drawer's rights are limited to requiring the drawee to recredit his account, the drawee will have the defenses noted above this and perhaps others; and the collecting bank or banks will have the defenses in Section 4-207 (4) . . . and Section 4-406 (5), and perhaps others. If the drawer is allowed in the present case to sue the collecting bank, the assertion of the defenses, for all practical purposes, would be difficult. The possibilities of such a result would tend to compel resort to litigation in every case involving a forgery of commercial paper. It is a result to be avoided. . . .

Order sustaining demurrer affirmed. . . .

The National Bank of Slatington v. Derhammer

1958, (Pa.) 16 D.&C.2d 286

The plaintiff bank alleged that on March 4, 1957, the defendant opened a joint account at the bank with one Paul M. Barry; that the only deposit to the account was a check drawn by Eli J. Brannon in favor of Paul M. Barry on a New York Bank; that plaintiff paid defendant or her consignatory $150 in cash, and that on March 6, 1957, $2,800 was paid to the "account owners" on a check signed by "one of the joint makers." It is further alleged that the check was drawn on a fictional bank and plaintiff therefore, sought to recover the deficit of $2,950.

HENNINGER, P. J. . . . Defendant filed preliminary objections (1) by way of demurrer and (2) by way of motion for a more specific pleading in that (a) deposit slip not attached (b) failure to state whether defendant was a party to any of the instruments involved (c) whether the $4,950 check was legally credited to the account and (d) on what theory defendant is being sued.

In passing upon a demurrer, we are limited to the facts as pleaded by plaintiff and we must accept them as verity. . . .

We find then from the facts pleaded and from the exhibits attached that, in addition to the above stated facts, the joint account was in the joint names of defendant and one Paul M. Barry, that, of the two, Barry's name alone appears on the invalid check upon which the deposit and subsequent withdrawals were based, but that the signature card states that the initial deposit was the joint property of both.

At the argument, defendant assumed that all of the chicanery was the work of Barry and that he reaped all of the fruits of it. That may well prove to be the case, but it is not the state of facts upon which we must decide the demurrer. We have no doubt of defendant's innocence of wrongdoing, but the complaint pleads that *she* deposited the invalid check and that *she* received the proceeds of the withdrawals against it.

If that be true, or if defendant participated even innocently in negotiation of the $4,950 check, she might be sued for the money lost by reason of the dishonored check. This would be true although, as we know, it was only Barry who endorsed the invalid check and although, as we have been informed, it was only he who signed the $2800 check. Whether or not plaintiff, through any act of its own, has forfeited its right to recover or whether or not defendant actually received any of the money is a matter of defense.

In the light of the motion for a more specific pleading, it becomes necessary for us to rule upon the proposition advanced by plaintiff that every cosignatory to an account is answerable out of his own funds over and above those entrusted to the joint account, for transactions made by his cosignatory which may result in an overdraft. If that were the law, plaintiff's complaint would be sufficient; if it is not the law, other facts must be specifically pleaded to impose liability upon defendant.

While Article 4 of the Uniform Commercial Code of April 6, . . . 4-101 to 4-407, is entitled "Bank Deposits and Collections," it deals almost exclusively with collections of checks and drafts. To rule as plaintiff would have us rule would endanger not only the cosignatory's balance in the account—to which he has consented—but all of his other assets as well—to which he has not consented. Every cosignature would constitute a partnership without limits as to the liability of one partner for the machinations of the other.

Although in Pennsylvania an overdraft is considered an involuntary loan to the one causing it . . . our attention has not been called to any Pennsylvania case, which holds that the cosignatory can be held *beyond the balance* in the account or that the joint deposit makes each cosignatory the agent of the other to borrow money from the bank in this irregular manner. . . .

We are not convinced that Article 4 of the Code intended to impose this new and additional responsibility upon the shoulders of a cosignatory or to change the law of agency, despite the language of Section 4-212 . . . subjecting a customer to refund upon dishonor of an item for collection and Section 4-104 . . . defining a customer as "any person having an account."

Exactly the same situation as in this case was ruled adversely to the bank in *Faulkner v. Bank of Italy*. . . . In that case, however, there was no allegation that the proceeds of charges against the invalid check had been received by the cosignatory.

When we come to the motion for a more specific complaint, it is clear that a litigant need not plead the *theory* upon which he sues. It is enough that he pleads facts which in law entitle him to a recover. Pleading theory might be helpful to Court and adversary, but we cannot demand it.

Plaintiff's complaint is obviously drawn so as to avoid showing that Barry and not defendant perpetrated the fraud. In our opinion, plaintiff's case must stand or fall upon some showing of defendant's responsibility for negotiation of the $4,950 check or upon her enrichment through Barry's fraud.

Under these circumstances, we believe that the complaint is not sufficiently specific. Defendant's signature does not appear upon the invalid check. We should know, therefore, what acts on her part, besides the mere fact of cosignature, are relied upon by plaintiff to fasten liability upon this defendant. If, on the other hand, she is to be held because she received monies based upon a dishonored check, we should have a full frank statement naming by name the person or persons who received the money.

. . . *defendant's preliminary objections by way of demurrer are overruled and her preliminary objections by way of motion for a more specific complaint are sustained and it is ordered that plaintiff file, within twenty (20) days after service of this order on its counsel, a more specific complaint in accordance with this opinion.* . . .

Peoples Savings Bank et. al v. Playdium Lanes, Inc.

1964, (Ohio) 203 N.E.2d 51

McNEILL, J. The Playdium Lanes, Inc., a corporation, in 1962 had opened an account at the Peoples Savings Bank. The signature card, covering all transactions, indicated that the account should be signed by any two officers, the president, vice president, or treasurer. Checks were usually stamped, "Pay to the Order of Playdium Lanes, Inc." with no signature being placed thereon; the checks then were placed in the bag and deposited in the account. The bank placed a certain designated amount of change in the bag for the registers.

In July, 1962, one Detwiler was working for Playdium, and one Self was Vice President and was named on the signature card. Self called Detwiler and told him to take a check which had been received that day and to cash it. Detwiler endorsed the check, Playdium Lanes, per himself, and got the money and took it back to the bowling alley. When Self came in that evening, Detwiler gave the money to Self. About a month later, in August, Self was discharged. Because of a change-over in accountants, it was not until January that it was determined that the account was short this $500.00.

Both sides claim that this case is controlled by *Butler Produce and*

Canning Company v. Edgerton State Bank, (91 Ohio App. 385, 108 N.E. 2d 324). However, before considering this case, one other matter should be examined.

This is not a forged instrument. It may be an unauthorized instrument, and the bank may be liable on an unauthorized instrument as well as a forged one. There was no intent to defraud on the part of Detwiler. He was told by a vice president of the corporation, his immediate superior, to take the action that he did. All officers of the corporation had indicated to him, he, of course, not being controlled by the signature card, that Self was in charge and was running the bowling alley. Therefore, from Detwiler's standpoint, he did only what any agent of the corporation would do; that is, followed the orders of a superior and obtained the money.

At the time Detwiler received the money, he took it immediately back to the Van Wert office of the corporation and placed it in the files, awaiting Self's return. When Self returned, Detwiler then gave the money to him. Self stated he was putting it in petty cash and showed it to others for at least two or three days.

Was Self guilty of embezzlement? Detwiler obtained it as corporation money and gave it to Self as corporation money. Self accepted it and stated it was for petty cash. Thus, it came into his possession as corporation money. If he then made off with it, it would be embezzlement. If it were otherwise, he might be guilty of no crime whatsoever.

It may be true that Self had the intention to embezzle the money at the time he called Detwiler; but intention is not sufficient to constitute a crime. The embezzlement was complete only when he accepted the money from Detwiler and then appropriated it to his own use.

Therefore, whether or not the bank could be liable is immaterial, as there was no damage as a result of this check. Five hundred dollars may have been properly withdrawn from the corporate funds; but the five hundred dollars was returned immediately to the corporation. The fact that it was thereafter embezzled does not change the fact that the corporation had received the money.

This is a case of one person defaulting, and one of two innocent persons must suffer. In this case, the bank may have been careless; but the corporation may have been more careless in hiring Self. He was an officer; he gave the directions. The Bank had dealt with Detwiler and its employees believed him to be honest, which he was. The Bank may foresee that if a check is wrongfully cashed the person presenting it may make off with the money. They aren't required to foresee that if money, even if incorrectly paid out, is returned to the corporation, a vice president will embezzle it.

Judgment for the bank.

Malphrus v. Home Savings Bank of City of Albany

1965, (N.Y.) 254 N.Y.S.2d 980

MARTIN SCHENK, J.   This is a motion by the plaintiff for summary judgment. One Carole Kuebler, a depositor in the defendant

Savings Bank, requested the defendant to issue a *teller's check* in the sum of $450.00 payable to the *order of the plaintiff*. She directed that the amount he deducted from her account. Thereupon, Miss Kuebler delivered the check to the plaintiff in part payment for an automobile which the plaintiff delivered to her. When the check was presented at the National Commercial Bank and Trust Company [drawee bank], upon which it was drawn by the defendant Savings Bank, [drawer] payment was refused on the ground that the defendant [bank] had stopped payment. Plaintiff now sues the defendant Savings Bank for the amount of the check.

The point of law raised here appears to be novel. The rights of the parties are governed by the Uniform Commercial Code which became effective in this State September 27th, 1964, just a few days before the series of transactions referred to above. That a customer may (provide certain rules are followed) stop payment on a check is clearly covered by Section 4-403(1) of the Uniform Code. Furthermore, Section 4-104(1) specifically defines a "customer" as including "a bank carrying an account with another bank." The question presented is whether or not payment on a teller's check may be stopped by the issuing bank within the purview of the Uniform Code. It seems that one purpose of granting authority and providing procedure to stop payment of a check is to afford protection to a party who may have discovered fraud or engaged in a disagreement as to terms or consideration in connection with the underlying contract pursuant to which the check was issued. Here the transaction for the sale and purchase of the automobile was between the plaintiff and Miss Kuebler. The defendant Savings Bank had no stake in that transaction whatsoever. The other purpose of prescribing procedure for payment stoppage is to protect the bank on which the check is drawn. The National Commercial Bank is clearly covered and protected by the Uniform Code so that it incurred no liability by refusing payment on its depositor's check. The question is: did the defendant Savings Bank have the authority to interject itself so as to defeat the plaintiff's claim herein? I am of the opinion that it did not have such right.

By issuing a *teller's check* the defendant Savings Bank gave to its depositor an instrument upon which the *plaintiff relied* in making the sale and delivery of an automobile. *The plaintiff did not rely on Miss Kuebler's credit but in good faith accepted the check of a savings bank.* The underlying transaction, as indicated above, was between the plaintiff and Miss Kuebler. The plaintiff accepted a bank check as in the nature of cash. This is a procedure that is widely followed in business transactions of many varieties throughout this area and presumably elsewhere in the State of New York. A teller's check has generally been treated as *"cash."* As a business practice such checks have been used and regarded on the same basis as *certified checks*. There are, of course, legal distinctions between certified checks and teller's checks. Their respective legal effects may be different under different circumstances. Here, however, there is no basis upon which to make a determination that the plaintiff should have considered the teller's check in any different light than he would have considered a certified check. This was a bank obligation which he received as consideration when he delivered his merchandise.

Although the foregoing conclusion is without precedent in this jurisdiction it receives support in other provisions of the Uniform Commercial Code. For example, Section 3-802 provides that ". . . *where an instrument is taken for an underlying obligation"*

(a) *the obligation is pro tanto discharged if a bank is drawer, maker or acceptor of the instrument and there is no recourse on the instrument against the underlying obligor.* It would seem from the foregoing that the plaintiff has no recourse now against the defendant Savings Bank. If the defendant Savings Bank is not liable to the plaintiff it would seem that he has no rights enforceable under the Uniform Commercial Code which was enacted to protect persons engaged in business transactions involving instruments for the payment of money including, of course, checks.

It seems to me that the defense urged by the defendant would be applicable *only where the bank issuing the teller's check is an actual party to a transaction.* For example, if the defendant Savings Bank were engaged in a contract for the purchase of property, equipment, etc. it would be regarded as the actual obligor in the transaction and could stop payment if it discovered fraud or a question arose as to the consideration, etc. in the same manner as any individual could stop payment. Here, however, the defendant Savings Bank, in effect, sold an *instrument* which was used exactly as one might use cash or a certified check. The defendant Savings Bank was in no sense a party to the transaction between the plaintiff and Miss Kuebler. The arguments raised by the defendant in reliance on Sections 4-403(1) and 4-104(1) (e) are not applicable here, at least as far as the rights of this plaintiff acting in good faith are concerned. *The motion for summary judgment is granted with costs and interest.* [Emphasis supplied.]

[The reason for giving the stop order is not explained in the opinion.]

Jackson v. First National Bank of Memphis, Inc.

1966 (Tenn.) 403 S.W.2d 109

This is an action to recover money from a bank, money which had been paid out on forged instruments. The suit was brought by Jackson, Trustee of a church, on behalf of the church against the bank. In 1963 the church opened an account which required two signatures for withdrawal—Cleve Jordan, Financial Secretary, and Jackson. For a period of about one year, Jordan forged Jackson's name on some fifty checks and used the money to gamble at the dog races. The Bank sent monthly statements to Jordan in his capacity as Financial Secretary. The church discovered the fraud and brought suit against the bank for the money. The trial court found for the church and the bank appealed.

BEJACH, J. . . . Some of the checks involved in this litigation were drawn and cashed prior to July 1, 1964 when the Uniform Commercial Code, enacted by the 1963 Tennessee Legislature, became effective in

Tennessee, and some of the checks were drawn and cashed after that date. The provisions of the Uniform Negotiable Instruments Law, which was in effect in Tennessee prior to the effective date of the Uniform Commercial Code, controls as to those checks drawn and cashed prior to July 1, 1964 and the Uniform Commercial Code controls as to those cashed subsequent to July 1, 1964. The provisions of these uniform laws applicable to the transactions here involved are 47-123 T.C.A., which is section 23 of the Uniform Negotiable Instruments Law, and sections 47-3-406 and 47-4-406 T.C.A., which are sections 3-406 and 4-406 of the Uniform Commercial Code. Section 47-123 T.C.A. provides:

> Forged or unauthorized signatures—Effect—When a signature is forged or made without the authority of the person whose signature it purports to be, it is wholly inoperative, and no right to retain the instrument, or give a discharge therefor, or to enforce payment thereof against any party thereto, can be acquired through or under such signature, unless the party against whom it is sought to enforce such right, is precluded from setting up the forgery or want of authority.

Sections of the Uniform Commercial Code, 47-3-406 and 47-4-406, T.C.A. are as follows:

> 47-3-406. Negligence contributing to alteration or unauthorized signature.— Any person who by his negligence substantially contributes to a material alteration of the instrument or to the making of an unauthorized signature is precluded from asserting the alteration or lack of authority against a holder in due course or against a drawee or other payor who pays the instrument in good faith and in accordance with the reasonable commercial standards of the drawee's or payor's business.
>
> 47-4-406. Customer's duty to discover and report unauthorized signature or alteration.—(1) When a bank sends to its customer a statement of account accompanied by items paid in good faith in support of the debit entries or holds the statement and items pursuant to a request or instructions of its customer or otherwise in a reasonable manner makes the statement and items available to the customer, the customer must exercise reasonable care and promptness to examine the statement and items to discover his unauthorized signature or any alteration on any item and must notify the bank promptly after the discovery thereof.
>
> If the bank establishes that the customer failed with respect to an item to comply with the duties imposed on the customer by subsection (1) the customer is precluded from asserting against the bank
>
> (a) his unauthorized signature or any alteration on the item if the bank also establishes that it suffered a loss by reason of such failure; and
>
> (b) an unauthorized signature or alteration by the same wrongdoer on any other item paid in good faith by the bank after the first item and statement was available to the customer for a reasonable period not exceeding fourteen (14) calendar days and before the bank receives notification from the customer of any such unauthorized signature or alteration.
>
> (3) The preclusion under subsection (2) does not apply if the customer establishes lack of ordinary care on the part of the bank in paying the item(s).
>
> (4) Without regard to care or lack of care of either the customer or the

bank a customer who does not within one (1) year from the time the statement and items are made available to the customer (subsection (1)) discover
and report his unauthorized signature or any alteration on the face or back
of the item or does not within three (3) years from that time discover and
report any unauthorized indorsement is precluded from asserting against
the bank such unauthorized signature or indorsement or such alteration.

(5) If under this section a payor bank has a valid defense against a claim
of a customer upon or resulting from payment of an item and waives or
fails upon request to assert the defense the bank may not assert against any
collecting bank or other prior party presenting or transferring the item a
claim based upon the unauthorized signature or alteration giving rise to the
customer's claim.

Under the above quoted statutes a drawee bank which pays the check
on a forged signature is deemed to have made the payment out of its own
funds and not the depositor's, provided the depositor has not been guilty
of negligence or fault that misled the bank.

In the instant case, the negligence of the depositor relied on by the
bank is its failure to examine the checks and report the forgery, thus
preventing a repetition thereof. The fallacy of this argument is that the
checks were mailed to Cleve Jordan, Financial Secretary of the Church,
who was the forger. He was an unfaithful servant, and obviously his
knowledge and information on the subject would not be reported by him
to the Church, nor imputed to it. He had been a faithful and trusted
member of the Church and one of its officers for about twenty years, and,
consequently, the Church cannot be held guilty of negligence in employing
an unfaithful agent. The contention is made, however, that the church
officials, other than Cleve Jordan, himself, should have called on Jordan
for an accounting from time to time, and that the Church was negligent
in its failure to perform this duty. The proof shows that the Church did
from time to time call on Cleve Jordan for production of the checks and
records of the Church, but that he made excuses, said he forgot to bring
them, or made other excuses. Under these circumstances, in view of his
previous good record and reputation, we cannot say that the Bank carried
the burden of showing negligence on the part of the Church.

Under the Negotiable Instruments Law, no time limit establishing a
reasonable period is fixed within which a depositor must examine the
canceled checks returned to him, but under the provisions of the Uniform Commercial Code, such limit is fixed at fourteen days. Under the
provisions of section 47-4-406, T.C.A. (Section 4-406 of the Uniform Commercial Code) subsection 2(b), a depositor is precluded by failure to
examine the checks within fourteen days from asserting liability against
the bank on account of unauthorized signature or alteration of a check
paid by the bank in good faith, but subsection (3) of the same Code
section provides: "The preclusion under subsection (2) does not apply
if the customer establishes lack of ordinary care on the part of the bank
paying the item(s)."

In *Farmers' and Merchants' Bank v. Bank of Rutherford* (905), 115
Tenn. 64, 88 S.W. 939, 112 Am.St.Rep. 817), the Supreme Court held that,

"It is negligence in a drawee bank to pay a forged check drawn on it in the name of its customer, whose signature is well known to it, where the cashier does not examine the signature closely, but relies on the previous endorsements." It is argued on behalf of the Bank that such examination of the signature card, which admittedly was not made in the instant case, is not practical under modern banking methods. Such may be true as a practical matter, but, if so, the Bank, because of that fact, cannot escape the consequences and must, under that decision, be held guilty of negligence.

We think, however, that the Bank must be held to be guilty of negligence in another and much stronger aspect of the instant case. The Bank account here involved was that of a church, which obviously involved trust funds, and the counter signature of Milton Jackson, Trustee, whose signature has been forged, was required on all checks. In the case of *Fidelity and Deposit Co. of Maryland v. Hamilton Nat'l Bank* (1938, 23 Tenn.App. 20, 126 S.W.2d 359), in an opinion written by McAmis, J., now presiding judge, this Court, Eastern Section, held that one who takes paper from a trustee importing upon its face its fiduciary character, is bound to inquire of the transferor the right to dispose of it. A long list of cases is cited as authority for this proposition. Any adequate inquiry made in the instant case by the Bank would have disclosed the situation that Cleve Jordan was forging the name of Milton Jackson, Trustee, and would have prevented a repetition of such forgery.

There is another and a stronger reason why the Bank must be held guilty of negligence and held responsible for the result of the forgery here involved. All of the checks, recovery for which was granted in the instant case, were made payable to Cleve Jordan, personally; and many of them bear the endorsement of the Southland Racing Company, which is the corporation operating the dog racing track in Arkansas across the Mississippi River from Memphis. These circumstances, and especially the one that the checks were made payable to Cleve Jordan, personally, should have put the bank on inquiry as to whether or not the funds represented by these checks were being withdrawn for unauthorized purposes. Any inquiry would have disclosed the true situation and prevented further depletion of the Church's bank account. The bank account being of a trust fund and the checks withdrawing same being made to one of the authorized signers of checks, was sufficient to put the bank on notice that the funds were being improperly withdrawn, or should at least have required the bank to make inquiry as to whether or not the withdrawals involved were authorized. In *Hartford Accident & Indemnity Co. v. Farmers Nat. Bank* (1940, 24 Tenn.App. 699, 149 S.W.2d 473), this Court, Middle Section, held that the withdrawal of funds from a trust account for personal benefit of the trustee charged the bank with knowledge that the funds were being illegally withdrawn and made it liable. . . .

The case of *Hartford Accident & Indemnity Co. v. Farmers Nat'l Bank* (1940, 24 Tenn.App. 699, 149 S.W.2d 473), is cited in volume 10 Am.Jur.2d.,—Banks,—Section 525, page 501, where it said:

It is held that where a bank knows that a fiduciary is drawing checks on the trust account for personal use, it is put upon inquiry and is liable as a participant in the misappropriation if it pays such checks without any inquiry.

For the reasons hereinabove stated, we think that all of the defendant's assignments of error must be overruled. The decree of the lower court, together with interest thereon, will be affirmed against the defendant First National Bank of Memphis, Inc. and its surety on the appeal bond. The costs of the cause will also be adjudged against the Bank and its surety.

CHAPTER 26
REVIEW QUESTIONS AND PROBLEMS

1. *A* is the holder of a check drawn by *B* on the Last National Bank. *A* also has an account at the Last National. The check is deposited at the bank on a Monday. On that day *B*'s account is overdrawn, but *B* has promised to make a substantial deposit, so the bank holds the check until Thursday. *B* does not make the deposit and on Friday the bank returns the check to *A* marked "Insufficient Funds." Can *A* require the bank to make good on the check?

2. A thief stole a blank check from *A* and forged *A*'s name as drawer. He made the check payable to his own order and cashed it at a tavern. The tavern owner deposited the check and it was paid by the drawee bank. *A* did not notify the bank of the forgery until a month later. The bank contends that the loss must fall on *A* or the tavern owner. Is the bank correct?

3. X Bank is preparing forms to be filled out by customers who wish to stop payment on checks. *B* Bank wishes to include a statement that the customer "agrees to hold the bank free of all liability should payment be made contrary to the stop order, if such payment occurs through accident or inadvertance only." Would this provision be enforceable?

4. *A* is the drawer of a check drawn on the Last National Bank. The check was drawn to the order of *B* in payment for a TV set. The set is defective and *A* stops payment on the check. However, the bank by mistake honors the check. Would it matter whether the check was presented by *B* rather than one to whom *B* had endorsed it, insofar as the bank's position is concerned?

5. *P*, the payee of checks drawn on *X* Bank, indorsed the checks on the

same day they were drawn and deposited the checks in *Y* Bank. *P* then drew checks against the deposit and depleted the entire balance of his account. Unknown to *X* Bank, the drawer had stopped payment on the checks. The drawee, *X* Bank, paid the *Y* Bank and debited the drawer's account. What are the respective rights of *X* Bank and *Y* Bank?

6. *A* and *B* maintained a joint account at *X* Bank. *A* issued a large check which created an overdraft in the joint account. *X* Bank seeks to recover from *A* and *B*. Should *B* be held liable?

7. *P* drew a check in favor of *X* Co. for materials purchased. *A*, an employee of *P*, stole the check from *P*'s office; forged the indorsement of *X* Co. and cashed the check at *C* Bank. *C* Bank forwarded the checks to the drawee, *Y* Bank, and received payment from that bank. What are *P*'s rights against *C* Bank? Against *Y* Bank?

8. *H* received a check by indorsement from *A* on June 1, 1966. On June 10 *H* deposited the check in his bank. The check was returned by the drawee bank marked "Insufficient Funds." Can *H* recover from *A*, the indorser?

9. A check drawn on *Y* Bank was deposited in *X* Bank. The depositor did not indorse the check. The check was honored by *Y* Bank and charged to the drawer's account. The drawer challenged the payment. What result?

10. A check was sent to *X* Bank for collection. *X* Bank, through the negligence of one of its employees, delayed in forwarding the check to the drawee bank. When the check was finally forwarded, the drawer's account was overdrawn and the check was returned. Would the *X* Bank be liable to the depositor of the check?

11. *A* Bank forwarded checks to its correspondent *B* Bank for collection. While the checks were in the possession of *B* Bank, it became insolvent. Is *A* Bank liable to the owners of the checks?

12. The drawer's signature to a check was forged. Neither the depositor nor any of the collecting banks has knowledge of the forgery. The payor bank honored the check. Against whom does the payor bank have recourse?

13. *A* draws on *D* Bank a check for $150 in favor of *P*. *P* holds the check for ninety days, and, when he presents it, he finds that *A* has no money in his account. At the time the check was drawn, *A* had more than sufficient funds there to meet it. May *P* recover from *A* on the check?

14. *M* drew a check on *D* Bank in favor of *P*. *P* presented the check to the bank, but the bank refused to make payment, although they had sufficient funds belonging to *M* to do so. Has *P* an action against the bank?

chapter 27

Secured Transactions: The Security Interest

3-130 Introduction. Prior to the promulgation of the Uniform Commercial Code, a great variety of devices were utilized and developed for the purpose of giving a creditor security interests in personal property of debtors. These devices were used in Code states prior to its adoption and continue to be used in those states which have not adopted the Code. The names given to these devices such as chattel mortgages, conditional sales contracts, trust receipts, factors liens and assignments of accounts receivable continue to be used in Code states even though these devices are technically eliminated. Common to all of them was their basic function—to provide security rights in personal property of a debtor so that a creditor could collect his debt out of the property in the event of nonpayment. Each device had its own peculiar characteristics, including many requirements which varied widely from one state to another.

Article 9–Secured Transactions replaces all of these security devices with a single security device known as a *security interest*. It should be noted, however, that the Code does not displace such state statutes as those which regulate consumer installment sales and consumer loans. Such transactions present special problems so that it was deemed more appropriate for them to be regulated by existing state statutes in those states which have such laws. While the Article deals primarily with secured transactions, its provisions also cover outright *sales* of accounts, contract rights, and chattel paper. (See Section 3-138) It will be recalled that these property items are expressly excluded from the coverage of Article 2–Sales.

Except for *sales* of accounts, contract rights, and chattel paper, the main test to be applied in order to determine whether a given transaction

591

falls within the purview of Article 9 is whether it was intended to have effect as *security*.[1] The application of this test may reveal that many transactions are actually within the scope of Article 9, although they might at first appear to be governed by some other Article or by some law not within the Code. For example, a consignment, which is a "sale or return" under Article 2–Sales, is a transaction in which the obvious intention is to give the seller a security interest in the consigned goods until he has been paid for the goods. Article 2, therefore, governs the relations between buyer and seller, but Article 9 has application to the rights of the seller when he is seeking to defend his security interest against *attaching creditors* of the buyer or the latter's *trustee in bankruptcy*. Thus, Article 9 applies to any transaction which is intended to create a security interest in personal property or fixtures, *except* those which are expressly excluded.[C1] The exclusions in general are transactions which are not really of a commercial character. One important exclusion is liens given by law for services and materials, as for example the lien given to a garage man who repairs a car. Certainly the garage man has a security right in the car, but except to the extent that a question of its relative priority with other security interests under the Code is involved, it is outside the scope of Article 9. Likewise, it has been held that the Code is inapplicable to situations arising out of the landlord-tenant relationship.

The basic policy of Article 9 is to provide a simple, effective, and unified arrangement to meet the needs of modern secured financing transactions. The Code provides rules which are tailored to meet the financing requirements which will vary according to the type of property and the relationship between the parties to the transaction. In particular, consumers and farmers for reasons of established public policy are afforded some special considerations in their role as debtors who give security interest in their personal property and the rules pertaining to these groups should be carefully noted.

 A "Security interest" is an interest in personal property or fixtures which secures either payment of money or performance of an obligation.[C2] The reference to fixtures is included because personal property is often affixed to real property in which event it is called a fixture. The security interest results from the execution by the parties of a "security agreement" covering the debtor's "collateral"—the personal property in which a security interest exists. The parties to the security agreement are the "debtor" who owes the obligation and is giving the security and the "secured party," lender, seller, or other person in whose favor there is a security interest.[C3] Before a security interest is effective, as between the parties, it must attach to the collateral and before it is effective to give priority over the rights of third parties, the security interest must be perfected. These matters are discussed in the sections which follow.

---

1 *In re Wheatland Electric Products Co.*, page 605.

C1 *U.C.C.* 9-102.   C3 *U.C.C.* 9-105.
C2 *U.C.C.* 1-201(37).

3-131 The Security Agreement.[C4] The security agreement must be in writing, unless the security arrangement is a possessory one and the secured party is in possession of the collateral. The only other formal requirement is that the agreement be signed by the debtor and that it contain a description of the collateral sufficient to reasonably identify it. The security agreement may contain many other provisions and the forms in general use include also a statement of the amount of the obligation and the terms of repayment, the debtor's duties in respect to the collateral such as insuring it, and the rights of the secured party on default. In general, the parties can include such terms and provisions as they may deem appropriate to their particular transaction, but there are a few limitations on this freedom to contract in the interest of fairness to the debtor.

3-132 Attachment.[C5] It is not sufficient to merely create a security interest; it must "attach" to the collateral. A security interest attaches only after three events have occurred: (1) the security agreement has been executed, (2) the secured party has given value and (3) the debtor has rights in the collateral. They may occur in any order. For example, a security agreement may be executed and the secured party may give value, e.g. loan money, to the debtor before the debtor acquires rights in the collateral. Attachment is the legal term used to describe the phenomenon whereby the secured party acquires rights in the collateral.

Value [C6] for purpose of attachment is defined somewhat differently than it is in Commercial Paper. Basically, value means that a secured party has furnished to the debtor any consideration sufficient to support a simple contract. The secured party also gives value if his rights are acquired in return for a binding commitment to extend credit to the debtor or if he acquires his rights as security for, or in total or partial satisfaction of, a pre-existing claim which he has against the debtor. In most cases the giving of value by the secured party will be quite obvious. A dealer sells a piece of equipment to a merchant: The delivery of the equipment is the value. A bank loans $10,000 to a merchant and takes a security interest in his inventory: The loan of money constitutes the value.

The third requirement for attachment is that the debtor have *rights in the collateral*. A debtor has no rights: (1) in crops until they are planted or otherwise become growing crops, or in the young of livestock until they are conceived; (2) in fish until they are caught; (3) in oil, gas, or minerals until they are extracted; (4) in timber until it is cut. A debtor has no rights in an account until it comes into existence—until goods have been sold there could not be an account receivable. While a merchant could enter into an agreement to assign future accounts to a secured party, the latter's security interest could not *attach* until the accounts actually came into existence.

[C4] *U.C.C.* 9-203(1).
[C5] *U.C.C.* 9-204.

[C6] *U.C.C.* 1-201(44).

The security agreement may provide that property acquired by the debtor at any later time shall also secure the obligation covered by the security agreement. This means that if such a clause were included in the security agreement, *after-acquired property* of the debtor would be additional security for the secured party—i.e., as soon as the debtor acquires rights in other property a security interest would attach to such property in favor of the secured party. This obviously binds a debtor quite severely and the Code places a limitation on the effect of after-acquired property clauses in relation to crops and to consumer goods (see Section 3-136) on the theory that such clauses are best suited to commercial transactions and might work an undue hardship on a consumer or a farmer. Thus, no security interest can attach under an after-acquired property clause: (1) to crops which become such more than one year after the execution of the security agreement; or (2) to consumer goods which are given as additional security unless the consumer obtains the goods within 10 days after the secured party gives value.

3-133 The "Floating Lien." As noted above, security agreements may provide for a security interest in after-acquired property.[2] The agreements may also provide that future advances made by the creditor to the secured party will be covered by the collateral in which the secured party has a security interest. In addition, a debtor may be allowed to have absolute control over the collateral without eliminating the lien of the secured party. Thus, a debtor may have the right to use, commingle, or dispose of the collateral, or to compromise claims and allow repossessions without voiding the lien of the secured party. These three provisions provide the basis for the so called "floating lien" concept. The amount of the debt and the actual collateral can be constantly revolving if the security agreement is so worded as to include after-acquired property and future advances of money. Businessmen can pledge property to be obtained in the future, but farmers and consumers are limited as noted above.

PERFECTION OF THE SECURITY INTEREST

3-134 In General. A security interest that has attached to the collateral, establishes the rights and liabilities as *between the secured party and the debtor* in relation to the collateral. However, the secured party is not necessarily protected against *other persons* who may claim an interest in the collateral. Creditors of the debtor may attach the collateral; other persons may have acquired a subsequent security interest in it; the debtor may have sold the collateral; or the debtor may be in bankruptcy. To have priority over such third persons or be able to recover the collateral from the trustee in bankruptcy,[3] the secured party must "perfect" his security interest. Perfection may be accomplished by: (1)

---

2 *Industrial Packaging Prod. Co. v. Fort Pitt Pack. Inc.*, page 606.
3 *In re United Thrift Stores*, page 608.

possession, (2) filing a financing statement, and (3) attachment; and each reflects the basic purpose of perfection which is to give proper notice to all persons who may be dealing with the debtor that the secured party has or may have a security interest in the collateral. In order to determine which of the methods is appropriate in a particular transaction, the following factors must be considered: (1) the kind of collateral in which a security interest was created, (2) the use which the debtor intends to make of the collateral, and (3) the status of the debtor in relation to the secured party. These factors which are also significant in the creation and attachment of the security interest, will be discussed prior to the methods of perfection in the next section.

Before discussing the various classifications of collateral, it is noted that even a *perfected* security interest is subordinate to some third party rights. For example, a person who repairs or improves the collateral may have a lien for his services and materials which will be superior to the secured party's interest. Obviously, a perfected security interest is generally inferior to another party's prior security interest. Also, in the case of collateral which is inventory, a buyer from the debtor in the ordinary course of business will obtain clear title although a purchaser out of the ordinary course of business will not.[4]

In the main, however, the holder of a perfected security interest will prevail in his rights in the collateral. On the other hand, an unperfected security interest is in general subordinate to the claims of others who acquire an interest in the collateral without knowledge of the unperfected security interest even though it is subsequently perfected.[5] Also, a "lien creditor" is preferred over the unperfected interest if he becomes such without knowledge of the security interest and before it is perfected.

A "lien creditor" is to be distinguished from an ordinary creditor. He is a creditor who by legal process has attached or levied upon the collateral and thereby acquired a lien against it. Trustees in bankruptcy, equity receivers, and assignees for the benefit of creditors are included within the definition.

3-135 Classifications of Collateral. Collateral may be classified according to its physical make-up into (1) tangible, physical property or goods, (2) purely intangible property such as an account receivable, and (3) property which has physical existence, such as a negotiable instrument, but which is simply representative of a contractual obligation. Each type of collateral presents its own peculiar problems and the framework of Article 9 is structured on the peculiarities of each type. There may be security interest not only in the collateral itself, but also in the proceeds of the collateral —that which the debtor receives when he sells or otherwise disposes of it. If the collateral is returned to the debtor or repossessed by him, the security interest which existed originally may be reinstated.

---

[4] *Al Maroone Ford, Inc. v. Manheim Auto Auction, Inc.,* page 611.
[5] *Main Investment Co. v. Gisolfi,* page 612.

3-136 Tangible Property: Goods.[C7] Four classifications are established: consumer goods, equipment, farm products, and inventory. In determining the classification of any particular item of collateral in the form of goods, it is necessary to take into account not only the physical attributes but also the status of the debtor who is either buying the property or using it as security for a loan.

Consumer goods.[C8] Goods fall into this classification if they are used or bought primarily for personal, family, or household purposes. The particular significance of the consumer status in a secured transaction stems from the public policy of protecting a person who is not generally accustomed to analyzing carefully all aspects of his transactions and reading carefully all the papers and documents involved. As noted previously, this public policy is reflected in a variety of state statutes regulating small loans and retail installment sales. Mention has already been made of the limitation of after-acquired property clauses in consumer purchases. The perfection of a security interest in such goods may be by attachment without the requirement of filing. Note should also be taken that special treatment is afforded upon default by a consumer.

Equipment.[C9] Goods which are used or bought for use primarily in a business, in farming, in a profession, or by a non-profit organization or government agency fall within this category. Also included are goods which do not meet the above specifications but also do not qualify as consumer goods, inventory, or farm products. Thus the category is something of a "catch-all" so that goods which otherwise defy classification will be treated as equipment. It is important to note that equipment as well as other goods may become attached to realty so as to constitute a "fixture." There may thus be questions of priority as between the holder of a security interest in the fixture and the party, such as a mortgagee, who has security in the land. Special rules relate to the method of perfecting a security interest in fixtures (see Section 3-149).

Inventory.[C10] Inventory is to be distinguished from equipment although both relate to goods which are used commercially. It comprises goods which are held by a person for sale or lease or to be furnished under a contract of service, whether they be raw materials, work in process, completed goods, or material used or consumed in a business.[6] The basic test to be applied in determining whether goods are inventory is whether they are held for immediate or ultimate sale or lease, but the test must be applied with caution. The reason for the inclusion of materials used or consumed in a business, e.g., supplies of fuel and boxes and other containers to be used in packaging the goods, is that they will soon be used up or consumed in a course of production which results in an end product which will be sold. Most often the inventory will be

---

[6] *Weisel v. McBride et al.,* page 614.

[C7] *U.C.C.* 9-105(f).   [C9] *U.C.C.* 9-109(2).
[C8] *U.C.C.* 9-109(1).   [C10] *U.C.C.* 9-109(4).

goods offered for sale by a merchant who is financing his business through the medium of a security interest in the inventory.

Farm products.[C11] This category includes: crops and live-stock, supplies used or produced in farming operations, the products of crops or livestock in their unmanufactured state, (e.g. ginned cotton, wool, milk, and eggs)—provided that such items are in the possession of a debtor who is engaged in farming operations. The Code specifies that farm products are *not* equipment or inventory. Note that goods cease to be farm products and must therefore be reclassified when: (1) They are no longer in the farmer's possession, or (2) they have been subjected to a manufacturing process. Thus, when the farmer delivers his farm products to a marketing agency for sale or to a frozen food processor as raw materials, the products in the hands of the other party are inventory. Likewise, if the farmer maintained a canning operation, the canned product would be inventory even though it remained in his possession.

It should be apparent that the proper classification of goods in other instances as well is to be determined on the basis of its nature and intended use to be made of it by the debtor. For example, a television set in a dealer's warehouse is inventory to the dealer and as such may be covered by an inventory-financing arrangement. When the set is sold on a conditional sale contract to a consumer-customer it is a consumer good in the consumer's hands. The customer is the debtor; the dealer is the secured party; and the collateral is the specific television set. If an identical set were sold on the same terms to the owner of a tavern to be used for entertaining his customers, the set would be equipment in the hands of the tavern owner.

3-137 "Semi-intangible" Collateral.[C12] Three types of property-paper are included for convenience under this heading: documents of title, chattel paper, and instruments. They comprise various categories of paper used in commerce which are either negotiable or to some extent dealt with as though negotiable. They are all evidenced by an "indispensable writing," and are representative of obligations and rights.

Documents of title. Included under this heading are bills of lading, warehouse receipts and any other document "which in the regular course of business or financing is treated as adequately evidencing that the person in possession of it is entitled to receive, hold, and dispose of the document and the goods it covers."

Chattel paper. Chattel paper refers to a writing or writings which evidence both (1) an obligation to pay money, and (2) a security interest in or a lease of specific goods. The chattel paper is *itself* a security agreement. A security agreement in the form of a conditional sale contract, for example, is often executed in connection with a negotiable note or a series of notes. The group of writings—the contract plus the note—taken together as a composite constitute "chattel paper." A typical situa-

[C11] *U.C.C.* 9-109(3).　　　　　　　[C12] *U.C.C.* 9-105(b)(e)(g).

tion involving chattel paper as collateral is one in which a secured party who has obtained it in a transaction with his customer may wish to borrow against it in his own financing. To illustrate: A dealer sells an electric generator to a customer on a conditional sales contract and the customer signs a negotiable installment note. At this point the contract is the security agreement: the dealer is the secured party; the customer is the debtor; and the generator is the collateral-equipment. The dealer needing funds for working capital transfers the contract and the note to a finance company as security for a loan. In the transaction between dealer and finance company, the contract and note are the collateral-chattel paper; the finance company is the secured party; the dealer is the debtor; and the customer is now designated as the "account debtor."

Instrument. To be distinguished from chattel paper, an instrument means (1) a negotiable instrument (2) a security such as stocks and bonds, or (3) any other writing which evidences a right to the payment of money and which is not itself a *security agreement or lease.* In order to qualify as an instrument, the "other writing" must also be "of a type which is in ordinary course of business transferred by delivery with any necessary indorsement or assignment." Thus, the classification includes in addition to negotiable instruments those which are recognized as having some negotiable attributes. It must be noted that Article 9 deals with transfers of instruments for the purpose of giving *security* to the transferee, and this Article controls that phase of the transaction. Article 3–Commercial Paper governs the matters relative to the rights and obligations of the parties to a negotiable instrument as among themselves and Article 8–Investment Securities governs such rights and duties in respect to stocks and bonds.

3-138 Intangibles.[C13] Under this heading are three items: (1) accounts, (2) contract rights, and (3) "general intangibles." Accounts and contract rights are related as each is frequently the subject of commercial financing transactions, but neither is required to be evidenced by a writing as are the "semi-intangibles" discussed above.

Account.   Account means any right to payment arising out of the sale of goods or the rendition of services which is not evidenced by either an instrument or chattel paper. It is an account receivable and represents a right to payment earned by the seller's performance—the sale of goods or services actually rendered.

Contract right.   This is a right to payment under a contract, which right has not yet been earned, but rather is to be earned by performance under an existing contract. A contract does exist and when the party performs his obligations under the contract, his potential account becomes an account receivable.

General intangibles.   This heading includes various miscellaneous types of intangible personal property and contractual rights which may be used as commercial security and which do not fall within

C13 *U.C.C.* 9-106.

any of the preceding five classifications of intangible or semi-intangible property. Examples are good will, literary rights, patents, and copyrights.

3-139 Perfection by Possession.[C14] The possession of the collateral by the secured party gives notice of his security-interest—hence no public filing is required. As noted previously, the possessory security interest does not require a written security agreement. Therefore, this is the simplest method of handling a security transaction but it has very definite limitations in practice. In most secured transactions the debtor will want to use the collateral either as a consumer or as a manufacturer or merchant. Accordingly, the possessory security interest is appropriate primarily in those situations where the debtor does not need or desire the use of the collateral; where the collateral is of such nature that it does not have a practical utility to the debtor; or where it is the only feasible method of giving the required notice and protection.

Possession is the required method of perfection of a security interest in instruments and is the optional method in the case of collateral consisting of goods, negotiable documents of title and chattel paper. However, possession is the only method whereby complete protection in documents and chattel paper can be obtained since: 1) the rights of holders to whom a document has been negotiated by the debtor will prevail over the secured party, even though there has been a filing; and, 2) the purchaser of chattel paper from the debtor is given such protection if he takes without *actual notice* of the security interest, gives new value, and takes possession in the ordinary course of his business.

When possession is the method of perfection, the security interest is perfected at the time when the secured party takes possession. However, the secured party is given a grace period of 21 days from the time the security interest attaches during which his interest is perfected even though he does not take possession. The grace period applies only if the secured party gave new value to the debtor—it would not apply if the security interest in the instrument were given to buttress an existing obligation. Also, for the grace period to apply it is necessary that there be a *written* security agreement. The grace period is a substantial benefit to the parties and is in keeping with normal commercial necessity, but, unless he takes possession of the instrument, the secured party's rights will be defeated if the debtor transfers the instrument to a holder in due course or a bona fide purchaser. It is to be recalled that the basic characteristic of instruments is their negotiability.

A 21-day grace period during which the security interest is protected against creditors of the debtor without possession or filing is also provided in the case of *negotiable documents.* The same risk exists that the documents may be negotiated to a holder, who, of course, would prevail and the same requirements of a written security agreement and new value by the secured party apply. Special considerations are required if a negotiable document of title has been issued covering goods, since there could

[C14] *U.C.C.* 9-302.

theoretically be a security interest in both the *goods* and a *document* such as a warehouse receipt or bill of lading which *represents the goods.* This problem is resolved by a provision that no separate security interest can exist in the goods and at the same time in the document, during the period that the goods are in the *possession of the issuer* of a negotiable document. Therefore the creditor with a security interest in the document prevails. Possession of goods by a bailee gives notice to any potential financer or purchaser that a document of title may be outstanding and that he should proceed with caution.

A different rule applies if the goods in the hands of a bailee are covered by a *non-negotiable* document or if no document has been issued. In these circumstances, a security interest in goods in the hands of a bailee may be perfected: 1) by issuance of a document in the name of the secured party, 2) by giving the bailee proper notice of the secured party's interest, or 3) by filing as to the goods themselves.

For a variety of commercial reasons it may be necessary or desirable that the secured party temporarily release possession of the collateral to the debtor. Since the release is of short duration, it would be cumbersome to require a filing and the Code therefore provides that a security interest *remains perfected* for a period of 21 days without filing where a secured party having a *perfected security interest* releases the collateral to the debtor. This grace period applies only to 1) an instrument, 2) a negotiable document, and 3) goods in the hands of a bailee and not covered by a negotiable document of title. It applies only to a secured party who already has a perfected security interest. The purposes for which the collateral may be released to the debtor, in the case of *goods* or *documents* representing the goods, are limited to making them available to the debtor, 1) for the purpose of ultimate sale or exchange, or 2) "for the purpose of loading, unloading, storing, shipping, transshipping, manufacturing, processing, or otherwise dealing with them in a manner preliminary to their sale or exchange."

In the case of a temporary release of an instrument to the debtor, the purpose must be to enable the debtor to make a presentation of it, collect it, renew it, obtain registration of a transfer or to make an ultimate sale or exchange. The risk attendant upon such a release—an improper or unauthorized negotiation to a holder or sale to a bona fide purchaser by the debtor—has been previously discussed.

3-140 Perfection by Filing—the "Financing Statement." [C15] The most common method of perfecting a security interest is by filing a "financing statement." The financing statement, which is to be distinguished from the *security agreement,* is a document signed by both the debtor and the secured party which contains a description of the collateral and indicates that debtor and secured party have entered into a security agreement. Simple forms are available which contain spaces for additional provisions as agreed upon by the parties, but this basic information is all

[C15] *U.C.C.* 9-402.

that is required. If crops or fixtures constitute the collateral, then the financing statement must include a description of the real estate concerned.

A financing statement is not a substitute for a security agreement but a security agreement may be filed as a financing statement if it contains the required information and is signed by both parties but the converse is not true.[7] However, filing the security agreement would make public information which the parties might prefer to have remain confidential and for this reason there will usually be a separate financing statement.

The Code is based upon a system of "notice filing," which means that the purpose of filing is only to give notice that the secured party who filed it may have a security interest in the described collateral. A person searching the records therefore obtains minimal information and further inquiry from the parties to the financing statement would be required to obtain more complete information. A procedure is established for such disclosure by the secured party at the request of the debtor.

The financing statement may provide a maturity or expiration date, but more often it is silent on this point, since the statement usually will not mention the debt or obligation. The Code provides that in the absence of such date the filing is effective for a period of five years, subject to being renewed by the filing of a continuation statement signed by the secured party. If so renewed, it continues the effectiveness of the original statement for another five years. The presence in the records of a financing statement constitutes a burden upon the debtor since it reveals to all persons with whom he may be dealing that his property is or may be subject to the claims of others. Therefore, the Code provides for the filing of a *termination statement* to clear the record when the secured party is no longer entitled to a security interest as where the debtor has completely satisfied the obligation for which the security interest was given. Failure of the secured party to send a termination statement within 10 days after written demand by the debtor subjects him to a $100 penalty and also renders him liable for any loss occasioned to the debtor.

Filing a financing statement is permissive in secured transactions involving chattel paper or negotiable documents; it is *required* in the following secured transactions in order to perfect a non-possessory security interest: 1) intangible collateral—accounts, contract rights, and general intangibles; and 2) goods—inventory and equipment (in general), farm products, and consumer goods. However, the statute exempts transactions concerning certain purchase money security interests involving consumers and farmers. This exemption is discussed in the next section dealing with perfection by attachment.

Filing is also not required in the case of "an assignment by accounts or contract rights which does not alone or in conjunction with other assignments to the same assignee transfer a significant part of the outstanding accounts or contract rights of the assignor." Thus, the isolated transaction is exempted.[8]

---

[7] *American Card Co. v. H.M.H. Co.*, page 616.
[8] *Citizens & Southern Nat. Bank v. Capital Const. Co.*, page 617.

The Code provides three alternative methods in regard to the place where the financing statement is to be filed. A state may select a central filing system, a local filing system, or a combination system.[C16]

In states which have adopted exclusive central filing, all financing statements (except for fixtures) will be filed in the office of the Secretary of State.

In states with the combination local-central filing, most "commercial" or "business type" secured transactions require both a central filing *and* local filing. The local filing is made in the county where the debtor has his business—if he maintains more than one place of business in the state, local filing is not required. Included within this category are the following types of collateral: non-farm equipment, inventory, accounts, contract rights, and general intangibles.

In these states, any secured transaction involving a consumer or farmer requires only a local filing and the place to file is the county where the debtor resides. In addition, if the security is crops, there must be a filing in the office in the county where the land on which the crops are growing or to be grown is located. The various transactions which require only local filing include those involving: (1) farm equipment; (2) farm products; (3) accounts, contract rights or general intangibles arising from or relating to the sale of farm products; and (4) consumer goods.

The rules as to places of local filing are also applicable to the states which have adopted the exclusively local system.

Regardless of which filing alternative has been adopted, when the collateral is goods, which, at the time the security interest attaches, are fixtures or are to become fixtures, the financing statement must be filed in the office "where a mortgage on the real estate concerned would be filed or recorded." Local state law relative to what constitutes a fixture and other matters relating thereto will be controlling, as the Code does not venture into this area. (See Sec. 7-29, Book 7–Real Property.)

3-141 Perfection by Attachment.[C17] Perfection based upon attachment

is a very restricted concept and is limited to transactions involving installment sales to consumers and sales of farm equipment which has a purchase price of $2,500 or less.

The basic concept is that the attachment of the security interest is also the perfection of it; and the practical reason for the exceptions is that the tremendous volume of such transactions would make a filing requirement extremely burdensome. The exemption from the filing requirement does not apply if the collateral is either a fixture or a motor vehicle which is required to be licensed. The only method of perfecting a security interest in a motor vehicle is by a notation of such interest on the certificate of title if the state has enacted a certificate of title law. If a state does not have such a law, the filing of a financing statement is required.

It must be remembered that the exemption is limited to a "purchase money security interest" and that perfection by attachment gives only

C16 *U.C.C.* 9-401.   C17 *U.C.C.* 9-302.

limited protection to the secured party. It protects him from creditors of the debtor and from others to whom the farmer-consumer debtor may give a security interest in the collateral, but it does *not* protect against the rights of a good faith purchaser from the debtor who buys the collateral from him "without knowledge of the security interest, for value and for his own family or household purposes or his own farming operation." The secured party can obtain complete protection only by filing a financing statement which he has the option of doing.

3-142 Purchase Money Security Interests.[C18] The purchase money concept has application to transactions other than in consumer goods and farm equipment. It relates to any transaction in which a security interest is taken or retained in collateral in connection with the purchase thereof. Such interest is available to either the seller or the party who makes the funds available for the purchase, provided the funds are actually so used. Several characteristics are peculiar to the purchase money transaction. A 10-day grace period, following the date upon which the secured party gives value, is provided during which a security interest is perfected without filing, in those cases where filing is required for perfection. The secured party must, however, file *within* the 10-day period. The protection during such pre-filing period is limited: it gives priority only over the rights of (1) transferees in bulk from the debtor and (2) lien creditors to the extent that such rights arise "between the time the purchase money security interest attaches and the time of filing." It is to be noted that the secured party is *not* protected against: 1) a sale by the debtor to another party, or 2) a secured transaction wherein the collateral is given as security for a loan. To prevail in these cases a filing prior to the time when the sale is made or the subsequent security interest attaches is required. Other significant features of the purchase money security interest will be discussed in the next chapter.

3-143 Proceeds.[C19] The debtor may sell or otherwise dispose of the collateral with or without the authority, as provided in the security agreement, to do so. In such event the secured party has an interest in the "identifiable proceeds"—that which the debtor receives when he sells, exchanges, collects, or otherwise disposes of the collateral. The proceeds are either, 1) "cash proceeds"—money, checks, etc., or 2) "non-cash proceeds." In the latter category is the account receivable which the debtor obtained when he sold the collateral on credit.

Two situations must be considered: 1) where the debtor has the authority under the security agreement to dispose of the collateral as in the case of inventory, and 2) where the debtor unauthorizedly disposes of it as in the case of a sale of equipment by the debtor. In either situation, the secured party has an interest in the *proceeds;* but in the former he loses his security interest in the *collateral* which is sold in the ordinary course of business, while in the latter he retains a security interest in the

---

[C18] *U.C.C.* 9-107.   [C19] *U.C.C.* 9-306.

collateral and thus has a security interest in *both* the collateral *and* the proceeds.

The security interest in proceeds is based upon the interest in the primary collateral, hence it comes into existence whether or not provision is made therefore in the security agreement; and even though the security agreement may have prohibited disposition.

The financing statement may provide for a security interest in proceeds in which event no further filing is required; the original filing constitutes all that is necessary for *perfection* of a security interest in the proceeds. If (1) the financing statement covering the original collateral did *not* provide for proceeds or (2) if the security interest was perfected by possession or attachment rather than by filing, a perfected security interest in proceeds continues for 10 days provided the secured party: 1) files a financing statement covering the proceeds *within* the 10-day period, or 2) he takes possession of the proceeds.

The debtor may in the course of his business have sold the collateral (inventory) and then received it back either 1) by voluntary act on the part of his customer who was not satisfied with it, or 2) by repossession from a defaulting customer, or 3) by exercising the rights given to him under Article 2–Sales to reclaim the goods or stop them in transit. (See Sec. 3-24.) In general, the secured party's security interest attaches to the return or repossessed goods and continues to be perfected in such goods without further action. However, there are significant priority problems in connection with returned or repossessed goods. Other persons may be financing the seller's business beside the party who has a security interest in his inventory—e.g. one who purchases the chattel paper arising from the sale and one who purchases the account receivable arising therefrom. These problems will be discussed in the next chapter.

Special provisions relate to the secured party's interest in proceeds if the debtor becomes involved in bankruptcy or other insolvency proceedings. In general, the secured party is entitled, under the Code, to reclaim from the trustee in bankruptcy proceeds which can be identified as relating to the original collateral including cash proceeds which are identifiable—i.e. have not been commingled with other money or deposited in a bank account prior to the insolvency proceedings. Checks which have not been deposited by the debtor can also be reclaimed. If the cash (money and checks) proceeds are no longer identifiable because they have been commingled or deposited, the secured party nonetheless has a perfected security interest in the debtor's cash or bank account, but subject to the following limitations: 1) it is limited to a maximum of the amount of any cash proceeds received by the debtor within 10 days prior to the commencement of the bankruptcy proceedings, 2) less the amount of any cash proceeds which the debtor may have paid to the secured party during the 10-day period, and 3) subject to any existing right of set-off, as where an obligation may be owing from the secured party to the debtor.

The foregoing constitutes a general picture of the secured transaction including the creation, attachment, and perfection of a security interest.

The specific application of the rules of Article 9 as well as a delineation of the rights, duties, and obligations of the secured parties and debtors is determined largely by (1) the nature of the collateral and the use to be made of it by the debtor, and (2) the type of transaction. The next chapter is concerned with priorities, default and the remedies of the parties.

SECURED TRANSACTIONS: THE SECURITY INTEREST CASES

In re Wheatland Electric Products Co.

1964, 237 F.Supp. 820

Burroughs Corp. leased a machine to Wheatland Electric Products Co. for a term of one year and to continue thereafter until terminated. In the lease, the list price was stipulated and a monthly rental was set. The lease contained an option to purchase with a provision that 75 per cent of the rentals would be applied toward the purchase. The lease was subsequently extended. Wheatland filed a petition in bankruptcy and Burroughs filed a petition for reclamation of the machine in the bankruptcy proceedings. The referee refused the petition on the ground that the lease was a security agreement and since it had not been filed was invalid against the trustee in bankruptcy.

John L. Miller, J. . . . The question presented by the Petition for Review is whether the lease was intended as security and is to be determined by the facts of the case. In determining the intent of the parties, we may look only to the language of the lease itself, which provided that "there are no understandings, agreements, representations or warranties, express or implied, not specified herein, respecting this lease or the equipment or served hereinabove described."

The Code provides that "the inclusion of an option to purchase does not of itself make the lease one intended for security."

This language of the Code describes what was formerly known in Pennsylvania as a bailment lease, a security device by which one desiring to purchase an article of personal property, but not wishing to pay for it immediately, could secure possession of it with the right to use and enjoy it as long as the rental was paid and with the further right to become the owner, upon completing the installment payments, by the payment of an additional nominal sum.

The Courts, in referring to the term "nominal consideration," frequently use it interchangeably with the sum of $1.00 or some other small amount.

In the instant case, the additional amount which Wheatland was to pay to secure ownership of the machinery should it choose to exercise the option was a minimum of 25 per cent of the list price, or $2,006.25. That amount is not a nominal consideration for the right to become the owner of the equipment, but represents a substantial proportion of the purchase price.

Because we find that the leasing agreement between Burroughs and Wheatland was not one intended for security within the terms of the Uniform Commercial Code, Burroughs was not required to file a financing statement to perfect its interest and to maintain its right to reclamation. *For this reason, the Order of the Referee in Bankruptcy will be reversed and the case remanded to the Referee for proceedings consistent with this Opinion.*

Industrial Packaging Prod. Co. v. Fort Pitt Pack. Inc.

1960, (Pa.) 161 A. 2d 19

JONES, J.   The Provident Trust Company of Pittsburgh, pursuant to Section 9-403 of the Uniform Commercial Code filed the following financing statement in the office of the Prothonotary of Allegheny County on August 18, 1955:

15110 of 1955
Financing Statement

This financing statement is presented to a filing officer for filing pursuant to the Uniform Commercial Code.

1. Debtor (or assignor)—Fort Pitt Packaging Co., Inc., 5615 Butler Street, Pittsburgh 1, Pa.

2. Secured Party (or assignee)—Provident Trust Co., 900 East Ohio St., Pittsburgh 1, Pa.

3. Maturity date of obligation _____.

4. The financing statement covers the following types of property: All present and future accounts receivable submitted.

Fort Pitt Packaging Co., Inc.
Leo A. Levy, Treas.
Provident Trust Company
A. W. Charlton
Executive Vice Pres.

Under Section 9-403 of the Code such a statement remains effective for a period of five years. On August 19, 1955, Provident Trust Company filed a similar statement in the office of the Secretary of the Commonwealth in Harrisburg.

On February 4, 1957, Fort Pitt Packaging International Inc. entered into a written contract with the United States Government for the maintenance, repair, and overhaul of vehicles. On March 26, 1957, Fort Pitt entered into a contract with Empire Commercial Corporation wherein Empire agreed to lend Fort Pitt $140,000 and Fort Pitt agreed to assign to the Provident Trust Company as Empire's agent its contract with the United States Government and any and all payments due or to become due thereunder. On the same day, March 26, Fort Pitt sold and assigned to the Provident Trust Company, the payments due or which may become due under the government contract. Notice of the assignment was given to the Contracting Officer of the Department of the Army, pursuant to the provisions of the Federal Assignment of Claims Act of 1940, as amended, 31 U.S.C.A. Section 203.

One year later, on March 27, 1958, Fort Pitt was placed in receivership and on May 27, 1958, upon petition of creditors, Robert Mellin, Esquire, was appointed receiver. On June 10, 1958, the said receiver petitioned the Court of Common Pleas of Allegheny County for a rule upon Empire to show cause why the assignments of the proceeds for Fort Pitt's services performed under the government contracts should not be declared null, void, and ineffective as against the receiver. After hearing held and argument, the court below dismissed the receiver's petition. From that order this appeal was taken. . . .

Appellant Mellin contends that the filing of the financing statement in 1955 was not sufficient to secure the amounts due under Fort Pitt's contract with the United States Government which was executed in 1957. The filing of the financing statement pursuant to Section 9-403 was entirely proper. The Uniform Commercial Code does not require that the secured party as listed in such statement be a principal creditor and not an agent. In this case, apparently, the Provident Trust Company filed the financing statement as a principal creditor, but in 1957, it became the collecting agent for the Empire Commercial Corporation. Neither the Provident Trust Company nor Empire had any reason to believe that it would be necessary to file a second financing statement which would in all respects duplicate the 1955 statement with the exception that the Provident Trust Company would be listed as an agent for Empire. The purpose of filing this financing statement is to give notice to potential future creditors of the debtor or purchasers of the collateral. It makes no difference as far as such notice is concerned whether the secured party listed in the filing statement is a principal or an agent, and no provision in the Uniform Commercial Code draws such a distinction.

The financing statement covered "all present and future accounts receivable submitted." Section 9-110 of the Uniform Commercial Code provides that "for the purposes of this Article any description is sufficient whether or not it is specific if it reasonably identifies the thing described." There is no doubt that the description in the financing statement reasonably identifies the collateral security. It is difficult under the circumstances to imagine how the description could be more complete without filing new and amended descriptions each time a new account receivable falls within the purview of the financing statement. Nowhere in the Uniform Commercial Code is such a requirement set forth.

Section 9-204 (3) provides that "except as provided in subsection (4) (which deals with crops and consumer goods) *a security agreement may provide that collateral, whenever acquired, shall secure any* advances made or other *value given at any time* pursuant to the security agreement. [Emphasis added.]

In the 1957 agreement between Fort Pitt and Empire, Fort Pitt agreed to assign to Provident Trust Company all payments to be received as they became due from the United States Government under Fort Pitt's contract of February 4, 1957 with the Government. These amounts due fell within the clause "future accounts receivable submitted" contained in the 1955 financing statement filed by Provident Trust Company. Comment 2 to Section 9-303 of the Code states that the "secured party is entitled to have his security interest recognized in insolvency proceedings instituted against the debtor." Therefore, the interest of the secured party, Provident Trust Company is superior to that of the receiver in bankruptcy and any funds which have been placed in the hands of Provident Trust Company pursuant to the Assignment by Fort Pitt need not be turned over to the receiver. These funds are properly being held by the Provident Trust Company for the benefit of its principal, Empire Commercial Corporation.

Order affirmed.

In re United Thrift Stores, Inc.

1965, 242 F.Supp. 714

AUGELLI, J. This matter is before the Court on petition of Redisco, Inc. (Redisco) for review of an order of the Referee in Bankruptcy (Referee), made on January 5, 1965, *which denied Redisco's petition for reclamation of certain property from the Bankrupt herein,* United Thift Stores, Inc. (United Thrift).

On October 30, 1964, United Thrift filed a petition for an *arrangement under Chapter XI of the Bankruptcy Act.* Redisco was listed in United Thrift's schedules as an *unsecured creditor* in the amount of $42,753.79. On November 13, Redisco filed its petition to reclaim from United Thrift certain *Kelvinator appliances,* or for the *proceeds* thereof, which totaled $36,816.44.

On November 24, the Referee . . . denied the petition for reclamation *on the ground that United Thrift bought the appliances in question on open account, and that therefore Redisco was not a secured creditor entitled to reclamation.* An order to this effect was entered on January 5, 1965. In the meantime, on December 16, United Thrift was adjudicated a bankrupt, and the receiver, Masterson, was thereafter appointed Trustee.

Redisco filed this petition for review on January 13, 1965, and the Referee's findings of fact and conclusions of law were filed on February 23, 1965. The following are the facts disclosed by the record in this case.

Redisco is a subsidiary of American Motors Corporation, and is engaged in the business of financing Kelvinator electrical home appliances sold to distributors by the American Motors Sales Corporation. United Thrift was engaged in the business of buying Kelvinator and other brand appliances, and selling them to retail dealers.

On March 12, 1963, a *financing statement,* pursuant to the Uniform Commercial Code (effective in New Jersey on January 1, 1963) (N.J.S.A. 12A:1-101 *et seq.*), was filed with the Secretary of State of New Jersey. This statement covered "(i)nventory of Kelvinator appliances and products including Kelvinator refrigerators, washers, dryers, freezers, and other Kelvinator gas and electrical appliances." United Thrift was named as *debtor,* and Redisco as the *secured party. Proceeds* of *collateral* were also noted as being covered. There is no indication of *termination* of financing on the statement before the Court.

On March 22, 1963, the Secretary of State certified that he had searched his files under the Uniform Commercial Code, and found four previously recorded, *secured parties* for United Thrift as *debtor.* Redisco thereupon duly *sent notices, informing the other secured party* that it "has or expects to acquire a *purchase money security interest* in *inventory* of Kelvinator electrical and gas appliances. . . , which (it) . . . will from *time to time deliver* or cause to be delivered to United Thrift. . . ."

Four separate *agreements* were thereafter entered into between the Kelvinator Division of the American Motors Sales Corporation, United Thrift, and Redisco. These agreements, on identical printed forms prepared by Redisco, are entitled "Redisco Wholesale Floor Plan." Each agreement contains three sections, as follows: (1) a bill of sale from the Kelvinator Division to Redisco for the articles listed by model and serial numbers; (2) a trust receipt from United Thrift to Redisco, covering the same articles and setting forth a release amount opposite each item; and (3) a signed, but incompleted, promissory note from United Thrift to Redisco, which bears the same identification number as the trust receipt.

In the section labeled "trust receipt," United Thrift acknowledges the receipt of the listed appliances, acknowledges that they are the property of Redisco and will be returned to Redisco on demand and agrees "not to sell, loan, deliver, pledge, mortgage, or otherwise dispose of said articles to any other person until after payment of amounts shown in Release Amount column below." The trust receipts do not indicate thereon that any payments have been made, or any appliances released, pursuant thereto.

While Redisco has raised a number of issues in its petition for review, this Court will address itself only to *the question of whether Redisco has a valid security interest,* and is therefore entitled to reclamation. Since the Court is of the opinion that the Referee's conclusion, that Redisco's security interest is invalid, is clearly erroneous, it becomes unnecessary to consider the other issues on this review. . . .

Under the Uniform Commercial Code as adopted in New Jersey (Code) (N.J.S.A. 12A:9-102(1) (a)) provides that the Code chapter dealing with secured transactions (N.J.S.A. 12A:9-101 *et seq.*) is applicable *"to any transaction (regardless of its form) which is intended to create a security interest in personal property. . . ."* N.J.S.A. 12A:9-102(2) specifically refers to said chapter applying to security interests created by a "trust receipt."

The term *"security agreement,"* which is defined in N.J.S.A. 12A:9-105(1) (h) as "an agreement which creates or provides for a security interest," is used in the Code in place of such terms as "trust receipt." A "security interest" is defined under N.J.S.A. 12A:1-201(37) as *an interest in personal property which secures payment of an obligation.* Finally, N.J.S.A. 12A:9-201 provides that "a security agreement is effective according to its terms *between the parties . . . and against creditors."*

The four trust receipts in this case meet the requirements of N.J.S.A. 12A:9-203(1) (b) for a valid security agreement, since they are *written agreements* signed by United Thrift, grant *security interests* in *collateral,* and contain a description of said collateral. The *financing statement* between Redisco and United Thrift also meets the *filing requirements* in N.J.S.A. 12A:9-401 *et seq.* Pursuant to N.J.S.A. 12A:9-204(1), the security interests herein *attached* when the agreements were made, value was given, and United Thrift received possession of the collateral. Under N.J.S.A. 12A:9-302 and N.J.S.A. 12A:9-303(1), *said security interests were perfected when they attached.*

The *financing statement* in this case between Redisco and United Thrift was executed and filed *prior* to the making of the *security agreements.* The Trustee contends that an agreement for the creation of a security interest must be in existence *prior* to the filing of a financing statement, because under N.J.S.A. 12A:9-204(1) a security interest cannot attach until there is an agreement that it attach.

This Court finds no such requirement in the Code. N.J.S.A. 12A:9-402(1) provides that "(a) financing statement may be filed *before* a security agreement is made or a security interest otherwise attaches." Under N.J.S.A. 12A:9-303(1), where the financing statement is filed *before* the security interest attaches, the security interest is *perfected* when it does so attach. *Thus, the Code clearly contemplates that the financing statement may be filed prior to the making of the security agreement, and that a security interest need not be in existence at the time the financing statement is filed.*

In holding Redisco's security interest invalid, the Referee concluded that

> The 4 separate trust receipt agreements were contradictory in that provisions for *credit* on a 30, 60 and/or 90 day basis were included therein. The fact that Redisco, Inc. made no effort to enforce the provisions of the agreements which set up a trust, and the fact that United Thrift Stores, Inc. made, and Redisco, Inc. accepted, payments on the 30, 60 and/or 90 day basis, show that the parties both understood that the agreements provided for *sales on open account.*

However, the Code contains no requirements with regard to method of payment affecting the validity of a security interest. (See N.J.S.A. 12A:9-203(1) (b)) In fact, N.J.S.A. 12A:9-205 provides that a "security interest is *not invalid* . . . by reason of the failure of the secured party to require the debtor to account for proceeds or replace collateral." Thus, under the Code, payment is not relevant to the question of validity of a security interest, and there is no requirement of "policing" of collateral by the secured party.

Moreover, this Court does not agree that payment of release amounts and payment on 30-60-90 day terms are contradictory methods of payment. The only testimony in this case regarding payment was given by James K. Marlowe, the authorized agent of Redisco in this matter, who was the sole witness at the hearing. He testified that each term payment

was applied to reduce the total indebtedness of the particular trust receipt, and not to release particular appliances. Thus, the release amount
of each appliance was *reduced proportionately* by the term payments that
were received, but *no single appliance was released* because none of the
trust receipts was fully paid. Redisco's security interest in the collateral
was thereby protected *while any part of the total indebtedness on each
agreement remained unpaid.*

Since Redisco's *security interests* are valid under the Code, and since
United Thrift is in default by reason of its failure to make payments as
provided in the *security agreements,* Redisco is entitled to take *possession
of the collateral,* or to obtain the *proceeds* thereof. (N.J.S.A. 12A:9-508
and N.J.S.A. 12A:9-306) Since Redisco's security interests *attached* and
were perfected prior to the filing of the Chapter XI petition, Redisco's
rights thereto take *priority* over the rights of the Trustee.

*Under the circumstances, the order of the Referee in denying Redisco's
reclamation will be reversed. . . .*

Al Maroone Ford, Inc. v. Manheim Auto Auction, Inc.

1965, (Pa.) 208 A.2d 290

Brown bought a new car from a New York dealer, Al Maroone Ford
Inc., under an installment sales contract under which the seller retained
title. The car was driven to Pennsylvania and sold to Manheim Auto
Auction, Inc. Brown executed a New York certificate of sale. The New
York dealer assigned the contract to the Bank of Buffalo and it was immediately recorded. All of the above transactions took place on April 6,
1961. Brown defaulted and the defendant repossessed the car. Al Maroone, for the benefit of the bank, brought an action against the defendant. Under New York law the reservation of title was effective
even though no notation of the sellers' interest appeared on the title
certificate. The lower court ruled in favor of Manheim and plaintiff
appealed.

FLOOD, J.   . . . [T]he court below held that the appellee [Manheim
Auto Auction, Inc.] was a "(b)uyer in ordinary course of business" under
1-201(9) of the Uniform Commercial Code and therefore took the car
free of the seller's perfected security interest under 9-307(1) of the Code.

A buyer in ordinary course of business is defined in 1-209(9) of the
Code as a "person who in good faith and without knowledge that the sale
to him is in violation of the ownership rights or security interest of a
third party in the goods buys in ordinary course from a person in the
business of selling goods of that kind. . . ." The appellant raises no
question as to the appellee's good faith or knowledge of the appellant's
rights. Therefore we shall assume its good faith and ignorance of the
appellant's rights and confine our consideration to the question of
whether it bought "in ordinary course from a person in the business of
selling goods of that kind."

There is no evidence that the appellee purchased from one "in the
business of selling goods of that kind," i.e., a dealer in automobiles. The

car was a new automobile when the Browns bought it the day before in New York. While the certificate of sale executed by Brown to appellee indicates that the car was used, the word "New" was inserted in the box for the listing of the last plate number of the vehicle.

Under these circumstances, we cannot find from the agreed statement that the appellee purchased from a dealer or a "person in the business of selling goods of that kind." The recitals in the certificate of sale give rise, at most, to an inference that Gordon Brown was the owner of the car and was trading it as a dealer in used cars. These self-serving recitals do not constitute proof that Brown owned the car or was a dealer. The evidence is that he and his wife were the owners. The transaction with the appellee appeared to be a sale to a dealer, not a consumer.

The definition of "buyer in ordinary course" as one who buys "in ordinary course" from a dealer is in part circular. Under our cases a sale in the ordinary course normally means a sale from inventory. The comment of the draftsmen of the Code likewise states that the definition of "(b)uyer in ordinary course of business," restricts it, for practical purposes, almost exclusively to inventory. It also states that in most of the cases covered the goods will in fact be inventory. Nothing in the case stated indicates that there was a sale from inventory here.

We conclude that the appellee was not a buyer in ordinary course. Moreover, the facts that the car was a substantially new car, purchased for resale many miles away from the place of business of the sellers by an auctioneer who has had experience with foreign security interests in automobiles, without any inquiry, so far as the agreed facts show, as to existence of any such interest, all tell against the contention that the appellee was a buyer in ordinary course.

Since Manheim is not a buyer in ordinary course under the Code, it may take against the appellant, the holder of a security interest, only "to the extent that (it) gives value and receives delivery of the collateral without knowledge of the security interests and before it is perfected." (Uniform Commercial Code, 9-301(10 (c). . . .) Here the security interest of the appellant was perfected when the appellee bought the car . . . and the appellee's purchase was subject to the security interest. Therefore, the sale of the car by the appellee was a conversion of the car as against the appellant.

The judgment is reversed and is entered in favor of the use-plaintiff, Bank of Buffalo, against the defendant, Manheim Auto Auction, Inc.

Main Investment Company v. Gisolfi

1964, (Pa.) 190 A.2d 535

The defendant, Gisolfi, bought an automobile from Casterline Auto Marts, a nonfranchised dealer in new and used automobiles. Casterline had purchased it from another dealer for resale. The defendant received a bill of sale. Shortly thereafter Casterline delivered to plaintiff finance company a security agreement for financing nine automobiles, and included in it the one it had sold to defendant, for a loan of $2,300. A certificate of title in the name of Casterline and listing an encumbrance of $2,300 in favor of Main was also delivered. There were conflicting claims to the automobile and it was tied up for about six months. The finance company brought a replevin action to recover the car. The lower court awarded the automobile to the defendant, Gisolfi, but denied him an award of damages. Both parties appealed.

MONTGOMERY, J.   In regard to the replevin action, we are constrained to agree with the lower courts summary of the facts, wherein it stated,

> that at the time of these events that Casterline had title to the vehicle, else a certificate in its name could not have been issued to Main as the lien holder, that the vehicle whether "new" or "used" was in Casterline inventory, that Main financed it as part of inventory, that Main had no security interest in the vehicle at the time of the sale to Gisolfi, and that as to this vehicle at least, Casterline perpetrated a fraud on Main in securing an advance on a vehicle which had passed out of Casterline's possession by a sale from inventory in the ordinary course of trade.

We further agree that the lower court correctly concluded that the Uniform Commercial Code 9-307 conclusively controls this matter. That section states: "(1) A buyer in ordinary course of business . . . other than a person buying farm products from a person engaged in farming operations takes free of a security interest created by his seller even though the security interest is perfected and even though the buyer knows of its existence.". . . (9-307) Gisolfi was a buyer in the ordinary course of business in this situation; he bought the car from a dealer in the business of selling cars from inventory. Thus Gisolfi was unaffected by any security interest in the automobile held by others.

Main relies on *Sterling Acceptance Co. v. Grimes* (194 Pa.Super. 503, 168 A.2d 600 (1961)) for the principle that, since the automobile in question was not a "new" car, Gisolfi was on notice that a certificate of title had been issued for the automobile; therefore, Gisolfi should have demanded that certificate of title before accepting delivery of the automobile. In that case, at page 509 of 194 Pa.Super., at page 603 of 168 A.2d, this Court stated, in construing the Uniform Commercial Code and The Vehicle Code, "We believe that the legislature did not intend to have the rights of buyers of new automobiles . . . defeated by lien creditors of the dealer, through the noting of encumbrances upon dealer's certificates of title which were not required and generally were not issued." (Emphasis supplied) Further, we stated, "The purchaser of a used automobile knows that a certificate of title has been issued for the automobile and expects to have it produced at the time of sale, but the purchaser of a new vehicle expects no such certificate to exist." Even if that be taken as a correct principle of law, we do not believe that it is applicable in this situation. When Gisolfi bought and accepted delivery of the automobile in question, no security interest had been placed on the automobile; and, in fact, Main never could have a security interest in this automobile because title and possession had passed to Gisolfi on October 28, 1961. The trust receipt security agreement was not executed until eleven days later, on November 8, 1961.

. . . Gisolfi seeks damages for his inability to use the automobile from October 28, 1961, until May 1, 1962. The lower court denied damages to Gisolfi on the theory that the detention of the automobile was due to the fraud of Casterline and not to any action of Main, who was only making an effort "to support a supposed legal right." However, we find that this reasoning is irrelevant to the issue of damages in this case. It is well established in Pennsylvania that the successful party in a replevin action has the right to establish damages.

Judgment for defendant. [Gisolfi]

Weisel v. McBride et al.

1959. (Pa. Super.) 156 A.2d 613

HIRT, J.   The plaintiff on June 6, 1957, bought a Studebaker Station Wagon from the defendant James McBride trading as McBride Motor Sales, who at the time was an authorized distributor or dealer for Studebaker cars. He paid this defendant the sale price in full, including the Pennsylvania Sales Tax and the fee for registration of title in his name. Thereupon, on the above date, possession of the automobile was given to the plaintiff and he then signed an application for title to the car in his name and delivered the application to McBride for forwarding to the proper authorities. Notwithstanding he had been paid the full consideration for the sale, McBride subsequently, on June 12, 1957, executed a collateral mortgage in favor of the County Trust Company under an existing floor plan agreement which McBride had with that bank. The mortgage covered the identical car sold and delivered to the plaintiff. Accompanying the mortgage McBride gave his note to the bank for $2,411.66, the amount of his debt as stated in the collateral mortgage. McBride then sent in his own application for title to the car, instead of the plaintiff's and a certificate of title was issued by the Commonwealth of Pennsylvania in the name of McBride Motor Sales with an encumbrance of $2,411.66 in favor of County Trust Company noted thereon. The Trust Company, subsequently, on May 1, 1958, assigned the above note and the collateral mortgage to the defendant John P. McNelly. Title to the car with the encumbrance noted thereon was also assigned to McNelly by McBride. In this action in equity the plaintiff sought a mandatory injunction directing McNelly to deliver to him, Charles A. Weisel Jr., a certificate of title in his name for the Studebaker Station Wagon, free and clear of all encumbrances, and without further cost to him. The court after hearing, refused relief and dismissed the complaint; hence this, the plaintiff's appeal.

On August 16, 1956, a financing statement had been filed by McBride Motor Sales in the Prothonotary's office of Somerset County under Section 9-302 of the Uniform Commercial Code of April 6, 1953, P.L. 3, 12A P.S. Section 9-302 for the wholesale "floor planning" of Studebaker and Packard automobiles not to exceed four cars at any one time, at factory delivered prices. Plaintiff has recently traded the Studebaker in on a new automobile in one of the Western States and it is important that he assign to the new owner his title to the station wagon here involved.

The Uniform Commercial Code in Section 9-307, 12A P.S. Section 9-307 provides: "(1) In the case of inventory, and in the case of other goods as to which the secured party files a financing statement in which he claims a security interest in proceeds, a buyer in ordinary course of business takes free of a security interest even though perfected and even though the buyer knows of the terms of the security agreement." And under the heading: "Power to Transfer; Good Faith Purchase of Goods; 'Entrusting'" the Code in Section 2-403, 12A P.S. Section 2-403 provides: "(1) A purchaser of goods acquires all title which his transferor has or has power to transfer except that a purchaser of a limited interest acquires rights only to the extent of the interest purchased. A person with voidable title has power to transfer a good title to a good faith purchaser for value. (2) Any entrusting of possession of goods to a merchant who deals in goods of that kind gives him power to transfer all rights of the entruster to a buyer in ordinary course of business. (3) 'Entrusting' includes any delivery and any acquiescence in retention of possession regardless of any condition expressed between the parties to the delivery or acquiescence and regardless of whether the procurement of the entrusting or the possessor's disposition of the goods have been such as to be larcenous under the criminal law." In the comment on this section it is said in 12A P.S. Section 2-403: "The many particular situations in which a buyer in ordinary course of business from a dealer has been protected against reservation of property or other hidden interest are gathered by subsections (2)-(4) into a single principle protecting persons who buy in ordinary course out of inventory. Consignors have no reason to complain, nor have lenders who hold a security interest in the inventory, since the very purpose of goods in inventory is to be turned into cash by sale." The instant case presents one of "the many situations" in which the Commercial Code intends to protect "persons who buy in ordinary course out of inventory" as did the plaintiff in this case. It was the obligation of McBride when he received the entire consideration for the sale from Weisel, to satisfy any outstanding "security interest" against the Studebaker Station Wagon. Instead, McBride fraudulently created a new debt with the identical automobile as security in an accompanying mortgage. The fraud was inexcusable on any ground for notwithstanding the appearance of regularity, he used the property of another—the automobile which had been sold to Weisel—as security for his debt. A transaction, even such as this, may be good between the parties but in this case the mortgage was wholly void as to Weisel under the above sections of the Commercial Code. . . .

The order is reversed and the action is remanded to the lower court for the entry of a mandatory decree directing the defendants James Mc-

Bride and John P. McNelly to deliver to the plaintiff the title to the 1957 Studebaker Station Wagon engine number 12223680 free and clear of all encumbrances and without further cost to him.

American Card Company v. H. M. H. Co.

1963, (R.I.) 196 A.2d 150

CONDON, J.   This is a partnership creditors' claim for priority as a valid security interest under the Uniform Commercial Code. . . .

The sole question for our determination is whether the superior court erred in holding that 6A-9-203(1) (b) of the Code requires in a case of this kind a written security agreement between the debtor and the secured party before a prior security interest in any collateral can attach. The claimants, Oscar A. Hillman & Sons, a co-partnership, contend that a separate agreement in writing is not necessary if the written financing statement which was filed contains the debtor's signature and a description of the collateral. In support of that position they point out that . . . 6A-9-402 recognizes that a security agreement and a financing statement can be one and the same document. They further argue that "under the unique circumstances that exist in this case" the minimum requirements of 6A-9-203 are satisfied. . . .

Those circumstances may be summarized as follows. On February 21, 1962 the debtor corporation executed a promissory note in the sum of $12,373.33 payable to claimants. On March 14, 1962 the corporation as debtor and claimants as secured parties signed a financing statement form provided by the office of the Secretary of State and filed it in that office in accordance with the provisions of the Uniform Commercial Code. . . . (6A-9-402)

On July 2, 1962 Melvin A. Chernick and George F. Treanor were appointed co-receivers of the debtor corporation. On October 6, 1962 claimants duly filed their proof of debt and asserted therein a security interest against certain tools and dies of the debtor which were mentioned in the financing statement as collateral.

The claimants argue that the Code requires no " 'magic words,' no precise, formalistic language which must be put in writing in order for a security interest to be enforceable." And they further argue that "the definition of a security agreement indicates, the question of whether or not a security interest is 'created or provided for' is a question of fact which must be decided upon the basis of the words and deeds of the parties." They rely on the definition of "agreement" in 6A-9-105(1) (h) for support of this latter contention.

Upon consideration of those provisions of the Code, we are of the opinion that they are not decisive of the special problem posed in the instant case. The receivers contend here, as they did successfully before the superior court, that the controlling section of the Code is, in the circumstances, 6A-9-203(1) (b) and that in order to establish a security interest in any collateral the secured party must show that "the debtor has signed a security agreement which contains a description of the collateral. . . ." They concede that such a signed agreement may serve as a financing statement if it also contains the requirements thereof, but they deny that a financing statement, absent an agreement therein, can be treated as the equivalent of a security agreement.

The pertinent language of 6A-9-402 in this regard is, "A copy of the security agreement is sufficient as a financing statement if it contains the above information and is signed by both parties." In other words, while it is possible for a financing statement and a security agreement to be one and the same document as argued by claimants, it is not possible for a financing statement which does not contain the debtor's grant of a security interest to serve as a security agreement.

In our opinion there is merit in the receivers' contention, and since the financing statement filed here contains no such grant it does not qualify as a security agreement.

In an article . . . (42 B.U.L.Rev. 187) entitled "Accounts Receivable Financing: Transition from Variety to Uniform Commercial Code," it is stated at page 189: "The financing statement does not of itself create a security interest. An agreement in writing signed by the debtor 'which contains a description of the collateral' is required." In the absence of any judicial precedent this commentary on the Code is worthy of consideration in the solution of the question here.

The financing statement which the claimants filed clearly fails to qualify also as a security agreement because nowhere in the form is there any evidence of an agreement by the debtor to grant claimants a security interest.

The claimants' appeal is denied and dismissed, the decree appealed from is affirmed, and the cause is remanded to the superior court for further proceedings.

Citizens & Southern Nat. Bank v. Capital Const. Co.

1965, (Ga.) 144 S.E.2d 465

One Mozley, doing business as Briarcliff Plumbing and Heating Co., assigned to the plaintiff bank an account owing him by the defendant. Mozley had written to the defendant, Capital, as follows:

> Re: Work completed at Buick, Oldsmobile, Pontiac Plant.
> Gentlemen: The work completed and billed to you in the amount of $13,-809.00 has been assigned to the Citizens And Southern National Bank. Please issue your checks payable to them and us when remitting.

This letter contained a notation that it was "Accepted by: Capital Construction Company, Guy H. Miles" and dated 8/31/64.

The money was not paid by defendant and plaintiff brought suit. Defendant alleged that it had defenses and counterclaims against Mozley. The bank alleged that it had loaned Mozley more than the amount of money due under the contract; that it had not been aware of defenses or counterclaims; and that it had relied on defendant's "acceptance."

The lower court ruled in favor of the defendant and the plaintiff appealed.

NICHOLDS, J. Under Code Ann. 109A-9-302(1) (e), the assignment of an account not embracing a loan or in connection with other assignments to the same assignee, a significant part of the outstanding accounts or contract rights of the assignor does not have to be perfected by the filing of a financing statement under the Uniform Commercial Code, and under Code Ann. 109A-9-203 the security agreement must be in writing but not in any particular form. The writing relied upon in the instant case stated that the "account" (right to payment for goods sold or services rendered, Code Ann. 109-A-106), had been assigned to the plaintiff, the defendant acknowledged such assignment and the writing was delivered to the plaintiff who on the strength thereof loaned money to the debtor (the defendant's creditor).

Under the decision of the Supreme Court in *Southern Mutual Life Insurance Ass'n v. Durdin* (132 Ga. 495, 64 S.E. 264, 131 Am.St.Rep. 210), the language used in the letter addressed to the defendant and "accepted" by it was sufficient to constitute an assignment of the indebtedness so as to create a security interest under the terms of the Uniform Commercial Code and there had been value given (the loan to the defendant's creditor) so as to bring it under the terms of Code Ann. 109-A-9-204 before the present action was filed.

As between the plaintiff and the defendant the petition set forth a cause of action and the trial court erred in sustaining the defendant's general demurrer and dismissing the petition.

Judgment reversed.

CHAPTER 27
REVIEW QUESTIONS AND PROBLEMS

1. *A,* a manufacturer, sold a machine used in the manufacture of boxes to *B* Co. The machine was installed in *B*'s plant. *A* retained a security interest in the machine and filed the security agreement only with the County Deeds Registrar. *B* thereafter filed a petition in bankruptcy. As between *A* and the trustee on bankruptcy, who should prevail?

2. *A* Co., wishing to obtain equipment, entered into an agreement with *B* Leasing Co. whereby the latter purchased the equipment from the manufacturer and leased it to *A*. *A* made a substantial initial payment and agreed to make fixed monthly payments for 5 years, the total payments equalling the cost of the equipment plus 7 per cent interest. Shortly thereafter, *A* Co. filed in bankruptcy, and *B* Leasing Co. wishes to obtain the equipment. Can *B* recover it from the trustee in bankruptcy?

3. *X* Bank financed the purchase of machinery used by a road con-

tractor. The items financed were diesel crawler tractors, a front end loader and a backhoe with a diesel engine. The contractor is bankrupt and the trustee claims the right to possession of the vehicles. Should the trustee prevail over X Bank?

4. *A* as debtor and *X* Bank as secured party entered into a security agreement. A financing statement was filed but it was not signed by the bank. In a controversy between *X* Bank and the trustee in bankruptcy, who should prevail?

5. *A* loaned *B* $500 to enable him to purchase a color TV set. *A* and *B* entered into a security agreement whereby *A* was given a security interest in the set. *A* wishes to know whether or not he should file a financing statement. Advise him.

6. *A*, a manufacturer of novelty items, delivered a large quantity to *B*, a retailer, on a consignment basis. *B* was to receive a commission on the sale of the goods and to return the unsold goods at the end of a specified period. *B* became insolvent. Can *B*'s creditors reach the consigned goods? How could *A* himself protect against the claims of these creditors?

7. *A* sold a TV set to a dentist for the waiting room in the dentist's office. What should *A* do to perfect a security interest in the set?

8. *A* is negotiating with *B* to furnish financing for *B*'s retail business. What should he do in order to determine the status of *B*'s assets?

9. *F*, a farmer, borrowed $10,000 from *L* and secured the loan by a security interest in growing crops. The lien was perfected by filing, but the crops were harvested and sold to *X* Co., who paid *F* for them. Does *L* have a claim against *X* Co., for the value of the crops as security for the $10,000, *F* being unable to pay?

10. *X* Co., a manufacturer of bicycles, borrowed money from time to time from a bank and gave as security its inventory of raw material and semi-processed or processed goods then on hand or to be found on hand from time to time in the future. Proper filing took place. Later *X* Co. became bankrupt. Is the bank's lien superior to that held by the trustee in bankruptcy on inventory acquired after the loan was made by the bank?

11. *A* is arranging with *B* to finance *B*'s business. It will be a secured financing plan and *A* will have a security interest in inventory, equipment, and accounts receivable belonging to *B*. What provisions should *A* require for inclusion in the security agreement? In the financing statement?

12. *F* Finance Co. has a security interest in *A*'s inventory. The financing statement and security agreement provide for a "floating lien" on *A*'s property. *A* wishes to finance with *X* Finance Co. which has offered more favorable terms than *F*. What problems exist with reference to financing with *X* Finance Co.? Can this problem be resolved?

chapter 28

Secured Transactions: Priorities, Default and Remedies

3-144 Introduction. As noted in the preceding chapter, problems as to the respective rights of secured creditors in a debtor's collateral arise when "proceeds" are involved and when returned or repossessed goods are the subject of claims by various financing parties. There are many other situations which present problems of priority as between creditors each of whom has or claims a security interest in the same collateral. This is especially true if the debtor is in bankruptcy.[1] Related problems arise (when the debtor has sold or otherwise disposed of the collateral) as to the rights of the purchaser vis-à-vis the secured creditors. Conflicting claims against collateral may also arise 1) when it becomes a fixture (see Sec. 3-149), 2) when it has become attached to *personal property* belonging to another, 3) when it has been repaired or improved by the services or materials of another, or 4) when it has been processed by another as where raw materials are manufactured into a finished product. In all of the foregoing situations it becomes necessary to "sort out" the conflicting interests and determine a priority among them.

The security agreement should contain provisions as to 1) the respective rights and duties of the *debtor and secured party* in connection with the collateral, 2) the rights of the secured party upon default or in the event that he has cause for concern as to the ability of the debtor to perform his obligations under the agreement, and 3) other pertinent factors relating to the course of action to be taken in fulfillment of the agreement. The parties may in general tailor the agreement to suit their particular needs, but there are certain limitations on this "free-

[1] *U.S. v. Lebanon Woolen Mills,* page 628.

dom of contract" which are designed to protect the debtor. In those situations in which the parties have not spelled out in the Security Agreement the procedures to be followed upon default the Code's provisions on default apply.

PRIORITIES

3-145 Priorities—In General.[C1] The secured party who has not filed a financing statement or otherwise perfected his security interest has only a very limited protection as against third parties but he will be protected in certain situations.[2] He has an interest in the collateral *as against the debtor* but little protection against third parties. As a general rule he will have priority over persons who acquire the property with *knowledge* of his interest or become lien creditors with such knowledge. For example, a person who buys equipment which he knows is subject to a security interest would not be protected. Where two secured parties are involved one may agree to subordinate his interest to that of the other.[3]

The Code provides a series of rules to determine priorities of perfected security interests where more than one party has or claims an interest in the same collateral. As in other areas of the law of secured transactions, the nature of the collateral, its intended use, and the relationship of the parties have an important bearing on priorities. The following sections discuss specific priority issues where perfection has occurred.

3-146 Chattel Paper as Proceeds. A merchant whose inventory is financed under a security agreement may sell items from inventory to a customer on an installment sale contract. Such contract (chattel) paper is now the collateral since it is the proceeds derived from the sale. If the secured party does not take possession of the chattel paper, the debtor is in a position to transfer the collateral to a third party. While the original secured party may have a perfected security interest in the chattel paper *as proceeds,* his interest is subordinate to that of the purchaser of the chattel paper even though the latter has knowledge that the specific paper is subject to the security interest of the inventory financer.

A different situation exists where a secured party's interest in the chattel paper is something other than a mere claim to it as proceeds of inventory. If the chattel paper was the *original collateral* and the secured party entrusts it to the debtor for purposes of collection, the wrongful disposition by the debtor will not subordinate the interest of the secured party.

---

[2] *Rodi Boat Co. v. Provident Trademens Bank & T. Co.,* page 631.
[3] *Philco Finance Corp. v. Mehlman,* page 634.

[C1] *U.C.C.* 9-312.

3-147 Returned or Repossessed Goods. Goods sold are occasionally returned or repossessed. As noted previously, any security interest in the goods prior to sale will revive and be effective as against the seller (debtor) or his trustee in bankruptcy. However, if the buyer had given *chattel paper*, such as a conditional sale contract, which the retailer has sold, the person holding the chattel paper has priority over the secured party having a security interest in inventory. This is *not* the result if an account receivable was transferred; the transferee of the account is subordinate to the party with a security interest in inventory with respect to the goods which were returned or repossessed. The purchaser of either an account or chattel paper will prevail as against the seller or his trustee in bankruptcy.

3-148 Purchase Money Security Interest. A distinction is to be noted between 1) a purchase money security interest in inventory and 2) such an interest in collateral other than inventory. As was discussed in the prior chapter, it is possible to have a continuing security in a floating stock of merchandise, i.e., goods to be acquired in the future may be the subject of a security contract. The holder of a purchase-money security interest in inventory has priority over a secured party who has a security interest in the inventory under an after-acquired clause contained in an earlier security agreement *provided* that 1) the purchase money secured party perfected his interest before the debtor took possession and 2) he notified prior parties known to have an interest or who had filed their financing statement.[4] Such notice must be given to these parties before the debtor receives possession of the inventory and must state that a purchase-money interest has been taken or will be taken in described inventory of the debtor. For collateral *other than* inventory, the purchase-money security interest is superior if perfected before the debtor receives possession of the collateral or within ten days thereafter.

3-149 Fixtures.[C2] Goods which are sold under a security agreement may *thereafter* become attached to real property in such a manner as to become a fixture.[5] If the security interest was perfected *before* the collateral was affixed, the secured party has priority as to the goods over those persons who have an interest in the real estate—e.g., mortgagors and purchasers. In general, if the secured party has not perfected, his security interest will be subordinate to the interest of a *subsequent* purchaser or mortgagee of the real estate to which the collateral has become attached. The unperfected security interest will be good as against *prior* mortgagees since it in theory increased the value of the property used as security. A security interest can attach to goods *after* they become fixtures and the same rules of priority will apply *except*

---

[4] *National Cash Register Co. v. Firestone & Co.,* page 636.
[5] *Cain v. Country Club Delicatessen,* page 639.

[C2] *U.C.C.* 9-313.

that it will be invalid as to mortgagees of the real estate whose lien was effective when the security interest attached to the goods, unless they agree in writing to subordinate status. The secured party who has priority is entitled, upon default, to remove his property from the real estate. He is required to reimburse any encumbrancer or owner other than the debtor for the cost of repair of any physical damage caused by the removal.

3-150 Accessions.[C3] Goods, in addition to being affixed to real estate, may become installed in or affixed to other *goods*. The goods so installed or affixed are called "accessions." In general, a perfected security interest which attaches to goods *before* they become accessions has priority as to such goods over a security interest in the whole, and subsequent purchasers of the whole. A security interest may attach to goods after they have become affixed. The secured party has the same priorities as those stated above, but his security interest will prevail over another security interest in the whole only if the holder of the security interest in the whole has consented in writing to the security interest. As in the case of fixtures, the secured party can upon default remove his collateral from the whole but he must make payment for the cost of repair of any physical damage caused by removal.

3-151 Commingled and Processed Goods.[C4] In a manufacturing process several items, including raw materials and components, each of which may be subject to different security interests, combine to make a finished product. The security to which the financing party is entitled will ultimately be the product which results from the combination of the materials in which he has a security interest. If a security interest in the raw materials was perfected, the security interest continues in the product if 1) the identity of the goods is lost, or 2) the original financing statement provided for a security interest which covered the "product." In a situation where component parts are assembled into a machine, the secured party would have a choice of either 1) claiming a security interest in the machine or 2) claiming an interest in a component part as provided for security interests in accessions. If he stipulates "products" in the financing statement he cannot claim an accession. Where more than one security interest exists in the product, the secured parties share in the product in proportion to the costs of their materials used.

3-152 Liens on Goods.[C5] The common law lien on goods which is allowed for repair, improvement, storage, or transportation is superior to a perfected security interest as long as the lien claimant retains possession of the property. Statutory liens also have such priority unless the statute expressly subordinates them.[6] Even though his lien is

[6] *Commonwealth Loan Co. v. Downtown Lincoln Mercury Co.*, page 642.

[C3] *U.C.C.* 9-314.
[C4] *U.C.C.* 9-315.

[C5] *U.C.C.* 9-310.

second in point of time, it is usually granted priority over a perfected security interest in the goods, presumably because the service rendered by the lienholder has added to or protected the value of the property.[7]

3-153 Miscellaneous. The foregoing is a compilation of rules for determining priorities among conflicting security interests in particular situations and involving particular collateral. The following general rules apply to all other situations: 1) If the conflicting interests are perfected by filing, the *first to file* will prevail even though the other interest attached first and whether it attached before or after filing; 2) Unless both are perfected by filing, the first *to be perfected* will have priority regardless of which one attached first; 3) If neither of the security interests is perfected, priority will be given to the first to attach.

RIGHTS AND REMEDIES OF THE SECURED PARTY

3-154 Before Default.[C6] A secured party has certain rights in the collateral during the period prior to default. These rights and duties of the parties are those set forth in the security agreement and those provided by the Code. The Code also contains limitations on the rights of the secured party and imposes certain duties upon him in respect to the collateral. The secured party who is in possession of the collateral is required to exercise reasonable care of it and the duty to do so may not be disclaimed. Reasonable care in the case of an instrument or chattel paper includes taking necessary steps to preserve rights against prior parties—e.g., in the case of a negotiable instrument, making a timely presentment to the primary party and giving notice of dishonor. The parties can agree, however, that this obligation shall rest with the debtor. *Unless the security agreement provides otherwise:* 1) all reasonable expenses related to the collateral are chargeable to the debtor and are secured by the collateral; 2) the risk of accidental loss or damage is on the debtor to the extent that it is not covered by insurance; 3) the secured party is entitled to hold as additional security any increase or profits, except money, received from the collateral—money so received shall be applied to reduce the secured obligation or remitted to the debtor; 4) the secured party is entitled to repledge—i.e., use the collateral as security in his own financing—but only on such terms as do not impair the debtor's right to redeem it, but 5) the secured party must keep the collateral identifiable except that fungible goods can be commingled. Should the secured party fail to meet his obligations in these respects, he is liable for any loss but he does not thereby lose his security interest. The security agreement may provide, when the collateral is accounts, chattel paper, contract rights, instruments, or gen-

---

[7] *Decker v. Aurora Motor Co.,* page 644.

[C6] *U.C.C.* 9-207.

eral intangibles, that the arrangement be on a "notification" basis or that it be on a "non-notification" basis. The former means that the secured party can notify the account debtor, for example, that the account has been transferred and direct such person to make payment directly to the secured party. In the latter, the debtor collects on the accounts and remits to the secured party—the party owing the account is not notified.

In most situations the collateral will remain in the possession of the debtor and he may be given wide latitude in using, commingling, or disposing of the property without thereby rendering the security interest invalid or fraudulent against creditors. The Code lists the following additional specific privileges which a debtor may exercise without infringing upon the validity of the security interest: He may (1) collect or compromise accounts, contract rights or chattel paper, (2) accept the return of goods or make repossessions, or (3) use, commingle, or dispose of proceeds. The security interest is not affected by reason of the failure of the secured party to require the debtor to account for proceeds or replace collateral. Note that the foregoing are permissive and that the security agreement may and usually will substantially restrict the debtor in possession. He may, for example, be required to obtain the secured party's permission prior to a sale of the collateral and be required to account for and surrender to the secured party all proceeds as they are received. Also, the security agreement should make appropriate provisions for insuring the collateral and all other matters relating to its preservation and protection.

Usually the financing statement will state only that a secured party may have a security interest in specified types of collateral owned by the debtor. Nothing is said about either the amount of the secured debt or the particular assets covered. The debtor for various reasons may need a detailed statement as to both the present amount of the obligation and the collateral which is covered. The Code provides that the secured party is obligated to furnish such information when so requested by the debtor.

3-155 After Default.[C7] In most respects the parties can specify in their agreement what steps are to be taken upon default. The Code sets forth applicable rules where the parties have not so specified.

When the debtor is in default under the security agreement—has failed to pay or satisfy the obligation which is secured—the secured party is given several remedies. What the secured party can do as well as the protection afforded the debtor in connection with the default procedures is determined by the terms of the security agreement and the rules set forth in the Code. The Code therefore both supplements the security agreement and limits it. The limitations are designed to protect not only the defaulting debtor but also other creditors of the debtor. The basic remedies of the creditor—secured party—on default are to repossess the collateral and to dispose of it. It is also possible for

[C7] *U.C.C.* 9-501 *et seq.*

the secured party to accept the collateral as discharge of the obligation and retain it rather than selling it. This remedy is discussed in the next section.

If the secured party is already in possession of the collateral as in the case of a possessory security interest, or has acquired possession in accordance with the security agreement or by other arrangement prior to default, he is of course entitled to retain possession. If he does not have possession, the right to take possession is specifically granted.[C8] The secured party can simply take the collateral into his possession without any judicial process if he can do so without "breaching the peace." If he meets with resistance in his effort to repossess, he can, of course, obtain judicial assistance in accomplishing it. The security agreement may contain provisions for possession by the secured party before or after default and may require the debtor after default to gather the collateral together and voluntarily make it available to the secured party at a place designated by the secured party. In some situations it is not practical to take possession or remove the collateral as where it is heavy equipment installed in the debtor's plant. The Code authorizes the secured party to render the equipment unusable pending resale or other disposition.

Somewhat different problems arise when the collateral is accounts, chattel paper, contract rights, instruments, or general intangibles. The Code in recognition of this provides that the secured party or assignee can simply proceed to collect whatever may become due on the collateral, e.g., direct the person who owes the account receivable to make payment directly to the secured party.[C9] Prior to default, the payments may have been coming to the debtor-assignor who was under a duty to remit collection to the secured party. In addition, the secured party is entitled to take control of any "proceeds." (See Sec. 3-143). As noted previously, Article 9 covers both outright *sales* and secured transactions where the property (collateral) is chattel paper, accounts or contract rights. If such collateral has been assigned to a secured party as security for a *loan,* then the secured party upon collection must account to the debtor for any surplus and the debtor (absent a contrary provision in the security agreement) is liable for any deficiency if the amount collected is not sufficient to satisfy the obligation. On the other hand, if the transaction is a *sale* of such items the assignee can retain any surplus and the assignor is not liable for any deficiency in the event that the items prove uncollectible. The purchase agreement can, however, provide for a different result.

If the secured party has repossessed the collateral or is otherwise in possession of it, the Code gives him broad powers to dispose of it in order to obtain satisfaction of the obligation.[C10] He may sell or otherwise dispose of it in its present condition or he may within "commercially reasonable" limits prepare the goods for sale. Any sale of the

---

[C8] *U.C.C.* 9-503.
[C9] *U.C.C.* 9-502.

[C10] *U.C.C.* 9-504.

goods is subject to the provisions of Article 2–Sales. The sale may be either public or private and is subject to the requirement that it be accomplished in a commercially reasonable manner. In general, the secured party is required to notify the debtor of the time and place of any public sale or of the time after which a private sale is to be made. The notification is not required where 1) the collateral is perishable or threatens to decline speedily in value, or 2) it is of a type "customarily sold on a recognized market." Notice must also be sent (except in the case of consumer goods) to any other person who has filed a financing statement covering the same collateral and who is known to have a security interest in the collateral. The secured party may buy at the public sale if he so desires. If the sale is private, the secured party's right to purchase is substantially restricted. The person who buys the collateral at a sale thereof receives it free of the security interest under which the sale was made and free, also, of any subordinate security interest. Thus, the good faith purchaser at a disposition sale receives substantial assurance that he will be protected in his purchase. After the sale has been made, the proceeds of the sale will be distributed and applied as follows and in that order: 1) the expenses of the secured party in connection with the repossession and sale including (if provided for in the security agreement) attorney's fees and legal expenses, 2) the satisfaction of the debt owing to the secured party, 3) satisfaction of the indebtedness owing to persons who have a subordinate security interest in the collateral; finally, if any surplus remains after satisfaction of all of the above, the secured party shall account for it to the debtor. Note that the debtor is liable for any deficiency unless the security agreement otherwise provides.

3-156 Acceptance in Discharge. The secured party may prefer to simply keep the collateral in satisfaction of the obligation rather than dispose of it. He is entitled to make such a proposition in writing and send it to the debtor. Except in the case of consumer goods, the proposal must also be sent to all persons who have filed a financing statement covering the collateral or who are known to have a security interest in it. Within prescribed time limits, the debtor, a secured party entitled to receive notification, or any other secured party can object in writing to the proposal in which event the collateral would have to be sold. If no such notice is forthcoming, the matter is closed and the secured party can retain the collateral in satisfaction. Special provisions relate to consumer transactions. Disposition of the goods is *compulsory* and a sale must be made within 90 days after possession is taken if, in the case of: 1) a purchase money security interest in consumer goods, 60 per cent of the cash price has been paid, or 2) a security interest based upon a loan against consumer goods, 60 per cent of the loan has been repaid. The consumer can, however, waive this right by signing a statement to that effect after default.[c11]

c11 *U.C.C.* 9-505.

3-157 Debtor's Right to Redeem.[C12] Except for the 90-day period for consumer goods, the secured party is not required to make disposition of the repossessed goods within any time limits. The right to redeem the property by the debtor or another secured party exists until such time as 1) the property has been sold, or contracted to be sold, or 2) the obligation has been satisfied by the retention of the property. The redeeming party must, as a condition to redemption, tender the full amount of the obligation secured by the collateral, plus the expenses incurred by the secured party in connection with the collateral and, if so provided in the agreement, attorney's fees and legal expenses.

3-158 Compliance by Secured Party.[C13] If the secured party fails to comply with provisions of the Code relating to default, a court may order disposition or restrain disposition as the situation requires. If the sale has already taken place, the secured party is liable for any loss resulting from his noncompliance and may lose his right to recover any deficiency.[8] If the collateral is consumer goods, the consumer-debtor is entitled to recover *in any event* an amount not less than the (1) credit service charge *plus* ten percent of the principal amount of the debt or (2) the time price differential *plus* ten percent of the cash price. The secured party is protected against claims that he did not obtain the best possible price for the goods if he has made the sale in a "commercially reasonable manner." The Code gives substantial latitude to the secured party in selecting the time for and method of the sale.

SECURED TRANSACTIONS: PRIORITIES, DEFAULT AND REMEDIES CASES

U.S. v. Lebanon Woolen Mills

1964 241 F. Supp. 393

CONNOR, J. This is a motion wherein Miller Auto Company, Inc. seeks a judgment granting its conditional sales contract priority over a federal tax lien, and an order permitting it to prove its claim as a secured creditor of Lebanon Woolen Mills Corporation. [Miller intervened in the proceedings.]

From the representations at the hearing and from the memoranda supplied thereafter, it appears that both Miller and the Government are in agreement as to the following facts. On October 4, 1961, Miller sold to Lebanon Woolen Mills Corporation a 1961 Pontiac Catalina Vista sedan automobile, Serial No. 361L-17631, under a conditional sales agreement which was not recorded until February 23, 1962. Sometime during October, 1961, Miller made an attempt to record the conditional

---

[8] *Associates Discount Corp. v. Cary,* page 646.

[C12] *U.C.C.* 9-506.   [C13] *U.C.C.* 9-507.

sales contract in Lebanon, New Hampshire, but for some reason the City Clerk of the City of Lebanon refused to record the contract.

The complaint alleges, and it is nowhere disputed by Miller, that the Commissioner of Internal Revenue made assessments against Lebanon Woolen Mills Corporation for income taxes, penalties, and interest, on January 24, 1962, and that notice and demand was made and refused two days later. The complaint further alleges that the District Director thereafter "duly filed notices of the tax lien . . . in the proper offices as provided by law." A *Receiver* for Lebanon Woolen Mills Corporation was appointed by order of this court on February 14, 1962.

The question to be determined on the above set of facts is whether the security interest of a conditional vendor is superior to a lien for federal taxes against the vendee, assessed and filed subsequent to the execution of the conditional sales contract, but prior to the filing of that contract. For the purposes of the present motion, no question is raised as to the validity of the federal tax lien or as to the amount claimed to be due under the conditional sales contract, or as to the priorities of other creditors.

In cases involving a contest as to the priority as between a federal tax lien and a lien or other interest arising under state law, there are, generally speaking, two main areas of inquiry. The first is to determine the nature and extent of the interest arising under state law; this is a question of state law. . . .

As a matter of state law, the conditional sales contract in question, though unfiled, was effective to create a security interest according to its terms between the parties. (NH RSA 382-A:9-201.) Although the form of the agreement prescribed the retention of title in the conditional vendor, Miller, it would be more appropriate, under the terminology of the Uniform Commercial Code (NH RSA ch. 382-A), to consider Miller as the holder of a purchase money security interest and to consider his status as analogous to that of a chattel mortgagee.

Due to the insolvency of the taxpayer corporation here involved, the question of priority is determined, in the first instance, by 31 U.S.C. § 191, which provides that "whenever any person indebted to the United States is insolvent . . . the debts due to the United States shall be first satisfied . . . . " "Debts," as used in this section, includes federal taxes. . . .

Despite the seemingly absolute priority thus attaching to federal tax liens in insolvency situations, it has long been recognized that certain classes of prior transfers and interests are exempt from the operation of the present statute and its predecessors. Thus, for example, a prior conveyance or mortgage executed by the taxpayer is not affected by the "absolute" priority of a federal tax lien or other subsequent debt owing to the United States; and, despite recent dicta of the United States Supreme Court to the contrary, the same may well be true of other classes of prior specific and perfected liens. (Cases cited.) The rationale of these cases appears to be that to the extent that the taxpayer has conveyed, mortgaged, or in any other way alienated a property interest, that property interest is no longer his and cannot be made subject to a subsequent lien for taxes owed by him.

The security interest held by Miller in the present cases appears to fit well within this judicially maintained exception. Whether the vendee taxpayer corporation be deemed to have mortgaged away a property interest in the automobile or never to have received the full property interest in the automobile, it is clear that the conditional sales contract operated to create in Miller a distinct and separate security interest. To the extent of this security interest, the automobile has been alienated from the assets of the taxpayer vendee and a lien for the unpaid taxes of the vendee cannot attach to it. Accordingly, the prior purchase money security interest of Miller takes priority over the subsequent attaching federal tax liens.

It is not always a simple matter . . . to determine what property belongs to the debtor and what interests rightfully belong to others. In order to afford a certain amount of protection to the collection of federal revenues and to facilitate the proper allocation of property interests involved, the federal courts have insisted that an intervening party claiming ownership of a property interest about to be subjected to the enforcement of taxes owing by the tax debtor, must establish that his asserted interest has been sufficiently segregated from the assets of the debtor or has become sufficiently segregated from the assets of the debtor or has become sufficiently earmarked among them. The word *choateness* has been used in recent years to describe that quality of completeness, perfection, and specificity of which an intervenor's interest must partake in order not to be considered a part of the debtor's property and subject to the lien for the debtor's unpaid taxes. Recent formulations of choateness have said that the identity of both the debtor and the intervenor must be certain, the extent of the intervenor's claim must be definite, and the property in which the intervenor's interest inheres must be specific. . . .

The thrust of the federal requirement of *choateness* then, is that the intervenor must show that the property interest he asserts has become sufficiently alienated from the assets of the tax debtor to satisfy the interests of federal tax policy. Whether the intervenor has also perfected his interest against *other third parties* is irrelevant. The New Hampshire recording statute, in its application to a conditional sale, however, concerns itself only with *perfection as against third* parties and adds nothing to the federally required perfection as against the conditional vendee tax debtor. Perfection as to third parties being superfluous, the statute becomes irrelevant. Miller's interest as against the tax debtor corporation was already as perfected as it could be. (See NH RSA 382-A:9-201.) [Emphasis supplied.]

This is not to say that the recording statute would not be of importance to the federal concept of perfection with respect to other types of intervening interests whose choateness may be in question. Either state law or sound federal policy, or both, may require recordation of certain types of interests as an integral step in the perfection of the respective liens arising therefrom. It is in this context that it is properly announced that in order to establish the choateness of his interest, an intervenor must comply with all the state requirements for the protection of his interest. Much of the litigation in this area concerns judgment creditors, statutory creditors' liens and statutory liens for state and local taxes. (Cases cited.)

As noted earlier, however, mortgages and purchases have traditionally remained aloof from this hassle over choateness. Both under state law (NH RSA 382-A:9-201) and in substantial reality, the properly executed sale or mortgage operates to conclude the rights of the parties to the transaction as between themselves. Inherent in the transaction is the creation and transfer of property interests so specific as to more than meet the requirements of the federal concept of choateness. Nothing more can be done under state law to perfect their interests as against each other.

While compliance with state recording statutes may in some instances, then, be considered a necessary prerequisite to the establishment of the choateness of some types of interests, compliance with NH RSA 382-A:9-302(1) (d) in the present case does not serve to add one whit of perfection to Miller's interest as against the corporation. The statute provides only the additional, and here superfluous, perfection as against third parties; it does not add to, or affect, the requisite federal perfection or choateness.

Turning, at length, from this rather extended discourse concerning factors deemed not controlling in the present case, it is, in sum, the holding of this court that the conditional sales contract executed on October 4, 1961, operated to vest in Miller a security interest which was valid, effective and perfected as between the parties; that recordation and the attendant perfection as to third parties was not necessary; and that as a prior valid security interest, analogous to that of a chattel mortgage, the interest of Miller fits well within the recognized exception to 31 U.S.C. § 191 in favor of such prior conveyances. No opinion is intended to be expressed herein with respect to the validity of the tax lien, the amount due under the conditional sales contract, or the relative priorities existing among the conditional sales contract and the interest of any creditors other than the Government.

Rodi Boat Company v. Provident Tradesmens Bank & Trust Co.

236 F. Supp. 935 (1964)

KIRKPATRICK, J. It is no longer open to question that in Pennsylvania a bank has no right to set off *identifiable funds* of a third party [Rodi Boat Company] in a depositor's account against a debt due it by the depositor. This is true even though the bank has no notice of any third party's interest in the debtor's account. . . .

The evidence before the Court on this motion for summary judgment shows that:

At all times from October 23, 1961, to and including November 8, 1961, William Stuempfig was indebted to the defendant Bank in an amount of $56,250—an amount which did not vary during that period.

On October 24, 1961, Stuempfig received some $60,000 from the sale of a Chris Craft boat which he had purchased from the plaintiff about a year earlier. When he bought the boat, he made a down payment and executed a "retail installment contract," agreeing to pay the plaintiff the balance, $52,028.24, in 36 monthly payments. As of October 23, 1961, $36,132.67 was still owing to the plaintiff. The contract provided that the boat should remain the personal property of the seller or its assigns until the balance was paid in full.

Stuempfig's sale of the boat was without permission from the plaintiff or from the discount company which had financed the transaction, and neither company has assented to nor ratified it.

From the proceeds of the sale Stuempfig deposited $29,500 on October 24, and $29,682 on November 1 in an account in the defendant Bank carried by him under the name of "W. Stuempfig and Co. Management Account," W. Stuempfig and Co. was simply a fictitious name under which William Stuempfig carried on his real estate management business.

On November 9, 1961, the Bank set off the sum of $43,313.04 in the Management Account identifiable as part of the proceeds of the boat against obligations of Stuempfig and W. Stuempfig and Co. held by it.

In this suit the plaintiff asks judgment against the Bank for $36,132.67, being the amount due it from Stuempfig on the boat.

The facts recited above are uncontroverted and are all the facts material to the decision of this motion.

The record contains a great deal of evidentiary matter which may have some value as furnishing a background for the transactions involved but which does not affect the issue before the Court. The following conclusions as to its immateriality are set out in order to deal with a number of contentions advanced by counsel.

Specifically, it is immaterial:

(1) That Stuempfig had another account with the Bank, carried in his individual name, and that it and the Stuempfig and Co. Management Account were used indiscriminately by him for general business and personal purposes.

(2) It is uncontroverted, but also immaterial, that the Bank, before it exercised its claimed right of set-off, was aware that the monies deposited by Stuempfig on October 24 and November 1 were the proceeds of the sale of the boat and that the boat was subject to a conditional sales contract.

(3) That neither Stuempfig nor the Bank intended to establish any trust in favor of the plaintiff in the deposits made of the proceeds of the boat.

(4) That the boat had never been kept at Stuempfig's Philadelphia address or that it was in Maryland when Stuempfig sold it. It does not appear whether or not the boat was in Broward County, Florida when the retail installment contract was recorded there, but its whereabouts at that time is immaterial.

(5) That the plaintiff did not comply with the provisions of the Uniform Commercial Code (12A P.S. 9-401 *et seq.*), in respect of filing a financing statement in Pennsylvania in connection with its sale of the

boat to Stuempfig. The filing provisions of the Code simply provide a system of notice of a reservation of title to purchasers, creditors, and others. They do not affect any rights or obligations *as between seller and buyer* and noncompliance with them does not, *as between those parties,* divest the seller's reserved title and vest it in the buyer.

DISCUSSION

Stuempfig's sale and delivery of the boat to the man who bought it from him was a conversion of it. As a result, the proceeds of the sale, when received by him and deposited in his account in the Bank, were impressed with a constructive trust in favor of the plaintiff who had retained title to the boat. "A constructive trust has been defined to be a relationship with respect to property subjecting the person by whom the title to the property is held to an equitable duty to convey it to another on the ground that his acquisition or retention of the property is wrongful and that he would be unjustly enriched if he were permitted to retain the property . . . a constructive trust is imposed not to effectuate intention but to redress wrong or unjust enrichment. . . . "

At the time the Bank exercised its claimed right of set-off the sum of $36,132.67 of the proceeds of Stuempfig's sale of the boat was still in his Management Account and identifiable as such. "Once the proceeds (resulting from the conversion of property) have been traced into some fund, the entire fund is subject to the trust until the amount wrongfully placed in it has been repaid. . . . " At no time between November 1, the date of the last deposit of the boat's proceeds, and November 9, the date of the set-off, had the Stuempfig account been reduced by withdrawals below $36,132.67. The person in whose favor a constructive trust has arisen is in equity the owner of the trust property, regardless of the form it has taken, provided it can be traced and identified. Thus, when the defendant Bank, through the medium of a set-off, applied the money due to the plaintiff by Stuempfig in the Management Account to the payment of his indebtedness to it, it appropriated property of a third person with whom it had had no dealings. This the Bank could not lawfully do and, consequently, it is bound to surrender the money to the plaintiff.

The defendant takes the position in its brief that the plaintiff "has certainly waived its rights under the contract and cannot now assert its violation against Mr. Stuempfig's other creditors."

The fact is that, whatever rights, if any, the plaintiff may have lost through failing to file a financing statement, it did not lose title to the boat as between it and Stuempfig. It is not questioned that in most jurisdictions, including Pennsylvania, failure to comply with the requirements of the recording statutes makes a conditional sale absolute and the reservation of title invalid as to the persons protected by the statutes. Such persons are *bona fide purchasers, creditors who have extended credit to the buyer* in reliance upon his possession of the collateral, and the like, but the Bank in this case is not such a party. It had not extended credit to Stuempfig in reliance upon his possession of the boat. Nor had it extended any credit at all to him after his account had been augmented by his deposit in it of the proceeds of the boat. This plaintiff's case does not depend upon its standing as a general creditor in competition with other general creditors. Its right is not created by statute nor by agreement to make a trust but is grounded upon an equitable title to money in the Bank's hands, arising entirely *in invitum* by operation of law through the device of a constructive trust.

An order for judgment in favor of the plaintiff may be presented.

Philco Finance Corporation v. Mehlman

1964, (S.C.) 139 S.E.2d 475

TAYLOR, J.　The Appellant, R. E. Mehlman (defendant) sold all of the capital stock in his radio and appliance business to Frank E. Brown in December, 1959, for $75,000. Mehlman, as a part of such sale, executed a note to the South Carolina National Bank for $25,000 which was endorsed by Brown, who received the proceeds and was to repay same. The entire sale of the business was on credit and Brown, in consideration of the above, executed his note to Mehlman for $75,000 and as security for these obligations, executed a chattel mortgage to Mehlman in the amount of $100,000 covering the capital stock and some equipment, inventory, fixtures, trucks, and other chattels.

After the above transaction, Brown commenced selling a large number of Philco appliances, financing such sales by selling or assigning his contracts to Philco Finance Corporation, Respondent (plaintiff) herein. In August, 1960, Philco and Brown requested Mehlman to execute a document denominated "Subordination and Assignment Agreement." This instrument was apparently intended to improve Brown's credit with Philco. In January, 1963, the affairs of Brown were placed in the hands of a receiver by Philco, and he was found to be insolvent. Brown's indebtedness to Philco arises out of advances by Philco to Brown on forged or fraudulent conditional sales contracts in the amount of $121,000, upon which the alleged purchasers' names were forged by Brown or contracts which Brown had fraudulently induced the purchasers to sign. Mehlman took possession of the property covered by the chattel mortgage and sold the same for the purpose of applying the proceeds to the unpaid debts secured thereby.

Philco brought this action against Mehlman asserting that its rights are prior to those of Mehlman and the sums realized by Mehlman through the sale of the property covered by the chattel mortgage by reason of the "Subordination and Assignment Agreement" are subordinate thereto.

The matter was referred to the Master in Equity for Richland County, who recommended the issuance of an Order declaring that Brown's obligation to Mehlman be subordinated to his obligation to Philco and that said subordination and assignment agreement effectively assigns all liens that Mehlman has on Brown's property to Philco as security for

Brown's obligation to Philco. Exceptions were taken to the Master's Report, but the Honorable John Grimball adopted the findings of fact and conclusions of the master and issued his Order implementing these recommendations. This appeal is from that Order.

Mehlman contends that the trial court erred in placing a construction on the Subordination and Assignment Agreement which would subordinate his right under the mortgage with Brown to Philco's claim for indebtedness to it by Brown arising out of Brown's fraudulent conduct.

Pertinent parts of the Subordination and Assignment Agreement appear as follows:

> To induce Philco Finance Corporation (hereinafter called "Philco Finance") to grant credit and financing accommodations to (Frank K. Brown doing business as) Brown-Dantzler Company (hereinafter called "Debtor"), Philco Finance, Debtor and R. E. Mehlman (hereinafter called "Creditor") mutually covenant and agree as follows:
> 1. Until all indebtedness and all obligations of Debtor to Philco Finance, whether now existing or hereafter acquired or incurred and whether individual, joint or several, primary, secondary, direct, or contingent or otherwise, have been fully paid or discharged in accordance with the terms thereof, Creditor will not demand or receive from Debtor any part or all of the moneys now owing by Debtor to Creditor, or that may hereafter be due and payable to Creditor by Debtor, or any security therefor, and Debtor will not make payment or give security to Creditor, except in accordance with this Agreement. . . .
> 2. Creditor hereby assigns, transfers and sets over to Philco Finance as collateral security for all such indebtedness and obligations of Debtor to Philco Finance all claims and demands of Creditor against Debtor, now owned or hereafter acquired and all interest accruing thereon at any time. . . .

Mehlman contends that the above agreement is a suretyship contract and as such should be construed strictly in his favor as he is a gratuitous surety.

In 72 C.J.S. Principal and Surety 1, p. 514, it is said that "Suretyship is a lending of credit to aid a principal who has insufficient credit of his own, and is a direct contract to pay the principal's debt or perform his obligation in case of his default." And in 2, p. 515, a surety is defined as follows: "In a broad sense a surety is one who becomes responsible for the debt, default, or miscarriage of another, but in a narrower sense, a surety is a person who binds himself for the payment of a sum of money, or for the performance of something else, for another who is already bound for such payment or performance."

The agreement here was entered into by Mehlman in order to improve Brown's credit with Philco; however, Mehlman did not contract to pay Brown's debts to Philco in case of default but rather agreed to subordinate his claims to those of Philco in order that Philco would continue to extend credit to Brown. Under these facts no personal obligation for Brown's indebtedness to Philco was entered into and the relationship of principal and surety did not arise.

For the foregoing reasons, we are of opinion that the Order appealed from should be affirmed; and it is so ordered. [Philco prevailed.] *Affirmed.*

National Cash Register Company v. Firestone & Co.

1963, (Mass.) 191 N.E.2d 471

WILKINS, J. . . . The underlying question is the relative standing of two security interests. Uniform Commercial Code . . . 9-105 reads: " 'Security agreement' means an agreement which creates or provides for a security interest.". . . " 'Security interest' means an interest in personal property or fixtures which secures payment or performance of an obligation. The retention or reservation of title by a seller of goods notwithstanding shipment or delivery to the buyer (Section 2-401) is limited in effect to a reservation of a 'security interest.' " On June 15, 1960, the plaintiff, a manufacturer of cash registers, and one Edmund Carroll, doing business in Canton as Kozy Kitchen, entered into a conditional sale contract for a cash register. On November 18, 1960, the defendant, which was in the financing business, made a loan to Carroll, who conveyed certain personal property to the defendant as collateral under a security agreement. The defendant filed a financing statement with the Town Clerk of Canton on November 18, 1960, and with the Secretary of State on November 22, 1960. Between November 19 and November 25 the plaintiff delivered a cash register to Carroll in Canton. On November 25, the contract of June 15 was canceled and superseded by a new contract for the same cash register but providing for different terms of payment. The plaintiff filed a financing statement with respect to this contract with the Town Clerk of Canton on December 20 and with the Secretary of State on December 21. Carroll subsequently became in default both on the contract with the plaintiff and on the security agreement with the defendant. In December the defendant took possession of the cash register, and although notified on January 17, 1961, of the Plaintiff's asserted right, sold it at auction on the following day.

The defendant's security agreement recites that Carroll in consideration of $1,911 paid by it does

> hereby grant, sell, assign, transfer and deliver to Grantee the following goods, chattels, and automobiles, namely: The business located at and numbered 574 Washington Street, Canton, Mass. together with all its good-will, fixtures, equipment and merchandise. The fixtures specifically consist of the following: *All contents of luncheonette including equipment such as: booths and tables; stand and counter; tables, chairs; booths; steam tables; salad unit; potato peeler; U. S. Slicer; range; case; fryer; compressor; bobtail; milk dispenser; silex; 100 Class air conditioner; signs; pastry case; mixer; dishes; silverware; tables; hot fudge; Haven Ex.; 2 door stationwagon 1957 Ford A57R107215* together with all property and articles now, and which may hereafter be, used or mixed with, added or attached to, and/or substituted for, any of the foregoing described property.

In the defendant's financing statement the detailed description of the "types (or items) of property" is the same as the words in supplied italics in the security agreement. There is no specific reference to a cash register in either document, and no mention in the defendant's financing statement of property to be acquired thereafter.

Under the Uniform Commercial Code . . . after-acquired property, such as this cash register, might become subject to the defendant's security agreement when delivered . . . 9-204 (With exceptions presented immaterial, "a security agreement may provide that collateral whenever acquired shall secure all obligations covered by the security agreement.") and likewise its delivery under a conditional sale agreement with retention of title in the plaintiff would not, in and of itself, affect the rights of the defendant. . . . ("Title to Collateral Immaterial. Each provision of this Article with regard to rights, obligations and remedies applies whether title to collateral is in the secured party or in the debtor.") although the plaintiff could have completely protected itself by perfecting its interest before or within ten days of the delivery of the cash register to Carroll. ("A purchase money security interest in collateral other than inventory has priority over a conflicting security interest in the same collateral if the purchase money security interest is perfected at the time the debtor receives possession of the collateral or within ten days thereafter.") It did not try to do so until more than ten days after delivery. Thus the principal issue is whether the defendant's earlier security interest effectively covers the cash register.

The trial judge gave no reasons for his ruling. The Appellate Division rested its decision upon the mere statement of the omission of the defendant's financing statement to refer to after-acquired property or to the cash register specifically. The Massachusetts Commissioners on Uniform State Laws in their brief as *amici curiae* argue that there need be no reference to after-acquired property in the financing statement. Before we reach that question, however, we must consider several matters raised by the plaintiff.

First, the plaintiff argues that the debtor could not have intended to grant a security interest to the defendant because the purchase was five months earlier, delivery was about to be made, and the cash register could be repossessed by the plaintiff for default within the period of twenty-one months provided for installment payments. It is also urged that, without the cash register, the defendant was well secured for its loan, a fact which cannot be inferred and which, in any event, would not be conclusive. The debtor's intent must be judged by the language of the security agreement.

In . . . 9-110, it is provided: "For the purposes of this Article any description of personal property or real estate is sufficient whether or not it is specific if it reasonably identifies what is described." In 9-203 it is provided: (1) ". . . a security interest is not enforceable against the debtor or third parties unless . . . (b) the debtor has signed a security agreement which contains a description of the collateral. . . ."

Contrary to the plaintiff's contention, we are of opinion that the security agreement is broad enough to include the cash register, which concededly did not have to be specifically described. The agreement covers "All contents of luncheonette including equipment such as," which we think covers all those contents and does not mean "equipment, to wit." There is a reference to "all property and articles now, and which may hereafter be, used . . . with, (or) added . . . to . . . any of the foregoing described property." We infer that the cash register was used with some of the other equipment even though the case stated does not expressly state that the luncheonette was operated.

We now come to the question whether the defendant's financing statement should have mentioned property to be acquired thereafter before a security interest in the cash register could attach. The Code, . . . 9-402(1), reads in part: "A financing statement is sufficient if it is signed by the debtor and the secured party, gives an address of the secured party from which information concerning the security interest may be obtained, gives a mailing address of the debtor and contains a statement indicating the types, or describing the items, of collateral."

In the official comment to this section appears the following:

> 2. This Section adopts the system of "notice filing" which has proved successful under the Uniform Trust Receipts Act. What is required to be filed is not, as under chattel mortgage and conditional sales acts, the security agreement itself, but only a simple notice which may be filed before the security interest attaches or thereafter. The notice itself indicates merely that the secured party who has filed may have a security interest in the collateral described. Further inquiry from the parties concerned will be necessary to disclose the complete state of affairs. Section 9-208 provides a statutory procedure under which the secured party, at the debtor's request, may be required to make disclosure. (The plaintiff contends that 9-208 is of no help if the debtor or named creditor is slow in giving, or refuses to give, the necessary information. See *Coogan, Public Notice* under the Uniform Commercial Code and other Recent Chattel Security Laws, including "Notice Filing" (47 Iowa L.Rev. 289, 318n). If so, the remedy lies with the Legislature.) Notice filing has proved to be of great use in financing transactions involving inventory, accounts and chattel paper, since it obviates the necessity of refiling on each of a series of transactions in a continuing arrangement where the collateral changes from day to day. Where other types of collateral are involved, the alternative procedure of filing a signed copy of the security agreement may prove to be the simplest solution. . . .

The framers of the Uniform Commercial Code, by adopting the "notice filing" system, had the purpose to recommend a method of protecting security interests which at the same time would give subsequent potential creditors and other interested persons information and procedures adequate to enable the ascertainment of the facts they needed to know. In this respect the completed Code [represents] a decision of policy reached after several years' study and discussion by experts. We conceive our duty to be the making of an interpretation which will carry out the intention of the framers of uniform legislation which already has been enacted in twenty-five States. That the result of their policy decision may be asserted to favor certain types of creditors as against others or that a different policy could have been decided upon is quite beside the point.

The case at bar is, for all practical purposes, one of first impression under the Code. There seem to be no decisions anywhere which specifically deal with the situation presented to us.

In view of the broad purposes of the act we do not give a restrictive construction to the provision which sets forth what constitutes a "sufficient" financing statement. The defendant's financing statement is signed by the debtor and the secured party and gives both the address of the letter from which information is to be obtained and the mailing address of the debtor. It is argued, however, that the "statement indicating the types, or describing the items, of collateral" is inadequate because it fails to include a reference to the after-acquired clause of its security agreement, and so is not a reasonable identification of the cash register. Based upon the last two sentences of comment 2 above quoted, the plaintiff emphasizes that the cash register is "equipment" (c. 106, 9-109(2)) and not "inventory" (9-109(4)) or an "account" (9-106) or "chattel paper" (9-105(1) (b)). We cannot agree that the distinction, unexpressed in the Code, is presently controlling. We observe nothing to exclude the cash register, or any "equipment" for that matter, from the system of "notice filing," the adoption of which the comment discloses to be the intent of the section for all purposes and not just for some. That "the alternative procedure of filing," a copy of the security agreement, may be the simple solution for some types of collateral does not bar notice filing. Filing a copy of the security agreement is not exclusive but is an alternative procedure.

The words, "All contents of luncheonette," including, as we have held, all equipment, were enough to put the plaintiff on notice to ascertain what those contents were. This is not a harsh result as to the plaintiff, to which, as we have indicated (9-312(4)) made available a simple and sure procedure for completely protecting its purchase money security interest.

The order of the Appellate Division is reversed. The finding for the plaintiff is vacated. Judgment is to be entered for the defendant.

So ordered.

Cain v. Country Club Delicatessen of Saybrook, Inc.

1964 Connecticut 203 A.2d 441

This is a motion of the receiver, Cain, for a determination of priority between two secured creditors. The First Hartford Fund, Inc. and General Electric Credit Corporation were both secured creditors of Country Club Delicatessen of Saybrook, Inc. By court order the assets of the delicatessen were sold and the entire proceeds were ordered held by the receiver until a determination of the parties' rights was made by the court. The funds held are not sufficient to satisfy both creditors. The delicatessen borrowed $35,000 from First Hartford giving a promissory note secured by a chattel-mortgage covering "All goods, personal property, equipment, machinery, fixtures, inventory, leasehold rights, including, but not limited to, the property described below, *including all after acquired property* of like kind," and there followed a description of specific property. First Hartford had filed a financing statement with the Secretary of State showing the defendant-delicatessen as debtor and itself as creditor. First Hartford also filed a similar statement with the clerk in the town of Old Saybrook. Hewitt Engineering, Inc., sold the defendant goods on a conditional sales contract and assigned the contract to General Electric. General Electric filed a financial statement with the clerk of the city but not with the Secretary of State, Uniform Commercial Code division. This statement was filed after First Hartford had filed its statement. Some of the same property was described in both parties' financial statements. First Hartford claims priority since it was the first to file. General Electric claims priority on the ground that First Hartford was not a secured creditor within the legal definition at the time First Hartford filed its financial statement. The receiver requested a ruling so that he would be able to distribute the funds.

Pastore, J. . . . Under . . . 9-204(1), a debtor must have "rights in the collateral" before a security interest may be created. The code does not clearly establish the meaning of this phrase, as for instance whether such rights arise when the debtor enters into a contract to buy goods, or only when he has an interest in the goods when identified with a contract under the Uniform Commercial Code, Article 2, "Sales." . . .

In the instant case, while it is shown that the personal property bought August 30, 1962, from Hewitt, called here the "Hewitt goods" for convenience, was in the possession of the defendant debtor by July 26, 1962, and at least before August 19, 1962, and that the conditional sale contract between defendant and Hewitt was executed August 30, 1962, there is no showing as to the circumstances or arrangement whereby the defendant had this possession. No legal authority has come, or been brought, to the notice of this court that such mere possession may constitute such "rights in the collateral." An inference that defendant was an unconditional owner of the Hewitt goods on August 15, 1962, would be speculation. . . . It is clear that as of the date, August 15, 1962, when First Hartford filed its financing statements, the conditions of . . . 9-204(1) had not been met by Hewitt so as to create a security interest in its favor and so constitute the Hewitt goods "collateral" . . . in which defendant debtor could have any "rights.". . .

The financing statements filed by First Hartford on August 15, 1962, with both the Secretary of State and the town clerk of Old Saybrook each had an after-acquired property clause in it expressly including in the description of the property covered "all after acquired property of like kind" to the type described and specifically mentioned therein. The description expressly includes certain specific items of the Hewitt goods, and where otherwise, the description of the types of property covered is sufficiently broad to cover any other of the Hewitt goods. A similar clause is also contained in the security agreement between First Hartford and defendant corporation. For the purposes of Article 9 of the Uniform

Commercial Code, any description of personal property or real estate is sufficient whether or not it is specific if it reasonably identifies what is described. (9-110)

Under Section 9-204(3), after-acquired property of the kind described in the conditional sale contract of Hewitt can become subject to the security agreement of First Hartford. . . . A conditional sale contract comes within the scope and policy of Article 9 of the Uniform Commercial Code as to secured transactions. (9-102(1), (2)) The retention or reservation of title by a seller of goods notwithstanding delivery to the buyer is limited in effect to a reservation of a "security interest." (1-201(37)) Also, the delivery of the "Hewitt goods" under the conditional sale contract with retention of title in Hewitt does not, in and of itself, affect the rights of First Hartford.

The conditional sale contract of August 30, 1962, between defendant corporation and Hewitt created a security interest in favor of Hewitt which attached to the property thereby sold. . . . To perfect this security interest, a financing statement was required to be filed . . . , which, as to goods which at the time the security attached were or were to become fixtures, would be filed in the office where a mortgage on the real estate would be filed, and in all other cases would be filed in the office of the Secretary of State. . . .

Included in this priority of First Hartford are such non-Hewitt goods as might be fixtures as of August 16, 1962, as to which First Hartford filed with the town clerk on August 16, 1962, and Hewitt and General Electric not until August 30, 1962, assuming, without deciding, that Hewitt had a security interest in such non-Hewitt goods.

A more fundamental reason for the priority of First Hartford in this non-Hewitt goods portion of the defendant corporation's collateral subject to First Hartford's security agreement, whether fixtures or otherwise, is that neither Hewitt nor General Electric has been shown to have a security interest in that portion of the defendant's property. While the financing statement of Hewitt attempts to be all embracing, there is no security agreement of Hewitt and defendant creating a security interest in that non-Hewitt portion of Defendant's property. Without a security agreement . . . , a security interest cannot attach. . . . Any conflicting security interest would thus relate to such portion of the defendant corporation's property as involved the goods sold by Hewitt to defendant.

The question of the priority of such of the Hewitt goods as at the time the security interest of Hewitt may have attached were fixtures is next considered. . . .

The question when and whether personal property becomes fixtures is determined by the law of the state other than the Uniform Commercial Code. . . . The conditional sale contract of Hewitt, assignor of General Electric, provided in part as follows: "The equipment shall remain personal property regardless of any affixation to the realty and title thereto shall not pass to buyer until the . . . balance has been fully paid in cash." The parties to the contract were competent to make such an agreement, which was binding as between them, even though any such equipment were to be permanently affixed to the realty. . . . On August 30, 1962, the "rights in the collateral" which defendant debtor had . . . with respect to any such fixtures were as personal property. When on that date, therefore, the rights of the defendant in the Hewitt collateral and said collateral came under the coverage of the after-acquired property clause of the first Hartford security agreement, the Hewitt goods were still personal property. On this basis, the failure of Hewitt and General Electric to file with the Secretary of State makes their security interest subordinate to that of First Hartford, whose prior filing gives First Hartford priority over that of General Electric. . . . Moreover, there is nothing to indicate that General Electric has any interest in the pertinent real estate which would subordinate the First Hartford security interest to the benefit of General Electric. . . .

In accordance with the foregoing, it is hereby found and adjudged that the secured claim of The First Hartford Fund, Inc., in its full amount has priority over the secured claim of General Electric Credit Corporation and is entitled to payment in priority to said General Electric Credit Corporation.

Commonwealth Loan Co. v. Downtown Lincoln M. Co.

1964, 4 Ohio App.2d4, 211 N.E.2d 57

HOVER, J. This is an appeal on a question of law from a judgment in a replevin action in the Municipal Court of Cincinnati, where it was found that the right of possession to a certain 1957 Mercury automobile was in the Commonwealth Loan Company, plaintiff below.

The sole assignment of error is whether the right to possession was in the holder of a mortgage on the chattel, the plaintiff loan company, or in the holder of an artisan's lien on the same chattel, the defendant garage. The facts are not in controversy, each party having a lawful lien on the chattel with only the question of priority between such liens to be determined.

It is claimed by the appellant garage that the adoption of the so-called Uniform Commercial Code changes and supercedes previously existing provisions for secured liens in the automobile title law and specifically directs a priority of liens under the circumstances contrary to *Metropolitan Securities Co. v. Orlow* (107 Ohio St. 583, 140 N.E. 396 . . . and related cases, with the result that the artisan now takes precedence over the mortgage creditor.

The alleged conflict between the priority provision of the Uniform Commercial Code, particularly Section 1309-29, Revised Code, and a similar provision in the automobile certificate of title law, particularly Section 4505-13, Revised Code, is more apparent than real, and a close scanning of the provision of each of the above statutes will so indicate. Section 1309-29, applied to the facts of this case, provides: "When a person (the garage here) furnishes services or materials with respect to goods subject to a security interest (the mortgage here), a lien upon goods in the possession of such person (the garage) *given by statute or rule of law* . . .

(a common-law lien) takes priority over a perfected security interest (the mortgage) *unless the lien is statutory and the statute expressly provides otherwise.*" [Emphasis added.]

A statute which "expressly provides otherwise" is Section 4505-13, Revised Code, which states as follows:

> . . . Any security agreement covering a security interest in a motor vehicle . . . in the case of a certificate of title, if a notation of such instrument has been made by the clerk of the court of common pleas on the face of such certificate, shall be valid as against the creditors of the debtor, whether armed with process or not, and against subsequent purchasers, secured parties, and other lienholders or claimants . . . .

Section 1309-29, Revised Code, in its simplest terms, seems to hold (1) that a statutory lien for labor and material is superior unless the lien is statutory and the statute denies the priority and (2) that a common-law (rule of law) is superior unless the lien is statutory and the statute denies the priority. Proposition (2) above does not make sense, although the statute is susceptible to this translation. Proposition (1) says that a statutory lien is superior unless the statute denies the superiority. (Query: Does this mean that the statute granting the lien must deny its priority, or may any applicable statute deny priority to the lien granted by some other statute?) On the other hand, proposition (2) above certainly says that a nonstatutory lien is superior unless the lien is statutory. (Query: What lien?)

While the question arising from proposition (1) above is not directly involved here because the instant artisan's lien is not statutory the uncertainty is patent and should be borne in mind in view of the comments following.

It is the duty of a court called upon to interpret a statute to breathe sense and meaning into it; to give effect to all its terms and provisions; and to render it compatible with other and related enactments whenever and wherever possible.

This can be done in regard to the seemingly built-in conflicts in Section 1309-29, Revised Code, only by considering that the first use of the word, "lien," in the statute refers to the claim of the laborer or materialman in possession, and the second use of the world, "lien," in the same statute refers to the claim of the secured interest. Such an interpretation would require the statute to be read as if it stated:

> When a person . . . furnishes services or materials with respect to goods subject to a security interest, a lien upon the goods . . . given by statute or rule of law takes priority over the security interest unless the security interest is statutory and the statute provides otherwise.

In this way only can meaning be read into Section 1309-29, Revised Code, and all its terms be given effect and rendered compatible with other existing statutes dealing with same or similar subject matter. Such another existing statute is Section 4505-13, Revised Code. It is clear that this is a statute which (1) provides a lien for a security interest and which (2) provides that the priority of the lien thus established is otherwise than the priority set out in Section 1309-29, Revised Code.

It appears accordingly that the enactment of Section 1309-29, as it must be interpreted, coupled with the re-enactment of Section 4505-13, has had the effect of carrying into the substantive statutory law the judicial rule previously laid down in the case of *Metropolitan Securities Co. v. Orlow, supra* (107 Ohio St. 583, 140 N.E. 2d 306, 32 A. L. R. 992) and subsequent and related cases. The judgment below recognizing the priority of the lien of the plaintiff is correct and, therefore, is affirmed.

Judgment affirmed. [For holder of security interest.]

Decker v. Aurora Motors, Inc.

1966 Alaska 409 P.2d 603

On July 9, 1963, the plaintiff, Aurora Motors, Inc., as seller, and one Lynn, as buyer, executed a "Retail Instalment Contract" for the sale of a used 1963 Pontiac. The agreement called for monthly payments of $111.13, commencing August 16, 1963. On July 31, 1963, a Certificate of Title was issued to Lynn noting a lien in the amount of $2,940.66. On July 9, 1964 Decker, doing business as Triangle Service, repaired the car at Lynn's request. Lynn did not pay for the repairs and Decker retained possession. On August 5, 1964, plaintiff brought a replevin action against Decker and Lynn. The plaintiff prevailed and Decker appealed.

RABINOWITZ, J.   The issues to be determined, as framed by the parties in this appeal, relate to a question of priority between a prior recorded security interest in a motor vehicle and a subsequent mechanic's lien. We are of the opinion that the trial court's resolution of these issues in favor of the security interest holder was correct. . . .

[T]he legislature in 1957 amended subsection (4) of section 7 of the Alaska Motor Vericle Act of 1951. As amended the subsection in question (AS 28.10.510) now reads as follows:

> The filing and the issuance of a new certificate of title is constructive notice of all liens and encumbrances against the vehicle described in the certificate to creditors of the owner, or to subsequent purchasers and encumbrancers. *However, an encumbrance or lien on a vehicle for work, labor, material, transportation, storage, or similar activity, whether or not dependent on possession for its validity, is subordinate only to mortgages, conditional sales contracts, or similar encumbrances or liens properly filed on or before the time that the vehicle is subject to, or comes into possession of, the encumbrance or lien claimant.* [Emphasized portion indicates the 1957 amendment.]

By virtue of the 1957 amendment, the Legislature clearly indicated its intent to subordinate the lien of a mechanic-artisan to the lien of a prior recorded security interest.

Analysis of the statutory provisions relating to mechanic's liens also supports our conclusion that the Legislature intended, by virtue of the

1957 amendment, to subordinate a mechanic's lien in a situation such as we have in this appeal. AS 34.35.175(a) provides:

A person who makes, alters, repairs or labors upon an article of personal property at the request of the owner or lawful possessor has a lien on the property for his just and reasonable charges for the labor performed and material furnished. The person may keep possession of the article until the charges are paid.

In regard to the priority of mechanic's liens, AS 34.35.200 states:

The lien provided in § 175 of this chapter, when filed as provided in that section, is superior to and preferred to . . .

(2) a lien, mortgage, or other encumbrance which attaches before that time, *when the person furnishing the material or performing the services did not have notice of the prior lien, mortgage, or encumbrance, or the prior lien, mortgage, or encumbrance was not recorded or filed in the manner provided by law.* [Emphasis furnished.]

AS 34.35.200(2) when read in conjunction with subsection (4) of section 7 (as amended) of the Alaska Motor Vehicle Act of 1951 further evidences the Legislature's intent to subordinate the mechanic's lien. The provisions of AS 28.10.510 furnish the notice which subordinates the mechanic's lien under the language of AS 34.35.200(2).

Since the Retail Instalment Contract in question was entered into on July 9, 1963, it is subject to the provisions of the Uniform Commercial Code which became law in this jurisdiction on December 31, 1962. In our opinion nothing contained in the Uniform Commercial Code alters our conclusion as to the question of priorities under AS 34.35.200(2) and AS 28.10.510.

Section 9-310 of the Uniform Commercial Code provides:

When a person in the ordinary course of his business furnishes services or materials with respect to goods subject to a security interest, *a lien upon goods in the possession of such person given by statute or rule of law for such materials or services takes priority over a perfected security interest unless the lien is statutory and the statute expressly provides otherwise.* [Emphasis furnished.]

(This section has been codified as AS 45.05.750. Appellee's interest under the July 9, 1963, Retail Instalment Contract is a "security interest" as that term is used in AS 45.05.750 and throughout the Uniform Commercial Code. AS 45.05.020(37), which is the general definition section of the Uniform Commercial Code, provides in part as follows:

"[S]ecurity interest" means an interest in personal property or fixtures which secures payment or performance of an obligation; the retention or reservation of title by a seller of goods notwithstanding shipment or delivery to the buyer (§ 126) is limited in effect to a reservation of a "security interest." . . .

The Official Code Comment to Section 9-310 of the Uniform Commercial Code states in part:

> . . . Under chattel mortgage or conditional sales law many decisions made the priority of such liens turn on whether the secured party did or did not have "title." This Section changes such rules and makes the lien for services or; materials prior in all cases where they are furnished in the ordinary course of the lienor's business and the goods involved are in the lienor's possession. *Some of the statutes creating such liens expressly make the lien subordinate to a prior security interest. This Section does not repeal such statutory provisions.* . . . [Emphasis furnished.]

From a reading of the text of Section 9-310 and the comment thereto, it is clear that the priority given to a mechanic's or artisan's lien by Section 9-310 (AS 45.05.750) is controlling unless our statute pertaining to a mechanic's lien "expressly provides otherwise." We are of the opinion that AS 34.35.200(2) expressly subordinates a mechanic's lien to a prior recorded (perfected) security interest under AS 28.10.510 and therefore the priority given to a mechanic's lien by Section 9-310 is not applicable here.

Appellant argues that despite any statutory priority that may have been accorded to appellee's security interest over his mechanic's lien appellee impliedly subordinated its security interest and impliedly consented to the repairs in question by allowing Lynn to have possession and use of the vehicle under the terms of the Retail Instalment Contract. In support of this contention appellant relies upon the wording of Section 9-316 of the Uniform Commercial Code, now codified as AS 45.05.762. AS 45.05.762 provides:

> Nothing in §§ 690-794 of this chapter prevents subordination by agreement by a person entitled to priority.

Paragraph 2 of the "Provisions" section of the Retail Instalment Contract states in part:

> The buyer shall keep said property free of all taxes, liens and encumbrances. . . .

In light of the above, and upon a reading of the entire text of the Retail Instalment Contract, we concur in the trial court's conclusion that appellee did not agree to subordinate the priority it was entitled to by virtue of AS 28.10.510 and AS 34.35.200(2). We are of the further opinion that AS 45.05.762 (§ 9.316), when read in conjunction with AS 28.10.510 and AS 34.35.200(2), precludes finding subordination by implication. . . .

Judgment for plaintiff, holder of security interest, affirmed.

Associates Discount Corp. v. Cary

1965 (N.Y.) 262 N.Y.S.2d 646

The defendant, Cary, purchased an automobile in Washington, D.C., on a conditional sales contract on September 8, 1959. The dealer assigned the contract to the plaintiff finance company, Associates, and the defendant was notified to make all installment payments directly to the plaintiff. The defendant moved to Boston and made some payments on the contract. He became delinquent in his payments; plaintiff repossessed the car, and resold it on March 18, 1960, at private sale without notice to defendant for $975. The original purchase price, including finance and insurance, was $2452.40. Defendant had paid in towards that amount a total of $842.08 and was credited with the $975 realized on the resale, so that plaintiff claimed a balance of $635.32 plus attorney's fees and expenses for a total of $747.86. The defendant had moved to New York and this action was brought there to recover the deficiency.

EDWARD J. GREENFIELD, J.   This case raises the question of which state's law applies in a multi-state transaction in which property is purchased subject to a security interest in one jurisdiction, repossessed and resold in another, and a deficiency judgment is sought in a third. New York appears to have no case squarely in point.

. . . It is the well-established law of New York, the forum where the deficiency judgment is sought, that if the repossession and resale are not in compliance with the law, no suit for any claimed deficiency will lie. (Cases cited.)

Clearly, however, New York's statutes in effect at the time governing repossession and resale procedure in conditional sales . . . can have no application to a District of Columbia contract which was sought to be enforced in Massachusetts, at a time when neither of the parties had any relation to New York. A New York court must then look to its own body of conflicts-of-law rules to determine which foreign law shall here be applied to each specific issue. (Cases cited.)

Plaintiff argues that there is no real problem—that the contract between the parties permitted repossession and resale without notice, and that this was perfectly permissible under the District of Columbia Code (Section 28-1409) where the contract was made. (It is to be noted that since that time, the District of Columbia has shifted from a permissive to a protective jurisdiction, and like New York, has adopted the Uniform Commercial Code (D.C.Code, Title 28, 9-504) which was already on the books in Massachusetts.) Defendant points out however that Massachusetts, where the repossession and resale took place, prohibited resale without notice . . ., and expressly provided that the notice requirement could not be waived or varied. . . .

In deciding whether or not to permit a suit for a deficiency, which presupposes a valid resale, which law is New York, as the forum, to apply? Plaintiff urges that the agreement between the parties must govern, and that as it was a valid contract in the District of Columbia, where made, it is valid everywhere. This is the tradition in the law of conflicts since Beale —that the law of the place of contracting governs the validity and effect of a contract of conditional sale, and will be enforced pursuant to its terms by a sister state unless it offends the public policy or positive statute of the sister state. . . . Even without express statutory command however, we have more and more been considering the law of that state with which

the contract has the most significant relationship, or grouping of contacts.
. . . The neat and simplistic solution—application of the *lex locus contractus*—fails to meet the problem head on. We are concerned here not with the validity of the contract, or interpretation of the contract, or ascertainment as to whether there has been a breach of the contract—all of which are indisputed—but with the rules governing the remedies for an admitted breach of an admittedly valid contract.

Pragmatic policy considerations would dictate that the local view of the jurisdiction where the remedies are sought to be invoked be accorded primacy. The self-help permitted in the area where the parties originally bargained may lead to a breach of the peace and worse in another place and another time. The "law west of the Pecos" has no place on the import lists of staid New England.

In seeking our answer . . . we need not rely solely on shifting principles of conflicts-of-law, or pursue the will-o'-the-wisp of public policy. The latter appears plain enough when the statute expressly forbids any waiver or variation of the notice requirements. But the Uniform Commercial Code, which is now the law in New York as well as in Massachusetts, has its own built-in conflicts rules, explicitly dealing with transactions which, before they have run their course, spill over state lines.

Section 1-105 deals generally with all commercial transactions covered by the code, and permits the parties to agree as to the law which will govern, provided that state bears a reasonable relation to the transaction. Failing such agreement, the Code would apply to all transactions bearing an "appropriate relation" to the state where it was in force. Express provision is made in subdivision (2) for the application for sections 9-102 and 9-103 on secured transactions, with any contrary agreement being effective only to the extent permitted by the law specified.

Section 9-102 makes it plain that the article on secured transactions (which includes a prohibition on waiving or varying the notice requirements) applies "so far as concerns any personal property and fixtures within the jurisdiction of this State" in which there is a security interest, including conditional sales. The Massachusetts Code Comment (Mass. Gen. Laws Annotated, Ch. 106, 9-102) says of this section: "It applies to any security interest or collateral within the Commonwealth." And Homer Kripke, in his commentary on the section, states:

> In general this Article adopts the position, implicit in prior law, that the law of the state where the collateral is located should be the governing law, without regard to possible contacts in other jurisdictions. (McKinney's Consolidated Laws of N.Y., Uniform Commercial Code, p. 326).

The only exception with which we need be concerned is in Section 9-103, dealing with multiple state transactions, in which it is provided that when property already subject to a security interest is brought into a state, the validity of that interest is determined by the law of the jurisdiction where the security interest attached. This is in accord with

the well-grooved traditions of *lex locus contractus*. . . . It has always
been recognized however that if, after a valid conditional sale, a chattel
is taken into another state, new interests may arise in the second state if
it has a law dealing with property within its territorial jurisdiction.

Thus, applying the statutory law to the facts in this case it is plain
(a) that the parties did not expressly agree as to which law would govern;
(b) the validity and interpretation of the conditional sales agreement
under District of Columbia law is unchallenged: (c) whether the property subject to the agreement had been removed to Massachusetts—
rightly or wrongly—is immaterial; (d) the parties dealt with the property and the obligations arising out of its sale in Massachusetts. Hence
the provisions of the Uniform Commercial Code in effect where the
property was located govern. No matter what the contract may say in
obviating the requirement of notice prior to resale, notice was required
in the state where the repossession took place. Notice never having been
given, the resale was illegal in Massachusetts, and New York will not
permit any recovery under those circumstances of any alleged deficiency.

Plaintiff's complaint is dismissed. Judgment for the defendant.

CHAPTER 28
REVIEW QUESTIONS AND PROBLEMS

1. *X* sold goods to *Y* and has a security interest in *Y*'s inventory. The
   financing statement provides for a security interest in after acquired
   property. *Y* is not negotiating for the purchase of additional inventory items from *Z* and wishes to give *Z* a security interest in the new
   inventory. *Z* is concerned over the status of his security interest if he
   sells goods to *Y*. Advise *Z* as to a proper course of action.
2. *A* finance Co. had a security interest in *B*'s car. *B* defaulted and *A*
   repossessed the car. *A* gave notice that the car would be sold at public
   sale to be held at *A*'s office. On the day of the sale no one appeared
   and the car was purchased for *A* by the company's manager. Can *A*
   obtain a judgment against *B* for the deficiency between the amount
   paid by *A* and the balance due on the car?
3. *S* sold a portable steel building to *B* and retained a security interest.
   B gave *S* a note indorsed by *X* in payment. *B* defaulted on the note
   and contract and *S* repossessed the building. Thereafter the building
   was sold for $5,000 less than the balance due. Is *X* liable for the
   deficiency?
4. *A*, a car dealer, sold a used car to *X* on an installment contract. The
   contract was sold to *B* Bank with provision that *A* would repurchase
   the car for the amount due thereon if *X* defaulted in his payments.
   The contract provided that *A* waived all notice. The bank repossessed

the car and sold it without notice to *A*. Can the bank recover the deficiency from *A*?

5. *A* entered into a security agreement with *B* Bank and a financing statement which described the collateral as "inventory and accounts receivable" was filed. Thereafter *A* entered into an agreement with *C* Finance Co. and a financing statement covering "accounts receivable now existing or to be hereafter created" was filed. As between the bank and the finance company, which has prior claim to the receivables?

6. *B* Bank has a perfected security interest in a bulldozer owned by *A*. *A* has taken the machine to *X* Garage for repairs. If *X* repairs it, will his lien for parts and services have priority over the bank's security interest?

7. *R*, a retail automobile dealer, at times borrowed money from *X* Co. and *Y* Co., each of whom had filed the necessary statements, *X* Co. being first to file. Thereafter on October 1, *R* borrowed $10,000 of *Y* Co. and used four cars as security. He later borrowed $8,000 of *X* Co. and used the same cars as security. *R* is now insolvent and *X* Co. took possession of the cars. Is this lien superior to that of *Y* Co.?

8. *R*, a retail farm implement dealer, sold a used tractor to *F*, a farmer, for $2,200, payable in installments, and retained a security interest in the tractor to secure the payments. After *F* had reduced the indebtedness to $1,800, he became bankrupt. *R* had not perfected his lien by filing. Is *R*'s security interest good as against the trustee in bankruptcy?

9. *F* Co. loaned *M* Co. money, taking a security interest in an inventory as security, the security contract providing that the lien carry over to the proceeds. If *M* Co. becomes bankrupt after selling several items of the inventory, having on hand notes receivable, checks, and accounts receivable growing out of sales, does the lien of *F* Co. carry over to these items, assuming proper filing had taken place?

10. *A*, an automobile dealer, by a valid security agreement retained a security interest in an automobile which he sold *B* on credit. No financing statement was filed, and *B* was given both the automobile and the certificate of title, which failed to show *A*'s interest. *B* resold the car to *C*. If *A*'s claim is not paid, may he possess the car?

11. *A*, a furniture dealer, by a valid security agreement retained a security interest in a $750 sofa sold to *B* on credit. No financing statement was filed. *B* resold the sofa to *C*, another consumer. If *A* is not paid, may he repossess the sofa?

12. *K* Piano Company consigned pianos to *R*, a retailer dealer. *R* sold one of the pianos to *X* for cash but did not account to *K* for the proceeds of the sale. *K* had filed a financing statement. *K* claims to be entitled to possession of the piano. Can *K* recover the piano from *X*?

BOOK FOUR

Agency and Employment

Introduction to Agency and Employment

4-1 Scope of the Subject Matter. The field of agency and employment transcends many areas of the law. Traditionally, the term "agency" has referred to the relationship that arises when one party authorizes another to create, to modify, or to terminate contractual relations between the former and third parties. The one granting the authority is known as the *principal,* whereas the one to whom the power is given is called the *agent.* Agency as defined in this limited sense excludes the relationship of master and servant, for the servant has no power to create or modify contractual relations. However, the importance of the law of torts and the thousands of cases which have arisen because an employee has allegedly committed a tort has resulted in the subject of tort liability being considered as an integral part of the law of agency. Since the same general principles control the tort liability of both principals and employers, the distinction between them has little significance. In the next chapter, the contractual aspects of the law of principal and agent are discussed. Chapter 31 is concerned with tort liability of principals and employers. Both chapters are also concerned with the proprietor-independent contractor relationship which may be broadly considered as a part of employment.

In addition to invading most areas of private law, the modern view is that the law of agency and employment has many connections with public law. The government has attempted to regulate the employment relationship and to define the rights of the parties. A study of this field of commercial law requires some mention of the role of government. For example, the 1964 Civil Rights Statute is directly concerned with the selection and discharge of agents and servants and the rights and duties of the employees and those who employ them must be analyzed in light of this statute. States have modified the tort liability of employers to employees by statutes and these must also be considered. While it is not the intention to cover all of the legal aspects of employment which are affected by public statutes, many of them will be mentioned in order that the legal environment of employment will be understood.

Agency problems are usually discussed within a framework of three parties—the principal (*P*), the agent (*A*), and the third party (*T*) with whom the agent contracts on behalf of *P* or against whom he commits a tort while in the employment of *P*. These letters—*P, A,* and *T*—will sometimes be used in the sections and chapters which follow to describe these parties.

4-2 Terminology. Agents are frequently classified by the functions which they perform and the rights and powers which they possess. Two common terms are *broker* and *factor*. A broker is an agent with special and limited authority to procure a customer to effect a sale or exchange of property which he does not possess or control. A factor is a person who has possession and control of another's property and is authorized to sell such property. A factor has a property interest and may sell the property in his own name while a broker may not.

Another common distinction is to classify agents either as *general* or *special*. While this distinction creates a great deal of confusion, most cases define a general agent as one authorized to conduct a series of transactions involving a continuity of service while a special agent conducts a simple transaction or a series of transactions without continuity of service. The importance of this distinction will be illustrated in the next chapter.

The term *employee* creates a great deal of difficulty in the law. Does the term cover all agents and servants? The meaning of each term depends on the sense in which it is being used. For example, an agent is not necessarily an employee subject to social security and withholding tax. Local fire insurance agents and commission houses are usually agents but not employees in this sense. It must also be recognized that a person may be an agent and create contractual liability and yet not be a servant for tort liability. For example, a real estate broker selling a house could create contractual liability but not tort liability if the broker negligently injured a prospect while driving an automobile. It is also obvious that a servant may create tort liability and yet have no authority or power to create contractual liability.

Some persons who perform services for others are known as *independent contractors*. A person may contract for the services of another in such a way as to have full and complete control over the manner in which the latter conducts the work, or he may simply contract for a certain end result. If the agreement provides merely that the second party is to accomplish a certain result and has full control over the manner and methods to be pursued in bringing about the result, he is deemed an independent contractor, and the one receiving the benefit of his services is generally not responsible to third parties for the independent contractor's actions. On the other hand, if the second party places his services at the disposal of the first in such a manner that the action of the second is controlled by the former, an agency relation is established.[1]

An agent may purport to be acting on behalf of a stated principal in which case the latter is called a *disclosed principal.* The agent may purport to be acting for himself and keep his agency a secret in which case the principal is called an *undisclosed principal.* A third term, *partially disclosed principal,* is used to describe the situation in which the agent admits that he is acting for a principal but does not disclose his identity.

4-3 Capacity of Parties. It is generally stated that anyone who may act for himself may act through an agent. To this rule there is one fairly well-reorganized exception. An infant may enter into a contract, and so long as he does not disaffirm, the agreement is binding. There is considerable authority to the effect that any appointment of an agent by an infant is void. Therefore, under this theory any agreement entered into by such an agent would be ineffective, and an attempted disaffirmance would be superfluous. Most recent cases hold, however, that the act of the agent who represents a minor is voidable only and is subject to rescission or ratification by the minor.

Nevertheless, an infant may act as an agent for someone else, and an agreement which he makes while acting for his principal is binding. Although the infant has a right to terminate his contract of agency at his will, as long as he continues in the employment his acts within the scope of the authority conferred become those of his principal.

Contracts in which authority is delegated to an agent, like other agreements, must have for their purpose a legal object. As in the case of other illegal contracts, the courts would not enforce an agency agreement with an illegal purpose, but would leave the parties without any legal redress.

4-4 Formal Requirements. Usually no particular formalities are essential to the appointment of an agent with two exceptions: The appointment may be either written or oral. First, where the purpose of the agency can be exercised only by the signing of a formal document under seal, the agency must be created under seal. Where a formal sealed instrument is used for conferring authority upon the agent, he is said to possess a *power of attorney.* A power of attorney may be general, giving the agent authority to act in all respects as the principal could act, or it may be special, granting to the agent only restricted authority. A power of attorney is customarily acknowledged before a notary public whose seal is affixed thereto. Second, the law in the majority of the states requires that any agent who is given power to sell or to convey any interest in or concerning real estate must obtain such power by a written authorization from the principal.[2] The ordinary real estate broker, however, in most

1 *King v. Young, Brown, and Beverly, Inc.,* page 658.
2 *Dineff v. Wernecke,* page 660.

states would not need a written agreement, as his authority is merely to find a buyer with whom the seller is willing to contract. Normally, he has no authority to enter into a binding contract to convey the property. However, in many states a "listing agreement" is required to be in writing.

A further exception exists in a few states where it is required that the authority must possess the same dignity as the act to be performed. In these states an agent who possesses authority to sign a contract which is required to be in writing must receive his appointment by an instrument in writing. Such is not the law in most states.

Insofar as the execution of a simple contract or commercial paper is concerned, the agent should execute it in such a fashion as to clearly indicate his representative capacity, but many contracts are ambiguous and fail to indicate the actual relationship of the parties. Although the signture does not indicate definitely who the real contracting party is, many of the states permit the use of parol evidence to show the intention of the agent and the third party when the signature is ambiguous—the agent is allowed to offer proof that it was not intended that he assume personal responsibility. However, the agent may be liable as a result of his failure to clearly indicate his representative capacity.[3]

4-5 Statutory Aspects of Employment. There are many legislative enactments which affect the employment relationship. First, there are the federal statutes which regulate labor-management relations and especially collective bargaining. These statutes, the judicial decisions interpreting them, and the actions of the administrative agency which enforces and administers them compose a major segment of the law relating to employment. This matter is discussed further in the next section.

Secondly, there are both federal and state statutes which regulate wages, hours, and working conditions. The Fair Labor Standards Act which controls such matters as minimum wages, hours, and the records to be kept by employers is an example of such a statute. State laws control such matters as child labor, safety devices, workmen's compensation, unemployment compensation, and fair employment practices. While we will not discuss most of these matters in detail, it must be recognized that many of the rights and duties of both employers and employees are determined by these statutes and the administrative agencies operating pursuant to them. The businessman must be familiar with these statutes and comply with those applicable to his business.

4-6 Labor-Management Relations. An examination of employment and the employer-employee relationship necessarily includes some mention of labor-management relations. Since many, if not most, employment contracts are actually entered into by unions on behalf of their members, a general understanding of laws affecting labor-management contracts is desirable.

---

3 *Universal Lightning Rod, Inc. v. Rischall Electric Company,* page 661.

While there had been several earlier statutes which had attempted to encourage collective bargaining by unions on behalf of workers, it was not until the adoption of the so-called Wagner Act in 1935 that the legal environment encouraged the growth of unions and collective bargaining and provided an administrative agency, the National Labor Relations Board (N.L.R.B.), to enforce the law and decide disputes arising thereunder.

The Wagner Act, to encourage collective bargaining and give equality of bargaining power to labor, declared certain activities of employers to be unfair labor practices. These included interference with efforts of employees to form, join, or assist labor unions; domination of labor organizations (company unions); discrimination in hire or tenure because of union affiliation; discrimination against employees who filed charges or testified under the Act; and refusing to bargain collectively with a duly designated union. These unfair labor practices have been the subject of numerous judicial decisions interpreting the Act and a whole body of labor law has developed concerning the duties of employers in bargaining with unions. While it is not the purpose of this discussion to cover these matters in detail, the student is cautioned that the common law principles discussed herein are subject to the limitations of these statutes as are the contracts entered into in the areas covered by them.

Unions, encouraged by the Wagner Act and the increased demand for labor caused by World War II, grew in power and importance until by the mid-1940's there was a feeling that laws were needed to curb the power of unions and to balance once again the bargaining power of labor and management. The Wagner Act had added strength to the union movement to give unions equal bargaining power with management but it had failed to create equality. In 1947, the so-called Taft-Hartley Act was enacted covering labor's unfair practices. It declared that certain activities by unions were unfair labor practices and, in addition, to protect the public interest, created legal machinery to postpone nation-wide strikes where the public interest would be adversely affected. This latter provision provides for an 80-day cooling-off period during which federal mediators attempt to resolve the differences between management and labor. Activities which are unfair labor practices by unions include coercing employees into joining a union, causing discrimination against non-union employees, refusing to bargain with the employer, engaging in secondary boycotts for illegal purposes, causing an employer to pay for work not performed, and picketing where the union is not certified. While this list is not complete, it indicates the type of activity which is prohibited in order to encourage collective bargaining and fair treatment. The avowed purpose of both statutes is to create equality of bargaining power between labor and management, while protecting the interest of the public, to the end that collective bargaining will settle disputes and controversies concerning employment.

In 1959, Congress enacted the Labor-Management Reporting and Disclosure Act, usually referred to as the Landrum-Griffin Act. This statute was adopted in order to protect union members from wrongful conduct by their officers. The statute also clarified and tightened the restrictions of the Taft-Hartley statute on secondary boycotts, hot cargo contracts, and organizational picketing. The statute is designed to give the rank and file union members control over the union affairs and to ensure that their rights are protected by federal intervention if necessary. The information which unions may furnish the Department of Labor concerning their activities is very substantial.

4-7 Job Discrimination. Many cities, most states, and the Federal government have enacted statutes which are designed to prevent discrimination in hiring, promotion, pay, or lay-offs because of race, color, creed, sex, or national origin. These statutes have modified the basic common law concept that an employer had a free choice in selecting his employees and in the absence of a contract, a free choice in discharging them. They have been passed as a part of the general philosophy of government that all persons should have equality of opportunity. These statutes frequently contain criminal sanctions and authorize civil suits for damages. Usually, administrative agencies called Fair Employment Practices Commissions are established to enforce these statutes.

These anti-job-discrimination laws are an example of private contract rights being superseded by an overriding public policy. Freedom of contract gives way to laws regulating the employment relationship because of the economic loss to the country caused by discrimination and because of the adverse effect it has on the minority groups directly affected.

The Federal statute is applicable to all employers of 25 or more employees, all employment agencies, and all labor organizations maintaining a hiring hall. Exceptions are created where there is a bona fide occupational qualification. For example, a university desiring to hire a football coach could legally limit the job to males without being subject to a suit for discrimination based on sex.

Most statutes require the keeping of records by employers which establish the reason for various actions in respect to employee relations. While testing is specifically allowed under the federal law, tests should not be used to defeat the goal of equal opportunity and if a test is more difficult than necessary to select qualified persons for a particular job, the employer may be guilty of discrimination.

INTRODUCTION TO AGENCY AND EMPLOYMENT CASES

King v. Young, Brown, and Beverly, Inc.

1958, (Fla. App.) 107 S.2d 751

King, the plaintiff, brought suit against Young, a trucker, Brown, a transportation broker, and Beverly, Inc., a supplier of vegetables, to recover for losses sustained in a two tractor-trailer collision caused by the negligence of Young's driver. The plaintiff alleged that Young was the agent of the other defendants. Beverly, Inc. called Brown to obtain transportation for a load of beans to a destination in Georgia and Brown in turn called Young. Young picked up the beans and upon the return of the receipted bill of lading was to receive from Brown $234.79, less a brokerage commission of 7 per cent. Brown and Beverly, Inc. both contend that Young was an independent contractor and that no agency relationship existed. The lower court found in their favor and King appealed so far as his claim against Brown was concerned. Young was held liable and no appeal was taken from that judgment.

KANNER, J. . . . The term *agency* may be defined as "a contract either express or implied upon a consideration, or gratuitous undertaking, by which one of the parties confides to the other the management of some business to be transacted in his name or on his account, and by which that other assumes to do the business and render an account of it." (2 Am. Jur., *Agency,* Section 2, p. 13) In an agency relationship, the party for whom another acts and from whom he derives authority to act is known and referred to as a principal, while the other party who acts for and represents the principal and who acquires his authority from him is known and referred to as an agent. Thus, the agent steps into the shoes of his principal and acts for him pursuant to the grant of authority vested in him by the principal. (2 Am. Jur., *Agency,* Section 2, p. 13)

In the instant case, Brown was merely the intermediary in the transaction between the shipper and the transportation medium. What he did was to procure transportation for the shipper through the trucker Young, for which he, Brown, was to receive as his brokerage commission a percentage of the total transportation price. Although Brown arranged for Young to haul the beans, Young was to pay his own expenses; he had the control and choice of routes to follow; and he was completely independent of Brown after the load was arranged, except that Young had to bring back a receipt so as to show delivery of the beans before he could collect his freight charge.

The status of an independent contractor, as distinguished from that of an agent, consists of a contractual relationship by one with another to perform something for him, but the one so engaged is not controlled or subject to the control of the other in the performance of the engagement but only as to the result. Conversely, a principal in an agency relationship retains the right to control the conduct of an agent in regard to the engagement intrusted to him. It may be said that the recognized distinction between an agent and an independent contractor relationship is determined by whether the person is subject to or whether he is free from control with regard to the details of the engagement. . . .

The position assumed by appellant is inconsistent, because the agency relationship as applied to the instant case can only contemplate that one person, that is, the principal, is superior and that the other person, the agent, is subordinate. There is no indication whatever that Brown was a principal to either the shipper of the commodity or of the trucker. He was called upon by the shipper as a transportation broker to procure

transportation and he then arranged with the trucker to haul the load, for which he was only to receive a commission for his services. . . .
Judgment affirmed.

Dineff v. Wernecke

1963 (Ill.) 190 N.E.2d 308

Prospective purchasers of realty brought suit against defendants, brother and sister, who owned realty, for specific performance of an alleged contract to sell jointly owned property with the sister in her own behalf and as agent for brother, and for damages for failure of brother and sister to convey. The Superior Court entered a decree adverse to the prospective purchasers after the defendants pleaded the Statute of Frauds and plaintiffs appealed. The brother had not authorized his sister in writing to enter into the contract on his behalf but had orally agreed to its terms.

HERSHEY, J. . . . The record is clear that Louis R. Wernecke did not sign any contract or letter of acceptance of an offer from Dineff. Nor is there in evidence any writing signed by any agent in behalf of Louis R. Wernecke. Further, there is no evidence that Louis R. Wernecke in writing authorized Elsie Wernecke or anyone else to act as his agent in selling or signing any contract. Section 2 of the Illinois Statute of Frauds provides: "No action shall be brought to charge any person upon any contract for the sale of lands, tenements or hereditaments or any interest in or concerning them, for a longer term than one year, unless such contract or some memorandum or note thereof shall be in writing, and signed by the party to be charged therewith, or some other person thereunto by him lawfully authorized in writing, signed by such party." As we stated in *Fletcher v. Underwood* (240 Ill. 554, 88 N.E. 1030): "Where an agent sells real estate for another, in order to bind the principal it is not only necessary that the authority of the agent should be in writing, but also that the contract made by the agent, or some memorandum thereof, should be in writing and signed by the agent."

Thus, it is clear that Louis R. Wernecke is in no way bound as to the plaintiffs.

The fact that Louis R. Wernecke did not sign any contract with the plaintiffs makes the contract unenforceable against Elsie Wernecke since the negotiations for the purchase of the property were intended to be with Elsie Wernecke and Louis R. Wernecke jointly. Plaintiffs intended to purchase the interests of both parties, not separate interests. The instant case is like that in *Madia v. Collins* (408 Ill. 358, at page 362, 97 N.E.2d 313, at page 315), wherein we said: "It is obvious that plaintiff knew with whom he was dealing; that he was not misled as to the ownership; and that his offer of purchase was made to both owners for the entire title. Without the signature of both owners, no contract was formed, and there could be no breach upon which plaintiff could base an action for specific performance. . . . One cannot have specific performance in such case where the contract contemplates the sale of all the interests in the property contracted for, or none. (*Spadoni v. Frigo,* 307 Ill. 32, 138 N.E. 226)"

The complaint nowhere alleges a separate price for the interests of each and there is no prayer for partial performance against Elsie Wernecke. At all times plaintiffs treated the Werneckes as a unit.

Decree affirmed.

Universal Lightning Rod, Inc. v. Rischall Electric Co.

1963 (Conn.) 192 A.2d 50

HOLDEN, J. This is an action, brought against the defendant Harold M. Rischall, seeking to hold him personally liable on a promissory note, in the amount of $590, which is dated April 9, 1962. The question presented is whether he is liable personally on the note. He signed the note in manner and form as follows: "Rischall Electric Co., Inc. (and under this designation) Harold M. Rischall."

The Rischall Electric Company, Inc., was a corporation which had been in business for more than twenty years. In the course of its business, certain lightning rods were ordered from the plaintiff in order to fill a contract for electrical work in a low-cost housing project. The note in question was prepared at the direction of Harold M. Rischall, hereinafter called the defendant, and none of its terms were demanded or suggested by the plaintiff.

In the course of the trial, the question of interpretation of the word "we" as used in the note was raised. Objection was made that such evidence was inadmissible under the parol evidence rule. The objection was sustained, not for the reasons stated, but because any attempt to describe the meaning of the word "we" would be, at best, self-serving. Where the parties have reduced their agreement to a writing, their intention is to be determined from its language and not on the basis of any intention either may have secretly entertained. Where a note contains the words, "I promise to pay," and is signed by two persons as makers, they are deemed to be and are jointly and severally liable thereon, and either of the makers is liable for the full amount of the note due and unpaid. Needless to say, the use of the word "we" would assess joint and several liability upon all makers. This interesting and academic question of semantics is not decisive of the issue.

The decision must be based upon the terms of § 42a-3-403 of the General Statutes, which is part of the commercial code enacted into law effective October 1, 1961. A liberal construction must be given to the sections of this law so as to secure to them a reasonable meaning and to effectuate the intention of its framers and make it workable and serviceable to the important business to which it relates. Section 42a-3-403 takes the place of § 39-21 (a section of the Negotiable Instruments Act, repealed) and states in part: "(2) An authorized representative who signs his own name to an instrument . . . (b) except as otherwise established between the immediate parties, is personally obligated if the instrument names the person represented but does not show that the representative signed in a representative capacity." When the defendant executed the note in question, he did not indicate that he did so in any representative capacity.

For the reasons stated above, the issues are found for the plaintiff and the claim of the defendant that he is not personally liable is overruled. . . .

Judgment for plaintiff.

CHAPTER 29
REVIEW QUESTIONS AND PROBLEMS

1. What is the difference between the principal-agent relationship and the master-servant relationship?
2. What is the technical distinction between a broker and a factor?
3. *A*, a real estate broker, while examining *D*'s property in order to list it for sale, negligently injures *P*. Is *D* liable to *P*?
4. What is the test to determine if a person performing services is an agent or an independent contractor?
5. *A*, a minor son of *P*, was authorized to act as *P*'s agent and entered into a contract with *T*. May *P* avoid the contract?
6. *P*, a resident of Florida, by telephone instructed *A*, his son, to sell the family home in Champaign for the best price available but not less than $14,000, its FHA appraised value, and to invest the proceeds in government bonds. *A* found *T*, a ready, willing and able buyer, at a price of $15,000 and entered into a written contract with him for the sale of the house. It was signed "by *A* as agent for *P*" and by *T*. *P* refuses to perform the contract. *T* sues *P* for breach of contract. What result?
7. John Jones, the President of *XYZ* Co., signed a note payable to the *ABC* Bank as follows: "John Jones, President." He intended for the company to pay the note but the company became insolvent. Is John Jones personally liable on the note?
8. *X*, a Negro, applied for a job at the *ABC* Co. *X* was given a test and the company refused to hire him because he allegedly failed the test. Does *X* have any recourse?

chapter 30

Contractual Liability of Principals and Agents

LIABILITY OF PRINCIPAL

4-8 Principal's Liability in General. A principal is liable on all contracts entered into by the agent within the scope of the agent's actual or apparent authority. The burden is on third parties dealing with an agent to prove the requisite authority. The principal does not have to prove lack of authority.

4-9 Actual Authority. While there are many terms used to describe various types of authority, actual authority consists of that expressly conferred or which is incidental thereto. Incidental powers are those required, or reasonably anticipated as necessary in order to carry out the major purpose for which the agency was created. The usual procedure in the creation of an agency is for the principal to expressly confer certain authority upon the agent (express authority). The agreement may be explicit, setting forth in detail the rights and duties of the respective parties, or it may consist of general terms, in which event the extent of the authority conferred depends upon various factors, such as general custom, business usage, and past practices of the particular principal (incidental authority).

The incidental powers of an agent often vary with local custom or usage. To illustrate: P appoints A as his agent to sell a certain used automobile for $900. As an incident to his authority to sell, A has authority to enter into a written contract with the purchaser and to sign P's name to the contract. Whether he has implied or incidental authority to sell on credit instead of cash or to warrant the condition of the car sold turns local custom. If it is customary for other agents in this locality to make warranties or sell on credit, this agent and the third party with whom he deals may assume he possesses such authority in the absence of knowledge to the contrary.

Customs often vary between different lines of business and between employers engaged in the same kind of endeavor. Where these customs are well established and known, third parties are bound to respect them.

Illustrating these general principles, let us assume that it is not customary for so-called departmental buyers in the department stores to buy, but merely to list needs. In such case, the purchasing office contracts for goods. This limitation being general, third parties would be bound by it. However, it might be customary for a particular department store to give their buyers authority to buy. In the latter case, an employee named as buyer would have authority to make binding contracts of purchase.

4-10 Apparent Authority. Apparent authority is that which the principal has held the agent out as possessing; it results from estoppel. It gives the agent *power* to bind his principal in many cases where he has no *right* to do so.[1]

The estoppel is created by some conduct of the "principal" which leads the third party to believe that a person is his agent or that an actual agent possesses the requisite authority. The purported agent cannot by his own conduct alone establish the relationship, and no statement of his, standing alone, can justify a third party in believing an agency exists. As was previously noted, the burden is on the third party to prove the agent's authority.

When conditions develop under which the principal, because of his conduct, is estopped to deny the existence of an agency, the agent is called an *ostensible* agent. For an agency by estoppel, the principal must conduct himself in such a manner as to lead third parties to reasonably believe that an agency exists and the third party must know of such conduct and act in reliance thereon. No estoppel can arise except where the third party relies upon facts known to him at the time he transacts business with the agent, which facts would have led a reasonably prudent person to assume that an agency existed.

An agency by estoppel or additional authority by estoppel may arise from a course of dealing on the part of an agent, which is constantly ratified by the principal, or it may result from a person's holding himself out as an agent without any dissent on the part of the purported principal and under conditions where such person owed a duty to speak. To illustrate: Upon several occasions *A* indorses his principal's name to checks and has them cashed at the bank. The principal has never given the agent such authority, but no protest is lodged with the bank until the agent appropriates to his own use the proceeds from one of the checks. The principal then attempts to recover from the bank. By approval of

---

[1] *Reusche v. California Pacific Title Insurance Company,* page 674.

the agent's previous unauthorized action, the principal has led the bank to reasonably assume that the agent possesses authority to indorse checks.

4-11 Authority Created by Necessity or Emergency. An existing emergency which necessitates immediate action may add sufficiently to the agent's powers to enable him to meet the situation. However, if time permits and the principal is available, any proposed remedy for the difficulty should be submitted to the principal for approval.[2] It is only when the principal is not available that the powers of the agent are extended. Furthermore, the agent receives no power greater than that sufficient to solve the difficulty. Thus, the power of an agent to borrow money on the strength of his principal's credit is rarely implied. Suppose, however, that a C.O.D. shipment arrives for the principal during his absence and money is not available to pay for the goods. Clearly, his representative in charge of the business may borrow sufficient funds to pay for the goods and avoid demurrage charges and other possible losses. The principal would not be liable for any excess borrowed beyond that required to pay for the particular shipment.

4-12 Ratification. A principal who is not bound by a contract because his agent lacks either actual or apparent authority may nevertheless decide that he desires to become bound. He may do so under certain circumstances by ratifying the agreement. Ratification consists of conduct which indicates approval of action taken by one party on behalf of another without authority to do so. Such approval cures the defect of lack of authority, and the relation of the parties assumes the status that would have existed had authority been granted before the one contract was executed.

4-13 Conditions Required for Ratification. Various conditions must exist before a ratification will be effective to bring about a contractual relation between the principal and the third party. First, ratification can be effective only where both the principal and the agent were capable of contracting at the time the contract was executed and are still capable at the time of ratification since ratification relates back to the time of the contract. For this reason a corporation may not ratify contracts made by its promoters before the corporation was formed. For the corporation to be bound by such agreements, a novation or assumption of liability must be shown. Ratification is impossible because the corporation was not in existence when the agreement was formed and could not possibly have entered into a contract as of that date.

Second, an agent's act may be ratified only when he holds himself out as acting for the one who is alleged to have approved the unauthorized agreement. In other words, the agent must have professed to act as an agent. A person who professes to act for himself and who makes a contract in his own name does nothing that can be ratified even though he

2 *Carlson v. Hannah et al.,* page 675.

intends at the time to let another have the benefit of his agreement. Therefore, an undisclosed principal may not ratify a contract.

Third, as a general principle, ratification does not bind the principal unless he acts with full knowledge of all the important facts. Of course, where ratification is expressed and the principal acts without any apparent desire to know or to learn the facts involved, he may not later defend himself on the ground that he was unaware of all the material facts. Where, however, ratification is to be implied from the conduct of the principal, he must act with complete understanding of all important details. *A,* a salesman with authority only to solicit orders, having no authority to sell, contracts to sell certain of his principal's goods to *T* and signs *P*'s name to the order. As an inducement to *T* to enter into the agreement, *A* sells all of the articles at a 10 per cent discount. *A* informs *P* of the sale, and files the duplicate sales slip without *P* having an opportunity to inspect it. At the time the order is ready to be shipped, it is noted for the first time that the discount is to be allowed. It would seem to be improper to find ratification under such circumstances.

The states are slightly in conflict as to whether the third party— the one with whom the agent dealt—may withdraw before ratification takes place. The better view, and that which apparently has the support of most of the states, is that the third party may withdraw from the transaction at any time before it is ratified by the principal. If not permitted to withdraw, he would be unable to hold the principal and at the same time would not be free to act with others concerning the subject matter until the principal had exercised his option. It seems only fair, therefore, to permit the third party to withdraw at any time before the principal has indicated his adoption of the transaction. However, it should be pointed out that ratification does not require notice to the third party. As soon as conduct constituting ratification has been indulged in by the principal, the third party loses his right to withdraw.

4-14 Conduct Constituting Ratification. What conduct on the part of the principal will amount to ratification? Ratification may be either express or implied. Where certain formalities, such as a writing or an authorization under seal, are required to create a particular agency, the ratification must follow the form required for the creation of the agency. Aside from this, any conduct which definitely indicates an intention on the part of the principal to adopt the transaction will constitute ratification.[3] It may take the form of words of approval to the agent, a promise to perform, or actual performance, such as delivery of the product called for in the agreement. Accepting the benefits of the contract or basing a suit on the validity of an agreement clearly amounts to ratification.

At this point it should be mentioned that an unauthorized act may not be ratified in part and rejected in part. The principal cannot ac-

---

[3] *Karetzkis v. Cosmopolitan National Bank,* page 677.

cept the benefits and refuse to assume the obligations. Because of this fact it is said that a principal, by accepting the benefits of an authorized agreement, ratifies the means used in procuring the agreement unless, within a reasonable time after learning of the true facts, he takes steps to return, so far as possible, the benefits which he has received.

Some conflict exists as to whether silence or inaction on the principal's part can be construed as ratification. Where the situation is such that failure to speak misleads the third party, causing him to rely upon the validity of the agent's acts, it seems that the principal is under a duty to speak and refute the impression. As soon as a principal learns of an unauthorized act by his agent, it is usually his duty to repudiate it with promptness.

4-15 Special Situations. There are many special problems which may arise in the law of agency. For example, is a summons served on a maid a valid service of process on the employer? Is a husband liable for his wife's purchase of a new mink coat? Many of these questions are answered by statutes on civil procedure and statutes relating to marriage. These statutes vary from state to state, and no general answer may be stated for these questions. There are, however, situations in which the general rules relating to a principal's liability and an agent's authority may be stated. These rules are discussed in the sections which follow.

4-16 Right to Collect. The power of an agent to collect a bill owed to his principal is not readily implied. It has been held that possession of a statement upon the principal's billhead and in the principal's handwriting did not justify an assumption of such authority.

A question of considerable difficulty is encountered concerning the apparent or implied power of a salesman to collect. Clearly the agent behind the counter or other agent who sells the goods has, under most circumstances, an implied power to collect for them at the time of the sale but not at a later date. If, however, the sale is on credit, no power exists to collect at a later date unless the business is a relatively small one in which the agent performs a rather general service.

The agent who delivers goods which have been sold for cash undoubtedly has a right to collect all payments due at the time of delivery. Other than such payments the ordinary delivery boy has no authority to collect unless it is expressly conferred or arises through custom.

The traveling salesman who covers certain designated territory and solicits orders for his principal has no authority to collect as payments fall due except those payments that are to be made at the time the order is obtained. In the absence of express authority, payments made to such agents, which fail to find their way into the principal's possession, may again be collected from the debtor.

Authority to collect gives the agent no authority to accept anything other than money in payment. He is not empowered to accept negotiable notes or property in settlement of an indebtedness unless expressly authorized.[4] It is customary to accept checks as conditional payment. Under such circumstances the debt is not paid unless the check is honored. If the check is not paid, the creditor-principal is free to bring suit on the contract which gave rise to the indebtedness or to sue on the check, at his option.

4-17 Agent's Power to Appoint Subagents. Agents are usually selected because of their personal qualifications. Owing to these elements of trust and confidence, a general rule has developed that an agent may not delegate his duty to someone else and clothe the latter with authority to bind the principal.[5] An exception has arisen to this rule in those cases in which the acts of the agent are purely ministerial or mechanical. An act that requires no discretion and is purely mechanical may be delegated by the agent to a third party. Such a delegation does not make the third party the agent of the principal or give him any action against the principal for compensation unless the agent was impliedly authorized to obtain this assistance. The acts of such third party become in reality the acts of the agent and bind the principal if they are within the authority given to the agent. Acts which involve the exercise of skill, discretion, or judgment may not be delegated without permission from the principal.

The case of authorized salesmen for local insurance agents seems to offer a slight exception to this rule. The local agent of an insurance company often authorizes his salesmen to accept fire insurance risks. Even though such action seems to involve a certain amount of judgment and discretion, the insurance companies are bound by the subagent's act, although they are in no respect obligated to compensate him, for the salesman must obtain his compensation from the local agent.

An agent may, under certain circumstances, have the actual or implied authority to appoint other agents for the principal, in which case they become true employees of the principal and are entitled to be compensated by him. Such a power on the part of the agent is not often implied, but if the situation is such that the major power conferred cannot be exercised without the aid of other agents, the agent is authorized to hire such help as is required. Thus, a manager placed in charge of a branch store may be presumed to possess authority to hire the necessary clerks and sales force demanded by the size of the business.

4-18 Purchase on Credit. An agent who is given special authority to purchase is limited to the quantity and quality of goods set forth by the principal. Such limitations imposed upon a general purchasing agent on a particular occasion would, however, amount to secret limitations and would not, therefore, be effective against innocent third parties. A general agent placed in charge of a business presumably has

[4] *Zazzaro v. Universal Motors,* page 679.

[5] *State ex rel. Kendrick v. Thormyer,* page 679.

power to purchase either on credit or for cash. If the principal provides a special purchasing agent with cash and instructs him not to purchase on credit, the majority holds that the principal is not liable for goods purchased on credit. This rule is applicable only where the agent has not in some manner been held out as possessing greater authority.

4-19 Secret Limitations. It is said that limitations imposed upon the usual and ordinary powers of an agent do not prevent the principal from being liable to third parties where the agent acts in violation of such limitations unless the attention of the third parties has been drawn to them.[6] In other words, the third party, having established that an agency exists and having determined in a general way the limits of the authority, is not bound to explore for unexpected and unusual restrictions. He is justified in assuming, in the absence of contrary information, that the agent possesses those powers which like agents customarily have.

An instruction to a sales agent not to sell to a certain individual or not to sell to him on credit, when credit sales are customary, cannot affect the validity of a contract made with this individual unless the latter was aware of the limitation at the time the contract was made. The principal, by appointing an agent normally possessed of certain authority, is estopped to set up the limitation as a defense, unless the limitation is made known to the third party prior to the making of the contract.

4-20 Real Estate Broker. The ordinary real estate broker possesses no authority, implied or apparent, in the absence of an express grant, to enter into a contract for the sale of property listed with him. It is his business to find a party who is willing to purchase the property upon the terms set forth in the "Listing Agreement." The owner reserves the right to contract, or not as he sees fit, at the time the broker presents a prospective buyer.

The same is true of many solicitors—often called salesmen—whose authority is limited to obtaining orders for merchandise—the orders being subject to approval by the principal. If such a limitation conforms to custom or usage, the contract of purchase is ineffective until it has been approved by the seller.

UNDISCLOSED PRINCIPAL

4-21 Undisclosed Principal's Contracts. For various reasons a principal may desire to hide his identity. To accomplish this he appoints an agent to act for him; the agent enters into all contracts in his own name, leaving the third party either unaware of the existence of *any*

---

[6] *Zager v. Gubernick,* page 680.

principal (undisclosed principal) or unaware of the principal's *identity* (partially disclosed principal). The law relating to partially disclosed principals is the same as that of disclosed principals and they are here treated together. Such agreements are always entered into on the strength of the agent's credit, and the agent is liable thereon until such a time as the third party elects to hold the principal. The third party, upon learning of the principal's existence or identity, may elect to enforce the contract against the principal rather than against the agent. The principal is responsible for all contracts entered into by the agent within the scope of the agent's authority and he may be sued when he is disclosed.

The undisclosed principal is never liable upon a negotiable instrument signed by his agent since his name does not appear thereon. The third party can waive the note and sue upon the agreement that furnished the consideration therefore and thus avoid the difficulty encountered by a suit on the note.

4-22 Settlement Between Principal and Agent. In the preceding section it was stated that the third party, after learning of a principal's interest in a transaction, might elect to look to the principal rather than the agent for performance. Suppose, however, that the undisclosed principal supplied the agent with money to purchase the goods but the agent purchased on credit and appropriated the money. In such a case the principal would be relieved of all responsibility. The same result obtains where the principal settles with the agent after the contract is made and the goods are received, but before his disclosure to the third party. Any bona fide settlement between principal and agent before disclosure apparently releases the principal. A settlement cannot have this effect, however, when it is made after the third party has learned of the existence of the principal and the principal is aware of that fact.

The settlement rule is fair to the third party, in that it gives him all the protection which he originally bargained for, and at the same time it aids the principal, since it protects him against a second demand for payment.

4-23 Election. Election means choice, and a choice becomes possible only when the third party learns of the existence of a principal. If a settlement has taken place previously, no election is possible; otherwise, the third party, when he learns of the existence of a previously undisclosed principal, may look either to the agent or to the principal for performance until such time as he definitely elects to hold one or the other. The election to hold one party releases the other from liability. No conduct on his part which precedes the disclosure of the principal can constitute an election. Because of this rule, it has been held that an unsatisfied judgment obtained against the agent before disclosure of the principal will not bar a later action against the principal.

After disclosure, the third party may evidence his election by obtaining a judgment against one of the parties, or by making an express declaration of his intention. It has been held that sending a bill to one of the parties does not indicate an election. Most states also hold that the receipt of a negotiable instrument from either principal or agent does not show an election. The mere starting of a suit against the principal or agent has been held insufficient to constitute an election, but if the case proceeds to judgment against either the agent or the principal, election has taken place although the judgment remains unpaid. From these illustrations it can be seen that definite action is essential to constitute an election. The third party is usually free at any time to sue the particular party, principal or agent, whose credit is best.

4-24 Notice to Agent. Notice or knowledge acquired by an agent while acting within the scope of his authority binds the principal.[7] This is true on the theory that the agent is the principal's other self, and, therefore, what the agent knows, the principal knows. The principal is not bound unless the notice is acquired by an agent who represented the principal in relation to the particular subject matter involved. An agent who is acquiring property for his principal and has knowledge of certain un-recorded liens against the property takes the property for his principal subject to those liens. Knowledge by an agent who did not represent the principal in the particular transaction and who did not receive the notice definitely for his principal could not be imputed to the principal.

Some question has arisen as to whether notice acquired by an agent before he became such can affect the principal. One view is that notice which is acquired by a person before the creation of the agency is notice to the principal who later hires the person as his agent.

Notice to the agent, when he is under a duty to some third party not to disclose the information, does not bind the principal. Furthermore, notice to the agent, combined with collusion or fraud between him and the third party that would defeat the purpose of the notice, would not bind the principal. Thus, an agent who receives notice of an unrecorded mortgage from the mortgagor, with request that the fact not be made known to the principal, has not received notice which is binding on the principal. If the principal purchases the property, it will not be subject to the mortgage.

LIABILITY OF AGENT

4-25 Contractual Liability. As a general rule, an agent is not personally liable on contracts which he has entered into on behalf of his disclosed principal and the liability is solely that of the principal.[8] To this rule, there are certain well-recognized exceptions. First, if the agent carelessly executes a written agreement he may fail to bind his principal and incur personal liability. To use an illustration suggested previously, the agent

[7] *Ivers and Pond Piano Company v. Peckham,* page 682.
[8] *Henderson v. Phillips,* page 683.

who signs a negotiable instrument for his principal, but fails to execute it in the principal's name by himself as agent or otherwise fails to show his representative capacity, is personally liable under the Uniform Commercial Code.

Second, the third party may request the agent to be personally bound because of the agent's credit rating or some other personal reason. Where the agent voluntarily assumes the burden of performance in his personal capacity, he unquestionably becomes liable in the event of nonperformance by his principal.

In addition to the above situations, the agent of an undisclosed principal always assumes personal liability. So far as the third party is informed, the contract is made with the agent, and he takes on full responsibility for its performance. As was previously noted, however, the third party may elect to hold either the agent or the principal, provided he acts within the proper time after he learns of the existence of the undisclosed principal. If the agent is held liable, he in turn has recourse against the principal.

4-26 Warranty of Authority. Occasionally an agent attempts to act for a principal when he possesses no power to bind the latter. In such instances he may or may not be aware of the limitation of his power; he may honestly think his authority extends to the act complained of, or he may be well aware that he was never appointed an agent. In either event he becomes liable to third parties for the damages resulting from his failure to bind the principal. His liability is said not to rest upon the contract itself, but to result from breach of an implied warranty. Every agent impliedly warrants to third parties that he possesses power to affect the contractual relations of his principal. If in any particular transaction he fails to bear such a relation to his principal, he violates this implied warranty. In addition, an agent who intentionally misrepresents his authority may be liable in an action of deceit. In such a case all the elements of fraud are present. Presumably, in either event, the damages would be those suffered because the agent failed to possess the authority that he attempted to exercise.

The agent may escape liability for damages arising from lack of authority by a full disclosure to the third party of all facts relating to the source of his authority. Where all the facts are available, the third party is as capable of judging the limits of the agent's powers as is the agent. In other words, the third party must rely upon the warranty in order to hold the agent for its breach. Where he has full knowledge of all particulars, he relies upon his own judgment and not upon the agent's representation of authority.

The liability of the agent is qualified in one other respect. He is not liable when, unknown to him, his agency has been cut short by the death of his principal. Such an event as death is usually accompanied by sufficient publicity to reach third parties. As indicated in an earlier section, the facts are equally available to both parties, so no warranty arises.

4-27 Competent Principal. Every agent who deals with third parties warrants that his principal is capable of being bound. Consequently, an agent who acts for a minor or a corporation not yet formed may find himself liable for the nonperformance of his principal. The same rule enables the third party to recover from the agent where his principal is an unincorporated association. In such a case, since there is no entity capable of being bound, a breach of the warranty results. The third party has a right to insist that the principal be a person, a firm, or a corporate entity capable of entering into an enforceable agreement. An unincorporated body has no legal entity, and only those voting for the particular transaction, or later adopting it, are liable.

Where, however, the third party is fully informed that the principal is an unincorporated organization, and he agrees to look entirely to it for performance, the agent is relieved. The evidence must clearly indicate such an agreement, as the normal presumption is that the third party expects to look to one party and not to the membership for performance.

In case the principal is a corporation, the agent does not warrant that his principal has legal capacity to enter into the particular transaction. In other words, the agent is not responsible if the contract made by him exceeds the authorized powers of the corporation. The limits of a corporation's powers are governed by its charter. Since charters are usually made a matter of public record, the powers of the corporation are equally available to the agent and to the third party.

4-82 To Account for Money Received. An agent who, in the course of his employment, receives money from third parties for the benefit of the principal owes no duty to account to the third parties. If such money does not find its way into the principal's hands, it may be recovered in an action by the principal against the agent. This rule adequately protects all parties. On the other hand, money paid to an agent who has no authority to collect it, and not turned over to the principal, may be recovered in an action by the third party. To illustrate: A traveling salesman normally has no authority to collect for his principal. Should he do so and surrender the money to his principal, the debtor has no cause of action. A failure on his part to account to his principal, however, subjects him to an action by the third party.

A different problem is presented when money is paid to an agent in error, such as occurs by overpayment of an account. If the agent has passed the money on to his principal before the mistake is discovered, it is clear that only the principal is liable. Nevertheless, money which is still in the possession of the agent when he is notified of the error should be returned to the third party. The agent does not relieve himself of this burden by subsequently making payment to his principal.

Any payment made in error to an agent and caused by his mistake or misconduct may always be recovered from him, although he may have surrendered it to his principal. Also, any overpayment may be recovered from the agent of an undisclosed principal. In such a case the agent is dealt with as the principal.

CONTRACTUAL LIABILITY OF PRINCIPALS AND AGENTS CASES

Reusche v. California Pacific Title Insurance Co.

1965 (Cal. D.C.) 42 Cal. Rptr. 262

Plaintiff sued to determine the validity of a promissory note and trust deed forged by her agent, George Husack. The title insurance company which had insured the title and the payees of the note answered contending that plaintiff was bound by the acts of her agent. The defendants obtained judgment but a new trial was ordered. Defendants appeal from the order granting a new trial.

Husack had acted as plaintiff's agent, cotenant, and manager of her properties for several years. In 1956, Husack arranged a loan secured by a mortgage on an apartment building of plaintiff. The lender called plaintiff about the loan and plaintiff said she would discuss it with Husack who had told all parties that he was authorized to consummate the transaction. The title company prepared the documents and Husack forged plaintiff's name to them and kept the $15,000 proceeds. Plaintiff by telephone agreed to have the check mailed to Husack. Later, she was shown the check by the bank after which she talked to Husack who told her it was for another transaction. Plaintiff then notified the bank that everything was regular and met with her approval. In addition she stated that Husack had a Power of Attorney to offer her signature which he in fact did not possess.

At the trial, Husack admitted the forgery, his lack of authority, and the fictitious explanation to Plaintiff.

TAYLOR, J., . . . The findings of the trial court indicate that the judgment holding respondent Reusche responsible on the forged note and deed of trust was based on . . . the agent's ostensible authority. If there is substantial evidence to support the judgment . . . the judgment must be sustained and the order granting the new trial reversed.

Ostensible Authority

Ostensible authority is defined by Section 2317 of the Civil Code as such authority ". . . as a principal, intentionally or by want of ordinary care, causes or allows a third person to believe the agent to possess." Liability of the principal for the ostensible agent's acts rests on the doctrine of estoppel and its essential elements are representation by the principal, justifiable reliance thereon by the third party and change of position or injury resulting from such reliance.

A principal who puts an agent in a position that enables the agent, while apparently acting within his authority, to commit a fraud upon third persons is subject to liability to such third persons for the fraud. The principal is liable although he is entirely innocent, although he has received no benefit from the transaction, and although the agent acts solely for his own purposes. Liability is based upon the fact that the agent's position facilitates the consummation of the fraud, in that, from the point of view of the third persons, the transaction seems regular on its face and the agent appears to be acting in the ordinary course of the business confided to him. The law reasons that where one of two innocent parties must suffer, the loss should be accepted by the principal who is responsible for the selection of the agent and for the definition of his authority.

In the instant case, Husack represented to the lenders and their agents that he had authority to negotiate the loan on the LaPlaya property. The telephone calls from Pels and the title company in which they disclosed this transaction to respondent and in which she failed to disavow, but rather impliedly confirmed Husack's agency, constituted a sufficient representation to justify the trial court's finding of ostensible authority.

. . .

We conclude that there is ample evidence to sustain the judgment and the order granting the new trial is therefore reversed.

Carlson v. Hannah et al.

1951, 6 N.J. 202, 78 A.2d 83

During the year 1940 Carlson and Galler Beverages, Inc. entered into a contract whereby the former was to act as distributor for "7-Up" in Paterson and certain territory north of the city. He was to supply his own truck, and was not to assign his contract without the approval of Galler. In 1942 Carlson, the plaintiff, was called into the service of the United States Army, so he made an agreement with the defendant to operate his route, with a certain amount being paid to the plaintiff for use of his truck. He then gave one McHugh power of attorney to act for him in those matters requisite and necessary to the distributorship. Business increased and the company demanded an additional truck, and a driver was found for it, he being given the outside city route. In 1944, the defendant threatened to quit unless he were protected when the plaintiff returned from the service, so McHugh agreed that the northern route was to be his upon the plaintiff's return, the latter being limited to the city route. This agreement had the approval of Galler. After plaintiff's return, he refused to approve the contract made by McHugh and demanded his entire territory although the defendant continued to operate the northern route as though it was his own. The plaintiff then instituted this suit to determine the effect of McHugh's contract and for an accounting. The lower court determined that McHugh exceeded his authority and gave plaintiff a judgment of $4,000.

ACKERSON, J. . . . The power of attorney which accompanied the contract made between Carlson personally and Hannah on May 22, 1942, conferred upon McHugh authority to act for the plaintiff during his absence ". . . in all matters pertaining to my distributorship of a carbonated beverage known as "7-Up," . . . giving my said attorney full power to do everything whatsoever, requisite and necessary to be done in said distributorship, . . ." McHugh's authority with respect to the operation of the accompanying contract itself is expressed in paragraph 8 thereof, hereinabove quoted, giving him power "to alter" the contract when deemed necessary with the consent of the other party thereto.

Attorneys in fact created by formal letters of attorney are merely agents and their authority and the manner of its exercise are governed by the principles of the law of agency. Such actual authority may be express or implied. Implied authority may be inferred from the nature or extent of the function to be performed, the general course of conducting the business, or from the particular circumstances of the case. Implication is but another term for meaning and intention; express authority given to an agent includes by implication, whether the agency be general or special, unless restricted to the contrary, all such powers as are proper and necessary as a means of effectuating the purposes for which the agency was created. Accordingly, it is well settled that, unless otherwise agreed, the authority of an agent to manage a business extends no further than the direction of the ordinary operations of the business, including authority to make contracts which are incidental to such business, are usually made in it, or are reasonably necessary in conducting it. But *prima facie* authority to manage a business does not include authority to dispose of it in whole or in part.

What, then, was the purpose of the instruments executed by plaintiff on the eve of entering the armed forces? Obviously he desired to preserve his business intact until his return and appointed McHugh to supervise it during his absence. Logically it is impossible to imply from the evidence before us any authority in the agent McHugh to dispose of any part of his principal's business by gift, sale or otherwise, and thereby defeat the very purpose for which such instruments were created. The grant of power was intended to aid and facilitate the operation of the distribution during plaintiff's absence and not to authorize its partition upon his return.

Appellant further contends that McHugh's authority to contract for the assignment of the territory in question was implied under the doctrine of "emergency power." This principle is defined in the Restatement (*Agency*) § 47, as follows:

> Unless otherwise agreed, if after the authorization is given, an unforeseen situation arises for which the terms of the authorization make no provision and it is impracticable for the agent to communicate with the principal, he is authorized to do what he reasonably believes to be necessary in order to prevent substantial loss to the principal with respect to the interests committed to his charge.

It is important to note, however, that this rule is expressly qualified in the Restatement as applicable only where it is "impracticable for the agent to communicate with the principal" and ascertain his wishes before acting. (*Sibley v. City Service Transit Co., supra,* 2 N.J. at page 463, 66 A.2d 864)

The claimed emergency relied upon the invocation of the foregoing rule is said to be the choice with which McHugh was confronted of either abandoning the entire route because of the uncertainty of replacing Hannah due to wartime shortage of manpower, or acceding to his demand for a part of the territory on plaintiff's return. We find no merit in this contention. Emergency in this connection means "a sudden or unexpected occurrence or condition calling for immediate action." (*Frank v. Bd. of Education of Jersey City,* 90 N.J.L. 273, 278, 100 A. 211, 213, L.R.A. 1917D, 206 (E. & A. 1916)) The evidence discloses that continuous pressure to procure the questioned contract had been exerted on McHugh by both Hannah and Galler for upwards of two months before it was finally signed. During all of this period and resistance, however, no attempt was made to communicate with Carlson and it was not impracticable to have done so. Furthermore there is no proof that Hannah could not have been replaced. While McHugh testified that he did not know where he could have picked up another driver, nevertheless it does not appear that he made any effort to do so. Significantly, only a month before the execution of the questioned contract, another driver was procured to help Hannah service the territory. No immediate urgency or necessity was presented other than an opportunity to demand a part of plaintiff's capital and that situation was of Hannah's own making.

We therefore conclude that the defendant McHugh was not authorized to make the executory assignment of territory attempted to be accomplished by the agreement of September 2, 1944 . . .

Judgment of the lower court affirmed.

Karetzkis v. Cosmopolitan National Bank

1962 (Ill. App.) 186 N.E.2d 72

Plaintiff had purchased a note and trust deed in January 1953. In July or August, the note was in default and plaintiff turned it over to McGuire, an attorney for collection. The attorney indicated that he would start foreclosure proceedings but did not do so. In August of 1956, the attorney sold the note for $5,000 after forging the plaintiff's name to the note, released the trust deed, and kept the proceeds. Plaintiff then filed this suit to foreclose the trust deed and in the alternative for $5,000 for misappropriation of funds. Plaintiff also filed a petition in bankruptcy and pressed criminal charges against McGuire.

McGuire then paid $5,000 to the plaintiff but plaintiff still seeks to recover the balance due on the note through foreclosure on the land covered by the trust deed and also seeks to eliminate the rights in the real estate of parties who had acquired an interest in the land after the trust deed was released by McGuire.

MURPHY, J. . . . We agree with plaintiff that authority to prosecute a suit does not involve authority to compromise it. Before an attorney can compromise a suit, he must have special authority for that purpose. He has no power to assign or sell a claim or judgment of his client without special authority. Similarly, in a case in which liability of a principal for the acts of another is sought to be predicated upon the apparent authority of the latter to act for the former, the rule is that the party dealing with the agent must prove that the facts giving color to the agency were known to him when he dealt with the agent. If he had no knowledge of such facts, he does not act in reliance upon them and is in no position to claim anything on account of them. However, the above rules are not determinative here.

We believe the decisive question is whether the activities of plaintiff constitute a ratification of the sale of the mortgage papers by McGuire. The master found that plaintiff ratified the sale of the mortgage by his collection, from McGuire, of the $5,000 proceeds of the sale and by "the pressing of criminal charges against McGuire for forgery of the checks," and that "the record shows . . . a desire and intention of plaintiff to ratify the sale by McGuire and to accept $5,000.00 in lieu of the note and trust deed."

It is the rule in Illinois that "if an agent acts for his principal outside the scope of his authority, the principal is not bound thereby, yet the principal may ratify such act and thus render it upon him[self]." "Such subsequent assent and ratification would be equivalent to an original authority, and confirm what was originally an unauthorized and illegal act." (*Hefner v. Vandolah,* 62 Ill. 483, 485 (1872))

Ratification may be express, or it may be inferred from circumstances which the law considers equivalent to an express ratification. In the latter sense, ratification may be found to have taken place when the principal, with knowledge of the material facts of the unauthorized transaction, takes a position inconsistent with nonaffirmation of the transaction. An example of such ratification is for the principal to seek or retain the benefits of the transaction. Thus, it is ratification if the principal, with knowledge of the facts, sues the third party or the agent "to enforce promises which were part of the unauthorized transaction or to secure interests which were the fruit of the transaction and to which he would be entitled only if the act had been authorized." (Restatement (Second), *Agency,* § 97(a) (1958)) . . .

We agree with the conclusion of the master that the actions of plaintiff, previously detailed, amount to a ratification of the sale of the mortgage papers. While plaintiff's complaint sought relief in the alternative, asking either foreclosure of the trust deed or payment of the $5,000 by McGuire, plaintiff actually did collect the $5,000 from McGuire. We think that this behavior, under the circumstances, is a ratification of the alleged unauthorized sale.

Plaintiff argues that no ratification occurred because he immediately tendered the $5,000 to defendants and has since remained ready to reimburse defendants upon their return of the mortgage papers to him. It is undoubtedly the rule that "receipt of these benefits with full knowledge of the material facts relating to the source of the benefits and the manner of acquisition, constitutes a ratification of such act [the agent's unauthorized act] unless the principal returns the benefits and repudiates the act within a reasonable time." [Emphasis supplied.]

However, this rule is inapplicable here, where plaintiff, from the beginning of these proceedings, over a period of months, took many affirmative steps, as "the true owner," to secure the funds of the alleged unauthorized sale. This was full and irrevocable ratification.

Affirmed.

Zazzaro v. Universal Motors

1938, (Conn.) 197 Atl. 884

This was an action by Anthony T. Zazzaro to recover possession of an automobile. The defendant had given one Horwitz special authority to sell it for $400 net. The plaintiff signed a contract to purchase, and gave his check for $100 and note for $300 in settlement. Horwitz, to induce the sale, promised personally to hold the note for a few days until the plaintiff could borrow $300 on his insurance. The note, however, was immediately turned over to the defendant. When the check arrived from the insurance company, the plaintiff indorsed and delivered it to Horwitz, who failed to surrender it to the defendant. The defendant, under the conditional sale contract, repossessed the car and plaintiff now seeks to recover it on the theory that he had paid for it in full.

BROWN, J. . . . The court has stated the implied powers incident to the agency relationship in these words: "The creation of an agency carries with it the usual and appropriate means of accomplishing its object and clothes the agent with such authority as is proper to effectuate its purpose." (*Kearns v. Nickse,* 80 Conn. 23, 25). . . . The American Law Institute, in dealing with the question as to the circumstances under which incidental authority is inferred, says: "Unless otherwise agreed, authority to conduct a transaction includes authority to do acts which are incidental to it, or are reasonably necessary to accomplish it." (Restatement, *Agency,* § 35, p. 89) And under Comment (a), it is further stated that "conversely to the rule . . . *prima facie,* an agent is not authorized to do acts not incidental to the transaction, nor usually done in connection therewith, nor reasonably necessary." The application of this principle to the undisputed facts in this case make evident that the court was warranted in concluding that Horwitz had no authority to accept payment of the note. As the defendant's agent for this isolated transaction only and pursuant to express instructions, he sold this car known by the plaintiff to belong to the defendant for $100 cash plus his note to its order for $300 due thirteen days later and secured by the conditional bill of sale, both of which instruments were forthwith turned over to the defendant, which kept them. Horwitz collected the note before maturity. Under these circumstances, authority in Horwitz to accept payment of the note was neither proper nor reasonably necessary to do the act directed or to accomplishing the result specified by the defendant. Nor was the acceptance of the payment either a usual or an appropriate means to that end.

Judgment for defendant affirmed.

State ex rel. Kendrick v. Thormyer

1958, (Ohio App.) 155 N.E.2d 66

This was a mandamus action brought against the defendant, Thormyer, by Kendrick to compel reinstatement of the latter as a state employee. Kendrick had been released by a notice signed with Thormyer's name by one Reiners, his assistant. By statute power of appointment and dismissal rested in the head of the department Thormyer, and plaintiff alleges that the dismissal was ineffective because action was taken without the personal knowledge of Thormyer.

MILLER, J. . . . The question presented is whether or not the suspension was by Thormyer, who had no personal knowledge of the transaction, even though his name appeared on the letter to the relator, which in fact was signed by his alleged authorized agent, Fred G. Reiners. Now, if there had been a proper delegation of authority to Reiners, clearly, the suspension order would have been that of Thormyer, but it is our opinion that such powers may not be delegated for the reason that the authority imposed upon Thormyer involved personal judgment or discretion. We are supported in our conclusion by 2 O. Jur.2d., 134, which says:

> It is a well-established general rule that when authority delegated to an agent involves personal trust or confidence reposed in the agent, and especially when the exercise of that delegated authority involves personal judgment, skill, or discretion, such authority cannot be delegated by the agent to another as subagent to represent the principal, unless the principal has given express authority to conduct a transaction . . . does not include authority to delegate the performance of the acts incidental to that transaction which involve the agent's discretion or skill, unless it is otherwise agreed as between the principal and the agent.

And in 9 C. Jur.2d, 420, it is said:

> Where the whole power of appointment to, and removal or suspension from, a particular position rests in one officer, an order of suspension issued by another officer is absolutely void and of no effect. An action for wrongful suspension of a civil service employee must be brought against the employing authority who made the actual suspension and not against a supervisor who caused the suspension.

In our case the sole power of appointment was in Thormyer who also possessed the sole power of suspension or removal under Section 143-26, Revised Code . . .

For the foregoing reasons we hold that the order of suspension was void and since the relator has no adequate remedy at law the writ of mandamus will be allowed in accordance with the prayer of the petition.

Judgment for the plaintiff.

Zager v. Gubernick

1965 (Pa.) 208 A.2d 45

Plaintiff sued an insurance adjuster (Gubernick) and an insurance company to recover on a settlement for an accident claim. After the accident, Plaintiff's attorney wrote the owner of the car at fault for the name of the insurance company. Gubernick then advised that he was handling the claim. A $4,200 settlement was negotiated and plaintiff signed releases prepared by the adjuster which were forwarded to the company with a request for payment. Payment was not made because the company contended the settlement was too high and that the adjuster had exceeded his authority. The company indicated that Gubernick was a good adjuster but that the authority of outside adjusters was limited. The company contended that the releases were executed subject to acceptance or rejection by the company. The trial court found for the plaintiff holding that the adjuster was authorized.

FLOOD, J. . . . The circumstances clearly warrant the conclusion that the company in authorizing Gubernick to handle this case for it, authorized him to make adjustment of the claims.

So far as the plaintiffs are concerned, the appellant had clothed Gubernick with all the appearances of authority to negotiate a settlement.

. . . (E)ven if Gubernick did not have actual authority to settle the claim, and we think there is evidence that he did, he had at least apparent authority to deal with the plaintiffs and make the settlement. Under such circumstances, the plaintiffs have the same rights with reference to the appellant as if Gubernick had been authorized.

Even if there were a limitation as to the amount for which Gubernick could settle, and he was aware of this, the appellant would still be bound. A limitation on his authority as to amount only, which was communicated to Gubernick but not to the parties with whom he is authorized to deal, does not affect his principal's liability. Such "secret instructions" have no effect upon dealings with a third person who had no notice of them.

. . . Moreover, there is no evidence that even Gubernick knew of any such limitation on his authority until the appellant attempted to repudiate it, or that the settlement or its amount was so far beyond what had been previously negotiated by him in other cases on behalf of the appellant as to negate the natural inference that his authority extended to it.

All the circumstances of the case taken together show that Gubernick had at least apparent authority to conclude the settlement and bind the company so far as the plaintiffs were concerned. An adjuster may occupy such a relation to the company by virtue of long continued employment, and long continued custom with relation to the conduct of certain matters, that his acts will bind it. When an insurance company delegates the power of adjustment, an adjuster so employed has the power to make arrangements with the insured after loss, and to bind the insurer thereby.

An affirmance of even an unauthorized transaction can be inferred from a failure to repudiate it. Here, there was a total failure to communicate to the plaintiffs or their attorney any dissent from, or repudiation of, the settlement for almost three months after Gubernick had made it on the appellant's behalf. . . .

The plaintiffs have performed their part of the accord by executing and delivering the releases, and therefore have the right to enforce the settlement instead of suing in trespass for their damages in the accident.

Judgment affirmed.

RHODES, P. J., and WOODSIDE, J., absent.

Ivers & Pond Piano Co. v. Peckham

1966 (Wis.) 139 N.W.2d 57

The defendant entered into a contract with plaintiff by which defendant guaranteed payment for pianos delivered to his son not to exceed $2,000. The son's account rose to $5,200 and an agent of plaintiff contacted the son about collecting the $2,000 from the defendant. Defendant gave his son a $2,000 check, payable to the son, which the son deposited in his own account. The son then mailed a check to the plaintiff for $2,000. Plaintiff's agent knew that the defendant had furnished the $2,000. The son and plaintiff continued business on a cash basis for a year at which time the balance of the account was discharged in bankruptcy. Plaintiff sued defendant on the guaranty and the defendant answered alleging payment. The trial found for the defendant and the plaintiff appeals.

HEFFERNAN, J.   The trial court found that Robert H. Hoyman, agent for the piano company, knew that the $2,000 paid on May 12, 1961, originating with the defendant, Ellsworth L. Peckham, was for the purpose of satisfying the guaranty contract and, therefore, held that the defendant discharged his guaranty by payment. We deem that the court applied the correct rule of law. Where a creditor accepts payment from a third person knowing it came from the guarantor, the payment must be applied in satisfaction of the guaranty.

> . . . if the creditor is aware of the source of the payment, he should apply it to the note guaranteed by the surety. . . .

However, though Hoyman, the agent, knew that the father in fact made the payment, was that knowledge imputable to the principal . . . ? We conclude that it was . . .

Where an agent has authority to deal in general with the subject matter of a transaction, knowledge that he gives in the course of that transaction is imputable to the principal, and he is charged with the consequences of that knowledge. . . .

The knowledge of an agent may be imputed to a principal irrespective of whether the agency is founded on express or implied authority.

. . . It is not denied that the representative . . . was the agent for sales purposes. It is equally obvious that his duties entailed the collection of past-due accounts . . .

The entire course of relations between Ivers & Pond, Peckham (the son), and Hoyman leads to the inescapable conclusion that Hoyman was at least clothed with the powers of a general agent under the doctrine of apparent authority. This court has stated that three elements are required to establish apparent authority: (1) Acts by the agent or principal justifying belief in the agency; (2) knowledge thereof by the party sought to be charged; and (3) reasonable reliance thereon by a third party.

The undisputed facts are sufficient to establish that Hoyman was clothed with apparent authority to negotiate generally in regard to all aspects of the dealings between the parties and, specifically, the piano company knew of, and through its credit manager directed, collection of the guaranty. Hoyman stated he was directed to not leave town until he got the $2,000.

While a finding of express agency is not necessary to the determination of this case, the facts are sufficient to establish an express agency to collect the guaranty.

. . . Hence, we conclude that Hoyman was an agent whose knowledge that the payment was made by the father was imputable to Ivers & Pond. We also conclude that the evidence supports the inference drawn by the trial judge that the piano company had actual knowledge of the payment.

We therefore conclude that Ellsworth Peckham's contract of guaranty was discharged by payment.

Judgment affirmed.

Henderson v. Phillips

1963 D.C. 195 A.2d 400

MYERS, J. The sole question upon appeal is whether appellee Phillips, president of Metropolitan Designed for Living, Inc., was personally liable under two contracts for plumbing services rendered by appellant.

Metropolitan Designed for Living, Inc., was a corporation engaged in the construction of new houses. Phillips was president of the company. Henderson was engaged in the plumbing business. Phillips telephoned Henderson requesting an estimate on the cost of doing some plumbing work on a particular house, identifying himself as president of the construction firm. Henderson admitted he might have so identified himself. After inspecting the house under construction, Henderson prepared two written contracts addressed to "Design for Modern Living" and mailed them to the corporation. Each was accepted under the signature of "James O. Phillips" and re-mailed to Henderson in an envelope bearing in the upper left corner the name "Designed for Living, Inc., 2814 Pennsylvania Avenue, N.W., Washington 7, D.C.," within the outline of a picture of a house. Thereafter, payment on account was made by checks mailed in a similar envelope. Printed on the first check in the upper lefthand corner was "Metropolitan Designed for Living, Inc.," showing the Pennsylvania Avenue address. It was signed by two persons, one of whom was Phillips, under the printed name of the corporation, with no indication as to the capacity of either signor. A second check, similarly drawn, was not paid upon presentment. Henderson then sued both the corporation and Phillips.

Phillips and Henderson had had one previous business dealing when Henderson completed plumbing work on another house built by the same corporation. On that occasion, three similar checks, drawn on the corporate account and signed by the same two persons, without identification of their official authority to co-sign the checks, were received in payment.

Upon this evidence, the trial judge, sitting without a jury, found that Phillips was not individually liable for the balance due under the contracts with Henderson.

In this jurisdiction, when an agent enters into a contract without disclosing both the identity of his principal as well as the fact of his agency relationship, he becomes personally liable on the contract. On the other hand, when his principal is disclosed and words are absent from the contract expressly binding him, the agent ordinarily does not incur personal liability. The law is well settled that when an agent acts in good faith on behalf of a disclosed principal, he is not held responsible in the event of his principal's default. A principal is disclosed if "at the time of a transaction conducted by an agent, the other party thereto has notice that the agent is acting for a principal and of the principal's identity . . ." (Restatement (Second) *Agency*, § 4 (1958))

The prior dealing between appellant and Phillips was sufficient to impute notice of the agency relationship of Phillips. The checks in payment for the work performed by Henderson were definitely revealing as to the corporate identity of the builder. The present contracts were again negotiated through Phillips who identified himself as president of the corporation. It is true that he "accepted" the written contracts without indicating his agency capacity, but he did the same when co-signing the corporation checks in payment for both jobs by Henderson. Henderson recognized that he was dealing with a corporate entity when he addressed his contracts to "Design for Modern Living." It is also significant that Henderson never testified that he thought he was dealing only with Phillips and intended to rely upon him for payment and not upon the corporate builder. Neither contract contained any words expressly binding Phillips personally or indicating any intent by him to be responsible for payment in the event the corporation defaulted.

The identity of the principal being known and the agency of Phillips being established at the time of the transaction, upon default of the disclosed principal, personal liability could not be imposed upon its agent.

The decision of the trial judge was substantiated by competent evidence, and we find no error requiring reversal.

Affirmed.

CHAPTER 30
REVIEW QUESTIONS AND PROBLEMS

1. *A* was authorized by *P* to purchase bowling alley equipment on credit. He told the seller he was acting as an agent, but was not at liberty to disclose his principal's name. The bill remaining unpaid and *P* being now disclosed, may the seller recover of *A*?

2. *B*, the secretary-treasurer of *C* Co., gave a company note to Bank, typed the signature of *C* Co. and immediately followed it with his own signature, there being no "by" or "per" or anything to indicate that he signed as agent. The bank sought to hold him as a co-maker. What result?

3. *A*, thinking he had authority to do so, signed *P*'s name to a contract whereby *T* was to drill an oil well for $7,000. It developed later that *A* had no authority to act for *P*. Is *A* liable if the contract was signed "*P* per *A*"?

4. *A*, acting for a corporation which is soon to be formed, orders two delivery trucks from *T*. The corporation is formed, but refuses to ratify the contract. Under what circumstances is *A* liable to *T*?

5. *T*, by reason of an error on the part of *A*, an agent for *P*, overpays to the extent of some $300 his account with *P*. Before *A* pays the money over to *P*, *T* discovers the error and demands the excess from *A*. Is *A* under a duty to return the money to *T*, or may he turn it over to *P*?

6. *A* was a traveling salesman for *P*. He sold and delivered to *T* goods amounting to $300. At the time of delivery, he collected the sale price, but failed to turn it in to *P*. Will *T* have to pay again? Would the result be the same if *P* had shipped the goods and *A* had collected at the end of the month? Suppose *A* had sold the goods in exchange for groceries and had used the groceries. Would *P* have been able to collect again of *T*?

7. *A* was the purchasing agent of *P* for the purpose of buying poultry and farm produce. In all his transactions with the farmers, *A* acted as the principal and purchased on the strength of his own credit. *A* failed to pay for certain of the produce purchased. The farmers, having ascertained that *P* was the true principal, seek to hold him. May they do so? Suppose *P* had previously settled with *A*?

8. *A*, an insurance salesman for *X* Company without authority to adjust losses, learned that *T*'s car had been badly damaged in an accident, and because he knew it was covered by insurance, he had it towed to *G*'s garage for immediate repairs. Some time later, the adjuster for *X* Company visited the garage to see the car and noticed that *G* was engaged in repairing it. He made no comment, and the company later refused to pay the repair bill, alleging lack of authority by *A*. Is *X* Company liable?

chapter 31

Tort Liability of Principals and Agents

4-29 Introduction. The law of Agency is concerned not only with the legal relations of the parties resulting from contracts but also with civil wrongs to persons or property (torts) and with injuries to employees (workmen's compensation). As a general rule a master is not liable for the *crimes* of his servant and this area of the law will not be discussed. This chapter is concerned with the general tort aspects of Agency and Employment and with the rights of the parties to reimbursement or indemnity from each other in the event that either incurs tort liability to third persons. In torts the master-servant relationship rather than the principal-agent relationship is used to describe the parties since there is no question of authority although some cases use the latter.

A servant is a person employed to perform a service for another subject to the latter's power or right to control the performance of the service. Neither compensation nor contract is required but both are usually present. A minor may be a servant but cannot be held to a master's liability. The master-servant relationship cannot as a general rule be established by estoppel. With a few exceptions, it would seem that a master would not be held to have ratified a tort concerning which he otherwise had no liability. For example, suppose a bartender assaults a customer as a result of a private quarrel. If the master fails to discharge the bartender, has he ratified the tort? Common sense and most courts would say "No."

4-30 Servants Tort Liability. Every person who commits a tort is personally liable therefore to the injured party. This includes servants who commit torts in the performance of the master's business since the liability is based on the wrongful conduct of the servant. The fact that the master may also have liability does not excuse the servant.

If the tort is committed by the servant without knowledge that his conduct is tortious and while following the master's instructions, the master is required to indemnify the servant for his loss. For example, a servant repossesses a car when ordered to do so but the repossession is wrongful because of lack of title in the master. The master must pay the claim which the third party has against the servant. Similarly, if the servant is at fault (he is negligent or commits an intentional tort) the master may recover his loss from the servant because all servants are required to exercise that degree of skill and diligence ordinarily expected of those who perform like undertakings.[1] A servant who agrees to perform a particular task implies that he possesses the requisite skill and training. However, his duty requires only that he exercise a reasonable degree of care; he is not liable for a failure to use the highest degree of care possible. Suits by masters against servants are not common since most losses are covered by insurance and the master does not actually have to pay the third party. In those few situations not covered by insurance, suits would seldom be useful because of the limited financial resources of most servants.

Occasionally, a master may have immunity from suit and the question arises as to whether this immunity also protects the servant. For example, a municipality may be immune from suit but does this immunity extend to a policeman working for the municipality? The usual view is that the servant is not protected by "personal" immunities such as in the above example but is protected by immunities which are general in nature. Thus a statute which makes a driver of a car immune from suit by a guest passenger would apply to a servant.

Another problem is whether the master must compensate the servant for injuries to the servant caused by third parties. Except for statutory liability under Workmen's Compensation later discussed, a master is not an insurer of the safety of his servant.[2] It is the duty of a master to use ordinary care in providing a safe place to work and reasonably fit appliances for his servant's use. Where the master fails to discharge his duties and injury to the servant proximately results therefrom, the master is liable absent some special defense.

4-31 *Respondeat Superior.* A master is liable to third persons for the torts committed by his servants *within the scope of their employment*. This concept frequently known as *respondeat superior* (let the master respond) imposes vicarious liability on employers as a matter of public policy. While negligence of the servant is the usual cause of liability the doctrine of *respondeat superior* is also applicable to intentional torts such as trespass, assault, libel and fraud.

The vicarious liability imposed on masters, which makes them pay

---

[1] *Holcomb v. Flavin,* page 692.
[2] *Hopkins v. Hacker,* page 692.

for wrongs they have not actually committed, is not based on logic and reason but on matters of business and social policy and the theory that the master is in a better position to pay for the wrong than is the servant. This concept is sometimes referred to as the "deep pocket" theory. The business policy theory is that injuries to persons and property are hazards of doing business, the cost of which the business should bear rather than to have the loss borne by the innocent victim of the tort or society as a whole.

There are two major difficulties in applying the doctrine of *respondeat superior*. The first involves the issue as to whether the party at fault is a servant as contrasted with an independent contractor. The tort liability of a proprietor for the acts of an independent contractor is discussed in section 4-33 of this chapter but it must be noted that as a general rule the doctrine of *respondeat superior* is not applicable to this relationship.

The second problem is whether the servant is *acting within the course of his employment* at the time of the commission of the tort. The law imposes liability on the master only when the master's business is being carried on as provided in the various theories of vicarious liability previously noted. It is not possible to state a simple test to determine if the tort is committed within the scope of the employment. However, factors which are considered in determining the scope of employment include the nature of the employment, the right of control, the ownership of the instrumentality such as an automobile, whether the instrumentality was furnished by the employer, whether the use was authorized, and the time of the occurrence. Most courts inquire into the intent of the servant and the extent of deviation from expected conduct involved in the tort. The issue is usually one of fact and is left to the jury.[3]

A servant is not acting within the scope of his employment if he is in a "frolic" of his own.[4] The deviation may sometimes be described as a detour, in which case, a problem is presented as to the point at which the detour ends and the course of employment resumes.[5] Another difficult situation is presented when the servant combines his own business with that of his master. As a general rule, this fact does not relieve the master of liability. The doctrine of *respondeat superior* has been extended to create liability for negligence of strangers while assisting a servant in carrying out the master's business, where the authority to obtain assistance is given or is required as in the case of an emergency.

The master cannot avoid liability by showing that he has instructed the servant not to do the particular act complained of. Neither is he released by evidence that the servant was not doing the work his master had instructed him to do, where the servant had misunderstood the instruction. As long as the servant is attempting to further his master's business, the master is liable.

A number of states have adopted what is known as the "family car doctrine." Under it, any member of the family is presumed to be an agent

[3] *Maple v. Tennessee Gas Transmission,* page 694.
[4] *Riley v. Standard Oil,* page 695.
[5] *Fiocco v. Carver,* page 697.

of the parent-owner when using the family car for his or her convenience or pleasure, if the car is made available generally for family use. The presumption may be rebutted, however.

Intentional or willful torts are not as likely to occur within the scope of the servant's employment as are those predicated upon a negligence theory. If the willful misconduct of the servant has nothing to do with his master's business and is animated entirely by hatred or a feeling of ill-will toward the third party, the master is not liable. Where the predominant motive is not to work off a personal grudge, but rather to advance his master's interests, it has been held that the master is liable.[6]

4-32 Procedure. Unlike the law of contracts in relation to principal-agent, the tort law of agency allows joinder of the master and servant as defendants in one cause of action or permits them to be sued separately. While the plaintiff is limited to one recovery, the master and servant are jointly and severally liable. The party may collect from either or both in any proportion until the judgment is paid in full.

Sometimes a jury with a bias against business will render a verdict against the master while at the same time holding the servant to be "not guilty." Such a verdict cannot stand since the master's liability is predicated on the servant's fault which the jury found to be non-existent. It should also be noted that if separate suits are brought, a finding for either the master or servant as a defendant would bar a subsequent suit against the other under the doctrine of *res ajudicata.*

4-33 Proprietor—Independent Contractor. An independent contractor is a person performing a service for an employer under an arrangement by which the employee has the power to control the details of the work being performed. Since he performance is within the control of the employee, he is not a servant and his only responsibility is to accomplish the result contracted for. To illustrate: *A* contracts to build a boat for *P* at a cost of $1,000 and according to certain specifications. In such a case it is clear that *A* is an independent contractor with the completed boat as the result. However, had *P* engaged *A* by the day to build the boat and had authorized *A* to purchase the necessary materials, it is equally clear that an agency would have been created.

The distinction is important because a proprietor is not liable for the contracts of the independent contractor and as a general rule, the doctrine of *respondeat superior* and the concept of vicarious liability in tort are not applicable to this relationship. There is no tort liability as a general rule because the theories which justify liability on the master for the servant's tort are not present when the employee is not a servant.

The hallmark of an employee-employer relationship is that the employer not only controls the result of the work but has the right to direct the manner in which the work shall be accomplished; the distinguishing feature of an independent contractee-contractor relationship is

---

[6] *Lockhart v. Friendly Finance Company,* page 699.

that person engaged in work has exclusive control of the manner of performing it, being responsible only for the result. In ascertaining whether a person is a servant or independent contractor, the basic inquiry is whether such person is subject to the alleged employer's control or right to control with respect to his physical conduct in performance of services for which he was engaged. If the facts as to alleged master and servant relationship are in dispute, the precise nature of relationship is for the jury,[7] but where facts are not in dispute, the question of the relationship is for the court.

The rule of insulation from liability in the independent contractor situation is subject to several well recognized exceptions. The most common of these is where the work involved is inherently dangerous to the public. The basis of this exception is that it would be contrary to public policy to allow an employer engaged in such an activitity to avoid his liability by selecting an independent contractor rather than a servant to do the work.

Another apparent exception (which is really not an exception at all) imposes liability on the employer where the employer is himself at fault as where the employer negligently selects the employee. For example, if a young boy without qualifications is hired to break a horse, the employer would be liable to the third parties injured by the horse. Fault may also exist where the employer actively participates in the work such as inspecting during performance or giving unsolicited advice. This exception is similar to the situation in which the independent contractor is a "dummy corporation" established to avoid liability and torts of the dummy impose liability upon the parent corporation.

Another exception to vicarious liability exists where the work being done is illegal although the logical connection between illegality and fault is frequently not present. A common exception involves employee's duties which are considered to be non-delegable. In the law of contracts, it was noted that personal rights and personal duties could not be transferred without consent of the other party. Many statutes impose strict duties on parties such as common carriers and innkeepers. If an attempt is made to delegate these duties to an independent contractor, it is clear that the employer upon whom the duty is imposed has liability for the torts of the employee, even if the relationship is that of proprietor-independent contractor.

Just as a servant is personally liable for his own torts, it should be remembered that the independent contractor has liability for his own torts.

4-34 Workmen's Compensation and F.E.L.A. Injuries may be suffered by employees as well as third parties. At common law, an employee who was injured at work could sue his employer but was confronted with overcoming three defenses available to the employer, one or all of which usually barred recovery. The first of these defenses was that the employee

---

[7] *Morain v. Lollis,* page 700.

was *contributorily negligent.* If the employee was even partially at fault, this defense was successful though the majority of the fault was the employer's. Second, if the injury was caused in part by some other employee, the *fellow-servant doctrine* excused the employer and limited recovery to a suit against the other employee who was at fault. Finally, in many jobs which by their very nature involved some risk of injury, the doctrine of *"assumption of risk"* would allow the employer to avoid liability.

The common law rules resulted for the most part in imposing on employees the burdens that resulted from accidental injuries, occupational diseases, and even death. Through the legislative process, society has rather uniformly determined that this result is undesirable as a matter of public policy and statutes usually known as Workmen's Compensation have been enacted to balance the interest of the parties by creating liability without fault (eliminated the defenses); but limiting the amount of the liability by creating definite and detailed schedules of amounts due for various injuries. At the federal level, there is a Federal Employee's Liability Act which accomplishes the same results for businesses engaged in interstate and foreign commerce such as railroads.[8] It does, however, require proof of negligence but does not limit the amount of recovery. Basically, F.E.L.A. merely eliminates the common law defenses.

The scheme of Workmen's Compensation in most states is to provide employer liability for accidental injuries, occupational diseases, and death *"arising out of and in the course of employment."* This liability is fulfilled by the employer paying all medical expenses and in addition requiring him to make periodic payments, usually weekly, during periods of disability based on prior earnings and size of the family to be supported. Many statutes provide for a specific number of weekly payments for specific losses such as an arm, finger, leg, or eyes. In addition, a fixed death benefit depending on earnings and number of dependents is provided. For permanent total disability, a lifetime pension may be allowed. Disfiguration and injuries such as those to the back create difficult questions as to the amount due. These are decided by the administrative agency, Industrial Accident Commission, which administers the compensation laws and fixes the benefits.

In recent years, the administrative agencies and the courts have tended to broaden the coverage and scope of Workmen's Compensation. For example, an employee who suffers a heart attack may have incurred a compensable injury based on recent standards.[9] Broken legs incurred in athletic contests during lunch periods have also been held to be compensable.

In some states, Workmen's Compensation is the exclusive remedy available to an injured employee. In others he may bring a common law tort action against his employer but the common law defenses are

---

[8] *Hopson v. Texaco, Inc.,* page 702.
[9] *Fattore v. Police and Fireman's Retirement System of N. J.,* page 704.

available. Some states have provisions comparable to F.E.L.A. which eliminate common law defenses of employers. In these states the employer can elect to reject Workmen's Compensation and carry private insurance. When the injury is caused by a third party, the employee may bring a tort suit in all states but the employer is subrogated to the extent of the Workmen's Compensation payments.

TORT LIABILITY OF PRINCIPALS AND AGENTS CASES

Holcomb v. Flavin

1962 (Ill.A.C.) 185 N.E.2d 716

Plaintiff brought an action for personal injuries sustained in an automobile collision. Defendants who were alleged to be employers of driver of vehicle involved in the collision sought leave to bring in such driver as a third party defendant, alleging that if they had liability to plaintiff, then the driver had liability to them.

CULBERTSON, J. . . . A master, not guilty of active participation in a tort may recover against his servant the amount which the master is required to pay for damages to a third person by reason of the servant's torts.

While the Illinois Act authorizing the third party complaint specifically provides that nothing in the Act creates any substantive right to contribute among tort-feasors, such provision obviously relates to joint tort-feasors, that is, those whose concurrent acts of omissions combine to cause the injury. If a master is active with the servant there may be a situation of joint tort-feasors involving a master and servant. The acts or omissions involved in the case before us, however, refer only to acts done by the servant, or the master by and through the servant. The ground of responsibility is solely that of *respondeat superior*. Such being the case, it is obvious that the complainants would have a right, if found responsible and required to pay, to recover against their servant. Under the third party practice this right is sanctioned without separate litigation under the terms of the statutory provisions referred to. The prohibition against recovery from the other tort-feasor who was the agent is not prohibited as a matter of law in this State. Contribution among tort-feasors is permissible and can be enforced so long as the parties do not stand *in pari delicto.*

. . . *Reversed and remanded, with directions.*

Hopkins v. Hacker

1963 (N.H.) 195 A.2d 587

DUNCAN, J. . . . The disputed issues relate to the verdict for Hopkins as defendant in the cross action of *Hacker v. Hopkins,* in which Hacker sought damages for personal injuries suffered in an assault by a third person.

As agent for Hopkins, Hacker leased certain premises at Seabrook Beach for the latter part of the summer of 1957, at a rental of $400, $100 of which was deposited with Hacker in advance. The tenant or tenants, who were residents of Massachusetts, took possession on July 27, paying the $300 balance by check. They were immediately dissatisfied with the condition and furnishings of the premises, and complained to Hacker. At Hacker's request Hopkins visited the premises on July 28 and 29 to adjust the oil burner and to repair a lock. The tenants occupied the premises through Labor Day.

On July 28, Hacker delivered the $300 check to Hopkins, and there was evidence that on the same day the tenants demanded their money back. However Hopkins deposited the check on July 29, and later in the week was notified by the bank that payment had been stopped. The agent was advised by letter of the tenant, received on July 29, that payment of the check had been stopped. On August 3, 1957, however, the $300 balance of the rental, was paid to Hopkins on behalf of the tenant, in cash, at Hopkins' residence.

On the evening of July 30, it came to the attention of Hacker, who resided nearby, that a trailer was being driven onto the Hopkins property. He went to the premises and advised the driver of the trailer that zoning requirements forbade trailers at this location. While he was so engaged, he was assaulted by one or more of the occupants of the rented cottage, as he stood by the highway.

There was conflict in the testimony as to whether the principal Hopkins was aware of any prior threat to the safety of the agent. The agent testified that he repeatedly asked the principal to refund the $300 paid, and that the principal refused to do so.

The liability of a principal for injuries suffered by his agent in carrying out the agency is defined in the Restatement (Second), *Agency*, s. 471 as follows: "A principal is subject to liability in an action of tort for failing to use care to warn an agent of an unreasonable risk involved in the employment, if the principal should realize that it exists and that the agent is likely not to become aware of it, thereby suffering harm." In the absence of special agreement, the principal is under no duty to indemnify his agent against the torts of third persons.

In this case the testimony of the agent plainly indicated that as early as July 28, 1957 he was apprehensive of violence at the hands of the tenants, and that his knowledge of the risk was at least as great as the principal's.

Hacker, as plaintiff, contends that Hopkins was under a duty to have refunded the rent, and that had he done so the assault would not have occurred. The answer to this contention is that payment of the $300 check had been stopped before July 30, so that the principal then had no rent which could be refunded. The down payment of $100 was made to the agent, and had not been paid over to the principal before the assault occurred. Further, there was evidence from which the Court could find that the agent himself resisted the principal's suggestion made on July 28, that the deposit should then be refunded and the letter of the tenant received by the agent on July 29 stated that the tenant would vacate the premises and forfeit the deposit.

We are satisfied that the verdicts returned by the Court were fully warranted by the law and the evidence. . . .

Judgment on the verdicts.

Maple v. Tennessee Gas Transmission

1963 (Ohio C.A.) 201 N.E.2d 299

BROWN, J. The plaintiff, while attempting to turn his car on a roadway adjacent to the defendant company's pumping station in icy weather, became stuck in the ditch adjacent to defendant company's driveway. Plaintiff walked onto the defendant's premises, talked with Stewart, one of the defendant company's employees, and told Stewart his problem. Stewart and he went in Stewart's car to one of the garages on the company's property intending to get a truck with which to pull plaintiff's car from the ditch.

While plaintiff and Stewart were attempting to open the garage door Stewart's driverless car proceeded forward pinning plaintiff to the garage doors and seriously injuring him.

The jury returned a verdict for the plaintiff, upon which judgment was rendered.

The fifth assignment of error questions whether the factual situation as demonstrated by the evidence, giving that evidence a construction most favorable to the plaintiff, gives rise to a jury question as to whether Mr. Stewart, defendant's agent, was acting in the course and scope of his agency at the time of the accident.

There was evidence that Stewart, the defendant's employee, was in charge of the pumping station generally in the absence of the superintendent, and that the superintendent was absent on this occasion. There was evidence that the plaintiff's car in the ditch was partly blocking one of the driveways by means of which entrance to and exit from the defendant company's plant was obtained. From this and other evidence in the record, we may presume that Stewart reasonably may have concluded that the defendant company had some interest, or would derive some benefit directly or indirectly from rendering assistance in this emergency. We can not say on this evidence as a matter of law that Stewart at the time of the accident was beyond the scope of his employment. Stewart was acting in an area in which he had some implied authority to exercise discretion in determining whether his rendering help in this emergency was in his company's interest.

We note the following well stated comment in 35 American Jurisprudence, Section 550, Page 981:

. . . whether any particular act is within the authority which has been impliedly conferred upon the employee is one which the courts have found oftentimes to be difficult of solution. In this respect, the decisions hold that where authority to act for another has been conferred without special limitation, it carries with it, by implication, authority to do all things that may be necessary to its execution; and where the authorization involves the exercise of the discretion of the employee, the use of such discretion is a part of the thing authorized and, where exercised, becomes, as to third persons, the discretion and act of the employer. . . .

Doubt as to whether or not a servant is acting within the course and scope of his authority when injuring another will be resolved against the master in an action to hold the latter liable for the act, at least to the extent of requiring the question to be submitted to the jury. Assigned error number five is therefore not well taken.

Judgment affirmed.

Riley v. Standard Oil Co.

1921 (N.Y.) 132 N.E. 97. 231 N.Y. 301

ANDREWS, J. Driving directly towards his master's mill; his master's truck loaded with his master's goods for which his master had sent him; his only purpose to deliver them as his master had commanded; with no independent object of his own in mind; Million, a chauffeur employed by the defendant, ran over the plaintiff, negligently, as the jury have said with some evidence to support their finding. Therefore, the complaint should not have been dismissed unless we can say as a matter of law that at the moment of the accident this chauffeur was not engaged in the defendant's business. We reach no such conclusion.

There could be no debate on this subject were not the essential facts obscured or modified by other circumstances. It appears, however, that the chauffeur had been ordered to go from the mill to the freight yards of the Long Island railroad, about two and one-half miles away, obtain there some barrels of paint and return at once. After the truck was loaded, Million discovered some waste pieces of wood. He threw them on the truck and on leaving the yards turned, not towards the mill, but in the opposite direction. Four blocks away was the house of a sister, and there he left the wood. This errand served no purpose of the defendant nor did the defendant have knowledge of or consent to the act of the chauffeur. Million then started to return to the mill. His course would lead him back past the entrance to the yards. Before he reached this entrance and when he had gone but a short distance from his sister's house, the accident occurred.

A master is liable for the result of a servant's negligence when the servant is acting in his business; when he still is engaged in the course of his employment. It is not the rule itself but its application that ever causes a doubt. The servant may be acting for himself. He may be engaged in an independent errand of his own. He may abandon his master's service permanently or temporarily. While still doing his master's work he may be also serving a purpose of his own. He may be performing his master's work but in a forbidden manner. Many other conditions may arise.

No formula can be stated that will enable us to solve the problem whether at a particular moment a particular servant is engaged in his master's business. We recognize that the precise facts before the court will vary the result. We realize that differences of degree may produce unlike effects. But whatever the facts, the answer depends upon a consideration of what the servant was doing, and why, when, where and how he was doing it.

A servant may be "going on a frolic of his own, without being at all on his master's business." He may be so distant from the proper scene of his labor, or he may have left his work for such a length of time as to evidence a relinquishment of his employment. Or the circumstances may have a more doubtful meaning. That the servant is where he would not be had he obeyed his master's orders in itself is immaterial except as it may tend to show a permanent or a temporary abandonment of his master's service. Should there be such a temporary abandonment the master again becomes liable for the servant's acts when the latter once more begins to act in his business. Such a re-entry is not effected merely by the mental attitude of the servant. There must be that attitude coupled with a reasonable connection in time and space with the work in which he should be engaged. No hard and fast rule on the subject either of space or time can be applied. It cannot be said of a servant in charge of his master's vehicle who temporarily abandons his line of travel for a purpose of his own that he again becomes a servant only when he reaches a point on his route which he necessarily would have passed had he obeyed his orders. He may choose a different way back. Doubtless this circumstance may be considered in connection with other facts involved. It is not controlling.

We are not called upon to decide whether the defendant might not have been responsible had this accident occurred while Million was on his way to his sister's house. That would depend on whether this trip is to be regarded as a new and independent journey on his own business, distinct from that of his master or as a mere deviation from the general route from the mill and back. Considering the short distance and the little time involved, considering that the truck when it left the yards was loaded with the defendant's goods for delivery to its mill and that it was the general purpose of Million to return there it is quite possible a question of fact would be presented to be decided by a jury. At least, however with the wood delivered, with the journey back to the mill begun, at some point in the route Million again engaged in the defendant's business. That point, in view of all circumstances, we think he had reached.

The judgment of the Appellate Division must be modified in so far as it directs the dismissal of the complaint and in so far as it fails to direct a new trial and as so modified affirmed, with costs to abide the event.

McLAUGHLIN, J. (dissenting). . . . This court is about to reverse the Appellate Division upon the ground that Million having left his sister's residence, and started back towards the yard, had as matter of law reached a point in the route when he again engaged in the defendant's business. I am unable to see how this conclusion can be reached as matter of law. Nor do I think that the facts would justify a finding to this effect. The uncontradicted facts show, as it seems to me, that Million, at the place where and time when the accident occurred, was not acting for defendant. His act at and immediately prior to the accident was not a mere deviation from his duty or an irregular method of its performance. He was doing an independent act of his own and outside of the service for which he had been employed. When he started from the yard to deliver the wood to his sister's residence, he broke the connection between himself and his master, temporarily terminated the employment, and did not re-enter the same until he had again reached the yard. The return from his sister's residence to the yard was just as much a part of his personal errand as was going to her residence. I cannot believe that the liability of the defendant here is to be determined by the way in which the truck was headed. Rights of property do not rest upon such a slender thread. . . .

Fiocco v. Carver

1922 (N.Y.) 137 N.E. 309. 234 N.Y. 219.

CARDOZO, J. The defendants, engaged in business in the city of New York, sent a truckload of merchandise from Manhattan to Staten Island. The duty of the driver when he had made delivery of the load was to bring the truck back to the garage at Twenty-third street and Eleventh avenue on the west side of the city. Instead of doing that, he went, as he tells us, to Hamilton street on the east side, to visit his mother. A neighborhood carnival was in progress in the street. A crowd of boys, dressed in fantastic costumes, as Indians, Uncle Sam, cowboys, and the like, were parties to the frolic. They asked the driver for a ride, and in response to the request, he made a tour of the district, going from Hamilton street to Catherine, then through other streets and back again to Catherine. At this point he stopped in front of a pool room, and left his truck for a moment to say a word to a friend. It is here that the plaintiff, a child of eleven years, arrived upon the scene. The merry-makers were still crowding about the truck. The plaintiff with a play-mate tried to join them. While he was climbing up the side, the driver came back and three times ordered him to get off. As the third order was given, the plaintiff started to come down, but before he could reach the ground, the truck, as he tells us, was started without warning, and his foot was drawn into a wheel. The driver gives a different story, insisting that the boy ran after the moving truck and climbed on the side when it was impossible to see him. All the witnesses agree that the truck as it left Catherine street was still carrying the boys. The driver adds that his purpose then was to go back to the garage. Upon these facts a jury has been permitted to find that he was in the course of his employment. The ruling was upheld at the Appellate Division by the divided court.

We think the judgment may not stand.

The plaintiff argues that the jury, if it discredited the driver's narrative of the accident, was free to discredit his testimony that there had been a departure from the course of duty. With this out of the case, there is left the conceded fact that a truck belonging to the defendant was in the custody of the defendant's servant. We are reminded that this without more sustains a presumption that the custodian was using it in the course of his employment. But the difficulty with the argument is that in this case there *is* more, though credit be accorded to the plaintiff's witnesses exclusively. The presumption disappears when the surrounding circumstances are such that its recognition is unreasonable. We draw the inference of regularity, in default of evidence rebutting it, presuming, until otherwise advised, that the servant will discharge his duty. We refuse to rest upon presumption, and put the plaintiff to his proof, when the departure from regularity is so obvious that charity can no longer infer an adherence to the course of duty. . . .

We turn, then, to the driver's testimony to see whether anything there, whether read by itself or in conjunction with the plaintiff's narrative, gives support for the conclusion that the truck was engaged at the moment of the accident in the business of the master. All that we can find there, when we view it most favorably to the plaintiff, is a suggestion that after a temporary excursion in streets remote from the homeward journey, the servant had at last made up his mind to put an end to his wanderings and return to the garage. He was still far away from the point at which he had first strayed from the path of duty, but his thoughts were homeward bound. Is this enough, in view of all the circumstances, to terminate the temporary abandonment and put him back into the sphere of service? We have refused to limit ourselves by tests that are merely mechanical or formal. Location in time and space are circumstances that may guide the judgment, but will not be suffered to control it, divorced from other circumstances that may characterize the intent of the transaction. The dominant purpose must be proved to be the performance of the master's business. Till then there can be no resumption of a relation which has been broken and suspended.

We think the servant's purpose to return to the garage was insufficient to bring him back within the ambit of his duty. He was indisputably beyond the ambit while making the tour of the neighborhood which ended when he stopped at Catherine street upon a visit to a pool room. Neither the tour nor the stop was incidental to his service. Duty was resumed, if at all, when ending the tour, he had embarked upon his homeward journey. It was in the very act of starting that the injury was done. The plaintiff had climbed upon the truck while it was at rest in front of the pool room, still engaged upon an errand unrelated to the business. The negligence complained of is the setting of the truck in motion without giving the intruder an opportunity to reach the ground. The self-same act that was the cause of the disaster is supposed to have ended the abandonment and reestablished a relation which till then had been suspended. Act and disaster would alike have been avoided if the relation had not been broken. Even then, however, the delinquent servant did not purge himself of wrong. The field of duty once forsaken, is not to be re-entered by acts evincing a divided loyalty and thus continuing the offense. . . .

The judgment of the Appellate Division and that of the Trial Term should be reversed, and the complaint dismissed, with costs in all courts.

Lockhart v. Friendly Finance Co.

1959, (Fla.) 110 S.2d 478

The plaintiff, Lockhart, purchased a television set from a third party, after which the defendant claimed to have security interest in it. It was orally agreed between plaintiff and defendant that plaintiff would pay $100 at the rate of $15 a week. The plaintiff failed to pay so the defendant sent its agent out to collect the account or repossess. Plaintiff, when approached by the agent and two detectives, told them not to enter since his wife was ill and very nervous. Nevertheless, they entered and threw a small radio and lamp on the floor, breaking them, and slamming a door so hard the glass in it was broken. They carried the television set away, and the plaintiff sued for trespass and damages sustained. The lower court directed a judgment for the plaintiff, but later ordered a new trial because he thought he erred. The plaintiff appealed from the order for a new trial.

WIGGINGTON, J. . . . We are now called upon to determine whether the undisputed facts recited above, construed in a light most favorable to the defendant, were reasonably susceptible of but the single conclusion that defendant was liable as a matter of law.

The problem here presented has been passed upon by our Supreme Court on many occasions. Basically it has been held that the determination of this question must turn upon the facts and circumstances of each case.

Actions for trespass committed by an agent are based upon the doctrine of *respondeat superior*. The master's liability does not arise unless the tortious act was committed as an incident to the master's business and while acting within the range of employment, or that the master directed the wrongful act or ratified it afterwards. The test of liability is whether the act constituting the trespass was within the general scope of the servant's employment while engaged in the employer's business, and was done with the view of furthering that business.

The latest decisions on this subject have followed the modern view that the liability of the master for intentional acts which constitute legal wrongs can only arise when that which is done is within the real or apparent scope of the master's business. It does not arise where the servant has stepped aside from his employment to commit a tort which the master neither directed in fact nor could be supposed, from the nature of his employment, to have authorized or expected the servant to do.

It is appellee's contention that the issues of whether its agent's act of trespass was committed within the real or apparent scope of defendant's business; whether the agent stepped aside from his employment to commit the act complained of; and whether defendant directed or could be supposed to have authorized or expected the agent to commit the tortious act, were all questions for the jury to determine. It is upon this premise that appellee insists the trial court committed error in directing a verdict on these issues in plaintiff's favor, and that the court's subsequent order granting a new trial because of such error is correct and should be sustained. . . .

The manager's instruction to the agent to go to plaintiff's house and get the television receiver, knowing as he did that the agent was not then armed with judicial process entitling him to lawfully take the security claimed by defendant, is susceptible of but one reasonable interpretation. These instructions, unqualified as they were, contemplated that the agent would take such action as he deemed necessary in order to carry them out. That the agent did not misinterpret these instructions is evidenced by the fact that he reinforced himself with the assistance of two city detectives before arriving at plaintiff's home with the obvious intention of retaking the receiver by whatever means appeared necessary. Defendant's manager knew, or is presumed to have known, that television receivers are customarily if not invariably kept inside people's homes, and cannot be seized by a lienor over the objection of the owner without the commission of a trespass. Defendant accepted and benefited from its agent's activities by retaining the receiver without offering to return it to its owner, knowing or being presumed to have known the manner in which possession of the instrument was obtained.

It is our view that the undisputed evidence established defendant's liability for the tortious act of its agent, and any contrary view that may have been taken by the jury could not have been sustained. There was no genuine issue of any material fact touching upon defendant's liability in this case, and the trial court was correct as a matter of law in directing a verdict in plaintiff's favor. It therefore follows that the court committed error by entering its order granting a new trial. . . .

The order granting a new trial is reversed.

Morain v. Lollis

1962 (Okl.) 371 P.2d 473

HALLEY, J.   Othel Lollis, plaintiff, filed an action for damages against Gordon Morain, defendant, for negligence in causing injury to his cattle. The matter was tried to a jury which returned its verdict for the plaintiff. Defendant appeals from the order of the trial court overruling his motion for new trial. The parties will be referred to as they appeared in the trial court.

Defendant's principal contention is that the trial court should have ruled as a matter of law that witness A. A. Wallace was an independent contractor and that defendant's motion for directed verdict at the close of the evidence should have been sustained.

A summary of the rules which we must use in making a determination concerning defendant's contentions is found in *Mistletoe Express Service v. Culp* (Okl., 353 P.2d 9) as follows:

> An independent contractor is defined as one who engages to perform a certain service for another, according to his own method and manner, free from control and direction of his employer in all matters connected with the performance of the service, except as to the result of the service. However, as a general rule, the line of demarcation between an independent contractor and a servant is not clearly drawn, but the question of such relationship must be determined upon the facts peculiar to each case, and if the evidence is such that the minds of reasonable men may differ as to whether the relationship established was that of contractee and independent contractor, or master and servant, the determination of such relationship is for the jury under proper instructions by the court.
>
> "From the above definition and cited authorities, we find that in the determination of whether the relationship between Wolfe and Mistletoe was that of a servant or independent contractor the many elements to be considered are: (1) the nature of the contract between the parties, whether written or oral; (2) the degree of control which by the agreement the employer may exercise on the details of the work or the independence enjoyed by the contractor or agent; (3) whether or not the one employed is engaged in a distinct occupation or business and whether he carries on such occupation or business for others; (4) whether the employer or the workman supplies the instrumentalities, tools and the place of work for the person doing the work; (5) the length of time for which the person is employed; (6) the method of payment, whether by the month or by the job; (7) whether or not the work is a part of the regular business of the employer; (8) whether or not the parties believe they are creating the relationship of master and servant; and (9) the right of either to terminate the relationship without liability.

The facts in the instant case are that plaintiff was the owner of 104 head of cattle which he kept on leased land in Marshall County. Defendant had a home and heating and air conditioning business at Norman, Oklahoma. A. A. Wallace was a welder by trade who built boathouses. Defendant contacted Wallace at Madill on January 9, 1957, concerning his building a boathouse like one which Wallace had built for another party a short time before. Wallace wrote down on a piece of paper the materials he would need to build the boathouse together with the cost of the items and the cost of labor. Defendant introduced the piece of paper into evidence. Testimony of defendant and Wallace showed that defendant advised Wallace he would furnish some of the materials written on the paper and the total price was lowered accordingly. Defendant agreed to and did deliver to Wallace the barrels, fire hose and paint which were part of the materials to be used to build the boathouse. There was some difference in the testimony of defendant and Wallace as to how the site was selected for the building of the boathouse. The effect of the testimony was, however, that it was agreed between defendant and Wallace that the construction would be done at a level point along a certain mile of shoreline of Lake Texoma with the specific location to be determined by Wallace. Wallace hired and paid other persons to help him. Wallace testified that defendant came to the location several times to check up on him or see if he was "doing it right"; and that although defendant did not tell him how to do the work on those occasions he could have, if Wallace had been doing it wrong. Wallace also testified that defendant had the right to fire him at any time. Defendant also assisted Wallace in towing the boathouse, after it was completed, across part of the lake to the cove where defendant had a cabin.

When the evidence in this case is viewed in the light of these rules, we find that there is room for a reasonable difference of opinion as to the proper inference concerning the relationship of defendant and A. A. Wallace from the known facts. It was therefore proper to submit the question to the jury for determination under proper instructions.

.   .   .

The effect of the verdict of the jury was that Wallace was an employee and not an independent contractor. There was competent evidence to support the verdict.

.   .   .

Defendant also argues that no negligence was shown on the part of defendant or his employee. We have discussed some of the evidence in reaching our conclusions above. Other evidence in this case shows that defendant's employee saw the red paint on heads of several of plaintiff's cattle, that he saw tracks of the cattle around the boathouse, and that he had to repaint some spots on the boathouse. The veterinarian performed autopsies on two of the three dead cattle and stated that they died of lead poisoning. He stated that all of the living ones exhibited symptoms of lead poisoning in varying degrees. Plaintiff's leased premises were fenced and there was no showing of any other painting on the premises at or around that time. The sickness and death of the cattle occurred immediately at and after the painting of the boathouse. Suffice it to say that there was competent evidence to support the verdict of the jury.

Affirmed.

Hopson *et al.* v. Texaco, Inc.
1966, 86 S.Ct. 765

PER CURIAM.   These actions were brought under the Jones Act . . . to recover damages for injuries sustained by one seaman and for the death of another, as a result of an automobile accident on the Island of Trinidad. Judgment on the jury's verdict was entered in United States District Court in favor of the plaintiffs, but the Court of Appeals reversed. (4 Cir., 351 F.2d 415) We grant a writ of certiorari and reverse.

The facts are not in dispute. The two seamen were members of the crew of respondent's tanker which was docked at respondent's refinery at Pointe-a-Pierre on the Island of Trinidad. Both fell ill and it was determined that they would be unable to continue the voyage. In order to discharge an incapacitated seaman in a foreign port, federal law requires that he be taken to a United States Consul where arrangements for his return to the United States can be made. The United States Consul's office was located in Port-of-Spain, some 38 miles distant. Although respondent had a fleet of motor vehicles used for transportation in the immediate vicinity of the refinery and docking areas, its practice was to utilize either of two local taxi companies for journeys to more distant points. The ship's Master procured one of these cabs, which set out for Port-of-Spain with the two ill seamen. En route, the taxi collided with a truck, killing the Master and one of the seamen; the other seaman was seriously injured. The jury found that the taxi driver had been negligent—a finding challenged neither in the Court of Appeals nor here. The Court of Appeals reversed the District Court's determination that respondent is liable to petitioners for this negligence of the taxi operator.

The Jones Act incorporates the standards of the Federal Employers' Liability Act which renders an employer liable for the injuries negligently inflicted on its employees by its "officers, agents, or employees." We noted in *Sinkler v. Missouri Pac. R. Co.* (356 U.S. 326, 78 S.Ct. 758, 2 L.Ed.2d 799) that the latter Act was "an avowed departure from the rules of the common law" (id., at 329, 78 S.Ct. at 762), which, recognizing "[t]he cost of human injury, an inescapable expense of railroading," undertook to "adjust that expense equitably between the worker and the carrier." (*Ibid*) In order to give "an accommodating scope . . . to the word 'agents'" (id., at 330-331, 78 S.Ct. at 762), we concluded that "when [a]n . . . employee's injury is caused in whole or in part by the fault of others performing, under contract, operational activities of the employer, such others are 'agents' of the employer within the meaning of § 1 of F.E.L.A." (id., at 331-332, 78 S.Ct. at 763.)

We think those principles apply with equal force here. These seamen were in the service of the ship and the ill-fated journey to Port-of-Spain was a vital part of the ship's total operations. The ship could not sail with these two men, nor could it lawfully discharge them without taking them to the United States Consul. Indeed, to have abandoned them would have breached the statutory duty to arrange for their return to the United States. Getting these two ill seamen to the United States Consul's office was, therefore, the duty of respondent. And it was respondent—not the seamen—which selected, as it had done many times before, the taxi service. Respondent—the law says—should bear the responsibility for the negligence of the driver which it chose. This is so because, as we said in Sinkler, "justice demands that one who gives his labor to the furtherance of the enterprise should be assured that all combining their exertions with him in the common pursuit will conduct themselves in all respects with sufficient care that his safety while doing his part will not be endangered." (356 U.S., at 330, 78 S.Ct. at 762.)

Reversed.

Fattore v. Police and Firemen's Retire. Syst. of N.J.

1963 (N.J. Sup. Ct., A.D.) 80 N.J. Super. 541, 194 A.(2) 363

Fattore, a fireman, was assisting in the replacement of a fire hose on a pumper apparatus. He was pulling and folding lengths of hose weighing 225 lbs. handed him by others. While doing the work, he felt a pain in the upper part of his chest which went down his left arm. This was later diagnosed as a myocardial infarction. He was off work some time and later tried to return to work but slight work caused precordial distress and he applied for a retirement pension. His doctor diagnosed his condition as an acute myocardial infarction due to arterosclerotic heart disease and coronary arteriosclerosis. The medical board for the retirement system agreed with the diagnosis but did not believe that it was precipitated by the work. An independent doctor was consulted who agreed that the work could have caused the condition.

CONFORD, S.J.A.D. . . . Of controlling effect in this case are the two prior decisions of this court in *Roth v. Board of Trustees, etc.* (49 N.J. Super, 309, 139, A.2d 761 (App.Div.1958)), and *Kochen v. Consolidated Pol., etc., Pension Fund Comm.* (71 N.J. Super. 463, 177 A.2d 304 (App.Div.1962)). In construing cognate public employee disability pension legislation, we held in these cases that such legislation was social in nature and purpose, should be liberally construed in favor of employees, and, specifically, that the principles of the Workmen's Compensation Act as construed should be applied in passing upon the issue of causal connection between the work effort and the alleged accidental injury. There is no reason why those decisions should not be held controlling here, the legislation in question being of the same general nature and purposes as that construed in the Roth and Kochen cases.

Viewed from this perspective, it is clear that the attitude and approach of the medical board in the present case, upon which the board of trustees substantially relied for its determination, was erroneous. The essence of the position of the medical board and of its testimonial representative, Dr. Eckstein, was that the work incident could not be taken to be the natural and proximate cause of the heart attack and disability because the work Fattore was then doing was an effort of the type to which he was accustomed. Also stressed is the fact that he had a pre-existing arteriosclerosis. This approach is the equivalent of the rule of "unusual strain," once accepted as a prerequisite criterion of compensable heart attacks, but in effect discarded as incorrect in *Ciuba v. Irvington Varnish & Insulator Co.* (27 N.J. 127, 141 A.2d 761 (1958)). As most recently restated in *Dwyer v. Ford Motor Co.* (36 N.J. 487, at p. 493, 178 A.2d 161, at p. 164 (1962)), the heart attack is compensable if the actual work effort (whether or not unusual for the workman) did in fact materially contribute to the precipitation, aggravation or acceleration of the heart attack, or of any pre-existing heart or circulatory disease, thereby culminating in an attack. The former presumption that a heart attack is the result of natural physiological causes is also rejected in that case.

The difficulty of deciding the issue of causality in a particular case does not excuse the adjudicating tribunal from making the effort. The claim cannot automatically be rejected because the work effort was such as the worker was accustomed to, or because of the contribution to the attack of pre-existing disease, factors clearly constituting the ratio decidendi of the medical board and the adjudicating agency in this case.

. . . The predominance of the credible proofs sustains the conclusion in terms of probability that the work effort caused the heart attack.

. . . *Reversed, with directions to the board of trustees to grant the accidental disability retirement allowance.*

CHAPTER 31
REVIEW QUESTIONS AND PROBLEMS

1. *S*, a bus driver for *X* Co., was operating his bus when it was struck by a truck of *T* Co., driven by *F*. *S* stopped the bus and attempted to get name of the truck driver and license number of the truck. At this point, *F* kicked and beat him up very badly. *S* sued *T* Co. for damages. What result?

2. *A* was *O*'s agent in charge of a lumber yard and of loading and unloading lumber. He had been instructed never to pile lumber outside the lumber yard, but because of ease in unloading, he piled some outside and near a sidewalk. Some of it fell on *C*, who was passing by on the sidewalk. Was *O* liable to *C*? If *O* was liable to *C*, did he have an action against *A*? Could *C* have recovered of *A*?

3. *M*, driving a gasoline truck, negligently ran into and killed *Z*. *M* was driving the truck for his brother, a distributor of *T* oil and gas products, the contract with *T* Co. providing that the truck carry the words "*T* Co." at certain places, that it be used for delivery of *T* Co. products to designated filling stations and that the driver, in collecting for deliveries made, sign the receipt in name of *T* Co. For these services *M*'s brother received a commission. When sued by *Z*'s executor for wrongful death, *T* Co. claimed *M*'s brother was an independent contractor rather than an agent. What result?

4. *G*, engaged by *F* Co. at 10 cents a mile to deliver a new truck to a buyer and to pick up a used one, was instructed to drive by the shortest route, not to drive on gravel roads, to check the oil on arrival and to replace any oil loss. *G* while en route was injured in an accident, but *F* Co.'s workmen's compensation insurer refused to pay, insisting that *G* was an independent contractor. *G* files a claim for compensation. What result?

5. X was drowned during a Saturday outing while boating on a South Korean lake. At the time of his death he was employed at a defense base in South Korea by Y, a government contractor. X had been transported to South Korea at Y's expense. Y paid his rent and provided him with a per diem expense allowance for each day of the year, including weekends and holidays, to cover "the necessary living expenses in the Korean economy." He worked on a "365 day per year basis . . . subject to call at the job site at any time." The employer considered all its employees to be "in the course of regular occupation from the time they leave the United States until they return." The employer expected the decedent and its other employees to seek recreation away from the job site on weekends and holidays. Is X's death covered by Workmen's Compensation?

6. P sued D for injuries sustained when P was struck by an automobile at D's business. D's employee X, directed a stranger, Y, who was sitting in the automobile which blocked D's business entrance, to move the car. Y indicated that she did not know how to drive. X told her to move it anyway, which she did, striking P. Is D liable?

7. D owned a beauty supply company. D employed X as a commission salesman in a state. X drove and maintained his own automobile and chose his own hours and places of work. In addition to commissions, he was paid $5 for each night spent "on the road." X injured P while driving his car. P sues D for the injuries. What result?

8. A was employed by D as a laundry route salesman. He was furnished a truck and uniform. A, after his usual working hours, while using his personal car to make a delivery which he forgot to make before he returned D's truck, negligently injured P. P sues D. What result?

9. P, a fireman, suffered a heart attack while fighting a fire. He had a heart condition prior to the attack. Is he entitled to Workmen's Compensation?

10. W was struck by a truck, operated by H, her husband. He was acting in the scope of his employment for D. W sues D for her injuries and D asserts immunity from suit based on the servants marital relation with W. What result?

11. P sued X and Y for damage to his automobile caused by a faulty oil filter installed by X. Y leased X his station and X honored Y's credit cards. Is Y liable?

chapter 32

Liability of
Third Parties

4-35 Introduction. The previous chapters contain a discussion of the contractual and tort liability of Principals, Agents, Masters, and Servants. The law of Agency deals with matters relating to the duties and obligations of these parties; it is also properly concerned with their rights against third parties which may arise *ex contractu* or *ex delicto*. This chapter is concerned with these rights.

4-36 Disclosed Principal on Contract. The disclosed principal may sue the third party upon any contract made by the agent for the former's benefit. This rule applies to all simple contracts in which the principal is the real party in interest, despite the fact that they are made in the agent's name. Furthermore, any contract made for the benefit of the principal, although the agent acted outside the scope of his authority, entitles the principal to performance, provided the contract has been properly ratified before withdrawal by the other party.

4-37 Undisclosed Principal on Contract. The undisclosed principal is also entitled to performance by third parties of all simple contracts made for his benefit by the agent. In the ordinary case, it is no defense for the third party to say that he had not entered into a contract with the principal.[1] When, however, the contract is one which involves the skill or confidence of the agent and which would not have been entered into but for this skill or confidence, its performance may not be demanded by the principal. In other words, whenever a contract made

[1] *Kelly Asphalt Block Co. v. Barber Asphalt Paving Co.*, page 709.

for the benefit of an undisclosed principal is such that it cannot be assigned or its duties delegated, the principal cannot demand its benefits.

In all cases, other than those involving commercial paper, the undisclosed principal takes over the contract subject to all defenses which the third party could have established against the agent.[2] For example, if the third party contracts to buy from such an agent and has a right of set-off against the agent, he has this same right to set-off against the undisclosed principal. He may also pay the agent prior to discovery of the principal [3] and such payment will discharge his liability.

4-38 Liability to Agent on Contract. Normally the agent possesses no right to bring suit on contracts made by him for the benefit of his principal because he has no interest in the cause of action. Where the agent binds himself to the third party, either intentionally or ineptly by a failure properly to express himself, he may, however, maintain an action. An agent of an undisclosed principal always binds himself. As a result, he may sue in his own name in the event of nonperformance by the third party. Under the circumstances outlined, either the agent or the principal might bring suit, but in case of a dispute the right of the principal is superior.

Custom has long sanctioned an action by the agent based upon a contract in which he is interested because of anticipated commissions. As a result, a factor may institute an action in his own name to recover for goods sold. He may also recover against a railroad for delay in shipment of goods sold or to be sold.

Similarly, an agent who has been vested with title to commercial paper may sue the maker thereof. The same is true of any claim held by the principal that he definitely places with the agent for collection and suit, where such is necessary. In all cases of this character, the agent retains the proceeds as a trust fund for his principal.

4-39 Tort Liability. Any person injured by the commission of a tort has a cause of action against the wrongdoer. This includes both principals and agents. As previously noted, if the employee is injured by a third party, the principal is entitled to recover his Workmen's Compensation payments from the sum which the agent recovered from the negligent third party.

There are two rather unusual tort situations that are mentioned because of their direct relation to the employment contract. First, any third party who maliciously or wrongfully influences the principal to terminate his agent's employment thereby commits a tort.[4] He must compensate the agent for any damages which result from such conduct. Second, any third person who influences another to breach a contract in which the agent is interested thereby renders himself liable to the

---

[2] *American Enameled Brick & Tile Co. v. Brozek,* page 710.

[3] *Darling-Singer Lumber Co. v. Commonwealth et al.,* page 711.

[4] *Herron v. State Farm Mutual Insurance Company,* page 712.

agent as well as the principal.[5] To illustrate: The agent has sold goods to *T* upon which he is entitled to a commission. Anyone who causes *T* to refuse to carry out the agreement thereby damages the agent and is correspondingly liable.

LIABILITY OF THIRD PARTIES CASES

Kelly Asphalt Block Co. v. Barber Asphalt Paving Co.

1914 (N.Y.C.A.) 211 N.Y.68, 105 N.E. 88

CARDOZO, J.   The plaintiff sues to recover damages for breach of an implied warranty. The contract was made between the defendant and one Booth. The plaintiff says that Booth was in truth its agent, and it sues as undisclosed principal. The question is whether it has the right to do so.

The general rule is not disputed. A contract not under seal, made in the name of an agent as ostensible principal, may be sued on by the real principal at the latter's election. . . . The defendant says that we should establish an exception to that rule, where the identity of the principal has been concealed because of the belief that, if it were disclosed, the contract would not be made. We are asked to say that the reality of the defendant's consent is thereby destroyed, and the contract vitiated for mistake.

The plaintiff and the defendant were competitors in business. The plaintiff's president suspected that the defendant might refuse to name him a price. The suspicion was not based upon any previous refusal, for there had been none; it had no other origin than their relation as competitors. Because of this doubt the plaintiff availed itself of the services of Booth, who, though interested to the defendant's knowledge in the plaintiff's business, was also engaged in a like business for another corporation. Booth asked the defendant for a price and received a quotation, and the asphalt blocks required for the plaintiff's pavement were ordered in his name. The order was accepted by the defendant, the blocks were delivered and payment was made by Booth with money furnished by the plaintiff. The paving blocks were unmerchantable, and the defendant, retaining the price, contests its liability for damages on the ground that if it had known that the plaintiff was the principal, it would have refused to make the sale.

We are satisfied that upon the facts before us the defense cannot prevail. A contract involves a meeting of the minds of the contracting parties. . . . Neither of the supposed parties was wanting in this case. The apparent meeting of the minds between determinate contracting parties was not unreal or illusory. The defendant was contracting with the precise person with whom it intended to contract. It was contracting with Booth. It gained whatever benefit it may have contemplated from his character and substance. . . . An agent who contracts in his own

[5] *Watson v. Settlemeyer*, page 714.

name for an undisclosed principal does not cease to be a party because of his agency. . . . Indeed, such an agent, having made himself personally liable, may enforce the contract though the principal has renounced it. . . . As between himself and the other party, he is liable as principal to the same extent as if he had not been acting for another. It is impossible in such circumstances to hold that the contract collapses for want of parties to sustain it. The contractual tie cannot exist where there are not persons to be bound, but here persons were bound, and those the very persons intended. If Booth had given the order in his own right and for his own benefit, but with the expectation of later assigning it to the plaintiff, that undisclosed expectation would not have nullified the contract. His undisclosed intention to act for a principal who was unknown to the defendant was equally ineffective to destroy the contract in its inception. . . .

The judgment should be affirmed, with costs. . . .

American Enameled Brick & Tile Co. v. Brozek

1930 (Mich.) 251 Mich. 7, 231 N.W. 45

BUTZEL, J.   Plaintiff, a New York corporation, manufactures enameled brick. Thomas Brothers & Co., Detroit, Michigan, its sales agent, sold defendant, Stanley Brozek, a builder, an order for the purpose of erecting a public building in Dearborn, Michigan. . . . There was some dispute as to whether defendant instructed Thomas Brothers & Co. to ship the order in March or whether only 20,000 bricks were to be shipped in March, and the remainder as and when called for. In the latter event, part of the order would have been filled prior to the time when it was to be sent and there might be a small balance due defendant on account of loss of discount in not being able to pay for brick that was shipped prior to the time for delivery. There was also a claim on the part of defendant that he was put to a small expense in building a shed to store high-priced brick which arrived prematurely.

The judge of the lower court ruled against defendant's contentions, and the record justifies him in so doing. . . . A judgment was rendered in favor of plaintiff for the full balance due, together with interest. The court held Thomas Brothers & Co. were the agents, and plaintiff the principal, and the proper party plaintiff, which could adopt the agent's contract and sue on it. There is some dispute as to whether plaintiff was the undisclosed principal or not, whether defendant did not know that Thomas Brothers & Co. were simply acting as agents. . . .

. . . Defendant claims that the court erred . . . in . . . refusing to exclude all testimony of plaintiff's witness showing that Thomas Brothers & Co. were merely acting as the agents of plaintiff. Defendant does not claim that he was put to any loss whatsoever through making his contract with plaintiff instead of Thomas Brothers & Co. There is no question of set-off, counterclaim, or any other showing of any disadvantage that defendant suffered through the order being executed by plaintiff instead of Thomas Brothers & Co. He simply claims a technical objection to the fact that plaintiff, instead of Thomas Brothers & Co.

brought suit. . . . Even if plaintiff was not a disclosed principal, it would have the right to bring the suit, for it is elementary that an undisclosed principal may bring in its own name to collect for goods furnished by it on contract made through its agent. The defendant may avail himself of any defense which existed in its favor against the agent at the time of the disclosure to him of the existence of the real principal. Defendant was not precluded from claiming any such defense. . . .

We find no error whatsoever in the case, and the judgment of the lower court is affirmed, with costs to plaintiff.

Darling-Singer Lumber Co. v. Commonwealth & Others

1953 290 Mass. 488, 195 N.E. 723

RUGG, J. This is a petition . . . to enforce a lien for the collection of the price of lumber furnished to Attilio D. Daddario, hereinafter called the defendant, who used it pursuant to two contracts with the Commonwealth for the construction of sections of the Metropolitan sewer. . . .

The facts pertinent to the grounds of this decision are: On November 3, 1950, the defendant purchased from one A. C. Place, doing business in Boston as the Place Lumber Company, 50,000 feet of fir plank to be shipped from the Pacific Coast, to be consigned to the defendant and to be delivered at site of job by Place. . . . In fact, Place was acting as agent for the plaintiff, Darling-Singer Lumber Co. of Portland, Oregon. He was authorized by it to sell lumber on commission and had been notified to have purchasers remit directly to F. P. Gram Co., Inc. of said Portland, to which corporation at that time the plaintiff was assigning its accounts receivable. Place, in conducting his business in Boston, used his own stationery, memoranda of sales, and held himself out to the defendant as conducting business on his own account. Place solicited the orders for this lumber from the defendant and the defendant believed and had every reason for believing that he was dealing with Place as principal. . . . This lumber was delievered by Place at the location indicated by the defendant. Accompanying the bill of lading was an invoice on the letterhead of Darling-Singer Lumber Co., Portland, Oregon. Also accompanying the invoice and bill of lading was a notice headed from F. P. Gram Co., Inc., reading "We enclose herewith duly assigned to us invoice and bill of lading covering cars containing lumber sold and shipped to you by Darling-Singer Lumber Company amounting to $1,459.36. We are entitled to the proceeds under this assignment and look to you for payment of the same. Please remit directly to us." . . . The defendant has paid Place in full for all this lumber shipped by the plaintiff and has paid all freight charges. Place deposited the checks thus received to his own credit and has not accounted for them to the plaintiff. In making these payments to Place, the defendant acted entirely in good faith. He regarded Place as the only one with whom he had contracted and the only one to whom he owed any obligation of payment. He failed to understand the legal significance of the documents mailed to him by F. P. Gram Co., Inc. . . . The trial judge found, "under the facts herein set forth," that the payments by the defendant to Place constituted payments of the accounts for which this petition was brought and denied a ruling to the contrary, requested by the plaintiff, subject to its exception. A final decree was entered dismissing the bill as to the defendant, with costs. The plaintiff appealed. . . .

The plaintiff was the undisclosed principal of Place in the sales of lumber to the defendant. Although Place purported to act as principal, he was in fact the agent for the plaintiff in making those sales. An undisclosed principal may sue on a single contract not under seal made by his agent even though the agent appeared as principal in the transaction without disclosing his agency. This rule is equally applicable to foreign and domestic principals. (*Barry v. Page,* 10 Gray, 398, 399.) When property is sold by an agent purporting to act as principal but in truth as agent for an undisclosed principal, if before payment the undisclosed principal gives notice to the purchaser to pay to him and not to the agent, the purchaser is bound to pay the principal subject to any equities of the purchaser against the agent. . . . The purchaser, however, is protected in making payment to the agent at any time previous to notice of the agency, but not in making payment after notice of the agency. . . . Difficulty may arise in determining under what circumstances the purchaser has notice of the agency so that thereafter at his own risk he pays the agent, and whether such notice means actual knowledge or reasonable cause to know. . . . That point need not here be determined.

. . . The invoice and bill of lading thus indicating the plaintiff as seller were accompanied by notice from F. P. Gram Co., Inc. as assignee of the invoice demanding payment for the lumber. This was express notice to the effect that the plaintiff was principal in the sale. It was given to the defendant before payment by him to Place. The question of reasonable cause to know that the plaintiff was principal in the transaction does not arise because the notice was direct and unequivocal. The circumstance that Place had told the defendant that he had a western mill or office from which the lumber would be shipped does not dull the effect of the notice. The documents sent by F. P. Gram Co., Inc., were unmistakable in their import that the plaintiff was the seller of the lumber and had assigned to F. P. Gram Co., Inc., the amount due for such lumber, and that payment must be made to F. P. Gram Co., Inc., alone. That the defendant failed to understand them does not exonerate him from the legal effect upon him of the terms of those documents. . . .

The result is that upon the facts found the decree in favor of the defendant could not rightly have been entered. The plaintiff was entitled to prevail. *The exceptions are sustained and the decree is reversed.* . . .

Herron v. State Farm Mutual Insurance Company

1961 (Cal.) 363 P.2d 310

GIBSON, J. Plaintiffs, attorneys at law, brought this action against Mr. and Mrs. Donald Halverson for breach of contract and against State Farm Mutual Insurance Company and its agent, Anthony Caruso, for intentional interference with contractual relations. The Halversons were not served, and a demurrer of State Farm and Caruso (who will be referred to as defendants) was sustained without leave to amend. Plaintiffs have appealed from the ensuing judgment.

The following is a summary of plaintiffs' allegations: The Halversons entered into a contingent fee contract with plaintiffs concerning claims reasonably worth $60,000 for personal injuries sustained in an automobile accident caused by the negligence of a person insured by State Farm. Plaintiffs were to advance all expenses necessary for the preparation of the case and for court costs and were to receive one-third of the amount of the recovery remaining after deduction of the costs. No settlement was to be made without the consent of plaintiffs and the Halversons, and in the event there was no recovery plaintiffs were to receive nothing for their services or for costs advanced. Plaintiffs notified defendants of the agreement immediately after its execution, and they proceeded to hire private investigators, photographers, and a draftsman, make an investigation, and incur expenses in the amount of $1,250. Defendants, by telling the Halversons that they did not need an attorney and that a satisfactory settlement would be made, induced them to breach the contingent fee contract and to discharge plaintiffs and deprive them of the benefits of the contract and the expenses incurred for investigation and preparation. Defendants assisted the Halversons in preparing letters which informed plaintiffs of their dismissal. The conduct of defendants was maliciously designed to injure plaintiffs' rights and lawful business, and it violated the rules of the National Conference Committee on Adjusters of which State Farm or its agents are members. The rules provide, in part, that an insurance company will not deal directly with any claimant represented by an attorney without the consent of the attorney and will not advise the claimant to refrain from seeking legal advice or retaining counsel to protect his interest. As a result of the conduct of defendants, plaintiffs suffered the loss of the expenses incurred in investigation and preparation and did not receive their one-third contingent fee.

Plaintiffs prayed for judgment against defendants for $20,000 or one-third of the judgment or settlement recovered by the Halversons, whichever is the lesser, and, in addition, for $25,000 punitive damages.

An action will lie for the intentional interference by a third person with a contractual relationship either by unlawful means or by means otherwise lawful when there is a lack of sufficient justification. . . . There is no valid reason why this rule should not be applied to an attorney's contingent fee contract. Such an agreement is a legal and valid contract entitled to the protection of the law, and an attorney who is wrongfully discharged is generally entitled to the same amount of compensation as if he had completed the contemplated services. . . . While a client is permitted to discharge his attorney without cause, this is allowed not because the attorney's interest in performing his services and obtaining his fee is unworthy of protection but because of the importance

of the client's interest in the successful prosecution of his cause of action.
. . . An attorney's interest in his contingent fee agreement is greater than
that of a party to a contract terminable at will, as to which it has been
held that an intentional and unjustifiable interference is actionable.

. . .

Whether an intentional interference by a third party is justifiable
depends upon a balancing of the importance, social and private, of the
objective advanced by the interference against the importance of the interest interfered with, considering all circumstances including the
nature of the actor's conduct and the relationship between the parties.
. . . Justification is an affirmative defense and may not be considered
as supporting the trial court's action in sustaining a demurrer unless it
appears on the face of the complaint. . . . The only allegation relied
upon by defendants as showing justification is that State Farm had
issued an automobile public liability insurance policy to the person
whose negligence caused the injuries to the Halversons. In our opinion
this allegation does not establish justification.

The conduct of an insurance company in inducing an injured person
to repudiate his contract with an attorney may be detrimental not only to
the interests of the attorney but also to the interests of the client since, as
we have seen, the client, in addition to being deprived of the aid and
advice of his attorney, may also be liable for the full contract fee.
Defendants argue that the policy of the law is to encourage settlement,
that an insurance company has a legal duty to effect a settlement of a
claim against its insured in an appropriate case . . . and that furtherance
of the actor's own economic interests will justify an intentional interference with a contractual relationship in some circumstances where his
interests are threatened by the contract. However, these considerations
standing alone cannot justify inducing the Halversons to repudiate the
contract and to deprive plaintiffs of its benefits. So far as appears from
the complaint, no cause for the dismissal of plaintiffs existed, no efforts
were made to negotiate with them, and there is no indication that State
Farm could not have protected its interests and obtained a satisfactory
settlement without interfering with the contract.

The judgment is reversed with directions to overrule the demurrer.

Watson v. Settlemeyer

1962 (Colo.) 372 P.2d 453

SUTTON. On December 23, 1955, in Colorado, Settlemeyer
sued Watson and two State of Washington corporations, the Bardahl
Manufacturing Corporation and its sales agent the Bardahl Oil Company, for alleged conspiracy to breach an oral distributorship contract
for the State of Colorado, which was granted in 1950 by the Bardahl
Manufacturing Corporation to Settlemeyer. Actual damages in the
amount of $42,529.68 and exemplary damages in the sum of $10,000.00
were sought. Watson, who was Bardahl's New Mexico distributor, re-

placed Settlemeyer in Colorado as distributor under a written contract dated July 1, 1955, though Settlemeyer was not notified of his dismissal until mid-July 1955.

Settlemeyer's attempts to procure service of process on the two Bardahl corporations has proved fruitless . . . He then elected to proceed to trial on June 30, 1959, against Watson without a jury on the theory of unlawful interference with his contract by Watson. Judgment entered in favor of Settlemeyer on April 24, 1961. This was after these unfortunate litigants had parts of their case, including various preliminary motions, heard by five separate judges over a period of almost six years. The hectic history of this case and the need to bring it to a belated but respectable conclusion restrains us from again returning it to the trial court so that the matter of damages can be properly determined. We elect to dispose of it at this time, however, only because Settlemeyer in his briefs filed with this court has expressly waived his rights in this respect and has consented to the award if the judgment can be otherwise affirmed.

Watson urges four grounds for reversal:

1. That the trial court erred in not allowing parol evidence to show what he calls the "true date" of the written contract between himself and Bardahl.

2. That the oral contract between Settlemeyer and Bardahl was terminable at will and therefore no possible damages could accrue when Bardahl elected to end it.

3. That the proof of damages was not only insufficient but was entirely speculative.

4. That the trial court's findings were contrary to both the evidence and the law because in substance no valid enforceable contract was shown by Settlemeyer to have been intentionally interfered with by Watson which resulted in damages to Settlemeyer.

. . . we find there is sufficient evidence to justify an award of $7500.00 to Settlemeyer, provided there is any basis upon which any damages at all may be awarded. Accordingly we address ourselves to the question of liability.

The evidence is that Watson had visited Bardahl in Seattle, Washington, at various times, the last trip being in June 1955. Also, Watson had attempted to trade part of his territory in New Mexico to Settlemeyer in Colorado prior to June 1955 so that more economical geographical units would be held by each of them. Prior to Bardahl discharging Settlemeyer, Settlemeyer's accounts with Bardahl were becoming delinquent and Bardahl was becoming dissatisfied with Settlemeyer. Nevertheless, Settlemeyer had expended considerable sums of his own money ($8,251.47) at Bardahl's request to advertise and promote the Bardahl products and had built up outlets of about 1500 filling stations in Colorado in five years time. At the time Watson took over, Settlemeyer had a considerable stock of Bardahl's products and promotional materials on hand—all purchased from Bardahl on the implied representation that Settlemeyer would be able to use them. Bardahl, however, instructed Watson not to buy these items from Settlemeyer, even though Watson had previously approached Settlemeyer about taking over his territory.

In addition to the above, the records show that regardless of the correct date of the written contract between Watson and Bardahl, both Watson and Bardahl recognized that Settlemeyer had some rights in his distributorship for this instrument expressly details many of Bardahl's dealings with Settlemeyer and for example states ". . . that Bardahl Manufacturing Corporation has now taken steps to discontinue any further right of C. V. Settlemeyer, as aforesaid, to continue as the distributor of said product . . . that if, however, said Manufacturing Corporation ultimately is unable to effect an effective cancellation and termination of the rights of said distributor, then First Party herein (Bardahl) incurs no liability unto Second Party (Watson) in that respect. . . ." Further on it is provided that ". . . the First Party expressly agrees to assume and pay the burden of any expenses to which Second Party may be put in connection with said litigation . . . ," i.e. if such results from Bardahl's attempt to oust Settlemeyer.

Suffice it to say, without detailing more of the events which occurred that it is immaterial whether the written agreement in fact was signed on July 1, as it states, or on August 1, 1955, as Watson asserts, for the unlawful interference of Watson with Settlemeyer's distributorship was his entire course of conduct as disclosed by this record. Though some conflicts appear in the evidence, the trier of fact found against Watson on these points by holding for Settlemeyer and we will not disturb such findings on review when supported by competent evidence. . . .

Though Bardahl may have had the right to terminate Settlemeyer's oral contract at will, a point which we need not decide here, Watson *had no right to induce such an act or to intentionally interefere* between Bardahl and Settlemeyer by promoting his purpose and intention to take over if Bardahl was successful in ousting Settlemeyer. . . . ". . . the general rule is that (in cases of employer-employee relationships) *it is immaterial that the contract is terminable at will.*". . .

The contract of July 1, 1955, alone admits knowledge and interference by Watson and, when coupled with other evidence before the trial court, properly led it to the conclusion that Watson was liable for the results which followed his course of conduct leading to the termination of Settlemeyer's sales agency contract. . . .

We hold that independent contractors or agents like Settlemeyer have the right to earn a livelihood and to continue their business unmolested by unwarranted activities of third persons and are entitled to protection in equity just like the employees of any business.

Of course, what is "unwarranted" interference depends on the facts of each case. Here the course of conduct of Watson, though in part disputed, justified the trial court in so holding as to Watson.

The judgment is affirmed.

CHAPTER 32
REVIEW QUESTIONS AND PROBLEMS

1. *T,* because of his dislike of *A,* persuades *P* to discharge *A.* Assuming that *A* does not have a contract for any definite period, may he recover damages from *T?*
2. *X* employed *P* as his attorney to sue *D* for personal injuries. *P* was to receive ⅓ of any amount collected. *D* told *X* that *D* would pay *X* $30,000 and to discharge *P. X* discharged *P* and *P* sues *D* for $10,000. What result?
3. *P* was employed by *X* as its agent. *D* encouraged *X* to break the contract with *P* and to employ *D* as its agent. *P* sues *D* for damages. What result?
4. *A* and *T* entered into a contract by which *T* agreed to serve as auctioneer at ½ of the usual rate at an auction to be held at *A's* farm. *A* had secretly agreed with *P* that *P* could bring his goods to the auction for sale in order that *P* could also take advantage of the special rate. *T* learns of the arrangement and refuses to perform. *P* sues *T* for breach of contract, alleging that *A* was acting as his agent in arranging the contract. What result?
5. *X* is injured by *T* while serving in the employment of *P. X* collects workmen's compensation from *P* and then sues *T* in tort for his injuries. *T* uses the workmen's compensation payment as a defense contending that *X's* suit would in effect give him a double recovery. What result?
6. *A* enters into a contract with *T* which is beyond *A's* authority from *P.* Before *P* learns of the contract, *T* notifies *A* that he wishes to cancel the contract. *A* asks *P* if he should allow *T* to do so and *P* informs *T* that he considers the contract binding. If *P* sues *T* for breach of contract, what result?
7. *A* enters into a contract with *T* on behalf of *P,* an undisclosed principal. As a result of the contract, *T* owes *P* $1,000. If *A* was indebted to *T* in the amount of $600, how much is *P* entitled to collect from *T* if he discloses his interest in the contract?

chapter 33

Duties of Principal and Agent to Each Other

DUTIES OF AGENT TO PRINCIPAL

4-40 Introduction. The extent of the duties imposed upon agents and servants is governed largely by the contract of employment. In addition to the duties expressly designated, certain others are implied by the nature of the relationship. These duties are divided roughly into five groups. The agent is: (1) to be loyal to his principal; (2) to obey all reasonable instructions; (3) not to be negligent; (4) to account for all money or property received for the benefit of the principal; and (5) to inform the principal of all facts which materially affect the subject matter of the agency. A duty arising under any specific circumstances will usually be found to fall within one of these groups.

4-41 Duty of Loyalty. An agent stands in a fiduciary relationship to his principal and thus has a duty of undivided loyalty to the principal. Because of the duty of loyalty it is held that he should undertake no business venture that competes or interferes in any manner with the business of his employer or make any contract for himself when he should have made it for his principal. The same rule forbids a sales agent to sell his principal's property to himself, unless the principal assents to the sale. The rule also prevents a purchasing agent from buying his own property or that in which he has an interest. Transactions violating these rules may always be rescinded by the principal, if he so desires, despite the fact the agent acted for the best interests of his principal and the contract was as favorable as could be obtained elsewhere. The general rule is applied without favor in order that every possible motive or incentive for unfaithfulness may be removed.

In addition to the remedy of rescission, a principal is entitled to treat any profit realized by the agent in violation of this duty as belonging to the principal. Such profits include rebates, bonuses, commissions, or divisions of profits received by an agent for dealing with a particular third party. Here again the contracts may have been favorable to the employer, but the result is the same, since the agent should not be tempted to abuse the confidence reposed in him.

An agent may deal with himself only if he obtains the permission of the principal. In any case in which the agent obtains the consent of the principal to deal with himself, the agent must disclose fully all facts which materially influence the situation. In such a case, agent and principal do not deal at "arm's length," and the circumstances demand the utmost good faith on the part of the agent.

The duty of loyalty denies a broker the right to represent both the seller and the buyer in the same transaction unless both have been informed of his dual relationship.[1] His desire to earn the commission is apt to cause him to disregard the best interests of one of his principals. Either party who is without knowledge of the dual representation may rescind the agreement and the agent is not entitled to any fee or commission.

Loyalty demands that information of a confidential character acquired while in the service of the principal shall not be used by the agent to advance his interests in opposition to those of the principal. An employee who learns of secret processes or formulas or comes into possession of lists of customers may not use this information to the detriment of his employer. The employer may obtain an injunction to prevent its use.[2] The rule relating to trade secrets is applied with equal severity whether the agent acts before or after he severs his connection with the principal. The knowledge must in fact be a trade secret.[3] Knowledge that is important but which does not amount to a trade secret may be used, although it affects his former employer injuriously. For this reason there is nothing to hinder a person who has made the acquaintance of his employer's customers from later circularizing those whom he can remember. His acquaintanceship is part of his acquired skill. The employer may protect himself in the latter case by a clause in the employment agreement to the effect that the employee will not compete with the employer or work for a competitor for a limited period of time after his employment is terminated, as discussed in the book on Contracts.

"Moonlighting" has in recent years become quite common. Many people work at two jobs in order to improve their standard of living. While such initiative may be very laudable, certain legal problems arise. If the second job is conducted during the time the agent is supposed to be working for the principal, the duty of loyalty is breached and the principal may recover any amounts paid to the agent. If the work is performed after hours or during a period when he is not expected to be

1 *Standard Realty & Development v. Ferrera,* page 724.
2 *Albert B. Cord Co. v. S & P Management Service, Inc.,* page 725.
3 *Town & Country House & Home Serv., Inc. v. Evans,* page 728.

working for his principal, the gain or money received unquestionably remains the property of the agent.

4-42 Duty to Obey Instructions. It becomes the duty of an agent to obey all instructions issued by his principal as long as they refer to duties contemplated by the contract of employment. Burdens not required by the agreement cannot be indiscriminately imposed by the employer. An instruction may not be regarded lightly merely because it departs from the usual procedure and seems fanciful and impractical to the employee. It is not his business to question the procedure outlined by his superior. Any loss which results while he is pursuing any other course makes him absolutely liable to the principal for any resulting loss.

Furthermore, an instruction of the principal does not become improper merely because the motive is bad. He may be well aware of the agent's distaste for certain tasks, yet, if those tasks are such as may be called for under the employment agreement, it becomes the agent's duty to perform them. Failure to perform often results in proper grounds for his discharge.

This obligation on the part of the agent to follow carefully his principal's orders applies to an agent who acts gratuitously, as well as to one who receives pay for his services. Although the former is under no duty to perform, even though he has promised to do so, yet if he undertakes to carry out his commission, he must follow explicitly the instructions received.

Closely allied to the duty to follow instructions is the duty to remain within the scope of the authority conferred. Because of the doctrine of estoppel, it often becomes possible for an agent to exceed his authority and still bind his principal. In case of such a violation of his contract, the employee becomes responsible for any resulting loss. He is in this instance failing to follow the instructions set forth in his contract with his employer. These instructions must be fully complied with, as well as those issued later by the principal.

Occasionally circumstances arise that nullify instructions previously given. Because of the new conditions, the old instructions would, if followed, practically destroy the purpose of the agency. Whenever such an emergency arises, it becomes the duty of the agent, provided the principal is not available, to exercise his best judgment in meeting the situation.

An instruction to do an illegal or immoral act, or an act that will impair the security or position of the agent, may be disregarded. To illustrate: A factor has a lien on goods in his possession for all money advanced to his principal. An order from the principal to return the goods or to sell them on credit could be disregarded until such time as all advances had been paid.

4-43 Duty Not to Be Negligent. As was discussed in Chapter 31, an agent or servant who commits a tort while acting within the scope of his employment creates liability for his principal or master. He therefore has a duty to exercise due care and caution for the safety of others and their property. If he fails to do so and the employer is held responsible he has liability to the principal or master for any loss incurred. For a further discussion, see Chapter 31.

4-44 Duty to Account. Money or property entrusted to the agent must be accounted for to the principal. Because of this fact, the agent is required to keep proper records showing receipts and expenditures, in order that a complete accounting may be rendered. Any money collected by an agent for his principal should not be mingled with funds of the former. If they are deposited in a bank, they should be kept in a separate account and so designated that a trust is apparent. Otherwise, any loss resulting from an insolvent bank must be borne by the agent.

The principal may follow any funds misappropriated by the agent until they fall into the hands of a third party. Even then the principal may follow the proceeds and impress a trust upon them, so long as they have not reached an innocent third party. Furthermore, if such proceeds can be shown to have increased the estate of the agent, a trust may be imposed upon the agent's estate to that extent.

4-45 Duty to Give Notice. It becomes the duty of an agent to tell his principal all facts which vitally affect the subject matter of the agency and which are obtained within the scope of the employment. Information learned while outside the scope of employment and which the agent never expects to use need not be communicated to the principal.

This rule extends beyond the duty to inform the principal of conflicting interests of third parties in a particular transaction, and it imposes upon the agent a duty to give his principal all information which materially affects the interest of the principal. Thus, knowledge of facts which have greatly advanced the value of property placed with an agent for sale should be communicated before the property is sold at a price previously established by the principal.

DUTIES OF PRINCIPAL TO AGENT

4-46 Duty to Compensate in General. The agent is entitled to be compensated for his services in accordance with the terms of his contract of employment. If no definite compensation has been agreed upon, there arises a duty to pay the reasonable value of such services. Whenever the party performing the services is a stranger to the employer, the obligation to compensate exists. However, where relatives are working for one another and no express agreement has been formulated, the courts are likely to infer that the services so rendered should be considered as gratuitous. This question frequently arises in claims against an estate for the value of care given the deceased prior to his death by a relative. Following this rule, the claims are usually denied in the absence of an express contract to pay for the care.

If the contract is silent on the amount of compensation, the reasonable value will be the customary rate in the community, if any. If no customary rate is available, opinion evidence is received in determining the value of the services.

4-47 Duty to Compensate–Brokers. Perhaps no single question of Agency law results in more litigation than the issue of the right of a broker to a real estate commission. In the absence of an express agreement, the real estate broker earns his commission at either one of two times. First, he will be entitled to it as soon as he finds a buyer who is ready, willing, and able to meet the terms outlined by the seller as per the Listing Agreement. The owner cannot deprive him of his compensation by refusing to deal with the prospective purchaser or by withdrawing the property from sale. He cannot relieve himself of the duty to pay the commission by terminating the agency and later contracting directly with the broker's prospect. The fee is earned if it is shown that the broker was the inducing cause of the sale.[4]

The commission is also earned as soon as the owner contracts with the purchaser (whether or not the price is less than the listed price), even though it later develops that the buyer is unable to meet the terms of the contract. The owner assumes the risk of performance if he is willing to, and does, contract with the buyer presented by the broker. The broker's commission is contingent on payment by the purchaser only when his contract of employment so states.[5] An owner who lists property with several brokers is obligated to pay the first one to find a satisfactory purchaser, at which time the agency of other brokers is automatically terminated, assuming a simple listing.

There are three distinct types of real estate listings—placing of property with real estate brokers for sale. First is the simple listing of the property for sale on the terms set forth by the seller, in which case the listing may be with several brokers and the right to withdraw or terminate the relationship at any time is reserved by the seller. Under such circumstances, the seller pays the commission to the first broker who finds a buyer. The owner is free to sell on his own behalf without a commission. The second type consists of an exclusive listing which usually gives to the broker the exclusive right to find a buyer for an agreed period of time. In this case the seller is not free to list the property with other brokers and a sale through other brokers would be a violation of the contract of listing, although the seller, himself, is free to find a buyer of his own. Third, a listing in which the broker is given an exclusive right to sell. In this case even the seller is not free to find a buyer of his own choosing. If the seller does sell on his own behalf, he is obliged to pay a commission to the broker holding an exclusive right to sell.

The right to a real estate commission is subject to statutory limitations in several states. Some of these require a written contract and others require a license before a person may engage in this activity. Some cases

[4] *Haymes v. Rogers,* page 731.
[5] *Richard v. Falleti,* page 733.

have gone so far as to hold that a broker selling property in a state in which he is licensed is not entitled to a fee if the buyer is found or the sale completed in another state. Strict adherence to the licensing statutes is usually required.

4-48 Duty to Compensate—Sales Representative. Salesmen who sell merchandise on a commission basis have problems confronting them that are similar to those of the broker, unless the employment contract is specific in its details. Let us assume that *X* Co. appoints *A* as its exclusive sales representative in a certain territory on a commission basis and that the employer is engaged in producing and selling electrical equipment. *T*, a businessman in the area involved, sends in a large order for merchandise directly to the home office of *X* Co. Is *A* entitled to a commission on the sale? It is generally held that such a salesman is entitled to a commission only on sales solicited and induced by him, unless his contract of employment gives him greater rights.

The salesman usually earns his commission as soon as an order from a responsible buyer is obtained, unless his contract of employment makes payment contingent upon delivery of the goods or collection of the sale's price. If payment is made dependent upon performance by the purchaser, the employer cannot deny the salesman his commission by terminating the agency prior to collection of the account. When the buyer ultimately pays for the goods, the seller is obligated to pay the commission.

An agent who receives a weekly or monthly advance against future commissions is not obligated to return the advance if commissions equal thereto are not earned. The advance, in the absence of a specific agreement, is considered by the courts as a minimum salary.

4-49 Duty to Reimburse and Indemnify. Money expended by the agent in behalf of the principal may be recovered. It must appear that the money was reasonably spent and that its expenditure was not necessitated by the misconduct or negligence of the agent.

The agent is justified in presuming that instructions given by the principal are such as he lawfully has a right to give and that performance resulting from such instructions will not injuriously affect third parties. Where this is not the case, and the agent incurs a liability to some third party because of trespass or conversion, the principal must indemnify the agent against loss. In like manner, it becomes the duty of the principal to make possible performance by the agent whenever the latter has entered into a contract in his own name for the former's benefit. The undisclosed principal must fully protect his agent.

4-50 Duty to Protect from Injury. At common law a master had a duty not to be negligent or a duty to use ordinary care under the circumstances. As was discussed in Chapter 3, this duty was subject to common law defenses and has been largely replaced by the Workmen's Compensation and F.E.L.A. statutes previously discussed.

DUTIES OF PARTIES CASES

Standard Realty & Development v. Ferrera
1957, (Cal.App.) 311 P.2d 855

The plaintiff, Standard Realty & Development Company, contacted McEvoy, a real estate broker, to see if he could aid it in obtaining certain property owned by the defendant. The broker approached the defendant and persuaded him to list the property with him for sale and, a few days later had a "straw" man pay defendant $500 for an option to purchase the property for $32,500, the option being assigned to the plaintiff. The defendant later learned that a new industrial plant was to be located nearby and refused to carry out the contract, alleging fraud because the broker was acting as an agent for both parties without defendant's knowledge. Plaintiff brought a suit for specific performance and the lower court gave judgment for defendant. The plaintiff appealed.

FOURT, J. . . . Appellant contends that granted arguendo the trial court was correct in its finding that McEvoy was acting in a dual capacity as agent for plaintiff and defendants, nonetheless, it is not grounds for a rescission of the contract even though he made no disclosure of this fact to the defendants. There is persuasive authority to the contrary in the recent Supreme Court case of *McConnell v. Cowan* (44 Cal.2d 805, 285 P.2d 261). In that case the court discusses a factual situation similar to the one presented in this case, where there was dual representation, the agent assuming to act in a double capacity without disclosing this fact to one principal. At page 809 of 44 Cal.2d, at page 264 of 285 P.2d, the court says:

> . . . Such conduct is a fraud upon his principal, and not only will the agent not be entitled to compensation for services so rendered, but the contract or dealings made or had by the agent, while so acting also for the other party without the knowledge or consent of the principal, are not binding upon the latter, and if they still remain executory, he may repudiate them on that ground, or, if they have been executed in whole or in part, he may by acting promptly and before the rights of innocent parties have intervened, restore the consideration received, rescind the contract and recover back the property or rights with which he has parted under it. . . .

The defendants in the case before us followed the prescribed procedure exactly, and the trial court did not err in finding that the defendants had a right to rescind the contract. Thus the defendants could not be required to specifically perform the option agreement, nor is plaintiff entitled to recover damages.

This Court having found defendants justified in rescinding the contract, the other points raised by appellant on appeal become immaterial and it is unnecessary to discuss them.

Judgment affirmed.

Albert B. Cord Co. v. S & P Management Services, Inc.

1963 (Ohio C.P.) 194 N.E.2d 173

Leis, J.   The plaintiff, Albert B. Cord Company, Inc., is an Ohio corporation engaged in management consulting. Mr. Albert B. Cord is the president of said corporation.

The defendant, S & P Management Service, Inc., is, likewise, a management consulting business and was organized some time after May 30, 1961. The individual defendants, Mr. Anthony M. Schummer and Mr. J. Paul Pickering, S & P's principal shareholders, were employed by the plaintiff prior to May 30, 1961. Mr. Schummer, an engineer, became a member of plaintiff's staff as a Staff Engineer at or about June 1948. In January 1950, he was promoted to the supervisory staff as Chief Engineer. In this capacity Mr. Schummer was recognized as Assistant General Manager with full power and authority to act in the event anything happened to the General Manager (Mr. Albert Cord), and he had full force and power to perform anything that, in his discretion, he saw fit. Mr. J. Paul Pickering was employed by the plaintiff as its Sales Manager prior to his resignation.

Management counsulting firms offer assistance to business concerns in solving various problems in such areas as labor relations, shop operations, wage plans, production, administration, sales promotion and related problems peculiar to modern business. Service is rendered upon a fee basis. One of the chief assets of a management consulting firm is its staff of well-trained engineers, accountants, administrators and salesmen; men who are qualified and trained both technically and through years of experience in all the phases of business activity in production control, sales and sales promotion, administration, accounting and cost control, statistics, engineering, etc. These assets are "human assets" and, as experts, their minds and mentality, and their ability to analyze the problems presented to them, apply their technical knowledge, experience and imagination and recommend a workable remedy to cure the business ailment are of intangible value to the management consulting firm. Another asset of relative and equal importance to the management consulting company is a knowledge of, and access to, companies which are likely to need its services.

In the case at bar Mr. Pickering was the person most relied upon to secure the clientele. He was continually "on the road" making business calls in the midwest—Ohio, Indiana, Michigan, Illinois, Missouri, Pennsylvania and West Virginia. Whenever he made a call he submitted a report to the office for filing in the customer's file (if the call merited such a file). These reports were variously entitled, per the exhibits before the Court as "Survey Authorization," "Sales Report," "Survey Report," "Client Reactivation Sales Report," "Memorandum." The contents of the reports included the name of the person or persons contacted, a summarization of any discussions with the prospective client, including observations of the manner in which he (the salesman) was received, the problems confronting the prospect, if any; information concerning employees, financial data and statistics, affiliation with other companies, contemplated plans of merger or sale, volume of business activity, D & B credit rating of the client or prospect, and many other items and facts pertinent and helpful to the plaintiff, for the present and for the future, in ascertaining whether or not the prospect is in need, or will be in need of service and if repeat calls should be made. All this data and these comprehensive reports were accumulated in the plaintiff's confidential file with the hope that at some future time it would or will be available in securing an engagement for the plaintiff. Much time, effort and money was spent by the plaintiff through its sales representatives, under the leadership of Mr. Pickering.

The plaintiff's plan followed a definite pattern, namely:

1. The first sales call, and
2. Follow-up calls (if deemed advantageous), leading to
3. An initial Survey, followed up by
4. Contract to perform service to cure the "business ill." A natural by-product of these contacts was a building of confidence, a relationship between the plaintiff and its personnel and a healthy atmosphere for a successful tenure if a contract was forthcoming.

This Court recognizes the unique character of this type of business as compared to the type of business which offers a commodity or product, or a common service. The Court also recognizes the fact that repeat business can result from a successful initial engagement. Another element of this business that entered into this Court's consideration is the fact that Cord Company personnel had to work closely with their client's management and personnel. Such close contact can result in relationships of confidence and trust in the personnel of the plaintiff. For this reason the plaintiff, in its contracts, included the following statement:

> In order to maintain a professional atmosphere it is our policy to consider your personnel ineligible for employment with our organization, and we require your commitment to similar conditions regarding the employment or engagement of our personnel by your organization.

All of these factors emphasize the unique character of the plaintiff's business service and of its intangible value, a value which cannot be measured accountingwise in money, but which is a valuable asset to the corporation in the nature of good will.

The defendants, Mr. Schummer and Mr. Pickering, were the top men in the plaintiff company. The evidence shows that while other employees had written contracts of employment none were required of Mr. Schummer and Mr. Pickering. Evidence was presented to show that Mr. Cord and the defendants worked closely together and freely interchanged information at all times and, as a result of membership in this "inner circle" the defendants had unlimited access to confidential information contained in the locked files of the Cord Company. The defendants had keys to all the locked confidential files except two drawers which contained private papers of Mr. Cord.

This case is categorized under the topic in law entitled "Trade Secrets." The Restatement of Torts, Section 757, comment (b) (1939) defines a "Trade Secret" as follows:

> A trade secret may consist of any formula pattern, device, or compilation of information which is used in one's business, and which gives him an opportunity to obtain an advantage over competitors who do not know or use it. It may be a formula for a chemical compound, a process of manufacturing, treating or preserving materials, a pattern for a machine or other device, or a list of customers. . . .

A trade secret, therefore, is almost anything and everything useful or advantageous in business activity that is not generally known or easily or immediately ascertainable to members of the trade. . . .

The plaintiff in its Second Amended Petition alleges that the defendants

> have solicited on behalf of S & P Management Services, Inc. the following clients or prospective clients of plaintiff, among others, with whom said individual defendants had dealt on behalf of plaintiff during the last three years of their employment by plaintiff and with respect to whom defendants possessed information secured in the course of their confidential employment by plaintiff and regarded as confidential;

the plaintiff then lists twenty-six company names. Included in the list is the Frick-Gallagher Mfg. Co., Wellston, Ohio, a client of the plaintiff and with whom the plaintiff had been negotiating additional service when defendants were plaintiff's employees, which company plaintiff alleges the defendants induced to retain defendant S & P Management Service, Inc. to perform management-consulting service on the basis of information available to Mr. Schummer and Mr. Pickering as a result of their confidential employment by plaintiff.

The Supreme Court of Ohio stated in *Curry v. Marquart* (133 Ohio St. 77, 11 N.E.2d 868 (1937)):

> The authorities are quite uniform that disclosures of trade secrets by an employee secured by him in the course of confidential employment will be restrained by the process of injunction, and in numerous instances attempts to use for himself or for a new employer information relative to the trade or business in which he has been engaged, such as lists of customers regarded as confidential, have been restrained."

In the case of *Soeder v. Soeder* (82 Ohio App. 71, 77 N.E.2d 474 (1947)) the Court held:

> Disclosure of secrets secured by an employee in the course of confidential employment, such as lists of customers, will be restrained by injunctive process.

In the 1960 case of *Hance v. Peacock* (Ohio Com.Pl., 169 N.E.2d 564) the Court held:

> Lists of customers obtained by defendant while in employ of plaintiff's bottle gas business was confidential information and its use by defendant after defendant terminated his employment with plaintiff and began his own business could be enjoined as unauthorized use of a trade secret.

A court of appeals of California case is very much in point to the matter now before this Court, namely, *Alex Food, Inc. v. Metcalfe* (137 Cal.App.2d 415, 290 P.2d 646 (1955)):

> Independent of an express contract, equity will enjoin the disclosure of confidential knowledge of trade secrets which a former employee learned in the course of his employment. The fact that a defendant was employed by plaintiff for years during which he learned the names, address, and requirements of plaintiff's customers justifies injunctive relief where the defendant undertook to use such information in unfair competition to the detriment of plaintiff. Such knowledge is a part of the good will of the business and is a trade secret. A list of customers is a trade secret if there is confidential information as to such customers. To act upon it is an improper use of confidential information and amounts to unfair competition.

This Court concludes that the information available to the defendants Mr. Schummer and Mr. Pickering was confidential information and was the property of the plaintiff, secured and paid for by the plaintiff with the aid and assistance of the defendants while they were employed by the plaintiff in a confidential capacity. The defendants were confidential employees intrusted with information, in the regular course of their employment, of such a nature that it was not necessary that there be a written customer list for an injunction to issue. The defendants are men of high intelligence and this Court concludes that their memories are as good as any written list. The information about the clients and prospective clients was available to the defendants up until the day of their termination of employment.

This Court grants the temporary injunction per the plaintiff's motion filed November 27, 1961.

Town and Country House & Homes Serv., Inc., v. Evans

1963 (Conn.) 189 A.2d 390

SHEA, J. The plaintiff conducts a housecleaning business and provides men and machinery for that purpose. The defendant was employed by the plaintiff from May, 1957, to March, 1960. It was the plaintiff's custom to require its employees to sign covenants binding them, under certain circumstances, not to engage in the housecleaning business after the termination of their employment with the plaintiff. The defendant was requested to sign such a covenant but refused to do so. He worked for the plaintiff at the homes of various customers in Fairfield County in this state and in Westchester County in New York.

During the latter part of his employment, he told a number of the plaintiff's customers that he was planning to enter the housecleaning business for himself, and he solicited business from them. Thereafter, the defendant terminated his employment and started his own house-cleaning business. At the time of the trial he had fifteen regular customers, some of whom were former customers of the plaintiff.

On these facts, the trial court concluded that the relationship between the parties was the ordinary one of employer and employee; that the defendant was not entrusted with any of the plaintiff's confidential communications and did not learn any peculiar secrets or gain any private information while he was in the plaintiff's employ; that there was nothing secret about the plaintiff's list of customers; that, in the absence of fraud or express contract, the defendant had a right to start his own business and could legally solicit business from his former employer's customers; and that judgment should be rendered for the defendant.

. . .

The plaintiff has also assigned error in the court's conclusions, on the ground that the facts set forth in the finding do not support them. He claims that the defendant was not entitled to solicit its customers for his rival business before the termination of his employment. The defendant, as an agent of the plaintiff, was a fiduciary with respect to matters within the scope of his agency. . . . The very relationship implies that the principal has reposed some trust or confidence in the agent and that the agent or employee is obligated to exercise the utmost good faith, loyalty and honesty toward his principal or employer. . . . In the absence of clear consent or waiver by the principal, an agent, during the term of the agency, is subject to a duty not to compete with the principal concerning the subject matter of the agency. . . .

Upon termination of the agency, however, and in the absence of a restrictive agreement, the agent can properly compete with his principal in matters for which he had been employed. "Thus, before the end of his employment, he can properly purchase a rival business and upon termination of employment immediately compete. He is not, however, entitled to solicit customers for such rival business before the end of his employment . . . in direct competition with the employer's business." (Restatement (Second), 2 *Agency* § 393, comment (e)). Knowledge acquired by an employee during his employment cannot be used for his own advantage to the injury of the employer during employment. . . .

The court found that the defendant solicited customers for his own business before his employment with the plaintiff was terminated. Such action was in direct competition with his employer and was contrary to the employer's interest. It was a betrayal of the employer's trust and confidence in the defendant. He is not entitled to the benefits resulting from this unlawful conduct, and he should account to the plaintiff for the profits received from any business done with former customers of the plaintiff who were solicited by him while he was in its employ. Moreover, the plaintiff is entitled to injunctive relief restraining the defendant from performing, either directly or indirectly, any service, in competition with the plaintiff, for any former customers of the plaintiff who were solicited by him prior to the termination of his employment.

The plaintiff also claims that the names of its customers constituted a trade secret and that the court erred in reaching a contrary conclusion. "A trade secret may consist of any formula, pattern, device or compilation of information which is used in one's business, and which gives him an opportunity to obtain an advantage over competitors who do not know or use it. It may be a formula for a chemical compound . . . or a list of customers." (Restatement, 4 *Torts* § 757, comment b; *Allen Mfg. Co. v. Loika, supra,* 516, 144 A.2d 306, 309) Matters of public knowledge or of general knowledge in an industry cannot be appropriated by one as his secret. A trade secret is known only in the particular business in which it is used. It is not essential that knowledge of it be restricted solely to the proprietor of the business. He may without losing his protection, communicate the secret to employees or to others who are pledged to secrecy. Nevertheless, a substantial element of secrecy must exist, to the extent that there would be difficulty in acquiring the information except by the use of improper means. Some of the factors to be considered in determining whether given information is a trade secret are (1) the extent to which the information is known outside the business; (2) the extent to which it is known by employees and others involved in the business; (3) the extent of measures taken by the employer to guard the secrecy of the information; (4) the value of the information to the employer and to his competitors; (5) the amount of effort or money expended by the employer in developing the information; (6) the ease or difficulty with which the information could be properly acquired or duplicated by others. . . .

Trade secrets are the property of the employer and cannot be used by the employee for his own benefit. The lack of any express agreement on the part of the employee not to disclose a trade secret is not significant. The law will import into every contract of employment a prohibition against the use of a trade secret by the employee for his own benefit, to the detriment of his employer, if the secret was acquired by the employee in the course of his employment. . . . A list of customers, if their trade and patronage have been secured by years of business effort and advertising and the expenditure of time and money, constitutes an important part of a business and is in the nature of a trade secret. It is the property of the employer and may not be used by the employee as his own property or to this employer's prejudice. . . . If in any particular business the list of customers is, because of some peculiarity of the business, in reality a trade secret and an employee has gained knowledge thereof as a matter of confidence, he will be restrained from using that knowledge against his employer. (1 Nims, op. cit. §157) On the other hand, where the identity of the customers is readily ascertainable through ordinary business channels or through classified business or trade directories, the courts refuse to accord to the list the protection of a trade secret. . . .

The plaintiff brought this action in equity requesting, in its prayer for relief, an accounting of profits, an injunction and damages. If the list of customers was a trade secret, the plaintiff would be entitled, in addition to any other proper relief, to an injunction restraining the defendant from performing services for customers on the list. . . . On the other hand, if the list of customers was not a trade secret, the right to injunctive relief and damages would apply only to business done with customers solicited before the end of the employment. Thus, the measure and extent of the relief to which the plaintiff may be entitled depends on a proper determination of whether the plaintiff's list of customers was a trade secret. The court's conclusion that there was nothing secret about the plaintiff's list of customers is not supported by any subordinate facts in the finding. We are unable to determine what factors were considered by the court in reaching this conclusion. Without the necessary facts to support it, it cannot stand.

There is error, the judgment is set aside and a new trial is ordered.

Haymes v. Rogers

1950, (Ariz.) 222 P.2d 789

DECONCINI, J.   In our former opinion, June 12, 1950 (70 Ariz. 257, 219 P.2d 339), we held that as a matter of law there was bad faith shown on the broker's part which precluded him from recovery of his commission. In the light of the motion for rehearing and a re-examination of the evidence and instructions we are constrained to change our view.

Kelley Rogers, hereinafter called appellee, brought an action against L. F. Haymes, hereinafter referred to as appellant, seeking to recover a real estate commission in the sum of $425.00. The case was tried before a jury which returned a verdict in favor of appellee. The said appellant owned a piece of realty which he had listed for sale with the appellee, real estate broker, for the sum of $9,500. The listing card which appellant signed provided that the commission to be paid appellee for selling the property was to be five (5%) per cent of the total selling price. Tom Kolouch was employed by the said appellee as a real estate salesman, and is hereinafter referred to as "salesman."

On February 4, 1948 the said salesman contacted Mr. and Mrs. Louis Pour, prospective clients. He showed them various parcels of real estate, made an appointment with them for the following day in order to show them appellant's property. The salesman then drew a diagram of the said property in order to enable the Pours to locate and identify it the next day for their appointment. The Pours, however, proceeded to go to appellant's property that very day and encountering the appellant, negotiated directly with him and purchased the property for the price of $8,500. The transcript of evidence reveals that the appellant knew the Pours had been sent to him through the efforts of appellee's salesman, but whether he knew it before they verbally agreed on a sale and appellant had accepted a $50 deposit was in dispute. Upon learning that fact he told the Pours that he would take care of the salesman.

Appellant makes several assignments of error and propositions of law directed against the appellee's requested instructions given by the trial court and the court's refusal to grant his requested instructions and a motion for an instructed verdict in favor of the defendant.

The trial court correctly refused defendant's motion for an instructed verdict in his favor, because the matter of bad faith on the part of the appellee broker should have been submitted to the jury.

The important proposition of law relied upon by the appellant is as follows:

The law requires that a real estate broker employed to sell land must act in entire good faith and in the interest of his employer, and if he induces the prospective buyer to believe that the property can be bought for less, he thereby fails to discharge that duty and forfeits all his right to claim commission and compensation for his work.

There is no doubt that the above proposition of law is correct. A real estate agent owes the duty of utmost good faith and loyalty to his principal. The immediate problem here is whether the above proposition is applicable to the facts in this instance.

The facts here are as follows: The salesman informed the purchasers that he had an offer of $8,250 for the property from another purchaser which he was about to submit to appellant. He further told them he thought appellant would not accept the offer, but they might get it for $8,500.

Mr. Rogers, the appellee broker, testified that appellant phoned him after he had accepted the $50 deposit from the purchasers and informed him that he had closed the deal himself and felt that he owed no commission but would split the commission with him, which he, the appellee, refused to do. He further testified that the appellant told him that if their other offer from a third person had been $8,500 he would have accepted it and paid a full commission.

The evidence in this case presents a close question as to good or bad faith on the part of the broker. The trial court should have submitted that matter for the jury to decide. This court has held in negligence cases where the question is close or is in the "shadow zone" that the trial court should not as a matter of law decide those things but rather submit the question to the jury. (*Dillon v. City of Yuma*, 55 Ariz. 6, 97 P.2d 535.) We feel that while the facts are not analogous, yet the principle of law is the same and decline to decide what is bad faith as a matter of law because that is within the province of the triers of fact. The appellant is entitled to have the jury weigh the evidence and inferences therefrom as to whether or not appellee acted in bad faith in the light of the foregoing.

We wish to reiterate that a broker or salesman owes the utmost good faith to his principal as does any other person acting as agent or in a fiduciary capacity. If an agent betrays his principal, such misconduct and breach of duty results in the agent's losing his right to compensation for services to which he would otherwise be entitled. . . .

In this case the appellant sold the property to a purchaser whom he knew was sent to him by the appellee's salesman. Therefore, in the absence of bad faith the broker is entitled to his commission when he is the procuring cause of sale. . . .

Judgment is reversed and the case remanded for a new trial with directions to submit the question of bad faith on the part of the appellee to the jury.

Judgment reversed.

Richard v. Falleti et ux.

1951, 13 N.J. Super. 534, 81 A.2d 17

BIGELOW, J. A. D. The appellant, Richard, a real estate broker, sues for the unpaid half of a commission earned on the sale of land. The trial court held that plaintiff's right was contingent on delivery of the deed and rendered judgment for defendants inasmuch as the deed had not been delivered.

By the contract between the parties to the action, the defendant agreed to pay a commission of $750 "in consideration of services rendered in connection with the sale" of defendants' premises; "said commission to be paid one-half on signing agreement for sale of property and the balance on delivery of deed." The agreement of sale was signed the same day and $3,000 on account of the purchase price was paid. At the same time, the defendants paid plaintiff $375, being one-half the stipulated commission. Two and one-half months later—time having been made of the essence —defendants tendered the deed, but the buyer failed to pay the purchase price, "stating that he did not have in hand funds necessary to perform on his part." And so there was no delivery of deed.

It is familiar law that in the absence of a special agreement, a broker earns his commission when he produces a customer able and willing to buy the property upon the seller's terms. The broker is entitled to a commission if the seller accepts the broker's customer and enters into a binding contract with him, even though the buyer eventually proves to be financially unable to carry out the purchase. (*Freeman v. Van Wagenen,* 90 N.J.L. 358, 101 A. 55 (Sup. Ct. 1917); *Matz v. Bessman,* 1 N.J. Misc. (Sup. Ct. 1923); *Brindley v. Brook,* 160 A. 398, 10 N.J. Misc. 612 (Sup. Ct. 1932).) The rule is the same in other jurisdictions. (12 C.J.S., Brokers, § 85, p. 188.) The broker and his employer may, however, by the use of appropriate language, make the broker's right to a commission depend upon a future happening, such as the actual passage of title from vendor to purchaser. . . .

Where a debt has arisen, liability will not be excused because, without fault of the creditor and due to happenings beyond his control, the time for payment, as fixed by the contract, can never arrive. (Restatement, *Contracts,* § 301; Williston, *Contracts,* § 799; *Goldfarb v. Cohen,* 92 Conn. 277, 102 A. 649 (Conn. 1917).) . . .

In the instant appeal, the broker completed performance on his part when he induced the purchaser to sign the agreement of sale. He was under no duty to assist at the closing of title. The promise to pay him a commission was not in form conditional. "We hereby agree to pay to

Carmine Richard a commission in the amount of $725." The clause fixing the time for payment is independent, separated by a semicolon from the agreement to pay, _____ "said commission to be paid one-half on signing of Agreement of Sale and the balance on delivery of deed." We are satified that the obligation to pay was not made contingent on delivery of the deed. The commission fell due when it became evident that the buyer could not or would not pay for the land.

The judgment is reversed.

CHAPTER 33
REVIEW QUESTIONS AND PROBLEMS

1. *P* sued *D,* his employer, in a common law action for injuries sustained by *P* when his clothes became entangled in the mechanism of a power-driven corn elevator which *P* was operating on *D*'s farm. *P* was aware of the danger present because of the machine. What result?

2. *D* gave *P,* a real estate broker, a single listing which provided that if the real estate was sold within one year after expiration of listing to anyone with whom *P* had negotiated, *P* would be entitled to a commission. After the listing expired, another broker sold the property to *B*. *B* had discussed the property with *P* during the period of *P*'s listing. Is *P* entitled to a commission?

3. *P* employed *A* as manager of his business and authorized him to buy such supplies and merchandise as was needed. Being a member of CO-OP, *A* purchased all of his supplies through it. At the end of the year, he received a personal dividend of $900 because of the purchases. Is he entitled to retain it? Assume that he purchased the supplies as advantageously as he could have at any other place.

4. *P* Co. was engaged in a wholesale business supplying goods to hospitals and novelty stores, *A* being its manager. *A,* while still working for *P* Co., agreed with a salesman of *P* Co. and a third party to enter a competing business and arranged to handle two lines for which *P* Co. previously held the exclusive agency. *A* quit and entered the competing business, but *P* Co. seeks to enjoin them from operation. What result?

5. *B,* appointed to sell merchandise in a certain area for *S,* was to receive a commission of 2 per cent on all sales. He received a weekly advance of $750 for ten weeks but his commissions averaged only $40 a week. Does he owe *S* the $350 difference?

6. *P,* a real estate broker, sold *D*'s house to *X*. *P* prepared a real estate contract to be executed by the parties. *P* sued *D* for commission and *D* defended on the ground that *P*'s action in preparing the contract

constituted unauthorized practice of law and therefore the whole transaction was illegal and *P* could not collect a commission. What result?

7. *D* listed his house for sale with *P*, a real estate broker. The contract provided that *P* would be paid his commission "at the time of final settlement." *P* sold *D*'s house to *X* and a contract was signed. *X* breached the contract. Is *P* entitled to a commission?

8. *P* sued *D*, his agent, for rental collected by *D*. *D* had rented a night depository, but *D* had kept the rent in his desk, from which two week's collections were stolen. What result?

9. *P* sold a car to *M*, relying on *M*'s statement that he was 21. *A*, who worked as a mechanic for *P*, knew *M* and was aware of the fact that *M* was only 19 years old. *M* seeks to avoid the contract. Is *P* chargeable with knowledge of *M*'s age? Is *A* liable to *P* for failure to tell *P M*'s age?

10. *A*, with proper authority, bought certain goods for cash from *T* on behalf of *P*. *T* gave *A* a bonus of $100 for making the purchase from him. Assume that *A* acted in the best interest of *P* and could not have procured a more favorable contract elsewhere. Is *P* entitled to recover the bonus from *A*?

11. *P* employed *A* as a general workman in his factory for one year at a salary of $500 per month. One of the tasks of general workmen was the washing of windows in the factory. *P* desired to induce *A* to quit his job, because *P* did not like *A*, although *A* always performed his duties as well as any other workman. Knowing that *A* had an extreme aversion to height of any kind, and a strong distaste for washing windows, *P* assigned *A* to that job, permanently. Under these circumstances, is *A* justified in not following *P*'s instructions, so that if he does, *P* may not discharge him without liability?

12. *A*, at *B*'s instruction, repossessed *C*'s car. *B* had no right to repossess the car. *C* sued *A* for wrongful conversion of his car. *A* seeks to join *B* in the suit and attempts to impose any liability on *B* which he, *A*, may have to *C*. May he do so?

13. *P* employed *A* as a sales representative in the State of Alaska. Is *A* entitled to a commission on all sales within Alaska including direct orders to *P*? If customers fail to pay *P* for credit purchases, is *A* still entitled to a commission?

14. *A*, while driving a company vehicle, negligently injures *X*. *X* sues *A*'s employer and collects $10,000. *A* inherits $15,000 and *A*'s employer demands that *A* reimburse the employer the $10,000. If *A* refuses, could the employer collect it by suit?

chapter 34

Termination of Agency

4-51 Introduction. Termination of the agency relationship involves basically two questions. First, what acts or facts are sufficient to terminate the authority of the agent insofar as the direct parties are concerned? Second, what is required to terminate the agent's authority insofar as third parties are concerned? The latter question recognizes that an agent may continue to have the *power* to bind the principal but not the *right* to do so. The methods of termination are usually divided into termination by act of the parties and termination by operation of law. The discussion which follows is limited to termination of the agency relationship. It should be remembered that termination of the master and servant relationship will frequently be subject to the terms of an applicable collective bargaining agreement and the employer does not necessarily have the right to terminate all employment relationship at will. In addition, the provisions of the Civil Rights laws relating to promotion and tenure of employment must be considered by employers but are beyond the scope of the discussion which follows.

4-52 By Act of the Parties. Termination by act of the parties includes termination by force of their agreement or by the act of one or both of the parties. An example of the former is an agency which is created to continue for a definite period of time. It ceases, by virtue of the terms of the agreement, at the expiration of the stipulated period. If the parties consent to the continuation of the relationship beyond such period, the courts imply the formation of a new contract of employment. The new agreement contains the same terms as the old one and continues for a like period of time, except that no implied contract can run longer than one year because of the Statute of Frauds.

Another example is an agency created to accomplish a certain purpose which automatically ends with the completion of the task assigned. In such case third parties are not entitled to notice of the termination. Furthermore, when it is possible for one of several agents to perform the task, such as selling certain real estate, it is held that performance by the first party terminates the authority of the other agents.

Any contract may be terminated by mutual agreement; therefore, the agency relationship may be severed in this manner. Furthermore, either party to the agreement has full *power* to terminate it whenever he desires although he possesses no *right* to do so.[1] Wrongful termination of the agency by either party subjects him to a suit for damages by the other party.[2] An exception to these rules exists in the case of so-called agencies coupled with an interest. Such agencies cannot be terminated without the consent of the agent, and a full discussion of them will be found in a subsequent section.

4-53 Wrongful Termination and Its Effect. An employment which continues at the will of the parties may be rightfully terminated by either party at any time.[3] On the other hand, if the employer wrongfully terminates a contract which was to continue for an agreed period, he becomes liable for damages. If the agent is discharged for cause, such as failure to follow instructions or to exercise proper care or for nonperformance of various other duties, he may not recover damages from his employer.

The employee whose employment has been wrongfully cut short is entitled to recover compensation for work done before his dismissal and an additional sum for damages. Most of the states permit him to bring an action either immediately following the breach, in which he recovers prospective damages, or after the period has expired in which event he recovers the damages actually sustained. In the latter case, he is compelled to deduct from the compensation called for in the agreement the amount which he has been able to earn during the interim.[4] Under such circumstances, the employee is under a duty to exercise reasonable diligence in finding other work of like character. Apparently this rule does not require him to seek employment in a new locality or to accept work of a different kind or more menial character. His duty is to find work of like kind, provided it is available in the particular locality.

4-54 Termination by Law. Certain acts are held by law to terminate the agency. Among these are death,[5] insanity, bankruptcy of either of the parties, or destruction of the subject matter of the agency. Bankruptcy has such an effect only in case it affects the subject matter of the agency.

It is said of such cases that the agency is immediately terminated and that no notice need be given to either the agent or the third parties.

---

1 *Sarokhan v. Fair Lawn Memorial Hospital, Inc.,* page 739.
2 *Shumaker v Hazen,* page 741.
3 *Brekken v. Reader's Digest Special Products, Inc.,* page 742.
4 *People v. Johnson,* page 743.
5 *Bowman v. Bowman,* page 744.

However, with reference to insanity, unless the principal has been publicly adjudged insane, it is believed that an agent's contracts are binding on the principal unless the third party is aware of the mental illness, especially where the contract is beneficial to the insane principal's estate.

4-55 Agency Coupled with an Interest. An agency coupled with an interest cannot be terminated without the consent of the agent. Such agencies are of two classes: those in which the agent has a legal or equitable interest in the subject matter, and those in which the agency is created as a source of reimbursement to the agent because of money owed him by the principal. This latter type is most often called an *agency coupled with an obligation.* Although it cannot be terminated by the principal during his lifetime, it is terminated by death. A true agency coupled with an interest is not terminated in either case. To illustrate: A mortgagee who receives a mortgage in which is included a provision giving him the right to sell in case of default could not have this right taken away during the lifetime or by the death of the principal. On the other hand, an agent who is given the right to sell a certain automobile and to apply the proceeds on a claim against the principal has his right cut off by the death of his principal.

Under either type of agency, it should be clear that the interest in the subject matter must be greater than the mere expectation of profits to be realized. In other words, a principal who has appointed an agent to sell certain goods on commission could certainly have the power to terminate the agency at any time although his conduct might constitute a breach of the agreement. See *Sarokhan v. Fair Lawn Memorial Hospital, Inc.* p. 739 for a discussion of contracts coupled with an interest.

4-56 Notice in Event of Termination. Termination of the agency, as explained above, may take place by act of the parties or by operation of law. If the parties by their own action have terminated the agency, it is the duty of the principal to notify all third parties, who have learned of the existence of the agency, of its termination. Without such notice the agent would still possess apparent authority to act for his principal. Those persons entitled to such notice may be divided into two groups: (1) those who have previously relied upon the agency by dealing with the agent; and (2) those who have never previously dealt with the agent, but who, nevertheless, have learned of the agency. The principal's duty to the first class can be satisfied only by the actual receipt of notice of the termination by the third party. The principal satisfies his duty to the second group by giving public notice, such as newspaper publicity, in the location involved. If any one of the second group, not having seen the newspaper account of the termination, relies upon the continuation of the agency to his detriment, he has no cause of action against the principal. If a member of the first group has not received direct notice from the principal, but has learned indirectly of the severance of relation or of facts sufficient to place him on inquiry, he is no longer justified in extending credit to the agent or otherwise dealing with him as a representative of the principal.

Where the agency is terminated by action of law, such as death, insanity, or bankruptcy, no duty to notify third parties is placed upon the principal. Such matters receive publicity through newspapers, official records, and otherwise, and third parties normally become aware of the termination without the necessity for additional notification. If the death of the principal occurs before an agent contracts with a third party, the third party has no cause of action against either the agent or the estate of the principal unless the agent is acting for an undisclosed principal. In the latter case, since the agent makes the contract in his own name, he is liable to the third party. Otherwise, the third party is in as good a position to know of the death of the principal as is the agent.

Two additional problems of notice need be considered. Must an undisclosed principal give notice of termination? Since the failure to give notice allows liability on a theory of apparent authority and there is no apparent authority in cases involving undisclosed principals, notice of termination is not required.

The other problem involves notice in cases of special agents as distinguished from general agents. Ordinarily, notice is not required to revoke the authority of a special agent since the agent possesses no continuing authority and no one will be in a habit of dealing with him. However, if the principal has directly indicated that the agent has authority in a certain matter or at a certain time, notice will be required to prevent reliance on the principal's conduct by a party dealing with the agent. This is especially true if the agent is acting under a special power of attorney. Actual notice of termination is required in these cases.

TERMINATION OF AGENCY CASES

Sarokhan v. Fair Lawn Memorial Hospital, Inc.

1964 N.J. 83 N.J. Super. 127, 199 A.2d 52

A doctor brought suit to enjoin a hospital from terminating his services as medical and surgery director of the hospital and for other relief. Plaintiff had no financial investment in the hospital but had a written contract for 10 years. The agreement provided that it could not be revoked or altered during the period. Plaintiff had organized the hospital and was given rather complete control over it. A controversy developed and the Board of Directors of the hospital sought to discharge the Plaintiff.

KILKENNY, J. A. D.   The contract herein was one for the rendition of personal services. This is so even though the duties of the job required a person "knowledgeable in the medical arts and in the processes of medical administration," as the contract noted. Personal service contracts are generally not specifically enforceable affirmatively. Equity will not compel performance of the personal services, even where the contract involves a "star" of unique talent, because equity will not make a vain decree. At most, equity will restrain violation of an express or implied negative covenant, thus precluding the performer from performing for somebody else.

So, too, it is a general rule that agency contracts are not specifically enforceable in a suit brought by the agent against his principal. Courts are not wont to force a principal to keep an agent against his will, "because the law has allowed every principal a power to revoke his deputation at any time." To do so would violate the basic concept in the law of agency, *viz.*, the right of a principal to select his own *alter ego,* to exercise his *delectus personarum.*

The mere fact that the appointment recites that it will be irrevocable during the term of the appointment does not preclude the principal from exercising the power to revoke it. So, too, "it is not necessary for the principal to have any good reasons for his action in revoking the agency, and he may cancel the agent's authority at his caprice, even though the instrument creating the agency contains an express declaration of irrevocability." This does not mean that the principal may breach such a contract with impunity. For a wrongful breach, the agent may sue at law and recover money damages. Normally, that is the only remedy available to him. The same rule is applicable to a partnership agreement, a mutual agency relationship in which co-owners carry on a business for profit. . . .

The trial court was concerned about the possible injury to plaintiff's professional reputation that might result from termination of the contract. This possible impairment of the agent's reputation, as a basis for ordering specific performance of a personal service contract, was considered by our then highest court in *Fiedler, Inc. v. Coast Finance Co., Inc., supra,* and rejected. (129 N.J.Eq., at p. 165, 18 A.2d at p. 270, 135 A.L.R. 273) Such an element of damage can be proved "with as much accuracy as any unliquidated claim can be ascertained." *(Ibid)* Similarly rejected in *Hewitt v. Magic City Furniture & Mfg. Co., supra,* was plaintiff's contention therein that specific performance would give him the opportunity to make a reputation for efficiency in the superintendence of defendant's business that would be of great future advantage to him in the business world.

Specific performance of personal services contracts is refused for the further reason that they lack mutuality of enforcement. The employee or agent, reinstated by judicial decree, might abandon his duties on the next day, and a court of equity could not compel him to perform. The wronged principal's only remedy would be an action at law for money damages. *Fiedler, Inc. v. Coast Finance Co., Inc., supra,* noted that a want of mutuality in the remedy warrants denial of specific performance. "If the enforcement of the obligation may not be granted to both contracting parties, it should not be enforced against one party."

The law has recognized, as an exception to the general rule, that "an agency coupled with an interest" cannot be revoked by the principal during the term fixed for its existence. Even the death of the principal does not terminate it. The best known case setting forth this exception is *Hunt v. Rousmanier* (8 Wheat. (U.S.) 174, 5 L.Ed. 589 (1823)). In that case, Hunt loaned money to Rousmanier and to secure repayment of the debt the borrower gave the lender a power of attorney to sell a vessel, with authority to deduct from the proceeds the balance due on the loan and turn over the residue to the borrower. The issue was whether the power survived the death of Rousmanier, the giver of the power. The rule was laid down that the death of the principal does not revoke an agency coupled with an interest.

Defendants concede that, if the contract herein created an agency coupled with an interest, they would not have the power to revoke it. They maintain that such an agency was not created. We agree. The test of an agency coupled with an interest is stated in 2 Williston, *Contracts* (3rd Ed.), § 280, pp. 301-302, as follows:

> Does the agent have an interest or estate in the subject matter of the agency independent of the power conferred, or does the estate or interest accrue by or after the exercise of the power conferred?
>
> If the former, it is an agency coupled with an interest, or as has been suggested, a proprietary power; if the latter, it is not.

If the agency is given as security for a debt or obligation, it is regarded as an agency coupled with an interest. "In order that a power may be irrevocable because coupled with an interest, it is necessary that the interest shall be in the subject matter of the power, and not in the proceeds which will arise from the exercise of the power." (3 Am.Jur.2d, *Agency*, § 62). The agency herein was not given as security for some obligation due plaintiff. He had no interest in the subject matter of the power independent of the power conferred. The power conferred by defendant hospital was not one "coupled with an interest." Accordingly, it is not irrevocable, despite the terminology used by the parties.

We conclude that the contract in issue did not create an agency coupled with an interest and that defendants had and have the *power* to terminate it. It becomes unnecessary for us to decide whether the contract contravenes public policy. We make no determination as to whether defendants breached any contractual *right* of plaintiff in terminating his relationship with the hospital. Those reserved issues will require a plenary trial for resolution, as will the tort claims set forth in the first two counts of the complaint.

The order under review is reversed and the injunction pendente lite *is dissolved. The matter is remanded to the Chancery Division for further proceedings not inconsistent herewith.*

Shumaker v. Hazen

1962 (Okl.) 372 P.2d 873

Plaintiff sued defendant alleging that defendant had employed plaintiff to sell 12,700 shares of stock in the Utex Exploration Co. at stated percentage commissions, that plaintiff could have sold the stock but defendant refused to allow him to do so. Plaintiff had been given an irrevocable power of attorney for one year but defendant had cancelled it during the year. Plaintiff contended that defendant had by this act prevented the performance of the contract.

JOHNSON, J. . . . The power of attorney in this case provided that it should be "irrevocable" for a period of one year. The law is well settled that a principal may revoke an agent's authority at any time and is not at all affected by the fact that there is an express or implied contract that the agency is irrevocable unless the power is coupled with an interest.

We hold that . . . this was not a power coupled with an interest.

Therefore, the power to revoke is beyond question but subject to the qualifications set forth in the fourth paragraph of the syllabus in the McKellop case, *supra.*

> The principal, having the power to revoke an agency, is liable in damages if, by the revocation, substantial injury is sustained by the agent.

The defendant was therefore answerable in damages.
Affirmed.

Brekken v. Reader's Digest Special Products, Inc.

1965, 353 F.2d 505

MERCER, J. Summary judgment was entered in this suit for damages arising out of the alleged improper termination by defendant of the plaintiffs' contracts of employment. This appeal followed:

Each of the plaintiffs was employed by defendant as a regional manager pursuant to the provisions of a written, form contract executed by the parties. Each plaintiff was discharged from employment within one year after his contract had been signed.

The controversy relates to the construction of the following provisions of the contracts, to-wit:

> This agreement shall be effective from the date of execution and shall remain in effect for a period of twelve months and will be automatically renewed for twelve-month terms unless sooner terminated.
> This agreement may be terminated by either party upon written notice or by Manager's death.

Plaintiffs do not question the adequacy of the notice given if defendant had the legal right to terminate the contracts within the first year of their life.

Plaintiffs argue that the words "unless sooner terminated" apply only to renewal periods subsequent to the expiration of the initial term. That argument is born from the contemplation of the plaintiffs' frustrated hopes, not from any tenable legal foundation.

The well established principles guiding the construction of ambiguous contract provisions are of no help to plaintiffs in the light of the plain provisions of these contracts. An employment contract for a stated term, which is expressly terminable by either party upon notice, must be recognized as a valid contract and its provisions must be given effect.

It cannot be doubted as plaintiffs assert that they expected their employment to continue for at least one year, but that was merely an expectation and not a right guaranteed by the contracts which they signed. The courts cannot rewrite the contracts which they made. Clearly the phrase "unless sooner terminated" relates to the whole sentence of which that phrase is a part. The court below correctly construed each of these contracts as being terminable at will.

Affirmed.

People v. Johnson

1965 (Ill.) 205 N.E.2d 470

A writ of mandamus was sought to compel City of Chicago officials to pay the back salary accrued during a period of wrongful discharge of one Jack F. Bourne, referred to as Relator. Relator was a civil service employee who was suspended from city employment because of his debts. The debts were incurred during the illness and death of his wife and the wrongfulness of the discharge had been established in a separate administrative hearing.

From March 5, 1962 to January 4, 1963, Relator worked from 5:00 P.M. to 2:00 A.M. at a liquor store for $105 a week. These hours were not during the hours of his city employment and he also worked the same hours at the liquor store prior to his discharge. The City had no rule against "moonlighting."

UNDERWOOD, J. . . . The defendant officials contend the courts erred in holding the monies earned in the liquor store employment should not be set off against the back salary. . . . Relator concedes that the right of setoff exists as to earnings by an employee during the period of wrongful discharge, but contends that this rule embraces only those earnings which would have been incompatible with the prior employment. The precise question for our consideration is, therefore, whether an employer who wrongfully discharges an employee is entitled to credit on a back-pay award for subsequent earnings of the employee from a secondardy job, compatible with, and held by the employee in conjunction with the principal employment.

We have previously and specifically held the employer entitled to set off the employee's earnings from other employment against the salary accruing during the period he was improperly prevented from performing his duties.

The theory underlying a suit for back salary is to make the employee whole—to compensate him to the extent that the wrongful deprivation of salary has resulted in financial loss. For that reason the amount recoverable is to be reduced by his other earnings during the period of separation insofar as such income would have been incompatible with performance of his duties to his erring employer. But this does not necessitate mitigation of the recoverable salary by earnings compatible with and being received during the employment from which the employee is wrongfully discharged. There is in this record no hint of incompatibility between Relator's liquor store employment and his obligation to the municipality, either in the form of regulatory proscriptions or conflicting hours or duties. In fact, relator held both jobs for a substantial period of time prior to his wrongful discharge. As was aptly observed by the Appellate Court, the industrious holder of two compatible jobs who is wrongfully discharged from one should not be penalized by permitting the wrongdoer to deduct from the damages for which he is liable the earnings of the second job during the period of wrongful discharge.

Embraced in defendants' argument is the contention that relator must establish his use of reasonable diligence to secure substitute employment before he may recover damages in the form of back salary, but we believe defendants misplace the burden. The defendants were here the wrongdoers, and the obligation to produce whatever proof existed in diminution of damages rested on them. The overwhelming weight of authority, in this State and elsewhere in this country, is that an employer in an action for lost wages must affirmatively show in order to reduce damages that the discharged employee could or did have other earnings subsequent to the wrongful discharge. (See cases collected in annotations in 150 A.L.R. 100, 121, and 17 A.L.R.2d 968, 978-982.) There is here no proof that Relator regarded his liquor store employment as a substitute for his municipal employment, except such probative value as may attach to the fact that the former terminated about the time of his reinstatement to the latter, and this scarcely serves to outweigh the fact that he performed the duties of both for a substantial period prior to the municipal discharge. Nor is there any showing of lack of diligence in seeking additional employment during the hours formerly occupied by the municipal work. We therefore conclude that where an employee simultaneously holds two compatible jobs and is wrongfully discharged from one, his employer may not set off the earnings from the remaining job against liability for lost wages in the absence of proof of a lack of diligence by the employee in seeking additional employment or that the remaining job was regarded as a complete substitute for the prior dual employment.

Bowman v. Bowman

1965 3 Ohio Misc. 161, 210 N.E.2d 920

Petitioner, the executrix of the will of her deceased husband, seeks construction of the will.

ANDREWS, C. R   . . . Item 2 reads as follows:

> I give, devise and bequeath any and all business enterprises that I may own or have the right to dispose of at the time of my decease, to my wife, IRMA B. BOWMAN, provided, however, that after six (6) months from the date of my decease, I make my daughter, Doris E. Briggs, a full partner in all such business enterprises with my wife, IRMA A. BOWMAN; provided further that upon the death of Irma Bowman then the business enterprises above mentioned are to be solely owned by my daughter, Doris E. Briggs.

It is evident that a "business enterprise," as referred to in the will, must consist of some sort of business capable of being transferred by will. For example, had testator owned, as an individual proprietor, a grocery store business, he could have transferred his ownership by will or, for that matter, by an *inter vivos* transaction.

However, the evidence shows that Mr. Bowman, the deceased, was a "manufacturer's representative," doing business under the name of Vince G. Bowman Company, with offices at 4500 Euclid Avenue, Cleveland, Ohio. The company was not incorporated. Mr. Bowman was "the company." Income tax returns were filed by him as sole proprietor. There was no written lease for the offices, and the tenancy was apparently from month to month.

At the time of Mr. Bowman's death, the company (meaning Mr. Bowman) was the sales representative for six manufacturing companies. As such, the company negotiated sales on behalf of the manufacturers. The buyers of the products paid the manufacturer directly, and the manufacturer, in turn, paid a monthly commission to the Vince G. Bowman Company.

Except in the case of one manufacturer, there was no written contract, and even with this manufacturer, as with the others, the arrangement was not for a fixed period. To the contrary, the relationship could be canceled by either party at any time. Moreover, there was testimony that the right to represent the various manufacturers was regarded as personal and nontransferable.

John Briggs, the testator's son-in-law, worked as a salesman for Vince G. Bowman Company, beginning in 1953. Before his employment by Mr. Bowman, the testator, the matter was cleared with the various manufacturers, who gave their consent thereto. Mr. Biggs was paid a salary by Vince G. Bowman Company, plus a year-end bonus when warranted.

After Mr. Bowman's death, Mr. Briggs became the manufacturer's representative for the six companies. This was through appointment by the companies. With permission of Mrs. Irma A. Bowman, the testator's wife, Mr. Briggs continues to use the name Vince G. Bowman Company. He is located at the same office and pays the rental.

The company has about one thousand dollars' worth of office furniture, which, of course, is part of Mr. Bowman's estate. By agreement among members of the family, Mr. Briggs is continuing to use the office furniture.

At the time of testator's death, the company also had funds on deposit in the bank, and there was money due it by way of accounts receivable. These items, too, were part of Mr. Bowman's estate.

The inventory and appraisement, under "Accounts and Debts Receivable," lists $18,000 due the testator as "Vince G. Bowman & Company, Manufacturer's Representative, unincorporated business." It is conceded that the $18,000 includes, in addition to actual accounts receivable, the furniture and bank accounts. . . .

It is obvious that Mr. Bowman did not own the type of "business enterprise" which can be transferred by will, sale, or otherwise. He was in legal effect an agent or broker for the firm he represented, and the law of agency governed the rights and liabilities of the parties.

The very definition of agency precludes the agent from transferring this sort of "business enterprise" by will or otherwise, as shown by Restatement, *Agency* 2d, Sec. 1:

> Agency is the fiduciary relation which results from the manifestation of consent by one person to another that the other shall act on his behalf and subject to his control, and consent by the other so to act.

There can be no agency without the consent of the principal. The principal appoints or employs the agent. And it is basic that death terminates the agency in the absence of a power coupled with an interest, which is not present here. The rule is so strict that even where the agent, with authority, has appointed a subagent, the death of the agent terminates the authority of the subagent to act for the principal.

It is clear that the testator had no power to transfer to another person by will or in any other manner his right to represent his principals as their agent. And this was the only "business enterprise" in which he was engaged.

Admitting, as we have seen, that the testator had no power to bequeath his agency, may we say that Item 2 is nevertheless effective to pass the assets of the Vince G. Bowman Company, consisting of the furniture, bank accounts, and accounts receivable? I think not. The wording of Item 2 indicates an intention to bequeath a going business, to be operated by the widow for six months; then by the widow and her daughter, Mrs. Doris E. Briggs, as partners; and after the death of Mrs. Bowman, the widow, by Mrs. Briggs alone.

Although had there been a "business enterprise" to bequeath, the assets would have passed as part of it, I think it would be completely illogical and unrealistic to interpret Item 2 as passing the mere furniture and other business assets when there was no devisable business enterprise. After all, it would be rather ludicrous to hold that Mrs. Bowman and her daughter could be partners in a desk. Moreover, desks, bank accounts, and accounts receivable are not, by themselves, "business enterprises."

For the reasons given, I hold that Item 2 is inoperative and that nothing passes by it. . . .

(The property then passed under the residuary clauses of the will.)

Judgment accordingly.

CHAPTER 34
REVIEW QUESTIONS AND PROBLEMS

1. *P* engaged *A* to operate a retail lumber business in the latter's name. *A* sold merchandise to *T* on credit. Later *P* notified *T* that *A*'s agency was terminated and directed *T* to pay the debt to *P*. *T* later disregarded

instructions and paid the obligation to *A*, who failed to account to *P*. May *P* collect from *T*?

2. *X* and *Y* had an employment contract which provided that it would remain in effect for 12 months and would be automatically renewed for 12-month terms unless sooner terminated. It also provided that the agreement could be terminated by either party on written notice or by employee's death. *X* gave written notice of termination within the initial 12-month period. *Y* sues *X* for breach of contract. What result?

3. *P* sued *D* for specific performance of a real estate contract and *D* defended on the ground that the purchase price had not been paid. *D* had employed *A* as its agent for several years and *A* had collected several payments on the real estate. *D* discharged *A* but failed to notify *P*, who continued to make payments to *A*. *A* kept the payments. What result?

4. *X* signed a note which contained a confession of judgment clause. *X* died and *P*, the holder, thereafter confessed judgment on the note. *X*'s executor moved to set the judgment aside on the ground that the death of *X* terminated the authority of any attorney to confess judgment against him. *P* contended that the agency was coupled with an interest and therefore survived. What result?

5. *A* gave two real estate brokers simple listings on his house. One broker, *X*, found a ready, willing, and able buyer one day and before *A* could notify the other broker, *Y*, *Y* also found a buyer. Is *Y* entitled to a commission?

6. *A* had been employed by *P* as general purchasing agent for *P*'s hardware store for a period of 10 years. *X* had done business with *P* through *A*. *P* discharged *A* for misappropriating funds and put a notice of termination in the paper which *X* did not see. If *A* makes a contract with *Y* for 200 pounds of nails in *P*'s name, is *P* bound?

7. *A*, the buyer for the *X* department store, was discharged. *Y* had never sold to *A* but knew that *A* was *X*'s buyer. After *A* was discharged, an article about his changing jobs was in the newspaper but *Y* did not read it. If *A* purchases goods on credit from *Y*, charging them to *X*, is *X* liable therefor?

BOOK FIVE

Business Organizations

Part One

Partnerships

General Principles

5-1 Definition. In general, organizations for the conduct of business are of three main types—individual proprietorships, partnerships, and corporations. There are some less important types which are discussed in Chapter 43. The law of partnership was introduced into the common law from the law merchant and was later codified in The Uniform Partnership Act, which is herein referred to as the Uniform Act or the Act. This statute adopted by a majority of the states defines a partnership as an association of two or more persons to carry on as co-owners, a business for profit.

A partnership is the result of an agreement. The agreement is not required to be in writing but good business judgment dictates that a partnership agreement should be most carefully prepared and reduced to writing.

One important provision that should be included in a partnership agreement is a "buy and sell" provision. Many problems arise upon the death or withdrawal of a partner and there are many possibilities of litigation and economic loss to all concerned. Many of these problems can be avoided by providing a method whereby the surviving partner can purchase the interest of the deceased partner or the remaining partner can purchase the interest of the withdrawing partner. A method of determining the price to be paid for such interest should be provided. The time and method of payment should be stipulated and the buy and sell agreement should specify whether a partner has an option to purchase the interest or a duty to do so. It is common for partners to provide for life insurance on each other's lives, and in the event of a partner's death the proceeds of the life insurance policy are utilized to purchase the deceased partner's interest.

The existence of a partnership depends upon the intention of the parties, manifested either by an interpretation of their words, spoken or written, or by their conduct.[1] The basic question is whether they intend a relationship which includes the essential elements of a partnership as defined above; not whether they intended to be partners.

If the essential elements of a partnership are present, the mere fact that the parties did not think they were becoming partners is immaterial. If the parties agree upon an arrangement that is a partnership in fact, it is immaterial that they call it something else or that they declare that they are not partners. On the other hand, the mere fact that the parties themselves call the relation a partnership will not make it so if they have not, by their contract, agreed upon an arrangement which by the law is a partnership in fact.

5-2 Partnerships Distinguished from a Corporation. There are three basic distinguishing features between a partnership and a corporation. First, a partnership is the result of an agreement between two or more parties, whereas a corporation comes into existence not by reason of a contract, but by reason of an act of the state. A partnership, therefore, is a creature of contract, whereas a corporation is a creature of the state. Second, the liability of the partners is unlimited; that is, each partner is individually liable for all the obligations of the organization created in pursuit of the partnership business because each partner is an agent for the partnership entity and for each individual partner; whereas the liability of a member of a corporation is limited to the extent of any unpaid balances due upon stock owned by him. Third, a corporation is a taxable entity and must pay an income tax upon its net profits, and the stockholders must also pay an individual income tax upon the dividends which they receive. In a partnership organization the partnership is not a taxable entity, but the individual partner pays a personal income tax upon his share of the profits. The partnership files an income tax return showing the net profit of the firm and the amount allocated to each partner. Each partner must pay an income tax on his share of the profits, even though the income is not distributed to the partners. This is true even if the partnership agreement provides that profits cannot be withdrawn but must remain in the partnership capital.

It should be noted that the shareholders of small business corporations may, by unanimous consent, elect to pay taxes on the corporate income in much the same way as a partnership. In a "tax option" corporation each shareholder pays a tax upon his proportionate share of the earnings, whether distributed or not, and the corporation itself does not pay a tax.

There are many aspects of partnership and corporation law which are similar under modern statutes. Both are legal entities capable of suing and being sued in the firm name. Both can hold title to property and contract in the firm name. The Code treats a partnership as a legal entity for purpose of endorsement of instruments. This, the historical distinc-

---

[1] *Grau v. Mitchell,* page 757.

tion that a corporation was a legal entity whereas a partnership was not, no longer exists.

5-3 Partner by Estoppel. Where a person by words spoken or written, or by conduct, represents himself or consents to another's representing him to be a partner in an existing partnership, or a partner with other persons not in a partnership, he is not a partner but is liable to any party to whom such representation has been made.[2] Such liability, created by estoppel, does not arise, however, unless the third party gives credit to the firm or other persons in reliance upon such representation. If the facts in any particular case indicate that such party knew the true facts, or should reasonably have known them, no liability on the basis of partnership is created. This liability is similar to that of a principal based on apparent authority of an agent or an ostensible agent.

The cases are not in accord as to whether a person is under a duty to affirmatively disclaim a reputed partnership where the representation of partnership was not made by or with the consent of the person sought to be charged as a partner. Some cases hold that if a person is held out as a partner and he knows it, he should be chargeable as a partner unless he takes reasonable steps to give notice that he is not, in fact, a partner. Other cases indicate that there is no duty to deny false representations of partnership where the ostensible partner did not participate in making the misrepresentation.

Estoppel frequently arises when one of the partners in an existing partnership is acting outside the scope of his authority. For example, if one partner, with knowledge of the other partner, uses the firm name for the purpose of giving credit on negotiable instruments for other persons on matters outside the scope of the partnership business, and this course of conduct is allowed by the other partner to continue for a long time, the firm will be bound on the unauthorized indorsement of the negotiable paper by the partner, under the doctrine of estoppel.

5-4 To Carry On As Co-owners a Business for Profit. The essential attributes of a partnership are a common interest in the business and management and a share in the profits and losses. The presence of a common interest in property and management is not enough to prove a partnership. Also, an agreement to share the gross returns of a business, sometimes called gross profits, does not of itself prove an intention to form a partnership. The Uniform Partnership Act provides that the receipt by a person of a share of the real or net profits in a business is *prima facie* evidence that he is a partner in the business.[3] The presumption that a partnership exists by reason of sharing net profits may be overcome by evidence that the share in the profits is received for some other purpose such as payment of a debt by installments, wages, rent, annuity to a widow of a deceased partner, interest on a loan, or as payment for goodwill by install-

---

[2] *Brown & Bigelow v. Roy,* page 758.
[3] *Troy Grain & Fuel Co. v. Rolston et al.,* page 759.

ments.[4] For example, bonuses are frequently paid as a percent of profit and such a payment does not make the employee a partner.

5-5 Partnership Property. It is obvious that a partnership may use its own property, the property of the individual partners, or the property of some third person. It frequently becomes important, especially on dissolution and where claims of firm creditors are involved, to ascertain exactly what property constitutes partnership property in order to ascertain the rights of partners and firm creditors to specific property.

As a general rule, the agreement of the parties will determine what property is properly classified as partnership property. In absence of an express agreement, what constitutes partnership property is ascertained from the conduct of the parties, the partnership agreement, and from the purpose for and the way in which property is used in the pursuit of the business.[5] The Uniform Partnership Act, in general terms, states: (1) All property originally brought into the partnership stock, or subsequently acquired by purchase or otherwise on account of the partnership, is partnership property. (2) Unless the contrary intention appears, property acquired with partnership funds is partnership property.

Since a partnership is a legal entity in some respects with the rights to acquire, own and dispose of personal property in the firm name, legal documents affecting the title to partnership personal property may be executed in the firm name by any partner. The Uniform Partnership Act also treats a partnership as a legal entity for the purposes of title to real estate which may be held in the firm name. Title so acquired can be conveyed in the partnership name, though without words of inheritance, passes the entire estate of the grantor, unless a contrary intent appears. Where title to real property is in the partnership name, any partner may convey title to such property by a conveyance executed in the partnership name. To be effective such a conveyance must be within the terms of the partnership agreement or within the pursuit of the partnership business.

5-6 Firm Name and Goodwill. Since a partnership is created by the agreement of the parties, they select the name to be used. Their right of selection is limited by statute in many states in two ways. First, they may not use the word "company" or other language that would imply the existence of a corporation and, secondly, if the name is other than that of the partners, they must comply with an assumed name statute which requires the giving of public notice as to the actual identity of the partners. Failure to comply with this statute may result in the partnership being denied access to the courts to sue its debtors. A firm name is an asset of the firm, and as such it may also be sold, assigned, or disposed of in any way that the parties agree upon.[6]

Goodwill, which is usually transferred with the name, is based upon the justifiable expectation of the continued patronage of old customers

---

4 *Trojnar v. Bihlman*, page 761.
5 *Sanderfur v. Ganter*, page 762.
6 *O'Hara v. Lance et ux.*, page 763.

and the probable patronage of new customers resulting from good reputation, satisfied customers, established location, and past advertising. It is usually considered in evaluation of the assets of the business, and is capable of being sold and transferred. Upon dissolution caused by the death of one of the partners, it must be accounted for by the surviving partner to the legal representative of the deceased partner unless the Buy and Sell Agreement is to the contrary.

When goodwill and the firm name are sold, an agreement not to compete is usually a part of the sales agreement.[7] See Chapter 12, Contracts, section 2-64. As was noted, these agreements may be implied but it is safer to have a specific provision.

5-7 Partnership Capital. Partnership capital consists of the total credits to the capital accounts of the various partners, provided the credits are for permanent investments in the business. Such capital represents that amount which the partnership is obligated to return to the partners at the time of dissolution, and it can be varied only with the consent of all the partners. Undivided profits which are permitted by some of the partners to accumulate in the business do not become part of the capital. They, like temporary advances by firm members, are subject to withdrawal at any time unless the agreement provides to the contrary.

The amount which each partner is to contribute to the firm, as well as the credit he is to receive for assets contributed, is entirely dependent upon the partnership agreement.

A person may become a partner without a capital contribution. For example, he may contribute services to balance the capital investment of the other partners. Such a partner, however, has no capital to be returned at the time of liquidation. Only those who receive credit for capital investments—which may include good will, patent rights, and so forth, if agreed upon—are entitled to the return of capital when dissolution occurs.

If the investment is in a form other than money, the property no longer belongs to the contributing partner. He has vested the firm with title and he has no greater equity in the property than any other party. At dissolution he recovers only the amount allowed to him for the property invested.

5-8 Property Rights of Partners. The Uniform Partnership Act enumerates the property rights of a partner as (1) his rights in specific partnership property, and (2) his interest in the partnership. A partner is a co-owner with his partners of specific partnership property and subject to any agreement between the partners, a partner has an equal right among his partners to possess partnership property for partnership purposes. He has no right to possess specific partnership property for other purposes without the consent of the other partners. A partner has a right that the property shall be used in the pursuit of the partnership business and

---

[7] *Bergum v. Weber,* page 765.

to pay firm creditors. A partner does not own any specific item of the partnership property. He, therefore, has no right in specific partnership property that is assignable, and any sale by him, as an individual, of a particular part of the partnership property does not pass title to the specific property. He has no right to use firm property in satisfaction of his personal debts [8] and he has no interest in specific partnership property that can be levied upon by his personal creditors.

When a partner dies his right in specific partnership property passes to the surviving partner or partners who possess the property only for partnership purposes subject to the partnership agreement and the rights of the estate of the deceased partner. The surviving partner may sell the property, real and personal, of the partnership in connection with the winding-up of the business.

A partner's interest *in the firm* consists of his rights to share in the profits which are earned and, after dissolution and liquidation, to the return of his capital and such profits as have not been distributed previously. This assumes, of course, that his capital has not been absorbed or impaired by losses.

The Act provides that a partner can assign his interest in the partnership and that such an assignment will not of itself work a dissolution of the firm. The assignee is not entitled to interfere in the management of the business or to require that the books of the firm be made available for his inspection. The only right of the assignee is to receive the profits to which the assignor would otherwise have been entitled and in the event of dissolution to receive his assignor's interest.

At common law a partner's interest could be levied upon by his separate creditors and sold at public sale, but under the Act a separate creditor of a partner must proceed by way of a "Charging Order," which is obtained by a judgment creditor who applies to the court for an order charging the interest of the debtor partner with the unsatisfied amount of the judgment debt.[9] The court will ordinarily appoint a receiver who will receive the partner's share of the profits and any other money due or to fall due to him in respect of the partnership and apply the same upon the judgment. Likewise, the court may order that the interest charged be sold. Neither the charging order nor the sale of the interest will cause a dissolution of the firm.

The Partnership Agreement including the Buy and Sell provisions determines the rights of the partners to such property as the proceeds of life insurance on the life of a partner. Since the insurance is usually intended for use in purchasing the interest of the deceased partner, the Agreement as well as the policy beneficiary provisions must be carefully prepared.

5-9 Powers of Partners over Property. Each partner has implied authority to sell to good-faith purchasers personal property that is held for the purpose of resale and to execute such documents as are necessary to

[8] *Windom National Bank et al. v. Klein et al.*, page 765.
[9] *Shirk v. Caterbone*, page 767.

effect a transfer of title thereof.[10] Of course, if his authority in this connection has been limited and such fact is known to the purchaser, the transfer of title will be ineffective or voidable. A partner has no power to sell the fixtures and equipment used in the business unless he has been duly authorized. Such acts are not a regular feature of the business and a prospective purchaser of such property should make certain that the particular partner has been given authority to sell. The power to sell, where it is present, gives also the power to make such warranties as normally accompany similar sales.

The right to sell firm real property is to be inferred only if the firm is engaged in the real estate business. In other cases, there is no right to sell and convey realty, except where such sale has been authorized by a partnership agreement.

Under the Uniform Act, title to real property may be taken in the firm name, and any member of the firm has power to execute a deed thereto by signing the firm name. In such a case, what is the effect of a wrongful transfer of real estate that has been acquired for use in the business and not for resale? The conveyance may be set aside by the other partners since the purchaser should have known that one partner has no power to sell without the approval of the others. However, if the first purchaser has resold and conveyed the property to an innocent third party, the latter takes good title.

If the title to firm property is not held in the firm name, but is held in the names of one or more of the partners, a conveyance by those in whose names the title is held passes good title, unless the purchaser knows or should know that title was held for the firm. There is nothing in the record title in such a situation to call the buyer's attention to the fact that the firm has an interest in the property.

The power to mortgage or pledge firm property is primarily dependent upon the power, later discussed, to borrow money and bind the firm. A partner with authority to borrow may, as an incident to that power, give the security normally demanded for similar loans. Since no one partner, without the consent of the others, has the power to commit an act that will destroy or terminate the business, the power to give a mortgage on the entire stock of merchandise and fixtures of a business is usually denied. Such a mortgage would make it possible, upon default, to liquidate the firm's assets and thus destroy its business. Subject to this limitation, the power to borrow carries the power to pledge or mortgage.

GENERAL PRINCIPLES CASES

Grau v. Mitchell

1964 (Colo.) 397 P.2d 488

DAY, J. . . . Plaintiff filed suit alleging a copartnership with the defendant in the operation of a business in Parshall, Colorado. He sought dissolution of the partnership, appointment of a receiver, an ac-

---

[10] *Lankford v. State,* page 768.

counting of the partnership assets, liabilities and profits, and distribution to the partners according to their respective rights and interests. . . .

Trial was to the court which entered findings of fact and conclusions of law and judgment of dismissal in favor of defendant. It held that the evidence failed to support this claim. . . .

No good purpose would be served in detailing the complete history of plaintiff's work in and around defendant's business establishment for the period involved. A reading of the record fails to disclose any of the elements of a partnership between the parties.

The real estate was owned by defendant, and there is nothing in the record to establish plaintiff's interest in the real property and improvements thereon. As to the operation of the business, the defendant kept the books, maintained the bank account in her name, paid all the bills, and compensated plaintiff either in cash or "in kind" for all the work that he did. No partnership returns were filed with either the federal or state government. Plaintiff's remuneration had no relationship with the business making or losing money. He was not able to establish any agreement for a share of the profits, and there was nothing to make him liable for any of the debts.

At one time in the relationship there was some talk of a partnership, and pursuant thereto, an agreement drawn up which plaintiff refused to consummate because, as he said, "he wasn't going to assume any part of the indebtedness; also, he wanted a half interest in the entire real estate." This evidence in itself would be sufficient to defeat the claim of a partnership.

This court has stated that a partnership is a contract, express or implied, between two or more competent persons to place their money, effects, labor or skill, or some or all of them, into a business, and to divide the profits and bear the losses in certain proportions.

In reading the record one cannot find any evidence of an agreement, oral or written, express or implied, wherein the parties were joined together to carry on the business for a profit and to share the losses. The . . . claim was properly dismissed. . . .

Affirmed.

Brown & Bigelow v. Roy

1955, (Ohio App.) 132 N.E.2d 755

MILLER, J. This is a law appeal from the judgment of the Municipal Court rendered in favor of the plaintiff-appellee for the sum of $413.66 and interests and costs. The action was one on an account for goods and merchandise sold and delivered to the F. & M. Truck Stop, an alleged partnership consisting of Clarence F. Roy, the appellant, and H. Fay Lucas, who was not a party to the action.

The answer was a general denial. Upon request being made the court filed separate findings and conclusions of law and fact. Those pertinent to the issues presented are:

(1) The merchandise was "purchased by the partnership, and sold to it."

(2) That the defendant-appellant "held himself out or permitted himself to be held out as a partner in the F. & M. Truck Stop."

(3) That the defendant-appellant is estopped from denying such partnership; and

(4) That no notice or publication pertaining to termination or dissolution of said partnership was made by the defendant.

All of the errors assigned relate to the sufficiency of the evidence to sustain the judgment, the appellant urging that his motion to dismiss at the close of plaintiff's case and again at the conclusion of all of the evidence, should have been sustained.

No direct proof of a partnership was offered, but the same was based upon the conduct of the appellant at the place of business; that a sum of money was advanced by the appellant which he testified was a loan to the other alleged partner and upon the further fact that a vendor's license was secured from the State of Ohio in the name of "Henry F. Lucas and Clarence F. Roy, DBA F. & M. Truck Stop." The application for this license was signed by both of the alleged partners and the license issued in response thereto was posted at the place of business of the alleged partnership. It is urged that the evidence does not disclose that the appellee had any knowledge of the information contained in the license and therefore there could have been no reliance placed on the statements it contained; that the doctrine of estoppel has no application. We concur with counsel for the appellant upon his factual conclusion and are of the opinion that his views as to the law would be correct were it not for the fact that our statutory law modifies the common-law rule. Section 1775-15 of the Revised Code provides:

> When a person, by words spoken or written or by conduct, represents himself, or consents to another representing him to any one, as a partner in an existing partnership or with one or more persons not actual partners, he is liable to any such person to whom such representation has been made, who has, on the faith of such representation, given credit to the actual or apparent partnership, and if he has made such representation or consented to its being made in a public manner he is liable to such person, whether the representation has or has not been made or communicated to such person so giving credit by or with the knowledge of the apparent partner making the representation or consenting to its being made.

Clearly the defendant represented that he was a partner in the business when he signed the application for a vendor's license and the posting of the license at the place of business was notice to the public of the nature of the business being conducted on the premises. The Court did not err in holding that the defendant was a partner.

Affirmed.

Troy Grain & Fuel Co. v. Rolston et al.

1950, (Mo. App.) 227 S.W.2d 66

The plaintiff, Troy Grain & Fuel Co. brought this action against Miller Howard and Jackson Rolston, as partners, for the unpaid balance due for corn and oats delivered. Howard owned two trucks and it was agreed that he would furnish the trucks and Rolston the labor in hauling grain. The profits from the operation were to be divided equally. A judgment was rendered in favor of the plaintiff and defendant Howard appealed.

SPERRY, Commissioner. . . . Howard stated that he and Rolston verbally agreed that Rolston should furnish the labor and use his trucks in hauling grain; that Rolston should keep books on the transactions, pay all expense of operation, and give Howard half of the profits as rent on the trucks; that Rolston kept books and delivered same to him, which he then had in court (but they were not offered in evidence); that Rolston kept the bank account in his own name and wrote all checks thereon; that they operated under this arrangement until shortly after these transactions occurred. He denied the existence of a partnership or that he was to bear any losses occuring in the operation.

The evidence made a submissible case on the question of partnership between Howard and Rolston. Partnership is a relation arising out of contract expressed or implied whereby two or more parties agree to engage in a common enterprise, each contributing capital or services and each sharing in the profits and losses. (47 C.J. 648 *et seq.*). In the absence of proof of an express contract a partnership may be proved by evidence of the entire transaction, and construed from that, in the light of surrounding circumstances. (*Willoughby v. Hildreth,* 182 Mo. App. 80, 91, 167 S.W. 639). The testimony of both Howard and Rolston was to the effect that they agreed that Howard should furnish his trucks, Rolston furnish the labor, and that Rolston should buy, transport, and sell grain, the profits thereof to be equally divided after payment of expenses. Sharing the profits of a business venture, where one furnishes capital and the other labor, constitutes *prima facie* evidence of the existence of a partnership. (*Willoughby v. Hildreth, supra,* 182 Mo. App. *loc. cit.* 91, 167 S.W. 639). While an agreement to share profits in such a venture is not conclusive proof of the existence of a partnership, it is *prima facie* proof thereof and raises a presumption of partnership. If such presumption is not overcome by other evidence tending to prove that, in fact, the parties intended there to be no partnership, such prima facie proof of the existence of a partnership becomes conclusive. It is true that there was no direct proof that the partners were to share the losses accruing in the venture, nevertheless their agreement to share profits implies a sharing of loss; and that presumption can only be overcome by evidence tending to prove the contrary. While a partnership relationship necessarily rests on contract, as between the parties themselves, the contracting parties are not required to know and fully understand all of the legal incidents flowing therefrom. Parties "entering into agreements and transactions which, by the law of the land constitute them partners, whatever they may please to say or think about it, or by whatever name they may choose to call it," will be held to be partners. (*Meyers v. Field,* 37 Mo. 434, 439). We hold that there was substantial evidence tending to prove that Howard and Rolston were partners; and the determination of that question was for the jury.

. . . *The judgment should be affirmed.*

Trojnar v. Bihlman

1964 (Ind. A.C.) 200 N.E.2d 227

HUNTER, J. This is an appeal from the Lake Circuit Court wherein the trial judge sustained a motion for a directed verdict filed by the defendant-appellee at the close of the plaintiff-appellant's evidence. The appellant alleged as a basis for the cause of action in the lower court that the appellee was liable to the appellant for additional compensation for overtime work in excess of forty (40) hours per week during the two and one-half (2½) years that the appellant was employed by the appellee, and further alleged that the appellee was liable to the appellant for a share of the profits of appellee Bihlman Enterprises, Inc., based upon the existence of a partnership agreement between the appellant and the appellee Bihlman. The defendant-appellee in his answer alleged full payment of any debt due the appellant, and denied the existence of a partnership agreement. . . .

In the pleadings filed in the trial court, the appellant inferentially alleged that a partnership agreement existed between the plaintiff-appellant and the defendant-appellee. The theory was raised also in the brief filed by the appellant in this court. The existence or non-existence of a partnership is controlled by the provisions of the Uniform Partnership Act. . . . Under this act, specific rules have been formulated to determine whether or not a partnership exists. . . . the following provisions have been established:

> In determining whether a partnership exists, these rules shall apply:
> (1) Except as provided by section 16, persons who are not partners as to each other are not partners as to third persons.
> (2) Joint tenancy, tenancy in common, tenancy by the entireties, joint property, common property, or part ownership does not of itself establish a partnership, whether such co-owners do or do not share any profits made by the use of the property.
> (3) The sharing of gross returns does not of itself establish a partnership, whether or not the persons sharing them have a joint or common right or interest in any property from which the returns are derived.
> (4) The receipt by a person of a share of the profits of a business is prima facie evidence that he is a partner in the business, but no such inference shall be drawn if such profits were received in payment:
>   (a) As a debt by installments or otherwise,
>   (b) As wages of an employee or rent to a landlord,
>   (c) As an annuity to a widow or representative of a deceased partner,
>   (d) As interest on a loan, though the amount of payment vary with the profits of the business,
>   (e) As the consideration for the sale of a goodwill of a business or other property by installments or otherwise. . . .

To afford himself the remedy of recovery under the theory of partnership, the appellant necessarily should have proved the existence of a partnership . . . by the evidence presented at the trial. The appellant failed, however, to bring himself within the provisions of the Uniform

Partnership Act, by the testimony presented. The record does not show the existence of a written partnership agreement, nor does it show the existence of an implied agreement, nor does it show a periodic sharing of the profits of the appellee's business, which would raise a presumption in favor of the appellant's allegation of the existence of a partnership agreement. The plaintiff-appellant having failed to prove a *prima facie* case of partnership, the directing of a verdict on the part of the trial court was correct with respect to the issue of partnership.

The appellant contends that the terms of his employment contract were based upon a forty-hour work week, and that any labor in excess of the forty hours constituted overtime, which required additional compensation. There is, however, no evidence of the existence of an hourly wage. The evidence further shows that the appellant worked varying numbers of hours in separate weeks while still receiving an identical salary for each week's labor. The appellant's salary was increased on two occasions during his two and one-half year term of employment, but the evidence introduced in the trial court fails to show any discussion between the appellant and appellee concerning an overtime rate and the actual number of hours of overtime labor. At no time during the term of employment did the appellant demand overtime compensation. At the termination of the employment, the appellant requested only his compensation for his final week's labor, and further that the appellee purchase a truck which the appellant had used in the business. No demand was made for compensation for alleged overtime labor during the two and one-half years that the appellant had been employed. In addition, there was no evidence of a demand for a sharing of the profits, which the appellant alleges was promised to him by the appellee at the inception of the term of employment. . . .

Judgment affirmed.

Sanderfur v. Ganter

1953, (Ky. Ct. App.), 259 S.W.2d 15

The plaintiff, Dr. Fred Ganter, is seeking to recover possession of office space from the defendant Dr. B. D. Sanderfur. Plaintiff's father had secured a 10-year lease on the space for the practice of optometry. Plaintiff was called into military service and during his absence the father entered into a partnership agreement with the defendant which gave the latter an option to purchase an interest in the office equipment, but which did not mention the lease or the office space. The office space was actually used for partnership purposes. Plaintiff's father died and the executrix assigned all interests in the lease to the plaintiff. The defendant continued in possession claiming under the right of a surviving partner. The trial court ruled in favor of the plaintiff and defendant appealed.

CULLEN, C.   This is an appeal by Dr. B. D. Sanderfur from a judgment which held that Dr. Fred Ganter is entitled to the exclusive possession of certain office space in a building in Glasgow, and which mandatorily enjoined Dr. Sanderfur to surrender possession of the office to Dr. Ganter.

. . . The only basis upon which Dr. Sanderfur claims to be entitled to occupy the offices is that the lease (or at least Dr. George Ganter's interest in the lease) was a partnership asset. The trial court found that it was not, so our concern is with the correctness of that finding.

. . . The question of whether property which was owned by a partner prior to the formation of the partnership has been contributed by him to the firm so as to become partnership property, is a question of the intention of the parties, and the mere fact that the property is used in the firm business will not of itself show that it is firm property. (Cases cited) As concerns real estate owned by a partner, it has been held that there is a presumption against its inclusion in the partnership, and in order that it be treated as belonging to the partnership, the intention must be clearly manifested. While a lease is technically not real estate, we think that the reasons behind the rule with respect to real estate may be equally as applicable to a lease.

We find nothing in the partnership agreement here, or in the conduct of the parties, to show that the lease was intended to be contributed by Dr. George Ganter to the partnership as an asset. The agreement shows clearly that Dr. Ganter was not contributing his equipment, and there is no reason to conclude that he intended to contribute or donate the lease, which, as evidenced by this lawsuit, was a valuable item of property.

It is our opinion that the trial court correctly found that the lease was not a partnership asset, and therefore Dr. Sanderfur has no basis for his claim of right to occupy the office.

O'Hara v. Lance et ux.

1954, 77 Ariz. 84, 267 P.2d 725

The defendant, General W. Lance, established a business known as the Ace-Lance Refrigeration Company in Phoenix in 1942. In 1946 the defendant and the plaintiff entered into a partnership agreement and continued in the same business as "Ace-Lance & O'Hara Refrigeration Company." In 1949 the partnership was dissolved, Lance selling all partnership assets, including goodwill, to O'Hara. Lance agreed not to compete for a period of two years and granted to O'Hara the exclusive right to the firm name except for the condition that after December 21, 1950, O'Hara might not further use Lance's name without his consent. In 1951 the plaintiff sued to enjoin the defendant from competing and to restrain him from using the word "Ace" in the firm name of any refrigeration business in Arizona. The lower court denied this relief and held that the defendant alone had the right to use the word "Ace." The plaintiff appealed.

TULLAR, J. . . . The first and primary step is to determine what was bought and sold at the time of the dissolution of the partnership. Happily, the agreement of the parties is explicit. Lance, "the retiring partner," is being paid, "for his share in the business and the capital, stock, equipment, effects and good will thereof." The agreement recites that valuations and estimates have been placed upon these items, and agreed to, specifically including the good will, and a balance has been struck.

In the law of partnership, it is the rule that, in the absence of agreement to the contrary, a sale of assets and good will of a commercial partnership carries with it the right to use the partnership name. (Cases cited.) We are not here dealing with a "professional" partnership (see, e.g., *Hunt v. Street,* 182 Tenn. 167, 184 S.W.2d 553), wherein the law is quite different.

A conveyance of the good will of a business carries with it an implied covenant to do nothing which would derogate from the grant. If the vendor of the good will re-engage in business, it is his duty to conduct his new business in such a way that it will not appear to be a continuation of the business that he has sold. The vendor has a duty not only to his vendee, but to the public, not to confuse or deceive the customer into thinking he is in one place of business when he is in another. This type of confusion and deceit is the keystone of unfair competition. And, we have previously pointed out, this is the universal test for the presence of unfair competition: Is the public likely to be deceived? (Cases cited.)

So in this case, when Lance included in his sale the good will of the business, he sold to O'Hara the right to the use of the firm name, Ace-Lance & O'Hara Refrigeration Company. And, as the agreement recites, this was "to hold the same unto O'Hara absolutely."

This does not necessarily mean, in law, that Lance has parted with the right henceforth to use his own personal name. Indeed, there is a presumption that no one intends to part with this right, and that an assignment of good will does not, ipso facto, confer upon the assignee the exclusive right to the use of assignor's personal name. While one may sell his own name as a trade name servient to the business to which it is attached, the intent so to divest oneself must clearly be shown.

Lance . . . sold to O'Hara the exclusive use of his personal name as a trade name in the refrigeration business, but only for a limited time. The time limit having expired, there is now no restraint upon Lance's use of his personal name for any lawful purpose he may desire, so long as he does not transgress his obligation not to interfere with O'Hara's right to receive the benefits of his purchase.

. . . Fact and law conclusively show O'Hara's right in and to the use of the word "Ace," in the refrigeration business in his trade area. Lance does not have the same right.

O'Hara has prayed for state-wide restraint. He is, however, entitled to protection only in the territory from which he received business or might reasonably be expected to receive business in the future. His protection should extend as far as his business reputation and his goods have become known.

The judgment of the trial court is reversed with directions to dissolve the restraining order and enter judgment in favor of plaintiff, Richard O'Hara and against the defendants, General W. Lance and Vera Lance, his wife, granting to plaintiff the right to use the name, "Ace," and granting to plaintiff an injunction restraining the defendants, General W.

*Lance and Vera Lance, his wife, or either of them, and all persons act-
ing for them or under them, from using the name, "Ace," in any refrigeration business within the area served by the Phoenix metropolitan
area telephone directory.*

Bergum v. Weber

1955, 136 Cal. App.2d 389, 288 P.2d 623

Plaintiff, Bergum, bought the entire interest of defendant, his former
partner, in the partnership including goodwill. The defendant thereafter
solicited business from customers of the old partnership and the plaintiff
sought to enjoin such solicitation. The trial court dismissed the action
and plaintiff appealed.

NOURSE, J. pro tem. . . . Did the defendant, by the contract alleged
in the complaint, impliedly covenant not to directly solicit the customers
of plaintiffs who had been customers of the business he had sold to
them[?]

We have come to the conclusion that this question must be answered
in the affirmative.

The goodwill of a business is property and may be transferred. The
customers of a business are an essential part of its goodwill. In fact, without their continued custom goodwill ceases to exist, for goodwill is the
expectation of continued public patronage.

When the goodwill of a business is sold, it is not the patronage of the
general public which is sold, but that patronage which has become an
asset of that business. It follows that one who has sold his interest in the
goodwill of a business can no more act directly to destroy that asset than
he could to destroy or make useless any other asset which he had for
value transferred to the purchaser.

The law implies in every contract a covenant that neither party will
do anything that will deprive the other of the fruits of his bargain.

The direct solicitation by the seller of the customers of the business,
the goodwill of which he has sold, is a violation of this covenant.

This implied covenant does not prevent the seller from engaging in a
competing business and by fair means soliciting the business of the public
generally. It does prevent him from directly soliciting the patrons of the
business he has sold.

Relief sought by plaintiff was granted.

Windom National Bank et al. v. Klein et al.

1934, 191 Minn. 447, 254 N.W. 602

Four brothers owned and operated as partners a dairy farm under the
firm name of Bender Bros. The plaintiff bank had an unsatisfied personal
judgment against two of the brothers and in conformity with the provisions of the Uniform Partnership Act had a receiver appointed over all
the right and interest of the two brothers in the partnership. The court
also gave an order charging *their interest* in the firm with payment of the
judgment debt. The two brothers had mortgaged certain specific partner-

ship property to the defendants, Klein and others, and this action by the bank was for the purpose of annulling these mortgages. The defendants demurred and the lower court sustained the demurrer. Plaintiffs appealed.

STONE, J. . . . The tenancy in partnership created by the statute is an innovation on the common law. Its genesis was in the "inequitable results" of the long established judicial habit of applying to partnership property the analogies of joint tenancy. Some of them (particularly a joint tenant's unrestrained power of disposition) did not fit. The result was "very great confusion" where separate creditors of a partner tried to reach specific partnership property or where a partner attempted to dispose of it for his own purposes. ("Commissioners' Note," 7 U.L.A. 33) Thus it appears that tenancy in partnership is a restricted adaptation of common-law joint tenancy to the practical needs of the partnership relation. One of those needs arose from the formerly conflicting claims to specific partnership property of (1) separate creditors of a partner and (2) assignees of a partner's share in an aliquot part of the firm assets. To meet that need, two simple "incidents" have been attached to the tenancy in partnership: (1) Expressly, the interest of each tenant or partner in specific partnership property is put beyond reach of his separate creditors; and (2) it has been made nonassignable. That means simply that the partner owner is deprived of all power of separate disposition even by will.

All a partner has now, subject to his power of individual disposition, and all that is subject to the claims of his separate creditors, is his interest, not in specific partnership property, but in the partnership itself. Plain is the purpose that all partnership property is to be kept intact for partnership purposes and creditors. The statutory incidents of the partnership cotenancy are attached thereto for that purpose, which will be pro tanto thwarted as effect is given to an attempted disposition of a partner's interest in specific partnership property. The aim of the statute is to prevent such an assignment.

. . . Dean William Draper Lewis, one of the commissioners who drafted the Uniform Partnership Act, has said, in explanation of its purpose to "avoid the consequences of regarding partners as joint tenants" that "while any partner has an equal right with his copartners to possess partnership property for partnership purposes" and while he "may assign partnership property for a partnership purpose, . . . if he attempts to assign the property for his own purposes he makes no assignment at all, because the act destroys the quality of assignability for any but a partnership purpose."

. . . It follows that a receiver, such as plaintiff Gillam, of a partner's "share of the profits," acting under a charging order and § 28 (Mason's Minn. St. 1927, § 7411), has the right in a proper action to have adjudicated the nullity of any mortgage or other assignment by some but not all of the partners of their interest in specific property of the partnership less than the whole. Such a receiver is entitled to any relief under the language of the statute "which the circumstances of the case may require" to accomplish justice under the law. Obviously, a part of such relief is the avoidance of any unauthorized attempt to dispose of partnership property. Such a receiver is entitled to the "share of profits and surplus" (§ 26, Mason's Minn. St. 1927, § 7409) of the partner who happens to be the judgment debtor. While he is not entitled to share in the management of the firm as a partner, the receiver would be of little use if he could not protect "profits and surplus" by preventing such unauthorized and illegal dissipations of firm assets as the complaint alleges in this case.

The complaint states a cause of action. It was error to sustain the demurrer.

The order sustaining the demurrer was reversed because the partners could not lawfully mortgage partnership property to secure personal indebtedness.

Shirk v. Caterbone

1963 (Penn.) 193 A.2d 664

FLOOD, J. . . . We have examined the question raised in the appeal and find no merit in the appellant's position. The appellant seeks priority for a charging order entered in his favor upon a judgment against a member of a partnership, as against a levy, made later, upon personal property of the partnership under a judgment obtained against the partnership by the plaintiff. The court below properly held that the charging order has priority. The levy against the partnership reached all the tangible personal property of the partnership levied upon, and was a lien upon the property. The charging order, on the other hand, reached only the distributive share of the judgment-defendant Caterbone, one of the partners, in the assets of the partnership after all its debts had been paid and was not a lien upon any specific property of the partnership.

Section 28 of the Uniform Partnership Act of March 26, (1915, P.L. 18, 59 P.S. § 75) provides that upon due application to a competent court by any judgment creditor of a partner the court which entered the judgment may "charge the interest of the debtor partner with payment of the unsatisfied amount of such judgment debt with interest thereon; and may then or later appoint a receiver of his share of the profits, and of any other money due or to fall due to him in respect of the partnership. . . ." It is obvious from this language that the creditor of the individual partner is entitled only to his debtor's share of the profits or of the net assets upon liquidation. It is equally obvious that the amount due a partnership creditor is a liability that must be discharged before the amount of net assets is determined out of which profits are due to a partner. The partnership creditor who has obtained judgment is entitled to be paid out of partnership assets and may levy upon its tangible property. The creditor of the individual partner, on the other hand, can be paid only out of what remains to the individual partner as his share of the profits after the partnership obligations, including those of any judgment creditor of the partnership have been satisfied. He cannot reach partnership property in execution.

Appeal quashed.

Lankford v. State
1965 Ga. 144 S.E.2d 463

This action upon an open account was brought by Universal Creditors Association, Inc., as assignee of a firm composed of several medical doctors, against Leonard R. Wood and Joan C. Wood. The defendants except to the trial court's judgment overruling their general demurrer. Defendants contend . . . that the petition fails to state a cause of action because plaintiff is not a real party in interest due to the assignment by only one doctor of the firm.

BELL, J. . . . Defendants argue that the assignment of the claim to plaintiff fails to show that the assignor is a legal entity; and that the plaintiff corporation "can stand in no better position than its transferor." The assignment of the claim, a copy of which is annexed to the petition as an exhibit, shows that it was executed by one member of a named "firm" composed of several medical doctors, on behalf of the firm. In common acceptation the word "firm" is synonymous with "partnership." Any member of a partnership may in its behalf transfer in writing choses in action belonging to the firm. The assignment to the corporation, the plaintiff in this case, being valid, there is no merit in the defendants' contention that the plaintiff is not a real party in interest.

The trial court properly overruled defendants' general demurrer to plaintiff's petition.

Judgment affirmed.

CHAPTER 35
REVIEW QUESTIONS AND PROBLEMS

1. *A* and *B* as partners rented a cannery for one season. They entered into a contract with *P*, a broker, whereby it was agreed to label all products with *P*'s label, to allow *P* the exclusive right to sell their entire output and to pay him 5 per cent of gross sales. *P* guaranteed the cannery a supply of cans and other material and promised to advance money for operating expenses and payroll. For this advance *P* was to receive as "extra compensation" one-half the net profits of the cannery for the season. *P* had the right to control wages and payroll for the cannery. Is *P* a partner?

2. *A* is hired to operate a store owned by *P*. It is agreed that *A* shall receive for his services one-third of the net profits. No profits result, but losses are incurred. Must *A* share in these losses? Is he a partner?

3. *M* wished to purchase a tract of land, plat it, and sell the lots. He

needed capital, and *P* loaned him $6,000. *M* gave *P* a note and it was understood that when the lots were sold the proceeds would first be used to pay the $6,000 to *P*. Any profits above the $6,000 would be divided equally. Was there a partnership?

4. *P* and *D* entered into an agreement for trading in grain futures. *P* furnished the funds for margin requirements and profits and losses were to be shared. No partnership income tax return was ever filed. The authorization for *D* to trade on *P*'s account with the brokerage company referred to *D* as *P*'s "agent." Do these last two facts prevent a holding that a partnership existed?

5. *A*, a grain broker, and *B*, his brother, a farmer, entered into an agreement whereby each was to pay to the other annually for three years one-half the profits of his business, and also to make good one-half the losses that might be suffered by the other. The ownership of each individual business was to be distinct. *B* became bankrupt. To what extent, if any, could *A* be made to satisfy the claims of *B*'s creditors?

6. *A* agreed to loan money to *P* and to indorse notes for him in order that *P* might operate a lumber mill. For this consideration, *A* was to receive one-third of the profits. Was there a partnership?

7. *A* and *B* formed a partnership, and *A* contributed an unpatented invention. He later took out the patent in his own name. To whom does the patent belong upon dissolution?

8. *A* invests $10,000 and *B* $5,000 in a certain business for profit. With the investment they purchase 15 pianos. What is the interest of each one in the pianos?

9. *A* and *B* were equal partners in the transfer and drayage business. They owned six trucks with which they conducted their business. *C*, a creditor of *A*, levied on three of the trucks and had them sold to *H*. Did *H* obtain good title to the trucks?

10. *A* and *B* are partners. *A* dies, and *B* continues the business in his own name. In accounting for the firm assets, he refuses to make any allowance for good will. May the executrix of *A* recover an additional sum for the good will of the business? Give a definition of good will.

11. *A*, *B*, and *C* formed a partnership to purchase and develop a subdivision of suburban real estate. Title to some of the property was taken in the name of College Crest Realty Company, other portions of the realty were taken in the name of *A*, *B*, and *C* jointly, and some in *C*'s name. In each of the above situations what will be necessary to convey proper legal title to a purchaser?

12. A partner assigned his interest in the partnership to *X* as collateral security. The partner continued to be active in the partnership affairs. What are the rights of the assignee, *X*?

chapter 36

Rights, Duties and Powers of Partners

RELATIONS OF PARTNERS TO ONE ANOTHER

5-10 In General. The rights that a partner has as against his co-partners, as well as his duties to them, will generally be defined by the partnership agreement. For example, the amount of his investment, his right to interest thereon, and the share of the profits to be credited to him, along with his right to share in the management of the business or to receive compensation for such, are matters usually controlled by the articles of copartnership. When the agreement is silent on these matters, the rules found in the Uniform Partnership Act which has been adopted by almost all of the States will control. These are set forth in the sections immediately following. In those few states which have not adopted the U.P.A., other statutes or common law will control. The powers of a partner are essentially those of an agent and these will be discussed in the latter portion of this chapter.

5-11 Sharing of Profits and Losses. Unless the Agreement is to the contrary, each partner has a right to share equally in the profits of the enterprise, and each partner is under a duty to contribute equally to the losses. Capital contributed to the firm is a liability owing by the firm to the contributing partners. If, on dissolution, there are not sufficient assets to repay each partner his capital, such amount is considered as a loss and must be met like any other loss of the partnership. For example, a partnership is composed of *A, B,* and *C. A* contributed $20,-000, *B* contributed $10,000, and *C* contributed $4,000. The firm is dissolved, and upon the payment of firm debts there remains only $10,000 of firm assets. Since the total contribution to capital was $34,000, the operating loss is $24,000. This loss must be borne equally by *A, B,* and *C,* so that the loss for each is $8,000. This means that *A* is entitled to be reimbursed to the extent of his $20,000 contribution less $8,000, his share of the loss, or net of $12,000. *B* is entitled to $10,000, less $8,000, or $2,000. Since *C* has contributed only $4,000, he must now contribute to the firm an additional $4,000 in order that his loss will equal $8,000. The additional $4,000 contributed by *C,* plus the $10,000 remaining, will now be distributed so that *A* will receive $12,000 and *B* $2,000.

Occasionally articles of copartnership specify the manner in which profits are to be divided, but neglect to mention possible losses. In such cases, the losses are borne in the same proportion that profits are to be shared. In the event that losses occur when one of the partners is insolvent and his share of the loss exceeds the amount owed him for advances and capital, the excess must be shared by the other partners. They share this unusual loss, with respect to each other, in the same ratio that they share profits.

Thus in the above example, if *C* is insolvent, *A* and *B* would each bear an additional $2,000 loss.

In addition to the right to be repaid his contributions, whether by way of capital or advances to the partnership property, the partnership must indemnify every partner in respect of payments made and personal liabilities reasonably incurred by him in the ordinary and proper conduct of its business, or for the preservation of its business or property.

5-12 Partner's Right to Interest. Contributions to capital are not entitled to draw interest unless they are not repaid when the repayment should be made. The partner's share in the profits constitutes the earnings upon his capital investment. In absence of an expressed provision for the payment of interest, it is presumed that interest will be paid only on advances above the amount originally contributed as capital. Advances in excess of the prescribed capital, even though credited to the capital account of the contributing partners, are entitled to draw interest from the date of the advance.

Unwithdrawn profits remaining in the firm are not entitled to draw interest. Such unwithdrawn profits are not considered advances or loans by the mere fact that they are left with the firm. However, custom, usage, and circumstances may show an intention to treat such unwithdrawn profits as loans to the firm.

5-13 Right to Participate in Management. All partners have equal rights in the management and conduct of the firm business. The partners may, however, by agreement, place the management within the control of one or more partners. The right to an equal voice in the management and conduct of the business is not determined by the share that each partner has in the business.

In regard to ordinary matters arising in the conduct of the partnership business, the opinion of the majority of the partners is controlling. If the firm consists of only two persons, and they are unable to agree, and the articles of partnership make no provision for the settlement of disputes, dissolution is the only remedy.

The majority cannot, however, without the consent of the minority, change the essential nature of the business by altering the partnership agreement or by reducing or increasing the capital of the partners; or embark upon a new business; or admit new members to the firm.

There are certain acts other than those enumerated above which require the unanimous consent of the partners, in order to bind the firm, namely: (1) assigning the firm property to a trustee for the benefit of creditors; (2) confessing a judgment; (3) disposing of the goodwill of the business; (4) submitting a partnership agreement to arbitration; and (5) doing any act which would make impossible the conduct of the partnership business.

5-14 Partner's Right to Be Compensated for Services. It is the duty of each partner, in absence of an agreement to the contrary, to give his entire time, skill, and energy to the pursuit of the partnership affairs. No partner is entitled to payment for services rendered in the conduct of the partnership business, unless an agreement to that effect has been expressed or may be implied from the conduct of the partners.[1] Often one of the partners does not desire to participate in the management of the business. The partnership agreement in such case usually provides that the active partners receive a salary for their services in addition to their share in the profits. A surviving partner is entitled to reasonable compensation for his services in winding up the partnership affairs.

5-15 Right to Information and to Inspection of Books. Each partner, whether active or inactive, is entitled to full and complete information concerning the conduct of the business and may inspect the books to secure such information. The partnership agreement usually provides for a bookkeeper and each partner is under a duty to give the bookkeeper whatever information is necessary efficiently and effectively to carry on the business. It is the duty of the bookkeeper to allow each partner access to the books and to keep them at the firm's place of business. No partner has a right to remove the books without the consent of the other partners. Each partner is entitled to inspect the books and make copies therefrom, provided he does not make such inspection or copies to secure an advantageous position or for fraudulent purposes.

5-16 Fiduciary Relation of the Partners. A partnership is a fiduciary relationship[2] and each partner owes the duty of undivided loyalty to

---

[1] *Waagen v. Gerde et ux.*, page 775.
[2] *Hurst v. Hurst*, page 776.

the other. Therefore, every partner must account to the partnership for any benefit, and hold as a trustee for it any profits gained by him without consent of the other partners from any transaction connected with the formation, conduct, or liquidation of the partnership, and account for any use by him of the partnership property. This duty also rests upon representatives of deceased partners engaged in the liquidation of the affairs of the partnership.

The partnership relation is a personal one, and each partner is under duty to exercise good faith, and to consider the mutual welfare of all the partners in his conduct of the business. If one partner attempts to secure an advantage over the other partners, he thereby breaches the partnership relation, and he must account for all benefits that he obtains. This includes transactions with partners and with others.

5-17 Partner's Right to an Accounting. The partners' proportionate share of the partnership assets or profits, when not determined by a voluntary settlement of the parties, can only be ascertained by a bill in equity for an accounting. A partner cannot maintain an action at law against other members of the firm upon the partnership agreement, because, until there is an accounting and all the partnership affairs are settled, the indebtedness between the firm members is undetermined.[3] Partners ordinarily have equal access to the partnership books, and there is no reason why they should be subject to formal accountings to determine their interest. An accounting will not be permitted to settle incidental matters of disputes between the partners, however, unless the disputes are of such a grievous nature as to make impossible the continued existence of the partnership.

In all cases a partner is entitled to an accounting upon the dissolution of the firm. In addition he has a right to a formal accounting without a dissolution of the firm in the following situations:

1. Where there is an agreement for an accounting at a definite date.
2. Where one partner has withheld profits arising from secret transactions.
3. Where there has been an execution levied against the interest of one of the partners.
4. Where one is in such a position that he does not have access to the books.
5. Where the partnership is approaching insolvency and all parties are not available.

Upon an agreement between themselves, the partners may make a complete accounting and settle their claims, without resort to a court of equity.

[3] *Weiser v. Burick,* page 776.

POWERS AND LIABILITIES OF PARTNERS

5-18 Powers in General. A partner is an agent of the partnership for the purpose of its business and the general laws of Agency are applicable to his conduct. It is suggested that Chapter 30 be reviewed. He has the power to bind the partnership both in tort and in contract. The Act provides for contractual liability whenever the partner is apparently carrying on in the usual way the business of the partnership of which he is a member, unless the partner so acting has in fact no authority to act for the partnership in the particular matter, and the person with whom he is dealing has knowledge of the fact that he has no such authority. An act of a partner which is not apparently for the carrying on of the business of the partnership in the usual way does not bind the partnership unless authorized by the other partners.[4]

However, unless authorized by the other partners or unless they have abandoned the business, one or more but less than all the partners have no authority to do those things set forth in Section 5-13.

The Act imposes tort liability upon the partnership for all wrongful acts or omissions of any partner acting in the ordinary course of the partnership.

The rules of Agency relating to authority and secret limitations on the authority of a partner are applicable to partnerships but the extent of implied authority is generally greater for partners than for ordinary agents. Each partner has implied power to do all acts necessary for carrying on the business of the partnership. The nature and scope of the business and what is usual in the particular business determine the extent of the implied powers.

The concept of ratification is also fully applicable to partnerships.

5-19 Trading and Nontrading Partnerships. For the purpose of determining the limit of a partner's powers, partnerships may be divided into two general classes—trading and nontrading partnerships. A trading partnership is one which has for its primary purpose the buying and selling of commodities. In such a trading firm, each partner has an implied power to borrow money and to extend the credit of the firm, in the usual course of business, by signing negotiable paper.[5]

A nontrading partnership is one that does not buy and sell commodities, but that has for its primary purpose the production of commodities or is organized for the purpose of selling services, such as professional partnerships. In such partnerships a partner's powers are more limited and a partner does not have implied power to borrow money or to bind the firm on negotiable paper. However, where the act is within

---

[4] *Bole v. Lyle et al.,* page 777.
[5] *Holloway v. Smith et al.,* page 778.

the scope of the partnership business, a member of a nontrading partnership may bind the firm by the exercise of implied authority just the same as a partner in a trading partnership.

5-20 Notice and Admissions. Each partner has implied authority to receive notice for all of the other partners concerning matters within the pursuit of the partnership business; and knowledge, held by any partner in his mind, but not revealed to the other partners, is notice to the partnership. Knowledge of one partner is knowledge of all. This knowledge, however, must be knowledge obtained within the scope of the partnership business. If the partner could have and should have communicated knowledge to the other partners and fails to do so, his failure would be chargeable to the firm. This rule does not apply, however, if fraud is perpetrated on the partnership by the partner having such knowledge.

Admissions or representations pertaining to the conduct of the partnership business and made by a partner may be used as evidence against the partnership.

RIGHTS, DUTIES AND POWERS OF PARTNERS CASES

Waagen v. Gerde et ux.

1950, 36 Wash.2d 563, 219 P.2d 595

The plaintiff and the defendants were partners in the ownership and operation of a fishing vessel. The plaintiff brought this action for an accounting and alleged that the defendants had wrongfully withheld partnership earnings from the plaintiff. The defendant Karl Gerde perfected a new type of net for catching sharks and contended that he was entitled to compensation for the time and effort expended in constructing the shark nets. The lower court held in favor of the plaintiff and the defendants appealed.

DONWORTH, J. . . . Appellant's final assignment of error is that the trial court erred in refusing to allow appellant any credit for work done by him in constructing the shark nets.

The evidence shows that appellant with some help from his two sons designed and built the shark nets. Respondent did not in any way assist him in this job. According to appellant, the value of this work was $2,-500 and he claims that he should be compensated for this work.

The general rule is clear that one partner is not entitled to extra compensation from the partnership, in the absence of an express or an implied agreement therefor. Each case must depend largely upon its own facts, and thus other cases are generally of little or no assistance in deciding the case at hand.

The exception to the general rule is well stated in 1 Rowley, Modern Law of Partnership 412, § 354, as follows: "Where it can be fairly and justly implied from the course of dealing between the partners, (or) from circumstances of equivalent force, that one partner is to be compensated for his services, his claim will be sustained." *(Emerson v. Durand,* 64 Wis. 111, 24 N.W. 129, 54 Am. Rep. 593) The partnership may be of such a peculiar kind, and the arrangements and the course of dealing of the partners in regard to it may be such as pretty plainly to show an expectation and understanding, without an express agreement upon the subject, that certain services of a copartner should be paid for. Such cases, presenting unusual conditions, are exceptions to the general rule. *(Hoag v. Alderman,* 184 Mass. 217, 68 N.E. 199)

While appellant's ingenuity and industry were largely responsible for the success of the Princess in shark fishing, we cannot find anything in the record from which an agreement to pay him special compensation could be implied. Appellant did inform respondent that he was busy getting the nets ready and that it would "be lots of work to fix" them, but never at any time did he inform respondent what the work actually entailed or that he expected any compensation for it. Since respondent had so little knowledge of the conduct of the net operations, there could not be any implied agreement for compensation. The trial court found no factual basis for such an allowance, and we can find none in the record.

Affirmed.

Hurst v. Hurst

1965 (Ariz.) 405 P.2d 913

HATHAWAY, J.   . . . We shall consider the question of certain "unidentified deposits" in appellee's bank account prior to dissolution. Appellee Lee Hurst had deposited both partnership funds and personal funds in his own personal account. The accounting report prepared for the trial court excluded these unidentified deposits in computing the undistributed cash assets belonging to the dissolved partnership. We hold that this was partially erroneous.

A partner stands in a fiduciary relationship to his co-partner. If a trustee mixes trust funds with his own, the entire commingled mass should be treated as trust property except in so far as the trustee may be able to distinguish what is his. The evidence having established that part of the money deposited in Lee Hurst's account was partnership or trust funds, it was incumbent upon the trustee-partner, Lee Hurst, to distinguish his personal funds. He failed to do this and the unidentified deposits for 1951, 1952, and 1953 should have been treated as a partnership cash asset.

So ordered.

Weiser v. Burick

1965 (N.Y.) 263 N.Y.S.2d 506

DEMPSEY, J.   Plaintiff sued defendant in the county court to receive $2000 alleged to have been advanced by plaintiff for the partnership and on behalf of the same. Defendant, in addition to denying the alleged partnership agreement, has interposed an affirmative defense plus several counterclaims. . . .

(The court has challenged its jurisdiction over the subject matter of the suit.)

The test of jurisdiction of a cause must be resolved by the nature of the action. Though the prayer for relief seeks recovery of purported money damages, the documentation of jurisdiction stands or falls upon the factual allegations in the complaint. . . .

For resolution is the question whether the complaint is based in equity or at law. Distinctions in pleadings on equity and law actions have been abolished by the Legislature. Jurisdictional questions of equity actions, however, persist. The County Court is a court of limited equity jurisdiction . . .

The instant action is as heretofore stated, a suit by one partner against another. The pleading is replete with reference (Paragraphs "Second, Third, Fourth, Fifth and Sixth") with claim of a partnership and an advance for the benefit of the partnership. It is almost universally recognized that absent statutory authorization one partner may not maintain an action at law based upon partnership transactions which involves an accounting of the partnership affairs until there has been a final settlement of the business of the partnership. In the absence of an accounting, one partner cannot maintain a suit at law for contributions or advances made by him to the firm, or for money paid on debts (or assumption of obligations as herein alleged) settled by him for the firm out of his private funds. Breach of special covenants may give rise to law actions under special circumstances, but these are not here present.

This is an equity action before our court. This court does not have jurisdiction of the dissolution and accounting of partnerships. The procedures should be utilized for removal of the case to the proper forum. . . . The application should be made in thirty days. *If no such application is made, this Court will then entertain a motion to dismiss for lack of jurisdiction over the subject matter.*

Bole v. Lyle et al.

1956, (Tenn. App.), 287 S.W.2d 931

Lyle, Peters, and Barton were partners operating a business of manufacturing packing crates and other wood products. The partnership had purchased a tract of timber and were cutting it into lumber to supply their needs. Barton, the managing partner, entered into a contract to sell lumber to the plaintiff and received payment therefor. The lumber was never delivered to plaintiff and Barton never accounted to the partnership for the money received. Plaintiff sought to hold the partnership accountable. The lower court held that Lyle and Peters were not liable. The plaintiff appealed.

McAmis, Presiding Judge. . . . The general rule is that each partner is a general agent of the firm but only for the purpose of carrying on the business of the partnership. Any sale by a partner to be valid must be in furtherance of the partnership business, within the real scope of the business or such as third persons may reasonably conclude, from all the circumstances, to be embraced within it. If the act is embraced within the partnership business or incident to such business according to the ordinary and usual course of conducting it, the partnership is bound regardless of whether the partner, in performing the act, proceeds in good faith or bad faith toward his copartners.

Sales made by a partner in a trading firm are, of course, not viewed with the same strictness as in nontrading firms such as here involved because in trading firms sales are usually within the scope of the business while in nontrading firms they are exceptional and only incidental to the main business. A priori, in determining whether an act is within the scope of the business it is of importance, first, to determine the character of the partnership operations. (Cases cited.)

We think the case here presented is simply that of a nonresident, unfamiliar with the partnership operations, being defrauded by one of the partners acting in a matter beyond both the real and apparent scope of the business and beyond the real or apparent scope of the agency. There was nothing in the firm name to suggest that it was in the business of selling lumber. Complainant chose to deal with one of the partners without knowing anything of the nature of the partnership operations and we agree with the Chancellor that the nonparticipating partners were in no way responsible for his loss and that recovery should be against Barton alone.

Affirmed.

Holloway v. Smith et al.

1955, 197 Va. 334, 88 S.E.2d 909

The defendants Smith and Ten Brook were partners in the automobile business under the name of Greenwood Sales and Service. Defendant Ten Brook borrowed $6,000 from the plaintiff and gave a partnership note in return. It is contended by the Smiths that Ten Brook borrowed the money to make his initial capital contribution to the partnership and that the obligation to repay was solely that of Ten Brook. They also contended that Ten Brook lacked the authority to bind the partnership on the note. The lower court held that the Smiths were not liable on the note.

SPRATLEY, J. Greenwood Sales & Service was a trading or commercial partnership, and in the course of its business, it borrowed money for carrying on its business in the usual way.

. . . It is settled law in Virginia, both by statute and in numerous decisions that a partner is an agent of the firm for the purpose of the partnership business, and may bind all partners by his acts within the scope of such business. It is of no consequence whether the partner is acting in good faith with his copartners or not, provided the act is within the scope of the partnership's business and professedly for the firm, and third persons are acting in good faith.

. . . Pertinent here is this statement from 40 Am. Jur., *Partnership,* § 11 at p. 134:

> The character and nature of partnerships ordinarily determine the powers and liabilities of different classes of partners. In this connection, the most important distinction exists between trading or commercial partnerships and those which are not organized for the purpose of trade or commerce. Greater powers are impliedly given to members of the former as compared with the second type of partnerships, such as in the matter of drawing or endorsing negotiable instruments.

The Smiths selected Ten Brook as their partner. The partnership was a going concern when the $6,000 note was executed. In the absence of a restriction on his authority, known to Mrs. Holloway, Ten Brook had the same power to bind the partnership as his copartners had. Ten Brook, as the agent of the partnership, solicited the loan professedly for the firm, and executed the note evidencing it, for "apparently carrying on in the usual way the business of the partnership" of which he was a member.

The court held that the Smiths as well as Ten Brook were liable on the note.

CHAPTER 36
REVIEW QUESTIONS AND PROBLEMS

1. *A* and *B* entered into a partnership for the purpose of conducting a grocery business. *A* invested $10,000 and *B* $5,000. At the end of the first year, no profits had been made and all capital had been lost. *A* desires to recover $2,500 from *B*. In the absence of any agreement concerning the division of profits and losses, is he entitled to recover?

2. *A* advances to a partnership, for a period of 60 days, the sum of $19,000 in addition to his agreed capital. Is he entitled to interest on the advance?

3. *A* and *B* were partners engaged in the operation of a jewelry business. *A* ran the business while *B* engaged in other activities not related to the firm business. Is *A* entitled to compensation for his services?

4. *A* was a partner in a retail grocery business and acted as the purchasing agent for the firm. He was also a partner in a certain milling industry. He purchased flour from the mill for the grocery: purchases that because of his interest in the mill netted him $500 during the year. Assuming that his partners were unaware of his interest in the

mill but later ascertained the true facts, should *A* be allowed to retain his profits?

5. *A* and *B* have been partners for a number of years. Upon *A*'s death, *B* spent considerable time in winding up the partnership affairs. Is he legally entitled to compensation for his services?

6. *A*, *B*, and *C* were partners operating a store under the name of Eufaula Cash Store. The store being in need of funds, *A* borrowed money from the bank and executed a note in the name of the firm. The note was not paid and the bank obtained a judgment against *A* and the firm. *A* paid the note and now wishes to bring action against his partners to require them to contribute their proportionate share. Should he succeed?

7. *A* and *B* are partners in the hardware business. It is expressly agreed in the partnership agreement that the full duties of management shall be entrusted to *A* and that he shall be the only purchasing agent of the firm. Despite this fact, *B* orders from the *X* Company certain hardware for the firm. *A* refuses to accept the goods for the firm. Is the firm liable in damages to the *X* company?

8. *A* and *B* are partners in the retail clothing business. Being short of funds in the business, *A*, without the consent or knowledge of *B*, borrowed $500 from *C* and signed a security agreement. Is the partnership property subject to the debt?

9. *P* and *D* were partners in the sawmill business. The partnership had ceased operations and *P* in an action at law before an accounting sues to recover his capital contribution to the firm. He contended that *D* had not contributed the agreed amount and that the court should order him to make such a contribution. What result?

10. *X*, a partner in an accountancy firm, borrowed $10,000 in the firm name and used the proceeds to pay an individual debt. Is the firm liable for the debt?

chapter 37

Dissolution

5-21 In General. Dissolution of a partnership is effected when the partnership relation is destroyed by any partner's ceasing to be a member of the firm.

Dissolution is not the equivalent of termination as will be noted later. Dissolution may occur either without violating the Partnership Agreement or in violation of it. Even though the Agreement provides for a definite term, dissolution is always possible because the relationshp is essentially a mutual agency not capable of specific performance and, therefore, each partner has the *power*, but not the right to revoke the relationship. In the event of wrongful dissolution, the wrongdoer is liable for damages.

Under the Uniform Act, dissolution may occur without violation of the partnership agreement; (a) by the termination of the stipulated term or particular undertaking specified in the agreement; (b) by the express will of any partner when no definite term or particular undertaking is specified; (c) by the express will of all the partners who have not assigned their interests or suffered them to be charged for their separate debts either before or after the termination of any specified term or particular undertaking; or (d) by the expulsion, in good faith, of any partner from the business, in accordance with such a power conferred by the partnership agreement.

5-22 By Operation of Law. If during the period of the partnership, events occur that make it impossible or illegal for the partnership to continue, it will be dissolved. Such events or conditions are: death or bankruptcy of one of the partners or a change in the law which makes the continuance of the business illegal.

A partnership is a personal relationship existing by reason of contract. Therefore, when one of the partners dies, the partnership is dissolved though not terminated. The former partners cannot bind the estate of the deceased partner by a new contract, even though it was expressly intended by the decedent that the partnership be continued. Although partnership agreements occasionally provide for the continued existence of the partnership after the death of the partner, the agreement does not bind the legal representatives of the deceased partner to continue the firm in existence. Occasionally articles of partnership provide that a deceased partner's interest in the firm may be retained by the survivors for a limited period. Such provision may be enforced and the partnership extended beyond the death of a partner. Although the authorities are not unanimous, it has been held that the estate of a deceased partner is liable for further transactions in such cases.

The bankruptcy of a partner will dissolve the partnership, because the control of his property passes to his assignee or trustee for the benefit of the creditors in somewhat the same way that the control of the property passes to the legal representatives upon the death of a partner. The mere insolvency of a partner will not be sufficient to justify a dissolution, unless there has been an assignment of his assets. The bankruptcy of the firm itself is a cause for dissolution, as is also a valid assignment of all the firm assets for the benefit of creditors.

5-23 Dissolution by Court Decree. Where a partnership, by its agreement, is to be continued for a term of years, circumstances may arise which might make the continued existence of the firm impossible and unprofitable. Therefore, upon the application of one of the partners to a court of equity, the partnership may be dissolved. The following are the circumstances and situations that will give a partner a right to go into a court of equity for dissolution:

1. Total incapacity of a partner to conduct business and to perform the duties required under the contract for partnership.

2. A declaration that a partner is insane by a judicial process.

3. Gross misconduct and neglect or breach of duty by a partner to such an extent that it is impossible to carry out the purposes of the partnership agreement. The court will not interfere and grant a decree of dissolution for mere discourtesy, temporary inconvenience, differences of opinion, or errors in judgment.[1] The misconduct must be of such gross nature that the continued operation of the business would be unprofitable.

4. Willful and persistent commitment of breach of the partnership agreement, misappropriation of funds, or commitment of fraudulent acts.

5. A partnership that was entered into by reason of fraud may be dissolved on the application of an innocent party. But, if the defrauded partner continues in the partnership with the knowledge of the fraud, no decree of dissolution will be granted.

[1] *Lunn v. Kaiser,* page 787.

EFFECT OF DISSOLUTION BETWEEN THE PARTNERS

5-24 Effect of Dissolution on Powers of Partners. Upon dissolution, a partnership is not terminated, but continues in existence for the purpose of winding up the partnership affairs. The process of winding up, except where the Agreement provides for continuation by purchase of a former partner's share, involves the liquidation of the partnership assets so that cash may be available to pay creditors and to make a distribution to the partners.

In general, dissolution terminates the authority of any partner to act for the partnership except so far as may be necessary to wind up partnership affairs, to liquidate the assets of the firm in an orderly manner, or to complete transactions begun but not then finished. There are two areas which must be considered—termination of authority as it relates to the partners, and the effect of such termination upon persons who are not partners but who have engaged in transactions with the firm. In respect to the former it is noted that different results obtained depending upon the cause of the dissolution: (1) where the dissolution is not caused by the act, bankruptcy, or death of a partner, and (2) where it is so caused.

If in situation (2) a partner enters into a contract or incurs a liability on behalf of the firm after dissolution, each partner will be liable to the other for his share of any liability the same as if the partnership had not been dissolved unless: (a) the dissolution was caused by the *act* of any partner and the partner incurring the liability had knowledge of the dissolution, (b) the dissolution being by the *death* or *bankruptcy* of a partner, the partner acting for the partnership had knowledge or notice of the death or bankruptcy. In these situations the partner is alone responsible and cannot require his fellow partners to share the burden of his unauthorized act.

In the event of dissolution resulting from the death of a partner, title to partnership property remains in the surviving partner or partners for purposes of winding up and liquidation. Both real and personal property is, through the survivors, thus made available to firm creditors. All realty is treated as though it were personal property; it is sold and the surviving partners finally account, usually in cash, to the personal representative of the deceased partner for the latter's share in the proceeds of liquidation.[2]

5-25 Right of Partners After Dissolution. Where the dissolution is caused in any way other than the breach of the partnership agreement, each partner, as against his copartners or their assignees, has a right to insist that all the partnership assets be used first to pay firm debts. After firm obligations are paid, remaining assets are used to return capital invest-

---

2 *Cultra et al. v. Cultra et al.,* page 788.

ments, proper adjustments for profits and losses having been made. All of the partners, except those who have caused a wrongful dissolution of the firm, have the right to participate in the winding up of the business. The majority may select the method or procedure to be followed in the liquidation, but the assets, other than real estate, must be turned into cash unless all the partners agree to distribution in kind.

If a partnership which is to continue for a fixed period is dissolved by the wrongful withdrawal, in contravention of the partnership agreement, of one of its members, the remaining members may continue as partners under the same firm name for the balance of the agreed term of the partnership if they have settled with the withdrawing partner for his interest in the partnership. The remaining partners, in determining the interest of the withdrawing partner, have the right to pay him his share in cash, less the damages caused by his wrongful withdrawal. In the calculation of his share, the good will of the business is not taken into consideration. If no accounting is made at the time that the partner withdraws, the remaining partners may continue the business for the agreed period by securing the payment of the ascertained value of such withdrawing partner's interest by a bond approved by the court, covering not only the partner's interest at the time of the withdrawal, but also indemnifying him against any future liabilities of the continuing partnership.

The right of the partners to expel one of their number is determined entirely by the partnership agreement. Thus, the right to continue after expulsion, as well as the amount which the expelled partner is to receive, depends exclusively upon the articles of copartnership.

EFFECT OF DISSOLUTION AS TO THIRD PARTIES

5-26 Liability Existing Prior to Dissolution. Although the dissolution of a partnership terminates the authority of the partners to create future liability, it does not discharge the existing liability of any partner. An agreement between the partners themselves that one or more of the partners will assume the partnership liabilities and that a withdrawing partner will be discharged does not bind the firm creditors. However, upon dissolution, a partner who withdraws may be discharged from any existing liability by an agreement to that effect with the creditors. If upon dissolution of a partnership, an incoming partner or the remaining partners promise to assume the liabilities of the dissolved partnership, such liabilities will be discharged as to the withdrawing partner if any creditor of the partnership, knowing of the agreement, changes or alters the character of the liability or the time of its payment by agreement with the new firm.

The individual estate of a deceased partner, where firm assets are insufficient to pay firm debts, is liable to third parties for all debts created while he was a partner, subject, however, to the payment of his separate debts.

5-27 Notice. Transactions entered into with former creditors of the firm who have not received actual knowledge of the dissolution continue to bind any partner who has withdrawn.[3] Notice of dissolution is required whether the dissolution is caused by an act of the parties or by law, except where a partner becomes bankrupt or the continuation of the business becomes illegal. Therefore, on death the personal representative of the deceased partner must give notice.

Where the dissolution is caused by an act of the parties, the partners will continue to be liable to all persons who formerly dealt with the firm but who are not creditors, unless public notice of such dissolution is given. Notice by publication in a newspaper in the community where the business has been transacted or notice of the dissolution by a properly addressed envelope placed in the mailbox is sufficient.

Where a partner has not actively engaged in the conduct of the partnership business and creditors had not learned that he was a partner and have not extended credit to the firm on the faith of such partner, he is under no duty to give notice to either of the groups mentioned above.

5-28 New Partners and New Firms. A person admitted as a partner into an existing partnership is, as a member of the firm, liable to the extent of his investment for all obligations created before his admission, as though previously he had been a partner. His separate estate is not liable for such obligations, and the creditors of the old firm can look only to the firm assets and to the members of the old firm.

If a business is continued without liquidation of the partnership affairs, creditors of the first, or dissolved, partnership are also creditors of the partnership continuing the business. Likewise, if the partners assign all their interest to a single partner, who continues the business without liquidation of the partnership affairs, creditors of the dissolved partnership are also creditors of the single person so continuing the business. Likewise, when all the partners or their representatives assign their rights in the partnership property to one or more third persons who promise to pay the debts and to continue the business, the creditors of the dissolved partnership are also creditors of the person or persons continuing the business.

5-29 Distribution of Firm Assets and Liabilities of Partners on Dissolution. Upon the dissolution of a solvent partnership and a winding up of its business, an accounting is had to determine its assets and liabilities. Before the partners are entitled to participate in any of the assets, whether such partners are owed money by the firm or not, all firm creditors other than partners are entitled to be paid. After firm creditors are paid, the assets of the partnership are distributed among the partners, as follows:

(1) Each partner who has made advances to the firm, or has incurred liability for or on behalf of the firm, is entitled to be reimbursed.

---

[3] *Letellier-Phillips Paper Co. v. Fiedler et al.,* page 789.

(2) Each partner is then entitled to the return of the capital which he has contributed to the firm.[4]

(3) Any balance is distributed as profits, in accordance with the partnership agreement.

When the firm is *insolvent* and a court of equity has acquired jurisdiction because of a bill for accounting, a petition by creditors, or an insolvency proceeding, etc., over the assets of the partnership, together with the assets of the individual partners, the assets are distributed in accordance with a rule known as "marshaling of assets."

Persons entering into a partnership agreement impliedly agree that the partnership assets shall be used for the payment of the firm debts before the payment of any individual debts of the partners. Consequently, a court of equity, in distributing firm assets, will give priority to firm creditors in firm assets as against the separate creditors of the individual partners and will give priority to private creditors of individual partners in the separate assets of the partners as against firm creditors. Each class of creditors is not permitted to use the fund belonging to the other until the claims of the other have been satisfied. Since the firm creditors have available two funds out of which to seek payment—firm assets and the individual assets of the partners—and individual creditors of the partners have only one fund, the personal assets of the partners, equity compels the firm creditors to exhaust firm assets before having recourse to the partners' individual assets.[5] This rule does not apply, however, if a partner conceals his existence and permits the other member of the firm to deal with the public as the sole owner of the business. Under these circumstances the dormant partner by his conduct has led the creditors of the active partner to rely upon firm assets as the separate property of the active partner, and by reason of his conduct the dormant partner is estopped from demanding an application of the equity rule that firm assets shall be used to pay firm creditors in priority and individual assets to pay individual creditors. Thus the firm assets must be shared equally with firm creditors and the individual creditors of the active partners. Since the firm assets may not be sufficient to pay all the firm debts when depleted by payments to individual creditors, there may be unpaid firm creditors, and dormant partners will be personally liable. Since the firm creditors' right to firm property rests upon the partners' right that firm assets be used to pay firm debts, the conduct that estops a dormant partner also denies the creditors such a preference. Furthermore, the creditors who relied upon the assets in the hands of the sole active partner cannot claim a preference when later they learn such assets were partnership assets.

Just as the individual creditors are limited to individual assets, firm creditors are limited to firm assets. Therefore, firm creditors are not entitled to payment out of the individual assets of the partners until the individual creditors have been paid. This rule applies, even though the

---

[4] *Gordon v. Ginsberg,* page 789.
[5] *Casey et al. v. Grantham et al.,* page 790.

firm creditors may, at the same time, be individual creditors of a member of the firm. There are two main exceptions to this general rule: (1) Where there are no firm assets and no living solvent partners. The rule for the limit of firm creditors to firm assets applies only where there are firm assets. If no firm assets or no living solvent partner exists, the firm creditors may share equally with the individual creditors in the distribution of the individual estates of the partners. (2) If a partner has fraudulently converted the firm assets to his own use, it follows that the firm creditors will be entitled to share equally with individual creditors in such partner's individual assets.

DISSOLUTION CASES

Lunn v. Kaiser

1955, (S.D.) 72 N.W.2d 312

Plaintiff and defendant were partners in the farming and livestock business. They became involved in a series of arguments over matters of a trivial nature and plaintiff brought this action to dissolve the partnership. The lower court ruled in favor of the plaintiff and the defendant appealed.

RUDOLPH, Presiding Judge . . . The evidence also discloses several minor incidents such as arguments about walking across the lawn, the amount of cream furnished plaintiff, the pounding on the house being remodeled while defendant's children were asleep, and perhaps other similar incidents.

It may be conceded that the relationship between the parties was not that of bosom friends but nevertheless the purpose for which the contract was entered into succeeded and the personal animosity, if such it may be called, existing between the parties did not detract from the successful conduct of the business.

. . . We find nothing in the record to support any determination that plaintiff was deprived of any right of direction he had under the contract. The real dispute here relates to discord over trivial matters, for which both parties were responsible. No doubt the bringing of this action only added to the discord, as plaintiff testified the parties were only on speaking terms during the two months preceding the trial, but defendant cannot be charged with commencing these proceedings.

The agreement expires by its own terms on March 1, 1956. It does not clearly appear that the plaintiff will suffer any loss by the continuation of the relationship during the existence of the agreement. The trial court stated in his memorandum opinion, "I am unable to determine that one is more responsible for this situation than the other. . . ." Under these circumstances we believe the harsh remedy of dissolution is unnecessary. We are inclined to agree with the Pennsylvania court, "Differences and discord should be settled by the partners themselves by the application of mutual forbearance rather than by bills in equity for dissolution. Equity is not a referee of partnership quarrels. A going and prosperous business will not be dissolved merely because of friction among the partners; it will not interfere to determine which contending faction is more at fault."

Reversed.

Cultra et al. v. Cultra et al.

1949, 188 Tenn. 506, 221 S.W.2d 533

Four people (Cultras) were partners doing business under the trade name "Morning Star Nursery." The partnership acquired several tracts of land. Two of the partners have died. A controversy arose as to the rights of a child of one of the deceased partners in the partnership real property. The lower court held that the interest of the deceased partners was personalty and that the surviving partner had a right to sell this land and then distribute the proceeds as other partnership property.

BURNETT, J.   This case presents the question of whether or not the real estate owned by a partnership, purchased by said partnership with partnership funds for partnership purposes, and not needed to pay partnership debts, descends to the heirs of a deceased partner or continues to be personalty and subject to the laws of distribution.

. . . Courts of other states, in construing the Uniform Partnership Act, adopt the rule of "out and out" conversion, that is, that when the property is acquired by the partnership, from the partnership fund, for partnership purposes, it becomes personalty for all purposes. The most notable of these cases is *Wharf v. Wharf* (306 Ill. 179, 137 N.E. 446, 449).

These cases, and the holdings last above referred to, in effect adopt the English rule. This rule is that partnership realty must be regarded as personalty for all purposes, including descent and distribution. Real estate purchased and used for partnership purposes is an "out and out" conversion to personalty so that it will be distributed as such.

. . . It is true that in the *Wharf* case the partnership was solely for the purpose of dealing in real estate and that the general rule is that real estate partnerships are considered as personalty, and must be distributed as such. We consider the reasoning in the *Wharf* case, that is, that the rule is changed as to all partnerships, whether real estate or otherwise, by reason of the passage of the Uniform Partnership Act, is the most reasonable rule and is one that we should adopt and do adopt as the applicable rule in this State.

In this construction and application of the Uniform Partnership Act, we are meeting and reaching the intent of the Legislature in passing this Act. By so doing the conversion of real estate into personalty for certain purposes and then when those purposes have been met, reconverting the real estate back into realty is done away with by this Act. By this construction, when a partnership once acquires real estate, with partnership funds and for partnership purposes, it then becomes personalty for all purposes and can be conveyed according to the terms of the Act as other partnership property. This seems a sound rule to apply and we are applying it here.

From what has been said above, it results that the decree of the Chancellor must be affirmed.

Letellier-Phillips Paper Co. v. Fiedler et al.

1949, 32 Tenn. App. 137, 222 S.W.2d 42

The plaintiffs brought this action to recover from the defendants as individuals and members of a partnership for merchandise sold and delivered to them. A corporation had been formed by the defendants which took over their individual and partnership assets. The plaintiffs alleged that they were not aware that the partnership had been converted into a corporation. From a judgment in favor of the plaintiffs, defendants appealed.

SWEPSTON, J.   The suit is on account for merchandise sold and delivered and the essential question in the trial below was whether there was partnership liability or corporate liability, the partners having operated as such for about a year and having later formed a corporation.

. . . The bill alleges that about December 24, 1945 complainant agreed to extend credit to defendants, Fiedler & Sullivan, individually and as partners trading as Fied-Sul Paper Mills. That upon the pledge of the individual credit of the defendants complainant began shipping them merchandise.

That the account about January 1, 1947 was current and amounted to $6,855.26. That subsequently the balance began to grow larger until on August 1, 1947, it amounted to $26,890.70, which later upon demand was reduced to $24,060.74 at which figure it has remained, because all purchases lately have been for cash.

That about August 1, 1947 complainant learned for the first time that a corporation had been formed by defendants and that it had taken over certain assets of the individuals and of the partnership all without notice to complainant.

That it had never dealt with the corporation and had relied upon the credit of the partnership and the individuals composing it and that said transfer of assets was fraudulent, etc.

. . . The cases show that the notice may be an express notice or may be implied from sufficient circumstances. However obtained, it must be sufficient to amount to actual knowledge where one who has been dealing with the firm before dissolution is involved. The knowledge may be constructive as to those who have not dealt with the firm before dissolution.

Affirmed.

Gordon v. Ginsberg

1964 (N.Y.S.C.) 255 N.Y.S.2d 966

PER CURIAM.   In an action for the dissolution of a partnership and for an accounting, defendant appeals from an interlocutory judgment of the Supreme Court, Kings County, entered July 30, 1963 after a nonjury trial, upon the opinion and decision of the court in plaintiff's favor. . . .

The parties, concededly, were partners in a leather goods business known as Ginsberg Brothers. The principal dispute between them is whether they were also partners in certain real estate ventures into which defendant entered in his own name. We are of the opinion that the proof was sufficient to support the finding of the learned trial court that the parties were partners in the real estate transactions. Each party, on the accounting which has been directed, may establish the amount of his capital contributions to the various ventures and each will be entitled to the return of such contributions before any division is made of the remainder of the assets.

We are also of the opinion, however, that an accounting of the leather goods business should have been ordered. Both parties requested such an accounting in their pleadings; the business allegedly was the source, at least in part, of the funds used for the purchase of the real estate; and, under the circumstances presented by this record, we believe such an accounting is required in order to determine, adequately, the respective rights of the parties.

Casey et al. v. Grantham et al.

1954, 239 N.C. 121, 79 S.E.2d 735

The plaintiff, Casey, brought this action against the defendant Harold J. Grantham, his partner in the sawmill and cotton gin business, for a partnership accounting and against the defendant Clarence Grantham to enjoin the foreclosure of a deed of trust on partnership property and on the home and farm of the plaintiffs until a partnership accounting is had. The deeds of trust had been given to secure a loan made to the partnership by the defendant Clarence Grantham. The plaintiffs contend that the partnership property is well worth the amount of the debt owed by the partnership to Clarence Grantham. The lower court sustained a demurrer to the complaint and the plaintiffs appealed.

PARKER, J. . . . G.S. § 59-68 (1) reads:

> When dissolution is caused in any way except in contravention of the partnership agreement, each partner, as against his copartners and all persons claiming through them in respect of their interest in the partnership, unless otherwise agreed, may have the partnership property applied to discharge its liabilities, and the surplus applied to pay in cash the net amount owing to the respective partners.

. . . It is said in 68 C.J.S., *Partnership*, § 185, p. 639, "The right, in equity, to have the partnership and individual assets marshaled is for the benefit and protection of the partners themselves, and, therefore, the equity of a creditor, to the application of this doctrine, is of a dependent and subordinate character, and must be worked out through the medium of the partners or their representatives"—citing in support of the text *Dilworth v. Curts* (139 Ill. 508, 29 N.E. 861, 865), where it is said "the right in equity to have the partnership and individual assets marshaled is one resting in the hands of the partners, and must be worked out through them."

Each partner has the right to have the partnership property applied to the payment or security of partnership debts in order to relieve him from personal liability.

It appears that under the general rule as to marshaling partnership and individual assets, or under the application of a principle of equity similar to that rule, the rule that partnership debts may be paid out of individual assets is subject to the modification that the individual assets may be so applied where, and only where, there are no firm assets, or where the firm assets have become exhausted. It would seem that the rationale for this modification to the rule rests upon the fact that the partners occupy the position of sureties in respect to their individual property being liable for the payment of partnership debts.

. . . It may be that the property of the partnership conveyed in the deed of trust may not sell for enough at a forced sale to pay Clarence Grantham's debt in full—though the demurrer admits that it will—but that Harold J. Grantham may be indebted to the partnership in an amount to make up such deficiency, if such a deficiency should exist. How can that be determined, until there is an accounting between the parties of the partrnership affairs?

Under the rules laid down above it would seem to be plain that the plaintiffs have alleged sufficient facts to enjoin a foreclosure sale under the deed of trust until there has been an accounting and settlement of the partnership affairs between the partners, Casey and Harold J. Grantham. Under such circumstances it is the rule with us that an injunction should be granted where the injury, if any, which the defendant Clarence Grantham, would suffer from its issuance would be slight as compared with the irreparable damage which the plaintiffs would suffer from the forced sale of their home and farm from its refusal, if the plaintiffs should finally prevail.

Reversed.

CHAPTER 37
REVIEW QUESTIONS AND PROBLEMS

1. *A, B,* and *C* are partners, and by the terms of the agreement the partnership is to continue for a period of five years. At the end of the third year conditions have arisen that indicate that the firm cannot continue except at a loss. *B* and *C* refuse to quit, and *A* files a bill to obtain an order for dissolution. Should he succeed?

2. *A* and *B* formed a partnership to operate a restaurant. *A* contributed a building and fixtures worth $8,500, and *B* contributed $3,000 cash. *A* obtained a dissolution of the firm on account of *B*'s wrongful

withholding of *A*'s share of the profits in the amount of $5,500. After dissolution but before final judgment on the accounting and termination of the partnership, *A* formed another partnership with *X* and *Y* which made a profit operating the restaurant. Is *B* entitled to a share therein?

3. *A*, *B*, and *C* are partners under an agreement whereby the firm is to continue in business for ten years. *A* causes a wrongful dissolution of the partnership and demands his interest therein. May he demand that firm assets be liquidated? Is there any asset in which he is not entitled to share?

4. *A* withdraws from a firm under an agreement with the surviving partners that they shall assume and pay all outstanding liabilities. *A* notified all creditors of his withdrawal from the firm. The surviving partners failed to pay the debts. Has *A* avoided liability therefor?

5. *A*, *B*, and *C* take a new partner, *D*, into their business. He invests $3,000. What is the extent of his liability, if any, to creditors of the old firm? What are the rights of creditors of the old firm, in comparison with creditors of the new firm, in the firm assets?

6. *A* agreed with *B* to share the profits and losses of a farming operation. *B* was to supervise and also to furnish a tractor and $2,500. *B* failed to furnish the tractor or money and was insolvent. There were no other joint funds available for harvest. *A* had already contributed more than he had agreed to contribute. What may *A* do?

7. *A* and *B* formed a partnership under written articles which provided that if either partner desired to dissolve the firm he was to give written notice to the other partner. The notice was to include a statement of the amount the partner was willing to pay for the interest of the other partner. The partner who received the notice was then to have his option of selling his interest for the sum so stated or else of buying the interest of the notifying partner for the same amount. *A* gave notice to *B*, and *B* elected to sell. *A* then attempted to withdraw the notice. What results?

8. *A*, *B*, *C*, and *D* formed a partnership to drill oil and gas wells. In 1960 it was dissolved by mutual consent. In 1961, still during the period of liquidation of partnership assets, *A*, who was in charge of liquidation, signed a note purporting to bind the partnership. This note was payable to *X*, who knew of the dissolution, and was given for an insurance premium payment that had become due in 1959. Against whom may *X* obtain a judgment on the note if it is not paid when due?

Part Two

Corporations

chapter 38

Characteristics

5-30 Essential Features. A corporation is a legal entity created by the state through which a collection of individuals may operate a business with their risk limited to their investment. A corporation may exist as a separate legal entity even though it has only one shareholder.

A corporation, being created by the state, has the rights and powers given to it by the state in its charter; but by its very nature as a legal entity, these would include the right to sue and be sued, existence for the period stated which is usually perpetual, the right to own property and the right to enter into contracts.

A corporation is a resident and a citizen of the state which creates it. When the word "person" or "persons" is used in constitutional and statutory provisions, corporations are usually deemed to be included when the circumstances in which they are placed are identical with those of natural persons expressly included within such statute. For example, a corporation is a person within the meaning of the Fourteenth Amendment to the Federal Constitution, which provides that "no state shall make or enforce any law which shall abridge the privileges or immunities of citizens of the United States; nor shall any state deprive any person of life, liberty, or property without due process of law, nor deny to any person within its jurisdiction the equal protection of the laws."

A corporation which is organized for the purpose of profit is known as a stock company because it issues stock to evidence ownership. A not-for-profit corporation does not issue stock and the rights of members are determined by the by-laws.

5-31 Domestic and Foreign Corporations. A corporation organized under the laws of a particular state or country is called within that particular state or country a "domestic corporation." When such a corporation does business within another state or country it is called a "foreign corporation" in such state or country. Domestic corporations become qualified to do business upon receipt and recording of their charter but foreign corporations doing business in *intrastate* commerce must "qualify" to do business in each state in which it is doing business and obtain a certificate of authority from such state. A foreign corporation engaged in wholly *interstate* commerce need not qualify in each state but there are usually sufficient local activities to require qualification. Section 5-33 of this chapter sets forth the circumstances in which a corporation is deemed to be "doing business." Failure to qualify usually results in a denial of access to the courts as a plaintiff [1] and other penalties.

5-32 Qualification of Foreign Corporations. Most state statutes require foreign corporations to register by filing a copy of their articles with the Secretary of State, to appoint an agent upon whom service of process may be served, to pay license fees, to designate and maintain an office in the state, to keep books and records. Some states further require the corporation to deposit bonds or securities with the treasurer of the state for the purpose of protecting any individual who might suffer loss by reason of the corporation's conduct. Refusal or failure by a foreign corporation to comply with these requirements justifies the state in denying the corporation the right of access to the courts. This has the net effect of preventing them from conducting business since the corporation contracts are not enforceable by suit and debtors would thus be able to avoid payment of their debts to the corporation. It must be noted that a corporation which has not qualified may still be sued and noncompliance cannot be used as a defense by the corporation when sued by a third party. If a contract is fully performed, neither party may seek restitution. Transacting business within the state without complying with the statute also subjects the corporation or its officers to penalties.

While a state may require compliance with the above requirements by a foreign corporation, a state may not impose arbitrary and unreasonable requirements and may not discriminate against foreign corporations in favor of domestic corporations in the fees and taxes charged and other burdens imposed on commerce. Foreign corporations are protected in this regard by the "commerce clause" of the Federal Constitution.

5-33 What Constitutes "Doing Business" by a Foreign Corporation. The term "doing business" is not reducible to an exact and certain definition. State statutes do not define the term "doing business." In order

---

[1] *Eli Lilly and Company v. Sav-On-Drugs, Inc.,* page 800.

to aid in determining whether a corporation is "doing business" within a state, the Model Foreign Corporation Act was drafted. It sets forth basic principles heretofore established by the courts. The Act defines the term to mean that a foreign corporation is "doing business" when "some part of its business substantial and continuous in character and not merely casual or occasional" is transacted within a state.[2] The Act states that a corporation is *not* "doing business" in a state merely because:

(a) It engaged in a single or isolated transaction in this state where its action in engaging in such single or isolated transaction indicates no intent or purpose of continuity of conduct in that respect; or . . .

(e) It does any act or acts which is or are merely preliminary to or looking toward the future transaction of business in this state, or

(f) It does any act or acts in this state relating solely to the management or control of the internal affairs of the corporation, such as the holding of corporate meetings, issuance of stock certificates, authorization of issue of bonds, making of calls on stock, or other acts of like nature; or

(g) It acquires and holds stock of domestic corporations and exercises in this state the incidents of such ownership unless through such stock ownership the domestic corporation is controlled by the foreign corporation and is in reality acting as the agent of the foreign corporation and doing business in this state for it and in its behalf . . .

The model Act states a foreign corporation shall not be required to obtain a license to do business by reason of the fact that:

(a) It is in the mail order or a similar business, receiving orders by mail or otherwise, in pursuance of letters, circulars, catalogs or other forms of advertisement, or solicitation, accepting such orders outside this state and filling them with goods shipped into this state from without same direct to the purchaser there, or his agent; or

(b) It employs salesmen, either resident or traveling, to solicit orders in this state, either by display of samples or otherwise (whether or not maintaining sales offices in this state), all orders requiring approval at the offices of the corporation without this state, and all goods applicable to such orders being shipped in pursuance thereof from without this state to the purchaser; provided that any samples kept within this state are for display or advertising purposes only, and no sales, repairs, or replacements are made from stock on hand in this state . . .

5-34 *De Jure* and *De Facto* Corporations. A *de jure* corporation is a corporation which has been formed in compliance with the law authorizing such a corporation. A *de facto* corporation is one which operates as a corporation for all practical purposes, but has failed to comply with some provision of the law with respect to its creation and thus

2 *Chesapeake Supply & Equipment Co. v. Manitowoc Engineering Corp.*, page 802.

has no legal right to its corporate existence. Its corporate existence can be challenged only by the state itself, and not by third parties. A *de facto* corporation results where there is a valid law authorizing such a corporation; a bona fide attempt to organize and comply with the statute; and the exercise of corporate power. The *de facto* corporation can make contracts, purchase and hold real estate, sue and be sued in its corporate name, and do any and all things necessary to its corporate existence that a *de jure* corporation may do but the State may challenge its continued existence or impose other penalties.

If persons hold themselves out as a corporation and create liability, and such organization is less than a *de facto* corporation, they are generally held liable as partners. In some jurisdictions the stockholders even of a *de facto* corporation are held personally liable like partners for debts incurred by the corporation. Some courts, however, hold that the liability rests not upon partnership relationship but upon the theory that such persons are agents for the other members of a pretended corporation.

5-35 Entity Disregarded. Occasionally, the courts look behind the corporate entity and take action as though no entity separate from the members existed. However, the corporate entity may not be disregarded simply because all of the stock is owned by the members of a family or by one person.[3] One of the basic advantages of the corporate form of business organization is the limitation of liability and corporations are formed for the express purpose of limiting one's risk to the amount of his investment in the stock.

There are certain situations in which the corporate entity is often disregarded. First, if the use of the corporation is to defraud or to avoid an otherwise valid obligation, the court may handle the problem as though no corporation existed.[4] To illustrate, let us assume that *A* and *B* sold a certain business and agreed not to compete with the buyer for a given number of years. Desirous of re-entering business in violation of the contract term, they organize a corporation, becoming the principal stockholders and managers. The buyer may have the corporation enjoined from competing with him as effectively as he could have enjoined *A* and *B* from establishing a competing business. Likewise, if the corporate device is used to evade a statute, the corporate entity may be disregarded.[5]

A parent corporation, owning a controlling interest in a subsidiary, often completely dominates the activity of the latter so that it becomes purely an agent or arm of the parent company. Under such circumstances, the courts have often held the parent company liable for torts committed by the subsidiary. Occasionally, if the finances of the two companies have been used somewhat indiscriminately to meet the obli-

---

[3] *Marks v. Green,* page 804.

[4] *Diamond Fruit Growers, Inc. v. Goe Co.,* page 805.

[5] *New Hampshire Wholesale Beverage Assn. v. New Hampshire State Liquor Comm.,* page 806.

gations of either company, ordinary contract creditors of the subsidiary are permitted to sue the parent company.

5-36 Procedure for Incorporation. A general law authorizing the formation of a corporation defines the purposes for which corporations may be formed, and prescribes the steps to be taken for the creation of the corporation. Such general law usually prescribes that any number of adult persons, usually not less than three, who are citizens of the United States and at least one of whom is a citizen of the state of incorporation, may file an application for a charter. The application usually requires the names and addresses of the incorporators; the name of the corporation; the object for which it is formed; its duration; the location of its principal office; the total authorized capital stock, preferred and common; the number of shares, with their value; and, if the statute provides for stock without par value, the number of shares of such stock. It also requires the names and addresses of the subscribers to the capital stock, and the amount subscribed and paid in by each subscriber. It further requires the amount and the character of capital stock proposed to be issued at once, and whether the stock is paid for in cash or in property. This application, signed by all the incorporators and acknowledged by a notary public, is usually forwarded to a state official. This official then issues a charter which contains all the information on the application, and usually sets out the powers, rights, and privileges of the corporation as prescribed by the general incorporation act. The law usually requires that, upon the receipt of the charter, it be filed in the proper recording office located in the same community as the principal office of the corporation. A fee is usually charged, payable in advance, for filing an application for a charter, and no charter will be issued until such fee is paid. Where the application is for a corporation not for pecuniary profit, no detailed information is required relative to issues of stock, shares, and so forth. The requirements for securing a charter vary greatly in the different states and in different types of business in the same state. The requirements of the statute must be satisfied and complied with in detail for the formation of a *de jure* corporation.

After the charter has been received and filed, the board of directors and stockholders meets, drafts by-laws, and elects officers. The receipt of the charter and its filing are the operative facts that bring the corporation into existence and give it authority and power to operate.

The charter of a corporation is a contract and cannot be repealed or amended by the legislature unless such power has been reserved by the state when the charter was granted. The charter may be amended, however, by the consent of all of the stockholders or a certain portion thereof, as provided by the statute of the state.

5-37 Promoters. A promoter is one who performs the preliminary duties necessary to bring a corporation into existence. A promoter calls together and supervises the first meeting of the organizers; enters into pre-incorporation contracts with brokers, bankers, and subscribers; arranges for the preparing of the preliminary articles of incorporation; and provides for registration and filing fees. He arranges for compliance with the applicable securities laws (Blue-Sky Laws) and causes any advertising desired to be prepared. He will arrange for a Prospectus to be prepared if required by the applicable securities laws. The corporation, after its creation, may become bound by "adoption" upon contracts made by its promoter.[6] The term "adoption" does not mean ratification as applied in the law of agency, because at the time the contract was made by the promoter with a third party the corporation as principal was not in existence. More accurately, what occurs is a novation. When the corporation assents to the contract, the third party agrees to discharge the promoter and to look only to the corporation. The discharge of the promoter by the third party is consideration to make binding the corporation's promise to be bound upon the contract.

In the absence of evidence to show that such a novation has occurred, the promoter will continue to be personally liable on the contract. Since the contract made with the promoter was made in anticipation of the formation of a corporation, the acceptance of the contract by the corporation after its creation is some evidence from which to draw an inference that a novation has occurred, but usually both the promoter and the corporation are liable, since the latter merely assumes, by implication, the obligation of the promoter without any agreement as to his release.

From the standpoint of the promoter, it is desirable that contracts entered into by him on behalf of the proposed corporation be so worded as to relieve him from personal liability. Thus it is possible in the contract to express an intent that the promoter shall not have personal liability.

Corporations are generally not liable for expenses and services of promoters, unless specifically made so by statute or by charter. However, a promise made after incorporation by the directors to pay for expenses and services of promoters will be binding and supported by sufficient consideration, on the theory of services previously rendered. It is held in some jurisdictions that corporations are liable by implication for the necessary expenses and services incurred by the promoters in bringing them into existence, and such expenses and services inure to the benefit of the corporation.

Promoters occupy a fiduciary relationship toward the prospective corporation and have no right, therefore, to secure any benefit or advantage over the corporation itself or over other stockholders, because of their position as promoters. A promoter cannot purchase property and then sell it to the corporation at an advance, nor has he a right to receive a commission from a third party for the sale of property to the corporation. In general, however, he may sell property acquired by

---

[6] *Knox et al. v. First Security Bank of Utah et al.,* page 808.

him prior to the time he started promoting the corporation, provided he sells it to an unbiased board of directors after full disclosure of all pertinent facts.

CHARACTERISTICS CASES

Eli Lilly and Company v. Sav-On-Drugs, Inc.

1961, 366 U.S. 276

BLACK, J.   The appellant Eli Lilly and Company, an Indiana corporation dealing in pharmaceutical products, brought this action in a New Jersey state court to enjoin the appellee Sav-On-Drugs, Inc., a New Jersey corporation, from selling Lilly's products in New Jersey at prices lower than those fixed in minimum retail price contracts into which Lilly had entered with a number of New Jersey drug retailers. Sav-On had itself signed no such contract but, under the New Jersey Fair Trade Act, prices so established become obligatory upon nonsigning retailers who have notice that the manufacturer has made these contracts with other retailers. Sav-On moved to dismiss this complaint under a New Jersey statute that denies a foreign corporation transacting business in the State the right to bring any action in New Jersey upon any contract made there unless and until it files with the New Jersey Secretary of State a copy of its charter together with a limited amount of information about its operations and obtains from him a certificate authorizing it to do business in the State.

Lilly opposed the motion to dismiss, urging that its business in New Jersey was entirely in interstate commerce and arguing, upon that ground, that the attempt to require it to file the necessary information and obtain a certificate for its New Jersey business was forbidden by the Commerce Clause of the Federal Constitution. Both parties offered evidence to the Court in the nature of affidavits as to the extent and kind of business done by Lilly with New Jersey companies and people. On this evidence, the trial court made findings of fact and granted Sav-On's motion to dismiss, stating as its ground that "the conclusion is inescapable that the plaintiff [Lilly] was in fact doing business in this State at the time of the acts complained of and was required to, but did not, comply with the provisions of the Corporation Act." On appeal to the Supreme Court of New Jersey, this constitutional attack was renewed and the State Attorney General was permitted to intervene as a party-defendant to defend the validity of the statute. The State Supreme Court then affirmed the judgment upholding the statute, relying entirely upon the opinion of the trial court. We noted probable jurisdiction to consider Lilly's contention that the constitutional question was improperly decided by the state courts.

The record shows that the New Jersey trade in Lilly's pharmaceutical products is carried on through both interstate and intrastate channels. Lilly manufactures these products and sells them in interstate commerce to certain selected New Jersey wholesalers. These wholesalers then sell the products in intrastate commerce to New Jersey hospitals, physicians and retail drug stores, and these retail stores in turn sell them, again in intrastate commerce, to the general public. It is well established that New Jersey cannot require Lilly to get a certificate of authority to do business in the State if its participation in this trade is limited to its wholly interstate sales to New Jersey wholesalers. Under the authority of the so-called "drummer" cases, such as *Robbins v. Shelby County Taxing District,* Lilly is free to send salesmen into New Jersey to promote this interstate trade without interference from regulations imposed by the State. On the other hand, it is equally well settled that if Lilly is engaged in intrastate as well as interstate aspects of the New Jersey drug business, the State can require it to get a certificate of authority to do business. In such a situation, Lilly could not escape state regulation merely because it is also engaged in interstate commerce. We must then look to the record to determine whether Lilly is engaged in intrastate commerce in New Jersey.

The findings of the trial court, based as they are upon uncontroverted evidence presented to it, show clearly that Lilly is conducting an intrastate as well as an interstate business in New Jersey. . . .

We agree with the trial court that "[t]o hold under the facts above recited that plaintiff [Lilly] is not doing business in New Jersey is to completely ignore reality." Eighteen "detailmen," working out of a big office in Newark, New Jersey, with Lilly's name on the door and in the lobby of the building, and with Lilly's district manager and secretary in charge, have been regularly engaged in work for Lilly which relates directly to the intrastate aspects of the sale of Lilly's products. These eighteen "detailmen" have been traveling throughout the State of New Jersey promoting the sales of Lilly's products, not to the wholesalers, Lilly's interstate customers, but to the physicians, hospitals and retailers who buy those products in intrastate commerce from the wholesalers. To this end, they have provided these hospitals, physicians and retailers with up-to-date knowledge of Lilly's products and with free advertising and promotional material designed to encourage the general public to make more intrastate purchases of Lilly's products. And they sometimes even directly participate in the intrastate sales themselves by transmitting orders from the hospitals, physicians and drugstores they service to the New Jersey wholesalers. . . .

Lilly also contends that even if it is engaged in intrastate commerce in New Jersey and can by virtue of that fact be required to get a license to do business in that State, New Jersey cannot properly deny it access to the courts in this case because the suit is one arising out of the interstate aspects of its business. In this regard, Lilly relies upon such cases as *International Textbook Co. v. Pigg,* holding that a State cannot condition the right of a foreign corporation to sue upon a contract for the interstate sale of goods. We do not think that those cases are applicable here, however, for the present suit is not of that kind. Here, Lilly is suing upon a contract entirely separable from any particular interstate sale and the power of the State is consequently not limited by cases involving such contracts.

Affirmed.

Chesapeake Supply & Equip. Co. v. Manitowoc Eng. Corp.

1963 Maryland 194 A.2d 624

This is a suit by a Maryland purchaser of a mobile truck crane against the Maryland distributor and the foreign manufacturer of the crane (Manitowoc) for damage suffered when the crane collapsed. The foreign manufacturer challenged the jurisdiction of the court on the ground that it was not doing business in Maryland nor had the contract been entered into within Maryland. The trial court and the appellate court each dismissed the suit as to the foreign corporation for lack of jurisdiction and plaintiff appeals.

HORNEY, J. . . . Manitowoc is a manufacturer of heavy equipment with its principal office and manufacturing facilities in Manitowoc, Wisconsin, and sells its products through distributorship agreements with local retail dealers. During the period between October of 1956 and July of 1964, Manitowoc entered into three such agreements (all of which were similar though not identical) with Chesapeake, which had its principal place of business in Baltimore City. Besides being a local distributor for Manitowoc, Chesapeake sold heavy equipment for some twenty other manufacturers.

The distributorship agreements provided in pertinent part that Chesapeake was not the agent of Manitowoc; that all orders taken by Chesapeake were to be submitted, together with a report on the financial condition of the purchaser, to Manitowoc for final acceptance or rejection; that Manitowoc had the right to fix the price and terms on which all sales were to be made on any other terms and conditions; and that Chesapeake was to stock an adequate supply of replacement parts for servicing the territory allotted to it by Manitowoc . . .

In January of 1957, Chesapeake entered into negotiations with Linder for the sale of a crane. As a result of a proposal made by Chesapeake and accepted by Linder on January 21, 1957, Chesapeake sent Manitowoc on January 28, 1957, a written purchase order for a crane, in which neither the price nor the terms of sale were mentioned. Manitowoc, acting in accordance with the distributorship agreement then in force, declined to "bill" or accept the order until it had been paid a deposit of 10 per cent and had been assured that payment of the balance of the purchase price would be made on presentation of sight draft with bill of lading attached. Thereafter, the negotiations between Chesapeake and Linder having been resumed, certain changes were made in some of the specifications relating to the crane which entailed an increase in the original purchase price quoted by the distributor to the purchaser in the first proposal. While the further preliminary negotiations were in progress between the distributor and the purchaser, the distributor communicated frequently with the manufacturer by mail, telephone and telegraph concerning the purchase price and terms of sale and with respect to expediting the order for the crane to meet the shipping date promised by the distributor. Finally, the revised specifications and purchase price were restated in a second proposal made by Chesapeake and accepted by Linder on February 25, 1957. On the same day, the distributor, in a letter to the manufacturer, confirmed the tele-communication revisions of the original purchase order, enclosed a check for the required 10 per cent deposit, advised the manufacturer that the purchaser had agreed to pay the balance upon presentation of sight draft at its bank, and instructed shipment of the crane by fast freight direct to the purchaser instead of to the distributor as previously directed.

Linder's revised offer to purchase the crane was not accepted by Manitowoc in writing and the record is silent as to when the construction or assembling of it was commenced. However, work thereon was in progress, and was nearing completion, when the president of Linder and a representative of Chesapeake visited the Manitowoc plant on March 5, 1957, to inspect the crane before it was shipped. The crane, having been shipped f.o.b. Manitowoc on March 7, 1957, arrived in Baltimore on March 25th, and Linder paid the sight draft and the freight due.

When the crane was delivered in Baltimore, an employee of Manitowoc was present and helped unload and reassemble it and instructed Linder's operator how to use it. Having done so, the employee immediately left the state. In May of 1957, after the crane had collapsed, another Manitowoc employee helped repair the damaged crane. The repairman came to Baltimore at the request of Chesapeake and was paid by it.

In February of 1959, Chesapeake sold another Manitowoc crane to the Arundel Corporation. During the preliminary negotiations for the sale, a district manager for Manitowoc residing in Pennsylvania (who often visited Chesapeake "just to make Chesapeake conscious of Manitowoc") came into Maryland and assisted in negotiating the sale. Other than not requiring a deposit and payment of balance on sight draft and shipment to Chesapeake, the sale to Arundel was accomplished in substantially the same manner as the sale to Linder. Upon delivery of the Arundel crane, an employee of Manitowoc was again present to supervise unloading and assembly, and to instruct Arundel's operator, after which the employee left the state. . . .

The question on appeal is whether the foreign corporation was "doing business" in Maryland and whether the contract was "made" in this state.

We think that Manitowoc was not "doing business" in this State within the meaning of Code (1957), Art. 23, § 92(a).

The general rule is that a foreign corporation is doing business within a state when it transacts some substantial part of its ordinary business therein. The question whether or not a foreign corporation is doing business within a state "must be largely determined upon the facts of each individual case." Necessarily, this requires careful consideration of the nature and extent of the business activities conducted by or on behalf of the foreign corporation in the forum state.

With respect to the claims of the appellants that certain activities on the part of the appellee constituted doing business in this State, we deem it sufficient to say that we find nothing in the record to show that Manitowoc exercised such domination and control over Chesapeake as would bring the activities of Manitowoc within the jurisdiction of the court. We think that the activities of the district sales manager, in regularly visiting Chesapeake to keep it "conscious of Manitowoc" and in assisting Chesapeake to negotiate the sale of the Arundel crane, were not such as would subject Manitowoc to suit in Maryland. We also think that the activities of Manitowoc employees, in unloading and assembling the Linder and Arundel cranes and in instructing the future operators thereof, were merely incidental to sales which had been made in interstate commerce and did not make Manitowoc amenable to suit in Maryland. Nor was Manitowoc amenable to suit because one of its employees came into Maryland and helped repair the Linder crane, for this activity was but an isolated act that did not constitute "doing business."

We hold that under the facts in this case Manitowoc was not doing business in Maryland. . . .

Affirmed.

Marks v. Green

1960, (Fla.) 122 So.2d 491

The plaintiff is the sole owner of all the outstanding shares in Sa-Rey-Mar, Inc., a Florida corporation whose assets consist principally of intangible property. The corporation paid an intangible tax on this property but the defendant did not include his stock in Sa-Rey-Mar in his personal return. The taxing authorities ordered him to do so. He refused to do so and brought this suit for equitable relief against imposition of the tax. The defendants include the State Comptroller, the County Tax Assessor and the County Tax Collector. From a judgment in favor of the defendants plaintiff appealed.

WIGGINGTON, C. J. . . . The principal ground for relief is predicated upon the premise that the intangible tax assessment against appellant's ownership of all outstanding shares of stock in the corporation duplicated the tax assessment in the same amount levied against the corporation based upon the value of the intangible property owned by it, and as such amounted to a four mill levy on intangible property within the prohibition of the Constitution and laws of Florida. . . .

Appellant does not dispute that the capital stock owned by him in Sa-Rey-Mar Inc., falls within the classification of Class B intangible property as defined by the statute. He contends, however, that since he is the sole owner of the corporation and the corporation has already paid the intangible tax assessed against it on its capital assets, that he should be relieved of the burden of again paying an intangible tax on the value of the same property for which the corporation has already once paid the identical tax. Such reasoning falsely assumes that there exists an identity between the property owned by appellant as represented by his shares of stock in Sa-Rey-Mar, and the property owned by the corporation on which it has already paid the intangible tax. Appellant asks the court to indulge in this assumption on the theory that for tax purposes the separate identity of the corporation should be disregarded, and he as an individual should be adjudged the owner of the intangible property held by the corporation on which the tax has already been paid.

Appellant fortifies his position by citing a number of decisions in which courts of equity have under particular circumstances disregarded the corporate entity, pierced the corporate veil, or regarded the corporation as the alter ego of its stockholders. Such principles, when properly applied, are sound and entitled to respect. The cited authorities indicate, however, that such course has been followed as a matter of necessity only for the purpose of promoting justice or preventing injustice or fraud. We do not conceive that such principles may logically be applied in resolving the issue raised by this appeal. . . . It is our judgment that a sounder concept of the principles which should be followed in making an equitable distribution of the tax burden among the property owners of this state requires that for purposes of taxation, the identity of the corporate entity must be kept separate and distinct from the identity of its stockholders, unless otherwise provided by statute. . . .

Appellant has seen fit to organize a domestic corporation and own all its outstanding capital stock. He has elected to do business through this corporate entity. The benefits of conducting one's business in such manner are obvious and too numerous to mention in this opinion. Having so elected, appellant is in no position to claim all benefits accruing to him by virtue of doing business as a corporation, and at the same time seek to disregard the existence of the corporate entity in order to avoid payment of a tax otherwise chargeable to him. If payment of the intangible tax on the value of his stock in the corporation is considered to be an onerous burden, appellant . . . may dissolve the corporation and distribute to himself in kind the intangible property held by it.

. . . In adopting the latter course appellant would lose the many benefits he now enjoys by conducting his business through a fictitious legal entity. The choice of alternatives is the appellant's, but he cannot eat his cake and have it too.

Affirmed.

Diamond Fruit Growers, Inc. v. Goe Co.
1966 (Ore.) 400 P.2d 909

PERRY, J. The plaintiff Diamond Fruit Growers, a cooperative association, brought this suit against the defendants to have a standard cooperative growers contract entered into with Goe Brothers, a partnership consisting of Joe, Merle and Donald Goe, specifically enforced.

The trial court entered its decree enforcing the provisions of the contract, and the defendants appeal.

The record discloses that the partnership was the owner of four separate parcels of land upon which fruit was produced; that on September 4, 1957, the partnership and the individual members of the partnership entered into a growers contract with the plaintiff association. This contract provided that:

> The said Grower hereby transfers and agrees to deliver to the Association his entire crop of merchantable apples, pears, strawberries and other fruit for the year 1957 and every year thereafter, continuously, provided that the Grower may cancel this contract on March 31st of any year by giving written notice to the Association on or before March 20th of such year that he desires the same cancelled, and delivering his copy of the contract to the Association and paying any indebtedness due to the Association from the Grower. The failure of the Grower to so notify the Association and comply with the provisions aforesaid shall operate to continue this contract in force until such notification shall be given at the proper time, and other stipulations aforesaid shall likewise be complied with.

Subsequently, and on the 4th day of February, 1963, a corporation known as "Goe Co." was organized by the Goe brothers and all of the real property except one parcel was conveyed by the partnership to the corporation. On February 28, 1963, the partnership notified the plaintiff association that they had sold the other three parcels of land and as to these properties the marketing agreement would no longer be recognized.

After the formation of the corporation and the transfer of the three parcels of land from the partnership to the corporation, the real property was managed and operated in exactly the same manner by the Goe brothers as they had under the partnership, and the income therefrom was used to pay personal bills of the brothers as they had done when operating as partners.

The trial court found "that the principal purpose of forming the corporation and transferring the partnership interest in three of the four partnership ranches to the corporation was to avoid the obligation to market through the Plaintiff as required in the contract of September 4, 1957." With this finding we agree.

Since the trial court held in effect that the creation of the corporation was but a subterfuge to avoid the marketing contract, and we agree, that a court of equity will look through the form of the transaction to the substance and enforce the contract sought to be avoided.

The decree of the trial court is affirmed.

New Hampshire Wholesale Beverage Assn. v. New Hampshire State Liquor Comm.

1955, (N.H.) 116 A.2d 885

The plaintiff is an association of individuals who hold wholesaler's liquor permits issued by the defendant commission under authority of a statute (R.C.L. 170). Sec. 76 of the statute provides, "No person shall directly or indirectly hold more than two off-sale permits at one time." The plaintiff alleges that the defendant has violated the statute by issuing one or two off-sale permits to each of certain corporations with knowledge that such corporations are owned, operated or controlled by the same person or the same group of persons. The plaintiff seeks an injunction and a declaratory judgment. The trial judge referred the case to the Supreme Court.

GOODNOW, J. . . . In applying this limitation to a corporation, the commission has treated the corporation as a separate entity, without regard to whether the person or persons who own or control it are the owners or in control of other corporate off-sale permittees. The plaintiffs contend that the same person or group of persons have thereby been permitted to hold "directly or indirectly . . . more than two off-sale permits at one time," in violation of § 76.

The fiction that the corporation is a being independent of those who are associated as its stockholders is not favored in this state.

It is to be disregarded "when justice demands it." In this case, it is not entitled to recognition as the basis for the issuance of off-sale permits if a means is thereby provided of avoiding a clear legislative purpose.

The defendants, relying on the fact that § 58 specifically authorizes the issuance of off-sale permits to corporations and that the word "person" in the statute in question should be construed as "corporation" in accordance with § 1, subd. III, contend that the Legislature did not intend that the issuance of off-sale permits to a corporation should in any way depend upon the identity of its stockholders. They further urge that if such had been the legislative purpose, that fact could have been spelled out as it is in the prohibitions concerning interlocking stock ownership between the holder of a wholesaler's permit and the holder of an on-sale or off-sale permit. We are unable to adopt this view of the Legislature's intention.

Chapter 170 has repeatedly been construed by this court as "intended to provide a complete and well-rounded system for the regulation and control of all intoxicating liquors."

By its terms, manufacturers, wholesalers and retailers of alcoholic beverages are separated into classes and "no control, direct or indirect and no interest, financial or otherwise, shall be exercised by one over the other." The statute now in question was designed to impose a similar regulation within one class of retailers.

The maximum number of off-sale permits is not only fixed at two but the limitation is to be applied so that "no person" shall hold more than that number either "directly or indirectly." By so limiting the number of off-sale permits we believe that the Legislature intended to prevent a concentration of such permits in the hands of the same persons. Not every case of interlocking stock ownership results in an indirect holding of an off-sale permit. Before the issuance of such permits to a corporation the facts must be determined by the commission as to whether the person or persons owning or controlling the corporation are also the holders of other off-sale permits, either individually or as the owners or those in control of other corporate off-sale permittees.

The relief sought by plaintiffs was granted.

Knox et al. v. First Security Bank of Utah et al.

1952, 196 F.2d 112

The plaintiffs as surviving heirs of Frank Knox brought this action against the bank as executor of the estate of A. C. Milner, deceased, and the Milner Corporation as defendants to recover damages for breach of contract. In 1909 Milner as a promoter entered into an agreement with the deceased Frank Knox whereby it was stipulated that the Milner Corporation would be organized and that when chartered the corporation would pay to Knox $25,000 from the first net profits derived by the corporation from the sale of the mining properties involved in the agreement. The corporation was subsequently organized and in 1924 Milner as president of the defendant corporation wrote a letter to the plaintiff, DeWitt Knox, stating that the corporation would live up to the terms of the agreement made with his father. The lower court sustained defendant's motion to dismiss and the plaintiffs appealed.

BRATTON, Circuit Judge. . . . The first contention urged by plaintiffs is that the complaint stated a cause of action against the defendant Milner Corporation, and that the court erred in dismissing the action as against that defendant. It is argued in support of the contention that the original undertaking entered into in 1909 was a promoters contract; that it was accepted and adopted by the defendant Milner Corporation; and that therefore such defendant is liable. It is well settled law in Utah that promoters or those contemplating the organization of a corporation do not have power to enter into a contract with binding effect upon the corporation after it is organized. They lack that power, either as agents or otherwise. But promoters or those contemplating the formation of a corporation may make a contract in furtherance of the corporation and for its benefit; and if the corporation after it comes into existence accepts or adopts the contract, it thereupon becomes the contract of the corporation and may be enforced against it. (Cases cited)

Under the law of Utah, a contract made by and with promoters which is intended to inure to the benefit of a corporation about to be organized is to be regarded as an open offer which the corporation may after its formation accept or adopt, as it chooses. And if it does in the exercise of its own judgment accept or adopt the contract and retain the benefits of it, it cannot reject liability under it. In the absence of acceptance or adoption of a contract of that kind, the corporation is not liable even though it may have been entered into with the understanding that the corporation would be bound. But it is not necessary that acceptance or adoption of a contract of that kind be by express action of the corporation entered in the minutes of the directors, or that it be effectuated in any other like formal manner. It may be inferred from acts, conduct, and acquiescence.

The original undertaking was an agreement in the nature of a promoter's contract. And from what has been said it is manifest that defendant Milner Corporation is not bound by it to make payment of the $25,000 unless it was accepted or adopted in an effective manner. Assuming for the moment that Milner, in his capacity as president of the corporation, was clothed with authority to act for it in accepting and adopting the undertaking, there can be little doubt that the letter written in 1924 constituted an effective acceptance and adoption. The letter referred at the beginning to the undertaking to pay $25,000 from the sale of the property or from profits derived from its operation. It stated in clear terms that the time when liquidation of the obligation would begin was dependent upon the volume of business done and the payment of advances made to an operating company. And it further stated without condition or qualification that the agreement was being kept in mind and would be reached at the proper time. Plainly, the last statement was intended to mean that the obligation would be reached for payment at the proper time. The letter constituted recognition of the original undertaking as an obligation on the part of the corporation to pay the amount specified in the contract at the proper time. And in the circumstances, that recognition amounted to an effective acceptance and adoption of the undertaking.

The judgment insofar as it dismissed the action against the defendant Milner Corporation is reversed.

CHAPTER 38
REVIEW QUESTIONS AND PROBLEMS

1. A corporation is formed under the name of Maybe Butter Company. Promoters for another concern desire to incorporate under the name of Mayby Butter Company. Will those responsible for granting charters grant them one under that name?

2. State X required building contractors to obtain a license to build. Access to the courts was denied if the license was not obtained. P entered into a contract with D in state X to build in state Y. When D failed to pay, P brought suit and D sought to have the case dismissed because P did not have a license. What result?

3. State X requires foreign corporations to qualify to do business or suffer the penalty of non-access to the courts. P maintains a warehouse for an inventory of goods which are shipped to customers within and without the state on orders received at its home office without the state. Must P qualify to do business in X?

4. If, in question 3, all the goods were shipped to out-of-state customers, would the result be the same?

5. *P* owns real and personal property in state *X*. *X* has a statute requiring qualification but *P* did not qualify. *P* leases its property to *D*, the lease being executed in state *Y*. If *D* fails to pay the rent, may *P* sue *D* in state *X*?

6. *D* Co. had qualified to do business in state *X* but its qualification had been suspended for non-payment of franchise taxes. *D* was sued by *P* in state *X*. May *D* defend the suit?

7. *X* Co. was formed but failed to have its charter recorded locally. *X* leased space to *D* and *D* failed to pay the rent. When *X* Co. sued *D* for the rent, *D* challenged the legality of *X*'s organization and contended that *X* Co. had no standing to sue. What result?

8. *D* is a promoter for the *X* Co. *X* Co. is guilty of fraud in several transactions with *P* in which *D* was not involved. *X* Co. is insolvent. *P* sues *D* for fraud. What result?

9. *D* was a promoter for *A* Co. He accepted $10,000 from *P*, a subscriber, who was told that the stock was $10 par value and that *P* would receive 1,000 shares. The corporation when formed issued no par stock. *P* sues *D* and the *A* Co. for the return of his purchase price. What result?

10. *A* Co. was the parent and *B* Co. a subsidiary. *A* Co. extended credit to *B* Co. Later *B* Co. became insolvent and the other creditors objected to *A* Co. sharing equally in the assets. Is *A* Co. entitled to its pro rata share of *B*'s assets?

11. *P* sued *D* Co. for a percentage of the net earnings of *D* Co. pursuant to an employment contract. *D* Co. had commingled its records and funds into a corporate maze. *P* seeks to hold all companies of the "mage" and to disregard the various corporate entities. May he do so?

chapter **39**

Powers of Corporations

5-38 In General. A corporation has only such powers as are conferred upon it by the state which creates it. States may grant to corporations any power requested by the corporation that is not prohibited by the Federal Constitution or a state constitution. The incorporators in the application for a charter request the powers desired and these are usually quite broad. The state then issues the charter and the charter together with the statute under which it is issued set forth the express powers of the corporation. In addition, all powers reasonably necessary to carry out the expressed powers are implied.[1]

The following powers are those usually provided in the statutes of most states: (1) to have a corporate name, to control, to own, to convey property, to sue and to be sued therein; (2) to have continued existence during the period for which created; (3) to have a common seal; (4) to make by-laws; (5) to purchase and to hold real estate for the purpose of the corporation, unless forbidden by its charter or statute; (6) to borrow money when necessary to carry out the corporate purpose.

The corporate name may not be deceptively similar to those of other business enterprises and by the law of many states must conclude with either the word "Company," "Corporation," or "Incorporated." The name may be changed by charter amendment at any time without affecting corporate contracts or title to corporate property in any way.

5-39 Power to Borrow. In connection with the power to borrow money, it should be noted that a corporation may give a mortgage or security

[1] *Edward v. Peabody Coal Co. et al.,* page 815.

interest in its property to secure a debt created for a corporate objective. In addition, the officers may, with the consent of a majority of the stockholders, when the corporation is insolvent, make an assignment of all the property for the benefit of creditors. In the absence of statutory authority, a corporation cannot sell or mortgage its franchise or charter. In addition, corporations vested with the public interest, such as public utilities, cannot mortgage or sell their property without authority from the state creating them.

A corporation has the power, in the absence of an express restriction, to borrow money and to evidence the same with bonds. The statute usually specifies the procedure necessary for issuing such bonds, and if the statute is not complied with, the bonds are invalid.

A corporation likewise has implied power to take or to indorse promissory notes and to accept or to indorse bills of exchange in the usual course of its business. A corporation has no implied power to loan money or become a surety or guarantor, in absence of express statutory authority, unless it is necessary for the purpose of carrying out the objects of the corporation. Statutes in some states authorize a corporation to enter into contracts of guaranty without limitation; others allow it only when the corporation has a direct interest in the subject matter of the contract guaranteed.[2]

5-40 Other Powers. A corporation is without power to enter into a partnership or combination with other corporations for the purpose of bringing the management of the partnership or corporations under one control. A corporation does not have authority to share its corporate management with natural persons in a partnership because it would expose the stockholders to risks not contemplated by the stockholders' contracts, although it may enter a joint-venture.

A corporation, in absence of statutory authority, has no implied power to subscribe to, purchase, or hold the stock of another corporation whose chartered purpose is totally foreign to its own. Many states allow such stock transactions; those who do not, feel that to permit such action would subject the stockholders to risks not anticipated by them. By court decision or statute, the corporations of most states are now empowered to subscribe for, or purchase, the stock of other corporations for the purpose of furthering their own objectives. It may invest idle funds in the stock of other corporations or accept such shares in settlement of an indebtedness owing to it. A certain phase of its business may be transacted by means of a subsidiary for whose organization it is responsible or whose control it has acquired by stock purchase.[3] In such cases, the parent company may, or may not, be a holding company organized for the express purpose of acquiring stock of other corporations.

Acquisitions of stock of other corporations are subject to the provisions of section 7 of the Sherman Antitrust Act as amended by the Celler-

---

[2] *Choctaw Lumber Co. v. Atlanta Band Mill, Inc.,* page 816.
[3] *Durham v. Firestone Tire & Rubber Co.,* page 817.

Kefauver amendment which prohibits the acquisition by one corporation of assets or stock of another, where, in any line of commerce, the effect may be substantially to lessen competition, or tend to create a monopoly.

5-41 Treasury Stock. A corporation is somewhat restricted in its power to purchase its own previously issued stock, because the purchase of its own stock might effect a reduction of its capital to the detriment of creditors and stockholders. In most states a corporation is permitted to purchase shares of its own stock only out of accumulated profits or surplus.[4] This retains an investment in the corporation by stockholders equivalent to the original capital as a protective cushion for creditors in case subsequent losses develop. A few states, however, permit a corporation to acquire treasury stock as long as the corporation is not insolvent. A corporation may also acquire its own stock in payment of, or in security for, an antecedent debt due the corporation. It may also take its own stock for nonpayment of an authorized assessment made by the company on the stock or it may take it as a gift. A corporation that has issued preferred stock has the power to redeem such stock, where there is no injury to, or objection by, creditors. Here again, many of the states require the preferred stock to be redeemed out of surplus or demand that authority to reduce the capital stock be obtained from the state.

Treasury stock—stock of its own issue acquired by a corporation—is not automatically canceled. It lies dormant in the treasury of the corporation without the right to vote or to share in dividends until it is again sold and transferred to a stockholder. It is to be noted that the capitalization of a corporation can be reduced only with the approval of the state of incorporation and the procedure outlined in the state corporation laws must be followed in effecting the reduction.

5-42 *Ultra Vires.* Any acts of a corporation that are beyond the authority express or implied given to it by the state are said to be *ultra vires* acts —"beyond the authority." If a corporation performs acts or enters into contracts to perform acts which are *ultra vires,* the state creating such corporation may forfeit its charter for misuse of its corporate authority. The extent of the misuse is controlling in determining whether the state will take away its franchise or merely enjoin the corporation from further *ultra vires* conduct.

While third parties have no right to object to the *ultra vires* acts of a corporation, a stockholder may bring court action to enjoin a corporation from performing an *ultra vires* contract. In addition, the corporation may recover from the directors who approved the *ultra vires* contracts any losses or damages sustained because of the *ultra vires* venture. When they exceed corporate powers, they may become personally liable for resulting losses.

---

[4] *Jarroll Coal Co., Inc. v. Lewis et al.,* page 818.

At common law, a corporation had no liability on contracts beyond its corporate powers because the corporation has capacity only to do those things expressly authorized within its charter or which were incidental thereto.[5] However, most modern statutes, including the Uniform Business Corporation Act, provide that all *ultra vires* contracts are enforceable. Neither party to such a contract may use *ultra vires* as a defense. *Ultra vires* conduct on the part of the corporation may be enjoined by the state or any stockholder as previously noted, but otherwise contracts previously made are binding whether they be wholly executory, partially executed, or fully performed. In such cases, the directors are liable for losses suffered as a result of engaging in *ultra vires* activities.

5-43 Power to Commit Torts. Like natural persons, a corporation has power to do wrong, such as commit torts and crimes, and is liable therefor. A corporation, being an artificial person and impersonal, cannot personally commit a tort. But a corporation is liable under the laws applicable to principal and agent for the contracts and for the torts of its agent committed in the pursuit of the corporate business.[6] Tort liability is created even though the act is *ultra vires* to the corporate charter.

A corporation is liable for fraud committed by its officers or agents within the scope of their authority. It is also liable if the fraudulent act is apparently within the general authority of the agents. Corporations are not only liable for acts committed by their agents in the pursuit of the corporate business, but they are likewise liable for injury caused by the failure of their agents to perform duties of the corporation. Thus a corporation is liable for acts of omission such as the negligence of an agent in failing to keep its property in safe condition.

A corporation cannot commit crimes which involve intent or personal violence. However, a corporation may be criminally liable for the violation of a law which imposes a duty upon the corporation to do, or not to do, an act. For example, a corporation may be fined for failure to comply with some statute that specifies certain things to be done by the corporation—such as supplying protection for employees and making reports—and for the violation of regulatory statutes under the police power of the state.

A corporation may be indicted for improperly performing an act that it may lawfully do. For example, a corporation may be indicted for conducting a perfectly legal business in such a manner as to be guilty of maintaining a nuisance. Corporations cannot be held liable for criminal acts involving personal violence, but may be held criminally responsible for failure to comply with statutes which have prohibited certain acts. Corporations have been criminally liable for unlawful conspiracies to restrain trade, for knowingly and fraudulently concealing property under the Bankruptcy Act, for giving rebates to shippers in violation

---

5 *Temple Lumber Co. v. Miller,* page 820.
6 *Poledna v. Bendix Aviation Corporation,* page 821.

of federal statutes, and for violations of other statutes. Corporations may also be held for contempt of court by reason of acts or omissions of their agents where they have violated an injunction. The court may punish such corporations by the levy of a fine, the same as against a natural person.

POWERS OF CORPORATIONS CASES

Elward v. Peabody Coal Co. et al.

1956, 9 Ill. App.2d 234, 132 N.E.2d 549

The plaintiff, a stockholder in the defendant corporation, brought this suit against the corporation and its seven directors for a declaratory decree that a stock option was invalid and for injunctive relief. The directors by resolution gave one of the employees of the corporation an option to purchase 40,000 shares at $3 per share. On the day that the option was given the market price of the common was $3 per share; in June, 1955, it was $8 per share. The plaintiff contended that under the corporate laws of Illinois the corporation was not authorized to grant the option. The lower court dismissed the complaint and plaintiff appealed.

BURKE, J. . . . The plaintiff asserts that the Business Corporation Act does not empower a corporation to issue a stock option; that this power is not granted in express terms or by implication; that a shareholder is entitled under the common law to preemptive rights; and that the Act should be construed strictly so as not to impair the preemptive rights of stockholders. The public policy of this state is found in the Constitution, the statutes and the decisions of the courts. Plaintiff cites cases pointing out the distinction between the power to sell and the power to give an option. The preemptive right of shareholders to share pro rata in any new issue of corporate stock so that their interest will not be diluted but continue proportionately, is part of the common law of this State. Section 24 of the Business Corporation Act, reads:

> The preemptive right of a shareholder to acquire additional shares of a cooporation may be limited or denied to the extent provided in the articles of incorporation. Unless otherwise provided by its articles of incorporation, any corporation may issue and sell its shares to its employees or to the employees of any subsidiary corporation, without first offering the same to its shareholders, for such consideration and upon such terms and conditions as shall be approved by the holders of two-thirds of its shares entitled to vote with respect thereto or by its board of directors pursuant to like approval of the shareholders.

The first sentence of § 24 provides that the charter of an Illinois corporation may limit or deny the preemptive right of a shareholder to acquire additional shares of stock. The second sentence of the section allows a corporation which does not have an express charter denial or limitation of preemptive rights, to issue and sell stock to its employees free of preemptive rights for such consideration and upon such terms and conditions as shall be approved by the holders of two-thirds of its shares entitled to vote with respect thereto or by its board of directors pursuant to like approval of the shareholders. Plaintiff inquires that, keeping in mind the doctrine that corporate powers are to be construed strictly and that no power is to be implied unless reasonably necessary to an express power, under what section or sections could the power to issue stock options be regarded as implied? Section 5 of the Business Corporation Act states that each corporation shall have power to make contacts and incur liabilities, to elect or appoint officers and agents of the corporation, to define their duties and fix their compensations, and to exercise all powers necessary or convenient to effect any or all of the purposes for which the corporation is formed. It cannot be doubted that Illinois corporations are empowered to enter into contracts relating to employment. The implied powers which a corporation has in order to carry into effect those expressly granted and to accomplish the purposes of its creation are not limited to such as are indispensable for these purposes, but comprise all that are necessary in the sense of appropriate and suitable, including the right of reasonable choice of means to be employed. (13 Am. Jur., Corporations, § 740). We are of the opinion that there is ample implied power in §§ 5 and 24 of the Business Corporation Act and in Article 9 of the amended charter to sustain the action of the defendant corporation in entering into a valid contract with an officer or employee for a stock option.

Reversed and remanded however, for other reasons.

Choctaw Lumber Co. v. Atlanta Band Mill, Inc.

1953, 88 Ga. App. 701, 77 S.E.2d 333

The plaintiff corporation filed suits on two contracts of guaranty against the defendant-guarantor, Atlanta Band Mill, Inc. The defendant had guaranteed payment of the notes issued by Atlanta Band Mill Sales, Inc. The resolution passed by the Board of Directors of the defendant corporation read in part as follows: "Whereas, Atlanta Band Mill Sales, Inc. is a sales agency for Atlanta Band Mill, Inc. and whereas, it is to the financial advantage of Atlanta Band Mill, Inc. that Atlanta Band Mill Sales, Inc. meet its obligations and maintain its financial integrity; Now, therefore, be it resolved that Atlanta Band Mill, Inc. authorize and direct its officers to execute a Guarantee in usual terms guaranteeing the payment of the following note." The case proceeded to trial and at the conclusion of the plaintiffs' evidence a motion to nonsuit was granted. Plaintiff appealed.

TOWNSEND, J.   . . . Prior to the Corporation Act of 1938 Ga. L. 1938, p. 214, the law, as stated in Code, § 22-701, was as follows: "Corporations created under Chapter 22-3 may exercise all corporate powers necessary to the purpose of their organization, but shall make no contract, or purchase or hold any property of any kind, except such as is necessary in legitimately carrying into effect such purpose, or for securing debts due to the company." Following such Act, Code Ann. Supp. § 22-1828 (c) gives to corporations the power "to guarantee, become surety upon or indorse the contracts or obligations of any other corporation, firm or individual as to matters in which the corporation guaranteeing has a direct interest but shall not have the right to enter into any contract of guaranty, suretyship or indorsement where the corporation guaranteeing has no direct interest in the subject matter of the contract guaranteed or to make any purely accommodation guaranty, indorsement or contract of suretyship, unless such right . . . is contained in the charter of the corporation or an amendment lawfully made thereto."

The latter Code section certainly enlarged the meaning of the former to some extent as to the power of corporations to enter into guaranty contracts executed upon a valid consideration. The contract here had such consideration. (Cases cited.) The question of the extent to which such powers were enlarged must be determined. It is no longer necessary to prove that the contract was "necessary in legitimately carrying into effect such purpose (of the corporate organization), or for securing debts due to the company," but it must be shown that the guarantor corporation has a "direct interest in the subject matter of the contract guaranteed." The contract guaranteed was one granting an extension of time to the sales agency to pay a debt, for the purpose of avoiding a lawsuit which would have the effect of injuring the credit of the defendant. The term direct interest has previously been the subject of judicial construction. It is defined in Black's Law Dictionary as meaning "not contingent or doubtful." An employee seeking unemployment compensation is "directly interested" in a labor dispute which would affect the amount of wages received by himself and other employees similarly situated, under an unemployment compensation statute.

Applying this definition to the proof offered by the plaintiff on the trial of the case, it appears that the defendant guarantor whose owners had created the sales agency for its convenience was financially involved in the latter's credit, to the extent that a failure of the debtor corporation would seriously impair both the guarantor's credit and the distribution of its products; that it entered into the contract to prevent a lawsuit being filed against the sales company, and that the sales company was either insolvent at that time or became so between the date of the contract and the date of the filing of this suit, approximately five months later.

. . . It follows, therefore, that the evidence in this record is sufficient to authorize the finding that the defendant corporation had a direct interest in the subject matter of the contracts guaranteed within the meaning of Code Ann. Supp. § 22-1828. The trial court erred in granting a nonsuit and in overruling the motion to reinstate the case.

Judgment reversed.

Durham v. Firestone Tire & Rubber Co. of California
1936, 47 Ariz. 280, 55 P.2d 648

The plaintiff, Firestone Tire and Rubber Company of California, brought action against Durham, the defendant, to recover on a promissory note executed by the defendant. The note was given in payment for stock in Firestone Service Stores, Inc. of Phoenix, an Arizona corporation. The incorporators of the Phoenix corporation included the California Corporation which by agreement was always to own at least 51 per cent of the stock. The defendant contended that one corporation may not organize or subscribe to the original stock of another and that the organization of the Phoenix Company was void, and its stock worthless so that there was no consideration for defendant's note. The lower court gave judgment to the plaintiff and defendant appealed.

LOCKWOOD, C. J. . . . There is undoubtedly considerable conflict in the authorities as to whether one corporation may participate in the organization of another. Among those cases holding that it may not are found such as *Nebraska Shirt Co. v. Horton* (3 Neb. (Unof.) 888, 93 N.W. 225); *Denny Hotel Co. v. Schram* (6 Wash. 134, 32 P. 1002, 36 Am. St. Rep. 130); *Moore v. Los Lugos Gold Mines* (172 Wash. 570, 21 P.2d 253); *Schwab v. E. G. Potter Co.* (194 N.Y. 409, 87 N.E. 670), and others. Apparently this is based, although not always so expressed, upon the idea set forth in *Nebraska Shirt Co. v. Horton, supra,* in the following language: "Corporations have quite enough power without allowing them to incorporate themselves in new companies." Stated as a general proposition, there may be merit in this theory, but we think there is at least one well-grounded exception thereto. Where the obvious purpose of the new corporation is merely to act as a subsidiary for the parent one, and to carry out the purposes for which the parent itself was formed, we see no reason why, in the absence of a statute forbidding it, a corporation, as a matter of principle, should not be permitted to participate in the organization of its subsidiary. Unless prohibited by law, if its articles are broad enough, it can purchase stock in another such corporation after the latter is organized, and, through such purchase, control the operations of the other company, and, if it may do this, it would be extremely technical to say that it may not, through its duly authorized agents, organize the new company in the beginning. If the new company were organized for the purpose of evading limitations placed on the rights and authority of the parent company, the situation might be very different, but in the present case there can be no doubt that the Phoenix company was organized for the purpose of assisting in the better and more profitable disposition of the very product which the California company was engaged in producing and distributing.

. . . We hold, therefore, that under the law of Arizona a corporation is not prohibited from subscribing to or holding the stock of a new corporation whose purpose is naturally subsidiary to, and in aid of, the business of the old corporation.

Jarroll Coal Co., Inc. v. Lewis et al.

1954, 210 F.2d 578

On March 1, 1949, E. L. Jarroll, Sr. and the members of his family owned all the stock of the mining company, defendant in this action. On that day he entered into a contract with the company by the terms of which the company purchased all of the stock from him paying him $4,000 in cash and giving him its note in the sum of $20,000. There was testimony that the note was to be secured by a chattel deed of trust but this was not executed until two years later. In March, 1949, the assets of the company, exclusive of good will, exceeded its liabilities, exclusive of the note by less than $15,000.

The plaintiffs, trustees of the United Mine Workers Welfare and Retirement Fund, had obtained a judgment against the company on a contract of March 1, 1949, whereby the company agreed to pay into the Welfare and Retirement Fund a certain amount per ton on coal mined by the company. This matter was brought before the court at the instance of the United States Marshal to have the court determine the conflicting claims to property of the coal company upon which he had levied execution. The trustees claimed it under their judgment and Mr. Jarroll claimed it under his trust deed.

. . . From a judgment in favor of the plaintiffs, execution creditors, holding the note and chattel deed of trust void as against them because violative of the West Virginia statute, Code of 1949, § 3051 (31-1-39), (forbidding a corporation to use its funds to purchase its own stock, where this results in an impairment of capital, the coal company has appealed.

PARKER, C. J. . . . The pertinent portion of § 3051 of the West Virginia Code of 1949 (31-1-39), which was taken from the general corporation law of the State of Delaware, is as follows:

> Every corporation organized under this chapter, or existing under the laws of this State, shall have the power to purchase, hold, sell and transfer shares of its own capital stock: Provided, that no such corporation shall use its funds or property for the purchase of its own shares of capital stock when such use would cause any impairment of the capital of the corporation.

Accepting, as we think we should, the finding of the trial judge that the good will of the company was without value, there can be no question but that payment of the $4,000 in cash and the execution of the $20,000 note on March 1, 1949, not only impaired the capital of the corporation but rendered it insolvent. Appellant contends that, even so, the trustees of the welfare and retirement fund were not creditors at that time and cannot complain of the transaction for that reason. It appears, however, that the contract under which the claim of the trustees arises was executed on the very day that the note was given and that the indebtedness had been incurred before the execution of the chattel deed of trust, two years later, transferring the assets of the corporation to secure the note. It was the transfer under this deed which was relied upon to defeat the levy under the execution; and there can be no question but that such transfer, made at a time when the corporation was insolvent and made to secure stockholders for the purchase price of stock theretofore purchased from them, is void as to claims of creditors existing at the time it was made. (*Boggs v. Fleming*, 4 Cir., 66 F.2d 859, 860). As said by this court in the case cited:

> While, in the absence of charter or statutory prohibition, it is well settled that a corporation may purchase its own stock, it can only do so provided the act is in good faith and without intent to injure its creditors. . . . The authorities are unanimous to the effect that, even though a corporation be solvent when it contracts to purchase its own stock, it may not later, upon insolvency, pay for it, until after the existing creditors have been paid . . .

We think, also, that, even though the trustees be regarded as subsequent creditors, they are in a position to attack the transaction here under consideration. It is a fraud on subsequent as well as upon existing creditors for the stockholders of a corporation to cause it to purchase their stock at a price rendering it insolvent, take an unrecorded lien upon all of its assets and allow it to continue doing business in its corporate name as if nothing had happened. Such creditors are unquestionably entitled to treat as void, because in fraud of their rights, a transaction which in effect gives stockholders a secret lien on corporate assets.

. . . There was no error and the judgment appealed from will be affirmed.

Temple Lumber Co. v. Miller

1943, (Tex. Civ. App.) 169 S.W.2d 256

The plaintiff, Miller, sued the defendant Temple Lumber Company, a corporation, for damages resulting from defective workmanship and the use of defective material in the construction of a house for the plaintiff. The defendant contended that it could not be held liable on the contract because it was *ultra vires*. The corporation's charter set out the purposes of the corporation as that of "manufacturing lumber and the purchase and sale of material used in such business and doing all things necessary and incident to such lumber business." The lower court ruled in favor of the plaintiff and defendant appealed.

SPEER, J. . . . It is insistently urged that since defendant's charter only authorized it to buy and sell lumber and building material, it could not be held to have made a contract to construct a building, as contended by plaintiff.

. . . It appears that the early English cases, as well as some by federal courts, and even the early cases decided by our state courts, are not in complete harmony with respect to the extent a corporation may go and bind itself. But the trend seems to be that even though the charter provisions do not, in so many words, authorize an act, the corporation may bind itself to do many things when not against public policy and are not forbidden by law. There is a clear distinction between acts which are void because of legal inhibitions, and those which are not prohibited but are those which are not enumerated in the purpose clause of the charter. In the latter class are to be found instances which include acts which are appropriate, convenient and suitable in carrying out the purposes for which the charter was expressly granted. These are termed implied powers and authority. (Cases cited)

To our minds, the contract involved here was not one prohibited by law nor by any principle of public policy. No good reason exists why defendant could not contract with plaintiff to sell him the materials to go into his house. We think it would logically follow that as an inducement to plaintiff to buy the materials from it, defendant could agree and bind itself to deliver the materials at its own expense, although its charter did not expressly authorize it to haul building materials. It could deliver, then could it not even cut the lumber into desired lengths? Carrying the thought further, it could with propriety obligate itself to do many things not expressly mentioned in its charter, when "appropriate," "convenient" and "suitable" in the prosecution of the line of business expressly mentioned in the charter. An act of a corporation is said to be *ultra vires* when beyond the scope either of the express or implied powers of its charter. If the acts are within the scope of the implied powers of the corporation, they cannot be said to be *ultra vires,* yet some of our courts deem them such if they are not within the express terms of the charter. We think that if the act is not one prohibited by law or public policy, and it inures to the direct benefit of the corporation, and is executed, it is not, strictly speaking, *ultra vires,* and this is apparently the view taken by the trial court.

. . . The court found as a fact (and there is an abundance of evidence to support it) that the house was in fact erected by defendant, and that plaintiff had paid to defendant the entire original contract price—the contract was fully executed on both sides; the controversy here being over defective workmanship and materials. It would appear that in such circumstances, defendant would be estopped to plead and rely upon *ultra vires,* and at the same time receive and retain the direct benefits of the contract it seeks to avoid. Such contention does not appeal to our sense of justice and equity. Estoppel was pleaded by plaintiff; the court found the facts as indicated, and concluded that defendant was estopped to rely upon its plea of *ultra vires.* In this we think he was correct.

. . . *We have concluded that no reversible errors are presented by any of the points raised, and we therefore order that the judgment of the trial court should be and is accordingly affirmed.*

Poledna v. Bendix Aviation Corporation

1960 (Mich.) 103 N.W.2d 789

EDWARDS, Justice.   Plaintiff Robert Poledna brought a libel and slander action against defendants Bendix Aviation Corporation and Walter Bare for certain allegations of theft made against him. After trial before Berrien County Circuit Court, the jury returned a verdict of $10,000 "past damage" and $2,500 "punitive" damage. . . .

Defendants appeal claiming . . . that defendant corporation may not be held responsible for slander by an employee. . . .

The action was occasioned by the circumstances of plaintiff's discharge from the employment of defendant Bendix Aviation Corporation by defendant Walter Bare, at that time the employment manager for Bendix' plant at St. Joseph, Michigan.

. . . The next of appellants' issues pertains to the claim that defendant corporation is not liable for the actions of defendant Bare. In support of this contention, they cite *Robertson v. New York Life Ins. Co.* (312 Mich. 92, 19 N.W.2d 498), and *Flaherty v. Maxwell Motor Co.* (187 Mich. 62, 153 N.W. 45). In this latter case, 187 Mich. at page 67, 153 N.W. at page 46, the Court said:

> Our examination of the cases satisfies us that the great weight of the authorities holds that a corporation is not liable for slander uttered by its servants unless it affirmatively appears that the agent was expressly authorized to speak the words in question or the corporation subsequently ratified the utterance.

The facts in our current record leave no doubt that Bare was functioning in his official capacity as employment manager of defendant corporation on the occasion of the slanderous utterance. The trial judge's charge included these words:

> And by the way, the defendant, Bendix Aviation Corporation, is responsible for any act of its personnel officer, who is the other defendant, Walter Bare, in this case.

Whatever the state of the law of libel and slander when Flaherty was decided, it seems apparent that the trial judge's charge comes far closer to representing the majority rule today.

> There is no longer any doubt that a corporation may be held liable for slander uttered by an agent while in the discharge of his duty as agent, and in relation to the matter about which his duty as agent permits or requires him to act, in the same way and to the same extent as an individual could be held liable for the same slander. (*Priest v. Central States Fire Ins. Co.,* 1928, 223 Mo.App. 122, 9 S.W.2d 543). . . .

Fletcher's *Cyclopedia Corporations* (Perm. Ed.) § 4888, says:

> The doctrine of nonliability based on the proposition that there can be no agency in slander has long been exploded.

(See, also, 55 A.L.R.2d 828.)

We approve the charge of the trial judge on this issue and overrule any language in the Flaherty and Robertson cases, *supra,* which conflicts with the views expressed herein.

The corporation was held to be liable.

CHAPTER 39
REVIEW QUESTIONS AND PROBLEMS

1. The *L & S* Lumber Co. was a corporation operating a mill in the woods. A highline used in the mill extended across a road and had

fallen. This highline had fallen once before, and *B,* who was a stock-holder-director and officer of the corporation and who worked at the mill, knew this and the continuing danger that the line might fall again. The line fell again, and *X* was struck. Is *B* liable to *X*? Is the corporation liable to *X*?

2. *X* corporation operated a market. The manager of the market falsely accused *A,* a customer, of taking groceries from the store without paying for them. *A* sued *X* corporation for false arrest, false imprisonment, and slander. Should he recover judgment?

3. *X* Co. was sued by an architect for services rendered in designing homes for resale. *X* Co.'s charter did not authorize it to deal in real estate. *X* Co. contended that the contract was *ultra vires.* What result?

4. *X* Co., a manufacturing concern, purchased some stock in the *A* Bank from another stockholder. The bank refused to issue a new stock certificate, contending that *X* Co. had no power to own stock and that the bank wanted only individual stockholders. *X* Co. sued *A* Bank to require the issuance of new stock certificates. What result?

5. What are the sources of a corporation's powers?

6. *X* Co. decided to donate $10,000 to the State College scholarship fund. *P,* a minority shareholder, objected and demanded that the sum be used for dividends. May *P* enjoin the gift?

7. Who may question an *ultra vires* action?

Stock and
Stock Ownership

5-44 Membership in Corporations. Where the corporation is a nonstock company, membership is regulated by the By-laws. Membership in a stock corporation is acquired by a contract with the corporation; this membership is evidenced by a certificate showing ownership of shares of stock. The right to membership may be acquired by a stock subscription before the corporation is created, or by a purchase of shares of stock from the corporation after it is organized, or by a transfer of shares from some person who owns the stock. This chapter is concerned with stock and stock ownership.

5-45 Terminology. The term capital stock creates confusion in the law because the *terms* capital and stock have a distinct meaning when not joined together. Technically, capital stock is the expressed equity of the stockholders in corporate assets resulting from their investments before the latter have been influenced by profits or losses. It should equal the amount of money, services, and property paid in or subscribed by the stockholders for the purposes of carrying on the corporate business. However, if the subscribed pays more than par value as stated on the face of the certificate to the corporation for his stock, the excess is usually credited to capital surplus or paid in surplus, rather than to the corporation's capital stock account. Capital stock is the sum fixed as such in the corporate charter. The capital stock would therefore always remain the same unless changed by an amendment of the charter. This viewpoint is generally considered to express correctly the true meaning of "capital stock," but other meanings have been given to the term.

The term "capital stock" has been loosely used to mean the representative interest of the shareholders in the total assets of the corporation, measured by its tangible and intangible property, franchise, and goodwill. The term capital stock, as used in some statutes for taxation purposes, refers to the total value of the property owned by the corporation.

The term "capital" means the net assets of the corporation, including not only the original investment, but also all gains and profits realized from the conduct of the corporate business. For example, if a corporation is incorporated with a capital stock of $50,000, fully paid, and it makes a profit of $20,000, which is kept in the business and is not distributed as dividends, it has a capital of $70,000. Its capital stock, however, is the $50,000 originally placed in the business.

The term "stock" refers to the ownership of rights in the corporation. These rights are primarily three in number: the right to share in profits, the right to participate indirectly in the control of the corporation, and the right to receive a portion of the assets at time of dissolution. A share of stock is representative of an investment made in the corporation, but it gives the holder no right to share in the active management of the business, and the general rules of law applicable to personal property are applicable to stock.

A certificate of stock is written evidence of the ownership of a certain number of shares of stock of a corporation which shows upon its face the character of the interest and the method of transfer, and may state a part of the contract existing between the shareholder and the corporation, or between him and the other shareholders. A subscriber often becomes a stockholder before the certificate is issued. The certificate is merely the physical evidence and indicates that the corporation recognizes a certain person as being a stockholder.

A bond, unlike stock, is an obligation of the corporation to pay a certain sum of money in the future at a specified rate of interest. It is comparable to a promissory note in which the corporation is the maker. Corporate bonds are often secured by a mortgage on the assets of the corporation but many corporate bonds called debentures do not have such security. A bondholder is a creditor of the corporation, whereas a stockholder is not. A stockholder has a right to receive dividends if declared by the board of directors and to participate in the assets of the corporation after all creditors have been paid. A bondholder has no right to vote or to participate in the management and control of a corporation, unless, upon insolvency, such rights are given by contract; whereas a shareholder, in the absence of contractual limitations, has a right to participate in the corporate control.

There are certain contracts with corporations which are difficult to classify. Is the holder of a preferred share of stock, which guarantees a dividend at a given rate and contains a promise of redemption at a given time, but which carries no right to vote, a shareholder or a creditor? Similarly, is a bondholder, whose bond draws interest payable only out of profits, and who is subordinate to the claims of general creditors in case of insolvency, and whose bond gives the holder the right to vote in case interest payments are not made, an investor in a corporation or a creditor? The answers are determined largely by the terms of the agreement between the corporation and the investor.

A stock warrant is a certificate which gives to the holder thereof the right to subscribe for and purchase a given number of shares of stock in a corporation at a stated price. It is usually issued in connection with the sale of other shares of stock or of bonds, although the law of some states permits the issuance of stock warrants entirely separate and apart from the sale of other securities. Usually the warrants are transferable, although in some cases they are personal only. The option to purchase contained in the warrant may or may not be limited as to time or otherwise conditioned. A warrant has value and can readily be sold on the market in the same fashion as other securities.

5-46 Kinds of Stock. *Common stock* is the simplest type of corporate stock, and entitles the owner to share in the control, profits, and assets of the corporation in proportion to the amount of common stock he holds. Such a stockholder has no advantage, priority, or preference over any other class of stockholders unless otherwise specified as to any particular class.

Preferred stock is stock that has a prior claim to dividends, or to assets on dissolution, over other classes of stock. The most important right given to a preferred stockholder is the right to receive a certain specified dividend, even though the earnings are not sufficient to pay a like dividend to common stockholders.

Preferred stock may be provided for by the charter; but, if no provision is made for the issuance of preferred stock by the charter or statute, such stock cannot be issued without the unanimous consent of the common stockholders.

Preferred stock may be *cumulative* or *noncumulative*. If the certificate of the preferred stock evidencing the contract provides not only that the preferred shares shall be entitled to a dividend of a certain per cent annually when earned, but that the arrears, if any, in one year or more are payable out of the earnings of the subsequent years, before payment of dividends on the common stock the dividends are said to be cumulative. If the dividends are to be paid out of current profits only, without provision for payment of arrearages, the preferred stock is said to be noncumulative. Whether preferred stock is cumulative or noncumulative depends upon the statute, the charter, or the contract set forth on the face of the certificate of stock. However, if nothing is said about the payment of the dividends, the preferred stock is cumulative,[1] and preferred dividends and all arrears thereon must be paid before a dividend is declared on common stock.

Preferred stock may be *participating* or *nonparticipating*. If the preferred stock is given the right to share in dividends equally with other classes of stock, after the payment of the preferred dividends, it is desig-

---

[1] *Arizona Power Co. v. Stuart,* page 839.

nated as participating preferred stock. Such participating preferred stock is entitled to additional dividends, however, only after the common stock has received a dividend equal to the preferred dividend for the current year. If, however, the preferred stock is limited in its dividend to a fixed amount, it is designated as nonparticipating preferred stock. The term "participating preferred stock" is also used to designate a preferred stock which receives a preference in the corporate assets on dissolution and liquidation of the corporation and may in addition enable the holder to share with other classes of stock in the assets that remain after the common and preferred stock have been fully satisfied by repayment of the stockholder's original investment. To determine whether preferred stock has equality in the participation in dividends and assets with other classes of stock, after the payment of its fixed dividend or return of investment, it is necessary to examine, not only the contract evidenced by the stock certificate, but also the articles of incorporation, the by-laws, and the state corporation statutes. In the absence of an agreement or other provision, preferred stock has no preference in corporate assets at dissolution.

The statutes of most states provide that a corporation may issue stock with *no par* value, the value of the stock being determined by its sale value in the open market or by the price set by the directors as a "stated value." Stockholders, creditors of the corporation, and the public will not be misled or prejudiced by this type of stock, because there is no holding out that the stock has any particular face value, and all persons dealing in such stock are put on notice that they should investigate the corporation's assets and its financial condition. Stock with no par value represents the proportionate part of the total assets of the corporation it stipulates but does not indicate the monetary value or par value of the share. The state law usually permits the directors to determine what portion of the amount received from the sale of no par stock shall be credited to the capital stock account and how much, if any, shall be credited to capital or paid-in surplus.

5-47 Watered Stock. Watered stock is stock that has been issued as fully paid, when in fact its full par value has not been paid in money, property, or services.[2] The capital stock of a corporation represents the total par value of all the shares of the corporation (plus the stated value of no par stock) and the public, including corporate creditors, has a right to assume that the capital stock issued has been paid for in full. The corporation represents that assets have been received in payment equal in amount to its issued capital stock. If stock is issued in excess of the actual assets in money value received for it by the corporation, it is said to be watered stock, and original holders of such stock are liable to corporate creditors for the difference between its par value and the amount they actually paid for the stock.

In suits by creditors against stockholders to force payment on watered stock, it is maintained by many jurisdictions that the capital stock is a

[2] *Bing Crosby Minute Maid Corp. v. Eaton,* page 839.

"trust fund" for the payment of the corporate debts and that the law implies a promise by the original stockholders to pay their stock in full when called upon by the creditors.

Another basis upon which creditors seek recovery against holders of such stock is called the "holding out" theory. Under this doctrine the right of creditors to compel the holders of bonus stock to pay for it, contrary to their actual agreement with the corporation, rests not upon an implied contract or upon any trust fund doctrine but simply upon the ground of fraud. This right applies only to those creditors who have relied upon the stock as representing actual capital paid in; therefore, payment cannot be enforced against stockholders in favor of those creditors who became such before the bonus stock was issued. In either case, only the original purchaser of the stock is liable. One who acquires it in good faith from the original stockholder has no additional liability.

5-48 Treasury Stock. "Treasury stock" is that which has been issued by the corporation for value and returned by gift or purchase to the corporation, or to trustees for the corporation to sell. It may be sold below par and the proceeds returned to the treasury of the corporation for working capital. It differs from stock originally issued below par, in that the purchaser is not liable for the difference between par and the sale price. It may be sold at any price the company sees fit to charge.

STOCK SUBSCRIPTIONS

5-49 Stock Subscriptions Before Incorporation. A stock subscription is an agreement to purchase stock in a corporation. It is a binding contract created among the subscribers for stock in a corporation to be formed, so that a subscriber cannot revoke his subscription. The subscription may be drafted in such a manner as to create a contract and some states by statute have provided that a pre-incorporation subscription constitutes a binding, irrevocable offer to the corporation, by reason of the mutual promises of the parties, and amounts to a subscription when the corporation is formed. Other states regard the subscription as a mere continuing offer which may be revoked at any time prior to acceptance by the corporation.

Certain conditions are inherent in the subscription contract. The subscriber will not be liable unless the corporation is completely organized as a *de jure* corporation; the full amount of the capital stock has been subscribed in absence of an express agreement to the contrary; and the purpose, articles, and by-laws of the corporation are as originally stated and relied upon by the subscriber. Conditions express or implied in the stock subscription agreement are often waived by the subscriber if, with knowledge of the nonperformance, he participates in stockholders' meetings, pays part or all of his subscription, or acts as an officer or director of the corporation.

Subscriptions for shares are often made subject to the happening of certain expressed conditions precedent. For example, the subscriber agrees to take shares conditioned upon the promoter's securing certain other persons to take shares, or upon a certain number of shares being subscribed. As between the corporation after it is chartered and the subscriber, the subscriber has no liability for the subscription if the conditions are not met. However, if the rights of third parties, such as creditors of the corporation, who do not have knowledge of the failure of the condition become involved, the subscription is enforceable under the doctrine of estoppel [3] and the subscriber's oral testimony of such condition and its nonperformance is not admissible. Therefore, for the protection of the subscriber any conditions should be made a part of the subscription agreement.

A distinction must be made between a subscription on a condition and a conditional delivery of a subscription contract. In an action against the subscriber to enforce the subscription agreement, oral evidence may be introduced by the subscriber to prove that the subscription contract was conditionally delivered and that in absence of the happening of the condition no subscription contract was to come into existence. Such evidence, however, cannot be introduced to show that the delivery of the subscription agreement was a conditional one if other parties such as creditors of the corporation have been misled thereby. These parties must occupy a position similar to that of a holder in due course of commercial paper if the conditional delivery is to be ignored.

5-50 Subscriptions After Incorporation. A subscription to stock of a corporation already in existence is a contract between the subscriber and the corporation, and such a contract may come into existence by reason of an offer either made by the corporation and accepted by the subscriber or made by the subscriber and accepted by the corporation. If the corporation opens subscription books and advertises its stock, it is seeking for an offer to be made by the subscriber. The corporation may, however, make a general offer to the public, which may be accepted by the subscriber in accordance with the terms of the general offer.

One must exercise care in distinguishing between a present subscription to stock, by which contract the subscriber immediately becomes liable as a stockholder, and a contract to purchase stock. Where the contract is for the purchase of stock, the purchaser does not become a stockholder until a certificate of stock has been delivered to him. Upon the breach of such contract and the tender of the stock certificate by the corporation, recovery is limited to damages for failure to purchase. Under a present subscription contract, however, the subscriber is liable upon his promise to pay for the full amount of the stock subscribed, even though the corporation has not tendered the stock certificate.

An underwriter's contract to place a certain block of stock, or, if unable to dispose of it, to purchase it himself, is not a subscription contract. Such an underwriter may, however, be held liable for as much of the stock as

---

[3] *Hoppe v. Rittenhouse*, page 841.

he guaranteed to dispose of but was unable to place. For his services in this connection, the underwriter receives a certain commission on stock sold.

TRANSFER OF STOCK
AND OTHER INVESTMENT SECURITIES

5-51 In General. A share of stock is personal property and the owner has a right to transfer his stock, just as he may transfer any other personal property. It is a marketable commodity and is bought and sold daily on the market. A share of stock is generally transferred by an indorsement and delivery of the certificate of stock. A share may be transferred or assigned by a bill of sale or by any other method that will pass title to a chose in action or other intangible property. Whenever a share of stock is sold and a stock certificate issued, the name of the new owner is entered on the stock book of the corporation. In a small corporation the secretary of the corporation is capable of handling all transfers of stock and the canceling and reissuing of new certificates. This method, however, is inadequate in large corporations where the business of transferring stock has become enormous and complicated. For the purpose of meeting this situation transfer agents are now established and employed by corporations. The transfer agents transfer stock, cancel old certificates, issue new ones, prepare and keep up to date the names of the stockholders of the corporation, distribute dividends, mail out stockholders' notices, and perform many of the functions normally performed by a corporation secretary. Stock Exchange rules provide that corporations listing stock for sale must maintain a transfer agency and registry, operated and maintained under the rules of the Stock Exchange. The registrar of stock is an agent of the corporation whose duty is to see that no stock certificates are issued in excess of the authorized capitalization of the corporation. For every share of stock transferred, the old certificate must be canceled and a new certificate issued.

The transfer of stock is an assignment, and in order to make a complete transfer a novation is necessary. A novation is executed when the old stock certificate is surrendered and canceled and a new certificate issued to the transferee and his name entered on the corporate stock book by the corporation through the transfer agent. Consequently, there are two distinct steps necessary to make a perfect transfer of the stock.

First, the certificate is assigned by the transferor to the transferee when the transferor signs his name in a blank provided on the back of the certificate, and delivers it to the transferee. Second, the transferred certificate is delivered to the corporation or transfer agent and the corporation enters upon the corporate stock transfer book that the transferee has acquired the stock, after which the corporation issues a new certificate of stock, certifying that the newly recorded stockholder owns the specified amount of stock. The corporation then cancels the old certificate of stock.

As between the transferor and the transferee, the registration of the transfer is not necessary. As between the stockholder and the corporation, a registration is necessary, in order that the corporation may know who is entitled to the rights of a stockholder.

The Code in Article 8 provides for the method of transfer indicated above. The Article is broad in coverage and includes bearer bonds formerly covered by the NIL, registered bonds which were not previously encompassed by any Uniform Law, and stock certificates which were previously covered by the Uniform Stock Transfer Act. Additional types of investment paper which have not been covered by any Uniform Act are also included within the coverage of Article 8.

Security instruments are governed by Article 8 even though they also meet the requirements of Article 3—Commercial Paper.

A "security" is an instrument which is:

1. issued in bearer or registered form, and
2. is a type commonly dealt in upon securities exchanges and markets or is commonly recognized as a medium for investment, and
3. evidences a share, participation or other interest in property or in an enterprise or evidences an obligation of the issuer.[C1]

Registered form is defined as a security which specifies the name of the owner and which may be transferred by registration upon books maintained by or on behalf of the issuer. A security is in bearer form when it runs to bearer according to its terms and not by reason of any indorsement.[C2]

It is to be noted that the definition of "security" is functional—based upon its use as a medium for investment—rather than formal as in the case of commercial paper. Transferable warrants (rights to subscribe for shares in a corporation) will usually satisfy the requirements of a security. The size of the organization issuing the securities is not significant. Stock certificates, bonds, debentures, script, certificates, and other instruments which evidence a share, participation, or other interest in property or an enterprise, or evidence an obligation of the issuer are included within the term security.

Negotiability is not affected under Article 8 by expressions that the instrument is "subject to" another agreement.

Overissue.[C3]   The power of a corporation to issue securities is controlled by statute, and the charter limits the number of shares that can be issued. The issue of securities in excess of the authorized amounts is prohibited. An "overissue" is defined as the issue of securities in excess of the amount which the issuer has the corporate power to issue. If a person is entitled to securities and the issue would exceed the authorized limit, he may insist that the corporation purchase the shares, where identical shares are reasonably available on the market or are available by purchase from other shareholders in order to fulfill its obligation to him. As an alternative, the party entitled to the shares can recover damages for failure to provide the shares.

C1 *U.C.C.* 8-102(1)(a).
C2 *U.C.C.* 8-102(1)(c)(d).

C3 *U.C.C.* 8-104.

Securities negotiable.[C4] The Code provides that securities are negotiable instruments and that bona fide purchasers thereof have greater rights than they would have "if the things bought were chattels or simple contracts." [C5] The particular rules of Article 3 relating to the establishment of preferred status for commercial paper are applied to securities. Defenses of the issuer are in general not effective against a purchaser for value who has taken without notice of the particular defense.

5-52 Issuer.[C6] The issuer may impose restrictions on the transfer of stock —that is, limiting the right to dispose of the stock. Such restrictions even though lawful are ineffective against a person unless he has actual knowledge of the restriction. If the restriction is not noted on the certificate the issuer can be compelled to register the transfer. In most jurisdictions, corporations are authorized to impose restrictions on transfer to the extent that the corporation or stockholders of the issuing corporation have the option to purchase the stock at a specified price before it is offered to third parties. The right to transfer freely one's share in the ownership of the business is inherent in corporate organization. It is one of those features of corporate life which distinguishes it from a partnership. Unmindful of this principle, "closed" corporations often attempt by agreement or by-law to limit the group of potential purchasers. In this effort they are only moderately successful. A corporate by-law which provides that the shares of stock can be transferred only to the corporation or to those approved by the board of directors is unenforceable. It places too severe a restraint upon the alienation of property. Society is best protected when property may be transferred freely from hand to hand. However, an agreement or a by-law approved by all stockholders, to the effect that no transfer of stock shall be made until it has first been offered to the other members of the corporation, is generally enforced. Notice of the by-law or agreement should be set forth in the stock certificate, since an innocent purchaser without notice of the restriction on alienation takes free from it.

Occasionally an officer of a corporation is appointed upon the condition that he will purchase a certain amount of corporate stock. The agreement usually stipulates that, upon the termination of his official relationship, he will resell the stock at a stipulated price to the corporation. Such an agreement has generally been enforced, although, if it is clear that the corporation promises to purchase the stock, some courts suggest that the agreement is illegal. Since a corporation may acquire treasury stock only out of surplus, an agreement to purchase when no surplus exists is of doubtful validity.

Unauthorized signature on issue.[C7] A corporation may entrust its securities to an employee or transfer agent to prepare them for issue. This process includes affixing the corporate seal and adding a sig-

C4 *U.C.C.* 8-105.   C6 *U.C.C.* 8-201, 8-204.
C5 *U.C.C.* 8-301.   C7 *U.C.C.* 8-205.

nature necessary for issue. If the person entrusted with the securities or who has access to them forges a signature or signs without authority "prior to or in the course of issue," such signature is ineffective except that "the signature is effective in favor of a purchaser for value and without notice of the lack of authority. . . ." The purpose of this is to place upon the issuer the duty to avoid negligent entrusting of securities to employees or others in the course of issue. This rule deals with signatures placed upon securities prior to or in the course of issue and does not apply to forged indorsements. A related problem is that of completion or alteration of an instrument. A purchaser for value without notice can enforce an incorrectly completed instrument and that a complete security which is wrongfully altered is enforceable but only according to its original terms. Nondelivery of an incomplete instrument is not a defense against a holder for value without notice.

Rights of issuer—registered owners.[C8] When a security in registered form is transferred, the new owner should present it to the issuer for registration of the transfer. Prior to such presentment, the issuer may "treat the registered owner as the person exclusively entitled to vote, to receive notifications, and otherwise to exercise all the rights and powers of an owner." Stock that is being paid for by installments that fall due at the demand or call of the board of directors may be sold before all of the calls have been made. In such cases the purchaser is deemed to have assumed responsibility for all future calls, and the transferor is relieved of liability. In other words, as soon as the transfer is recorded on corporate records, a novation has been consummated. This is not true when the transfer is made to a financially irresponsible person for the express purpose of eliminating the liability for stock of doubtful value.

As to the calls made previous to the transfer, but that remain unpaid at that time, the transferor remains liable. The liability of the transferee in such a case doubtless depends upon his knowledge or lack of knowledge of the unpaid calls. If the corporation issues a certificate prior to the time when all calls are made, it should not be marked "fully paid and nonassessable." An innocent purchaser of stock thus erroneously marked takes it free from any liability to the corporation for unpaid calls. The Code does not affect the liability of the registered owner of a security for calls, assessments, or the like. Likewise, the Code does not preclude a holder of record from denying ownership when assessments are levied if he is otherwise entitled to do so under state law.

5-53 Purchaser.[C9] A bona fide purchaser is defined as one who purchases in good faith and without notice of any adverse claim takes delivery of a security in bearer form or of one in registered form issued to him or indorsed to him or in blank. One who takes from a bona fide purchaser is given the rights of a bona fide purchaser. This is comparable to the "shelter provision" of Article 3—Commercial Paper. A bona fide purchaser takes free of "adverse claims" which include a claim that a

---

[C8] *U.C.C.* 8-207.   [C9] *U.C.C.* 8-301, 8-302.

transfer was wrongful or that some other person is the owner of, or has an interest in, the security.

5-54 Transfer. A person who transfers a security for value warrants that his transfer is effective and rightful; that the security is genuine and has not been materially altered; and that he knows of no fact which might impair the validity of the security. A broker makes all the warranties of a transferor.[C10]

A transfer is accomplished when the transferor delivers the security to the purchaser. Such transfer is complete upon delivery. If the security is in registered form and has been transferred without any necessary indorsement, the purchaser has a specifically enforceable right to have any necessary indorsement supplied. He does not attain the status of a bona fide purchaser until the indorsement is received.

Indorsement.[C11] The transfer may be accomplished by the signature of the transferor on the back of a security or by a separate document signed by the transferor. An indorsement may be in blank or special; an indorsement to bearer is a blank indorsement. A special indorsement specifies the person to whom the security is transfered. A holder may convert a blank indorsement into a special indorsement. The indorser does not assume any obligation that the security will be honored by the issuer unless the indorser has agreed to assume this obligation. Unlike commercial paper, an indorser may transfer only a part of a security representing units. Thus 50 shares may be transferred where the certificate represents 100 shares. There are two steps in the transfer—indorsement and delivery. The transfer is not accomplished until delivery has taken place. Since the concept of indorsement is applicable to registered securities, the indorsement of a security in bearer form is normally of no effect.

If an indorsement is forged, the owner may assert the ineffectiveness of the indorsement to deprive the owner of his ownership against the issuing corporation or any purchaser other than a bona fide purchaser who has in good faith received a new, reissued, or reregistered security on registration of transfer. The issuer who registers the transfer of a security upon a forged indorsement is subject to liability for improper registration.[4] Any person guaranteeing a signature of an indorser of a security makes certain warranties.[5]

5-55 Registration.[C12] Though a transfer, as between transferor and purchaser, is complete when a registered security is indorsed and delivered, the remaining step is to register the transfer. This means that the new owner's name is placed on the stock register and the transferor's name is removed. Registration is of vital importance to the purchaser. Where a security in registered form is presented to the issuer with a request to

---

[4] *LeSavoy Industries v. Pennsylvania General Paper Corp.*, page 842.
[5] *Love v. Pennsylvania R. R. Co.*, page 844.

[C10] *U.C.C.* 8-306.	[C12] *U.C.C.* 8-401.
[C11] *U.C.C.* 8-308.	

register transfer, the issuer is under a duty to do so provided the security is properly indorsed, reasonable assurance is given in a manner satisfactory to the corporation at the time of presentment that the indorsements are genuine, tax requirements have been satisfied, and the transfer is in fact rightful or is to a bona fide purchaser.

Lost, destroyed and stolen securities.[C13] When a security has been lost, apparently destroyed, or wrongfully taken, the owner must notify the issuer of such fact within a reasonable time. Should he fail to do so and the issuer registers a transfer, the owner is precluded from asserting the ineffectiveness of a forged indorsement and the wrongfulness of the registration of the transfer. If the lost security had been indorsed by the owner the registration is not wrongful unless notice has been given to the issuer.

Where the owner of a security claims that the security has been lost, destroyed or wrongfully taken, the issuer must issue a new security in place of the original security if the owner

(a) so requests before the issuer has notice that the security has been acquired by a bona fide purchaser; and

(b) files with the issuer a sufficient indemnity bond; and

(c) satisfies any other reasonable requirements imposed by the issuer.

If, after the issue of the new security, a bona fide purchaser of the original security presents it for registration of transfer, the issuer must register the transfer unless registration would result in overissue, in which event the issuer's liability is governed by the provisions previously discussed as to overissue. In addition to any rights on the indemnity bond, the issuer may recover the new security from the person to whom it was issued or any person taking under him except a bona fide purchaser.

Right of transferee to dividends.   Dividends on stock belong to the person who is owner of the stock at the time the dividends are declared. As to the corporation, the ownership of the stock is determined by the stock register, and the dividends will be paid to the person whose name appears upon the stock book. In the absence of an agreement to the contrary, dividends declared before a transfer of stock, although not payable until a future time, belong to the transferor. But dividends declared after the transfer of the stock, although earned before the transfer, belong to the transferee. However, by agreement between the transferor and the transferee, upon notice to the corporation, the corporation must pay the dividends in compliance with the agreement.

Dividends are often declared as of a certain date and payable to stockholders of record as of a later date. In such cases a transfer after declaration, but before the record date, carries the dividends to the transferee. There is also some authority to the effect that a stock dividend passes to the transferee unless the contract of sale provides otherwise. Dividends normally become a debt as of the time they are declared, but stock dividends may be rescinded, according to many courts, after they have been

C13 *U.C.C.* 8-405.

declared. Consequently, in the case of cash dividends, the debt is owed to the stockholder at the date of declaration, or record date, whereas in reference to stock dividends, no debt exists since the new issue of stock is transferred to the owner at the time it is issued. "No interference is intended with the common practice of closing the transfer books or taking a record date for dividend, voting, and other purposes as provided for in by-laws, charters, and statutes."

RIGHTS OF STOCKHOLDERS

5-56 In General. A shareholder has the following rights usually created by statute and reiterated in the by-laws: (1) the right to inspect the books and papers of the corporation, (2) the right to attend stockholders' meetings and to vote for directors and on certain other matters such as dissolution or merger, (3) a right to share in the profits when a dividend is declared, (4) the preemptive right, and (5) the right to bring a shareholder's derivative suit. In some states, a stockholder has the additional right of cumulative voting or voting all of his votes for one or more directors by accumulating them.

The right to inspect the books and papers is limited to inspections for proper purposes at the proper time and the proper place. The inspection, however, must be made with a justifiable motive and not through idle curiosity or for purposes which in any way interfere with the corporate management. The business hours of the corporation are the reasonable and proper hours in which a stockholder is entitled to inspect the books. Some courts hold that the motive of inspecting the books is immaterial and that the corporation has no right to question the reason for which the books are being inspected.

5-57 Dividends. While a stockholder has a right to his share of dividends when declared, whether or not a dividend is declared is within the discretion of the board of directors. The stockholders of a corporation are not entitled to the payment of a dividend whenever an earned surplus exists. The board of directors, at its discretion, may see fit to continue the profits in the business for the purpose of extension and improvements. A board of directors, however, must act reasonably and in good faith. Where such is not the case and there are profits out of which dividends may be declared, the stockholders may compel the board of directors to declare dividends.[6] It must be clear, however, that the board of directors has, illegally, wantonly, and without justification, refused to declare a dividend before the stockholders have a right to interfere.

When a dividend is declared, it becomes a debt of the corporation and will be paid to the person whose name appears on the corporate stock books as the owner of the share, unless the corporation has received notice of a transfer. A cash dividend, once its declaration has been made public,

---

[6] *Knapp et al. v. Bankers Securities Corp., et al.*, page 845.

may not be rescinded, although there is some authority for rescinding a stock dividend.

The statutes of the various states governing the declaration of dividends appear to follow two distinct patterns. The first group of states, apparently codifying the common law, provide that dividends can be declared only out of net profits. Under this rule it seems safe to say that dividends may be declared out of current profits, even though a deficit has arisen from the operation of previous years. Capital surplus or surplus arising from the appreciation of fixed assets would not appear to be available under the law of these states.

The other group of states, representing perhaps a majority, determine the legality of a dividend by its effect upon the capital stock. A declaration of dividends is proper so long as it does not impair the capital stock. Any declaration, however, which reduces the net assets of the corporation below the outstanding capital stock is illegal. Under this view it would seem that capital or paid-in surplus might be available for dividends. The law in this regard is not at all definite, but the Uniform Business Corporation Act, which has accepted the majority view, makes capital surplus available for dividends. However, it limits the use of surplus arising from appreciation of fixed assets to stock dividends.

Under either theory, dividends are permissible only after provision has been made for all expenses, including depreciation. In those industries dealing with wasting or depleting assets, such as mines and oil wells, it is not necessary to care for the depletion before declaring dividends.

The directors in many states are personally liable to creditors for dividends improperly declared in case the corporation later becomes insolvent. Also, the stockholders who receive such dividends may be compelled to return them. In a few of the states, statutes make the stockholders liable only if they received them in bad faith and directors liable only if they acted carelessly or in bad faith.

Dividends may be paid in cash, property other than cash including the stock of another corporation, or scrip which is a certificate representing property which will later be redeemed in cash from the sale of the property or stock.

A stock dividend is a transfer of surplus to capital and is used where the earnings are required for growth of the business. Stock dividends of the issuing company are not taxable income to stockholders. A stock split differs from a stock dividend in that in the former there is no transfer of surplus to capital but only a reduction in par value and an increase in the number of shares.

5-58 Preemptive Right. The capital stock of a corporation is fixed by the charter, and it cannot be increased except by express authority from the state creating the corporation. The stockholders and not the directors must authorize an increase in the capital stock. Such an authorization must be made by amendment of the charter in compliance with the statute providing for changes in the corporation.

When an increase in the capital stock has been properly authorized, the existing stockholders have a prior right against third parties to subscribe to the increased capital stock. This right is called the stockholder's *preemptive* right and is based upon the stockholder's right to protect and maintain his proportionate control and interest in the corporation.[7] Thus, if a class of stock has no voting power and is nonparticipating, it is questionable whether such preemptive right exists. This right may be limited or waived by contract and by provisions in the charter or by-laws of the corporation. In many states it is not applicable to treasury stock.[8] It is applicable to new authorization of stock and perhaps to new allotments of stock previously authorized, particularly if the new allotment of an original authorization takes place some time after the original issue. Some states approve the issuance of stock to employees without regard to the preemptive right. Whether or not a stockholder must pay more than par value for the increased stock varies in the different states. Some states hold that he can be compelled to pay more, and other states hold that he cannot.

5-59 Derivative Suits. A stockholder cannot maintain an *action at law* for injuries to the corporation, because the corporation is a legal entity and by law has a right to bring a suit in its own name. A stockholder cannot bring a suit at law for and in behalf of the other stockholders for injury to the corporation. Neither can a stockholder bring a suit in law against the directors or other officers of the corporation for negligence, waste, and mismanagement in the conduct of the corporate business, although such conduct is injurious to the stockholder. The right to sue for injuries to the corporation rests strictly with the corporation itself.

A stockholder may, however, bring a *suit in equity* known as a shareholder's derivative suit to enjoin the officers of a corporation from entering into *ultra vires* contracts or from doing anything that would impair the stockholders' rights in the corporate assets. Likewise, the stockholder has a right to bring suit in equity for, or on behalf of, the corporation itself if the officers are acting outside the scope of their authority, are guilty of negligent conduct, or are engaging, or about to engage, in fraudulent transactions with other stockholders in such a way as to be injurious to the corporation itself.[9]

Before a stockholder may enter into a suit in equity for and on behalf of the corporation, he must show that he has done everything possible to secure action by the managing officers and directors and that they have refused to act. Any judgment received in such an action benefits the corporation and only indirectly the stockholder who initiates the action. He is permitted, however, to recover the expenses involved in the suit.

It has been held that mere dissatisfaction by some of the stockholders as to the management of the corporation will not justify the liquidation of the company.

---

[7] *Ross Transport, Inc. et al. v. Crothers et al.,* page 846.
[8] *Runswick et al. v. Floor et al.,* page 848.
[9] *Ramsburg et al. v. American Investment Co. of Illinois et al.,* page 849.

STOCK AND STOCK OWNERSHIP CASES

Arizona Power Co. v. Stuart

1954, 212 F.2d 535

The plaintiff corporation brought this action against the defendant, Collector of Internal Revenue, to recover income taxes allegedly overpaid. The question presented to the court was whether the plaintiff could deduct dividends paid on preferred stock for the purpose of computing the corporate surtax. This in turn depended upon whether the stock fell within the definition of preferred stock in the Internal Revenue Code as being stock the dividends of which are cumulative. The lower court ruled against the plaintiff and plaintiff appealed.

LEMMON, D. J. . . . A preferred stockholder is not creditor of the corporation in which he holds his stock. The dividends thereon are not payable absolutely but only out of the net earnings or net assets in excess of capital and only when and as declared. A dividend is that which the corporation has set aside from its net earnings or profits to be divided among the stockholders. The preference is limited to profits when earned. The agreement to pay dividends on preferred stock is to be construed as an agreement to pay them from profits. This is the rule unless corporations are expressly authorized by statute to resort to capital in payment of such dividends.

Dividends on preferred stock are ordinarily regarded as cumulative.

. . . This brings into focus the distinction between a cumulative and a non-cumulative dividend. A cumulative dividend survives as a senior charge on earnings. A non-cumulative dividend disappears if not declared and ceases to be a preferential right.

. . . Appellee [Collector of Internal Revenue] reminds us that there is no specific statement in the articles that the preferred stock is cumulative. But references are made in the articles to "accumulated and unpaid dividends" on the preferred stock.

. . . It is unnecessary that the word "cumulative" be used. It is sufficient if the stipulated preferences make it such.

. . . *Reversed and remanded with directions to enter judgment in favor of appellant.*

Bing Crosby Minute Maid Corp. v. Eaton

1956, (Cal.2d) 297 P.2d 5

The plaintiff corporation was a judgment creditor of a corporation in which the defendant Eaton was the principal stockholder. The judgment was not paid and the plaintiff brought this action to recover from the defendant. The defendant had received 4,500 shares of stock having a par value of $10 in return for consideration from the defendant of $34,780.83. The lower court rendered a judgment against the defendant in the amount of $10,219.17. The lower court granted a new trial and the plaintiff appealed.

SHENK, J. . . . In this state a shareholder is ordinarily not personally liable for the debts of the corporation; he undertakes only the risk that his shares may become worthless. (Cases cited.) There are, however, certain exceptions to this rule of limited liability. For example, a subscriber to shares who pays in only part of what he agreed to pay is liable to creditors for the balance.

. . . The plaintiff seeks to base its recovery on the only other exception to the limited liability rule that the record could support, namely, liability for holding watered stock, which is stock issued in return for properties or services worth less than its par value Accordingly, this case calls for an analysis of the rights of a creditor of an insolvent corporation against a holder of watered stock. Holders of watered stock are generally held liable to the corporation's creditors for the difference between the par value of the stock and the amount paid in.

. . . The liability of a holder of watered stock has been based on one of two theories; the misrepresentation theory or the statutory obligation theory. The misrepresentation theory is the one accepted in most jurisdictions. The courts view the issue of watered stock as a misrepresentation of the corporation's capital. Creditors who rely on this misrepresentation are entitled to recover the "water" from the holders of the watered shares. (Cases cited.)

Statutes expressly prohibiting watered stock are commonplace today. In some jurisdictions where they have been enacted, the statutory obligation theory has been applied. Under that theory the holder of watered stock is held responsible to creditors whether or not they have relied on overvaluation of corporate capital.

. . . In his answer the defendant alleged that in extending credit to the corporation the plaintiff did not rely on the par value of the shares issued, but only on independent investigation and reports as to the corporation's current cash position, its physical assets and its business experience. At the trial the plaintiff's district manager admitted that during the period when the plaintiff extended credit to the corporation, (1) the district manager believed that the original capital of the corporation amounted to only $25,000, and (2) the only financial statement of the corporation that the plaintiff ever saw showed a capital stock account of less than $33,000. These admissions would be sufficient to support a finding that the plaintiff did not rely on any misrepresentation arising out of the issuance of watered stock. The court made no finding on the issue of reliance. If the misrepresentation theory prevails in California, that issue was material and the defendant was entitled to a finding thereon. If the statutory obligation theory prevails, the fact that the plaintiff did not rely on any misrepresentation arising out of the issuance of watered stock is irrelevant and accordingly a finding on the issue of reliance would be surplusage.

It is therefore necessary to determine which theory prevails in this state. The plaintiff concedes that before the enactment of § 1110 of the Corporations Code in 1931, the misrepresentation theory was the only one available to creditors seeking to recover from holders of watered stock.

. . . In view of the cases in this state adopting the misrepresentation theory, it is reasonable to assume that the Legislature would have used clear language expressing an intent to broaden the basis of liability of holders of watered stock had it entertained such an intention. In this state the liability of a holder of watered stock may only be based on the misrepresentation theory.

The plaintiff contends that even under the misrepresentation theory a creditor's reliance on the misrepresentation arising out of the issuance of watered stock should be conclusively presumed. This contention is without substantial merit. If it should prevail, the misrepresentation theory and the statutory obligation theory would be essentially identical. This court has held that under the misrepresentation theory a person who extended credit to a corporation (1) before the watered stock was issued, or (2) with full knowledge that watered stock was outstanding, cannot recover from the holders of the watered stock. These decisions indicate that under the misrepresentation theory reliance by the creditor is a prerequisite to the liability of a holder of watered stock. The trial court was therefore justified in ordering a new trial because of the absence of a finding on that issue.

. . . *The order granting the new trial is affirmed.*

Hoppe v. Rittenhouse

1960, 279 F.2d 3

The Trustee in Bankruptcy (Hoppe) challenged as a voidable preference a secured creditor's claim filed by one of the creditors. The creditor, Gammill, had assigned his claim to Rittenhouse. The bankrupt, Los Gatos Lumber Products, Inc., had been hampered by lack of adequate working capital. Morton, president of the bankrupt, had advanced substantial sums of money to it but this had not been sufficient. The creditor had also advanced money and had obtained a mortgage on the property of the bankrupt. The Trustee's contention was that the corporation was insolvent at the time the mortgage was given and that this was known to the creditors. The creditor contends that the corporation was not insolvent because Morton was not a creditor—that his advances were not "as loans but as equity capital in the form of subscriptions to the capital stock." The lower court ruled in favor of the creditor and the Trustee appealed.

KOELSCH, C. J. . . . The undisputed evidence is thus that the Mortons had orally agreed to exchange their notes for stock in the corporation on the condition that additional working capital be obtained from some outside source, and that the corporation, through its president, Carl Morton, not only agreed to this proposal but actively sought additional financing from prospective lenders by positively asserting that the apparent indebtedness of the corporation to the Morton family would be erased as a liability when additional financing was obtained. There is little doubt that the Mortons intended to and did enter into a conditional subscription agreement. The critical question, then, is whether this agreement was binding and enforceable, for on it hinges the validity of the referee's finding that the Mortons' advances were "subscriptions," not "loans.". . .

Under California law an agreement by prospective shareholders to purchase stock in a proposed corporation, or unissued shares in an existing corporation, is a binding and enforceable contract. . . . The proposal made by such subscribers must be accepted by the corporation before they are finally bound, and it is clear in the present case that Carl Morton, acting on behalf of the corporation, did so accept. . . .

The trustee argues that because no stock was issued to the Mortons, they remained creditors and did not become subscribers of stock; but as in most cases, their status as subscribers is determined by the intention of the parties to the agreement. . . . Here the intention to convert notes into stock if additional capital was obtained is established by an abundance of testimony, and it is clear that the mere mechanical act of issuing stock certificates is not necessary to constitute the subscribers shareholders. . . .

It is true that the agreement was subject to a condition precedent, i.e., obtaining additional working capital, but that condition occurred when the Gammills began advancing considerable sums, which eventually exceeded $29,000.00, to the corporation. The condition thus having occurred, the contract became binding and constituted the Mortons shareholders instead of creditors, and as such "beneficial owners" of the corporate assets. . . .

Moreover, should we assume that the agreement was subject to some infirmity rendering it invalid, it is clear under California law that as between the Gammills and the Mortons, the latter would be estopped to deny their status as subscribers where, as here, the Gammills relied upon the agreement in making loans. . . .

The fact that the Mortons presented creditors' claims in the bankruptcy proceeding is not conclusive but at most creates a conflict in the evidence. Indeed, such behavior by subscribers follows a familiar pattern where efforts to continue the corporation in operation have failed: subscribers oftentimes endeavor to salvage something of their investment by attempting to qualify as creditors. . . .

Affirmed.

Lesavoy Industries v. Pennsylvania Gen. Paper Corp.

1961, 404 Pa. 161, 171 A.2d 148

The owner of all the stock in Lesavoy Industries, plaintiff, executed a general power of attorney to Allen Daniels. Plaintiff corporation was the owner of all the outstanding stock in the defendant corporation. Daniels entered into an agreement with one Price whereby Price was to receive 52 per cent of the stock in defendant corporation and a certificate was to be issued in the name of Price. Plaintiff corporation contends that it did not give the power to Lesavoy (its sole shareholder) or to Daniels to enter into this agreement. A certificate was issued to Price and is now in his possession. Plaintiff asked the court to declare null and void the transfer of shares from defendant corporation to Price and that defendant corporation be ordered to reassign and retransfer to plaintiff the shares of stock. The lower court ruled for plaintiff.

COHEN, J. . . . The lower court, in order to support its finding that the defendant corporation was a principal defendant, ruled that the plaintiff had alleged a proper cause of action against the defendant corporation on the theory that the defendant corporation breached its duty to protect its stockholder from an unauthorized transfer of shares.

It is generally accepted that a corporation owes its shareholders the duty to protect them from fraudulent transfers. A corporation also owes its shareholders a duty to protect them from unauthorized transfers. This court impliedly recognized such a duty where a corporation had been informed in advance of conflicting claims to the stock in question. We need not now decide if this duty extends beyond cases involving forgeries or notice to the corporation of irregularities, since here a wholly owned subsidiary relied upon a general power of attorney given to an agent by the parent corporation's sole shareholder. There can be no greater justification for a finding that the agent was clothed, at least, with apparent authority, thus effectuating an estoppel against the principal (plaintiff corporation).

Plaintiff has failed to allege a cause of action against the defendant corporation and thus that defendant is only a passive party in a dispute between two claimants to the same stock. As such the defendant corporation is not a principal defendant (cases cited).

The situs of the stock in question is determined by the Uniform Stock Transfer Act (now embodied in the Uniform Commercial Code), the policy of which is to make the certificate represent the shares of stock.

In *Crane v. Crane* (1953, 373 Pa. 1, 95 A.2d 199), this court did consider the situs of stock to be that of the corporation and permitted an action against the corporation to transfer shares on its books. However, such actions will be permitted only where the outstanding certificates are either seized, surrendered or their transfer enjoined unless it is unnecessary to enjoin transfer; e.g., the defendant cannot convey title of the certificate without the joinder of the attaching creditor. It is admitted that the outstanding shares in this case are located in New York and that they have not been seized or surrendered nor their transfer enjoined. We must therefore find that property which is the subject matter of the action is not within the jurisdiction of the court below.

Extra-territorial service upon Price, failing to qualify under either of the criteria set forth in Pa. R.C.P. 1504 (b), was unauthorized and ineffectual to subject him to the jurisdiction of the court below.

Decree reversed.

Love v. Pennsylvania Railroad Co.

1961 (Pa.) 200 F. Supp. 563

The plaintiff and her father jointly owned stock, with the right of survivorship, in the Pennsylvania Railroad Company. The father prepared an assignment whereby the stock was transferred to him individually and forged plaintiff's name to the assignment. The railroad transferred the shares from the joint names of plaintiff and her father to the sole name of the father. Plaintiff sued the railroad and two banks were added as defendants on the basis that they had guaranteed the signatures of plaintiff and her father on a stock assignment and dividend request. Plaintiff seeks to amend her complaint to assert a claim against the additional defendants.

KRAFT, D. J. . . . Plaintiff relies in part upon Section 8-312 of the Uniform Commercial Code, as that section provided at the time of the guarantee:

> Section 8-312. Effect of Guaranteeing Signature or Indorsement
> (1) Any person guaranteeing a signature as being that of an indorser of a security warrants to any person taking or dealing with the security in reliance on the guaranteed signature that
>   (a) the signature is not forged; and
>   (b) the signer is the holder or has authority to sign in the name of the holder; and
>   (c) the signer has legal capacity to sign.
> But the guarantor does not warrant the rightfulness of the particular transfer.
> (2) . . .
> (3) The guarantor of a signature or an indorsement shall be liable to any person, including an issuer who registers a transfer in reliance on the guarantee, for any loss resulting from breach of the warranties stated in this section but no issuer may require an indorsement guarantee as a condition to registration or transfer of a security.

Plaintiff emphasizes the phrase "to any person" in subsection (3), and contends that these words establish the third-party defendants' liability to her for her loss resulting from the breach of the warranty that "the signature is not forged." While a literal reading of the provision lends some support to the plaintiff's contention, we think it clear that its language must be read in conjunction with that contained in subsection (1). So read, the signature guarantor's liability "to any person" must be deemed co-extensive merely with his warranty, which runs only "to any person taking or dealing with the security in reliance on the guaranteed signature." That this was the real meaning of subsection (3) seems apparent from the fact that the subsection was amended in 1959 to express, in clear and unequivocal language, that precise meaning. Since, under the averments of the complaint, plaintiff did not take or deal with the security in reliance on the guaranteed signature, the third-party defendants' warranty did not extend to her, and they are not liable to her for any loss resulting from its breach.

The industry of counsel and our own research have disclosed a singular dearth of authority on the precise question. However, the few cases in point establish the principle that the guarantee of a signature does not run to the owner of the security unless the signature guarantor had actual knowledge of the impropriety of the transaction. It was so held in *Eulette v. Merrill, Lynch, Pierce, Fenner and Beane* (101 So. 2d 603, 606, Fla. App. 1958).

> The guarantee of the forged signature of the appellant (owner) on the stock certificate could not, in our opinion, afford the appellant any basis for recovery. The guarantee would run only to those persons who, subsequent to the guarantee, dealt with the stock in reliance upon the guarantee. There has been no showing that the appellant acted to his detriment, or, for that matter, acted at all, in reliance upon the appellee's guarantee.

It is the uniform rule in Pennsylvania that a person making a general guarantee to warranty is liable only to those parties who have acted in reliance thereon (cases cited).

We conclude, therefore, that the averments of the proposed amended complaint fail to state a legal claim against either third-party defendant, and the motion for leave to amend must be denied.

Knapp et al. v. Bankers Securities Corporation et al.

1956, 230 F.2d 717

The plaintiffs, shareholders in defendant corporation, brought this action against the corporation and its directors to compel the declaration of dividends. The lower court held in favor of the plaintiffs.

MARIS, C. J. . . . The present action was brought in the district court for the eastern district of Pennsylvania by shareholders, New York residents, against the Bankers Securities Corporation, a Pennsylvania corporation, and its directors, charging that Albert M. Greenfield, one of the directors and the majority shareholder, and the other directors were acting unreasonably in failing to eliminate accumulated arrearages of dividends of approximately $3,000,000 on the common stock in order that the preferred and common stockholders might participate in the earnings of the corporation, that the distribution of earnings was being arbitrarily withheld for the benefit of the majority shareholder.

. . . It is an elementary principle of corporation law that the declaration of dividends out of net profits rests in the discretion of the board of directors. However, there are circumstances under which shareholders may compel the declaration of dividends. If directors have acted fraudulently or arbitrarily in refusing to declare a dividend when the corporation has a surplus which it can divide among the shareholders without detriment to the business, a shareholder may invoke the equitable powers of a court for relief. It is just such equitable power which the plaintiffs seek to invoke in this case. The question then is whether in such an action the shareholder is seeking relief from a personal wrong done to him and thus is enforcing a primary or personal right of his own or is seeking to redress a wrong done to the corporation and thus is enforcing a secondary right derived from the corporation.

. . . The right to dividends is an incident of the ownership of stock. The fact that the distribution of profits cannot ordinarily be enforced until after a dividend has been declared does not detract from the shareholders' fundamental right to share in the net profits of the corporation. This right is the basis of his suit to compel the declaration of dividends. If the directors have wrongfully withheld the declaration of dividends the shareholder is the injured party. He shows an injury to himself which is quite apart from any which the corporation might be thought to suffer. Even if the corporation might under some circumstances have a right of action that fact would not affect the authority of its shareholders to enforce by suit their personal and individual rights to the declaration of a dividend.

It is suggested that the right here asserted must be regarded as one vested in the corporation because the mechanics of relief have to be worked out by a decree against the directors rather than against the corporation. Our answer to this proposition was made by Judge Goodrich in *Kroese v. General Steel Castings Corporation* (3 Cir., 1950, 179 F.2d 760, 763-764, 15 A.L.R.2d 1117), when he said:

> It is to be observed that when a court steps in and orders the payment of a dividend, the corporate affairs have reached the point where the judgment of the directors is no longer controlling. The set of facts presented is such that the court substitutes its judgment, based on a rule of law, for the ordinary business judgment of those in charge of the business enterprise. . . .
>
> In such a case, even though the individual directors are joined as parties, they are not called upon to exercise any business discretion. The case has passed that point. As said before, the court is declaring rights protected by a rule of law, not calling upon the directors to exercise judgment. . . . The duty of a corporation to pay dividends then and there has been imposed by the judgment of the court, not by the ayes and nays of the members of the board. The situation becomes in substance the same as that in which any corporate creditor sues the enterprise in the corporate name to recover from it what it owns him; he does not need any meeting of the corporation's board to make his judgment good. Nor does a shareholder whose claim to dividends is based on his showing of fiduciary mismanagement need a directors' meeting to make his rights good. The judgment of a court is enough in either case.

. . . The order of the district court will be affirmed.

Ross Transport Inc. et al. v. Crothers et al.

1946, 185 Md. 573, 45 A.2d 267

The plaintiff Crothers and other stockholders brought this action against the corporation, its directors and certain stockholders to set aside the issuance of certain shares of stock. The stock was sold to a director and to the family of the president and director. The lower court decreed that the stockholders who had received the additional stock must repay to the corporation the dividends received by them and the stock declared to be illegally issued and ordered cancelled. The defendants appealed.

MARBURY, C. J. . . . The sale of this additional stock to a director and to the family of the president and director . . . without opportunity to buy given to other stockholders, is sought to be justified on the ground that it was originally planned, and that the money was needed to purchase additional buses at a cost of about $16,000. The facts, however, show no such need. The company was an immediate financial success.

. . . The appellees give two reasons for their contention that the stock sales of August 26th were void: First, because they deprive them and the other original stockholders of their pre-emptive rights to purchase a proportionate amount of the remaining shares, and, second, because, in selling to themselves and their nominees, Williams and Ross have abused their trust as officers and directors. They claim to be injured in two ways. Their voting powers have been proportionately lessened, and the control of the company has passed to Williams and Ross. And the amount paid in dividends has to be divided among 365 more shares of stock to the consequent financial loss of the holders of the original shares.

. . . The doctrine known as the pre-emptive right of shareholders is a judicial interpretation of general principles of corporation law. Existing stockholders are the owners of the business, and are entitled to have that ownership continued in the same proportion. Therefore, when additional stock is issued, those already having shares, are held to have the first right to buy the new stock in proportion to their holdings. This doctrine was first promulgated in 1807 in the case of *Gray v. Portland Bank,* 3 Mass. 364, 3 Am. Dec. 156. At that time, corporations were small and closely held, much like the one before us in this case. But in the succeeding years, corporations grew and expanded. New capital was frequently required. New properties had to be acquired for which it was desirable to issue stock. Companies merged, and new stock in the consolidation was issued. Stock was issued for services. Different kinds of stock were authorized—preferred without voting power but with prior dividend rights— preferred with the right to convert into common—several classes of both common and preferred with different rights. Some stock had voting rights. Other stock did not. Bonds were issued, convertible into stock. All of these changes in the corporate structure made it impossible always to follow the simple doctrines earlier decided. Exceptions grew, and were noted in the decisions.

Only one of these exceptions is involved in the present case. It has been held that pre-emptive rights do not exist where the stock about to be issued is part of the original issue. This exception is based upon the fact that the original subscribers took their stock on the implied understanding that the incorporators could complete the sale of the remaining stock to obtain the capital thought necessary to start the business. But this gives rise to an exception to the exception, where conditions have changed since the original issue. The stock sold the Williams family and Ross was part of the original issue and it is claimed by the appellants that it comes within the exception, and the appellees and the other stockholders have no pre-emptive rights.

The appellees, on the other hand, contend, and the chancellors found that changed conditions made it unnecessary to use the remaining unsold stock to obtain capital, and pre-emptive rights exist in it just as they would exist in newly authorized stock.

It is unnecessary for us to decide which of these two conflicting points of view applies to this cause, because another controlling consideration enters. The doctrine of pre-emptive right is not affected by the identity of the purchasers of the issued stock. What it is concerned with is who did not get it. But when officers and directors sell to themselves, and thereby gain an advantage, both in value and in voting power, another situation arises, which it does not require the assertion of a pre-emptive right to deal with.

It has long been the law in this State that trustees cannot purchase at their own sale, and trustees, in this sense, include directors of corporations.

. . . *The decree will be affirmed.*

Runswick et al. v. Floor et al.

1949, 116 Utah 91, 208 P.2d 948

The plaintiff and other stockholders of the New Quincy Mining Company, a corporation, brought this action against Floor and other defendants to set aside the sale of treasury stock to the defendant Floor. The lower court ruled in favor of the defendants and plaintiffs appealed.

LATIMER, J. . . . The principal issue to be decided by this court is as to the validity or invalidity of the sale of the treasury shares to defendant Floor. In proceeding to determine this question, it should initially be pointed out that the shares of stock involved had been once fully paid for and had been returned to the treasury of the company. Officers of a corporation may reissue this type of stock for value and in good faith without first offering it pro rata to existing shareholders. (Cases cited) We quote from *Borg v. International Silver Co.* (D.C.S.D.N.Y., 11 F.2d 143, 11 F.2d 147): "The distinction may appear tenuous, but rests upon the effect which a new issue has upon the voting control of the company. When a person buys into a company with an authorized capital, he accepts that proportion of the voting rights which his purchase bears to the whole. This applies certainly so far as the other shares are issued at the same time, and perhaps, also, though they are issued much later. But treasury shares have by hypothesis once been issued, and have diluted, as it were, the shareholder's voting power *ab initio*. He cannot properly complain that he is given no right to buy them when they are resold, because that merely restores the status he originally accepted. All he can demand is that they shall bring to the corporate treasury their existing value. If they do, his proportion in any surplus is not affected. However, when the capital stock is increased beyond the original amount authorized, the voting power is diluted along with it; the shareholders who had not originally bought into so large an issue may insist that the old proportions be observed. To deprive them of their right of pre-emption is to change their contract. At any rate it is only on this theory that any right of pre-emption exists, and since the shares at bar were never bought to be retired, and the capital was not increased, the right does not exist."

Hence, the sale of the 150,000 shares to Floor was not objectionable by reason of the fact that the shares were not first offered to existing shareholders on a pro rata basis.

Affirmed.

Ramsburg et al. v. American Investment Company of Illinois et al.

1956, 231 F.2d 333

The plaintiffs as stockholders of defendant Domestic Finance Corporation brought this suit for an injunction to restrain a proposed merger of that Company with defendant American Investment Company of Illinois. Both are incorporated under the laws of Delaware. The complaint averred that American had, through divers means, obtained some 80 per cent of the common stock of Domestic thereby gaining control; that American had utilized its stock to effectuate election of a board of directors of Domestic composed of officers of American, who were serving as Domestic's officers, and that American, through its control, had so operated Domestic as to reduce its effective position as a competitor of American in various cities and states where both corporations transact business. On August 17, 1955, Domestic mailed to its stockholders a notice of a special meeting to be held September 15, 1955, to consider and vote on a proposed merger of the two corporations. The complaint herein was filed September 7, 1955, charging that the merger would constitute a violation of § 7 of the Clayton Act, in that its effect would be to lessen substantially competition in commerce. It was further averred that Domestic would be seriously injured by the proposed action.

The complaint prayed a preliminary injunction restraining American from voting its Domestic stock in favor of the merger at the September 15 meeting or at any other time, and that, after hearing on the merits, the temporary injunction be made final, and a decree entered directing American to divest itself of the Domestic stock it owns and granting such other and further relief as to the court might seem just. The lower court denied the injunction and plaintiffs appealed. The defendants moved to dismiss the appeal on the ground that the cause was moot since the merger had been accomplished.

LINDLEY, C. J. . . . The question before us is reduced to an inquiry as to whether a stockholders' derivative suit will lie under § 7 of the Clayton Act. We frame our answer to that question on the teachings contained in a recent opinion by the Court of Appeals for the Second Circuit in *Fanchon & Marco, Inc. v. Paramount Pictures, Inc.* (202 F.2d 731, 36 A.L.R.2d 1336), which involved an appeal from a judgment dismissing a stockholders' derivative, antitrust suit for treble damages and injunctive relief. The court held that the action would lie and reversed the judgment of dismissal, saying (202 F.2d at p. 734): "Now there does not seem real doubt but that an antitrust derivative suit will lie; indeed, that seems to follow from the nature of such suits. '. . . Equity . . . traditionally entertains the derivative or secondary action by which a single stockholder may sue in the corporation's right when he shows that the corporation on proper demand has refused to pursue a remedy, or shows facts that demonstrate the futility of such a request. . . . The cause of action which such a plaintiff brings before the court is not his own but the corporation's. . . .' Mr. Justice Jackson in *Koster v. (American) Lumbermen's Mutual Casualty Co.* (330 U.S. 518, 522, 523, 67 S.Ct. 828, 91 L.Ed. 1067)." After discussing the applicable authorities, the court continued (202 F.2d at p. 735): "There is an occasional flat statement . . . that no derivative antitrust suit will lie, as in *Kalmanash v. Smith* (291 N.Y. 142, 157, 51 N.E.2d 681, 688); but, as indicated, the precedents actually look the other way and we can see no reason for such a view." We agree with this reasoning and hold that plaintiffs were competent parties when this suit was brought and have remained so throughout pendency of the litigation.

Motion to dismiss appeal denied.

CHAPTER 40
REVIEW QUESTIONS AND PROBLEMS

1. *A* bought stock in *X* Corporation from the corporation. He did not receive certificates at the time, but did pay the price. Is *A* a stockholder if the transaction was entirely oral?

2. The *X* Company has both preferred and common stock. The preferred stock is 7 per cent stock. The company declares a 7 per cent dividend on the preferred stock and then declares a 10 per cent dividend on the common stock. Under such conditions, have the preferred stockholders a right to demand 10 per cent?

3. *A,* along with a number of others, subscribes for stock in anticipation that a corporation will later be formed. Before incorporation takes place, he notifies the incorporators that he withdraws his subscription. May he legally do so? Suppose the subscription had been made after incorporation?

4. The *X* Company purchased an invention from *A* and paid for it by the issuance of $100,000 of common stock. As a matter of fact the invention was worth only $50,000, but the directors honestly believed that it was worth $100,000. May the creditors recover an additional $50,000 from *A*?

5. *A* became a transferee of sixty shares of stock in a corporation which

issued its stock marked fully paid and nonassessable upon the payment of 70 per cent of its par value. Assuming that *A* knew the conditions surrounding its issuance, is he liable to creditors in case of insolvency? Suppose he had been an innocent purchaser?

6. *Y* Company on March 1 declared a cash dividend of 5 per cent, payable on June 1 to all stockholders of record on May 1. On April 10, *A* sold ten shares of stock in *Y* Company to *B*, although the transfer was not recorded on the corporation's books until May 15. To whom will the company pay the dividend? As between *A* and *B*, who is entitled to the dividend?

7. *P* sold shares he owned in a corporation to *X* but the corporation refused to transfer ownership on its books to *X*. The corporation claimed it was holding the shares to answer for a debt *P* owed the corporation. May the corporation succeed in its attempt to collect in this way?

8. The directors of a corporation, by reason of misconduct and negligence, have wasted the assets of the corporation. May a stockholder of the corporation recover from them in the name of the corporation for the losses caused by the directors' negligence? What should he do first?

9. *P* was a stockholder in *X* Corp. He desired to obtain a list of stockholders so that he could contact them before the annual stockholders meeting to persuade them to vote for a corporate merger to which the board of directors of *X* Corp. was opposed. If the clerk required by the by-laws to keep the books refuses *P* the opportunity to inspect them, what may *P* do?

10. The directors of *X* Corporation declared a dividend but at a later meeting rescinded this action. Are the stockholders entitled to the dividend?

11. The directors of *X* Co. authorized the issuance of par value stock for 90 cents. The shareholders at a special meeting ratified the issuance. The company later became insolvent and suit was brought against the purchasers of the aforesaid stock. What result?

12. *X* Co. decided to establish an employee incentive program and adopted a policy of allowing employees to purchase treasury stock in the company at its par value which was 50 per cent of its actual value. *P*, a 10 per cent shareholder, files suit to enjoin the sale on the alternative that he be allowed to purchase 10 per cent of all stock sold at the same price. What result?

chapter **41**

Management of Corporations

5-60 In General. There are three distinct groups which participate in the management of a corporation. The stockholders comprise the basic governing body and their control is exercised by electing the Board of Directors, by approving the By-Laws and by voting on such matters as merger, consolidation or dissolution. The Board of Directors is the policy making group and in addition has the responsibility for electing the officers who carry out the policies. The duties and powers of the Board of Directors and the various officers are set forth in the by-laws which every corporation has the power to enact.

5-61 By-Laws. The by-laws usually provide for the number of officers and directors, the method of electing them, and the enumeration of their duties. They also specify the time and place of the meetings of the directors and the stockholders. If the corporation is a nonstock corporation, the by-laws specify the requirements and the method for membership.

A by-law is a rule for governing the corporation which is binding upon all stockholders but the provisions of the by-laws are not binding on third persons unless the third person has knowledge of them.

The stockholders have power to amend, to add to, and to repeal the by-laws to the same extent that they have power to create by-laws in the first instance. They cannot, however, repeal, amend, or add to the by-laws, where such change will affect the vested rights of a stockholder.

The stockholders may delegate to the board of directors the right to adopt new by-laws or to repeal or to add to them. The board of directors, however, cannot change the by-laws with respect to limitation of their powers or to eliminate a duty imposed upon them by the stockholders.

5-62 Stockholders' Meetings. Action by the stockholders normally binds the corporation only when taken in a regular, or properly called, special meeting, after such notice as is required by the by-laws or statute has been given. However, it is generally conceded and some states so provide by statute that action approved informally by *all stockholders* will bind the corporation.

Notice of a special meeting must include a statement concerning the matters to be acted upon at the meeting, and any action taken on other matters will be ineffective. If unusual action, such as a sale of corporate assets, is to be taken at a regular meeting, notice of the meeting must call specific attention to that fact; but otherwise any business may be transacted at the annual meeting.

Failure to give proper notice of a meeting generally invalidates the action taken at the meeting. A stockholder who, having failed to receive notice, attends and participates in a meeting is said to waive the notice by his presence.

A quorum of stockholders must be present in order to transact business, such quorum being a majority of the voting shares outstanding, unless some statute or the by-laws provide for a larger or smaller percentage. Affirmative action is approved by majority vote of the shares represented at a meeting, provided a quorum exists. There are certain unusual matters, such as merger or sale of all corporate assets, which, at common law, required unanimous vote. Today, statutes usually provide that such action can be taken by vote of two-thirds or three-fourths of the stockholders. Many of these statutes also provide that the dissenting shareholders have the right to surrender their shares and receive their fair value in case they disapprove of the action taken.

5-63 Voting. Every member of a corporation is entitled to vote. In nonstock companies the members are entitled to one vote. In stock companies the members are entitled to as many votes as they own shares of stock. The stockholder whose name appears upon the corporate record is usually designated by the by-laws as the person entitled to vote. Preferred stockholders, by their contract with the corporation, may not be entitled to a vote. All jurisdictions hold, however, that every stockholder, whether preferred or not, is entitled to vote unless agreed otherwise. A stockholder cannot be deprived of a right to vote by a by-law. However, unless expressly prohibited by statute, the corporation may issue stock in the future, either common or preferred, and specify that the holder shall not vote.

The statutes of some states provide that a stockholder, in the election of directors by cumulative voting, may cast as many votes for one candidate for a given office as there are offices to be filled, multiplied by the number of his shares of stock; or he may distribute this same number of votes among the candidates as he sees fit.

A stockholder is entitled to vote only by virtue of his ownership in the stock, and, under the common law, this right can only be exercised in person. However, by statute, or the charter, or the by-laws, a stockholder may specifically authorize another to vote his stock. This authorization is made by power of attorney and must specifically state that the agent of the stockholder has power to vote his principal's stock. This method of voting is called voting by proxy. It is a personal relationship, and may be revoked at any time by the stockholder before the authority is exercised. The laws relative to principal and agent control this relationship.

A stockholder, unlike a director, is permitted to vote on a matter in which he has a personal interest. In certain respects he represents the corporation welfare in his voting, whereas in other respects he votes in such a manner as he thinks will best serve his interest. The majority of stockholders may not take action, however, that is clearly detrimental to the corporation and minority interests. This becomes particularly significant when the majority of the shareholders also own most of the stock of an allied or related enterprise and seek to operate the first corporation in such a manner as to profit the second at the expense of the first. If it is clear that the affairs of the first corporation are being mishandled in order to benefit the second, such action may be enjoined by the minority interests.

5-64 Voting Pools and Trust Agreements. Various devices have been used whereby minority interests or a group of stockholders may effectively control a corporation. The creation of a holding company, the issuance of non-voting shares or the issuance of shares with voting rights, but with a small or nominal par value, voting pools and voting trusts, have all been utilized for this purpose, and in general all of them are effective means for obtaining control. A voting pool arises whenever a number of stockholders agree to vote their stock as a unit in accordance with a certain plan. Such an agreement is enforceable unless the purpose to be accomplished is improper.

A voting trust develops from the transfer of title of their shares by various stockholders to a trustee for the purpose of voting the stock. The stock is then registered in his name, he votes at the meetings of shareholders, and receives dividends as they are declared. He issues to each stockholder, whose stock he holds, a certificate of beneficial interest which entitles the owner thereof to have his shares returned at the termination of the trust and to receive dividends within a given time after they are paid. Some courts have held voting trust unenforceable because they tend to separate ownership from control and management. Many of the courts, including most of those rendering recent decisions, enforce the trust agreement unless its objectives are improper or the period of its continuance unreasonably long.[1] The Uniform Business Corporations Act sets a limit of ten years upon voting trusts.

---

[1] *Alderman et al. v. Alderman et al.*, page 857.

DIRECTORS

5-65 Qualifications and Powers. The directors of a corporation are elected by the stockholders. In the absence of a provision in the charter, by-laws, or statute, it is not essential that directors hold stock in the corporation. Since they are to supervise the business activities, select key employees, and plan for the future development of the enterprise, they are presumably elected because of their business ability.

The directors have power to take such action as is necessary or proper consistent with the charter in the ordinary business activities of enterprises of the type being managed. They may not amend the charter, approve a merger, or bring about a consolidation with another corporation without the approval of the stockholders.

Directors are presumed to be free to exercise their independent judgment upon all matters presented to them. Consequently, their management of the business cannot be interfered with by action on the part of the stockholders.[2] Similarly, any contract made by a director with a stockholder concerning a particular matter before the board is contrary to public policy and unenforceable. Free and independent action by directors is required for the best interests of the corporation itself as distinct from the interests of a few stockholders.

5-66 Meetings. The statute, charter, and by-laws usually provide for the number of directors. In most cases, not less than three directors are required. Since the board of directors must act as a unit, it is usually necessary that it assemble at board meetings.[3] The by-laws usually provide for the method of calling directors' meetings and for the time and the place of meeting. A record is usually kept of the activities of the board of directors, and the evidence of the exercise of its powers is usually stated in resolutions kept in the corporate record book. A majority of the members of the board of directors is necessary to constitute a quorum. Special meetings are proper only when all directors are notified or are present at the meeting. Directors may not vote by proxy, having been selected as agents because of their personal qualifications.

Modern statutes provide for informal action by a Board of Directors (usually by telephone) providing the action taken is subsequently reduced to writing and signed by the Directors. This gives a Board the flexibility and capability to make decisions when needed without delay.

5-67 Compensation. In the absence of a stipulation in the charter or by-laws or resolution of the stockholders, directors receive no compensation for their services as such. If they do work not recognized as falling within the duties of a director, they may recover for the reasonable value

[2] *Petition of Avard,* page 859.
[3] *Tuttle v. Junior Bldg. Corp.,* page 860.

of their services. Directors who are appointed as officers of the corporation should have their salaries fixed at a meeting of the shareholders or in the by-laws. Since directors are not supposed to vote on any matter in which they have a personal interest, director-officers of small corporations usually vote on salaries for each other but not their own and the action to determine salaries should be ratified by the stockholders in order to insure the validity of the employment contracts.

5-68 Liabilities of Directors. Directors are said to stand in relation to the corporation as trustees, for both the corporation and the stockholders.[4] However, they are not trustees in the strict sense. They are agents with more than the usual authority of an agent. Therefore, a director occupies a position of trust and confidence with respect to the corporation, and cannot, by reason of his position, directly or indirectly derive any personal benefits that are not enjoyed by the corporation or the stockholders.[5] All secret profits obtained by a director in the pursuit of the corporate business must be accounted for to the corporation.

A director may contract with the corporation that he represents, but he is subject to the same limitations that an agent is in dealing with his principal. He is required to disclose his interest in all contracts and, because of his fiduciary relation, to volunteer all pertinent information regarding the subject matter involved. Furthermore, he is forbidden to vote as a director on any matter in which he has a personal interest. Even though his vote is not necessary to carry the proposition considered, most courts consider the action taken to be voidable. Some courts go so far as to hold that, if he is present at the meeting, favorable action will not be binding. Clearly, if his presence is required to make a quorum, no transaction in which he is interested should be acted upon. These rather severe rules are enforced so that directors will not be tempted to use their position to profit at the expense of the corporation.

Directors are personally liable when they willfully misuse their power and misapply the funds of the corporation. They are also personally liable where they issue stock as fully paid when it is not paid in full. Directors are required to perform the duties of their office in a reasonable manner and in good faith. The standard of care required of directors cannot be exactly defined. It is generally held that directors are bound to exercise that degree of care which men of prudence exercise in the management of their own affairs. The standard of care varies with the size and type of the corporation. In large corporations many duties must be delegated, thus intimate knowledge of details by the directors is not possible. In corporations invested with a public interest such as insurance companies, banking, building and loan, and public utilities, rigid supervision and specific obligations are imposed upon directors. If a director fails to exercise the requisite degree of care and skill, the corporation will have a right of action against him for resulting losses. When directors by their negligent misconduct involve the corporation in an *ultra vires* transaction which causes a loss, the directors may be liable to the corporation.

[4] *Mardel Securities, Inc. v. Alexandria Gazette Corp.*, page 861.
[5] *Vulcanized Rubber & Plastics Company v. Scheckter*, page 862.

They are not liable, however, for accidents and mistakes of judgment or for losses, if they have acted in good faith and have exercised ordinary care, skill, and diligence.

The directors, although holding a fiduciary relation to the corporation, have no such relationship with the individual stockholders. In a sale of stock by a stockholder to a director, they deal at arm's length. The director who, because of his relation to the corporation, is in a position to know many factors which affect the value of the stock, is not obligated to volunteer such information to the stockholder. There is a strong minority view and a tendency in recent decisions to support a fiduciary relationship in such cases.

MANAGEMENT OF CORPORATIONS CASES

Alderman et al. v. Alderman et al.

1935, 178 S.C. 9, 181 S.E. 897

The plaintiffs had assigned their stock in the D. W. Alderman & Sons Company to the defendants R. J. and Paul R. Alderman in a voting trust. The plaintiffs sought to have the trust declared null and void. The lower court ruled in favor of the defendants and the plaintiffs appealed.

BAKER, J. . . . It is a universally known fact to lumbermen that the operation of a sawmill and lumber plant, small or large, is a business in which one can lose heavily unless well managed. Indeed, this is so well recognized that it has become an adage among lumbermen, "Never to wish an enemy in torment but wish such enemy owned a sawmill."

Realizing, no doubt, that the success of the corporations, especially D. W. Alderman & Sons Company, depended upon the management, D. W. Alderman, Sr., requested that upon his death R. J. and Paul R. Alderman should be continued in the active management and control of the corporations in order that his well-known policies would be continued, and therefore, in deference to the wishes of the said D. W. Alderman, Sr., and having little if any experience with the operation and management of the business of said corporations, Mrs. Rice, Mrs. Shaw, Miss Martha Alderman, and D. W. Alderman, Jr., severally executed trust deeds or contracts conveying their stock in trust in the said corporations to the said R. J. and Paul R. Alderman.

. . . The position of appellants is that the instruments placing R. J. and Paul R. Alderman in the control of the corporation constituted what is known to the law as "voting trusts"; that they are void and voidable; being without consideration, illegal, and against public policy.

Therefore, the natural approach to a decision is to first inquire what constitutes a voting trust. There are various definitions of a voting trust given by the textbook and text-writers, among such definitions being as follows:

A voting trust agreement is an agreement which cumulates in the hands of a person or persons the shares of several owners of stock in trust for the purpose of voting them in order to control the corporate business and affairs. [14 C. J. 915]

A voting trust may be comprehensively defined as one created by an agreement between a group of the stockholders of a corporation and the trustee, or by a group of identical agreements between individual stockholders and a common trustee, whereby it is provided that for a term of years, or for a period contingent upon a certain event, or until the agreement is terminated, control over the stock owned by such stockholders, either for certain purposes or for all, shall be lodged in the trustee, with or without a reservation to the owner or persons designated by them of the power to direct how such control shall be used. [Fletcher's *Cyclopedia of Corporations*, No. 1705, vol. 3.]

The definitions given by the various leading text-writers are practically in accord, and the whole theory of voting trusts is built up on the idea that a group or a portion of the stockholders of a corporation unite and execute an instrument to a trustee for the purpose of voting and controlling the policies of the corporation, but in no definition, nor reported case, do we find the entire stock of the corporation pooled in the same trustee or trustees. The instruments executed in the case at bar, while containing practically every element going to make up what is commonly known as a voting trust, in fact go farther, and constitute in addition thereto a managing trust and trust deed, and the voting power given under the instruments has been treated as only one of the many powers conveyed by the instruments and as incidental to governing the management of the corporations. The instruments before the court convey the certificates of stock in the corporations to these trustees with full power and authority to control the corporations, and for a definite time, the lifetime of the trustees or the survivor. On their face, the instruments have all the earmarks of a complete contract. The parties thereto were competent to contract. There was a subject-matter, there was a legal consideration, and there was mutuality of agreement and mutuality of obligation.

We come then to the question first if the instruments before the court are void or voidable as being against public policy.

. . . If the instruments create nothing more than voting trusts, are they void as against public policy? There are two distinct lines of cases, the one holding that the separation of the voting power in stock from its beneficial ownership is contrary to public policy and void, the other, that any voting trust which is entered into in good faith and for the promotion and good of the corporation, and thereby necessarily for the welfare and good of all of the stockholders, is valid and enforceable.

> . . . It is very generally held or said that voting trusts are not per se unlawful; and one of the most familiar illustrations of a voting trust which may be lawful is where the object is to carry out a particular policy, with a view to promote the best interest of all of the stockholders. It is said that the validity of the trust is to be determined by the propriety and justness of the ultimate purposes sought to be accomplished . . . (14 C. J. 915).

The instruments herein sought to be declared null and void are not against the public policy of the state, not contravening any statute, and there being a total lack of evidence that they were entered into to serve any illegal purpose, but, to the contrary, to better serve the interests of all of the stockholders and benefit them and the corporations.

Judgment affirmed.

Petition of Avard

1955, 144 N.Y.S. 2d 204

The petitioners, minority stockholders of Oneita Knitting Mills, a corporation, brought this action against the corporation to recover the value of their stock in the corporation. The corporation, which manufactured knit goods, was operating at a loss in its plant in New York and it desired to shift its operations to a low-cost plant in South Carolina where it was believed that the business could be profitably conducted. The petitioners contended that the sale by the company of its property in New York could not be made without the consent of two thirds of the stockholders. The lower court dismissed the petition and the stockholders appealed.

GORMAN, J. . . . Section 20 of the Stock Corporation Law in substance requires the approval of two-thirds of the stockholders entitled to vote if a corporation desires to sell or convey its property, rights, privileges and franchises, or any interest therein or any part thereof, if such sale, lease or exchange is not made in the regular course of its business and involves all or substantially all of its property, rights, privileges and franchises, or an integral part thereof essential to the conduct of the business of the corporation. Section 21 of the same law prescribes the procedure to be followed by duly objecting stockholders. If, in view of the purposes and objects of a corporation, a particular sale may be regarded as within the regular and normal course of the business of the corporation and as not involving an integral part thereof, it is not within the purview of the statute. If the sale is such as to deprive the corporation of the means of accomplishing the ends for which it was incorporated; that is, if the business, and assets sold were essential to the ordinary conduct of the business, it is within the statute.

The present controversy squarely poses the question of whether the conduct of the respondent was such as to bring it within the scope of § 20. The management of a corporation is entrusted to its board of directors. It is well established that the directors have power, in the ordinary course of business, to do any act permitted by the charter or certificate of incorporation. There is no serious suggestion that the actions of the board of directors were tainted by fraud, deceit or bad faith in any of the contested transactions. Although the statute has been held inapplicable to the actions of a corporation pursuing a business advantage (*Matter of Leventall,* 241 App. Div. 277, 271 N.Y.S. 493), the courts have rarely been called upon to construe the applicability of its terms to the actions of a solvent corporation motivated by business conditions to pursue somewhat far-reaching measures in the manipulation of its assets in an effort to continue its business.

If corporate management determines that a business is unprofitable, it may dispose of the property or business to eliminate further loss without the consent of its stockholders.

The time-honored test to determine the need for stockholder consent "is not the amount involved, but the nature of the transaction, whether the sale is in the regular course of the business of the corporation and in furtherance of the express objects of its existence, or something outside of the normal and regular course of the business."

The instant transactions do not involve the investment of respondent's assets in a substantially different business of a kind in which it was not authorized to engage, nor the exchange of its stock for the stock of another corporation, nor were they *pro tanto* going out of business in any vital department or branch of respondent's business.

"What in the instance of one corporation may be a sale or lease of all its assets requiring consent of stockholders, may, in the case of another corporation, depending upon its purposes, methods of operation and past history, and the industry practices and pattern, represent usual, normal and ordinary activity which does not require consent." (*Schreiber v. Butte Copper & Zinc Co.,* D.C., 98 F. Supp. 106, 111.) Respondent has shown that it has long been the custom in the knit goods industry in general and its own operations in particular to discontinue unprofitable production and to sell equipment and machinery no longer needed in the ordinary course of its business. Subsequent to 1920, respondent found it expedient to reduce the production of men's and, particularly, women's heavy-weight underwear, the volume of which had previously been much greater than the aggregate of all its other production. This procedure constituted a normal operation of its business and was affected without specific stockholder approval. Respondent's present decision to concentrate upon the profitable production of light-weight underwear, T-shirts and outerwear would seem to be in accord with accepted business practice. Respondent has not relinquished any of its franchises nor has it prohibited itself from engaging in any branch of the knitted goods business which may now, or in the future, prove acceptable to consumers and profitable to it. None of the acts of the respondent can practicably be called acts of complete or partial self-destruction. It has not deprived itself of its ability to carry out its corporate purposes as exemplified in its amended charter by alienating an integral part of its business and has not altered the avowed purpose of the corporation— to manufacture, process, sell and otherwise deal in knit goods of any character. Since the charter further specifically provides that the corporate purpose is to do all acts and things as may be necessary, convenient or incidental to the foregoing, the board of directors may not be held to have acted in excess of their declared powers.

Affirmed.

Tuttle v. Junior Bldg. Corporation

1948, 228 N.C. 507, 46 S.E.2d 313

The directors and stockholders of the defendant Junior Building Corporation met informally and discussed plaintiff's offer to purchase the building owned by the corporation. It was informally agreed to sell to the plaintiff, and the defendant's attorney, who was also a director, was instructed to prepare a deed. There was no formal vote and no record of the meeting was entered in the corporate minutes. The deed was delivered to the bank in escrow and later withdrawn without the consent of the plaintiff and before he tendered the balance of the purchase price. The plaintiff brought this suit to compel specific performance of the contract of purchase and sale. From a judgment for defendant, plaintiff appealed.

BARNHILL, J. . . . A corporation is bound by the acts of its stockholders and directors only when they act as a body in regular session or under authority conferred at a duly constituted meeting. "As a rule authorized meetings are prerequisite to corporate action based upon deliberate conference, and intelligent discussion of proposed measures." (*O'Neal v. Wake County,* 196 N.C. 184, 145 S.E. 28, 29.)

. . . "The separate action, individually, without consultation, although a majority in number should agree upon a certain act, would not be the act of the constituted body of men clothed with corporate powers." Angel & Ames on Corporations, § 504. "Indeed, the authorities upon this subject are numerous, uncontradicted, and supported by reason." (*Duke v. Markham,* 105 N.C. 131, 10 S.E. 1017, 18 Am. St. Rep. 889.)

. . . If stockholders and directors cannot bind the corporation by their individual acts and declarations, *a fortiori* an unauthorized act performed in the name of the corporation by its officers cannot thereafter be ratified by such acts or declarations. Hence the court below properly excluded the evidence of declarations made by stockholders and directors after the sale had been repudiated and the deed withdrawn from escrow.

Affirmed.

Mardel Securities, Inc. v. Alexandria Gazette Corp.

1960, 183 F.Supp. 7

WALTER E. HOFFMAN, D. J. Mardel Securities, Inc. has instituted this secondary action in its capacity as a 48% minority stockholder of the Alexandria Gazette Corporation, publishers of a newspaper advertised as "America's Oldest Daily Newspaper," against the Gazette and its principal officer, Charles C. Carlin, Jr., the latter being the owner of 52% of the outstanding stock issued by the Gazette. Plaintiff contends that Carlin is indebted to the Gazette in substantial amounts allegedly occasioned by reason of Carlin's ownership and operation of a newspaper known as the "Arlington Daily Sun," hereinafter referred to as the "Sun," which said newspaper Carlin caused to be printed at, and partially operated from, the physical plant of the Gazette at Alexandria, Virginia, only a few miles from Arlington where the Sun had its principal office but possessed no facilities for printing the newspaper. Plaintiff contends that the amounts charged to the Sun by the Gazette resulted in substantial losses to the Gazette for which Carlin, by reason of his fiduciary capacity, is liable to the Gazette. In short, the action, while maintained by the minority stockholder, is actually for the use and benefit of the Gazette corporation.

. . . We have no difficulty applying the controlling principles of law to the facts here presented. As was said in *Rowland v. Kable* (174 Va. 343, 6 S.E.2d 633, 642):

> The authorities are agreed that a director of a private corporation cannot directly or indirectly, in any transaction in which he is under a duty to guard the interests of the corporation, acquire any personal advantage, or make any profit for himself, and if he does so, he may be compelled to account therefor to the corporation. This does not mean that he may not deal with his corporation or sell his property to the corporation if the transactions are open, fair and honest, and the corporation is represented by competent and authorized agents. The unbending rule is that the director must act in the utmost good faith, and this good faith forbids placing himself in a position where his individual interest clashes with his duty to his corporation. The purpose of the law is to secure fidelity in the director. If, in violation of the general rule, he places himself in a position in which he may be tempted, by his own private interest, to disregard that of the corporation, his transactions are voidable at the option of the corporation and may be set aside without showing actual injury. One who is entrusted with the business of anoher cannot be allowed to make that business an object of interest to himself.

To the same effect will be found . . . *Wight v. Heublein* (4 Cir., 238 F. 321, 324). In the last cited case, the Court pointed out that directors are:

> . . . (precluded) from doing any act, or engaging in any transaction in which their own private interest will conflict with the duty they owe to the stockholders and from making any use of their power or of the corporation property for their own advantage.

In *Solimine v. Hollander* (128 N.J.Eq. 228, 16 A.2d 203, 217), we are told that

> a director or officer of a corporation cannot use corporate assets to acquire, finance, or develop his own individual business project or venture and insist that either the venture or the profits thereof are his own property.

It is clear that Carlin, in his fiduciary capacity as officer and director of the Gazette, has violated the cardinal rules applicable to his position.

Vulcanized Rubber & Plastics Company v. Scheckter
1960 (Pa.) 162 A.2d 400

COHEN, J. On August 20, 1959, the appellee corporation moved for and was granted a temporary order restraining the appellants, two of whom had been both lawyers and accountants of the appellee and a third a former director, from voting any of appellee's stock owned, held or controlled by appellants at any future stockholder's meeting. After holding several hearings, the chancellor, finding that certain stock was acquired by appellants in breach of their fiduciary responsibilities, decreed that the restraining order be continued as a preliminary injunction pending final hearing and determination of the case. From this order appellants have taken these appeals.

The instant suit involves another round in the struggle between the present management group of the appellee, Vulcanized Rubber & Plastics Company, and a group headed by the individual appellants, Scheckter, Fish and Redland, for managerial control of the appellee corporation. . . .

The chancellor found that from about March 1, 1956, until approximately the commencement of this action, a Weatherly Steel Castings Company and its successor, the appellant Dutron Plastics, Inc., made numerous purchases of the appellee's common stock, causing the price of the stock to increase from about $25 per share to more than $60 per share. Throughout this period, appellants Scheckter and Fish held majority control of both Weatherly Steel Casting Company and Dutron Plastics. They did not reveal their interest in these companies to the appellee. . . .

. . . Generally speaking, a corporation as such has no interest in its outstanding stock, or in dealings by its officers, directors, or shareholders with respect thereto. (*Howell v. McCloskey,* 1953, 375 Pa. 100, 99 A.2d 610; *Bisbee v. Midland Linseed Products Co.,* 8 Cir., 1927, 19 F.2d 24.) As a result, in and of itself, there can be nothing improper so far as the corporate entity is concerned with one of its fiduciaries, be he officer, director or otherwise, buying up a controlling number of shares. . . . Nor can it be of any consequence, therefore, if the control is secretly acquired (which as a practical matter will usually be the case, for to do so otherwise will result in a rise in the market price).

On the other hand, if there should exist some reason or necessity for the corporation to purchase its outstanding shares, the situation is necessarily altered. There is no doubt that the relationship between a corporation and its officers and directors, as well as its lawyers and accountants, is such that these "fiduciaries" cannot act contrary to or complete with the interests of the corporation. Predominantly for the protection of shareholders, there has developed in corporation law a doctrine of "corporate opportunity" under which a corporation has the right to legal redress where one of its fiduciaries has in some way usurped some advantageous opportunity in which the corporation has an existing interest or where the opportunity is necessary for corporate existence or prosperity. . . .

It becomes evident that the basis of appellee's action here must be that the appellant fiduciáries, in purchasing the stock in issue, regardless of the secrecy in doing so, have acted in competition with some existing corporate interest in the stock, or have pre-empted a corporate purchase which was necessary for the appellee's prosperity or existence. . . . Upon an examination of the record, and upon analysis of the applicable doctrines of corporate law, we find that the appellee corporation, as a corporate entity separate and apart from its management group, had no interest in purchasing the stock in issue . . . which could result in the appellee being legally harmed by the conduct of the appellants. . . .

There being no indication in the record that the board of directors as a body ever considered purchasing any stock, there could not be any existing corporate interest therein. Accordingly, it cannot be held that appellants' purchases were in competition with the corporation itself. . . .

The order granting the preliminary injunction is reversed.

CHAPTER 41
REVIEW QUESTIONS AND PROBLEMS

1. *A* is a director of a corporation operating an automobile dealership. The corporation owes him $21,000. It also owes *X*, a third party creditor, $50,000. Both debts cannot be paid and insolvency is imminent. *A* persuades the other directors to join him in authorizing payment to himself. May *X* require *A* to pay over to him the amount received?

2. The directors of the *X* Company declared a dividend when there were insufficient profits and surplus to pay it, although, at the time, the remaining assets were more than sufficient to pay liabilities if stock was not regarded as a liability. The corporation soon became insolvent. Could the creditors have recovered the amount of the dividend from the directors?

3. *X*, *Y*, and *Z* entered into a voting trust by the terms of which they authorized their trustee to vote their stock in the *AB* Co. The agreement was to last for 11 years but the State of Incorporation by statute limited such agreements to a maximum of 10 years. Can *X* withdraw from the voting pool?

4. The holders of a corporate mortgage were given trust certificates representing stock which allowed the mortgagee to vote the stock at shareholders' meetings. The mortgagee controlled the management of the corporation and made sure that the mortgage payments were made. Was the arrangement legal?

5. *P*, a minority stockholder in *X* Co., demanded to inspect the corporate records in order to conduct a proxy fight with management. Is he entitled to do so?

6. If all directors are present and voting at a meeting, is the action binding without formal notice of the meeting?

7. *P* sued *D* Co. under a contract. *P* was a director of *D* Co. and his presence and vote were necessary to the approval of the contract. *D* Co. contends that the contract was void. Is *D* Co. correct?

8. *P* owned stock in *X* Bank. *P* went to the bank, informed the officers of his desire to sell his stock and inquired as to its value. He was informed

that the stock was worth its par value, $100 per share. The book value was $149 and a merger was in process. *P* signed his certificates in blank and delivered them to the officers. On merger, the stock brought $187 per share. *P* seeks to rescind the sale. May he do so?

9. In what situation are directors of a corporation personally liable?

chapter 42

Dissolution of
a Corporation

5-69 Expiration of Charter. Corporate existence may be terminated by the expiration of its charter, through dissolution by the attorney general, by consolidation, or by action of the stockholders.

Where the charter provides that the corporation shall exist for a definite period, it automatically terminates at the expiration of the period. However, upon application, a rule for the continued existence of the corporation may be made.

5-70 Dissolution by Attorney General. The state, having brought the corporation into existence, has a right to forfeit the charter. Suits to forfeit a charter, known as Quo Warranto proceedings, may only be instituted by the states legal official known as the Attorney General and may not be instituted by private parties. Such a suit may be brought by the Attorney General if a corporation misuses its power, or enters into illegal acts, such as combinations in restraint of trade, or ceases to perform its corporate functions for a long period of time. The Attorney General may also, without charter forfeiture, by proper proceedings enjoin a corporation from engaging in a business not authorized by its charter.[1]

5-71 Consolidation and Merger. Consolidation is the uniting of two or more corporations, by which a new corporation is created and the old entities are dissolved. The new corporation takes title to all the property, rights, powers, and privileges of the old corporations, subject to the liabilities and obligations of the old corporations.

[1] *State ex. rel. Safeguard Ins. Co. v. Vorys,* page 868.

In a merger, however, one of the corporations continues its existence, but absorbs the other corporation, which is merged into it. The continuing corporation may expressly or impliedly assume and agree to pay the debts and liabilities of the absorbed corporation. If so, such creditors become third party creditor beneficiaries. By statutes in many states the surviving corporation is deemed to have assumed all the liabilities and obligations of the absorbed corporation. The statutes of the various states provide the methods for corporate consolidation and merger.

5-72 Dissolution by the Stockholders. A corporation can be dissolved by the consent of all the stockholders and by less than all of the stockholders if it is insolvent. If the corporation is insolvent, it may be dissolved upon application to the state that created it. Under these circumstances, a court usually appoints a receiver to marshal the assets and to make distribution to the creditors.

Upon dissolution all the corporate property, both personal and real, is first used to pay corporate debts. After the debts are paid, the remainder is to be distributed among the stockholders in proportion to the capital stock they own. The liability of the stockholders, upon dissolution, ceases as to any further business. Where a receiver has been appointed and it is necessary to carry out contracts not yet completed, the corporation still remains liable for the performance of its executory contracts.

RIGHTS OF CREDITORS

5-73 Right Against Corporate Assets. The corporation stands in the same position as a natural person, with respect to creditors. A suit may be brought against it, and upon judgment being obtained, an execution may be levied against its property, which may then be sold. Likewise, corporate assets may be attached, and if the corporation has no property subject to execution, its assets may be traced by a bill in a court of equity.

The creditors have no right, because they are creditors, to interfere with the management of the business. A creditor who has an unsatisfied judgment against a corporation, because there is no corporate property upon which a levy can be made, may bring a bill in equity to set aside conveyances and transfers of corporate property which have been fradulently transferred for the purpose of delaying and hindering creditors.[2] Creditors may also, under the above circumstances, ask for a receiver to take over the assets of the corporation and to apply them to the payment of debts.

5-74 Right Against Stockholders. Stockholders are not liable for the debts of the corporation. This distinction is the essential difference between a corporation and a partnership. Each member of a partnership is liable for the debts of the firm. The members of a corporation, on the other hand, are not liable for the debts of the firm.[3]

[2] *State et al. v. Simmer Oil Corp. et al.,* page 869.
[3] *Shaw v. Bailey-McCune Company,* page 870.

If the members of a corporation have not paid their stock in full, however, the creditors, after exhausting the assets of the firm, may look to the stockholders for their unpaid balance. This is the limit of the liability of the members of a corporation.

But the statutes of many states have increased the liabilities of stockholders to corporate creditors. That is, the statutes provide that the stockholders shall be liable for a sum in addition to the par value of their stock. This additional liability is known as the statutory liability of stockholders. A few states, by statute, attach additional liability to stockholders of manufacturing corporations. Some attach liability equal to the par of the shares in banking and trust companies. The stockholders will be liable to the creditors if the capital stock has been distributed among the stockholders before the creditors have been paid, and the creditors can reach the assets of the corporation in the hands of the stockholders on the theory that the assets have been transferred in fraud of creditors.

DISSOLUTION OF A CORPORATION CASES

State ex rel. Safeguard Ins. Co. v. Vorys

1960 (Ohio) 167 N.E.2d 910

The relator (Safeguard Ins. Co.) brought an action in mandamus against Vorys, Superintendent of Insurance, to require the latter to release to relator $53,000 in securities which had been deposited by an insurer which had since merged into relator. Safeguard had deposited with the Superintendent for the security and benefit of all its policy holders the requisite amount of securities required. The relator filed a demurrer to the Superintendent's answer.

TAFT, J. . . . Generally, where there is an assumption by one legal entity of the liability or obligation of another legal entity, such assumption will not represent a payment or an extinguishment of such liability or obligation. However, the extent of the liability or obligation of a corporation may be dependent upon and measured by the law which establishes its existence as a legal entity. Thus, that law may authorize the substitution, for the liability and obligation of a corporation that it has created as a corporate entity, of the liability of another solvent legal entity into which it lawfully merged. . . .

Certainly, a creditor who voluntarily deals with such a corporation in the light of constitutional provisions such as those found in Section 2 of Article XIII of the Ohio Constitution ("corporations may be formed under general laws: but all such laws may, from time to time, be altered or repealed") is in no position to complain where the law which created the corporation provides that (on the happening of certain events and without interfering with any pending legal proceedings) such corporation's obligations and liabilities shall cease to be the obligations and liabilities of such corporation and instead shall become the obligations and liabilities of a solvent legal entity into which said corporation merges. . . .

Thus, after the merger, any obligations and liabilities secured by the $53,000 deposits made with the respondent superintendent by the indemnity company, which were not the subject of pending legal proceedings (none apparently were) were no longer obligations and liabilities of the indemnity company as a legal entity separate from relator but were obligations and liabilities of relator, although still secured by those $53,000 of deposits; and those deposits belong to relator, subject to any claims or liens against such deposits in favor of those to whom the indemnity company had been before the merger and to whom relator was thereafter obligated or liable. . . .

It follows that relator's demurrer to the amended answer must be sustained. . . .

Writ allowed.

State et al. v. Simmer Oil Corporation et al.

1942, 231 Iowa 1041, 2 N.W.2d 760

The plaintiff, State of Iowa, obtained a judgment against the defendant corporation. This judgment was not paid and the plaintiff is seeking to set aside certain transfers of property made by the corporation in order that the property may be made available to satisfy the plaintiff's claim. The corporation deeded the property to Leonard Simmer and his wife, the principal stockholders of the defendant corporation. The trial court ruled that the transfer would not be set aside and the plaintiff appealed.

SAGER, J. . . . Appellants insist that they are entitled to have these properties subjected to the unpaid debts of the oil corporation. Appellees deny, urging that they legally have claim to these properties because transfers were made in satisfaction of money advanced by them to the corporation; and they say that even though the corporation deeded to Leonard, president and director, this was a valid legal transaction. The trial court took this view and we think therein erred. It must be admitted that some of our earlier cases tend to support the decision below. (Cases cited)

These cases do declare generally the right to give such preference but our later cases, while not overlooking the prior decisions, have limited their apparent scope. In discussing the so-called "trust fund" doctrine we said in *Luedecke v. Des Moines Cabinet Co.* (140 Iowa 223, 118 N.W. 456, 458, 32 L.R.A., N.S., 616):

> We do not recognize the trust-fund doctrine to the extent that it has obtained in some of the courts; but are of opinion that corporate creditors are entitled in equity to the payment of their debts before any distribution of corporate property is made among the stockholders, and recognize the right of a creditor of a corporation to follow its assets or property into the hands of any one who is not a good-faith holder in the ordinary course of business.

Certainly the appellees Simmer are not good-faith holders "in the ordinary course of business." We do not wish to be understood as charging that they were guilty of any actual or intentional fraud. The record excludes this. Agnes Simmer put into this corporation upwards of twenty thousand dollars even mortgaging the homestead to keep the business going. If there be any fraud in the transaction it is in a strictly legal sense and not actual fraud with which we are dealing.

. . . Under the authorities cited the properties above described should be made subject to the debts held by appellants and other creditors, if any there be.

. . . As to these, any equities there may be above existing mortgages should be applied to the payment of unpaid creditors of the Simmer Oil Corporation.

It follows that the cause must be and it is remanded for further proceedings in accordance herewith. Other creditors, if there are any, should be brought in as parties so their interests may be protected.

Shaw v. Bailey-McCune Company

1960 (Utah) 355 P.2d 321

The defendant, Bailey-McCune Company, leased real property from the plaintiffs and also purchased certain items of merchandise on credit. The individual defendants are stockholders in the corporation. The corporation failed financially and the plaintiffs contending that the corporate structure is a sham, seek to hold the stockholders personally liable for the unpaid rent and merchandise. The plaintiffs contend that the corporation was under-capitalized. The lower court dismissed the action against the individual defendants. The plaintiffs appealed.

CALLISTER, J. . . . The mere relation of being a stockholder in a debtor corporation does not under the law make a stockholder liable for the debts and obligations of the corporation. A corporation is a statutory entity which is regarded as having an existence and personality distinct from that of its stockholders even though the stock is owned by a single individual.

Under some circumstances the corporate entity may be disregarded in the interest of justice in such cases as fraud, contravention of law or contract, or public wrong. However, great caution should be exercised by the courts in disregarding the entity.

Moreover, the conditions under which the corporate entity may be disregarded or the corporation be regarded as the alter ego of the stockholders vary according to the circumstances in each case inasmuch as the doctrine is essentially an equitable one and for that reason is particularly within the province of the trial court.

The lower court found that the corporation was not a sham or the alter ego of the Baileys and refused to disregard the corporate entity. These findings of the trial court should not be overturned unless the evidence clearly preponderates against them. We have carefully examined the record and find no reason to reverse the trial court's determination.

Affirmed.

CHAPTER 42
REVIEW QUESTIONS AND PROBLEMS

1. *X* Corporation entered into a contract to purchase linseed oil from *Y*. Subsequently, *X* Corporation merged with *Z* Corporation and the latter refused to purchase linseed oil from *Y*. Does *Y* have a cause of action against *Z* Corporation?

2. A corporation had not made a profit for 20 years and no dividends had been paid for that period. The preferred stockholders brought suit to obtain a decree of dissolution. Should they succeed?

3. *A* owned a minority of the stock in *X* Corporation. He could not agree with the majority on the way they desired to conduct the business. Specifically they desired to merge with another corporation over his vehement objection. What may be done? If *A*'s stock is ordered sold to the majority, how will the price be fixed?

4. *D* owed *X* Corporation $10,000. *X* Corporation's directors and shareholders voted to dissolve. Thereafter, *X* co-sued *D*, and *D* contended that he had no liability because of the dissolution. What result?

5. *X* Co. owed *P* $500. *X* Co. voted to dissolve and thereafter distributed its assets to its shareholders. Does *P* have any remedy?

6. What is the difference between a consolidation and a merger?

7. *X* Co. failed to pay its franchise taxes to the state of incorporation. The state commenced involuntary dissolution proceedings. *X* Co. objected, contending that the state could sue for the taxes but could not take away its charter. What result?

Part Three

Miscellaneous
Business
Organizations

5-75 Introduction. Most of our business is conducted by individual proprietorships, partnerships, and corporations. A few of the other types should, however, be given some consideration. The most important of these are the limited partnership, the joint stock company, and the business trust. In the sections that follow, it is proposed to consider briefly their organization and the extent to which the owners have personal responsibility for obligations which are incurred.

5-76 Limited Partnerships. A limited partnership, just as other partnerships, comes into existence by virtue of an agreement. However, a limited partnership is like a corporation in that it is authorized by statute and because the liability of one or more of the partners, but not of all, is limited to the amount of capital contributed at the time of the creation of the partnership. This latter characteristic supplies the name for this type of business organization which is in effect a hybrid between the partnership and the corporation. A limited partnership may be formed by two or more persons, having one or more general partners and one or more limited partners. To create a limited partnership under the Uniform Limited Partnership Act the parties must sign and swear to a certificate containing the following information: the name of the partnership; the character of the business, its location; the name and place of residence of each member; those who are to be the general and those who are to be the limited partners; the term for which the partnership is to exist; the amount of cash or the agreed value of property to be contributed by each partner; the additional contributions, if any, to be made from time to time by each partner; the time that any such contributions are to be returned to the limited partner; the share of profit or compensation which each limited partner shall receive; the right that a limited partner has to substitute an assignee of his interest; the right to admit additional limited partners; the right given to one or more of the limited partners to priority over other limited partners as to contributions, and compensation by way of income; the right of a limited partner to demand property rather than cash in return for his contribution; and the right of the remaining general partners to continue the business on the death, retirement, or incapacity of other partners.

The certificate must be recorded in the county where the partnership has its principal place of business, and a copy must be filed in every community where it conducts business or has a representative office. In addition, most states require notice by newspaper publication. In the event of any change in the facts contained in the certificate as filed, such as a change in the name of the partnership, the capital, or other matters, a new certificate must be filed. If such a certificate is not filed and the partnership continues, the limited partners immediately become liable as general partners.

The statutes of most states require the partnership to conduct its business in a firm name which does not include the name of any of the limited partners or the word "Company." Some states specify that the word "Limited" shall be added. In some jurisdictions no liability will attach to the limited partners unless creditors are misled or injured by the failure of the firm to use the word "Limited" or by the use of the word "Company." A limited partner is not liable beyond his contribution to creditors of the partnership in the pursuit of the partnership business, unless the limited partner participates in the management and control of the business.[1] Participation in management makes the limited partner a general partner with unlimited liability notwithstanding the certificate. A limited partnership cannot be dissolved voluntarily before the time for its termination as stated in the certificate, without the filing and publication of the notice of the dissolution. Upon dissolution, the distribution of the assets of the firm is prescribed in the statute which gives priority to limited partners over general partners after all creditors are paid.

5-77 Joint Stock Companies. A joint stock company is a business arrangement which provides for the management of the business to be placed in the hands of trustees or directors. Under the constitution or by-laws of the organization, shares represented by certificates are issued to the various members who are joint owners in the enterprise. These shareholders elect the board of directors or trustees. The shares are transferable, the same as the shares of a corporation, and such transfer does not cause dissolution. Likewise, the death of one of the shareholders does not dissolve the organization as in a partnership.[2] It exists for the period

---

1 *Filesi v. United States,* page 876.
2 *Hammond et al. v. Otwell et al.,* page 877.

of time designated in the by-laws. Such an association is a partnership, even though the primary purpose of such an arrangement is to secure many of the advantages of a corporation. Unlimited liability continues, but in many other respects the features of a corporation are present. In many states by statute a suit may be brought against a joint stock company as an entity.

5-78 Business Trusts. The business trust is an organization formed by trustees under a contract, called a declaration of trust, executed by the trustees. Under the agreement, the trustees issue certificates of beneficial interest, which are sold to investors.

The trustees take the capital in compliance with the agreement and operate the business, whatever it may be, as principals, for the benefit of the shareholders. Such an organization has many of the characteristics of a corporation, in that the trustees elect officers from among themselves, and in some states the shareholders at stated meetings, by virtue of the trust agreement, are permitted to elect the trustees.

Such an organization avoids the statutory regulations of a corporation, in that it is not a creature of the state, and seeks as well to avoid partnership liability on the part of the investors. The courts in most of the states, however, have held that if the investors under the trust agreement have a right to exercise some control over the management of the business, by way of election of trustees or otherwise, such shareholders are liable as partners. It is clear, on the other hand, that if such shareholders have no control over, or no right to interfere in any way with, the management of the business, they are beneficiaries under a trust agreement and are not liable as partners.[3] This business organization has been called different names, such as "Business Trust," "Massachusetts Trust," and "The Common Law Trust." As a substitute for a corporation, it has lost many of its advantages, owing to statutory regulation by the various states; as a method to avoid partnership liability, it is ineffective, in that a shareholder whose money is being risked in a business venture naturally desires to have some control over the policy and conduct of the business, and such reservations carry with them the obligation of partnership.

The trustees are usually held to have unlimited liability for all obligations of the business trust unless the contracts restrict the rights of the creditors to the assets of the trust. It is customary for business trusts to place this limiting clause in all contracts, particularly if there is any possible question about the solvency of the trust. Generally those organizations known as "Business Trusts" engage in the investment business. Investors purchase shares or certificates which entitle the holders to income from and increased value of stocks and bonds purchased by the trustees or directors of trust.

[3] *Commercial Casualty Insurance Co. v. North et al.,* page 880.

MISCELLANEOUS BUSINESS ORGANIZATIONS CASES

Filesi v. United States

1965, 352 F.2d 339

BOREMAN, C. J. The Commissioner of Internal Revenue, asserting that the Jolly Tavern had been operated as a cabaret because dancing had been permitted to the music of a juke box, assessed deficiencies in cabaret excise taxes, penalties and interest in the amount of $46,567.28 against the taxpayer, Alfred Filesi, based on the receipts from the operation of the tavern. One assessment for the sum of $33,651.87 was against Henry Muller, deceased, and Filesi, as partners, in the operation of the tavern for the period from the first quarter of 1954 through the first quarter of 1957. . . .

In the District Court Filesi readily admitted that no excise tax returns had been filed for the periods covered by the assessments. He contended, however, that no excise tax was due and no returns were required because the Jolly Tavern had not been operated as a cabaret at any time as dancing had not been permitted, tolerated or regularly engaged in. Further, assuming the tavern was a cabaret, he contended that he was not liable for excise tax for the period from the first quarter of 1954 through the first quarter of 1956 as he was a "limited partner" during this period and did not become a general partner until a written partnership agreement was executed on April 4, 1956. . . .

At the close of all the evidence the District Court ruled as a matter of law that Filesi was a general partner for the period in dispute. The remaining issues were then submitted to the jury. The jury found that there was dancing at the tavern and that the total tax liability for the entire period from 1954 through the third quarter of 1958 should have been $28,854.95 rather than the $46,567.28 assessed by the Commissioner. Judgment was accordingly entered.

The principal errors assigned on appeal relate to rulings of the court: first, that the court erred in ruling as a matter of law and instructing the jury that Filesi was a general partner for the period from the first quarter of 1954 through the first quarter of 1956.

In his testimony Filesi admitted he and Muller were partners but contended he was a "limited partner" and not liable for the tax for the periods before the second quarter of 1956. The facts upon which this contention is based are these. From 1949 when Filesi first became associated with the management of the Jolly Tavern until April 14, 1951, Filesi along with Muller and John Marshall were the only shareholders of a corporation organized to operate the tavern. Marshall wanted out of the business and on April 14, 1951, the corporation was dissolved and Muller assumed to purchase Marshall's interest but to do so Muller borrowed money from an outside source and the loan was subsequently repaid from the profits of the Jolly Tavern before Filesi and Muller received their shares as partners. The effect of this transaction was that Filesi became the purchaser of one half of Marshall's interest. According to Filesi, Muller did not have funds to buy Filesi's interest also so Muller persuaded him to leave his investment in the tavern. In return, Filesi testified, it was orally agreed that he was to manage the business at a stipulated salary and receive 50 percent of all profits but was not to be liable for any losses. The liquor license was transferred to Muller's name and the business was operated under this arrangement until April 4, 1956. On that date Muller and Filesi executed a written partnership agreement under which both were to share gains and losses equally. From April 4, 1956, to April 4, 1957, the tavern was operated under this written agreement. On the latter date the partnership was dissolved and Muller sold his interest to Filesi who has since owned and operated the tavern.

Filesi argues that he was a limited partner from April 14, 1951, to April 4, 1956, and as such he was not liable for any losses of the partnership during this period; that, as the excise tax from the first quarter of 1954 through the first quarter of 1956 would constitute a loss he should not be held accountable for the tax. We cannot agree. It is well settled that to obtain the protections and privileges of limited liability a person must comply with the statutory requirements regulating the formation of limited partnerships or otherwise be held liable as a general partner. The Annotated Code of Maryland specified the acts which must be performed by a person desiring to become a limited partner in the operation of a business within that State. It was clearly shown that Filesi did not comply with these provisions and, therefore, he cannot now claim the protection of a limitation of liability. It is clear from the evidence generally and from Filesi's own testimony that he openly and publicly took an active part in the management and control of the business. We think the District Court was correct in holding as a matter of law that Filesi was liable as a general partner for any excise tax properly assessed for the period in dispute.

Even assuming that Filesi was a limited partner his argument is unsound. According to applicable law a limited partner is liable for any losses of the partnership to the extent of his invesment in the assets of the business. On this point, however, no evidence was produced to show what Filesi's investment was for the period, although in 1951 it was slightly in excess of $10,000.

Cause reversed for other reasons.

Hammond et al. v. Otwell et al.

1930, 170 Ga. 832, 154 S.E. 357

The plaintiffs, Hammond and others, brought this action against the defendants who were allegedly members of a joint stock association, People's Bank. The plaintiffs all have claims against the now defunct bank. The defendants contended that the bank was a partnership which had been dissolved by the prior death of some of the partners. The lower court granted a non-suit as to all of the defendants except one, and the plaintiffs excepted.

HINES, J. . . . The question whether a joint-stock company can be legally created in this state by agreement of parties, without legislative action, has been discussed by counsel for the defendants; but in the view which we take of this case we deem it unnecessary to pass upon this question. The controlling question is whether the articles of association, the substance of which is above set out, created a partnership or a joint-stock company. It is difficult to frame an exact definition of a joint-stock company, one sufficiently comprehensive to embrace every essential element, and sufficiently exclusive to exclude every irrelevant factor. It has been held that at common law joint-stock companies are regarded as partnerships. It has been said that unincorporated joint-stock companies are governed by the same general principles as are applicable to partnerships. It has been said that such companies are partnerships except in form. It has been held that they are partnerships with some of the powers of corporations. But such companies are not entirely controlled by the legal rules and principles which govern ordinary partnerships. (*Spotswood v. Morris,* 12 Idaho 360, 85 Pac. 1094, 6 L.R.A. (N.S.) 665.) In a joint-stock company there is no delectus personae as in the ordinary partnership. It has been declared that one distinction between a joint-stock company and a partnership is that the death of a member of the former does not ordinarily dissolve a joint-stock company, whereas it does have that effect in an ordinary partnership. Another distinction is that in a partnership each member speaks and acts as the agent of the firm, while this is not true in a joint-stock company. It has been declared that a joint-stock company at common law lies midway between a corporation and a partnership, and partakes of the nature of both. The changeability of membership or transferability of shares is often used as a determining criterion between ordinary partnerships and joint-stock companies. (*Haiku Sugar Co. v. Jonstone* (C.C.A.) 249 Fed. 103.) "The fundamental distinction between ordinary partnerships and joint-stock companies is that the partnership consists of a few individuals known to each other, bound together by ties of friendship and mutual confidence, and who therefore are not at liberty, without the consent of all, to retire from the firm, and substitute other persons in their places, and the decease of a member works a dissolution of the firm; whereas, a joint-stock company consists of a large number of individuals not necessarily or indeed usually acquainted with each other at all, so that it is a matter of comparative indifference whether changes are made among them or not, and consequently the certificates and shares in such associations may be transferred at will, without the consent of other members, and the decease of a member does not work a dissolution of the association or entitle the personal representative to an accounting. In joint-stock companies there is no delectus personae."

In view of these fundamental distinctions between ordinary partnerships and joint-stock companies, in which class does the association with which we are dealing fall? The answer to this question is not entirely free from doubt. We cannot say that this association consisted of such a large number of individuals as to hold that it falls within the class of joint-stock companies. The articles of association limit the transferability of the shares of the members of the association. In the first place, a member desiring to withdraw from the business must give 60 days notice in writing of his intention to do so. In the second place, a member can only sell, transfer, and convey his interest in the bank to some individual, corporation, or firm who is acceptable to the finance committee in charge of said business, as a shareholder in the bank. Here the right of delectus personae is reserved to the members composing the association. In joint-stock companies the members have no right to decide what new members shall be admitted; on the other hand, the right of delectus personae is an inherent quality of an ordinary partnership. The provision that the shares shall be of the par value of $100, and that certificate shall be issued to the members, indicating the amount paid and the amount of interest that each subscriber has in the business of the bank, is not conclusive of the fact that the association is a joint-stock company. Such provision is consistent with the formation of a partnership. The shares are issued to indicate the amounts paid in by the members and the amount of interest the subscriber has in the bank. Of course, this provision can be looked to in determining the character of the association. Again, the provision that the business shall be conducted by a finance committee to be elected or appointed by the subscribers, and that each subscriber shall be entitled to one vote for each $100 or for each share paid in by him, does not conclusively establish the character of the association as a joint-stock company. It can be looked to in the solution of this question. All of the above provisions are consistent with the view that the association established by this agreement was a partnership and not a joint-stock company. The articles of association expressly declare that it is the purpose of the members signing the same to establish a partnership. Again, the articles of association declare that the committee appointed to conduct the business of the bank shall select a cashier and general manager who shall "be in charge of disbursing the funds belonging to the partnership hereby formed."

. . . We hold that under the articles of association a partnership was formed by the defendants for the purpose of conducting a banking business.

Having reached the conclusion that the association formed by the defendants under the articles of agreement constituted a partnership, we are next to consider the question whether the death of three of the members of the partnership dissolved it; these deaths occurring prior to the contraction of the debts upon which the plaintiffs sue in this case. Every partnership is dissolved by the death of one of the parties. A dissolution puts an end to all the powers and rights resulting from the partnership. As to third persons, it absolves the partners from all liability for future contracts and transactions, but not for transactions that are past. (Civil Code 1910, §§ 3162, 3164.) After dissolution, a partner has no power to bind the firm by a new contract, or to revive one already for any cause extinct, nor to renew or continue an existing liability. (§ 3188) When one of the partners dies, it is not necessary that notice should be given to third persons or to the world of the dissolution of the partnership. (*Bass Dry Goods Co. v. Granite City Mfg. Co.,* 116 Ga. 177, 42 S.E. 415.) The death of a partner supplies such notice. So, when the debts sued on in this case were contracted, the partnership doing business as the People's Bank had been dissolved by the death of several of its members; and members of the partnership who had no part in creating these debts could not be held liable by reason of their membership in the dissolved partnership.

Applying the principles above ruled, the trial judge did not err in granting a nonsuit as to all the defendants except M. W. Webb.

Commercial Casualty Insurance Co. v. North et al.

1943, 320 Ill. App. 221, 50 N.E.2d 434

The plaintiff brought this action against the defendants, who were the beneficiaries of a business trust in the construction business. The plaintiff had furnished a performance bond for the business trust and had been required to defend a legal action for an alleged breach of the construction contract. The plaintiff seeks to recover the expenses incurred in defending the suit. The lower court ruled in favor of the defendants and the plaintiff appealed.

Dove, J. . . . Appellant invokes the rule that when the beneficiaries of an alleged trust are given control over the management of the trust property, the so-called trust agreement, as a matter of law, creates a partnership.

. . . In *Schumann-Heink v. Folsom* (328 Ill. 321, 327, 159 N.E. 250, 253, 58 A.L.R. 485), the court sets out in the opinion the well-established rule in such cases, in the following language: "There are also essential differences between a business trust and a partnership, but there are times when it is difficult to determine whether the declaration of trust relieves the trustees and shareholders from liability as partners. A partnership is, in effect, a contract of mutual agency, each partner acting as a principal in his own behalf and as agent for his copartner. Where, under the declaration of trust, the unit holders retain control over the trustees and have authority to control the management of the business the partnership relation exists. On the other hand, where the declaration of trust gives the trustees full control in the management of the business of the trust and the certificate holders are not associated in carrying on the business and have no control over the trustees, then there is no liability as partners."

We agree with the claim of appellees that the trust agreement in this case goes further than a positive vesture of powers in the trustees, and negatives any right of control in the beneficiaries. After generally and in detail vesting complete control of the business and the property in the trustees, too voluminously set out to be repeated here, Paragraph

Fourth (F) concludes with these words: "and the right of said Trustees to manage, control and administer the said trust estate shall be absolute and unconditional, free from the control or management of the Certificate Holders." And Paragraph Ninth (C) provides: "The ownership of interests hereunder shall not entitle the Certificate Holder to any title in or to the trust property whatsoever, or . . . for an accounting, or for any voice or control whatsoever of the trust property or of the management of said property or business connected therewith by the trustees."

. . . Our conclusion is that the trust agreement is valid, and appellees are not liable to appellant individually or as partners for any of the reasons urged.

Affirmed.

CHAPTER 43
REVIEW QUESTIONS AND PROBLEMS

1. Ten doctors formed a limited partnership to operate a clinic. Dr. *A* was the sole general partner. A contractor, *C,* was hired to construct a building for the clinic and was paid $9,000 in advance, but he failed to construct it. The partnership sued *C* for the money. *C* attempted to assert a counterclaim based on the fact that Dr. *X,* one of the ten, owed him that much for construction of a private cabin in the mountains. Will *C* be allowed to balance this claim against Dr. *X* over against the claim of the limited partnership to which Dr. *X* belongs?

2. A limited partnership was dissolved and the contribution of *A,* limited partner, was returned to him before the partnership creditors were paid. Is *A* obligated to restore the sum received in order to meet the claims of creditors?

3. *A, B,* and *C* invest money in a joint enterprise and place this money in the hands of certain trustees. From time to time they offer suggestions to the trustees and at times they elect new trustees. What are the liabilities of the investors?

4. *X* invests in a limited partnership in which *Y* is the general partner. A major policy decision needs to be made and *Y* seeks to consult with *X*. Should *X* give *Y* advice?

BOOK SIX

Creditors' Rights

General Rights

6-1 In General. The element of rights of creditors pervades the entire field of commercial transactions. The Code contains numerous provisions relating to these rights. Virtually every Article has provisions relating either directly or indirectly to the problem and many sections relate specifically to rights and remedies of creditors. Mention has already been made of devices available to creditors to obtain security so that they are not relying simply upon the debtor's willingness and ability to pay. Article 9–Secured Transactions sets forth a battery of arrangements for security in personal property under the single lien of the security interest. Article 2–Sales also contains provisions relative to protection afforded a creditor, particularly in the event of his debtor's insolvency. Article 3–Commercial Paper makes provision for "accommodation parties" who lend their credit to negotiable paper and assume liability in the event that the primary party does not pay. Article 6–Bulk Transactions is designed specifically to protect creditors. An examination of all of the other Articles likewise reveals the importance which is attached to rights and remedies of creditors.

It must not be concluded, however, that the Code provides the exclusive privileges of creditors. There are numerous arrangements outside the Code which relate to creditors' rights. These must be considered in juxtaposition to the Code provisions—they are often intimately connected therewith.

As will be noted in later chapters, interests in land may furnish security to a creditor by means of a mortgage or trust deed which secures a promissory note. The mechanics lien offers security to a creditor who has performed services on real property or furnished supplies and materials.

One who performs services on the personal property of another is entitled to an artisan's lien. The priority problems in this connection were discussed in the material on Secured Transactions.

The security to a creditor may be in the form of a contract of suretyship or guaranty in which a third party, surety, agrees to assume responsibility for the debt or other obligation in the event of a default by the principal debtor. This has been discussed previously in connection with accommodation parties to commercial paper and the Statute of Frauds.

When a debtor is in default, legal action can be brought against him by the creditor and other legal remedies are available in connection with such legal action. The debtor may be involved in bankruptcy or other insolvency proceedings and this brings other rights of creditors into play.

It should be evident that the insolvency of debtors presents a very serious problem to persons extending credit, and that it is only natural that the law has developed many arrangements for the protection of creditors. At the same time the law jealously protects a debtor's rights so that a compromise has been necessary between rights of a creditor and relief to a debtor.

In ensuing sections there will be discussed additional security arrangements for creditors and security in personal property for those who perform services in connection with such property; methods of proceeding against recalcitrant debtors; bankruptcy; and subsequently, security in real property. Throughout this discussion the reader should bear in mind the rights, remedies, and security for which provision is made in the Code.

ARTISAN'S LIENS

6-2 Liens on Personal Property. From a very early date, the common law permitted one who expended labor or material upon the personal property of another to retain possession of such property as security for his compensation. The right arose when the task was completed and was not assignable since it was personal. The lien did not arise in a credit transaction. The lien also existed in favor of public warehousemen and common carriers of goods entrusted to their care; it has been extended by statute in many states to cover all cases of storage or repair.

The artisan's lien may be superior to prior liens of record or the claim of a conditional vendor. Since it is based on possession, surrender of possession terminates the lien, unless the surrender is only temporary with an agreement that the property will be returned. Even in such case, if the rights of a third party arise while the lienholder is not in possession, the lien is lost. Surrender of part of the goods will not affect the lien on the remaining goods. In some states, surrender of possession will not terminate the lien if a notice of lien is recorded.

At common law, the lienholder retained the property until a judgment was obtained at which time he levied execution on the property. Modern statutes, however, permit the lienholder to foreclose and the property is sold to satisfy the claim. Any surplus proceeds after the claim is satisfied are paid to the owner of the property.

Note again the Code provisions relating to the priority status of an artisan's lien. Reference must also be made to the law of the particular state with reference to liens on personal property.

JUDGMENTS–EXECUTION

6-3 Legal Procedures. If a creditor does not have a security interest in collateral, a lien, a suretyship arrangement, or any other protective provision, it may be necessary to bring legal action. Of course, the creditor would prefer not to resort to this, as it is an expensive and time-consuming process. The creditor would ordinarily be much better off if he could, for example, recover from the debtor that which he had sold to him. As noted, however, this remedy is greatly restricted and in many instances there is no available avenue other than legal action. It is to be assumed that the creditor has exhausted all of the nonlegal approaches such as conferences and attempts to persuade the debtor to make payment.

Frequently there is a problem of obtaining jurisdiction if the defendant-debtor is in a different state. Jurisdiction may be obtained by "attaching" property of the defendant within the state.[1]

The lawyer for the creditor will prepare the necessary pleadings describing the obligation and the amount due. The case will be filed and papers served on the defendant debtor. Often, this service of process will produce a salutary result and the debtor will pay rather than face a trial. If the debtor ignores the proceedings, a default judgment can be taken against him. If he answers and contests the creditor's claim, there will be a trial resulting in a judgment. In either event the creditor, if he prevails in the lawsuit, will now have a judgment against the debtor, which judgment, incidentally, can be enrolled and constitutes in many states a lien upon the judgment debtor's real property.

In many states the statutes provide for "confession of judgment," also known as a "cognovit" judgment. Reference has been made to this in the material on Commercial Paper where it was noted that a provision in an instrument allowing the holder to confess a judgment against the maker or other primary party does not impair negotiability. This special remedy for creditors may be included in many types of contracts and agreements other than commercial paper. The debtor at the time of the agreement and as a part thereof agrees that if he becomes in default he appoints an attorney to represent him and to confess the debt to any court. The creditor, or his assignee, can file a complaint with an answer

---

[1] *Hobgood v. Sylvester,* page 889.

admitting the debt, signed by a friendly attorney on behalf of the debtor and obtain a judgment against the debtor summarily without a trial, and without the debtor even being aware of the fact that the judgment was rendered against him. The judgment, of course, will be brought to his attention when the judgment creditor enforces his judgment against the debtor's property.

The attorney for the creditor has little or no difficulty in obtaining the signature of another attorney to the answer on behalf of the debtor admitting liability. The instrument authorized any attorney to so act, and it is done as an accommodation among attorneys. A confessed judgment includes principal, interest, costs, and a reasonable attorney's fee for the creditor's attorney.

It should be noted that in many states a confession of judgment is not an allowable procedure. Also, it will be recalled that several of the cases studied previously involve attempts on the part of a defendant against whom a judgment has been confessed to have such judgment set aside.

In any event the debtor may, and usually will if he is able, satisfy the judgment, thereby ending the entire unfortunate affair. However, he may be unwilling or unable to satisfy the judgment, in which event the creditor is then in a position to bring a battery of ancillary remedies into action against the debtor and his property.

6-4 Remedies to Enforce Judgment. The creditor, now called a "judgment creditor," can obtain a writ of execution whereby the sheriff will be directed to seize property belonging to the debtor and sell it at public sale, the proceeds being applied against the judgment. The creditor can "garnish" the wages of the debtor, or his bank account, or any other obligation owing to the debtor from a third party. In the process of garnishment the person owing money to the judgment debtor—the employer, bank of deposit, third party—will be directed to pay the money into court rather than to the judgment debtor and such money will be applied against the judgment debt. In all states there are certain limitations on garnishment and certain property of the debtor is exempt from execution—e.g. a "homestead" exemption is a specified dollar amount obtained from the sale of the family home as, for example, some states provide that on the sale of the family home to pay a judgment debt, the first $5000 of the sale price belongs to the debtor free of the judgment.

In spite of this impressive array of weapons it frequently develops that the judgment is of little value because of the lack of assets which can be reached. It is also to be expected that other creditors may have taken like action against the debtor. It must be remembered that a judgment standing alone has little value.

The ultimate result may be that the debtor files a voluntary petition in bankruptcy or if he has committed an "act of bankruptcy" that his creditors may file an involuntary petition against him.

GENERAL RIGHTS CASE

Hobgood v. Sylvester

1965, (Ore.) 408 P.2d 925

The plaintiff brought suit to recover judgment on a debt allegedly owed by non-resident of Oregon defendants. Process could not be served on the defendants in Oregon, so the plaintiffs attempted to attach "Property" of the defendants in Oregon and thereby obtain *quasi in rem* jurisdiction over the defendants so that process could properly be served outside the state. The "property" was a debt owing to defendants and a garnishment had been served on this debtor. The local court quashed the return of service upon defendants and plaintiff appealed.

GOODWIN, J. Plaintiff commenced an action to recover an alleged debt from nonresident defendants. To obtain *quasi in rem* jurisdiction over the defendants, plaintiff sought to attach a debt owed them by third-party Oregon residents. From an order quashing the return of service upon motion made by way of a special appearance, plaintiff appeals.

The debt sought to be attached in these proceedings was the unpaid balance of the purchase price of land, which debt had been evidenced by a negotiable promissory note and secured by a mortgage on the land. In answer to the notice of garnishment, the garnishees eventually acknowledged the installment debt, described the note, and correctly stated that no payment was due as of the date of the return. (The first return had stated: "Nothing due now.")

The issue is whether, for jurisdictional purposes, a debt which is evidenced by a negotiable instrument can be attached under ORS 29.170 (Manner of executing writ.)

"The sheriff to whom the writ is directed and delivered shall note upon the writ the date of such delivery, and shall execute the writ without delay, as follows:

(1) To attach real property. . . .

(2) Personal property capable of manual delivery to the sheriff and not in the possession of a third person, shall be attached by taking it into . . . (the sheriff's) custody.

(3) Other personal property shall be attached by leaving a certified copy of the writ, and a notice specifying the property attached, with the person having possession of the same, or if it be a debt, then with the debtor. . . .

by simply serving the debtor with the notice described in subsection (3). The alternative would require the instrument itself to be brought under a sheriff's control as "property" described in subsection (2). The plaintiff was unable to effect the seizure of the note, which reposed in a California bank.

The underlying theory of *quasi in rem* jurisdiction does not contemplate a typical personal judgment against the defendant, but only a judgment to the extent of the defendant's property within the state. The concept, classically illustrated in *Pennoyer v. Neff* (95 U.S. 714, 24 1.Ed. 565 (1878)), is that, where the court controls the disposition of a defendant's property through attachment, as an exercise of the sovereign's power over property found within its borders, the court can also adjudicate unrelated personal rights of the nonresident property owners, and enter judgment up to the value of their property within the court's control. Due process is satisfied by the presumption that a person ordinarily keeps track of his property, and will come in and defend the case. The property may be tangible or intangible (*Harris v. Balk,* 198 U.S. 215, 25 S.Ct. 625, 49 L.Ed. 1023 (1905)), but it must be brought under the control of the court so that it can be sold, if need be, on execution. Thus, *quasi in rem* jurisdiction is not to be confused with personal jurisdiction that may be obtained under ORS 14.035.

The inquiry involves two questions: (1) whether the attachment attempted under ORS 29.170(3) which did not effect a change in the possession of the negotiable instrument was an effective attachment of the debt; and (2) if not an effective attachment, was it nonetheless sufficient to confer jurisdiction?

If the court should, in a case like the one now pending, enter judgment against the defendants, it would be asked to order execution of the judgment. The purchaser of the debt at the execution sale would, presumably, demand payment of the next installment to fall under the terms of the note. . . . Assuming that the garnishee should pay an installment under the compulsion of such an execution, however, such a payment would not be a defense to an action against the garnishee by a holder in due course. (ORS 73.3020–Uniform Commercial Code.)

If a holder in due course acquires a negotiable instrument, he takes it free of all defenses of any party to the instrument with whom the holder has not dealt (except for certain statutory defenses not relevant here). (ORS 73.3020 to 73.3050) Even payment is no defense against a holder in due course, and a maker of a negotiable instrument who pays the original payee all or part of the debt evidenced thereby may be compelled by a holder in due course to pay again. (See *Whitney v. Day,* 86 Or. 268, 168 P. 295 (1917); *Nordyke v. Charlton,* 108 Iowa 414, 79 N.W. 136 (1899)). . . .

In *Whitney v. Day, supra,* this court held that when a debt is evidenced by a negotiable instrument, attempted levy of execution against the debt without reduction of the instrument to the sheriff's possession gives the judgment creditor no interest in the note as against a holder in due course of the note. This rule seems to be in harmony with authority elsewhere. . . . *Whitney v. Day* appears to assume, without deciding, that the debt evidenced by the note would not be payable without surrender of the note.

In *Fishburn v. Londershausen* (50 Or. 363, 92 P. 1060 (1907)) this court held that a negotiable instrument was "personal property capable of manual delivery." We believe that when a debt has been evidenced by such an instrument, because of the peculiar incidents of negotiability, the debt cannot be attached effectively without bringing the instrument under the court's control. The reason given for this rule in other jurisdictions is that without obtaining control of the instrument, the court cannot protect the maker against double liability. (Cases cited)

An attempted attachment under subsection (3) obviously is not effective to enable the court to issue a writ of execution upon the note. If execution is attempted upon the debt without surrender of the instrument, the execution would be either an empty gesture or, if it produced a payment, the payment could work substantial injustice upon the garnishee. The garnishee is, between the litigants, an innocent third person. Accordingly, we hold that where the return of a garnishee shows that a debt has been evidenced by a negotiable instrument, an attachment of the debt does not confer *quasi in rem* jurisdiction upon the court until the instrument itself is reduced to the possession of the sheriff. The only purpose of *quasi in rem* jurisdiction is defeated if the court cannot dispose of the property sought to be attached without invading the rights of innocent third persons. (There is no need to decide in this case what procedure would suffice to bring resident parties in possession of a note before the court so that the rights of all interested parties could be protected. In the case at the bar the instrument and those apparently entitled to its possession were all beyond the reach of Oregon process).

The order quashing the return of service is affirmed.

CHAPTER 44
REVIEW QUESTIONS AND PROBLEMS

1. *A* took his watch to *B*'s jewelry store for repairs. What security does *B* have for payment for the parts and services furnished by him?
2. *B* repaired *A*'s automobile and installed a new engine. He wished to retain a lien on the car for parts and labor. How can he accomplish this?
3. *G* held a security interest in a certain automobile. The owner of the car took it to *H*'s garage for repairs. The owner paid neither *G* or *H* and *H* is now in possession of the car. *G* seeks to obtain possession of the car from *H*. Should he succeed?
4. Debtor *A* lives in Illinois but owns property in Oregon. Creditor *B* wishes to bring legal action to recover from *A*. In what state may he bring his legal action?
5. A note contained a confession of judgment clause. Can the note be negotiable?

6. *A* has a judgment against *B* for $10,000. *B* refuses to pay the judgment. What further action can be taken by *A*?

7. *A* owes *B* $500 and *B* is indebted to *C* in the same amount. *B* has refused to pay *C* and *C* has obtained a judgment against *B*. What can *C* now do?

8. *H* and *W*, husband and wife, have a joint bank account at the Last National Bank. *X* has a judgment against *H* resulting from a tort action for negligence. Can *X* garnish the Last National Bank? To what extent?

9. *A* is employed by *X* Manufacturing Company at a salary of $600 per month. *B* has a judgment against *A* in the amount of $10,000. To what extent can *B* have *A*'s wages garnished?

10. *A* has a $10,000 judgment against *B*. A writ of execution has been issued on the judgment. Can the sheriff levy upon and sell all of *A*'s property?

11. *A, B,* and *C* have formed a corporation to engage in the sale and repair of television sets, radios and electronic equipment. They have a limited amount of capital and will need to arrange financing. What arrangements might they make to obtain loans and credit which would be acceptable to suppliers and banks or other lending institutions?

12. One of the features of a corporation is the limited liability of stockholders. How does this feature affect a corporation's ability to borrow money or obtain credit? How can this difficulty be overcome?

13. Debtor *A* and Creditor *B* both of California have done business for many years. *A* has operated a retail store in Los Angeles. Would *B* have cause for concern if *A* sold his store? If *A* leased his store to *C* and moved to San Francisco? If *A* made a gift of the store to his son and moved to New York?

14. *A* Department Store sold several appliances to *B* on an installment contract. *B* moves to another state and takes the appliances with him. If *B* defaults in his payments what remedy is available to the store?

chapter 45

Suretyship

6-5 Introduction. Although security often takes the form of a lien on property, credit may be extended upon the combined financial standing of the debtor and some third person. The agreement whereby the third party extends his financial standing as security for the debtor is known as a contract of suretyship or guaranty.

Since much of business today is conducted by agents, it becomes necessary for the principal to exact the utmost honesty and good faith of his agent in the performance of his duties. Whenever the principal is unwilling to repose such confidence in the agent alone, he usually obtains what is known as a *bond* for faithful performance that is signed by the agent and some third party. This bond also amounts to a *contract of suretyship.* A contract of suretyship, therefore, appears to have for its objective, security either for the payment of money or for the faithful performance of some other duty, in the latter case often being known as fidelity insurance.

The person primarily bound to perform is known as the *principal* or *principal debtor;* the party secondarily liable is called the *surety* or *guarantor;* and the party entitled to performance is customarily spoken of as the *creditor.*

6-6 Nature of Relation. Whenever, as between two parties, one of them is primarily liable and the other secondarily or collaterally liable for the faithful performance of an obligation, in the broad sense a suretyship relation exists. As soon as interested third parties learn of it, they are bound to treat it as such. To illustrate, let us assume that Jones sells his retail lumber business to Smith with the latter assuming and agreeing to pay, as part of the purchase price, all outstanding liabilities. It is clear as between Smith and Jones, that Smith has now become the primary debtor with Jones being collaterally liable. As soon as the creditors are notified of the change, they are obligated to respect the new relationship that exists. This does not mean, as is indicated later, that the creditors must first attempt to recover of Smith before looking to Jones.

6-7 Distinction Between Guarantor and Surety. In a general way the term suretyship is broad enough to encompass both guaranty and suretyship, and for the purposes of this chapter the term surety will be considered to include both surety and guarantor except as otherwise indicated. While the courts have in some cases made a technical distinction between the two, the importance of the distinction is becoming less significant.[1]

A surety, in the technical sense, is liable on the same obligation with the principal debtor. His promise is made jointly or jointly and severally with the principal debtor to the creditor. Thus an accommodation co-maker of a note is a surety rather than a guarantor.

A guaranty is by language a secondary promise, a promise to pay or perform if the principal debtor defaults—a promise that another will perform, but if he fails, the guarantor will perform. It is separately made, but impresses a duty on the guarantor to perform as soon as the principal defaults. Since he has not joined in the principal's promise to perform, his liability is secondary, but effective as soon as the principal defaults. A guaranty of collectibility guarantees the solvency of the debtor at the time the obligation matures. In such a case, the guarantor is not liable unless the creditor first sues the debtor and is unable to collect or presents convincing evidence it would have done no good to do so. The creditor is also obligated to notify such a guarantor, usually called a conditional guarantor, of a default. Failure to do so releases the guarantor to the extent he is injured by failure to receive prompt notice of default.

Although in a few states all guarantors are entitled to notice, in most of the states absolute guarantors and sureties are not entitled to notice of default. It becomes their duty to keep informed and to make good where the principal fails unless their contract with the creditor has provided for notice.

6-8 Contract of Suretyship. Although suretyship may result by operation of law because of a change in the relationship of parties, as was indicated in the previous illustration, it most often develops as a result of an express contract between the surety and the creditor whereby the former assumes a secondary responsibility for the principal's performance. He agrees that he may be called upon to perform in case the principal defaults. Like all other contracts, the agreement consists of

---

[1] *Timberlake v. J. R. Watkins Company*, page 902.

offer and acceptance supported by consideration, although in the majority of instances the consideration is the same as that received by the principal. Thus, one who promises to pay for goods supplied to *A* in case *A* fails to pay for them gets no beneficial consideration. The creditor who supplies the goods to *A* on the strength of *A*'s promise to pay and the surety's secondary promise supplies the needed consideration to both by delivery of goods to *A*. In reliance upon the two promises, the creditor did an act he was not otherwise obligated to do. However, if the goods had been delivered before the surety made his promise, some new consideration would have been essential to bind the surety. Likewise, if money has been loaned, a guaranty that the borrower will repay, made subsequent to the loan, lacks consideration.[2]

As indicated in the study of contracts, contracts of suretyship–agreements to become secondarily liable for the debt or default of another–are required by the Statute of Frauds to be evidenced by writing. As suggested at that point, if the debt really becomes that of the promisor–let *P* have goods and I will pay for them–no writing is required. Likewise, if the main purpose of the surety's promise is to derive some substantial benefit for himself from the performance of the creditor, no writing is necessary in most states. The benefit in such a case must be something other than mere consideration for becoming a surety.

The duties assumed by the surety are largely determined by the contract terms as expressed by the parties, but, in the interpretation of ambiguous language, historically the courts have favored the voluntary or accommodation–unpaid–surety at the expense of the creditor. Currently, the courts incline so far as possible to give words their normal meaning even though it works a hardship on the surety, but, where the meaning is uncertain, courts construe ambiguous language against the person who used it. Since in the case of unpaid sureties, the language is usually framed by the creditor and signed by the surety, this serves to benefit the surety.

6-9 Fiduciary Relation. A suretyship relation is, within limits, fiduciary in character, involving special trust and confidence between the parties. As a consequence, a creditor in possession of extremely vital information affecting the risk should volunteer such information to the surety at the time the contract is made. This applies only to information so significant and unusual that the surety normally would not think to inquire concerning it.

Since the contract is between the surety and the creditor, any misconduct of the principal which induces the surety to become such does not permit the surety to avoid the contract.[3] However, if the creditor is aware, when the contract is being formed, of the principal's misconduct, he is obligated to inform the surety.

Because of these rules, an employer who is aware of past defalcations of an employee and who seeks a bond assuring faithful performance by

[2] *Vaccaro v. Andresen*, page 904.
[3] *Watkins Co. v. Brund et al.*, page 905.

the employee of his duties is bound to notify the surety at the time the contract is being formed of such misconduct. Similarly, a creditor who learns that the principal has misrepresented his financial condition to a prospective surety is obligated to warn the surety that he is assuming a risk not anticipated. Otherwise, the creditor will not be able to enforce the surety's promise.

An employer who discovers that his employee has been guilty of misappropriation of funds should immediately discharge him unless the surety assents to his continued employment. To continue the employee at his task subjects the surety to a risk not contemplated, so if a second opportunity to make good is to be offered the employee, it should be done with the approval of his surety.

6-10 Immediate Recourse to Surety. As indicated in an earlier section, the surety or absolute guarantor becomes liable to the creditor as soon as the principal defaults in the performance of his obligation, and the creditor need not exhaust his remedies against the principal before looking to them. This rule seems to apply even though the creditor is in possession of collateral provided by the principal debtor. He may resort to the surety without disposing of the collateral unless the surety requests the sale of the collateral in order to avoid unreasonable hardship. In a case of extreme hardship the surety may require the creditor to dispose of the collateral before looking to him.

Where several sureties are jointly or severally liable, they may be joined in one action and, after obtaining judgment, the creditor may recover the entire amount from any one of them. If these obligations are several, he may sue any one for the full amount unless it exceeds the particular surety's maximum liability. The claim, unless the creditor has agreed otherwise, is entire and need not be divided for the benefit of the sureties.

6-11 Duration of Liability. A guarantor or surety for a particular debt naturally continues liable until the obligation has been satisfied unless released by the Statute of Limitations. Similarly, one who agrees to be liable for the default of an employee or an elected official continues liable as long as the employee works under his original contract or the official remains in office, unless the contract sets its own period of liability.

Ambiguous language often causes difficulty where a guarantor guarantees payment of goods supplied a principal debtor. "Let bearer have what leather he needs and if he fails to pay for it, I will," may be construed to apply to a single purchase or to be a continuous guaranty of credit. Usually in the absence of a time or an amount limitation, the courts tend to limit the liability to one transaction unless it is clear from other evidence that the parties intended otherwise. Where there is a limit as to time the courts tend to construe the guaranty as continuous for that period up to any reasonable amount, and when a limit on amount is indicated the guaranty is likewise continuous,[4] with the maximum liability being the figure established. In the latter case, the guar-

---

[4] *Frell v. Dumont-Florida, Inc.*, page 906.

anty of credit continues on various obligations until it is withdrawn, being much like a continuing offer. Receipt of the withdrawal notice or death of the guarantor terminates liability for credit thereafter extended to the principal. Difficulty in all these cases could be eliminated by a careful phrasing of the contract terms relating to liability.

Confusion exists as to whether a creditor who relies upon a letter of guaranty is obligated to notify the guarantor that he accepts, that he has acted or will act in reliance upon it. If it is a general letter addressed "to whom it may concern," the better view is that the creditor must notify the guarantor within a reasonable time after credit has been extended. Because of existing uncertainty, it is a wise business policy in all cases to give notice that the guaranty has been or will be relied upon. Although the offer is unilateral and accepted by the act of extending credit, if the act is one knowledge of which when performed is not readily available, notice of performance should be given.

6-12 Subrogation. Literally, subrogation means the substitution of one person in place of another, and as used in this section it refers to the creditor's right to step into the shoes of the surety so far as they relate to the surety's right against the principal. Security of any kind given to the ⸝urety by the principal for the protection of the former in case the latter defaults may be available to the creditor. To the extent of his claim, the creditor may substitute his position for that of the surety, with reference to the securities. Thus, it has been held that, in the event of the return of securities by the surety to the principal, the creditor is entitled to follow them into the hands of the debtor and subject them to a lien in his favor. This rule applies only where the rights of innocent third parties have not intervened. He may also secure an injunction against their return to the principal, thus having the securities impounded by the court until the principal debt falls due, at which time they may be sold for the benefit of the creditor.

Collateral posted with a surety to protect him against loss on any one of several obligations upon which he is surety does not necessarily give a particular creditor the right of subrogation. In the event of the surety's insolvency, the collateral is apportioned among the various creditors to whom the surety was obligated.

The right of subrogation does not exist where the securities are left with the surety by some third party. The theory is that securities placed with the surety form a trust of that portion of the estate of the principal which he sets aside for the payment of his debt. Securities belonging to third parties do not form part of the principal's estate, and, therefore, are not subject to subrogation.

RIGHTS OF SURETIES

6-13 Extension of Time. The creditor should be careful not to extend the time for performance without the consent of the surety. A contract between the principal and the creditor, which definitely extends the time within which performance may be demanded, releases the surety. The reason for this rule is that the financial status of the principal may become less sound during the period of the extension. Such a change in his financial condition would work to the disadvantage of the surety. The court does not consider in each case whether the position of the surety has been injured by the extension, but merely applies the general rule that an extension of time releases the surety.

Mere indulgence upon the part of the creditor or passively permitting the debtor to take more time than the contract calls for does not release the surety.[5] The latter is in no sense injured by such conduct, because he is free at any time to perform on his part and immediately start suit against the principal. The surety is not discharged unless there is a binding agreement between the principal and the creditor for a definite period of extension.

The consent of the surety may be obtained either before or after the extension has been granted. Consent given after the extension amounts to a waiver of the right to rescind and is valid, although it is not based upon any new consideration. Notice to the surety that an extension has been granted or a failure on the part of the surety to reply to a request seeking permission to extend is not equivalent to consent. In the latter case, silence should act as a warning not to grant the extension since the surety is apparently unwilling to extend the risk.

6-14 Extension with Rights Reserved. An extension of time by the creditor, in which the extension agreement stipulates reservation of rights against the surety, does not release the surety. Such an extension binds only the creditor. It does not bind the surety. He is free at any time to complete performance for the principal and immediately to sue him for damages suffered, since to him the arrangement is quite similar to mere indulgence. To illustrate: *S* becomes surety for *P* on a note in favor of *C*. The note falls due on a certain date, and *P* requests from *C* an extension of ninety days. The extension is granted with the express stipulation that *C* reserves all rights against *S*. *S* is not released, although he receives no notice of the extension. His right to pay the debt at any time he desires and to turn to *P* for reimbursement is not impaired.

To the extent that a surety is protected by securities placed with him by his principal debtor, an extension of time does not effect a discharge. An extension of time cannot injure a fully secured surety, and one who is only partially secured is released to the extent the security is inadequate.

A paid surety—one who has received some compensation for the risk that he assumes—is not released unless he is damaged as a result of the extension of time granted to the principal.[6] In such a case the surety is released only when he can show that the ability of the principal to perform has perceptibly weakened during the period of extension.

---

[5] *Bayer & Mingolia Const. Co. v. Deschens,* page 907.
[6] *Supra.*

An extension of time on an obligation arising out of a continuous guaranty does not release the guarantor except that the maximum liability is not thereby extended. To illustrate, let us assume that *G* guaranteed payment of goods sold to *P* by *C* up to a maximum of $10,000. If a claim for $3,000 falls due, an extension of time by *C* will not release *G*. *C* is still protected by the $10,000 maximum liability of *G*.

6-15 Change in Contract Terms. Any material change in the terms of the contract between the principal and the creditor, without the consent of the surety, discharges him.[7] Inasmuch as the principal contract governs the surety's liability, any change in its terms must be assented to by him. Likewise, the creditor's failure to comply with the terms of the contract of suretyship will result in the discharge of the surety.[8]

A discharge of the principal debtor, or any one of them if there are two or more, unless assented to, releases the surety. This rule is subject to those exceptions existing in the case of an extension of time; that is, the surety is not released if the principal debtor is discharged with reservation of rights against the surety, or if the surety is protected by securities or is a paid surety and is not injured.

6-16 Payment. Payment of the principal obligation by the debtor or someone in his behalf discharges the surety, although a payment later avoided causes the surety's liability to revive. This situation is likely to occur in bankruptcy, where a creditor may be compelled in certain cases to surrender a preference received.

A valid tender of payment by either the principal or the surety that is rejected by the creditor releases the surety. In such a case it is not necessary that the tender be kept good or continuously available in order for the surety to be released. Since the creditor has had an opportunity to receive his money, the surety is no longer liable.

Whenever payment is made by a debtor who owes several obligations to the creditor, unless the debtor has indicated where it is to be applied, the creditor is free to apply it on any matured obligation. However, if the money is in reality supplied by the surety, and this fact is known to the creditor, he must apply it on the one for which the surety is liable. If the creditor makes no specific application, in court the money will be applied where the court feels it is equitable, but a tendency to apply it on the unsecured obligations is reasonably clear from court decisions.

The mere receipt of a note or check of the principal debtor by the creditor does not release the surety, as the debt is not paid until the note or check is honored. If a new note is given in settlement of an old one, the old one being canceled and returned, an extension of time has taken place, which releases the surety. Where both notes are retained by the creditor, the courts hold that the second is merely collateral to the first and the surety is not released.

---

7 *Magazine Digest Pub. Co., Limited v. Shade et al.,* page 907.
8 *George E. Failing Co. v. Cardwell Investment Co.,* page 908.

6-17 Defenses of Principal. Many of the defenses available to the principal may be asserted by the surety against the creditor, particularly where the principal is willing to have the defenses so used. Such defenses as mutual mistake, fraud, illegality, lack or failure of consideration, or undue influence, if available to the principal, may be used by the surety. Infancy and bankruptcy form exceptions to the rule, and may not be used by the surety, since he is employed in the first instance to protect the creditor against the inability of the debtor to perform.

Although a minor may avoid his contract and return the consideration he received, the surety is, in perhaps the majority of the states, required to make up any deficiency between the value of the item returned and the amount of the indebtedness. Other states hold that avoidance by the minor releases the surety.

Generally, if the debtor is insolvent or the principal and surety are jointly sued, the surety is entitled to use set-offs that are available to the principal debtor.

Similarly, the surety may set off against the creditor any claim which the creditor owes him if the debtor is insolvent or the creditor is solvent. If the creditor calls upon the surety to pay the principal's obligation of $500, the surety may deduct any amount which is due him from the creditor. Thus, it may be said that the surety can interpose either his own or his principal's defenses against the creditor.

The Statute of Limitations available to the principal debtor may not be used by the surety.[9] Each has his own period after which he is no longer liable to the creditor, and the period may be longer for one than the other. Thus, the debtor may be liable on an oral contract while the surety is liable on a written contract, or the debtor may have made a part payment which extends the period of his liability but which has no effect upon the liability of the surety.

6-18 Subrogation. This is another aspect of subrogation to be distinguished from the subrogation rights of the creditor in collateral held by the surety for the latter's protection. The surety who fully performs the obligation of his principal is subrogated to the creditor's rights against the principal. The surety who pays his principal's debt becomes entitled to any securities which the principal has placed with the creditor to secure that particular debt. Likewise, if the creditor has obtained a judgment against the principal, the surety receives the benefit of the judgment when he satisfies the principal's debt. Where the creditor has collateral as general security for a number of obligations, the surety's right of subrogation does not arise unless all of the obligations are satisfied. It should be noted that subrogation applies only to rights of the creditor against the principal. If some third person, to secure the principal's debt, also pledges collateral to the creditor, the surety has no equity in the security although the creditor calls upon him to satisfy the debt.

---

[9] *Bomud Company v. Yockey Oil Company and Osborn,* page 909.

A creditor in possession of collateral given to him by the principal is not at liberty to return it without the consent of the surety. Any surrender of securities releases the surety to the extent of their value, his loss of subrogation damaging him to that extent. Failure of the creditor to make use of the securities, however, does not relieve the surety, since the latter is free to pay the indebtedness and to obtain the securities for his own protection. However, if the creditor loses the benefit of collateral by inactivity–failure to record a mortgage or notify an indorser–the surety is released to the extent he is injured. In general, if the person who is entitled to protection under the contract of suretyship does anything that will materially prejudice the rights of the surety, the surety will to that extent, at least, be discharged.[10]

6-19 Recovery from Principal. One who becomes a surety at the request, or with the approval, of the principal is entitled to reimbursement for any loss caused by the principal's default. Normally, the surety is not permitted to add any attorney's fees that he has been compelled to pay on his own behalf by way of defense or fees paid to the creditor's attorney. All attorney's fees can be avoided by performance of contract terms; when the principal fails to perform, it becomes the immediate duty of the surety to act. Attorney's fees incurred in a bona fide attempt to reduce the amount of the recovery form an exception to this general rule.

The surety may recover only the amount paid by him. Thus, if he settles a claim for less than the full amount owing the creditor, his right to recover is limited to the sum paid under the settlement. Furthermore, bankruptcy on the part of the principal, although it takes place before the surety is called upon to perform, releases him from further liability to the surety.

Any securities falling into the possession of the surety at the time he settles his principal's obligation may be disposed of as far as is necessary to extinguish the surety's claim for indemnity.

The surety also possesses the right to be exonerated, which makes it possible for him to go into court and compel the principal to perform in order to save the surety harmless. Naturally, this right of exoneration has little value where the principal is financially unable to make payment or to take such other action as his contract requires.

6-20 Cosureties' Liability. Whenever two or more sureties become secondarily liable for the same obligation of the principal, they become cosureties whether they know of each other's liability or not at the time they become sureties. If the creditor compels one surety to meet the obligation in full, that particular surety takes on the burden of recovering from his cosureties the portion they should contribute.

An extension of time to or a release of one surety releases other sureties only to the extent the released surety would have been obli-

---

[10] *Board of Education v. Hartford Accident & Ind. Co.*, page 910.

gated to contribute. There is an implied contract between cosureties that they will share any loss equally unless they have agreed otherwise or have fixed different maximum amounts for their liability. In the latter event, they are assumed to have agreed to share in proportion to their maximum liability. This right to contribution from cosureties provides initially for a sharing between solvent cosureties within the state. Each contributing surety then possesses an independent action against the insolvent or nonresident surety for the amount which he paid on behalf of the insolvent or nonresident surety.

So long as the balance of a claim remains outstanding and unpaid, a cosurety has no right to contribution unless he has paid more than his share of the claim, and then only to the extent of the excess. This he may recover from any cosurety unless it compels the latter to pay more than his full share.

No surety has a right to profit at the expense of a cosurety. Neither has he a right to reduce his personal risk by secretly procuring collateral from the principal debtor. Any such collateral, obtained either before or after he became a surety, must be held for the benefit of all the sureties. It is possible, of course, for all the sureties at the time they become such to agree that one of them may be favored by receiving collateral for his protection, but in the absence of such an arrangement, all have a right to share in the collateral held by one.

SURETYSHIP CASES

Timberlake v. J. R. Watkins Company
1965 (Ind.) 209 N.E.2d 909

The Watkins Company, plaintiff, entered into a written agreement with Timberlake whereby he became a distributor of the company's products. Timberlake, defendant, purchased the products from the plaintiff, and his wife, Stella, also a defendant, signed an agreement to guarantee payment by her husband of amounts due to the company up to $3000. In the agreement she was called "surety." Timberlake received credit and did not pay; and the company brought action against both him and his wife. The lower court entered judgment for the plaintiff and the Timberlakes appealed.

WICKENS, J. Appellants [defendants] declare that the second agreement is a "suretyship agreement" and is void because, they say, it was executed on Sunday, and that there is "lack of mutuality, want of consideration, failure to create a valid suretyship agreement for the reason that no tripartite relation of principal creditor, principal debtor or obligor, and surety, existed at the time the alleged Suretyship Agreement was signed; . . ."

Appellants' demurrer and most of appellants' argument on the merits hinge on the question of whether these agreements create a "suretyship" as appellants use this term. Appellants contend that when Stella signed an agreement in 1952 no obligation then existed on the part of Everett [Timberlake] moving to appellee. It is insisted that this situation constitutes a failure to establish the tripartite relationship essential to a surety agreement.

We find that similar agreements have been construed by the courts of this State to be those of suretyship. . . .

It is a frequent general holding that suretyship involves a tripartite arrangement, that is, a principal debtor or obligor and a valid subsisting debt or obligation for which the principal is responsible and an undertaking by the surety to make himself collaterally liable. . . .

No reason has been advanced to show that the agreement in question cannot be more than merely one of suretyship, as that word has been used in a limited or strict sense. We think it is capable of being a contract of suretyship under certain facts (i.e., where a debt already exists) and under a different set of facts, being one of guaranty or one of indemnity. It appears that was the theory on which the trial court proceeded.

Authorities have attempted with some success to differentiate beween contracts of suretyship, guaranty, indemnity, and in some instances, insurance. At the same time we have not found any that indicate a contract might not be capable of having the attributes of more than one of these classifications. In fact the Restatement of the Law of Security, sec. 82, p. 231, says "the term 'guaranty' is used in this Restatement as a synonym for suretyship." It further says:

> The possible convenience of having certain terms denote only particular types of surety obligations has resulted in some jurisdictions in the use of 'suretyship' as a general term and 'suretyship' with a restricted meaning. There has never been general agreement as to which term is to be the broader and which the narrower. Moreover, if both of the two terms are used with a restricted meaning, they do not suffice to cover even the main types of surety obligations.
>
> Suretyship obligations are contractual, and the important point of inquiry should be the precise undertaking of the surety and the duty of the principal. The recognition of the existence of different forms of contractual suretyship and the emphasis upon the obligation assumed in a particular case, are of greater significance than the distribution of labels to the various types of contracts.

Following that suggestion, we proceed to ignore the label and place emphasis on the obligation assumed. Stella Timberlake executed an agreement which appellee accepted. This contract specified that if appellee would extend credit to Everett Timberlake, in consideration thereof, she promised to pay up to $3000 of the indebtedness thereafter incurred and owing by Everett. Such an agreement is not contrary to public policy; it contravenes no statute known to us; being in writing it is not within the statute of frauds. In this case it is not being attacked for fraud and no question was properly raised affecting its execution. We conclude with the trial court that it is a valid and enforceable agreement.

As to the consideration for the contract, the extension of credit to Everett Timberlake constitutes sufficient consideration. Consideration need not be of benefit to the party making the promise. . . .

We find no merit in appellant's argument that there is no tripartite relationship here. As we understand that arrangement, all elements are present except an existing obligation which we hold to be unnecessary since after incurred indebtedness is covered by the agreement.

Finding no error, the judgment is affirmed.

Vaccaro v. Andresen

1964 (D.C.) 201 A.2d 26

HOOD, C. J.   Michael P. Vaccaro [plaintiff], one of the appellants here, and appellee [defendant] Andresen were officers and stockholders in a corporation engaged in the florist business. The corporation was in financial difficulties and on March 31, 1961, Vaccaro and his wife executed an "installment discount" note to a bank in the sum of $2,556. The net proceeds of the note amounted to $2,009.54 and Vaccaro paid $2,000.00 of it to the corporation. According to Vaccaro the note was executed and the money paid to the corporation at the request of Andresen, who orally guaranteed payment of the note. According to Andresen, he merely asked Vaccaro "to put some money in the corporation." After receiving $2,000 the corporation carried the note on its books as a corporate liability and the corporation made some payments on it.

In June 1961 Andresen executed a paper guaranteeing payment of the Vaccaro note, promising to make the future installment payments on it and agreeing to reimburse Vaccaro for payments he had made on the note. In October 1961 the corporation went into bankruptcy and Vaccaro filed a claim against the bankrupt estate for money loaned "to the bankrupt corporation on March 31, 1961." The present action was brought by Vaccaro and his wife against Andresen on the guaranty agreement of June 1961, alleging that Andresen had paid $568 on the note and seeking recovery of the balance of $1,988. The trial court found that Vaccaro made a loan to the corporation on March 31 and that the guaranty agreement of June 7 lacked consideration, and the court denied recovery.

An enforceable contract of guaranty or suretyship requires, as do all contracts, a valid consideration; and where the guaranty is given subsequent to the original contract, the guaranty must be supported by a new consideration, separate and independent from the original contract. Here there was no evidence of any new consideration to Andresen for execution of the agreement of 1961.

It is true that the agreement recites a consideration of "One Dollar ($1.00) and other good and valuable consideration," but appellants did not even press the argument that this recitation established a sufficient consideration. They do argue, however, that the agreement was under seal and that a sealed instrument imports a consideration. Although the current tendency is to minimize the distinction between sealed and unsealed instrument, this jurisdiction continues to recognize the distinction. (Note, however, that the Uniform Commercial Code, enacted for the District of Columbia on December 30, 1963, to become effective January 1, 1955 Public Law 88-243, in 28:2-203 provides:

> The affixing of a seal to a writing evidencing a contract for sale or an offer to buy or sell goods does not constitute the writing a sealed instrument and the law with respect to sealed instruments does not apply to such a contract or offer.

However, we do not agree with appellants that the agreement here in question is an instrument under seal. It does conclude with the words: "Witness my hand and seal," but this recital, in the absence of a seal, does not operate to make the instrument one under seal. It is the attachment or adoption of a seal that is the operative fact. Here, no word, symbol or scroll indicative of a seal follows the signature. There is a single dot or period immediately after the signature, but we are not willing to rule that this minute mark constitutes a seal, in the absence of proof that it was deliberately placed there to serve as a seal.

Affirmed. [Defendant, Andresen, was not liable as a surety.]

Watkins Co. v. Brund et al.

1931, 160 Wash. 183, 294 Pac. 1024

Action by J. R. Watkins Company against Joseph Buerkli, one of the defendants, the latter having signed a bond which guaranteed the payment by one Brund of $988.54 to plaintiff and such additional sums as arose out of a certain sales agreement between the plaintiff and Brund. The bond was signed by Buerkli with the definite understanding between him and Brund that it was not to be delivered to the plaintiff until the signature of one Kalb had been obtained. Disregarding this agreement, Brund procured Heim, financially irresponsible, to sign the agreement, and mailed it to the plaintiff. Brund defaulted and plaintiff seeks to recover from Buerkli. The lower court gave judgment for the plaintiff.

BEELER, J. . . . The trial court found, which finding is supported by the record, that respondent knew nothing whatever of the understanding or agreement between Brund and Buerkli, and furthermore, that it had no means of obtaining any knowledge concerning the negotiations between them. . . . It was wholly a secret understanding between appellant and Brund. [Here he quotes the rule as found in 21 R.C.L. 968.]

Hence, the rule sustained by the great weight of authority is that the agreement of a surety with his principal that the latter shall not deliver a bond until the signature of another be procured as a cosurety will not relieve the surety of liability on his bond although the cosurety is not obtained, where there is nothing on the face of the bond, or in the attending circumstances, to apprise the taker that such further signature was called for in order to complete the instrument. In such cases the surety, having vested his principal with apparent authority to deliver the bond, is estopped to deny his obligation to the innocent holder, on the principle that where one of two innocent persons must suffer, the loss must fall upon him who puts it in the power of a third person to cause the loss.

The judgment is affirmed.

Frell v. Dumont-Florida, Inc.

1959 (Fla. App.) 114 S.2nd 311

PEARSON, J. The appellant [Frell] was defendant in an action on a written guaranty. He appeals from a final judgment for the plaintiff which was based upon a jury verdict. The letter of guaranty contained the following:

> You have been requested to open a line of credit not to exceed Ten Thousand Dollars ($10,000.00), in favor of: Best Appliance Sales & Service Ltd.
> You have indicated that you are unwilling to extend this line of credit to this dealer without other, and further, security of payment thereof.
> In consideration of this agreement to extend this dealer a line of credit in question, the undersigned, hereby undertakes to, and does guarantee payment of any, and all, credit granted by you not to exceed Ten Thousand Dollars ($10,000.00). . . .

The appellant contends first that the guaranty was, by its terms, limited to $10,000 and after that total amount had been purchased the guaranty did not cover new purchases even though the indebtedness was not as much as $10,000. This argument overlooks the ordinary meaning of "a line of credit," which is a limit of credit to cover a series of transactions. (*Pittinger v. Southwestern Paper Co.,* Tex. Civ. App. 1941, 151 S.W.2d 922.)

It is further argued that the guaranty was rendered ineffective as to purchases from the plaintiff after the date that the principal-debtor changed its name and one of the partners withdrew. The trial judge correctly found that the appellant as guarantor was estopped to claim this defense because the guarantor 1) participated in the change of name, 2) participated in the profits (if any) of the original debtor after the change, which business both before and after the name change was dependent upon the purchases made under the continuing guaranty, and 3) the guarantor at no time disclaimed responsibility under the guaranty until suit. (See *Wilson & Toomer Fertilizer Co. v. American Cyanamid Co.,* 5 Cir. 1929, 33 F.2d 812.)

The appellant also assigns and argues certain other alleged errors. They have been considered and are found not well taken. The judgment of the trial court is therefore affirmed.

Affirmed.

Bayer & Mingolia Construction Co. v. Deschenes

1965 (Mass.) 205 N.E.2d 208

The plaintiff, Bayer, was the general contractor on a State highway contract and the defendant, Deschenes, was a subcontractor engaged by plaintiff to do certain excavation work as specified in the prime contract. Under the subcontract all work was to start not later than November 24, 1958, and be completed on or before March 1, 1959. Deschenes was required to furnish a bond of $91,000 for faithful performance. The bond was written by Aetna Insurance Co. Deschenes did not start work until December 1, 1958, and on June 22, 1959, when he quit, he had completed only about half of the work. During this time Bayer made efforts to get Deschenes to do the work but finally completed the job himself. He brought action against Aetna on the bond and the lower court rendered judgment for the plaintiff. The defendants appealed.

CUTTER, J. Aetna contends that it is discharged as surety by the extensions of time for performance given by Bayer to Deschenes, despite Aetna's knowledge of these extensions, and the absence of any finding of injury to Aetna caused thereby. Aetna, however, "is a compensated surety and is not entitled to invoke the ancient doctrine of *strictissimi juris.* . . ."

In the case of an *accommodation* surety, "where the principal and creditor, without the surety's consent, make a binding agreement to extend . . . time . . . the surety is discharged unless the creditor in the extension agreement reserves his rights against the surety. . . ." The modern rule, however, with respect to a *compensated* surety (see Restatement: *Security*, 129(2)) is that such a surety "is discharged only to the extent that he is harmed by the extension."

In any event, it is only by a binding, enforceable agreement for new consideration for an extension, which cannot be rescinded or disregarded, that the discharge of a surety will be effected. . . . The auditor's finding concerning the extensions of time for performance is merely that they were made "by mutual agreement of Bayer . . . and Deschenes." This finding does not import to us an enforceable agreement for consideration but merely Bayer's effort to obtain even dilatory performance by Deschenes.

We hold that Aetna, which has not shown itself to have been harmed by the extensions of time, was not thereby discharged as surety.

The order for judgment against Aetna is affirmed.

Magazine Digest Pub. Co., Limited v. Shade et al.

1938, 330 Pa. 487, 199 Atl. 190

DREW, J. This suit in assumpsit was brought [by Magazine Digest] to recover money alleged to be due under a contract between plaintiff and Mutual Magazine Distributors, Inc., on which contract defendants were guarantors. In their affidavit of defense defendants denied liability on the ground that they were discharged by a subsequent oral agreement which altered the original contract without their knowledge or consent. . . .

Under its original contract Mutual Distributors agreed to buy plaintiff's magazines at 14½¢ a copy for resale to retailers at 16½¢. Defendants guaranteed Mutual's obligation to pay plaintiff, with the additional stipulation that:

> . . . the publisher (plaintiff) may in his absolute discretion and without diminishing the liability of the guarantors (defendants), grant time or other indulgence to the distributor and may accept or make any composition or arrangements when and in such manner as the publisher may think expedient.

The parties continued under this contract until September 19, 1933, when Mutual was in arrears to the extent of $1,162.12. On that date it was orally agreed between plaintiff's president and the president of Mutual that if plaintiff refrained from terminating the contract, Mutual would pay the increased price of 15¢ a copy for the magazines. . . .

We cannot agree that defendants are liable for Mutual's debts under the substituted agreement of September 10, 1933. Even compensated guarantors—and defendants are not shown to be such—are not liable when the original contract on which their undertaking was made is materially changed without their assent. (*Sall B. & L. Ass'n v. Heller,* 314 Pa. 237, 171 Atl. 464). A gratuitous or accommodation guarantor is discharged by any change, material or not, and "even if he sustains no injury by the change, or if it be for his benefit, he has a right to stand upon the very terms of his obligation and is bound no farther." (100 Pa. 500, 505). But there can be no doubt here the alteration was material. To the distributor it meant 25 per cent less in its sale profit, to the plaintiff it made the difference between the terminating and continuing contractual relations with the distributor, and to the defendants it meant an increase in their obligation of $1,118.05 on 223,609 magazines received from the publisher after the new contract was in force. . . . Nor can the legal effect of alteration be escaped by limiting recovery against guarantors to the rate set in the original contract. The very theory of their defense is that after the change there is a new contract on which the guarantor has not agreed to be liable to any extent. . . .

Defendants are not relieved, however, from Mutual's debts which accrued while the original contract remained in force. The subsequent variation of that contract had no effect upon the liability that had already become fixed. Consequently defendants were not discharged as to it.

George E. Failing Co. v. Cardwell Investment Co.

1962 (Kansas) 376 P.2d 892

The defendant, Cardwell Investment Co., was guarantor of the payment of McPeters, drilling contractors, purchasers from the plaintiff. The guaranty agreement required plaintiff to submit all invoices to the contractor for approval and at the same time mail to defendant copies of all invoices. The plaintiff delayed seven months in mailing a copy of a particular invoice to defendant. The lower court ruled that the guarantor was discharged from liability and the plaintiff, Failing Co., appealed.

SCHROEDER, J.   Even compensated guarantors are not liable when the original contract on which their undertaking was made is materially changed without their assent. A gratuitous or accommodation guarantor is discharged by any change, material or not, and even if he sustains no injury by the change, or if it be for his benefit, he has a right to stand upon the very terms of his obligation and is bound no further. The guarantor is at least entitled to notice of change and the attempt to increase his burden and his chances of loss. . . .

In the instant case the terms of the guaranty contained in the letters are neither ambiguous nor inconsistent. The law views with a jaundiced eye any attempt to vary by parol evidence the terms of a written contract. This is particularly true with respect to a written contract of guaranty, inasmuch as the nature of the transaction makes it subject to the statute of frauds. . . . If the language of the contract of guaranty is clear and leaves no doubt as to the parties' intention concerning the measure of the guarantor's liability, the guarantor cannot be held liable in excess of the limitations that the contract language imposes. The character of the credit given in a written guaranty which is complete in itself cannot be explained by parol evidence. . . .

By the terms of the contract Failing agreed to submit all invoices to Mr. McPeters for his approval, and at the same time mail copies of all invoices to Cardwell "as made" for Cardwell's knowledge of McPeters' purchases through Failing.

We hold that Failing was required under the written terms of the guaranty to make a reasonably prompt submission of all invoices by sending a copy to Cardwell for his knowledge of McPeters' purchases through Failing, if Failing sought to obligate Cardwell on the guaranty.

It may be conceded that the contract of guaranty specified no limitation as to the amount McPeters might purchase through the Failing Company or the time during which such purchases could be made, but this does not preclude a reasonably prompt submission of copies of invoices for which purchases were made through Failing.

An analogous situation is found with respect to the time for presentment of a check for payment which has been drawn upon a bank. . . . A check must be presented for payment within a reasonable time after its issuance or the drawer will be discharged from liability thereon to the extent of the loss caused by the delay.

Accordingly, the judgment of the trial court is affirmed.

Bomud Company v. Yockey Oil Company and Osborn

1958 (Kan.) 142 P.2d 148

Osborn in a letter guaranteed payment by Yockey of oil well supplies which the plaintiff, Bomud, in reliance on the letter sold to Yockey on credit. Yockey is no longer liable because of the short Statute of Limitations for oral agreements but the five year statute applying to written accounts has not run. Osborn contends that he is released because Yockey is no longer liable and the lower court awarded judgment in favor of Osborn, against whom the plaintiff has taken this appeal.

FATZER, J. A guarantor, to be relieved from his obligation to pay, must establish one of three facts: (1) the debt has been paid or extinguished; (2) a valid release or discharge; or (3) the bar of the statute of limitations as to himself. It is conceded that the debt has not been paid. The fact that the statute bars recovery against Yockey does not extinguish the debt. . . . It is also conceded that the statute of limitations has not run as to Osborn's individual liability on his written contract if he has not been released or discharged. Did the failure to bring the action upon the open account, until the statute had run in favor of Yockey, release or discharge Osborn from his guarantee to pay under his written contract? We think it did not. . . . The contract of a guarantor is his own separate contract. It is in the nature of a warranty by him that the thing guaranteed to be done by the principal shall be done, and is not an engagement jointly with the principal to do the thing. A guarantor, not being a joint contractor with the principal, is not bound like a surety to do what the principal has contracted to do, but answers only for the consequence of the default of the principal. . . . When default occurs on the part of the principal, the guarantor's liability becomes primary and is absolute. . . .

Osborn's contract with Bomud was based upon a valid consideration. It was a separate undertaking to pay if Yockey defaulted. When Osborn's liability became primary and absolute, the open account was then enforceable against Yockey, and it is of no consequence to Osborn if since that time the statute has run in Yockey's favor. Osborn's liability was fixed and determined by his written guaranty and that obligation has not been discharged. That the Statute of Limitations (G.S.1949, 60-306, *First*) had not run in Osborn's favor when suit was filed is conceded. The debt has not been paid. Bomud is entitled to recover from Osborn in accordance with the terms and conditions of his contract.

The judgment is reversed with directions to set aside the order entering judgment for Osborn on the pleadings, and to proceed in accordance with the views expressed in this opinion. It is so ordered.

Board of Education (Anning-Johnson Co.) v. Hartford Accident & Ind. Co.

1965 (Ill.) 208 N.E.2d 51

Anning-Johnson Co., plaintiff, was a subcontractor on a project for the Board of Education. The prime contractor was bonded by Hartford by arrangement of the Board of Education. The parties stipulated as to the following facts: plaintiff upon completion of the subcontract delivered waivers of lien to the general contractor certifying that he had been paid $6,840 on his claim of $9,600, that plaintiff to the extent of $6,840 released the Board of his right of lien against public money in its hands; that in fact he had been paid nothing; that the general contractor was thereby enabled to receive a payment of $6,840 from the Board. Anning-Johnson sought to recover $9,600 from Hartford. In an action on the bond, the court held that Hartford, surety, was obligated to pay only $2,760. The plaintiff appealed.

CORYN, J. The judgment held, in effect, that plaintiff is barred from recovery against Hartford on the performance bond to the extent of amounts for which plaintiff delivered partial waiver of lien. The trial court found that by reason of plaintiff's conduct, its claim, to the extent of $6,840, was not a just claim within the meaning of the act in relation to bonds of contractors entering into contracts for public construction.

Defendant, Hartford, argues that the ruling of the trial court is correct, in that the partial waivers of lien delivered by plaintiff induced payment by the School District as plaintiff intended; that these waivers therefore operated as a relinquishment of rights to which defendant was entitled to be *subrogated* in the event of its payment to plaintiff; *that defendant's position was materially prejudiced by this conduct of plaintiff which reduced the amount of public moneys available as security for defendant's commitment as surety;* and that plaintiff's claim is not therefore a just claim within the meaning of said Payment Bond Statute.

In *Alexander Lumber Co. v. Aetna Co.* (296 Ill. 500, 129 N.E. 871), it was held that where the bond of a building contractor covers obligations for material furnished for the building, a subcontractor supplier of material who refrained from filing a lien against a building fund for a portion of his claim, so that the right thereto was lost, to that extent released the surety on the bond. Such failure was held to be a violation of a duty arising from the relationship of surety and assured. "It is an equitable rule," said the court at page 509, 129 N.E. at page 874, "that, where a creditor releases or permits to be lost a security for a debt, other sureties are thereby released to that extent." In *Northbrook Supply Co. et al. v. Thumm Construction Co. et al.* (39 Ill.App.2d 267, 188 N.E.2d 388), plaintiff was a supplier to a subcontractor and had delivered lien waivers to the subcontractor by which the latter was enabled to obtain payment from the general contractor. When the subcontractor subsequently failed to pay the plaintiff, a complaint was filed against the surety on the general contractor's performance bond delivered in compliance with 15 and 16 of ch. 29, Ill. Rev.Stat. Although the facts of this case are substantially different from those in the case at bar, the Appellate Court there held plaintiff's claim barred, not because the general contractor had paid the claim once and had not defaulted, but because plaintiff was estopped by its conduct and its claim was not therefore a just one. At 50 Am. Jur., Suretyship, 109, 110, it is stated that a surety by operation of principles of equity is entitled to be subrogated to the benefit of all the securities and means of payment under a creditor's control.

Defendant, Hartford, in the case at bar, by reason of the relationship of the parties here as surety and assured, had a right exercisable at any time, to pay plaintiff's claim and to be subrogated thereby to its rights of lien against public moneys in the hands of the School District. By extinguishing this right through the delivery of partial waivers certifying payment, which induced the release of public moneys, as plaintiff intended, plaintiff is estopped by its own conduct, *pro tanto,* from recovering against Hartford. We agree with the finding of the trial court that plaintiff's claim is not a just one within the meaning of the statute. Irrespective of whether the statute contemplates liability on the part of a surety in cases where final settlement may have been made, and rights of subrogation therefore lost, it is also evident that the claim asserted must be a just one. The statute does not contemplate liability, in our judgment, in a case where a claimant has voluntarily prejudiced the rights of the surety.

The judgment of the trial court is accordingly affirmed.

CHAPTER 45
REVIEW QUESTIONS AND PROBLEMS

1. *S* wrote a letter to *C,* a material man, saying he would be liable for "any bill my son makes for material." A dispute arose later as to whether this covered one purchase or a series of purchases. What is your answer?

2. Suppose *S* signs a statement to the effect that he will be secondarily liable for groceries, not exceeding $300, furnished to *X.* How long will such a guaranty continue?

3. *G,* by contract, guaranteed prompt payment of a certain note owing by *P* to *C.* The note fell due at a time when the maker was solvent, but *C* made no attempt to collect and gave *G* no notice of the default. Later *P* became insolvent and *C* desires to collect of *G.* May he do so?

4. Davis was surety for his brother on a $1,152 note in favor of Bank, the brother giving Davis a mortgage on real property to protect him against loss. Davis and his brother are insolvent and are thinking about releasing the mortgage. The court held Bank could have the mortgage impounded for its benefit. Why?

5. *S* was surety upon *P*'s obligation to *C.* Some time after the debt fell due, *P,* with the knowledge and consent of *S,* made a payment on the obligation. Did this payment toll the statute of limitations for *S* as well as *P*?

6. *C* held an obligation of *P*'s upon which *S* was surety. *C* permitted the obligation to run several years past its maturity date, although the interest was always paid. No definite extension period was ever agreed upon between *P* and *C.* After a number of years, although within

the period required by the Statute of Limitations, C attempted to recover from S. Should he have been allowed to recover?

7. C, A, E, and M were sureties upon a $4,000 obligation of B to W. The obligation provided for attorney fees of 10 per cent if placed with an attorney for collection. B defaulted and C, upon demand, paid the $4,000 note to W. He then sued A, E, and M for $3,000 and attorney fees in an action against them jointly. The court refused to allow any attorney fees and refused to give a joint judgment against the three. Why?

8. A and B are sureties upon an obligation of P. At the time A became a surety, he obtained a mortgage from P upon certain personal property to protect himself in case P defaulted. P failed to perform, and A and B were compelled to carry out the agreement. Did A hold the mortgage for his own protection alone or for the mutual protection of the sureties? If you were A, how would you arrange the matter to protect yourself only?

9. The mother and wife of P became cosureties on P's note for $5,000, the note being secured by a chattel mortgage on P's household furniture. The wife settled the claim for $3,500 and released the chattel mortgage on furniture worth $2,500. She now seeks contribution from the mother, her mother-in-law. How much should she recover?

10. C Co. loaned J Co. $68,000, $59,280 of the amount being guaranteed in writing by W and his wife. As security for the guaranty, they pledged a note for $59,280 owing to them as joint tenants by X. The $68,000 debt fell due and in settlement a new note for a lesser amount and a different rate of interest was given C Co. by J Co. W guaranteed the new debt and repledged the $59,280 note as security, his wife not joining in the guaranty or pledge. J Co. is again in default and C Co. proposes to use the $59,280 note as a means of collection, when W's wife claims one-half of it because she did not join in the pledging. Was her original pledge still good?

11. A and S signed a mortgage note in favor of P for $15,000, it being known to P that S was merely a surety. Some time later, A became insolvent, and P accepted $7,000, discharging A from further liability. May P recover the $8,000 balance from S?

12. S wrote a letter to C in which he promised to be liable as a continuous guarantor on all goods sold to P until the guaranty was withdrawn by notice. Before any goods had been sold, S died, but this fact being unknown to C, he sold goods to P on credit. Since P has failed to pay for the goods, C seeks to recover of the estate of S. Is the estate liable?

chapter 46

Bankruptcy

6-21 In General. The problems which arise when a person, firm or corporation becomes financially involved so that their obligation to creditors cannot be satisfied have been mentioned previously. In the Book on Contracts, mention was made of a composition of creditors—an informal arrangement between a financially involved debtor and his creditors whereby the creditors agree to accept a pro rata part of their claims in complete discharge of the debtor's obligations. Other methods of handling insolvency problems have also been developed, the most significant of which is bankruptcy.

Bankruptcy was discussed also in the material dealing with Secured Transactions. Questions arise as to whether or not a security interest will "stand up" in bankruptcy where the debtor party is involved in such proceedings. It is to be noted that bankruptcy is a federal function and that federal statutes control it.

6-22 Kinds of Bankruptcy. The federal government has by statute—the Bankruptcy Act—provided a procedure whereby, under certain conditions, one may be discharged of his obligations. He is permitted to start his business life anew, unfettered by weighty obligations assumed in the past. The filing of a voluntary petition in bankruptcy usually accomplishes this result. The federal court, through its designated officers, takes control of all property involved, turns it into cash, pays all expenses, and uses the balance to pay off creditors as far as possible.

At the same time the Bankruptcy Act has made it possible for a creditor of an insolvent debtor to get his full share of the insolvent's estate by filing an involuntary petition in bankruptcy against the debtor. A person cannot be forced into involuntary bankruptcy unless his liabilities equal at least $1,000. If twelve or more creditors exist, the petition must be signed by at least three of them—otherwise, only one need sign. The petitioning creditors as a group must also own definite unsecured claims totalling $500 or more. Relatives, persons holding fully secured claims, and other biased creditors are not counted in determining the number of creditors required to sign the petition. If there are only eleven creditors other than relatives, one creditor may bring about involuntary bankruptcy regardless of the total number of creditors involved.

Any person, firm, or corporation may become a *voluntary* bankrupt, with the exception of five types of corporations. Railway, banking, insurance, municipal, and building and loan corporations may not become voluntary bankrupts, but an insolvent railway may petition a bankruptcy court for confirmation of a reorganization plan, provided the plan has first been approved by the Interstate Commerce Commission.

Any natural person, except a farmer or wage earner, any partnership, and any moneyed business or commercial corporation except the five previously mentioned, may be adjudged an *involuntary* bankrupt for proper cause. It should be noted that three new groups are exempt from involuntary bankruptcy, namely, farmers, wage earners, and nonbusiness corporations.

A farmer is defined as anyone engaged in the tillage of the soil, raising poultry or livestock and their products, or operating a dairy. If he spends most of his time on the farm and expects to derive most of his income from it, he is deemed a farmer although he is incidentally engaged in other enterprises. A wage earner is one who works for another at a rate of pay of $1,500 a year or less.

6-23 Acts of Bankruptcy. The purpose of involuntary bankruptcy is to force an equal distribution of an insolvent debtor's assets. In this connection it should be noted that mere insolvency affords no basis for a petition in involuntary bankruptcy. Unless a debtor has committed some act which indicates an intention to abuse or to prefer certain creditors, or has done something which shows a willingness to have his assets distributed, involuntary bankruptcy is impossible. The Bankruptcy Act sets forth six acts, one of which must be committed within four months prior to the petition before involuntary bankruptcy proceedings are possible.

Acts of bankruptcy by a person shall consist of his having:

1. Conveyed, transferred, concealed, or removed, or permitted to be concealed, or removed, any part of his property with intent to hinder, delay, or defraud his creditors, or any of them;

2. Transferred, while insolvent, any portion of his property to one or more of his creditors with intent to prefer such creditors over his other creditors;

3. Suffered or permitted, while insolvent, any creditor to obtain a lien upon his property through court action and not having vacated or discharged such lien within thirty days from the date thereof or at least five

days before the date set for any sale or other disposition of such property;

4. Made a general assignment for the benefit of creditors;

5. While insolvent or unable to pay his debts as they mature, procured, permitted, or suffered voluntarily or involuntarily the appointment of a receiver or trustee to take charge of his property;

6. Admitted in writing his inability to pay his debts and his willingness to be adjudged a bankrupt.

Attention should be called to the fact that the second, third, and fifth acts must be accompanied by insolvency at the time they are committed. With respect to the first, fourth, and sixth acts, insolvency is not required. Another provision of the act, however, makes solvency at the time the petition is filed a good defense to the first act of bankruptcy. In none of the other acts is solvency at the time the petition is filed important. In the first three instances mentioned, it is a matter of insolvency at the time the act is committed. *Insolvency,* as used in bankruptcy, refers to a situation in which the debtor's assets valued on the basis of a voluntary sale fail to equal his liabilities.

It should be emphasized, concerning the third act, that it is not the lien which constitutes the act of bankruptcy, but it is the failure to vacate it within the time allotted to the debtor.

The petition in involuntary bankruptcy must be filed within four months of some act of bankruptcy. Whenever recording is required in order to render a transfer fully effective, the four months' period is calculated from the date of recording and not from the date of the transfer.

6-24 Officers of the Court. The bankruptcy petition is filed with the clerk of the Federal District Court and is then referred to the referee, who is appointed by the court to hear the evidence and to submit his findings to the court. All dividends are ordered paid by the referee, he being a semiadministrative and judicial officer.

A trustee is elected by the creditors at the first meeting, a majority in number and amount of claims held by those present at the meeting being necessary for election. The trustee then takes title to all non-exempt property, both real and personal, owned by the bankrupt at the time the petition was filed. It becomes his duty to dispose of the property as best he can, under the supervision of the court, for the benefit of creditors. Personal property, purchased by an innocent party from the bankrupt after the filing of the petition but before the trustee or receiver takes possession, remains with the purchaser. Any property received by the bankrupt after the filing of the petition belongs to his new estate, except that all devises, bequests, or inheritances received within six months thereafter belong to the trustee. Executory contracts may be accepted or rejected within 60 days after the petition in bankruptcy has been passed upon. If the trustee chooses to reject a long-term contract, the other party is then permitted to file a claim for damages against the bankrupt estate. In case of leases, however, the landlord may file a claim for all past due rentals and for damages caused by breach of the lease agreement, but the latter claim shall not be in excess of one year's rental.

A receiver is a temporary officer appointed by the court to take charge of a bankrupt's property until a trustee is appointed. He is appointed only when someone is required to care for the property in this intervening period in order to avoid waste or loss.

6-25 Recoverable Preferences. Any transfer of property by an insolvent person to a particular creditor that has the effect of preferring that creditor above the others constitutes a preference. A preferential transfer may be recovered by the trustee if it took place within the four months preceding the filing of the bankruptcy petition, and if the creditor, at the time of the transfer, knew, or had cause to believe, that he was obtaining a greater percentage of his claim than other creditors could recover.[1] The transfer may consist of the payment of money or the transfer of property as payment of, or as security for, a prior indebtedness. A mortgage or pledge may be set aside as readily as payment, providing it is received by the creditor with knowledge of the debtor's insolvency. Such pledge or mortgage can be avoided, however, only if it was received within the immediate four months prior to the filing of the petition of bankruptcy and was obtained as security for a previous debt. In the case of the mortgage, the four months' period dates from the recording of the mortgage rather than from its signing.

If the property received by a preferred creditor has been sold to an innocent third party, recovery of the property may not be had, but its value may be obtained from the creditor. A creditor, however, who in good faith extends additional credit after having received a preference, may deduct from the recoverable preference the amount of any new unpaid credit items. In this manner, a creditor who attempts to help an insolvent debtor out of his financial difficulties is not penalized if, after obtaining payment, he extends no greater credit than the old claim amounted to.

Any judgment lien obtained within the four months' period is void, irrespective of knowledge, so long as it continues to maintain the character of a lien at the time the petition in bankruptcy is filed, if the judgment was obtained while the debtor was insolvent.

Payment of a fully secured claim does not constitute a preference and, therefore, may not be recovered.

Transfers of property for a present consideration may not be set aside. A mortgage given to secure a contemporaneous loan is valid although the mortgagee took the security with knowledge of the debtor's insolvency. An insolvent debtor has a right to extricate himself, as far as possible, from his financial difficulty.

Any debtor of a bankrupt may set off against the amount he owes the bankrupt estate any sum which the estate owes him. To the extent of

[1] *Riccio, Trustee v. G.M.A.C.*, page 922.

his set-off against the estate, he becomes a preferred creditor, legally entitled to his preference. This rule is not applicable where the claim against the bankrupt has been purchased or created with the express purpose of set-off. A bank that has loaned a bankrupt $2,000 and happens to have $1,500 of the bankrupt on deposit at the time of bankruptcy, is a preferred creditor to the extent of the deposit. This set-off must be allowed, unless the evidence discloses that the deposit was made with the express purpose of preferring the bank. In such a case the deposit becomes part of the bankrupt estate.

6-26 Provable Claims. Not all claimants against a bankrupt may share in his assets. Those claims upon which dividends are paid are called provable claims and must be filed within six months after notice of the first creditors' meeting. All judgments, workmen's compensation awards, and claims founded upon a contract are provable; thus, any debt or claim for damages because of breach of contract may be filed. Disputed contract claims that have not been made definite at the time for filing are made certain by court decree or agreement prior to the payment of dividends by the trustee.

Tort claims—demands made because of injury to person or property—are not provable unless they have been reduced to contract or judgment prior to the petition in bankruptcy, except that, in torts involving negligence, the injured party may prove his claim if he has instituted suit prior to the filing of bankruptcy proceedings. Thus, *A*, who has an action against *B* because of an assault by the latter, is deprived of any share in *B*'s bankrupt estate, provided the petition in bankruptcy is filed before *A* has reached an agreement with *B*. As noticed in the succeeding section, however, the claim is not discharged, and may be enforced against any new assets *B* may acquire.

Claims for costs in suits started against the bankrupt or in cases started by him and abandoned by the trustee are also provable. Taxes also represent provable claims.

A claim by a creditor who has received a recoverable preference is not allowed until he has returned the preference. If a creditor has knowingly received payment of a claim from an insolvent debtor within four months of bankrupty, he is not entitled to prove other claims until he has surrendered the preference that he received.

6-27 Claims That Are Discharged. All provable claims, with a few exceptions, are discharged by a discharge in bankruptcy. The most important of these exceptions are claims for taxes, losses resulting from breach of trust by one acting in a fiduciary capacity, liability resulting from willful or malicious tort,[2] wages earned within three months of filing of the petition in bankruptcy, and liabilities for property or money obtained under false pretenses or by fraudulent representations. Nonprovable claims, not being discharged, also continue as claims against the bankrupt

2 *First National Bank of Lansing v. Padgen,* page 923.

after his discharge. An amendment to the Bankruptcy Act effective October 3, 1966 makes "dischargeable in bankrupty debts for taxes which became legally due and owing more than 3 years preceding bankruptcy." The discharge does not release or affect any tax lien, however.

It becomes the duty of the bankrupt, as soon as a petition in bankruptcy is filed, to schedule all his creditors and the amount due each. The claim of any creditor who is not listed and who does not learn of the proceedings in time to file his claim is not discharged. The bankrupt, under such circumstances, remains liable.

In addition to providing that certain claims are not discharged, the Bankruptcy Act provides a number of circumstances under which the bankrupt may not obtain a discharge. In such a case the assets of his present estate are distributed among his creditors, but he remains liable out of future assets for that portion of the claims that remains unpaid after all assets have been liquidated and distributed. The Bankruptcy Act states the following about the discharge of bankrupts:

> The court shall grant the discharge unless satisfied that the bankrupt has (1) committed an offense punishable by imprisonment as provided under this Act; or (2) destroyed, mutilated, falsified, concealed, or failed to keep or preserve books of account or records, from which his financial condition and business transactions might be ascertained, unless the court deems such acts or failure to have been justified under all the circumstances of the case; or (3) while engaged in business as a sole proprietor, partnership, or as an executive of a corporation,[3] obtained for such business money or property or credit, or obtained an extension or renewal of credit, by making or publishing or causing to be made or published, in any manner whatsoever, a materially false statement in writing respecting his financial condition or the financial condition of such partnership or corporation; or (4) at any time subsequent to the first day of the twelve months immediately preceding the filing of the petition in bankruptcy, transferred, removed, destroyed, or concealed or permitted to be removed, destroyed, or concealed, any of his property, with intent to hinder, delay, or defraud his creditors; or (5) has within six years prior to bankruptcy been granted a discharge . . . ; or (6) in the course of a proceeding under this Act refused to obey any lawful order, or to answer any material question approved by the court; or (7) has failed to explain satisfactorily any losses of assets or deficiency of assets to meet his liabilities.

Any of the circumstances mentioned may be set up by a creditor as a bar to a discharge, or they may be set up by the trustee, when he has been authorized to do so by the creditors. Furthermore, if any creditor can show reasonable cause for believing that the bankrupt has done any of the things mentioned, the burden shifts to the bankrupt to show that he has not committed an act that will bar discharge. In addition, it should be suggested that the discharge of a partnership does not act as a discharge of the individual members of the firm. They are discharged only upon action of the court in their behalf as individuals.

The third ground for barring the discharge has been recently limited to businessmen. Prior to 1960, persons not in business who furnished

[3] *Branch v. Mills and Lupton Supply Co.*, page 925.

false financial statements to obtain property or credit would also be denied a discharge. Because of the fact that false financial statements are frequently submitted to short-term lending institutions which loan relatively small amounts of money, Congress decided that such action should not bar discharge but should only prevent discharge of the debt which arose out of the transaction in which the fraudulent financial statement was submitted. Therefore, a false financial statement by a businessman is a complete bar to a discharge but a false financial statement by a person not engaged in business is only a bar to discharge of the debt involved.

6-28 Exemptions. The bankrupt is allowed the exemptions provided by the law of the state in which he resides. Such laws usually provide for a certain sum in cash or personal property and, if the bankrupt owns his homestead, some additional amount.

6-29 Priority of Claims. Since the trustee's title to property is only the title previously held by the bankrupt, any valid lien against the property continues after bankruptcy and must be paid first if the trustee desires to dispose of the property free of encumbrances; otherwise, the lienholder merely enforces his lien. Should a sale of the property fail to pay the entire secured debt, the creditor then becomes an unsecured creditor for the deficit.

The Bankruptcy Act provides a definite order for the payment of provable claims as follows:

1. Cost of preserving and administering the bankrupt estate.
2. Claims of wage earners not exceeding $600 to each claimant, provided the wages have accrued within the three months preceding bankruptcy.[4]
3. Claims for money expended in defending against or setting aside arrangements of the bankrupt debtor.
4. Claims for taxes.

The 1966 amendment limits "the priority accorded to taxes in the distribution of bankrupt estates to those taxes which became legally due and owing within 3 years preceding bankruptcy."

5. Claims for rent granted priority by state statute and any claims allowed priority by federal law. Many of the claims held by the federal government have been given priority under this provision.

The 1966 amendment restricts the priority for rent to not more than three months rent owing at the time of bankruptcy.

6. Claims of general creditors.

In case funds are insufficient to pay in full any particular class of creditors, the funds available for such group are distributed in proportion to the amount of each claim, all classes falling lower in the list receiving no payment. For example, if the assets are insufficient to pay in full the claims of wage earners amounting to $600 per person and earned within

---

[4] *U.S. v. Munro-Van Helms Company, Inc.*, page 926.

the previous three months, the wage earners would share proportionately the amount available, but the claims for taxes and general creditors would not share, no payment being made on them.

6-30 Fraudulent Conveyances. Conveyances of property to relatives or friends that are made for the purpose of hindering, delaying, or defrauding creditors may usually be set aside by the creditors.[5] This rule applies whether or not bankruptcy has intervened. In any case where the conveyance leaves the transferor without sufficient assets with which to pay his debts, the transfer is said to be fraudulent.[6] The courts insist that one must be "just before he is generous."

If property has been fraudulently transferred to an innocent third party, it can be avoided only if the consideration given for it was inadequate, and then only if the third party is reimbursed to the extent he gave consideration for it. Property may be taken from a person who receives it with knowledge of the fraud, in which case the person becomes an ordinary creditor of the debtor.

The states usually impose no time limit in which an action may be brought by creditors to set aside a fraudulent conveyance. Whenever creditors discover that such a transfer has been effected, they are free to institute an action for the purpose of restoring the property to the debtor's estate, in which it may be attached and sold by his judgment creditors or used by a bankruptcy court in paying creditors.

6-31 Reorganizations. At one time the law made it possible for a small minority of creditors to jeopardize the interests of the majority whenever a debtor became financially embarrassed. They could force the debtor into bankruptcy and insist upon liquidation at unfavorable times; they could demand, in many instances, foreclosure of mortgages or threaten lengthy and expensive receiverships unless the other creditors purchased their claims at exorbitant figures; or they could effectively block any plan for rehabilitation of the debtor until their demands had in large measure been satisfied. Amendments to the Bankruptcy Act were made to relieve this situation and have been woven together in such a way as to meet several distinct needs. In general, the method chosen by this legislation is to coerce the minority interests to follow a plan that has been approved by a large group and sanctioned by the court.

The reorganization chapters of the Bankruptcy Act provide for four distinct situations: (1) an arrangement which modifies only the claims of unsecured creditors; (2) one which alters only the claims held against debtors other than corporations of creditors secured by real estate; (3) one by which wage earners who earn no more than $5,000 a year may reorder their affairs; or (4) a complete reorganization of a corporation which is in financial difficulty. In this latter situation, the corporation is usually permitted to continue operation under court supervision until

[5] *Cross v. Commons et al.,* page 927.
[6] *Priebe v. Svehlek,* page 929.

some plan of reorganization is approved or it is determined that no plan can secure the requisite support for its approval. If such support cannot be obtained, the court proceeds to liquidate the corporation as in any other case of bankruptcy.

The procedure for reorganization is somewhat similar in each of the four types, since the plan must be approved by the court and by a stipulated percentage of the creditors who are affected by the plan. The percentage varies from a simple majority in number and amount to two-thirds of the claims in each class affected, depending on the type of arrangement which is involved.

6-32 Wage-earner Plans. One section of the federal Bankruptcy Act provides an arrangement whereby a "wage-earner" who qualifies can work out a plan to pay off his creditors over a period of time rather than filing an ordinary petition in bankruptcy. In this connection a "wage-earner" is a person whose wages or salary and other income do not exceed $5,000 per year. Such a plan enables a person who has financial problems and who is being pressed by his creditors to work out a long-range program to pay off his debts. If the plan is not carried out, the wage-earner may be entitled to convert it to straight bankruptcy.[7]

BANKRUPTCY CASES

Riccio v. General Motors Acceptance Corporation
1963 (Conn.) 203 A.2d 92

This is an action by the trustee in bankruptcy to recover the proceeds of the sale of an automobile.

In 1960, Jamarc entered into a contract with Michael J. Cozy, Inc. for the purchase of a new 1960 Oldsmobile. The terms called for payment of $100.76 monthly in twenty-four installments. To secure payment the seller reserved the title and retained a security interest in the automobile until the amount due was fully paid in cash. The seller assigned the contract to the defendant. Jamarc defaulted in the payment due on January 21, 1961, and continued to be in default. On February 3, 1961, the defendant exercised its rights under the contract and repossessed the automobile. The car was then sold. On February 7, 1961, Jamarc was adjudicated a bankrupt. The bankrupt's trustee brought this suit to recover the money on the grounds that it was a preferential transfer. The trial court found for the defendant and the trustee appealed.

JACOBS, J. . . . Briefly stated, the elements of a preference under Sec. 60a consist of the following: a debtor (1) making or suffering a transfer of his property, (2) to or for the benefit of a creditor, (3) for or on account of an antecedent debt (resulting in a depletion of the estate, (4) while insolvent, and (5) within four months of bankruptcy . . . , (6) the effect of which will enable the

7 *In the Matter of Hendren,* page 930.

creditor to obtain a greater percentage of his debt than some other creditor of the same class. The creditor's knowledge or reasonable cause to believe that a preference is effected by a transfer to him is no longer an element in determining whether such transfer constitutes a preference under subdivision a or Sect. 60. However, under subdivision b a preference is voidable by the trustee in bankruptcy only upon proof of the additional element that (7) the creditor receiving or to be benefited by the preference had reasonable cause to believe that the debtor was insolvent. If any one of the elements of a preference as enumerated in Sect. 60a is wanting, there is no necessity of considering an avoidance of the transfer under Sect. 60b, since a preference under the terms of Sect. 60 itself has not been established.

In order to prove that a preference be effected under Sect. 60 of the Act, a transfer of property must be made or suffered by the debtor "while insolvent." . . . As in the other elements of a preference, the burden of proof is on the trustee to show insolvency at the time of the transfer. . . . The transfer may be voluntary or involuntary. The term "suffered," as used in the act, does not require any conscious participation by the debtor. . . . The insolvency must be in the bankruptcy sense, as defined by Sect. 1(19) of the Bankruptcy Act (30 Stat. 544, Sect. 1(15), as amended, 11 U.S.C. Sect. 1(19), which reads as follows: "A person shall be deemed insolvent within the provisions of this title whenever the aggregate of his property, exclusive of any property which he may have conveyed, transferred, concealed, removed, or permitted to be concealed or removed, with intent to defraud, hinder, or delay his creditors, shall not at a fair valuation be sufficient in amount to pay his debts.

Applying the foregoing principles to the controverted issue of insolvency at the time of the transfer in the present case, we point out that it was incumbent on the trustee to introduce into evidence a statement of the assets and liabilities of the bankrupt. . . . There is nothing in the record before us showing the financial condition of the bankrupt; such as inventories, bankruptcy appraisals, trustee's reports, orders confirming bankruptcy sales, or even the bankrupt's own schedules. . . . It was the duty of the trustee not only to plead but to prove, and for the court to make a finding, that on February 3, 1961—the date of the alleged transfer —the bankrupt's debts exceeded the aggregate fair value of its assets. A failure to prove and find this indispensable and essential element must result in a finding that the preference, if any, is not voidable. It becomes unnecessary, in the view which we have taken of his case, to consider other legal propositions argued and briefed by the trustee.

Judgment for Defendant affirmed.

First National Bank of Lansing v. Padjen
1965 (Ill.) 210 N.E.2d 332

BURKE, J. This action was brought by plaintiff-mortgagee (First National Bank) against defendants-mortgagors for the conversion of chattels covered by a chattel mortgage. The defense of discharge in bankruptcy was raised, which was sustained by the trial court. The mortgagee appeals.

On April 7, 1962, defendants executed a chattel mortgage covering restaurant equipment to plaintiff. The mortgage was duly recorded and covered, among other items, two heat lamps and a glass chiller. Defendants later filed a petition in bankruptcy, individually and in their business capacity, in the United States District Court. A receiver was appointed and plaintiff obtained an order from the federal court directing that the receiver turn over to plaintiff all chattels in his possession which were covered by the chattel mortgage. All of the chattels were turned over except the two heat lamps and the glass chiller; it was at this time that plaintiff first learned that these chattels had been previously disposed of by defendants. It appears that on July 30, 1963, the glass chiller was returned to the seller from whom it had been purchased and $300 credited to defendants' account; when and to whom the two heat lamps were disposed of does not appear on record.

Plaintiff thereupon filed this action in the Circuit Court for damages for the conversion of the chattels. Judgment was rendered in favor of the defendants on the ground that the defendants' act of disposing of the chattels did not constitute a conversion within the meaning of Section 17 of the Bankruptcy Act (11 U.S.C.A. 35) and consequently was not within those debts of a bankrupt not discharged by bankruptcy. The trial court certified the following question to this court: whether or not the return of the chattel-mortgaged property to the original seller for which money is received by the chattel-mortgagors, without securing the release or consent of the chattel-mortgage holder, is tantamount to willful conversion of property which would not be discharged under Section 17 of the Bankruptcy Act (11 U.S.C.A. 35). It does not appear that this matter was presented in the bankruptcy court so that the question of *res judicata* does not arise. . . .

Section 17 of the Bankruptcy Act states:

(a) A discharge in bankruptcy shall release a bankrupt from all of his provable debts, whether allowable in full or in part, except such as . . . (2) are liabilities for . . . willful and malicious injuries to the person or property of another. . . . (11 U.S.C.A. 35.)

The question certified to this court and raised by this appeal is one of first impression in the State of Illinois. Only two other states have passed upon this question. . . .

The United States Supreme Court has held that to deprive another of his property by deliberately disposing of it without semblance of authority is an injury thereto within the common meaning of the words used in the Bankruptcy Act. . . . Furthermore, the converter need not act with actual malice or ill will, nor with the specific intent to injure a particular person, but only that he act without legal cause or justification. . . .

The Illinois Commercial Code provides that the conversion of the security of a loan by a mortgagor without the assent of the mortgagee will subject the mortgagor to criminal penalties. . . . The same was true under the statutes predating the present Code. . . . The purpose of these criminal penalty provisions is to prevent the disposition of the security by the mortgagor to the injury of the mortgagee. . . . That the mortgagee's interest in the chattel securing a loan is a protectible property cannot be doubted.

In the instant case, defendants disposed of the chattels in question without the consent of the plaintiff. In so doing, they deprived plaintiff of property to which it had a right to look in the event that defendants failed to meet the payments on the loan. It would be an absurd result to say that plaintiff, upon defendants' bankruptcy, has a right to those chattels covered by the mortgage which are still in defendants' possession, but has no right to seek the value of those chattels covered by the mortgage wrongfully disposed of, on the grounds that the liability for the wrongful disposition was discharged by the bankruptcy proceedings. We are of the opinion that the unauthorized disposition of the two heat lamps and the glass chiller constituted a "willful and malicious injury to property" within the meaning of Section 17 of the Bankruptcy Act. The question certified to this court by the trial court is answered in the affirmative.

The judgment is reversed and the cause is remanded with directions to enter judgment for plaintiff and against defendants in the amount of $550 and costs.

Judgment reversed and cause remanded with directions.

Branch v. Mills & Lupton Supply Company

1965, 348 F.2d 901

Branch had made false statements in writing for the purpose of obtaining a loan from a creditor. Thereafter he was involved in bankruptcy proceedings and a creditor objected to his receiving a discharge. The referee allowed the objection and his decision was upheld by the federal district court. Branch appealed.

PER CURIAM. The bankrupt, who was engaged in the business of building shell homes, admitted that he furnished false affidavits for the purpose of obtaining a loan. One of the creditors filed specifications of objections to his discharge.

The referee in bankruptcy sustained the objections to the discharge in a memorandum opinion containing findings of fact and conclusions of law, saying:

> One of the objects of the Act is to release an honest and insolvent person from his debts. From this evidence it does not appear that this bankrupt was honest in his dealings with his creditors and the public. While he claims that it was a recognized practice of the trade and that he had made this same affidavit in many other cases, that does not cure the fact that he swore falsely to a material fact for the purpose of obtaining a loan. The giving of an oath, either written or oral, should be treated as sacred. This bankrupt's act of swearing falsely for the purpose of obtaining a loan is not indicative of such honesty as Congress intended to protect.
>
> I find as a fact that the bankrupt swore falsely, or made a false statement in

writing, to material fact for the purpose of obtaining credit or property from
Family Pride Homes, Inc., in Atlanta, Georgia, and that they knew at the time
these statements were made they were false. I further find that Family Pride
Homes, Inc., to whom the statements were made, relied upon them in
extending the credit.

We find that the pertinent facts and applicable law are correctly set
forth in the opinion of the district court.
Affirmed.

United States v. Munro-Van Helms Company, Inc.

1957, 243 F.2d 10

Munro-Van Helms Company, Inc. is involved in a bankruptcy proceeding during which a question is raised as to the priority to be given, if
any, of claims by laborers for vacation pay which had been earned over
a period of a year based upon a percentage of their earnings, the vacation
pay for the year having been accrued within the past three months. The
lower court allowed the vacation pay for the full year, while creditors
contended that only that portion of the vacation pay actually earned
within the last three months was entitled to priority.

JONES, J.   . . . Vacation pay is, by all of the decisions, regarded as
wages. (6 Remington on Bankruptcy, 382, § 2807.) The courts are not in
accord as to extent of the priority which claims for vacation pay should
be accorded by courts of bankruptcy. It has been held that full priority
should be given to claims for vacation pay which accrued during the
three months' period even though part of the services upon which the
right to the pay is conditioned was rendered prior to the beginning of
the three months' period. (In re *Kinney Aluminum Co.,* D.C.S.D. Cal.
1948, 78 Supp. 565; Supp. Vol. 3 Moore's Collier on Bankruptcy, 192,
§ 64.203.) This theory is based upon the assumption that the purpose of
the priority granted to wage claimants is to benefit those who have lost
employment by reason of the bankruptcy and need the protection of the
statute. (In re *Kinney Aluminum Co., supra.*) It has been said, however,
that the priority was intended to provide that those who created assets
immediately prior to the filing of the petition and had not received payment for such creations should be set apart in a privileged class. (In re
Raiken, D.C.N.J. 1940, 33 F. Supp., 88.) This purpose would not be served
by allowing priority for the full amount of vacation pay.

The better reasoned rule is, we think, that announced by the Ninth
Circuit where Judge Healy, speaking for the court, said:

"Under the terms of the statute the compensation claimed must have
been earned within the three months' period and also must be due. If
any employee here had not, prior to bankruptcy, completed a year's continuous service no compensation for vacation time would have been due
him, regard being had to the wage agreement. All having completed the
required year's service prior to bankruptcy, vacation compensation may
fairly be regarded as due even though the vacation was not to be taken
until some later time; but the vacation had been earned by the perfor-

mance of the entire year's service, and only one-fourth of it earned during the three months preceding bankruptcy. We see no more justification for giving priority to vacation pay conditionally accruing prior to such three months' period than for giving priority to straight wages earned prior thereto." (Division of Labor Law Enforcement, *State of Cal. v. Sampsell,* 9 Cir., 1949, 172 F.2d 400, 401.)

We decide that the vacation pay of those entitled to it under the contract constituted wages earned over the period of a year but such wages are entitled to priority only to the extent of one-fourth of the annual vacation pay. In reaching this conclusion we are aware that some of the employees will perhaps have put in more time during the yearly period than others whose vacation pay would be the same, and we recognize the possibility that some, perhaps all, will have worked more in some of the quarter-annual periods than in others. Vacations, and their equivalents in vacation pay, result from arrangements to secure the well-being of employees and are factors in maintaining harmonious employer-employee relations. Each employee's status as such, under the vacation article of the agreement, continues even though there is an illness, a lay-off or other work interruption, and while continuing the inchoate vacation right accumulates. (Priority allowed for only that portion earned during the last three months.)

Cross v. Commons et al.

1953, Mich., 59 N.W.2d 41

This suit was initiated by plaintiff Cross, trustee in bankruptcy of defendant, to recover part of the value of property alleged to have been conveyed in fraud of creditors. The lower court gave judgment for defendant, and plaintiff has appealed.

BUTZEL, J.   George D. Commons was purchasing the home in which he resided in the township of Laketon, county of Muskegon, State of Michigan, on land contract. From time to time he had borrowed sums of money from Mark Jones who, on November 10, 1950, loaned him an additional amount so as to make the aggregate owing $5,000, which amount Commons agreed to pay to Jones in one year, with interest at 6 per cent. As security for the loan, Commons pledged his vendee's interest in the land contract to Jones. The debt became due on November 10, 1951. Commons was unable to pay and in lieu of foreclosure he assigned his equity in the property to Jones. At the time of the transfer there was $5,300 due Jones and $2,756.62 still owing to the vendors in the land contract, so that the total indebtedness was $8,056.62. It is conceded that the fair market value of the property was $10,000. Jones thereupon paid off the balance due the land contract vendors and transferred the premises to Charles O. White and Martha White, his wife, who sold the property for $10,000.

On November 23, 1951, an involuntary petition in bankruptcy was filed against Commons, and six days later he was adjudged a bankrupt. George H. Cross, as trustee in bankruptcy, brought the instant suit against Commons, Jones and wife, and White and wife, to recover the sum of $1,943.38, the difference between the $10,000 realized from the sale of the property and the sum of $5,300 due Jones and $2,756.38 due the vendors on the land contract. Plaintiff claims recovery on the theory that the transfer to Commons' equity in the property to Jones and wife and by them to White and wife was either a preference under the bankruptcy act or an unlawful, fraudulent conveyance, without consideration and in fraud of creditors. No consideration is shown to have been paid by White and wife to Jones and wife. The record indicates that over $500 was paid out for taxes, repairs and improvements after Commons assigned the contract and prior to the sale to third parties. The trial judge did not deem it necessary to consider additional amounts but based his opinion and decrees on the ground that Commons owned a homestead interest in the property at the time he conveyed to Jones and, as his equity was of a value of less than $2,500, the amount of homestead interest exempt under the law, such interest was immune from the claims of his creditors and his trustee in bankruptcy. He held that Commons had a right to do whatever he saw fit with his exempt property.

In our discussion we view the facts as found by the trial judge. He found that Commons was insolvent at the time he assigned the contract; that Jones and his wife knew of his financial condition notwithstanding the fact that bankruptcy proceedings had not been begun; that the fair value of the property was $10,000; and that Commons' equity, after deducting the amount due Jones and the balance still owing the vendors on the contract, was $1,943.38 for the recovery of which amount only suit was brought. . . .

In 6 Am. Jur., *Bankruptcy,* § 1102, it is said that:

> Creditors cannot complain of transfers of exempt property. A transfer of such property, although made within four months of bankruptcy and made while the debtor is insolvent, does not deplete the assets available for administration by the trustee in bankruptcy for the benefit of the general creditors. Therefore, a transfer of exempt property cannot constitute a preference.

. . . The Bankruptcy Act § 6, as amended (11 U.S.C.A. § 24), provides as follows:

> Sec. 6. Exemptions of bankrupts. This title shall not affect the allowance to bankrupts of the exemptions which are prescribed by the laws of the United States or by the State laws in force at the time of the filing of the petition in the State wherein they have had their domicile for the six months immediately preceding the filing of the petition, or for a longer portion of such six months than in any State. . . .

The trial judge also based his opinion on *Kleinert v. Lefkowitz* (271 Mich. 79, 259 N.W. 871, 875), wherein the history of the homestead exemption and the rights of the trustee in bankruptcy are carefully considered and where we said:

. . . The homestead exemption did not pass to the trustee in bankruptcy. Defendants could do with it what they pleased. Creditors were not defrauded by reason of any dealings therewith. By the terms of the bankruptcy statute the bankruptcy courts and the state courts have concurrent jurisdiction. Homestead exemptions are governed by the law of the state. The exemption involved is not necessarily the exemption of the bankrupt, but involves the right of his wife to claim a homestead exemption. The trustee in bankruptcy authorized by the referee to institute this suit invoked the jurisdiction of the state court, and in the courts of the state he has available to him he remedies conferred by the laws of the state. Defendants are entitled to the homestead rights of the real estate used and occupied by them as such.

. . . *The decree of the lower court, dismissing the bill, is affirmed, with costs to defendants.*

Priebe, Trustee of Estate of Giles Svehlek, Bankrupt v. Svehlek

1965 (Wisconsin) 245 F.Supp. 743

This is an action by the trustee in bankruptcy to set aside as fraudulent a conveyance of $10,000 made by the bankrupt to his wife. The bankrupt and his wife were joint tenants in a piece of real estate which served as their homestead. The defendant-wife was given a weekly allowance for running the household while the home was occupied. The house was sold in 1961 and the defendant and her husband received $19,000 after all encumbrances were paid. The husband transferred $10,000 to his wife, the defendant. Shortly thereafter he declared bankruptcy. It is the position of the plaintiff-trustee that the defendant made, without fair consideration, the conveyance of $10,000 which left him without sufficient funds to pay his debts and was therefore fraudulent as to his creditors. The defendant contends that the bankrupt was solvent when he purchased the property and made the gift of one-half interest in the property by means of a joint tenancy and that the $10,000 represents her share as joint tenant in the real estate.

GRUBB, D. J. The Wisconsin Supreme Court recently discussed the interests of joint tenants in the case of *Jezo v. Jezo* (23 Wis.2d 399, 406, 127 N.W.2d 246, 250 (1964)) as follows:

> The rule is, therefore, that the interests of joint tenants being equal during their lives, a presumption arises that upon dissolution of the joint tenancy during the lives of the cotenants, each is entitled to an equal share of the proceeds. This presumption is subject to rebuttal, however, and does not prevent proof from being introduced that the respective holdings and interests of the parties are unequal. The presumption may be rebutted by evidence showing the source of the actual cash outlay at the time of acquisition, the intent of the cotenant creating the joint tenancy to make a gift of the half interest to the other cotenant, unequal contribution by way of money or services, unequal expenditures in improving the property or freeing it from encumbrances and clouds, or other evidence raising inferences contrary to the idea of equal interest in the joint estate.

Considering the facts of this case in light of the principle expressed in the Jezo case, it is clear that the defendant did not have an interest in the property which would be sufficient consideration for $10,000. In this regard, it should be noted that the $10,000 is more than half of the $19,000 realized from the sale of the property.

The record in this case does not support the contention that a gift of one-half interest in the property was made in 1958 when the deed was executed to the defendant and her husband as joint tenants. The record does not demonstrate that the property was placed in joint tenancy for any reason other than mere convenience and in accordance with common practice.

The conveyance by the bankrupt of the $10,000 was one made without fair consideration. It is now necessary to decide whether the conveyance was one which left the bankrupt without sufficient funds to pay his debts as they matured.

In the latter part of 1960, the bankrupt decided to go into the restaurant business. As a result of this decision, he negotiated a lease of a building and personally guaranteed performance of the lease. He also entered into contracts for the purchase of equipment for the restaurant, which contracts were also guaranteed personally. The restaurant was operated for approximately three months before a gas explosion ended operations. At the time of the transfer of the $10,000, the total amount of these obligations from the restaurant, together with federal tax liabilities for 1958 and 1960, was approximately $55,000.

At the time of the transfer involved here, the assets of the bankrupt consisted of the equity in the home and stock in two corporations— Golden Chicken, Inc., and Golden Chicken Products, Inc. After the restaurant explosion and in February 1961, these two corporations had no income and paid no salary or dividends to the bankrupt. In March 1963, when the petition in bankruptcy was filed by the defendant, this stock was listed as worthless.

The conveyance of the $10,000 by the bankrupt to the defendant was one without fair consideration, which left the bankrupt without sufficient funds to pay his debts as they matured, and was fraudulent as to his creditors under Chapter 242, Wisconsin Statutes.

Judgment for the plaintiff.

In the Matter of R. C. Hendren, Debtor

1965 (Ohio) 240 F.Supp. 807

This is an appeal from a referee's decision denying a debtor the conversion from a Chapter XIII proceeding (Wage-Earner Plan) to a straight bankrupt. The debtor had filed in 1962. He, at that time, chose to proceed under the Wage-Earner Plan pursuant to Chapter XIII in which he made regular payments to a trustee in order to pay off his creditors on a long term basis. When Hendren found himself unable to continue making the monthly payments he petitioned to convert to a straight bankruptcy. The referee denied the petition and the debtor appealed.

PECK, J.   . . . Chapter XIII was intended as a rehabilitating device by which a debtor could be sheltered from his creditors while applying his future earnings to the payment of his debts. Straight bankruptcy envisages the liquidation of the bankrupt's estate for the payment of his creditors. The Act provides that a wage-earner is not subject to involuntary proceedings (11 U.S.C. Sect. 22, sub. b), so a debtor in financial difficulty may only seek relief under Chapter XIII or in voluntary bankruptcy proceedings.

The question presented here is whether a debtor who is in arrears in making payments pursuant to his confirmed Wage-Earner Plan has the right, under the provisions of the Act, to convert his plan to straight bankruptcy or whether such conversion lies within the discretion of the Referee. . . .

As relevant here, Section 1066 provides for certain failures of a plan ". . . if after confirmation a debtor defaults in any of the terms of the plan . . . the court shall . . . (2) where the petition has been filed under (Chapter XIII), enter an order dismissing the proceeding under this chapter or, with the consent of the debtor, adjudging him a bankrupt and directing that bankruptcy be proceeded with pursuant to the provisions of this title.". . .

In the case at bar . . . the debtor has fallen behind on his payments made pursuant to his plan and must be held to be in default. In view of the mandatory language of 11 U.S.C. Sect. 1066 . . . it is here concluded that when a debtor is in default under the provisions of his plan and the Referee does not dismiss it on his own motion, the debtor may convert to straight bankruptcy as a matter of right. . . .

To deny one who has sought to honorably pay his creditors in full under a Chapter XIII proceeding the right to convert to voluntary bankruptcy when the obligations of a wage-earner plan become intolerable would be inconsistent with the intent of the Bankruptcy Act, repugnant to the philosophy of this Court, and would substantially destroy the attraction of such a plan to the foundering but well intentioned wage earner. Accordingly,

It is ordered that the petition for review should be and it hereby is granted and sustained. . . .

CHAPTER 46
REVIEW QUESTIONS AND PROBLEMS

1. *A* is a farmer and owes many creditors. He has made some unwise investments and is now insolvent. One of his large creditors, *B*, is pressing for payment and in order to relieve this pressure *A* gave *B* a mortgage on his farm. May *A*'s other creditors force him into involuntary bankruptcy?

2. *A* is insolvent. His assets are $50,000 in value and his liabilities are $100,000. State whether the following transactions would 1) justify the filing of a petition in involuntary bankruptcy by his other creditors and 2) if so, they would be "recoverable preferences":

   a) *A* paid creditor *X* in full on an open account.
   b) *A* gave creditor *Y* a mortgage on part of *A*'s property.
   c) *A* paid creditor *Z* in full a debt secured by a mortgage on property owned by *A*.
   d) *A* borrowed $10,000 from creditor *R* and gave a mortgage on *A*'s property to secure the loan.

3. *C* sued *T* to recover on an indebtedness of $500, which *T* claimed was discharged in bankruptcy. *K* had sold the goods to *T* but had assigned the $500 claim to *C* and *T* had received notice of the assignment to *C*. *T* listed *K* as a creditor and notice of bankruptcy was sent to *K* but not to *C*. Consequently, *C,* not learning of bankruptcy, failed to file a claim. Because of this, *C* contends the claim is not discharged. Is *C* correct in his contention?

4. *A,* while insolvent, paid an obligation for $300 in favor of *B*. Although *A* was insolvent at the time, he was clearly unaware of the fact. Has he committed an act of bankruptcy?

5. A petition in involuntary bankruptcy was filed against *K* on Nov. 29. On Nov. 30 *K* sold to *M* $16,000 in accounts receivable for $15,600, *M* knowing of the petition in bankruptcy. *K* used these funds to meet payroll and taxes. On Dec. 10, *K* was adjudicated a bankrupt, and the trustee sought to obtain the return of the accounts. The court allowed the trustee to recover. Was this decision sound?

6. *B* owed *C* a past due indebtedness of $500 and induced the latter to extend the maturity of the indebtedness three years at 6 per cent interest by giving a chattel mortgage as security. Sixty days after the mortgage was given, *B* filed a petition in voluntary bankruptcy. Under what conditions, if any, will the trustee in bankruptcy be able to avoid the mortgage?

7. *A* became a voluntary bankrupt. At the time the petition was filed, he owed *B* the sum of $2,000, which was to fall due 60 days later. *B* owed *A* on a separate transaction the sum of $1,000, which was due at the time the petition was filed. May the trustee collect the $1,000 and force *B* to become an ordinary creditor as to the $2,000?

8. An insurance agent collected premiums but failed to remit to the company. The agent became a bankrupt and obtained his discharge. Is he still liable to the company for the premium? Was the agent a fiduciary?

BOOK SEVEN

Property

The Concept of Property

7-1 The Significance of Property. All life is concerned with and affected by property. It is the motive for economic activity, the subject matter of succession and inheritance, the substance with which debts are settled, and the mark of prestige. It is that with which businessmen deal and is the measure of wealth.

Property, whether communal or private, can exist only in an ordered society. Property depends upon the economic pattern and social structure of the community. In a communistic society, communal property predominates and individual interests are subordinated to the interests of the group. In an individualistic society, private property predominates and group interests are subordinate. Private property is made secure by rules of law which impose duties upon people not to interfere with the liberty, person, or property of the individual.

In Anglo-American law, the right of private property and freedom of contract stimulated by the ideals of individualism became the basis of the dominant economic philosophy of western civilization. The security of personal liberty and private property was the principal function of common law. Government under common law was limited to the preservation of order, thus permitting the pursuit of business and liberty of contract to enjoy unhampered activity. Property became more than things: it became rights created by contract. Contract rights—enforceable promises —became valuable and represented wealth. Thus, the contract in the free enterprise system was the effective instrument by which property was created.

Since our economic structure rests upon various concepts of property, some consideration of its history, nature, and function is of primary importance. During the course of its history, the term *property* has had different meanings. In one context the word means things—land and movables—and in another the word means rights or claims that are invisible, that "can neither be seen nor handled; are creatures of the mind and exist only in contemplation." The term may also mean the union of both physical and non-physical concepts. The term *property* is also said to connote an aggregate of legal relationships existing between persons with respect to or concerning physical things like land and automobiles, and intangibles such as contract rights, debts, wave-lengths, news, patent rights, and weather expectations. In order that businessmen may communicate accurately and have a "meeting of the minds" when dealing in the area of property law, it is important that the term *property* mean the same thing to different persons at different times. It will be the purpose of the following sections to set out in detail some of the variant meanings given to the term *property*.

7-2 The Components of Property. The term *property* or property itself is meaningless except as it is associated with individuals. The terms used in expressing this association are *ownership, title,* and *possession.*

Ownership is a word signifying degrees; it is a "more or less" word. To *own* is to have. But the question is, what must one have to be an owner? Ownership denotes the *quantum* of property interest one has. An owner may have all the legal relations or interests concerning the subject matter of property, or an owner may have less than all the legal interests in a particular thing, tangible or intangible, while at the same time another may have legal interests in the same thing. Thus, a lessor has an interest in land which is limited by the interest held by the lessee. The lessor is said to hold the fee and the lessee the leasehold. Both own property and are in a position under the proper circumstances to exclude the other. The meaning of the word "owner" is dependent upon the context in which it is used.[1]

The word *title* is often used synonymously with *ownership*. The word signifies the method by which ownership is acquired, whether by gift, by purchase, or by other methods. It also indicates the evidence by which the claim of ownership is established—the deed or other written instrument. It includes not only the method and the evidence, but the result. The result which obtains from the method, the evidence, and the documents used is characterized by such words as *legal title, equitable title, good title, marketable title, tax title, fee simple title,* and so forth.

The word *possession* is difficult to define precisely. It links together the concept of physical control or dominion by a person over property with his personal and mental relationship to it. It is distinguished from mere custody, since the latter is limited to physical control only, without any interest therein adverse to the true owner. Possession, however, means not only physical control or the power to have physical control, but also legal sanctions therewith to enforce continued relation with the thing, or, if deprived of such relation, to have the same restored.

[1] *Robinson v. Walker,* page 943.

In determining whether the legal consequence "possession" is present, the court must examine in each particular case the claimant's intent and physical relation to the thing in question. Possession may be actual; that is, physically held by the owner, or physically held by one over whom the owner has control, such as a servant or agent. Possession may be constructive; that is, physical control may be in one person while another has a better right. *X* finds *B*'s watch, knowing it to be *B*'s watch. *X* appropriates it to his own use, and sells and delivers it to *C*. *X* is guilty of larceny because he dispossessed *B* of the watch, although at the time *B* was not in physical possession of the watch. *B* is entitled to the return of the watch from *C*. A thief cannot pass title to stolen goods even to an innocent purchaser. A finder of lost things as against the true owner has no property right but as to all others he has a better right.

The meanings found in the word *possession* depend upon the fact situation involved and the end to be achieved. Thus, the fact situation and policy reasons resulting in possession in a finder case, abandoned property, acquisition of wild animals, trespass, crimes, attachments by sheriffs, and illegal holding under statutes are all different.

7-3 Property as Things. In early law it was difficult to understand how there could be ownership, possession, and transfer of rights, with respect to things, without possessing and transferring the thing itself. A thing could be seen, touched, possessed, and delivered; hence the *thing* was the property. Rights to the thing were embodied in the physical object, so that the handing over of the physical object was essential to endowing another with property, ownership, title, possession, and all the other attributes one could have in a thing.[2] Things owned and possessed were of two kinds: land and chattels. Land, a fixed, immovable thing, could not be handed over or delivered. In England under the feudal system, in order to satisfy the requirement of physical delivery, land was transferred by a symbolic process called *feoffment,* by which a twig or clod taken from the land by the grantor was delivered to the grantee. This symbol is said, in the proper case, to have seised the grantee with fee simple title. This historical symbolism is reflected in our present method of conveying land. Today the transfer of land is accomplished by the execution, and delivery, of a thing—a written instrument—called a *deed.*

No difficulty was experienced in owning, possessing, and manually delivering a movable thing. The most significant movable things in early civilization were cattle. Their mobility facilitated their use as a medium of exchange. From the term *cattle* is derived the word *chattel.* These two types of things, land and chattels, became known as two different kinds of property. Land became real property and chattels became personal property. Such designation arose out of the types of remedies developed to protect rights with respect to land and chattels.

One seeking a remedy against interference with the land, such as eviction or dispossession, brought an action to recover the land itself;

2 *City of Atlanta v. J. J. Black & Co.,* page 946.

that is, the ousted plaintiff sought to recover the thing—the *res*. The action was called an action *in rem,* or a real action. Thus, the thing protected—land—derived its name *real property*.

Since a movable thing—a chattel—could be stolen, destroyed, or transferred away, a remedy other than the recovery of the thing or *res* was necessary. An action against the wrongdoer for restitution by way of damages was instituted. This action was against the wrong-doing person, and was called an action *in personam,* or a personal action. Thus, the things protected—movable chattels—derived their name, *personal property*.

Land has a fixed location. Therefore, its title, ownership, method of transfer, inheritance, and succession are governed by the law of the place where it is located. The law which controls movables, however, is highly influenced by the law of the domicile of the owner of the chattels.

Land and chattels as "things" are designated as "property" not only in common parlance, but also in court opinions, legal texts, and statutes. The following examples are illustrative. "The term 'property' as commonly used denotes an external object over which the right of property is exercised." "A man's property consists of lands, buildings, automobiles, and so on." "Property is of a fixed and tangible nature, capable of being had in possession and transmitted to another, such as houses, lands and chattels." By statutes in many states, "dogs are hereby declared to be personal property."

There are certain things incapable of being included within the term "property" in this context. Such things as light, air, clouds, running water, and wild animals by reason of their nature are not subject to exclusive dominion and control and hence are not property in this sense. However, wild animals when caught and reduced to possession as physical things are included within the term *property*. Although the owner of land may have no natural rights to "light" and "air," he may acquire, by way of easement, the right to have light and air come onto his land from that of an adjacent owner. Likewise, an owner of land has the right that the air over his land be free from pollution. Property rights in running water may be acquired by use of the water or by ownership of the abutting land.

Commercial necessities and historical considerations have endowed many printed and written instruments, such as commercial paper, bills of lading, warehouse receipts, and certificates of stock, with attributes of a thing or chattel. Thus, as things, their physical delivery is often essential to serve as objective evidence of transfer of the rights which they represent.

7-4 Property as Non-physical or Incorporeal. The concept that only things were the subject of property and that property was more than the thing itself developed during the days of feudal land tenure in England. Out of the English feudal land system there developed many intangible and invisible inheritable rights called "incorporeal hereditaments." "These rights grew out of, touched or concerned the land, but they were not the substance of the thing itself." Among such rights were the right to use common pasture land and parks, called "the commons," and rights to annuities and rents. Such incorporeal interests are recognized in our law today. A lease granting the right to explore for oil accompanied by a duty to pay royalties, if oil is found, creates no property in a thing, but an invisible, intangible right concerning the land. Such right is property. For example, easements, leases, and various types of restrictive covenants which touch and concern land are property interests protected by the courts.

7-5 Property as Relationships. In the preceding paragraphs land, chattels, commercial paper, bonds, negotiable instruments, and written and printed documents are considered things, called *property*.

In order to have a more complete idea of the meaning of the term *property*, we shall in this section refer to things—land, chattels, commercial paper, bonds, written and printed documents, contracts, debts, and choses in action—not as property, but as the *subject matter* of property. The term *property* as here used means a part or the totality of relationships existing between persons with respect to either physical things, or with respect to the non-physical such as contracts, debts, choses in action, patent rights, news, and pensions. The particular relationships with which we are concerned are "rights," "powers," "privileges," and "immunities."

These legal relations are defined by the Restatement of the Law of Property [3] as follows:

"A right is a legally enforceable claim of one person against another, that the other shall do a given act or shall not do a given act." For every right there is a corresponding duty. A's right concerning the ownership, possession, and use of his land, home, and chattels places B under a duty not to interfere with or deny A his rights.

A power is an ability on the part of a person to produce a change in a given legal relation by doing or not doing a given act. For every power there is a corresponding liability. A gives B, his agent, authority to transfer his, A's land. B has the power to change A's legal relation with respect to the land; thus A is under a liability that such change will be made. *Liability* here does not mean duty. One often says "liability to pay money." What is meant in this situation is, duty to pay money.

"A privilege is a legal freedom on the part of one person as against another to do a given act or legal freedom not to do a given act." For every privilege there is an absence of a right. A has the privilege of painting his house; all others have no right or concern with his privilege.

"An immunity is a freedom on the part of one person against having a legal relation altered by a given act or omission to act on the part of another person." For every immunity on one side there is a disability on the other. A owes B money, secured by a mortgage. A pays B. A is now immune from any legal right of B's to foreclose, and B is under a disability.

[3] *American Law Institute, Restatement of Property*, Sec. 1-5 (1936).

If a person has all the rights, powers, privileges, and immunities that one is capable of having with one person or with all the persons in the world with respect to or concerning land or chattels, tangible and intangible, then such aggregate of legal relations constitutes *property*.

One may, however, have property with respect to a thing or intangible situation and not have all the relationships. These relationships are continually changing. If *A* exercises a power and mortgages his land to *B*, *A* has cut down his right relations and endowed *B* with right relations concerning the land. Again, if the state passes restrictive legislation concerning the use of A's land, his legal relations have been diminished.

In order to identify the relationships termed "property" concerning things, the Restatement of the Law of Property uses the word *interest*. "The word interest includes . . . varying aggregates of legal rights, powers, privileges, and immunities and distributively [means] any one of them." Thus, rights, powers, privileges, and immunities with respect to land are "interests in land," or likewise, interests in things.

If property is to be considered as "legal relations" it is necessary to consider how such relationships came into existence and how they will be protected. Land and things are just things capable of being subjects of property until relations arise between people which will be given recognition by a government. No legal relationships or property interest can be said to exist unless some method is afforded to enforce them. This, of course, is the function of government and law—the courts and other agencies of society will protect the relations of rights, power, privileges, and immunities with which the government has endowed the person. Thus, if there is a trespass upon one's land the trespasser can be compelled to cease trespassing by a court and in addition can be required to make restitution for damages.

It is fundamental that a person who has "property"—an enforceable legal right-duty relation—has a power of destroying his own relation and creating relations in others. Thus, he has the power to enter into contracts and transfer all his legal interests by a sale or he can give them to someone else. He may part with some of his interests and reserve to himself those which remain. For example, he may lease his land or he may borrow money and give a mortgage on the land as security for the mortgagee-lender. In each case he has divided his legal interests by creating legal interests in a lessee and a mortgagee and retaining legal interests in himself. When the lease expires the interest of the lessee terminates; when the debt is paid the interest of the mortgagee no longer exists; there is now an immunity from the interests of either the tenant or the creditor. The courts will give recognition to the interests of tenant and creditor during the period of their existence; likewise protection will be afforded to the "owner" upon their termination.

If a person has a totality of all the relationships regarding the land, he then has complete ownership or property. He may, however, from time to time have less than all the relationships or interests in land. When he leases the land, grants an easement over, above, or below the land, or dedicates portions to the city for streets, he diminishes his legal relationships. Likewise a person may have his relationships reduced by government through its exercise of the police power by way of zoning or its power of eminent domain or of taxation.

A person's interests in land and in things can be said to consist of a "bundle of rights"—he may have all of the elements of the bundles or some may be vested in others. Just how few relationships one may have and still have property cannot be definitely ascertained. If a court gives a judgment in favor of the particular relationships asserted, then it may be said that a "property interest" exists. As we have seen, the term *property* connotes a multiplicity of rights, duties, powers, and immunities. The term may include all or some of the relationships. One may have or create all of these elements in another, or one may have or be endowed with a very limited number of these elements and still have a property interest. Thus, a person in possession of illegal goods as against the state may have no property; however, he may have a property interest as against third persons. Even though a statute makes ownership and possession of slot machines illegal, "there yet exists certain rights [sic: privileges] in the individual who may possess such a contraband article as against any one other than the state. The owner [sic: person in possession] at least has the privilege of destroying the machine, he also has the right to surrender it to the authorities. It is true his right to the possession of the slot machine is by law very limited; nevertheless, he has certain claims and powers not possessed by any other, which invests in him something real and tangible. . . . There are no property rights innate in objects themselves. Such rights as there are are in certain persons as against others with respect to the particular objects in question. Since property or title is a complex bundle of rights, duties, powers, and immunities, the taking away of some or a great many of these elements does not entirely destroy the property.

The right to be free from unreasonable noise of low-flying planes and the privilege of quiet use and enjoyment of land are forms of property. The "continuing and frequent low flights over the appellant's land constituted a taking of property. . . . Property in a thing consists not merely in its ownership and possession, but in the right of its use, enjoyment and disposal.

The change of the grade of a street which lessens the enjoyment of an easement of ingress and egress by abutting property owners is the taking of property.[4]

Injunctive relief has been granted to restrain the chemical seeding of clouds, because such seeding dissipated and scattered the clouds, preventing rain. Such conduct is an interference with a property right, namely, the right to a possibility that it may rain.[5]

Which legal relations in the total bundle are most significant, important, and decisive cannot be given a uniform fixed determination. The relationship concept of the term *property* is used by the court as a tool

4 *In re Forsstrom et ux.*, 44, page 946.
5 *Southwest Weather Research v. Rounsaville,* page 948.

to solve the particular problem before it. Whether particular relations are legally protected interests and called "property" or the "thingified" concept of property will depend upon the circumstances, the purpose and intention of the parties, and the result sought to be obtained by the court.

Thus, in construing statutes involving crimes and tort liability, the court may emphasize a "thingified" concept of property. In our technological and complex society, new relationships are continually being established and asserted which demand protection. When these new relationships are given judicial protection, they become legal interests or property. For example, in advertising and marketing, when ideas expressed in word, form, shapes, or modes of packaging acquire an economic value, the right to use and exploit such ideas becomes a property interest protected by the courts. The right to exclude others from the use of collected news items, the rebroadcasting of radio and television programs, the right to have unimpaired the rain potential of clouds over one's land, and the privilege of unhampered entrance to and from the street by an abutting landowner are illustrations of newly created property interests. The courts are frequently called upon to rule as to whether or not a given situation gives rise to property rights.[6]

7-6 Property in a Legal Environment. The foregoing discussion of the concepts of property must be considered in their proper perspective. They are simply the tools used by the courts in arriving at decisions when conflicting claims regarding land and things are brought before them. It remains true that in common parlance people think of "property" as being the thing itself rather than their relationships in connection with the thing. Thus, when a business man states that he "owns" his business he is conveying the notion that the building, furniture and fixtures, delivery equipment, and inventory belong to him *in toto*. He regards these *things* as his "property" and is not likely to give consideration to the more philosophical aspects of the theories relating to the nature of his interests. It is necessary therefore in business transactions to give recognition to the "thingified concept" and the word "property" is often used loosely—personal property; real property—without spelling out its true significance. However, a true understanding of the law relating to business transactions requires an understanding of what lies behind the commonly used word. It is particularly important to recognize that property encompasses much more than physical things—that contract rights and other intangibles are "property"; and that more than one person may have interests in the same property.

The law is flexible and is constantly in a process of change and development as new social, economic, and business needs arise. Codifications such as the Uniform Commercial Code do not constitute a straightjacket in business; they rather give a needed certainty yet allow room for growth. Business does need an element of certainty in its legal environment and

---

[6] *Davies v. Carnation Company*, page 950.

sudden changes in the law with respect to business transactions and "property" used in such transactions could be disastrous. The Code has been said to constitute not a *revolution* or an upheaval in the commercial law, but rather that it is a major *evolutionary* development in the law. It does affect property relationships between buyers, sellers, financers, and others but it is based upon commercial understandings and recognized customs and usages of business people.

The concept of "property" is an expanding one and the development of new techniques in business and technological changes may result in new concepts of property as yet not conceived in the mind of man.

7-7 Kinds of Property. Property is classified as either personal property or real property from the standpoint of its physical characteristics. Land and things affixed to or growing upon the land come under the heading of real property; and as will be noted a separate body of real property law has developed, both for historical reasons and reasons associated with the peculiar characteristics of land. All other property is said to be personal property and, in general, it is subject to different treatment under the law than is real property.

The Uniform Commercial Code, as has been noted, covers only personal property and sets forth rules and principles concerned with its sale and transfer and security interests in such property. The Code does, however, refer to three situations in which real property is involved: priority rights where personal property is so attached to land as to become a fixture; the sale of goods such as timber to be severed from the realty; and the sale of or a security interest in crops to be grown upon land. Aside from this the law relating to real property—its sale and transfer and security interests in it—must be found in other sources. However, the interrelationship of real property law and personal property law such as the Code must be borne in mind as for example where a note, personal property, is secured by a mortgage on land as a part of the purchase transaction or a loan.

It must also be noted that the Code by no means encompasses all of the law relating to personal property—its focus is simply upon commercial transactions involving the various types and kinds of personal property described in the Code.

THE CONCEPT OF PROPERTY CASES

Robinson v. Walker

1965 (Ill.) 211 N.E.2d 488

Plaintiff, Faye Robinson, brought this suit for personal injuries allegedly resulting from an armed assault upon her by the defendant, Henry Walker. She bases her claim against the defendant on the Dram Shop Act (Ill. Rev. Stat., Ch. 43, 135 (1961), set forth below). She sought recovery against the land trustees who held title to the real estate upon which the taverns were respectively located. (A land trustee is one who is involved in a security interest in land.) One land trustee, defendant, Central National Bank in Chicago, moved for summary judgment in its favor. Judgment in favor of the Bank was ordered by the trial court. Plaintiff appealed from that order.

BURMAN, J.   The portion of the Dram Shop Act relevant to this appeal provides:

> Every person, who shall be injured, in person or property by any intoxicated person, shall have a right of action in his or her own name, severally or jointly, against any person or persons who shall, by selling or giving alcoholic liquor, have caused the intoxication, in whole or in part, of such person; and any person owning, renting, leasing or permitting the occupation of any building or premises, and having knowledge that alcoholic liquors are to be sold therein, . . . shall be liable, severally or jointly, with the person or persons selling or giving liquors aforesaid, . . . (Ill., Rev. Stat. ch. 43, 135 (1961)

Basing her claim against the Bank upon this language, plaintiff alleges that the Bank, as land trustee, is the "owner" of the property upon which one of the taverns is located, and that the Bank had knowledge of the sale of alcoholic liquors on the premises. Defendant contends that as a land trustee it holds "naked" title to the property, without any accompanying right to manage or to control its use; that it had disclosed to plaintiff the beneficiaries of the land trust, who are in active control of the premises; and that the Dram Shop Act, in imposing liability upon an owner, did not intend to impose liability upon a land trustee under these circumstances.

On the question of who had the right to manage and to control the use of the real estate, the Trust Agreement pertaining to that real estate, which was attached to defendant's motion for summary judgment, provides:

> The beneficiary or beneficiaries here under shall in his, her or their own right have the full management of said real estate and control of the selling, renting and handling thereof, and any beneficiary or his or her agent shall handle the rents thereof and the proceeds of any sales of said property, and said Trustee shall not be required to do anything in the management of control of said real estate.

The Trust Agreement also sets forth the names and addresses of the beneficiaries.

Appellant (Plaintiff) principally contends that the Dram Shop Act simply imposes liability upon the "owner" of the premises and makes no requirement that he have the right to manage or to control. We have not been referred to, nor have we found, any Illinois cases which are directly in point.

In cases arising under statutes other than the Dram Shop Act, the word "owner" as applied to land has been held to have no fixed meaning which can be declared to be applicable under all circumstances. (*Coombs v. People,* 198 Ill. 586, 64 N.E. 1056.) The word usually signifies one who has the legal or rightful title, but this is not always the sense in which it is employed. It is not rigid in meaning, especially in ordinances and statutes, and frequently is used to denote one in control, but having less than absolute title. The meaning usually depends, in great measure, upon the context and the subject matter to which it is applied. (*De Luxe Motor Cab Company v. Dever,* 252 Ill.App. 156) In *Woodward Governor Company v. City of Loves Park* (335 Ill.App. 528, 82 N.E.2d 387), the court was required to determine whether a railroad having an easement over certain property was the "owner" of that property within the meaning of a statute relating to the disconnection of land from a city. In holding that the railroad was such an owner, the court said: ". . . there is no uniform guide as to what meaning shall be ascribed to the term 'owner' and . . . consideration must be given to the nature and purpose of the statute involved." (335 Ill.App., at 535, 82 N.E.2d, at 390)

Mr. Justice Schwartz, speaking for this court in the recent case of *Osinger v. Christian* (43 Ill.App.2d 480, 193 N.E.2d 872), addressed himself to the question of the purpose of the Dram Shop Act:

> The dramshop act is designed to fulfill a need for discipline of traffic in liquor and to provide a remedy for the evils and dangers which flow from such traffic. (43 Ill.App.2d, at 485, 193 N.E.2d, at 875.)

Almost half a century earlier in the U.S. Supreme Court, in upholding the constitutionality of the Illinois Dram Shop Act as applied to the lessor of the premises, characterized the statute as, ". . . for the regulation of the traffic in intoxicating liquors, . . . with a view to repress the evil consequences which may result therefrom." (*Eiger v. Garrity,* 246 U.S. 97, at 102, 38 S.Ct. 298, at 300, 62 L.Ed. 596.)

We conclude that the purposes of the Dram Shop Act would in no way be served by imposing liability upon one who, as defendant here, holds "naked" title and has no right to exercise any control over the use of the property for the sale of intoxicating liquors; and that such a title holder was not intended to be included within the provision imposing liability upon an owner. Holding a land trustee liable would not provide "discipline of traffic in liquor," for the trustee neither participates in nor has control over such traffic.

Plaintiff devotes much of her argument to the problem of whether the judgment against defendant should be in its representative capacity or in its individual capacity. Another point raised by her is that the interest of the beneficiaries of the land trust is personal property, not real property. Finally, she contends that the pleadings raise an issue of fact as to the knowledge of defendant of the sale of liquor on the premises. The view we take of the case, however, makes it unnecessary for us to resolve these questions.

The judgment is therefore affirmed.

City of Atlanta v. J. J. Black & Company
1964 (Ga.) 139 S.E.2d 515

J. J. Black & Co., plaintiff, brought an action against the City of Atlanta and the architects and structural engineers employed by the city. He alleged that because of an unusual and unconventional roof design on the high school building on which he was contractor he could not pour the concrete for the roof in a manner acceptable to the architects. He claimed that he had been put to unnecessary and extra losses and expenses. The contract price was paid and accepted but he brought action to receive his extra expenses. The city claims that the statute requires *ante litem* notice (notice before suit is brought) and demurred on the ground that such notice had not been given.

FELTON, J. The plaintiff in error city, in arguing its general demurrer, contends that the petition was fatally defective in that it failed to allege compliance on the part of the plaintiff contractor with the *ante litem* notice, therefore, it must be strictly construed and not extended beyond it plain and explicit terms. . . . The statute requires the *ante litem* notice for claims "on account of injuries to person or *property.*" "Property" at common law was limited to tangible realty or personalty, therefore, cannot be extended to include property rights in contracts. The purpose of the law, as expressed in *Mayor &c. of Buford v. Light* (65 Ga.App. 99, 100, 15 S.E.2d 459, 460) "was simply to give to the municipality notice that the citizen or property owner has a grievance against it. It is necessary only that the city shall be put on notice of the general character of the complaint, and, in a general way, of the time, place, and extent of the injury. . ." In the case of claims arising out of contracts, as contrasted with torts, the city, being a party to the contract, is already on notice as to the existence and the circumstances of the contract which is the basis of the claim, therefore the reason for such notice does not exist. [The plaintiff prevailed in spite of the adverse ruling on injury to "property."]

In re Forsstrom et ux.
1934, 44 Ariz. 472, 38 P.2d 878

LOCKWOOD, J. The question is solely one of law, and the facts may be briefly stated as follows: The main tracks of the Southern Pacific Railroad cross North Stone Avenue near an intersection of Sixth Street at the present grade of said Avenue. The authorities of the City of Tucson, believing that such grade crossing is a menace and hazard to public travel on the street determined to abolish it by the construction of an underpass or subway below the tracks. . . . (By so doing) ingress and egress to the premises of the abutting property owners will be made more difficult. . . .

We come then to the question as to whether the proposed action of the City of Tucson, insofar as it affects petitioners at all, is a ["taking of property"] within the meaning of the statute. . . .

In order that we may understand the better what is meant by a "taking" of property, we should have a clear knowledge of what property really is. The word is used at different times to express many varying ideas. Sometimes it is taken in common parlance to denote a physical object, as where one says an automobile or a horse is his property. On careful consideration, however, it is plain that "property" in the true and legal sense does not mean a physical object itself, but certain rights over the object. A piece of land in an unexplored and uninhabited region which belongs to no one does not necessarily undergo any physical change merely by reason of its later becoming the property of any person. A wild animal may be exactly the same physically before and after it is captured, but, when it is running free in the forest, no one would speak of it as property. We must therefore look beyond the physical object itself for the true definition of property. Many courts and writers have attempted to define it, using different words, but meaning in essence the same thing. One of the great writers on jurisprudence says:

"Property is entirely the creature of the law. . . . There is no form, or color, or visible trace, by which it is possible to express the relation which constitutes property. It belongs not to physics, but to metaphysics; it is altogether a creature of the mind." (Bentham: *Works* (Ed. 1843), Vol. 1, p. 308.)

> (Other authorities say) . . . Property itself, in a legal sense, is nothing more than the "exclusive right of possession, enjoying and disposing of a thing. . . ." (*Chicago & Western, etc. R.R. Co. v. Englewood, etc. Co.*, 115 Ill. 375, 4 N.E. 246, 249, 56 Am. Rep 173.)
>
> Property, in its broader and more appropriate sense, is not alone the chattel or the land itself, but the right to freely possess, use, and alienate the same; and many things are considered property which have no tangible existence, but which are necessary to the satisfactory use and enjoyment of that which is tangible. (*City of Denver v. Bayer*, 7 Colo. 113, 2 P. 6.)
>
> It is used in the constitution in a comprehensive and unlimited sense, and so it must be construed. . . . It need not be any physical or tangible property which is subject to a tangible invasion. . . . The right to light and air, and access is equally property. . . . (*State v. Superior Court*, 26 Wash. 278, 66 P. 385, 388.)

It would follow from these definitions and explanations of the meaning of the term "property" that since it consists, not in tangible things themselves, but in certain rights in and appurtenant to them, it would logically follow that, when a person is deprived of any of these rights, he is to that extent deprived of his property, and that it is taken in the true sense, although his title and possession of the physical object remains undisturbed. Any substantial interference, therefore, with rights over a physical object which destroys or lessens its value, or by which the use and enjoyment thereof by its owner is in any substantial degree abridged or destroyed, is both in law and in fact a "taking" of property. It is apparently only of recent years that the meaning of the word "taking" when used in regard to eminent domain has been properly understood by the majority of the courts, although it would seem obvious that a careful analysis of the true nature of "property" would have shown it long since. . . .

From the very nature of these rights of user and of exclusion, it is evident that they cannot be materially abridged without, *ipso facto,* taking the owner's property. If the right of indefinite user is an essential element of absolute property or complete ownership, whatever physical interference annuls this right takes "property"—although the owner may still have left to him valuable rights (in the article) of a more limited and circumscribed nature. He has not the same property that he formerly had. Then, he had an unlimited right; now, he has only a limited right. His absolute ownership has been reduced to a qualified ownership. Restricting *A*'s unlimited right of using one hundred acres of land to a limited right of using the same land, may work a far greater injury to *A* than to take from him the title in fee simple to one acre, leaving him the unrestricted right of using the remaining ninety-nine acres. Nobody doubts that the latter transaction would constitute a "taking" of property. Why not the former? . . .

> Property in land must be considered, for many purposes, not as an absolute, unrestricted dominion, but as an aggregation of qualified privileges, the limits of which are prescribed by the equality of rights, and the correlation of rights and obligations necessary for the highest enjoyment of land by the entire community of proprietors. . . .

. . . The changing of the street grade which lessens the enjoyment of the easement of ingress and egress is within the true meaning of the constitutional provision [and a "taking"] which injuriously affects the value of adjoining property [and] is "damage." The damage is to the easement of the ingress and egress.

Southwest Weather Research v. Rounsaville

1958 (Tex. Civ. App.) 320 S.W.2d 211 Affirmed; 327 S.W.2d 417

PER CURIAM.   This is an appeal from an injunction issued by the Eighty-third District Court, Jeff Davis County, Texas, which said injunction commands the appellants "to refrain from seeding the clouds by artificial nucleation or otherwise and from in any other manner or way interfering with the clouds and the natural conditions of the air, sky, atmosphere and air space over plaintiffs' lands and in the area of plaintiffs' lands to in any manner, degree or way affect, control or modify the weather conditions on or about said lands. . . ."

Appellees are ranchmen residing in West Texas counties, and appellants are owners and operators of certain airplanes, and equipment generally used in what they call a "weather modification program" and those who contracted and arranged for their services.

It is not disputed that appellants did operate their airplanes at various times over portions of lands belonging to the appellees, for the purpose of and while engaged in what is commonly called "cloud seeding." Appellants do not deny having done this, and testified through the president of the company that the operation would continue unless restrained. He stated, "We seeded the clouds to attempt to suppress the hail." The controversy is really over appellants' right to seed clouds or otherwise modify weather conditions over appellees' property. . . .

We have carefully considered the voluminous record and exhibits that were admitted in evidence, and have concluded that the trial court had ample evidence on which to base his findings and with which to justify the issuance of the injunction. . . .

Appellants maintain that appellees have no right to prevent them from flying over appellees' lands; that no one owns the clouds unless it be the state, and that the trial court was without legal right to restrain appellants from pursuing a lawful occupation; also that the injunction is too broad in its terms. . . .

Appellees urge here that the owner of land also owns in connection therewith certain so-called "natural rights," and cites us the following quotation from (*Spann v. City of Dallas,* III Tex. 350, 235 S.W. 513, 514), in which Chief Justice Nelson Phillips states:

> Property in a thing consists not merely in its ownership and possession, but in the unrestricted right of use, enjoyment and disposal. Anything which destroys any of these elements of property, to that extent destroys the property itself. The substantial value of property lies in its use. If the right of use be denied, the value of the property is annihilated and ownership is rendered a barren right. . . .
>
> The very essence of American constitutions is that the material rights of no man shall be subject to the mere will of another. (*Yick Wo v. Hopkins,* 118 U.S. 356, 6 S.Ct. 1064, 30 L.Ed. 220.)

In Volume 34, *Marquette Law Review,* at page 275, this is said:

> Considering the property right of every man to the use and enjoyment of his land, and considering the profound effect which natural rainfall has upon the realization of this right, it would appear that the benefits of natural rainfall should come within the scope of judicial protection, and a duty should be imposed on adjoining landowners not to interfere therewith.

In the *Stanford Law Review,* November 1948, Volume 1, in an article entitled, "Who Owns the Clouds?", the following statements occur:

> The landowner does have rights in the water in clouds, however, the basis for these rights is the common law doctrine of natural rights. Literally, the term "natural rights" is well chosen; these rights protect the landowner's use of his land in its natural condition. . . .
>
> All forms of natural precipitation should be elements of the natural condition of the land. Precipitation, like air, oxygen, sunlight, and the soil itself, is an essential to many reasonable uses of the land. The plant and animal life on the land are both ultimately dependent upon rainfall. To the extent that rain is important to the use of land, the landowner should be entitled to the natural rainfall.

In *California Law Review,* December 1957, Volume 45, No. 5, in an article, "Weather Modification," are found the following statements:

> "What are the rights of the landowner or public body to natural rainfall? It has been suggested that the right to receive rainfall is one of those natural rights' which is inherent in the full use of land from the fact of its natural contact with moisture in the air. . . .
>
> "Any use of such air or space by others which is injurious to his land, or which constitutes an actual interference with his possession or his beneficial use thereof would be a trespass for which he would have remedy." (*Hinman v. Pacific Air Transport,* 9 Cir. 83 F.2d 755, 758.)

Appellees call our attention to various authorities that hold that although the old *ad coelum* doctrine has given way to the reality of present-day conditions, an unreasonable and improper use of the air space over the owner's land can constitute a trespass (*Guity v. Consumers Power Co.,* D.C., 36 F. Supp. 21; Restatement of the Law of Torts, paragraph 194 etc.; *United States v. Causby,* 328 U.S. 256, 66 S.Ct. 1062, 90 L.Ed. 1206). Other cases are cited, also, and apparently hold that the landowner, while not owning or controlling the entire air space over his property, is entitled to protection against improper or unreasonable use thereof or entrance thereon. . . .

We believe that under our system of government the landowner is entitled to such precipitation as nature deigns to bestow. We believe that the landowner is entitled, therefore and thereby, to such rainfall as may come from clouds over his own property that nature in her caprice may provide. It follows, therefore, that this enjoyment of or entitlement to the benefits of nature should be protected by the courts if interfered with improperly and unlawfully.

Davies v. Carnation Company
1965 352 F.2d 393

The plaintiff, claiming to be a researcher in the food industry, had written an unsolicited letter to one D. D. Peebles who had develped a powdered milk product which was distributed by the Carnation Company under the name, Carnation Instant Milk. In the letter she expressed interest in testing the product in her "home test kitchen." The letter was referred to Carnation Company and she subsequently wrote that in testing Carnation Instant Milk, she had "found a value and property therein, which is both unexpected and extremely important from the marketing and promotional aspect." She inquired as to whether she should discuss the matter with Mr. Peebles or "contact the Carnation Company directly." She concluded, "The marketing ideas we develop we assign to an interested company, in consideration of a fee or a retainer arrangement." Thereafter, the general manager of Carnation's commercial sales division advised her of his plan to visit New York City, and expressed interest in meeting with her at her convenience. This brought a written reply, in which she offered the following:

(a) I am ready to make written disclosure to you which if you accept or use in connection with Patent protection, or any other purpose, you would compensate me the sum of $3500. And, I am also ready to serve in a consulting capacity to your firm, or advertising agency, for an amount to be discussed. (b) If you do not use the subject of my disclosure, you will not be obligated to me.

Thereafter, a representative of Carnation's corporate department wrote a letter informing her that because of certain considerations, Carnation had adopted a policy not to consider any suggestion or idea of this type unless the person wishing to submit the idea or suggestion first signs a release form. After receiving this letter, she replied, protesting that the nature of her work demanded an arrangement opposed to Carnation's general policy. The company replied, stating, in effect, that the policy was inflexible. Later the plaintiff wrote: "To facilitate your evaluating the project and its timeliness with respect to your competition and to determine your position, I am enclosing a complete disclosure, as I have faith and trust in the fair dealings of your company." The enclosed "disclosure" was a document containing a recommendation as to an approach by which Carnation's advertisement of its product could be improved. The only unique idea which the appellant claims to have included within her "disclosure" is that of advertising and promoting the "pouring or sprinkling" of "dry milk into warm or hot liquids, or food mixtures, during the usual cooking processes." Promptly, in a letter Carnation stated that it had "no interest in acquiring whatever rights you may have to these ideas," and pointed out, in effect, that while Carnation had not chosen to advertise the use of its products with heated liquids, the company had conducted tests and was familiar with the product's properties for such use.

Approximately eight years later, she instituted her suit and her complaint alleged that Carnation failed to return the report which she voluntarily forwarded on July 27, 1955 and thereby wrongfully converted property belonging to her to its own use and benefit.

The District Court dismissed the complaint and she appealed.

ELY, C. J. . . . The District Court was correct in its conclusion that the contents of the report revealed no substantial uniqueness or novelty to Carnation. The record reveals that Mr. Peebles, during the development of his process, tried and tested the product in warm and heated mixtures and that, as a matter of fact, the label affixed to the product before its distribution was undertaken by Carnation recommended "To hot and cold beverages, soups, etc., add PEEBLES INSTANT MILK to taste. In cooking and baking, for extra nourishment, extra richness, simply use more dry PEEBLES INSTANT MILK." A mere idea without novelty is not a property right to which one may claim exclusive ownership. (Cases cited) This most certainly is true when the one against whom the right is asserted has already entertained the idea and shared it with the general public. The fact that Carnation, at a time subsequent to its receipt of appellant's report, commenced to advertise the product for use with warm and heated liquids, as Peebles had done before, as Carnation had not done, and as appellant had recommended, did not create in appellant a property right which she had not previously enjoyed. . . .

Appellant's claim, under federal antitrust law, of a right to recover for Carnation's alleged conspiracy with others to interfere with the use of her services by defendant's competitors is baseless. Violations of the prohibitions of the antitrust laws are subject to complaint by "any person who shall be injured in his business or property" by reason of such violations. . . . The allegations, coupled with the facts and their legal effect, make it clear that there can be no support for a conclusion that if Carnation and others did conspire in the alleged manner, appellant was thereby "injured" in her "business or property."

Affirmed.

CHAPTER 47
REVIEW QUESTIONS AND PROBLEMS

1. *A* stores merchandise in *B*'s warehouse and receives a negotiable warehouse receipt as evidence of the bailment. What property concepts are involved in this transaction? How would these relationships be changed if *A* indorsed the warehouse receipt to *C*?

2. *A* is the owner of real property—a business building. He borrows $100,000 from *B* and gives *B* a mortgage on the building. Who now has title to the building?

3. *A* steals goods from *B* and stores the stolen goods in a warehouse in another state. He receives a warehouse receipt from the warehouse operator who is unaware of the theft. The warehouse receipt is then sold to *B* who purchases in good faith and in the belief that *A* owns the stored goods. Does *B* become the owner of the goods?

4. *A* operates a dairy farm. Fumes from a smelter nearby permeate the air and cause the fields to become tainted with chemicals. As a result the milk produced by *A*'s cows who graze on the fields is not marketable. Have *A*'s property rights been violated? Does he have any legal remedy?

5. *A* Co. is engaged in the lumber business and operates a large sawmill in Forest City. The company plans to build a paper mill at the site in order to utilize sawdust and other waste products produced by the mill. The new paper mill would be an economic advantage to Forest City but would produce vile odors. What property problems are raised by these facts?

6. *A* Co. manufactures a soft drink called "Paz-Zaz." *B* Co., a rival is now preparing to market a drink called "Zaz-Paz." Does *A* Co. have any legal remedy?

7. *A* is the owner of a large tract of land upon which there is a stand of timber. *A* sells the timber to *B*. Does this transaction fall within the provisions of the Uniform Commercial Code?

8. *A* purchases refrigeration equipment from *B* for installation in a grocery store and meat market owned by *A*. Would this equipment be classified as real property or personal property? What difference would the classification make?

9. *A* Co. operates a chemical plant and requires a large volume of pure water in its operations. A stream flows through the plant property and supplies the water. *B* who owns land upstream from *A*'s plant diverts the stream so that its flow through *A*'s land is diminished. Have *A*'s property rights been infringed?

10. *A* has operated a "slaughter house" and meat packing plant on the outskirts of a city for many years. Now the city has grown and his property is within the city limits. The plant area is now residential and the noise and odors of the operation are offensive to people living in the vicinity. What conflicts of "property interests" do you see in this situation?

chapter 48

Personal Property

7-8 In General. It has been noted previously that the word property refers to the rights that a person has in things both tangible and intangible. The denomination "personal property" clearly encompasses those rights connected with moveable, physical objects—chattels—such as "goods" and it is customary to refer to such objects as personal property. The term is not limited to physical objects but includes also such items as "goodwill." Goodwill is an intangible item, yet it has value—is bought and sold—and is personal property.[1] Patents are personal property, as are copyrights and trade-marks. The designation *chattels personal in action,* often called "choses in action" includes those things to which one has a right to possession, but concerning which it may be necessary to bring some legal action in order eventually to enjoy possession. Any contract right may be said to be a chose in action. A common form of chose in action is a negotiable instrument. While the instrument itself may be said to be property, it really is simply evidence of a right to money, and it may be necessary to maintain an action to reduce the money to possession.

The foregoing relates to interests in things, tangible or intangible, *other than land.* While most interests in land fall within the classification of real property, there are some which partake of the flavor of personal property. Such interests in land are called "chattels real." Usually, leases of land for a period of years are considered chattels real and upon the death of the lessee pass to his executor or administrator as personal property of the estate.

[1] *Bergum v. Weber, supra,* page 765.

7-9 Personal Property: Real Property—Importance of Distinction. When a person dies without leaving a will directing how his property shall pass upon his death, he is said to die "intestate" and his property will pass in conformity with the laws of intestate succession, which are included as part of the probate law of every state. When he dies leaving a will, he dies "testate." There is a substantial variation among the states with regard to intestate laws. In general, *real property* passes in accordance with the law of the situs—the law of the state where such property is located—while *personal property* intestate succession is controlled by the domicile of the owner without regard to the physical location of the property. Real property descends to the persons designated as heirs by the law of the situs; personal property passes to the person appointed by the court as administrator of the estate of the deceased to be distributed by him in accordance with the laws of the state of domicile of the deceased. Where there is a will, the property passes to the executor to be distributed in accordance with the terms of the will.

Not only is the distinction significant in the case of the death of the owner, but it is significant also during his lifetime. The methods of transferring personal property and real property are substantially different. Formal instruments such as deeds are required to transfer an interest in land, whereas few formalities are required in the case of personal property. A bill of sale *may* be used in selling personal property, but it is not generally required and does not in any event involve the technicalities of a deed. A motor vehicle transfer may require the delivery of a certificate of title, but in the main the transfer of personal property is quite simply accomplished. Thus the distinction between real and personal property is significant in connection with the determination of which law is applicable to a transaction; to matters of intestate succession; and to the methods of transfer.

It will be recalled that the Uniform Partnership Act provided: "A partner's interest in the partnership is *personal property*." It also provides that on death of a partner his right in *specific partnership property* vests in the surviving partners and is not a part of his estate. The estate has a general claim for the value of his interest only.

7-10 Methods of Acquiring Title. Title to personal property may be acquired through any of the following methods: original possession, transfer, accession or confusion.

        Original possession. Personal property which is in its native state and over which no one as yet has taken full and complete control belongs to the first person reducing such property to his exclusive possession. Although most property today may be said to belong definitely to someone, there are still some kinds of property, especially wild animals, fish, and other property of like kind, that are still available for appropriation by any individual. Property once reduced to ownership, but later discarded, belongs to the first party taking possession.

In addition to the above, it might be said that property created through mental or physical labor belongs to the creator unless he has agreed to create it for someone else, being induced to do so because of some compensation that has been agreed to by the interested parties. Under this heading might be included such items as books, inventions, and trademarks. This kind of property is usually protected by the government through means of copyrights, patents, and trade-marks.

Transfer.   Personal property may be transferred through sale, gift, will, or operation of law.

The law relating to transfer by sale has previously been discussed in connection with Article 2 of the Uniform Commercial Code. It will be recalled that other Articles of the Code specify the methods of transfer for intangibles such as negotiable instruments, accounts receivable, stock certificates, and the like. Since title to personal property may be encumbered as by way of an outstanding security interest, the records must be searched in order to determine the nature of the title.

Gift.   A transfer by gift may be made effective with the consent of the owner by an actual physical change in possession of the property. Normally, the gift is not complete until the change in possession has been effected. In the case of choses in action, the transfer of possession usually takes place by means of an assignment; the exception being negotiable instruments which may be transferred either by assignment or negotiation. It will be recalled that a promise to make a gift is ordinarily not enforceable because no consideration is present to support the promise. However, an executed gift—one accomplished by delivery of the property to the donor, does not present this problem. The delivery can be either actual or constructive as the situation may demand. Thus, if the property is in storage, the donor could make a delivery by giving the donee the warehouse receipt. A donor may in general make an irrevocable gift by delivering to the donee something which is a token representing the latter's dominion and control. A key to a strong box especially if it were the only key, given to a person with words indicating an intent to make a gift of the contents, could constitute the requisite delivery.

Special tax problems arise when a donor makes a gift in lieu of a testamentary disposition of his property. Gifts may be used to reduce federal income and estate taxes. For example, a gift of income-producing securities will reduce the income taxable to the donor and upon his death the securities would not be included in his estate. While a federal gift tax is imposed on gifts, it is at a lower rate than the estate tax, and there are substantial exemptions and exclusions from the gift tax. Thus the tax laws encourage living gifts as contrasted with testamentary dispositions of property or gifts in contemplation of death which are treated as testamentary for tax purposes. The details of this subject are left to texts concerned with taxation.

Another aspect of the gift in contemplation of death is that in which a person who is, or who believes that he is, facing death makes a gift on the assumption that death is imminent. A person about to embark on a perilous trip or to undergo a serious operation, or one who has an apparently incurable and fatal illness might make a gift and deliver the item to the donee on the assumption that he is not long for this world.

If he returns safely, the operation is successful, or the illness is miraculously cured, the donor is allowed to revoke the gift and recover the property from the donee.

Will.   A person has the privilege of providing for the disposition of his property upon his death by executing a will. The requirements of a valid will vary from state to state but in all states it is required that a person who signs his will be of sound mind and not acting under duress or undue influence. The person who leaves his property by will is called a testator and the persons receiving it are called legatees, while the persons receiving real property are called devisees. Subject to the rights of spouses, testators can make whatever disposition of their property they desire.

Operation of law.   As noted previously, when the deceased leave no will, the property is distributed as provided by the laws of the particular state involved. In the case of personal property, the law of the state in which the deceased was domiciled controls. If the deceased has no heirs and does not leave a will, his property will escheat to the state.

Foreclosure sale offers another illustration of transfer of title by operation of law.

7-11 Nature of Title.   In most cases of transfer of property, the transferee takes no better title than his transferor had. This is true even though the transferee believes that his transferor has a good title. Thus, an innocent purchaser from a thief obtains no title to the property purchased, and no subsequent purchaser stands in any better position. However, if the transferor of the property has a voidable title, and he sells property to an innocent purchaser, the transferee may obtain good title to the property. This topic is discussed in the Book on the Uniform Commercial Code from the standpoint of the "purchaser in the ordinary course of business" and the "good faith purchaser for value." (See Sec. 3-13). Also, refer to Sec. 3-7 dealing with warranty of title and Sec. 3-155 concerning the rights of a purchaser at a sale following default in a secured transaction.

7-12 Accession.   *Accession,* taken literally, means "adding to." Personal property permanently added to other property and forming a minor portion of the finished product becomes part and parcel of the larger unit. Accession is the legal term used to signify the acquisition of title to personal property by its incorporation into other property or its union with other property. The problem of accessions has been discussed in connection with Secured Transactions (Sec. 3-150), wherein the rights of parties with a security in the accession and in the whole are discussed together with the right of removal of the accession in the event of default. The rights of secured parties when goods are commingled or processed are discussed in Sec. 3-151.

The problems relating to accession also arise in situations other than security transactions. The general rule is that when the goods of two different owners are united together, the title to the resulting product goes to the owner of the principal goods. The owner of the minor unit may recover damages if such property were wrongfully taken from him, but he cannot recover the property.

Another type of accession may arise when personal property owned by one person is increased in value by skill or material added by another. Generally, the increased value passes to the one who retains title to the raw material. If raw material is wrongfully taken and is greatly increased in value after the taking by the expenditure of labor and materials, the owner is clearly entitled to some relief, but the nature of the relief is dependent upon several factors.

An increase in value by an intentional wrongdoer through the expenditure of labor and materials always passes to the true owner of the property, and he may successfully bring suit to reduce it to his possession, although the raw material has been enhanced in value many times. A sale of the property in its improved state by the wrongdoer and increased in value by the bona fide purchaser follows a different rule. An innocent purchaser of stolen goods who greatly increases the property in value by the expenditure of skill and materials becomes liable to the true owner for the value of the goods in their original state only. In effect, title passes to the bona fide purchaser, provided he pays to the original owner the former value of the property. The original owner, however, may reclaim the property unless the bona fide purchaser has greatly increased its value—at least two or three times its original value.

An unintentional wrongdoer who greatly improves the value of the property wrongfully taken, if sued for the value of the property, is always liable for the original value of the property. If he has improved the value of the property to a great extent by the expenditure of skill and labor, the original owner may not replevin the article from him. There are a few courts, however, which seem to permit the original owner to recover the improved article.

7-13 Confusion. Property of such a character that one unit may not be distinguished from another unit and that is usually sold by weight or measure is known as fungible property. Grain, hay, logs, wine, and other similar articles afford illustrations of property of this nature. Such property, belonging to various parties, often is mixed by intention of the parties, and occasionally by accident or by the misconduct of some wrongdoer. Confusion of fungible property belonging to various owners, assuming that no misconduct is involved, results in an undivided ownership of the total mass. To illustrate: grain is stored in a public warehouse by many parties. Each owner holds an undivided interest in the total mass, his particular interest being dependent upon the amount stored by him. Should there be a partial destruction of the total mass, the loss would be divided proportionately.

Confusion of goods which results from the fraudulent conduct of one of the parties causes the title to the total mass to pass temporarily to the innocent party. If the wrongdoer is unable to show that the resultant mass is equal in value per unit to that of the innocent party, he loses his interest in the resulting mass. Where the new mixture is worth no less per unit than that formerly belonging to the innocent party, the wrongdoer may claim his portion of the new mass by presenting convincing evidence of the amount added by him.

7-14 Abandoned and Lost Property. Property is said to be abandoned whenever it is discarded by the true owner, who, at that time, has no intention of reclaiming it. Such proprety belongs to the first individual again reducing it to possession.[2]

Property is lost whenever, as a result of negligence, accident, or some other cause, it is found at some place other than that chosen by the owner. Title to lost property continues to rest with the true owner. Until the true owner has been ascertained, the finder may keep it, and his title is good as against everyone except the true owner. The rights of the finder are superior to those of the person in charge of the property upon which the lost article is found. Occasionally, state statutes provide for newspaper publicity concerning articles which have been found. Under these statutes, if the owner cannot be located, the found property reverts to the state or county if its value exceeds an established minimum.

Mislaid or misplaced property is such as is intentionally placed by the owner at a certain spot in such a manner as to indicate that he merely forgot to pick it up. In such a case the presumption is that he will later remember where he left it and return for it. The owner of the premises upon which it is found is entitled to hold such property until the true owner is located.

7-15 Extent of Ownership. Title to personal property may be held in common with others. Normally, in such a case, the owners are entitled to an equal use of the property or to their portion of the income derived from its use. In the event of the death of one of the co-owners, his share in the property passes to the executor or administrator of his estate.

Under the laws of many states, personal property, as well as real estate, may be held in joint tenancy. The interest of a deceased owner passes automatically to his joint owner without the necessity of probate. Because of this fact, husband and wife in many cases hold personal property jointly in order to avoid the expense of administration of an estate in the event of the death of either. Joint tenancy of personal property does not arise unless a contract between the co-owners states clearly that such is the case and that the right of survivorship is to apply.

BAILMENTS OF PERSONAL PROPERTY

7-16 Definition of Bailments. Possession of property is often temporarily surrendered by the owner. In such cases the person taking possession may perform some service pertaining to the goods, after which he returns

---

[2] *Nippon Shosen Daisha, K.K. v. United States,* page 965.

them to the owner. Upon many occasions one person borrows or rents an article which belongs to another. A contract whereby possession of personal property is surrendered by the owner with provision for its return at a later time forms a *bailment*. The owner of the goods is known as the *bailor,* whereas the one receiving possession is called the *bailee*. From the foregoing definition it appears that three distinct requisites of a bailment exist. If these essentials are thoroughly understood, the student should encounter no difficulty in distinguishing a bailment from other contractual relationships. The three requisites are (1) retention of title by bailor; (2) possession and temporary control of the property by the bailee; (3) ultimate possession to revert to the bailor unless he orders it transferred to some designated third person. It is to be noted that a mere change in the form of the property while in the hands of the bailee does not affect the relationship. Thus, *A* floats logs downstream to *B,* to be sawed into lumber by the latter. *B* is as much a bailee of the lumber as he was of the logs.

7-17 Types of Bailment. Bailments group naturally into three classes: bailments for the benefit of the bailor; bailments for the benefit of the bailee; and bailments for the mutual benefit of the bailer and the bailee. Typical of the first group are those cases in which the bailor leaves goods in the safekeeping of the bailee under circumstances that negative the idea of compensation. Inasmuch as the bailee is not to be paid in any manner, the bailment is for the exclusive benefit of the bailor. A bailment for the benefit of the bailee is best exemplified by a loan of some article. Thus, *A* borrows *B*'s watch to carry for the day. The bailment is one for the sole benefit of *A*.

The most important type of bailment is the one in which both parties are to benefit. Contracts for repair, carriage, storage, or pledge of property fall within this class. The bailor receives the benefit of some service; the bailee benefits by the receipt of certain agreed compensation; thus both parties profit as a result of the bailment.

7-18 Degree of Care Required. Provided that proper care has been exercised by the bailee, any loss or damage to the property bailed follows title and consequently falls upon the bailor. Each type of bailment requires a different degree of care. In a bailment for the benefit of the bailor, the bailee is required to exercise only slight care, while, in one for the benefit of the bailee, extraordinary care is essential.[3] A bailment for the mutual benefit of the parties demands only ordinary care on the part of the bailee. *Ordinary care* is defined as that care which the average individual usually exercises over his own property.[4] Slight care and extraordinary care vary from ordinary care in that the one is a lower, and the other a higher, degree of care than ordinary care.

The Uniform Commercial Code, Article 7–Documents of Title pro-

---

3 *Clack-Nomah Flying Club v. Sterling Aircraft Inc.,* page 966.
4 *Althoff v. System Garages Inc.,* page 967.

vides: "A warehouseman is liable for loss of or injury to the goods caused by his failure to exercise such care in regard to them as a reasonably careful man would exercise under like circumstances but unless otherwise agreed he is not liable for damages which could have been avoided by the exercise of such care." However, provision is made for the continued effective operation of any statute (state or federal) which imposes more rigid standards of responsibility for some or all failures.

Furthermore, the amount of care demanded varies with the nature and value of the article bailed. The care found to be sufficient in the case of a carpenter's tool chest would probably not be ample for a diamond ring worth $10,000. A higher standard of protection is required for valuable articles than for those less valuable.

Property leased by the bailor to the bailee must be reasonably fit for the service desired. For this reason it is the duty of the bailor to notify the bailee of all defects in the property leased, of which he might reasonably have been aware.[5] The bailor is responsible for any damage suffered by the bailee as the result of such defects, unless he notifies the bailee of them. This rule holds true even though the bailor is not aware of the defect if, by the exercise of reasonable diligence, he could have discovered it. If, on the other hand, the article is merely loaned to the bailee —a bailment for the benefit of the bailee—the bailor is in duty bound to notify the bailee only of known defects. A bailor who fails to give the required notice of a defect is liable to any person who he might anticipate would be using the defective article as a result of the bailment. Employees of the bailee and members of the bailee's family might well recover of the bailor for injuries received as a consequence of the defect.

7-19 Contracts Against Required Care. Certain classes of bailees have found it desirable to provide in the bailment agreement against any liability resulting from their negligence or that of their employees. Such a provision found in the contract of a quasi-public bailee, such as a railway public warehouse or a hotel, is illegal and, therefore, ineffective. The ordinary private bailee, however, may insert in the contract any provision which he desires, as long as the bailor is willing to enter into the agreement under the particular terms. If the latter is unwilling to accept the particular terms, he is at liberty to contract eleswhere. Where the provision is such as to defeat the real purpose of the contract and to shock the sense of justice of the court, the provision will not be enforced. Thus, *A* stored apples in *B*'s private warehouse to protect them against the winter weather. The agreement provided that they were left at the owner's risk. *B* failed to heat the building, and the apples were frozen. It was held that such a provision did not relieve *B* from liability. The Uniform Commercial Code provides that damages may be limited by a term in the warehouse receipt or storage agreement limiting the amount of liability in case of loss or damage. However, a warehouseman cannot disclaim the obligations of reasonable care by such agreement.

[5] *Perry v. Richard Chevrolet, Inc.*, page 969.

7-20 Rights and Duties of Bailee. The bailment agreement governs the duties and rights of the bailee. Should he treat the property in a different manner, or use it for some purpose other than that contemplated by the contract, he becomes liable for any loss or damage to the property in the interim. This result appears to be true, although the damage can in no sense be attributed to the conduct of the bailee. To illustrate: Let us assume that *A* stores his car in *B*'s public garage for the winter. *B,* because of a crowded condition, has the car temporarily moved to another garage without the consent of *A*. As the result of a cyclone, the car is destroyed while at the second location. The loss falls upon *B*, as he exceeded the terms of the bailment contract. In a restricted sense, the bailee is guilty of conversion of the bailor's property during the period in which the contract terms are being violated.

The bailee has no right to deny the title of the bailor unless he has yielded possession to one having paramount title. In other words, the bailee has no right to retain, possession of the property merely because he is able to prove that the bailor does not have title. In order to defeat the bailor's right to possession, the bailee must show that he has returned the property to someone having better title, or is holding the property under an agreement with the true owner.

7-21 Insurance. Property which is in the hands of a bailee may be covered by insurance policies issued to either the bailor or the bailee. The policies of insurance should be carefully arranged so that proper coverage will be effected. It is not enough to assume that because a bailee has insurance on his own goods that such coverage extends to goods held under bailment.

Only property which is definitely described in the policy is protected. Furthermore, the policy often limits its application to property owned by the insured, unless the applicant clearly states his desire to have other property in his care protected by the insurance. The interest of the insured in the property should be clearly set forth where such is pertinent according to policy terms. Thus, a policy which covers the goods of the insured located at a certain place does not cover goods held on consignment, unless the agreement is expressly so drawn.

A policy may be issued that covers property regardless of where it is located, although most insurance contracts protect property only so long as it remains at a certain location, the particular location being one of the elements of the risk. In this latter situation, a removal of the property without notice to the insurer terminates the protection.

COMMON CARRIERS AS BAILEES

7-22 Definition. A common carrier of freight is defined as one who holds himself out as being ready and willing to carry goods for anyone who presents them. A common, or public, carrier is distinguished from a private carrier in that the former stands ready to serve anyone desiring the service, while the latter operates under a contract only. A common carrier usually operates between definite termini or over a definite route. A private carrier transports freight from point to point, as demanded by his contract with the shipper. A private carrier becomes a public one as soon as it begins to cover definite territory at somewhat regular intervals and carries goods for anyone desiring to ship them. An ordinary drayman is a private carrier, but the operator of a truck between two cities on a regular schedule would, under most circumstances, be a common carrier.

A common carrier rests under a duty to accept goods for transportation whenever they are presented. It may, however, limit its business to a particular kind of property. The mere fact that a truck owner limits his business to the transportation of milk does not render him a private carrier if he stands ready to carry milk for anyone. An express company is not bound to accept any or all personal property presented. Its business is limited to somewhat small and valuable articles.

7-23 Care Required of the Common Carrier. The contract for carriage of goods constitutes a mutual benefit bailment, but the care required of the carrier greatly exceeds that of the ordinary bailee. A common carrier is an absolute insurer of the safe delivery of the goods to their destination. This rule is subject to only five exceptions. Any loss or damage which results from (1) an act of God, (2) action of an alien enemy, (3) order of public authority, (4) inherent nature of the goods, or (5) misconduct of the shipper must fall upon the one possessing title. Thus, any loss which results from an accident or the wilful misconduct of some third party must be borne by the carrier. For example, *A,* in order to injure a certain railway company, sets fire to several boxcars loaded with freight. Any damage to the goods falls upon the carrier. On the other hand, if lightning, an act of God, had set fire to the cars, the loss would have fallen upon the shipper.

Any damage to goods in shipment which results from the very nature of the goods or from the failure properly to crate or protect the property must be suffered by the shipper. Thus, the damage to a shipment of fresh strawberries, caused by excessive heat during the period of shipment, must be borne by the shipper, provided the carrier has offered proper refrigeration.

Goods may be damaged while in the possession of either the receiving or a connecting carrier. Damages arising while goods are being transported by a connecting carrier may be recovered by the shipper from either of the two carriers. If the shipper files his claim against the original carrier, it, in turn, demands restitution from the connecting carrier. The burden is on the shipper to prove that the goods were in good condition at the time and place of shipment.[6]

7-24 Contract Against Liability of Carrier. A common carrier may not contract away its liability for goods damaged in shipment by the negli-

[6] *Florence Banana Corp. v. Pennsylvania Railroad,* page 969.

gence of its employees. Such a provision in a bill of lading is illegal. It may, however, where lower rates are granted, relieve itself from the consequences of causes or of conduct over which it has no control. Thus, a provision which relieves a carrier from damage caused by fire is effective, where the fire is not caused by any misconduct on the part of employees.

The Uniform Commercial Code provides: "A carrier who issues a bill of lading whether negotiable or non-negotiable must exercise the degree of care in relation to the goods which a reasonably careful man would exercise under like circumstances." However, it must be noted that federal legislation will control interstate shipments and the Code stipulates that the section quoted "does not repeal of change any law or rule of law which imposes liability upon a common carrier for damages not caused by its negligence."

Furthermore, the company may limit its liability to an agreed valuation. The shipper is limited in his recovery to the value asserted in the bill of lading. The rate charged for transportation may vary with the value of the property shipped. It is for this reason that the agreed valuation is binding.

7-25 Beginning of the Relation. The liability of the carrier attaches as soon as the goods are delivered to it. The receipt of the goods is usually acknowledged by a bill of lading, which sets forth the terms and conditions of shipment. The carrier becomes responsible for a carload shipment as soon as the car has been delivered to it. If the car is loaded while located upon railroad property, the carrier becomes liable at the moment the car is fully loaded.

7-26 Termination of the Relation. The extreme degree of care required of the carrier may be terminated before the goods are actually delivered to the consignee. Three views prevail in this country as to when the relationship of carrier ceases. Some states hold that the duties of the carrier end and those of a warehouseman begin as soon as the local shipment is unloaded from the car into the freight house. Others hold the carrier to strict liability until the consignee has had a reasonable time in which to inspect and remove the shipment. Still other states hold that the consignee is entitled to notice and that he has a reasonable time after notice in which to remove the goods before the liability of the carrier as a carrier is terminated. To illustrate: Let us assume that goods arrive at their destination and are unloaded in the freight house. Before the consignee has had time to take them away, the goods are destroyed by fire, although the carrier has exercised ordinary care. Under the first of these views, the loss would fall upon the shipper, as at the time of the fire the railway was no longer a carrier but a warehouseman. Under the other two views, the loss would fall on the carrier, as the extreme liability had not yet terminated, inasmuch as no time had been given for delivery.

The carload shipment is delivered as soon as it is placed on the private switch of the consignee or "spotted" at the unloading platform. Any subsequent loss, unless it results from the negligence of the carrier, must fall upon the owner of the goods.

7-27 Rates. Rates charged by common carriers must be reasonable. Carriers engaged in interstate business are subject to the regulation of the Interstate Commerce Commission and all tariffs or rate schedules must be filed with it. Almost all the states have railroad commissions for the purpose of establishing rates for intrastate business. These commissions also require tariffs to be filed with them. Any rate either higher or lower than that shown in the tariff is illegal. Discriminatory rates by the use of rebates are also forbidden, and the giving or receiving of rebates constitutes a crime.

A railway may insist upon the payment of the charges at the time it accepts the delivery. Since it has a lien upon the goods as security for the charges, however, it customarily waits until the goods are delivered, before collecting. The carrier usually refuses to surrender the goods unless the freight is paid, and, if the freight remains unpaid for a certain period of time, it may advertise the property for sale. Any surplus, above the charges, realized from the sale reverts to the owner of the goods.

Any undue delay on the part of the consignee in removing the goods from the warehouse or the tracks of the railway permits the carrier to add a small additional charge known as demurrage.

PERSONAL PROPERTY CASES

Nippon Shosen Daisha, K.K. v. United States
1964, 288 F.Supp 55

A vessel, the S.S. Kokoku Maru, collided with another ship in the Pacific Ocean and it became necessary for the crew to abandon the vessel. The cargo was phosphate rock and was insured by the Sumitomo Marine and Fire Insurance Co., Ltd. The insurance company had paid the consignee the full value of the cargo. Under a federal statutory procedure instituted by the owner of the vessel, the vessel and its cargo were sold to the highest bidder and the federal court appointed a Trustee to represent all persons who had legal claims against the vessel. The Trustee would then make a distribution to such claimants. Sumitomo claimed that it was entitled to the proceeds of the sale allocable to the phosphate rock. The representatives of Sumitomo, according to an affidavit submitted by one Chick, had surveyed the vessel and cargo and had concluded that it would be too expensive to try to remove the cargo.

THOMAS, D. J. Court is of the opinion that Sumitomo is not entitled to the proceeds for the phosphate rock cargo because the uncontradicted evidence conclusively shows that both Sumitomo and its insured abandoned said phosphate rock cargo.

Abandonment is the intentional relinquishment of property. (1 C.J.S. *Abandonment* 1 (1936)) The letter of Chick dated July 9, 1963, with the enclosed letters of Sumitomo and of the consignees of the phosphate rock cargo, clearly evidence the intent and the act sufficient to constitute an intentional relinquishment of all right or interest in the phosphate rock cargo.

Sumitomo contends that to be legally effective an abandonment must be voluntary, and that the fact that the parties involved, including Sumitomo and its insured, were mistaken as to the value of the cargo rendered the abandonment legally ineffective.

However, the fact that the parties were mistaken as to the value of the cargo does not render the abandonment by Sumitomo and its insured any less voluntary. The affidavit of Chick, filed on behalf of Sumitomo, shows that Sumitomo and its insured made their decision to abandon the cargo only after careful consideration of information provided by those who made investigations on the scene. The fact that such information and/or their conclusion as to the value of the cargo turned out to be in error does not affect the voluntariness of the decision by Sumitomo and its insured to abandon the cargo.

Sumitomo correctly points out that one cannot abandon property to a particular person. One becomes the owner of abandoned property by subsequently appropriating it. The files and records in the case at bar at present do not reveal any appropriation of the phosphate rock cargo prior to the time when the Trustee, Arimori, acting on behalf of all legally-entitled claimants, listed the cargo in his Notice of Ship Sale. Under this view of the case, therefore, the ownership in the phosphate rock cargo passed directly to the Trustee Arimori, acting on behalf of the legally-entitled claimants. Once abandoned property has been appropriated by another, the former owner who relinquished such property cannot reclaim it. . . . (*Wiggins v. 1100 Tons, More or Less, Of Italian Marble,* 186 F.Supp. 452, ED.Va. 1960)

On the basis of the record presently before the Court, including the affidavits and exhibits filed on behalf of petitioner Sumitomo, the Court concludes that there is no genuine issue of fact with respect to Sumitomo's claim to the $12,467.76 in the registry of the Court representing the proceeds from the sale of the phosphate rock cargo and that the uncontradicted evidence established that Sumitomo and its insured abandoned said cargo.

Accordingly, the petition of Sumitomo for the payment from the registry of the Court of the sum of $12,467.76 is hereby denied, said order, however, is without prejudice to the rights of claimants or Shipowner in said proceeds.

Clack-Nomah Flying Club v. Sterling Aircraft, Inc.

1965 (Utah) 408 P.2d 904

The plaintiff's airplane was flown to Salt Lake City where it landed at defendant's airport. The pilot instructed the caretaker to look after the airplane and told him that it would probably be there for a day. The day in question was a gusty, windy day. About 3 P.M. a sudden heavy wind commenced to blow, the gusts of which were estimated at about 95 miles per hour. The airplane was soon turned over onto its back and destroyed, along with the other equipment.

The defendant contends that the facts merely show that there was a violent wind which caused the accident and that the plaintiff has completely failed to show any negligence which caused or contributed in causing the accident. The trial court took the view that the plaintiff had made a sufficient showing of negligence against the defendant and instructed the jury that the burden of proof was on the plaintiff to prove by a preponderance of the evidence that the defendant was guilty of negligence which proximately caused or contributed in causing the accident, and if the jury so found their verdict should be in favor of the plaintiff and the damages sustained should be determined by it. The jury rendered a verdict for the plaintiff.

WADE, J. This court has consistently held that a bailee for hire is responsible for the value of goods entrusted to him which he fails to return, reasonable wear and tear excepted, and that in such case the burden is on the bailee, defendant here, to show that he is free from negligence in the care of such goods which are placed for hire in his custody. This is the relationship of the parties which the evidence conclusively shows existed here. The plaintiff brought the airplane to defendant's old Salt Lake City airport and left it with the defendant as a bailee for hire for about a day. Under these circumstances, the defendant as the bailee had the burden of proving that the destruction of the airplane was not caused by its negligence and the plaintiff did not have the burden of proving that the defendant was guilty of negligence which proximately caused the destruction of the airplane and the other property. Thus the court's instructions to the jury covered the issue which was directly presented to the jury of whether defendant was guilty of negligence. This instruction was more favorable to the defendant airport, the bailee, than it was entitled to have. It placed the burden of proof on the plaintiff bailor instead of on the defendant bailee.

The fact that the court instructed the jury on the wrong theory of the case, as long as the instructions were more favorable to the defendant than they were entitled to, does not require a new trial.

Judgment affirmed. Costs to respondent.

Althoff v. System Garages, Incorporated

1962 (Wash.) 371 P.2d 48

ROSELLINI, J. Damages resulting from the theft of the plaintiff's automobile from the defendant's parking garage, in Seattle, were sought in the instant action.

On the evening of December 19, 1959, the plaintiff left his 1958 Ford Thunderbird at the defendant's garage, where he had often parked before, and received a claim check. According to the custom of the place, he left the key in the ignition.

An intoxicated person was seen by the defendant's employee Lou

Kranda at the garage at approximately 12:30 the following morning.

When the plaintiff returned to claim his automobile at approximately 2:38 A.M., it was discovered that it had been stolen. Later it was learned that it had been stolen by the intoxicated man, a sailor, who had driven it into a house in Marysville, severely wrecking it. He was killed in the accident.

This action followed and was tried to the court, which found in favor of the plaintiff. The defendant, appealing, contends that the court was not justified in finding that its employees were negligent. It is urged that the case is not distinguishable from the case of *Ramsden v. Grimshaw* (23 Wash.2d 864, 162 P.2d 901), which involved the theft of an automobile from a parking lot.

Speaking of the applicable rule of law, we said:

> The rule on bailment for hire in such a case as the instant one is that a prima facie case of negligence is made out when the bailee is unable to deliver the bailed article. But if the bailee shows the theft of the bailed article under circumstances that do not indicate the negligence of the bailee, the prima facie case fails and the bailor must go forward with proof that the theft resulted from negligence, that is to say from the want of due care of the bailee.

We also observed that, as applied to bailments, ordinary care means such care as ordinarily prudent men, as a class, would exercise in caring for their own property under like circumstance. Also, the usages of a particular business may be presumed to have entered into and formed a part of the contracts and understandings of persons engaged in such business and those who deal with them, and so such usages may have the effect of enlarging or qualifying the liability of a bailee the same as a special contract. . . .

The trial court in this case was justified in finding that the surveillance of the garage at night fell below the standard of reasonable care, and that, had all of the parking levels been kept under observation, the theft could have been prevented.

The defendant makes some argument that its liability should be limited to the sum of $250, because of the following words which appeared on the claim check:

> Company shall not be responsible for: Cars after closing time, Loss of Use of cars; Value of or damage to car, or liability to customer, exceeding $250.00.

It is conceded by the defendant that we have adopted the general rule . . . that a professional bailee cannot contract away responsibility for his own negligence or fraud. It was so held in *Ramsden v. Grimshaw, supra.* But the defendant suggests that we should adopt a rule allowing a limitation of liability to a "reasonable amount." Inasmuch as there was no showing in this case that the words on the claim check were ever brought to the plaintiff's attention, and no showing that the amount to which the liability was limited was reasonable under the circumstances, we do not have before us facts which would justify a consideration of the question whether such a modification of the rule should be adopted.

The judgment is affirmed.

Perry v. Richard Chevrolet, Inc.
1962 (Mass.) 182 N.E.2d 297

WILKINS, J. The plaintiff sues in tort for personal injuries allegedly caused by the negligence of the defendant in furnishing the plaintiff an automobile in which a radiator hose clamp was defectively installed.

The subsidiary facts . . . were as follows. The plaintiff was planning on November 19, 1957 to purchase an automobile from the defendant, a dealer in motor vehicles. Pending alterations on the car he was to purchase, the defendant turned over to him a 1946 model sedan. The plaintiff was unable to start the motor because of insufficient gasoline in the tank. An employee of the defendant put gasoline in, but the motor still would not turn over. Finally, the employee started the engine, telling the plaintiff that the car was "O.K. now." The plaintiff drove the car from the defendant's premises, a distance of five or six miles, when he heard a "bang" and saw a ball of fire coming from the engine and under the dashboard. His arms and eyebrows were singed by flames. He threw himself into the street and sustained bruises. The fire department extinguished the fire. The plaintiff then noticed that the clamp used to fasten the hose running between the radiator and the engine block was off, and that alcohol was coming out of the radiator. The clamp was found at the bottom of the pan below the radiator hose. The plaintiff was using the automobile for a purpose incidental to the defendant's business. . . .

The defendant owed the duty to the plaintiff to use ordinary care in the circumstances. There is, however, nothing in the subsidiary facts to indicate that the defendant knew or should have known that the hose clamp was defective, if in fact it was defective. Certainly difficulty in starting an automobile in mid-November is no such indication. The finding of negligence in furnishing the vehicle, being based exclusively upon knowledge of or negligent failure to discover a defective hose clamp, cannot stand. On the auditor's report the cause of the accident is unexplained. It is left a matter of conjecture whether the hose clamp becoming detached was the cause of, or was caused by, the explosion.

Exceptions sustained.

Judgment for the defendant.

Florence Banana Corp. v. Pennsylvania Railroad
1963 (D.C.) 195 A.2d 309

MYERS, A. J. Florence Banana Corporation appeals from a judgment upon a directed verdict for appellee in a suit seeking the value of a carload of apples alleged to have been spoiled by negligence in transportation by the carrier.

In early January, 1960, appellant bought four carloads of apples in the state of Washington for shipment east by railroad. Inspections were made of the fruit by the U.S. Department of Agriculture on January 6, 1960, and on April 12, 1960. The apples were shipped at different times; the last carload here involved was moved on May 27, 1960. Appellant claims that the apples in this carload were unspoiled when delivered for shipment, but as a result of the negligence of the carrier in icing and checking the car enroute, they arrived here in improper condition.

The only evidence offered by appellant was the testimony of one witness, the owner of the corporate shipper, who was not present when the apples were purchased, or inspected, or shipped, and who was held by the trial judge, and properly so, incompetent to testify as to his understanding of the contents of certain official inspection reports from the Agriculture Department. Neither the inspectors nor any person who had examined or handled the apples immediately precedent to shipment on May 27, 1960, was called as a witness. The inspection reports, although denied admission at trial because "too remote in time to be material," were thereafter considered by the trial judge in passing upon the sufficiency of all evidence to make a *prima facie* case for appellant, and found to be of little probative value without a fair explanation of their contents.

It is conceded that the railroad as carried of perishable goods was subject to the rule, applicable to all bailees, that if goods arrived at their destination in a damaged state, proof of their delivery to the carrier in good condition establishes a *prima facie* case of negligence, which must be rebutted by competent evidence from the carrier.

We are in accord with the ruling of the trial judge that the evidence, considered in the light most favorable to the appellant, was insufficient in law to prove delivery to the carrier in good condition. Absence of this essential element was fatal to appellant's claim. To submit to the jury upon this meager evidence the question of whether the apples were in good condition at time of their delivery to the shipper would have required mere conjecture or guesswork on their part in order to reach an answer.

We hold that the general testimony of the one witness, plus the inspection reports, unexplained, and the fact that appellant did not make a satisfactory showing that the fruit was delivered to the carrier in good condition (the inspection six weeks before did not suffice for that purpose), failed to establish a *prima facie* case warranting submission to the jury. The directed verdict was therefore proper and is

Affirmed.

CHAPTER 48
REVIEW QUESTIONS AND PROBLEMS

1. *A* is the owner of a drug store. He sells the store which he has operated for many years to *B* and as part of the transaction agrees not to engage in a pharmacy operation in the city for a period of 5 years. Can *A* enforce this agreement not to compete?

2. *A,* who is a resident of Illinois, owns real property in Michigan and personal property which is stored in Virginia. If *A* dies without leaving a will which state law will determine how his property passes to his heirs?

3. *A* operates an appliance business. His inventory is financed by *F* Finance Company which has a security interest in it. If *A* sells a refrigerator to *B* will *B* receive a good title?

4. *A* has a security interest in lumber owned by *B*. If *B,* who is in the boat-building business, constructs boats out of this lumber will *A*'s security interest continue in the boats?

5. *A* installed a replacement motor in *B*'s automobile. *C* had sold the automobile to *B*, but *B* had not paid *C* in full. In the event that *C* should reclaim the automobile from *B*—which he has a right to do under the sales contract for nonpayment of the purchase price—does *C* or *A* have a better right to the new motor?

6. *A* intentionally took corn belonging to *B* and distilled it into whisky. *B* had the sheriff seize the whisky, but *A* contends that the whisky belongs to him because of the great increase in its value. Is *A* correct?

7. *A* owns some lumber which he fraudulently mixes with lumber owned by *B*. The quality of the two piles of lumber was entirely different, but the contents of the two amounts cannot now be distinguished. May *B* retain title to both amounts?

8. *A,* employed by *P* Hotel Company to paint certain rooms, lifted a rug and found $750 in old bills. Being told by the hotel that the owner was known, he surrendered the money to *P* Company. The hotel was unable to locate the owner, and *A* demands the money. Is he entitled to it?

9. A bill of lading of a common carrier contains a clause relieving it of liability for all loss to property in transit caused by fire. A fire, caused by the negligence of the carrier's agent, destroyed goods in shipment belonging to *B*. Has *B* an action against the carrier?

10. *A* takes to *B*'s mill certain wheat to be ground into flour. After the wheat is ground into flour, but before the flour is returned to *A,* creditors of *B* levy upon the flour. Are their rights superior to those of *A*?

chapter **49**

Real Property

7-28 The Nature of Real Property. The preceding chapter dealt with personal property; the following discussion concerns land and the particular rules of law concerning real property. These rules may consider real property as "a thing" or property as "the subject matter of relationships." Whichever meaning is intended will be manifested by the purposes sought to be accomplished through the use and application of particular rules.

Real property includes not only the land but also things permanently affixed thereto including buildings, fences, trees and shrubbery, and the like. As noted previously, the Uniform Commercial Code–Article 2–Sales makes special provision for the sale of goods to be severed from the realty; and its provisions apply to contracts for the sale of timber, minerals or the like, or a structure if they are to be severed by the seller. In other words such transactions, together with a sale of growing crops or other things attached to realty which can be severed without material harm, fall under the heading of personal property. However, these transactions are subject to any third party rights as disclosed by realty records. The Code also provides that a contract for sale of such items may be recorded as a document transferring an interest in land and it shall then "constitute notice to third parties of the buyers' rights under the contract for sale."

Another area in which there is an overlapping of personal and real property concepts relates to fixtures. Provisions relating to security interests in things attached to or to become attached to realty are dealt with in Secured Transactions (Book 3—see Sec. 3-149). However, fixture problems do arise in areas other than those involving security interests.

7-29 Fixtures. The Code does not contain a definition of "fixtures"—it simply provides that the rules of Article 9 do not apply and that no security interests exists in "goods incorporated into a structure in the manner of lumber, bricks, tile, cement, glass, metal work and the like. . . ." The law of the particular state determines when and whether other goods become fixtures. It therefore becomes significant, whether or not the transaction is under the Code, to inquire into the rules generally applicable in making such a determination whether or not personal property has become so affixed to realty as to be a fixture.

There are many definitions of the term *fixtures*. In a broad sense, a fixture is an article that formerly had the characteristic of personal property, but upon becoming attached, annexed, or affixed to real property becomes a part of the real property. In order to determine in a particular case whether personal property attached to realty has become part of the realty the following rules and tests have been developed by the courts:

1. *Actual annexation to the realty.* The old English law required the chattel to be "let into" or "united" to the land, or to some substance that is a part of the land. A chattel that lies upon the ground is not attached by force of gravity. The test of annexation alone is inadequate, for many things attached to the soil or buildings are not fixtures and many things not physically attached to the soil or buildings are considered fixtures. For example, articles of furniture or plumbing substantially fastened but capable of easy removal are not necessarily fixtures. Physical annexation may be only for the purpose of more convenient use. On the other hand, machinery that has been annexed, but detached for repairs or other temporary reason, may still be considered a fixture although severed.

Keys, doors, windows, window shades, screens, storm windows and the like, although readily detachable, are generally considered fixtures because they are an integral part of the building and pertain to its function. The mode and degree of attachment and whether the article can be removed without material injury to the article, the building, or land are often important considerations in determining whether the article is a fixture. Electric ranges connected to a building by a plug or vent pipe under the material injury test are not fixtures, but the removal of wainscoting, wood siding, fire place mantels, and water systems, including connecting pipes, would cause a material injury to the building and land.

2. *Adaptation test.* Since the annexation test alone is inadequate to determine what is a fixture, there has been developed the adaptation test. Adaptation means that the article is used in promoting the purpose for which the land is used. Thus, if an article is placed upon or annexed to land to improve it, make it more valuable, and extend its use, it is a fixture. Windmills, pipes, pumps and electric motors for irrigation systems, and fruit dryers are examples of chattels which may be so adapted as to become fixtures. This test alone is not adequate because rarely is an article attached or placed upon land except to advance the purpose for which the land is to be used.

3. *Intention test.* Annexation and adaptation as tests to determine whether a chattel has become realty are only part of the more inclusive

test of intention. Annexation and adaptation are evidence of an intention to make a chattel a fixture. In addition to annexation and adaptation as evidence of an intention, the following situations and circumstances are also used from which intention is deduced: (1) the kind and character of the article affixed; (2) the relation and situation of the parties making the annexation; for example, the relation of landlord and tenant suggests that such items as show cases and machinery, acquired and used by the tenant, are not intended to become permanently part of the real property. Such property called trade fixtures is generally intended to be severed at the end of the term; (3) the structure, degree, and mode of annexation; (4) and the purpose and use for which the annexation has been made.[1] Purchasers, lienees, and mortgagees who have no notice of the conditional sale agreement will not be affected, and as to them the article will be treated as a fixture.[2]

7-30 How Title to Real Property Is Acquired. Title to real property may be acquired in several different ways: (1) by original entry, called title by occupancy; (2) by transfer through, and with the consent of, the owner; (3) by transfer upon sale by a sheriff; (4) by possession of a party under claim of title for the period of the Statute of Limitations, usually 20 years, called adverse possession; (5) by will; (6) by descent, regulated by statute; and (7) by accretion, as when a river or a lake creates new land.

7-31 Original Entry, or Title by Occupancy. Except in those portions of the United States where the original title to the land was derived from grants that were issued by the King of England and other sovereigns who took possession of the land by conquest, title to all the land in the United States was derived from the United States government. Private individuals who occupied land for the period of time prescribed by federal statute and met such other conditions as were established by law acquired title by patent from the federal government.

7-32 Transfer with the Consent of the Owner. The title to real property is most commonly transferred by the owner's executing a deed to his transferee. A deed is generally a formal instrument under seal. The deeds most generally used are warranty and quit claim. A warranty deed conveys the fee simple title to the grantee, his heirs, or assigns and is so called because of the covenants on the part of the grantor by which he warrants: (1) that, at the time of the making of the deed, he has fee simple title therein and right and power to convey the same; (2) that the property is free from all encumbrances, except those encumbrances enumerated therein; (3) that his grantees, heirs, or assigns will have the quiet and peaceful enjoyment thereof and that he will defend the title to the property against all persons who may lawfully claim it. In most states the above warranties are implied from the words written in the deed.

[1] *Dean Vincent Inc. v. Redisco,* page 993.
[2] *Merchants & Mech. Fed. Sav. & Loan Assn. v. Herald,* page 995.

There may be circumstances under which the grantor would not wish to make warranties with respect to the title, and under such conditions he may execute a quitclaim deed. Such a deed merely transfers his existing legal and equitable rights in the premises described in the deed to the grantee. A quitclaim deed would be used under circumstances where an heir, owning an undivided interest in real property, wished to make a conveyance of his rights in the land, or where the interest of a person in land is questionable, a quitclaim deed would be used to clear the title. In the latter case, if he had title, he has parted with it, and if he had none, no injury has been done to him by the execution of the deed.

7-33 Transfer upon Sale by Sheriff. Title to land may be acquired by a vendee at a sale conducted by a sheriff or other proper official. Such sale is one made under the jurisdiction of a court having competent authority to order the sale. In order to secure the money to pay a judgment secured by a successful plaintiff, it may be necessary to sell the property of the defendant. Such a sale is called a judicial sale. A tax sale is a public sale of land, owned by a delinquent taxpayer, for the collection of unpaid taxes. The purchaser at such sale acquires a tax title. A mortgage foreclosure sale is a proceeding in equity by which a mortgagee secures by judicial sale money to pay the obligation secured by the mortgage. The word foreclosure is applied to the proceedings for enforcing other types of liens such as mechanics liens, assessments against realty to pay public improvements, and other statutory liens. The character of title acquired by a purchaser at such judicial sale is determined by statute.

7-34 Title Acquired by Adverse Possession. Title to land may be acquired under a principle known as adverse possession. Thus one who enters into actual possession of land and remains thereon openly and notoriously for the period of time prescribed in the Statute of Limitations, claiming title thereto in denial of, and adversely to, the superior title of another, will at the end of the statutory period acquire legal title. A person may acquire title to land even though he is not in actual possession of all the land claimed under what is called the doctrine of constructive adverse possession. Such a person must assert in good faith as evidence of his title, a writing describing the total property claimed and purporting to convey the land to the claimant. Such writing, although defective and imperfect, may be adequate as some evidence of ownership if it is a sign, semblance, token, or color of title. Before possession of a part of the land is sufficient to sustain a valid claim to the whole, the area claimed must have some relation in size, proximity, and use to that portion actually occupied. Actual knowledge by the true owner that his land is occupied adversely is not essential. However, the possession must be of such a nature as to charge a reasonably diligent legal owner with knowledge of the adverse claim. It has also been held that adverse possession will not run against a municipal corporation.

7-35 Title by Will or Descent. As previously noted, a person may make disposition of his property after death by an instrument in writing called a will. The person who carries out the provisions of the will is called an *executor*. The words "last will and testament" are usually used together. When the will operates to transfer real property, it is often called a devise, and the beneficiary a devisee. Who may make a will, how it may be executed, who may or may not be excluded as beneficiaries, how a will may be revoked, and what rules are to be used in construing a will are controlled by state statute.

A will is effective only when it has been drawn by one of sufficient mental capacity to realize fully the nature and effect of his act. The law usually requires that the signature to the will be witnessed by at least two, and in some states three, persons who are not interested in the estate. In a few states, a will written entirely in the handwriting of the deceased is probated even if it has not been witnessed. It should be understood that a will has no effect on the right of the owner to dispose of property during his lifetime. A will takes effect only at death and only then if it has not been revoked by the testator prior to his death.

If a person dies without making a will his real property will pass to his heirs or those entitled to receive the same according to the Statute of Descent.

7-36 Title Acquired by Accretion. An accretion is the accumulation of land to the land of an owner by action of water. If land is added to that of an owner by reason of an imperceptible gradual deposit by water, so that the shore or bank is extended, such increase is called alluvion. If a gradual increase in the land of an owner is caused by the receding of water, such increase is called reliction. If an addition to an owner's land be caused suddenly by reason of a freshet or flood, even though boundaries are changed, no change in ownership occurs. However, if such change in boundaries is slow and gradual by alluvion or reliction, the newly-formed land belongs to the owner of the bed of the stream in which the new land is formed. If the opposite bank of a private stream belongs to different persons, it is a general rule that each owns the bed to the middle line of the stream. In public waters, such as navigable streams, lakes, and the sea, the title of bed of the water, in absence of special circumstances, is in the United States. Accretion to the land belongs to the riparian owner; islands created belong to the government.

7-37 Covenants and Conditions. Quite often the grantor places restrictions upon the use that may be made of the land conveyed. He may, for instance, provide that the land shall be used exclusively for residential purposes, that the style and cost of the residence meet certain specifications, that certain fences and party walls shall be maintained, that building lines shall be established, that ways and roads shall be open and parks established. These restrictions inserted in the deed are covenants or promises on the part of the grantee to observe them and are said to run with the land. Even though the grantee fails to include them in a subsequent deed made by him, the new owner is nevertheless subject to them. They remain indefinitely as restrictions against the use of the land. Such restrictions will not be enforced, however, if the neighborhood has changed substantially since the inception of the covenants.[3]

Most of these covenants are inserted for the benefit of surrounding property and may be enforced by the owners of such property. This is particularly true where the owner of land which is being divided into a subdivision inserts similar restrictions in each deed. The owner of any lot which is subject to the restrictions is permitted to enforce the restrictions against the other lot owners located in the same subdivision. Occasionally a covenant is inserted for the personal benefit of the grantor, and will not run with the land. If a grantee *A* as part of the consideration covenants to repair a dam on land owned by the grantor *B*, such covenant will not run with the land and place a duty upon a grantee of *A*. The promise does not touch and concern the land granted from *A* to *B*, but is only a personal covenant for the benefit of *B*.

An estate on condition is an estate in fee, for life or for years, but its beginning or its continuation is dependent upon the happening of or the doing of an act by some person. If before an estate can begin, an event must occur, the event is a condition precedent. Thus, if *A* is to have an estate in land upon his marriage and his arrival at 25 years of age, such event is a condition precedent. If an estate may be terminated by the grantor or his successors, upon the happening of an event (a condition), an estate subject to a condition subsequent has been created. Thus, if *A* conveys to *B* and his heirs land on condition that if liquor is sold upon the premises conveyed, *A* may enter and terminate the estate, *B* has a fee simple estate, subject to a condition subsequent.

7-38 Execution of Deeds. The statutes of the various states provide the necessary formal requirements for the execution and delivery of deeds. A deed ordinarily is required to be signed, sealed, acknowledged, and delivered. A deed is not effective until it is delivered to the grantee: that is, placed entirely out of the control of the grantor. This delivery usually occurs by the handing of the instrument to the grantee or his agents. Where property is purchased on installment contract and occasionally in other cases, the deed is placed in the hands of a third party to be delivered by him to the grantee upon the happening of some event, usually the final payment by the grantee. Such delivery to a third party is called delivery in escrow and takes control over the deed entirely out of the hands of the grantor. Only if the conditions are not satisfied is the escrow agent at liberty to return the deed to the grantor. The owner of land may deed it to another, but reserve to himself certain rights as, for example, mineral rights.

7-39 Recording of Deeds. In order that the owner of real estate may notify all persons that he has title to the property, the statutes of the

---

[3] *Paschen v. Pashkow,* page 996.

various states provide that deeds shall be recorded in the recording office of the county in which the land is located. Failure to record a deed by a new owner who has not entered into possession makes it possible for the former owner to convey and pass good title to the property to an innocent third party, although the former owner has no right to do so and would be liable to his first grantee in such a case.

7-40 Abstracts of Title. Every deed, mortgage, judgment, lien, or other proceeding that affects the title to real estate must be filed and recorded in the recording office of the county within which the real estate lies to give constructive notice. In order for an owner to know the history and nature of the title to be obtained by him, title companies examine such records and prepare abstracts of the record. A purchaser of real estate should demand such abstract of title and have it examined in order to determine whether there are any existing claims against the property, or any outstanding interests that might in any way affect his title. The abstract of title must be supplemented from time to time, in order to show the chain, so that all court proceedings, such as foreclosures, partitions, transfers by deed, and probate proceedings, may be shown. Title companies are organized for the purpose of preparing such abstracts, and, after their preparation, examination of them should be made by a competent attorney before a purchaser accepts the title from the grantor. In many communities title companies are now organized as title insurance companies and upon the purchase of land, the grantor usually secures for the grantee from the title insurance company a land-title insurance policy which has for its purpose the protection of the grantee from claims against the title.

ESTATES IN REAL PROPERTY

7-41 Estates in Fee Simple. A person who owns the entire estate in real property is said to be an owner in fee simple.

7-42 Life Estates. An owner of land may create, either by will or by deed, a life estate therein. Such a life estate may be for the life of the grantee or it may be created for the duration of the life of some other designated person. Unless the instrument that creates the life estate places limitations upon it, the interest can be sold or mortgaged like any other interest in real estate. The buyer or mortgagee takes into consideration the fact that he receives only a life estate and that it may be terminated at any time by the death of the person for whose life it was created. For full protection, the mortgagee should carry insurance upon the life of the life tenant.

The life tenant is obligated to use reasonable care to maintain the property in the condition in which it was received, ordinary wear and tear excepted. It is his duty to repair, to pay taxes, and out of the income received, to pay interest on any mortgage that may have been outstanding at the time the life estate was created. The life tenant has no right to make an unusual use of the property if such a use tends to deplete the value of the property, unless the property was so used at the time the estate was created. For instance, a life tenant would have no right to mine coal or to cut and mill timber from land in which he held only a life estate unless such operations were being conducted or contemplated at the time the life estate was created.

7-43 Remainders and Reversions. After the termination of a life estate, the remaining estate may be given to someone else, or it may revert to the original owner or his heirs. If the estate is to be given to someone else upon the termination of a life estate, it is called an estate in remainder. If it is to revert back to the original owner, it is called a reversion. If the original owner of the estate is dead, the reversion comes back to his heirs. A remainder or a reversionary interest may be sold, mortgaged, or otherwise disposed of in the same manner as any other interest in real property.

7-44 Dower and Curtesy. At common law, a wife is entitled, upon the death of her husband, to a life estate in one third of any real property that her husband owned at the time of his death. The common law provided that, if there was a child born alive, upon the death of the wife the husband was entitled to a life estate in the whole of the wife's property. This was known as curtesy.

Curtesy has quite generally been abolished by statute, although in some of the states the husband is given a right comparable to the wife's dower. Some of the states have also abolished dower, making some other provision for the surviving wife or husband. In those states where dower or curtesy is provided for, the husband or wife cannot defeat the other by conveying his or her property prior to his or her death. A purchaser acquires good title only if the wife and husband join in the deed, unless the statute makes some other provision. Dower and curtesy are now generally controlled by statute. The student is advised to investigate the statute of the state, in order to ascertain the extent of the wife's dower interest.

7-45 Easements. An easement is a right, granted by the grantor to the grantee, to use real property. For example, the grantor may convey to the grantee a right of way over his land, the right to erect a building that may shut off light or air, the right to lay drain tile under the land, or the right to extend wires over the land. If these rights of easement are reserved in the deed conveying the property, or granted by a separate deed, they pass along with the property to the next grantee and are burdens upon the land. Such easements may be made separate and distinct by contract and are binding only on the immediate parties to the agreement. If such right to use another's land is given orally, it is not an easement but a license, and the owner of the land may revoke it at any time; unless it has become irrevocable by estoppel; whereas an easement given by grant cannot be revoked or taken away, except by deed, as such a right of way is considered a right in real property. An easement, like title to property, may be acquired by prescription which is similar to adverse possession.

7-46 Tenancies—Joint Tenancy and Tenancy in Common. An estate in land may be owned by several persons. Such persons may hold the real estate, either as tenants in common or as joint tenants, according to the nature of the granting clause in the deed by which the title is transferred. In a joint tenancy each person owns an undivided interest in the real property. Upon the death of any one of the owners, the remaining owners take the property, and upon the death of all the owners except one, the entire property passes to such survivor if the joint tenancy has not been terminated by some act of the parties. In tenancies in common, however, upon the death of one of the several owners, the title to his share passes to his heirs, and the heirs, therefore, become tenants in common with the surviving tenants in common. A joint tenancy can be created only by a specific statement in the granting clause of the deed, which usually states that the grantees shall hold title to said premises as joint tenants with the right of survivorship, and not as tenants in common. In the absence of such clause, grantees are tenants in common.

7-47 Tenancy by Entirety and Community Property. Since at common law a husband and wife are considered as one person, a conveyance of land to a husband and wife, in absence of words to the contrary, creates presumably an estate called a "tenancy by the entirety." To the extent that upon the death of either the survivor takes the entire estate, a tenancy by the entirety is similar to a joint tenancy. Tenancy by the entirety, however, differs from a joint tenancy in that the estate by entirety cannot be determined without the consent of both parties. A joint tenancy, however, can be destroyed by either cotenant transferring his interest to a third party, thus making the transferee a tenant in common with the other owner.

Several of the southwestern and western states have what is known as community property, having inherited it in part from their French and Spanish ancestors. In these states all property acquired after marriage other than by devise, bequest, or from the proceeds of noncommunity property becomes the joint property of husband and wife. Control of the property is vested primarily in the husband, and he is authorized, in most states, to sell or to mortgage it. The proceeds of the sale or mortgage in turn become community property. Upon the death of one of the parties, title to at least half of the community property passes to the survivor. In most of the states, the disposition of the remainder may be by will or under the rules of descent.

ENCUMBRANCES ON REAL ESTATE

7-48 Security Interests in Land. Article 9–Secured Transactions of the Uniform Commercial Code provides for the utilization of the security agreement to give a security interest in *personal property* in connection with transactions involving the sale of such property or borrowing against it. Prior to the Code this could be accomplished for example, by the chattel mortgage and the conditional sale contract. Similar provisions are found in statutes *other than the Code* for creating security interests in land. As noted previously conflicts may arise between secured parties claiming an interest in land and secured parties with an interest in chattels where the chattels have become attached to the land as fixtures.

Aside from such conflicts which are to be resolved under the priorities provisions of Article 9, the rules and principles relating to the encumbrance of real property are found in the state statutes relating to liens and mortgages. Three situations are to be considered: (1) mortgages on land, (2) land sale contracts, and (3) mechanic's liens on land. The first two will be considered together in the following sections from the point of view of their utilization in connection with the financing of the purchase of land. The lien of those who supply materials and services for the improvement of land will be discussed separately.

REAL ESTATE MORTGAGES

7-49 Nature of Mortgages and Essential Requirements Under the Common Law. A real estate mortgage is now generally considered a lien on land, created by contract, for the purpose of securing the performance of an obligation, usually the payment of money. The party who makes the mortgage is the mortgagor; the party to whom it is made—the one who lends the money—is the mortgagee. Under the common law, the early form of a mortgage on land consisted of an absolute conveyance of the title of the land by the owner to the mortgagee, upon a condition that the title would revert to the mortgagor when the obligation was performed or the money was repaid. The mortgagee secured the absolute right to the land and could take possession and collect the rents and profits. If the mortgagor failed to pay the money on or before the day set, the property would never revert to the mortgagor.

7-50 Growth of Equitable Theory. Under the common-law theory, the owner often lost his land if he was unable to repay a small loan on the due date, as required under his contract. In order to avoid the harshness of this rule, courts of equity began to allow the mortgagor to redeem his land after he had made a default. This right of the mortgagor, first recognized by a court of equity, is called his *equity of redemption*. Upon default, the mortgagee, by a process called a bill to foreclose the mortgage, asked the court to fix a date within which time the mortgagor must exercise his right to redeem his land. On the mortgagor's failure to redeem within the fixed time, the property became the absolute property of the mortgagee.

Also at common law, during the time that the land was encumbered by the mortgage, the mortgagee had the absolute right to take possession of the property and to secure the income from it. On account of these unjust advantages given to the mortgagee, courts of equity have taken the view that, since the transaction is intended by the parties only as a security transaction, such intention should be carried out. Under modern statutes regulating mortgages, the mortgagor is now regarded as the real owner of the land. He has the right to exercise all the powers of an owner, subject, however, to the limitations contained in the mortgage.

7-51 Legal and Equitable Theories of Mortgages. Many of the states still hold to the old legal theory and regard the title and the right of possession as passing to the mortgagee. This theory is called the title theory of mortgages, since title passes to the mortgagee. In the states where the title theory prevails, courts of equity permit the mortgagor to have a right of accounting against the mortgagee for any income obtained from the property while it is in his possession. In the law courts in the title-theory states, the mortgagor today is regarded as the real owner as to everyone except the mortgagee.

In a majority of the states the equitable theory prevails; in these states the title remains in the mortgagor, and the mortgagee has only a lien against the property as a security for his loan. Such view is called the lien theory of mortgages.

7-52 Property Capable of Being Mortgaged. In general, any interest in land, an equitable as well as a legal interest, can be mortgaged.

Property that one does not own cannot be mortgaged, but a mortgage may be so drawn as to cover property to be acquired in the future. Although no mortgage exists at the time, equity will recognize a lien against the property as soon as it is acquired. This lien is good as to all persons who acquire rights in the property, except bona fide purchasers for value without notice.

A mortgage may be given prior to the time when the money is advanced to the mortgagor. It has been held that when the mortgagee makes the payment the mortgage is a valid lien as of the date when the mortgage was recorded.

7-53 Form of Mortgage. The form of mortgage in common use still reflects the title theory, and as in a deed, states that it conveys the property to the mortgagee, subject to the conditions set forth in the mortgage. Such a conveyance of real property must be in writing, under seal, and executed with all the formalities of a deed. The contract between the parties with respect to the loan need not be included in the deed of conveyance, but may be set forth on a separate sheet of paper. In the title-theory states, a mortgage is a very formal instrument. In the lien-theory states, short forms of mortgages are usually authorized by statute and are not of such a technical nature.

7-54 Recording Mortgages. In order that the mortgagee may give notice to third parties that he has an interest in the real estate covered by the mortgage, it is necessary that the mortgage be recorded in the recording office of the county where the real estate is situated. This recording protects the mortgagee against subsequent bona fide purchasers of the land from taking the real estate free from the mortgage. The statutes of the various states specify the requirements necessary for recording mortgages.

7-55 An Absolute Conveyance May Be a Mortgage. An absolute deed made by a landowner to a person may be shown by parol evidence to be a mortgage, if such evidence indicates that the intention of the parties was to make the transfer a security for a loan.[4] The landowner must prove, however, by clear, precise, and positive evidence that it was the intention of the parties to draw up the deed for the purpose of securing a loan.

Likewise, a landowner may sell his land and give an absolute deed, with an agreement that he retain the right to repurchase for a certain price within a specified time. Parol evidence may be introduced in such a case to establish that the deed was given for the purpose of securing a loan. If the evidence is convincing, a court of equity will declare such a deed to be a mortgage. For example, a man may convey his farm worth $30,000 for a consideration of $10,000. The so-called buyer then gives the seller an option to repurchase at a figure approximating $10,000 and interest. If the evidence is clear that the parties intended to make a loan, even though the option period has expired, it is not too late for the grantor to redeem his property, because the court will treat the deed as if it had been a mortgage.

7-56 Deed of Trust in the Nature of a Mortgage. A deed of trust as a security instrument is often used as a substitute for a mortgage for the purpose of securing debts. The property is conveyed by the borrower who executes the deed of trust to a trustee to hold in trust for the benefit of creditors. If the debt is paid at the time required by the contract, the trustee reconveys the property to the grantor, the borrower. If there is a default in the payment, the trustee forecloses the trust deed and applies the proceeds to the payment of the debt secured. Deeds of trust are used where numerous notes are secured by the same property and are also used to secure bonds held by many different persons. For example, where it is desired to issue bonds secured by railroad or other corporate property, a trust deed may be executed to secure the entire bond issue. This method is necessary, because it would be impractical to execute a separate mortgage to secure each bond. An important feature of the deed of trust in many jurisdictions is that the note secured by it can be freely negotiated separate and apart from the deed of trust. When the mortgagor pays the note he surrenders it to the trustee under the trust deed and the latter makes it a matter of record that the obligation has been satisfied.

7-57 Purchase Money Mortgages. A purchase money mortgage is given for a part or the whole of the purchase price of land. For example, *A*

---

[4] *Davis v. Stone,* page 997.

wishes to purchase real estate worth $30,000. He has $10,000 in cash. Upon securing title from the vendor, he can complete his purchase by giving back to the vendor a mortgage on the real estate to secure a note for the remaining purchase price of $20,000. This type of mortgage is normally used in the buying and selling of real estate. In many jurisdictions a deficiency decree obtained upon the foreclosure of a purchase money mortgage will not be enforced.

7-58 Land Sale Contract. In the above illustration, the transaction could have been handled differently. The vendor and purchaser could have entered into a land sale contract whereby the vendor retained title and the purchaser would not receive a deed until he had paid the purchase price. The security of the vendor here lies in his retention of title. Often in the land sale contract an *escrow* will be established whereby the vendor executes a deed which is placed with some third party such as a bank with instruction to deliver it to the purchaser when he has completed his obligations under the contract. Under such an arrangement it is customary for the purchaser to make his payments to the escrow agent who in turn remits to the vendor. This method of handling a real estate purchase is often used where the purchaser makes a small down payment. There are many possible variations one of which is to provide for delivery of the deed with a mortgage back when a certain amount has been paid on the contract. In general the foreclosure of a purchaser's interest under a land sale contract is more easily accomplished than is the foreclosure of a mortgage.

7-59 Rights of Mortgagor. The mortgagor is personally liable for the mortgage debt, not by reason of the mortgage, but because he makes a note, a bond, or other contract which evidences the debt secured by the mortgage. A mortgage may be made to secure the performance of an obligation other than the payment of money. The mortgagor under the lien theory of modern statutes is regarded as the owner of the land. He has the same right to control the property as he had before making the mortgage, and he may sell the land, lease it, or make other mortgages, subject, however, to the agreement creating the already existing mortgage. Upon his death, interest in the real estate passes to his heirs, or, if he leaves a will, to his devisees under the will. His interest may be sold by a judgment creditor under an execution, subject to the prior right of the mortgagee. The mortgagor is entitled to retain possession of the property, cultivate the land, and secure the income therefrom. Since he is the owner of the mortgaged property, the mortgagor has an insurable interest in the property and can insure it for full value, regardless of the amount for which it is mortgaged. By the terms of the mortgage, the mortgagor is usually required to keep up the insurance for the benefit of the interest represented by the mortgage for, and on behalf of, the mortgagee. Upon a loss the insurance company pays the mortgagor and the mortgagee, as their interests may appear, if the insurance policy is so drawn as to protect both parties.

7-60 Rights and Liabilities of the Mortgagee. In the title-theory states, the mortgagee has legal title and theoretically the right to possess the mortgaged property during the period of the mortgage, unless the contract grants to the mortgagor the right to remain in possession. In the lien-theory states, the mortgagor is entitled to possession unless a different arrangement is provided for in the mortgage. In both the lien- and title-theory states, the mortgagee is protected against any person who commits waste or impairs the security. Even the mortgagor may not use the property in such a manner as to reduce materially its value. Mining ore, pumping oil, or cutting timber are operations which must be provided for in the mortgage agreement. Perhaps, if they were being conducted at the time the mortgage was created, the mortgagor might continue without authorization in the mortgage.

A mortgagee has a right to pay off or to redeem from any superior mortgage in order to protect his security, and he can charge the amount so paid to the mortgagor. Likewise, he may pay taxes or special assessments, which are a lien on the land, defend suits which threaten the title of the mortgagor, and recover the sum so expended. The mortgagor is under a duty to protect the security, but, should he fail to do so, the mortgagee has the right to make any reasonable expenditures necessary to protect the security for a debt.

Just as in the case of security agreements in personal property, a mortgage can provide for future advances to be made by the mortgagee. If the mortgagor gives a second mortgage prior to the future advances under the first, a priorities problem is presented. Generally, it is held that the first mortgagee prevails unless he had actual knowledge of the second when he made the further advances.[5]

7-61 Transfer of Mortgaged Property. The mortgagor may sell, will, or give away the mortgaged property, subject, however, to the rights of the mortgagee. A transferee from a mortgagor occupies the position of a grantee; he stands in the same position as the mortgagor and has no greater rights. Such grantee of the mortgagor's interest may redeem the land and require the mortgagee, if the latter is in possession, to account for rents and profits. A grantee of mortgaged property is not personally liable for the mortgage debt, unless he impliedly or expressly assumes and agrees to pay the mortgage. Such obligation must be established by clear and conclusive evidence. If he merely purchases "subject to" the mortgage, he pays the mortgage debt only when he deems the real estate to have a value greater than the amount of the mortgage, and he is not personally liable on the obligation. If he assumes the mortgage, he becomes personally liable for the debt, although the land is worth less than the mortgage. For example, if *A* purchases real estate worth $8,000 which is subject to a mortgage of $5,000 and assumes and agrees to pay the mortgage, he pays the former owner $3,000 and assumes responsibility for the ultimate payment of the mortgage. If he merely purchases the

[5] *Blaustein v. Aiello,* page 999.

real estate subject to the mortgage, he again pays the owner $3,000, but pays the $5,000 mortgage only if the land is worth that much when the mortgage matures. Otherwise, he permits the land to be foreclosed without any personal liability on his part for the deficit: whereas, if he had assumed the debt, he would have been liable for it.

7-62 Liability of Mortgagor After Transfer. If the grantee of the mortgaged property assumes and agrees to pay the indebtedness, he thereby becomes the person primarily liable for the debt; as between himself and the mortgagor, by virtue of his promise to the mortgagor to pay the debt, he is the principal debtor and the mortgagor is the surety. This assumption by the grantee, however, does not relieve the mortgagor of his obligation to the mortgagee, and such mortgagor continues liable unless he is released from his indebtedness by the mortgagee. Such a release must comply with all the requirements for a novation. In those states which recognize the relationship of principal and surety between the mortgagor and his grantee, an agreement made by the mortgagee with the grantee, to extend the time of payment, will release the mortgagor from liability. If the grantee takes "subject to" the mortgage, the original debtor is not released, since suretyship is not involved directly. Many states, however, release the mortgagor of responsibility for any loss resulting from a decline in value of the mortgaged property during the period of extension.

7-63 Insurance. As noted, both the mortgagor and the mortgagee have an insurable interest in the mortgaged property. The destruction of mortgaged property by fire gives the mortgagee no interest in the proceeds recovered under a fire insurance policy unless the mortgage required the mortgagor to insure the property for the benefit of both parties. Since the vast majority of mortgages require insurance, insurance companies have formulated various mortgage clauses for insertion when insurance is issued on mortgaged property.

One of these clauses provides that in case of loss, payment shall first be made to the mortgagee until his debt is satisfied, any balance being paid to the insured. Such a provision is a simple loss-payable clause and gives the mortgagee no greater rights against the insurer than those possessed by the mortgagor. Thus, if property mortgaged for $7,000 is fully insured, and a $9,000 loss occurs, $7,000 is payable to the mortgagee and $2,000 to the mortgagor. The amount paid to the mortgagee effectively reduces the amount owed by the mortgagor. In this manner both parties are adequately protected by a single policy.

In many states the insurer, when requested, inserts in the policy what has become known as the "standard mortgage clause." In effect, a policy with such a clause creates two contracts, one with the mortgagor and one with the mortgagee. Consequently, if for any reason the policy is not enforceable by the mortgagor, it nevertheless is enforceable by the mortgagee to the extent of his interest. Misconduct or violation of policy terms by the mortgagor does not destroy the mortgagee's protection unless he is aware of such conduct and fails to report it to the insurance company. To terminate the policy as to the mortgagee, ten days' written notice is required. However, if at any time the insurer pays the mortgagee when under no duty to the mortgagor, the latter having violated some policy term, the mortgage debt is not reduced. To the extent payment is made to the mortgagee under these conditions, the insurer takes over that portion of the claim against the owner under the doctrine of subrogation.

7-64 Transfer of Debt. A debt that is secured by the mortgage is a chore in action, usually evidenced by notes or bonds. If the notes or bonds are nonnegotiable, the assignee of such notes or bonds takes title subject to all defenses that are available against the assignor. If, however, the notes or bonds are negotiable instruments and are transferred by negotiation as required under the Code, the holder takes free of personal defenses that would have been available against the transferror. The holder of the negotiable instrument secured by the mortgage has the right, upon default, to enforce the mortgage for the purpose of securing payment of the debt, as evidenced by the notes or bonds. If the mortgagee transfers the note without any formal transfer or mention of the mortgage, the transferee of the note is entitled to the benefit of the mortgage, because the security follows the debt. Since a debt secured by the mortgage is the principal and the mortgage only an incident, it would appear that an assignment of the mortgage without the debt is a nullity. Since a mortgage without a debt is difficult to comprehend, an assignment of the mortgage without the assignment of the debt accomplishes nothing. The debt cannot be assigned to one and the mortgage security to another.

If an assignment of the mortgage is made, the assignment should be recorded in order to give notice of the rights of the assignee to all subsequent purchasers. However, failure to record the assignment will not aid a purchaser or later mortgagee who has notice of the assignment. Actual notice should also be given to the mortgagor; otherwise, payment by the mortgagor to the mortgagee may discharge the mortgage.

7-65 Payment Before Default. Payment of the mortgage debt terminates the mortgage. Upon payment by the mortgagor a release or satisfaction is secured from the mortgagee, and this release should be recorded in order to clear the title to the land. Otherwise, the unreleased mortgage will remain a cloud on the title. If the mortgagee refuses voluntarily to give a release, he can be compelled to do so in a court of equity by a bill to remove a cloud on the title or by other proceeding provided for by statute.

A tender of the principal by the mortgagor before the due date does not terminate the lien evidenced by the mortgage, because the mortgagee cannot be forced to lose his investment before maturity. However, a tender of principal and interest upon the due day terminates the lien, although such a tender does not discharge the debt, and the mortgagee may still enforce it personally against the mortgagor until absolute payment has taken place. Under the common-law title theory, a tender on the due date satisfies the condition and reinvests the title in the mortgagor, but a tender after the due day does not have such an effect. The condition not having been performed, a reconveyance by the mortgagee is necessary. Thus, in the title theory states, a tender at maturity reinvests the title in the mortgagor, although in the lien theory states, a tender at or after maturity terminates the lien. The mortgagor's only remedy in title theory states is that of placing his money in court and bringing a suit in equity for redemption. Such tender does, however, forestall recovery for interest and court costs.

7-66 Right to Redeem Before Foreclosure Sale. At any time after default, but before sale of the land on foreclosure, a mortgagor may exercise his right to redeem from the mortgage or foreclosure sale, unless this right has been barred by a period of time specified by the statute. The mortgagor or any person who has an interest in the mortgaged land is entitled to redeem from the mortgage before foreclosure sale; but, in order to do so, he must pay the entire mortgage debt, with interest, and all other sums, including costs, to which the mortgagee may be entitled by reason of the mortgage. If the mortgagee is in possession of the mortgaged property and refuses to consent to a redemption, the mortgagor or any party entitled to redeem may file a bill in equity for the purpose of redeeming the mortgaged property. Such person, however, must be ready and willing to pay whatever the court finds due, or tender to the court all moneys due on said mortgage.

7-67 Right to Redeem After the Foreclosure Sale. By statute in most states, any person interested in the premises, through or under the mortgagor, may, within a specified period of time from the foreclosure sale of said property, redeem the real estate so sold. To do so, he must pay to the purchaser thereof, to the sheriff or to the court officer who sold the property for the benefit of the purchaser, the sum of money, with interest and costs, for which the premises were sold or bid off. The period of time allowed for redemption varies greatly from state to state. Generally, the redeeming mortgagor is required to pay in addition costs incurred by the purchaser at the foreclosure sale in protecting and preserving the property. In some states the redemption price includes the value of improvements made by the purchaser on possession.[6]

MORTGAGE FORECLOSURES

7-68 Right to Foreclose. If the mortgagor fails to perform his obligation—that is, to pay the debt when it falls due or to perform any of the covenants set forth in the mortgage, such as the payment of principal by installment, of interest, insurance, or taxes—or if he defaults in other obligations, the mortgagee may declare the whole debt due and payable, and foreclose for the purpose of collecting the indebtedness.

[6] *Ladd v. Pavmer,* page 1000.

7-69 Types of Foreclosure. The statutes of the various states specify the procedure by which mortgages are foreclosed. There are four types of foreclosure proceedings for the purpose of using the mortgaged property to pay the mortgage debt; strict foreclosure, foreclosure by suit in equity, foreclosure by exercise of the power of sale, and foreclosure by entry and writ of entry.

7-70 Strict Foreclosure. Strict foreclosure is one by which the mortgagee gets the land free from the right of redemption after the date specified in the foreclosure decree; that is, the decree provides that, if the debt is not paid by a certain date, the mortgagor loses the realty and the mortgagee takes it free from the rights of junior mortgagees and lienholders. This is a harsh rule and is used only where it is clear that the mortgaged property is not worth the mortgage indebtedness, the mortgagor is insolvent, and the mortgagee accepts the property in full satisfaction of the indebtedness.

Strict foreclosure as a remedy for the mortgagee-creditor is not only used under limited circumstances in mortgages, but may also be used as a remedy by the vendor in installment land sale contracts. In many contracts for the sale of land, the vendee is put in possession by making a down payment of part of the purchase price with the remainder to be paid in stated installments. The title is reserved by way of security by the vendor with a deed placed in escrow. The contract usually provides that all payments must be promptly made, otherwise the vendor may declare all payments due, terminate the contract, and cause the vendee to forfeit all previous payments and improvements as liquidated damages or as rent for the use of the property.

That such strict foreclosure might work a hardship on a purchaser is apparent. Since the relationship created is similar to that of mortgagee-mortgagor, the courts upon proper application will not permit the vendee to lose his equity of redemption and will order a foreclosure and sale of the land. Whether a land sale contract will be strictly foreclosed lies within the discretion of an equity court. If the vendee has made only a small payment, is guilty of gross laches, or has been negligent in the performance of his contract and it is not inequitable to place the vendor in his original position, strict foreclosure will be permitted. However, if the vendee has made only a slight default as to the amount and time of payment, or has largely completed his payments, and the amount of the unpaid purchase price is much less than the value of the property involved, strict foreclosure will be denied.

7-71 Foreclosure by Suit in Equity. The usual method of foreclosing a mortgage is a proceeding in equity, such proceeding being provided for by statute. A bill for foreclosure is filed in a court of equity; this bill sets up the mortgagee's rights, as provided for in the mortgage, and shows such breaches of the covenants in the mortgage as will give a right of foreclosure. The court will issue a certificate of sale authorizing the master in chancery or some other officer of the court to sell the land at public auction. Following the sale, he gives the purchaser a deed to the land and accounts for the funds realized as a result of the sale. To the extent that funds are available, they are used to pay court costs, the mortgage indebtedness, and inferior liens in the order of their priority. If any surplus remains, it is paid to the former owner of the property. Foreclosure by a second mortgagee is made subject to all superior liens. The buyer at the foreclosure sale takes title, and the first mortgage remains a lien on the property. All inferior liens are cut off by foreclosure except as the holders thereof have an equity in a surplus if such exists. As stated in § 7-67, the statutes in many states provide a short period of time after the sale within which the mortgagor or other persons in interest are entitled to redeem the property. Where such statutes are in force, the purchaser is not entitled to his deed until after the expiration of the period within which redemption may be made.

7-72 Foreclosure by Exercise of Power of Sale. The mortgage often provides that, upon default by the mortgagor, the mortgagee may sell the land without judicial process. This method of foreclosure can only be made in strict conformity with the terms of the mortgage. The power of sale makes the mortgagee the agent of the mortgagor to sell the land. In some states, however, a power of sale in the mortgage is expressly forbidden by statute, and foreclosures must be effected by judicial proceeding. A power of sale granted in a mortgage or a deed of trust is not revocable, since the agency is coupled with an interest; therefore, the death or insanity of the mortgagor will not revoke the power. In those states where the exercise of power is regulated by statute, the sale must be public after the prescribed notice is given. In the absence of statute or mortgage agreement, however, the sale may be private. Since a mortgagee, in selling the land under a power of sale, is acting as an agent for the mortgagor, he is not allowed to purchase at the sale, because an agent cannot himself purchase that which he has been given authority by his principal to sell. The purchaser at such a sale secures only such title as the mortgagor had when he made the mortgage.

When a deed of trust, in which the trustee is empowered to sell the land and to apply the proceeds to the mortgage debt, is given to secure the payment of a debt, the same rules apply as are set forth above.

7-73 Foreclosure by Entry and by Writ of Entry. In a very few states, the mortgagee may foreclose by entry upon the land, after default, after publication of notice and advertisement, and in the presence of witnesses; or by the possession of the premises for a period of time. If, after a limited period, the mortgagor does not redeem, the foreclosure is said to be completed and the title to rest in the mortgagee.

7-74 Deficiency Decree. Since the mortgage debt is usually represented by a bond or a note, the mortgagor is personally liable for such debt, and the mortgagee may sue the mortgagor for it. If the land that is the security for the debt does not sell for a sum sufficient to pay the mortgage indebtedness, by statute in most states the court may enter a deficiency decree for that part of the unsatisfied debt. This decree will stand as a judgment against the mortgagor, and his other property may be levied on to satisfy such judgment. For example: *A*, the mortgagee, owns a mortgage which is security for an indebtedness of $10,000 against *B*'s land. If, on foreclosure and sale of the land, the sum of only $7,000 is secured, *A* may obtain a deficiency judgment against *B* for $3,000, which will be a lien against any other property that *B* may own. Such other property may then be levied on and sold to satisfy the $3,000 deficiency judgment.

In order not to impose too great a hardship on mortgagor-debtors, different schemes have been devised to limit the amount of deficiency decrees. A revaluation of the property at the time of the foreclosure is sometimes used if its value is less than the total debt, and this amount is deducted from the judgment. Many states have statutes limited to purchase money mortgages that provide in part that when a decree is granted for the foreclosure of any mortgage given to secure payment of the balance of the purchase price of real property, the decree shall provide for the sale of the real property covered by such mortgage for the satisfaction of the decree, but the mortgagee shall not be entitled to a deficiency judgment if the property sells for less than the amount due on the debt. The elimination of deficiency decrees rests on several theories: that the mortgagee loaned his money on the security of the land and not the personal credit of the purchaser-debtor; that a mortgagee-creditor should share with the debtor the risk of declining land value; and that if the land is the limit of the security, fewer inflationary and sounder loans will be made.

7-75 Priorities. In general the recorded mortgage will have priority over general creditors of the mortgagor. However, if obtained for a pre-existing obligation, a judgment creditor who obtained his judgment prior to the mortgage will prevail.[7]

MECHANICS' LIEN LAWS

7-76 Nature. Mechanics' lien laws are the result of legislation that makes possible liens upon real estate where such real estate has been improved. The purpose of such legislation is to protect the laborer and materialman in the event of the insolvency of the owner or the contractor. The laws of the states vary slightly in the protection accorded and the procedure required to obtain it. For these reasons, the laws of the individual state should be consulted in a particular instance. The sections which follow relate to provisions which are generally found in the various state laws.

7-77 Persons Entitled to Lien. Those persons are entitled to a lien, who, by either express or implied contract with the owner of real property,

[7] *Sterlington Bank v. Terzia Lumber & Hardware, Inc.,* page 1001.

agree: (1) to deliver material, fixtures, apparatus, machinery, forms, or form work to be used in repairing, altering, or constructing a building upon the premises; (2) to fill, sod, or do landscape work in connection with the same; (3) to act as architect, engineer, or superintendent during the construction of a building; or (4) to furnish labor for repairing, altering, or constructing a building.

Those parties who contract with the owner, whether they furnish labor or material, or agree to construct the building, are known as contractors. Thus, practically any contract between the owner and another that has for its purpose the improvement of real estate gives rise to a lien on the premises in favor of those responsible for the improvement. To illustrate: a contract to attach a permanent fixture to a building or one to beautify a lawn would create a lien in favor of the contractor.

In addition to contractors, anyone who furnishes labor, materials, or apparatus to contractors, or anyone to whom a distinct part of the contract has been sublet, has a right to a lien. These parties are customarily referred to as subcontractors. Their rights differ slightly from those of contractors, and some of these differences will be considered in later sections.

In order that a lien for materials may be maintained, the material must be furnished to the contractor or subcontractor. In addition, a record of the material furnished on each job is usually required. This procedure is necessary for two reasons: first, the record is essential to accuracy in the determination of the amount of the lien; and, second, it is evidence that the contractor is not his own materialman. If the material is sold on the general credit of the contractor and no record of the deliveries is kept, title passes to the contractor, and he becomes his own materialman so that the original materialman is not entitled to the lien.

The lien of a party furnishing building material arises as soon as the material is delivered to the premises. On the other hand, one who supplies equipment or machinery receives a lien only if he can show that the goods delivered have become a part of the completed structure.

7-78 Against Whom Does the Lien Arise? Any interest in real estate may be subjected to a lien. A fee simple, a life estate, or a lease for years may have a lien against it, depending on the nature of the contract. If the owner of the fee simple contracts for the construction, or authorizes or knowingly permits the improvement to be made, the lien is good against his interest as well as against the improvement. If a lessee, without the consent or knowledge of the owner, contracts for the construction or improvement of property, the lien arises only upon the interest of the lessee. To illustrate: *A* leases a vacant lot from *B*, with the understanding that *A* is to construct a building on the premises. Any lien created will affect the interests of both *A* and *B*. If *A* had not obtained *B*'s consent to erect the building, the lien would have been created only against the interest of *A*.

The improvement of real property should not give to the lien holder a right to disturb or destroy a prior mortgage. At the same time, there is no occasion to increase the protection of the mortgagee at the expense of the lien holder. Consequently, an existing mortgage is always given a superior lien on the value of the property in its unimproved state. In many states, however, if the improvement, or its value, can be segregated, the mechanic's lien will be superior on the improvement. Where separation is not feasible, a method of appraisal is usually provided for, to determine what portion of the proceeds, at time of sale, are derived from the improvement.

7-79 Formalities Required to Perpetuate Lien. Under the law of most states the contractor's lien arises as soon as the contract is entered into. In order to protect the contractor against claims of innocent third parties who might purchase the property or obtain a mortgage thereon, the law provides that the lien must be made a matter of record within a certain time, usually three to four months after all work is completed. Failure on the part of the materialman to register his claim as required by the statute will result in the loss of the lien as against subsequent bona fide purchasers or encumbrancers. As between the owner and the contractor, however, the time limit may be extended somewhat beyond this period. During the four months' period, the lien is good against innocent third parties even though it is not recorded.

To establish their liens, the subcontractors—materialmen, laborers, and others—must, within a relatively short period of time after they have furnished the last of their materials or labor, either make the liens a matter of record, or serve written notice thereof on the owner, according to the particular state statute. The period most frequently mentioned by the various states is 60 days.

7-80 Protection Accorded the Owner. The mechanics' lien law usually states that the owner shall not be liable for more than the contract price, provided he follows certain procedure outlined in the law. The law further provides that it shall be the duty of the owner, before making any payments to the contractor, to obtain from the latter a sworn statement setting forth all the creditors and the amounts due, or to become due, to them. It is then the duty of the owner to retain sufficient funds at all times to pay the amounts indicated by the sworn statements, provided they do not exceed the contract price. In addition, if any liens have been filed by the subcontractors, it is the owner's duty to retain sufficient money to pay them. He is at liberty to pay any balance to the contractor. If the amount retained is insufficient to pay all the creditors, they share proportionately in the balance, except that most of the states prefer claims of laborers. The owner has a right to rely upon the truthfulness of the sworn statement. If the contractor misstates the facts and obtains a sum greater than that to which he is entitled, the loss falls upon the subcontractors rather than upon the owner. Under such circumstances, the subcontractors may look only to the contractor to make good their deficit. Payments made by the owner, without first obtaining a sworn statement, may not be used to defeat the claims of subcontractors, materialmen, and laborers. Before making any payment, it is the duty of the owner to require the sworn statement and to withhold the amount necessary to pay the claims indicated.

Where the contractor is willing, the owner may also protect himself by stipulating in the construction contract a waiver of the contractor's lien. A waiver of lien by the contractor also waives the lien of the subcontractors, as they derive their rights through those of the contractor. Certain states require the owner to record such a contract before subcontractors begin work, in order that the agreement may bar their right to a lien.

REAL PROPERTY CASES

Dean Vincent, Inc. v. Redisco, Inc.

1962 (Ore.) 373 P.2d 995

GOODWIN, J. This is a contest for priority between secured creditors. It arises out of the building of an apartment house. The plaintiff holds a first mortgage on the real property. The defendant, Redisco, Inc., holds a conditional sales contract and a second mortgage for the price of the floor coverings and the installation charges therefor. From a decree according priority to the plaintiff's mortgage, Redisco appeals. . . .

Carpeting, like electrical ornaments, plumbing bowls, hardware, and an infinite variety of other personal property, may or may not be so annexed to the real property as to lose its identity as personal property . . . Whether such property retains its character as personal property or loses its separate identity in the real property depends upon a combination of factors. These factors are usually spoken of as annexation, adaptation, and intention. Intention is the most important and the most difficult factor to apply. It must be objective, and not some secret plan or mental reservation. . . .

Except for the semantical influence of cases concerning "rugs," there is no reason to say that installed floor covering is any more or less movable than installed plumbing fixtures, as either may be removed by experts, properly outfitted with tools, without doing appreciable harm to the freehold. See *Roseburg Nat. Bank v. Camp*, 89 Or. 67, 73-74, 173 P. 313, 315, where we said:

> The old rule that all things annexed to the realty become a part of it has been much relaxed. Annexation is not the sole test for determining whether a fixture is removable or irremovable. The line between removable and irremovable fixtures is sometimes so close and difficult to ascertain that it is impossible to frame a precise, unbending and infalliable rule which can be applied to all cases. Each case must depend largely upon its own special facts and peculiar circumstances. . . .

The record shows that the trial judge had our former cases in mind when he ruled upon the question below. His ruling was based upon a careful consideration of the intention of the parties as disclosed by their behavior. He also considered the manner of installation (annexation), and the actual as well as the intended adaptation and adaptability of the material installed. Insofar as his evaluation of the facts is concerned, we can find no basis for reaching a different conclusion.

It may well be true that Redisco did not intend to give up the security title it retained under its conditional sales contract. However, no vendor is likely to intend to forfeit any security. The important question is not what the vendor intended, but what an objective bystander would make of the total factual situation. . . .

The controlling intent would seem to be that of the buyer and seller concerning the function of the floor covering. Did the parties intend that the floor covering be installed in the building, there to remain during its useful life, or did they intend to put down the floor covering to be used as such only until someone might see fit to take it out and use it elsewhere?

Since it is reasonable to assume that all parties expected the financial aspects of the transaction to proceed according to plan, the principal intention of the parties, from a functional point of view, was to put the carpet down and leave it there until it wore out. If such was their intention, then the nature of the order to the factory for custom-made carpet and the cutting and fitting within the seventy units is completely consistent with the view taken by the trial court that the floor covering was intended to become a permanent part of the building.

The possibility of a miscarriage in the financial arrangements no doubt occurred to the sellers, at least, and may have prompted their employment of a title-retaining contract of sale. This type of contract is not unusual, however, in the sale of fixtures of all kinds. The Legislative Assembly has devoted attention to the security aspects of sales of fixtures. (ORS 76.010 to 76.030 (applicable during the period covered by the transactions now before the court) and ORS 79.3130 (scheduled to take effect September 1, 1963, as part of the Uniform Commercial Code)). Under both sections of the code, the old and the new, the results in a given case may differ, but the determination of the character of the goods sold as either real or personal property is left to the common law. A thing does not become, or fail to become, a fixture by reason of the type of contract under which it is sold. If the merchandise does become a fixture, and if it was sold under a title-retaining contract, then the rights of the parties may be subject to certain statutory rules, e.g., ORS 76.010. However, in the case at bar there was no attempt to comply with the statutory law on the subject, and we need not concern ourselves with hypothetical questions that might have arisen under the code. We have only to decide whether the floor covering became a fixture under the common-law rules found in our cases.

There is no particular policy or equitable reason to favor either party in a transaction of this character. To permit the conditional seller of merchandise to go into the building and remove part of the building is no better or no worse than to wash out the security of the seller by forbidding such relief. The parties were dealing at arms' length at all times.

The first mortgage is a prior lien on the building and its fixtures. The carpet is a fixture under all the tests of annexation, adaptation, and function intention. We concur in the trial court's analysis of the factual situation, and in its application of the law of fixtures.

Affirmed.

Merchants & Mech. Fed. Sav. & Loan Assn. v. Herald

1964, Ohio 201 N.E.2d 237

Herald constructed a house and installed wall-to-wall carpeting which had been purchased from the Gaier Furniture Co. He gave the furniture company a note and chattel mortgage which were assigned to the First National Bank of Springfield. The mortgage was recorded. The plaintiff savings and loan association brought suit to foreclose on a *real property mortgage* given to it by Herald and the First National Bank intervened in the proceedings and filed a cross-petition seeking to foreclose its *chattel mortgage.* The property had been sold to Taggart Coal and Supply Co. which company moved to dismiss the First National Bank's petition. The record indicates that Taggart did not have actual notice of the chattel mortgage. The motion was granted and the bank appealed.

CRAWFORD, J. . . . It is our opinion that the principles enunciated in the case of *Holland Furnace Co. v. Trumbull Savings & Loan Co.* (1939, 135 Ohio St. 48, 19 N.E.2d 273) are dispositive of this case. While there is some variation in the facts, the same reasoning will apply.

The tests for determining whether a chattel has become a fixture are set forth in . . . that case as follows:

A fixture is to be determined by the consideration of a combination of the following tests: (1) To become a fixture it is essential that the chattel in question be annexed to some extent to realty. (2) The chattel must have an appropriate application to the use or purpose to which the realty to which it is attached is devoted. (3) There must be an actual or apparent intention upon the part of the owner of the chattel in affixing it to realty to make such chattel a permanent part of such realty. . . .

We proceed to apply these tests in their numerical order to the facts in the present case.

(1) Concerning annexation of a chattel to real estate, the court said in the course of its opinion, "The annexation may be very slight." In that case a furnace was involved. It was attached to the warm-air registers or pipes of the house with metallic sleeves or sections of pipe. In our case the attachment of the padding with staples to the floor and of the carpeting by being mechanically stretched and engaged with the smoothing strips, appears to us to be comparable.

It is doubtful that the carpeting and padding were as vital to the habitability of this house as was the furnace to that in the case cited. Nevertheless, these items "have an appropriate application to the use or purpose to which the realty to which it is (they are) attached, is devoted,". . .

The intent of the owner to make these chattels part of the realty, to be sold with it, is apparent and consistent throughout except for his execution of the chattel mortgage. However, in almost all such controversies, including the Holland Furnace case, the owner has executed a chattel mortgage or conditional sales agreement, else the question would not arise. Hence, this circumstance is not determinative. The property is a chattel or chattels when the mortgage is executed. Its annexation to the real estate is subsequent.

This decision of the Supreme Court also disposes of the only other important question in the case: Whether the purchaser was charged with notice of the chattel mortgage which had been made a matter of public record. As already noted, there is nothing to show that it had actual notice. The Holland Furnace case holds that in such a situation the chattel mortgage, filed as such and apparently containing no legal description of the real estate and no reference thereto except as to the location of the chattel property, does not constitute notice to a purchaser of the real estate

As between the chattel mortgagor and chattel mortgagee, we would have an entirely different question. But in the case of a bona fide purchaser of the real estate without actual notice of the chattel mortgage, the purchaser will prevail against the fully informed chattel mortgagee.

The judgment is affirmed.

Paschen v. Pashkow

1965 (Ill.) 211 N.E.2d 576

SULLIVAN, J.   This is an appeal from a declaratory judgment in favor of the defendants entered at the close of plaintiff's case declaring that a covenant entered into in 1896 restricting Castlewood Terrace in the city of Chicago to single-family residences was binding and enforceable. Plaintiff had sought the removal of the restriction in order to construct high-rise apartments.

Castlewood subdivision was subdivided and platted in 1896.

All of the deeds to the Castlewood Terrace lots contained the following restrictions: . . .

That "no apartment or flat building or structure built, used or adapted for the separate housekeeping of more than one family shall at any time be built or maintained upon said premises."

Plaintiff acquired title to the lots in question in 1916. Between 1930 and 1935 Lincoln Park was extended from Montrose to Foster by reclaiming submerged land. Marine Drive was constructed along what was previously the water's edge. There had been 14 high-rise buildings erected on Marine Drive between Irving Park and Foster avenue, which streets are respectively 12 blocks to the south of and five blocks to the north of Castlewood Terrace. At the southwest corner of Ainslie and Marine Drive an 8-story high-rise apartment has been erected. . . .

The record also indicates that the defendants and the owners of other lots on Castlewood Terrace have been vigilant in maintaining and enforcing the restrictive covenants. . . .

The question squarely confronting the court is whether the evidence showed such a substantial change in the character of the surrounding neighborhood as to make it impossible any longer to secure in a substantial degree the benefits sought to be realized through the performance of the building restriction. (American Law Property, Vol. 2, sec. 9.39, p. 445). . . .

Plaintiff properly states the law that the court will not uphold a restrictive covenant where the property and the neighborhood have, since the inception of the covenants, so changed in character or environment that the objects of the covenants are defeated or cannot be accomplished, and their enforcement would be harsh, inequitable or oppressive. . . . But each case involving restrictive covenants must be decided on its own facts. . . .

In the instant case the residential character of Castlewood Terrace has never been violated. The street is only 1200 feet long without intersections. The changes around this block caused by the construction of highrise apartments, a motel and hospitals along Marine Drive have not affected Castlewood Terrace.

We conclude that Castlewood Terrace and the neighborhood have not so changed in character and environment that the object of the covenants are defeated or cannot be accomplished, and the restrictions are reasonable and not contrary to public policy or any positive rule of law.

Judgment affirmed.

Davis v. Stone

1964, 236 F.Supp. 553

The plaintiffs purchased properties in Washington, D.C. The purchasers assumed an existing mortgage and gave the seller a second mortgage to secure a trust note for the purchase price. The note was sold to Stone, the defendant. Thereafter, the plaintiffs were in default and in lieu of foreclosure by Stone, the plaintiffs deeded the property to him under an agreement that the property would be deeded back if the plaintiffs completed all payments due under the mortgage note. The plaintiffs defaulted in their payments again. Stone contended that he was entitled to the property under the deed. The plaintiffs claimed that the deed should be declared an equitable mortgage.

KEECH, D. J. It has been pointed out by no less authority than Chief Justice Marshall that neither the policy nor the letter of the law prohibits the sale of property with the right to repurchase reserved to the vendor. (*Conway's Executors and Devisees v. Alexander,* 7 Cranch 218, 237, 11 U.S. 218, 237, 3 L.Ed. 321 (1812).) That a mortgagor may convey his equity of redemption to the mortgagee in satisfaction of a debt is also well established. . . . But courts of equity will carefully scrutinize such a transaction between mortgagor and mortgagee, to determine what was really intended. The policy of the law will not permit the conversion of a mortgage into a sale, and, because of the debtor's relative position, doubtful cases will be construed as mortgages. . . .

In these cases in which the mortgagor transfers to the mortgagee with a condition of defeasance reserved to the mortgagor, all the authorities agree that the test by which to determine whether the transaction is intended as a mortgage or as a sale is whether or not a personal debt is created or continues to exist. . . . This test applies even where the conveyance is in lieu of foreclosure. No consideration of law or public policy prevents a transfer of mortgaged property to the mortgagee in satisfaction of the debt, but the debt must be cancelled thereby. . . .

The presumption is that a deed is what it purports to be on its face and one who seeks to establish the contrary has the burden of doing so by clear and convincing evidence. But the condition of defeasance and creation or subsistence of a debt need not be on the face of the deed, but may be established by contemporaneous agreement. . . .

In the instant case, the court finds that there was no cancellation of the debt, but that the Davises continued to be indebted to Stone after delivery of the deeds.

Where evidence of the debt is retained by the grantee, the continued existence of the debt is presumed. . . . But there is no need here to resort to presumptions. Not only did the grantee retain the notes evidencing the grantor's obligations, but he continued to record Davis's payments on the second trust note itself as well as in the payment book incident to this note. . . . There was no notation on either the notes or the payment books of any cancellation or reduction of the debt on account of the transfer of the property. The only consideration on the face of the deed was ten dollars. Moreover, the intent to secure rather than cancel the existing debt, or to create a new one, is evident from the face of the agreement signed contemporaneously with the delivery of the deeds. The transfer is there limited, i.e., it is made only ". . . until all monies advanced by the party of the second part for delinquent payment on first trust, second trust on above described properties and taxes has been reimbursed, . . . It is further agreed that upon final payment of this obligation the party of the second part will reconvey the above described properties in fee simple. . . ." In conformance with this intent, plaintiffs remained in possession of the properties until they defaulted, almost a year after the transfer.

Ingersoll v. Tyler (47 App.D.C. 328, 331 (1918)) suggests that the keeping alive of the debt is not conclusive but only a strong indication of an intended mortgage. This court, however believes that it is controlling in view of the language in *Dollar v. Land, supra,* and practically unanimous authority elsewhere. This is especially true where there is no other sufficient consideration. In any event, the continuation or creation of a debt requires the grantee to show that the transaction was in fact a sale. This has not been done.

The court finds that the two deeds must be construed as mortgages when read in the light of the agreement of March 20, 1959, and the actions of the parties thereto.

Judgment for plaintiffs.

Blaustein v. Aiello

1963 (Md.) 190 A.2d 639

Home Federal Savings & Loan Association (Home) entered into two construction loan agreements with Forest Knolls, Inc., a corporation engaged in building dwellings. By the terms of these agreements, Forest Knolls agreed to construct six residences upon vacant lots; in return, Home agreed to lend Forest Knolls $84,000 to be advanced in the future in accordance with schedules set forth in the agreements. These schedules provided that the final portions of the loans, amounting to $2,800 for each house, were to be made "when (the dwellings were) FULLY COMPLETED, graded and landscaped; Release of Liens for all labor and materials submitted in proper form." The agreements further provided that if the real estate were encumbered without the consent of the lender, the lender would be under no obligation to make "further payments."

In accordance with these agreements, a note and deed of trust were executed by Forest Knolls. The trust was recorded.

Thereafter a second trust note was executed and recorded. Blaustein, assignee of the second trust note brought action against Aiello, the trustee under the first trust deed to establish his priority. The lower court ruled that the first trust deed prevailed as to advances made to Forest Knolls after the execution and recordation of the second. Blaustein appealed.

PRESCOTT, J. The appellant contends: (1) that the first deed of trust was one to secure future advances; (2) that the lien of the trust under which he claims attached before the "final payments" of $2,800 each were made; (3) that the final payments were voluntary and not obligatory under the terms of the trust, as the houses had not been completed nor had releases of liens been obtained; and (4) that Home, the holder of the first trust, had actual knowledge of the second trust at the time of the voluntary payments. From these premises, he argues that his claim is superior to that of the holder of the first trust.

For the purposes of this case, we shall assume, without deciding, that appellant's contentions (1), (2), and (3) above are correct. In *Frank M. Ewing Co. v. Krafft Company* (222 Md.21, 158 A.2d 654) we held, in accordance with the great weight of authority, that a voluntary advance, as distinguished from one that was obligatory, by the holder of a first trust after actual notice of the attaching of intervening liens ranks behind those liens. We were careful to point out in that case that the appellant had actual notice, i.e., such notice as actually imparts and brings home knowledge of the existence of a fact to a party to be affected thereby, or his authorized agent. There are several sound reasons for the above rule. Among these are that it would be inequitable to permit a prior lienor, with actual knowledge of subordinate liens, to diminish, voluntarily and at his whim or caprice, the security of subordinate lienors. And a contrary view would place an owner who is unable to demand advances from the holder of the first deed of trust in the unfortunate position of also being unable to borrow on his property from another by reason of the possibility that, after the giving of a later deed of trust to the latter, the holder of the prior deed of trust might make advances to the owner, which would take priority over the claim of such latter.

We hold that constructive notice by the recording of the second deed of trust was not sufficient to bring the instant case within the scope of the Ewing case. (We did not quite reach this specific question in Ewing.)

. . .

In the instant case, there is not a scintilla of evidence that Home, or any authorized agent of it, had actual knowledge of the second trust when it made the final payments. Since the appellant failed to establish one of the necessary factors to place him within the ambit of our holding in Ewing, he cannot prevail.

Order affirmed, appellant to pay the costs.

Ladd v. Parmer

1965 (Ala.) 178 So.2d 829

PER CURIAM. This is an appeal from a final decree of the Circuit Court of Mobile County, in Equity, fixing the amount appellants (Mortgagors) should pay to redeem their real property sold to appellees at a mortgage foreclosure sale.

The trial court fixed the sum at $9,081.35, but did not in the decree break down or itemize the items composing the same. We are left to an ascertainment of the items by reading the text of the evidence. This we have done. The briefs of the parties were very helpful in this respect.

Section 727, Title 7, Code of Alabama 1940, provides for the redemption of real estate from a mortgage foreclosure sale (as here), while Section 732 of the same title lists the items and charges that must be paid in order to effect such redemption.

Our review of the evidence and an examination of the contentions of the parties rule out any dispute as to the purchase price paid at the foreclosure sale, taxes, paving and sewage assessments. The latter (paving and sewage assessments) was a lien against the real property that was foreclosed. Neither is there any quarrel with the calculation of interest on these items.

There is a dispute about the amount claimed for repairs and improvements on the property made by appellees [purchasers at foreclosure sale] during the redemptive period of two years; also an item of $6.50, for recording the foreclosure deed, is challenged.

There was substantial evidence that appellees made repairs and permanent improvements on the buildings on the foreclosed property during the redemptive period in the sum of $3,202.66. Appellees testified the value was $3,202.66. Another witness for appellees testified that such market value of the improvements and repairs was $3,950.00. The evidence being *ore tenus,* the trial court evidently accepted the figure of $3,202.66 without interest.

But included in this figure of $3,202.66 was $350.00 allowed appellee for supervising and helping in the repairs and improvements while being made; and also for time consumed, and economy effected for making purchases of materials.

We held in *Ewing v. First National Bank of Montgomery* (227 Ala. 46, 148 So.836):

> The statute, Code 1923, 10153, does not deal with the cost, but "the value of all permanent improvements made on the land since the foreclosure sale," and, while the cost of improvements is related to the value, the reasonable value is made the basis of payment by the redemptioner.

There was evidence before the court that the value of these improvements was $3,202.66. While the cost of the improvements did include an item of $350.00 for services of appellee in supervising the work and in purchasing materials, such inclusion should not necessarily be eliminated or deducted from the value of the improvements to which the value is related. Such value is not circumscribed or limited by the cost, but only related thereto. If work, economy of purchases at a discount, and the supervision of labor by appellee contributed to the value of the improvements, then redemptioner cannot complain. The value of the improvements must be paid and not particularly the cost.

We do not think the item of $6.50 for recording the foreclosure deed is a proper charge to be paid by the redemptioner. We do not find any provision in Sec. 732, *supra,* for such charge.

The final decree of the trial court should be modified by eliminating therefrom the sum of $6.50. To this extent the decree is modified, but otherwise is affirmed.

Sterlington Bank v. Terzia Lumber & Hardware, Inc.

1965 (La.) 180 So.2d 16

The Sterlington Bank was the holder of notes and mortgages executed by Terzia Lumber and Hardware, Inc., and by the Terzias personally. Among the notes was a collateral mortgage note for $35,000 signed by F. C. Terzia, Sr., and F. C. Terzia, Jr. The bank brought foreclosure proceedings on the mortgages and another bank, the First National Bank of El Dorado; Arkansas, intervened requesting that the $35,000 mortgage be revoked as fraudulent against the Arkansas Bank. That bank had obtained a judgment against the Terzias which was unsatified. The Arkansas bank claimed that its rights as a judgment creditor should prevail over the other bank's mortgage interest. The lower court held the foreclosure proceedings in abeyance pending a determination of this question, and decided in favor of the Arkansas bank. The Sterlington Bank appealed.

BOLIN, J.   The principal ground for the revocatory actions is that the Terzias were insolvent at the time the mortgage was granted; that this circumstance was known, or should have been known, by the officers of the plaintiff bank; that the mortgage embraced all remaining property of value belonging to the Terzias; that the mortgage was not granted in the ordinary course of business but for the purpose of securing prior indebtedness for which the Terzias received no consideration, and, therefore, the mortgage was gratuitous and did not constitute security for further advances to the Terzias as mortgagors.

Answering the intervention, plaintiff asserted the $35,000 collateral note secured by the mortgage was executed and delivered in consideration of plaintiff's agreement to pay certain obligations amounting to a total principal sum of approximately $14,000 and was given in good faith in the regular course of business. Plaintiff further denied any knowledge of the interest of intervenor or the relationship existing between it and the Terzias, or any indebtedness by the latter to the Arkansas bank.

The court found that the Terzias were insolvent at the time of executing the mortgage of November 4, 1960; that officials of plaintiff bank inspected the property of the Terzias, requested an inventory and demanded the $35,000 mortgage on the individual property, all of which indicated the bank had knowledge of the insolvency of the Terzias; that the mortgage was not granted in the ordinary course of business, had no relation to the individual obligations of the Terzias who received nothing therefor. For these reasons, the plaintiff's mortgage was subordinated to intervenor's judicial mortgage.

From our study of the record we are in accord with the findings of the trial court.

Affirmed.

CHAPTER 49
REVIEW QUESTIONS AND PROBLEMS

1. The owner of two adjoining buildings sold one of them to *A*. The deed provided that *A* should have the privilege of passage from the other building to the one which he purchased. Subsequently, the owner sold the remaining building to *X*. *X* tore down the building and built a new one. Does *A* have a right of passage in the new building?

2. A power company cleared a right of way across *A*'s land and suspended a power line which had been constantly maintained. No poles or towers, however, were on the property. Many years later the company replaced the old power line with a new one and part of the installation was on *A*'s land. Can *A* require the company to remove the line?

3. *H* died leaving a will which gave *W*, the wife, the "use during her lifetime" of a 400-acre farm and upon *W*'s death the farm to go to *X*

and *Y,* a niece and nephew. Instead of putting half the income back into the farm in the nature of barns, ponds and fertilizer as had been previously done by *H,* her husband, she spent the entire income of the farm on herself. Who, if anyone, may object?

4. An outdoor advertising company ADCO signed an agreement with a hotel owner which granted ADCO "the exclusive right and privilege to maintain an advertising sign" on an exterior wall of the hotel. ADCO installed the sign. May the owner remove the sign during period agreed? Is the privilege conferred a license or easement?

5. *A* willed certain land to *W* for life with the remainder to *W*'s minor children. *A* died, and sometime thereafter *W* leased the property to *X* Coal Company, which stripped the land of coal and destroyed it for other useful purposes. Have the children a good cause of action against the coal company?

6. *A* loaned money to *B* and gave a note secured by a mortgage. It was provided that the mortgage would also be security for future advances which *A* might make to *B,* but *A* was not obligated to make any further advances. If *A* loaned additional amounts to *B* would the security of the mortgage extend to such amounts?

7. In April *M* gave *P* a note secured by a mortgage on his house. *P* on October 14 delivered the mortgage to the county recorder of deeds. On October 18 a mechanic's lien was filed with the recorder for materials furnished by *X* for improvement of the house over a period beginning August 31. On August 20 *Y* filed a lien for drilling an outside well that was begun on June 23. Which party has priority of lien assuming each was ignorant of the other? What effect would *P*'s recording of the mortgage in April have had? When did the mortgage become effective to prevent claims of other creditors becoming precedent to it?

8. *A,* desiring to borrow $15,000, gives *B* an absolute deed as security for a loan of this amount. *B* executes an agreement to reconvey the property upon the payment of the debt and interest three years later. Is this a sale or a mortgage?

9. *A* mortgaged his hotel to *B.* The mortgage contained a provision that *A* would replace the furniture in the hotel as it became necessary and that the mortgage would cover any furniture thereafter purchased. *A* purchased furniture and gave a chattel mortgage to *X.* As between *B* and *X* who has a better claim to the furniture?

10. *A* sells *B* property which has a $10,000 mortgage on it in favor of *C.* *B* purchases the property subject to the mortgage. The property declines in value and, at the maturity of the mortgage debt, is foreclosed and sells for $8,000. May *C* recover the deficit from *B?* May he recover from *A,* assuming that *A* is the mortgagor? Would the result differ if *B* had assumed the mortgage debt?

APPENDIX
HOW TO STUDY A CASE

When reading and studying the cases which are footnoted and appear at the end of each chapter, the student should attempt to analyze the court's reasoning in terms of the discussion in this section and other sections in the Introduction. Also, he should note the relevance of the case to the particular point under discussion. The student will thereby enhance his comprehension of the cases and also improve his own reasoning powers.

In order to understand a case, it is necessary to understand how a legal issue is presented by the use of the rules of procedure called adjective law, and how this legal issue is resolved by the application of appropriate rules of substantive law.

The case of *Levitz Furniture Company v. Fields* (Court of Common Pleas of Lebanon County, Pa., 1958, 6 Leb. 385) is here used to illustrate the method of abstracting or "briefing" a case. Note that in this case and many of the others in the book, the facts have already been digested by the authors in the paragraphs preceding the verbatim report of the judge's opinion. In other cases the facts have not been set forth in this fashion and the student must do this for himself as the facts are often interwoven into the opinion written by the judge.

The plaintiff, Levitz Furniture Company, entered into a contract to sell a television set to the defendant, Harold Fields. The contract contained a provision for a confession of judgment whereby the plaintiff was authorized to obtain a judgment against the defendant if he should be in default of any terms of the contract. The defendant stopped making payments under the contract and the plaintiff applied for and obtained a judgment against him. An execution was issued on the judgment and the sheriff has levied upon defendant's property. The defendant filed a petition to set aside the judgment and to be allowed to defend the case. He alleged that the set had never performed properly and that there was a warranty that the set would perform satisfactorily. At the hearing on the petition he testified that the plaintiff had been unable to make the set work after repeated efforts, and that he had therefore attempted to cancel the contract. The contract contained another provision that "no warranties of any kind with respect to the property have been made by the seller."

EHRGOOD, J. . . . The defendant contends that under the evidence produced and heretofore referred to, and under the law of Pennsylvania, that there is an implied warranty that the sale and installation of the Spartan TV set as contracted for under the instalment agreement between the parties, was suitable and would function for the purpose for which it was sold, wherefore, parol evidence is admissible and properly received by the court at the hearing in this matter.

It also seems clear to the court that inasmuch as the instalment contract is dated December 29, 1956, the question involved is controlled by the provisions of the Commercial Code which became effective July 1, 1954.

Article 2 of said Code pertains to sales, being Section 315, relating to implied warranties, being Title 12-a, P.S., 2-315, and provides as follows:

Where the seller at the time of contracting has reason to know any particular purpose for which the goods are required and if the buyer is relying on seller's skill or judgment to furnish suitable goods, there is, unless excluded or modified under the next section, an implied warranty that the goods shall be satisfactory for such purpose.

The plaintiff contends that the court erred in admitting testimony of the defendant and wife with respect to alleged warranties, either expressly or implied, because the best evidence thereof was the writing itself which contained the following:

Buyer acknowledged that he has received delivery of the property, having first examined and tested it, and found it to be in first class condition, and as represented by seller. No warranties of any kind with respect to the property and this transaction have been made by the seller (except that seller hereby warrants that it has a right to enter into this contract), unless endorsed hereon by writing.

Plaintiff cites *Kull v. General Motors* (311 Pa. 508), in which the court held, *inter alia:*

Where the parties have integrated their understanding and agreements into a formal, explicit contract, and excluded from the contract all previous communications not contained in the contract and provide that no modification shall be binding unless in writing, it cannot be permitted, in a suit brought on the contract, to prove parol modification of that contract in the absence of an averment of fraud, accident, or mistake in omitting from the writing sued upon on the terms afterwards offered in evidence.

In the instant case there was no averment of fraud, accident, or mistake, nor was there any evidence of fraud, accident, or mistake submitted at the time of the hearing. However, the plaintiff has overlooked the provisions of the Commercial Code hereinafter referred to by the court. Wherefore, the court will now refer to the court decisions and authorities applicable to the oral evidence produced by the defendant and the law relating thereto.

The aforesaid Section of the Commercial Code replaced and restated Section 15 of the Uniform Sales Act of 1915 (69 P.S. 124), relating to implied warranties, and which provides as follows:

Where a buyer, expressly or by implication, makes known to the seller the particular purpose for which the goods are required, and it appears that the buyer relies on the seller's skill or judgment (whether he be the employer or manufacturer or not), there is an implied warranty that the goods shall be reasonably fit for the purpose.

. . . Wherefore, it seems clear to the court, after considering the foregoing evidence produced by defendant and his wife, and the law applicable thereto, that the defendants have been diligent and timely in presenting their petition

to open judgment and that they have produced sufficient evidence to indicate a meritorious defense to the plaintiff's claim in that there is an implied warranty created by operation of law, which was not fulfilled by the plaintiff, notwithstanding the provisions in the contract that any changes of warranty had to be in writing.

. . . Further, it seems clear to the court that the defendants were unfamiliar with the construction and operation of TV sets and relied upon the judgment of the plaintiff and his employees that they would receive a set which was in a reasonably good condition to be usable for the purpose for which they agreed to purchase the same. The question as to whether or not the TV set which the plaintiff sold to the defendant complied with such requirements is a question of fact for a jury or a fact-finding body to determine.

The first step in case analysis is to set forth a brief statement of the facts—the basic essential facts which gave rise to the dispute.

1. *Statement of facts:* Fields, the defendant, purchased a TV set from Levitz Furniture Company, the plaintiff. The sales agreement provided that no warranties were made by the seller and that if the buyer defaulted the seller could confess a judgment against him. The defendant alleged that the set did not perform satisfactorily, and accordingly stopped making payments. The plaintiff took judgment against him. The defendant seeks to have the judgment set aside and wants to introduce evidence that the set was not satisfactory.

2. *Legal procedure by which is raised the question of law:* The defendant filed a petition asking that the judgment obtained by confession be set aside and that he be allowed to defend the action and introduce evidence that the set was faulty; to assert breach of warranty by way of defense.

3. *Question of law:* By this process an issue of substantive law was raised. Does a retail seller of goods impliedly warrant the goods that are sold?

4. *Plaintiff's argument:* The plaintiff contended that the agreement disclaims any warranties and that since the best evidence of warranty is the written agreement, the court should not admit the defendant's testimony.

5. *Defendant's argument:* The defendant claims that despite the disclaimer an implied warranty exists under the law of the state and that he should be allowed to introduce evidence of breach of warranty by way of defense.

6. *The opinion and decision of the court:* The court, Judge Ehrgood, held that under the Commercial Code there was an implied warranty created by operation of law. This warranty existed notwithstanding the contract provision that any changes of warranty had to be in writing. The defendant justifiably relied on the plaintiff to furnish a set that would be usable for the purpose for which it was purchased. Therefore, the judgment was set aside and the defendant at the ensuing trial may in-

troduce evidence to court or jury to establish that the warranty was breached. The court indicated that defendant's lack of knowledge of the workings of a TV set also justified this result.

This case was decided in 1958 by the Court of Common Pleas of Lebanon County Pennsylvania. The case can be found in Volume 6 of the reports of the courts of that county at page 385. This is a trial court opinion and does not appear in other case reports.

Most of the cases in this book are decisions of appellate courts. Decisions of state intermediate appellate courts and supreme courts are generally reported in two sources. One of these is the official state reports and the other the regional reporters published by the West Publishing Company, St. Paul, Minnesota. Each Regional Report is a collection of cases decided in the appellate courts of the states in a particular region of the country. For example, cases decided by the Oregon Supreme Court will be found in the Oregon Reports and also in the Pacific Reporter along with cases decided in a number of other western states.

For example, at page 119 of the text will be found the case of *Galati v. Potamkin Chevrolet Co.* ((1962) 198 Pa. Super. 533, 181 A.2d 900). This case which was decided on appeal in 1962, can be found in Volume 198 of the Pennsylvania Superior Court Reports at page 533. The same case can be found in the second series of the *Atlantic Reporter,* Volume 191 at page 900. The letter "A" here means *Atlantic Reporter.* This reporter includes cases decided by the state courts in Connecticut, Delaware, District of Columbia, Maine, Maryland, New Hampshire, New Jersey, Pennsylvania, Rhode Island, and Vermont. The figure "2d" after the letter "A" indicates that the *Atlantic Reporter* is now in a second series. The first series ran to 300 and instead of the next volume being called 301 it is designated as 1 A.2d.

In addition to the above *Reporter,* there are: the Pacific, cited as Pac. or P.2d: the Southeastern, cited as S.E. or S.E.2d: the Southwestern, cited as S.W. or S.W.2d; the Southern, cited as So. or S.2d; the Northwestern, cited as N.W. or N.W.2d; the Northeastern, cited as N.E. or N.E.2d. In addition to these reporters there are special reporters; for example, the State of New York has a *Reporter,* the New York Supplement, cited N.Y.S. and N.Y.S.2d. In this *Reporter* are found trial court cases and cases decided by the intermediate appellate courts of the State of New York.

Cases decided by United States courts are found in the West's National Federal Reporter System. U. S. district court cases are found in the *Federal Supplement Reporter,* cited as F. Supp. or F.Supp.2d. United States Court of Appeals cases are found in the *Federal Reporter,* F. or F.2d Cases decided by the United States Supreme Court are found in the *Supreme Court Reporter,* cited S.Ct. Also, cases decided by the United States Supreme Court are found in the official *U. S. Reporter* published by the U. S. Government Printing Office, cited as U.S. In addition, special

United States courts and administrative boards, such as the Court of Tax Appeals, Courts of Claims, Referees in Bankruptcy, the National Labor Relations Board, and others have their own special bound volumes for the publication of their cases.

In connection with the "briefing" of cases there are several techniques which should be kept in mind. First, be sure to identify the parties properly. At the trial court level the complaining party is called the plaintiff and the party being sued is the defendant. At the appellate court level the party who lost at the trial and who is therefore appealing and asserting that an error was committed by the trial court, is called the *appellant.* The party who prevailed in the lower court is now called the *appellee* or *respondent.* In some, but not all of the states, the citation or title of the case in the appellate court is *appellant v. appellee* (respondent). This can be confusing as where the trial defendant is appealing so that in some states the title of the case on appeal would make it appear at first glance that the defendant (appellant) is suing the plaintiff (respondent).

In briefing cases it is very helpful to use proper descriptive terms to further identify the parties and their respective roles both in the transaction which gave rise to the dispute and in the litigation. Thus, in a contract case one party can be identified as the offeror (the party who made an offer) and the other as offeree (the person to whom the offer was made). If one of the parties has performed his part of a contract, he is called an obligee, one entitled to performance by another, while the other party who has not yet performed is referred to as the obligor. In cases involving agency, one party can be described as principal, another as agent, and the party with whom the agent dealt as "the third party." Other descriptive terms will be apparent as the materials in the various books are studied.

There are some general observations that aid in understanding legal terminology. The suffixes "or" and "er" have special significance. "Or" refers to a party who is doing something or who has an obligation to another party; a mortgag*or* owes an obligation to the mortgag*ee* secured by a mortgage on the mortgagor's property; a promiss*or* makes a promise to the promiss*ee*; an oblig*or* owes an obligation to the oblig*ee*; an offer*or* is obligated by an offer made to the offer*ee* so that the latter can create a contract by accepting the offer; a pledg*or* delivers property to a pledg*ee* as security for a loan; a bail*or* entrusts property to a bail*ee*; an assign*or* transfers a right to an assign*ee*.

Sometimes the suffix "er" is used instead of "or"—for example, an indors*er* transfers a negotiable instrument to an indors*ee*; an entrust*er* places property with a trust*ee* for the former's benefit.

Glossary

Abandonment: The term applies to many situations. Abandonment of property is the giving up of the dominion and control over it with the intention to relinquish all claim to the same. Losing property is an involuntary act; abandonment is voluntary.

When used with duty, the word abandonment is synonymous with repudiation.

Abandonment of a child by its parents may be a criminal offense when such parents fail to perform their parental duty.

Abandonment in divorce law means the voluntary separation or desertion of one spouse from the other.

Abatement of a nuisance: An action to end any act detrimental to the public, such as a suit to enjoin a plant from permitting the escape of noxious vapors.

Ab initio: Latin phrase meaning, "from the beginning." A person who enters upon the land of another by permission and thereafter abuses the permission becomes a trespasser ab initio; that is, he becomes a trespasser from the time he first entered upon the land.

Acceptance *: Under Article 3–Commercial Paper this is the drawee's signed engagement to honor a draft as presented. It must be written on the draft, and may consist of his signature alone. It becomes operative when completed by delivery or notification.

Account *: Any right to payment for goods sold or leased or for services rendered which is not evidenced by an instrument or chattel paper.

Account *: Under Article 4–Bank Deposits and Collections this means any account with a bank and includes a checking, time, interest, or savings account.

Account Debtor: The person who is obligated on an account, chattel paper, contract right, or general intangible.

Action ex contractu: An action at law to recover damages for the breach of a duty arising out of contract. There are two types of causes of action; those arising out of contract, ex contractu, and those arising out of tort, ex delicto.

---

* The terms followed by an asterisk are defined in the Uniform Commercial Code and therefore these terms have significance in connection with Code materials. They are often given a particular meaning as related to the Code and the definitions are therefore not necessarily in conformity with meanings outside the framework of the Code.

Action ex delicto: An action at law to recover damages for the breach of a duty existing by reason of a general law. An action to recover damages for an injury caused by the negligent use of an automobile is an ex delicto action. Tort or wrong is the basis of the action. See *Action ex contractu.*

Ad damnum clause: A clause in a declaration or complaint of the plaintiff that makes the demand for damages and sets out the amount.

Ad hoc: Latin words meaning, "for this." An ad hoc refers to a limited or particular situation. An ad hoc decision means, for this purpose only. An ad hoc committee is one limited to a special purpose. An ad hoc attorney is one appointed to do a special task in a particular case.

Adjective law: The rules of procedure used by and in courts for enforcing the duties and maintaining the rights defined by the substantive law. Adjective law primarily involves matters of evidence, procedure, and appeals. It is also called remedial law.

Adjudicate: The exercise of judicial power by hearing, trying, and determining the claims of litigants before the court.

Administrator: A person to whom letters of administration have been issued by a probate court, giving such person authority to administer, manage, and close the estate of a deceased person.

Adverse possession: To acquire, by adverse possession, the legal title to another's land, the claimant must be in continuous possession during the period prescribed in the statute. This possession must be actual, visible, known to the world, with an intention by the possessor to claim the title as owner as against the rights of the true owner. The claimant usually must pay the taxes and liens lawfully charged against the property. Cutting timber or grass from time to time on the land of another is not such adverse possession as to confer title.

Advising Bank *: A bank which gives notification of the issuance of a credit by another bank.

Affidavit: A voluntary statement of facts formally reduced to writing, sworn to, or affirmed before, some officer authorized to administer oaths. Such officer is usually a notary public.

A fortiori: Latin words meaning "by a stronger reason." The phrase is often used in judicial opinions to say that, since specific proven facts lead to a certain conclusion, there are for this reason other facts that logically follow which make stronger the argument for the conclusion.

Agency coupled with an interest: When an agent has possession or control over the property of his principal and has a right of action against interference by third parties, an agency with an interest has been created. *A*, an agent, advances freight for goods sent him by his principal. He thus has an interest in the goods.

Agent: An agent is a person authorized to act for another (a principal). The term may apply to a person in the service of another, but in the strict sense an agent is one who stands in place of his principal. *A* works for *B* as a gardener and is thus a servant; but he may be an agent. If *A* sells goods for *B*, he becomes more than a servant. He acts in the place of *B*.

Agreement *: This means the bargain of the parties in fact as found in their language or by implication from other circumstances including course of dealing or usage of trade or course of performance as provided in the Uniform Commercial Code.

Aliquot: A subdivision or portion of the whole. An aliquot part.

Alter ego: Latin words literally meaning, "the other I." In law an agent is the alter ego or other person for his principal. When members of a corporation misuse the corporate entity, the courts look behind the entity that is the alter ego of the members.

Annuity: A sum of money paid yearly to a person during his lifetime, which sum arises out of a contract by which the recipient or another had previously deposited sums in whole or in part with the grantor—the grantor to return a designated portion of the principal and interest in periodic payments upon the arrival of the beneficiary at a designated age.

A priori: A generalization resting on presuppositions and not upon proven facts.

Architect's certificate: A formal statement signed by an architect that a contractor has performed under his contract and is entitled to be paid. The construction contract provides when and how such certificates shall be issued.

Arguendo: A Latin word which means to make the case by way of argument or in an argument.

Artisan's lien: One who has expended labor upon or added to another's property is entitled to the possession of such property as security until reimbursed for the value of labor or material. *A* repairs *B*'s watch. *A* may keep the watch in his possession until paid by *B* for such repairs.

Assignee: An assign or assignee is one to whom an assignment has been made.

Assignment: An assignment is the transfer by one person to another of a right that usually arises out of a contract. Such rights are called choses in action. *A* sells and assigns his contract right to purchase *B*'s house to *C*. *A* is an assignor. *C* is an assignee. The transfer is an assignment.

Assignment *: A transfer of "the contract" or of "all my rights under the contract" or an assignment in similar general terms is an assignment of rights, and unless the language or the circumstances (as in an assignment for security) indicate the contrary, it is a delegation of performance of the duties of the assignor; and its acceptance by the assignee constitutes a promise by him to perform those duties. This promise is enforceable by either the assignor or the other party to the original contract.

Assignment for the benefit of creditors: *A*, a debtor, has many creditors. An assignment of his property to *X*, a third party, with directions to make distribution of his property to his creditors is called an assignment for the benefit of creditors. See *Composition of creditors.*

Assignor: An assignor is one who makes an assignment.

Assumpsit: An action at common law to recover damages for the breach of contract. Historically it was based upon an implied undertaking (the word "assumpsit" is a Latin word meaning, "undertaking") to properly perform a duty.

Attachment: A legal proceeding accompanying an action in court by which a plaintiff may acquire a lien on a defendant's property as a security for the payment of any judgment which the plaintiff may recover. It is provisional and independent of the court action, and is usually provided for by statute. *A* sues *B*. Before judgment, *A* attaches *B*'s automobile in order to make sure of the payment of any judgment that *A* may secure.

Attorney at law: A person who has been granted a license by the state giving him the privilege of practicing law.

Attorney in fact: A person acting for another under a grant of special power created by an instrument in writing. *B*, in writing, grants special power to *A* to execute and deliver for *B* a conveyance of *B*'s land to *X*.

Bad faith: The term means "actual intent" to mislead or deceive another. It does not mean misleading by an honest, inadvertent, or careless misstatement.

Bail (verb): To set at liberty an arrested or imprisoned person upon security's being given to the state by himself or at least two other persons that will appear at the proper time and place for trial.

Bailee: A person into whose possession personal property is delivered.

Bailee *: The person who by a warehouse receipt, bill of lading, or other document of title acknowledges possession of goods and contracts to deliver them.

Bailment: A bailment is the delivery of personal property to another for a special purpose. Such delivery is made under a contract, either expressed or implied, that upon the completion of the special purpose, the property shall be redelivered to the bailor or placed at his disposal. *A* loans *B* his truck. *A* places his watch with *B* for repair. *A* places his furniture in *B*'s warehouse. *A* places his securities in *B* Bank's safety deposit vault. In each case, *A* is a bailor and *B* is a bailee.

Bailor: One who delivers personal property into the possession of another.

Banking Day *:   Under Article 4–Bank Deposits and Collections this means that part of any day on which a bank is open to the public for carrying on substantially all of its banking functions.

Bearer *:   The person in possession of an instrument, document of title, or security payable to bearer or indorsed in blank.

Bearer Form *:   A security is in bearer form when it runs to bearer according to its terms and not by reason of any indorsement.

Bench: A term often used to designate a court or the judges of a court. Sometimes used to name the place where the judges sit. The term "bench and bar" means the judges and attorneys of the profession.

Beneficiary: A person (not a promisee) for whose benefit a trust, an insurance policy, a will, or a contract promise is made.

Beneficiary *:   A person who is entitled under a letter of credit to draw or demand payment.

Bequest: A term used in a will to designate a gift of personal property. It is used synonymously with "devise" and often is construed to include real property.

Between Merchants *:   Any transaction with respect to which both parties are chargeable with the knowledge or skill of merchants.

Bid: An offering of money in exchange for property placed for sale. At an ordinary auction sale a bid is an offer to purchase. It may be withdrawn before acceptance is indicated by the fall of the hammer.

Bilateral contract: One containing mutual promises with each party being both a promisor and promisee.

Bill of Lading *:   A document evidencing the receipt of goods for shipment issued by a person engaged in the business of transporting or forwarding goods, and includes an airbill. "Airbill" means a document serving for air transportation as a bill of lading does for marine or rail transportation, and includes an air consignment note or air waybill.

Bill of sale: A written evidence that the title to personal property has been transferred from one person to another. It must contain words of transfer and be more than a receipt.

Binder: A memorandum evidencing temporary insurance issued by the insurer to the insured to cover a period of time during which the insured is considering formal application for a policy. Although incomplete as to specific terms, it is understood to include the normal provisions found in regular policies of insurance.

Bona Fide Purchaser *:   A purchaser of a security for value in good faith and without notice of any adverse claim who takes delivery of a security in bearer form or of one in registered form issued to him or indorsed to him or in blank.

Bond: A promise under seal to pay money. The term is generally used to designate the promise made by a corporation, either public or private, to pay money to bearer. U.S. Government Bonds; Illinois Central Railroad Bonds.

The term also describes an obligation by which one person promises to answer for the debt or default of another—a surety bond.

Book account: A record of the debits and credits between persons evidenced by entries in a book. The record usually contains detailed statements of the transactions between the parties. It indicates rights and duties and is an assignable chose in action.

Broker: A person employed to make contracts with third persons on behalf of his principal. Such contracts involve trade, commerce, buying and selling for a fee (called brokerage or commission).

Broker *:   A person engaged for all or part of his time in the business of buying and selling securities, who in the transaction concerned acts for, or buys a security from or sells a security to a customer. Nothing in this Article determines the capacity in which a person acts for purposes of any other statute or rule to which such person is subject.

Bulk Transfer *:   Any transfer in bulk and not in the ordinary course of the transferor's business of a major part of the materials, supplies, merchandise or other inventory of an enterprise subject to this Article.

Burden of Establishing *:   The burden of persuading the triers of fact that the existence of the fact is more probable than its non-existence.

Buyer *:   A person who buys or contracts to buy goods.

Buyer in Ordinary Course of Business *:   A person who in good faith and without knowledge that the sale to him is in violation of the ownership rights or security interest of a third party in the goods buys in ordinary course from a person in the business of selling goods of that kind but does not include a pawnbroker. "Buying" may be for cash or by exchange of other property or on secured or unsecured credit and includes receiving goods or documents of title under a pre-existing contract for sale but does not include a transfer in bulk or as security for or in total or partial satisfaction of a money debt.

By-laws: The rules adopted by the members or the board of directors of a corporation or other organization for its government. These rules must not be contrary to the law of the land, and they affect only the rights and duties of the members of the corporation or organization. They are not applicable to third persons.

Call: An assessment upon a subscriber for partial or full payment on shares of unpaid stock of a corporation. The term may also mean the power of a corporation to make an assessment, notice of an assessment, or the time when the assessment is to be paid.

Call-in pay: Pay guaranteed by contract to workers called for work, who report and are ready, but to whom no work is made available. Sometimes used to designate pay for "featherbedding." See *Featherbedding*.

Cancellation *:   When either party puts an end to the contract for breach by the other. Its effect is the same as that of "termination" except that the cancelling party also retains any remedy for breach of the whole contract or any unperformed balance.

Capital: The net assets of an individual enterprise, partnership, joint stock company, corporation, or business institution, including not only the original investment, but also all gains and profits realized from the continued conduct of the business.

Carrier: A natural person or a corporation who receives goods under a contract to transport for a consideration from one place to another. A railroad, a truck line, a bus line, an air line.

Cashier's check: A bill of exchange drawn by the cashier of a bank, for the bank, upon the bank. After the check is delivered or issued to the payee or holder, the drawer bank cannot put a "stop order" against itself. By delivery of the check, the drawer bank has accepted, and thus becomes the primary obligor. Note that an ordinary depositor after drawing a check, but before it is paid by the drawee bank, may countermand the same with a "stop order."

Cause of action: When one's legal rights have been invaded either by a breach of a contract or by a breach of a legal duty toward one's person or property, a cause of action has been created.

Caveat emptor: These words express an old idea at common law—"let the buyer beware"—and mean that when goods are sold without an express warranty by the vendor as to their quality and capacity for a particular use and purpose, the buyer must take the risk of loss as to all defects in the goods. The rule of caveat emptor applies at judicial sales. The buyer takes no better title than that held by the debtor or defendant.

Caveat venditor: These words mean "let the seller beware" (in contradistinction to caveat emptor—"let the buyer beware"). Caveat venditor means that unless the seller by express language disclaims any responsibility, he shall be liable to the buyer if the goods delivered are different in kind, quality, use, and purpose from those described in the contract of sale.

Certiorari: An order issuing out of an appellate court to a lower court, at the request of an appellant directing that the record of a case pending in the lower court be transmitted to the upper court for review.

Cestui que trust: A person who is the real or beneficial owner of property held in trust. The trustee holds the legal title to the property for the benefit of the cestui que trust.

Charter: As to a private corporation, the word "charter" includes the contract between the created corporation and the state, the act creating the corporation, and the articles of association granted to the corporation by authority of the legislative act. The word is also used to define the powers and privileges granted to the corporation by the legislature. The states have enacted general laws for the purpose of the creation and organization of corporations. Formerly many corporations were created by special acts of legislatures.

As to municipal corporations, charter does not mean a contract between the legislature and the city created. A city charter is a delegation of powers by a state legislature to the governing body of the city. The term includes the creative act, the powers enumerated, and the organization authorized.

Chattel: The word "chattel" is derived from the word "cattle." It is a very broad term and includes every kind of property that is not real property. Movable properties, such as horses, automobiles, choses in action, stock certificates, bills of lading, and all "goods, wares, and merchandise," are chattels personal. Chattels real concern real property, such as a lease for years—in which case the lessee owns a chattel real. A building placed on real property by a lessee is a chattel real.

Chattel mortgage: A formal instrument used prior to the Uniform Commercial Code executed by a debtor called the mortgagor transferring an interest in a chattel to a creditor called a mortgagee, for the purpose of giving security for a debt. If the debt is not paid, the mortgagee may sell the chattel and use the proceeds to pay the debt. This proceeding is called a foreclosure.

Chattel Paper *: A writing or writings which evidence both a monetary obligation and a security interest in or a lease of specific goods. When a transaction is evidenced both by such a security agreement or a lease and by an instrument or a series of instruments, the group of writings taken together constitutes chattel paper.

Chose in action: Words used to define the "right" one person has to recover money or property from another by a judicial proceeding. Such right arises out of contract, claims for money, debts, and rights against property. Notes, drafts, stock certificates, bills of lading, warehouse receipts, insurance policies are illustrations of choses in action. They are called tangible choses. Book accounts, simple debts, and obligations not evidenced by formal writing are called intangible choses. Choses in action are transferred by assignment.

Circumstantial evidence: If from certain facts and circumstances, according to the experience of mankind, an ordinary, intelligent person may infer that other connected facts and circumstances must necessarily exist, the latter facts and circumstances are considered proven by circumstantial evidence. Proof of fact A from which fact B may be inferred is proof of fact B by circumstantial evidence.

Civil action: A proceeding in a law court or a suit in equity by one person against another for the enforcement or protection of a private right or the prevention of a wrong. It includes actions on contract, ex delicto, and all suits in equity. Civil action is in contradistinction to criminal action in which the state prosecutes a person for breach of a duty.

Clearing Corporation *: A corporation all of the capital stock of which is held by or for a national securities exchange or association registered under a statute of the United States such as the Securities Exchange Act of 1934.

Clearing House *: Under Article 4–Bank Deposits and Collections this means any association of banks or other payors regularly clearing items.

Cloud on title: Words used to express the idea that there is some evidence of record which shows a third person has some prima facie interest in another's property.

Code: A collection or compilation of the statutes passed by the legislative body of a state. Such codes are often annotated with citations of cases decided by the State Supreme Courts. These decisions construe the statutes. Examples—Oregon Compiled Laws Annotated, United States Code Annotated.

Codicil: An addition to or a change in an executed last will and testament. It is a part of the original will and must be executed with the same formality as the original will.

Cognovit: The name of a plea by which the defendant for the purpose of avoiding a trial admits the right of the plaintiff. It is an answer to the complaint often called a "narr" in a confession of judgment action. This remedy is often used to secure judgments on promissory notes.

Co-insurer: A term in a fire insurance policy that requires the insured to bear a certain portion of the loss when he fails to carry complete coverage. For example, unless the insured carries insurance which totals 80 per cent of the value of the property, the insurer shall be liable for only that portion of the loss that the total insurance carried bears to 80 per cent of the value of the property.

Collateral: With reference to debts or other obligations, the term "collateral" means security placed with a creditor to assure the performance of the obligator. If the obligator performs, the collateral is returned by the creditor. *A* owes *B* $1,000. To secure the payment, *A* places with *B* a $500 certificate of stock in *X* Company. The $500 certificate is called collateral security.

Collateral *: The property subject to a security interest, and includes accounts, contract rights and chattel paper which have been sold.

Collecting Bank *: Under Article 4–Bank Deposits and Collections is any bank handling the item for collection except the payor bank.

Commercial Unit *: Such a unit of goods as by commercial usage is a single whole for purposes of sale and division of which materially impairs its character or value on the market or in use. A commercial unit may be a single article (as a machine) or a set of articles (as a suite of furniture or an assortment of sizes) or a quantity (as a bale, gross, or carload) or any other unit treated in use or in the relevant market as a single whole.

Commission: The sum of money, interest, brokerage, compensation, or allowance given to a factor or broker for carrying on the business of his principal.

Commission merchant: An agent or factor employed to sell "goods, wares, and merchandise" consigned or delivered to him by his principal, for a compensation called a commission.

Common carrier: One who is engaged in the business of transporting personal property from one place to another for a compensation. Such person is bound to carry for all who tender their goods and the price for transportation. A common carrier operates a public utility and is subject to state and federal regulations.

Community property: All property acquired after marriage by husband and wife other than separate property acquired by devise, bequest, or from the proceeds of non-community property. Community property is a concept of property ownership by husband and wife inherited from the civil law. The husband and wife are somewhat like partners in their ownership of property acquired during marriage.

Complaint: The first paper a plaintiff files in a court in a law suit. It is called a pleading. It is a statement of the facts upon which the plaintiff rests his cause of action.

Composition of creditors: An agreement between creditors and their debtors by which they agree that the creditors will take a lesser amount in complete satisfaction of the total debt due. *A* owes *B* and *C* $500 each. *A* agrees to pay *B* and *C* $250 each in complete satisfaction of the $500 due each. *B* and *C* agree to take $250 in satisfaction. Such agreement is called a composition of creditors.

Compromise: An agreement between two or more persons, usually opposing parties in a law suit, to settle the matters of the controversy without further resort to hostile litigation. An adjustment of issues in dispute by mutual concessions before resorting to a law suit.

Condemnation proceedings: An action or proceeding in court authorized by legislation (federal or state) for the purpose of taking private property for public use. It is the exercise by the judiciary of the sovereign power of eminent domain.

Condition: A clause in a contract, either expressed or implied, that has the effect of investing or divesting the legal rights and duties of the parties to the contract. In a deed, a condition is a qualification or restriction providing for the happening or nonhappening of events that on occurrence will destroy, commence, or enlarge an estate. "*A* grants Blackacre to *B* so long as said land shall be used for church purposes." If it ceases to be used for church purposes, the title to Blackacre will revert to the grantors.

Condition precedent: A clause in a contract providing that immediate rights and duties shall vest only upon the happening of some event. Securing an architect's certificate by a contractor before he (the contractor) is entitled to payment is a condition precedent.

A condition is not a promise; hence, its breach will not give rise to a cause of action for damages. A breach of a condition is the basis for a defense. In the above illustration, if the contractor sues the owner without securing the architect's certificate, the owner has a defense.

Conditions concurrent: Conditions concurrent are conditions that are mutually dependent and must be performed at the same time by the parties to the contract. Payment of money and delivery of goods in a cash sale are conditions concurrent. Failure to perform by one party permits a cause of action upon tender by the other party. If *S* refuses to deliver goods in a cash sale, *B*, upon tender, but not delivery of the money, places *S* in default and thus may sue *S*. *B* does not part with his money without getting the goods. If *S* sued *B*, *B* would have a defense.

Condition subsequent: A clause in a contract providing for the happening of an event that divests legal rights and duties. A clause in a fire insurance policy providing that the policy shall be null and void if combustible material is stored within ten feet of the building is a condition subsequent. If a fire occurs and combustible material was within ten feet of the building, the insurance company is excused from its duty to pay for the loss.

Confession of judgment: A voluntary submission to the jurisdiction of the court by a debtor permitting judgment to be taken against him without a formal trial. Such permission often appears in promissory notes giving consent that the judgment may be taken immediately upon default. See *Cognovit.*

Confirming Bank *: A bank which engages either that it will itself honor a credit already issued by another bank or that such a credit will be honored by the issuer or a third bank.

Conforming *: Goods or conduct including any part of a performance are "conforming" or conform to the contract when they are in accordance with the obligations under contract.

Consideration: An essential element in the creation of contract obligation. A detriment to the promisee and a benefit to the promisor. One promise is consideration for another promise. This creates a bilateral contract. An act is consideration for a promise. This creates a unilateral contract. Performance of the act asked for by the promisee is a legal detriment to the promisee and a benefit to the promisor.

Consignee: A person to whom a shipper usually directs a carrier to deliver goods. Such person is generally the buyer of goods and is called a consignee on a bill of lading.

Consignee *: The person named in a bill to whom or to whose order the bill promises delivery.

Consignment: The delivery, sending, or transferring of property, "goods, wares, and merchandise" into the possession of another, usually for the purpose of sale. Consignment may be a bailment or an agency for sale.

Consignor: The person who delivers freight to a carrier for shipment and who directs the bill of lading to be executed by the carrier is called a consignor or shipper.

Such person may be the consignor-consignee if the bill of lading is made to his own order.

Consignor *: The person named in a bill as the person from whom the goods have been received for shipment.

Conspicuous *: A term or clause is conspicuous when it is so written that a reasonable person against whom it is to operate ought to have noticed it. A printed heading in capitals (as: NON-NEGOTIABLE BILL OF LADING) is conspicuous. Language in the body of a form is "conspicuous" if it is in larger or other contrasting type or color. But in a telegram any stated term is "conspicuous." Whether a term or clause is "conspicuous" or not is for decision by the court.

Constitution: The Constitution of the United States constitutes the rules of organization of the United States and enumerates the powers and duties of the federal government thereby created. The constitutions of the several states prescribe the organization of each of the states and in general enumerate those powers not delegated to the federal government.

Constructive delivery: Although physical delivery of personal property has not occurred, yet by the conduct of the parties, it may be inferred that as between them possession and title has passed. *A* sells large and bulky goods to *B*. Title and possession may pass by the act and conduct of the parties.

Consumer Goods *: Goods that are used or bought for use primarily for personal, family, or household purposes.

Contract *: The total obligation which results from the parties' agreement as affected by the Code and any other applicable rules of law.

Contract Right *: Any right to payment under a contract not yet earned by performance and not evidenced by an instrument or chattel paper.

Conversion *: Under Article 3–Commercial Paper an instrument is converted when a drawee to whom it is delivered for acceptance refuses to return it on demand; or any person to whom it is delivered for payment refuses on demand either to pay or to return it; or it is paid on a forged indorsement.

Conveyance: A formal written instrument usually called a deed by which the title or other interests in land (real property) is transferred from one person to another. The word expresses also the fact that the title to real property has been transferred from one person to another.

Corporation: A collection of individuals created by statute as a legal person, vested with powers and capacity to contract, own, control, convey property, and transact business within the limits of the powers granted.

Corporation de facto: If persons have attempted in good faith to organize a corporation under a valid law (statute) and have failed in some minor particular, but have thereafter exercised corporate powers, such is a corporation de facto. Failure to have incorporators' signatures on applications for charter notarized is an illustration of noncompliance with statutory requirements.

Corporation de jure: A corporation that has been formed by complying with the mandatory requirements of the law authorizing such a corporation.

Corporeal: Physical things that are susceptible to the senses are corporeal. Automobiles, grain, fruit, and horses are corporeal and tangible and are called "chattels." The word corporeal is used in contradistinction to incorporeal or intangible. A chose in action (such as a check) is corporeal and tangible; or a chose in action may be a simple debt, incorporeal and intangible.

Costs: Costs, in litigation, are an allowance authorized by statute to a party for the expenses incurred in prosecuting or defending a law suit. The word "costs," unless specifically designated by statute or contract, does not include attorney's fees.

Counter-claims: A claim of the defendant by way of cross-action that the defendant is entitled to recover from the plaintiff. It must arise out of the same transaction set forth in the plaintiff's complaint, and be connected with the same subject matter.

S sues *B* for the purchase price. *B* counter-claims that the goods were defective, and that he thereby suffered damages.

Course of Dealing *: This is a sequence of previous conduct between the parties to a particular transaction which is fairly to be regarded as establishing a common basis of understanding for interpreting their expressions and other conduct.

Covenant: A promise in writing under seal. It is often used as a substitute for the word contract. There are covenants (promises) in deeds, leases, mortgages, and other instruments under seal. The word is used sometimes to name promises in unsealed instruments such as insurance policies and conditional sale contracts.

Covenant (action on): The name of remedy at early common law for the breach of a promise under seal.

Cover *: After a breach by a seller the buyer may "cover" by making in good faith and without unreasonable delay any reasonable purchase of or contract to purchase goods in substitution for those due from the seller.

Credit *: ("Letter of credit") This means an engagement by a bank or other person made at the request of a customer and of a kind within the scope of Article 5–Letters of Credit that the issuer will honor drafts or other demands for payment upon compliance with the conditions specified in the credit. A credit may be either revocable or irrevocable. The engagement may be either an agreement to honor or a statement that the bank or other person is authorized to honor.

Creditor *: This includes a general creditor, a secured creditor, a lien creditor and any representative of creditors, including an assignee for the benefit of creditors, a trustee in bankruptcy, a receiver in equity and an executor or administrator of an insolvent debtor's or assignor's estate.

Creditor beneficiary: If a promisee is under a duty to a third party, and, for a consideration, secures a promise from a promisor which promise, if performed, discharges the promisee's duty to the third party, such third party is a creditor beneficiary. *A* owes *C* $100. *B*, for a consideration, promises *A* to pay *A*'s debt to *C*. *C* is a creditor beneficiary.

Creditor's bill: A bill filed by a judgment creditor in a court of equity to have set aside previous fraudulent conveyances, in order to find property upon which to levy execution.

Cumulative voting: A stockholder in voting for a director may cast as many votes for one candidate for given office as there are offices to be filled multiplied by the number of shares of his stock, or he may distribute this same number of votes among the other candidates as he sees fit.

Curtesy: If a child, issue of the husband, has been born alive, then upon the death of the wife, the husband will be entitled to a life estate called "curtesy" in the whole of the wife's property. Such estates are now generally abolished by statute.

Custodian Bank *: Any bank or trust company which is supervised and examined by state or federal authority having supervision over banks and which is acting as custodian for a clearing corporation.

Custody (personal property): The word custody and possession are not synonymous. Custody means in charge of, to keep and care for under the direction of the true owner, without any interest therein adverse to the true owner. A servant is in custody of his master's goods. See *Possession*.

Customer *: Under Article 4–Bank Deposits and Collections this means any person having an account with a bank or for whom a bank has agreed to collect items and includes a bank carrying an account with another bank.

Customer *: As used in Letters of Credit a customer is a buyer or other person who causes an issuer to issue a credit. The term also includes a bank which procures issuance or confirmation on behalf of that bank's customer.

Damages: A sum of money the court imposes upon a defendant as compensation for the plaintiff because the defendant has injured the plaintiff by breach of a legal duty.

Debenture: A term used to name corporate obligations that are sold as investments. It is similar to a corporate bond. However, it is not secured by a trust deed. It is not like corporate stock.

Debt (action on): A common law remedy for the recovering of a sum certain in money.

Debtor *: The person who owes payment or other performance of the obligation secured, whether or not he owns or has rights in the collateral, and includes the seller of accounts, contract rights or chattel paper. Where the debtor and the owner of the collateral are not the same person, the term "debtor" means the owner of the collateral in any provision of the Article dealing with the colateral, the obligor in any provision dealing with the obligation, and may include both where the context so requires.

Deceit: A term to define that conduct in a business transaction by which one man, through fraudulent representations, misleads another who has a right to rely on such representations as the truth, or, who by reason of an unequal station in life, has no means of detecting such fraud.

Decision (judicial): The word "decision" may mean a final judgment of a court of last resort, a conclusion of law or facts, the opinion of the court, or the report of the court. Generally speaking, a decision means the judgment of the court as to the disposition of the case—for the plain, for the defendant, or for neither. Decision must be distinguished from opinion. An opinion of the court constitutes the reasons given for its decision or judgment. The report of the case is a printing of the opinion and decision.

Declaration: At common law, a word used to name the plaintiff's first pleading in which are set out the facts upon which the cause of action is based. The word "complaint" is used synonymously with declaration.

Decree: The judgment of the chancellor (judge) in a suit in equity. Like a judgment at law, it is the determination of the rights between the parties and is in the form of an order that requires the decree to be carried out. An order that a contract be specifically enforced is a decree.

Deed: A written instrument in a special form signed, sealed, and delivered, that is used to pass the legal title of real property from one person to another. See *Conveyance.* In order that the public may know about the title to real property, deeds are recorded in the Deed Record office of the county where the land is situated.

Deed of trust: An instrument by which title to real property is conveyed to a trustee to hold as security for the holders of notes or bonds. It is like a mortgage except the security title is held by a person other than the mortgagee-creditor. Most corporate bonds are secured by a deed of trust.

De facto: Arising out of, or founded upon, fact, although merely apparent or colorable. A de facto officer is one who assumes to be an officer under some color of right, acts as an officer, but in point of law is not a real officer. See *Corporation de facto.*

Defalcation: A person occupying a trust or fiduciary relation who, by reason of his own fault, is unable to account for funds left in his hands, has committed a defalcation. The word often means to embezzle or misappropriate funds.

Defamation: The use of words that are generally understood to impute some disreputable conduct or moral delinquency about the person of whom they are spoken.

Defendant: A person who has been sued in a court of law; the person who answers the plaintiff's complaint. The word is applied to the defending party in civil actions. In criminal actions, the defending party is referred to as the accused.

Defense: The word "defense" applies to all methods of procedure used by the defendant and to all facts alleged by way of denial by the defendant in his response to the plaintiff's complaint. Demurrers, set-offs, pleas in abatement, answers, denial, confession, and avoidance are procedural means of defense.

Deficiency judgment: If, upon the foreclosure of a mortgage, the mortgaged property does not sell for a sufficient amount to pay the mortgage indebtedness, such difference is called a "deficiency" and is chargeable to the mortgagor or to any person who has purchased the property and assumed and agreed to pay the mortgage. Illus.: *M* borrows $10,000 from *B*, and as security gives a mortgage on Blackacre. At maturity *M* does not pay the debt. *B* forecloses and at a public sale Blackacre sells for $8,000. There is a deficiency of $2,000, chargeable against *M*. If *M* had sold Blackacre to *C* and *C* had assumed and agreed to pay the mortgage, he would also be liable for the deficiency.

Defraud: To deprive one of some right by deceitful means. To cheat or withhold wrongfully that which belongs to another. Conveying one's property for the purpose of avoiding payment of debts is a transfer to "hinder, delay, or defraud creditors."

Del credere agency: When an agent, factor, or broker undertakes to guarantee to his principal the payment of a debt due from a buyer of goods, such agent, factor, or broker is operating under a del credere commission or agency.

Delectus personae: A Latin phrase used to designate a chosen or selected person. Partners are chosen persons—"a copartnership cannot be compelled to receive strangers . . ." since such "association is founded on personal confidence and delectus personarum." Delectus personae is absent in joint stock companies.

Delivery: A voluntary transfer of the possession of property, actual or constructive, from one person to another with the intention that title vests in the transferee. In the law of sales, delivery contemplates the absolute giving up of control and dominion over the property by the vendor, and the assumption of the same by the vendee.

Delivery *: With respect to instruments, documents of title, chattel paper, or securities this means voluntary transfer of possession.

Delivery order *: A written order to deliver goods directed to a warehouseman, carrier, or other person who in the ordinary course of business issues warehouse receipts or bills of lading.

Demand: A request by a party entitled, under a claim of right, that a particular act be performed. In order to bind an endorser on a negotiable instrument, a demand must first be made by the holder on the primary party and such person must dishonor the instrument. Demand notes mean "due when demanded." The word "demand" is also used to mean a claim or legal obligation.

Demurrage: Demurrage is a sum, provided for in a contract of shipment, to be paid for the delay or detention of vessels or railroad cars beyond the time agreed upon for loading or unloading.

Demurrer: A procedural method used in a law suit by which the defendant admits all the facts alleged in the plaintiff's complaint, but denies that such facts state a cause of action. It raises a question of law on the facts, which must be decided by the court.

Dependent covenants (promises): In contracts, covenants are either concurrent or mutual, dependent or independent. Dependent covenants mean the performance of one promise must occur before the performance of the other promise. In a cash sale, the buyer must pay the money before the seller is under a duty to deliver the goods.

Depositary bank *: Under Article 4—Bank Deposits and Collections this means the first bank to which an item is transferred for collection even though it is also the payor bank.

Descent: The transfer of the title of property to the heirs upon the death of the ancestor; heredity; succession. If a person dies without making a will, his property will "descend" according to the Statute of Descent of the state wherein the property is located.

Destination: The "destination of goods" is the place of delivery as provided for in the shipping contract. The carrier is under a duty to deliver the goods at such a place unless ordered otherwise by the consignee.

Detinue: A common law action to recover property. It is to be distinguished from trover, which is an action to recover damages for taking property, not the recovery of the actual property.

Detriment: Legal detriment that is sufficient consideration, constitutes change of position or acts of forbearance by a promisee at the request of a promisor. See *Consideration.*

Devise: A gift, usually of real property, by a last will and testament.

Devisee: The person who receives title to real property by will.

Dictum: An expression of an idea, argument, or rule in the written opinion of a judge that has no bearing on the issues involved and that is not essential for their determination. It lacks the force of a decision in a judgment.

Directed verdict: If it is apparent to reasonable men and the court that the plaintiff by his evidence has not made out his case, the court may instruct the jury to bring in a verdict for the defendant or himself direct a verdict for the defendant. If, however, different inferences may be drawn from the evidence by reasonable men, then the court cannot direct a verdict.

Discharge: Th word has many meanings. A servant or laborer upon being released from his employment is discharged. A guardian or trustee, upon termination of his trust, is discharged by the court. A debtor released from his debts is discharged in bankruptcy. A person who is released from any legal obligation is discharged.

Dishonor: A negotiable instrument is dishonored when it is presented for acceptance or payment, and acceptance or payment is refused or cannot be obtained.

Dissolution: Of a corporation—The termination of a corporation at the expiration of its charter, by the Attorney General of the state under proper statutory authority, by consolidation, or by the action of the stockholders, is dissolution.

Of a partnership—The termination of a partnership by the express will of the partners at a fixed or indefinite time, or by operation of law due to the incapacity, death, or bankruptcy of one of the partners, is dissolution.

Dividend: A dividend is a stockholder's pro rata share in the profits of a corporation. Dividends are declared by the board of directors of a corporation. Dividends are cash, script, property, and stock.

Document of title *: This term includes bill of lading, dock warrant, dock receipt, warehouse receipt, or order for the delivery of goods, and also any other document which in the regular course of business or financing is treated as adequately evidencing that the person in possession of it is entitled to receive, hold and dispose of the document and the goods it covers. To be a document of title a document must purport to be issued by or addressed to a bailee and purport to cover goods in the bailee's possession which are either identified or are fungible portions of an identified mass.

Documentary draft *: Under Article 4–Bank Deposits and Collections this means any negotiable or non-negotiable draft with accompanying documents, securities or other papers to be delivered against honor of the draft.

Documentary draft *: ("Documentary demand for payment".) A draft the honor of which is conditioned upon the presentation of a document or documents. "Document" means any paper including document of title, security, invoice, certificate, notice of default, and the like.

Domicile: That place that a person intends as his fixed and permanent home and establishm‿nt and to which, if he is absent, he intends to return. A person can have but one domicile. The old one continues until the acquisition of a new one; thus, while in transit the old domicile exists. One can have more than one residence at a time, but only one domicile. The word is not synonymous with residence. See *Residence.*

Dominion: As applied to the delivery of property by one person to another, the word means the separation by the transferor or donor from all control over the possession and ownership of the property and the endowing of the transferee or donee with such control of possession and ownership. See *Gift.*

Donee beneficiary: If a promisee is under no duty to a third party, but for a consideration secures a promise from a promisor for the purpose of making a gift to a third party, such third party is a donee beneficiary. *A,* promisee for a premium paid, secures a promise from the insurance company, the promisor, to pay *A's* wife $10,000 upon *A's* death. *A's* wife is a donee beneficiary.

Dormant partner: A partner who is not known to third persons, but is entitled to share in the profits and is subject to the losses. Since credit is not extended upon the strength of such partner's name, he may withdraw without notice and is not subject to debts contracted after his withdrawal.

Dower: A right for life held by a married woman in part of the lands owned by her husband, which right becomes vested upon his death.

Due care: The words express that standard of conduct which is exercised by an ordinary, reasonable, prudent person. See *Negligence.*

Due process of law: The words have a broad meaning. The constitutions of the United States and the states create and guarantee to every person the right to life, liberty, and property. These rights cannot be denied by government, except by the exercise of a fair and impartial legal procedure that is proper and appropriate. Legislation that confiscates one's property without just compensation is in the absence of due process of law. Under due process, a person accused of a crime is entitled to a trial by jury.

Duly negotiated *: A negotiable document of title is "duly negotiated" when it is negotiated in the proper manner to a holder who purchases it in good faith without notice of any defense against or claim to it on the part of any person and for value, unless it is established that the negotiation is not in the regular course of business or financing or involves receiving the document in settlement or payment of a money obligation.

Duress (of person): Duress means a threat of bodily injury, criminal prosecution, or imprisonment of a contracting party or his near relative to such extent that the threatened party is unable to exercise freely his will at the time of entering into or discharging a legal obligation.

Duress (of property): The seizure by force, or the withholding of goods by one not entitled, and the demanding by such person of something as a condition for the release of the goods.

Duty (in law): A legal obligation imposed by general law or voluntarily imposed by the creation of a binding promise. For every legal duty there is a corresponding legal right. By general law, A is under a legal duty not to injure B's person or property. B has a right that A not injure his person or property. X may voluntarily create a duty in himself to Y by a promise to sell Y a horse for $100. If Y accepts, X is under a legal duty to perform his promise. See *Right.*

Earnest money: A term used to describe money that one contracting party gives to another at the time of entering into the contract in order to "bind the bargain" and which will be forfeited by the donor if he fails to carry out the contract. Generally, in real estate contracts such money is used as part payment of the purchase price.

Easement: An easement is an interest in land—a right that one person has to some profit, benefit, or use in or over the land of another. Such right is created by a deed, or it may be acquired by prescription (the continued use of another's land for a statutory period).

Ejectment: An action to recover the possession of real property. It is now generally defined by statute, and is a statutory action. See *Forcible entry and detainer.*

Eleemosynary: A word used to classify corporations and institutions engaged in public charitable work, such as a hospital or children's home owned and operated by a church.

Embezzlement: The fraudulent appropriation by one person, acting in a fiduciary capacity, of the money or property of another. See *Conversion.*

Eminent domain: The right that resides in the United States, state, county, city, school, or other public body, to take private property for public use, upon the payment of just compensation. Eminent domain is to be distinguished from governmental power to take private property by limiting its use in order to eliminate nuisances. Abating a nuisance is the exercise of police power. No compensation is given for limiting the use of property under the police power.

Entirety (estate by): Property acquired by husband and wife whereby upon the death of one, the survivor takes the whole estate. The estate is called "entirety" because the law regards the husband and wife as one. They are vested with the whole estate so that the survivor takes no new title upon death of the other but remains in possession of the whole as originally granted. Such estate must be distinguished from a joint tenancy. Neither the husband nor wife may by conveyance destroy the right of survivorship. The words in a deed, "To John Smith and Mary Smith, his wife, with the right of survivorship," and not as tenants in common, will create an estate by the entirety. For the legal effect of such estate, the state statute should be consulted. See *Joint tenants.*

Entity: The word means "in being" or "existing." The artificial person created when a corporation is organized is "in being" or "existing" for legal purposes; thus, an entity. It is separate from the stockholders. The estate of a deceased person while in administration is an entity. A partnership for many legal purposes is an entity. The marriage status is an entity.

Equipment*: Goods that are used or bought for use primarily in business (including farming or a profession) or by a debtor who is a non-profit organization or a governmental subdivision or agency or if the goods are not included in the definitions of inventory, farm products or consumer goods.

Equitable action: In Anglo-American law there have developed two types of courts and procedures for the administration of justice: law courts and equity courts. Law courts give as a remedy money damages only, whereas equity courts give the plaintiff what he bargains for. A suit for specific performance of a contract is an equitable action. In many states these two courts are now merged.

Equitable conversion: An equitable principle that, for certain purposes, permits real property to be converted into personalty. Thus real property owned by a partnership is, for the purpose of the partnership, personal property because to ascertain a partner's interest, the real property must be reduced to cash. This is an application of the equitable maxim, "equity considers that done which ought to be done."

Equitable mortgage: A written agreement to make certain property security for a debt, and upon the faith of which the parties have acted in making advances, loans, and thus creating a debt. Example: an improperly executed mortgage, one without seal where a seal is required. An absolute deed made to the mortgagee and intended for security only is an equitable mortgage.

Equity: Because the law courts in early English law did not always give an adequate remedy, an aggrieved party sought redress from the king. Since this appeal was to the king's conscience, he referred the case to his spiritual adviser, the chancellor. The chancellor decided the case according to rules of fairness, honesty, right, and natural justice. From this there developed the rules in equity. The laws of trusts, divorce, rescission of contracts for fraud, injunction, and specific performance are enforced in courts of equity.

Equity of redemption: The right a mortgagor has to redeem or get back his property after it has been forfeited for nonpayment of the debt it secured. By statute, within a certain time before final foreclosure decree, a mortgagor has the privilege, by paying the amount of the debt, interest, and costs, of redeeming his property.

Escrow: An agreement under which a grantor, promisor, or obligor places the instrument upon which he is bound with a third person called escrow holder, until the performance of a condition or the happening of an event stated in the agreement permits the escrow holder to make delivery or performance to the grantee, promisee, or obligee. *A* (grantor) places a deed to *C* (grantee) accompanied by the contract of conveyance with *B* Bank, conditioned upon *B* Bank delivering the deed to *C* (grantee) when *C* pays all moneys due under contract. The contract and deed have been placed in "escrow."

Estate: A word used to name all the property of a living, deceased, bankrupt, or insane person. It is also applied to the property of a ward. In the law of taxation, wills, and inheritance, the word has a broad meaning. Historically, the word was limited to an interest in land: i.e., estate in fee simple, estate for years, estate for life, and so forth.

Estoppel: When one ought to speak the truth, but does not, and by one's acts, representations, or silence intentionally or through negligence induces another to believe certain facts exist, and such person acts to his detriment on the belief that such facts are true, the first person is estopped to deny the truth of the facts. *B*, knowingly having kept and used defective goods delivered by *S* under a contract of sale, is estopped to deny the goods are defective. *X* holds out *Y* as his agent. *X* is estopped to deny *Y* is not his agent. Persons are estopped to deny the legal effect of written instruments such as deeds, contracts, bills and notes, court records, judgments, and the like. A man's own acts speak louder than his words.

Et al.: Literally translated means "and other persons." Words used in pleadings and cases to indicate that persons other than those specifically named are parties to a law suit.

Et cetera—etc.: Literally translated means "and other things" or "and so forth." When a number of things of the same class have been listed and others exist, it is customary to add the word "etc." in order to avoid full enumeration. Example: "There are many items of junk, old cars, wagons, plows, etc."

Et uxor: The words mean "and wife." Sometimes used in the name of cases. Smith v. Jones et ux.

Eviction: An action to expel a tenant from the estate of the landlord. Interfering with the tenant's right of possession or enjoyment amounts to an eviction. Eviction may be actual or constructive. Premises made uninhabitable because the landlord maintains a nuisance is constructive eviction.

Evidence: In law the word has two meanings. First, that testimony of witnesses and facts presented to the court and jury by way of writings and exhibits, which impress the minds of the court and jury, to the extent that an allegation has been proven. Testimony and evidence are not synonymous. Testimony is a broader word and includes all the witness says. Proof is distinguished from evidence in that proof is the legal consequence of evidence. Second, the rules of law, called the law of evidence, that determine what evidence shall be introduced at a trial and what shall not; also what importance shall be placed upon the evidence.

Ex contractu: See *Action ex contractu.*

Ex delicto: See *Action ex delicto.*

Executed: As applied to contracts or other written instruments, means signed, sealed, and delivered. Effective legal obligations have thus been created. The term is also used to mean that the performances of a contract have been completed. The contract is then at an end. All is done that is to be done.

Execution: Execution of a judgment is the process by which the court through the sheriff enforces the payment of the judgment received by the successful party. The sheriff by a "writ" levies upon the unsuccessful party's property and sells it to pay the judgment creditor.

Executor (of an estate): The person, named or appointed in a will by a testator (the one who makes the will), who by authority of the will has the power to administer the estate upon the death of the testator and to dispose of it according to the intention of the testator. The terms executor and administrator are not synonymous. An executor is appointed by the deceased to administer an estate. An administrator is appointed by the court to administer the estate of a person who dies without having made a will. See *Intestate.*

Executory (contract): Until the performance required in a contract is completed, it is said to be executory as to that part not executed. See *Executed.*

Exemplary damages: A sum assessed by the jury in a tort action (over and above the compensatory damages) as punishment in order to make an example of the wrong-doer and to deter like conduct by others. Injuries caused by wilful, malicious, wanton, and reckless conduct will subject the wrongdoers to exemplary damages.

Exemption: The condition of a person who is free or excused from a duty imposed by some rule of law, statutory or otherwise. A workman against whom a judgment has been secured is by statute exempt from a writ of execution upon his working tools. A portion of a soldier's pay is exempt from the imposition of federal income tax.

Express warranties *:   Any affirmation of fact or promise made by the seller to the buyer which relates to the goods and becomes part of the basis of the bargain creates an express warranty that the goods shall conform to the affirmation or promise.

Any description of the goods which is made part of the basis of the bargain creates an express warranty that the goods shall conform to the description. Any sample or model which is made part of the basis of the bargain creates an express warranty that the whole of the goods shall conform to the sample or model.

Express warranty: When a seller makes some positive representation concerning the nature, quality, character, use, and purpose of goods, which induces the buyer to buy, and the seller intends the buyer to rely thereon, the seller has made an express warranty.

Factor: A factor is an agent for the sale of merchandise. He may hold possession of the goods in his own name or in the name of his principal. He is authorized to sell and to receive payment for the goods. The law concerning factors is codified in some states by legislation, and is called "Factors' Acts." See *Agent*.

Factor's lien: A lien or right that a factor has to keep the possession of goods consigned to him for the purpose of reimbursing himself for all advances previously made to the consignor.

Farm products *:   Goods that are crops or livestock or supplies used or produced in farming operations or if they are products of crops or livestock in their unmanufactured states (such as ginned cotton, wool-clip, maple syrup, milk and eggs), and if they are in the possession of a debtor engaged in raising, fattening, grazing or other farming operations. If goods are farm products they are neither equipment nor inventory.

Featherbedding: A term used in labor relations to describe the situation in which demand is made for the payment of wages for a particular service not actually rendered.

Fee simple estate: A term describing the total interest a person may have in land. Such an estate is not qualified by any other interest and passes upon the death of the owners to the heirs free from any conditions.

Felony: At common law, a felony was a criminal offense, and upon conviction the criminal forfeited his lands and goods to the crown and was subject to death. Today, by statute, the term includes all those criminal offenses that are punishable by death or imprisonment.

Fiduciary: In general a person is a fiduciary when he occupies a position of trust or confidence in relation to another person or his property. Trustees, guardians, and executors are illustrations of persons occupying fiduciary positions.

Fieri facias: Literally means "you cause it to be made." A writ or order issued by a court directing the sheriff to levy on goods or personal property of the defendant, in order to satisfy the judgment of the plaintiff.

Financing agency *:   A bank, finance company or other person who in the ordinary course of business makes advances against goods or documents of title or who by arrangement with either the seller or the buyer intervenes in ordinary course to make or collect payment due or claimed under the contract for sale, as by purchasing or paying the seller's draft or making advances against it or by merely taking it for collection whether or not documents of title accompany the draft. "Financing agency" includes also a bank or other person who similarly intervenes between persons who are in the position of seller and buyer in respect to the goods.

Fine: A sum of money collected by a court from a person guilty of some criminal offense. The amount may be fixed by statute or left to the discretion of the court. The term "fine" is to be distinguished from "penalty," which means a sum of money exacted for the doing of or failure to perform some act. Payment of a penalty of $5 for failure to secure a license to sell tobacco is different from paying a $5 fine for committing the offense of larceny.

Firm offers *:   An offer by a merchant to buy or sell goods in a signed writing which by its terms gives assurance that it will be held open.

Floating policy: An insurance policy that covers a class of goods located in a particular place that the insured has on hand at the time the policy was issued, but which goods at the time of fire may not be the identical items that were on hand at the time the policy was issued. A fire policy covering the inventory of a grocery store is an example.

Forbearance: Giving up the right to enforce what one honestly believes to be a valid claim in return for a promise is called forbearance and is sufficient "consideration" to make binding a promise.

Forcible entry and detainer: A remedy given to a landowner to evict persons unlawfully in possession of his land. A landlord may use such remedy to evict a tenant in default.

Forfeiture: Loss of money or property by way of compensation and punishment for injury or damage to the person or property of another or to the state. One may forfeit his citizenship upon the commission of a felony. One may forfeit interest earnings for charging a usurious rate.

Forgery: Forgery is the false writing or alteration of an instrument with the fraudulent intent of deceiving and injuring another. Writing, without his consent, another's name upon a check for the purpose of securing money, is a forgery.

Franchise: A right conferred or granted by a legislative body. It is a contract right and cannot be revoked without cause. A franchise is more than a license. A license is only a privilege and may be revoked. A corporation exists by virtue of a "franchise." A corporation secures a franchise from the city council to operate a water works within the city. See *License*.

Franchise tax: A tax on the right of a corporation to do business under its corporate name.

Fraud: An intentional misrepresentation of the truth for the purpose of deceiving another person. The elements of fraud are: (1) false representation of fact, not opinion, intentionally made; (2) intent that the deceived person act thereon; (3) knowledge that such statements would naturally deceive; and (4) that the deceived person acted to his injury.

Fraudulent conveyance: A conveyance of property by a debtor for the intent and purpose of defrauding his creditors. Such conveyance is of no effect, and such property may be reached by the creditors through appropriate legal proceedings.

Freehold: An estate in fee or one for life is a "freehold." A freeholder is usually a person who has a property right in the title to real estate amounting to an estate of inheritance (in fee), or one who has title for life, or for an indeterminate period. A grant by a city to a corporation to use the sidewalks for 30 years is not a freehold. "Householder" is not synonymous with "freeholder." See *Householder*.

From and to: Generally the word "from" is a word of exclusion, and the word "to" a word of inclusion. "From May 5 to May 10," in computing time means May 5 is excluded and May 10 included; thus, the period of time is 5 days.

Funded debt: The term applies to a debt where provision is made for a method of paying off the debt and its interest at fixed periods. A funded debt of a municipality is one where provision is made for the annual raising by tax of the sum necessary to pay the interest and principal as they respectively mature.

Funding: The procedure by which the outstanding debts of a corporation are collected together and the re-issuing of new bonds or obligations for the purpose of paying the debts. Thus 10 year 3 per cent bonds may be called and paid by issuing 20 year 3 per cent bonds. This process is called funding.

Fungible *: With respect to goods or securities this means goods or securities of which any unit is, by nature or usage of trade, the equivalent of any other like unit. Goods which are not fungible shall be deemed fungible for the purposes of this Act to the extent that under a particular agreement or document unlike units are treated as equivalents.

Fungible goods: Fungible goods are those "of which any unit is from its nature of mercantile usage treated as the equivalent of any other unit." Grain, wine, and similar items are examples.

Future goods *:   Goods which are not both existing and identified.

Futures: Contracts for the sale and delivery of commodities in the future, made with the intention that no commodity be delivered or received immediately.

Gambling: An arrangement between two or more persons to risk money or other things of value in any type of contest or game of chance wherein one of the parties wins at the expense of another.

Garnishee: A person upon whom a garnishment is served. He is a debtor of a defendant and has money or property that the plaintiff is trying to reach in order to satisfy a debt due from the defendant.

Garnishment: A proceeding by which a plaintiff seeks to reach the credits of the defendant that are in the hands of a third party, the garnishee. A garnishment is distinguished from an attachment in that by an attachment an officer of the court takes actual possession of property by virtue of his writ. In a garnishment, the property or money is left with the garnishee until final adjudication.

General agent: An agent authorized to do all the acts connected with carrying on a particular trade, business, or profession.

General intangibles *:   Any personal property (including things in action) other than goods, accounts, contract rights, chattel paper, documents and instruments.

Gift: A gift is made when a donor delivers the subject matter of the gift into the donee's hands, or places in the donee the means of obtaining possession of the subject matter, accompanied by such acts as show clearly that the donor intends to divest himself of all dominion and control over the property.

Gift causa mortis: A gift made in anticipation of death. The donor must have been in sickness and have died as expected; otherwise, no effective gift has been made. If the donor survives, the gift is revocable.

Gift inter vivos: A gift inter vivos is an effective gift made during the life of the donor. By a gift inter vivos, property vests immediately in the donee at the time of delivery; whereas, a gift causa mortis is made in contemplation of death and is effective only upon the donor's death.

Good faith *:   In the case of a merchant this means honesty in fact and the observance of reasonable commercial standards of fair dealing in the trade.

Good faith *:   Honesty in fact in the conduct or transaction concerned.

Good title: A title free from incumbrances, such as mortgages and liens, as disclosed by a complete abstract of the title as taken from the records in the recorder's office.

Goods *:   All things which are treated as movable for the purposes of a contract of storage or transportation.

Goods: This includes all things which are movable at the time the security interest attaches or which are fixtures but does not include money, documents, instruments, accounts, chattel paper, general intangibles, contract rights, and other things in action. "Goods" also include the unborn young of animals and growing crops.

Goods: All things (including specially manufactured goods) which are movable at the time of identification to the contract for sale other than the money in which the price is to be paid, investment securities and things in action. "Goods" also includes the unborn young animals and growing crops and other identified things attached to realty as described in the section on goods to be severed from realty.

Grant: A term used in deeds for the transfer of the title to real property. The words "convey," "transfer," and "grant" as operative words in a deed to pass title are equivalent. The words "grant, bargain, and sell" in a deed, in absence of statute, mean the grantor promises he has good title to transfer free from incumbrances and warrants it to be such.

Grantee: A grantee is a person to whom a grant is made; one named in a deed to receive title.

Grantor: A grantor is a person who makes a grant. The grantor executes the deed by which he divests himself of title.

Gross negligence: The lack of even slight or ordinary care.

Guarantor: One who by contract undertakes "to answer for the debt, default, and miscarriage of another." In general, a guarantor undertakes to pay if the principal debtor does not; a surety, on the other hand, joins in the contract of the principal and becomes an original party with the principal. See *Suretyship.*

Guardian: A person appointed by the court to look after the property rights and person of minors, insane, and other incompetents or legally incapacitated persons.

Guardian ad litem: A special guardian appointed for the sole purpose of carrying on litigation and preserving the interests of a ward. He exercises no control or power over property.

Habeas corpus: A writ issued to a sheriff, warden or official having custody of a person, directing the official to return the person, alleged to be unlawfully held, before a court in order to determine the legality of the imprisonment.

Hearsay evidence: Evidence that is learned from someone else. It does not derive its value from the credit of the witness testifying, but rests upon the veracity of another person. It is not good evidence because there is no opportunity to cross-examine the person who is the source of the testimony.

Hedging contract: A contract of purchase or sale of an equal amount of commodities in the future by which brokers, dealers, or manufacturers protect themselves against the fluctuations of the market. It is a type of insurance against changing prices. A grain dealer, to protect himself, may contract to sell for future delivery the same amount of grain he has purchased in the present market.

Heirs: Those persons upon whom the statute of descent casts the title to real property upon the death of the ancestor. See Statutes of descent for the particular state. See *Descent.*

Holder *: A person who is in possession of a document of title or an instrument or an investment security drawn, issued or indorsed to him or to his order or to bearer or in blank.

Holding company: A corporation organized for the purpose of owning and holding the stock of other corporations. Shareholders of underlying corporations receive in exchange for their stock, upon an agreed value, the shares in the holding corporation.

Homestead: A parcel of land upon which a family dwells or resides, and which to them is home. The statute of the state or federal governments should be consulted to determine the meaning of the term as applied to debtor's exemptions, federal land grants, and so forth.

Honor *: This means to pay or to accept and pay, or where a credit so engages to purchase or discount a draft complying with the terms of the credit.

Idem sonans: Absolute accuracy in spelling names is not required in legal documents. If a name spelled in a document is different from the correct name, it is still legally effective as sufficient name of a person, if, when pronounced, it sounds to the ear the same as the correct name. This is called the doctrine of idem sonans. For example: Smythe and Smith. Mackey and Macky.

Illegal: Conduct that is contrary to public policy and the fundamental principles of law is illegal. Such conduct includes not only violations of criminal statutes, but also the creation of agreements that are prohibited by statute and the common law.

Illusory: That which has a false appearance. If that which appears to be a promise is not a promise, it is said to be illusory. For example: "*A* promises to buy *B*'s horse, if *A* wants to," is no promise. Such equivocal statement would not justify reliance; thus, it is not a promise.

Immunity: Fredom from the legal duties and penalties imposed upon others. The "privileges and immunities" clause of the United States Constitution means no state can deny to the citizens of another state the same rights granted to its own citizens. This does not apply to office holding. See *Exemption*.

Implied: The finding of a legal right or duty by inference from facts or circumstances. See *Warranty*.

In personam: A legal proceeding, the judgment of which binds the defeated party to a personal liability.

In rem: A legal proceeding, the judgment of which binds, affects, or determines the status of property.

Insolvency proceedings *: Any assignment for the benefit of creditors or other proceedings intended to liquidate or rehabilitate the estate of the person involved.

Insolvent *: Refers to a person who either has ceased to pay his debts in the ordinary course of business or cannot pay his debts as they become due or is insolvent within the meaning of the federal bankruptcy law.

Installment contract *: One which requires or authorizes the delivery of goods in separate lots to be separately accepted, even though the contract contains a clause "each delivery is a separate contract" or its equivalent.

In statu quo: The conditions existing at the time of the commencement of an action, or, in case of rescission of contract, the position of the parties just prior to the creation of the contract.

Instrument *: This means a negotiable instrument or a security or any other writing which evidences a right to the payment of money and is not itself a security agreement or lease and is of a type which is in ordinary course of business transferred by delivery with any necessary indorsement or assignment.

Instrument *: Under Article 3—Commercial Paper this means a negotiable instrument.

Intermediary bank *: Under Article 4—Bank Deposits and Collections is a bank to which an item is transferred in course of collection except the depositary or payor bank.

In toto: In the whole amount. All together. As the persons were liable in toto.

Inalienable: The word means not capable of transfer or sale. The right to sue for a tort is inalienable. Contracts for personal service are inalienable choses in action. The word means nonassignable.

Inchoate: Incomplete situations out of which rights and duties may later arise. It also means "as yet not perfect." For example: a wife's dower is inchoate until her husband's death.

Incidental beneficiary: If the performance of a promise would indirectly benefit a person not a party to a contract, such person is an incidental beneficiary. *A* promises *B*, for a consideration, to plant a valuable nut orchard on *B*'s land. Such improvement would increase the value of the adjacent land. *C*, the owner of the adjacent land, is an incidental beneficiary. He has no remedy if *A* breaches his promise with *B*.

Incontestable: As applied to insurance, a clause in an insurance policy which states that after a certain period of time the policy may not be contested except for nonpayment of the premiums.

Incorporeal: Not manifest to the senses. The right of an owner of land to take the water of a stream for irrigation is an incorporeal hereditament.

Incumbrance: A burden on either the title to land or thing, or upon the land or thing itself. A mortgage or other lien is an incumbrance upon the title. A right of way over the land is an incumbrance upon the land and affects its physical condition.

Indebtedness: To be under a duty to another, usually for the payment of money. It is not a contract, but it may be the result of a contract.

Indemnity: A duty resting on one person to make good a loss or damage another has suffered. *A* contracts to build a house for *B*. *B* contracts with *C* for a premium to answer for any loss *B* may suffer by reason of *A*'s default. If *A* defaults and *B* suffers loss, *C* will indemnify *B*.

Indenture: A deed executed by both parties, as distinguished by a deed poll that is executed only by the grantor.

Independent contractor: The following elements are essential to establish the relation of independent contractor in contradistinction to principal and agent. An independent contractor must: (1) exercise his independent judgment as to the means used to accomplish the result; (2) be free from control or orders from any other person; (3) be responsible only under his contract for the result obtained.

Indictment: An indictment is a finding by a grand jury that it has reason to believe the accused is guilty as charged. It informs the accused of the offense with which he is charged in order that he may prepare its defense. It is a pleading in a criminal action.

Indorsement: Writing one's name upon paper for the purpose of transferring the title. When a payee of a negotiable instrument writes his name on the back of the instrument, such writing is an indorsement.

Infringement: Infringement of a patent on a machine is the manufacturing of a machine that produces the same result by the same means and operation as the patented machine. Infringement of a trademark consists in the reproduction of a registered trademark and its use upon goods in order to mislead the public to believe that the goods are the genuine, original product.

Inherit: The word is used in contradistinction to acquiring property by will. See *Descent*.

Inheritance: An inheritance denotes an estate that descends to heirs. See *Descent*.

Injunction: A writ of judicial process issued by a court of equity by which a party is required to do a particular thing or to refrain from doing a particular thing.

Injunction pendente lite: A provisional remedy granted by a court of equity before a hearing upon the merits of a suit, for the purpose of preventing the doing of any act whereby the rights in the controversy may be materially changed.

Insolvent: An insolvent debtor is one whose property is insufficient to pay all his debts, or out of which his debts may be collected. Within the Bankruptcy Act, "Whenever the aggregate of his property . . . shall not at a fair valuation be sufficient in amount to pay his debts."

Insurable interest: A person has an insurable interest in a person or property if he will be directly and financially affected by the death of the person or the loss of the property.

Insurance: By an insurance contract, one party, for an agreed premium, binds himself to another, called the insured, to pay to the insured a sum of money conditioned upon the loss of life or property of the insured.

Intent: A state of mind that exists prior to or contemporaneous with an act. A purpose or design to do or forbear to do an act. It cannot be directly proven, but is inferred from known facts.

Interim certificate: An instrument negotiable by statute in some states payable in stocks or bonds, and given prior to the issuance of the stocks or bonds in which payable.

Interlocutory decree: A decree of a court of equity that does not settle the complete issue, but settles only some intervening part, awaiting a final decree.

Interpleader: A remedy available to a stakeholder whereby he can require rival claimants to the thing or fund, to litigate their rival claims and thus relieve him of the risk of being sued twice.

Inter sese: Between or among themselves.

Intestate: The intestate laws are the laws of descent or distribution of the estate of a deceased person. A person dies intestate who has not made a will.

Inventory *: Goods that are held by a person who holds them for sale or lease or to be furnished under contracts of service or if he has so furnished them, or if they are raw materials, work in process or materials used or consumed in a business. Inventory of a person is not to be classified as his equipment.

Irreparable damage or injury: Irreparable does not mean such injury as is beyond the possibility of repair, but it does mean that it is so constant and frequent in occurrence that no fair or reasonable redress can be had in a court of law. Thus, the plaintiff must seek a remedy in equity by way of an injunction.

Issue (in a will): The word, as applied to a will, means descendants of whatever degree.

Issue (in pleading): The purpose of pleadings in a court proceeding is to find the "issue"; that is, a point which is affirmed on one side and denied on the other.

Issue *: Under Article 3–Commercial Paper "Issue" means the first delivery of an instrument to a holder or a remitter.

Issuer *: A bank or other person issuing a letter of credit.

Issuer *: A bailee who issues a document except that in relation to an unaccepted delivery order it means the person who orders the possessor of goods to deliver. Issuer includes any person for whom an agent or employee purports to act in issuing a document if the agent or employee has real or apparent authority to issue documents, notwithstanding that the issuer received no goods or that the goods were misdescribed or that in any other respect the agent or employee violated his instructions.

Item *: Under Article 4—Bank Deposits and Collections this means any instrument for the payment of money even though it is not negotiable but does not include money.

Jeopardy: A person is in jeopardy when he is regularly charged with a crime before a court properly organized and competent to try him. If acquitted, he cannot be tried again for the same offense.

Joint adventure: When two persons enter into a single enterprise for their mutual benefit without the intention of continuous pursuit, they have entered a joint adventure. They are essentially partners.

Joint contract: If two or more persons promise upon the same consideration for the same purpose to another party, they are joint obligors to the other party to the contract and have formed a joint contract.

Joint ownership: The interest that two or more parties have in property. Such interest has no existence in the absence of the interest of the other parties. The parties together own the total interest. *A, B,* and *C* as a unit own the property. See *Joint tenants.*

Joint tenants: Two or more persons to whom is deeded land in such manner that they have "one and the same interest, accruing by one and the same conveyance, commencing at one and the same time, and held by one and the same undivided possession." Upon the death of one joint tenant, his property passes to the survivor or survivors. Some states have abolished joint tenancy; other states make joint tenants, tenants in common.

The Statute of Descent does not apply to this type of estate so long as there is a survivor. See *Entirety.*

Joint tort-feasors: When two persons commit an injury with a common intent, they are joint tort-feasors.

Joint will: A joint will is a single will of two or more persons. A mutual will is one by which each testator makes a testamentary disposition in favor of the other.

Judgment (in law): A judgment is the decision, pronouncement, or sentence rendered by a court upon an issue in which it has jurisdiction.

Judgment in personam: A judgment against a person directing the defendant to do or not to do something, is a judgment in personam. See *In personam.*

Judgment in rem: A judgment against a thing, as distinguished from a judgment against a person. See *In rem.*

Judicial sale: A judicial sale is a sale authorized by a court that has jurisdiction to grant such authority. Such sales are conducted by an officer of the court. See *Sale.*

Jurisdiction: The authority conferred upon a court by the constitution to try cases and determine causes.

Jury: A group of persons, usually twelve, sworn to declare the facts of a case as they are proved from the evidence presented to them, and, upon instructions from the court, to find a verdict in the cause before them.

Kite checks: To execute and deliver a check in payment of a debt at a time when the drawer has insufficient money in the bank, but with the intention of making a deposit to cover the shortage before the check is presented for payment.

Laches: Laches is a term used in equity to name that conduct which is neglect to assert one's rights or to do what by the law a person should have done and did not do. Such failure on the part of one to assert a right will give an equitable defense to another party.

L.S.: The letters are an abbreviation for the Latin phrase "locus sigilli," meaning "place of the seal."

Latent defect: A defect in materials not discernible by examination. Used in contradistinction to patent defect which is discernible.

Lease: A contract by which one person divests himself of possession of lands or chattels and grants such possession to another for a period of time. The relationship where land is involved is called landlord and tenant.

Leasehold: The land held by a tenant under a lease.

Legacy: Personal property disposed of by a will. Sometimes the term is synonymous with bequest. The word "devise" is used in connection with real property distributed by will. See *Bequest, Devise.*

Legal incapacity: A person who has no power to sue except by a guardian, or a person such as an infant or insane person who has the power of avoidance of contract liabilities.

Legatee: A person to whom a legacy is given by will.

Letters testamentary: The orders or authority granted by a probate court to an administrator or representative of an estate whereby such person has power to reduce to money the estate of a deceased and make proper disposition. There are two kinds of letters. "Domiciliary letters" are issued at the domicile of the testator. When property is found in places other than at the domicile of the testator, the courts of such places issue "ancillary letters." Examples: *A* lives in state *B*. At his death, he owned property in state *C*. "Ancillary letters" will be issued in state *C*.

Levy (taxes): The word as applied to taxation means to impose or assess, or to charge and collect, a sum of money against a person or property for public purposes.

Levy (writ of): The literal use refers to the seizure of the defendant's property by the sheriff to satisfy the plaintiff's judgment. The word sometimes means that a lien has been attached to land and other property of the defendant by virtue of a judgment.

Liability: In its broadest legal sense, the word means any obligation one may be under by reason of some rule of law. It includes debt, duty, and responsibility.

Libel: The malicious publication of a defamation of a person by printing, writing, signs, or pictures, for the purpose of injuring the reputation and good name of such person. "The exposing of a person to public hatred, contempt, or ridicule."

License (privilege): A license is a mere personal privilege given by the owner to another to do designated acts upon the land of the owner. It is revocable at will, creates no estate in the land, and such licensee is not in possession. "It is a mere excuse for what otherwise would be a trespass."

License (governmental regulation): A license is a privilege granted by a state or city upon the payment of a fee, which confers authority upon the licensee to do some act or series of acts, which otherwise would be illegal. A license is not a contract and may be revoked for cause. It is a method of governmental regulation exercised under the police power. Examples: license to keep dogs in the city, to sell commodities in the street.

Lien: A right one person, usually a creditor, has, to keep possession of or control the property of another for the purpose of satisfying a debt. There are many kinds of liens: judgment liens, attorneys' liens, innkeepers' liens, loggers' liens, vendors' liens. Consult Statute of state for type of liens. See *Judgment*.

Lien creditor *: A creditor who has acquired a lien on the property involved by attachment, levy or the like and includes an assignee for benefit of creditors from the time of assignment, and a trustee in bankruptcy from the date of the filing of the petition or a receiver in equity from the time of appointment. Unless all the creditors represented had knowledge of the security interest, such a representative of creditors is a lien creditor without knowledge even though he personally has knowledge of the security interest.

Limitation of actions: Statutes of limitations exist for the purpose of bringing to an end old claims. Because witnesses die, memory fails, papers are lost, and the evidence becomes inadequate, stale claims are barred. Such statutes are called statutes of repose. Within a certain period of time, action on claims must be brought; otherwise, they are barred. The period varies from 6 months to 20 years.

Lineal descendant: A lineal descendant is one descended in a direct line from another person such as son, grandson, great-grandson, etc.

Liquidated: A claim is liquidated when it has been made fixed and certain by the parties concerned.

Liquidated damages: A fixed sum agreed upon between the parties to a contract, to be paid as ascertained damages by that party who breaches the contract. If the sum is excessive, the courts will declare it to be a penalty and unenforceable.

Liquidation: The process of winding up the affairs of a corporation or firm for the purpose of paying its debts and disposing of its assets. May be done voluntarily or under the orders of a court.

Lis pendens: The words mean, "pending the suit nothing should be changed." The court, having control of the property involved in the suit, issues notice "lis pendens," that persons dealing with the defendant regarding the subject matter of the suit, do so subject to final determination of the action.

Lot *: A parcel or a single article which is the subject matter of a seperate sale or delivery, whether or not it is sufficient to perform the contract.

Magistrate: A public officer, usually a judge, "Who has power to issue a warrant for the arrest of a person charged with a public offense." The word has wide application and includes justices of the peace, notaries public, recorders, and other public officers who have power to issue executive orders.

Maintenance (in law suits): The assisting of either party to a law suit by a person who has no interest therein. An officious intermeddling in a law suit.

Mala in se: Acts that are "bad in themselves" and are void of any legal consequences. A contract to do immoral acts is illegal and void because mala in se. Such acts are in contradistinction to acts "mala prohibita," which means illegal because prohibited by statute.

Malice: Malice is a term to define a wrongful act done intentionally without excuse. It does not necessarily mean ill will, but it indicates a state of mind that is reckless concerning the law and the rights of others. Malice is distinguished from negligence in that in malice there is always a purpose to injure, whereas such is not true of the word "negligence."

Malicious: Possessed of a willful and purposeful intent to injure another without just cause.

Malicious prosecution: The prosecution of another at law with malice and without probable cause to believe that such legal action will be successful.

Mandamus: A writ issued by a court of law, in the name of the state, directed to some inferior court, officer, corporation, or person commanding them to do a particular thing that appertains to their office or duty.

Mandatory: As applied to statutes, a mandatory provision is one, the noncompliance with which creates no legal consequences. For example, city bonds, issued in violation of statutory requirements that are mandatory, are void.

Mandatory injunction: An injunctive order issued by a court of equity that compels affirmative action by the defendant.

Margin: A sum of money deposited by a principal, buyer, or seller, with his broker to protect the broker against any loss due to price fluctuation in buying and selling.

Marketable title: A title of such character that no apprehension as to its validity would occur to the mind of a reasonable and intelligent person. The title to goods in litigation, subject to incumbrances, in doubt as to a third party's right, or subject to lien, is not marketable.

Marshalling assets: A principle in equity for a fair distribution of a debtor's assets among his creditors. For example, when a creditor of A, by reason of prior right, has two funds X and Y belonging to A out of which he may satisfy his debt, but B, also a creditor of A, has a right to X fund, the first creditor will be compelled to exhaust Y fund before he will be permitted to participate in X fund.

Master in chancery: An officer appointed by the court to assist the court of equity in taking testimony, computing interest, auditing accounts, estimating damages, ascertaining liens, and doing such other tasks incidental to a suit, as the court may require. The power of a master is merely advisory and his task largely fact-finding.

Maxim: A proposition of law that because of its universal approval needs no proof or argument, and the mere statement of which gives it authority. Example: "A principal is bound by the acts of his agent, when the agent is acting within the scope of his authority."

Mechanics' lien: A mechanics' lien is created by statute to assist laborers in collecting their wages. Such lien has for its purpose to subject the land of an owner to a lien for material and labor expended in the construction of buildings, which buildings having been placed on the land become a part thereof by the law of accession.

Mens rea: The term means "guilty mind." It is an element that has to be proven to sustain a verdict of guilty for a criminal offense. It is generally presumed from the proven facts.

Merchant *: A person who deals in goods of the kind or otherwise by his occupation holds himself out as having knowledge or skill peculiar to the practices or goods involved in the transaction or to whom such knowledge or skill may be attributed by his employment of an agent or broker or other intermediary who by his occupation holds himself out as having such knowledge or skill.

Merger: Two corporations are merged when one corporation continues in existence and the other loses its identity by its absorption into the first. Merger must be distinguished from consolidation, in which case both corporations are dissolved, and a new one created which takes over the assets of the dissolved corporations.

Midnight deadline *: Under Article 4—Bank Deposits and Collections with respect to a bank this is midnight on its next banking day following the banking day on which it receives the relevant item or notice or from which the time for taking action commences to run, whichever is later.

Ministerial duty: The performance of a prescribed duty that requires the exercise of little judgment or discretion. A sheriff performs ministerial duties.

Minutes: The record of a court or the written transactions of the members or board of directors of a corporation. Under the certificate of the clerk of a court or the secretary of a corporation, the minutes are the official evidence of court or corporate action.

Misdemeanor: A criminal offense, less than a felony, that is not punishable by death or imprisonment. Consult the local statute.

Misfeasance: The improper performance of a duty imposed by law or contract which injures another person. It is distinguished from nonfeasance which means doing nothing of an imposed duty.

Misrepresentation: The affirmative statement or affirmation of a fact that is not true; the term does not include concealment of true facts or nondisclosure or the mere expression of opinion.

Mistake of fact: The unconscious ignorance or forgetfulness of the existence or nonexistence of a fact, past or present, which is material and important to the creation of a legal obligation.

Mistake of law: An erroneous conclusion of the legal effect of known facts.

Mitigation of damages: A plaintiff is entitled to recover damages caused by the defendant's breach, but the plaintiff is also under a duty to avoid increasing or enhancing such damages. Such is called a duty to mitigate damages. If a seller fails to deliver the proper goods on time, the buyer, where possible, must buy other goods, thus mitigating damages.

Money *: A medium of exchange authorized or adopted by a domestic or foreign government as a part of its currency.

Monopoly: The exclusive control of the supply and price of a commodity that may be acquired by a franchise or patent from the government; or, the ownership of the source of a commodity or the control of its distribution.

Moot case: A judgment in advance of a presumed controversy, the decision of which has no legal effect upon any existing controversy.

Mortgage: A conveyance or transfer of an interest in property for the purpose of creating a security for a debt. The mortgage becomes void upon payment of the debt, although the recording of a release is necessary to clear the title of the mortgaged property.

Mutual assent: In every contract each party must agree to the same thing. Each must know what the other intends; they must mutually assent or be in agreement.

Mutuality: A word used to describe the situation in every contract that it must be binding on both parties. Each party to the contract must be bound to the other party to do something by virtue of the legal duty created.

Negligence: The failure to do that which an ordinary, reasonable, prudent man would do, or the doing of some act which an ordinary, prudent man would not do. Reference must always be made to the situation, the circumstances, and the knowledge of the parties.

Negotiation *: Under Article 3–Commercial Paper this is the transfer of an instrument in such form that the transferee becomes a holder. If the instrument is payable to order it is negotiated by delivery with any necessary indorsement; if payable to bearer it is negotiated by delivery.

Net assets: The property or effects of a firm, corporation, institution, or estate, remaining after all its obligations have been paid.

Nolle prosequi: A discharge of a particular indictment against the accused by the court upon request of the prosecuting officer. It is not an acquittal nor a pardon. The accused may be indicted again and tried for the same offense.

Nolo contendere: This plea by an accused in a criminal action is an implied confession of the offense charged. It virtually equals a plea of guilty. A judgment of conviction follows such plea.

Nominal damages: A small sum assessed as sufficient to award the case and cover the costs. In such case, no actual damages have been proven.

Non compos mentis: One who does not possess understanding sufficient to comprehend the nature, extent, and meaning of his contracts or other legal obligations.

Non obstante verdicto: A judgment given to the moving party notwithstanding the verdict already obtained. If upon re-examination, the court finds the plaintiff's pleadings demurrable, he will enter a judgment "non obstante verdicto" even though the plaintiff has a verdict.

Nonfeasance: The failure to perform a legal duty. See *Misfeasance*.

Nonresident: The citizen of another state.

Nonsuit: A judgment given against the plaintiff when he is unable to prove his case or fails to proceed with the trial after the case is at issue.

Notary: A public officer authorized to administer oaths by way of affidavits and depositions; also to attest deeds and other formal papers in order that such papers may be used as evidence and be qualified for recording.

Notation Credit *: A credit which specifies that any person purchasing or paying drafts drawn or demands for payment made under it must note the amount of the draft or demand on the letter or advice of credit.

Notice *: A person has "notice" of a fact when (a) he has actual knowledge of it; or (b) he has received a notice or notification of it; or (c) from all the facts and circumstances known to him at the time in question he has reason to know that it exists.

A person "knows" or has "knowledge" of a fact when he has actual knowledge of it. "Discover" or "learn" or a word or phrase of similar import refers to knowledge rather than to reason to know.

Notifies *: A person "notifies" or "gives" a notice or notification to another by taking such steps as may be reasonably required to inform the other in ordinary course whether or not such other actually comes to know of it. A person "receives" a notice or notification when: (a) It comes to his attention; or (b) it is duly delivered at the place of business through which the contract was made or at any other place held out by him as the place for receipt of such communications.

Novation: The substitution of one obligation for another. When debtor *A* is substituted for debtor *B*, and by agreement with the creditor *C*, debtor *B* is discharged, a novation has occurred.

Nuisance: The word nuisance is generally applied to any continuous or continued conduct that causes annoyance, inconvenience, and damage to person or property. It usually applies to the unreasonable and wrongful use of property that produces material discomfort, hurt, and damage to the person or property of another. Example: Fumes from a factory.

Obligee: A creditor or promisee.

Obligor: A debtor or promisor.

Option: A right secured by a contract to accept or reject an offer to purchase property at a fixed price within a fixed time. It is an irrevocable offer sometimes called a "paid-for offer."

Order *: Under Article 3–Commercial Paper this means a direction to pay and must be more than an authorization or request. It must identify the person to pay with reasonable certainty. It may be addressed to one or more such persons jointly or in the alternative but not in succession.

Ordinance: An ordinance is, generally speaking, the legislative act of a municipality. A city council is a legislative body and passes ordinances that are the laws of the city.

Ordinary care: That care that a prudent man would take under the circumstances of the particular case.

Overt act: Overt means open. Overt act is any motion, gesture, conduct, or demonstration that evidences a present design to do a particular act that will lead to a desired result.

Par value: The words mean face value. The par value of stocks and bonds on the date of issuance is the principal. At a later date, the par value is the principal plus interest.

Pari materia: Latin words that mean "related to the same matter or subject." Statutes and covenants concerning the same subject matter are in pari materia, and as a general rule, for the purpose of ascertaining their meaning, are construed together.

Partition: Court proceedings brought at the request of a party in interest, that real property be taken by the court and divided among the respective owners as their interests appear. If the property is incapable of division in kind, then the property is to be sold and the money divided as each interest appears.

Party *: A person who has engaged in a transaction or made an agreement within the Uniform Commercial Code. To be distinguished from a "third party."

Patent ambiguity: An uncertainty in a written instrument that is obvious upon reading.

Payor Bank *: Under Article 4–Bank Deposits and Collections a bank by which an item is payable as drawn or accepted.

Penal bond: A bond given by an accused, or by another person in his behalf, for the payment of money if the accused fails to appear in court on a certain day.

Penalty: The term has two different meanings. In criminal law it means the punishment imposed for the commission of a crime. It is used with the word "fine." In civil law, it may mean a sum agreed upon as payable for the breach of promise. The word is sometimes used as synonymous with "forfeiture." See *Liquidated damages.*

Pendente lite: A Latin phrase which means "pending during the progress of a suit at law."

Per curiam: A decision by the full court in which no opinion is given.

Peremptory challenge: An objection, by a party to a law suit, to a person serving as a juror, for which no reason need be given.

Perjury: False swearing upon an oath properly administered in some judicial proceedings. See *Oath.*

Perpetuity: The taking of any subject matter out of the channel of commerce by limiting its capacity to be sold for a period of time longer than that of a life or lives in being and 21 years thereafter plus the period of gestation.

Persona ficta: The Latin phrase for a fictitious person which refers to the corporate entity or artificial legal person.

Personal property: The rights, powers, and privileges a person has in movable things such as chattels, and choses in action. Personal property is used in contradistinction to real property.

Personal representative: The administrator or executor of a deceased person. The term also means the heir, next of kin, or descendant of a deceased person. The meaning of the term must be ascertained from the context.

Personal service: The term means that the sheriff actually delivered to the defendant in person a service of process.

Plaintiff: In an action at law, the complaining party or the one who commences the action is called the plaintiff. He is the person who seeks a remedy in court.

Plea: An allegation or answer in a court proceeding.

Pleading: The process by which the parties in a lawsuit arrive at an issue.

Pledge: The deposit or placing of personal property as security for a debt or other obligation with a person called a pledgee. The pledgee has the implied power to sell the property if the debt is not paid. If the debt is paid, the right to possession returns to the pledgor.

Plenary: Fully attended or constituted.

Policy of insurance: In insurance law, the word policy means the formal document delivered by the insurance company to the insured, which evidences the rights and duties between the parties.

Polling jury: To poll the jury is to call the name of each juror and inquire what his verdict is before such is made a matter of record.

Possession: The method, recognized by law, of holding, detaining, or controlling by one's self or by another, property, either personal or real, which will exclude others from holding, detaining, or controlling such property.

Precedent: A previously-decided case that can serve as an authority to help decide a present controversy. The use of such case is called the doctrine of "stare decisis," which means to adhere to decided cases and settled principles. Literally, "to stand as decided."

Preference: The term is used most generally in bankruptcy law. Where a bankrupt makes payment of money to certain creditors enabling them to obtain a greater percentage of their debts than other creditors in the same class, and the payment is made within four months prior to the filing of a bankruptcy petition, such payment constitutes illegal and voidable preference. An intention to prefer such creditors must be shown. An insolvent person may lawfully prefer one creditor to another, if done in good faith and without intent to defraud others.

Preferred stock: Stock that entitles the holder to dividends from earnings before the owners of common stock can receive a dividend.

Premises: As applied to the occupancy of real property, the word includes a definite portion of land, the building and appurtenances thereto over which the occupant exercises control. As applied to a controversy, the word means the general statement of a proposition.

Preponderance: Preponderance of the evidence means that evidence which in the judgment of the jurors is entitled to the greatest weight, which appears to be more credible, has greater force, and overcomes not only the opposing presumptions, but also the opposing evidence.

Prerogative: Rights, powers, privileges, and immunities, which one person has that others do not possess. Ambassadors of foreign countries have certain prerogatives. A senator has the prerogative of making remarks that would be slanderous if used by an ordinary citizen.

Presenting Bank *: Under Article 4–Bank Deposits and Collections, this is any bank presenting an item except a payor bank.

Presentment *: Under Article 3–Commercial Paper, "presentment" is a demand for acceptance or payment made upon the maker, acceptor, drawee, or other payor by or on behalf of the holder.

Presumption *: "Presumed" means that the trier of fact must find the existence of the fact presumed unless and until evidence is introduced which would support a finding of its non-existence.

Presumption: A presumtion is an assumed fact. It may serve as evidence until actual facts are introduced. In absence of actual facts, the person in whose favor a presumption exists prevails. A holder of a negotiable instrument is presumed to be a holder in due course until facts are introduced to the contrary. A disputable presumption makes a prima facie case. See local statute for a list of rebuttable and nonrebuttable presumptions.

Prima facie: The words literally mean "at first view." Thus, that which first appears seems to be true. A prima facie case is one that stands until contrary evidence is produced.

Privilege: A legal idea or concept of lesser significance than a right. An invitee has only a privilege to walk on another's land because such privilege may be revoked at will; whereas, a person who has an easement to go on another's land has a right, created by a grant which is an interest in land and cannot be revoked at will. To be exempt from jury service is a privilege.

Privity: Mutual and successive relationship to the same interest. Offeror and offeree, assignor and assignee, grantor and grantee are in privity. Privity of estate means that one takes title from another. In contract law, privity denotes parties in mutual legal relationship to each other by virtue of being promisees and promisors. At early common law, third party beneficiaries and assignees were said to be not in "privity."

Probate: The word means proof of a will by the proper court.

Proceeds *: Whatever is received when collateral or proceeds is sold, exchanged, collected or otherwise disposed of. The term also includes the account arising when the right to payment is earned under a contract right. Money, checks and the like are "cash proceeds." All other proceeds are "non-cash proceeds."

Process: In court proceeding, a process is an instrument issued by the court in the name of the state before or during the progress of the trial, under the seal of the court, directing an officer of the court to do, act, or cause some act to be done incidental to the trial.

Process of Posting *: Under Article 4–Bank Deposits and Collections, "Posting" is the usual procedure followed by a payor bank in determing to pay an item and in recording the payment including one or more of the following or other steps as determined by the bank: verification of any signature; ascertaining that sufficient funds are available; affixing a "paid" or other stamp; entering a charge or entry to a customer's account; correcting or reversing an entry or erroneous action with respect to the item.

Promise *: Under Article 3–Commercial Paper, it is an undertaking to pay and must be more than an acknowledgment of an obligation.

Properly Payable *: Under Article 4–Bank Deposits and Collections, this includes the availability of funds for payment at the time of decision to pay or dishonor.

Property: All those rights, powers, privileges, and immunities which one has concerning tangibles and intangibles. The term includes everything of value subject to ownership.

Pro tanto: "For so much." Persons are liable pro tanto or for such an amount.

Proximate cause: The cause that sets other causes in operation. The responsible cause of an injury.

Proximate damage: Damages that are direct, immediate, and the natural result of negligence or wrong, and which might reasonably have been expected.

Proxy: Authority to act for another; used by absent stockholders or members of legislative bodies to have their votes cast by others.

Public policy: There can be no strict definition for the term "public policy." Any conduct or any contract, the performance of which is against public morals or injurious to the public good, is in violation of public policy.

Punitive damages: Damages by way of punishment allowed for an injury caused by a wrong that is wilful and malicious.

Purchase *: This includes taking by sale, discount, negotiation, mortgage, pledge, lien, issue or re-issue, gift or any other voluntary transaction creating an interest in property.

Purchase Money Security Interest *: A security interest that is taken or retained by the seller of the collateral to secure all or part of its price; or taken by a person who by making advances or incurring an obligation gives value to enable the debtor to acquire rights in or the use of collateral if such value is in fact so used.

Purchaser *: A person who takes by purchase.

Quantum meruit (in pleading): An allegation that the defendant owes the plaintiff for work and labor a sum for as much as the plaintiff reasonably is entitled.

Quasi contracts: The term "quasi contracts" is used to define a situation where a legal duty arises that does not rest upon a promise, but does involve the payment of money. In order to do justice by a legal fiction, the court enforces the duty as if a promise in fact exists. Thus, if *A* gives *B* money by mistake, *A* can compel *B* to return the money by an action in quasi contract.

Quit claim: A deed that releases a right or interest in land, but which does not include any covenants of warranty. The grantor transfers only that which he has.

Quo warranto: A proceeding in court by which the state, city, county, or other governmental body tests or inquires into the legality of the claim of any person to a public office, franchise, or privilege. It is a proceeding to oust persons from public office.

Ratification: The confirmation of one's own previous act or act of another: e.g., a principal may ratify the previous unauthorized act of his agent. *B*'s agent, without authority, buys goods. *B*, by keeping the goods and receiving the benefits of the agent's act, ratifies the agency.

Ratify: To ratify means to confirm or approve.

Real property: The term means land with all its buildings, appurtenances, equitable and legal interests therein. The word is used in contradistinction to personal property which refers to moveables or chattels.

Reasonable care: The care that prudent persons would exercise under the same circumstances.

Rebuttal evidence: The evidence that is given to explain, repel, counteract, or disprove the testimony in chief given by the adverse party.

Receipt *: In the case of goods, means taking physical possession of them.

Receiver: An officer of the court appointed on behalf of all parties to the litigation to take possession of, hold, and control the property involved in the suit, for the benefit of the party who will be determined to be entitled thereto.

Recognizance: A recognizance is a contract of record or obligation made before a court by which the parties thereto obligate themselves to perform some act. It is different from a bail bond, in that a bail bond is under seal and creates a new debt. A recognizance is in the nature of a conditional judgment and acknowledges the existence of a present obligation to the state.

Recoupment: A right to deduct from the plaintiff's claim any payment or loss that the defendant has suffered by reason of the plaintiff's wrongful act. The words mean "a cutting back."

Redemption: To buy back. A debtor buys back or redeems his mortgaged property when he pays the debt.

Registered Form *: A security is in *registered form* when it specifies a person entitled to the security or to the rights it evidences and when its transfer may be registered upon books maintained for that purpose by or on behalf of an issuer as security so states.

Re-insurance: A contract of re-insurance is where one insurance company agrees to indemnify another insurance company in whole or in part against risks which the first company has assumed. The original contract of insurance and the re-insurance contract are distinct contracts. There is no privity between the original insured and the re-insurer.

Release: The voluntary relinquishing of a right, lien, or any other obligation. A release need not be under seal, nor does it necessarily require consideration. The words "release, remise, and discharge" are often used together to mean the same thing.

Remand: To send back a cause for the appellate court to the lower court in order that the lower court may comply with the instructions of the appellate court. Also to return a prisoner to jail.

Remedy: The word is used to signify the judicial means or court procedures by which legal and equitable rights are enforced.

Remedy *: Any remedial right to which an aggrieved party is entitled with or without resort to a tribunal.

Remise: The word means discharge or release. It is also synonymous with "quit claim."

Remitting Bank *: Under Article 4—Bank Deposits and Collections is any payor or intermediary bank remitting for an item.

Replevin: A remedy given by statute for the recovery of the possession of a chattel. Only the right to possession can be tried in such action.

Representative *: This includes an agent, an officer of a corporation or association, and a trustee, executor, or administrator of an estate, or any other person empowered to act for another.

Res: A Latin word that means "thing."

Res adjudicata: The doctrine of "res adjudicata" means that a controversy once having been decided or adjudged upon its merits is forever settled so far as the particular parties involved are concerned. Such a doctrine avoids vexatious lawsuits.

Respondent: One who answers another's bill or pleading, particularly in an equity case. Quite similar, in many instances, to defendant in law cases.

Respondeat superior: Latin words that mean the master is liable for the acts of his agent.

Responsible bidder: The word "responsible," as used by most statutes concerning public works in the phrase "lowest responsible bidder," means that such bidder has the requisite skill, judgment, and integrity necessary to perform the contract involved, and has the financial resources and ability to carry the task to completion.

Restraining order: An order issued by a court of equity in aid of a suit to hold matters in abeyance until parties may be heard. A temporary injunction is a restraining order.

Restraint of trade: Monopolies, combinations, and contracts that impede free competition are in restraint of trade.

Retainer: The payment in advance to an attorney to cover future services and advice.

Return of a writ: A sheriff's return of a writ is an official statement written on the back of a summons or other paper that he has performed his duties in compliance with the law or a statement as to why he has not complied with the law.

Right: The phrase "legal right" is a correlative of the phrase "legal duty." One has a legal right if, upon the breach of the correlative legal duty, he can secure a remedy in a court of law.

Right of action: The words are synonymous with "cause of action"; a right to enforce a claim in a court.

Rights *:   This includes remedies.

Riparian: A person is a riparian owner if his land is situated beside a stream of water, either flowing over or along the border of the land.

Robbery: The stealing or taking away from a person his money or other property either by force and violence or by putting him in fear of force and violence.

Rule (as a noun):   The regulation or direction of an administrative body is a rule. A rule of law is a general statement as to what the law is. "Every contract must be supported by consideration," is a rule of law. Rules of court are the rules for practice and procedure in a particular court.

Rule (as a verb):   The act of a court issuing an order that a defendant file a pleading is called a rule or command of the court.

Sanction: The penalty for the breach of a rule of law. Redress for civil injuries is called civil sanction; punishment for violation of criminal law is called penal sanction. The word literally means "enforcement."

Satisfaction: The term "satisfaction" in legal phraseology means the release and discharge of a legal obligation. Such satisfaction may be partial or full performance of the obligation. The word is used with accord. Accord means a promise to give a substituted performance for a contract obligation; satisfaction means the acceptance by the obligee of such performance.

Scienter: Knowledge by a defrauding party of the falsity of a representation. In a tort action of deceit, knowledge that a representation is false must be proved.

Scintilla of evidence: A very slight amount of evidence which aids in the proof of an allegation. If there is a "scintilla of evidence," the court generally presents the case to the jury.

Scrip: As applied to corporation law, "scrip" is a written certificate or evidence of a right of a person to obtain shares in a corporation.

Seal: A seal is to show that an instrument was executed in a formal manner. At early common law sealing legal documents was of great legal significance. A promise under seal was binding by virtue of the seal. Today under most statutes any stamp, wafer, mark, scroll, or impression made, adopted, and affixed, is adequate. The printed word "seal" or the letters "L.S." is sufficient.

Seasonably *: An action is taken "seasonably" when it is taken at or within the time agreed or if no time is agreed at or within a reasonable time.

Secondary Party *: Under Article 3–Commercial Paper this means a drawer or indorser.

Security: Security may be bonds, stocks, and other property placed by a debtor with a creditor, with power to sell if the debt is not paid. The plural of the term, "securities," is used broadly to mean tangible choses in action such as promissory notes, bonds, stocks, and other vendible obligations.

Security *: An instrument which is issued in bearer form or registered form; and is of a type commonly dealt in upon securities exchanges or markets or commonly recognized in any area in which it is issued or dealt in as a medium for investment; and is either one of a class or series or by its terms is divisible into a class or series of instruments; and evidences a share, a participation or other interest in property or in an enterprise or evidences an obligation of the issuer.

Security Agreement *: An agreement which creates or provides for a security interest.

Security Interest *: This means an interest in personal property or fixtures which secures payment or performance of an obligation. The retention or reservation of title by a seller of goods notwithstanding shipment or delivery to the buyer is limited in effect to a reservation of a "security interest." The term also includes any interest of a buyer of accounts, chattel paper, or contract rights which is subject to Article 9. The special property interest of a buyer of goods on identification of such goods to a contract for sale is not a "security interest," but a buyer may also acquire a "security interest" by complying with Article 9. Unless a lease or consignment is intended as security, reservation of title thereunder is not a "security interest" but a consignment is in any event subject to the provisions on consignment sales. Whether a lease is intended as security is to be determined by the facts of each case; however, (a) the inclusion of an option to purchase does not of itself make the lease one intended for security, and (b) an agreement that upon compliance with the terms of the lease the lessee shall become or has the option to become the owner of the property for no additional consideration or for a nominal consideration does make the lease one intended for security.

Secured Party *: A lender, seller, or other person in whose favor there is a security interest, including a person to whom accounts, contract rights or chattel paper have been sold. When the holders of obligations issued under an indenture of trust, equipment trust agreement or the like are represented by a trustee or other person, the representative is the secured party.

Sell: The words "to sell" mean to negotiate or make arrangement for a sale. A sale is an executed contract. "Sell" is the name of the process in executing the contract.

Seller *: A person who sells or contracts to sell goods.

Send *: In connection with any writing or notice this means to deposit in the mail or deliver for transmission by any other usual means of communication with postage or cost of transmission provided for and properly addressed and in the case of an instrument to an address specified thereon or otherwise agreed, or if there be none to any address reasonable under the circumstances. The receipt of any writing or notice within the time at which it would have arrived if properly sent has the effect of a proper sending.

Servant: A person employed by another and subject to the direction and control of the employer in performance of his duties.

Served or service: The delivery of a writ issued out of a court to a proper officer, usually the sheriff, by which a court secures jurisdiction over the defendant. See *Process.*

Set-off: A matter of defense, called a cross-complaint, used by the defendant for the purpose of making a demand on the plaintiff and which arises out of contract, but is independent and unconnected with the cause of action set out in the complaint. See *Counter-claims* and *Recoupment.*

Settle *: Under Article 4–Bank Deposits and Collections this means to pay in cash, by clearing house settlement, in a charge or credit or by remittance, or otherwise as instructed. A settlement may be either provisional or final.

Severable-contract: A contract, the performance of which is divisible. Two or more parts may be set over against each other. Items and prices may be apportioned to each other without relation to the full performance of all of its parts.

Several: A contract in which each promissor makes a separate promise and is separately liable thereon. There may be several promises. If the promissors make a single promise the obligation is joint. A joint and several promissory note consists of the joint promise of all and the separate promise of each. "We jointly and severally promise" is an illustration.

Share of stock: A proportional part of the rights in the management and assets of a corporation. It is a chose in action. The certificate is the evidence of the share.

Sheriff: A public officer whose authority and duties are created by legislation. His duties are to execute and administer the law.

Signed: This includes any symbol executed or adopted by a party with present intention to authenticate a writing.

Situs: Situs means "place, situation." The place where a thing is located. The "situs" of personal property is the domicile of the owner. The "situs" of land is the state or county where it is located.

Slander: Slander is an oral utterance that tends to injure the reputation of another. See *Libel.*

Solvent: A person is solvent when he is able to pay his debts.

Sovereignty: The word means the power of a state (organized government) to execute its laws, and its right to exercise dominion and authority over its citizens and their property subject only to constitutional limitations.

Special appearance: The appearance in court of a person through his attorney for a limited purpose only. A court does not get jurisdiction over a person by special appearance.

Special verdict: A special verdict is one in which the jury finds the facts only, leaving it to the court to apply the law and draw the conclusion as to the proper disposition of the case.

Specialty: The word "specialty" in commercial law means a promise under seal to pay money—a bond. In early law there were two kinds of specialties." "Common law specialties" were formal instruments under seal—bonds and covenants; "mercantile specialties" included bills and notes, insurance policies, and other unsealed commercial papers.

Specific performance: A remedy in personam in equity that compels such substantial performance of a contract as will do justice among the parties. A person who fails to obey a writ for specific performance may be put in jail by the equity judge for contempt of court. Such remedy applies to contracts involving real property. In absence of unique goods or peculiar circumstances, damages generally are an adequate remedy for the breach of contracts involving personal property. See Specific Performance under the Uniform Sales Act.

Stare decisis: Translated, the term means "stand by the decision." The law should adhere to decided cases. See *Precedent.*

Statute: A law passed by the legislative body of a state is a statute.

Stock: The word has several meanings. When applied to "goods, wares, and merchandise," it means goods in a mercantile house that are kept for sale. As applied in corporation law, the word means the right of an owner of a share of stock to participate in the management and ownership of a corporation. See *Capital Stock.*

Stock dividend: The issue by a corporation of new shares of its own stock to its shareholders as dividends.

Stockholders: Those persons whose names appear on the books of a corporation as the owners of the shares of stock and who are entitled to participate in the management and control of the corporation.

Stock split-up: A type of readjustment of the financial plan of a corporation whereby each existing share of stock is split into such number of new shares as may be determined by the managers of the corporation.

Stoppage in transitu: The right of a seller of goods, which have not been paid for, upon learning of the insolvency of the buyer, to stop the goods in transit and hold the same as security for the purchase price. It is an extension of the unpaid seller's lien.

Subpoena: A process issued out of a court requiring the attendance of a witness at a trial.

Subsequent Purchaser *: A person who takes a security other than by original issue.

Subrogation: The substitution of one person in another's place, whether as a creditor or as the possessor of any lawful right, so that the substituted person may succeed to the rights, remedies, or proceeds of the claim. It rests in equity on the theory that, where a party is compelled to pay a debt for which another is liable, such payment should vest the paying party with all the rights the creditor has against the debtor. For example: *X* insurance company pays *Y* for an injury to *Y*'s car by reason of *Z*'s negligent act. *X* insurance company will be subrogated to *Y*'s cause of action against *Z*.

Substantial performance: The complete performance of all the essential elements of a contract. The only permissible omissions or deviations are those which are trivial, inadvertent, and inconsequential. Such performance will not justify repudiation. Compensation for defects may be substituted for actual performance. See *Breach*.

Substantive law: A word applied to that law which regulates and controls the rights and duties of all persons in society. It is used in contradistinction to the term adjective law, which means the rules of court procedure or remedial law which prescribe the methods by which substantive law is enforced.

Succession: The word means the transfer by operation of law of all the rights and obligations of a deceased person to those who are entitled to take.

Succession tax: This tax is not a burden on property, but a tax upon the privilege of taking property, whether by will or descent.

Suit: The term refers to any type of legal proceeding for the purpose of obtaining a legal remedy; the term "suit" generally applies to "suit in equity," whereas, at law, the term is "action at law."

Summons: A writ issued by a court to the sheriff directing him to notify the defendant that the plaintiff claims to have a cause of action against the defendant and that he is required to answer. If the defendant does not answer, judgment will be taken by default.

Surety *: This term includes guarantor.

Suspends Payments *: Under Article 4–Bank Deposits and Collections with respect to a bank this means that it has been closed by order of the supervisory authorities, that a public officer has been appointed to take it over or that it ceases or refuses to make payments in the ordinary course of business.

Tacit: That which is understood from the nature of things. Those rules that are generally understood to be the law by reason of customs and mores.

Talisman: A juror summoned to fill up a panel for the trial of a particular case. Such person is not bound to serve the term.

Tangible: Tangible is a word used to describe property that is physical in character and capable of being moved. A debt is intangible, but a promissory note evidencing such debt is tangible. See *Chose in action, Chattel.*

Telegram *: This includes a message transmitted by radio, teletype, cable, any mechanical method of transmission, or the like.

Tenancy: The interest in property that a tenant acquires from a landlord by a lease is called a tenancy. It may be at will or for a term. It is an interest in land.

Tenant: The person to whom a lease is made. A lessee.

Tender: To offer money in satisfaction of a debt or obligation by producing the same and expressing to the creditor a willingness to pay. See *Legal tender.*

Tender of Delivery *: This means that the seller must put and hold conforming goods at the buyer's disposition and give the buyer any notification reasonably necessary to enable him to take delivery.

Tenement: The word has historical significance as applied to real property. In a broad sense it means an estate in land or some interest connected therewith, such as houses, rents, profits, and rights, to which a holder of the title is entitled. It is used with the word "hereditaments."

Tenure: The word is used to designate the means by which title is held to real property. For example, "tenure in fee simple," "tenure for life." It also is used to indicate the time limit of a person's right to public office. "Term" means limited time. "Tenure" means indefinite.

Term *: That portion of an agreement which relates to a particular matter.

Termination: This occurs when either party pursuant to a power created by agreement or law puts an end to the contract otherwise than for its breach. On "termination" all obligations which are still executory on both sides are discharged but any right based on prior breach or performance survives.

Term of court: That period of time prescribed by statute within which a court may legally hold its sessions and transact its business.

Testament: A testament is the declaration of a person's intention as to what disposition he desires to be made of his property after his death. The word is synonymous with will. The word is so used because a will is a testimonial of one's intention.

Testamentary capacity: A person is said to have testamentary capacity when he understands the nature of his business, the value of his property, knows those persons who are natural objects of his bounty, and comprehends the manner in which he has provided for the distribution of his property.

Testator: A male person who has died leaving a will. A female person is called a testatrix.

Testimony: Those statements made by a witness under oath or affirmation in a legal proceeding. See *Evidence.*

Title: This word has different meanings. It may be limited or broad in its meaning. When a person has the exclusive rights, powers, privileges, and immunities to property, real and personal, tangible and intangible, against all other persons, he may be said to have the complete title thereto. The aggregate of legal relations concerning property is the title. The term is used to describe the means by which a person exercises control and dominion over property. A trustee has a limited title. See *Possession.*

Tonnage: In marine insurance, registered tonnage means the vessel's carrying capacity as stated in the ship's papers at the date of the policy, and not the tonnage fixed by the law of the government under which the vessel is registered.

Tort: A wrongful act committed by one person against another person or his property. It is the breach of a legal duty imposed by law other than by contract. The word tort means "twisted" or "wrong." *A* assaults *B*, thus committing a tort. See *Right, Duty.*

Total disability: In a contract of insurance, these words do not mean "absolute helplessness." Their meaning is relative, depending on the circumstances of each case, the occupation, and capabilities of the insured.

Trade fixtures: Personal property placed upon or annexed to leased land by a tenant for the purpose of carrying on a trade or business during the term of the lease. Such property is generally to be removed at the end of the term, providing it can be so removed without destruction or injury to the premises. Trade fixtures include show cases, shelving, racks, machinery, and the like.

Trade-mark: No complete definition can be given for a trade-mark. Generally it is any sign, symbol, mark, word, or arrangement of words in the form of a label adopted and used by manufacturer or distributor to designate his particular goods, and which no other person has the legal right to use. Originally, the design or trade-mark indicated origin, but today it is used more as an advertising mechanism.

Trade union: A combination of workmen usually (but not necessarily) of the same trade organized for the purpose of securing by united action the most favorable working conditions for its members.

Transfer: In its broadest sense, the word means the act by which an owner sets over or delivers his right, title, and interest in property to another person. A "bill of sale" to personal property is evidence of a transfer.

Treasury stock: Stock of a corporation that has been issued by the corporation for value, but that is later returned to the corporation by way of gift or purchase or otherwise. It may be returned to the trustees of a corporation for the purpose of sale.

Trespass: An injury to the person, property, or rights of another person committed by actual force and violence, or under such circumstances that the law will imply that the injury was caused by force or violence.

Trial: A proceeding by the properly authorized officials into the examination of the facts and for the purpose of determining an issue presented according to proper rules of law.

Trust: A relationship between persons by which one holds property for the use and benefit of another. The relationship is called fiduciary. Such rights are enforced in a court of equity. The person trusted is called a trustee. The person for whose benefit the property is held is called a beneficiary or "cestui que trust."

Trustee in bankruptcy: An agent of the court authorized to liquidate the assets of the bankrupt, protect them, and to bring them to the court for final distribution for the benefit of the bankrupt and all the creditors.

Trustee (generally): A person who is intrusted with the management and control of another's property and estate. A person occupying a fiduciary position. An executor, an administrator, a guardian.

Ultra vires: Literally the words mean "beyond power." The acts of a corporation are ultra vires when they are beyond the power or capacity of the corporation as granted by the state in its charter.

Unauthorized *: Refers to a signature or indorsement made without actual, implied, or apparent authority and includes a forgery.

Undertaking: A so-called informal bond without a seal is called an "undertaking."

Unfair competition: The imitation by design of the goods of another for the purpose of palming them off on the public, thus misleading the public by inducing it to buy goods made by the imitator. It includes misrepresentation and deceit; thus, such conduct is fraudulent not only as to competitors but as to the public.

Unilateral contract: A promise for an act or an act for a promise; a single enforceable promise. *A* promises *B* $10 if *B* will mow *A*'s lawn. *B* mows the lawn. *A*'s promise now binding is a unilateral contract. See *Bilateral contract*.

Usage: When conduct has been long continued and is of uniform practice, it will fall within the category of "usage." Usage is a fact, not opinion. In trade, it is a course of dealing. Customs are the rules of law that arise from usage. Customs rest on usage.

Usage of Trade *: Any practice or method of dealing having such regularity of observance in a place, vocation or trade as to justify an expectation that it will be observed with respect to the transaction in question. The existence and scope of such a usage are to be proved as facts. If it is established that such a usage is embodied in a written trade code or similar writing the interpretation of the writing is for the court.

Usurious: A contract is usurious if made for a loan of money at a rate of interest in excess of that permitted by statute.

Utter: The word means to put out or pass off. To utter a check is to offer it to another in payment of a debt. The words "utter a forged writing" mean to put such writing in circulation, knowing of the falsity of the instrument with the intent to injure another.

Vacancy: As applied to a fire insurance policy, the words "vacancy," "vacant," or "unoccupied" mean, "that if the house insured should cease to be used as a place of human habitation or for living purposes, it would then be vacant or unoccupied." The period of time is unimportant. Vacant property increases the risk of the insurer, hence violates the policy.

Valid: That which is sufficient to satisfy the requirements of the law. A valid judgment is one lawfully obtained under the proper rules of procedure and evidence.

Valuable consideration: Any consideration that will support a simple contract. A classic definition is, "valuable consideration consists of some right, interest, profit, or benefit or value accruing to the promisor, and some forbearance, detriment, loss, or responsibility given or suffered by the promisee."

Value: The term has many meanings in law. Value is any consideration sufficient to support a simple contract. Although an antecedent debt would not be value to support a simple contract, it is considered adequate to support a negotiable instrument by the Law Merchant. A "bona fide purchaser," called a "B.F.P.," gives up something of value, either money, property, or services. Value in a business sense means market value. The money equivalent of property is value.

Value *: Except as otherwise provided with respect to negotiable instruments and bank collections a person gives "value" for rights if he acquires them
(a) in return for a binding commitment to extend credit or for the extension of immediately available credit whether or not drawn upon and whether or not a charge-back is provided for in the event of difficulties in collection; or
(b) as security for or in total or partial satisfaction of a pre-existing claim; or
(c) by accepting delivery pursuant to a pre-existing contract for purchase; or
(d) generally, in return for any consideration sufficient to support a simple contract.

Valued policy: As used in fire insurance, a valued policy is one in which the sum to be paid in case of loss is fixed by the terms of the policy. No reference can be made to the real value of the property that is lost.

Vendee: A purchaser of property. The term is generally applied to the purchaser of real property. The word "buyer" is usually applied to the purchaser of chattels.

Vendor: The seller of property. The term is usually applied to the seller of real property. The word "seller" is applied to the seller of personal property.

Vendor's lien: An unpaid seller's right to hold possession of property until he has recovered the purchase price. See *Seller's lien*.

Venire: To come into court; a writ used to summon a jury. The word is used sometimes to mean jury.

Venue: The geographical area over which a court presides. Venue designates the county in which the action is tried. Change of venue means a move to another county.

Verdict: The decision of a jury, reported to the court, on matters properly submitted to it for its consideration.

Vested: The word generally applies to the title to or interests in land. The word strictly means "there is an immediate right of present enjoyment, or a present fixed right of future enjoyment." A life estate is a vested interest. Dower right of a wife, however, is not vested until the death of the husband.

Vis major: The force of nature, sometimes called "act of God," which excuses persons from liability. If the ordinary exertion of human skill and prudence cannot avoid the effect of the force of nature, then an obligor may be excused under the doctrine of impossibility of performance.

Void: That which has no legal effect. A contract that is void is a nullity and confers no rights or duties.

Voidable: That which is valid until one party, who has the power of avoidance, exercises such power. An infant has the power of avoidance of his contract. A defrauded party has the power to avoid his contract. Such contract is voidable.

Voucher: A written instrument that bears witness or "vouches" for something. Generally a voucher is an instrument showing services have been performed or goods purchased, and is presented to a disbursing officer authorizing him to make payment and charge the proper account.

Wager: A relationship between persons by which they agree that a certain sum of money or thing owned by one of them will be paid or delivered to the other upon the happening of an uncertain event, which event is not within the control of the parties and rests upon chance. Consult state statutes.

Wages: Compensation or reward, usually money, paid at stated times for labor. If compensation is paid at completion of a job or task, or if compensation is earned as a profit from the labor of others, such compensation is not wages.

Waive (verb): To "waive" at law, is to relinquish or give up intentionally a known right or to do an act which is inconsistent with the claiming of a known right.

Waiver (noun): The intentional relinquishment or giving up of a known right. It may be done by express words or conduct which involve any acts inconsistent with an intention to claim the right. Such conduct creates an estoppel on the part of the claimant. See *Estoppel.*

Warehouseman *: A person engaged in the business of storing goods for hire.

Warehouse Receipt *: A receipt issued by a person engaged in the business of storing goods for hire.

Warehouse receipt: An instrument showing that the signer has in his possession certain described goods for storage, and which obligates the signer, the warehouseman, to deliver the goods to a specified person or to his order or bearer upon the return of the instrument. Consult Uniform Warehouse Receipts Act.

Warrant (noun): An order in writing in the name of the state and signed by a magistrate directed to an officer commanding him to arrest a person.

Warrant (verb): To guarantee, to answer for, to assure that a state of facts exists.

Warranty: An undertaking, either expressed or implied, that a certain fact regarding the subject matter of a contract is presently true or will be true. The word has particular application in the law of sales of chattels. The word relates to title and quality. The word should be distinguished from "guaranty" which means a contract or promise by one person to answer for the performance of another. See *Suretyship, Guarantor.*

Waste: Damage to the real property so that its value as security is impaired.

Watered stock: Corporate stock issued by a corporation for property at an over valuation, or stock issued for which the corporation receives nothing in payment therefor.

Wharfage: A charge against a vessel for lying at a wharf. It is used synonymously with "dockage" and "moorage."

Wholesale: The usual meaning of the word is the sale of goods in gross to retailers who, in turn, sell to consumers.

Will (testament): The formal instrument by which a person makes disposition of his property to take effect upon his death. See *Testament.*

Witness: A person who testifies under oath in a legal proceeding.

Working capital: The amount of cash necessary for the convenient and safe transaction of present business.

Writ: An instrument in writing under seal in the name of the state, issued out of a Court of Justice the commencement of, or during a legal proceeding, directed to an officer of the court commanding him to do some act, or requiring some person to do or refrain from doing some act pertinent or relative to the cause being tried.

Writing obligatory: These words refer to writings under seal.

Written or Writing *: This includes printing, typewriting or any other intentional reduction to tangible form.

Zoning ordinance: An ordinance passed by a city council by virtue of the police power which regulates and prescribes the kind of buildings, residences, or businesses that shall be built and used in different parts of a city.

Index

Abandoned personal property, 959
"Abandonment," defined, 1010
"Abatement of a nuisance," defined, 1010
"Ab initio," defined, 1010
Abstracting of cases, 1005–9
Acceptance, 113, 137–41 (see also Commercial paper: liabilities; Secured transactions)
  of bilateral offer, 139
  defined, 137, 1010
  to follow offer, 140–41
  by offeree, 140
  presentment of commercial paper for, 530–31
  silence as, 139
  time of taking effect, 141
  of unilateral offer, 137–39
Acceptance of goods, 393–94
  and remedies of sellers, 398–99
Accessions, 623
  of personal property, 957–58
Accommodation parties, liability of, 508–9
Accord, 305–6
"Account debtor," defined, 1010
Accounting:
  agents and duty regarding, 673, 721
  partners' rights to, 773
Accounts:
  as collateral, 598
  defined under UCD, 109

Accretion of real property, 976
Acker v. First Fed. Savings & Loan Assn. of St. Petersburg, 480–81
"Action ex contractu," defined, 1011
"Action ex delicto," defined, 1011
"Act of God," defined, 1048
"Ad damnum clause," defined, 1011
Additional hardship, and nonperformance of contract, 287–88
"Ad hoc," defined, 1011
Adjective law, 7, 1011
  need for, 80–81
"Adjudicate," defined, 1011
Administrative law, 7–8, 45, 55–58
  judicial functions, 56–58
  legislative functions, 56
"Administrator," defined, 1011
Administrators, contracts of, 245
"Adverse possession," defined, 1011
Adverse possession of real property, 975
Advertisements for bids, 132–33
"Advising bank," defined, 1011
"Affidavit," defined, 1011
"A fortiori," defined, 1011
After-acquired property, 594
Agency and employment, 652–747
  capacity of parties in, 655
  contractual liability of agents, 671–73
    to account for money received, 673
    competent principal, 673
    warranty of authority and, 672

Agency and employment (*Cont.*):
 contractual liability of principals, 663–69
  actual authority and, 663–64
  and agents' power to appoint subagents, 668
  apparent authority and, 664–65
  authority created by necessity and, 665
  conditions for ratificaiton, 665–66
  conduct constituting ratification, 666–
   67
  in general, 663
  and purchase on credit, 668–69
  and ratification, 665
  real estate brokers, 669
  and right to collect, 667–68
  secret limitations and, 669
  in special situations, 667
 duties of agent to principal, 718–21
  to account, 721
  to give notice, 721
  loyalty, 718–20
  not to be negligent, 720–21
  to obey instructions, 720
 duties of principal to agent, 721–23
  brokers, 722–23
  to compensate, 721–23
  to protect from injury, 723
  to reimburse and indemnify, 723
  sales representatives, 723
 formal requirements, 655–56
 introduction to, 653–62
 labor-management relations, 656–58
 liability of third parties, 707–17
  cases, 709–16
  and disclosed principal, 707
  and liability to agent, 708
  tort liability, 708–9
  and undisclosed principal, 707–8 (*see
   also* Undisclosed principal)
 statutory aspects of employment, 656
 termination of, 736–47
  by act of parties, 736–37
  agency coupled with interest and, 738
  cases, 739–46
  introduction to, 736
  by law, 737
  notice of, 738–39
  wrongful, 737
 terminology, 654–55 (*see also* specific
  terms)
 tort liability of principals and agents,
  686–706
  cases, 692–705
  introduction to, 686
  procedure in, 689
  proprietor—independent contractor,
   689–90
  respondeat superior, 687–89

Agency and employment (*Cont.*):
 tort liability of principals (*Cont.*):
  servants and, 686–87
  third parties and, 708–9
  workmen's compensation and F.E.L.A.,
   690–92
 undisclosed principals, 669–71
  election and, 670–71
  and notice to agent, 671
  and settlement between principal and
   agent, 670
"Agency coupled with an interest," defined, 1011
"Agent," defined, 1011
Agreement, 113, 130–49 (*see also* Contracts:
 specific types)
 acceptance, 137–41
 cases, 142–59
 defined, 1011
 duration of offers, 134–37
  cases, 251–62
  introduction to, 242–43
  parol evidence rule, 243–44
  statute of frauds and, 244–51
 formation of offers, 130–32
 form of, 242–63
 offers in special situations, 132–34
"Airbill," defined, 1013
*Albert B. Cord Co. v. S & P Management
 Services, Inc.,* 725–28
Alderman et al. v. Alderman et al., 857–59
"Aliquot," defined, 1011
Allen v. Allen, 170–71
Allonge, 436
*Al Maroone Ford, Inc. v. Manheim Auto
 Auction, Inc.,* 611–12
"Alter ego," defined, 1011
Altex Aluminum Supply Co. v. Asay, 489–
 91
Althoff v. System Garages, Incorporated,
 967–69
*American Bridge Co. et al. v. City of
 Boston,* 272–73
American Card Company v. H. M. H. Co.,
 616–17
*American Enameled Brick & Tile Co. v.
 Brozek,* 710–11
Analytical school, 5–6
Anderson v. Copeland, 118–19
"Annuity," defined, 1011–12
Anticipatory breach, 284–85
Anticipatory repudiation, 391
Appeals in lawsuits, 92–94
Approval sales, 345
"A priori," defined, 1012
Arbitration, 101–5, 116–17
 statutory aspects of, 102–5
"Architect's certificate," defined, 1012

Arcur v. Weiss, 259–60
"Arguendo," defined, 1012
Arizona Power Co. v. Stuart, 839
Artisan's liens, 886–87
    defined, 1012
"Assignee," defined, 1012
"Assignment," defined, 1012
"Assignment for the benefit of creditors,"
    defined, 1012
Assignments, 264–68, 1012
    and claims for money, 266
    duties of assignees, 267–68
    nature of, 264
    notice of, 268
    requisites of, 264–65
    rights of assignees, 266–67
    unassignable contracts, 265–66
"Assignor," defined, 1012
*Associated Hardware Supply Co. v. Big
    Wheel Distributing Co.,* 377–80
Associates Discount Corp. v. Cary, 646–49
"Assumpsit," defined, 1012
"Assumption of risk," 691
"Attachment," defined, 1012
Attachment, secured transactions and,
    593–94
    perfection by, 602–3
Attorney, power of, 655
"Attorney at law," defined, 1012
Attorney General, and dissolution of cor-
    poration, 866
"Attorney in fact," defined, 1012
Auctions, 132–33

Babcock Poultry Farm, Inc. v. Shook, 408–
    10
"Bad faith," defined, 1012
"Bail," defined, 1012
"Bailee," defined, 1012
"Bailment," defined, 1012–13
Bailments of personal property, 959–65
    common carriers as bailees, 962–65
    contracts against required care, 961–62
    definitions, 959–60, 1012–13
    degree of care required, 960–61
    insurance, 962
    types of, 960
"Bailor," defined, 1013
Bank drafts, 414, 417 (*see also* Drafts)
Banker's acceptance, 417
*Banker's Guarantee Title and Trust Co.
    v. Fisher,* 236–40, 485–88
"Banking day," defined, 1013
Bank notes, 413 (*see also* Promissory notes)
Bank of Marin v. England, Trustee, 574–76
Bankruptcy, 307, 914–31
    acts of, 115–16
    cases, 922–31

Bankruptcy (*Cont.*):
    discharge claims, 918–20
    and dissolution of partnerships, 781, 782
    and exemptions, 920
    fraudulent conveyances, 921
    in general, 914
    and holders of commercial paper, 468
    kinds of, 914–15
    officers of the court and, 916–17
    priority of claims, 920–21
    provable claims, 918
    recoverable preferences, 917–18
    reorganizations, 921–22
    and termination of agency, 737
    terminology of (*see* specific terms)
    wage-earner plans, 922
Banks (*see also* Commercial paper; specific
        terminology, transactions)
    deposits and collections, 326, 556–89
        cases, 567–89
        collection of items: depositary, collect-
            ing banks, 558–60
        collection of items: payor banks, 561–
            63
        introduction, 556–58
        relationship between payor bank and
            customer, 563–67
    instruments "payable through," "pay-
        able at," 433–34
    and liability, 501
Banks v. Crescent Lumber & Shingle Co.,
    147–49
Barrett Associates, Inc. v. Aronson, 208–9
Batchelder v. Granite Trust Co., 545–46
*Bayer & Mingolia Construction Co. v.
    Deschenes,* 907
"Bearer," bearer paper, 428–29, 431–32,
    1013
"Bearer form," defined, 1013
Beltone Electronics Corporation v. Smith,
    234–36
"Bench," defined, 1013
"Bench and bar," defined, 1013
"Beneficiary," defined, 1013
"Bequest," defined, 1013
Bergum v. Weber, 765
"Between merchants," defined, 1013
"Bid," defined, 1013
Bids, contract, 132–33
Bilateral contract, 111
    defined, 1013
Bilateral mistake, 204
Bilateral offer, acceptance of, 139
"Bill of sale," defined, 1013
Bills obligatory, 413
Bills of exchange, 413–14 (*see also* Com-
    mercial paper; Drafts; specific
    types)

Bills of lading (*see also* Documents of title):
defined, 1013
"Binder," defined, 1013
Bing Crosby Minute Maid Corp. v. Eaton, 839–41
Blank indorsement, 437, 438
Blaustein v. Aiello, 1001–2
Blow v. Ammerman, 456–57
Board of Education (Anning-Johnson Co.) v. Hartford Accident & Ind. Co., 910–12
Bole v. Lyle et al., 777–78
Bomud Company v. Yockey Oil Company and Osborn, 909–10
Bonadelle Construction Co. v. Hernandez, 291–92
"Bona fide purchaser," defined, 1013
"Bond," defined, 1013
Bonds, 413, 419, 825
suretyship (*see* Suretyships)
"Book account," defined, 1013
Books:
partners and right to inspect, 772 (*see also* Accounting; Accounts)
Borrowing:
corporations and power of, 811–12 (*see also* Debts; specific legal papers, terminology, etc.)
Boulevard Nat. Bank of Miami v. Air Metal Indus., 274–76
Bowman v. Bowman, 744–46
Branch v. Mills & Lupton Supply Company, 925–26
Breach of contract, 16 (*see also* Contracts; Performance of contracts; Sales; etc.)
anticipatory, 284–85
judicial remedies for, 113–17
Brekken v. Reader's Digest Special Products, Inc., 742–43
Brennan v. Brennan, 126–27
Briefing cases, 1005–9
"Broker," defined, 1013–14
Brokers, 654 (*see also* Agency and employment; Real estate brokers)
Brown & Bigelow v. Roy, 758–59
Bryant v. Troutman, 209–11
"Bulk transfer," defined, 1014
Bulk transfers, 328, 404–6
problem of, 404–5
requirement for compliance, 405–6
"Burden of establishing," defined, 1014
Burden of proof, holders of commercial paper and, 470–71
Burgamy v. Davis, 310–11
Business organizations, 749–881
corporations, 793–871

Business organizations (*Cont.*):
miscellaneous, 873–81
cases involving, 876–81
partnerships, 750–93
Business torts, 10–19
and judicial intervention, 10–12
retail price control, 12–19
Business trusts, 875
"Buyer," defined, 1014
"Buyer in ordinary course of business," defined, 1014
By-laws:
corporation, 852
defined, 1014

Cain v. Country Club Delicatessen of Saybrook, Inc., 639–42
"Call," defined, 1014
"Call-in pay," defined, 1014
Camp v. Bank of Bentonville, 193–94
"Cancellation," defined, 1014
Cancellation of commercial paper, 543
Capacity (competence) of parties, 113, 183–99 (*see also* specific terminology used in regard to)
and agency, employment, 655, 673
cases, 189–98
and holders of commercial paper, 467
and liability for necessaries, 187–88
and ratification, 187
and relationships between banks and customers, 565
requirements and right to disaffirm, 185–86
Capital (*see also* specific types):
defined, 825, 1014
of partnerships, 755
"Capital stock," 824–25
Carlson v. Hannah et al., 675–77
"Carrier," defined, 1014
Casey et al. v. Grantham et al., 790–91
Cashier's checks, 417
defined, 1014
"Cash proceeds," defined, 1039
"Cause of action," defined, 1014
"Caveat emptor," defined, 1014
"Caveat venditor," defined, 1014
Century Appliance Company v. Broff, 443–44
"Certificate of stock," 825
Certificates of deposit, 416, 419
Certified checks, 417, 565 (*see also* Checks)
"Certiorari," defined, 1015
"Cestui que trust," defined, 1015
Chairaluce v. Stanley Warner Management Corp. et al., 363–66
Chancery (*see* Equity)

Channel Master Corporation v. Aluminium Limited Sales, Inc., 206–7
Charge-back, right of, 560
"Charter," defined, 1015
Chatham Pharmaceuticals, Inc. v. Angier Chemical Co., Inc. et al., 273–74
Chattel, 937
  defined, 1015
"Chattel mortgage," defined, 1015
Chattel mortgage notes, 419
Chattel paper:
  as collateral, 597–98
  defined, 1015
  as proceeds, 621
Checks, 414, 416, 417 (*see also* Banks; specific terminology used in regard to checks)
  certification of, 505–6 (*see also* Certified checks)
  computers and, 323–24
  dishonoring (*see* Banks: deposits and collections)
  forged (*see* Forgery)
  stale, 565
Cherry v. Crispin, 211–12
Chesapeake Supply & Equip. Co. v. Manitowoc Eng. Corp., 802–4
Children (*see* Infants, infancy)
Choctaw Lumber Co. v. Atlanta Band Mill, Inc., 816–17
"Chose in action," defined, 1015
"C.I.F.," 345
"Circumstantial evidence," defined, 1015
Citizens & Southern Nat. Bank v. Capital Const. Co., 617–18
Citizens National Bank of Englewood v. Fort Lee Savings and Loan Association et al., 569–71
City of Atlanta v. J. J. Black & Company, 946
"Civil action," defined, 1015
Civil law, 45 (*see also* specific applications, terminology)
Clack-Nomah Flying Club v. Sterling Aircraft, Inc., 966–67
Claims (*see also* Breach of contract; specific instruments, terminology, transactions):
  discharge of, and consideration, 162–63
Classifications, legal, 7
"Clearing corp.," defined, 1015
"Clearing house," defined, 1015
"Cloud on title," defined, 1015
"Code," defined, 1016
"Codicil," defined, 1016
"Cognovit," defined, 1016
"Co-insurer," defined, 1016

Collateral (*see also* Secured transactions):
  defined, 1016
  impairment of right of, 543–44
Collateral notes, 418
"Collecting bank," defined, 1016
Collection, bill (*see* Agency and employment)
Commercial Casualty Insurance Co. v. North et al., 880–81
Commercial Credit Equipment Corporation v. Reeves, 461–62
"Commercial law," history of, 321–24
Commercial paper, 326, 412–89 (*see also* Holders; holders in due course; Secured transactions; specific terminology)
  additional terms regarding omissions, 432–36
  bank deposits and collections, 556–89
  concept of negotiability, 414–16
  condition's precedent, discharge, 529–54
    cases, 545–54
    discharge, 538–39, 540–45
    presentment, notice of dishonor, protest, 529–40
  creation, transfer of, 423–47
  defenses, 464–95
  history of, 412
  introduction to, 412–21
  language, words required to create, 423–27
  liability of parties regarding, 497–527
    cases, 515–27
    contractual liability of parties, 504–9
    warranty liability, 509–14
  negotiation by indorsement, 437–40
  origin of bill of exchange, 413–14
  origin of promissory note, 412–13
  payable to order or bearer, 428–32
  scope of Article 3, 416
  time of payment must be certain, 427–28
  transfer, negotiation, 436–37
  types, uses of negotiable instruments, 416–19
"Commercial unit," defined, 1016
Commingled goods, 623
"Commission," defined, 1016
"Commission merchant," defined, 1016
"Common carrier," defined, 1016
Common carriers as bailees, 962–65
  beginning of relation, 964
  care required of, 963
  contract against liability of, 963–64
  definitions, 962–63, 1016
  rates, 965
  termination of relation, 964–65
Common law, 44, 45, 51–55 (*see also* specific applications, terminology)

Common law trust, 875
Common stock, 826
Commonwealth Loan Co. v. Downtown Lincoln M. Co., 642–44
Community property, 980
  defined, 1016
Compensation *(see also* Agency and employment):
  of corporation directors, 855–56
  partners' right to, 772
Competence *(see* Capacity of parties)
Competition, 11–12, 221–22
"Complaint," defined, 1016
Composition of creditors, 307
  defined, 1015
"Compromise," defined, 1016
Computers, 323–24
"Condemnation proceedings," defined, 1017
"Condition," defined, 1017
Conditional sale notes, 419
Condition precedent, 282–83
  commercial paper and, 529–40, 545ff.
  defined, 1017
  time as, 283
"Conditions concurrent," defined, 1017
Conditions of contract performance, 281–86
  concurrent conditions, 283–84
  condition precedents, 282–83
  divisible and installment contracts, 285–86
  introduction to, 281–82
  money tender, 284
"Condition subsequent," defined, 1017
"Confession of judgment," defined, 1017
"Confirming bank," defined, 1017
"Conforming," defined, 1017
Confusion of goods, 958–59
Consideration, 113, 158–82
  adequacy of, 159–60
  cases involving, 166–81
  commercial paper and, 468–69
  defined, 1017
  and discharge of debts and claims, 162–63
  and existing obligations, 161–62
  introduction to, 158–59
  and moral obligation, past consideration, 163–65
  mutuality of, 165–66
  special concepts, 161–66
  and unforeseen difficulties, 162
"Consignee," defined, 1017
"Consignment," defined, 1017
"Consignor," defined, 1017–18
Consolidation of corporations, 866
"Conspicurus," defined, 1018

"Constitution," defined, 1018
Constitutional law, 7
Constitutions, 45–46
"Constructive delivery," defined, 1018
Consumer goods *(see also* Sales):
  defined, 1018
  secured transactions and, 596
Contemporary legal climate, 34
"Contract," defined, 1018
"Contract right," defined, 1018
Contracts, 8, 109–317, 1018 *(see also* Uniform Commercial Code; specific contracts; terminology regarding)
  agreement, form of, 242–63
  agreement—offer and acceptance, 130–59
  assignments, 264–68
  breach of, 16 *(see also* Breach of contract; Contracts: performance of)
  and capacity of parties, 183–99
  classification of, 111–12
  conditions of performance, 281–86
  and consideration, 158–82
  construction, interpretation of, 117–18
  discharge of, 304–17
  elements of, 113
  excuses for nonperformance of, 286–91
  frauds, statute of, 244–51
  and illegality, 218–41
  as intangible collateral, 598
  introduction to, 109–29
  judicial remedies for breach of, 113–17
  nature, importance of, 109–11
  performance of, 281–303
  quasi, 112–13
  and reality of assent, 200–17
  and rights of third parties, 264–81
"Contributory negligence," 691
"Conversion," defined, 1018
"Conveyance," defined, 1018
Cook Grain, Inc. v. Paul Fallis, 347–48
Co-ownership *(see also* Joint ownership):
  versus partnership, 753–54
Corneliuson v. Arthur Drug Stores, Inc. et al., 354–55
Corporate public obligations, 34
"Corporation," defined, 1018
Corporations, 793–871, 1018 *(see also* specific terminology used in regard to corporations)
  characteristics of, 794–810
    cases involving, 800–9
  de jure and de facto, 796–97, 1018
  dissolution of, 866–71
    by Attorney General, 866
    cases involving, 868–70
    consolidation, merger, 866–67
    expiration of charter and, 866

Corporations (*Cont.*):
  dissolution of (*Cont.*):
    rights of creditors regarding, 867–68
    by stockholders, 867
  domestic and foreign, 795–96
  entity disregarded, 797–98
  essential features, 794
  management of, 852–65
    by-laws, 852
    cases involving, 857–64
    directors, 855–57
    in general, 852
    stockholders' meetings, 853
    voting, 853–54
    voting pools, trust agreements, 854
  partnerships distinguished from, 752–53
  powers of, 811–23
    to borrow, 811–12
    cases involving, 815–22
    to commit torts, 814–15
    in general, 811
    and treasury stock, 813
    ultra vires, 813
  procedure for incorporation, 798
  promoters, 798–800
  stocks, stock ownership, 824–51 (*see also* Stocks, stock ownership)
  cases involving, 839–50
"Corporeal," defined, 1018
"Costs," defined, 1018
"Counter-claims," defined, 1018–19
"Course of dealing," defined, 1019
Courts (*see also* Judicial system; Lawsuits; Written law; etc):
  case demonstrating judicial system, 73–78
  of equity, 69–79
  federal system, 66–68
  function of, 63–65
  jurisdiction of, 70–72
  state systems, 65
  and venue, 72–73
Courts of Appeals, U. S., 68
"Covenant," defined, 1019
"Covenant" (in action), defined, 1019
Covenants and conditions, real property and, 975–76
"Cover," by buyer, 394–95
"Cover," defined, 1019
"Credit," defined, 1019
"Creditor beneficiary," defined, 1019
Creditors (*see* Composition of creditors; Creditors' rights; Sales; etc.; specific terms, transactions)
"Creditor's bill," defined, 1019
Creditors' rights, 884–931 (*see also* Commercial paper; Sales; Secured transactions; etc.)

Creditors' rights (*Cont.*):
  artisan's liens, 886–87
  and bankruptcy, 914–31 (*see also* Bankruptcy)
    cases involving, 922–31
  general rights, 885–91
  judgments—execution, 887–88
  suretyships, 893–912
    cases involving, 902–12
    change in contract terms, 899
    contract of, 894–95
    cosureties' liability, 901–2
    defenses of principal, 900
    distinction between guarantor and surety, 894
    duration of liability, 896–97
    extensions of time, 897–99
    fiduciary relationship, 895–96
    and immediate recourse, 896
    nature of relation, 893–94
    payment, 899
    recovery from principal, 901
    rights of, 897–902
    and subrogation, 897, 900–901
Credit purchase, agents and, 668–69
Criminal law, 8
Cross v. Commons et al., 927–29
Cultra et al. v. Cultra et al., 788–89
Cumulative stock, 826
"Cumulative voting," defined, 1019
Curtesy, 979
  defined, 1019
Custis v. Valley National Bank of Phoenix, 260–61
"Custodian bank," defined, 1019
"Custody" (personal property), defined, 1019
"Customer," defined, 1019

Damage, damages, 113, 114–16 (*see also* specific terminology, transactions)
  buyers and, 394–95
  defined, 1019
  fraud and, 203
  and remedies of sellers, 397, 398
  rules concerning, 115–16
  special types, 114–15
  theory of, 114
D'Andrea v. Feinberg, 444–45
Darling-Singer Lumber Co. v. Commonwealth & Others, 711–12
Dating of negotiable instruments, 432–33
Davies v. Carnation Company, 950–52
Davis v. Stone, 998–1000
Davis v. Western Union Telegraph Co., 522
Dean Vincent, Inc. v. Redisco, Inc., 994–96

Death (*see also* Administrators; Property; Wills; specific terminology):
and dissolution of partnerships, 781–82
excuse for nonperformance of contracts, 289
and relationship between customer and bank, 565
and termination of agency, 737
and title to real property, 976
"Debenture," defined, 1020
"Debt" (action on), defined, 1020
"Debtor," defined, 1020
Debts (*see also* Bankruptcy; Creditors' rights; Mortgages; etc.; specific terms, transactions):
discharge of, and consideration, 162–63
usury, 223–24 (*see also* Usury)
"Deceit," defined, 1020
"Decision" (judicial), defined, 1020
Decker v. Aurora Motors, Inc., 644–46
"Declaration," defined, 1020
"Decree," defined, 1020
Decrees, enforcements of, 94–95
"Deed," defined, 1020
"Deed of trust," defined, 1020
Deeds, 937 (*see also* Real property)
defined, 1020
execution of, 977
recording of, 977–78
"De facto," defined, 1020
De facto corporations, 796–97
defined, 1018
"Defalcation," defined, 1020
"Defamation," defined, 1020
Default, secured transactions and (*see* Secured transactions: priorities)
"Defendant," defined, 1020
"Defense," defined, 1020
Defenses (*see* specific instruments, types)
Deferred posting, bank collections and, 561
Deficiency decree, 990–91
"Deficiency judgment," defined, 1020–21
Definitions of law, 3–4
"Defraud," defined, 1021
De jure corporations, 796–97
defined, 1018
"Del credere agency," defined, 1021
"Delectus personae," defined, 1021
Delivery (*see also* specific terminology regarding deliveries; specific transactions):
defined, 1021
and holders of commercial paper, 469–70
sales contracts and, 344
"Delivery order," defined, 1021

Delta Airlines, Inc. v. Douglas Aircraft Company, Inc., 356–58
"Demand," defined, 1021
Demand paper, 427 (*see also* Checks; etc.)
"Demurrage," defined, 1021
"Demurrer," defined, 1021
Department of Public Works v. Halls, 149–51
"Dependent covenants," defined, 1021
"Depositary bank," defined, 1021
Descent, 976
defined, 1021
"Destination," defined, 1021
Destroyed commercial paper, 545
"Detinue," defined, 1021
"Detriment," defined, 1021
Devise (*see also* Bequest):
defined, 1022
Devisee:
Diamond Fruit Growers, Inc. v. Goe Co., 805–6
Diamos v. Hirsch, 295–96
"Dictum," defined, 1022
Dineff v. Wernecke, 660–61
"Directed verdict," defined, 1022
Directors, corporation, 855–57
compensation for, 855–56
liabilities of, 856–57
meetings of, 855
qualifications, powers of, 855
Discharge:
of claims in backruptcy (*see* Bankruptcy)
of commercial paper, 538–39, 540–45ff.
cancellation and renunciation, 543
in general, 540–41
and holders, 468
impairment of right of recourse or of collateral, 543–44
lost, destroyed, stolen instruments, 545
payment or satisfaction, 541–42
tender of payment, 542
and underlying obligation, 544
of contracts, 304–17 (*see also* Performance of contracts)
accord and satisfaction, 305–6
bankruptcy, composition of creditors, 307
cases, 307–16
introduction to, 304–5
novation and, 306
statute of limitations and, 306–7
defined, 1022
secured transactions, acceptance in discharge, 627
"Disclosed principal," 655
Discrimination, job, 658
Dishonor (*see also* Banks: deposits and collections):

Dishonor (*Cont.*):
  of commercial paper, 534–38ff.
    evidence of, 538
    notice of, 536–37, 538
    and protest, 537–38
  defined, 1022
Disparagement, 15–16
"Dissolution," defined, 1022
District courts, 66–68
"Dividend," defined, 1022
Dividends (*see* Investment securities;
  Stocks, stock ownership)
Divisible contracts, 285–86
Dluge v. Robinson, 551–54
"Dockage," defined, 1049
Documentary drafts, 417 (*see also* Docu-
  ments of title)
  defined, 1022
Documents of title, 328, 399–404 (*see also*
    Holders; holders in due course; spe-
    cific documents, terminology)
  defined, 1022
  general concepts; definitions, 399–401
  liability of indorser or transferor, 402–3
  negotiation, transfer of, 401–2
  obligations of bailee, 403–4
  as semi-intangible collateral, 597
Dollak v. Educational Aids Company,
  526–27
Dollar damages, 113, 114–15
Domestic Loan, Inc. v. Peregoy, 315–16
"Domicile," defined, 1022
"Dominion," defined, 1022
"Donee beneficiary," defined, 1022
"Dormant partner," defined, 1023
Dower, 979
  defined, 1023
Drafts, 417–18 (*see also* Banks; specific
  types)
  and orders to pay, 424–25
  presentment for acceptance (*see* Present-
    ment of commercial paper)
Drennan v. Star Paving Company, 145–47
"Due care," defined, 1023
Due process, 26–30
  defined, 1023
"Duly negotiated," defined, 1023
Duress:
  contracts and, 205
  and holders of commercial paper, 467
  of person, defined, 1023
  of property, defined, 1023
Durham v. Firestone Tire & Rubber Co.
  of California, 817–18
Durkin v. Siegel, 546–48
"Duty" (in law), defined, 1023

"Earnest money," defined, 1023

Easements, 979–80
  defined, 1023
"Ejectment," defined, 1023
Election (*see also* Voting):
  third parties and undisclosed principals,
    670–71
"Eleemosynary," defined, 1023
Elephant Lumber Co. v. Johnson, 225–26
*Eli Lilly and Company v. Sav-On-Drugs,
  Inc.,* 800–802
Elward v. Peabody Coal Co. et al., 815–
  16
"Embezzlement," defined, 1023
"Eminent domain," defined, 1023
Employees, 654 (*see also* Agency and em-
  ployment)
Employment (*see* Agency and employment)
English law, 53–54 (*see also* specific appli-
  cations, aspects)
Entirety (estate by), 980
  defined, 1024
"Entity," defined, 1024
Entry, foreclosure by, 990
Equipment:
  defined, 1024
  secured transactions and, 596
"Equitable action," defined, 1024
"Equitable conversion," defined, 1024
Equitable Discount Corp. v. Fischer, 472–
  75
"Equitable mortgage," defined, 1024
Equity, 69–70 (*see also* specific applica-
  tions, terms)
  defined, 1024
"Equity of redemption," defined, 981, 1024
Error (*see* Mistake)
Escrow, 984
  defined, 1024
Estate (*see also* Real property)
  defined, 1024
Estoppel:
  defined, 1025
  partners by, 753
  promissory, 159
"Et al.," defined, 1025
"Et cetera," "etc.," defined, 1025
Ethics, 36–39
"Et uxor," defined, 1025
"Eviction," defined, 1025
"Evidence," defined, 1025
"Ex contractu" (*see* "Action ex contractu")
Exculpatory clauses, 220
"Ex delicto" (*see* "Action ex delicto")
"Executed," defined, 1025
Executed contract, 111
"Execution," defined, 1025
"Executor," defined, 1025
Executors, contracts of, 245

Executory contract, 111
  defined, 1025
"Exemplary damages," defined, 1025
"Exemption," defined, 1025–26
Existing obligations, consideration and, 161–62
Express warranties, 337–38
  defined, 1026

Factors, 654
  defined, 1026
"Factor's lien," defined, 1026
Factory-wage earner period, 24
Fair-trade laws, 12–15 (*see also* Restraint of trade)
Falconer v. Mazess, 156
"Family car doctrine," 688–89
Farm products:
  defined, 1026
  secured transactions and, 597
"F. A. S. vessel," 344–45
Fattore v. Police and Firemen's Retirement Syst. of N. J., 704–5
"Featherbedding," defined, 1026
Federal Employees Liability Act, 691, 692
Federal government (*see also* specific cases, interests):
  big government, 35–36
  court system, 66–68
  limitations on free enterprise, 32–34
Federal Security Administrator v. Quaker Oats Co., 59–61
Federal Security Insurance Company v. Smith, 251–52
Fee simple, estates in, 978
  defined, 1026
Feinberg v. Pfeiffer Company, 168–70
F.E.L.A., 691, 692
"Felony," defined, 1026
Feoffment, 937
Ferri v. Sylvia, 442
Fictitious payees, 501–3
"Fieri facias," defined, 1026
Filesi v. United States, 876–77
Filing of financing statement, 600–602
"Financing agency," defined, 1026
Financing statement, filing of, 600–602
"Fine," defined, 1026
Fiocco v. Carver, 697–99
Firm offers, 133–34
  defined, 1026
First Nat. Bank of Boston v. Fairhaven Amuse. Co., 255–56
First National Bank of Lansing v. Padjen, 923–25
First National Bank of McAlester v. Mann, 519–20

(The) First National Bank of Philadelphia v. Anderson, 459–61
Fixtures, 622–23
  real property and, 973–74
Floating liens, 594
"Floating policy," defined, 1027
Florence Banana Corp. v. Pennsylvania Railroad, 969–70
"F.O.B.," 344
Foley v. Weaver Drugs, Inc., 374–77
Forbearance, 160
  defined, 1027
"Forcible enter and detainer," defined, 1027
Foreign corporations, 795–96
  and "doing business," 795–96
  qualification of, 795
"Forfeiture," defined, 1027
Forgery, 465, 500–501, 511, 513–14
  defined, 1027
"Franchise," defined, 1027
"Franchise tax," defined, 1027
"Fraud," defined, 1027
Fraud and misrepresentation, 200–204, 1027 (*see also* specific terminology used regarding fraud)
  bankruptcy and fraudulent conveyances, 921
  and commercial paper, 467–68
  and confusion of goods, 959
  defined, 200, 1027
  impostors and fictitious payees, 501–3
  and injury or damage, 203
  intention to mislead, 201
  justifiable reliance and, 202–3
  misstatement of fact, 201–2
  remedies, 203–4
  silence and, 202
  statute of frauds, 244–51
    concepts applicable to all provisions of, 250–51
    contracts involving real property and, 246–47
    contracts involving sale of personal property and, 248–49
    contracts involving two or more sections of, 249–50
    contracts of executors or administrators and, 245
    contracts of long duration and, 247–48
    guaranty contracts and, 245–46
    historical development of, 244–45
    nature of the writing of, 250
Fraudulent conveyances, 921
  defined, 1027
Freedom of contract, 219
Free enterprise, 25–34 (*see also* Fair-trade laws)

Free enterprise (*Cont.*):
  period of limitation on, 29–34
  period of unlimited, 25–29
"Freehold," defined, 1026
"Free will," contracts and, 205
  duress and undue influence and, 205
Frell v. Dumont-Florida, Inc., 906
"From" and "to," defined, 1027
Frustration of contract performance, 290–91
"Funded debt," defined, 1027
"Funding," defined, 1027
"Fungible," defined, 1027
"Fungible goods," defined, 1027–28
"Future goods," defined, 1028
"Futures," defined, 1028

Galati v. Potamkin Chevrolet Co., 119–21
"Gambling," defined, 1028
"Garnishee," defined, 1028
"Garnishment," defined, 1028
"General agent," defined, 1028
"General intangibles," defined, 1028
General Refrigerator and Store Fixture Company v. Fry, 524–26
George E. Failing Co. v. Cardwell Investment Co., 908–9
Gibbs v. Gerberich, 576–78
"Gift," defined, 1028
"Gift causa mortis," defined, 1028
"Gift inter vivos," defined, 1028
Gifts, 956–57
  defined, 1028
Gissen v. Goodwill, 197–98
Glossary, 1010–50
Good faith:
  defined, 1028
  holders in due course and, 453–54
"Goods," defined, 1028
"Good title," defined, 1028
Goodwill, partnerships and, 754–55
Gordon Supply Co. v. South Sea Apts., Inc., 441
Gordon v. Ginsberg, 789–90
Government (*see* Federal government)
Grange National Bank v. Conville, 518–19
"Grant," defined, 1028
"Grantee," defined, 1028
"Grantor," defined, 1029
Grau v. Mitchell, 757–58
Greater Valley Terminal Corp. v. Goodman, 483
Greeno v. Clark Equipment Company, 371–73
Gresham State Bank v. O & K Construction Co., 493–95
Grombach v. Oerlikon Tool and Arms Corp. of America, 171–72

"Gross negligence," defined, 1029
Grubb v. Rockey, 252–54
Guarantees (*see* Warranties)
"Guarantor," defined, 1029
Guarantors of commercial paper, 509
Guaranty contracts, 245–46 (*see also* Suretyships)
"Guardian," defined, 1029
"Guardian ad litem," defined, 1029

"Habeas corpus," defined, 1029
Hamilton and Spiegel, Inc. v. Board of Education of Montgomery County, 278–79
Hammond et al. v. Otwell et al., 877–80
Harvey v. Hadfield, 189–90
Haveg Corporation v. Guyer, 258–59
Hayes v. Guy, 254–55
Hayes v. Parklane Hosiery Co., Inc., 230–32
Haymes v. Rogers, 731–33
"Hearsay evidence," defined, 1029
Heating Acceptance Corporation v. Patterson, 481–82
"Hedging contract," defined, 1029
"Heirs," defined, 1029
Henderson v. Phillips, 683–84
Hendrickson v. International Harvester Co. of America, 153
Herron v. State Farm Mutual Insurance Company, 712–14
Hill's, Inc. v. William B. Kessler, Inc., 152–53
Hipskind Heating & Plumb. Co. v. General Industries, 302
Historical role of law in business, 24–34
Historical school, 4–5
Hobgood v. Sylvester, 889–91
Hogan v. Norfleet, 125–26
Holcomb v. Flavin, 692
"Holder," defined, 1029
Holders; holders in due course, 449–62 (*see also* Commercial paper)
  banks as, 560
  before overdue, 455–56
  cases involving, 456–62
  definitions, 449, 1029
  good faith and due notice, 453–55
  holder distinguished from holder in due course, 451–52
  requirements for holders in due course, 449–51
  value, 452–53
"Holding company," defined, 1029
Holloway v. Smith et al., 778–79
Hollywood Credit Clothing Company v. Gibson, 212–13
"Homestead," defined, 1029
"Honor," defined, 1029

Hopkins v. Hacker, 692–94
Hoppe v. Rittenhouse, 841–42
Hopson v. Texaco, Inc., 702–3
How to study a case (Appendix), 1005–6
Huber Glass Co. v. First National Bank of Kenosha, 475–78
Hunter v. Amer. Rentals, Inc., 226–27
Hurst v. Hurst, 776
Hydrocarbon Processing Corp. v. Chemical Bank N. Y. T. Co., 567–69

"Idem sonans," defined, 1029
Identification and salvage as seller's remedy, 398
"Illegal," defined, 1029
Illegality (*see also* specific illegal acts, terminology, transactions):
  contracts and, 218–41
    cases involving, 225–40
    and competition, 221–22
    concept of, 218–19
    effect of, 224
    exculpatory clauses and, 220
    as excuse for nonperformance of contracts, 288–89
    freedom of contract, public interest, 219–20
    restraint of trade, 220–21
    and unconscionable bargains, 222–23
    usury, 223–24
  and holders of commercial paper, 467
Illness as excuse for nonperformance of contracts, 289
"Illusory," defined, 1029
"Immunity," defined, 1029–30
"Implied," defined, 1030
Implied warranties, 338–40
Impostors, 501–2
Impracticability and contract performance, 291
"Inalienable," defined, 1030
Incapacity (*see* Capacity of parties)
"Inchoate," defined, 1030
"Incidental beneficiary," defined, 1030
"Incontestable," defined, 1030
"Incorporeal," defined, 1030
"Incumbrance," defined, 1030
"Indebtedness," defined, 1030
Indemnification of agents, 723
"Indemnity," defined, 1030
"Indenture," defined, 1031
Independent contractors, 654–55, 689–90
  (*see also* Agency and employment)
  defined, 1031
Independent News Co. v. Williams, 383–84
"Indictment," defined, 1031
Indorsement (*see also* Commercial paper):
  defined, 1031

Indorsement (*Cont.*):
  kinds of, 437
  negotiation by, 437–40
Industrial Packaging Prod. Co. v. Fort Pitt Pack. Int., 606–8
Infants, infancy:
  and agency, employment, 655
  and contracts, 183, 184–88
    and liability for necessaries, 187–88
    parents' liability, 188
    and ratification, 187
    requirements and right to disaffirm, 185–86
    and time of disaffirmance, 186
    torts, 188
  and holders of commercial paper, 467
"Infringement," defined, 1031
"Inherit," defined, 1031
"Inheritance," defined, 1031
"Injunction," defined, 1031
"Injunction pendente lite," defined, 1031
Injuries:
  agents and (*see* Workmen's compensation)
  fraud and, 203
"In personam," defined, 1030
In re Eton Furniture Co., 550–51
In re Forsstrom et ux., 946–48
In re Jacobs, 27
In re Laskin, 515–16
"In rem," defined, 1030
In re United Thrift Stores, Inc., 608–11
In re Wheatland Electric Products Co., 605–6
Insanity:
  and contracts, 188–89
  and termination of agency, 737, 738
Insdorf v. Wil-Avon Merchandise Mart, Inc., 483–84
Insolvency, 916 (*see also* Bankruptcy; specific terminology)
  and bank collection, 560
  of buyers, 398–99
  composition of creditors and, 307
  and holders of commercial paper, 468
  of sellers, 395–96
"Insolvency proceedings," defined, 1030
"Insolvent," defined, 1030, 1031
Installment contracts, 285–86 (*see also* Chattel paper)
  and buyer's rejection, 394
  defined, 1030
"In statu quo," defined, 1030
Instructions, agents' duty to obey, 720
"Instrument," defined, 1030
"Insurable interest," defined, 1031
Insurance (*see also* specific kinds, terminology used in regard to insurance):
  and bailment of personal property, 962

Insurance (*Cont.*):
   defined, 1031
   mortgages and, 986–87
"Intent," defined, 1031
Interest (*see also* specific uses):
   agency coupled with, 738
   partners' right to, 771
"Interim certificate," defined, 1031
"Interlocutory decree," defined, 1031
"Intermediary bank," defined, 1030
"Interpleader," defined, 1031
"Inter sese," defined, 1031
"Intestate," defined, 1031
In the Matter of R. C. Hendren, Debtor,
   930–31
"In toto," defined, 1030
Intoxicated persons and contracts, 189
Inventory (*see also* Secured transactions):
   defined, 1031
   secured transactions and, 596–97
Investment securities, 328 (*see also* Hold-
   ers; holders in due course; specific
   terminology, types)
   as collateral (*see* Secured transactions)
   transfer of, 830–36
      in general, 830–31
      issuers and, 832–33
      lost, destroyed, stolen, 835
      and overissue, 831
      purchasers and, 833–34
      and right to dividends, 835–36
"Irreparable damage or injury," defined,
   1032
"Issue," defined, 1032
"Issue" (in pleading), defined, 1032
"Issue" (in a will), defined, 1032
"Issuer," defined, 1032
"Item," defined, 1032
Ivers & Pond Piano Co. v. Peckham, 682–
   83

*Jackson v. First National Bank of Mem-
   phis, Inc.,* 585–89
James v. Jacobsen, 178–79
James Talcott, Inc. v. Kolberg, 482–83
Jamison v. Encarnacion, 58–59
Jarroll Coal Co., Inc. v. Lewis et al., 818–
   20
"Jeopardy," defined, 1032
Jobs (*see also* Agency and employment):
   discrimination in, 658
"Joint adventure," defined, 1032
"Joint contract," defined, 1032
Joint ownership (*see also* Co-ownership):
   defined, 1032
Joint stock companies, 874–75
Joint tenancy, 980
   defined, 1032

"Joint tort-feasors," defined, 1032
"Joint will," defined, 1032
Jorgensen v. Nudelman, 196–97
Judges, 87–88 (*see also* Courts; Judicial
   system)
"Judgment" (in law), defined, 1032
"Judgment in personam," defined, 1032
"Judgment in rem," defined, 1032
Judgment notes, 418
Judgments, enforcements of, 94–95
Judicial process, nature of, 95–99
Judicial reasoning, 95–99
Judicial review, 47–48
"Judicial sale," defined, 1032
Judicial system, 63–78 (*see also* Lawsuits;
   specific terminology used in regard
   to)
   case illustrating, 73–78
   federal system, 66–68
   function of courts, 63–65
   jurisdiction of courts, 70–72
   law and equity, 69–70
   state system, 65
   and venue, 72–73
Juries, 88–90 (*see also* specific terminology)
   defined, 1033
"Jurisdiction," defined, 1032
Justifiable reliance, 202–3

Karetzkis v. Cosmopolitan National Bank,
   677–78
*Kelly Asphalt Block Co. v. Barber Asphalt
   Paving Co.,* 709–10
Kergald v. Armstrong Transfer Exp. Co.,
   144
King Motors v. Delfino, 122–23
King v. Young, Brown, and Beverly, Inc.,
   658–60
"Kite checks," defined, 1033
*Knapp et al. v. Bankers Securities Corpo-
   ration et al.,* 845–46
*Knox et al. v. First Security Bank of Utah
   et al.,* 808–9
Kolias v. Colligan, 215–16
Kuschy v. Norris, 369–70

Labor-management relations, 556–58
Labor-Management Reporting and Disclo-
   sure Act, 657–58
Labor unions, 35
   definition of trade union, 1047
   and management relations, 656–58
"Laches," defined, 1033
Ladd v. Parmer, 1001–2
Laissez-faire, 25
Landrum-Griffin Act, 657–58
Lankford v. State, 768
"Latent defect," defined, 1033

Law (*see also* Illegality; Lawsuits; specific applications, terminology, etc.):
  functions and procedures of, 2–105
    judicial system, 63–78
    lawsuits, 80–99
    and nonjudicial conflict-solving, 101–5
    and society, 21–43
    sources of, 44–62
  history of commercial, 321–24
Lawsuits, 80–99 (*see also* specific cases, terminology)
  appeals, 92–94
  enforcements of judgments and decrees, · 94–95
  judges in, 87–88
  juries in, 88–90
  lawyers and, 90–92
  nature of the judicial process, 95–99
  need for adjective law, 80–81
  pleadings, 81–83
  pre-trial stage, 83
  trials, 84–87
Lawyers, 90–92
Leahy v. McManus, 516–18
"Lease," defined, 1033
"Leasehold," defined, 1033
"Legacy," defined, 1033
"Legal incapacity," defined, 1033
"Legal right," defined, 1042
"Legatee," defined, 1033
Legislation (*see* Written law)
Lesavoy Industries v. Pennsylvania Gen. Paper Corp., 842–43
Lesnick et al. v. Pratt, 192–93
Letellier-Phillips Paper Co. v. Fiedler et al., 789
Letters of credit, 327–28, 417–18
"Letters testamentary," defined, 1033
Levitz Furniture Company v. Fields, 1005–9
"Levy" (taxes), defined, 1033
"Levy" (writ of), defined, 1033
Lewis and Lewis v. Root and Root, 151–52
"Liability," defined, 1033
"Libel," defined, 1033
Liberty Aluminum Products Company v. John Cortis et ux., 441–42
"License" (governmental regulation), defined, 1033
"License" (privilege), defined, 1033
"Lien creditor," defined, 1034
Liens, 623–24 (*see also* Attachment; Secured transactions; specific types)
  artisans', 886–87, 1012
  defined, 1033–34
  mechanic's lien laws, 991–94
Life estates in real property, 978–79
"Limitation of actions," defined, 1034

Limitations, statute of, 306–7
Limited partnerships, 873–74
"Lineal descendant," defined, 1034
"Liquidated," defined, 1034
"Liquidated damages," defined, 1034
"Liquidation," defined, 1034
"Lis pendens," defined, 1034
Litigation (*see* Lawsuits)
Loans (*see* Debts; Secured transactions; etc.; specific terminology)
Lochner v. New York, 27–28
Lockhart v. Friendly Finance Co., 699–700
Long duration, contracts of, 247–48
Lonzrick v. Republic Steel Corp., 366–69
Lost commercial paper, 545
Lost goods:
  risk of, 387–89
  and seller's remedy, 398
Lost personal property, 959
Lost securities, and transfer, 835
"Lot," defined, 1034
Love v. Pennsylvania Railroad Co., 844–45
Loyalty, agents and, 718–20
"L.S.," defined, 1033
Lunn v. Kaiser, 787–88

McGinn v. American Bank Stationery Co., 142–43
McGuire Act, 13–14
McKenna v. Commissioner of Mental Health, 123–24
Magazine Digest Pub. Co., Limited v. Shade et al., 907–8
"Magistrate," defined, 1034
Main Investment Company v. Gisolfi, 612–14
"Maintenance" (in lawsuits), defined, 1034
"Mala in se," defined, 1034
"Malice," defined, 1034
"Malice prosecution," defined, 1034
"Malicious," defined, 1034
Malphrus v. Home Savings Bank of City of Albany, 583–85
Management (*see also* Corporations; Labor-management relations):
  partners and participation in, 771–72
"Mandamus," defined, 1034
"Mandatory," defined, 1034
"Mandatory injunction," defined, 1035
Mansion Carpet, Inc. v. Marinoff, 549–50
Maple v. Tennessee Gas Transmission, 694–95
Mardel Securities, Inc. v. Alexandria Gazette Corp., 861–62
"Margin," defined, 1035
"Marketable title," defined, 1035
Marks v. Green, 804–5
"Marshalling assets," defined, 1035

Massachusetts trust, 875
"Master in chancery," defined, 1035
Material alteration of commercial paper, 465–67
"Maxim," defined, 1035
Mead v. Collins Realty Co., 296–98
Mechanic's liens, 991–92
   against whom, 992–93
   defined, 1035
   nature of, 991
   to perpetuate, 993
   persons entitled to, 991–92
   protection accorded to owner, 993–94
"Mens rea," defined, 1035
"Merchant," defined, 1035
Merchant-middleman period, 24
Merchants & Mech. Fed. Sav. & Loan Assn. v. Herald, 996–97
Merger:
   corporate, 866–67
   defined, 1035
"Midnight deadline," defined, 1035
"Ministerial duty," defined, 1035
Minnesota Linseed Oil Co. v. Collier White Lead Co., 144–45
Minors *(see* Capacity of parties)
"Minutes," defined, 1035
"Misdemeanor," defined, 1035
"Misfeasance," defined, 1035
Misrepresentation *(see also* Fraud and misrepresentation):
   defined, 1035–36
Mistake, and assent to contracts, 204–5
   bilateral, 204
   and reformation of written contracts, 205
   unilateral, 204–5
"Mistake of fact," defined, 1036
"Mistake of law," defined, 1036
Mitchell v. The Campbell and Fetter Bank, 194–96
"Mitigation of damages," defined, 1036
Money *(see also* Promissory notes; specific terminology, uses):
   defined, 1036
"Monopoly," defined, 1036
Monroe v. Bixby, 174–76
"Moorage," defined, 1049
"Moot case," defined, 1036
Morain v. Lollis, 700–702
Morality, 36–39 *(see also* specific applications, terminology)
Moral obligation, and consideration, 163–65
"Mortgage," defined, 1036
Mortgages, 419, 981–92, 1036 *(see also* specific terminology used in regard to mortgages)

Mortgages *(Cont.):*
   absolute conveyances as, 983
   deeds of trust in the nature of, 983
   foreclosures of, 988–91
      deficiency decree and, 990–91
      by entry, writ of entry, 990
      by exercise of power of sale, 990
      priorities, 991
      rights to, 988
      strict, 989
      by suit in equity, 989–90
      types of, 989
   forms of, 982
   growth of equitable theory, 981–82
   insurance, 986–87
   land sale contract and, 984
   legal, equitable theories of, 982
   liability of mortgagor after transfer, 986
   nature of, essential requirements, 981
   payment before default, 987–88
   property capable of being mortgaged, 982
   purchase money, 983–84
   recording, 982–83
   rights, liabilities of mortgagee, 985
   rights of mortgagor, 984
   right to redeem after foreclosure sale, 988
   right to redeem before foreclosure sale, 988
   transfer of debt, 987
   transfer of mortgaged property, 985–86
"Mutual assent," defined, 1036
"Mutuality," defined, 1036
"Mutual will," defined, 1032

Names, firm:
   limited partnerships and, 874
   partnerships and, 754–55
Nardine v. Kraft Cheese Co., 176–77
Narr, 1016
(The) National Bank of Slatington v. Derhammer, 580–82
National Cash Register Company v. Firestone & Co., 636–39
National Labor Relations Board, 657
Natural law, 5–6 *(see also* Ethics)
Negligence *(see also* specific terminology, types):
   agents and duty regarding, 720–21
   and defenses in commercial paper cases, 471–72
"Negotiation," defined, 1036
"Net assets," defined, 1036
New Hampshire Wholesale Beverage Assn. v. New Hampshire State Liquor Comm., 806–8

Niebergall v. A. B. A. Contracting & Supply Co., 523–24
Nilsson et al. v. Kielmann et al., 313
Nippon Shosen Daisha, K. K. v. United States, 965–66
"No arrival, no sale," 345
"Nolle prosequi," defined, 1036
"Nolo contendere," defined, 1036
"Nominal damages," defined, 1036
"Non compos mentis," defined, 1036
Noncumulative stock, 826
"Nonfeasance," defined, 1036
Nonjudicial solving of conflicts, 101–5
"Non obstante verdicto," defined, 1036
Nonparticipating stock, 826–27
"Nonresident," defined, 1036
Nonsignor clause, 13–15
"Nonsuit," defined, 1037
Nontrading partnerships, 774–75 (*see also* Partnerships)
Norman v. World Wide Distributors, Inc. et al., 457–59
"Notary," defined, 1037
"Notation credit," defined, 1037
Notes (*see* Promissory notes)
Notice:
   agents' duty to give, 721
   defined, 1037
   in event of termination of agency, 738–39
   partnerships and, 775
"Notifies," defined, 1037
Novation, 306
   defined, 1037
Nuisances, 9–10
   abatement of, defined, 1010
   defined, 1037

"Obligee," defined, 1037
"Obligor," defined, 1037
O. C. Kinney, Inc. v. Paul Hardeman, Inc., 143
Offers, contract, 130–37 (*see also* Acceptance)
   communication of, 131–32
   construction of, 132
   duration of, 134–37
   formation of, 130–32
   lapse of, 134–35
   rejection of, 136
   revocation of, 135–36
   in special situations, 132–34
O'Hara v. Lance et ux., 763–65
Options, 133–34
   defined, 1038
Oral statements (*see* Contracts; Parol evidence)
"Order," order paper, 428–31, 1037

Orders to pay, drafts and, 424–25
"Ordinance," defined, 1037
"Ordinary care," defined, 1037
Ostensible authority, 674–75
Overdrafts, 564
"Overt act," defined, 1037
Overton v. Vita-Food Corporation, 298–99
"Ownership," 936
Ozier et al. v. Haines, 261–62

Parents, liability of, 188 (*see also* Infants, infancy)
"Parimateria," defined, 1037
Park County Implement Co. v. Craig, 406–7
Parol evidence, 243–44
"Partially disclosed principal," 655
Participating stock, 826–27
Particular fund, the, 425–26
"Partition," defined, 1037
Partnerships, 750–93 (*see also* specific terminology regarding partnerships)
   capital of, 755
   co-ownership versus, 753–54
   corporations and, 812
   definition, 751–52
   dissolution of, 781–93
      cases involving, 787–91
      by court decree, 782
      effects of, 783–87
      in general, 781
      by law, 781–82
      and powers of partners, 783
      and rights of partners, 783–84
      and third parties, 784–87
   distinguished from corporations, 752–53
   by estoppel, 753
   firm name and goodwill, 754–55
   general principles of, 751–69
      cases involving, 757–68
   limited, 873–74
   property of, 754–57
   rights, duties, powers of partners, 770–80
      cases involving, 775–79
      fiduciary relation of partners, 772–73
      in general, 770
      notice and admissions, 775
      powers and liabilities, 774–75
      relations of partners to one another, 770–73
   and right to accounting, 773
   and right to compensation, 772
   and right to information, 772
   and right to interest, 771
   and right to participate in management, 771–72
   sharing of profits and losses, 770–71

Partnerships (*Cont.*):
    trading and nontrading, 774–75
"Party," defined, 1038
"Par value," defined, 1037
Pascali v. Hempstead, 177–78
Paschen v. Pashkow, 997–98
Past consideration, 163–65
"Patent ambiguity," defined, 1038
"Payor bank," defined, 1038
"Penal bond," defined, 1038
"Penalty," defined, 1038
"Pendente lite," defined, 1038
Peoples Savings Bank et al. v. Playdium Lanes, Inc., 582–83
People v. Johnson, 743–44
"Per curiam," defined, 1038
"Peremptory challenge," defined, 1038
Performance of contracts, 281–303 (*see also* Discharge; specific types of contracts)
    additional hardship and, 287
    anticipatory breach and, 284–85
    cases involving, 291–302
    conditions of, 281–86
    divisible and installment, 285–86
    excuses for nonperformance, 286–91
    frustration and, 290–91
    impossibility of, 287–90
    impracticability and, 291
    money tender and, 284
    prevention of, 287
    and right to recover for part performance, 290
    waiver and, 287
"Perjury," defined, 1038
"Perpetuity," defined, 1038
Perry v. Richard Chevrolet, Inc., 969
"Persona ficta," defined, 1038
Personal property, 325, 938, 943, 954–70 (*see also* Property; specific terminology, transactions)
    abandoned and lost, 959
    bailments of, 960–65
    cases involving, 965–70
    contracts involving sale of, 248–49
    creditors and (*see* Creditors' rights)
    defined, 1038
    distinction between personal and real property, 955
    extent of ownership, 959
    in general, 954
    methods of acquiring title, 955–59
        accession, 957–58
        confusion, 958–59
        original possession, 955–56
        transfer, 956–57
    nature of title in transfers of, 957
"Personal representative," defined, 1038

"Personal service," defined, 1038
Petition of Avard, 859–60
Philco Finance Corporation v. Mehlman, 634–36
Pitillo v. Demetry, 488–89
Pittsburgh Testing Lab. v. Farnsworth & Chambers Co., Inc., 172–74
"Plaintiff," defined, 1038
"Plea," defined, 1038
Pleadings, 81–83
    defined, 1038
"Pledge," defined, 1038
"Plenary," defined, 1038
Poledna v. Bendix Aviation Corporation, 821–22
"Policy of insurance," defined, 1038
"Polling jury," defined, 1038
Possession, 936–37
    defined, 1038
Posting, 561
    defined, 1040
Power of attorney, 655
Precedent (*see also* Unwritten law):
    defined, 1038
Preemptive right, 837–38
"Preference," defined, 1039
Preferred stock, 826–27
    defined, 1039
"Premises," defined, 1039
"Preponderance," defined, 1039
"Prerogative," defined, 1039
"Presenting bank," defined, 1039
"Presentment," defined, 1039
Presentment of commercial paper, 529–40ff.
    for acceptance, 530–31
    discharge, 538–39
    dishonor, 534–38
    in general, 530
    how made, 532
    for payment, 531–32
    rights of party to whom made, 534
    time allowed for payment or acceptance, 535–36
    time of, 533–34
    when conditions need not be performed, 539–40
Presentment warranties, 510–12
"Presumption," defined, 1039
Prevention, performance of contracts and, 287
Price, recovery of, as remedy, 398
Pricing, 11, 12–15 (*see also* specific terminology)
    sales contracts and, 343
Priebe, Trustee of Estate of Giles Svehlek, Bankrupt v. Svehlek, 929–30
"Prima facie," defined, 1039

Private law, 8 (*see also* specific fields)
Private nuisances, 9–10
"Privilege," defined, 1039
"Privity," defined, 1039
"Probate," defined, 1039
Procedural due process, 26
Procedural law (*see* Adjective law)
"Proceeds," defined, 1039
"Process," defined, 1039–40
Processed goods, 623
"Process of posting," defined, 1040
Product liability, 340–42
"Promise," defined, 1040
Promises, negotiable notes and, 424–25
Promissory estoppel, 159
Promissory notes, 412–13, 418–19 (*see also*
    Commercial paper; specific types)
Promoters, 798–800
"Properly payable," defined, 1040
Property, 934–1003 (*see also* specific ter-
    minology; types)
  components of, 936–37
  concept of, 935–52
    cases involving, 943–52
  defined, 1040
  kinds of, 943
  in a legal environment, 942–43
  as non-physical or incorporeal, 938–39
  partnerships and, 754, 755–57 (*see also*
    Partnerships)
  personal, 954–70 (*see also* Personal prop-
    erty)
  real, 972–1003 (*see also* Real property)
  as relationships, 939–42
  significance of, 935–36
  as things, 937–38
Proprietors, 689–90 (*see also* Agency and
    employment)
"Pro tanto," defined, 1040
Protest, certificate of, 537–38ff.
"Proximate cause," defined, 1040
"Proximate damage," defined, 1040
"Proxy," defined, 1040
Public carriers (*see* Common carriers)
Public interest, contracts and the, 219–20
Public law, 7–8 (*see also* Administrative
    law)
Public nuisances, 10
"Public policy," defined, 1040
"Punitive damages," defined, 1040
"Purchase," defined, 1040
Purchase money mortgages, 983–84
Purchase money security interests, 603, 622
  defined, 1040
"Purchaser," defined, 1040

Qualified indorsement, 437
"Quantum merit" (in pleading), defined,
    1040

Quasi contract, 112–13
  defined, 1040
"Quit claim," defined, 1040
"Quo warranto," defined, 1040
Q. Vandenberg & Sons, N. V. v. Siter, 348–
    50

*Ramsburg et al. v. American Investment
    Company of Illinois et al.,* 849–50
"Ratification," defined, 1040
"Ratify," defined, 1041
Ray v. Deas, 356
Real estate (*see* Real property; specific
    terminology)
Real estate brokers, 669 (*see also* Agency
    and employment)
  and compensation, 722–23
Real estate mortgage notes, 419
Real property, 325, 938, 943, 972–1003
    (*see also* Property; Real estate
    brokers; Secured transactions;
    specific terminology)
  accretion of, 976
  adverse possession of, 975
  cases involving, 994–1003
  contracts involving, 246–47
  covenants and conditions, 976–77
  defined, 1041
  distinction between real property and
    personal property, 955
  dower and curtesy, 979
  easements, 979–80
  encumbrances on, 980–94 (*see also*
    Mortgages)
    mechanic's lien laws, 991–94
  estates in, 978–80
  execution of deeds to, 977
  fixtures to, 973–74
  how title is acquired, 974
  life estates in, 978–79
  nature of, 972
  original entry to; occupancy of, 974
  remainders, reversions of, 979
  tenancies of, 980
  transfer of, with consent of owner, 974–
    75
  transfer upon sale by sheriff, 975
  wills, descent, and, 976
Reality of assent, 200–217
  cases involving, 206–16
  fraud and, 200–204
  and lack of free will, 205
  mistake and, 204–5
"Reasonable care," defined, 1041
"Rebuttal evidence," defined, 1041
"Receipt," defined, 1041
"Receiver," defined, 1041
"Recognizance," defined, 1041
"Recoupment," defined, 1041

Recourse, impairment of right of, 543–44
"Redemption," defined, 1041
Refund, right of, 560
"Registered form," defined, 1041
Registration of securities, 833, 834–35
Reimbursing of agents, 723
"Re-insurance," defined, 1041
"Release," defined, 1041
"Remand," defined, 1041
Remedial law (*see* Adjective law)
"Remedy," law, 1041
"Remise," defined, 1041
"Remitting bank," defined, 1041
Renunciation of commercial paper, 543
"Replevin," defined, 1041
Repossessed goods, 622
"Representative," defined, 1041
"Res," defined, 1041
"Res adjudicata," defined, 1041
Resale, 397
Rescission, 113–14 (*see also* specific transactions)
   and negotiation of commercial paper, 440
Residue, negotiable paper and, 437
Respondeat superior, 687–89
   defined, 1042
"Respondent," defined, 1042
"Responsible bidder," defined, 1042
"Restraining order," defined, 1042
Restraint of trade, 220–21 (*see also* Fair-trade laws)
   defined, 1042
Restrictive indorsements, 437, 438–40
Retail price control, 12–15
"Retainer," defined, 1042
Returned goods, 622
"Return of a writ," defined, 1042
Reusche v. California Pacific Title Insurance Co., 674
Riccio v. General Motors Acceptance Corporation, 922–23
Richard v. Falleti et ux., 733–34
"Right," defined, 1042
"Right of action," defined, 1042
"Rights," defined, 1042
Riley v. Standard Oil Co., 695–97
"Riparian," defined, 1042
Risk of loss, 387–89
Robbery (*see also* Theft and stolen goods)
   defined, 1042
Robinson v. Walker, 943–45
Rock Island Auction Sales v. Empire Packing Co., 572–74
Rodi Boat Company v. Provident Tradesmens Bank & Trust Co., 631–34
Role of law, 21–24
Ross Transport Inc. et al. v. Crothers et al., 946–48

Roto-Lith, Ltd. v. F. P. Bartlett & Co., 154–56
Rufo v. Bastian-Blessing Company, 407–8
"Rule," defined, 1042
Runswick et al. v. Floor et al., 848–49
Rushlight Auto Sprinkler Co. v. City of Portland, 213–15

Sales, 326 (*see also* Agency and employment; Contracts; Secured transactions; specific terminology, etc.)
   bulk transfers, 404–6
   the contract, 331–84
      cases involving, 347–84
      construction of contracts, 342–43
      contract principles, 333–34
      formation of contract, 334–37
      obligation of parties, 337
      product liability, 340–42
      rights of third parties, creditors, 346–47
      Sales Article, 331–33
      terms of contracts, 343–46
      warranties, 337–40
   documents of title, 399–404
   performance and breach; remedies, 386–96ff.
      and adequate assurance, 391–92
      and anticipatory repudiation, 391
      cases involving, 406–10
      excuses of performance, 390–91
      title to goods; risk of loss, 386–87
   rights, remedies, obligations of buyer, 392–96
      acceptance by buyer, 393–94
      and damages, 394–95
      installment contracts, 394
      and rejection by buyer, 392–93
      and seller's insolvency, 395–96
   rights, remedies, obligations of seller, 396–99
      damages, 397
      identification and salvage, 398
      insolvency of buyer, 398–99
      limitation of actions, 399
      loss or damage, 398
      recovery of price, 398
      resale, 397
      stoppage of goods, 396–97
Salesmen (*see also* Agency and employment; Sales):
   duty to compensate, 723
"Sanction," defined, 1042
Sanderfur v. Ganter, 762–63
Sandler v. United Industrial Bank, 571–72
Sarokhan v. Fair Lawn Memorial Hospital, Inc., 739–41
Satisfaction:
   commercial paper and, 541–42
   of contracts, 305–6

Satisfaction (*Cont.*):
   defined, 1042
Schools of legal thought, 4–7
Schwegmann Brothers et al. v. Calvert Distillers Corporation, 13
"Scienter," defined, 1042
"Scintilla of evidence," defined, 1042
"Scrip," defined, 1042
"Seal," defined, 1042
"Seasonably," defined, 1043
"Secondary party," defined, 1043
"Secured party," defined, 1043
Secured transactions, 328–29, 591–649 (*see also* specific terminology, types of secured transactions)
   agreement, 593
   attachment, 593–94
   cases involving, 605–18, 628–49
   classification of collateral, 595
   floating liens, 594
   intangible, 598–99
   introduction to, 591–92
   perfection by attachment, 602–3
   perfection by filing, 600–602
   perfection by possession, 599–600
   perfection of security interest, 594–605
   priorities, default and remedies, 620–49
   proceeds, 603–5
   purchase money security interests, 603
   rights, remedies of secured party, 624–28
   semi-intangible collateral, 597–98
   tangible property goods, 596–97
Securities (*see* Investment securities; specific types)
"Security," defined, 1043
"Security agreement," defined, 1043
Security interest, 328, 591–618
   agreement, 593
   attachment, 593–94
   cases involving, 605–18
   classification of collateral, 595
   of collecting bank, 559–60
   defined, 1043
   floating liens, 594
   intangible, 598–99
   introduction to, 591–92
   perfection by attachment, 602–3
   perfection by filing, 600–602
   perfection by possession, 599–600
   perfection of, 594–605
   proceeds, 603–5
   purchase money, 603
   semi-intangible collateral, 597–98
   tangible property goods, 596–97
"Sell," defined, 1043
"Seller," defined, 1043
Semi-intangible collateral, 597–98
   chattel paper, 597–98

Semi-intangible collateral (*Cont.*):
   documents of title, 597
   instruments, 598
"Send," defined, 1043
Separation of powers, 46–47
Servants (*see also* Agency and employment)
   defined, 1043
   tort liability of, 686–92
      procedure, 689
      and respondeat superior, 687–89
      and workmen's compensation, 690–92
"Served" or "service," defined, 1043
"Set-off," defined, 1043
"Settle," defined, 1044
"Severable contract," defined, 1044
"Several," defined, 1044
"Share of stock," defined, 1044
Shares (*see* Stocks, stock ownership)
Shaw v. Bailey-McCune Company, 870
Sheriff:
   defined, 1044
   and sale of real property, 975
Shirk v. Caterbone, 767
Shumaker v. Hazen, 741–42
Signatures (*see also* Forgery; Indorsements; specific instruments):
   and liability of parties to negotiable instruments, 497–503
   and transfer of securities, 832–33, 834
"Signed," defined, 1044
Silence:
   as acceptance, 139
   as fraud, 202
Simpson v. Union Oil Company of California, 228–30
Singer v. Walker, 73–78
"Situs," defined, 1044
"Slander," defined, 1044
Slaughter-House cases, 26
Smith v. Lenchner, 479–80
Smith v. Russ, 127–28
Snyder v. Town Hill Motors, Inc., 445–46
Society, law and, 21–43
   cases, 39–42
   and ethics, 36–39
   historical role of law, 24–36
   role of law, 21–24
Sociological school, 6–7
Solicitors (*see* Agency and employment)
"Solvent," defined, 1044
Sources of law, 44–62
   administrative law, 55–58
   cases involving, 58–61
   introduction to, 44–45
   unwritten law, 51–55
   written law, 45–51
Southwest Distributors, Inc. v. Allied Paper Bag Corp., 352–54

*Southwest Weather Research v. Rounsa-
    ville,* 948–50
"Sovereignty," defined, 1044
"Special appearance," defined, 1044
Special indorsement, 437, 438
"Specialty," defined, 1044
"Special verdict," defined, 1044
Specific performance, 113, 116
    defined, 1044
Stale checks, 565
*Standard Realty & Development v.
    Ferrera,* 724
Stare decisis, 51–55
    defined, 1044
State court systems, 65
State ex rel. Kendrick v. Thormyer, 679–
    80
State ex rel. Safeguard Ins. Co. v. Vorys,
    868–69
*State et al. v. Simmer Oil Corporation et
    al.,* 869–70
State laws, uniformity of, 49–51
"Statute," defined, 1044
Statutes (*see also* specific applications,
    terminology):
    interpretation of, 48–49
Statutory law (*see* Written law)
Stelmack et al. v. Glen Alden Coal Co.,
    166–68
*Sterlington Bank v. Terzia Lumber &
    Hardware, Inc.,* 1002–3
"Stock," defined, 825, 1044
"Stock dividend," defined, 1044
Stockholders (*see also* Stocks, stock owner-
    ship):
    defined, 1045
"Stock split-up," defined, 1045
Stocks, stock ownership, 824–51 (*see also*
    Corporations; specific terminology)
    cases involving, 839–50
    corporations' power to deal in, 812, 813
    joint stock companies, 874–75
    kinds of, 826–27
    rights of stockholders, 836–38
        derivative suits, 838
        dividends, 836–37
        in general, 836
        preemptive, 837–38
        subscriptions, 828–30
    terminology, 824–26 (*see also* specific
        terms)
    transfer of, 830–36
        in general, 830–31
        issuers and, 832–33
        of lost, destroyed, or stolen securities,
            835
        and overissue, 831
        purchasers and, 833–34

Stocks (*Cont.*):
    transfer of (*Cont.*):
        registration, 833, 834–35
        and right to dividends, 835–36
    treasury (*see* Treasury stock)
    watered, 827–28
Stolen goods (*see* Theft and stolen goods)
*Stone & Webster Engineering Corp. v.
    First National Bank & Trust Co.
    of Greenfield,* 578–80
Stop orders, banks and, 562–63
    customer's right on, 564–65
"Stoppage in transitu," defined, 1045
Strauss v. West, 350–52
Streich v. General Motors Corp., 179–81
Strict foreclosure, 989
Strunk Chain Saws, Inc. v. Williams, 311–
    13
Subagents, 668
"Subpoena," defined, 1045
Subrogation:
    defined, 1045
    suretyships and, 897, 900–901
"Subsequent purchaser," defined, 1045
"Substantial performance," defined, 1045
Substantive due process, 26–27ff.
Substantive law, 7, 80, 1045
"Succession," defined, 1045
"Succession tax," defined, 1045
"Suit," defined, 1045
Suits (*see* Lawsuits)
"Summons," defined, 1045
Sundet v. Olin Matheson Chemical Corp.,
    374
*Sunshine Cloak & Suit Co. v. Roquette et
    al.,* 294–95
Supreme Court, U.S., 68 (*see also* specific
    cases)
"Surety," defined, 1045
*Surety Development Corporation v.
    Grevas,* 292–94
Suretyships, 893–912
    cases involving, 902–12
    and change in contract terms, 899
    contract of, 894–95
    cosureties' liability, 901–2
    defenses of principal, 900
    distinction between guarantor and
        surety, 894
    duration of liability, 896–97
    extensions of time, 897–99
    fiduciary relationship, 895–96
    and immediate recourse, 896
    nature of relation, 893–94
    payment, 899
    recovery from principal, 901
    rights of, 897–902
    and subrogation, 897, 900–901

"Suspends payments," defined, 1045
Sutton v. Wright & Sanders, 256–58
Suvada v. White Motor Company, 361–63

"Tacit," defined, 1045
"Talisman," defined, 1045
"Tangible," defined, 1045
Tangible property goods, 596–97
  consumer goods as, 596
  equipment as, 596
  farm products as, 597
  inventory as, 596–97
Taxes, taxing powers, 33–34 (*see also*
    specific taxes, terminology)
"Telegram," defined, 1045
Temple Lumber Co. v. Miller, 820–21
Tenancy (of real property), 980
  defined, 1045–46
"Tenant," defined, 1046
"Tender," defined, 1046
Tender, money, and condition of con-
    tract performance, 284
"Tender of delivery," defined, 1046
Tender of payment, and commercial
    paper, 542
"Tenement," defined, 1046
"Tenure," defined, 1046
"Term," defined, 1046
Terminal Vegetable Co., Inc. v. Beck,
    232–34
"Termination," defined, 1046
"Term of court," defined, 1046
"Testament," defined, 1046
"Testamentary capacity," defined, 1046
"Testator," defined, 1046
"Testimony," defined, 1046
Theft and stolen goods (*see also* specific
    terminology):
  commercial paper, 545
  and holders of commercial paper, 470
  and transfer of securities, 835
Third parties (*see also* Agency and em-
    ployment):
  dissolution of partnerships and, 784–87
    distribution of assets and liabilities
      of partners, 785–87
    and liabilities prior to, 784
    new partners and new firms, 785
    and notice, 785
  holders of commercial paper and claims
    of, 470
  liability regarding law of agency, 707–17
    cases involving, 709–16
    and disclosed principal on contract,
      707
    and liability to agent on contract, 708
    tort liability, 708–9
    and undisclosed principal, 707–8

Third parties (*Cont.*):
  rights of, contracts and, 264–81
    assignments to, 264–68
    cases involving, 270–79
    contracts for benefit of, 268–70
  sales contracts and, 346–47
Tickets, 133
Timberlake v. J. R. Watkins Company,
    902–4
Title, 386–87 (*see also* Documents of title;
    Property; specific terminology,
    types)
  defined, 936, 1046
"Tonnage," defined, 1046
Torts, 8–19
  agents and principals and (*see* Agency
    and employment)
  business, 10–19
  corporations and power to commit,
    814–15
  defined, 1046
  infants and, 188
"Total disability," defined, 1046
*Town and Country House & Homes Serv.,
    Inc. v. Evans*, 728–31
"Trade fixtures," defined, 1046
Trade-marks, 17–18
  defined, 1047
Trade unions (*see* Labor unions)
Trade values, 16–19
Trading partnerships, 774–75 (*see also*
    Partnerships)
"Transfer," defined, 1047
Transfer warranties, 512–13
Traveller's checks, 417
Treasury stock, 813, 828
  defined, 1047
Trespass:
  defined, 1047
  tort of, 10
Trials, 84–87
  defined, 1047
Trojnar v. Bihlman, 761–62
Troy Grain & Fuel Co. v. Rolston et al.,
    759–60
"Trust," defined, 1047
"Trustee," defined, 1047
"Trustee in bankruptcy," defined, 1047
Trusts, business, 875
Tuckel et al. v. Jurovaty, 307–9
Tuttle v. Junior Bldg. Corporation, 860–61

Ultra vires, 813
  defined, 1047
Umani v. Reber, 484–85
"Unauthorized," defined, 1047
Unauthorized signatures, 500–501
Unconscionability, 337

Unconscionable bargains, 222–23
"Undertaking," defined, 1047
Undisclosed principal, 655, 669–71
  contracts of, 669–70
  election, 670–71
  and liability of third parties, 707–8
  notice to agent, 671
  settlement between principal and agent, 670
Undue influence, contracts and, 205
Unexcused delay, and discharge of commercial paper, 538–39
"Unfair competition," defined, 1047
Unforeseen difficulties, consideration and, 162
Uniform Commercial Code, 50–51, 319–649
  and commercial paper, 412–89
  definitions having significance in connection with, 1009ff.
  introduction to, 321–24
  overlapping of articles of, 329
  purposes of, 324–25
  and sales, 331–410
  scope of, 325–29
  and secured transactions, 591–649
Unilateral contract, 111
  defined, 1047
Unilateral mistake, 204–5
Unilateral offer, acceptance of, 137–39
(The) Union Bank v. Joseph Mobilla, 522–23
Unions (*see* Labor unions)
United Securities Corporation v. Bruton, 491–92
United States v. Darby Lumber Co., 39–42
United States v. Munro-Van Helms Company, Inc., 926–27
Universal C.I.T. Credit Corporation v. Hudgens, 420–21
Universal Lightning Rod, Inc. v. Rischall Electric Co., 661–62
Unwritten law, 44, 45, 51–55
"Usage," defined, 1046
"Usage of trade," defined, 1047
"Usurious," defined, 1047
Usury, 223–24, 467
U.S. v. Lebanon Woolen Mills, 628–31
"Utter," defined, 1047–48

"Vacancy," defined, 1048
Vaccaro v. Andresen, 904–5
"Valid," defined, 1048
"Valuable consideration," defined, 1048
"Value," defined, 1048
"Valued policy," defined, 1048
"Vendee," defined, 1048
"Vendor," defined, 1048

"Vendor's lien," defined, 1048
"Venire," defined, 1048
Venue, 72–73
  defined, 1048
"Verdict," defined, 1048
"Vested," defined, 1048
"Vis major," defined, 1048
Visnov et ux. v. Levy, 548–49
"Void," defined, 1048
"Voidable," defined, 1048–49
Voting, stockholders and, 853–54
Voting pools, 854
Voting trusts, 854
"Voucher," defined, 1049
Vulcanized Rubber & Plastics Company v. Scheckter, 862–64

Waagen v. Gerde et ux., 775–76
Wage-earner plans, and bankruptcy, 922
"Wager," defined, 1049
"Wages," defined, 1048
Wagner Act, 657
"Waive," defined, 1049
Waiver:
  contract, 287
  defined, 1049
"Warehouseman," defined, 1049
Warehouse receipts (*see also* Documents of title):
  defined, 1049
"Warrant," defined, 1049
Warranties, 337–40, 1049
  of authority for agents, 672
  and bank collections, 559
  express, 337–38, 1026
  implied, 338–40
"Warranty," defined, 1049
Warranty liability, 509–14
  conversion of instrument; forged indorsements, 513–14
  finality of payment or acceptance, 513
  presentment warranties, 510–12
  transfer warranties, 512–13
Wasserman Theatrical Enterprise, Inc. v. Harris, 299–302
"Waste," defined, 1049
Watered stock, 827–28
  defined, 1049
Watkins Co. v. Brund et al. 905–6
Watson v. Settlemeyer, 714–16
Weisel v. McBride et al., 614–16
Weiser v. Burick, 776–77
Wesley v. Electric Auto-Lite Co., 276–78
Wetherell Bros. Co. v. United States Steel Co., 270–72
W. H. McCune, Inc. v. Revzon, 309–10
Whale Harbor Spa, Inc. v. Wood, 314–15
"Wharfage," defined, 1049

White Const. Corp. v. Jet Spray Cooler, Inc., 121–22

White v. First National Bank of Scotia, 520–22

"Wholesale," defined, 1049

Williams v. Walker-Thomas Furniture Company, 380–83

Wills (*see also* specific terminology regarding wills)
  defined, 1049
  and disposition of property, 957
  and real property, 975

Windom National Bank et al. v. Klein et al., 765–67

Wire & Textile Machinery, Inc. v. Robinson, 207–8

"Witness," defined, 1049

Wooldridge v. Hill, 190–92

"Working capital," defined, 1049

Workmen's Compensation, 690–92

Wrappers, 17, 18

Wright v. Massey-Harris Inc., 359–61

"Writ," defined, 1049

Writing (*see also* Signatures; etc.; specific instruments):
  defined, 1050

"Writing obligatory," defined, 1049

"Written," defined, 1050

Written law, 44, 45–51

Wrongful dishonor, banks and, 564

Wyoming Discount Corporation v. Harris, 446–47

Zager v. Gubernick, 680–81

Zazzaro v. Universal Motors, 679

"Zoning ordinance," defined, 1050